# THE

## GUIDE TO
# THE HOUSE OF
# COMMONS
## JUNE 2001

*Edited by*
# Tim Austin and Tim Hames

*Associate Editor*
## Ruth Winstone

TIMES BOOKS
London

First published in 2001 by
Times Books
HarperCollins*Publishers*
77–85 Fulham Palace Road
London W6 8JB

*Compiled by*
Clive Cardy, Richard Dixon, Steve Gibbs, Robert Hands,
Ralph Hawkins, Judy Hobson, Rachel Jenkinson, Mark
Jerome, Kay Mudge, Tony Norbury and Wendy Showell

*Cartoons by*
Jonathan Pugh

*Pictures predominantly supplied by*
Flying Colours

*Map by*
Times Graphics

*Special acknowledgements and thanks to*
Dr Michael Hart of Exeter College, Oxford; and Robert Waller
and Byron Criddle for their invaluable *Almanac of British
Politics* (Sixth Edition, 1999)

Printed and bound in Great Britain by the Bath Press Ltd.

British Library Cataloguing in Publication Data. A Catalogue
record for this book is available from the British Library.

ISBN 0 0071 2676 X

# CONTENTS

# GENERAL ELECTION 2001

Blair: gamble won

Hague: battle lost

Kennedy: on the up

FOUR YEARS and five weeks after Labour swept to power on May 1, 1997, Tony Blair led his party back for a second term with a slightly reduced overall majority — 167 seats compared with 179 at the dissolution of Parliament. The Prime Minister's twin gamble on the timing of the election — to go to the country a year early in a potential five-year term and then to postpone the poll by a month from the targeted date in May to June 7 because of the rampant outbreak of foot-and-mouth disease in parts of rural Britain — had paid off handsomely.

What was not so encouraging for Mr Blair, and indeed for all politicians, was the abysmally low turnout in this election. Down to 59.4 per cent of the electorate from the unimpressive 71.4 per cent who voted in 1997, this represented the lowest proportion of people going to the polling stations since 1918. Commentators ascribed this apparent apathy to a combination of public disillusionment at the perceived slow pace of reform in Labour's first term and an increasing dislike, or even distrust, of politicians generally.

However, if the result was satisfactory enough for Labour and encouraging too for the Liberal Democrats under Charles Kennedy (who increased their total of MPs from 46 to 52), it represented a second successive disaster for the Conservative Party despite a doughty and well-conducted campaign by William Hague. The party finished with 166 MPs, only one more than after the 1997 meltdown.

Mr Hague duly resigned as Tory leader on the morning after the election even as results were still coming in, precipitating a new leadership election just as John Major had done in the wake of the 1997 collapse. The candidates who declared themselves for the subsequent contest were Michael Portillo, Iain Duncan Smith, David Davis, Michael Ancram and Kenneth Clarke.

BY THE standards of the 1997 election, however, there were relatively few fresh faces to be seen when the Commons reassembled. Only 99 MPs were technically "new", although that figure included a clutch of seven Conservatives who returned to Parliament after four years of enforced absence. The majority of this gang of 99 assumed their seats from retiring Members rather than ousting a representative of another political party at the ballot box.

The new recruits confirmed trends that have been established across and within the major parties. Most of them could be labelled as "professional politicians" in that they had served either as local councillors, trade union advisers or senior policy advisers before being selected as the parliamentary candidate.

Labour is now prone to select far more middle-class candidates than those horny-handed sons of toil originating in the trade union movement. But whereas these professionals used to be predominantly teachers or polytechnic lecturers with a smattering of journalists, they are gradually being displaced by lawyers and others with a private sector background.

Only four of Labour's 38 new MPs are female and only one new Labour Member, Parmjit Dhanda of Gloucester, is from an ethnic minority. He won an overwhelmingly white seat and is, at 29, also the youngest of the 2001 intake.

Most of the victorious new Tories are either ex-MPs or smart young men in their thirties, while the principal common features of the successful Liberal Democrats — with a few exceptions such as David Laws, who succeeded Sir Paddy Ashdown in Yeovil — were their local roots and strong records of local achievement.

Overall, the number of women in the Commons dropped from 120 to 118, the first such fall since Margaret Thatcher became Prime Minister in 1979.

The state of the parties in the Commons after this election, compared with dissolution in May 2001 and the result of the 1997 election, is:

## STATE OF THE PARTIES

| Party | Election June 2001 | Dissolution May 2001 | Election May 1997 |
|---|---|---|---|
| Labour | 412 | 418 | 418 |
| Conservative | 166 | 162 | 165 |
| Liberal Democrat | 52 | 47 | 46 |
| Ulster Unionist | 6 | 9 | 10 |
| Scottish Nationalist | 5 | 6 | 6 |
| Plaid Cymru | 4 | 4 | 4 |
| Social Democratic & Labour | 3 | 3 | 3 |
| Democratic Unionist | 5 | 3 | 2 |
| Sinn Fein | 4 | 2 | 2 |
| UK Unionist | 0 | 1 | 1 |
| Independent | 1 | 3* | 1 |
| The Speaker | 1 | 1 | 1 |
| Vacant seats | 0 | 0 | 0 |
| Total | 659 | 659 | 659 |

*Tommy Graham and Ken Livingstone lost the Labour whip in the course of the 1997-2001 Parliament. Peter Temple-Morris (Leominster) and Shaun Woodward (Witney) defected from the Conservatives to Labour during the 1997-2001 Parliament.
In this Parliament, totals were affected by the by-election changes at Romsey and Antrim South. Details, pages 291-293.

# Her Majesty's Government

Prime Minister, First Lord of the Treasury and Minister for the Civil Service
**TONY BLAIR**

Deputy Prime Minister and First Secretary of State
**JOHN PRESCOTT**

Chancellor of the Exchequer
**GORDON BROWN**

President of the Council and Leader of the House of Commons
**ROBIN COOK**

Lord Chancellor
**Lord IRVINE of LAIRG**

Secretary of State for Foreign and Commonwealth Affairs
**JACK STRAW**

Secretary of State for the Home Department
**DAVID BLUNKETT**

Secretary of State for Environment, Food and Rural Affairs
**MARGARET BECKETT**

Secretary of State for International Development
**CLARE SHORT**

Secretary of State for Works and Pensions
**ALISTAIR DARLING**

Secretary of State for Transport, Local Government and the Regions
**STEPHEN BYERS**

Secretary of State for Health
**ALAN MILBURN**

Secretary of State for Northern Ireland
**JOHN REID**

Secretary of State for Wales
**PAUL MURPHY**

Secretary of State for Defence
**GEOFF HOON**

Chief Secretary to the Treasury
**ANDREW SMITH**

Secretary of State for Scotland
**HELEN LIDDELL**

Lord Privy Seal and Leader of the House of Lords
**Lord WILLIAMS of MOSTYN**

Secretary of State for Trade and Industry
**PATRICIA HEWITT**

Secretary of State for Education and Skills
**ESTELLE MORRIS**

Secretary of State for Culture, Media and Sport
**TESSA JOWELL**

Parliamentary Secretary, Treasury and Chief Whip
**HILARY ARMSTRONG**

Minister Without Portfolio and Party Chairman
**CHARLES CLARKE**

# DEPARTMENTS OF STATE AND MINISTERS

**CABINET OFFICE**
*Deputy Prime Minister and First Secretary of State*
JOHN PRESCOTT
*Minister for the Cabinet Office and Chancellor of the Duchy of Lancaster*
LORD MACDONALD of TRADESTON
*Ministers of State:*
BARBARA ROCHE; BARONESS MORGAN
*Parliamentary Secretary*
CHRISTOPHER LESLIE

**CULTURE, MEDIA AND SPORT**
*Secretary of State*
TESSA JOWELL
*Minister of State for Sport*
RICHARD CABORN
*Minister of State for Arts*
BARONESS BLACKSTONE
*Under-Secretary of State*
KIM HOWELLS (tourism, film, broadcasting)

**DEFENCE**
*Secretary of State*
GEOFF HOON
*Minister of State for the Armed Forces*
ADAM INGRAM (defence policy and planning, operations, intelligence and security)
*Under-Secretaries of State:*
*Minister for Defence Procurement*
LORD BACH (acquisition, defence exports and disposal)
*Minister for Veterans*
LEWIS MOONIE (veterans' issues, science and technology strategy, service personnel casework)

**EDUCATION AND SKILLS**
*Secretary of State*
ESTELLE MORRIS
*Minister of State for School Standards*
STEPHEN TIMMS
*Minister of State for Lifelong Learning and Higher Education*
MARGARET HODGE
*Under-Secretaries of State:*
BARONESS ASHTON of UPHOLLAND (school standards); IVAN LEWIS (young people); JOHN HEALEY (adult skills and workforce development)

**ENVIRONMENT, FOOD AND RURAL AFFAIRS**
*Secretary of State*
MARGARET BECKETT
*Minister of State for the Environment*
MICHAEL MEACHER
*Minister of State for Rural Affairs*
ALUN MICHAEL
*Under-Secretaries of State:*
ELLIOT MORLEY; LORD WHITTY

**FOREIGN AND COMMONWEALTH OFFICE**
*Secretary of State*
JACK STRAW
*Minister of State for Trade (also DTI)*
BARONESS SYMONS of VERNHAM DEAN (British Trade International, trade policy, N America)
*Minister of State for Europe*
PETER HAIN (European Union, global issues, economic policy, Russia, Eastern Europe)

*Under-Secretaries of State:*
BEN BRADSHAW (Middle East and North Africa, South Asia, SE Asia, international security); BARONESS AMOS (Sub-Saharan Africa, overseas territories, Caribbean, Commonwealth); DENIS MacSHANE (SE Europe, Latin America, NE Asia and Pacific, public diplomacy, British Council)

**HEALTH**
*Secretary of State*
ALAN MILBURN
*Minister of State for Health*
JOHN HUTTON (the NHS and delivery)
*Minister of State for Mental Health and Social Care*
JACQUI SMITH (social care, long-term care, disability and mental health)
*Under-Secretaries of State:*
LORD HUNT of KINGS HEATH (performance and quality); HAZEL BLEARS (emergency care and public involvement); YVETTE COOPER (public health)

**HOME OFFICE**
*Secretary of State*
DAVID BLUNKETT
*Minister of State for Crime Reduction, Policing and Community Safety*
JOHN DENHAM
*Minister of State for Criminal Justice, Sentencing and Law Reform*
KEITH BRADLEY
*Minister of State for Citizenship and Immigration*
LORD ROOKER
*Under-Secretaries of State:*
BEVERLEY HUGHES (community and custodial sentences); ROBERT AINSWORTH (anti-drugs co-ordination, and organised crime); ANGELA EAGLE (Europe, community and race equality)

**INTERNATIONAL DEVELOPMENT**
*Secretary of State*
CLARE SHORT
*Under-Secretary of State*
HILARY BENN (development awareness with non-governmental organisations and trade unions in the UK)

**LAW OFFICERS**
*Attorney-General*
LORD GOLDSMITH
*Solicitor-General*
HARRIET HARMAN
*Advocate-General for Scotland*
LYNDA CLARK

**LORD CHANCELLOR'S DEPARTMENT**
*Lord Chancellor*
LORD IRVINE of LAIRG
*Under-Secretaries of State:*
BARONESS SCOTLAND of ASTHAL (civil justice, legal aid, immigration and asylum, international policy); MICHAEL WILLS (Court Service, EU policy, IT and e-government policy, magistrates' courts, freedom of information); ROSIE WINTERTON (family policy, tribunals policy, social exclusion)

## NORTHERN IRELAND OFFICE
*Secretary of State*
JOHN REID
*Minister of State for Security, Prisons and Policing*
JANE KENNEDY
*Under-Secretary of State*
DESMOND BROWNE (criminal justice, victims and human rights)

## PRIVY COUNCIL OFFICE
*President of the Council and Leader of the House of Commons*
ROBIN COOK
*Parliamentary Secretary*
STEPHEN TWIGG
*Lord Privy Seal and Leader of the House of Lords*
LORD WILLIAMS of MOSTYN

## SCOTLAND OFFICE
*Secretary of State*
HELEN LIDDELL
*Minister of State for Scotland*
GEORGE FOULKES

## TRADE AND INDUSTRY
*Secretary of State*
PATRICIA HEWITT
*Ministers of State:*
*Minister for E-Commerce and Competitiveness*
DOUGLAS ALEXANDER
*Minister for Trade (and FCO)*
BARONESS SYMONS of VERNHAM DEAN
*Minister of State for Industry and Energy*
BRIAN WILSON
*Minister of State for Employment Relations and Regions*
ALAN JOHNSON
*Under-Secretaries of State:*
LORD SAINSBURY of TURVILLE (science and innovation); MELANIE JOHNSON (consumers and competition); NIGEL GRIFFITHS (small business issues, export controls)

## TRANSPORT, LOCAL GOVERNMENT AND THE REGIONS
*Secretary of State*
STEPHEN BYERS
*Minister for Transport*
JOHN SPELLAR
*Minister of State for Local Government and Minister for London*
NICK RAYNSFORD (electoral law, fire, health and safety)
*Minister of State for Housing and Planning*
LORD FALCONER of THOROTON (urban policy, regeneration, neighbourhood renewal, the Dome)
*Under-Secretaries of State:*
DAVID JAMIESON (railways, roads, road safety, aviation, shipping and ports, European policy); SALLY KEEBLE (housing, planning, urban policy, neighbourhood renewal); ALAN WHITEHEAD (local government, English regions, electoral law, regulatory reform)

## TREASURY
*Prime Minister, First Lord of the Treasury and Minister for the Civil Service*
TONY BLAIR
*Chancellor of the Exchequer*
GORDON BROWN
*Chief Secretary to the Treasury*
ANDREW SMITH (spending issues)
*Paymaster General*
DAWN PRIMAROLO (tax issues)
*Financial Secretary*
PAUL BOATENG (business, environmental issues, Welfare to Work)
*Economic Secretary*
RUTH KELLY (financial services)

## WALES OFFICE
*Secretary of State*
PAUL MURPHY
*Under-Secretary of State*
DON TOUHIG

## WORK AND PENSIONS
*Secretary of State*
ALISTAIR DARLING
*Minister of State for Work*
NICK BROWN (structural unemployment policy, Welfare to Work, JobCentre Plus)
*Minister of State for Pensions*
IAN McCARTNEY (pensions, National Insurance, older people)
*Under-Secretaries of State:*
*Minister for Children and the Family*
BARONESS HOLLIS of HEIGHAM (Child Support Agency, poverty and social exclusion, asylum, maternity and paternity pay); MALCOLM WICKS (work issues, housing benefit, income support); MARIA EAGLE (pensions, disability policy, long-term care)

## WHIPS
## HOUSE of LORDS
*Lord Chief Whip and Captain of the Gentlemen-at-Arms*
LORD CARTER
*Captain of the Yeomen (Deputy Chief Whip)*
LORD McINTOSH of HARINGEY
*Lords in Waiting:*
LORD DAVIES of OLDHAM; LORD GROCOTT; LORD FILKIN; LORD BASSAM of BRIGHTON
*Baroness in Waiting:* BARONESS FARRINGTON of RIBBLETON

## HOUSE OF COMMONS
*Parliamentary Secretary to the Treasury (Government Chief Whip)*
HILARY ARMSTRONG
*Treasurer of HM Household (Deputy Chief Whip)*
KEITH HILL
*Comptroller of HM Household*
THOMAS McAVOY
*Vice-Chamberlain of HM Household*
GERRY SUTCLIFFE
*Lords Commissioners (Whips):*
ANNE McGUIRE; JOHN HEPPELL; TONY McNULTY; NICK AINGER; GRAHAM STRINGER
*Assistant Whips:*
FRASER KEMP; IAN PEARSON; ANGELA SMITH; IVOR CAPLIN; JIM FITZPATRICK; PHIL WOOLAS; DAN NORRIS

*Second Church Estates Commissioner*
STUART BELL

# The House of Commons

The following have been elected Members of the House of Commons in the 2001 general election: Abbreviations to designate political parties:

Lab — Labour
Lab Co-op — Labour and Co-operative
C — Conservative
LD — Liberal Democrat
SNP — Scottish National Party
PC — Plaid Cymru
UUP — Ulster Unionist Party
SDLP — Social Democratic and Labour Party
DUP — Democratic Unionist Party
UKU — United Kingdom Unionist
SF — Sinn Fein
Ind — Independent
KHHC — Kidderminster Hospital and Health Concern

## A

**Abbott, Ms Diane**;
    Hackney North & Stoke Newington ...................Lab
**Adams, Gerry**; Belfast West ........................................SF
**Adams, Ms Irene**; Paisley North ..........................Lab
**Ainger, Nick**;
    Carmarthen West & Pembrokeshire South ........Lab
**Ainsworth, Bob**; Coventry North East ................Lab
**Ainsworth, Peter**; Surrey East .............................C
**Alexander, Douglas**; Paisley South .....................Lab
**Allan, Richard**; Sheffield Hallam ..........................LD
**Allen, Graham**; Nottingham North ....................Lab
**Amess, David**; Southend West .................................C
**Ancram, Michael**; Devizes ......................................C
**Anderson, Donald**; Swansea East .......................Lab
**Anderson, Ms Janet**; Rossendale & Darwen ......Lab
**Arbuthnot, James**; Hampshire North East ...........C
**Armstrong, Ms Hilary**; Durham North West ...Lab
**Atherton, Ms Candy**; Falmouth & Camborne ....Lab
**Atkins, Ms Charlotte**; Staffordshire Moorlands .Lab
**Atkinson, David**; Bournemouth East ....................C
**Atkinson, Peter**; Hexham .......................................C
**Austin, John**; Erith & Thamesmead ....................Lab

## B

**Bacon, Richard**; Norfolk South ..............................C
**Bailey, Adrian**; West Bromwich West ........Lab Co-op
**Baird, Ms Vera**; Redcar .........................................Lab
**Baker, Norman**; Lewes ............................................LD
**Baldry, Tony**; Banbury ...........................................C
**Banks, Tony**; West Ham .........................................Lab

**Barker, Greg**; Bexhill & Battle ...................................C
**Barnes, Harry**; Derbyshire North East ...............Lab
**Baron, John**; Billericay ............................................C
**Barrett, John**; Edinburgh West .............................LD
**Barron, Kevin**; Rother Valley ...............................Lab
**Battle, John**; Leeds West .......................................Lab
**Bayley, Hugh**; York, City of ................................Lab
**Beard, Nigel**; Bexleyheath & Crayford ...............Lab
**Beckett, Mrs Margaret**; Derby South ...............Lab
**Begg, Ms Anne**; Aberdeen South ........................Lab
**Beggs, Roy**; Antrim East .......................................UUP
**Beith, Alan**; Berwick-upon-Tweed ..........................LD
**Bell, Stuart**; Middlesbrough ..................................Lab
**Bellingham, Henry**; Norfolk North West ..............C
**Benn, Hilary**; Leeds Central ..................................Lab
**Bennett, Andrew**; Denton & Reddish .................Lab
**Benton, Joe**; Bootle ...............................................Lab
**Bercow, John**; Buckingham ....................................C
**Beresford, Sir Paul**; Mole Valley ..........................C
**Berry, Dr Roger**; Kingswood ...............................Lab
**Best, Harold**; Leeds North West .........................Lab
**Betts, Clive**; Sheffield Attercliffe .........................Lab
**Blackman, Ms Liz**; Erewash .................................Lab
**Blair, Tony**; Sedgefield ...........................................Lab
**Blears, Ms Hazel**; Salford ....................................Lab
**Blizzard, Bob**; Waveney .........................................Lab
**Blunkett, David**; Sheffield Brightside .................Lab
**Blunt, Crispin**; Reigate ............................................C
**Boateng, Paul**; Brent South ..................................Lab
**Borrow, David**; Ribble South ................................Lab
**Boswell, Tim**; Daventry ..........................................C
**Bottomley, Peter**; Worthing West ..........................C
**Bottomley, Mrs Virginia**; Surrey South West .......C
**Bradley, Keith**; Manchester Withington ..............Lab
**Bradley, Peter**; Wrekin, The ................................Lab
**Bradshaw, Ben**; Exeter .........................................Lab
**Brady, Graham**; Altrincham & Sale West ...............C
**Brake, Tom**; Carshalton & Wallington .................LD
**Brazier, Julian**; Canterbury ....................................C
**Breed, Colin**; Cornwall South East .......................LD
**Brennan, Kevin**; Cardiff West ..............................Lab
**Brinton, Mrs Helen**; Peterborough ...................Lab
**Brooke, Ms Annette**;
    Dorset Mid & Poole North ...................................LD
**Brown, Gordon**; Dunfermline East .....................Lab
**Brown, Nick**;
    Newcastle upon Tyne East & Wallsend .............Lab

**Brown, Russell**; Dumfries .....................Lab
**Browne, Desmond**; Kilmarnock & Loudoun ......Lab
**Browning, Mrs Angela**; Tiverton & Honiton ........C
**Bruce, Malcolm**; Gordon .......................LD
**Bryant, Chris**; Rhondda .....................Lab
**Buck, Ms Karen**;
    Regent's Park & Kensington North ....................Lab
**Burden, Richard**; Birmingham Northfield .........Lab
**Burgon, Colin**; Elmet .....................Lab
**Burnett, John**; Devon West & Torridge ................LD
**Burnham, Andrew**; Leigh .....................Lab
**Burns, Simon**; Chelmsford West .............C
**Burnside, David**; Antrim South .........UUP
**Burstow, Paul**; Sutton & Cheam ...........LD
**Burt, Alistair**; Bedfordshire North East ..................C
**Butterfill, John**; Bournemouth West .......C
**Byers, Stephen**; Tyneside North .........Lab

## C

**Cable, Dr Vincent**; Twickenham ...........LD
**Caborn, Richard**; Sheffield Central .....................Lab
**Cairns, David**; Greenock & Inverclyde ................Lab
**Calton, Ms Patsy**; Cheadle .....................LD
**Cameron, David**; Witney .........................C
**Campbell, Alan**; Tynemouth .....................Lab
**Campbell, Ms Anne**; Cambridge .........Lab
**Campbell, Gregory**; Londonderry East ............DUP
**Campbell, Menzies**; Fife North East ....................LD
**Campbell, Ronnie**; Blyth Valley .........Lab
**Cann, Jamie**; Ipswich .....................Lab
**Caplin, Ivor**; Hove .....................Lab
**Carmichael, Alistair**; Orkney & Shetland ..........LD
**Casale, Roger**; Wimbledon .....................Lab
**Cash, Bill**; Stone .....................C
**Caton, Martin**; Gower .....................Lab
**Cawsey, Ian**; Brigg & Goole .....................Lab
**Challen, Colin**; Morley & Rothwell .....................Lab
**Chapman, Ben**; Wirral South .....................Lab
**Chapman, Sir Sydney**; Chipping Barnet ...............C
**Chaytor, David**; Bury North .....................Lab
**Chidgey, David**; Eastleigh .....................LD
**Chope, Christopher**; Christchurch .....................C
**Clapham, Michael**; Barnsley West & Penistone ..Lab
**Clappison, James**; Hertsmere .....................C
**Clark, Dr Lynda**; Edinburgh Pentlands .....................Lab
**Clark, Paul**; Gillingham .....................Lab
**Clarke, Charles**; Norwich South .....................Lab
**Clarke, Kenneth**; Rushcliffe .....................C
**Clarke, Tom**; Coatbridge & Chryston ..................Lab
**Clarke, Tony**; Northampton South .......Lab

**Clelland, David**; Tyne Bridge .....................Lab
**Clifton-Brown, Geoffrey**; Cotswold .....................C
**Clwyd, Ms Ann**; Cynon Valley .....................Lab
**Coaker, Vernon**; Gedling .....................Lab
**Coffey, Ms Ann**; Stockport .....................Lab
**Cohen, Harry**; Leyton & Wanstead .....................Lab
**Coleman, Iain**; Hammersmith & Fulham ............Lab
**Collins, Tim**; Westmorland & Lonsdale ....................C
**Colman, Tony**; Putney .....................Lab
**Connarty, Michael**; Falkirk East .....................Lab
**Conway, Derek**; Old Bexley & Sidcup ....................C
**Cook, Frank**; Stockton North .....................Lab
**Cook, Robin**; Livingston .....................Lab
**Cooper, Ms Yvette**; Pontefract & Castleford ........Lab
**Corbyn, Jeremy**; Islington North .....................Lab
**Cormack, Sir Patrick**; Staffordshire South ...........C
**Corston, Ms Jean**; Bristol East .....................Lab
**Cotter, Brian**; Weston-super-Mare .........................LD
**Cousins, Jim**; Newcastle upon Tyne Central ........Lab
**Cox, Tom**; Tooting .....................Lab
**Cran, James**; Beverley & Holderness .....................C
**Cranston, Ross**; Dudley North .....................Lab
**Crausby, David**; Bolton North East .....................Lab
**Cruddas, Jon**; Dagenham .....................Lab
**Cryer, Ms Ann**; Keighley .....................Lab
**Cryer, John**; Hornchurch .....................Lab
**Cummings, John**; Easington .....................Lab
**Cunningham, Dr Jack**; Copeland .....................Lab
**Cunningham, Jim**; Coventry South .....................Lab
**Cunningham, Tony**; Workington .....................Lab
**Curry, David**; Skipton & Ripon .....................C
**Curtis-Thomas, Ms Claire**; Crosby ....................Lab

## D

**Daisley, Paul**; Brent East .....................Lab
**Dalyell, Tam**; Linlithgow .....................Lab
**Darling, Alistair**; Edinburgh Central ..................Lab
**Davey, Edward**; Kingston & Surbiton ..................LD
**Davey, Ms Valerie**; Bristol West .....................Lab
**David, Wayne**; Caerphilly .....................Lab
**Davidson, Ian**; Glasgow Pollok ................Lab Co-op
**Davies, Denzil**; Llanelli .....................Lab
**Davies, Geraint**; Croydon Central .....................Lab
**Davies, Quentin**; Grantham & Stamford ................C
**Davis, David**; Haltemprice & Howden .....................C
**Davis, Terry**; Birmingham Hodge Hill .............Lab
**Dawson, Hilton**; Lancaster & Wyre .....................Lab
**Dean, Ms Janet**; Burton .....................Lab
**Denham, John**; Southampton Itchen ....................Lab
**Dhanda, Parmjit**; Gloucester .....................Lab

**Dismore, Andrew**; Hendon .....................................Lab
**Djanogly, Jonathan**; Huntingdon ..........................C
**Dobbin, Jim**; Heywood & Middleton .........Lab Co-op
**Dobson, Frank**; Holborn & St Pancras ...............Lab
**Dodds, Nigel**; Belfast North ...............................DUP
**Doherty, Pat**; Tyrone West ...................................SF
**Donaldson, Jeffrey**; Lagan Valley .....................UUP
**Donohoe, Brian**; Cunninghame South ...............Lab
**Doran, Frank**; Aberdeen Central .........................Lab
**Dorrell, Stephen**; Charnwood .................................C
**Doughty, Ms Sue**; Guildford ...............................LD
**Dowd, Jim**; Lewisham West .................................Lab
**Drew, David**; Stroud ....................................Lab Co-op
**Drown, Ms Julia**; Swindon South .......................Lab
**Duncan, Alan**; Rutland & Melton ...........................C
**Duncan, Peter**; Galloway & Upper Nithsdale .........C
**Duncan Smith, Iain**;
   Chingford & Woodford Green ..............................C
**Dunwoody, Mrs Gwyneth**;
   Crewe & Nantwich ...............................................Lab

## E

**Eagle, Ms Angela**; Wallasey .................................Lab
**Eagle, Ms Maria**; Liverpool Garston ...................Lab
**Edwards, Huw**; Monmouth .................................Lab
**Efford, Clive**; Eltham ...........................................Lab
**Ellman, Ms Louise**; Liverpool Riverside ..Lab Co-op
**Ennis, Jeff**; Barnsley East & Mexborough .............Lab
**Etherington, Bill**; Sunderland North ...................Lab
**Evans, Nigel**; Ribble Valley .....................................C
**Ewing, Ms Annabelle**; Perth .............................SNP

## F

**Fabricant, Michael**; Lichfield ..................................C
**Fallon, Michael**; Sevenoaks ....................................C
**Farrelly, Paul**; Newcastle-under-Lyme .................Lab
**Field, Frank**; Birkenhead ....................................Lab
**Field, Mark**; Cities of London & Westminster .........C
**Fisher, Mark**; Stoke-on-Trent Central ..................Lab
**Fitzpatrick, Jim**; Poplar & Canning Town ............Lab
**Fitzsimons, Ms Lorna**; Rochdale .......................Lab
**Flight, Howard**; Arundel & South Downs ..............C
**Flint, Ms Caroline**; Don Valley ...........................Lab
**Flook, Adrian**; Taunton ...........................................C
**Flynn, Paul**; Newport West .................................Lab
**Follett, Ms Barbara**; Stevenage ..........................Lab
**Forth, Eric**; Bromley & Chislehurst ........................C
**Foster, Derek**; Bishop Auckland .........................Lab
**Foster, Don**; Bath ...................................................LD

**Foster, Michael J.**; Hastings & Rye .....................Lab
**Foster, Michael**; Worcester ..................................Lab
**Foulkes, George**;
   Carrick, Cumnock & Doon Valley ...........Lab Co-op
**Fox, Dr Liam**; Woodspring .......................................C
**Francis, Hywel**; Aberavon ...................................Lab
**Francois, Mark**; Rayleigh .......................................C

## G

**Gale, Roger**; Thanet North .......................................C
**Galloway, George**; Glasgow Kelvin .....................Lab
**Gapes, Mike**; Ilford South ..........................Lab Co-op
**Gardiner, Barry**; Brent North .............................Lab
**Garnier, Edward**; Harborough ...............................C
**George, Andrew**; St Ives .......................................LD
**George, Bruce**; Walsall South .............................Lab
**Gerrard, Neil**; Walthamstow ...............................Lab
**Gibb, Nick**; Bognor Regis & Littlehampton ..............C
**Gibson, Dr Ian**; Norwich North .........................Lab
**Gidley, Mrs Sandra**; Romsey ..............................LD
**Gildernew, Ms Michelle**;
   Fermanagh & South Tyrone ..................................SF
**Gillan, Mrs Cheryl**; Chesham & Amersham ..........C
**Gilroy, Mrs Linda**; Plymouth Sutton ........Lab Co-op
**Godsiff, Roger**;
   Birmingham Sparkbrook & Small Heath .........Lab
**Goggins, Paul**; Wythenshawe & Sale East ..........Lab
**Goodman, Paul**; Wycombe ....................................C
**Gray, James**; Wiltshire North .................................C
**Grayling, Chris**; Epsom & Ewell .............................C
**Green, Damian**; Ashford ........................................C
**Green, Matthew**; Ludlow ....................................LD
**Greenway, John**; Ryedale .......................................C
**Grieve, Dominic**; Beaconsfield ...............................C
**Griffiths, Ms Jane**; Reading East .......................Lab
**Griffiths, Nigel**; Edinburgh South .....................Lab
**Griffiths, Win**; Bridgend ....................................Lab
**Grogan, John**; Selby .............................................Lab
**Gummer, John**; Suffolk Coastal .............................C

## H

**Hague, William**; Richmond, Yorks .........................C
**Hain, Peter**; Neath ................................................Lab
**Hall, Mike**; Weaver Vale ....................................Lab
**Hall, Patrick**; Bedford .........................................Lab
**Hamilton, David**; Midlothian .............................Lab
**Hamilton, Fabian**; Leeds North East ..................Lab
**Hammond, Philip**; Runnymede & Weybridge .......C
**Hancock, Mike**; Portsmouth South .....................LD

**Hanson, David**; Delyn .............................Lab
**Harman, Ms Harriet**; Camberwell & Peckham  Lab
**Harris, Dr Evan**; Oxford West & Abingdon .........LD
**Harris, Tom**; Glasgow Cathcart .............................Lab
**Harvey, Nick**; Devon North ...................................LD
**Haselhurst, Sir Alan**; Saffron Walden ...................C
**Havard, Dai**; Merthyr Tydfil & Rhymney ...........Lab
**Hawkins, Nick**; Surrey Heath ...............................C
**Hayes, John**; South Holland & The Deepings .........C
**Heal, Ms Sylvia**; Halesowen & Rowley Regis .....Lab
**Heald, Oliver**; Hertfordshire North East ................C
**Healey, John**; Wentworth ....................................Lab
**Heath, David**; Somerton & Frome .......................LD
**Heathcoat-Amory, David**; Wells ...........................C
**Henderson, Doug**; Newcastle upon Tyne North  Lab
**Henderson, Ivan**; Harwich ..................................Lab
**Hendrick, Mark**; Preston .........................Lab Co-op
**Hendry, Charles**; Wealden ...................................C
**Hepburn, Stephen**; Jarrow .................................Lab
**Heppell, John**; Nottingham East .........................Lab
**Hermon, Sylvia**; Down North ............................UUP
**Hesford, Stephen**; Wirral West ..........................Lab
**Hewitt, Ms Patricia**; Leicester West ...................Lab
**Heyes, David**; Ashton under Lyne .......................Lab
**Hill, Keith**; Streatham .......................................Lab
**Hinchliffe, David**; Wakefield .............................Lab
**Hoban, Mark**; Fareham ........................................C
**Hodge, Mrs Margaret**; Barking ..........................Lab
**Hoey, Ms Kate**; Vauxhall ...................................Lab
**Hogg, Douglas**; Sleaford & North Hykeham .........C
**Holmes, Paul**; Chesterfield .................................LD
**Hood, Jimmy**; Clydesdale ..................................Lab
**Hoon, Geoff**; Ashfield ........................................Lab
**Hope, Phil**; Corby .................................Lab Co-op
**Hopkins, Kelvin**; Luton North ............................Lab
**Horam, John**; Orpington ......................................C
**Howard, Michael**; Folkestone & Hythe .................C
**Howarth, Alan**; Newport East ............................Lab
**Howarth, George**;
        Knowsley North & Sefton East .........................Lab
**Howarth, Gerald**; Aldershot ..................................C
**Howells, Dr Kim**; Pontypridd ............................Lab
**Hoyle, Lindsay**; Chorley ...................................Lab
**Hughes, Ms Beverley**; Stretford & Urmston ......Lab
**Hughes, Kevin**; Doncaster North ........................Lab
**Hughes, Simon**;
        Southwark North & Bermondsey .......................LD
**Humble, Ms Joan**;
        Blackpool North & Fleetwood ...........................Lab
**Hume, John**; Foyle ............................................SDLP
**Hunter, Andrew**; Basingstoke ...............................C

**Hurst, Alan**; Braintree ......................................Lab
**Hutton, John**; Barrow & Furness .......................Lab

# I

**Iddon, Dr Brian**; Bolton South East ...................Lab
**Illsley, Eric**; Barnsley Central ............................Lab
**Ingram, Adam**; East Kilbride ..............................Lab

# J

**Jack, Michael**; Fylde ...........................................C
**Jackson, Ms Glenda**; Hampstead & Highgate ...Lab
**Jackson, Ms Helen**; Sheffield Hillsborough .......Lab
**Jackson, Robert**; Wantage ...................................C
**Jamieson, David**; Plymouth Devonport ..............Lab
**Jenkin, Bernard**; Essex North ...............................C
**Jenkins, Brian**; Tamworth .................................Lab
**Johnson, Alan**; Hull West & Hessle ....................Lab
**Johnson, Boris**; Henley ........................................C
**Johnson, Ms Melanie**; Welwyn Hatfield ..........Lab
**Jones, Ms Helen**; Warrington North ..................Lab
**Jones, Jon Owen**; Cardiff Central .............Lab Co-op
**Jones, Kevan**; Durham North ..............................Lab
**Jones, Dr Lynne**; Birmingham Selly Oak ...........Lab
**Jones, Martyn**; Clwyd South ..............................Lab
**Jones, Nigel**; Cheltenham ...................................LD
**Jowell, Ms Tessa**; Dulwich & West Norwood .....Lab
**Joyce, Eric**; Falkirk West ...................................Lab

# K

**Kaufman, Gerald**; Manchester Gorton ..............Lab
**Keeble, Ms Sally**; Northampton North ...............Lab
**Keen, Alan**; Feltham & Heston ...................Lab Co-op
**Keen, Ms Ann**; Brentford & Isleworth ................Lab
**Keetch, Paul**; Hereford ......................................LD
**Kelly, Ms Ruth**; Bolton West ............................Lab
**Kemp, Fraser**; Houghton & Washington East .....Lab
**Kennedy, Charles**; Ross, Skye & Inverness West .LD
**Kennedy, Ms Jane**; Liverpool Wavertree ...........Lab
**Key, Robert**; Salisbury ........................................C
**Khabra, Piara**; Ealing Southall ...........................Lab
**Kidney, David**; Stafford .....................................Lab
**Kilfoyle, Peter**; Liverpool Walton .......................Lab
**King, Andy**; Rugby & Kenilworth .......................Lab
**King, Ms Oona**; Bethnal Green & Bow ...............Lab
**Kirkbride, Miss Julie**; Bromsgrove .......................C
**Kirkwood, Archy**; Roxburgh & Berwickshire .......LD
**Knight, Greg**; Yorkshire East ................................C
**Knight, Jim**; Dorset South ..................................Lab
**Kumar, Dr Ashok**;
        Middlesbrough South & Cleveland East ...........Lab

# L

**Ladyman, Dr Stephen**; Thanet South ................Lab
**Laing, Mrs Eleanor**; Epping Forest .......................C
**Lait, Mrs Jacqui**; Beckenham ....................................C
**Lamb, Norman**; Norfolk North ............................LD
**Lammy, David**; Tottenham ...................................Lab
**Lansley, Andrew**; Cambridgeshire South ...............C
**Lawrence, Ms Jackie**; Preseli Pembrokeshire ....Lab
**Laws, David**; Yeovil .................................................LD
**Laxton, Bob**; Derby North .....................................Lab
**Lazarowicz, Mark**;
 Edinburgh North & Leith ...................................Lab
**Leigh, Edward**; Gainsborough ..................................C
**Lepper, David**; Brighton Pavilion .............. Lab Co-op
**Leslie, Christopher**; Shipley ..................................Lab
**Letwin, Oliver**; Dorset West ....................................C
**Levitt, Tom**; High Peak .........................................Lab
**Lewis, Ivan**; Bury South ......................................Lab
**Lewis, Dr Julian**; New Forest East .........................C
**Lewis, Terry**; Worsley ...........................................Lab
**Liddell, Ms Helen**; Airdrie & Shotts ..................Lab
**Liddell-Grainger, Ian**; Bridgwater ........................C
**Lidington, David**; Aylesbury ...................................C
**Lilley, Peter**; Hitchin & Harpenden .........................C
**Linton, Martin**; Battersea ....................................Lab
**Lloyd, Tony**; Manchester Central ..........................Lab
**Llwyd, Elfyn**; Meirionnydd Nant Conwy ...............PC
**Lord, Michael**; Suffolk Central & Ipswich North ....C
**Loughton, Tim**; Worthing East & Shoreham ..........C
**Love, Andy**; Edmonton .................................Lab Co-op
**Lucas, Ian**; Wrexham ...........................................Lab
**Luff, Peter**; Worcestershire Mid ..............................C
**Luke, Iain**; Dundee East ......................................Lab
**Lyons, John**; Strathkelvin & Bearsden .................Lab

# M

**MacDonald, Calum**; Western Isles ....................Lab
**MacDougall, John**; Fife Central ...........................Lab
**MacKay, Andrew**; Bracknell ....................................C
**Mackinlay, Andrew**; Thurrock .............................Lab
**Maclean, David**; Penrith & The Border .................C
**MacShane, Denis**; Rotherham .............................Lab
**Mactaggart, Ms Fiona**; Slough .............................Lab
**McAvoy, Thomas**; Glasgow Rutherglen ...Lab Co-op
**McCabe, Stephen**; Birmingham Hall Green .......Lab
**McCafferty, Mrs Christine**; Calder Valley ........Lab
**McCartney, Ian**; Makerfield ..................................Lab
**McDonagh, Ms Siobhain**;
 Mitcham & Morden .............................................Lab

**McDonnell, John**; Hayes & Harlington ..............Lab
**McFall, John**; Dumbarton ..........................Lab Co-op
**McGrady, Eddie**; Down South .........................SDLP
**McGuinness, Martin**; Ulster Mid .......................SF
**McGuire, Ms Anne**; Stirling ..............................Lab
**McIntosh, Miss Anne**; Vale of York ......................C
**McIsaac, Ms Shona**; Cleethorpes .......................Lab
**McKechin, Ms Ann**; Glasgow Maryhill .............Lab
**McKenna, Ms Rosemary**;
 Cumbernauld & Kilsyth ......................................Lab
**McLoughlin, Patrick**; Derbyshire West ................C
**McNamara, Kevin**; Hull North ...........................Lab
**McNulty, Tony**; Harrow East ...............................Lab
**McWalter, Tony**; Hemel Hempstead ........Lab Co-op
**McWilliam, John**; Blaydon ..................................Lab
**Mahmood, Khalid**; Birmingham Perry Barr ......Lab
**Mahon, Ms Alice**; Halifax ..................................Lab
**Malins, Humfrey**; Woking ......................................C
**Mallaber, Ms Judy**; Amber Valley .....................Lab
**Mallon, Seamus**; Newry & Armagh ................SDLP
**Mandelson, Peter**; Hartlepool ............................Lab
**Mann, John**; Bassetlaw ........................................Lab
**Maples, John**; Stratford-on-Avon ...........................C
**Marris, Rob**; Wolverhampton South West ..........Lab
**Marsden, Gordon**; Blackpool South ...................Lab
**Marsden, Paul**; Shrewsbury & Atcham ..............Lab
**Marshall, David**; Glasgow Shettleston ...............Lab
**Marshall, Jim**; Leicester South ..........................Lab
**Marshall-Andrews, Bob**; Medway ....................Lab
**Martin, Michael**; Glasgow Springburn ........Speaker
**Martlew, Eric**; Carlisle ........................................Lab
**Mates, Michael**; Hampshire East ...........................C
**Maude, Francis**; Horsham .......................................C
**Mawhinney, Sir Brian**;
 Cambridgeshire North West ...................................C
**May, Mrs Theresa**; Maidenhead ...........................C
**Meacher, Michael**; Oldham West & Royton .......Lab
**Meale, Alan**; Mansfield ........................................Lab
**Mercer, Patrick**; Newark .........................................C
**Merron, Ms Gillian**; Lincoln ..............................Lab
**Michael, Alun**; Cardiff South & Penarth ...Lab Co-op
**Milburn, Alan**; Darlington ...................................Lab
**Miliband, David**; South Shields ..........................Lab
**Miller, Andrew**; Ellesmere Port & Neston .......Lab
**Mitchell, Andrew**; Sutton Coldfield ........................C
**Mitchell, Austin**; Great Grimsby ........................Lab
**Moffatt, Ms Laura**; Crawley ...............................Lab
**Moonie, Dr Lewis**; Kirkcaldy ...................Lab Co-op
**Moore, Michael**;
 Tweeddale, Ettrick & Lauderdale ..........................LD
**Moran, Ms Margaret**; Luton South ...................Lab

**Morgan, Ms Julie**; Cardiff North ........................ Lab
**Morley, Elliot**; Scunthorpe ........................ Lab
**Morris, Ms Estelle**; Birmingham Yardley .......... Lab
**Moss, Malcolm**; Cambridgeshire North East ........ C
**Mountford, Ms Kali**; Colne Valley .................... Lab
**Mudie, George**; Leeds East .................................. Lab
**Mullin, Chris**; Sunderland South ........................ Lab
**Munn, Ms Meg**; Sheffield Heeley ...................... Lab
**Murphy, Denis**; Wansbeck ................................ Lab
**Murphy, Jim**; Eastwood .................................... Lab
**Murphy, Paul**; Torfaen .................................... Lab
**Murrison, Dr Andrew**; Westbury ........................ C

# N

**Naysmith, Dr Doug**;
    Bristol North West ................................ Lab Co-op
**Norman, Archie**; Tunbridge Wells ........................ C
**Norris, Dan**; Wansdyke .................................... Lab

# O

**Oaten, Mark**; Winchester ................................ LD
**O'Brien, Mike**; Warwickshire North .................. Lab
**O'Brien, Stephen**; Eddisbury ............................ C
**O'Brien, Bill**; Normanton ................................ Lab
**O'Hara, Eddie**; Knowsley South ........................ Lab
**Olner, Bill**; Nuneaton .................................... Lab
**O'Neill, Martin**; Ochil .................................... Lab
**Opik, Lembit**; Montgomeryshire ........................ LD
**Organ, Ms Diana**; Forest of Dean ...................... Lab
**Osborne, George**; Tatton .................................. C
**Osborne, Ms Sandra**; Ayr ................................ Lab
**Ottaway, Richard**; Croydon South ...................... C
**Owen, Albert**; Ynys Mon ................................ Lab

# P

**Page, Richard**; Hertfordshire South West .............. C
**Paice, James**; Cambridgeshire South East .............. C
**Paisley, the Rev Ian**; Antrim North ................ DUP
**Palmer, Dr Nick**; Broxtowe .............................. Lab
**Paterson, Owen**; Shropshire North ...................... C
**Pearson, Ian**; Dudley South .............................. Lab
**Perham, Ms Linda**; Ilford North ...................... Lab
**Picking, Mrs Anne**; East Lothian ...................... Lab
**Pickles, Eric**; Brentwood & Ongar ...................... C
**Pickthall, Colin**; Lancashire West ...................... Lab
**Pike, Peter**; Burnley .................................... Lab
**Plaskitt, James**; Warwick & Leamington .............. Lab
**Pollard, Kerry**; St Albans .............................. Lab

**Pond, Chris**; Gravesham .................................. Lab
**Pope, Greg**; Hyndburn .................................... Lab
**Portillo, Michael**; Kensington & Chelsea .............. C
**Pound, Stephen**; Ealing North .......................... Lab
**Powell, Sir Raymond**; Ogmore ........................ Lab
**Prentice, Ms Bridget**; Lewisham East .............. Lab
**Prentice, Gordon**; Pendle .............................. Lab
**Prescott, John**; Hull East .............................. Lab
**Price, Adam**; Carmarthen East & Dinefwr .......... PC
**Primarolo, Ms Dawn**; Bristol South .................. Lab
**Prisk, Mark**; Hertford & Stortford ...................... C
**Prosser, Gwyn**; Dover .................................... Lab
**Pugh, John**; Southport .................................... LD
**Purchase, Ken**;
    Wolverhampton North East .................... Lab Co-op
**Purnell, James**; Stalybridge & Hyde .................. Lab

# Q

**Quin, Ms Joyce**;
    Gateshead East & Washington West ................ Lab
**Quinn, Lawrie**; Scarborough & Whitby .............. Lab

# R

**Rammell, Bill**; Harlow .................................. Lab
**Randall, John**; Uxbridge ................................ C
**Rapson, Syd**; Portsmouth North ...................... Lab
**Raynsford, Nick**; Greenwich & Woolwich .......... Lab
**Redwood, John**; Wokingham ............................ C
**Reed, Andrew**; Loughborough .................. Lab Co-op
**Reid, Alan**; Argyll & Bute .............................. LD
**Reid, Dr John**; Hamilton North & Bellshill ........ Lab
**Rendel, David**; Newbury ................................ LD
**Robathan, Andrew**; Blaby .............................. C
**Robertson, Angus**; Moray .............................. SNP
**Robertson, Hugh**; Faversham & Kent Mid .......... C
**Robertson, John**; Glasgow Anniesland .............. Lab
**Robertson, Laurence**; Tewkesbury ...................... C
**Robinson, Geoffrey**; Coventry North West ........ Lab
**Robinson, Mrs Iris**; Strangford .................... DUP
**Robinson, Peter**; Belfast East ........................ DUP
**Roche, Ms Barbara**;
    Hornsey & Wood Green ............................ Lab
**Roe, Mrs Marion**; Broxbourne .......................... C
**Rooney, Terry**; Bradford North ...................... Lab
**Rosindell, Andrew**; Romford .......................... C
**Ross, Ernie**; Dundee West .............................. Lab
**Roy, Frank**; Motherwell & Wishaw .................... Lab
**Ruane, Chris**; Vale of Clwyd .......................... Lab
**Ruddock, Mrs Joan**; Lewisham Deptford .......... Lab

**Ruffley, David**; Bury St Edmunds ............................C
**Russell, Bob**; Colchester ..........................................LD
**Russell, Ms Christine**; Chester, City of ..............Lab
**Ryan, Ms Joan**; Enfield North ...........................Lab

## S

**Salmond, Alex**; Banff & Buchan ...........................SNP
**Salter, Martin**; Reading West ................................Lab
**Sanders, Adrian**; Torbay .........................................LD
**Sarwar, Mohammed**; Glasgow Govan ...............Lab
**Savidge, Malcolm**; Aberdeen North ....................Lab
**Sawford, Phil**; Kettering .........................................Lab
**Sayeed, Jonathan**; Bedfordshire Mid .....................C
**Sedgemore, Brian**;
    Hackney South & Shoreditch ............................Lab
**Selous, Andrew**; Bedfordshire South West ..............C
**Shaw, Jonathan**; Chatham & Aylesford ..............Lab
**Sheerman, Barry**; Huddersfield ...............Lab Co-op
**Shephard, Mrs Gillian**; Norfolk South West ........C
**Shepherd, Richard**; Aldridge-Brownhills ..............C
**Sheridan, James**; Renfrewshire West ..................Lab
**Shipley, Ms Debra**; Stourbridge ..........................Lab
**Short, Ms Clare**; Birmingham Ladywood ...........Lab
**Simmonds, Mark**; Boston & Skegness ...................C
**Simon, Sîon**; Birmingham Erdington ..................Lab
**Simpson, Alan**; Nottingham South ......................Lab
**Simpson, Keith**; Norfolk Mid ..................................C
**Singh, Marsha**; Bradford West ...........................Lab
**Skinner, Dennis**; Bolsover .....................................Lab
**Smith, Andrew**; Oxford East ................................Lab
**Smith, Ms Angela**; Basildon .....................Lab Co-op
**Smith, Chris**; Islington South & Finsbury .............Lab
**Smith, Ms Geraldine**;
    Morecambe & Lunesdale .....................................Lab
**Smith, Ms Jacqui**; Redditch ................................Lab
**Smith, John**; Vale of Glamorgan ..........................Lab
**Smith, Llew**; Blaenau Gwent ...............................Lab
**Smith, Sir Robert**;
    Aberdeenshire West & Kincardine ......................LD
**Smyth, the Rev Martin**; Belfast South ..............UUP
**Soames, Nicholas**; Sussex Mid ...............................C
**Soley, Clive**; Ealing Acton & Shepherd's Bush ......Lab
**Southworth, Ms Helen**; Warrington South .......Lab
**Spellar, John**; Warley ..........................................Lab
**Spelman, Mrs Caroline**; Meriden ..........................C
**Spicer, Sir Michael**; Worcestershire West ..............C
**Spink, Dr Robert**; Castle Point ..............................C
**Spring, Richard**; Suffolk West ................................C
**Squire, Ms Rachel**; Dunfermline West ..............Lab
**Stanley, Sir John**; Tonbridge & Malling ................C

**Starkey, Dr Phyllis**;
    Milton Keynes South West ................................Lab
**Steen, Anthony**; Totnes ..........................................C
**Steinberg, Gerry**; Durham, City of ....................Lab
**Stevenson, George**; Stoke-on-Trent South ..........Lab
**Stewart, David**;
    Inverness East, Nairn & Lochaber ....................Lab
**Stewart, Ian**; Eccles ...............................................Lab
**Stinchcombe, Paul**; Wellingborough ..................Lab
**Stoate, Dr Howard**; Dartford .............................Lab
**Strang, Dr Gavin**;
    Edinburgh East & Musselburgh ........................Lab
**Straw, Jack**; Blackburn .........................................Lab
**Streeter, Gary**; Devon South West ..........................C
**Stringer, Graham**; Manchester Blackley ............Lab
**Stuart, Ms Gisela**; Birmingham Edgbaston ........Lab
**Stunell, Andrew**; Hazel Grove .............................LD
**Sutcliffe, Gerry**; Bradford South ........................Lab
**Swayne, Desmond**; New Forest West .....................C
**Swire, Hugo**; Devon East ........................................C
**Syms, Robert**; Poole .................................................C

## T

**Tami, Mark**; Alyn & Deeside ...............................Lab
**Tapsell, Sir Peter**; Louth & Horncastle ..................C
**Taylor, Mrs Ann**; Dewsbury ...............................Lab
**Taylor, Ms Dari**; Stockton South .........................Lab
**Taylor, David**;
    Leicestershire North West ......................Lab Co-op
**Taylor, Ian**; Esher & Walton ...................................C
**Taylor, John**; Solihull ..............................................C
**Taylor, Matthew**; Truro & St Austell ...................LD
**Taylor, Dr Richard**; Wyre Forest ..................KHHC
**Taylor, Sir Teddy**; Rochford & Southend East ........C
**Thomas, Gareth**; Clwyd West .............................Lab
**Thomas, Gareth R**; Harrow West ........................Lab
**Thomas, Simon**; Ceredigion ...............................PC
**Thurso, (Viscount) John**;
    Caithness, Sutherland & Easter Ross .................LD
**Timms, Stephen**; East Ham .................................Lab
**Tipping, Paddy**; Sherwood ..................................Lab
**Todd, Mark**; Derbyshire South ............................Lab
**Tonge, Dr Jenny**; Richmond Park ........................LD
**Touhig, Don**; Islwyn ...................................Lab Co-op
**Tredinnick, David**; Bosworth ................................C
**Trend, Michael**; Windsor .......................................C
**Trickett, Jon**; Hemsworth .....................................Lab
**Trimble, David**; Upper Bann .............................UUP
**Truswell, Paul**; Pudsey .........................................Lab
**Turner, Andrew**; Isle of Wight ...............................C

**Turner, Dennis**;
    Wolverhampton South East .................... Lab Co-op
**Turner, Dr Desmond**; Brighton Kemptown ...... Lab
**Turner, Neil**; Wigan ................................. Lab
**Twigg, Derek**; Halton ............................... Lab
**Twigg, Stephen**; Enfield Southgate ..................... Lab
**Tyler, Paul**; Cornwall North .................................. LD
**Tynan, Bill**; Hamilton South ............................... Lab
**Tyrie, Andrew**; Chichester ......................... C

# V

**Vaz, Keith**; Leicester East ......................... Lab
**Viggers, Peter**; Gosport ............................... C
**Vis, Rudi**; Finchley & Golders Green .................... Lab

# W

**Walley, Ms Joan**; Stoke-on-Trent North ............. Lab
**Walter, Robert**; Dorset North ................................. C
**Ward, Ms Claire**; Watford ................................ Lab
**Wareing, Bob**; Liverpool West Derby ................... Lab
**Waterson, Nigel**; Eastbourne ................................. C
**Watkinson, Mrs Angela**; Upminster .................... C
**Watson, Tom**; West Bromwich East ..................... Lab
**Watts, Dave**; St Helens North ............................... Lab
**Webb, Steve**; Northavon ........................................ LD
**Weir, Michael**; Angus ........................................ SNP
**White, Brian**; Milton Keynes North East ............ Lab
**Whitehead, Dr Alan**; Southampton Test ........... Lab
**Whittingdale, John**; Maldon & Chelmsford East ...C
**Wicks, Malcolm**; Croydon North ......................... Lab
**Widdecombe, Miss Ann**;
    Maidstone & The Weald ......................... C
**Wiggin, Bill**; Leominster ............................. C
**Wilkinson, John**; Ruislip-Northwood ..................... C
**Willetts, David**; Havant ............................. C
**Williams, Alan**; Swansea West ............................. Lab
**Williams, Mrs Betty**; Conwy ................................ Lab
**Williams, Hywel**; Caernarfon ................................ PC
**Williams, Roger**; Brecon & Radnorshire ............. LD
**Willis, Phil**; Harrogate & Knaresborough ............ LD
**Wills, Michael**; Swindon North ........................... Lab
**Wilshire, David**; Spelthorne ................................. C
**Wilson, Brian**; Cunninghame North ................... Lab
**Winnick, David**; Walsall North .......................... Lab
**Winterton, Mrs Ann**; Congleton ......................... C
**Winterton, Nicholas**; Macclesfield ..................... C
**Winterton, Ms Rosie**; Doncaster Central .......... Lab
**Wishart, Peter**; Tayside North .......................... SNP
**Wood, Mike**; Batley & Spen ................................ Lab

**Woodward, Shaun**; St Helens South ................. Lab
**Woolas, Phil**; Oldham East & Saddleworth ........ Lab
**Worthington, Tony**; Clydebank & Milngavie ..... Lab
**Wray, James**; Glasgow Baillieston ........................ Lab
**Wright, David**; Telford ........................................ Lab
**Wright, Tony**; Great Yarmouth ........................... Lab
**Wright, Dr Tony**; Cannock Chase ...................... Lab
**Wyatt, Derek**; Sittingbourne & Sheppey .............. Lab

# Y

**Yeo, Tim**; Suffolk South ............................... C
**Young, Sir George**; Hampshire North West ......... C
**Younger-Ross, Richard**; Teignbridge ................ LD

# ANALYSIS
# & COMMENT

# BLAIR'S DATE WITH HISTORY KEPT HIM CLEAR OF PITFALLS

## *by* Peter Riddell

### *Assistant Editor (Politics) of The Times*

TONY BLAIR took office in May 1997 with one overriding objective — to be the first Labour Prime Minister to win a second full term. Mr Blair and Gordon Brown were preoccupied, almost obsessed, with avoiding the mistakes of the Labour Governments of the 1960s and 1970s which were dogged by economic crises before defeat at the polls. Above all, the new Government was determined to prove to voters that Labour could be competent in office, particularly in managing the economy, after voter mistrust had condemned the party to 18 years in opposition.

This approach affected both the Government's strategy and its tactics, avoiding any risks that might imperil its chances of a second term.

This was despite having a commanding position in the Commons with a majority over all other parties of 179. At times, the Government behaved as if it had a tiny majority and was in danger of losing power.

The leading ministers — Prime Minister, Chancellor and Foreign Secretary — as well as their close advisers were also the least experienced to hold office since at least the first MacDonald administration in 1924. They were unfamiliar with handling the levers of power, and they carried into office the techniques of media management and policymaking by small groups which they practised in opposition.

Mr Blair broke with previous Whitehall practices. Membership of the Cabinet itself was largely a mark of status, not an opportunity to discuss, let alone decide, the main questions facing the Government.

Informality was adopted, both in style of addressing each other and in the Cabinet's business. Weekly meetings were often short, of less than an hour, and merely covered what was on Mr Blair's mind.

Moreover, while the formal structure of Cabinet committees existed, their use was patchy and uneven. Lord Irvine of Lairg, the Lord Chancellor, chaired a series of committees dealing with the constitutional reform legislation during the first hectic year. By contrast, other committees dealing with economic strategy or welfare reform hardly met.

Critics accused Mr Blair of presidentialism, but this was an oversimplification. Mr Blair was presented in a presidential manner, as a national rather than a parliamentary leader. This reflected his One Nation/big tent strategy of appealing outside Labour's traditional working-class core as well as specific media techniques.

But power was never concentrated in 10 Downing Street. There was always a dual leadership. Gordon Brown was in effective charge of much of the domestic agenda, notably the Welfare to Work programme, welfare and pensions reform, and many other aspects of training and industrial policy. Moreover, in relations with departmental ministers, Mr Blair adopted a bilateral rather than a presidential approach. Collective decision-making was out, apart from where issues crossed departmental boundaries. But Mr Blair had to work with the departmental baronies. He, and his advisers in the Downing Street policy unit, worked closely with relevant ministers pressing the Blairite agenda. Students of the Blair Downing Street — and that included many permanent secretaries — talked of a court atmosphere with a tight group of courtiers competing for the leader's attention. But the sharp increase in the number of political appointees in Downing Street — including two, Jonathan Powell, chief of staff, and Alastair Campbell, chief press spokesman, with special powers to give orders to civil servants — complicated decision-making. There were competing political and Civil Service hierarchies, and this confusion was compounded by Mr Blair's indecisiveness.

The main exceptions were Northern Ireland and Kosovo. Mr Blair discovered, like his predecessors, that he had to devote considerable amounts of time to Northern Ireland. The appointment of Mo Mowlam as Northern Ireland Secretary promised a fresh approach, though she lost the confidence of the Ulster Unionists before long. But Mr Blair took risks, including meeting Gerry Adams, the Sinn Fein leader. His personal involvement led to the Good Friday agreement of April 1998 between the British and Irish Governments and the main parties in Northern Ireland, including Sinn Fein but excluding the Democratic Unionists. The subsequent power-sharing agreement and cross-party administration just about survived, despite continuing problems over arms decommissioning and changes to the police. But Mr Trimble's resignation three weeks after polling day plunged the Province into fresh crisis.

Mr Blair proved to be decisive in committing British troops to combat — in bombing Iraq to enforce the no-fly zones, in Sierra Leone and, above all, in Kosovo in spring 1999 when Nato launched air attacks on Serbia. Mr Blair depicted this conflict in moral terms, developing a doctrine of humanitarian intervention, and clashing with President Clinton over the possible use of ground forces to push the Serbians out of Kosovo. Mr Blair was in danger of being out on a limb, but the issue never had to be resolved because President Milosevic backed down. The episode was striking because Mr Blair was prepared to take a high risk.

By contrast, Mr Blair was much more cautious on his European policy, and particularly over the euro. On taking office, he rapidly took steps to improve Britain's relations with its EU partners which had been strained at the end of the Major Government. Britain signed up to the social chapter and agreed to what became the Amsterdam treaty.

But after a series of press stories in the autumn of 1997, Mr Brown and he decided that the economic and political conditions were not right for entry into the euro — especially as Labour had promised a referendum. So, to the dismay of allies like Lord Jenkins of Hillhead, and the Liberal Democrats, as well as Labour euro supporters, entry was effectively ruled out for the first term. Apart from the divergence between Britain and the eurozone economies, he judged it was too great a political task, and risk, for the first term when his priority was to show that Labour could be trusted in government again. So, in October 1997, Mr Brown announced five economic tests which had to be passed before a decision would be made on entry. Mr Brown used this statement to squash any further debate in the Parliament, despite occasional tensions with some of his Cabinet colleagues.

The central achievement of the Blair Government was a growing economy with low inflation and low interest rates. Mr Brown was helped by a relatively benign inheritance from Kenneth Clarke, his predecessor, but he acted boldly in May 1997 to prevent any revival in inflation and to reduce a stubbornly high level of borrowing. His first, and most important, move, within four days of taking office, was to make the Bank of England responsible for setting interest rates within an inflation target set by him. This arms-length relationship proved to be highly successful and reassured financial markets, so long-term interest fell to the lowest level for three decades. Mr Brown also tightened fiscal policy, both by sticking to the public expenditure limits inherited from Mr Clarke (with exceptions for his New Deal Welfare to Work programme) and by raising taxes. He stuck to Labour's manifesto pledge not to raise the higher or basic rates of income tax (indeed the latter was cut by 1p to 22p in the pound) or extend VAT. But he raised around £5 billion from a windfall tax on privatised utilities (as promised in the Labour manifesto) and then much more from a tax on dividends received by pension funds and in various other small ways, aptly dubbed "stealth taxes" by the Conservatives. The tax burden rose during the Parliament. So, following lower than planned levels of public spending, the Budget moved into a sizeable surplus.

The early austerity on public spending led, despite some limited extra amounts for health and education, to increasing complaints that the public services were being squeezed. The Treasury undertook a Comprehensive Spending Review of all departments in July 1998, but Mr Brown oversold the results by announcing a £40 billion rise in spending for health and schools. This turned out to be triple-counting, adding together the rises for each of three years, including the amounts needed for inflation. More money was provided in the March 1999 Budget, but a severe shortage of hospital beds during a flu outbreak in January 2000 led to a promise by Mr Blair to raise NHS spending more rapidly. Again, more money was announced in the March 2000 Budget and the second spending review that July led to promises of record increases in health and schools spending as well as a ten-year plan for transport. The latter was one of the most criticised failures of the Blair Government since travelling conditions seemed to get worse both for drivers and rail passengers (particularly after a series of rail crashes, culminating in a fatal derailment at Hatfield in October 2000, led to severe disruptions as track was repaired).

Mr Brown was able to afford these spending increases over the three years to 2004 by reallocating money saved on social security benefits from the fall in unemployment and lower debt interest payments, and by using up the earlier Budget surplus. So there was a shift from famine to feast in public spending. But little of the impact was felt before the run-up to the 2001 general election.

Not only did public spending policy change during the first term, but the Blair Government also came to recognise that its initial approach to public services had to be revised. In health, a concentration on a pre-election pledge to cut waiting lists by 100,000 proved to be counter-productive as resources were diverted from more pressing clinical needs. Gradually this priority was downgraded, only to be abandoned just after the June 2001 election. The Government produced a ten-year plan for the NHS in July 2000 which sought to improve, rather than to change, the existing system by providing more resources, concentrating on cutting deaths from cancer and heart disease and giving more power to GPs in primary-care trusts. In education, the drive to raise standards in primary schools, via numeracy and literacy hours, did produce measurable improvements, but this was not matched at the secondary level. David Blunkett, Education and Employment Secretary for the whole of the first term, changed emphasis by accepting the need for greater diversity in provision, encouraging more specialist schools and reviving the Tory idea of City Technology Colleges under the new title of City Academies. There was fierce controversy over the introduction of tuition fees for students and over the funding of universities.

The record was patchier on law and order where Jack Straw, the Home Secretary, discovered how hard it is to affect levels of crime. While some progress was made in streamlining the youth justice system, attempts to tighten controls on disorder made little impact and violent crime rose. A sharp rise in the number of asylum-seekers also produced controversy with criticism from Right and Left, the former for allowing too many into Britain and the latter for being too tough. Mr Straw was a favourite target of the libertarian Left.

The most substantial legislative achievement was in the far-reaching programme of constitutional reform, though this attracted little public attention. After referendums in Scotland and Wales in September 1997, legislation led to the creation of a Parliament in Edinburgh and a National Assembly in Cardiff, elected for the first time in May 1999. Both were elected under a system of proportional representation so Labour, while the largest party in both cases, did not have an overall majority. London gained an elected Mayor and Assembly from summer 2000, also following a referendum. The European elections in June 1999 were also under PR for the first time. The European Convention on Human Rights was incorporated into British law and the Human Rights Act became an important constraint on the behaviour of public officials. A Freedom of Information Act also granted rights of access to public documents, though less than the reformers sought. And elections were sub-

" REMEMBER IT'S NOT THE WINNING, IT'S THE TAKING PART THAT COUNTS "

ject to national regulation, disclosure of contributions and controls over levels of spending for the first time with the creation of an Electoral Commission.

In political terms, the Blair Government's first term was often troubled. Many of the problems could be traced to the infighting of the courtiers and the lack of formal procedures. For instance, within six months of taking office, Mr Blair was engulfed in fierce controversy after Labour granted an exemption from a ban on tobacco advertising to Formula One after having accepted a pre-election donation of £1 million from Bernie Ecclestone, and discussing another £1 million donation. Mr Blair escaped by making a "trust me" appeal but this controversy was followed just over a year later by a row over a large loan made by Geoffrey Robinson, then Paymaster General in the Treasury, to Peter Mandelson, then Trade and Industry Secretary, to buy a house. Mr Robinson, who had been criticised by the Standards and Privileges Committee of the Commons for his failure to disclose some business interests, and Mr Mandelson both resigned in December 1998.

**M**r Mandelson returned to office within ten months as Northern Ireland Secretary, but resigned for the second time in January 2001 after allegations that he had misled ministers, and thus Parliament, over his involvement in the Hinduja brothers' applications for British passports. Mr Mandelson was later cleared of any wrongdoing over the applications. The Conservatives argued that these episodes — and allegations against Keith Vaz, Europe Minister from 1999 until 2001, over his business interests — showed that Labour was "sleazy", the very charge that had so damaged the Major Government before 1997.

The Mandelson/Robinson affair was part of a long-running saga of Mr Mandelson's feud with Mr Brown, dating back to the 1994 Labour leadership contest. The mutual suspicion was fuelled by the infighting between their advisers and by the appearance of books which were fiercely partisan on one side or the other.

Mr Blair was unable to control the animosity between his two close friends, but, at the same time, he had to face criticism for being a "control freak". This reflected both the general attempt to control what ministers said, and did, to ensure that they were "on message", but also, more specifically, to the attempts by Downing Street to influence the choice by Labour of its candidates to lead the party's campaign in Wales and to be Mayor of London. Both were embarrassing fiascos. Alun Michael, Mr Blair's candidate, duly became First Secretary in Wales after the first elections in May 1999, but Labour lost several previously safe seats in the Valleys and Mr Michael was forced to resign nine months later. In London, Frank Dobson, Health Secretary from 1997 until 1999, was eventually chosen as Labour candidate after some unsavoury fixing but he was beaten into a poor third place by Ken Livingstone in the elections of May 2000.

Labour was also beaten badly by the Conservatives in the European Parliament elections in June 1999, and came second in the local council elections in the following May. But these proved to be only temporary blips. The only time that the Tories went into the lead over Labour in the opinion polls was for a week or two in September 2000 when a series of protests against high fuel prices and taxes by some hauliers and farmers provided a lightning rod for popular dislike of Mr Blair and his Government and threatened to paralyse the country for a day or two. The Government had also become unpopular over a 75p rise in the basic state pension in April 2000. While this was in line with the official formula linking pension rises to inflation, the increase appeared miserly and was widely unpopular.

Labour also suffered at the same time from low attendances at, and widespread criticism of, the costly Millennium Dome project in the London Docklands.

This was supposed to a symbol of the new millennium, but proved to be a long-running embarrassment for the Government, and particularly for Mr Blair and close allies like Mr Mandelson and Lord Falconer of Thoroton, his successor as Dome minister and a close personal friend of the Prime Minister.

Yet despite these and other troubles — including an outbreak of foot-and-mouth disease which caused the election to be delayed from May to June 2001 — the Blair Government's cautious strategy ensured that Labour retained the political initiative and always looked like winning a second full term.

# VOTERS WELCOMED LABOUR FOR WHAT IT WAS NOT

## by Alice Miles

### Political Columnist of The Times

E VERY Parliament tends to have a defining moment. The 1992-97 Parliament saw the humiliation of Black Wednesday, the 1987-92 Parliament the disposal of Margaret Thatcher by a Conservative Party greedy for a fourth term in office. In 1983-87 the battle with the miners stood out, and in 1979-83 the Falklands conflict transformed Mrs Thatcher's fortunes.

It is a measure of the cautiously incremental approach from Labour's first Government for nearly two decades that its defining moment is difficult to discern. There were many candidates: the fuel protests in autumn 2000 which saw Labour's ratings slip behind the Conservatives for the only time in the Parliament; the moment of public humiliation when Tony Blair was slow-handclapped by the doughty ladies of the Women's Institute; the first resignation from the Cabinet of Mr Blair's close friend and fellow architect of new Labour, Peter Mandelson; the "winter crisis" in the NHS at the turn of the millennium; perhaps the dog that didn't bark, the failure of the world recession in 1998 to hit Britain.

The events following the death of Diana, Princess of Wales, in a Paris car crash on August 31, 1997 were significant.

When the Prime Minister delivered his "People's Princess" encomium later that morning, he did more than enunciate the mood of the nation: he expropriated it as his own. New Labour became the party in touch with 1990s Britain: emotional, guilt-ridden and sentimental. It was a quintessentially Blairite, bold and opportunistic move — Mr Blair grabbed a weeping Britain and hugged it to his breast. There, for most of the rest of the Parliament, it stayed, wriggling.

But the only event in the 1997-2001 Parliament comparable to Mrs Thatcher's battles with the miners or the Argentinians, where Mr Blair's credibility was similarly on the line, was the Balkans conflict in spring 1999 — an exercise which could have destroyed the Government but which instead saw the Prime Minister make his mark as a world statesman and imprinted the Blairite "Third Way" on the cartography of international politics.

The "Kosovo war" was a peculiarly "new Labour" conflict. As a strangely fuzzy defining moment, it bore all the hallmarks of "Blairism".

First, it wasn't quite what it said it was. It was not, technically, a "war". In perhaps the most extreme example of the Blair Government's ability to frame traditional policies in new language and brand them a "Third Way", new Labour rebranded war "humanitarian intervention".

Secondly, in common with so much else in Mr Blair's first term in office, it was a very "safe" war. No British or American soldiers were to be killed.

Britain would bomb Serbia, but she would do so from a sufficient height that risks to her airmen would be minimal.

Thirdly, defining moments of an administration tend also to be turning points: to reverse the fortunes of government, for better or worse.

The Kosovo war did neither. Like so much else in Mr Blair's first term, it had little impact on the popularity of new Labour. Few voters

PUGH

" IT'S A BIT BLURRED — HE WASN'T WEARING HIS GLASSES "

would even mention it if asked their impression of the 1997-2001 Parliament.

But the adventure in the Balkans was Mr Blair's first, and possibly only, big risk.

It confirmed the Prime Minister, not least in his own mind, as a man of absolute resolve under fire. When European allies threatened to desert and the US began to waver, Mr Blair travelled to Chicago to stiffen the backbone of the Clinton Administration. He used the occasion to set out a new "doctrine of international community" — a classic example of Blairism: turning adversity into opportunity.

Adversity suits Mr Blair. He appears to thrive on it. Whether driving through the Good Friday agreement in Northern Ireland, confronting the fuel protesters who threatened to bring Britain to a halt, or battling with foot-and-mouth in the run-up to the 2001 general election, the Prime Minister was at his best in an emergency. In part the Government's reliance on one man in times of crisis was a product of Mr Blair's much-criticised style of government: a neutered Cabinet and an administration tightly centralised in 10 Downing Street found itself impotent or afraid to act decisively when it mattered. Everything had to come back to the Prime Minister.

T he lack of any effective Opposition and an easy ride from the electorate throughout most of the Parliament left Mr Blair, the fine adversary, rootless. Nobody cared more about seeking a definition of new Labour than the Prime Minister himself. New Labour had grown out of the electorate's rejection both of the traditional Labour Party and of the modern Conservative Party. It thus came to office a party framed in the negative: not old Labour, not the Tories. In government, in pursuit of a more concrete identity, it sought definition from its opponents: if new Labour wasn't sure what it was, it could be defined by what it was not. This was the propulsion behind Mr Blair's 1999 speech to the Labour Party conference, in which he attacked the "forces of conservatism" which he claimed had been holding Britain back.

But the restless search for "opposition", of people and causes to fight, sat uneasily with the Government's relentless pursuit of popularity.

Only once in four years did Labour fall behind the Conservatives in the polls.

The public rebellion in autumn 2000, when Labour lost a 20-point lead in the polls in a month, was only on the surface about the high cost of fuel.

The real problem was that a Government perceived as arrogant and complacent — but which was actually insecure and paranoid — momentarily lost touch with public opinion and lost control of the country. It took Mr Blair, displaying a combination of toughness and humility, a matter of weeks to win them both back. The blackmail from parts of the electorate was answered with fuel tax cuts in the next Budget. The events demonstrated that while Labour's support might be broad, it was also shallow.

Many voters were sticking with new Labour in the hope of something better to come from it. Mr Blair had arrived in office promising a "new dawn"; nothing less than the complete transformation of Britain. His specific policy promises were limited, but the language they were dressed up in was extreme. The public quickly grew sick of the gap between the rhetoric of the Prime Minister and other ministers, and the reality of public services on the ground. A spending freeze in the first two years of office may have been necessary to ensure economic stability and the confidence of the City; its dressing up as vast spending increases which would rescue public services from their post-Thatcherite malaise was a huge error. The Government, as impatient for visible change as the electorate, tried to fill the gap between expectation and delivery with rhetorical flourish. Every initiative, however minor, became "radical"; each "czar" or quango a part of the Blair "vision" for Britain.

As a result, Blairism became derided as an insubstantial creed created by "spin". The blighted Dome stood at Greenwich, an apparent embodiment of new Labour — an impressive but essentially empty construct, filled with pap.

Mr Blair tried to combat the growing frustration by redoubling his efforts to enunciate a positive purpose for his administration. The electorate grew tired of hearing about Mr Blair's vision, message, mission, as things on the ground stayed the same. The health service remained on the verge of collapse; the transport system did collapse, flooding and train accidents combining to paralyse the road and rail network. Only in education, in primary schools, through the Government's relentless focus on literacy and numeracy, was progress clear.

Confronting failure, new Labour took refuge in long-term "plans": three-year spending plans, a ten-year plan for transport, a National Plan for the NHS.

It took almost the entire term for Labour to realise that the opposition it initially sought had been staring it in the face: within the public sector unions guarding the train drivers, nurses, teachers and policemen; the professional bodies protecting the interests of doctors and lawyers; the Civil Service minding the paths to delivery within government itself. The enemy was within: in the establishment of which new Labour was now a part; in the professional bodies to which Labour Cabinet ministers themselves belonged; and in the stroppy, curmudgeonly, idealistic Labour Party and the broader Labour movement.

Mr Blair never expected an easy ride from the Labour movement just because he had got it back into power. His programme for constitutional reform almost imploded as the Prime Minister attempted to fashion the paradox of implementing devolution while simultaneously keeping control of everything.

His attempts to impose favoured candidates in Wales and for the London mayoralty saw him derided as an autocratic "control freak". Labour members, who had entrusted Mr Blair with the party leadership, now wanted the Prime Minister to entrust them with some power of their own. Years of bitter experience had convinced Mr Blair that the last place power ought to reside was with activists within his own party.

Rarely can a government have been so publicly dogged by bitter internal rivalry as was new Labour. It reached into the highest echelons of the Cabinet. The farce of the relations between characters such as Gordon Brown, Robin Cook and Peter Mandelson was played out on the front pages of national newspapers, as briefing and counter-briefing fought to score points off one another.

And then there was "Gordon and Tony", the most brilliant, difficult, impenetrable but devastatingly effective two-man act ever to play for such a long run in Numbers 10 and 11 Downing Street. Their relationship dominated the Government; to both of them should be attributed its success.

The Chancellor kept the economy not just stable but sufficiently buoyant, and reaped enough tax revenues without unduly upsetting the voters to maintain low interest rates and repay debt while investing in public services. It is not sufficient to claim, as many have done, that Mr Brown was "lucky" with the economy. His immediate decision to hand control of interest rates to the Bank of England ensured their security from political manipulation. And Mr Brown correctly forecast, at odds with all the analysts and the commentators, that Britain would escape the 1998 recession. His projections for growth, universally derided at the time they were made, proved cautious rather than destructively optimistic.

At the same time, the Chancellor steered through many of Labour's unsung achievements: a minimum wage, a million extra people in work and the fundamental reform of the welfare state that eluded the Conservatives.

Mr Brown also wrested control of Labour's policy on the European single currency from the Foreign Office and 10 Downing Street. His October 1997 Commons statement, ruling out euro entry during the Parliament and refining the five economic tests which would have to be met before Britain would hold a referendum, just about held firm through to the election.

In Mr Brown's gift now rests Mr Blair's dream of taking Britain into the single currency.

The Government's cautious approach to the euro was typical. Much of Mr Blair's first term was devoted to reassuring a sceptical electorate that Labour could be trusted in government. The economy was absolutely essential to this. And trust was absolutely essential to the truly defining moment of new Labour's first term — its landslide re-election for its second.

" I'VE GOT A TEN YEAR PLAN TO READ IT IN 2011 "

# FRAGILE TORIES WERE KEPT FOR EVER ON DEFENSIVE

## *by* Tim Hames

### *Comment Editor of The Times*

WITH the exception of perhaps two weeks in the autumn of 2000, the 1997-2001 Parliament was a miserable experience for Conservative MPs, party activists and many supporters through the country. Labour retained a large lead in the opinion polls and the Tory leadership appeared to switch, almost desperately, from one strategy to another in the hope of alighting upon a solution. In the process, the party meandered between a political approach which might enthuse its core or another which could conceivably appeal to the uncommitted voter. In the end, neither section of the electorate seemed satisfied. The Tories entered the new Parliament with 166 MPs, an advance of precisely one over where they had stood at the outset of the old one. A cruel observer would note that even this risible advance was the consequence of Martin Bell's decision to honour his pledge not to seek re-election in Tatton — an act which handed that seat back to the Conservatives.

It should be acknowledged that the parliamentary party suffered from a miserable inheritance in May 1997. It had endured an intellectual crisis coupled with deep uncertainty as to its immediate political strategy. Europe had been the catalyst of deep internal divisions. National membership had fallen consistently for a decade before John Major was finally ejected from office. The average age of Tory stalwarts was therefore inevitably increasing. A series of adverse local election results between 1993 and 1997 had removed thousands of Conservative councillors. Once the Tories had fallen from 336 MPs in 1992 to 165 five years later, their institutional rout was completed. The party lost access to its remaining resources — patronage and therefore the prospect of raising funds to support its political activities.

It was against this unfavourable backdrop that five men — Kenneth Clarke, William Hague, Michael Howard, Peter Lilley, and John Redwood — fought for the leadership of the party in 1997. This shortlist would almost certainly have been different if fate had been less cruel to Conservatives at that year's election. Michael Portillo and Sir Malcolm Rifkind had been removed from the scene by the electorate, Michael Heseltine suffered health problems almost immediately after polls closed, Chris Patten remained the Governor of Hong Kong and Stephen Dorrell, once considered a highly plausible possibility, withdrew from the race once it became obvious that he did not have enough support to merit his efforts.

Mr Clarke led after the first ballot (on 48 votes) with Mr Hague not far behind (41) while the three supposed "right-wing" aspirants — Redwood (27), Lilley (24) and Howard (23) — sliced up the remaining MPs between them. Mr Clarke maintained a slim two-vote advantage over Mr Hague in the second ballot with Mr Redwood a distant third. To widespread surprise, Clarke and Redwood then struck a deal in an attempt to prevent the 35-year-old former Welsh Secretary storming to power. The ruse failed spectacularly as Mr Hague won by the relatively comfortable margin of 92 votes to 72 in the final ballot. His options for his first Shadow Cabinet were, though, limited and he retained a number of old stalwarts. Mr Lilley became Shadow Chancellor, Sir Brian Mawhinney, the

PLEASE GIVE UP THIS SEAT FOR SOMEONE WHO NEEDS IT. YOUR TORY MP FOR INSTANCE

Shadow Home Secretary, Michael Howard served as Shadow Foreign Secretary while Cecil Parkinson began his second spell as party chairman.

Mr Hague seemed to start with the view that the Conservative Party would require substantial modernisation were it to take on new Labour. He had campaigned on the basis of a thorough constitutional and organisational reform allied with an additional element of internal democracy. This initiative was allied with a set of symbolic moves towards younger electors, ethnic minorities and homosexuals. In public relations terms, however, this exercise was executed ineptly. Criticism of his decision to wear a baseball cap at a theme park, his attendance at the Notting Hill Carnival, his message of support for a Gay Pride march and his stiff response to the death of Diana, Princess of Wales, mounted within his party.

Mr Hague did, nevertheless, stick with the modernisation theme for the first year of his leadership. He was assisted at his first party conference as leader by Mr Portillo, who offered a moving mea culpa and reassessment of Conservatism. Mr Hague made a series of speeches which, cautiously perhaps, distanced himself from his party's immediate past. In 1998 he conducted a Shadow Cabinet reshuffle in which a number of senior figures made way for new blood. In addition, Francis Maude replaced Mr Lilley as Shadow Chancellor, allowing the former Social Security Secretary to become deputy leader and take charge of a sweeping policy review. Michael Ancram replaced Mr Parkinson as the Conservative Party chairman.

T he initial burst of modernisation came to an end with the publication of a new constitution for the party. Adverse polls left Mr Hague in a vulnerable position. Traditionalists demanded that he should not unduly disturb party orthodoxy in several areas. The uncertainty in East Asia in late 1998 was seized upon by the Shadow Chancellor. The possibility of an economic downturn or outright recession appeared to offer the Tories a painless route back to political credibility. This was the unspoken theme of the 1998 party conference — an event preceded by an internal referendum on Mr Hague's stance on the single currency (ruled out for the present and forthcoming Parliament) which was easily carried but on a low turnout.

Mr Hague entered 1999 still attempting to balance reform and reaction. His first major speech of the year, entitled "The British Way", seemed to be a partial retreat from radicalism. He made a highly publicised visit to the United States in February, the highlight of which was a short meeting with George W. Bush, then Governor of Texas and overwhelming favourite for the Republican presidential nomination. On his return he endorsed a new shift in strategy called "kitchen table conservatism" by its author, Andrew Cooper, then an influential Conservative Central Office official. He recommended that the party dissociate itself forcefully from the past and concentrate on forming new ideas on bread-and-butter domestic political questions.

A series of events then conspired to force another shift in direction. Amanda Platell, the former Editor of the *Sunday Express*, was recruited as the senior press adviser. Her instinct was to build up Mr Hague's personal image rather than concentrate on the details of policy. The recession that was supposed to destroy the Labour Party was averted by the Chancellor. Mr Lilley then delivered an extremely controversial speech which appeared to repudiate Thatcherite principles in social policy without outlining any new philosophy or policies to replace them. The address therefore annoyed almost everybody. If the Tories had performed badly in the local elections of May 1999 then Mr Hague could easily have been deposed from the leadership.

As matters evolved, low turnout (29 per cent) at the ballot box saved the Conservative leader. An even more miserable rate of participation in the European Parliament elections one month later (23 per cent) allowed the Tories to claim a victory in that campaign. Mr Hague won a breathing space during which he conducted his third reshuffle, with John Maples, the Shadow Defence Secretary during the Kosovo conflict, assuming the role of Shadow Foreign Secretary. Matters were not to remain peaceful for long, unfortunately. The contest for the Tory nomination as Mayor of London between Lord Archer of Weston-super-Mare and Steven Norris was becoming increasingly acrimonious. Michael Ashcroft, who was a Belize-based businessman whom Mr Hague had appointed as party treasurer in 1998, became a source of controversy and a leaked memo by Ms Platell on how to improve her leader's image ("Project Hague") became the object of ridicule.

The Conservative Party conference that year witnessed the launch of a policy document — the *Common Sense Revolution*. The title and many of the themes were borrowed from the progressive Conservative Party of Ontario in Canada. The text appeared to be a compromise between the intellectual instincts of advisers such as David Willetts and Danny Finkelstein and the more populist pretensions of others, notably Andrew Lansley and Tim Collins, two former Central Office directors who became MPs in 1997 and who were credited with masterminding the Conservative triumph in the European elections. It did, however, pass the muster of critical scrutiny.

A series of events in the last three months of 1999 were to send Mr Hague and the Conservative Party reeling. The most serious involved Lord Archer's withdrawal from the mayoral contest after newspaper allegations that he had asked witnesses to lie for him during his libel victory over the *Daily Star* in 1987. Mr Hague had been warned that Lord Archer was a potential liability but had allowed him to stand and endorsed him in glowing terms.

The Tories then compounded their agony by first discarding Mr Norris from the shortlist of contenders before having to reinstate him to avoid further humiliation.

With the Archer affair still hanging over him, Mr Hague acquired one new MP and lost an existing one. Michael Portillo was elected to serve for Kensington and Chelsea in place of the late Alan Clark. Shaun Woodward, the MP for Witney, was first sacked from the front bench in a row over his liberal stance on homosexuality and then he defected to the Labour Party.

Mr Hague entered 2000 in a distinctly fragile political position. He bought himself some time with a snap reshuffle which saw Mr Portillo become Shadow Chancellor, Francis Maude move to the post of Shadow Foreign Secretary and Archie Norman, the former Asda supremo, become Shadow Environment Secretary. Mr Maples and, more spectacularly, Mr Redwood were sacked. Mr Portillo wasted little time in dropping his party's opposition to the independence of the Bank of England and the minimum wage. He would later persuade Mr Hague that the "tax guarantee" (a pledge to reduce the share of taxation as a proportion of national income in the course of a Parliament) would have to be redefined as well.

The Government was, however, beginning to encounter difficulties of its own which took some of the pressure off the Tory leadership. Sensing a switch in national mood, Mr Hague opted for yet another strategic shift — towards high-profile populism. He made a controversial speech offering sympathy to Tony Martin, a Norfolk farmer convicted of murdering a teenage burglar while allegedly defending his property, and then attacked the Government on asylum-seekers. The Tories also announced a new policy on pensions in the hope of embarrassing ministers.

The local election results in May 2000 were mixed. The Tories again benefited from low turnout and made some sweeping gains in councillors. The distinctly liberal Mr Norris performed well in the mayoral election in the capital which implied to some that Mr Hague had embraced the wrong brand of Conservatism. That impression was compounded by the stunning Liberal Democrat victory over the Tories in a by-election held in Romsey, Hampshire.

The next six weeks were, nonetheless, quite encouraging for the Conservatives. The Government's poll lead shrank, down to 3 per cent in one survey. Mr Hague decided to plump for populism with few reservations. Yet a popular Comprehensive Spending Review produced by Gordon Brown in July and a staggering public relations mistake in August, when Mr Hague appeared to boast of having drunk 14 pints of beer a day in his youth, threw the Tories back on the defensive. They were then rescued by the petrol protests which allowed them to take a lead in the polls just before their own party conference.

That conference also suffered from an element of strategic confusion. A draft manifesto, *Believing in Britain*, was produced which smacked strongly of populism while retaining some of the more intellectual themes which had been highlighted 12 months earlier. But Mr Hague also wanted to reach out to other voters, notably Asians, by emphasising his interest in social policy. Mr Portillo made a very liberal speech while Ann Widdecombe outlined a new policy on automatic fines for cannabis use which had to be discarded within days. It was all very typical of the plight of the Conservative Party.

The petrol effect soon disappeared. A cunning Pre-Budget Report from the Chancellor in November appeased some motorists and enriched pensioners. The Government regained a large lead in the polls and headed towards victory. The Conservatives could do little more than press their preferred themes of tax, the euro, violent crime and asylum policy and hope to invigorate their own core vote. Matters were not helped by Mr Hague delivering a controversial speech in which he accused Labour of plotting to turn Britain into a "foreign land" if re-elected. This would later spark a damaging row over race and multiculturalism led by John Townend, a right-wing MP set to retire at the election anyway, and Lord Taylor of Warwick, the most prominent black member of the Conservative Party.

A technically competent campaign could not overcome the strategic errors and inconsistency which had preceded it. The scale of the Tory defeat in 2001 would therefore mirror that of 1997. And once again Conservative MPs would begin a new Parliament with the search for a new leader.

# KENNEDY FOUND WORDS TO MAKE A DIFFERENCE

## *by* Greg Hurst
### *Parliamentary Correspondent of The Times*

I N THE second week of the 2001 election campaign Charles Kennedy, the Liberal Democrat leader, introduced the phrase that became his byword until polling day: effective opposition.

Having conceded, with disarming and characteristic frankness, that he did not expect to form the next government, he set his sights on leading a "more effective and principled opposition" in the next Parliament.

The tactic was twofold. It signalled an honest dialogue with the electorate about the realistic scale of the third party's ambitions.

It also struck a contrast with the Conservatives. With little doubt that Labour was heading for re-election, Mr Kennedy sought to portray the likely official Opposition as riven by internal divisions and lacking empathy with voters' wishes for better public services.

There was, however, another undercurrent at play. The concept of effective opposition is qualitatively different from "constructive opposition", the guiding light by which his predecessor Paddy Ashdown led the Liberal Democrats into the 1997-2001 Parliament.

Constructive opposition, which provoked controversy among some party members, appeared initially to work well after the 1997 general election as the Labour Government began a series of constitutional reforms supported by the Liberal Democrats.

The two parties had in opposition forged an agreement, named after its principal authors Robin Cook and Robert Maclennan, on a shared programme encompassing devolution for Scotland, Wales and London, removing hereditary peers' voting rights in the Lords and incorporating the European Convention on Human Rights into United Kingdom law.

But tensions developed over its remaining planks. The first crack was the Government's muted response to the Jenkins Commission on proportional representation for the Commons. Relations deteriorated as ministers reneged on a commitment to a referendum on PR, diluted a Freedom of Information Bill and refused to engage the third party in developing fuller plans to reform the House of Lords.

As progress faltered and the Government's popularity waned, Liberal Democrats began to reap the downside of constructive opposition. Party members bridled at speculation that the two parties might eventually merge and Conservatives mocked them as poodles of Labour.

When Charles Kennedy took over the leadership of the party in August 1999 he cooled relations with Labour but struggled for the remainder of the Parliament to establish a distinctive alternative voice without a mandate of his own. He was consistently poor in the Commons, particularly at Prime Minister's Questions.

By fighting his first general election as leader under a banner of effective opposition he attempted finally to shake off the charge that the Liberal Democrats were too close to Labour to hold its ministers effectively to

" CAN I HAVE ANOTHER 20 MINUTES ? I STILL CAN'T DECIDE ...."

account. Was constructive opposition a failure? Cast in its harshest light the policy yielded a single concrete gain of proportional representation for elections to the European Parliament.

The European Parliament Elections Act was probably the sole constitutional reform to which the Government would not have committed itself without its working agreement with the Liberal Democrats, through the forum of a Joint Cabinet Committee drawn from both parties.

Even the new voting method introduced, using regional candidates' lists, was arguably the least defensible form of PR because it gave political parties more power than voters in ranking candidates in order of preference.

Constructive opposition did serve its purpose in providing a credible platform for Ashdown to fight the 1997 general election against a Conservative Party that had alienated large sections of the electorate and Labour, which offered a series of policies with which Liberal Democrats agreed wholeheartedly.

Equally it was central to the Liberal Democrats' longer-term aim of eroding two-party tribalism in British politics to give principled support to legislation it endorsed.

It was the scale of Tony Blair's first-term majority that swamped a strategy designed with tighter Commons voting arithmetic in mind, should Liberal Democrat votes have been needed to survive revolts from the Labour Left or even as a precursor to a Lab-Lib coalition.

After seeing through parts of the programme where the parties shared common ground — the devolution Acts, Human Rights Act, and so on — the Liberal Democrats were thus unable to keep Labour to calling a referendum on PR for Westminster or to more radical democratic reform of the Lords.

The same obstacle of Labour's 179-seat majority cast its giant shadow over the converse task for the Liberal Democrats of opposing the Government and challenging its record.

This illusive task spanned frontline combat in the Commons chamber and media studios to the largely unseen toil in standing committees where the duty of opposition parties is not simply to resist legislation but to improve its detail.

Liberal Democrats claimed some successes in outwitting and embarrassing ministers over policy, the chief weapons left to them.

Malcolm Bruce, the party's Treasury spokesman from 1997 to 1999, coined the phrase that Gordon Brown, the Chancellor, had a "war chest" of surplus revenue. Steve Webb, Social Security spokesman, led criticism of an annual inflation-linked uprating of the basic state pension by 1.1 per cent with the calculation that it amounted to 75p a week.

Menzies Campbell, Liberal Democrat spokesman on Foreign Affairs and Defence, was also widely regarded for his contributions on both. Generally the party's longer serving MPs, such as Mr Campbell, Alan Beith and Simon Hughes, who had less reason for anxiety about their majorities, were the more effective parliamentarians.

T hese tended, however, to be the exception and the 1997-2001 Parliament was characterised by accusations of an arrogant Government able to bypass the Commons and held in check only in the Lords, where Labour lacked a majority and Liberal Democrats held the balance of power.
The party's peers, led for most of the period by Lord Rodgers of Quarry Bank, grew in number to 62 by dissolution and were able to operate much more effectively to block, amend or improve legislation. They proved a highly disciplined force skilled at mustering their numbers for critical whipped divisions.

The marginal nature of many Liberal Democrat MPs' seats and the party's penchant for constituency activism meant that their attendance in the Commons was patchy and contributions from the back benches were frequently on local, not national, issues.

This tendency towards constituency-orientated politics was reflected in free votes on banning handguns and the unsettled question of foxhunting in which Liberal Democrat MPs split, largely reflecting the rural or urban profiles of their seats.

Again there were exceptions. David Heath, MP for Somerton and Frome, was an assiduous attender and active participant in the chamber, while Norman Baker, MP for Lewes, rapidly earned notoriety for determined questioning of policies spanning animal welfare to expenses of Anglican bishops.

It was Mr Baker who took the Government's greatest scalp, but on an issue of probity not policy. His parliamentary questions revealed the intervention by Peter Mandelson in a passport application by Srichand Hinduja, a wealthy sponsor of the Millennium Dome, which led to his resignation as Northern Ireland Secretary.

Tellingly, the outcome caused discomfort among some senior Liberal Democrats, who regretted the fall of the Government's greatest advocate of Lib-Lab co-operation and voting reform.

A nother weakness was the failure to develop convincing policy. This left Liberal Democrats contesting the 2001 election on a platform essentially the same as four years previously, advocating 1p more on basic income tax and a top rate of 50 per cent for those earning more than £100,000 to outspend Labour on core public services. Details altered but the thrust was the same.

The change in leadership was one reason but the party also betrayed a reluctance to embrace radicalism. Mr (now Lord) Ashdown ordered a policy review early in 1998 some of whose ideas deliberately challenged the monopoly provision of public services but proved too much for his members. These crystallised around a proposal to remove the running of schools from local authorities, which was defeated at that year's party conference.

His resignation the following January, which was delayed as the European Parliament Elections Bill hit turbulence in the Lords, caused a hiatus of eight months which left less time for his successor to develop, consult on and communicate new policy before the general election.

Yet the story of how the Liberal Democrats saw several long-held policy goals enacted but saw others elude them before they recoiled from the fire — lest, like Icarus, they flew too close to the sun — should not eclipse their development as an opposition force.

Having doubled the parliamentary party's size from 20 in 1992 to 46 in 1997, Liberal Democrats symbolically claimed a front bench on the Opposition side of the chamber below the gangway shared with the Father of the House, Sir Edward Heath. To do that they had to endure a series of amusing skirmishes with backbench Tory MPs who rose at dawn and put in prayer cards to claim seats on the bench.

More significantly the party's revenue was enhanced by the decision to raise taxpayers' contributions, known as Short money payments, after the former Leader of the Commons, Ted Short, who introduced taxpayer subsidy for parliamentary parties, together with state assistance for opposition parliamentary researchers, whips and leaders' offices, on the recommendation of the Committee for Standards in Public Life. The Liberal Democrats' allocation increased from £410,000 to £1 million.

On becoming leader Charles Kennedy recast his front bench into a "shadow cabinet" supported by junior frontbench spokesmen and left a handful of his MPs as backbenchers, ending the oddity of giving every MP a policy portfolio regardless of ability.

Nonetheless, Mr Kennedy spent the final days of the election campaign pointing to the role of Liberal Democrat peers, rather than his MPs in the last Parliament, as a model for his concept of effective opposition.

Its success will be judged on whether his MPs can, despite the return of a Labour Government with a near-identical majority, shake off the constraints which bound them in the previous Parliament and operate better in the Commons at holding ministers to account.

# TO WIN OUR LOVE, TONY, YOU STILL HAVE TO DELIVER

## *by* Philip Webster

### *Political Editor of The Times*

THE general election of 2001 was never meant to be on June 7. Tony Blair and his allies had planned for at least two years on May 3, the date set down for the local elections, as their day of destiny, the moment when Labour could make history and secure a second, consecutive full term. Labour was to take its place in the history books — but only after Mr Blair's plans were thrown awry by an outbreak of foot-and-mouth disease. As the epidemic took hold in the countryside Mr Blair became consumed by the need to beat it. It took all his energy and time and, against the wishes of most of his Cabinet and party, he postponed the election. It was an agonising decision but one that was to be completely vindicated.

Even more than the previous one, Election 2001 was Mr Blair's victory.

If the enduring image of the 1997 election campaign was the defeat of Michael Portillo at Enfield Southgate, a left-arm jab from John Prescott on an egg-throwing protester will last as the most arresting memory of 2001.

And how the campaign needed it. The democratic process owes a lot to the man who, after the election, was given a strengthened role of Deputy Prime Minister to ease him towards the end of an honourable parliamentary career.

Until Mr Prescott's encounter in Rhyl with the unfortunate Craig Evans, the country seemed barely aware that an election was under way. And although turnout was eventually to be a record low, who knows what would have happened had Mr Prescott not jolted an indifferent electorate into life? The bonus for Mr Prescott was that he did neither himself nor his party any harm. The polls suggested that the public backed his attack on his assailant.

Mr Prescott may have been Labour's unexpected card. But they were handed another gift in the shape of a quiet, unassuming, exceedingly clever, and, unfortunately for him, utterly straightforward West Country Tory MP.

Few would have heard of Oliver Letwin, the Shadow Chief Secretary to the Treasury and MP for Dorset West, before hostilities began. But he committed the cardinal sin, during a chat with journalists from the *Financial Times*, of putting a figure — £20 billion — on the Conservatives' long-term tax-cutting ambitions.

The problem for his party was that William Hague and Michael Portillo had announced plans for tax cuts of only £8 billion, and had painstakingly outlined the spending cuts that would have to be made to pay for them.

It was a gaffe that Gordon Brown, Chancellor of the Exchequer and Labour's chief election strategist again as in 1997, seized with relish. The indefatigable Mr Brown, who managed to chair all but one of Labour's daily press conferences while managing to pop up in all parts of the country, was one of his party's stars, managing those gatherings with the discipline of the "Headmaster from Hell" and exploiting ammuni-

" AH, YOU MUST BE THE BOY WHO WANTS TO GO INTO POLITICS "

tion to the full. Mr Letwin's indiscretion was a severe blow to the Conservatives. And when he went to ground in his constituency, with an excited press pack in full cry in pursuit of him, things got even worse. After the Tories made a strong start on the issue of taxation, the charge that there was a hidden Tory agenda of cuts was hard to handle and put them badly on the back foot. The focus groups showed, as the campaign wore on, that the Labour lead on the economy and taxation, two traditionally strong Conservative areas, was widening. Mr Letwin's honesty cost his party dear in terms of momentum in the campaign. The Tory taxation attack had given Labour a first, uncomfortable weekend. After the £20 billion "bombshell", the Conservatives were never able to regain the initiative.

The consolation for Mr Letwin is that, however embarrassing it seemed at the time, his slip-up would have had no impact on the overall result.

For the 2001 election will be remembered most as the poll which changed very little.

In the aftermath of Labour's 1997 landslide there were many startled new MPs who had won seats that the party had never remotely considered as targets. Many of them assumed that after one Parliament they would be trying to get back their old jobs. But astonishingly nearly all of them got back in. The Conservatives went through the Parliament without any great expectations of getting back to power in one go. But all of them, without exception, expected to make considerable strides on their 1997 performance when they achieved the paltry tally of 165 seats.

In 2001 they went a miserly one better, throwing the party into yet another leadership crisis. They began the 2001 Parliament in a worse state than 1997 because Labour, although suffering from the apathy factor in its heartlands, consolidated its position in the marginal seats that the Conservatives needed to grab back to make any impact.

The story of the campaign was of the Labour Party sticking rigidly (with one notable exception) to its grid, drawn up in the months beforehand; and the Conservatives playing their core issues for all they were worth in the early days, before concluding that they were making no headway and moving leftwards. It was to no avail. Mr Hague bowed out with dignity and speed.

But things had seemed more promising for them at the start. Mr Blair took a lot of flak from the press for the way he launched the campaign. After going to see the Queen on May 8 Mr Blair went to the St Saviour's and St Olave's church school in Southwark where he was televised, cross behind him and sacred stained glass above him, and announced the election to an audience of children. It looked faintly ridiculous and, in the eyes of some, sinister.

**M**r Hague was straight out of the traps. The manifestos had been expected the following week. But the Tories published theirs straightaway, with an eye-catching 6p reduction in petrol the centrepiece of their £8 billion tax-cutting plans.

With the independent Institute of Fiscal Studies helpfully pointing out that Mr Brown would have to raise taxes by £5 billion a year if he was to maintain his current level of spending in the latter years of the new Parliament, Labour was suddenly on the defensive.

There was no wobble at Millbank, just a tremor. And for once they departed from prelaid plans. They rushed forward the publication of their five-point "pledge card", a repeat of their 1997 tactic, in an attempt to seize back the early initiative in the race. There were other developments of use to the Tories — the spectacle of the defector Shaun Woodward being forced on a reluctant northern Labour seat among them. But the campaign had not settled down. A Tory Eurosceptic maverick, Sir Peter Tapsell, provided some weekend entertainment by comparing the European vision of Gerhard Schröder, the German Chancellor, to Hitler's personal manifesto. In campaign terms the Tories were ahead on points. Then came the *FT* report suggesting £20 billion of Conservative tax cuts. No source was included in the story. But before long Mr Letwin was named and could not demur. He disappeared to avoid the press. Mr Brown went into overdrive. "Wanted" posters were published, promising a £20 billion reward for finding Mr Letwin.

It was the perfect springboard for Labour's manifesto launch, staged, according to the grid, on Wednesday, May 16. Labour staked its appeal for a second term on a pledge of five years of unrelenting reform of the public services, with increasing use of the private sector if necessary. The middle classes were kept sweet with a promise that the standard and top rates of tax would not be raised, but overall it was a bolder document than 1997, building on the reputation for economic competence the party had gained in the first term. But it did not make the top story in the following morning's newspapers. "Events" conspired to relegate the manifesto to the inside pages. First of all Mr Blair's choreographed visit to a Birmingham hospital was ambushed by Sharron Storer, who vented her anger at him over the treatment received by her partner, a cancer patient. The stories were being rewritten when, suddenly, that Prescott punch was landed in North Wales. The balloon went up; manifestos were forgotten. At last the country took notice. The election had started with Labour holding a lead, according to surveys, of between 15 and 20 per cent, and nothing seemed to be having an impact. At Conservative Central Office the mood of the young workers was remarkably upbeat. For many it was their first election and they were going to enjoy it. The reports that kept coming in from the campaign suggested that the situation was far better than polls suggested.

C harles Kennedy, meanwhile, was having an excellent campaign. Criss-crossing the country, he clocked up a staggering 15,500 miles, far more than his rivals. Any who doubted his capacity to last out the gruelling campaign were proved severely in error as he promoted his policies of free long-term care for the elderly, the abolition of university tuition fees and, with less fanfare, raising the top rate of tax to 50 per cent and putting 1p on income tax to increase spending on public services. As so often the Liberal Democrats improved their position as the contest proceeded. It was time for Mr Kennedy to prove that there was life after Paddy Ashdown. He succeeded and fulfilled his own hopes and expectations that he could beat Sir Paddy's record tally of 46 seats.

Back in the Labour-Tory battle, routine cards were being played — for the Tories, asylum and a threat that Mr Brown would raise national insurance; for Labour, schools and hospitals.

With two weeks to go Mr Hague, with no obvious sign of an improvement in his position, made a desperate last-ditch attempt to turn the tide. There were two weeks to save the pound, he declared. In what was clearly a gamble, he apparently accepted that a future referendum on the euro would be lost by the Tories and that the election was the last chance.

He began a countdown; 13 days to save the pound, 12 days to save it, and so on. Baroness Thatcher made her usual, colourful appearance, breaking Conservative policy on the euro, but no one really seemed to care. Mr Hague used an interview with *The Times* to soften slightly his view that the election was the last chance to save sterling. The fight would carry on after the election. With a week to go the Liberal Democrats were still on the move, but the main parties were very much where they had been at the start. In a last throw the Tory leader, having shored up his core vote, tried to broaden his appeal, reaching out to floating voters in the language of Conservative One Nationism. Finally, in a belated damage-limitation exercise he began warning of a Labour landslide, calling on people to burst Mr Blair's bubble. It was all too late, and no one close to Mr Hague really believed it would make any difference. An air of desperation hung over Central Office even though the mantra that it was "better on the ground" continued to be preached. In the end the polls turned out to be right. As the results came in on the night of Thursday, June 7, it was clear that Mr Blair would be back in Downing Street, safer than ever. The result from Torbay — won by the Liberal Democrats in 1997 by 12 votes but now in 2001 with a majority of more than 6,000 — sent despondency through the Conservative ranks. It was not to be their night; if anything it was worse. The Liberal Democrats ended with 52 seats.

Mr Hague had made up his mind months before that he would go straightaway if he did not improve his party's position. He flew down from Yorkshire to Central Office and quietly bade farewell in front of tearful staff. For Mr Blair it was a very different morning after. This time there was no triumphalism. He was well aware that Labour had won the voters' cautious respect rather than affection in its first term. Next time it would be judged more harshly, probably with a more effective Opposition up against it. He saw the Queen, went back to Downing Street and thanked the voters for their trust. He had been given an "instruction to deliver", he said, and went back to work.

# STAY-AT-HOME ELECTION THAT CHANGED LITTLE

## *by* Peter Riddell
### *Assistant Editor (Politics) of The Times*

THE 2001 general election will be remembered as much for the number of registered voters who did not turn out as for the decisions of those who did. On the surface little apparently changed. A mere 21 seats changed hands between the parties in mainland Britain — the least for a century — though six out of 18 did in the more volatile politics of Northern Ireland. The already mammoth Labour majority of 179 over all other parties in the House of Commons slipped slightly to 167.

Some decline in turnout had been widely forecast on the basis of opinion polls, but no one expected as large a drop as occurred, from 71.4 per cent in 1997, already a postwar low, to 59.4 per cent. This was the lowest since the introduction of the adult franchise in 1918 (for all men over 21 and women over 30). This drop meant that, for the first time, many more people, 41 per cent of the registered electorate, did not vote than voted for the winning party, roughly 25 per cent of the electorate. This compares with a previous low of 29 per cent of the electorate backing Labour in the October 1974 election and nearly a third supporting Margaret Thatcher in her 1983 landslide and Tony Blair in his 1997 victory.

Seats were exchanged between the parties (all figures are by comparison with 1997). Labour ended up with 413 seats after losing six overall, gaining two (one from the Tories and one from Plaid Cymru), but losing eight (five to the Tories, one to the Liberal Democrats, one to Plaid Cymru and one to the Independent Kidderminster Hospital candidate).

The Conservatives finished with 166, after gaining just one seat overall, losing eight seats (seven to the Liberal Democrats and one to Labour) and gaining nine (five from Labour, two from the Liberal Democrats, one from the Scottish Nationalists and one from the Independent in Tatton). The Liberal Democrats advanced to 52 after gaining a net six seats, winning eight (seven from the Tories and one from Labour), while losing two to the Tories.

Otherwise, Plaid Cymru exchanged seats with Labour to end up unchanged on four, while the Scottish Nationalists lost one, to the Tories, to finish with five.

Yet this picture of little overall change in the political landscape is in itself remarkable in view of the extent of Labour gains in 1997. Constituencies which had never been Labour before then were retained comfortably. The drop in Labour support in its safe seats did not matter electorally, and was matched by a strengthening of support for the party from the middle classes, particularly in the key suburban marginals.

In the United Kingdom as a whole, Labour won 40.7 per cent of the vote, down 2.5 percentage points since 1997. This was a lower share than Margaret Thatcher won in any of her three victories when the Tories had a smaller Commons majority. Labour won 10.72 million votes, down from 13.52 million in 1997. This is the lowest absolute number of votes won by a winning party in the postwar era, less even than the 11.46 million that Labour won in October 1974 when the party had a bare overall majority. Labour's total on June 7, 2001, is smaller than the party won in the 1979 and 1992 elections which it lost.

" To THINK I DID THIS JOB BECAUSE I WANTED TO MEET PEOPLE "

The Conservatives raised their share by one point to 31.7 per cent, but this was still the second lowest in the modern mass franchise era. This was just above the 30.8 per cent gained by Labour in 1987, even though the Tories won 43 fewer seats than the 229 that Labour achieved then. This reflects the bias of the electoral system against the Tories, and in favour of Labour, which is now more successful in concentrating its vote in the key seats where it matters most for the party.

After seeing their vote share drop at each election from 1987 until 1997, the Liberal Democrats increased their share by 1.5 points to 18.3 per cent.

Among the minority parties on the mainland, the UK Independence Party won most votes (390,575 or 1.5 per cent), though this was less than half the combined total won by the UKIP and the other main Eurosceptic party, the old Referendum Party, combined in 1997.

The Greens won 166,477 votes, or 0.6 per cent of the national vote, up 0.4 points on 1997. The hard-left parties (Scottish Socialist, Socialist Alliance and Socialist Labour) together won 187,000 votes, or 0.7 per cent of the total. The far Right, notably the British National Party, made an impact only in the two Oldham seats.

Overall, the share of the vote of others fell from 4.8 to 4 per cent (excluding the three main parties, the Scottish and Welsh Nationalists and Northern Ireland parties). This largely reflects the decline in support for the Eurosceptic parties.

These figures suggest that public disenchantment with the main parties was mainly reflected in the sharp drop in turnout rather than in any large-scale switching to fringe parties, with the exception of the Greens in a handful of mainly middle-class seats with a high proportion of voters involved in higher or further education. For instance, Green candidates won 3.5 per cent of the vote in Bristol West, around the university; 3.3 per in Cambridge; 2.8 per cent in Oxford West and Abingdon; and 4.7 per cent in Hampstead and Highgate.

T he most striking statistic of the election was the fall in turnout. This has been attributed to a belief that the result was a foregone conclusion, that the result did not matter anyway, disappointment with Labour's performance in office (particularly among its traditional working-class supporters), and a longer-term detachment from the political process (especially among young people). All these factors probably contributed to the drop, as suggested by the particularly low turnout among young people and in Labour bastions in northern industrial cities. The proportionate drop in turnout was much higher in safe Labour seats than marginal ones.

Yet the drop in turnout is also worrying for the Tories. If much of the decline on the Labour side can be explained by disenchantment or regarding the result as a foregone conclusion, the Tories have no such comfort. The tiny rise in their percentage share masks a drop of 1.24 million people voting Tory since 1997 to 8.35 million, and of a huge 5.69 million, or two fifths, since the record peak won by John Major in 1992.

While there was little change in the overall distribution of voters between the parties — a mere 1.9 per cent swing from Labour to the Tories nationally — there were marked regional variations. The Tories performed better than average either in safe Labour seats or in seats they were defending rather than in constituencies they were trying to capture.

Labour did worst in terms of share of the vote in its northern strongholds, even though it did not lose any seats north of Chesterfield. There was a 3.1 per cent swing from Labour to the Tories in the North East, 2.8 per cent in Yorkshire and Humberside and 3.8 per cent in Wales. But in none of these three regions did Labour lose a seat. The two were co-related since the fall in Labour's share of the vote and turnout were partly linked to the safeness of the seats. In parts of Liverpool, Manchester and Newcastle upon Tyne, there were swings from Labour to the Liberal Democrats.

By contrast, Labour performed best in its most marginal seats. Defending Labour MPs with majorities of less than 10 per cent increased their share of the vote by 1.8 points, while the Tories in these seats improved their share by only 0.5 points.

This differential pattern was seen most clearly in the South East of England, where many of its most marginal seats are concentrated. The swing from Labour to the Tories was just 0.8 per cent in London and 0.3 per cent in the rest of the South East. This enabled Labour to see off Tory challenges in most places with the exception of the eastern edge of London and Essex, where the Tories won three seats (Romford, Upminster and Castle Point). By contrast, the expected Tory gains in the highly marginal seats of Kent affected by the influx of asylum-seekers failed to materialise.

The Tories' overall plight was summed up by their failure to make any headway in North London or around the M25 belt. Indeed, in several of the seats which Labour won in 1997, there were further swings from the Tories to Labour, of 3 per cent in Harrow East, 5.4 per cent in Harrow West, and 1.5 per cent in Wimbledon, to take just a few examples.

These regional trends were linked to a shift in the social pattern of support for the parties. Labour made further gains among the middle classes while losing ground among the working classes. The Tory lead in the middle classes slipped from five to two points (38 to 36 per cent), according to analyses by ICM. Among professionals and managers (ABs), the Tories have fallen since 1997 from 41 to 40 per cent, with Labour improving from 31 to 33 per cent.

Labour has lost ground among the working classes, mainly because more of its supporters stayed at home. Its lead over the Tories among this group has fallen from 31 to 21 per cent since 1997. Among skilled workers (C2s) Labour is three percentage points down to 47 per cent, with the Tories two points up at 29 per cent. This was reflected in the swing to the Tories in Essex, where there is a heavy concentration of C2s. Among unskilled workers and unemployed (DEs), the Labour share was down seven points to 50 per cent, with the Tories six points up on 27 per cent. The Liberal Democrats have gained particularly among DEs.

But the breakdown of class support is only part of the story. According to the exit polls, there were sharp differences in turnout depending on age. Roughly twice as many people aged over 65 turned out to vote as did 18 to 24-year-olds — 79 to 38 per cent, with 35 to 64-year-olds in the middle on 62 per cent. The Tories enjoyed a lead among the 65-pluses, of 42 to 37 per cent over Labour. In every other age group, Labour was ahead — by 47 to 29 per cent among 18 to 34-year-olds.

The implication is that, if the Tories were still ahead among pensioners, then Labour must have done very well among the working-age middle classes, particularly in key marginal seats. Millions of people in suburban and new town constituencies in the southern half of England who had voted Tory in 1992 deserted the party in 1997 and 2001, and many switched to Labour.

Consequently, the election result was more complicated than it appeared at first hand: a conditional endorsement for Labour, and a second rout in a row for the Tories, despite the slight increase in the party's share of the vote.

# REFORM FAILED TO KILL OFF OLD CAMPAIGN HABITS

□ *THE 2001 general election was the first to take place after a set of constitutional reforms which were clearly the most substantial package since the legislation enacted by William Gladstone in the first of his four terms as Prime Minister (1868-74) and could legitimately be considered the most far-reaching since the Glorious Revolution of 1688 and its aftermath. Scotland acquired its own Parliament for the first time in almost 300 years while Wales assumed a less-powerful Assembly. Northern Ireland had experienced devolution before during the unhappy Stormont period (1922-72) but the institution established through the Good Friday agreement was radically different from its predecessor. The fact that the three different chambers all enjoyed distinct electoral systems and particular legislative authority further complicated matters. In the Westminster election, therefore, a set of "national" issues might not apply in any one of, pair of, or all of Scotland, Wales, and Northern Ireland. It had been assumed that the 2001 campaign would therefore need to be different to take account of these developments. In fact, as the following essays demonstrate, old habits died hard and the election contest was conducted much as if devolution had never happened. Whether or not the Westminster political class will be able to sidestep their own constitutional handiwork at the next general election is, however, extremely debatable.*

## Fraser Nelson

### *on the campaign in Scotland*

JUST before being caught on tape denouncing John Reid as a "patronising bastard", Helen Liddell was privately congratulating herself on burying the Scottish National Party.

"It's the worst SNP result since I was general secretary of the party," she confided to Henry McLeish, the First Minister, who had forgotten about the live microphone on his tie. "It shows devolution works." Neither would have admitted this in public. Officially, Labour in Scotland did not care about the SNP. Its strategy was to defeat the nationalists by ignoring them, concentrating instead on the already-vanquished Scottish Tories. This seemed to work. The SNP vote fell for the first time since 1983 and it became the only party in Scotland to lose a seat — to the Tories.

The Scottish election 2001 was a strategists' nightmare. Devolution had put entirely new political dynamics in play. Promises on schools and hospitals could not be kept by any MP. Both are now run by Scotland's devolved Lib-Lab coalition government which has its own elections in May 2003. Fighting a campaign while respecting these realities would be difficult. So all parties, without exception, ignored them. The result was a brazen campaign of half-truths which ignored Scotland's new constitutional settlement. All parties agreed that schools and hospitals were too powerful as election weapons to be left stacked at Hadrian's Wall.

The new lines across Scottish government were deemed an irrelevance. Brian Wilson, one of Labour's most senior Scots MPs, said the distinction was "theological". Labour's pledge card demonstrated this point. Of its five promises, three (hospitals, crime and education) could not be carried out from Westminster and were thus irrelevant. Labour excused itself by saying its theme was the "partnership" between London and Edinburgh. So in Scotland the manifesto mutated. It mixed policies ("we'd like to do this in Scotland, but we can't") with promises ("we will raise pensions").

The Tory manifesto was no better. Policies on health and education sat alongside promises on Europe and pensions. Sir Malcolm Rifkind, who led the campaign, explained that he was "fighting Labour on all levels of government". The Liberal Democrat UK manifesto gave English voters a taste of the half-truths being peddled north of the border.

"In Scotland, where Liberal Democrats are part of the government, we have already guaranteed free personal care," its front page boasted. "We have also abolished tuition fees." Both claims are untrue. The Lib Dems in Scotland voted against free personal care — twice. A "review" had been set up thanks to a Labour U-turn. Nothing had been "guaranteed". Neither had the Scottish tuition fee been "abolished". It was reduced to a flat £2,000, renamed and made payable on graduation.

The SNP was the only party which could have exposed the duplicity coming from its London-based rivals. Instead, it joined in. It brought out all its policies on police, health, education. It intended to use the 2001 campaign as a dress rehearsal for its main target: the Holyrood 2003 election. Its main offensive was a call for fiscal autonomy. It placed a letter in *The Scotsman* from 11 academics arguing that Scotland should cut its financial ties from the Treasury, collect its own taxes and spend only what it raised. This debate lit up the political sky briefly then died after two days.

The Tories tried a similar tactic: accusing Labour of secret plans to abolish the Barnett formula, a 26-year-old mechanism that automatically decides Scotland's share of UK public spending. It was Alastair Campbell who set the record straight. Barnett would stay for the next parliamentary session. The Tories' Plan B was to accuse Labour of secret plans to abolish the Scottish Secretary job. Tony Blair poured scorn on this.

The Tory victory in Galloway and Upper Nithsdale was a shock to its high command. It was predicted by no one and showed how adrift the party had become. It had no idea what it was doing right. Several Scots Tory grassroot workers believe that this shows it must mass-produce Peter Duncan, now the lone Scots Tory, and find more "real people" with "real" jobs forming an antidote to the spun politician.

Not only had the SNP lost Galloway, it had held Perth against the Tories with a gossamer majority of 48. The party had recalled five of its six MPs to Holyrood and had put up a B-team of new faces — most of them party apparatchiks. But the SNP has also given Westminster its most talented politician: Alex Salmond. The former party leader plans to use guerrilla political tactics to ensure that his cadre of four MPs punch above their weight. Although only one Scottish seat was lost in the Scottish campaign, 21 changed hands. Mass retirement to Holyrood has seen the largest single influx of new Scottish politicians in one session. Those who moan about Westminster's McMafia have one comforting thought. Scotland's over-representation in the House of Commons will end at the next general election as the Boundary Commission redivides the country into about 58 constituencies.

This means about 14 Scottish seats will disappear completely, MPs and all. Lesser-known Scots MPs must spend the next session persuading their parties, not their constituents, that they deserve to hold on to their seats.

# Valerie Elliott

## *on the campaign in Wales*

The striking feature of the election campaign in Wales was that its focus was on national UK-wide issues. Campaigning itself, except for the infamous Prescott punch in Rhyl, was also low-key, and voters appeared to have little appetite for the whole process.

There had been fears that North Wales farmers and hauliers, who had played a significant role during last autumn's fuel protests, would create some sparks. But if there were some grand plans to block roads and encourage mutiny they did not pay off. Some believe that the devastation and despair of foot-and-mouth on Anglesey and parts of Mid Wales dented enthusiasm for further trouble.

The only issue which surfaced and which threatens to bring division between the Government and the Assembly is GM crops. On this a curious stand-off has emerged. It is government policy to continue with the scientific tests. Yet clearly the Government's collective responsibility does not extend to the Assembly or even Welsh Labour MPs. Labour candidates joined in protests against trials in Pembrokeshire and Clwyd with no rebuke from the Labour leadership. The Welsh Assembly is certain to exert pressure on the centre to keep trials away from the Principality, but ministers will have to explain this dichotomy.

Senior Labour Party figures in Wales were delighted with the conduct of their election campaign. The folk-hero appeal of Rhodri Morgan, the Assembly's First Secretary, did much to halt the progress of Plaid Cymru support from North and Mid Wales and into the traditional Labour territory, the South Wales Valleys.

This was the prime target area for Plaid and its new leader, Ieuan Wyn Jones, to flaunt their growing band of followers. After all, they had prevented Labour gaining an overall majority in the Assembly two years before. But Labour's core vote held up and Wales returned 34 out of its 40 MPs to Westminster, the same figure as 1997.

Labour also scored a coup by seizing Ynys Mon (Anglesey), the seat being vacated by Mr Wyn Jones. In a four-way marginal, Plaid had expected to hold the seat. It was compensated, however, by wresting control of Carmarthen East and Dinefwr from Labour, part of which used to be held by the veteran Welsh Nationalist Gwynfor Evans. The party still has four MPs in the House of Commons.

More importantly for Labour the Conservatives failed again to clinch a single seat. Roger Evans, the former Tory MP trying to regain Monmouth, put up a valiant campaign but was defeated by Labour's Huw Edwards, who secured a majority of 384.

The Liberal Democrat Party managed to hold on to its two seats, Montgomery and Brecon and Radnor. The latter seat was vigorously contested as a four-way marginal following the retirement of Richard Livesey.

Devolution had little impact in the election, but it will be interesting to see if Rhodri Morgan secures more powers for his fiefdom by 2003.

# Tim Hames

## *on the campaign in Northern Ireland*

The general election campaign in Northern Ireland differed from that on mainland Britain in at least four crucial respects: the political landscape had altered dramatically since May 1997; the Westminster results in 2001 were plainly unpredictable; the electorate was sufficiently inspired to vote in its usual numbers; and a large proportion of parliamentary seats would ultimately change hands.

On the day in 1997 that Tony Blair became Prime Minister the IRA was still conducting a military campaign, having abandoned a ceasefire in spectacular style at Docklands 15 months earlier. The process of political negotiations between the parties was thus frozen. Mr Blair swiftly travelled to Northern Ireland and with Mo Mowlam, his first Northern Ireland Secretary at his side, called on the IRA to still its arsenal and take part in another round of discussions. The election of Bertie Ahern and his Fianna Fail party in the Republic of Ireland helped to convince the IRA Army Council that it should announce a second ceasefire. With the assistance of the former US Senator George Mitchell a political accord, the Good Friday or Belfast agreement, was reached in 1998 although that treaty relied on textual ambiguity in many areas to achieve consensus. The document was endorsed by 72 per cent of Ulster's adult residents in a referendum shortly afterwards. Elections for an Assembly were held and David Trimble emerged as First Minister with Seamus Mallon of the SDLP as his deputy. A row over the terrorists' weapons forced Peter Mandelson, Mr Blair's second Northern Ireland Secretary, to suspend the various institutions created by the Good Friday agreement in February 2000. A further compromise allowed for their restoration five months later.

The fact that the agreement did not result in IRA decommissioning, or at least not in a form recognised as valid by Unionists or most neutral observers, inevitably cast a long shadow over the 2001 elections. Mr Trimble's opponents within his own party and, especially, the Democratic Unionist Party (DUP), were determined to turn the Westminster contest into a de facto referendum on the peace process. On the nationalist side, Sinn Fein sought to displace the SDLP as the premier political party.

In truth, though, the election was more complicated than a simple referendum on the constitutional question. The quality of individual candidates mattered more than in Great Britain and a variety of local issues — education, health, transport and pensions — also entered the equation. Their power was reinforced by the set of district council elections, originally scheduled for May 17 but postponed because of the foot-and-mouth outbreak and also held on June 7. Voters seemed to like devolution even if they were dissatisfied about police reform or decommissioning.

The campaign proved lively and the only major poll, conducted on behalf of *The Belfast Telegraph*, indicated that the established parties, the Ulster Unionists and SDLP, should be able to hold off their opponents. A series of electoral understandings, notably the willingness of the non-sectarian Alliance Party to stand down for pro-agreement Unionists, also appeared to provide the UUP with more secure political foundations. Mr Trimble had threatened to quit as First Minister 24 days after the election if no progress was recorded in decommissioning. That stance, while infuriating nationalists, seemed likely to pacify most Unionist electors. This did not prove to be an accurate assessment of the events to follow.

The election produced a series of upsets. The DUP won Belfast North by a surprisingly large margin from a pro-agreement Ulster Unionist and also picked up the seat of Strangford where John Taylor, the UUP deputy leader, had decided to retire. In an entirely unexpected development the party also snatched Londonderry East from William Ross, an anti-agreement Ulster Unionist. Mr Trimble saw his own majority in Upper Bann slashed by the DUP. The UUP extracted some revenge by taking Antrim South back from the DUP (who had won it from them in a by-election in 2000) and by defeating Robert McCartney, an independent anti-agreement Unionist, in North Down.

This set of results was not, in itself, devastating for Mr Trimble. But his party also lost two seats to Sinn Fein. The first was in West Tyrone, where an anti-agreement Unionist was defeated in a seat with a substantial majority of nationalist electors. The second occurred in Fermanagh and South Tyrone where James Cooper, a supporter of Mr Trimble, lost an acrimonious battle by 58 votes and threatened to ask the courts to annul the outcome. Sinn Fein thus finished with four seats compared with three for the SDLP, and won a slightly higher number of votes.

T his set of outcomes radically altered the structure of Ulster politics. The Ulster Unionists had entered the contest holding nine seats (but five of these MPs had turned against the Good Friday agreement), the DUP held three (including its by-election triumph in Antrim South), while Robert McCartney had the remaining Unionist slot. After polling day the UUP found itself with a mere six MPs (only two of whom, Mr Trimble and Lady Hermon, the new Member for North Down, could be considered pro-agreement), while the DUP had five. As the district council elections were disappointing for mainstream Unionism as well, severe internal strife was inevitable. A series of meetings was held in London and Belfast as John Reid, the third Northern Ireland Secretary in less than three years, considered how best to respond to the new situation.

Ulster had again returned to political crisis. Ministers and local politicians alike were surprised at the DUP performance. The eclipse of the SDLP by Sinn Fein was no less awkward. Mr Trimble survived his party's annual general meeting but his long-term prospects look bleak. It appeared even more implausible that he could stay First Minister for long if the IRA did not deliver a decommissioning package. Barely hours after having kissed hands again with the Queen, the Prime Minister was presented with what would be his first and most complicated second-term political crisis.

# WARY POLLSTERS EMERGE UNSCATHED THIS TIME

## by Michael Hart
### of Exeter College, Oxford

**T**HE election was called on May 8. From the outset the opinion polls were unanimous — Labour was going to win, and by a wide margin. On May 9 the *Daily Express* declared on its front page "Blair by 250" (NOP). As the campaign progressed, Labour's lead was inexorable. No event occurred to change public attitudes, nor did any issue seize the imagination enough to alter polls.

The pollsters had something to prove. They were ridiculed in 1992 when they predicted a Labour victory. They overestimated Labour in 1997. In 2001 they repeated this, but now there are more reasons to excuse a small statistical error. It became evident during the course of the election that there would, again, not be a national uniform swing and that the turnout was likely to decline. Although these features cannot be reflected in overall figures they were correctly identified in the commentaries accompanying many polls, especially later in the campaign. Fewer people said they were "very interested" or "fairly interested" in the election than in 1997, but nevertheless the proportion saying that they would definitely vote was always substantially higher than the 59 per cent who did turn out.

The national polls were dominated by MORI, NOP, ICM, Gallup and Rasmussen. Their findings suggested dramatically different Labour majorities, but this may have had more to do with their different sampling methods than with fluctuations in opinion. Most polls were conducted by telephone, only MORI collecting its data face to face. Differences emerged between polls which asked the blunt question of their interviewees "Who do you intend to vote for?" and those which, before asking the question, made mention of the parties contesting the election. Questions could be made more precise after the nominations closed and the list of candidates was known. MORI changed its methodology to reflect this and its polls began to suggest a slight narrowing of Labour's lead. Polls which asked questions about attitudes and issues also found slightly different outcomes according to whether interviewees were presented with a menu of issues or whether they were asked to name issues themselves. The latter method suggested that the Conservatives' emphasis on Europe and the future of the pound had failed to ignite the electorate, and this was a contributory factor in the shift of emphasis of their campaign in its closing stages.

Opinion polls can only represent a snapshot in time, reflecting views at the actual time of sampling. Over the timescale of a general election they can identify trends, but not until the last few days of an election can they be said to have a predictive capacity. Viewed in this way the polls were relatively consistent. Indeed, ever since 1997 Labour had enjoyed a lead, usually in double figures, over the Conservatives — something not achieved by any other government of modern times. It was an open secret that the election had been pencilled-in for May 3, only to be delayed because of foot-and-mouth disease. The delay did nothing to harm Labour. Just before the delay became apparent, MORI in *The Sunday Telegraph* suggested Labour leading by 48 per cent to 32 per cent (April 1) and ICM in *The Guardian* agreed (49 per cent to 34 per cent). By the be-

" JUST AN 'X' HERE IN THE LABOUR BOX, THERE'S A GOOD BOY "

ginning of the campaign proper Labour's lead, if anything, was even bigger

Throughout the month of May 8 to June 7 the Conservative percentage seldom varied. Seven polls put them at under 30 per cent. Only one put them as high as 34 per cent. Averaging all polls (itself slightly risky because of different sample sizes), the Conservatives stood at 30.3 per cent. It has become a common observation that Conservative supporters are more likely to decline to disclose their voting intention than supporters of other parties, and some polls were weighted to try to take account of this. An equally plausible claim in an election with such a low turnout is that Conservatives were more likely to vote than their Labour opposite numbers and that this marginally increased the actual Conservative percentage on polling day. This claim is strengthened by pollsters' findings during the campaign that Conservative support, although lagging far behind Labour, was also firmer.

Labour's vote appeared to be more fluid. From a high point of 55 per cent to a low of 43 per cent in the polls, the party's alleged support shifted not only more than the Conservatives' but also in a patternless way (except that all the final polls put Labour at 47 per cent or less). During the campaign Labour lost support overall to the Liberal Democrats, but this disguises a triangular movement. Labour did lose support to the Liberal Democrats, partly because of the willingness of Labour voters to shift to the Liberal Democrats in constituencies in which Labour entered the contest in third place — again something very difficult for polls to identify precisely because of the late decisions which such voters often make. But Labour also lost a small amount directly to the Conservatives, and even more from those who declared themselves Labour supporters who ultimately did not vote. Even from the fieldwork conducted on June 2 - 3, with the resulting polls published on June 5, 6, or 7, Labour's final support was overestimated by between 2 per cent and 6 per cent.

T he final polls for the Liberal Democrats and the smaller third parties were accurate predictions, even though support outside the two main parties is notoriously softer. The Liberal Democrats gained support modestly but firmly during the course of the election, and their leader Charles Kennedy was recognised by nearly twice as many respondents by June 7 as on May 8. As coverage of the Liberal Democrats increased in all the media, so did their poll ratings — a feature which was also true of the 1997 election.

The politics of Scotland and Wales involve a different pattern, (and Northern Ireland even more so, which is omitted from the table of polls published opposite), and in each country Labour maintained a bigger lead over the Conservatives than in England. The polls published exclusively for Scotland slightly overestimated SNP support and failed to detect the rise in support for the Liberal Democrats, while those in Wales also overestimated Plaid Cymru. The Labour lead in both was, however, so great that such a difference mattered little.

Even the last polls showed a Labour lead over the Conservatives of between 11 per cent and 17 per cent. In the event it was just short of 9 per cent. The different effects of regional and sub-regional voting make predicting a translation of percentages into seats hazardous. The closest estimate was ICM, published in *The Guardian* on June 6, which predicted a vote of 43 per cent to Labour, 32 per cent to the Conservatives and 19 per cent to the Liberal Democrats. On this basis ICM predicted an overall majority of 165. In fact it was 167. Peter Kellner, in the London *Evening Standard* as early as May 29, predicted Labour on 412 (it was 413), Conservatives on 163 (actually 166) and Liberal Democrats on 53 (actually 52), an overall majority of 165. It would be impossible in the world of polling, in changing electoral geography, to expect anything more accurate than these two forecasts.

The polls emerged relatively unscathed from the election. The errors they reported were not of their own making. In military history it is often remarked that generals prepare to fight the last war, not the next one. With such a disparate, changing and unpredictably local voting pattern in Britain today, pollsters can hardly be blamed for anything different.

# THE POLLS BY THE POLLSTERS 2001

| Pollster | Date | Published | C | Lab | LD | Other | Lab lead |
|---|---|---|---|---|---|---|---|
| Gallup | May 17 | D Telegraph | 32 | 48 | 13 | 7 | 16 |
| Gallup | May 24 | D Telegraph | 32 | 48 | 15 | 5 | 16 |
| Gallup | May 31 | D Telegraph | 31 | 47 | 16 | 6 | 16 |
| Gallup | Jun 07 | D Telegraph | 30 | 47 | 18 | 5 | 17 |
| ICM | May 13 | Observer | 32 | 48 | 15 | 5 | 16 |
| ICM | May 14 | Standard | 32 | 48 | 14 | 6 | 16 |
| ICM | May 16 | Guardian | 31 | 46 | 16 | 7 | 15 |
| ICM | May 23 | Guardian | 32 | 45 | 17 | 7 | 13 |
| ICM | May 30 | Guardian | 28 | 47 | 17 | 8 | 19 |
| ICM | Jun 01 | Channel 4 | 31 | 43 | 19 | 7 | 12 |
| ICM | Jun 03 | Observer | 34 | 46 | 15 | 5 | 12 |
| ICM | Jun 04 | Standard | 30 | 47 | 18 | 5 | 17 |
| ICM | Jun 06 | Guardian | 32 | 43 | 19 | 6 | 11 |
| MORI | May 09 | The Times | 30 | 54 | 13 | 3 | 24 |
| MORI | May 13 | S Telegraph | 31 | 51 | 13 | 5 | 20 |
| MORI | May 17 | Economist | 26 | 54 | 14 | 6 | 28 |
| MORI | May 18 | The Times | 28 | 54 | 12 | 6 | 26 |
| MORI | May 24 | The Times | 30 | 55 | 11 | 4 | 25 |
| MORI | May 31 | The Times | 30 | 48 | 16 | 6 | 18 |
| MORI | Jun 03 | S Telegraph | 27 | 50 | 17 | 6 | 23 |
| MORI | Jun 07 | The Times | 30 | 45 | 18 | 7 | 15 |
| NOP | May 13 | S Times | 32 | 49 | 13 | 6 | 17 |
| NOP | May 20 | S Times | 30 | 49 | 14 | 7 | 19 |
| NOP | May 27 | S Times | 30 | 49 | 14 | 7 | 19 |
| NOP | Jun 03 | S Times | 30 | 47 | 16 | 7 | 17 |
| Rasmussen | May 15 | Independent | 32 | 46 | 13 | 9 | 14 |
| Rasmussen | May 25 | Independent | 32 | 44 | 16 | 8 | 12 |
| Rasmussen | May 29 | Independent | 32 | 44 | 17 | 7 | 12 |
| Rasmussen | Jun 05 | Independent | 33 | 44 | 16 | 7 | 11 |
| **The result** | **Jun 07** | | **31.7** | **40.7** | **18.3** | **9.3** | **9** |

# FLEET STREET AVALANCHE TO BACK THE LANDSLIDE

## *by* Brian MacArthur
### *Associate Editor of The Times*

W ITH nine of the ten national daily newspapers — with British sales of 12.3 million (95 per cent of circulation) — and seven of the nine Sundays declaring against William Hague's Conservative Party, Tony Blair attracted an avalanche in Fleet Street to back his landslide in the country. It was the most overwhelming endorsement by newspapers for Labour in the party's history. Editors had not delivered so monolithic a verdict against a party since 1983, in the aftermath of the Falklands war, when Margaret Thatcher won her second election against a Labour Party led by Michael Foot whose only supporter was the *Daily Mirror*.

The 2001 election saw several historic switches of political allegiance, most notably by *The Times* which endorsed Labour for the first time in the newspaper's history. Another equally cautious convert to Labour was *The Sunday Times*. The *Daily Express* and *Sunday Express* were more enthusiastic. Both titles are now owned by Richard Desmond's Northern & Shell, which publishes *OK!* and a string of soft-porn magazines, and were also endorsing Labour for the first time. According to MORI, *The Times*, *Financial Times* and *Daily Express* voted against their readers — but the only titles where anti-Tory voters were not in a majority were *The Daily Telegraph* and *Daily Mail*.

The daily newspapers for Labour were *The Sun*, *The Mirror*, *Daily Star*, *Daily Express*, *The Times* and the *Financial Times* (for the third election in succession). *The Guardian* supported both Labour and tactical voting for the Liberal Democrats. *The Independent* said the Tories should be rejected but made no endorsement. The *Daily Mail* did not endorse Hague.

Sunday newspapers for Labour were the *News of the World*, *Sunday Mirror* and *Sunday People* (both stablemates of *The Mirror*), *Sunday Express*, *The Sunday Times* and *The Observer*, which also supported tactical voting against the Tories. *The Independent* said that Labour "just about" deserved to win but commended sizeable votes for the Greens, Liberal Democrats and the "sane" wing of the Tory party. Only *The Daily Telegraph*, *Sunday Telegraph* and the *Mail on Sunday* endorsed Hague with any degree of enthusiasm. That obvious lack of enthusiasm for Hague and anxiety about Blair among the electorate was perhaps best captured by the *Daily Mail*, a newspaper which commentators often describe as the authentic voice of the shires or Middle England. The proportion of hostile coverage of Blair and new Labour in the *Daily Mail* was the highest of any national newspaper, according to Echo Research, which analyses media coverage for major companies and government departments and which made a special study of "bias" in newspaper election reporting and comment. Yet the *Daily Mail* could not bring itself to endorse Hague, in spite of its "long-held and deeply felt conservative instincts" and its belief that Labour was "intent on destroying the vibrant message of Thatcherism". His party, it said, seemed timid, incoherent, lacking in the vision and confidence that once made Margaret Thatcher seem unstoppable. Where had been the core Tory beliefs that the State was too big or taxation too high? The Tories hadn't done enough to win — but Labour didn't merit an overwhelming victory.

The endorsement most prized by Blair in 1997 and made on the day the election was announced was from *The Sun*, Britain's biggest-selling daily newspaper with a readership of more than nine million. In the previous four elections it had supported Thatcher's and Major's Tories and derided Labour's leaders. In 2001 its endorsement of Blair for a second term was made even earlier, after Gordon Brown's

Budget in March. "It's in the bag, Tony," *The Sun* declared, albeit with a powerful warning that it would oppose him if he backed the euro. By its standards in past elections, *The Sun* was nevertheless notably fair to Hague, at frequent intervals praising his robust qualities, declaring that a Tory rout would be a "hammer blow" for democracy, and ensuring balanced reporting of his campaign. One in four of its election reports on the Tories was favourable compared with 6 per cent in *The Mirror*. According to Echo, *The Times* published the highest proportion of balanced articles on both parties, the *Financial Times* had the highest proportion of favourable articles on both and *The Guardian* published the highest number of unfavourable articles on both.

Although the tabloids, aware that many voters were allegedly bored by the election, tended to keep the election off their front pages, newspapers did their duty to democracy — 4,280 reports and comments were published by the nationals during the campaign. The presidential style of modern British election campaigns was reflected in the newspaper reporting which was utterly dominated by Tony Blair, William Hague, Gordon Brown and Charles Kennedy (see table below). The fracas in Rhyl, where John Prescott punched a protester, made him the third most mentioned Labour politician — and was a welcome fillip to newspaper sales which were up next morning by 150,000 (although the credit was also shared by the Liverpool football team which won the Uefa Cup on the same night). Sales of the daily tabloids fell by nearly 130,000 in May; the only exception was the least enthusiastic reporter of the campaign, the *Daily Star*, which recorded a sales increase of 6,500.

The question asked at every election is whether newspapers help to influence the votes of their readers. MORI's polling between the 1997 and 2001 elections suggests that they may in the longer term if not during the short election campaign. After 1997, the *Daily Express* became Blairite instead of the Tory propagandist it had been for the previous 97 years — the swing to Labour among its readers between 1997 and 2001 was 5 per cent. There was a similar swing to the Tories among the two titles most hostile to Blair, *The Daily Telegraph* and *Daily Mail*.

## LEADERS IN THE GREAT PUBLICITY STAKES

| Labour | Mentions | Conservative | Mentions | Lib Dem | Mentions |
|---|---|---|---|---|---|
| Tony Blair | 1697 | William Hague | 1230 | Charles Kennedy | 457 |
| Gordon Brown | 727 | Michael Portillo | 387 | Paddy Ashdown | 65 |
| John Prescott | 378 | Baroness Thatcher | 363 | Simon Hughes | 29 |
| Alastair Campbell | 197 | Ann Widdecombe | 218 | Matthew Taylor | 18 |
| Peter Mandelson | 185 | John Major | 171 | Menzies Campbell | 12 |

©Echo Research May 2001

# STRAIGHT LEFT THAT JOLTED
# JADED CAMPAIGN VIEWERS

## by Nicholas Wapshott
## of The Times

THE general election was announced on television when the Prime Minister addressed an audience of mostly bewildered schoolgirls. It ended on television as Tony Blair re-entered Downing Street with his family, holding in his arms the baby Leo, whom he kissed for the first time for the benefit of the cameras. In between, although the campaign was mainly fought over the airwaves, there were fewer set-piece speeches, less drama and fewer unscripted incidents than in elections in recent years. The close control upon what the press could see and therefore report, introduced to such effect by the Conservatives under Margaret Thatcher, held good under new Labour. This made the rare unscheduled outbreaks of reality seem even more vivid.

The attention of the broadcast media was focused mostly upon a procession of interviews taken in turn for the benefit of the main established political programmes. The first of any note was a highly abrasive encounter between the Prime Minister and John Humphrys on *Today*, Radio 4's morning news flagship. For a full ten minutes Humphrys pressed home a single point: that before the 1997 election Blair had promised a government free of the sleaze which had dogged the outgoing Major administration. Yet, said Humphrys, Blair had tolerated the continued presence in the Government of a number of high-profile figures, among them the Treasury Minister Geoffrey Robinson, the Northern Ireland Secretary Peter Mandelson and, above all, the Europe Minister Keith Vaz, all of whom had become enmeshed in dubious financial dealings. The Prime Minister's irritation at the tone of the questioning was evident and the interview ensured that the unsuitability of Vaz's presence in the Government remained a prominent issue for the rest of the campaign.

The Prime Minister was not to receive such a grilling again. By the time of his final interview, with Jeremy Paxman on BBC2's *Newsnight*, it appeared so evident that he would enjoy a second landslide that the questions were concerned less with the campaign than with exploring the tenor of the new Government. This was in sharp contrast to Paxman's barren interview with William Hague, the Tory leader, which became so embroiled in the inadequacies of the Conservatives' case and the inability of the Opposition Leader to make any progress with the electorate, politically or personally, that it almost ground to a halt.

More telling for the voter than the machismo evident in the interviewing duels were the elaborate and often awkward encounters between the party leaders and selected members of the electorate moderated by the brothers Dimbleby. While the elder brother, David, oozed charm and urbanity on BBC1, on ITV Jonathan applied more edge to the questioning. Each approach provided the nearest the television audience would see of what used to be traditional hustings. Blair, an established master at charming a controlled semi-public meeting, employed a blokey style of speech and alternately wore a concerned frown and a smile. Charles Kennedy's repertoire was more natural and exhibited his easy rapport with voters. For William Hague, however, these events were the closest

"DAD, I DON'T WANT A
TELLY IN MY ROOM ANYMORE"

he came to being at ease. He displayed a genuine sense of humour and was able to display his considerable natural gifts as a debater, qualities which in all other forms of electioneering he found difficult to summon. Above all, the aggressive and negative tone of the Tory party election broadcasts showed the serious flaw in Hague's election strategy. He had directed his party to frighten the electorate into voting Tory. Their efforts were gloomy and lamentable and announced to the press with suitable shame by Tim Collins, the vice-chairman in charge of campaigning, who insisted on remaining anonymous.

In an effort to reignite the alarm and despondency spread by the protests against high petrol prices the previous year, actors appeared as car-owners who could no longer afford to buy fuel, leaving the old isolated, the disabled housebound and the country-dweller starving for want of the price of a gallon. More extreme was an advertisement aimed at highlighting the dangers of Labour's prisoners' early release scheme based directly upon a notorious television campaign to discredit the Massachusetts Governor Michael Dukakis's parole policy. The American original featured a revolving door representing the liberal prison system which had allowed a killer, Willie Horton, to be freed early but who went on to rape and maim. The Tories revived the revolving door but could not find an exact British Horton parallel, making the broadcast both offensive and ineffective. The Conservatives' final broadcast concentrated far too late on trying to portray Hague as likeable.

By contrast, Labour's broadcasts were concerned with trying to counter voter complacency and apathy, particularly among Labour's traditional working-class supporters. To encourage voters to the polls, the final broadcast featured a young couple who on their return from voting were surprised to find themselves thanked by a formerly unemployed young man, a pensioner, two policemen and others who believed that the Labour Government had done them good, ending, like a Frank Capra movie, with a whole street full of people saying thank you. The Liberal Democrats, too, adopted a positive, though noticeably more old-fashioned, approach, introducing voters to their new leader, Charles Kennedy, against the picturesque backdrop of his Scottish Highlands constituency.

More interesting were the rare slips of public relations when things went wrong on camera, chief among them an extraordinary incident in which the Deputy Prime Minister punched a protester in Rhyl in full view. An egg was thrown point-blank at John Prescott; he replied with a left hook. The two burly men crashed to the ground in one of the ugliest, and in many ways most humorous, scuffles of modern electoral history. The Sky News camera had the best view and the pictures were soon passed on to the other news organisations. That evening and throughout the next day the punch was thrown and rethrown a thousand times as television news editors at last had something to show their jaded viewers.

A similar incident, in which a distressed woman whose partner was receiving tardy cancer treatment bearded the Prime Minister on his way into a Birmingham hospital, also received endless repetition. By this time, however, there were suspicions, voiced by the Labour general secretary Margaret McDonagh, that the media, in their irritation at being too closely confined, had encouraged angry voters to breach the security. After that there was but a single unexpected encounter, when a student, who was working as a student journalist, tackled Blair on student loans.

The low turnout on election day suggested that the power of broadcasting to engage voters, and thus involve them in the democratic process, was waning. But the parties and the broadcasting companies must share some of the blame for that. The Government was eager to motivate its own supporters but did not wish to rouse the voters in general. It concentrated most of its efforts in maximising the appeal of the Prime Minister. Some senior Labour figures, like Gordon Brown, Jack Straw and David Blunkett, were given minor roles. Similarly the Tories placed their faith almost wholly in William Hague, Michael Portillo and Ann Widdecombe.

Only Baroness Thatcher proved to be irrepressible. She was determined to go on the stump and Hague, although conscious that she was a mixed blessing, was obliged to acquiesce. Her message was predictable, strident and barely worth reporting in itself. But the broadcasters were so glad to find a seam of embarrassment to counter the rigorous party control that she was hurried on to the screen.

# LAW LIGHTING UP SHADOWY WORLD OF CAMPAIGN FUNDS

## by Tom Baldwin

### Deputy Political Editor of The Times

T HE muddy ground where politics meets money can rarely, if ever, have been so trampled over as during the previous Parliament.

The main political parties discovered that having first granted limited public access to this once-secret world, they were unable to resist pressure for full disclosure of the way they are funded.

The Labour and Conservative parties faced accusations that they were in the pocket of a few rich men who were buying access, influence and honours from the political system in return for donations.

The result was a new law, the Political Parties, Elections and Referendums Act 2000, which for the first time puts party fundraising and national election expenditure under statutory regulation.

In the 2001 election, political parties had to declare the exact amount of all donations above £1,000 and the names of their benefactors. The Act makes it a criminal offence to take money from overseas and caps each party's expenditure on a general election campaign at around £20 million.

An early indication of the success of this legislation is that the Electoral Commission, set up to enforce these rules, encountered few problems during the 2001 campaign.

Even in the weeks leading up to February 16 when the Act came into force, Labour and the Conservatives decided to disclose the names of multimillion-pound donors rather than risk accusations that they were seeking to circumvent the new rules by banking their money before the deadline.

In January, amid intense speculation about the identity of Labour's "mystery benefactors", the party named three donors who had each given it £2 million: Lord Hamlyn, the publisher, Lord Sainsbury of Turville, the former supermarket chief who is now Science Minister, and Christopher Ondaatje, a financier who once funded the Tory party.

At the same time, the Conservatives unveiled a record-breaking £5 million gift from Stuart Wheeler, the chairman of the IG Index online betting firm. After the election, the party disclosed that it had received another donation worth the same amount from Sir Paul Getty, the American-born billionaire who became a British citizen in 1997.

None of these donations can be seen as an attempt to buy favours from the parties that received them. Lord Hamlyn and Mr Ondaatje are both of an age when they have no desire to gain access or influence. Lord Sainsbury, who had already given Labour at least £3 million in recent years, has earned his spurs as a minister in his own right.

Mr Wheeler, who has said he does not want an honour and whose betting company was correctly forecasting a second Labour landslide at the time of his donation, would appear to have handed over a slice of his fortune in an act of altruism bordering on eccentricity.

The same seems to be true of Sir Paul, whose earlier donations to the miners' strike fund in the 1980s suggests his gifts are motivated more by a sentimental Anglophile attachment towards losing causes than any political ambition or, indeed, ideology.

"THE GOOD NEWS IS WE HAVENT GOT MONEY LEFT FOR ANY POLITICAL FUNDING"

The purity of intention behind the beneficence bestowed on the main parties before the 2001 election may well be a direct consequence of the scrutiny to which it was being subjected.

Before the 1997 election, the Tories received around £9 million from undisclosed overseas sources. This figure emerged only subsequently in the course of the investigation by Lord Neill of Bladen's Committee on Standards in Public Life, whose subsequent recommendations led to the new laws on funding.

The identity and motivation for such donations will probably never be known. After all, the link between Conservative fundraising, the receipt of peerages and knighthoods, and access to, as well as influence over, Tory ministers had long since been subject to more rumour and speculation than hard facts.

What was different about the 1997 campaign was that Labour, for the first time in its history, was also picking up seven-figure donations from sources other than trade unions.

Some of these were announced at the time with the agreement of the donors themselves. For instance no secret was made of £1 million gifts from the late Matthew Harding, the Chelsea Football Club vice-chairman, and the Political Animal Lobby.

But others wished to remain in the shadows. Although Labour already had its own voluntary code under which it disclosed the names of those who had given more than £5,000, the list was not published until the party conference season and even then it did not specify the amount.

As Lord Neill was to point out later, without knowing if a donor has given £5,000 or £5 million, it is difficult to assess whether someone has bought access or influence.

In November 1997, the Government announced that the proposed ban on tobacco sponsorship of sport would not include Formula One. This exemption had been secured at a Downing Street meeting between Tony Blair and Bernie Ecclestone, the motor racing tycoon.

When journalists began asking if it were true that Mr Ecclestone had given the party £1 million before the election, Labour was either unwilling, or unable, to make a clean breast of it.

The categorical denials initially issued by Mr Ecclestone's lawyers, Herbert Smith, only fuelled suspicions that he and Labour had something to hide.

It took five days after the first inquiry for Labour to admit to receiving the donation, and even then it was only because the party had received an unexpectedly robust reply from Lord Neill to a letter asking whether it should take further gifts from Mr Ecclestone.

To Downing Street's dismay, Lord Neill said Labour should not only refuse any more donations from the Formula One chief but should also repay the £1 million it had already received.

If it had not been for his verdict, Labour could have left the matter until the next autumn when it would have published Mr Ecclestone's name as just one of those who had given more than £5,000.

**B**ut even that would have been more open than the rules governing Mr Blair's "blind trust" for his office expenses before the 1997 election, under which donors were guaranteed complete anonymity. By the time of the 2001 campaign, such a system had been outlawed.

Instead, the scrutiny over party funding turned back to the Tory party and, in particular, the role of Lord Ashcroft, its treasurer from 1998.

The years that followed the Conservatives' removal from office in 1997 saw many of its traditional sources of income dry up. Lord Ashcroft's donations, thought to be worth a total of up to £5 million, topped up with interest-free loans of up to £2 million at any one time, may have kept the party afloat.

However, if it had not been for the party's impoverished state, he would not have been the obvious choice for the post of treasurer. There was a steady stream of allegations about Lord Ashcroft's business reputation and his financial interests in Belize, for whom he worked as its United Nations Ambassador and enjoyed a 30-year tax-free deal.

While he was eligible to vote in British elections through his dual nationality, many of the donations to the Tory party through the Belize Bank Trust Company would almost certainly have fallen foul of the new legislation banning gifts from foreign firms. It was not until he promised to return to Britain and stop being a diplomat for Belize that the Political Honours Scrutiny Committee ended its veto of William Hague's nomination of the Tory treasurer for a peerage.

Concerns were also raised about Lord Ashcroft's dual role of the party's chief benefactor for much of the previous Parliament and that of treasurer.

Under Lord Neill's reforms of political funding, party treasurers are expected to perform a key role in complying with rules on the eligibility of donations.

It was not until the Act came into force that Lord Ashcroft ended his dual role, with the Tories appointing David Prior to the post of compliance officer. And it was no surprise to anyone that after the election, Lord Ashcroft resigned from his post altogether on the same day that Mr Hague announced he was stepping down from the leadership.

The Electoral Commission, set up to enforce the new laws, is expected to recommend further changes to clean up the system of party funding.

Among the measures it will examine are proposals for a cap on individual donations, possibly at a level of no more than £150,000. Sam Younger, the commission's chairman, has stated that such measures might have to be linked to the introduction of state subsidies for parties to make up for any shortfall in their income.

However, for all this concentration on big donors in the past few years, Labour insists that such gifts make up no more than 20 per cent of its income, with the rest coming from members and small donations, the trade unions, as well as merchandising and sponsorship.

The Conservatives are probably slightly more reliant on big donors, but not exclusively so. The Tories, who already receive around £4 million a year of subsidy in the form of "Short money", have cut their running costs to around £15 million a year. Labour, as the governing party, receives no help from the taxpayer, but still needs an annual income of £25 million.

At the election, campaign expenditure for each party was eventually capped at £15.8 million. This is far less than the figure spent by Labour and the Conservatives in 1997.

But there is scant evidence that this reduction made any difference to the parties' ability to campaign and, even in 2001, much of the spending on billboard advertising was probably wasted.

Indeed, the controversies over the big gifts have arguably done more harm to the reputation of the donors and the recipients than benefit received by either of them.

Labour and the Tories have too often found themselves in the gutter over political funding. From that perspective they should be better placed to see if such donations are, in fact, a case of money going down the drain.

# E-MAIL CAMPAIGN SHOTS STILL LOST IN CYBERSPACE

## *by* **Roland Watson**

### *of The Times*

I

T WAS billed as the e-election, the first campaign in which parties would take the fight for votes into cyberspace.

Labour and the Conservatives certainly invested much time, effort and attempted humour in trying to turn technological advances to electoral effect.

The websites of the main parties became forums for day-to-day, even hour-by-hour, jousting. Claim and counter-claim were exchanged and rebutted via home pages. Voters found themselves, whether they liked it or not, being wooed online.

Internet adventurers could even log their mobile telephone numbers, and those of a friend, on to Labour's website, earning them a series of largely incomprehensible polling-related text messages.

There was a suggestion, halfway through the campaign, that the absence of party posters in front windows and gardens was a testament to how fiercely the tussle for hearts and minds was being fought on personal computer screens. But that was before the final turnout figures revealed how turned off most of the electorate were.

Immediately after the campaign, none of the parties was making great claims for its e-efforts. And for all the wizardry, the strong suspicion remains that the vast majority of Internet traffic was for the politically motivated whose party sympathies were already entrenched.

The parties were not to know that at the outset. They did, though, show varying degrees of commitment to the medium, reflecting their relative optimism about whether Britons were ready to be canvassed by e-mail.

The Tories showed most enthusiasm for the notion of the Internet as a vote-winning tool.

There was an element of faddishness in the approach, of following the trend of the United States where using the Internet to deliver party political messages became an established part of the 2000 presidential elections.

But there was also a harder-nosed logic to the Tory effort. It centred on the 180 "key seats" identified by the Tories as their targets. Many of those that had been lost to Labour in 1997 had significant suburban, middle-class elements.

Many of them had families. And for many of those families, the Internet was becoming part of the household's everyday communication with the outside world. So why not use it to solicit votes?

But they needed to know where to send their message. From a standing start, the Tories went about gathering e-mail addresses with zeal. In the Keep the Pound campaign launched by William Hague in 2000, they had a ready vehicle.

As Mr Hague's famed white Keep-the-Pound lorry toured the country, Tory supporters collected nearly a million signatures from sterling supporters. On the petition, people were asked for an e-mail address as well as a postal address, and many thousands of them supplied one. And by

" IT's SO EMBARRASSING — MY WIFE CAUGHT ME LAST NIGHT DOWNLOADING THE TORY MANIFESTO "

analysing postcodes, Tory officials were able to build up what they hoped would be a database of e-mail addresses in marginal seats.

A similar exercise was conducted during the fuel protests and their aftermath. A series of "days of action" organised by the Tories netted them tens of thousands more signatures, and with them valuable e-mail addresses.

The Tories launched their website at the 2000 party conference, and began gearing up for the election in earnest.

In line with many of the recruits staffing the Tories' "war room", the party turned to two former journalist to spearhead their Internet drive.

Steve Brine, formerly of the BBC, was put in charge of the operation. Henry Macrory, a Fleet Street veteran who knew Westminster's political lobby inside out thanks to berths at the *Sunday Express* and *Daily Star*, was put in charge of filling the website with news.

Macrory's touch was evident in the presentation of "news". Parts of the home page were designed to look like a newspaper front page, with teasers for what was inside. The days' events were presented as newspaper stories, with headlines, crossheads and sharp first paragraphs.

When the campaign was in full swing, Macrory was filing up to ten stories a day, trumpeting policy announcements from the Tories and exploiting gaps opened during Labour's morning press conference.

The constant updating gave the website an up-to-the-minute feel, but only to those who either sought it out or strayed on to it by mistake from one of its 1,000-plus links from other websites.

The party also broadcast several webcasts, with Michael Portillo, Ann Widdecombe, Michael Ancram and Francis Maude all answering questions live.

But the key to the drive was to take the Internet campaign into people's living rooms. The e-mail addresses collected from the Keep the Pound and fuel petitions were added to those from individuals visiting the Tory and Keep the Pound websites. Together, the Tories claimed a database approaching 100,000 e-mail addresses.

During the campaign, Central Office sent two e-mails a day to each of these addresses, highlighting their message for that day's campaigning.

Labour took a more sceptical view of the likely impact of e-campaigning. One party official said: "I think we all know the Internet is mostly used for shopping, sex and sport. Less than 2 per cent of surfers click on to political websites, so they are of limited use in reaching out to the unconverted."

But that did not stop the party's Millbank headquarters plunging into e-campaigning with glee.

Unlike the Tories' attempt to bring the news to life, Labour used its website as a drier, library-like resource. All the main speeches, press releases and party election broadcasts were there to be accessed and viewed. But there was no effort to bring them to life.

D uring the heat of campaigning, the website was updated up to 16 times a day, but that was chiefly to place the latest speech or press release.

The most notable aspect of the website was the way it was used to poke fun at the Tories and cheer up the party faithful struggling through a lifeless campaign.

A series of interactive games were placed, keeping pace with events in the run-up, and the campaign itself. Visitors to the website could join William Hague in a 14-pint drinking game in the Last Chance Saloon, or play "boom and bust" with "Michael Plotillo", or a version of Pacman involving £20 billion and Oliver Letwin.

Labour's other trick, thanks to its e-campaigns unit, was to localise the campaigning e-mails it did send out. Although the exercise was not on the same scale as the Tories', limited to a few tens of thousands, it was more sophisticated.

Of the tens of thousands of e-mail addresses Labour officials had, they knew where most of them were geographically; and the messages they dispatched were directly relevant to the recipient's community.

If the message was about health and education, it mentioned the names of local schools and local hospitals and how much money they had received during the past four years.

Labour also claimed the prize for the gimmick of the campaign, sending thousands of text messages to young voters. One ran: "d:*0 WUCIWUG #:-) VTE LBR 2MORO". The first four characters purported to display a sideways picture of William Hague wearing a baseball cap with small eyes, a "squiffy nose" and big mouth, followed by "what you see is what you get", "oh no!" and "vote Labour tomorrow".

Whether any recipients understood it without the benefit of explanatory notes is unclear; turnout among the youth vote, at which it was aimed, was low.

The Liberal Democrats ran a more focused operation under Mark Pack which concentrated on potentially critical voters. In the weeks and months before the campaign, they collected e-mail addresses on the doorstep from voters who said they wanted to learn more about the party's policies. Those households received between one and five e-mails during the campaign, depending on where they lived.

T he Lib Dems saw enough potential in the campaign to see a future for the Internet, not least because 1.5 per cent of their national membership are individuals who joined via the Internet since the begining of 2001.

The trend for using the Internet as a campaigning tool came from the US, and on the evidence of previous imports from across the Atlantic it is unlikely to go away.

Although all parties made noises about using it to win votes, their efforts were largely experimental.

The Internet allowed them all to make their manifestos, candidates and campaigning posters readily available to Internet browsers, particularly those living in rural areas or safe seats which, with canvassing increasingly targeted on a small number of potential swing voters, would not expect to see a political activist in any five years.

It also provided them with a means of rapidly distributing information to their teams in the field. But their campaigning was largely either gimmick-led or directed to the sympathetic or committed, rather than the swing voters needed to change the course of a campaign.

Another innovation came in the shape of two tactical voting websites. One of them, set up by the Labour-supporting singer Billy Bragg, was designed to encourage anti-Tory tactical voting in Dorset. But although Ian Bruce, the former Tory MP in Dorset South, was ousted by Labour, Oliver Letwin in Dorset West hung on against the Liberal Democrats.

The other site, which claimed 150,000 hits, was nationwide and provided a forum for voters whose party sympathies meant that their votes were wasted in their own seats to "swap" them with others where they could make a difference.

However, all their efforts may have been misplaced. According to research by the Industrial Society, cyber citizens were less likely to vote, expressed less interest in direct contact with political parties, and generally ignored political party websites. Its survey suggested that far from offering a powerful new political tool, only 2 per cent of Internet users said they were certain to use it to get information about the campaign; and 84 per cent said they would avoid politics altogether online.

All parties will review the effectiveness of their Internet efforts before working out how to improve them for next time.

But for all the expense involved, it was notable that none of those involved was claiming its efforts had won a single vote.

# MEDICAL WHITE COAT HAS REPLACED THE WHITE SUIT

## *by* Andrew Pierce
### *of The Times*

The decisive victory of Richard Taylor, a single-issue politician in Wyre Forest, ensured that an Independent would take over the mantle of the man in the white suit. While Martin Bell, the only Independent in the retiring Parliament, suffered predictable defeat in one of the Tories' safest seats, Dr Taylor's success on a platform of opposition to the rundown of a local hospital confirmed the rise of consumerist politics.

The election also saw the best Green performance, the best far-left performance for 50 years, and more worryingly, the strongest ever showing by the far-right British National Party.

But it was Dr Taylor's remarkable 17,630-vote majority over a Labour minister, on the issue of the downgrading of Kidderminster Hospital, which was one of the few upsets in an otherwise utterly predictable election result.

David Lock, the defeated Labour MP, was compelled to defend the unpopular hospital scheme because he had been a member of the payroll vote as a junior minister in the Lord Chancellor's Department. He complained bitterly afterwards that the rise of "consumerist" politics discriminated against politicians who had the courage to "tell uncomfortable truths about service provision" to a hostile electorate.

Dr Taylor, 66, will inevitably be compared to Mr Bell. The former consultant, while declining to complete the symbolism by donning his white medical overalls for life at Westminster, struck a chord with the electorate when he declared his victory a protest against an overmighty Government that had stopped listening.

"My election shows that people are desperately angry that their voice has not been heard," he said. "Many of my supporters have made it clear to me the hospital is not the only issue on their mind and they just want a voice that will speak for them with all honesty."

Dr Taylor's Health Concern group now has a majority of 17 seats on the Wyre Forest District Council and reduced the Labour vote to 22 per cent.

Mr Bell, a former BBC foreign correspondent, had resisted pressure to stand against high-profile Labour candidates who have been embroiled in sleaze such as Peter Mandelson, Geoffrey Robinson or Keith Vaz. He insists he does not regret his decision despite being defeated in Brentwood & Ongar, the Tories' ninth safest seat,where he came within 3,000 votes of toppling Eric Pickles who has held the seat since 1992. In 1997 Mr Bell had electrified the campaign when he stood against the disgraced Tory Neil Hamilton as the anti-sleaze candidate in Tatton.

Mr Bell had decided to oppose Mr Pickles after being approached by local Conservatives who were worried about the impact a Brentwood evangelical church was having on their association. The issue failed to make the same impact sleaze had made four years ago. Mr Bell's political career is now at an end and he is unemployed for the first time.

THERE ARE CASES OF APATHY SPREADING ALL OVER THE COUNTRY

More than 3,200 candidates paid £500 each to get their names on the ballot paper in the UK's 659 constituencies. Around 2,000 failed to clear the 5 per cent hurdle required for reimbursement of deposits, thereby providing a £1 million windfall for the Treasury.

Yet again the smaller political parties failed to win a seat because of the first-past-the-post voting system. The Green Party, which fielded 145 candidates, saved deposits in ten constituencies for the first time. Its 166,000 votes amounted to 2.45 per cent of the turnout. The party's strongest showing attracted 9 per cent of the vote in Brighton Pavilion and 8 per cent in Leeds West. The Greens had benefited from PR to secure the election of two MEPs, Members of the Scottish Parliament and London Assembly.

Tony Benn once claimed that the trouble with socialism was too many socialist parties and not enough socialists. Many old Left groupings saw the point of his comment and gathered under the Socialist Alliance umbrella. The result was the best for the far Left since 1950.

Socialists gained the backing of prominent long-term Labour supporters such as Harold Pinter, the playwright, and Ken Loach, the film-maker, who lost faith in new Labour.

In St Helens South, where the Tory defector Shaun Woodward was parachuted in at the eleventh hour, the Socialist Alliance polled 2,325 votes, 7 per cent of the total. In Coventry North East the city's former Labour MP Dave Nellist, who is chairman of the Socialist Alliance, retained his deposit, finishing in fourth place with 7.08 per cent.

The SA's sister party in Scotland, the Scottish Socialist Party, outstripped expectations and retained nine deposits with just over 3 per cent of the vote. Led by Tommy Sheridan, an MSP, the party failed, however, to hit its target of 100,000 votes and polled 70,000.

But there was no such success for Arthur Scargill, the former miners' leader who suffered a crushing defeat at the hands of Peter Mandelson, the architect of new Labour. Scargill, the old titan of old Labour who went to Hartlepool to bury its modern version, was humiliated. The leader of the Socialist Labour Party, who no longer sports the furious frizz of red hair to hide his bald patch on windy days, polled 912 votes compared with 22,500 for Mandelson.

T he United Kingdom Independence Party, which is now financed by Paul Sykes, the multimillionaire Yorkshire businessman, failed miserably to achieve its stated aim of three Westminster seats. But with 1.5 per cent of the vote it still boasts that it is the fourth largest party in Britain. It had high hopes of achieving a breakthrough at Westminster after picking up three Euro-seats in 1999, albeit on the back of proportional representation.

The party failed to win its main target seat of Bexhill and Battle in Sussex. Charles Wardle, the retiring Conservative MP, had lent his support to Nigel Farage, the UKIP candidate. Mr Farage, the UKIP's main spokesman and one of the party's MEPs, polled only 3,474 votes. The victorious Conservatives were swept back with 21,555 votes, a majority of 10,500.

But the party, which is committed to Britain's withdrawal from the EU, contributed to the downfall of at least one Conservative candidate and prevented some Eurosceptic Tories winning seats they expected to regain. Paul Simison, the UKIP candidate in Norfolk North, polled 608 votes. The Liberal Democrats, the most Europhile party, snatched the seat from David Prior, a Tory vice-chairman, with a majority of just 483 votes. In Braintree, Brooks Newmark, a close friend of William Hague, came within 358 votes of recapturing the seat from Labour. The UKIP siphoned off 748 of the votes which would otherwise have gone to the Tory.

The surprise of the election was the 11,643 votes — 16 per cent of those cast — across both Oldham constituencies for the BNP. Phil Woolas, the re-elected Labour MP for Oldham East & Saddleworth, described it as a "dangerous sign for the town". The BNP last had a councillor elected in 1993 in Millwall, East London; he was rejected after a year. The unexpectedly strong showing came after race-related riots. The two BNP candidates, Nick Griffin, the Cambridge-educated leader, and Mick Treacy, a minicab driver, wore gags at the official announcement of their results in protest at a ban on speeches imposed for fear of candidates inciting racial tension.

# SOME LEFT WITH A TEAR, AND ONE WITH A SULK

## *by* Melissa Kite

### *Political Correspondent of The Times*

SIR EDWARD HEATH led an exodus of political giants from the Commons at the 2001 election, leaving the House a younger but arguably less colourful place. The departure too of John Major, Tony Benn, Mo Mowlam, Sir Paddy Ashdown and Michael Heseltine was sorely felt as Parliament struggled to maintain its popular appeal.

At least the veteran Members went of their own accord, unlike 1997 when a record 132 MPs, almost all of them Tories, lost their seats. This time only six sitting Conservatives were routed, all of them Eurosceptics. In true-blue Guildford, the heart of Surrey's stockbroker belt, voters woke up to a Liberal Democrat MP after Nick St Aubyn, Michael Portillo's former parliamentary private secretary, was defeated. Patrick Nicholls saw the end of his political ambitions in Teignbridge, as did David Prior in Norfolk North, Ian Bruce in Dorset South, Christopher Fraser in Mid Dorset and Stephen Day in Cheadle.

Seven Labour members lost their seats, including the junior minister David Lock, who suffered a shock defeat at the hands of an NHS protest candidate, Richard Taylor, a retired hospital consultant who overturned Mr Lock's 6,946 majority at Wyre Forest.

But the real exodus occurred before the campaign even began. Twenty-three Conservatives, 33 Labour MPs and seven Liberal Democrats announced their resignation in the months before the election. The loss of experience was most profoundly felt on the Tory benches.

Former ministers including Sir Norman Fowler, John MacGregor, Tom King, Peter Brooke, a former Northern Ireland Secretary, and Mr Heseltine, former Deputy Prime Minister, all stood down, although the Commons' loss was the Upper House's gain.

Sir Peter Emery, Sir Peter Lloyd, Charles Wardle, an Immigration Minister who resigned over Europe, and Sir Geoffrey Johnson Smith, a former Defence Minister, also bowed out.

The former "whipless" Euro-rebels from the Major era, Teresa Gorman, Sir Richard Body and Christopher Gill, stood down, along with the colourful old-timers Bowen Wells and Sir David Madel.

The retirement of Sir Archie Hamilton, the chairman of the 1922 Committee, left a vacancy for a key post crucial to organising the imminent Tory leadership election.

Some of Labour's most senior MPs stood down, including Jeff Rooker, the former minister who was sent to the Lords. Giles Radice, chairman of the Treasury Select Committee, Robert Sheldon, chairman of the Standards and Privileges Committee, and the outspoken Dale Campbell-Savours, once a scourge of the Thatcher Government. All went to the Lords. Lord Campbell-Savours was the second longest-serving MP behind Sir Edward. His departure meant that the post of Father of the House passed to his Labour colleague Tam Dalyell.

Retiring Labour backbenchers included Joe Ashton, Gerry Bermingham, Eric Clarke, Lawrence Cunliffe, Maria Fyfe, Norman Godman, John Gunnell, Jenny Jones, Lynne Jones, John Maxton, Bill Michie,

Tom Pendry, Allan Rogers, Ted Rowlands and Peter Snape. Peter Temple-Morris, who defected from the Tories to Labour, was rewarded with a peerage, as was Bruce Grocott, Tony Blair's parliamentary aide for five years. However, the predicted loss of women was not as pronounced as expected. Of the record 117 intake of 1997, 106 returned to the Commons, 88 on the Labour benches. Some of the unfortunately branded "Blair Babes" did throw in the towel beforehand, making plain their grievances over the long working hours and gentlemen's club ethos of the Commons. Judith Church, 47, quit Parliament to spend more time with her young sons. Tess Kingham, 38, described Parliament as "stuck in the Dark Ages". Labour's Fiona Jones lost her seat to a delighted Patrick Mercer in Newark. Ms Jones, who was convicted two years ago then cleared of falsifying election expenses during a high-profile court case, blamed a vendetta by people in the town for her defeat and claimed that the Tory victory was tainted.

Of the retiring Labour women, Llin Golding was given a peerage after 15 years in the Commons.

Sir Paddy led six Liberal Democrats out of the Commons. He and Robert Maclennan, briefly leader of the SDP, went to the Lords with Ronnie Fearn, Richard Livsey and Ray Michie. Jim Wallace and Donald Gorrie departed for the Scottish Parliament.

Countryside campaigners claimed credit for deposing Jackie Ballard, the anti-foxhunting Lib Dem MP in Taunton. Her doctor colleague Peter Brand, a campaigning Member who rose to prominence after admitting he allowed a two-year-old leukaemia victim to die at the request of his parents, was deposed when the Tories pulled off a surprise victory in the Isle of Wight.

Members of the devolved Parliament and Assemblies were obliged to stand down, depriving the Commons of Henry McLeish and Rhodri Morgan, First Ministers in Scotland and Wales, Dafydd Wigley, former leader of the Welsh Nationalists, and other leading lights of the Scottish National Party who were also MSPs including Roseanna Cunningham, Margaret Ewing, Alasdair Morgan, Andrew Welsh, and the SNP leader John Swinney.

The Ulster Unionists were deprived of several veteran MPs and supporters of the Good Friday peace agreement with the defeat of Cecil Walker and Willie Ross and the retirement of Ken Maginnis and John Taylor, deputy leader of the party, who went to the Lords.

Ken Livingstone formally resigned from the Commons to continue as Mayor of London.

Mr Benn, 76, whose son Hilary carries on the family legacy as MP for Leeds Central, said that letting go of the Commons would be difficult. "I will miss the friends. But I hope I will still be able to visit and have dinner there from time to time." He cried as he listened to cross-party tributes, before lighting his pipe and leaving the Commons for the last time.

Mr Heseltine and Mr Major, meanwhile, were looking forward to spending more time with their beloved arboretum and Trollope respectively.

Mr Major, 58, took a job in banking and said he would divide his time between cricket, charity work and a newfound passion for writing. He left the Commons with a plea for MPs to resist Labour's "undemocratic" modernisation plans.

After 33 hectic years, during which time he helped to topple Margaret Thatcher, Mr Heseltine, 68, was content to dedicate his time to the trees he has been nurturing at his estate in Oxfordshire for a quarter of a century.

"Life as a backbench MP at my stage is not very pleasant," he said. "You are just sitting there hour after hour after hour with no real role to play."

Such tranquil pursuits could not have been further from the mind of Dr Mowlam, 51, who set government nerves jangling with rumours of a volume of memoirs with enough revelations to sink a Government. The former Cabinet Office Minister said she was standing down to look for something different to do "in the time I have left".

The departure of Sir Edward, 84, whose general election defeat in 1974 led to his bitter replacement as Tory leader by Mrs Thatcher, was hailed as the end of the longest political sulk in history.

He left Westminster with a characteristic sideswipe at the Tory party's hardline stance on Europe.

# STRESSED BLAIR BABES SET A DOWNWARD TREND

## *by* Jill Sherman

*Whitehall Editor of The Times*

I n May 1997 Tony Blair proudly boasted about securing a record number of female Labour MPs as he posed with his 102 "Blair Babes".

But on June 8, 2001, the Prime Minister paid the price for dropping the party's policy of all-women shortlists by witnessing a fall in Labour's female MPs, with only 95 elected out of a total 413 MPs.

The other two main parties fared little better, with the Tories maintaining 14 women out of a total of 166 MPs. The Liberal Democrats gained one from a derisory base of four, but still less than 10 per cent of their 52 MPs are women. The Scottish National Party returned only one female MP.

Overall the number of women MPs in the House of Commons dropped from 120 to 118, the first fall since Margaret Thatcher became Prime Minister in 1979. The figures would have been even worse but for a strong performance by women in Northern Ireland.

Michelle Gildernew (Sinn Fein), Iris Robinson (Democratic Unionist Party) and Sylvia Hermon (Lady Hermon, Ulster Unionist Party) were the first women to win seats in Northern Ireland for more than 25 years. In 1993, when John Smith was leader, Labour adopted a policy where all-women short-lists were drawn up in 50 per cent of marginal constituencies and in seats where MPs were retiring.

The policy was fiercely opposed in some areas with male would-be candidates accusing the party of unfair discrimination. Peter Jepson finally took the issue to an industrial tribunal in 1995 and won. Labour's National Executive Committee decided against an appeal and the policy came to an abrupt end in 1996.

Mr Blair was always uncomfortable with the policy, wincing at accusations of "political correctness", and was relieved when it was finally abandoned.

By then, however, most female candidates were in place and more than expected entered the House of Commons in May 1997 owing to Labour's historic landslide.

Mr Blair looked at the carefully groomed young women on his back benches and relaxed. There was no attempt to amend legislation to allow positive discrimination and as a result Labour fielded only six women in the 37 seats where MPs were retiring in 2001.

I'M AFRAID YOU'VE LOST YOUR SEAT

Under pressure from his female colleagues Mr Blair had a change of heart earlier this year and Labour's manifesto included a commitment to change the law to allow political parties to take positive action to increase female representation. The new "Blair Babes" had a difficult ride in the previous Parliament. Some of those elected in 1997 did not expect to make it to the House of Commons and were unprepared for the long hours and non-family-friendly conditions.

Many of the 1997 female intake did excel and more established women MPs were rewarded with senior government posts.

The stars of the 1997 intake were Yvette Cooper (Pontefract and Castleford), Patricia Hewitt (Leicester West) and Melanie Johnson (Welwyn Hatfield), who rapidly reached the first rung of the ministerial ladder.

Female members of the 1992 intake also did well, with Tessa Jowell and Estelle Morris moving swiftly up the ministerial ranks.

But in the end Mr Blair did not have the courage in the previous Parliament to promote many to the most senior spending departments. Harriet Harman was sacked after a disastrous spell at the Social Security Department and Margaret Beckett was moved from Trade and Industry Secretary to become Leader of the Commons. Ann Taylor moved from Leader of the Commons to Chief Whip and Baroness Jay of Paddington became Leader of the Lords. Clare Short surprised everyone by hanging on to her job as International Development Secretary but moved no further.

Mo Mowlam, who became the darling of the party during her spell as Northern Ireland Secretary, had a difficult last year. Despite overcoming a benign brain tumour, she was moved to the Cabinet Office in 1999 and was never really happy there. She left the Government with little fanfare on June 8.

The absence of key female Cabinet ministers was particularly obvious during the election campaign. Although women ministers appeared almost daily at Labour's early morning press conference they were rarely allowed to speak or answer questions. The most senior Labour women such as Dr Mowlam, Mrs Taylor and Lady Jay were nowhere to be seen, mainly because all were on their way out of Government.

T he next Tory leader will have to confront the party's failure to increase its proportion of female MPs over the past decade. While the party has never favoured all-women shortlists, the meagre sprinkling of females on the Conservative benches now looks embarrassing.

Before the election William Hague had toyed with forcing Tory selection boards to include women on their lists of candidates. Other senior members of the party made clear that they backed Labour's position on changing the law to allow positive action. But the Tory manifesto contained no such pledge.

The Liberal Democrats are also surprisingly behind the times. The liberal wing of the party has always opposed all-women shortlists on the ground that it smacks of interference from the centre. Some Liberal Democrats are pushing for a "cluster" policy, which is similar to the twinning policy in Scotland and Wales but covers a larger number of constituencies. This, however, has already been proposed at party conferences and defeated.

The Liberal Democrats still cannot agree on the best way forward and will need a two-thirds majority to change policy at the party conference, which could prove too big an obstacle.

On June 8, 2001, Mr Blair at last listened to his critics and used his reshuffle to put women into some of the most important posts in Government, including key spending departments.

Ms Morris was promoted to Education Secretary, covering an area which Mr Blair considers a top priority. Ms Hewitt, a former aide to Neil Kinnock, becomes the new Trade and Industry Secretary after only four years in Parliament. Ms Jowell, the new Culture, Media and Sport Secretary, won her spurs after overseeing a massive expansion of Labour's New Deal programme to get the jobless into work. Mrs Beckett, who was sidelined in the last Parliament, has made a surprise comeback and takes charge of the new Department of Environment, Food and Rural Affairs.

The Cabinet includes three other women: Ms Short, who stays at International Development; Hilary Armstrong, who was promoted to Chief Whip; and Helen Liddell, who stays as Scottish Secretary.

Ms Hewitt has also been appointed Women's Minister in the Commons while Sally Morgan, Mr Blair's former political secretary, is sent to the Lords and takes the same role there and oversees a women's unit at the Cabinet Office. Some ministers felt the rush to promote women was merely a reaction to criticism during the election campaign that Mr Blair had sidelined his female colleagues. Time will tell if the exercise was just window-dressing or a real commitment by the Prime Minister to giving women an influential role in Government.

# SILK TO SMOOTH RUFFLED LORDS' REFORM DOUBTS

## *by* James Landale

### *Political Correspondent of The Times*

TONY BLAIR earned a reputation in his first term for distrusting the House of Lords but he never hesitated giving substantial ministerial jobs to peers of the realm.

When he formed his second Government in June 2001, the Prime Minister continued this trend by placing peers in more high-profile positions within Government. The number of Lords ministers also rose from 22 to 24.

The most significant change was the appointment of Lord Williams of Mostyn as the new Leader of the House of Lords and Lord Privy Seal, replacing Baroness Jay of Paddington who stood down.

Mr Blair had deployed Lady Jay's uncompromising — if not blunt — manner to force through the expulsion of most hereditary peers in the first stage of his reforms to the upper chamber.

But he chose the forensic wit and ruthless efficacy of a Welsh libel silk to try to persuade their Lordships to accept further — and perhaps more radical — reforms promised at some stage in the second term.

Lord Williams, Deputy Lords Leader since 1998 and Attorney-General since 1999, has the respect of the House — a vital attribute in a chamber where *politesse* still obliges.

But his charm and agility at the dispatch box hide the inner steel of a committed and somewhat old Labour reformer whom opposition peers have learnt not to underestimate.

When Lord Williams, 60, the first member of a Cabinet to have been born in a taxi, once described himself as having "barking egomania, allied to rat-like cunning", he was only half-joking.

The new Deputy Leader of the Lords is Baroness Symons of Vernham Dean. Formerly a Defence Minister, she becomes Minister for Trade at both the Foreign Office and the Department of Trade and Industry, answering to both Secretaries of State.

Lord Irvine of Lairg remains Lord Chancellor, with a new responsibility for constitutional affairs, inherited from the Home Office.

Baroness Scotland of Asthal, the former junior Foreign Office Minister and QC, joins him as a junior minister at the Lord Chancellor's Department.

Lord Goldsmith, QC, the Prime Minister's special representative on the panel which drew up the new EU Charter of Fundamental Rights, replaces Lord Williams as Attorney-General.

Lord Macdonald of Tradeston, the former Transport Minister, is given an important role as Minister for the Cabinet Office and Chancellor of the Duchy of Lancaster. As deputy to John Prescott, he is effectively the minister responsible for ensuring that Labour delivers on its promises to improve the public services.

Lord Falconer of Thoroton, the Prime Minister's former flatmate, leaves the Cabinet Office for the newly formed Department for Transport, Local Government and the Regions. In a surprisingly modest appointment, he has become the Minister for Housing and Planning with

" MY DAD KNOWS A HEREDITARY PEER TONY BLAIR BROUGHT BACK FROM THE DEAD "

responsibility for the Millennium Dome. A new entrant to the House of Lords is Sally Morgan, former-ly the Prime Minister's Political Secretary at Downing Street. She was created a peer — without being vetted by the Appointments Commission — so that she could become a Minister of State at the Cabinet Office with responsibility for women's issues.

Jeff Rooker, the former Minister of State at Social Security who was given a peerage in the Dissolu-tion Honours List, moves to the Home Office with responsibility for asylum.

Baroness Blackstone, formerly Minister of State for Education and Employment, becomes the new Arts Minister at the Department for Culture, Media and Sport.

Lord Whitty, formerly at Environment, Transport and the Regions, moves over to become a junior minister at the new Department for Environment, Food and Rural Affairs.

Baroness Hollis of Heigham, formerly a junior Social Security Minister, effectively keeps the same job in the renamed Department for Work and Pensions. Lord Hunt of Kings Heath remains a junior minister at the Department of Health. Lord Sainsbury of Turville remains Science Minister (unpaid) at the Trade Department.

Baroness Amos is promoted from the Whips' Office to be a junior Foreign Office Minister. Lord Bach is promoted from the Lord Chancellor's Department to be a junior Defence Minister.

B aroness Ashton of Upholland, former health authority chairman, ex-CND organiser, and wife of the journalist Peter Kellner, enters Government for the first time as a junior Education Min-ister.

The Whips' Office sees some changes. The much respected Lord Carter remains Chief Whip, or as he is known in the Lords, Captain of the Honourable Corps of Gentlemen-at-Arms.

The Deputy Chief Whip — or Captain of the Queen's Bodyguard of the Yeoman of the Guard — re-mains Lord McIntosh of Haringey.

Lord Davies of Oldham and Baroness Farrington of Ribbleton continue as whips, known as Lords and Baronesses in Waiting.

But there are three new additions to the Whips' Office: Lord Bassam of Brighton, sacked from the Home Office; Bruce Grocott, Mr Blair's former parliamentary private secretary, given a peerage in the Dissolution Honours List; and Lord Filkin, the local government expert.

Apart from Lady Jay, four other Lords ministers stood down voluntarily. They were Baroness Hay-man, former junior Agriculture Minister, and the former whips, Lord Burlison, Baroness Ramsay of Cartvale and Baroness Gould of Potternewton.

# THE HOUSE OF COMMONS? THAT'S ENTERTAINMENT

### *by* Matthew Parris
*Columnist of The Times*

A S THE great Victorian constitutionalist Walter Bagehot remarked, we British are in the occasional habit of directing several hundred people to pack their bags and go down to London to represent us for a number of years — and the question arises: "What are they to do?" Bagehot never quite solved the puzzle.

Nor can I. The two Parliaments in which I served and the three I have subsequently sketched for *The Times* offer me no reassurance that the 21st century will come any closer than the 19th to answering Bagehot's question. The first of many errors into which we tend to slip when agonising about a "decline" in the House of Commons' "relevance" to modern government is to suppose this is a modern problem.

It is ancient. Bemoaning the decline of the House of Commons is one of our most hallowed British political traditions, and a fresh outbreak of it takes place in almost as ceremonial a way as the Queen's Speech, at the start of each new Parliament. A great wail goes up, led by senior newspaper columnists, greying leader-writers and respected elder statesmen (usually in the Lords) and supported by a chorus of lesser MPs and hacks. Parliament (like *Punch*) "isn't what it used to be". Backbenchers have become bootlicking poodles. Ministers are bypassing the chamber and leaking announcements to the media. There are no great orators any more. Parliamentarians are second-rate. The Commons, runs the insistent refrain, "has become marginalised".

Become? Westminster slipped from the centre of the administrative map long before any of our grandfathers were born, and it must be at least a couple of centuries since it was even imaginable that what is essentially a place where people posture and shoot their mouths off could, in any normal sense of that term, supervise the executive.

The Commons is a place of conflict. So long as it is composed of competing parties it must remain so. You cannot govern a country by means of an institutionalised dogfight.

Besides, when not baying at the moon, baring their teeth and barking at the passing pantechnicon of government, snapping at each other's legs or jumping tamely through the whips' hoops, MPs are sitting up and begging to their constituents. Each of the 659 Members must pretend, to every voter in their little patch of our country, to be answerable for the whole sweep of government policy in every field. It is a necessary charade conducted by people who are necessarily amateurs at policy and outsiders to practical administration.

Look, after all, at the likely crop brought in by the combine harvester of a British general election. They are never going to be a crack team of analysts and troubleshooters. The ballot box is random. Constituency selection committees are not professional headhunters. Specialisation is difficult; attention is divided; concentration is distracted; calibre is mixed.

In no methodical or structured way could an assembly of such persons, in a state of perpetual war with each other, "steer", "provide a

"D'YOU EVER WORRY YOUR KIDS MIGHT DRIFT INTO POLITICS?"

check on", "hold the reins of" or "hold to account" (all favourite, lazy metaphors) the whole fiendishly intricate circuitry of a modern administration. In most areas of government, for most of the time, most Members of Parliament haven't the least idea what's going on. This is inevitable and nobody's fault.

In the Parliament of 1997-2001 I sat at William Hague's request on a small committee chaired by Lord Norton of Louth to examine some of these supposed defects and ask whether and how they might be remedied. I do not resile from the conclusions we reached, which I think were, in a modest way, useful. We felt it was a pity that the career path of any ambitious and capable modern MP lay mainly through promotion within the government or opposition machine. That is where the power and glory, the pay and perks, and the excitement lie. This simple truth gives the party whips all the clout they need to subdue or suborn many backbenchers, for they can honestly remind their charges that it is upon their recommendation or censure that preferment will be offered or withheld.

With the examples of distinguished parliamentarians, living and dead, like Enoch Powell, Tam Dalyell, John Biffen or Robin Maxwell-Hyslop in mind, we asked how lustre and satisfaction might be added to a career outside the party or ministerial machine. We proposed that better pay, better offices, better training and staff — and perhaps even official limos — might be offered to (for instance) select committee chairmen; we looked for ways of getting the whips' tentacles out of their work. We hoped that as a result the idea might gain ground that being a parliamentarian could be an honoured and well-rewarded career in itself, rather than a stepping-stone to government. This might attract more expertise, more serious-mindedness, more independence, into politics, and offer an alternative career-path to capable people.

I am sure this was good advice. We were not alone in offering it. There is some chance that it may be acted upon. One would welcome that. It would make a constructive contribution.

But as I look back over some 25 years in and around Westminster, first as one of Margaret Thatcher's clerks, then for seven years as MP for West Derbyshire, then as a political interviewer for LWT's *Weekend World*, and finally as a columnist and, for some 14 years, parliamentary sketchwriter for *The Times*, a small insistent voice tells me that making a constructive contribution to the business of government will never be Parliament's principal or distinctive task, and never be what the House does best.

In the end, the Commons is a destroyer of men and governments, or it is nothing. The spirit is gladiatorial. The place must be, always and at least, a spectacle, and often a cruel one.

That, anyway, is what this sketchwriter would distil from those of his memories which stand out from that quarter century.


I watched from the gallery as, in 1979, after the Winter of Discontent, Jim Callaghan's Labour Government fell on a single vote on a motion of no confidence. It was nail-biting. The debate was noisy, sometimes angry, often humorous. For the Government Michael Foot made one of the funniest, finest parliamentary speeches of the century. As the whips advanced to the table with their count, one felt, perhaps melodramatically, that into the moment had been concentrated all the tensions and failures of many months, preceded by many years, of a tottering democratic socialist epoch. Parliament killed it off.

I listened (an MP now) as in the early 1980s Mrs Thatcher and Geoffrey Howe came quite close to losing their economic and political nerve in the Commons, as factories closed, unemployment soared, and the "wets" on the Conservative back benches muttered and plotted. Mrs Thatcher was being tested by incipient mutiny.

I listened as, one Saturday morning in 1982, the whole Commons left her in no doubt that she must order the invasion of the Falkland Islands or end her career in ignominy. Probably that was anyway her wish but nobody who heard the Commons then could have supposed she had any alternative. In that spectacle I learnt (to my mild surprise) how warlike were the British and their representatives.

Neither of these Commons dramas was, on cold analysis, anything more than a pantomime. The House lacked the economic expertise to understand the "monetarist" experiment the early Thatcher Government was running, but it was able to feel and dramatise the pain. The House could not have organised a croquet match let alone a war in the South Atlantic and was thoroughly ill-equipped to assess the risks; but as a conductor for popular anger and national defiance, the place did its democratic duty. The pantomime was a necessary pantomime: it instructed, as theatre often can.

Still an MP, I watched this and later Thatcher Governments win the argument as well as the votes over trade union reform, and begin the process of undermining "old" Labour's self-belief: a process that has led to almost everything which is important about post-Tory Labour government. I watched Thatcher and her ministers win the divisions but persistently fail to win the Commons argument about poll tax. Those who complain that a government with a good majority can ignore Parliament should pause a moment and look at what the Commons can eventually do to such a government.

For it was Parliament which brought down Mrs Thatcher: not in a vote, but in a billowing of smoke-signals and a cacophony of whispers. It is no coincidence Sir Geoffrey's final thrust against her was made in the chamber. None of us who watched it (I from the Press Gallery now) had any doubt that a parliamentary tribe was dispatching its chieftainess in a very traditional Commons way.

And it was Parliament which brought down John Major. The narrowness (finally the disappearance) of his majority did much to heighten the tension but he could have survived lost divisions if his party had not been fracturing around him. A principled argument about Europe was the sledgehammer, but if the party had not been weakened in resolve and confidence by a sense of haemorrhaging democratic mandate — a sense of having outlived its Thatcherite purpose and stayed too long — Mr Major could have ridden Parliament. Instead, Parliament threw him from his saddle. The election which followed in 1997 was certainly a cause but also a consequence of Tory parliamentary collapse.

We had, throughout, watched from the Press Gallery as, beneath the noise of Tories scrapping, the quieter sound of an Opposition rediscovering the will — and the way — to live, began to swell. New Labour was born at Westminster, even if electoral adversity was the midwife.

And at Westminster it will die, as all ascendancies finally do. Blairism's present hegemony need not be seen as a rebuff for Parliament, but as a playing out, on the stage which Parliament provides, of the many scenes of one act in the political play. When as a political force new Labour has outlived its usefulness, the Commons will dramatise, and by dramatising help to drive, its decline and fall. How this will happen we cannot know; when it will happen we can only guess; but, though the tale will be a national tale, the actors will be MPs and the stage set Neo-Gothic.

And all this will be watchable and watched: watched by millions of people. Yes, the Commons is crude, vulgar and ignorant; yes, it hardly begins to do justice to the intricacies of the argument; yes, the language is unrefined and the behaviour appalling . . . the British public have been aghast at the way their legislators carry on since (relatively recently) a written report was permitted to be made (and, more recently still) the proceedings heard, and finally seen on television. Aghast they may be, but the pantomime retains for them a horrible fascination. Almost alone among the peoples of Europe, the daily proceedings of their legislature remain, at least in their more sensational aspects, a matter of household knowledge. That is why I would, concluding, attempt a small, limited defence of the parliamentary sketch.

We sketchwriters are pantomime critics, comic-book artists, or we are nothing. If you doubt whether the House of Commons ought to be a pantomime, or its characters caricatures, then you will see the sketchwriters' art as degrading to its subject. But if, like me, you have concluded that to hold before the attention of the nation a comic-strip representation of the interplay of political forces and personalities, performed in an often Punch and Judy way, renders some sort of a democratic service, then you will suffer the sketchwriter to ply his (or her) trade.

That, anyway, is what I think. Parliament will never be a symposium, and the parliamentary sketch will never be a literary critique. The case for a rough-and-tumble Commons is the case for a knockabout sketch. Long may both thrive.

# RESULTS BY CONSTITUENCY

# HOUSE OF COMMONS, JUNE 2001

T HIS section of *The Times Guide to the House of Commons* lists in alphabetical order by constituency the full results of the general election held on June 7, 2001. All the 659 constituencies in England, Wales, Scotland and Northern Ireland are listed with statistical data on voting figures, turnout and swings compared with the results in May 1997, as well as brief biographies of the new Members and, for the first time in the *Times Guide*, a demographic and geographic profile of each seat.

The reason for these new constituency profiles is simple. Many constituency names, particularly since the pre-1997 boundary revision, bear little or no resemblance to the towns on which they are centred, so that many people outside the areas concerned are understandably confused. Where are Wansbeck and Wansdyke, Ochil and Ogmore, Elmet and Halton, Amber Valley and Mole Valley?

By providing these location paragraphs as well as a brief demographic sketch and a cross-reference to the fold-out map at the end of the book, the *Guide* attempts to address this problem. For much of the information here we are indebted to Robert Waller and Byron Criddle and their excellent *Almanac of British Politics* (6th edition 1999, published by Routledge).

In the following pages, constituencies in cities, boroughs or towns are listed under that city, borough or town, eg, Edgbaston will be found under Birmingham Edgbaston. The "St" constituencies (St Albans etc) come between Saffron Walden and Salford. On the sometimes contentious question of whether a seat should be Wiltshire North or North Wiltshire, for example, the *Guide* follows the precedent of previous editions, which in turn have followed the Press Association listing convention.

As there has been no constituency boundary change since the 1997 general election, the statistical comparisons — the swings and percentages of the vote, for example — are straightforward. The figures in the results tables have been calculated to two decimal points.

In the biographical details, directorships are not generally listed if they are in the Register of Members' Interests, available on the parliamentary website **(www.parliament.uk)**. See websites, page 294. MPs' fax numbers, e-mail addresses and websites are as provided by Members themselves.

A full list of the abbreviations used in the biographies can be found at the end of this section on pages 289 and 290. The list of party abbreviations used in the results tables is given below.

**Tim Austin and Tim Hames**

## PARTY ABBREVIATIONS

**Major parties: C** - Conservative; **Lab** - Labour; **Lab Co-op** - Labour and Co-operative; **LD** - Liberal Democrat; **PC** - Plaid Cymru; **SNP** - Scottish National Party; **UUP** - Ulster Unionist Party; **DUP** - Democratic Unionist Party; **SDLP** - Social Democratic and Labour Party; **SF** - Sinn Fein

**Minor parties: AL** - Asian League; **Alliance** - Alliance; **Anti-Corrupt** - Anti-Corruption Forum; **BNP** - British National Party; **Bean** - New Millennium Bean; **CPA** - Christian Peoples Alliance; **Ch D** - Christian Democrat; **Choice** - People's Choice; **Comm** - Communist Party; **Community** - Independent Community Candidate Empowering Change; **Country** - Countryside Party; **Customer** - Direct Customer Service Party; **Def Welfare** - Defend The Welfare State Against Blairism; **Elvis** - Church of the Militant Elvis Party; **Ext Club** - Extinction Club; **FDP** - Fancy Dress Party; **FP** - Freedom Party; **Green** - Green Party; **Grey** - Grey Party; **IOW** - Isle of Wight Party; **Ind** - Independent; **Ind B** - Independent B; **Ind Batch** - Independent Batchelor; **Ind Bell** - Independent Bell; **Ind Booth** - Independent Booth; **Ind Br** - Independent Br; **Ind Braid** - Independent Braid; **Ind Cam** - Independent Cam; **Ind Haines** - Independent Haines; **Ind Hill** - Independent Hill; **Ind Hunt** - Independent Hunt; **Ind J** - Independent J; **Ind K** - Independent K; **#** - Independent Kl; **Ind L** - Independent L; **Ind M** - Independent M; **Ind N** - Independent N; **Ind Nazir** - Independent Nazir; **Ind P** - Independent P; **Ind Pev** - Independent Pev; **Ind Pr** - Independent Pr; **Ind Prachar** - Independent Prachar; **Ind R** - Independent R; **Ind Sh** - Independent Sh; **Ind Sib** - Independent Sib; **Ind T** - Independent T; **Ind UU** - Independent United Unionist; **Ind Vote** - Independent Vote for Yourself Party; **Ind X** - Independent X; **Indep Braid** - Independent Braid; **JLDP** - John Lilburne Democratic Party; **JP** - Justice Party; **KHHC** - Kidderminster Hospital and Health Concern; **LCA** - Legalise Cannabis Alliance; **LP** - Liberated Party; **Left All** - Left Alliance; **Lib** - Liberal; **Loony** - Monster Raving Loony Party; **Low Excise** - Lower Excise Duty Party; **Marxist** - Marxist Party; **Meb Ker** - Mebyon Kernow; **Muslim** - Muslim Party; **NBP** - New Britain Party; **NF** - National Front; **NI Unionist** - Northern Ireland Unionist; **PF** - Pathfinders; **PJP** - People's Justice Party; **PUP** - Progressive Unionist Party; **Pacifist** - Pacifist Party for Peace, Co-operation, Environment; **Pensioner** - Pensioner Coalition; **Pro Euro C** - Pro Euro Conservative Party; **ProLife** - ProLife Alliance; **Prog Dem** - Progressive Democratic Party; **R & R Loony** - Rock & Roll Loony Party; **RP** - Rate Payer; **Ref UK** - Reform UK; **Reform** - Reform 2000; **Res Motor** - Residents and Motorists of Great Britain; **SSP** - Scottish Socialist Party; **Scot Ref** - Scottish Freedom Referendum Party; **Scot U** - Scottish Unionist; **Soc** - Socialist Party; **Soc All** - Socialist Alliance; **Soc Alt** - Socialist Alternative Party; **Soc Lab** - Socialist Labour Party; **Socialist** - Socialist; **Stuck** - Stuckist; **Sunrise** - Chairman of Sunrise Radio; **Tatton** - Tatton Group; **Third** - Third Way; **Truth** - Truth Party; **UK Ind** - UK Independence Party; **UKU** - United Kingdom Unionist; **Unrep** - Unrepresented People's Party; **WFLOE** - Women for Life on Earth; **WRP** - Workers' Revolutionary Party; **Wessex Reg** - Wessex Regionalist; **Women's Co** - Women's Coalition; **WP** - Workers' Party; **Wrestling** - Jam Wrestling Party

## ABERAVON | Lab hold

| Electorate | %Turnout | | 49,660 | 60.79% | 2001 | 50,025 | 71.89% | 1997 |
|---|---|---|---|---|---|---|---|---|
| **Francis H** | **Lab** | **19,063** | **63.14%** | **-8.18%** | **25,650** | **71.32%** | **Lab** |
| Turnbull Ms L | PC | 2,955 | 9.79% | 3.98% | 4,079 | 11.34% | LD |
| Davies C | LD | 2,933 | 9.72% | -1.62% | 2,835 | 7.88% | C |
| Miraj A | C | 2,296 | 7.61% | -0.27% | 2,088 | 5.81% | PC |
| Tutton A | RP | 1,960 | 6.49% | | 970 | 2.7% | Ref |
| Beany C | Bean | 727 | 2.41% | | 341 | 0.95% | Beanus |
| Chapman M | Soc All | 256 | 0.85% | | | | |
| **Lab to PC swing** | **6.08%** | **30,190** | Lab maj 16,108 | | **35,963** | Lab maj 21,571 | |
| | | | 53.36% | | | 59.98% | |

**HYWEL FRANCIS,** b June 6, 1946. Elected 2001. Inherits seat from the retiring Sir John Morris, former Welsh Sec and Attorney General. Univ professor and special adviser to Welsh Sec. Former dir, adult and continuing ed dept, Univ of Wales, Swansea. Ed Whitchurch GS; Univ of Wales, Swansea.

This is the sort of constituency which would once have been described as classic South Wales steel-making and Labour-voting. Two decades of job cuts have reduced the influence of steel in the area around Port Talbot but the loyalty to the Labour Party remains unshaken. An urban seat surrounded by a gritty industrial landscape. English, and not Welsh, is by far the dominant local language. Map 1

## ABERDEEN CENTRAL | Lab hold

| Electorate | %Turnout | | 50,098 | 52.75% | 2001 | 54,257 | 65.64% | 1997 |
|---|---|---|---|---|---|---|---|---|
| **Doran F** | **Lab** | **12,025** | **45.5%** | **-4.32%** | **17,745** | **49.82%** | **Lab** |
| Gault W | SNP | 5,379 | 20.35% | 4.16% | 6,944 | 19.5% | C |
| Anderson Ms E | LD | 4,547 | 17.2% | 3.96% | 5,767 | 16.19% | SNP |
| Whyte S | C | 3,761 | 14.23% | -5.27% | 4,714 | 13.24% | LD |
| Cumbers A | SSP | 717 | 2.71% | | 446 | 1.25% | Ref |
| **Lab to SNP swing** | **4.24%** | **26,429** | Lab maj 6,646 | | **35,616** | Lab maj 10,801 | |
| | | | 25.15% | | | 30.32% | |

**FRANK DORAN,** b April 13, 1949. Elected here 1997; MP for Aberdeen S 1987-92. PPS to Ian McCartney at DTI and Cabinet Office, 1997-2001. Lab spokesman, energy, 1988-92. Contested Scotland NE, 1984 Euro elections. Asst editor, Scottish Legal Action Grp Bulletin, 1975-78. Solicitor. Ed Ainslie Park Sec; Leith Acad; Dundee Univ. tel: 01224 252715 fax: 01224 252716

The core of the so-called Granite City and an area which has been equally firmly attached to the Labour Party. The lure of oil has led to an expansion of the population of northeastern Scotland and this seat was radically redrawn to accommodate those trends. A highly polarised constituency between a traditional working class and a comfortable middle class on the fringe that leans towards the Tories or the SNP. Map 2

## ABERDEEN NORTH | Lab hold

| Electorate | %Turnout | | 52,746 | 57.55% | 2001 | 54,302 | 70.74% | 1997 |
|---|---|---|---|---|---|---|---|---|
| **Savidge M** | **Lab** | **13,157** | **43.34%** | **-4.53%** | **18,389** | **47.87%** | **Lab** |
| Allan Dr A | SNP | 8,708 | 28.69% | 6.88% | 8,379 | 21.81% | SNP |
| Donaldson J | LD | 4,991 | 16.44% | 2.33% | 5,763 | 15.0% | C |
| Cowling R | C | 3,047 | 10.04% | -4.96% | 5,421 | 14.11% | LD |
| Forman Ms S | SSP | 454 | 1.5% | | 463 | 1.21% | Ref |
| **Lab to SNP swing** | **5.70%** | **30,357** | Lab maj 4,449 | | **38,415** | Lab maj 10,010 | |
| | | | 14.66% | | | 26.06% | |

**MALCOLM SAVIDGE,** b May 9, 1946. Elected 1997. Contested Kincardine and Deeside 1992 and 1991 by-election. Convener, all-party grp on global security and non-proliferation; vice-chairman of World Gvt grp; member, Environmental Audit Sel Cttee. Aberdeen city cllr, 1980-97 (dep leader, 1992-96). Member EIS; TGWU. Teacher. Ed Wallington County GS; Aberdeen Univ; Aberdeen Coll of Ed. tel: 01224 252708 fax: 01224 252712

Signs of the prosperity of Aberdeen are most starkly evident in this seat which combines a traditional working-class Labour base with suburban enclaves more willing to contemplate voting for one of the other three main parties in Scotland. The heartland of the seat remains, however, a set of huge council estates where poverty and unemployment, even in good times, remain stubbornly high. Map 3

## ABERDEEN SOUTH — Lab hold

| Electorate | %Turnout | | 58,907 | 62.62% | 2001 | 60,490 | 72.84% | 1997 |
|---|---|---|---|---|---|---|---|---|
| **Begg Ms A** | **Lab** | **14,696** | **39.84%** | **4.57%** | **15,541** | **35.27%** | **Lab** |
| Yuill I | LD | 10,308 | 27.94% | 0.31% | 12,176 | 27.63% | LD |
| Macdonald M | C | 7,098 | 19.24% | -7.13% | 11,621 | 26.37% | C |
| Angus I | SNP | 4,293 | 11.64% | 1.88% | 4,299 | 9.76% | SNP |
| Watt D | SSP | 495 | 1.34% | | 425 | 0.96% | Ref |
| **LD to Lab swing** | **2.13%** | **36,890** | **Lab maj 4,388** | | **44,062** | **Lab maj 3,365** | |
| | | | 11.89% | | | 7.64% | |

**ANNE BEGG,** b Dec 16, 1955. Elected 1997. Member, Scottish Affairs Select Cttee, 1997-2001; oil and gas industry grp; board of management, Scottish Physically Handicapped-Able Bodied; fellowship, Industry and Parly Trust; member, Scottish General Teaching Council; patron, Nat Fed of Shopmobility; Scottish Motor Neurone Disease Soc; Angus Special Playscheme. Disabled Scot of the Year, 1988. Confined to wheelchair suffering from rare blood disease. Teacher. Ed Brechin HS; Aberdeen Univ; Aberdeen Coll of Ed. e-mail: begga@parliament.uk tel: 01224 252704 fax: 01224 252705

This is by far the most competitive seat in Aberdeen. The Conservatives won the old constituency of the same name in 1992, one of only three places where they regained a seat they had lost five years earlier. The Liberal Democrats are also strong and benefited from boundary changes. It will always have the potential to perform as a three-way marginal with the final result dependent on middle-class sentiment. Map 4

## ABERDEENSHIRE WEST & KINCARDINE — LD hold

| Electorate | %Turnout | | 61,180 | 61.97% | 2001 | 59,123 | 73.05% | 1997 |
|---|---|---|---|---|---|---|---|---|
| **Smith Sir R** | **LD** | **16,507** | **43.54%** | **2.46%** | **17,742** | **41.08%** | **LD** |
| Kerr T | C | 11,686 | 30.82% | -4.1% | 15,080 | 34.92% | C |
| Hutchens K | Lab | 4,669 | 12.31% | 3.23% | 5,639 | 13.06% | SNP |
| Green J | SNP | 4,634 | 12.22% | -0.84% | 3,923 | 9.08% | Lab |
| Manley A | SSP | 418 | 1.1% | | 805 | 1.86% | Ref |
| **C to LD swing** | **3.28%** | **37,914** | **LD maj 4,821** | | **43,189** | **LD maj 2,662** | |
| | | | 12.72% | | | 6.16% | |

**SIR ROBERT SMITH,** b April 15, 1958. Elected 1997; contested Aberdeen N for SDP/All, 1987. LD spokesman, Scottish Affairs; Member, Scottish Affairs Select Cttee; LD whip for Scottish MPs, Scottish ed spokesman, 1995-97; vice-chairman, all party grp, UK offshore oil and gas industry. Managed family estate in Aberdeenshire. Aberdeenshire cllr, 1995-97. Member, Electoral Reform Soc; European Movement. Ed Merchant Taylors', London; Aberdeen Univ. e-mail: bobsmith@cix.co.uk tel: 020-7219 3531 fax: 020-7219 0907

A distinctly desirable and affluent seat consisting of rural dwellers and many who commute into the booming business sector of Aberdeen. Local opinion is polarised between the Liberal Democrats and the Conservatives, who were once entirely dominant in this area. A very high level of owner-occupation and professional/managerial employees when compared with the rest of Scotland. Map 5

## AIRDRIE & SHOTTS — Lab hold

| Electorate | %Turnout | | 58,349 | 54.39% | 2001 | 57,673 | 71.4% | 1997 |
|---|---|---|---|---|---|---|---|---|
| **Liddell Ms H** | **Lab** | **18,478** | **58.22%** | **-3.6%** | **25,460** | **61.82%** | **Lab** |
| Lindsay Ms A | SNP | 6,138 | 19.34% | -5.06% | 10,048 | 24.4% | SNP |
| Love J | LD | 2,376 | 7.49% | 3.32% | 3,660 | 8.89% | C |
| McIntosh G | C | 1,960 | 6.18% | -2.71% | 1,719 | 4.17% | LD |
| Dempsey Ms M | Scot U | 1,439 | 4.53% | | 294 | 0.71% | Ref |
| McGuigan K | SSP | 1,171 | 3.69% | | | | |
| Herriot C | Soc Lab | 174 | 0.55% | | | | |
| **SNP to Lab swing** | **0.73%** | **31,736** | **Lab maj 12,340** | | **41,181** | **Lab maj 15,412** | |
| | | | 38.88% | | | 37.42% | |

**HELEN LIDDELL,** b Dec 6, 1950. Elected here 1997; MP, Monklands East, 1994-97, having won by-election caused by death of Lab leader, John Smith. Sec of State, Scotland Office, June, 2001-; Min of State, DTI, 1999-2001; Min for Transport, 1999; Min of State, Scotland Office, 1998-99; Economic Sec to the Treasury, 1997-98. Lab spokeswoman on Scotland, 1995-97, dealing with ed and social work. Vice-chairwoman, all-party Scottish Opera grp, 1996-97. Ed St Patrick's HS, Coatbridge; Strathclyde Univ. e-mail:timmonsj@parliament.uk tel: 01236 748777 fax: 01236 748666

The successor constituency to Monklands East which was represented by John Smith before his untimely death in 1994. The heart of the seat is the town of Airdrie in Central Scotland. Religion still plays a part in local politics here and the preferred flavour in this seat is Protestantism. A solidly working-class seat with a strong attachment to the Labour Party. Map 6

# ALDERSHOT

**C hold**

| Electorate | %Turnout | | 78,262 | 57.9% | 2001 | 76,189 | 71.07% | 1997 |
|---|---|---|---|---|---|---|---|---|
| **Howarth G** | | C | **19,106** | **42.16%** | **-0.53%** | **23,119** | **42.69%** | C |
| Collett A | | LD | 12,542 | 27.68% | -2.79% | 16,498 | 30.47% | LD |
| Akehurst L | | Lab | 11,391 | 25.14% | 1.03% | 13,057 | 24.11% | Lab |
| Rumsey D | | UK Ind | 797 | 1.76% | 0.29% | 794 | 1.47% | UK Ind |
| Stacey A | | Green | 630 | 1.39% | | 361 | 0.67% | Ind |
| Pendragon A | | Ind | 459 | 1.01% | 0.34% | 322 | 0.59% | BNP |
| Hope A | | Loony | 390 | 0.86% | | | | |
| **LD to C swing** | **1.13%** | | **45,315** | | **C maj 6,564** | **54,151** | | **C maj 6,621** |
| | | | | | 14.49% | | | 12.22% |

**GERALD HOWARTH,** b Sept 12, 1947. Elected here 1997. MP, Cannock and Burntwood, 1983-92. Vice-chairman, C Home Affairs Cttee, 2000-; joint sec, C Defence Cttee, 1999-; member, Home Affairs Select Cttee, 1997-2001; Sound Broadcasting, 1987-92; member, Exec, 1922 Cttee, 1999-; vice-chairman (chairman, 1998-99) Parly aerospace grp. PPS to Margaret Thatcher, 1991-92; Sir George Young, Min. for Housing and Planning, 1990-91. Ed Bloxham Sch, Banbury; Southampton Univ.
tel: 020-7219 5650 fax: 020-7219 1198

An extremely pleasant Hampshire seat with a very strong connection to the Armed Forces. The extent to which the military vote is decisive now, however, is very much the stuff of fiction. Its inclusion largely depresses overall turnout figures. This northeastern corner of the county, which includes Farnborough, famous for its annual air show, has been reliably Conservative and was represented for many years by the colourful figure of Julian Critchley. Map 7

# ALDRIDGE-BROWNHILLS

**C hold**

| Electorate | %Turnout | | 62,388 | 60.6% | 2001 | 62,441 | 74.26% | 1997 |
|---|---|---|---|---|---|---|---|---|
| **Shepherd R** | | C | **18,974** | **50.18%** | **3.05%** | **21,856** | **47.13%** | C |
| Geary I | | Lab | 15,206 | 40.22% | -1.47% | 19,330 | 41.69% | Lab |
| Howes Mrs M | | LD | 3,251 | 8.6% | -2.58% | 5,184 | 11.18% | LD |
| Rothery J | | Soc All | 379 | 1.0% | | | | |
| **Lab to C swing** | **2.26%** | | **37,810** | | **C maj 3,768** | **46,370** | | **C maj 2,526** |
| | | | | | 9.97% | | | 5.44% |

**RICHARD SHEPHERD,** b Dec 6, 1942. Elected 1979. Member, Select Cttees: Modernisation of Commons, 1997; Severn Bridges Bill, 1991; Treasury and Civil Service, 1979-83. Introduced Public Interest Disclosure Bill, 1997. Joint vice-chairman, C Backbench Constitutional Affairs, Scotland and Wales Cttee, 1997-. Parliamentarian of Year, *Spectator*, 1995. Non-exec director, Partridges of Sloane Street Ltd, food retailing, 1972-, and Shepherd Foods (London) Ltd, 1970-. Member of Lloyd's, 1974-94. Ed Isleworth GS; LSE; Johns Hopkins Univ, Sch of Advanced International Studies.

This is a distinctive and independently minded West Midlands constituency. It is formed by the amalgamation of two very different towns. Aldridge contains some of the wealthiest residents of this region and is habitually Conservative. Brownhills, a former mining town many years ago, is reliably Labour. An almost entirely white seat in an otherwise multiracial area. Map 8

# ALTRINCHAM & SALE WEST

**C hold**

| Electorate | %Turnout | | 71,820 | 60.66% | 2001 | 70,625 | 73.32% | 1997 |
|---|---|---|---|---|---|---|---|---|
| **Brady G** | | C | **20,113** | **46.16%** | **3.0%** | **22,348** | **43.16%** | C |
| Baugh Ms J | | Lab | 17,172 | 39.41% | -0.84% | 20,843 | 40.25% | Lab |
| Gaskell C | | LD | 6,283 | 14.42% | 1.8% | 6,535 | 12.62% | LD |
| | | | | | | 1,348 | 2.6% | Ref |
| | | | | | | 313 | 0.6% | ProLife |
| | | | | | | 270 | 0.52% | UK Ind |
| | | | | | | 125 | 0.24% | NLP |
| **Lab to C swing** | **1.92%** | | **43,568** | | **C maj 2,941** | **51,782** | | **C maj 1,505** |
| | | | | | 6.75% | | | 2.91% |

**GRAHAM BRADY,** b May 20, 1967. Elected 1997. Ed and Employment Select Cttee, 1997-2000. PPS to Michael Ancram (chairman, Conservative Party), 1999-2000; Opposition whip, 2000-; 1922 Cttee Executive, 1998-2000; chairman, Northern area C students, 1987-89. Dir, Waterfront Partnership, transport and strategic consultancy, 1992-97; previously asst dir, Centre for Policy Studies. Ed Altrincham GS; Durham Univ (chairman, univ C assoc, 1987-88). e-mail: altsale@tory.org www.traffordconservatives.org.uk
tel: 020-7219 1260 fax: 020-7219 1649

An extremely affluent constituency which contains much of the Cheshire middle-class fringe surrounding the Manchester area. Altrincham and Sale themselves are rather more typical of the region but the leafy suburbs which envelop them have traditionally provided the Conservatives with a large number of supporters. Labour has historically relied on a small number of council estates for a political base. Map 9

## ALYN & DEESIDE — Lab hold

| Electorate | %Turnout | | 60,478 | 58.57% | 2001 | 58,091 | 72.21% | 1997 |
|---|---|---|---|---|---|---|---|---|
| **Tami M** | Lab | | **18,525** | **52.3%** | **-9.57%** | **25,955** | **61.87%** | Lab |
| Isherwood M | C | | 9,303 | 26.26% | 3.49% | 9,552 | 22.77% | C |
| Burnham D | LD | | 4,585 | 12.94% | 3.22% | 4,076 | 9.72% | LD |
| Coombs R | PC | | 1,182 | 3.34% | 1.58% | 1,627 | 3.88% | Ref |
| Armstrong-Braun K | Green | | 881 | 2.49% | | 738 | 1.76% | PC |
| Crawford W | UK Ind | | 481 | 1.36% | | | | |
| Cooksey M | Ind | | 253 | 0.71% | | | | |
| Davies G | Comm | | 211 | 0.6% | | | | |
| **Lab to C swing** | **6.53%** | | **35,421** | Lab maj 9,222 | | **41,948** | Lab maj 16,403 | |
| | | | | 26.04% | | | 39.10% | |

**MARK TAMI,** b Oct 3, 1962. Elected 2001. Inherits seat from Barry Jones, who held it from 1983. Member, Lab nat policy forum. National head of policy, AEEU headquarters for past 15 years; member, of campaign team to bring Airbus project to Broughton, N Wales; member, TUC General Council, 1999-2001 and the First Past the Post campaign. Author, Fabian pamphlet on compulsory voting. Ed Enfield GS; Univ Coll, Wales, Swansea.

This is a relatively small constituency which is located on the Welsh border adjacent to Chester. It has traditionally been an industrial area demonstrating the sort of loyalty to the Labour Party that is more commonly associated with seats in South Wales. It is still struggling to overcome the long-term impact of the closure of the vast steelworks at Shotton almost 20 years ago. Map 10

## AMBER VALLEY — Lab hold

| Electorate | %Turnout | | 73,798 | 60.32% | 2001 | 72,005 | 76.07% | 1997 |
|---|---|---|---|---|---|---|---|---|
| **Mallaber Ms J** | Lab | | **23,101** | **51.9%** | **-2.77%** | **29,943** | **54.67%** | Lab |
| Shaw Ms G | C | | 15,874 | 35.66% | 2.2% | 18,330 | 33.46% | C |
| Smith Ms K | LD | | 5,538 | 12.44% | 4.74% | 4,219 | 7.7% | LD |
| | | | | | | 2,283 | 4.17% | Ref |
| **Lab to C swing** | **2.49%** | | **44,513** | Lab maj 7,227 | | **54,775** | Lab maj 11,613 | |
| | | | | 16.24% | | | 21.21% | |

**JUDY MALLABER,** b July 10, 1951. Elected 1997. Member, Ed and Employment Select Cttee, 1997-2001; Treasury Select Ctte. Research Fellow, Local Gvt info unit and its dir, 1987-95. Advisory council member, Northern Coll for Adult Ed, Barnsley. Research officer, Nupe, 1975-85. Member, Unison; Action for Southern Africa; Liberty; SEA; Friends of the Earth; Amnesty. Ed N London Collegiate Sch; St Anne's Coll, Oxford.

An intriguing bellwether seat. Amber Valley itself is a largely industrial area of Derbyshire which once depended on coalmining for employment. The surrounding villages are very different in physical and political character. It was held by the Conservatives, perhaps somewhat surprisingly, between 1983 and 1997. It is difficult to imagine how Labour could lose a seat such as this and still retain power. Map 11

## ANGUS — SNP hold

| Electorate | %Turnout | | 59,004 | 59.34% | 2001 | 59,708 | 72.14% | 1997 |
|---|---|---|---|---|---|---|---|---|
| **Weir M** | SNP | | **12,347** | **35.26%** | **-13.01%** | **20,792** | **48.27%** | SNP |
| Booth M | C | | 8,736 | 24.95% | 0.34% | 10,603 | 24.61% | C |
| McFatridge I | Lab | | 8,183 | 23.37% | 7.74% | 6,733 | 15.63% | Lab |
| Nield P | LD | | 5,015 | 14.32% | 4.88% | 4,065 | 9.44% | LD |
| Wallace B | SSP | | 732 | 2.09% | | 883 | 2.05% | Ref |
| **SNP to C swing** | **6.67%** | | **35,013** | SNP maj 3,611 | | **43,076** | SNP maj 10,189 | |
| | | | | 10.31% | | | 23.66% | |

**MICHAEL WEIR,** b March 24, 1957. Elected 2001. Inherits seat from Andrew Welsh, who stood down after five terms as MP to concentrate on the Scottish Parliament. Contested Aberdeen S, 1987. Campaign spokesman, rural affairs. Solicitor. Ed Arbroath HS; Aberdeen Univ.

A large and very rural seat which ranges from the edges of the Highlands and the Grampians while attracting some Dundee commuters. With an unusually high dependence on agriculture and forestry for employment, it is mostly a patchwork of small rural towns. In a more deferential era, this was natural Conservative territory. It has become very solid in its support for the Scottish National Party. Map 12

## ANTRIM EAST  UUP hold

| Electorate | %Turnout | | 60,897 | 59.12% | 2001 | 58,963 | 58.26% | 1997 |
|---|---|---|---|---|---|---|---|---|
| **Beggs R** | | **UUP** | **13,101** | **36.39%** | **-2.38%** | **13,318** | **38.77%** | **UUP** |
| Wilson S | | DUP | 12,973 | 36.04% | 16.59% | 6,929 | 20.17% | Alliance |
| Mathews J | | Alliance | 4,483 | 12.45% | -7.72% | 6,682 | 19.45% | DUP |
| O'Connor D | | SDLP | 2,641 | 7.34% | 2.75% | 2,334 | 6.79% | C |
| Mason R | | Ind | 1,092 | 3.03% | -0.3% | 1,757 | 5.11% | PUP |
| Graffin Ms J | | SF | 903 | 2.51% | 0.93% | 1,576 | 4.59% | SDLP |
| Greer A | | C | 807 | 2.24% | -4.55% | 1,145 | 3.33% | Ind |
| | | | | | | 543 | 1.58% | SF |
| | | | | | | 69 | 0.2% | NLP |
| **UUP to DUP swing** | **9.48%** | | **36,000** | UUP maj 128 | | **34,353** | UUP maj 6,389 | |
| | | | | 0.36% | | | 18.60% | |

**ROY BEGGS,** b Feb 20, 1936. Elected 1983; resigned seat 1985 in protest at Anglo-Irish agreement and retained it in 1986 by-election. Party spokesman on ed and employment, community relations, and culture, media and sport. Member, NI Affairs Select Cttee, 1997-2001; member, Public Accounts Cttee, 1984-86 and 1987-97; sec/treas, all-party older people grp, 1997-; joint vice-chairman, Denmark grp, 1997-; sec, Gibraltar grp, 1997-. Member for N Antrim, NI Assembly, 1982-86; chairman, Economic Development Cttee, 1982-84. Ed Ballyclare HS; Stranmillis Training Coll.

**This is a diverse and intriguing seat in most respects with the exception of the predictability of sectarian affiliation. It is predominantly a coastal constituency resting between the Antrim hills and the sea. It contains a mixture of heavy and light industry, some rural voters, and has an element of tourism. The overwhelming majority of the local population are Protestant but with no fixed loyalty to one brand of Unionism. Map 13**

## ANTRIM NORTH DUP hold

| Electorate | %Turnout | | 74,451 | 66.11% | 2001 | 72,411 | 63.78% | 1997 |
|---|---|---|---|---|---|---|---|---|
| **Paisley The Rev I** | | **DUP** | **24,539** | **49.86%** | **3.32%** | **21,495** | **46.54%** | **DUP** |
| Scott L | | UUP | 10,315 | 20.96% | -2.69% | 10,921 | 23.65% | UUP |
| Farren S | | SDLP | 8,283 | 16.83% | 0.95% | 7,333 | 15.88% | SDLP |
| Kelly J | | SF | 4,822 | 9.8% | 3.53% | 2,896 | 6.27% | SF |
| Dunlop Miss J | | Alliance | 1,258 | 2.56% | -3.6% | 2,845 | 6.16% | Alliance |
| | | | | | | 580 | 1.26% | NI Women |
| | | | | | | 116 | 0.25% | NLP |
| **UUP to DUP swing** | **3.01%** | | **49,217** | DUP maj 14,224 | | **46,186** | DUP maj 10,574 | |
| | | | | 28.90% | | | 22.89% | |

**THE REV IAN PAISLEY,** b April 6, 1926. Leader DUP. MP for Antrim N since 1970. Resigned seat 1985 in protest at Anglo-Irish agreement and retained it in 1986 by-election. Member of NI Assembly, 1998-, 1982-86 and 1973-75; NI Forum; NI Constitutional Convention, 1975-76; Stormont, 1970-72. MEP, 1979-. Pres, Whitefield Coll of the Bible, 1979-. Minister, Martyrs Memorial Free Presbyterian Church, Belfast, 1946-. Ed Model Sch, Ballymena; Ballymena Tech Coll; S Wales Bible Coll; Reformed Presbyterian Theological Hall, Belfast.

**Although represented by the Rev Ian Paisley for many years, this constituency should not be seen as one that mirrors the views of its elected representative. With a much larger minority of Roman Catholics than the other Antrim seat, it is also more rural and agricultural and includes the tourist attraction of the Giant's Causeway on the north coast. The core vote is supplied by the largely Unionist towns of Ballymena, Ballymoney and Moyle. Map 14**

## ANTRIM SOUTH UUP hold

| Electorate | %Turnout | | 70,651 | 62.5% | 2001 | 69,414 | 57.91% | 1997 |
|---|---|---|---|---|---|---|---|---|
| **Burnside D** | | **UUP** | **16,366** | **37.06%** | **-20.43%** | **23,108** | **57.49%** | **UUP** |
| McCrea The Rev R | | DUP | 15,355 | 34.77% | | 6,497 | 16.16% | SDLP |
| McKee S | | SDLP | 5,336 | 12.08% | -4.08% | 4,668 | 11.61% | Alliance |
| Meehan M | | SF | 4,160 | 9.42% | 3.87% | 3,490 | 8.68% | PUP |
| Ford D | | Alliance | 1,969 | 4.46% | -7.15% | 2,229 | 5.55% | SF |
| Boyd N | | NI Unionist | 972 | 2.2% | | 203 | 0.51% | NLP |
| **No swing applicable** | | | **44,158** | UUP maj 1,011 | | **40,195** | UUP maj 16,611 | |
| | | | | 2.29% | | | 41.33% | |

**DAVID BURNSIDE,** b Aug 24, 1951. Won seat back for UUP from Willie McCrea, DUP, the victor in the Sept 2000 by-election. Founding patron, Friends of the Union. Member, Ulster Unionist Council. Former dir of public affairs, British Airways. Dir, international PR consultancy. Ed Queen's Univ, Belfast.
*Details of 2000 by-election on page 291*

**A large seat which stretches from Lough Neagh and the River Bann to the fringe of Belfast. It contains a balance between agricultural and industrial interests. It is largely Protestant and broadly middle-class by the standards of Northern Irish politics. It had historically aligned itself with mainstream Unionism, an association rudely interrupted by a by-election in 2000, but it returned safely to the UUP fold in 2001. Map 15**

## ARGYLL & BUTE — LD hold

| Electorate | %Turnout | | 49,175 | 62.95% | 2001 | 49,451 | 72.23% | 1997 |
|---|---|---|---|---|---|---|---|---|
| **Reid A** | **LD** | | **9,245** | **29.86%** | **-10.34%** | **14,359** | **40.2%** | **LD** |
| Raven H | Lab | | 7,592 | 24.52% | 8.85% | 8,278 | 23.17% | SNP |
| Petrie D | C | | 6,436 | 20.79% | 1.83% | 6,774 | 18.96% | C |
| Samuel Ms A | SNP | | 6,433 | 20.78% | -2.39% | 5,596 | 15.67% | Lab |
| Divers D | SSP | | 1,251 | 4.04% | | 713 | 2.0% | Ref |
| **LD to Lab swing** | **9.60%** | | **30,957** | **LD maj 1,653** | | **35,720** | **LD maj 6,081** | |
| | | | | 5.34% | | | 17.03% | |

**ALAN REID,** b Aug 7, 1954. Elected 2001. Inherits seat from Mrs Ray Michie, who was MP for 14 years. Contested Paisley S by-election, 1990 and 1992; Dumbarton, 1997. Renfrew dist cllr, 1988-96. Party activist since 1981, serving at various levels, including period as vice-convener, Scottish LDs. Computer programmer. Ed Ayr Acad; Strathclyde Univ.

An unusually beautiful seat containing a huge number of islands and inlets on the West Coast of Scotland. It is the fourth largest constituency in the country, with no dominant population centre. The personal vote matters enormously. It relies on agriculture and, increasingly, tourism. The Tories were strong here but have been taken on by Liberal Democrats and the Scottish National Party. Map 16

## ARUNDEL & SOUTH DOWNS — C hold

| Electorate | %Turnout | | 70,956 | 64.67% | 2001 | 67,641 | 75.9% | 1997 |
|---|---|---|---|---|---|---|---|---|
| **Flight H** | **C** | | **23,969** | **52.23%** | **-0.85%** | **27,251** | **53.08%** | **C** |
| Deedman D | LD | | 10,265 | 22.37% | -3.37% | 13,216 | 25.74% | LD |
| Taylor C | Lab | | 9,488 | 20.68% | 2.42% | 9,376 | 18.26% | Lab |
| Perrin R | UK Ind | | 2,167 | 4.72% | 1.81% | 1,494 | 2.91% | UK Ind |
| **LD to C swing** | **1.26%** | | **45,889** | **C maj 13,704** | | **51,337** | **C maj 14,035** | |
| | | | | 29.86% | | | 27.34% | |

**HOWARD FLIGHT,** b June 16, 1948. Elected 1997. Shadow Economic Sec to Treasury, 2001-. Ex-member of Environment and Social Security Select Cttees. Joint chairman, all-party Hong Kong grp. Ex-member of Gvt's Tax Consultative Cttee. Worked for Hong Kong Bank, 1977-79 in Hongkong and India. Joint chairman of Investec Asset Management Ltd. Ed Brentwood Sch; Magdalene Coll, Cambridge; Univ of Michigan Business Sch.
e-mail: flighth@parliament.uk www.the-flight-site.org

A new seat created in 1997 as a consequence of the rising population of West Sussex. It was patched together from five different seats but despite this has a reasonable commonality of character. This is an extremely prosperous area consisting of middle-class towns and even more middle-class villages. If the Tories ever lose this seat then they will have become all but extinct as a political force. Map 17

## ASHFIELD — Lab hold

| Electorate | %Turnout | | 73,428 | 53.59% | 2001 | 72,269 | 70.02% | 1997 |
|---|---|---|---|---|---|---|---|---|
| **Hoon G** | **Lab** | | **22,875** | **58.13%** | **-7.04%** | **32,979** | **65.17%** | **Lab** |
| Leigh J | C | | 9,607 | 24.41% | 4.15% | 10,251 | 20.26% | C |
| Smith B | LD | | 4,428 | 11.25% | 1.6% | 4,882 | 9.65% | LD |
| Harby M | Ind | | 1,471 | 3.74% | | 1,896 | 3.75% | Ref |
| Watson G | Soc All | | 589 | 1.5% | | 595 | 1.18% | BNP |
| Howse Ms K | Soc Lab | | 380 | 0.97% | | | | |
| **Lab to C swing** | **5.60%** | | **39,350** | **Lab maj 13,268** | | **50,603** | **Lab maj 22,728** | |
| | | | | 33.72% | | | 44.91% | |

**GEOFF HOON,** b Dec 6, 1953. Elected 1992. Sec of State for Defence, 1999; confirmed June, 2001. Min, FCO, May-July, 1999. Min for Europe, 1999. Junior Min, Lord Chancellor's Dept, 1997-99. Lab spokesman, trade and industry, 1995-97, responsibile for information superhighway; Lab whip, 1994-95; chairman, all-party friends of music grp, 1992-97; MEP for Derbyshire and Ashfield, 1984-94. Barrister and law lecturer. Ed Nottingham HS; Jesus Coll, Cambridge.
tel: 020-7218 6432 fax: 020-7218 7140

A surprisingly fascinating Nottinghamshire constituency. Recent election returns are entirely in keeping with the bald facts concerning this seat, its historic links with coalmining. But it also has a high rate of owner-occupation and was aligned with the breakaway Union of Democratic Mineworkers in the 1980s when it swung to the right. It now seems to have returned to its established political loyalties. Map 18

## ASHFORD | C hold

| Electorate | %Turnout | | 76,699 | 62.5% | 2001 | 74,149 | 74.57% | 1997 |
|---|---|---|---|---|---|---|---|---|
| **Green D** | | **C** | **22,739** | **47.44%** | **6.03%** | **22,899** | **41.41%** | **C** |
| Adams J | | Lab | 15,380 | 32.08% | 0.35% | 17,544 | 31.73% | Lab |
| Fitchett K | | LD | 7,236 | 15.09% | -4.62% | 10,901 | 19.71% | LD |
| Boden R | | Green | 1,353 | 2.82% | 1.63% | 3,201 | 5.79% | Ref |
| Waller D | | UK Ind | 1,229 | 2.56% | | 660 | 1.19% | Green |
| | | | | | | 89 | 0.16% | NLP |
| **Lab to C swing** | | **2.84%** | **47,937** | | **C maj 7,359** | **55,294** | | **C maj 5,355** |
| | | | | | 15.35% | | | 9.68% |

**DAMIAN GREEN,** b Jan 17, 1956. Elected 1997. C spokesman on environment, 1999-; employment & higher ed, 1998-99. Member, Culture, Media and Sport Select Cttee, 1997-98. Vice-chairman, Parliamentary Mainstream; vice-president, Tory Reform Grp. Worked in Prime Minister's Policy Unit, 1992-94. Presenter/City editor of Channel 4 business daily programme, 1987-92; news editor, *The Times* Business News, 1984-85. Ed Reading Sch; Balliol Coll, Oxford (Pres of Union, 1977).
e-mail: greend@parliament.uk tel: 020-7219 3911 fax: 020-7219 0904

A large town by Kent standards, linked to a pleasant rural area which has tended to support the Conservatives by a solid margin. There are, however, pockets of solid Labour support in the London overspill estates that are also a significant factor in this pluralist social mix. The opening of the Channel Tunnel has provided major economic opportunities as well as serious environmental concerns. Map 19

## ASHTON UNDER LYNE | Lab hold

| Electorate | %Turnout | | 72,820 | 49.11% | 2001 | 72,206 | 65.48% | 1997 |
|---|---|---|---|---|---|---|---|---|
| **Heyes D** | | **Lab** | **22,340** | **62.47%** | **-5.04%** | **31,919** | **67.51%** | **Lab** |
| Charlesworth T | | C | 6,822 | 19.08% | 0.14% | 8,954 | 18.94% | C |
| Fletcher Mrs K | | LD | 4,237 | 11.85% | 2.11% | 4,603 | 9.74% | LD |
| Woods R | | BNP | 1,617 | 4.52% | | 1,346 | 2.85% | Ref |
| Rolland N | | Green | 748 | 2.09% | | 458 | 0.97% | Loony |
| **Lab to C swing** | | **2.59%** | **35,764** | | **Lab maj 15,518** | **47,280** | | **Lab maj 22,965** |
| | | | | | 43.39% | | | 48.57% |

**DAVID HEYES,** b April 2, 1946. Elected 2001. Inherits seat from Robert Sheldon, who held it since 1964. Spent over 30 years as local gvt officer for Manchester city and Greater Manchester councils, and latterly served as a member of Oldham MBC. Service manager. Ed Blackley Tech HS, Manchester; OU (social sciences).

This seat straddles the Tameside and Oldham areas of Greater Manchester. It is relatively small and cohesive in character. There is a significant Asian minority. It is also reliably Labour. The reliance on traditional industrial activity makes this the sort of seat which southerners would consider typical of northwest England, which is true here but far from so in much of the rest of the region. Map 20

## AYLESBURY | C hold

| Electorate | %Turnout | | 80,002 | 61.36% | 2001 | 79,047 | 72.81% | 1997 |
|---|---|---|---|---|---|---|---|---|
| **Lidington D** | | **C** | **23,230** | **47.32%** | **3.14%** | **25,426** | **44.18%** | **C** |
| Jones P | | LD | 13,221 | 26.93% | -2.62% | 17,007 | 29.55% | LD |
| White K | | Lab | 11,388 | 23.2% | 1.03% | 12,759 | 22.17% | Lab |
| Harper J | | UK Ind | 1,248 | 2.54% | | 2,196 | 3.82% | Ref |
| | | | | | | 166 | 0.29% | NLP |
| **LD to C swing** | | **2.88%** | **49,087** | | **C maj 10,009** | **57,554** | | **C maj 8,419** |
| | | | | | 20.39% | | | 14.63% |

**DAVID LIDINGTON,** b June 30, 1956. Elected 1992. Front bench spokesman, home affairs, 1999-. PPS to William Hague, 1997-99; to Michael Howard, when Home Sec. Former joint sec, C Backbench Home Affairs Cttee; member, Ed Select Cttee, 1992-96. Special adviser to Douglas Hurd, Home Sec and Foreign Sec, 1987-90, when on secondment from Rio Tinto-Zinc. Ed Haberdashers' Aske's Sch, Elstree; Sidney Sussex Coll, Cambridge (chairman, Univ C Assoc, 1978).
www.aylesbury.tory.org.uk

An affluent and attractive town in mid-Buckinghamshire allied to an equally prosperous rural fringe. Over the past few decades it has attracted new residents, employed in light industry or the service sector. Unemployment is very low and likely to remain so regardless of wider economic conditions. Although strongly Conservative in the past, the combined anti-Tory vote was surprisingly high in 1997. Map 21

## AYR — Lab hold

| Electorate | %Turnout | | 55,630 | 69.32% | 2001 | 55,829 | 80.17% | 1997 |
|---|---|---|---|---|---|---|---|---|
| **Osborne Ms S** | **Lab** | | **16,801** | **43.57%** | **-4.87%** | **21,679** | **48.44%** | **Lab** |
| Gallie P | C | | 14,256 | 36.97% | 3.15% | 15,136 | 33.82% | C |
| Mather J | SNP | | 4,621 | 11.98% | -0.59% | 5,625 | 12.57% | SNP |
| Ritchie S | LD | | 2,089 | 5.42% | 0.69% | 2,116 | 4.73% | LD |
| Stewart J | SSP | | 692 | 1.79% | | 200 | 0.45% | Ref |
| Smith J | UK Ind | | 101 | 0.26% | | | | |
| **Lab to C swing** | **4.01%** | | **38,560** | **Lab maj 2,545** | | **44,756** | **Lab maj 6,543** | |
| | | | | 6.60% | | | 14.62% | |

**SANDRA OSBORNE,** b Feb 23, 1956. Elected 1997. PPS, George Foulkes, Min, Scotland Office, 2001-. Worked for Kilmarnock Women's Aid. S Ayrshire cllr; former Kyle and Carrick cllr. Member, TGWU, Scottish Women's Cttee. Ed Campshill HS, Paisley; Anniesland Coll; Jordanhill Coll; Strathclyde Univ.

An intriguing social mixture has made for a distinctive political constituency. This was once as reliable territory for Scottish Conservatives as, for example, Bournemouth, might be considered for their English counterparts. It remains polarised between very Tory wards and equally hostile components. New boundaries introduced for the 1997 election pushed the seat in the direction of the Labour Party. Map 22

## BANBURY — C hold

| Electorate | %Turnout | | 83,392 | 61.77% | 2001 | 77,456 | 75.46% | 1997 |
|---|---|---|---|---|---|---|---|---|
| **Baldry T** | **C** | | **23,271** | **45.17%** | **2.27%** | **25,076** | **42.9%** | **C** |
| Sibley L | Lab | | 18,052 | 35.04% | 0.24% | 20,339 | 34.8% | Lab |
| Worgan T | LD | | 8,216 | 15.95% | -0.75% | 9,761 | 16.7% | LD |
| Cotton B | Green | | 1,281 | 2.49% | 1.58% | 2,245 | 3.84% | Ref |
| Harris S | UK Ind | | 695 | 1.35% | 0.73% | 530 | 0.91% | Green |
| | | | | | | 364 | 0.62% | UK Ind |
| | | | | | | 131 | 0.22% | NLP |
| **Lab to C swing** | **1.02%** | | **51,515** | **C maj 5,219** | | **58,446** | **C maj 4,737** | |
| | | | | 10.13% | | | 8.10% | |

**TONY BALDRY,** b July 10, 1950. Elected 1983. Agriculture, Fisheries and Food Min, 1995-97. Under-Sec for Foreign and Commonwealth Affairs, 1994-95; Environment, 1990-94; Energy, 1990. Member, Select Cttee, Trade and Industry, 1997-2001. PPS to John Wakeham, Leader of Commons and then Energy Sec, 1987-90; and to Lynda Chalker, Min of State for Transport and then FCO, 1985-87. Non-exec dir, Merchant International Grp 1997-. Barrister and co dir. Ed Leighton Park, Reading; Sussex Univ. e-mail: baldryt@parliament.uk tel: 020-7219 4476 fax: 020-7219 5826

This is a boom area of Oxfordshire. The traditional market town has almost been engulfed by new employment-seekers, housed privately. This is also largely true of Bicester, the other significant town in the seat. The closure of the US Air Force base at Upper Heyford has diluted the military influence on local politics. A solidly Tory seat with a significant minority of council-estate Labour voters. Map 23

## BANFF & BUCHAN — SNP hold

| Electorate | %Turnout | | 56,496 | 54.53% | 2001 | 58,493 | 68.69% | 1997 |
|---|---|---|---|---|---|---|---|---|
| **Salmond A** | **SNP** | | **16,710** | **54.24%** | **-1.53%** | **22,409** | **55.77%** | **SNP** |
| Wallace A | C | | 6,207 | 20.15% | -3.65% | 9,564 | 23.8% | C |
| Harris E | Lab | | 4,363 | 14.16% | 2.35% | 4,747 | 11.81% | Lab |
| Herbison D | LD | | 2,769 | 8.99% | 3.02% | 2,398 | 5.97% | LD |
| Rowan Ms A | SSP | | 447 | 1.45% | | 1,060 | 2.64% | Ref |
| Davidson E | UK Ind | | 310 | 1.01% | | | | |
| **C to SNP swing** | **1.06%** | | **30,806** | **SNP maj 10,503** | | **40,178** | **SNP maj 12,845** | |
| | | | | 34.09% | | | 31.97% | |

**ALEX SALMOND,** b Dec 31, 1954. Elected 1987. Member of the Scottish Parliament, 1999-; National convener, SNP, 1990-2000; SNP spokesman, Treasury and economic affairs, energy, fishing, environment, 1988-97. Member, Energy Select Cttee. Founder, Scottish Centre for Economic and Social Research. Energy economist with Royal Bank of Scotland, 1980-87. Senior vice-convener (dep leader and former senior vice-chairman) SNP, 1987-90; SNP vice-chairman (publicity) 1985-87; member, SNP nat exec, 1981-. Ed Linlithgow Acad; St Andrews Univ.

A highly distinct constituency in East Aberdeenshire. The sitting Member, Alex Salmond, surprised Scottish political commentators when he decided to stand down from the leadership of the Scottish National Party and then said he would nonetheless stand again for the Westminster Parliament. This is a largely rural seat with a number of towns, including Fraserburgh and Peterhead, which expanded on the back of the oil boom. Map 24

## BARKING — Lab hold

| Electorate | %Turnout | | 55,229 | 45.49% | 2001 | 53,682 | 61.41% | 1997 |
|---|---|---|---|---|---|---|---|---|
| **Hodge Mrs M** | | **Lab** | **15,302** | **60.9%** | **-4.92%** | **21,698** | **65.82%** | **Lab** |
| Weatherley M | | C | 5,768 | 22.96% | 5.36% | 5,802 | 17.6% | C |
| Keppetipola A | | LD | 2,450 | 9.75% | 0.26% | 3,128 | 9.49% | LD |
| Toleman M | | BNP | 1,606 | 6.39% | 3.68% | 1,283 | 3.89% | Ref |
| | | | | | | 894 | 2.71% | BNP |
| | | | | | | 159 | 0.48% | ProLife |
| **Lab to C swing** | **5.14%** | | **25,126** | Lab maj 9,534 | 37.94% | **32,964** | Lab maj 15,896 | 48.22% |

**MARGARET HODGE,** b Sept 8, 1944. Elected 1994 by-election. Min for Universities, June 2001-; Parly Under-Sec, DfEE, 1998-2001. Member, Ed and Employment Select Cttee and chairwoman of its Ed Sub Cttee, also member of its Employment SubCttee, 1997-2001; Deregulation Select Cttee, 1996-97. Ex- chairwoman, London grp of Lab MPs. Islington cllr, 1973-94 (leader, 1982-92); chairwoman, Assoc of London Authorities, 1984-92. Ed Bromley HS; LSE (governor, 1990-).
tel: 020-7219 6666 fax: 020-7219 3640

An outer East End of London seat that retains many of its traditional features despite some dramatic industrial and social changes. A mixture of light industry and a steadily advancing service sector, it became highly competitive in the 1980s as sections of the white, skilled, working class became disenchanted with Labour. That flirtation with the Tories appears to have ended in the 1990s. Map 25

## BARNSLEY CENTRAL — Lab hold

| Electorate | %Turnout | | 60,086 | 45.84% | 2001 | 61,133 | 59.68% | 1997 |
|---|---|---|---|---|---|---|---|---|
| **Illsley E** | | **Lab** | **19,181** | **69.64%** | **-7.35%** | **28,090** | **76.99%** | **Lab** |
| Hartley A | | LD | 4,051 | 14.71% | 5.17% | 3,589 | 9.84% | C |
| McCord I | | C | 3,608 | 13.1% | 3.26% | 3,481 | 9.54% | LD |
| Rajch H | | Soc All | 703 | 2.55% | | 1,325 | 3.63% | Ref |
| **Lab to LD swing** | **6.26%** | | **27,543** | Lab maj 15,130 | 54.93% | **36,485** | Lab maj 24,501 | 67.15% |

**ERIC ILLSLEY,** b April 9 1955. Elected 1987. Lab spokesman on NI, 1995-97; local gvt, 1995; health, 1994-95. Member, Select Cttees: Foreign Affairs, 1997-2001; Procedure, 1991-2001; Energy, 1987-91; Broadcasting, 1988-91. Lab whip, 1991-94. Member, Environment and Social Security Backbench Cttees. Chairman, all-party glass grp, 1989-97; joint vice-chairman, occupational pensions grp, 1997-. Parly adviser to Caravan Club. Patron, Barnsley Alzheimer's Disease Society-. Ed Barnsley Holgate GS; Leeds Univ.
e-mail: illsleye@parliament.uk tel: 020-7219 3501 4863 fax: 020-7219 4863

A very traditional Yorkshire Labour coalmining seat which has suffered persistent social problems. Almost entirely white in a region where ethnic minorities have become more of a political presence, it was represented for many years by Roy Mason; his combination of economic populism and social conservatism is a reasonably accurate microcosm of the constituency as a whole. Map 26

## BARNSLEY EAST & MEXBOROUGH — Lab hold

| Electorate | %Turnout | | 65,655 | 49.51% | 2001 | 67,840 | 63.88% | 1997 |
|---|---|---|---|---|---|---|---|---|
| **Ennis J** | | **Lab** | **21,945** | **67.5%** | **-5.65%** | **31,699** | **73.15%** | **Lab** |
| Brook Mrs S | | LD | 5,156 | 15.86% | 5.5% | 4,936 | 11.39% | C |
| Offord M | | C | 4,024 | 12.38% | 0.99% | 4,489 | 10.36% | LD |
| Robinson T | | Soc Lab | 722 | 2.22% | -0.58% | 1,213 | 2.8% | Soc Lab |
| Savage G | | UK Ind | 662 | 2.04% | | 797 | 1.84% | Ref |
| | | | | | | 201 | 0.46% | SEP |
| **Lab to LD swing** | **5.57%** | | **32,509** | Lab maj 16,789 | 51.64% | **43,335** | Lab maj 26,763 | 61.76% |

**JEFF ENNIS,** b Nov 13, 1952. Elected here 1997; won Barnsley E in 1996 by-election. PPS to Tessa Jowell, Min for Employment, 1999-2001, and to Min for Public Health, DoH, 1997-99. Barnsley MBC, 1980- (leader of council, 1995-). Chairman, S Yorks Fire and Civil Defence Authority, 1995-. Ed Hemsworth GS; Redland Coll, Bristol.

This is a former coal industry seat which has been obliged to adapt to much harsher times. The constituency is a collection of small, overwhelmingly Labour, towns with a strong sense of shared culture. This is also an almost entirely white constituency. It is difficult to imagine any set of circumstances in which it would not return a Labour MP by a very large margin. Map 27

## BARNSLEY WEST & PENISTONE — Lab hold

| | | 65,291 | 52.94% | 2001 | 64,894 | 65.04% | 1997 |
|---|---|---|---|---|---|---|---|
| Electorate %Turnout | | | | | | | |
| Clapham M | Lab | 20,244 | 58.57% | -0.7% | 25,017 | 59.27% | Lab |
| Rowe W | C | 7,892 | 22.83% | 4.47% | 7,750 | 18.36% | C |
| Crompton M | LD | 6,428 | 18.6% | 0.56% | 7,613 | 18.04% | LD |
| | | | | | 1,828 | 4.33% | Ref |
| Lab to C swing | 2.59% | 34,564 | Lab maj 12,352 | 35.74% | 42,208 | Lab maj 17,267 | 40.91% |

**MICHAEL CLAPHAM,** b May 15, 1943. Elected 1992. PPS to Alan Milburn, Health Min until Nov 1997, when he resigned over proposed cut in benefit to lone parents. Member, Trade and Industry Select Cttee, 1992-97. Vice-chairman, all-party fire safety grp, 2000-; chairman, all-party coalfield communities grp, 1997-, and all-party safety and health grp, 1996-. Joint vice-chairman, PLP Trade and Industry Cttee, 1995-97. Ed Barnsley Tech Coll; Leeds Univ; Leeds Poly; Bradford Univ.
e-mail: claphamm@parliament.uk tel: 01226 731244 fax: 020-7219 5015

By Barnsley standards this is a relatively diverse seat, although it remains as racially monolithic as the other two Barnsley constituencies. Some extensive sheep-farming moorland provides relief from industrial conformity. There are pockets of Tory support and the Liberal Democrats put on a spurt in 1997 but this remains a solid Labour constituency nonetheless. Map 28

## BARROW & FURNESS — Lab hold

| | | 64,746 | 60.27% | 2001 | 66,960 | 72.03% | 1997 |
|---|---|---|---|---|---|---|---|
| Electorate %Turnout | | | | | | | |
| Hutton J | Lab | 21,724 | 55.67% | -1.62% | 27,630 | 57.29% | Lab |
| Airey J | C | 11,835 | 30.33% | 3.1% | 13,133 | 27.23% | C |
| Rabone B | LD | 4,750 | 12.17% | 3.33% | 4,264 | 8.84% | LD |
| Smith J | UK Ind | 711 | 1.82% | | 1,995 | 4.14% | PLP |
| | | | | | 1,208 | 2.5% | Ref |
| Lab to C swing | 2.36% | 39,020 | Lab maj 9,889 | 25.34% | 48,230 | Lab maj 14,497 | 30.06% |

**JOHN HUTTON,** b May 6, 1955. Elected 1992. Min of State for Health, 1999-. Under-Sec of State, Dept of Health, 1998-99; PPS to Leader of House, 1998-99; and to Sec State for Trade & Industry, 1997-98. Member, Home Affairs Select Cttee, 1992-97; Unopposed Bills Panel, 1992-97. Chairman, PLP Home Affairs Cttee, 1995-97; all-party welfare of pet home owners grp. Trustee, Furness Animal Rescue. Senior lecturer, Newcastle Poly, 1981-92. Lecturer. Ed Westcliff HS, Essex; Magdalen Coll, Oxford.
e-mail: huttonj@parliament.uk tel: 01229 431204 fax: 01229 432016

This is an unusual seat by far northwestern England standards. It is less rural Cumbria than an industrial enclave with an economy based on the Vickers port and shipbuilding centre. Labour had been strong here in the 1970s but a decade later, with the perception that the party had become "anti-defence", it swung to the Tories. This was reversed in the 1990s but the seat remains competitive. Map 29

## BASILDON — Lab hold

| | | 74,121 | 55.15% | 2001 | 73,989 | 71.74% | 1997 |
|---|---|---|---|---|---|---|---|
| Electorate %Turnout | | | | | | | |
| Smith Ms A | Lab Co-op | 21,551 | 52.72% | -3.13% | 29,646 | 55.85% | Lab |
| Schofield D | C | 13,813 | 33.79% | 2.96% | 16,366 | 30.83% | C |
| Smithard Ms J | LD | 3,691 | 9.03% | 0.35% | 4,608 | 8.68% | LD |
| Mallon F | UK Ind | 1,397 | 3.42% | | 2,462 | 4.64% | Ref |
| Duane D | Soc All | 423 | 1.03% | | | | |
| Lab Co-op to C swing | 3.04% | 40,875 | Lab Co-op maj 7,738 | 18.93% | 53,082 | Lab Co-op maj 13,280 | 25.02% |

**ANGELA SMITH,** b Jan 7, 1959. Elected 1997. Asst gvt whip, June 2001. PPS to Paul Boateng, Min of State, Home Office, 1999-2001. Vice-chairwoman, International Development Backbench Cttee. Member, all party grps, animal welfare, voluntary sector; chairwoman, all-party Cuba grp; vice-chairwoman, all-party hospices grp. Patron, Basildon Age Concern, Basildon Women's Refuge. Ed Chalvedon Sch, Basildon; Leicester Poly.
e-mail: flackk@parliament.uk www.angelasmithmp.org
tel: 020-7219 6273 fax: 020-7219 0926

Became synonymous with "Essex Man" — the skilled working-class convert to Thatcherism — in the 1980s and early 1990s. In many ways "New Town Man" would have been more accurate. Some boundary changes made the seat less secure for the Tories even before 1997. This will remain, however, a seat scrutinised for signs of broader political trends among the C2 section of the electorate. Map 30

## BASINGSTOKE — C hold

| Electorate | %Turnout | | 79,110 | 60.67% | 2001 | 77,035 | 74.16% | 1997 |
|---|---|---|---|---|---|---|---|---|
| **Hunter A** | | C | **20,490** | **42.69%** | **-0.63%** | 24,751 | 43.32% | C |
| Hartley J | | Lab | 19,610 | 40.86% | 1.73% | 22,354 | 39.13% | Lab |
| Sollitt S | | LD | 6,693 | 13.95% | -3.05% | 9,714 | 17.0% | LD |
| Graham Mrs K | | UK Ind | 1,202 | 2.5% | | | 310 | 0.54% | Ind |
| **C to Lab swing** | **1.18%** | | **47,995** | | **C maj 880** 1.83% | **57,129** | | **C maj 2,397** 4.19% |

**ANDREW HUNTER,** b Jan 8, 1943. Elected 1983. Chairman, 1992-97, and vice-chairman, 1997-, C backbench NI Cttee. Member, Select Cttees: NI, 1994-2001; Environment, 1986-92; Agriculture, 1985 and 1993-94. Joint vice-chairman, C Agriculture Cttee, 1987-91. Dep chairman, Monday Club, 1990- . Hon member, Soc of Sealed Knot; chairman, British Field Sports Soc, 1988-92. Vice-pres, Nat Prayer Book Soc. TA, 1973-84; commission; retired major. Ed St George's, Harpenden; Durham Univ; Jesus Coll, Cambridge.

Basingstoke was once a relatively small county town in north Hampshire much like the rest of that county. Proximity to London and the expansion of local service industries have drawn huge numbers of new residents to the area. They initially adopted the staunchly Conservative sympathies of more established residents. Labour made a huge advance, nonetheless, in 1997 and has now turned the seat into a tight marginal. Map 31

## BASSETLAW — Lab hold

| Electorate | %Turnout | | 68,302 | 56.95% | 2001 | 68,101 | 70.37% | 1997 |
|---|---|---|---|---|---|---|---|---|
| **Mann J** | | Lab | **21,506** | **55.29%** | **-5.84%** | 29,298 | 61.13% | Lab |
| Holley Mrs A | | C | 11,758 | 30.23% | 5.53% | 11,838 | 24.7% | C |
| Taylor N | | LD | 4,942 | 12.71% | 2.38% | 4,950 | 10.33% | LD |
| Meloy K | | Soc Lab | 689 | 1.77% | | | 1,838 | 3.84% | Ref |
| **Lab to C swing** | **5.68%** | | **38,895** | | **Lab maj 9,748** 25.06% | **47,924** | | **Lab maj 17,460** 36.43% |

**JOHN MANN,** b Jan 10, 1963. Elected 2001. Takes over from Joe Ashton. Bassetlaw has returned a Labour MP at every election since 1929. Contested E Midlands in the Euro election, 1999. Co dir and Lab Party trade union liaison officer. Previously national training officer, TUC, and head of research and ed, AEEU. Ed Manchester Univ.

The most northern aspect of Nottinghamshire based on the industrial town of Worksop, this seat (like many others in this county and neighbouring Derbyshire) used to be sustained by the coal industry. That influence disappeared but the working-class electorate remains loyal to Labour. The areas of the seat that border Lincolnshire, though, provide Conservatives with a reasonable pool of support. Map 32

## BATH — LD hold

| Electorate | %Turnout | | 71,372 | 64.87% | 2001 | 70,815 | 76.24% | 1997 |
|---|---|---|---|---|---|---|---|---|
| **Foster D** | | LD | **23,372** | **50.48%** | **2.01%** | 26,169 | 48.47% | LD |
| Fox A | | C | 13,478 | 29.11% | -2.1% | 16,850 | 31.21% | C |
| Hawkings Ms M | | Lab | 7,269 | 15.7% | -0.65% | 8,828 | 16.35% | Lab |
| Boulton M | | Green | 1,469 | 3.17% | 2.1% | 1,192 | 2.21% | Ref |
| Tettenborn A | | UK Ind | 708 | 1.53% | 0.95% | 580 | 1.07% | Green |
| | | | | | | 315 | 0.58% | UK Ind |
| | | | | | | 55 | 0.1% | NLP |
| **C to LD swing** | **2.06%** | | **46,296** | | **LD maj 9,894** 21.37% | **53,989** | | **LD maj 9,319** 17.26% |

**DON FOSTER,** b March 31, 1947. Elected 1992. LD chief spokesman, environment, transport and regions, 1999-; confirmed June, 2001. Member, Employment Select Cttee, 1996-99. Former ed and employment spokesman. Pres, national campaign, nursery ed. Avon cllr, 1981-89 (Alliance grp leader, 1981-86) and chairman, ed cttee, 1987-89. Member, exec cttee, ACC, 1985-89. Senior ed lecturer, Bristol Univ, 1981-89. Ed Lancaster Royal GS; Keele, Bath Univs. e-mail: fosterd@parliament.uk www.donfoster.co.uk tel: 020-7219 5001 fax: 020-7219 2695

An extraordinarily attractive South West spa town with a perhaps surprising bent for middle-class radicalism. The seat is a mixture of the historic West Country city itself and surrounding villages. In the 1970s the Labour Party presented the Tories with a real challenge. Its role was later usurped by the Liberal Democrats who snatched it from Chris Patten, then Conservative Party chairman, in 1992, and now seem solidly entrenched. Map 33

## BATLEY & SPEN — Lab hold

| Electorate | %Turnout | | 63,665 | 60.54% | 2001 | 64,209 | 73.14% | 1997 |
|---|---|---|---|---|---|---|---|---|
| Wood M | Lab | **19,224** | **49.88%** | 0.45% | 23,213 | 49.43% | Lab |
| Peacock Mrs E | C | 14,160 | 36.74% | 0.39% | 17,072 | 36.35% | C |
| Pinnock Ms K | LD | 3,989 | 10.35% | 1.55% | 4,133 | 8.8% | LD |
| Lord C | Green | 595 | 1.54% | 0.72% | 1,691 | 3.6% | Ref |
| Burton A | UK Ind | 574 | 1.49% | | 472 | 1.01% | BNP |
| | | | | | 384 | 0.82% | Green |
| C to Lab swing | 0.03% | 38,542 | Lab maj 5,064 13.14% | | 46,965 | Lab maj 6,141 13.08% | |

**MIKE WOOD,** b March 3, 1946. Elected 1997. Member, all-party grps: aids; homelessness and Indo-British affairs. Setting up parly grp on dystonia, a paralysing disease. Kirklees district cllr, 1980-87; dep council leader, 1987. Founder member of newspaper and food workers' co-operatives. Social worker. Ed Nantwich and Acton GS, Cheshire; Leeds Poly; Southampton Univ.
e-mail: mike.wood@geo2.poptel.org.uk www.mikewood.org.uk
tel: 01274 335233 fax: 01274 335235

An intriguing constituency. This is a predominantly working-class West Yorkshire seat with a solid Labour core based on the town of Batley. The Tories fare better in Spen and the villages. Against long odds Elizabeth Peacock, an independently minded Conservative MP, captured the seat in the 1980s and clung on until overwhelmed in 1997. It is likely to remain a distinctive political entity. Map 34

## BATTERSEA — Lab hold

| Electorate | %Turnout | | 67,495 | 54.53% | 2001 | 66,928 | 70.82% | 1997 |
|---|---|---|---|---|---|---|---|---|
| Linton M | Lab | **18,498** | **50.26%** | -0.48% | 24,047 | 50.74% | Lab |
| Shersby Mrs L | C | 13,445 | 36.53% | -2.9% | 18,687 | 39.43% | C |
| Vitelli Ms S | LD | 4,450 | 12.09% | 4.74% | 3,482 | 7.35% | LD |
| Barber T | Ind | 411 | 1.12% | | 804 | 1.7% | Ref |
| | | | | | 250 | 0.53% | UK Ind |
| | | | | | 127 | 0.27% | Dream |
| C to Lab swing | 1.21% | 36,804 | Lab maj 5,053 13.73% | | 47,397 | Lab maj 5,360 11.31% | |

**MARTIN LINTON,** b Aug 11, 1944 (in Stockholm). Elected 1997. Member, Home Affairs Select Cttee, 1997-2001. Joint-treas, all-party Swedish grp, 1997-. Wandsworth cllr, 1971-82. Ex *Guardian* journalist. Ed Christ's Hospital, Sussex; Université de Lyon; Pembroke Coll, Oxford.

A constituency which summarises the dramatically evolving political fortunes of the two major parties in London. It was once a reliable Labour seat until enormous social change, notably the arrival of young professionals in the Tory flagship council of Wandsworth, allowed the Tories to win in 1987 and extend their majority in 1992. The same professionals moved en masse to Tony Blair in 1997. Map 35.

## BEACONSFIELD — C hold

| Electorate | %Turnout | | 68,378 | 61.49% | 2001 | 68,959 | 72.8% | 1997 |
|---|---|---|---|---|---|---|---|---|
| Grieve D | C | **22,233** | **52.88%** | 3.66% | 24,709 | 49.22% | C |
| Lathrope S | Lab | 9,168 | 21.81% | 0.09% | 10,722 | 21.36% | LD |
| Lloyd S | LD | 9,017 | 21.45% | 1.76% | 10,063 | 20.05% | Lab |
| Moffatt A | UK Ind | 1,626 | 3.87% | 2.97% | 2,197 | 4.38% | Ref |
| | | | | | 1,434 | 2.86% | CASC |
| | | | | | 451 | 0.9% | UK Ind |
| | | | | | 286 | 0.57% | ProLife |
| | | | | | 193 | 0.38% | NLP |
| | | | | | 146 | 0.29% | B Ind |
| Lab to C swing | 0.95% | 42,044 | C maj 13,065 31.07% | | 50,201 | C maj 13,987 27.86% | |

**DOMINIC GRIEVE,** b May 24, 1956. Elected 1997. Opposition spokesman for Scotland and constitutional affairs, 1999-. Member, Select Cttees: Environmental Audit; Statutory Instruments, 1997-2001. Member, British-Irish parly body, 2000-. Member, John Major's campaign team, 1992. Hammersmith and Fulham cllr, 1982-86. Member, Lloyd's. London Diocesan Synod of C of E, 1994-2000. Barrister. Ed Westminster; Magdalen Coll, Oxford (pres, univ C assoc, 1977). Son of Percy Grieve, QC, ex-MP, Solihull.
e-mail: grieved@parliament.uk tel: 020-7219 6220 fax: 020-7219 4803

This remains one of the most Conservative seats in the country. It is based on Buckinghamshire towns such as Beaconsfield itself and Gerrards Cross, and smaller communities such as Denham, Iver and Taplow, that are prototypical Home Counties affluent commuter areas with a large retired population. Thus it is ideal territory for the Conservative Party. Tony Blair fought the seat in his first outing for Labour in a by-election in 1982. Map 36

# BECKENHAM

**C hold**

| Electorate | %Turnout | | 72,241 | 63.07% | 2001 | 72,807 | 74.65% | 1997 |
|---|---|---|---|---|---|---|---|---|
| **Lait Mrs J** | | **C** | **20,618** | **45.25%** | **2.78%** | **23,084** | **42.47%** | **C** |
| Watts R | | Lab | 15,659 | 34.37% | 1.01% | 18,131 | 33.36% | Lab |
| Feakes A | | LD | 7,308 | 16.04% | -2.1% | 9,858 | 18.14% | LD |
| Moran Ms K | | Green | 961 | 2.11% | | 1,663 | 3.06% | Ref |
| Pratt C | | UK Ind | 782 | 1.72% | 0.79% | 720 | 1.32% | Lib |
| Winfield R | | Lib | 234 | 0.51% | -0.81% | 506 | 0.93% | UK Ind |
| | | | | | | 388 | 0.71% | NF |
| **Lab to C swing** | | **0.89%** | **45,562** | | **C maj 4,959** | **54,350** | | **C maj 4,953** |
| | | | | | 10.88% | | | 9.11% |

**JACQUI LAIT,** b Dec 10, 1947. Elected here 1997 by-election; MP for Hastings & Rye, 1992-97. Spokeswoman, social security. Asst gvt whip, 1996-97, the first woman in the C Whips' Office. PPS to William Hague, when Welsh Sec, 1995-96; and formerly to social security mins. Ran Westminster and Euro parly consultancy, 1984-92. Parly adviser, Chemical Industries Assoc, 1980-84. Chairwoman, European Union of Women (British section) and vice-chairwoman, C Women's Nat Cttee, 1990-92. Ed Paisley GS; Strathclyde Univ.
*Details of 1997 by-election on page 291*

A seat with something of an identity crisis. It is, strictly speaking, in the London Borough of Bromley but most residents would consider themselves Men of Kent. It was once solidly Conservative but the Tory majority was rocked in 1997 not least because of a sex scandal involving the MP, Piers Merchant. A by-election in late 1997 produced an even smaller Tory win, though the 2001 result was almost identical to the last general election's. Map 37

# BEDFORD

**Lab hold**

| Electorate | %Turnout | | 67,763 | 59.88% | 2001 | 66,560 | 73.53% | 1997 |
|---|---|---|---|---|---|---|---|---|
| **Hall P** | | **Lab** | **19,454** | **47.94%** | **-2.68%** | **24,774** | **50.62%** | **Lab** |
| Attenborough Mrs N | | C | 13,297 | 32.77% | -0.89% | 16,474 | 33.66% | C |
| Headley M | | LD | 6,425 | 15.83% | 3.48% | 6,044 | 12.35% | LD |
| Rawlins Dr R | | Ind | 973 | 2.4% | | 1,503 | 3.07% | Ref |
| Lo Bianco Mrs J | | UK Ind | 430 | 1.06% | | 149 | 0.3% | NLP |
| **Lab to C swing** | | **0.89%** | **40,579** | | **Lab maj 6,157** | **48,944** | | **Lab maj 8,300** |
| | | | | | 15.17% | | | 16.96% |

**PATRICK HALL,** b Oct 20, 1951. Elected 1997. Member, Consolidation Bills Select Cttee, 1997-2001. Bedfordshire county cllr, 1989-97. Member, Chartered Inst of Public Finance and Accountancy; North Beds Community Health Council; chairman, Bedfordshire Door to Door dial-a-ride. Management cttee, Hillrise Urban Nature Park. Member, Nalgo. Ex-planning officer and town centre co-ordinator for Bedford. Ed Bedford Mod Sch.

This constituency, based on the town of the same name, was redrawn in boundary changes brought on by the notable expansion in the population of Bedfordshire. This is a mixed seat in several senses: between light industry and the service sector, town and village and with a surprisingly large Asian population. All of which factors render it, in a close election nationally, electorally competitive. Map 38

# BEDFORDSHIRE MID

**C hold**

| Electorate | %Turnout | | 70,594 | 66.07% | 2001 | 66,979 | 78.41% | 1997 |
|---|---|---|---|---|---|---|---|---|
| **Sayeed J** | | **C** | **22,109** | **47.41%** | **1.37%** | **24,176** | **46.04%** | **C** |
| Valentine J | | Lab | 14,043 | 30.11% | -2.42% | 17,086 | 32.53% | Lab |
| Mabbutt G | | LD | 9,205 | 19.74% | 2.94% | 8,823 | 16.8% | LD |
| Laurence C | | UK Ind | 1,281 | 2.75% | | 2,257 | 4.3% | Ref |
| | | | | | | 174 | 0.33% | NLP |
| **Lab to C swing** | | **1.89%** | **46,638** | | **C maj 8,066** | **52,516** | | **C maj 7,090** |
| | | | | | 17.29% | | | 13.51% |

**JONATHAN SAYEED,** b March 20, 1948. Elected here 1997; MP for Bristol E 1983-92. Appointed to Chairmen's Panel. Member, Select Cttees: Broadcasting, 1997-2001; Defence, 1987-91; Environment, 1987. PPS to Lord Belstead, Paymaster General and NI Min, 1990-92. Chairman (1991-92), vice-chairman (1985-91) and former sec, C backbench Shipping and Shipbuilding Sub-Cttee. Treas, all-party Pakistan grp. Ed Wolverstone Hall, Suffolk; RNC, Dartmouth; Royal Naval Engineering Coll, Manadon.
tel: 020-7219 2355 fax: 020-7219 1670

This is a prosperous seat which is more similar politically to others in Buckinghamshire rather than Bedforshire. It lost about 20,000 electors as a result of the last boundary review but that has not really altered its predominant characteristics. A mixture of small-town commuters and rural residents, with both groups usually inclined to support the Conservative contender. Map 39

## BEDFORDSHIRE NORTH EAST — C hold

| Electorate | %Turnout | | 69,451 | 65.15% | 2001 | 64,743 | 77.83% | 1997 |
|---|---|---|---|---|---|---|---|---|
| Burt A | | C | 22,586 | 49.92% | 5.64% | 22,311 | 44.28% | C |
| Ross P | | Lab | 14,009 | 30.96% | -1.64% | 16,428 | 32.6% | Lab |
| Rogerson D | | LD | 7,409 | 16.37% | 2.12% | 7,179 | 14.25% | LD |
| Hill Ms R | | UK Ind | 1,242 | 2.74% | | 2,490 | 4.94% | Ref |
| | | | | | | 1,842 | 3.66% | Ind C |
| | | | | | | 138 | 0.27% | NLP |
| Lab to C swing | 3.64% | | 45,246 | | C maj 8,577 | 50,388 | | C maj 5,883 |
| | | | | | 18.96% | | | 11.68% |

**ALISTAIR BURT,** b May 25, 1955. Elected here 2001. Inherits seat from Sir Nicholas Lyell, QC. Previously MP for Bury, 1983-97. Former Social Security Min and Min for Disabled People, 1995-97. Social Security Under-Sec, with responsibility for Child Support Agency, 1992-95. PPS, Kenneth Baker, 1985-90. Haringey cllr, 1982-84. Solicitor. Ed Bury GS; St John's Coll, Oxford, where he was president of Oxford Univ Law Society, 1976.

This is a new constituency assembled largely from Conservative-inclined wards of already Tory territory. It is a mixture of small and very appealing towns, such as Biggleswade and Sandy, with distinctly rural stretches. The strength of the Conservative Party is similarly consistent. The Tories were impeded in 1997, however, by a vigorous Referendum Party campaign and an Independent Conservative candidate; not so in 2001. Map 40

## BEDFORDSHIRE SOUTH WEST — C hold

| Electorate | %Turnout | | 72,126 | 60.8% | 2001 | 69,781 | 75.76% | 1997 |
|---|---|---|---|---|---|---|---|---|
| Selous A | | C | 18,477 | 42.13% | 1.4% | 21,534 | 40.73% | C |
| Date A | | Lab | 17,701 | 40.36% | -0.13% | 21,402 | 40.49% | Lab |
| Pantling M | | LD | 6,473 | 14.76% | 0.46% | 7,559 | 14.3% | LD |
| Wise T | | UK Ind | 1,203 | 2.74% | 1.9% | 1,761 | 3.33% | Ref |
| | | | | | | 446 | 0.84% | UK Ind |
| | | | | | | 162 | 0.31% | NLP |
| Lab to C swing | 0.76% | | 43,854 | | C maj 776 | 52,864 | | C maj 132 |
| | | | | | 1.77% | | | 0.24% |

**ANDREW SELOUS,** b April 27, 1962. Elected 2001. Takes over seat from Sir David Madel, MP for 30 years. Contested Sunderland N, 1997. Former TA officer, Honourable Artillery Company, 1981-94. Dir, CNS Electronics, 1988-94 and underwriter, Great Lakes, 1991-. Ed LSE.

An interesting constituency. This section of Bedfordshire borders Buckinghamshire and it might be assumed that it would be similarly Conservative. But the heart of this seat is Dunstable, a bastion of the white, skilled, working class. During the 1980s a large section of these votes aligned with rural residents to back Mrs Thatcher. In recent contests, the two sections appear to be at loggerheads; it is now one of the tightest marginals in the UK. Map 41.

## BELFAST EAST — DUP hold

| Electorate | %Turnout | | 58,455 | 63.0% | 2001 | 61,744 | 63.21% | 1997 |
|---|---|---|---|---|---|---|---|---|
| Robinson P | | DUP | 15,667 | 42.54% | -0.09% | 16,640 | 42.63% | DUP |
| Lemon T | | UUP | 8,550 | 23.22% | -2.11% | 9,886 | 25.33% | UUP |
| Alderdice Dr D | | Alliance | 5,832 | 15.84% | -7.96% | 9,288 | 23.8% | Alliance |
| Ervine D | | PUP | 3,669 | 9.96% | | 928 | 2.38% | C |
| O'Donnell J | | SF | 1,237 | 3.36% | 1.28% | 810 | 2.08% | SF |
| Farren Ms C | | SDLP | 880 | 2.39% | 0.78% | 629 | 1.61% | SDLP |
| Dick T | | C | 800 | 2.17% | -0.21% | 541 | 1.39% | NIFT |
| Bell J | | WP | 123 | 0.33% | -0.28% | 237 | 0.61% | WP |
| Weiss R | | Ind Vote | 71 | 0.19% | | 70 | 0.18% | NLP |
| UUP to DUP swing | 1.01% | | 36,829 | | DUP maj 7,117 | 39,029 | | DUP maj 6,754 |
| | | | | | 19.32% | | | 17.30% |

**PETER ROBINSON,** b Dec 29, 1948. Elected 1979, but resigned 1985 in protest at Anglo-Irish agreement; retained seat in 1986 by-election. Member, NI Assembly, 1998- and 1982-86 and Min, regional development, 1999-. NI Forum, 1997-1998; Select Cttee on NI, 1994-2001. Dep leader, DUP, 1980-87, gen sec, 1975-79. Member, all-party Cttee, Shipbuilding. Castlereagh borough cllr, 1977-; mayor, 1986. Dir (unpaid), Crown Publications, Belfast. Married to Iris Robinson, MP for Strangford. Ed Annadale GS; Castlereagh CFE. e-mail: info@dup.org.uk tel: 028-9047 3111 fax: 028-9047 1797

This seat would appear to be, even by Ulster standards, one of the least typical constituencies in the United Kingdom. A mere 5 per cent or so of the population is Roman Catholic. A substantial redistribution of electors in 1997 has, however, made the seat more diverse. There is now a middle-class fringe to a predominantly working-class core. This might produce a different brand of Unionism. Map 42.

## BELFAST NORTH

| Electorate | %Turnout | 60,941 | 67.17% | 2001 | 64,577 | 64.19% | 1997 |
|---|---|---|---|---|---|---|---|
| **Dodds N** | **DUP** | **16,718** | **40.84%** | | **21,478** | **51.81%** | **UUP** |
| Kelly G | SF | 10,331 | 25.24% | 5.04% | 8,454 | 20.39% | SDLP |
| Maginness A | SDLP | 8,592 | 20.99% | 0.6% | 8,375 | 20.2% | SF |
| Walker C | UUP | 4,904 | 11.98% | -39.83% | 2,221 | 5.36% | Alliance |
| Delaney Ms M | WP | 253 | 0.62% | -0.1% | 539 | 1.3% | Green |
| Weiss R | Ind Vote | 134 | 0.33% | | 297 | 0.72% | WP |
| | | | | | 88 | 0.21% | NLP |
| **No swing applicable** | | **40,932** | **DUP maj 6,387** | | **41,452** | **UUP maj 13,024** | |
| | | | 15.60% | | | 31.42% | |

**NIGEL DODDS,** b Aug 20, 1958. Elected 2001. Member for Belfast N in NI Assembly, 1998-, where he served as Min of Social Development. Member; NI Forum, 1996-98. DUP party sec, 1993-; Belfast city cllr, 1985-; Lord Mayor of Belfast, 1988-89, and 1991-92. Barrister. OBE. Ed Portora Royal Sch, Enniskillen; St John's Coll, Camb Univ.

The most diverse of the four Belfast constituencies. There is a substantial Catholic minority although one that seems to be split between the SDLP and Sinn Fein. The seat itself contains appalling slum conditions in and around the legendary "Orange" Shankill Road and some extremely desirable neighbourhoods as well. Formerly solidly UUP until the 2001 election. Map 43

## BELFAST SOUTH

| Electorate | %Turnout | 59,436 | 63.85% | 2001 | 63,439 | 62.24% | 1997 |
|---|---|---|---|---|---|---|---|
| **Smyth The Rev M** | **UUP** | **17,008** | **44.81%** | **8.84%** | **14,201** | **35.97%** | **UUP** |
| McDonnell Dr A | SDLP | 11,609 | 30.59% | 6.27% | 9,601 | 24.32% | SDLP |
| McWilliams Prof M | Women's Co | 2,968 | 7.82% | | 5,687 | 14.4% | PUP |
| Maskey A | SF | 2,894 | 7.63% | 2.52% | 5,112 | 12.95% | Alliance |
| Rice Ms G | Alliance | 2,042 | 5.38% | -7.57% | 2,019 | 5.11% | SF |
| Purvis Ms D | PUP | 1,112 | 2.93% | -11.47% | 1,204 | 3.05% | NI Women |
| Lynn P | WP | 204 | 0.54% | -0.18% | 962 | 2.44% | C |
| Weiss R | Ind Vote | 115 | 0.3% | | 292 | 0.74% | Ind Lab |
| | | | | | 286 | 0.72% | WP |
| | | | | | 120 | 0.3% | NLP |
| **SDLP to UUP swing** | **1.29%** | **37,952** | **UUP maj 5,399** | | **39,484** | **UUP maj 4,600** | |
| | | | 14.23% | | | 11.65% | |

**THE REV MARTIN SMYTH,** b June 15, 1931. Elected 1982 by-election; resigned 1985 in protest at Anglo-Irish agreement and held seat in 1986 by-election. UUP chief whip, 1995-2000; spokesman, health and family policy. Joint treas, all-party pro-life grp; treas, child abduction grp. NI Assembly, 1982-86. Member, NI Constitutional Convention, 1975. Ed Methodist Coll, Belfast; Magee Univ Coll, Londonderry; Trinity Coll, Dublin; Presbyterian Col, Belfast; San Francisco Theological Seminary.

This constituency has traditionally been regarded as the most middle-class and least brazenly sectarian of the Belfast seats. This reputation is based partly on the influence exercised by Queen's University lecturers and students. It is, nonetheless, solidly Protestant, although with space for the SDLP in particular to make a reasonable showing. Map 44

## BELFAST WEST

| Electorate | %Turnout | 59,617 | 68.74% | 2001 | 61,785 | 74.27% | 1997 |
|---|---|---|---|---|---|---|---|
| **Adams G** | **SF** | **27,096** | **66.12%** | **10.19%** | **25,662** | **55.93%** | **SF** |
| Attwood A | SDLP | 7,754 | 18.92% | -19.77% | 17,753 | 38.69% | SDLP |
| Smyth The Rev E | DUP | 2,641 | 6.44% | | 1,556 | 3.39% | UUP |
| McGimpsey C | UUP | 2,541 | 6.2% | 2.81% | 721 | 1.57% | WP |
| Lowry J | WP | 736 | 1.8% | 0.23% | 102 | 0.22% | HR |
| Kerr D | Third | 116 | 0.28% | | 91 | 0.2% | NLP |
| Weiss R | Ind Vote | 98 | 0.24% | | | | |
| **SDLP to SF swing** | **14.98%** | **40,982** | **SF maj 19,342** | | **45,885** | **SF maj 7,909** | |
| | | | 47.20% | | | 17.24% | |

**GERRY ADAMS,** b Oct 6, 1948. Regained seat 1997 which he held 1983-92. President of Sinn Fein since 1983; vice-president, 1978-83. Has not taken his seat at Westminster. Member for W Belfast, NI Assembly, 1998- and 1982. Interned 1971, released 1976. Thorr Award, Switzerland, 1995. Publications include *Before the Dawn*, 1996, (autobiog); *An Irish Voice, the quest for peace*, 1997, and *Politics of Irish Freedom*, 1988. Ed St Mary's GS, Belfast.

A truly exceptional seat and the home of the notorious Falls Road made familiar by Ulster's Troubles. Overwhelmingly nationalist or republican in sentiment but with enough Protestants to make the difference on those occasions when the SDLP and Sinn Fein are closely matched; in 2001, however, Sinn Fein surged ahead. This is a seat which contains some of the worst poverty in Europe. Map 45

## BERWICK-UPON-TWEED — LD hold

| Electorate | %Turnout | | 56,918 | 63.79% | 2001 | 56,428 | 74.08% | 1997 |
|---|---|---|---|---|---|---|---|---|
| **Beith A** | **LD** | | **18,651** | **51.37%** | **5.9%** | **19,007** | **45.47%** | **LD** |
| Sanderson G | C | | 10,193 | 28.07% | 4.01% | 10,965 | 26.23% | Lab |
| Walker M | Lab | | 6,435 | 17.72% | -8.51% | 10,056 | 24.06% | C |
| Pearson J | UK Ind | | 1,029 | 2.83% | 1.99% | 1,423 | 3.4% | Ref |
| | | | | | | 352 | 0.84% | UK Ind |
| **C to LD swing** | **0.94%** | | **36,308** | **LD maj 8,458** | | **41,803** | **LD maj 8,042** | |
| | | | | 23.30% | | | 19.24% | |

**ALAN BEITH,** b April 20, 1943. Dep leader LDs since 1992; confirmed June, 2001. Won as Lib, 1973 by-election; LD MP from 1988. Responsible for LDs strategy in Parliament. Spokesman, home affairs, 1997- and 1992-95; police, prison and security, 1995-97; Treasury, 1987-94. Member, Intelligence and Security Cttee 1994-96. Joint vice-chairman, all-party grps: arts and heritage; Iceland; Sweden and Norway, 1997-. Dep leader, Lib Party, 1985-88. Consultant, Bourne Leisure Grp. Methodist local preacher. Ed King's Sch, Macclesfield; Balliol and Nuffield Colls, Oxford.

On the face of it this is an odd seat to have returned a Liberal to Westminster for almost three decades. It has a large slice of rural Northumberland, including tourist attractions such as Holy Island, which might be expected to support the Tories. There are a number of ex-mining villages that should be sympathetic to the Labour Party. But Alan Beith has managed to turn a by-election victory in 1973 into a solid personal (not partisan) vote ever since. Map 46

## BETHNAL GREEN & BOW — Lab hold

| Electorate | %Turnout | | 79,192 | 48.58% | 2001 | 73,008 | 61.2% | 1997 |
|---|---|---|---|---|---|---|---|---|
| **King Ms O** | **Lab** | | **19,380** | **50.38%** | **4.06%** | **20,697** | **46.32%** | **Lab** |
| Faruk S | C | | 9,323 | 24.23% | 3.17% | 9,412 | 21.06% | C |
| Ludlow Ms J | LD | | 5,946 | 15.46% | 3.46% | 5,361 | 12.0% | LD |
| Bragga Ms A | Green | | 1,666 | 4.33% | 2.51% | 3,350 | 7.5% | BNP |
| Davidson M | BNP | | 1,267 | 3.29% | -4.21% | 2,963 | 6.63% | Lib |
| Delderfield D | NBP | | 888 | 2.31% | | 1,117 | 2.5% | R Lab |
| | | | | | | 812 | 1.82% | Green |
| | | | | | | 557 | 1.25% | Ref |
| | | | | | | 413 | 0.92% | Soc Lab |
| **C to Lab swing** | **0.44%** | | **38,470** | **Lab maj 10,057** | | **44,682** | **Lab maj 11,285** | |
| | | | | 26.14% | | | 25.26% | |

**OONA KING,** b Oct 22, 1967. Elected 1997. Vice-chairwoman, British Council, 1999-. Member, International Development Select Cttee, 1997-2001. Joint vice-chairwoman, London grp Lab MPs, 1997-. Founder, Parly grp on prevention of genocide in Rwanda and the Great Lakes. Former asst to Glyn Ford, MEP, and Glenys Kinnock, MEP. Ex-reg organiser, GMB southern region. Ed Haverstock Comp, London; York and Berkeley Univs. e-mail:silverv@parliament.uk fax: 020-7219 2798

A large, poor constituency in East London which has witnessed some gentrification in the past decade. It remains dominated by the tower blocks of Tower Hamlets, however. There are significant Afro-Caribbean and Bangladeshi minorities. The fact that Labour's new candidate in 1997 was of the former group appears to have led some Asian voters to abandon their Labour loyalties then; they seem to have returned in 2001. Map 47

## BEVERLEY & HOLDERNESS — C hold

| Electorate | %Turnout | | 75,146 | 61.71% | 2001 | 71,916 | 73.62% | 1997 |
|---|---|---|---|---|---|---|---|---|
| **Cran J** | **C** | | **19,168** | **41.33%** | **0.48%** | **21,629** | **40.85%** | **C** |
| Langford Ms P | Lab | | 18,387 | 39.65% | 0.33% | 20,818 | 39.32% | Lab |
| Willie S | LD | | 7,356 | 15.86% | -2.44% | 9,689 | 18.3% | LD |
| Wallis S | UK Ind | | 1,464 | 3.16% | 1.85% | 695 | 1.31% | UK Ind |
| | | | | | | 111 | 0.21% | NLP |
| **Lab to C swing** | **0.08%** | | **46,375** | **C maj 781** | | **52,942** | **C maj 811** | |
| | | | | 1.68% | | | 1.53% | |

**JAMES CRAN,** b Jan 28, 1944. Elected here 1997; represented Beverley 1987-97. Opposition whip, 1997-. PPS to Sir Patrick Mayhew, NI Sec, 1995-96. Member, Select Cttees: Selection; NI Affairs, 1994-95; Trade and Industry, 1987-92. Member, Trustee Forum Council, 1992-1995. West Midlands dir, CBI, 1984-87; northern dir, 1979-84. Vice-chairman, all-party Order of St John grp, 1994-. Sec, and then chief exec, Nat Assoc of Pension Funds, 1971-79. Member, court, Hull Univ, 1987-. Ed Ruthrieston Sch, Aberdeen; Aberdeen Coll of Commerce; Kings Coll; Aberdeen Univ; Heriot-Watt Univ.

This is an extremely pleasant slice of East Yorkshire. The majority of the electorate reside in Holderness, a coastal district that has preferred Independents to party operatives in local elections. Much of the rest is composed of the market town of Beverley along with a rural element. All had been solidly Tory, so it proved something of a surprise that Labour came within 1,250 votes in the 1997 election and cut the deficit even further in 2001. Map 48

## BEXHILL & BATTLE — C hold

| Electorate | %Turnout | | 69,010 | 64.89% | 2001 | 65,584 | 74.7% | 1997 |
|---|---|---|---|---|---|---|---|---|
| **Barker G** | | C | **21,555** | **48.13%** | **0.02%** | **23,570** | **48.11%** | C |
| Hardy S | | LD | 11,052 | 24.68% | -0.77% | 12,470 | 25.45% | LD |
| Moore-Williams Ms A | | Lab | 8,702 | 19.43% | 1.33% | 8,866 | 18.1% | Lab |
| Farage N | | UK Ind | 3,474 | 7.76% | 6.16% | 3,302 | 6.74% | Ref |
| | | | | | | 786 | 1.6% | UK Ind |
| **LD to C swing** | | **0.40%** | **44,783** | | **C maj 10,503** | **48,994** | | **C maj 11,100** |
| | | | | | 23.45% | | | 22.66% |

**GREGORY BARKER,** b March 8, 1966. Elected 2001. Inherits seat from Charles Wardle. Vice-chairman, Hammersmith C assoc, and Wandsworth and Tooting C assoc. Served in TA; former primary sch governor. Previously worked for Centre for Policy Studies; Brunswick PR; Siberian Oil Co and as dir of Daric. Ed Steyning GS; London Univ.

A largely rural South Coast seat based on two stereo-typical East Sussex towns, seaside Bexhill and inland Battle, situated between Eastbourne and Hastings. It is homogenously white and with a very large number of retired residents. Those who do work are engaged mostly in agriculture or tourism. It is an extremely safe Conservative seat and one where the Referendum Party performed unusually well in 1997. Map 49

## BEXLEYHEATH & CRAYFORD — Lab hold

| Electorate | %Turnout | | 63,580 | 63.51% | 2001 | 63,334 | 76.14% | 1997 |
|---|---|---|---|---|---|---|---|---|
| **Beard N** | | Lab | **17,593** | **43.57%** | **-1.93%** | **21,942** | **45.5%** | Lab |
| Evennett D | | C | 16,121 | 39.93% | 1.51% | 18,527 | 38.42% | C |
| O'Hare N | | LD | 4,476 | 11.09% | -0.09% | 5,391 | 11.18% | LD |
| Smith C | | BNP | 1,408 | 3.49% | 2.6% | 1,551 | 3.22% | Ref |
| Dunford J | | UK Ind | 780 | 1.93% | 1.14% | 429 | 0.89% | BNP |
| | | | | | | 383 | 0.79% | UK Ind |
| **Lab to C swing** | | **1.72%** | **40,378** | | **Lab maj 1,472** | **48,223** | | **Lab maj 3,415** |
| | | | | | 3.65% | | | 7.08% |

**NIGEL BEARD,** b Oct 10, 1936. Elected 1997. Member, Treasury Select Cttee, 2000-01; Science and Tech, 1997-2000. Chairman, Woking CLP, 1981-82, and Surrey W Euro constituency, 1984-92. Member, Southern region, Lab Party exec; board, Royal Marsden Hospital, 1982-90, and Inst of Cancer Research, 1981-. Former grp research and development manager, Zeneca. FRSA. Ed Castleford GS; Univ Coll London.
e-mail: nigel.beard@geo2.poptel.org.uk www.mymp.org.uk/nige
lbeard tel: 01322 332261 fax: 01322 332279

An Outer London seat created by the Boundary Commission in 1997. While it is solidly suburban, it is not noticeably affluent. The electorate consists largely of homeowners on moderate incomes who commute into Central London. It is, though, lower middle-class rather than wealthy. There is thus a reasonable basis of support for both of the major political parties, though Labour just holds the whiphand at present. Map 50

## BILLERICAY — C hold

| Electorate | %Turnout | | 78,528 | 58.07% | 2001 | 76,550 | 72.4% | 1997 |
|---|---|---|---|---|---|---|---|---|
| **Baron J** | | C | **21,608** | **47.39%** | **7.63%** | **22,033** | **39.76%** | C |
| Campbell Ms A | | Lab | 16,595 | 36.39% | -0.92% | 20,677 | 37.31% | Lab |
| Bellard F | | LD | 6,323 | 13.87% | -1.94% | 8,763 | 15.81% | LD |
| Yeomans N | | UK Ind | 1,072 | 2.35% | | 3,377 | 6.09% | LC |
| | | | | | | 570 | 1.03% | ProLife |
| **Lab to C swing** | | **4.27%** | **45,598** | | **C maj 5,013** | **55,420** | | **C maj 1,356** |
| | | | | | 10.99% | | | 2.45% |

**JOHN BARON,** b June 21, 1959. Elected 2001. Inherits seat from retiring anti-Euro MP, Teresa Gorman. Contested Basildon, 1997. Member, Streatham Conservatives, 1995-96. Previously fund manager, dir of Henderson Private Investors, and captain, Royal Regiment of Fusiliers. Charity fundraiser for Crisis and Barnardo's. Ed Jesus Coll, Cambridge and RMC, Sandhurst.

A stereotypical Essex constituency with a record of sending colourful and controversial characters to Westminster. Harvey Proctor won the new seat in 1983 and was succeeded by Teresa Gorman. The constituency itself is a mixture between new towns and more sedate county. It is a land of owner-occupiers and commuters. It also produced one of Labour's best and least expected showings in 1997, but the party failed to capitalise further in 2001. Map 51

## BIRKENHEAD — Lab hold

| Electorate | %Turnout | | 60,726 | 47.7% | 2001 | 59,782 | 65.78% | 1997 |
|---|---|---|---|---|---|---|---|---|
| Field F | Lab | | 20,418 | 70.49% | -0.27% | 27,825 | 70.76% | Lab |
| Stewart B | C | | 4,827 | 16.66% | 1.45% | 5,982 | 15.21% | C |
| Wood R | LD | | 3,722 | 12.85% | 3.83% | 3,548 | 9.02% | LD |
| | | | | | | 1,168 | 2.97% | Soc Lab |
| | | | | | | 800 | 2.03% | Ref |
| Lab to C swing | 0.86% | | 28,967 | Lab maj 15,591 | | 39,323 | Lab maj 21,843 | |
| | | | | 53.82% | | | 55.55% | |

**FRANK FIELD,** b July 16, 1942. Elected 1979. Min, Social Security for Welfare Reform, 1997-98. Chairman, Social Security Select Cttee, 1991-97; Social Services, 1987-91; member, Ecclesiastical Select Cttee. Lab spokesman on health and social security, 1983-84; ed, 1979-81. Member, TGWU. Author, *The State of Dependency: Welfare under Labour* (2000). Writer and journalist. Ed St Clement Danes GS; Hull Univ.
e-mail: hendeyj@parliament.uk/forsythb@parliament.
uk tel: 020-7219 5193 fax: 020-7219 0601

A Labour stronghold associated with a range of social problems and located across the Mersey from Liverpool. There is a small middle-class enclave but otherwise this seat is a classic example of the industrial North, based on the struggling shipyards and strongly working-class districts such as Tranmere. Labour was split in the 1980s as the hard Left tried, ultimately unsuccessfully, to deselect an equally determined Frank Field as the sitting MP. Map 52

## BIRMINGHAM EDGBASTON — Lab hold

| Electorate | %Turnout | | 67,405 | 56.0% | 2001 | 70,204 | 69.03% | 1997 |
|---|---|---|---|---|---|---|---|---|
| Stuart Ms G | Lab | | 18,517 | 49.05% | 0.45% | 23,554 | 48.6% | Lab |
| Hastilow N | C | | 13,819 | 36.61% | -2.0% | 18,712 | 38.61% | C |
| Davies Ms N | LD | | 4,528 | 12.0% | 2.32% | 4,691 | 9.68% | LD |
| Gretton J | Pro Euro C | | 454 | 1.2% | | 1,065 | 2.2% | Ref |
| Brackenbury S | Soc Lab | | 431 | 1.14% | | 443 | 0.91% | BDP |
| C to Lab swing | 1.23% | | 37,749 | Lab maj 4,698 | | 48,465 | Lab maj 4,842 | |
| | | | | 12.45% | | | 9.99% | |

**GISELA STUART,** b Nov 26, 1955. Elected 1997; contested Worcestershire and S Warwickshire 1994 Euro elections. Under-Sec of State for Health, 1999-2001. Member, Social Security Select Cttee, 1997. PPS to Paul Boateng, Home Office, 1998-99. Ex-deputy dir, London Book Fair and publishing marketing manager. Postgraduate research on occupational pensions, Birmingham Univ. Member, Charter 88; Fabian Soc. Law lecturer; publisher. Ed in Germany; Manchester Poly; London Univ.

Most observers would contend that this is probably the most middle-class constituency in Britain's second city but it is also starkly polarised between high-income affluence in the Calthorpe Estate on the edge of the inner city, plus Harborne, and suburban postwar estates near the city boundaries. It fell to Labour for the first time in 1997. That process may have been aided by pockets of middle-class radicalism associated with Birmingham University. Map 53

## BIRMINGHAM ERDINGTON — Lab hold

| Electorate | %Turnout | | 65,668 | 46.6% | 2001 | 66,380 | 60.87% | 1997 |
|---|---|---|---|---|---|---|---|---|
| Simon S | Lab | | 17,375 | 56.77% | -2.04% | 23,764 | 58.81% | Lab |
| Lodge O | C | | 7,413 | 24.22% | -3.27% | 11,107 | 27.49% | C |
| Johnson Ms S | LD | | 3,602 | 11.77% | 1.59% | 4,112 | 10.18% | LD |
| Shore M | NF | | 681 | 2.23% | | 1,424 | 3.52% | Ref |
| Goddard S | Soc All | | 669 | 2.19% | | | | |
| Nattrass M | UK Ind | | 521 | 1.7% | | | | |
| Sambrook-Marshall Ms J | Soc Lab | | 343 | 1.12% | | | | |
| C to Lab swing | 0.62% | | 30,604 | Lab maj 9,962 | | 40,407 | Lab maj 12,657 | |
| | | | | 32.55% | | | 31.32% | |

**SIÔN LLEWELYN SIMON,** b Dec 23, 1968. Elected 2001. Inherits seat from Robin Corbett. Columnist since 1997, *The Daily Telegraph*, *News of the World* and *Spectator*. Freelance speechwriter, 1995-97. Senior manager, Guinness plc, 1993-95. Member, AEEU, NUJ and the Fabians. Research assistant, George Robertson MP, 1990-93. Ed Magdalen Coll, Oxford

This is a mixed constituency in the northeast of the city. The amalgam of tower blocks, numerous council houses sold to their owners in the 1980s and suburbia used to make for the classic West Midlands marginal. Boundary changes made life easier for Labour even before the 1997 election. Erdington is the home of Spaghetti Junction and notorious traffic delays on the M6. Map 54

## BIRMINGHAM HALL GREEN — Lab hold

| Electorate | %Turnout | | 57,563 | 57.47% | 2001 | 58,767 | 71.16% | 1997 |
|---|---|---|---|---|---|---|---|---|
| McCabe S | | Lab | 18,049 | 54.56% | 1.06% | 22,372 | 53.5% | Lab |
| White C | | C | 11,401 | 34.46% | 1.1% | 13,952 | 33.36% | C |
| Singh P | | LD | 2,926 | 8.84% | -0.81% | 4,034 | 9.65% | LD |
| Johnson P | | UK Ind | 708 | 2.14% | | 1,461 | 3.49% | Ref |
| Lab to C swing | 0.02% | | 33,084 | | Lab maj 6,648 | 41,819 | | Lab maj 8,420 |
| | | | | | 20.09% | | | 20.14% |

**STEPHEN McCABE,** b Aug 4, 1955. Elected 1997. Member, NI Affairs Select Cttee. Vice-chairman, all-party European secure vehicle alliance, 1997-. Sec, all-party police and ME grps; treas, all-party transport telematics grp. Former adviser, central council for the ed and training of social workers. Birmingham city cllr, 1990-97. Climbed Himalayan peak to raise money for Rainer Foundation. Ed Port Glasgow Senior Sec; Moray House Coll of Ed; Bradford Univ.

This seat on the southern edge of Birmingham is a lot less like the city as a whole than most of its neighbours. It is largely white and certain wards have extremely high levels of home ownership. They are balanced against pockets of unusually high municipal housing. The Conservatives clung on here until 1992 and would retain some hope of recapturing the constituency in a national recovery. Map 55

## BIRMINGHAM HODGE HILL — Lab hold

| Electorate | %Turnout | | 55,254 | 47.9% | 2001 | 56,066 | 60.91% | 1997 |
|---|---|---|---|---|---|---|---|---|
| Davis T | | Lab | 16,901 | 63.86% | -1.73% | 22,398 | 65.59% | Lab |
| Lewis Mrs D | | C | 5,283 | 19.96% | -4.05% | 8,198 | 24.01% | C |
| Dow A | | LD | 2,147 | 8.11% | -0.36% | 2,891 | 8.47% | LD |
| Windridge L | | BNP | 889 | 3.36% | | 660 | 1.93% | UK Ind |
| Hussain P | | PJP | 561 | 2.12% | | | | |
| Cridge D | | Soc Lab | 284 | 1.07% | | | | |
| Vivian H | | UK Ind | 275 | 1.04% | -0.89% | | | |
| Khan A | | Muslim | 125 | 0.47% | | | | |
| C to Lab swing | 1.16% | | 26,465 | | Lab maj 11,618 | 34,147 | | Lab maj 14,200 |
| | | | | | 43.90% | | | 41.58% |

**TERRY DAVIS,** b Jan 5, 1938. Elected here 1983; MP Birmingham Stechford 1979-83; Bromsgrove 1971-74. Member, exec cttee, British grp, IPU, 1997-; joint vice-chairman, all-party Danish and Swedish grps, 1997-; leader of delegation to Council of Europe and WEU, 1997-; member, public accounts cttee, 1987-94; advisory council on public records, 1989-94. Former manager in motor industry. Ed King Edward VI GS, Stourbridge; London Univ; Michigan Univ.

This constituency, the successor to the Stechford seat, lies to the east of the city centre and appears to be more polarised by racial profile than partisan allegiance. A mixture of traditional "old Labour" - white, working-class - and a rapidly expanding Asian minority. There are some middle-class pockets which would allow the Tories a modest presence. The seat as a whole is, however, considered very secure for the Labour Party. Map 56

## BIRMINGHAM LADYWOOD — Lab hold

| Electorate | %Turnout | | 71,113 | 44.29% | 2001 | 70,013 | 54.24% | 1997 |
|---|---|---|---|---|---|---|---|---|
| Short Ms C | | Lab | 21,694 | 68.89% | -5.19% | 28,134 | 74.08% | Lab |
| Prentice B | | C | 3,551 | 11.28% | -2.02% | 5,052 | 13.3% | C |
| Chaudhry M | | LD | 2,586 | 8.21% | 0.26% | 3,020 | 7.95% | LD |
| Ditta A | | PJP | 2,112 | 6.71% | | 1,086 | 2.86% | Ref |
| Virdee S | | Soc Lab | 443 | 1.41% | | 685 | 1.8% | Nat Dem |
| Hussain M | | Muslim | 432 | 1.37% | | | | |
| Caffery J | | ProLife | 392 | 1.24% | | | | |
| Nattrass Dr A | | UK Ind | 283 | 0.9% | | | | |
| Lab to C swing | 1.59% | | 31,493 | | Lab maj 18,143 | 37,977 | | Lab maj 23,082 |
| | | | | | 57.61% | | | 60.78% |

**CLARE SHORT,** b Feb 5, 1946. Elected 1983. International Development Sec of State, 1997-; confirmed June, 2001. Shadow Overseas Development Min, 1996-97; Shadow Transport Sec, 1995-96. Elected to Shadow Cabinet, 1995. Spokeswoman, women's issues, 1993-95; environmental protection, 1992-93; social security, 1989-91; employment, 1985-88. Member, Home Affairs Select Cttee, 1983-85; chairwoman, all-party race relations grp, 1985-86. Vice-chairwoman, Lab Party, 1997-98; Lab Party NEC, 1988-98. Ed St Paul's GS; Keele, and Leeds Univs.

A solid Labour seat which covers much of Birmingham city centre (including the redeveloped Bull Ring and New Street station) as well as the north and east of the centre. It has witnessed a huge social transformation triggered by immigration and rebuilding, including the regeneration of the canalside around Brindleyplace and much new housing. A majority of voters are now non-white, and away from the city centre poverty and unemployment persist. Map 57

## BIRMINGHAM NORTHFIELD  Lab hold

| Electorate | %Turnout | 55,922 | 52.81% | 2001 | 56,842 | 68.34% | 1997 |
|---|---|---|---|---|---|---|---|
| Burden R | Lab | 16,528 | 55.96% | -1.49% | 22,316 | 57.45% | Lab |
| Purser N | C | 8,730 | 29.56% | 1.57% | 10,873 | 27.99% | C |
| Sword T | LD | 3,322 | 11.25% | 0.75% | 4,078 | 10.5% | LD |
| Rogers S | UK Ind | 550 | 1.86% | | 1,243 | 3.2% | Ref |
| Walder C | Soc All | 193 | 0.65% | | 337 | 0.87% | BNP |
| Carpenter Z | Soc Lab | 151 | 0.51% | | | | |
| Chaffer A | Comm | 60 | 0.2% | | | | |
| Lab to C swing | 1.53% | 29,534 | Lab maj 7,798 26.40% | | 38,847 | Lab maj 11,443 29.46% | |

**RICHARD BURDEN,** b Sept 1, 1954. Elected 1992. Former PPS to Jeff Rooker, Min of State, Dept of Social Security. Vice-chairman, Lab campaign for electoral reform, 1997-; chairman, all-party electoral reform grp, 1997-; treas, H of C motor club; treas, sec, 1995-97, and vice-chairman, 1994-95, Yemen grp; vice-chairman, Lab Middle East Council, 1994-. Founder and sec, joint action for water services, 1985-90. Nalgo officer, 1979-92. Ed Wallasey Tech GS; Bramhall Comp; St John's CFE, Manchester; York and Warwick Univs.

This seat was once regarded as the model marginal constituency. It changed hands four times between the 1979 and 1992 elections but swung decisively to Labour in 1997 and stayed that way in 2001. It is evenly divided between owner-occupiers and council tenants, middle-class commuters, the skilled working class and poorer residents. The Longbridge car factory lies within its borders. Map 58

## BIRMINGHAM PERRY BARR Lab hold

| Electorate | %Turnout | 71,121 | 52.61% | 2001 | 71,031 | 64.6% | 1997 |
|---|---|---|---|---|---|---|---|
| Mahmood K | Lab | 17,415 | 46.54% | -16.49% | 28,921 | 63.03% | Lab |
| Binns D | C | 8,662 | 23.15% | 1.44% | 9,964 | 21.71% | C |
| Hunt J | LD | 8,566 | 22.89% | 13.03% | 4,523 | 9.86% | LD |
| Singh Jouhl A | Soc Lab | 1,544 | 4.13% | | 843 | 1.84% | Ref |
| Johnson Ms C | Soc All | 465 | 1.24% | | 718 | 1.56% | Lib |
| Nattrass Ms N | UK Ind | 352 | 0.94% | | 544 | 1.19% | BNP |
| Roche M | Marxist | 221 | 0.59% | | 374 | 0.82% | Fourth P |
| Davidson R | Muslim | 192 | 0.51% | | | | |
| Lab to C swing | 8.96% | 37,417 | Lab maj 8,753 23.39% | | 45,887 | Lab maj 18,957 41.32% | |

**KHALID MAHMOOD,** b July 13, 1961. Elected 2001. Takes over from Jeff Rooker, who held seat from 1974. Local cllr and chairman, race relations cttee, 1990-93. Member, AEEU, Soc Health Assoc and Soc Ed Assoc. Governor, local primary sch, further ed coll, neighbourhood forum and S Birmingham CHC. Adviser, Pres of Olympic Council, Asia, 1993-95. Project manager, Birmingham Coll. Engineer. Ed Golden Hillock Comp, Birmingham; Birmingham Poly.

A seat that is a stark and not entirely comfortable mixture of two very different social constituencies. One section is dominated by the skilled, white working class, intuitively Labour in sentiment but not a hopeless cause for the right sort of populist Conservative candidate. The other segment is strikingly non-white. The net result is a solid Labour seat but one with considerable internal tension. Map 59

## BIRMINGHAM SELLY OAK Lab hold

| Electorate | %Turnout | 71,237 | 56.29% | 2001 | 72,049 | 70.16% | 1997 |
|---|---|---|---|---|---|---|---|
| Jones Dr L | Lab | 21,015 | 52.41% | -3.22% | 28,121 | 55.63% | Lab |
| Hardeman K | C | 10,676 | 26.62% | -1.14% | 14,033 | 27.76% | C |
| Osborne D | LD | 6,532 | 16.29% | 4.18% | 6,121 | 12.11% | LD |
| Smith B | Green | 1,309 | 3.26% | | 1,520 | 3.01% | Ref |
| Williams Mrs B | UK Ind | 568 | 1.42% | | 417 | 0.82% | ProLife |
| Lab to C swing | 1.04% | 40,100 | Lab maj 10,339 25.78% | | 50,550 | Lab maj 14,088 27.87% | |

**LYNNE JONES,** b April 26, 1951. Elected 1992. Member, Science and Tech Select Cttee, 1992-2001; co-chairwoman, all-party grp on mental health; chairwoman, parly forum on transexualism. Birmingham city cllr, 1980-94. Member, MSF. Ex-housing manager. PhD biochemistry and worked for 12 years in medical research. Ed Bartley Green Girls GS, Birmingham; Birmingham Univ; Birmingham Poly.

A south Birmingham seat that remained Tory throughout the 1980s but one in which demographic change has ultimately proved decisive. Much of the constituency is middle-class with a strong skilled working-class component. A growing non-white population has made matters easier for the Labour Party. The Cadbury chocolate factory and former model community of Bournville are located here. Map 60

## BIRMINGHAM SPARKBROOK & SMALL HEATH — Lab hold

| Electorate | %Turnout | | 74,358 | 49.28% | 2001 | 73,130 | 57.11% | 1997 |
|---|---|---|---|---|---|---|---|---|
| **Godsiff R** | | **Lab** | **21,087** | **57.54%** | **-6.73%** | **26,841** | **64.27%** | **Lab** |
| Afzal Q | | LD | 4,841 | 13.21% | 3.9% | 7,315 | 17.51% | C |
| Hussain S | | PJP | 4,770 | 13.02% | | 3,889 | 9.31% | LD |
| Hussain I | | C | 3,948 | 10.77% | -6.74% | 959 | 2.3% | Green |
| Mohammed G | | Ind | 662 | 1.81% | 0.64% | 737 | 1.76% | Ref |
| Vincent W | | UK Ind | 634 | 1.73% | | 538 | 1.29% | Fourth P |
| Aziz A | | Muslim | 401 | 1.09% | | 513 | 1.23% | PAYR |
| Mirza S | | Soc All | 304 | 0.83% | | 490 | 1.17% | Ind |
| | | | | | | 483 | 1.16% | Soc Lab |
| **Lab to LD swing** | **5.31%** | | **36,647** | Lab maj 16,246 | | **41,765** | Lab maj 19,526 | |
| | | | | 44.33% | | | 46.76% | |

**ROGER GODSIFF,** b June 28, 1946. Elected here 1997; MP for Birmingham Small Heath 1992-97. Chairman, British-Japanese parly grp; all-party British/Kashmir grp. Lewisham cllr, 1971-90, mayor, 1977. Political officer, Apex, 1970-90; senior research officer, GMB, 1990-92. Bank clerk, 1965-70. Ed Catford Comp.
tel: 020-7219 5191 fax: 020-7219 2221

Britain's second city has declined in population over recent years; as a result it lost one seat in the most recent boundary review in 1997. This section of inner southeast Birmingham is a mixture of traditional working-class, Victorian terrace housing and a large immigrant population. A majority of the constituency is now non-white. It is also very secure territory for the Labour Party. Map 61

## BIRMINGHAM YARDLEY — Lab hold

| Electorate | %Turnout | | 52,444 | 57.23% | 2001 | 53,058 | 71.22% | 1997 |
|---|---|---|---|---|---|---|---|---|
| **Morris Ms E** | | **Lab** | **14,085** | **46.93%** | **-0.12%** | **17,778** | **47.05%** | **Lab** |
| Hemming J | | LD | 11,507 | 38.34% | 5.36% | 12,463 | 32.98% | LD |
| Roberts B | | C | 3,941 | 13.13% | -4.7% | 6,736 | 17.83% | C |
| Ware A | | UK Ind | 329 | 1.1% | 0.67% | 646 | 1.71% | Ref |
| Wren C | | Soc Lab | 151 | 0.5% | | 164 | 0.43% | UK Ind |
| **Lab to LD swing** | **2.74%** | | **30,013** | Lab maj 2,578 | | **37,787** | Lab maj 5,315 | |
| | | | | 8.59% | | | 14.07% | |

**ESTELLE MORRIS,** b June 17, 1952. Elected 1992. Sec of State for Ed and Skills, June 2001-; Min of State for Ed and Employment, 1998-2001. Under-Sec of State for Sch Standards, 1997-98. Lab spokeswoman, ed and employment, 1995-97; Lab whip, 1994-95. Warwick district cllr, 1979-91 (grp leader, 1981-89). Teacher. Ed Whalley Range HS, Manchester; Coventry Coll of Ed.
e-mail: estelle@morrisrthon.freeserve.co.uk tel: 0121-789 7356

This is the most unusual and in many ways the most politically intriguing of the Birmingham constituencies. It lies in the southeast of the city, bordering prosperous Solihull, and an unusual social mixture has allowed all three parties the hope of victory in recent years. Indeed, this is one of the very few seats in the West Midlands where the Liberal Democrats can muster any noticeable strength. Map 62

## BISHOP AUCKLAND — Lab hold

| Electorate | %Turnout | | 67,377 | 57.23% | 2001 | 66,754 | 68.88% | 1997 |
|---|---|---|---|---|---|---|---|---|
| **Foster D** | | **Lab** | **22,680** | **58.82%** | **-7.21%** | **30,359** | **66.03%** | **Lab** |
| McNish Mrs F | | C | 8,754 | 22.7% | 2.49% | 9,295 | 20.21% | C |
| Foote-Wood C | | LD | 6,073 | 15.75% | 6.57% | 4,223 | 9.18% | LD |
| Bennett C | | Green | 1,052 | 2.73% | | 2,104 | 4.58% | Ref |
| **Lab to C swing** | **4.85%** | | **38,559** | Lab maj 13,926 | | **45,981** | Lab maj 21,064 | |
| | | | | 36.12% | | | 45.82% | |

**DEREK FOSTER,** b June 25, 1937. Elected 1979. Member, Select Cttee on Ed and Employment, 1997-2001. Min of State, Office of Public Service, May 4, 1997, but resigned two days later. Shadow Chancellor, Duchy of Lancaster, 1995-97. Lab Chief Whip, 1985-95; Northern reg whip, 1981-82. Chairman, 1988-89, and vice-chairman, 1987-88, Northern grp of Lab MPs. PPS to Neil Kinnock, 1983-85. Asst dir of ed in Sunderland, 1974-79. Member, Salvation Army. Ed Bede GS, Sunderland; St Catherine's Coll, Oxford.

A pleasing Co Durham constituency including some rural areas of exceptional charm. The seat divides fairly simply into the town of Bishop Auckland itself and the former coalfield country, which has long been allied to the Labour Party, and the rural hinterland which provides a reasonable bounty of votes for the Conservatives without ever actually threatening the likely overall result. Map 63

## BLABY — C hold

| Electorate | %Turnout | | 73,907 | 64.46% | 2001 | 70,471 | 76.05% | 1997 |
|---|---|---|---|---|---|---|---|---|
| Robathan A | C | | 22,104 | 46.4% | 0.57% | 24,564 | 45.83% | C |
| Morgan D | Lab | | 15,895 | 33.36% | -0.39% | 18,090 | 33.75% | Lab |
| Welsh G | LD | | 8,286 | 17.39% | 2.46% | 8,001 | 14.93% | LD |
| Scott E | BNP | | 1,357 | 2.85% | 1.87% | 2,018 | 3.77% | Ref |
| | | | | | | 523 | 0.98% | BNP |
| | | | | | | 397 | 0.74% | Ind |
| Lab to C swing | 0.48% | | 47,642 | | C maj 6,209 | 53,593 | | C maj 6,474 |
| | | | | | 13.03% | | | 12.08% |

**ANDREW ROBATHAN,** b July 19, 1951. Elected 1992. Member, International Development Select Cttee, 1997-2001; vice-chairman, C Backbench NI and Defence Cttees. PPS to Ian Sproat, 1995-97. Joint vice-chairman, all-party renewable and sustainable energy grp, 1997-; chairman, all-party cycling grp, 1994-97. Hammersmith and Fulham cllr, 1990-92. Officer, Coldstream Guards. Rejoined Army to serve in Gulf War. Freeman, City of London. Ed Merchant Taylors', Northwood; Oriel Coll, Oxford; Sandhurst; Army Staff Coll, Camberley.

A seat dominated by Leicester's suburban, middle-class and predominantly Conservative electors. It was represented by Nigel Lawson, the former Tory Chancellor, for almost two decades. It ranges from open countryside, with a surprisingly low population density for a constituency in the East Midlands, to the edge of the city itself. **Map 64**

## BLACKBURN — Lab hold

| Electorate | %Turnout | | 72,621 | 55.75% | 2001 | 73,058 | 65.01% | 1997 |
|---|---|---|---|---|---|---|---|---|
| Straw J | Lab | | 21,808 | 53.87% | -1.17% | 26,141 | 55.04% | Lab |
| Cotton J | C | | 12,559 | 31.02% | 6.41% | 11,690 | 24.61% | C |
| Patel I | LD | | 3,264 | 8.06% | -2.45% | 4,990 | 10.51% | LD |
| Baxter Mrs D | UK Ind | | 1,185 | 2.93% | | 1,892 | 3.98% | Ref |
| Morris P | Ind | | 577 | 1.43% | | 671 | 1.41% | Nat Dem |
| Cullen T | Soc Lab | | 559 | 1.38% | 0.04% | 637 | 1.34% | Soc Lab |
| Nichol F | Socialist | | 532 | 1.31% | | 608 | 1.28% | Green |
| | | | | | | 506 | 1.07% | KBF |
| | | | | | | 362 | 0.76% | CSSPP |
| Lab to C swing | 3.79% | | 40,484 | | Lab maj 9,249 | 47,497 | | Lab maj 14,451 |
| | | | | | 22.85% | | | 30.43% |

**JACK STRAW,** b Aug 3, 1946. Elected 1979. Foreign Sec, June, 2001-; Home Sec, 1997-2001; Shadow Home Sec, 1994-97. Lab spokesman, local govt, 1992-94; ed, 1987-92; housing and local govt, 1983-87; special adviser, Barbara Castle, Social Services Sec, 1974-76 and Peter Shore, Environment Sec, 1976-77. Member, Lab NEC, 1994-95. A Master of Inner Temple Bench, 1997. Visiting Fellow, Nuffield Coll, Oxford. Pres, Nat Union of Students, 1969-71. Non-practising barrister. Ed Brentwood Sch, Essex; Leeds Univ; Inns of Court Sch of Law.

A starkly divided Lancashire constituency which was once regarded as a textile town but which has had to adapt to harsher economic circumstances. It can crudely be divided into three sections: an inner city with a substantial concentration of ethnic minority electors, a skilled working class which has not always welcomed its new neighbours, and a network of middle-class residential wards which provide the Conservatives with an electoral base. **Map 65**

## BLACKPOOL NORTH & FLEETWOOD — Lab hold

| Electorate | %Turnout | | 74,456 | 57.19% | 2001 | 74,989 | 71.67% | 1997 |
|---|---|---|---|---|---|---|---|---|
| Humble Ms J | Lab | | 21,610 | 50.75% | -1.44% | 28,051 | 52.19% | Lab |
| Vincent A | C | | 15,889 | 37.31% | 1.76% | 19,105 | 35.55% | C |
| Bate S | LD | | 4,132 | 9.7% | 1.14% | 4,600 | 8.56% | LD |
| Porter C | UK Ind | | 950 | 2.23% | | 1,704 | 3.17% | Ref |
| | | | | | | 288 | 0.54% | BNP |
| Lab to C swing | 1.60% | | 42,581 | | Lab maj 5,721 | 53,748 | | Lab maj 8,946 |
| | | | | | 13.44% | | | 16.64% |

**JOAN HUMBLE,** b March 3, 1951. Elected 1997. Member, Social Security Select Cttee, 1997-2001. Chairwoman, all-party social services panel. Sec, Culture, Media and Sport Backbench Cttee, 1997-; NW Lab MPs grp. Lancs county cllr, 1985-97. JP. Christian Soc. Member, Co-op and TGWU. Ed Greenhead GS, Keighley; Lancaster Univ.
e-mail: sue@humblemp.freeserve.co.uk tel: 020-7219 5025 fax: 020-7219 2755.

As the name implies, this seat encompasses the northern part of Blackpool proper and adds the coastal strip which runs up to Fleetwood, a noted fishing and container port. It is a largely affluent seat with a high rate of owner-occupation. It was also regarded as the most Conservative of the Blackpool seats and therefore a surprise that Labour captured it so easily in 1997. **Map 66**

## BLACKPOOL SOUTH — Lab hold

| Electorate | %Turnout | | 74,311 | 52.2% | 2001 | 75,720 | 67.8% | 1997 |
|---|---|---|---|---|---|---|---|---|
| Marsden G | Lab | | 21,060 | 54.29% | -2.75% | 29,282 | 57.04% | Lab |
| Morris D | C | | 12,798 | 32.99% | -1.42% | 17,666 | 34.41% | C |
| Holt Ms D | LD | | 4,115 | 10.61% | 2.06% | 4,392 | 8.55% | LD |
| Cowell Mrs V | UK Ind | | 819 | 2.11% | | | | |
| Lab to C swing | 0.67% | | 38,792 | Lab maj 8,262 | | 51,340 | Lab maj 11,616 | |
| | | | | 21.30% | | | 22.63% | |

**GORDON MARSDEN,** b Nov 28, 1953. Elected 1997; contested seat 1992. Member, Ed and Employment Select Cttee and its Ed Sub-Cttee, 1997-2001; joint vice-chairman, Backbench Ed and Employment Cttee, 1997-. Treas, all-party arts and heritage grp, 1997-. Editor of *History Today*, 1985-97. Trustee, Inst of Historical Research. Chairman, Fabian Soc. Pres, British Resorts Assoc. Co-chairman, Future of Europe Trust. Ed Stockport GS; New Coll, Oxford; London and Harvard Univs. tel: 01253 344143 fax: 01253 344940

The vast majority of what outsiders would regard as Blackpool proper is now contained in this seat, including the famed Golden Mile. Tourism, naturally enough, is the dominant source of employment and income. Like its neighbour, this seat swung to Labour for the first time in 1997. Labour's decision to abandon Blackpool for annual conferences in the course of the previous Parliament did, however, prompt fierce local resentment. Map 67

## BLAENAU GWENT — Lab hold

| Electorate | %Turnout | | 53,353 | 59.46% | 2001 | 54,800 | 72.32% | 1997 |
|---|---|---|---|---|---|---|---|---|
| Smith L | Lab | | 22,855 | 72.04% | -7.43% | 31,493 | 79.47% | Lab |
| Rykala A | PC | | 3,542 | 11.16% | 5.93% | 3,458 | 8.73% | LD |
| Townsend E | LD | | 2,945 | 9.28% | 0.55% | 2,607 | 6.58% | C |
| Williams H | C | | 2,383 | 7.51% | 0.93% | 2,072 | 5.23% | PC |
| Lab to PC swing | 6.68% | | 31,725 | Lab maj 19,313 | | 39,630 | Lab maj 28,035 | |
| | | | | 60.88% | | | 70.74% | |

**LLEWELLYN (LLEW) SMITH,** b April 16, 1944. Elected 1992; MEP for SE Wales 1984-94. Served on Euro Parly Cttees on Energy, Research and Tech, Economic and Monetary Affairs and Industrial Policy. Ex-labourer with Pilkington Glass and George Wimpey; computer operator with British Steel; tutor-organiser, WEA. Member, Soc Campaign Grp. Former chairman, Abertillery CLP and exec member, Welsh Lab Party. Ed Greenfield Sec Mod, Newbridge; Harlech Coll; Univ Coll of Wales, Cardiff.

For years this constituency at the head of the South Wales Valleys was known as Ebbw Vale and was represented first by Aneurin Bevan and then Michael Foot. The seat was renamed in 1983 and was moderately reshaped but with little impact on the utter hegemony enjoyed by the Labour Party. The local economy has had to adapt rather more sharply to the decline of the coal and steel industries. Map 68.

## BLAYDON — Lab hold

| Electorate | %Turnout | | 64,574 | 57.43% | 2001 | 64,699 | 70.98% | 1997 |
|---|---|---|---|---|---|---|---|---|
| McWilliam J | Lab | | 20,340 | 54.85% | -5.11% | 27,535 | 59.96% | Lab |
| Maughan P | LD | | 12,531 | 33.79% | 9.99% | 10,930 | 23.8% | LD |
| Watson M | C | | 4,215 | 11.37% | -1.8% | 6,048 | 13.17% | C |
| | | | | | | 1,412 | 3.07% | Ind Lab |
| Lab to LD swing | 7.55% | | 37,086 | Lab maj 7,809 | | 45,925 | Lab maj 16,605 | |
| | | | | 21.06% | | | 36.16% | |

**JOHN McWILLIAM,** b May 16. Elected 1979. Chairman, Selection Cttee, 1997-2001; member, Chairmen's Panel and Liaison Select Cttee; member, Defence Select Cttee, 1987-99. Chairman, all-party IT grp, 1997-; former member, Parly Ecclesiastical Cttee. Chairman, computer sub-cttee 1983-87; Lab Whip, 1984-87. Unpaid dir, EURIM, a non-profit making IT organisation in Europe for MPs. Ex-PO engineer. Member, Edinburgh Corp, 1970-75. Ed Leith Acad; Heriot-Watt Coll; Napier Coll of Science and Tech.

This seat, home of the Blaydon Races of song and folklore, lies at the western end of the Metropolitan Borough of Gateshead, near Newcastle upon Tyne. It is a collection of small industrial towns with the legacy of coalmining as part of its heritage. It is in no sense an especially poor or deprived constituency, but although the Liberal Democrats make a respectable showing, it is as loyal to the Labour Party as other such areas. Map 69

## BLYTH VALLEY — Lab hold

| Electorate | %Turnout | | 63,274 | 54.6% | 2001 | 61,761 | 68.78% | 1997 |
|---|---|---|---|---|---|---|---|---|
| Campbell R | | Lab | 20,627 | 59.7% | -4.51% | 27,276 | 64.21% | Lab |
| Reid J | | LD | 8,439 | 24.43% | 1.97% | 9,540 | 22.46% | LD |
| Daley W | | C | 5,484 | 15.87% | 2.53% | 5,666 | 13.34% | C |
| Lab to LD swing | 3.24% | | 34,550 | Lab maj 12,188 | | 42,482 | Lab maj 17,736 | |
| | | | | 35.28% | | | 41.75% | |

**RONNIE CAMPBELL,** b Aug 14, 1943. Unemployed miner when elected in 1987. NUM sponsored. Member, Public Administration Select Cttee, 1997-2001; Parly Commissioner for Admin, 1987-97; Lab Dept Cttees, Health and Office of Public Service, 1997-. Member, Lab, vice-chairman, Blyth Valley, 1967; Blyth borough cllr, 1969-74; Blyth Valley cllr, 1974-88. Patron ME Assoc. Worked from age of 15 at Bates Pit, Blyth. Ed Ridley HS, Blyth.
e-mail: ronnie@campbellmp.abelgratis.com tel: 020-219 4216 fax: 020-219 4358

The constituency lies in the southeast corner of Northumberland and is a mixture between traditional ex-mining communities and the dockyards at Blyth, and privately housed new town developments. Eddie Milne, then sitting Labour MP, was deselected shortly before the February 1974 election, stood and won as an Independent and narrowly lost eight months later. The seat then became a Labour/SDP marginal. It is solidly Labour again now. Map 70

## BOGNOR REGIS & LITTLEHAMPTON — C hold

| Electorate | %Turnout | | 66,903 | 58.25% | 2001 | 66,480 | 69.86% | 1997 |
|---|---|---|---|---|---|---|---|---|
| Gibb N | | C | 17,602 | 45.17% | 0.95% | 20,537 | 44.22% | C |
| O'Neill G | | Lab | 11,959 | 30.69% | 2.23% | 13,216 | 28.46% | Lab |
| Peskett Ms P | | LD | 6,846 | 17.57% | -6.44% | 11,153 | 24.01% | LD |
| Stride G | | UK Ind | 1,779 | 4.57% | 1.26% | 1,537 | 3.31% | UK Ind |
| Haggard Cheyne Ms L | | Green | 782 | 2.01% | | | | |
| C to Lab swing | 0.64% | | 38,968 | C maj 5,643 | | 46,443 | C maj 7,321 | |
| | | | | 14.48% | | | 15.76% | |

**NICK GIBB,** b Sept 3, 1960. Elected 1997. Contested Rotherham by-election 1994. Frontbench spokesman, trade and industry, 1999; Treasury spokesman, 1998. Joint vice-chairman, all-party grps on occupational pensions; ageing and older people, 1997-. Chairman, Bethnal Green and Stepney C Assoc, 1989-90. Member, C Social Security Cttee, 1997-. Tax consultant and senior manager with KPMG Peat Marwick; with NatWest Bank, 1982-83. Ed Maidstone GS; Roundhay Sch, Leeds; Thornes House Sch, Wakefield; Durham Univ.

This is a popular stretch of the West Sussex coastline which became a seat in its own right only in 1997. It consists of a large, retired community in the Bognor area and surrounding villages, combined with a somewhat more industrial centre at Littlehampton. The Conservatives are strong in both portions of the constituency. Map 71

## BOLSOVER — Lab hold

| Electorate | %Turnout | | 67,537 | 56.67% | 2001 | 66,476 | 71.32% | 1997 |
|---|---|---|---|---|---|---|---|---|
| Skinner D | | Lab | 26,249 | 68.59% | -5.38% | 35,073 | 73.97% | Lab |
| Massey S | | C | 7,472 | 19.52% | 2.81% | 7,924 | 16.71% | C |
| Bradley Ms M | | LD | 4,550 | 11.89% | 2.57% | 4,417 | 9.32% | LD |
| Lab to C swing | 4.10% | | 38,271 | Lab maj 18,777 | | 47,414 | Lab maj 27,149 | |
| | | | | 49.06% | | | 57.26% | |

**DENNIS SKINNER,** b Feb 11, 1932. Elected 1970. Member, NEC, 1978-93 and 1994-96; chairman, Lab Party, 1988-89; vice-chairman, 1987-88. Unsuccessfully contested PLP chair, 1990. Chairman, miners grp of Lab MPs, 1977-78. Pres, Derbyshire miners (NUM), 1966-70; NE Derbyshire CLP, 1968-71. Clay Cross cllr, 1960-70; Derbyshire county cllr, 1964-70. Miner, 1949-70. Ed Tupton Hall GS; Ruskin Coll, Oxford.

One of those rare constituencies that has become synonymous with the sitting Member of Parliament. The economic base of the seat has, though, changed radically in the three decades since Dennis Skinner entered the House of Commons. It was once one of the leading mining areas in Britain but has been obliged to diversify radically. The rock-solid loyalty to the Labour Party in this Derbyshire seat, however, remains undiminished. Map 72

## BOLTON NORTH EAST — Lab hold

| Electorate | %Turnout | | 69,514 | 56.03% | 2001 | 67,930 | 72.44% | 1997 |
|---|---|---|---|---|---|---|---|---|
| Crausby D | Lab | | 21,166 | 54.34% | -1.79% | 27,621 | 56.13% | Lab |
| Winstanley M | C | | 12,744 | 32.72% | 2.33% | 14,952 | 30.39% | C |
| Perkins T | LD | | 4,004 | 10.28% | 0.4% | 4,862 | 9.88% | LD |
| McIvor K | Green | | 629 | 1.61% | | 1,096 | 2.23% | Ref |
| Lowe Ms L | Soc Lab | | 407 | 1.04% | -0.33% | 676 | 1.37% | Soc Lab |
| Lab to C swing | 2.06% | | 38,950 | Lab maj 8,422 | | 49,207 | Lab maj 12,669 | |
| | | | | 21.62% | | | 25.74% | |

**DAVID CRAUSBY,** b June 17, 1946. Elected 1997; contested seat 1992; Bury N 1987. Member, Social Security Select Cttee, 1997-2001. Chairman, housing and environmental health cttee, Bury Council, 1985-92 (district cllr, 1979-92); chairman, Bury North CLP, 1987. Engineer. AEU convener. Ed Derby GS, Bury; Bury Tech College.

This is the sort of seat that is normally saturated at election time with visiting reporters attempting to discern broader trends. It is, at least in close general elections, a classic marginal with a Conservative–inclined north evenly matched against a Labour-leaning southern section. There are few better bellwethers than this Lancashire former textile town constituency - and for now at least it appears reliably Labour. **Map 73**

## BOLTON SOUTH EAST — Lab hold

| Electorate | %Turnout | | 68,140 | 50.12% | 2001 | 66,459 | 65.23% | 1997 |
|---|---|---|---|---|---|---|---|---|
| Iddon Dr B | Lab | | 21,129 | 61.86% | -7.01% | 29,856 | 68.87% | Lab |
| Rashid H | C | | 8,258 | 24.18% | 4.47% | 8,545 | 19.71% | C |
| Harasiwka F | LD | | 3,941 | 11.54% | 2.76% | 3,805 | 8.78% | LD |
| Kelly Dr W | Soc Lab | | 826 | 2.42% | | 973 | 2.24% | Ref |
| | | | | | | 170 | 0.39% | NLP |
| Lab to C swing | 5.74% | | 34,154 | Lab maj 12,871 | | 43,349 | Lab maj 21,311 | |
| | | | | 37.69% | | | 49.16% | |

**BRIAN IDDON,** b July 5, 1940. Elected 1997. Member, Science and Tech Select Cttee, 2000-01; Environmental Audit, 1997-2000. Chairman, all-party drugs misuse grp; dep chairman, Parly and Scientific Cttee. Member, Ed and Employment, Environment, Transport and the Regions and Health and Social Services Backbench Cttees. Reader in chemistry, Salford Univ. Ed Christ Church Boys' Sch, Southport; Southport Tech Coll; Hull Univ.
e-mail: iddonb@parliament.uk tel: 020-7219 2096/4064 fax: 020-7219 2653

A very different seat in character from its neighbour. This part of Bolton is solidly working-class with a significant proportion of non-white voters. It remained loyal to Labour in the depths of the 1980s when the other two seats in the town defected to the Conservatives. It is likely to remain thus attached for decades to come. **Map 74**

## BOLTON WEST — Lab hold

| Electorate | %Turnout | | 66,033 | 62.41% | 2001 | 63,535 | 77.37% | 1997 |
|---|---|---|---|---|---|---|---|---|
| Kelly Ms R | Lab | | 19,381 | 47.03% | -2.49% | 24,342 | 49.52% | Lab |
| Stevens J | C | | 13,863 | 33.64% | -1.49% | 17,270 | 35.13% | C |
| Ronson Ms B | LD | | 7,573 | 18.37% | 7.57% | 5,309 | 10.8% | LD |
| Toomer D | Soc All | | 397 | 0.96% | | 1,374 | 2.79% | Soc Lab |
| | | | | | | 865 | 1.76% | Ref |
| Lab to C swing | 0.50% | | 41,214 | Lab maj 5,518 | | 49,160 | Lab maj 7,072 | |
| | | | | 13.39% | | | 14.39% | |

**RUTH KELLY,** b May 9, 1968. Elected 1997. Economic Sec, Treasury, June, 2001-. PPS, Nick Brown, MAFF, 1998-2001. Member, Treasury Select Cttee, 1997-98. Economist and former dep head of inflation report div, Bank of England. Economics writer, The Guardian, 1990-94; established The Guardian's panel of "seven wise women" economists. Publicity officer for Tower Hamlets anti-racist cttee. Ed Sutton HS; Westminster; Queen's Coll, Oxford; LSE.
e-mail: kellyr@parliament.uk tel: 020-7219 3496 fax: 020-7219 2211

This seat combines some of the most desirable districts in this part of Lancashire with a few significant pockets of urban poverty. Almost four in five residents are owner-occupiers and around 97 per cent are white. This should be highly favourable territory for the Conservatives and it has been their best constituency in Bolton. It was snatched by Labour in 1997 and the party held firm in 2001. **Map 75**

## BOOTLE — Lab hold

| Electorate | %Turnout | | 56,320 | 49.0% | 2001 | 57,284 | 66.73% | 1997 |
|---|---|---|---|---|---|---|---|---|
| **Benton J** | **Lab** | | **21,400** | **77.55%** | **-5.3%** | **31,668** | **82.85%** | **Lab** |
| Murray J | LD | | 2,357 | 8.54% | 2.81% | 3,247 | 8.49% | C |
| Symes Miss J | C | | 2,194 | 7.95% | 0.54% | 2,191 | 5.73% | LD |
| Flynn D | Soc Lab | | 971 | 3.52% | | 571 | 1.49% | Ref |
| Glover P | Soc All | | 672 | 2.44% | | 420 | 1.1% | Soc |
| | | | | | | 126 | 0.33% | NLP |
| **Lab to LD swing** | **4.05%** | | **27,594** | **Lab maj 19,043** | | **38,223** | **Lab maj 28,421** | |
| | | | | 69.01% | | | 74.36% | |

**JOE BENTON,** b Sept 28, 1933. Elected 1990 by-election. Member, Chairmen's Panel, 1998; Ed and Employment Select Cttee, 1997-98. Lab whip, 1994-97. Member, British-Irish inter-parly body and British-Spanish grp, 1997-. Joint sec, all-party pro-life grp, 1992-. Sefton borough cllr, 1970-90 (grp leader, 1985-90). Chairman, governors, Hugh Baird Coll of Tech, 1972-93. Employed Girobank, 1982-90; ex-personnel manager, Pacific Steam Navigation Co. Ed St Monica's Primary and Sec Mod; Bootle Tech Coll.

This is the one of the very safest Labour seats in the United Kingdom. It is almost uniformly white and the only social pluralism is the division between the working class and the underclass. A very tough and depressed former docks town on Merseyside that has scarcely benefited from economic prosperity in the past decade. Even by the standards of the region this is one-party political territory. Map 76

## BOSTON & SKEGNESS — C hold

| Electorate | %Turnout | | 69,010 | 58.42% | 2001 | 67,623 | 68.87% | 1997 |
|---|---|---|---|---|---|---|---|---|
| **Simmonds M** | **C** | | **17,298** | **42.91%** | **0.5%** | **19,750** | **42.41%** | **C** |
| Bird Ms E | Lab | | 16,783 | 41.63% | 0.61% | 19,103 | 41.02% | Lab |
| Moffatt D | LD | | 4,994 | 12.39% | -4.19% | 7,721 | 16.58% | LD |
| Wakefield C | UK Ind | | 717 | 1.78% | | | | |
| Harrison M | Green | | 521 | 1.29% | | | | |
| **C to Lab swing** | **0.06%** | | **40,313** | **C maj 515** | | **46,574** | **C maj 647** | |
| | | | | 1.28% | | | 1.39% | |

**MARK SIMMONDS,** b April 12, 1964. Elected 2001. Inherits seat from Eurosceptic, Sir Richard Body, MP for 36 years. Contested Ashfield, 1997. Chartered surveyor; managing dir, Mortlock Simmonds, 1999. Royal Institution of Chartered Surveyors, 1987. Ed Worksop Coll, Trent Univ.

The county of Lincolnshire has enjoyed a quiet population boom in recent years and as a result was awarded an extra parliamentary seat by the Boundary Commissioners in 1995. This marginal seat, in the low countryside bordering the Wash, was the result of the various revisions. It is moderately prosperous with a large rural component. Tourism is the key industry for Skegness. The Tories have just sneaked home in 1997 and 2001. Map 77

## BOSWORTH — C hold

| Electorate | %Turnout | | 69,992 | 64.44% | 2001 | 68,113 | 76.57% | 1997 |
|---|---|---|---|---|---|---|---|---|
| **Tredinnick D** | **C** | | **20,030** | **44.41%** | **3.78%** | **21,189** | **40.63%** | **C** |
| Furlong A | Lab | | 17,750 | 39.35% | 0.69% | 20,162 | 38.66% | Lab |
| Ellis J | LD | | 7,326 | 16.24% | -1.56% | 9,281 | 17.8% | LD |
| | | | | | | 1,521 | 2.92% | Ref |
| **Lab to C swing** | **1.54%** | | **45,106** | **C maj 2,280** | | **52,153** | **C maj 1,027** | |
| | | | | 5.05% | | | 1.97% | |

**DAVID TREDINNICK,** b Jan 19, 1950. Elected 1987; contested Cardiff S and Penarth 1983. Chairman, Joint Cttee and Select Cttee on Statutory Instruments, 1997-2001. PPS to Sir Wyn Roberts, Welsh Office Min, 1991-94. Chairman, British-Atlantic grp of young politicians, 1989-91; Member of Lloyd's; chairman, Anglo-East European Trading Co, 1990-98; dir, Ukraine Business Agency, 1992-97. Marketing manager. Ed Ludgrove Sch, Wokingham; Eton; Mons Officer Cadet Sch; Graduate, Business Sch, Cape Town Univ; St John's Coll, Oxford.

A pleasant seat set in the Leicestershire countryside. It is speckled with new, usually private, housing developments. These have now eclipsed the influence once held by the mining industry. The seat was made more competitive by the loss of 14,000, mostly Conservative, electors to the neighbouring seat of Charnwood before the 1997 election, but the Tories have since hung on. Map 78

## BOURNEMOUTH EAST       C hold

| Electorate | %Turnout | | 60,454 | 59.22% | 2001 | 61,862 | 70.2% | 1997 |
|---|---|---|---|---|---|---|---|---|
| **Atkinson D** | **C** | | **15,501** | **43.3%** | **1.86%** | **17,997** | **41.44%** | **C** |
| Garratt A | LD | | 12,067 | 33.71% | 2.28% | 13,651 | 31.43% | LD |
| Nicholson P | Lab | | 7,107 | 19.85% | -1.29% | 9,181 | 21.14% | Lab |
| Chamberlaine G | UK Ind | | 1,124 | 3.14% | 1.32% | 1,808 | 4.16% | Ref |
| | | | | | | 791 | 1.82% | UK Ind |
| **C to LD swing** | **0.21%** | | **35,799** | | **C maj 3,434** | **43,428** | | **C maj 4,346** |
| | | | | | 9.59% | | | 10.01% |

**DAVID ATKINSON,** b March 24, 1940. Elected 1977 by-election. Member, Science and Tech Select Cttee, 1997-99. Chairman, Euro democratic grp, Council of Europe, 1998-. Leader, C delegation, Council of Europe and WEU, 1997-; vice-chairman, all-party British-Russia grp, 1997-; member, C Backbench Health Cttee, 1988-97. Ed St George's Coll, Weybridge; Southend Coll of Tech; Coll of Automobile and Aeronautical Engineering. e-mail: atkinsond@parliament.uk tel: 020-7219 3598 fax: 020-7219 3847

Despite the name, this seat is less the east of town than the area to the east of it. This is balmy South Coast territory with numerous retired residents and a strikingly low number of council house tenants. While the constituency invariably returns a Conservative to Westminster it has not done so in quite the crushing manner that the social profile of the area might suggest. Map 79

## BOURNEMOUTH WEST       C hold

| Electorate | %Turnout | | 62,038 | 54.24% | 2001 | 62,028 | 66.22% | 1997 |
|---|---|---|---|---|---|---|---|---|
| **Butterfill J** | **C** | | **14,417** | **42.85%** | **1.18%** | **17,115** | **41.67%** | **C** |
| Stokes D | Lab | | 9,699 | 28.82% | 4.25% | 11,405 | 27.77% | LD |
| Hornby Ms F | LD | | 8,468 | 25.17% | -2.6% | 10,093 | 24.57% | Lab |
| Blake Mrs C | UK Ind | | 1,064 | 3.16% | 2.48% | 1,910 | 4.65% | Ref |
| | | | | | | 281 | 0.68% | UK Ind |
| | | | | | | 165 | 0.4% | BNP |
| | | | | | | 103 | 0.25% | NLP |
| **C to Lab swing** | **1.54%** | | **33,648** | | **C maj 4,718** | **41,072** | | **C maj 5,710** |
| | | | | | 14.02% | | | 13.90% |

**JOHN BUTTERFILL,** b Feb 14, 1941. Elected 1983. Member, Trade and Industry Select Cttee, 1992-2001; Unopposed Bills Panel, 1997-2001; Chairmen's Panel and Court of Referees. Chairman, C Backbench European Affairs Cttee, 1995-97; joint vice-chairman, all-party building socs grp, 1997-. Partner, Butterfill Associates. Member, Council of Management, PDSA, 1990-. Ed Caterham Sch; Coll of Estate Management, London. e-mail: butterfillj@parliament.uk tel: 020-7219 6375 fax: 020-7219 3899

This constituency encompasses most of the Bournemouth that would be familiar to the millions of visitors to this Dorset seaside resort. It is largely affluent and with a sizeable number of retired residents. There is, though, enough of an urban core to allow the Labour and Liberal Democrat parties some hope of offering a repectable challenge. Map 80

## BRACKNELL       C hold

| Electorate | %Turnout | | 81,118 | 60.68% | 2001 | 79,292 | 74.52% | 1997 |
|---|---|---|---|---|---|---|---|---|
| **MacKay A** | **C** | | **22,962** | **46.65%** | **-0.71%** | **27,983** | **47.36%** | **C** |
| Keene Ms J | Lab | | 16,249 | 33.01% | 3.23% | 17,596 | 29.78% | Lab |
| Earwicker R | LD | | 8,424 | 17.11% | 1.67% | 9,122 | 15.44% | LD |
| Boxall L | UK Ind | | 1,266 | 2.57% | 1.61% | 1,909 | 3.23% | N Lab |
| Roberts Ms D | ProLife | | 324 | 0.66% | 0.19% | 1,636 | 2.77% | Ref |
| | | | | | | 569 | 0.96% | UK Ind |
| | | | | | | 276 | 0.47% | ProLife |
| **C to Lab swing** | **1.97%** | | **49,225** | | **C maj 6,713** | **59,091** | | **C maj 10,387** |
| | | | | | 13.64% | | | 17.58% |

**ANDREW MacKAY,** b Aug 27, 1949. Elected here 1997; MP Berks E 1983-97. Shadow NI Sec, 1997-. Govt dep chief whip, 1996-97; senior whip and pairing whip, 1993-96; assist whip, 1992-93. Ex-member, Finance and Services Select Cttee. PPS, Tom King, NI and Defence Sec, 1986-92. Sec, C friends of Israel grp, 1986-92. Privy Counsellor, 1998. Dir, Cabra Estates plc, 1989-92. Former estate agent. Husband of Julie Kirkbride, MP for Bromsgrove. Ed Solihull Sch.

This east Berkshire seat is actually rather more Conservative than an initial reading of its demographic characteristics would suggest. It is a mixture of aspirational new town, rural "old money", the high-tech industries that have sprung up alongside the M4 and a dash of military influence via Sandhurst. The Tories have, though, at least in this part of the Home Counties, solid support in each of these sections. Map 81

## BRADFORD NORTH                                           Lab hold

| Electorate | %Turnout | 66,454 | 52.69% | 2001 | 66,228 | 63.26% | 1997 |
|---|---|---|---|---|---|---|---|
| **Rooney T** | **Lab** | **17,419** | **49.74%** | **-6.34%** | **23,493** | **56.08%** | **Lab** |
| Iqbal Z | C | 8,450 | 24.13% | -1.46% | 10,723 | 25.59% | C |
| Ward D | LD | 6,924 | 19.77% | 5.25% | 6,083 | 14.52% | LD |
| Brayshaw J | BNP | 1,613 | 4.61% | | 1,227 | 2.93% | Ref |
| Schofield S | Green | 611 | 1.74% | | 369 | 0.88% | Loony |
| **Lab to C swing** | **2.44%** | **35,017** | **Lab maj 8,969** | | **41,895** | **Lab maj 12,770** | |
| | | | 25.61% | | | 30.49% | |

**TERRY ROONEY,** b Nov 11, 1950. Elected 1990 by-election. PPS to Michael Meacher, Environment Min, 1997-2001. Chairman, PLP Social Security Cttee, 1991-97; ex-member, Broadcasting Select Cttee. Sec, Yorks grp of Lab MPs. Bradford cllr, 1983-90; chairman, Lab grp, 1988-90; dep council leader, 1990. Ex-welfare rights advice worker and commercial insurance broker. Ed Buttershaw Comp; Bradford Coll.
e-mail: terryrooney01@genie.co.uk fax: 01274 777817

A slightly odd constituency in that, despite the name, Bradford North is actually largely to the east of this West Yorkshire city. It contains a lot of older housing stock and a large and expanding Asian population. It shifted briefly to the Tories in the mid-1980s, largely because of the division of the non-Tory vote. It has recently taken on the look of a secure prospect for Labour. Map 82

## BRADFORD SOUTH                                           Lab hold

| Electorate | %Turnout | 68,450 | 51.33% | 2001 | 68,391 | 65.88% | 1997 |
|---|---|---|---|---|---|---|---|
| **Sutcliffe G** | **Lab** | **19,603** | **55.79%** | **-0.93%** | **25,558** | **56.72%** | **Lab** |
| Tennyson G | C | 9,941 | 28.29% | 0.28% | 12,622 | 28.01% | C |
| Wilson-Fletcher A | LD | 3,717 | 10.58% | -0.72% | 5,093 | 11.3% | LD |
| North P | UK Ind | 783 | 2.23% | | 1,785 | 3.96% | Ref |
| Kelly T | Soc Lab | 571 | 1.63% | | | | |
| Siddique A | Soc All | 302 | 0.86% | | | | |
| Riseborough G | Def Welfare | 220 | 0.63% | | | | |
| **Lab to C swing** | **0.61%** | **35,137** | **Lab maj 9,662** | | **45,058** | **Lab maj 12,936** | |
| | | | 27.50% | | | 28.71% | |

**GERRY SUTCLIFFE,** b May 13, 1953. Elected 1994 by-election. Gvt asst whip, 1999-. PPS to Harriet Harman, Social Security Sec, 1997-99. Member, Public Accounts Cttee, 1996-97; Unopposed Bills Panel, 1997. Chairman, all-party S Pennines grp, 1996-; vice-chairman, Yorks grp Lab MPs, 1995-. Capt, Parly Football Club XI, 1997-. Former dep sec, Sogat; display advertising clerk. *Bradford Telegraph and Argus*, 1971-75. Ed Cardinal Hinsley GS; Bradford Coll.
e-mail: sutcliffeg@parliament.uk tel: 01274 400007 fax: 01274 400020

This is potentially quite a competitive constituency. There are notable middle-class enclaves and the Asian population is smaller and less monolithically Labour than in other parts of Bradford. The white working class here has, though, tended to stick with its traditional Labour loyalties. Map 83

## BRADFORD WEST                                            Lab hold

| Electorate | %Turnout | 71,620 | 53.57% | 2001 | 71,961 | 63.32% | 1997 |
|---|---|---|---|---|---|---|---|
| **Singh M** | **Lab** | **18,401** | **47.96%** | **6.41%** | **18,932** | **41.55%** | **Lab** |
| Riaz M | C | 14,236 | 37.1% | 4.06% | 15,055 | 33.04% | C |
| Robinson J | Green | 2,672 | 6.96% | 5.07% | 6,737 | 14.78% | LD |
| Khan A | LD | 2,437 | 6.35% | -8.43% | 1,551 | 3.4% | Soc Lab |
| Hussain I | UK Ind | 427 | 1.11% | | 1,348 | 2.96% | Ref |
| Khokhar F | AL | 197 | 0.51% | | 861 | 1.89% | Green |
| | | | | | 839 | 1.84% | BNP |
| | | | | | 245 | 0.54% | Soc |
| **C to Lab swing** | **1.17%** | **38,370** | **Lab maj 4,165** | | **45,568** | **Lab maj 3,877** | |
| | | | 10.85% | | | 8.51% | |

**MARSHA SINGH,** b Oct 11, 1954. Elected 1997. Member, Home Affairs Select Cttee, 1997-2001. Treas, all-party Kashmir grp. Successfully introduced Private Member's Bill on Community Care, 1998. NHS senior development manager. Chairman, Bradford CLP, 1992-. Ed Bellevue GS, Bradford; Loughborough Univ.
e-mail: singhmp@parliament.uk tel: 020-7219 4516 fax: 020-7219 0965

This seat produced arguably the single most peculiar result of the 1997 election and the explanation lies in racial politics. Almost 40 per cent of the population is Asian. Labour selected a Sikh rather than a Muslim candidate and provoked a backlash from the Asian community. The seat is a mixture of some of the poorest and most affluent parts of Bradford. Although Labour's majority was slightly up in 2001, this will remain a highly distinctive seat. Map 84

# BRAINTREE                                          Lab hold

| Electorate | %Turnout | | 79,157 | 63.56% | 2001 | 72,772 | 76.37% | 1997 |
|---|---|---|---|---|---|---|---|---|
| **Hurst A** | | **Lab** | **21,123** | **41.98%** | **-0.72%** | **23,729** | **42.7%** | **Lab** |
| Newmark B | | C | 20,765 | 41.27% | 1.18% | 22,278 | 40.09% | C |
| Turner P | | LD | 5,664 | 11.26% | -0.29% | 6,418 | 11.55% | LD |
| Abbott J | | Green | 1,241 | 2.47% | 1.19% | 2,165 | 3.9% | Ref |
| Nolan M | | LCA | 774 | 1.54% | | 712 | 1.28% | Green |
| Cole C | | UK Ind | 748 | 1.49% | | 274 | 0.49% | New Way |
| **Lab to C swing** | | **0.95%** | **50,315** | | **Lab maj 358** | **55,576** | | **Lab maj 1,451** |
| | | | | | 0.71% | | | 2.61% |

**ALAN HURST,** b Sept 2, 1945. Elected 1997. Member, Agriculture Select Cttee, 1997-2001. Southend borough cllr, 1980-95; Lab grp leader, 1990-95; Essex county cllr, 1993-. Solicitor. Member, Law Soc. Ed Westcliffe HS; Liverpool Univ.
tel 020-7219 4068 fax: 01376 517709

A large constituency occupying much of the heart of Essex. It is a combination of an urban electorate based in Braintree (which usually leans towards Labour) and some smaller towns and villages (invariably loyal to the Tories). It was represented by Tony Newton, a long-serving Cabinet minister under John Major, until his tiny defeat in 1997. But Labour's tiny majority in 2001 has turned this into a very tight marginal. Map 85

# BRECON & RADNORSHIRE                              LD hold

| Electorate | %Turnout | | 52,247 | 71.81% | 2001 | 52,142 | 82.24% | 1997 |
|---|---|---|---|---|---|---|---|---|
| **Williams R** | | **LD** | **13,824** | **36.85%** | **-4.0%** | **17,516** | **40.85%** | **LD** |
| Aubel Dr F | | C | 13,073 | 34.85% | 5.89% | 12,419 | 28.96% | C |
| Irranca-Davis H | | Lab | 8,024 | 21.39% | -5.25% | 11,424 | 26.64% | Lab |
| Parri B | | PC | 1,301 | 3.47% | 2.02% | 900 | 2.1% | Ref |
| Mitchell I | | Ind M | 762 | 2.03% | | 622 | 1.45% | PC |
| Phillips Mrs E | | UK Ind | 452 | 1.2% | | | | |
| Nicholson R | | Ind N | 80 | 0.21% | | | | |
| **LD to C swing** | | **4.94%** | **37,516** | | **LD maj 751** | **42,881** | | **LD maj 5,097** |
| | | | | | 2.00% | | | 11.89% |

**ROGER WILLIAMS,** b Jan 22, 1948. Elected 2001. Inherits seat from retiring Richard Livsey. Chairman, Mid-Wales agri-food partnership. Former chairman, Brecon and Radnor NFU. Member, Farmers' Union of Wales. Farmer. Ed Christ Coll, Brecon; Selwyn Coll, Cambridge.

This large Mid Wales seat centred on the Black Mountains is one of those rarities, a potential three-way marginal where the personal vote still matters. It is largely rural, with agriculture and forestry the main employers, although it has a southern fringe whose values were shaped by coalmining. The main towns are Brecon, Builth Wells, Llandrindod Wells and Hay-on-Wye. A wonderfully unpredictable constituency just held by the Lib Dems in 2001. Map 86

# BRENT EAST                                        Lab hold

| Electorate | %Turnout | | 58,095 | 49.9% | 2001 | 53,548 | 65.87% | 1997 |
|---|---|---|---|---|---|---|---|---|
| **Daisley P** | | **Lab** | **18,325** | **63.21%** | **-4.12%** | **23,748** | **67.33%** | **Lab** |
| Gauke D | | C | 5,278 | 18.21% | -4.09% | 7,866 | 22.3% | C |
| Bhatti Ms N | | LD | 3,065 | 10.57% | 2.77% | 2,751 | 7.8% | LD |
| Aspis Ms S | | Green | 1,361 | 4.69% | | 466 | 1.32% | Soc Lab |
| Macken Ms S | | ProLife | 392 | 1.35% | 0.73% | 218 | 0.62% | ProLife |
| Cremer Ms I | | Soc Lab | 383 | 1.32% | 0.0% | 120 | 0.34% | Dream |
| Tanna A | | UK Ind | 188 | 0.65% | | 103 | 0.29% | NLP |
| **Lab to C swing** | | **0.01%** | **28,992** | | **Lab maj 13,047** | **35,272** | | **Lab maj 15,882** |
| | | | | | 45.00% | | | 45.03% |

**PAUL DAISLEY,** b July 20, 1957. Elected 2001. Takes over from Ken Livingstone, who was elected Mayor of London in 2000, and who sat as an Independent after his expulsion from the Lab Party. Brent cllr since 1990 and leader, Brent Council, for the past five years. Former finance dir.

A highly distinctive North London seat. Brent East contains neighbourhoods such as Kilburn which have traditionally been associated with large numbers of Irish immigrants as well as many more recent new Commonwealth constituents. It was represented by Ken Livingstone from 1987 to 2001. The seat has, over the past decade, become solidly Labour. Map 87

## BRENT NORTH — Lab hold

| Electorate | %Turnout | | 58,789 | 57.73% | 2001 | 54,149 | 70.5% | 1997 |
|---|---|---|---|---|---|---|---|---|
| Gardiner B | Lab | | 20,149 | 59.37% | 8.7% | 19,343 | 50.67% | Lab |
| Allott P | C | | 9,944 | 29.3% | -10.84% | 15,324 | 40.14% | C |
| Lorber P | LD | | 3,846 | 11.33% | 3.2% | 3,104 | 8.13% | LD |
| | | | | | | 204 | 0.53% | NLP |
| | | | | | | 199 | 0.52% | Dream |
| C to Lab swing | 9.77% | | 33,939 | Lab maj 10,205 | | 38,174 | Lab maj 4,019 | |
| | | | | 30.07% | | | 10.53% | |

**BARRY GARDINER,** b March 10, 1957. Elected 1997. Member, Broadcasting and Public Accounts Select Cttees. Chairman, all-party grps: leasehold reform and commonhold, and the leisure industry. Chairman, Lab friends of India. Partner of Mediterranean Average Adjusting Co; occasional lecturer for Acad of Nat Economy, Moscow. Cambridge city cllr, mayor, 1992. Member, MSF/GMB, Co-op Party. Ed Glasgow HS; Haileybury; St Andrews Univ; Corpus Christi Coll, Camb; Harvard (Kennedy Scholar).

An exceptional swing delivered what once appeared to be an extremely secure Conservative seat to Labour in 1997 and the trend was confirmed in 2001. This has always been, however, a rather complicated North London constituency, starkly polarised along class and racial lines. Some 42 per cent of the population are not white. It is perhaps surprising, therefore, that it had not become competitive earlier. Map 88

## BRENT SOUTH — Lab hold

| Electorate | %Turnout | | 55,891 | 51.24% | 2001 | 53,505 | 64.48% | 1997 |
|---|---|---|---|---|---|---|---|---|
| Boateng P | Lab | | 20,984 | 73.28% | 0.29% | 25,180 | 72.99% | Lab |
| Selvarajah C | C | | 3,604 | 12.59% | -3.32% | 5,489 | 15.91% | C |
| Hughes H | LD | | 3,098 | 10.82% | 3.08% | 2,670 | 7.74% | LD |
| McDonnell M | Soc All | | 491 | 1.71% | | 497 | 1.44% | Ref |
| Mac Stiofain T | Res Motor | | 460 | 1.61% | | 389 | 1.13% | Green |
| | | | | | | 175 | 0.51% | Dream |
| | | | | | | 98 | 0.28% | NLP |
| C to Lab swing | 1.81% | | 28,637 | Lab maj 17,380 | | 34,498 | Lab maj 19,691 | |
| | | | | 60.69% | | | 57.08% | |

**PAUL BOATENG,** b June 14, 1951. Elected 1987. Fin Sec, Treasury, June 2001-; Min of State, Home Office and Dep Home Sec, 1998-2001, and Min for Young People, 2000-01. Under-Sec for Health, 1997-98. Lab spokesman, Lord Chancellor's Dept, 1992-97. Privy Counsellor. Ex-joint sec, all-party Council of Christians and Jews; member, GLC, 1981-86; World Council of Churches Commission on programme to combat racism, 1984-91. Ed Ghana International Sch; Accra Acad; Apsley GS; Bristol Univ Coll of Law. tel: 020-7219 6816 fax: 020-7219 4970

At the time of the 1991 census this was the most heavily non-white constituency in the United Kingdom. The electorate is nonetheless divided between voters of Afro-Caribbean and Asian backgrounds on the one hand, and between a white working class and distinctly affluent (if small) middle class concentrated in certain wards. The predictable result is again strongly Labour. Map 89

## BRENTFORD & ISLEWORTH — Lab hold

| Electorate | %Turnout | | 84,049 | 52.96% | 2001 | 79,058 | 71.0% | 1997 |
|---|---|---|---|---|---|---|---|---|
| Keen Ms A | Lab | | 23,275 | 52.29% | -5.16% | 32,249 | 57.45% | Lab |
| Mack T | C | | 12,957 | 29.11% | -2.64% | 17,825 | 31.75% | C |
| Hartwell G | LD | | 5,994 | 13.47% | 5.25% | 4,613 | 8.22% | LD |
| Ferriday N | Green | | 1,324 | 2.97% | 1.75% | 687 | 1.22% | Green |
| Ingram G | UK Ind | | 412 | 0.93% | -0.16% | 614 | 1.09% | UK Ind |
| Faith D | Soc All | | 408 | 0.92% | | 147 | 0.26% | NLP |
| Khaira A | Ind | | 144 | 0.32% | | | | |
| Lab to C swing | 1.26% | | 44,514 | Lab maj 10,318 | | 56,135 | Lab maj 14,424 | |
| | | | | 23.18% | | | 25.70% | |

**ANN KEEN,** b Nov 26, 1948. Elected 1997. PPS to Gordon Brown, Chancellor of the Exchequer, 2001-; former PPS to Sec of State for Health. Member, Health Select Cttee, 1997-2001. Member, all-party cancer and Aids grps. Vice-chairwoman, PLP TU grp. Member, PLP Health Cttee. Awarded Parly Figure of the Year by Ovarian Cancer Grp. Moved amendment to Age of Consent Bill to bring equality to gay community. Ed Elfed Sec Mod, Clwyd; Surrey Univ. Husband, Alan, is MP for Feltham and Heston. tel: 020-7219 5623 fax: 020-7219 2233

This is the eastern section of the borough of Hounslow in West London. It contains such picturesque spots as Kew Gardens and the Old Deer Park. The constituency as a whole is more mixed in terms of housing patterns with a relatively low rate of owner-occupation for a seat held by the Conservatives from 1974 to 1997. A rising number of non-white electors may also help to entrench the Labour Party for the foreseeable future. Map 90

## BRENTWOOD & ONGAR — C hold

| Electorate | %Turnout | | 64,695 | 67.3% | 2001 | 66,005 | 76.85% | 1997 |
|---|---|---|---|---|---|---|---|---|
| Pickles E | | C | 16,558 | 38.03% | -7.37% | 23,031 | 45.4% | C |
| Bell M | | Ind Bell | 13,737 | 31.55% | | 13,341 | 26.3% | LD |
| Kendall D | | LD | 6,772 | 15.55% | -10.75% | 11,231 | 22.14% | Lab |
| Johnson Ms D | | Lab | 5,505 | 12.64% | -9.5% | 2,658 | 5.24% | Ref |
| Gulleford K | | UK Ind | 611 | 1.4% | 0.48% | 465 | 0.92% | UK Ind |
| Pryke P | | Ind Pr | 239 | 0.55% | | | | |
| Bishop D | | Elvis | 68 | 0.16% | | | | |
| Appleton T | | Ind T | 52 | 0.12% | | | | |
| No swing applicable | | | 43,542 | C maj 2,821 | | 50,726 | C maj 9,690 | |
| | | | | 6.48% | | | 19.10% | |

**ERIC PICKLES,** b April 20, 1952. Elected 1992. Opposition spokesman, Social Security. Member, Select Cttees: Environment, Transport and Regions, 1997-2001; Transport, 1995-97; Environment 1992-93. Joint vice-chairman, C Backbench Environment, Transport and Regions Cttee, 1997-98. Leader, Bradford council, 1988-90; member, 1979-91; leader, C grp, 1987-91. Local gvt editor, Conservative *Newsline*, 1990-92. Ed Greenhead GS, Keighley; Leeds Poly.

An Essex seat on the fringes of the capital. It is a mixture of largely middle-class commuter towns alongside more rural villages. The Conservatives have historically benefited from this combination. The seat attracted controversy in the previous Parliament with the allegation that a supposed religious cult had infiltrated the Conservative Association. This prompted Martin Bell, the former Independent MP, to stand; he failed to dislodge the Tories. Map 91

## BRIDGEND — Lab hold

| Electorate | %Turnout | | 61,496 | 60.17% | 2001 | 59,721 | 72.44% | 1997 |
|---|---|---|---|---|---|---|---|---|
| Griffiths W | | Lab | 19,422 | 52.49% | -5.56% | 25,115 | 58.05% | Lab |
| Brisby Ms T | | C | 9,377 | 25.34% | 2.53% | 9,867 | 22.81% | C |
| Barraclough Ms J | | LD | 5,330 | 14.4% | 2.92% | 4,968 | 11.48% | LD |
| Mahoney Ms M | | PC | 2,652 | 7.17% | 3.36% | 1,662 | 3.84% | Ref |
| Jeremy Ms S | | ProLife | 223 | 0.6% | | 1,649 | 3.81% | PC |
| Lab to C swing | 4.05% | | 37,004 | Lab maj 10,045 | | 43,261 | Lab maj 15,248 | |
| | | | | 27.15% | | | 35.24% | |

**WIN GRIFFITHS,** b Feb 11, 1943. Elected 1987. Under-Sec, Welsh Office, 1997-98. Lab spokesman, Wales, 1994-97; ed, 1992-94; environmental protection, 1990-92. Chairman, Backbench Ed, Science and Arts Cttees, 1988-90. MEP, S Wales, 1979-89; a vice-president, European Parliament, 1984-87. Vale of Glamorgan borough cllr, 1973-76; Dinas Powys community cllr, 1974-79. Methodist lay preacher. Teacher. Ed Brecon Boys' GS; Univ Coll, Cardiff.

By the standards of Mid-Glamorgan this must be considered a reasonably diverse and competitive seat. There is not much of a mining influence here and the constituency consists of the market centre of Bridgend itself, some smaller towns such as the seaside resort of Porthcawl, and picturesque villages. It returned a Conservative to the House of Commons in 1983 but has been firmly aligned with Labour subsequently. Map 92

## BRIDGWATER — C hold

| Electorate | %Turnout | | 74,079 | 64.59% | 2001 | 73,038 | 74.79% | 1997 |
|---|---|---|---|---|---|---|---|---|
| Liddell-Grainger I | | C | 19,354 | 40.45% | 3.52% | 20,174 | 36.93% | C |
| Thorn I | | LD | 14,367 | 30.03% | -3.62% | 18,378 | 33.65% | LD |
| Monteith W | | Lab | 12,803 | 26.76% | 2.01% | 13,519 | 24.75% | Lab |
| Gardner Ms V | | UK Ind | 1,323 | 2.77% | | 2,551 | 4.67% | Ref |
| LD to C swing | 3.57% | | 47,847 | C maj 4,987 | | 54,622 | C maj 1,796 | |
| | | | | 10.42% | | | 3.28% | |

**IAN LIDDELL-GRAINGER,** b Feb 23, 1959. Elected 2001. Inherits seat from Tom King. Stood for Devon W & Torridge, 1997 and Tyne & Wear in Euro election, 1994. Managing dir, construction co, previously working on family farm in Berwickshire. Chairman, Countryside Alliance in Devon. Major in TA. Ed Millfield Sch, Somerset; S of Scotland Agriculture Coll, Edinburgh.

This Somerset constituency, stretching across the Quantocks up to the coast at Minehead, is an interesting mixture of political traditions. Bridgwater itself is firmly Labour, strikingly so by West Country standards. The surrounding areas are largely Tory but with heavy inroads made of late by the Lib Dems. If the anti-Tory vote had not been fractured so badly in 1997 then Tom King, the Conservative former Defence Secretary, would probably have lost. Map 93

## BRIGG & GOOLE — Lab hold

| Electorate | %Turnout | | 63,536 | 64.62% | 2001 | 63,648 | 73.53% | 1997 |
|---|---|---|---|---|---|---|---|---|
| Cawsey I | Lab | | 20,066 | 48.88% | -1.32% | 23,493 | 50.2% | Lab |
| Stewart D | C | | 16,105 | 39.23% | 2.68% | 17,104 | 36.55% | C |
| Nolan D | LD | | 3,796 | 9.25% | -0.78% | 4,692 | 10.03% | LD |
| Bloom G | UK Ind | | 688 | 1.68% | | 1,513 | 3.23% | Ref |
| Kenny M | Soc Lab | | 399 | 0.97% | | | | |
| Lab to C swing | 2.00% | | 41,054 | Lab maj 3,961 | | 46,802 | Lab maj 6,389 | |
| | | | | 9.65% | | | 13.65% | |

**IAN CAWSEY,** b April 14, 1960. Elected 1997. PPS to Lord Williams of Mostyn, Leader of the House of Lords, June 2001-. Member, Home Affairs Select Cttee, 1999-2001; chairman, PLP Home Affairs Cttee, 1997-. Ex-research asst, Elliot Morley, MP. Humberside cllr, 1989-96; council leader, North Lincs UA, 1995-97; chairman, Humberside police authority, 1993-97. Ex-dir, Humberside International Airport. Member, Friends of the Earth. Systems analyst. Ed Wintringham Sch, Grimsby.

This North Lincolnshire/East Yorkshire seat is an uneasy amalgam of two quite different areas. Brigg, a relatively Tory town, was once partnered with Scunthorpe, then Cleethorpes (also quite sympathetic to the Conservatives) and now Goole. But the inland port of Goole on the Ouse is considerably larger than Brigg and has quite strong Labour sympathies. The intervening areas slightly arrest this trend, creating an intriguing marginal seat. Map 94

## BRIGHTON KEMPTOWN — Lab hold

| Electorate | %Turnout | | 67,621 | 57.97% | 2001 | 65,147 | 70.81% | 1997 |
|---|---|---|---|---|---|---|---|---|
| Turner Dr D | Lab | | 18,745 | 47.82% | 1.26% | 21,479 | 46.56% | Lab |
| Theobald G | C | | 13,823 | 35.26% | -3.64% | 17,945 | 38.9% | C |
| Marshall Ms J | LD | | 4,064 | 10.37% | 0.66% | 4,478 | 9.71% | LD |
| Miller H | Green | | 1,290 | 3.29% | | 1,526 | 3.31% | Ref |
| Chamberlain-Webber Dr J | UK Ind | | 543 | 1.39% | | 316 | 0.68% | Soc Lab |
| McLeod J | Soc Lab | | 364 | 0.93% | 0.25% | 172 | 0.37% | NLP |
| Dobbs D | Free | | 227 | 0.58% | | 123 | 0.27% | Loony |
| Cook Ms E | ProLife | | 147 | 0.37% | | 93 | 0.2% | Dream |
| C to Lab swing | 2.45% | | 39,203 | Lab maj 4,922 | | 46,132 | Lab maj 3,534 | |
| | | | | 12.56% | | | 7.66% | |

**DESMOND TURNER,** b March 17, 1939. Elected 1997; contested Mid-Sussex 1979. Member, Science and Tech Select Cttee, 1997-2001. Founder, Wage-Line, campaign for minimum wage. E Sussex cllr, 1985-97; Brighton borough cllr, 1994-97; Brighton and Hove unitary cllr, 1996-99. Concerns: older people, social exclusion and animal welfare. Teacher and biochemist. Ed Luton GS; Imperial Coll and University Coll, London.
e-mail: turnerd@parliament.uk www.desturnermp.co.uk
tel: 01273 330610 fax: 01273 500966

This seat contains what is perhaps the less fashionable half of Brighton. It incorporates some quite rough council estates alongside plush districts that include Roedean School. The seat also contains one of the largest and most politically mobilised homosexual communities in the UK. This has to be balanced against a rural fringe which takes a very different view of lifestyle matters. This was Labour's first Sussex seat and its first there before 1997. Map 95

## BRIGHTON PAVILION — Lab hold

| Electorate | %Turnout | | 69,200 | 58.85% | 2001 | 66,431 | 73.69% | 1997 |
|---|---|---|---|---|---|---|---|---|
| Lepper D | Lab Co-op | | 19,846 | 48.73% | -5.89% | 26,737 | 54.62% | Lab |
| Gold D | C | | 10,203 | 25.05% | -2.64% | 13,556 | 27.69% | C |
| Berry Ms R | LD | | 5,348 | 13.13% | 3.64% | 4,644 | 9.49% | LD |
| Taylor K | Green | | 3,806 | 9.35% | 6.8% | 1,304 | 2.66% | Ref |
| Fyvie I | Soc Lab | | 573 | 1.41% | | 1,249 | 2.55% | Green |
| Dobbs B | Free | | 409 | 1.0% | | 1,098 | 2.24% | Ind C |
| Hutchin S | UK Ind | | 361 | 0.89% | 0.52% | 179 | 0.37% | UK Ind |
| Paragallo Ms M | ProLife | | 177 | 0.43% | | 125 | 0.26% | SG |
| | | | | | | 59 | 0.12% | Dream |
| Lab Co-op to C swing | 1.63% | | 40,723 | Lab Co-op maj 9,643 | | 48,951 | Lab maj 13,181 | |
| | | | | 23.68% | | | 26.93% | |

**DAVID LEPPER,** b Sept 15, 1945. Elected 1997; contested seat 1992. Member, Public Administration and Broadcasting Select Cttees, 1997-2001. Chairman, all-party grp on town centre management issues; vice-chairman, leasehold and commonhold reform and wildlife protection grps. Sec, Co-op housing grp. Mayor of Brighton, 1993-94. Lab leader, Brighton council, 1986-93. Retired teacher. Ed Wimbledon County Sec; Kent and Sussex Univs; Central London Poly.
tel: 01273 551532 fax: 01273 550617

This seat was once considered very favourable territory for the Conservative Party. The Tory position has been undermined by social change in the seat, which contains most of urban Brighton, including the elegant seafront and Sussex University. The critical new political players have been homosexual electors, a large number of social security claimants and the many casual, often young, workers linked to tourism. Labour now seems quite secure. Map 96

## BRISTOL EAST | Lab hold

| Electorate | %Turnout | | 70,279 | 57.39% | 2001 | 68,990 | 69.87% | 1997 |
|---|---|---|---|---|---|---|---|---|
| **Corston Ms J** | Lab | **22,180** | **54.99%** | -1.89% | **27,418** | **56.88%** | Lab |
| Lo-Presti J | C | 8,788 | 21.79% | -1.57% | 11,259 | 23.36% | C |
| Niblett B | LD | 6,915 | 17.14% | 2.37% | 7,121 | 14.77% | LD |
| Collard G | Green | 1,110 | 2.75% | | 1,479 | 3.07% | Ref |
| Marsh R | UK Ind | 572 | 1.42% | | 766 | 1.59% | Soc Lab |
| Langley M | Soc Lab | 438 | 1.09% | -0.5% | 158 | 0.33% | NLP |
| Pryor A | Soc All | 331 | 0.82% | | | | |
| **Lab to C swing** | **0.16%** | **40,334** | Lab maj 13,392 | | **48,201** | Lab maj 16,159 | |
| | | | | 33.20% | | | 33.52% |

**JEAN CORSTON,** b May 5, 1942. Elected 1992. Former PPS to David Blunkett, Sec of State for Ed and Employment. Member, Select Cttees: Home Affairs, 1995-97; Agriculture, 1992-95. Vice-chairwoman, PLP, 1997-98 and 1999-2000. Worked, Lab reg office, Bristol, 1976-85; Lab Party HQ, 1985-86. Non-practising barrister. Unpaid dir, Tribune Publications Ltd. Ed Yeovil Girls' HS, Somerset; OU; LSE; Inns of Court Sch of Law.
e-mail: jeancorstonmp@hotmail.com tel: 020-7219 1568 fax: 020-7219 4878

Much of this seat was once represented by Tony Benn when he was the Member for Bristol South East. At the 1997 election it returned to being a solidly Labour constituency. This is, though, a very mixed constituency socially, capable of producing different results depending on the political mood of the skilled working class of the city. Map 97

## BRISTOL NORTH WEST | Lab hold

| Electorate | %Turnout | | 76,756 | 60.83% | 2001 | 75,009 | 73.65% | 1997 |
|---|---|---|---|---|---|---|---|---|
| **Naysmith D** | Lab Co-op | **24,436** | **52.33%** | 2.42% | **27,575** | **49.91%** | Lab |
| Hansard C | C | 13,349 | 28.59% | -0.72% | 16,193 | 29.31% | C |
| Tyzack P | LD | 7,387 | 15.82% | 2.67% | 7,263 | 13.15% | LD |
| Carr Miss D | UK Ind | 1,149 | 2.46% | -0.08% | 1,718 | 3.11% | Ind Lab |
| Horrigan V | Soc Lab | 371 | 0.79% | | 1,609 | 2.91% | Ref |
| | | | | | | 482 | 0.87% | Soc Lab |
| | | | | | | 265 | 0.48% | BNP |
| | | | | | | 140 | 0.25% | NLP |
| **C to Lab Co-op swing** | **1.57%** | **46,692** | Lab Co-op maj 11,087 | | **55,245** | Lab maj 11,382 | |
| | | | | 23.74% | | | 20.60% |

**DOUG NAYSMITH,** b April 1, 1941. Elected 1997; contested seat 1992. Member, Select Cttees, Social Security, 1999-2001; Deregulation, 1998-2001. Vice-chairman, PLP Health Cttee, 1997-; chairman, Science in Parly Editorial Cttee, 2000-. Council of Europe and WEU delegate, 1997-99. Medical scientist/lecturer. Bristol city cllr, 1981-89. Ed Musselburgh Burgh Sch; George Heriot Sch Edinburgh; Edinburgh and Yale Univs.
e-mail: naysmithd@parliament.uk tel: 020-7219 4187 fax: 020-7219 2602

This is the sort of evenly divided constituency which makes or breaks electoral aspirations. There are substantial clusters of working class, skilled working class and middle class. This part of Bristol has swapped partisan loyalties on seven occassions in the postwar era. It has been represented by eight different Members of Parliament since 1950, but for the present Labour seems well settled. Map 98

## BRISTOL SOUTH | Lab hold

| Electorate | %Turnout | | 72,490 | 56.52% | 2001 | 72,393 | 68.87% | 1997 |
|---|---|---|---|---|---|---|---|---|
| **Primarolo Ms D** | Lab | **23,299** | **56.87%** | -3.08% | **29,890** | **59.95%** | Lab |
| Eddy R | C | 9,118 | 22.26% | 1.08% | 10,562 | 21.18% | C |
| Main J | LD | 6,078 | 14.84% | 1.42% | 6,691 | 13.42% | LD |
| Vowles G | Green | 1,233 | 3.01% | 1.56% | 1,486 | 2.98% | Ref |
| Drummond B | Soc All | 496 | 1.21% | | 722 | 1.45% | Green |
| Prasad C | UK Ind | 496 | 1.21% | | 355 | 0.71% | Soc |
| Shorter G | Soc Lab | 250 | 0.61% | | 153 | 0.31% | Glow |
| **Lab to C swing** | **2.08%** | **40,970** | Lab maj 14,181 | | **49,859** | Lab maj 19,328 | |
| | | | | 34.61% | | | 38.77% |

**DAWN PRIMAROLO,** b May 2, 1954. Elected 1987. Paymaster General, 1999-; confirmed June, 2001. Financial Sec to the Treasury, 1997-99. Lab spokeswoman on Treasury matters, 1994-97; health, 1992-94. Member, Select Cttee, Members' Interests, 1988-92. Avon county cllr, 1985-87. Ex-researcher. Ed Thomas Bennett Comp, Crawley; Bristol Poly; Bristol Univ.

This is easily the most working-class of the Bristol constituencies. There are a large number of working-class estates forming the bedrock of support for the Labour Party. There are enough affluent electors to offer the Tories some sort of base but it would take an extraordinary result at the national level to shift this seat away from Labour. Map 99

## BRISTOL WEST — Lab hold

| Electorate | %Turnout | | 84,821 | 65.63% | 2001 | 84,870 | 73.81% | 1997 |
|---|---|---|---|---|---|---|---|---|
| Davey Ms V | | Lab | 20,505 | 36.84% | 1.61% | 22,068 | 35.23% | Lab |
| Williams S | | LD | 16,079 | 28.89% | 0.87% | 20,575 | 32.85% | C |
| Chesters Mrs P | | C | 16,040 | 28.82% | -4.03% | 17,551 | 28.02% | LD |
| Devaney J | | Green | 1,961 | 3.52% | 2.16% | 1,304 | 2.08% | Ref |
| Kennedy B | | Soc Lab | 590 | 1.06% | 0.67% | 852 | 1.36% | Green |
| Muir S | | UK Ind | 490 | 0.88% | | 244 | 0.39% | Soc Lab |
| | | | | | | 47 | 0.08% | NLP |
| LD to Lab swing | 0.37% | | 55,665 | Lab maj 4,426 | | 62,641 | Lab maj 1,493 | |
| | | | | 7.95% | | | 2.38% | |

**VALERIE DAVEY,** b April 16, 1940. Elected 1997. Member, Ed and Employment Select Cttee and its Ed Sub Cttee, 1997-2001. Chairwoman, PLP ed grp. Member, all-party grps, disablement, human rights and cycling. Avon county cllr, 1981-86; leader, Lab grp, 1992-96. Member, NUT; SEA; Amnesty; Lab Campaign for Electoral Reform. Teacher. Ed Birmingham and London Univs. e-mail:valdavey@labourbriswest.demon.co.uk tel: 0117-907 7464 fax: 0117-907 7465

This has traditionally been the most affluent and desirable of the Bristol constituencies. It also contains a large section of the university population. The leafy suburbs such as Clifton, however, disguise a seat which contains much of the deprived St Paul's ward, once associated with race riots. Although Labour is now in the ascendancy, the whole mixture produces a seat which could be captured at different times by any of the three main parties. Map 100

## BROMLEY & CHISLEHURST — C hold

| Electorate | %Turnout | | 68,763 | 62.87% | 2001 | 71,104 | 74.17% | 1997 |
|---|---|---|---|---|---|---|---|---|
| Forth E | | C | 21,412 | 49.53% | 3.21% | 24,428 | 46.32% | C |
| Polydorou Ms S | | Lab | 12,375 | 28.63% | 3.39% | 13,310 | 25.24% | Lab |
| Payne G | | LD | 8,180 | 18.92% | -4.84% | 12,530 | 23.76% | LD |
| Bryant R | | UK Ind | 1,264 | 2.92% | 0.69% | 1,176 | 2.23% | UK Ind |
| | | | | | | 640 | 1.21% | Green |
| | | | | | | 369 | 0.7% | NF |
| | | | | | | 285 | 0.54% | Lib |
| C to Lab swing | 0.09% | | 43,231 | C maj 9,037 | | 52,738 | C maj 11,118 | |
| | | | | 20.90% | | | 21.08% | |

**ERIC FORTH,** b Sept 9, 1944. Elected here 1997; MP for Worcestershire Mid 1983-97; MEP, N Birmingham 1979-84. Ed and Employment Min, 1995-97; Ed Min, 1994-95; Ed Under-Sec, 1992-94, and Employment, 1990-92; Consumer Affairs Under-Sec, 1988-90. Member, House of Commons Commission, 2000-; Standards and Privileges Cttee, 1999-2001; Cttee on Procedures, 1999-2001. PPS to Ed and Science Min, 1986-87. Brentwood cllr 1968-72. Ed Jordanhill Coll Sch, Glasgow; Glasgow Univ.

This part of Kent is extremely favourable territory for the Conservative Party. It consists mostly of smallish and affluent towns with numerous commuters. There are a few council estates which provide a modest number of reliable votes for the Labour Party. In the rest of the constituency, however, the Liberal Democrats provide what opposition there is to the Tories. Map 101

## BROMSGROVE — C hold

| Electorate | %Turnout | | 68,115 | 67.07% | 2001 | 67,744 | 77.07% | 1997 |
|---|---|---|---|---|---|---|---|---|
| Kirkbride Miss J | | C | 23,640 | 51.75% | 4.59% | 24,620 | 47.16% | C |
| McDonald P | | Lab | 15,502 | 33.93% | -3.85% | 19,725 | 37.78% | Lab |
| Rowley Mrs M | | LD | 5,430 | 11.89% | 0.01% | 6,200 | 11.88% | LD |
| Gregory I | | UK Ind | 1,112 | 2.43% | 1.95% | 1,411 | 2.7% | Ref |
| | | | | | | 251 | 0.48% | UK Ind |
| Lab to C swing | 4.22% | | 45,684 | C maj 8,138 | | 52,207 | C maj 4,895 | |
| | | | | 17.81% | | | 9.38% | |

**JULIE KIRKBRIDE,** b June 5, 1960. Elected 1997. Member, Select Cttees, Culture, Media and Sport, 1999-2001; Social Security, 1997-99. Ex-social affairs editor, *The Sunday Telegraph*; previously political reporter, *The Daily Telegraph*. Member, Halifax YCs, 1974-78. Ed Highlands GS; Girton Coll, Cambridge (vice-pres of Union). Wife of Andrew MacKay, MP for Bracknell.

This seat constitutes the northeast corner of Worcestershire on the edge of the Clent Hills - an area that has experienced a rapid surge in population recently. It is quite polarised but in a manner that has operated to the benefit of the Conservative Party. The majority of the population are relatively affluent commuters or rural dwellers. The town of Bromsgrove itself contains some council estates that back Labour. Map 102

## BROXBOURNE — C hold

| Electorate | %Turnout | | 68,982 | 54.86% | 2001 | 66,720 | 70.41% | 1997 |
|---|---|---|---|---|---|---|---|---|
| Roe Mrs M | | C | 20,487 | 54.13% | 5.27% | 22,952 | 48.86% | C |
| Prendergast D | | Lab | 11,494 | 30.37% | -4.33% | 16,299 | 34.7% | Lab |
| Davies Ms J | | LD | 4,158 | 10.99% | -0.31% | 5,310 | 11.3% | LD |
| Harvey M | | UK Ind | 858 | 2.27% | | 1,633 | 3.48% | Ref |
| Cope J | | BNP | 848 | 2.24% | 0.94% | 610 | 1.3% | BNP |
| | | | | | | 172 | 0.37% | Third |
| Lab to C swing | 4.80% | | 37,845 | | C maj 8,993 23.76% | 46,976 | | C maj 6,653 14.16% |

**MARION ROE,** b July 15, 1936. Elected 1983. Member, Chairmen's Panel, 1997-; House of Commons Finance and Services Cttee, 1997-2001; chairwoman, Commons Administration Cttee, 1997-2001. Member, Select Cttees: Health, 1992-97; Procedure, 1991-92; Sittings of Commons, 1991-94; Social Services, 1988-89. Parly under sec, Environment, 1987-88. Joint chairwoman, all-party breast cancer grp, 1997. Freeman, City of London. Ed Bromley HS and Croydon HS (GPDST); English Sch of Languages, Vevey.

A pleasing corner of southeast Hertfordshire which borders Essex. It contains a network of affluent suburban communities linked more or less by the A10. While the southern end of Waltham Cross, which borders London, is fertile territory for the Labour Party, the rest of the constituency is staunchly Conservative and is likely to stay so. Map 103

## BROXTOWE — Lab hold

| Electorate | %Turnout | | 73,675 | 66.51% | 2001 | 74,144 | 78.41% | 1997 |
|---|---|---|---|---|---|---|---|---|
| Palmer N | | Lab | 23,836 | 48.64% | 1.61% | 27,343 | 47.03% | Lab |
| Latham Mrs P | | C | 17,963 | 36.66% | -0.78% | 21,768 | 37.44% | C |
| Watts D | | LD | 7,205 | 14.7% | 2.77% | 6,934 | 11.93% | LD |
| | | | | | | 2,092 | 3.6% | Ref |
| C to Lab swing | 1.20% | | 49,004 | | Lab maj 5,873 11.98% | 58,137 | | Lab maj 5,575 9.59% |

**NICK PALMER,** b Feb 5, 1950. Elected 1997; contested Chelsea 1983; E Sussex and Kent S in 1994 Euro elections. Member, NI Select Cttee. Chairman, fund for replacement of animals in medical experiments (all-party grp); vice-chairman, animal welfare all-party grp. Editor, *Flagship*, a magazine reviewing games played by post; hon chairman, Astro-Sprint Ltd, publishers of *Flagship* magazine. Ed London Univ; Copenhagen Univ.
e-mail: palmern@parliament.uk tel: 0115-943 0721 fax: 0115-943 1860

This is the home of many of the more affluent residents of the Nottingham area. It contains a mixture of desirable suburbs alongside smaller villages with a modest working-class base for Labour. The overall impression to an outsider would be that this is a seat destined to elect Conservatives and by a secure margin. It was, therefore, a real shock when this patch returned a Labour MP in 1997, though the shock had worn off by 2001. Map 104

## BUCKINGHAM — C hold

| Electorate | %Turnout | | 65,270 | 69.36% | 2001 | 62,945 | 78.48% | 1997 |
|---|---|---|---|---|---|---|---|---|
| Bercow J | | C | 24,296 | 53.67% | 3.88% | 24,594 | 49.79% | C |
| Seddon M | | Lab | 10,971 | 24.23% | -0.48% | 12,208 | 24.71% | Lab |
| Wilson Ms I | | LD | 9,037 | 19.96% | -4.69% | 12,175 | 24.65% | LD |
| Silcock C | | UK Ind | 968 | 2.14% | | 421 | 0.85% | NLP |
| Lab to C swing | 2.18% | | 45,272 | | C maj 13,325 29.43% | 49,398 | | C maj 12,386 25.08% |

**JOHN BERCOW,** b Jan 19, 1963. Elected 1997. C front-bench spokesman, ed and employment, 1999-2000; home affairs, 2000-. Member, Select Cttees: Welsh Affairs, 1997-98; Trade and Industry, 1998-99. Joint sec, C Backbench Home Affairs and Employment Committees, 1997-99. Special adviser, Nat Heritage Sec, 1995-96, and previously, Chief Sec to Treasury. Lambeth cllr, 1986-90. Ex-senior consultant, Westminster Strategy. Credit analyst with Hambros Bank, 1987-88. Ed Finchley Manorhill Sch; Essex Univ.
e-mail: danielsrj@parliament.uk tel: 020-7219 6346 fax: 020-7219 0981

This enviable patch of Buckinghamshire, the site of Britain's first private university, is an extremely safe seat for the Conservative Party. The constituency is based on the surprisingly small town of Buckingham and a myriad of small, attractive and staunchly Tory villages. The only surprise is that Labour and the Liberal Democrats between them are capable of attracting a reasonable number of votes. Map 105

## BURNLEY — Lab hold

| Electorate | %Turnout | | 66,393 | 55.55% | 2001 | 67,582 | 66.95% | 1997 |
|---|---|---|---|---|---|---|---|---|
| Pike P | | Lab | 18,195 | 49.33% | -8.6% | 26,210 | 57.93% | Lab |
| Frost R | | C | 7,697 | 20.87% | 0.65% | 9,148 | 20.22% | C |
| Wright P | | LD | 5,975 | 16.2% | -1.21% | 7,877 | 17.41% | LD |
| Smith S | | BNP | 4,151 | 11.25% | | 2,010 | 4.44% | Ref |
| Buttrey R | | UK Ind | 866 | 2.35% | | | | |
| Lab to C swing | | 4.62% | 36,884 | Lab maj 10,498 | 28.46% | 45,245 | Lab maj 17,062 | 37.71% |

**PETER PIKE,** b June 26, 1937. Elected 1983. Select Cttees: Commons Modernisation, 1997-2001; Deregulation, 1995-97; Procedure, 1995-97; Environment, 1985-90. Joint chairman, all-party grp, road passenger transport. Lab spokesman, housing, 1992-94; rural affairs, 1990-92. Merton and Morden cllr, 1962-63; Burnley borough cllr, 1976-84. Production worker (inspection), 1973-83. Lab Party organiser and agent, 1963-73; union shop steward, 1976-83. Former factory worker. Ed: Hinchley Wood Sec Sch; Kingston Tech Coll.

**This is a seat that has not changed much over the years either in its social composition or political inclinations. Like many Lancashire ex-cotton towns in the shadow of the Pennines, it consistently votes Labour because of its urban, industrial working class, though it also has a not insignificant middle class that has leant towards the Tories. The BNP established a presence here in 2001 and racial disturbances followed shortly after the election. Map 106**

## BURTON — Lab hold

| Electorate | %Turnout | | 75,194 | 61.78% | 2001 | 72,601 | 75.08% | 1997 |
|---|---|---|---|---|---|---|---|---|
| Dean Ms J | | Lab | 22,783 | 49.04% | -1.98% | 27,810 | 51.02% | Lab |
| Punyer Mrs M | | C | 17,934 | 38.6% | -0.8% | 21,480 | 39.4% | C |
| Fletcher D | | LD | 4,468 | 9.62% | 1.15% | 4,617 | 8.47% | LD |
| Crompton I | | UK Ind | 984 | 2.12% | | 604 | 1.11% | Nat Dem |
| Taylor J | | ProLife | 288 | 0.62% | | | | |
| Lab to C swing | | 0.59% | 46,457 | Lab maj 4,849 | 10.44% | 54,511 | Lab maj 6,330 | 11.62% |

**JANET DEAN,** b Jan 28, 1949. Elected 1997. Member, Commons Catering Cttee, 1997-. E Staffordshire county cllr, 1981-97 (mayor, 1996-97); Uttoxeter town cllr, 1995-97. Founder member, Uttoxeter crime prevention panel; chairman, Uttoxeter CAB. Ed Winsford Verdin GS, Cheshire.

**This is one of Britain's great brewing centres which consumes almost all of east Staffordshire. The town of Burton upon Trent itself is vociferously Labour, a loyalty reinforced in recent years by new Commonwealth immigrants, while the surrounding area is much more friendly to the Conservatives. This sort of split makes for the hardest fought of constituencies and it remains a marginal. Map 107**

## BURY NORTH — Lab hold

| Electorate | %Turnout | | 71,108 | 62.99% | 2001 | 70,515 | 78.07% | 1997 |
|---|---|---|---|---|---|---|---|---|
| Chaytor D | | Lab | 22,945 | 51.23% | -0.58% | 28,523 | 51.81% | Lab |
| Walsh J | | C | 16,413 | 36.65% | -0.87% | 20,657 | 37.52% | C |
| Hackley B | | LD | 5,430 | 12.12% | 3.88% | 4,536 | 8.24% | LD |
| | | | | | | 1,337 | 2.43% | Ref |
| C to Lab swing | | 0.15% | 44,788 | Lab maj 6,532 | 14.58% | 55,053 | Lab maj 7,866 | 14.29% |

**DAVID CHAYTOR,** b Aug 3, 1949. Elected 1997; contested Calder Valley 1987 and 1992. Member, Select Cttees, Environmental Audit, 2000-01; Deregulation, 1997-2001. Chairman, all-party grp for FE, 1999-; sec, Globe UK all-party grp, 2000-; sec, all-party adult ed grp, 1997-. Calderdale borough cllr, 1982-97. Member, full employment forum; member,TGWU. Ex-head of continuing ed, Manchester Coll of Arts and Tech. Ed Bury GS; London Univ, Leeds Univ.

**Bury North is an interesting Lancashire seat, both more prosperous and more sympathetic to the Conservative Party than might be expected. It is a mixture of the aspirational middle class and the more traditional working-class electorate. The Tories held it from 1983 to 1997 and will need to recapture it, at some point, if they are to obtain a parliamentary majority. Map 108**

## BURY SOUTH — Lab hold

| Electorate | %Turnout | | 67,276 | 58.77% | 2001 | 66,568 | 75.6% | 1997 |
|---|---|---|---|---|---|---|---|---|
| Lewis I | Lab | | 23,406 | 59.2% | 2.26% | 28,658 | 56.94% | Lab |
| Le Page Mrs N | C | | 10,634 | 26.89% | -5.35% | 16,225 | 32.24% | C |
| Pickstone T | LD | | 5,499 | 13.91% | 5.51% | 4,227 | 8.4% | LD |
| | | | | | | 1,216 | 2.42% | Ref |
| C to Lab swing | 3.80% | | 39,539 | Lab maj 12,772 | | 50,326 | Lab maj 12,433 | |
| | | | | 32.30% | | | 24.70% | |

**IVAN LEWIS,** b March 4, 1967. Elected 1997. Parly Sec, Ed and Skills, June 2001-. Member, Select Cttees: Deregulation, 1997-2001; Health, 1999-2001. PPS to Trade and Industry Sec, 1999-2001; vice-chairman, Lab friends of Israel, 1998-; chairman, all-party grp on parenting, 1999-. Chairman, Bury S CLP, 1991-96. Chief exec, Jewish Social Services, Greater Manchester (a charity). Ed William Hulme's GS; Stand Sixth-Form Coll.
e-mail: ivanlewis@burysouth.fsnet.co.uk tel: 0161-773 5500 fax: 0161-773 7959

This has been a competitive seat over the past two decades. Bury is one of the most prosperous of Lancashire's former textile towns, and this seat is socially divided in a similar fashion to Bury North but with some inherent advantages for Labour. There is also a strong Jewish flavour to both the electorate and the local political class (regardless of party affiliation). It swung decisively to Labour in 1997 and the majority was almost identical in 2001. Map 109

## BURY ST EDMUNDS — C hold

| Electorate | %Turnout | | 76,146 | 66.0% | 2001 | 74,017 | 75.02% | 1997 |
|---|---|---|---|---|---|---|---|---|
| Ruffley D | C | | 21,850 | 43.48% | 5.14% | 21,290 | 38.34% | C |
| Ereira M | Lab | | 19,347 | 38.5% | 0.82% | 20,922 | 37.68% | Lab |
| Williams R | LD | | 6,998 | 13.92% | -4.27% | 10,102 | 18.19% | LD |
| Howlett J | UK Ind | | 831 | 1.65% | | 2,939 | 5.29% | Ref |
| Brundle M | Ind | | 651 | 1.3% | | 272 | 0.49% | NLP |
| Benwell M | Soc Lab | | 580 | 1.15% | | | | |
| Lab to C swing | 2.16% | | 50,257 | C maj 2,503 | | 55,525 | C maj 368 | |
| | | | | 4.98% | | | 0.66% | |

**DAVID RUFFLEY,** b April 18, 1962. Elected 1997. Member, Public Administration Select Cttee, 1997-2001. Special adviser to Sec of State for Ed and Science, 1991-92; Home Office, 1992-93; and to Chancellor of the Exchequer, 1993-96. Consultant, Grant Maintained Schs Foundation, 1991-. Ed Bolton Sch; Queens' Coll, Cambridge.

The county of Suffolk has become increasingly popular in recent years and the historic market and cathedral town of Bury St Edmunds has grown as a consequence. The Boundary Commission created an additional seat here which necessitated substantial revision to several seats. This constituency is based on the town itself, where predominant Labour support contrasts with the villages, which lean towards the Conservatives. Map 110

## CAERNARFON — PC hold

| Electorate | %Turnout | | 47,354 | 61.35% | 2001 | 46,815 | 73.72% | 1997 |
|---|---|---|---|---|---|---|---|---|
| Williams H | PC | | 12,894 | 44.38% | -6.67% | 17,616 | 51.05% | PC |
| Eaglestone M | Lab | | 9,383 | 32.3% | 2.84% | 10,167 | 29.46% | Lab |
| Naish Ms B | C | | 4,403 | 15.16% | 2.9% | 4,230 | 12.26% | C |
| ab Owain M | LD | | 1,823 | 6.27% | 1.38% | 1,686 | 4.89% | LD |
| Lloyd I | UK Ind | | 550 | 1.89% | | 811 | 2.35% | Ref |
| PC to Lab swing | 4.75% | | 29,053 | PC maj 3,511 | | 34,510 | PC maj 7,449 | |
| | | | | 12.08% | | | 21.59% | |

**HYWEL WILLIAMS,** b May 14, 1953. Elected 2001. Inherits seat from Dafydd Wigley who held it since 1974. Caernarfon had only had four MPs in the last 111 years, including David Lloyd George from 1890 to 1945. Member, Welsh Assembly, 1999. Social worker, Glamorgan County Council, 1974-76; Gwynedd County Council, 1976-84; project worker, N Wales social work practice centre, and head of centre, 1985-2001. Author on social work and social policy. Lecturer. Ed Univ of Wales, Cardiff.

Caernarfon has been described as comfortably the most "Welsh" constituency in the whole of the Principality. It is easy to understand why. Almost 80 per cent of the residents speak Welsh and there is a fierce sense of local identity. This beautiful area — a mixture of coastland, rural villages and small towns such as Caernarfon itself, plus Portmadoc, Criccieth and Pwllheli extending along the Lleyn Peninsula — has become a Plaid Cymru stronghold. Map 111

## CAERPHILLY — Lab hold

| Electorate | %Turnout | | 67,593 | 57.45% | 2001 | 64,621 | 70.05% | 1997 |
|---|---|---|---|---|---|---|---|---|
| David W | Lab | | 22,597 | 58.19% | -9.62% | 30,697 | 67.81% | Lab |
| Whittle L | PC | | 8,172 | 21.05% | 11.37% | 4,858 | 10.73% | C |
| Simmonds D | C | | 4,413 | 11.36% | 0.63% | 4,383 | 9.68% | PC |
| Roffe R | LD | | 3,649 | 9.4% | 1.17% | 3,724 | 8.23% | LD |
| | | | | | | 1,337 | 2.95% | Ref |
| | | | | | | 270 | 0.6% | ProLife |
| Lab to PC swing | 10.49% | | 38,831 | Lab maj 14,425 | | 45,269 | Lab maj 25,839 | |
| | | | | 37.15% | | | 57.08% | |

**WAYNE DAVID,** b July 1, 1957. Elected 2001. Inherits seat from Ron Davies, who resigned as Welsh Sec after a "moment of madness" on Clapham Common in 1998. Former MEP for S Wales and S Wales Central. History teacher; adviser in youth policy. Ed Cynfig Comp; Univ Coll, Cardiff; Univ Coll, Swansea.

This seat has been shaped by the economics and politics of coalmining. A collection of towns in the lower Rhymney Valley north of Cardiff, it has demonstrated a consistent loyalty to the Labour Party. This solidarity masks the fact that this is not an especially poor area. Its traditional allegiance has hardly been shaken by the scandals associated with Ron Davies, MP, in 1998. Map 112

## CAITHNESS, SUTHERLAND & EASTER ROSS — LD hold

| Electorate | %Turnout | | 41,225 | 60.32% | 2001 | 41,566 | 70.18% | 1997 |
|---|---|---|---|---|---|---|---|---|
| Thurso Viscount J | LD | | 9,041 | 36.36% | 0.77% | 10,381 | 35.59% | LD |
| Meighan M | Lab | | 6,297 | 25.32% | -2.52% | 8,122 | 27.84% | Lab |
| Macadam J | SNP | | 5,273 | 21.2% | -1.8% | 6,710 | 23.0% | SNP |
| Rowantree R | C | | 3,513 | 14.13% | 3.34% | 3,148 | 10.79% | C |
| Mabon Ms K | SSP | | 544 | 2.19% | | 369 | 1.26% | Ref |
| Campbell G | Ind | | 199 | 0.8% | | 230 | 0.79% | Green |
| | | | | | | 212 | 0.73% | UK Ind |
| Lab to LD swing | 1.64% | | 24,867 | LD maj 2,744 | | 29,172 | LD maj 2,259 | |
| | | | | 11.03% | | | 7.75% | |

**JOHN THURSO,** b Sept 10, 1953. Elected 2001. Takes over seat from Robert Maclennan, who held it from 1966 as a rep of Lab, SDP and LDs. Viscount Thurso is the first hereditary peer from the reformed House of Lords to be elected to the House of Commons. Candidate, Highlands & Islands reg list, 1999, Scottish Parliament. Former spokesman, business, industry and tourism, House of Lords. Managing dir, Fitness and Leisure Holdings and chairman, Lochdu Hotels Ltd. Ed Eton.

This is a vast northern Scottish constituency, overwhelmingly rural, with a very small electorate and a strong tradition of the personal vote. It includes John o'Groat's, the granite fishing ports of Wick and Thurso and the seaside town of Tain. It has been represented by Labour, Tory, Liberal and Social Democratic parties as well as two Independents since 1945. Lib Dems hold it at present, but this is likely to remain extremely distinctive territory. Map 113

## CALDER VALLEY — Lab hold

| Electorate | %Turnout | | 75,298 | 62.98% | 2001 | 74,901 | 75.39% | 1997 |
|---|---|---|---|---|---|---|---|---|
| McCafferty Mrs C | Lab | | 20,244 | 42.69% | -3.44% | 26,050 | 46.13% | Lab |
| Robson-Catling Mrs S | C | | 17,150 | 36.16% | 1.1% | 19,795 | 35.06% | C |
| Taylor M | LD | | 7,596 | 16.02% | 1.28% | 8,322 | 14.74% | LD |
| Hutton S | Green | | 1,034 | 2.18% | 1.32% | 1,380 | 2.44% | Ref |
| Nunn J | UK Ind | | 729 | 1.54% | | 488 | 0.86% | Green |
| Lockwood P | LCA | | 672 | 1.42% | | 431 | 0.76% | BNP |
| Lab to C swing | 2.27% | | 47,425 | Lab maj 3,094 | | 56,466 | Lab maj 6,255 | |
| | | | | 6.52% | | | 11.07% | |

**CHRISTINE McCAFFERTY,** b Oct 14, 1945. Elected 1997. Member, Procedures Select Cttee, 1997-99. Member, all-party grps: social, health and family; population, development and reproductive health. Parly member, Council of Europe, 1999-; WEU 1999-. Member, Political Advisory Cttee, Environmental Industries Commission. Member, Calderdale MBC, 1991-97; served as chairwoman, social services, women's advisory grp, adoption panel. Ed Whalley Range GS for Girls; Footscray HS, Victoria, Australia. e mail: chrismccaffertymp@btinternet.com tel 01422 843713

An interesting constituency in the eastern Pennines. It has been a hard-fought Yorkshire marginal seat for some years. It consists of small towns and numerous villages with no single conurbation dominating the others. Once a hub of the textile industry, but now tourism - especially round Hebden Bridge - has become increasingly a crucial part of the local economy. Map 114

## CAMBERWELL & PECKHAM — Lab hold

| Electorate | %Turnout | 53,694 | 46.75% | 2001 | 50,214 | 56.71% | 1997 |
|---|---|---|---|---|---|---|---|
| **Harman Ms H** | **Lab** | **17,473** | **69.6%** | **0.29%** | **19,734** | **69.31%** | **Lab** |
| McCarthy D | LD | 3,350 | 13.34% | 2.11% | 3,383 | 11.88% | C |
| Morgan J | C | 2,740 | 10.91% | -0.97% | 3,198 | 11.23% | LD |
| Poorun S | Green | 805 | 3.21% | | 692 | 2.43% | Ref |
| Mulrenan J | Soc All | 478 | 1.9% | | 685 | 2.41% | Soc Lab |
| Adams R | Soc Lab | 188 | 0.75% | -1.66% | 443 | 1.56% | Lib |
| Sweeney F | WRP | 70 | 0.28% | -0.09% | 233 | 0.82% | Soc |
| | | | | | 106 | 0.37% | WRP |
| **Lab to LD swing** | **0.91%** | **25,104** | **Lab maj 14,123** | | **28,474** | **Lab maj 16,351** | |
| | | | 56.26% | | | 57.43% | |

**HARRIET HARMAN,** b July 30, 1950. Elected here 1997; MP, Peckham 1982-97. Solicitor-General, June, 2001-; Social Security Sec, 1997-98. Lab Shadow, Social Security, 1996-97; Health, 1995-96; Employment, 1994-95. Shadow Chief Sec to the Treasury, 1992-93, retaining post when defeated in 1993 Shadow Cabinet elections. Member, NEC, 1993-97. Legal officer, National Council for Civil Liberties, 1978-82; Brent Community Law Centre, 1975-78. Ed St Paul's Girls Sch; York Univ.
e-mail: harmanh@parliament.uk tel: 020-7219 4218 fax: 020-7219 4877

This is a very poor South London constituency with a predictable loyalty to the Labour Party. There are large numbers of council tenants and an expanding ethnic minority population. The gruesome murder of Damilola Taylor, a 10-year-old boy from Nigeria, in November 2000 focused national attention on the deprivation associated with this seat. Map 115

## CAMBRIDGE — Lab hold

| Electorate | %Turnout | 70,663 | 60.62% | 2001 | 71,669 | 71.63% | 1997 |
|---|---|---|---|---|---|---|---|
| **Campbell Ms A** | **Lab** | **19,316** | **45.09%** | **-8.35%** | **27,436** | **53.44%** | **Lab** |
| Howarth D | LD | 10,737 | 25.07% | 8.93% | 13,299 | 25.9% | C |
| Stuart G | C | 9,829 | 22.95% | -2.95% | 8,287 | 16.14% | LD |
| Lawrence S | Green | 1,413 | 3.3% | 2.03% | 1,262 | 2.46% | Ref |
| Senter H | Soc All | 716 | 1.67% | | 654 | 1.27% | Green |
| Baynes L | UK Ind | 532 | 1.24% | | 191 | 0.37% | ProLife |
| Underwood Ms C | ProLife | 232 | 0.54% | 0.17% | 107 | 0.21% | WRP |
| Courtney Ms M | WRP | 61 | 0.14% | -0.07% | 103 | 0.2% | NLP |
| **Lab to LD swing** | **8.64%** | **42,836** | **Lab maj 8,579** | | **51,339** | **Lab maj 14,137** | |
| | | | 20.03% | | | 27.54% | |

**ANNE CAMPBELL,** b April 6, 1940. Elected 1992. PPS to Patricia Hewitt, Sec of State for Trade & Industry, 2001-; also to John Battle, Trade and Industry Min of State, 1997-2001. Member, Select Cttee, Science and Tech, 1992-97; joint vice-pres, 1996-97 (chairwoman, 1994-97), Parly and Scientific Cttee; joint vice-chairwoman all-party energy studies grp, 1997-. Cambridgeshire cllr, 1985-89. Ed Newnham Coll, Cambridge.
e-mail: anne.campbell.mp@dial.pipex.com tel: 01223 506500 fax: 01223 311315

The seat contains not only the ancient university city itself but also a number of surrounding villages. All three parties have entertained hopes of capturing this seat over the past 20 years. Shirley Williams stood here for the then Alliance in 1987 and the Conservatives held it throughout the 1980s, but then academic sentiment moved sharply against them. Tactical voting is likely to prove an obstacle to their retaking the constituency. Map 116

## CAMBRIDGESHIRE NORTH EAST — C hold

| Electorate | %Turnout | 79,891 | 60.15% | 2001 | 76,056 | 72.87% | 1997 |
|---|---|---|---|---|---|---|---|
| **Moss M** | **C** | **23,132** | **48.14%** | **5.1%** | **23,855** | **43.04%** | **C** |
| Owen D | Lab | 16,759 | 34.88% | 1.04% | 18,754 | 33.84% | Lab |
| Renaut R | LD | 6,733 | 14.01% | -2.35% | 9,070 | 16.36% | LD |
| Stevens J | UK Ind | 1,189 | 2.47% | | 2,636 | 4.76% | Ref |
| Hoey T | ProLife | 238 | 0.5% | | 851 | 1.54% | Soc Lab |
| | | | | | 259 | 0.47% | NLP |
| **Lab to C swing** | **2.03%** | **48,051** | **C maj 6,373** | | **55,425** | **C maj 5,101** | |
| | | | 13.26% | | | 9.20% | |

**MALCOLM MOSS,** b March 6, 1943. Elected 1987. Opposition frontbench spokesman, Agriculture, 1999- and NI, 1997-99; C whip, July-Oct, 1997. NI Under-Sec, 1994-97. PPS to Tristan Garel-Jones, Foreign Office Min, 1991-94. Member, Energy Select Cttee, 1988-91; joint vice-chairman, 1989-91, and sec, 1987-89. Fenland district cllr, 1983-87; Cambridgeshire county cllr, 1985-87. Ed Audenshaw GS; St John's Coll, Cambridge.
e-mail: mossm@parliament.uk www.malcmoss.easynet.uk
tel: 020-7219 6933 fax: 020-7219 6840

This seat, at the very heart of the Fens and incorporating the small towns of Wisbech and March, was known for many years as the Isle of Ely. It was represented by Clement Freud, a prominent media personality of his time, for the Liberal Party until his surprise defeat in 1987. Since then his party has virtually collapsed in the constituency, a process that has assisted the Conservatives. Map 117

## CAMBRIDGESHIRE NORTH WEST

**C hold**

| Electorate | %Turnout | 70,569 | 62.29% | 2001 | 65,791 | 74.2% | 1997 |
|---|---|---|---|---|---|---|---|
| **Mawhinney Sir B** | **C** | **21,895** | **49.81%** | **1.7%** | **23,488** | **48.11%** | **C** |
| Cox Ms A | Lab | 13,794 | 31.38% | -0.85% | 15,734 | 32.23% | Lab |
| Taylor A | LD | 6,957 | 15.83% | 0.7% | 7,388 | 15.13% | LD |
| Hudson B | UK Ind | 881 | 2.0% | 1.45% | 1,939 | 3.97% | Ref |
| Hall D | Ind | 429 | 0.98% | | 269 | 0.55% | UK Ind |
| **Lab to C swing** | **1.27%** | **43,956** | | **C maj 8,101** | **48,818** | | **C maj 7,754** |
| | | | | 18.43% | | | 15.88% |

**SIR BRIAN MAWHINNEY,** b July 26, 1940. Elected here 1997. MP for Peterborough 1979-97. Shadow Home Sec, 1997-98. Min without Portfolio and chairman of C Party, 1995-97. Transport Sec, 1994; Health Min, 1992-94; NI Min, 1990-92; NI Under-Sec, 1986-90. PPS to Treasury Min, 1982-84; Employment Sec, 1984-85; and NI Sec, 1985-86. Member, Environment Select Cttee, 1979-82. Member, General Synod of C of E, 1985-90. Radiation biologist. Ed Royal Belfast Academical Inst; Queen's Univ, Belfast; Univ of Michigan, US; London Univ.

The county of Cambridge, like many others in eastern England, has become extremely popular of late and hence earned extra parliamentary representation. Much of this new constituency, which lies on the west and south sides of Peterborough, was borrowed from the Huntingdon seat of the former Prime Minister, John Major. While not as solidly Tory as his terrain, it is still a safe Conservative area. Map 118

## CAMBRIDGESHIRE SOUTH

**C hold**

| Electorate | %Turnout | 72,095 | 67.05% | 2001 | 69,850 | 76.85% | 1997 |
|---|---|---|---|---|---|---|---|
| **Lansley A** | **C** | **21,387** | **44.24%** | **2.19%** | **22,572** | **42.05%** | **C** |
| Taylor Ms A | LD | 12,984 | 26.86% | 1.04% | 13,860 | 25.82% | LD |
| Herbert Dr J | Lab | 11,737 | 24.28% | -0.84% | 13,485 | 25.12% | Lab |
| Saggers S | Green | 1,182 | 2.45% | | 3,300 | 6.15% | Ref |
| Davies Mrs H | UK Ind | 875 | 1.81% | 1.25% | 298 | 0.56% | UK Ind |
| Klepacka Ms B | ProLife | 176 | 0.36% | | 168 | 0.31% | NLP |
| **LD to C swing** | **0.58%** | **48,341** | | **C maj 8,403** | **53,683** | | **C maj 8,712** |
| | | | | 17.38% | | | 16.23% |

**ANDREW LANSLEY,** b Dec 11, 1956. Elected 1997. Shadow Min for Cabinet Office and Shadow Chancellor of the Duchy of Lancaster, 1999-; vice-chairman C Party, 1998-99; member, Health Select Cttee, 1997-98. Head of research dept, C Central Office, 1990-95; dir, Public Policy Unit, 1995. Principal private sec, Chancellor of Duchy of Lancaster, 1985-87; private sec, Trade and Industry Sec, 1984-85. Member, Nat Union Exec and Gen Purposes Cttees, C Party, 1990-95. Ed Brentwood Sch; Exeter Univ.
e-mail: lansleya@parliament.uk tel: 020-7219 2538 fax: 020-7219 6835

As the name implies, this seat stretches from Cambridge southwards. It includes the two most reliably Conservative wards within the city itself, plus several small towns and picturesque villages. It is solid Tory territory. This factor was reinforced by the Boundary Commission, which transferred a large slice of the ultra-Tory Huntingdon constituency to this patch. Map 119

## CAMBRIDGESHIRE SOUTH EAST

**C hold**

| Electorate | %Turnout | 81,663 | 63.54% | 2001 | 75,666 | 75.08% | 1997 |
|---|---|---|---|---|---|---|---|
| **Paice J** | **C** | **22,927** | **44.19%** | **1.24%** | **24,397** | **42.95%** | **C** |
| Brinton Ms S | LD | 13,937 | 26.86% | 1.78% | 15,048 | 26.49% | Lab |
| Inchley A | Lab | 13,714 | 26.43% | -0.06% | 14,246 | 25.08% | LD |
| Scarr N | UK Ind | 1,308 | 2.52% | | 2,838 | 5.0% | Ref |
| | | | | | 167 | 0.29% | Fair |
| | | | | | 111 | 0.2% | NLP |
| **C to LD swing** | **0.27%** | **51,886** | | **C maj 8,990** | **56,807** | | **C maj 9,349** |
| | | | | 17.33% | | | 16.46% |

**JAMES PAICE,** b April 24 1949. Elected 1987. Opposition spokesman, agriculture, fisheries and food, 1997-. Ed and Employment Under-Sec, 1994-97. PPS to John Gummer, Agriculture Min and Environment Sec, 1991-94, and Agriculture Min, 1989-91. Chairman, all-party racing and bloodstock grp, 1992-94. Suffolk Coastal cllr, 1976-87 (chairman, 1982-83). Non-exec dir, United Framlingham Farmers Ltd, 1989-94. Ed Framlingham Coll, Suffolk; Writtle Agricultural Coll, Essex (a governor).

This is probably the most rural of the several Cambridge constituencies. The flatlands contain dozens of small towns, villages and hamlets, plus the small and charming cathedral city of Ely. Agriculture is a significant component of life and the local economy. It is always likely to send a Conservative to Westminster. Indeed, it is something of a mystery as to where the votes for the other parties actually come from. Map 120

# CANNOCK CHASE

**Lab hold**

| Electorate | %Turnout | | 73,423 | 55.93% | 2001 | 72,362 | 72.37% | 1997 |
|---|---|---|---|---|---|---|---|---|
| **Wright Dr T** | **Lab** | | **23,049** | **56.13%** | **1.31%** | **28,705** | **54.82%** | **Lab** |
| Smithers G | C | | 12,345 | 30.06% | 2.89% | 14,227 | 27.17% | C |
| Reynolds S | LD | | 5,670 | 13.81% | 5.15% | 4,537 | 8.66% | LD |
| | | | | | | 1,663 | 3.18% | Ref |
| | | | | | | 1,615 | 3.08% | N Lab |
| | | | | | | 1,120 | 2.14% | Soc Lab |
| | | | | | | 499 | 0.95% | Loony |
| **Lab to C swing** | **0.79%** | | **41,064** | **Lab maj 10,704** | | **52,366** | **Lab maj 14,478** | |
| | | | | 26.07% | | | 27.65% | |

**TONY WRIGHT,** b March 11, 1948. Elected here 1997; MP for Cannock and Burntwood 1992-97. PPS to Lord Irvine of Lairg, Lord Chancellor, 1997-98. Member, Select Cttees: Liason, 1999-2001; Parly Commissioner for Administration, 1992-97; Public Service, 1995-97; chairman, Public Admin, 1999-2001. Joint editor, *Political Quarterly*; unpaid dir, Political Quarterly Publishing Co. Former exec member, Fabian Soc. Univ lecturer/reader in politics. Ed Kettering GS; LSE; Harvard Univ; Balliol Coll, Oxford.

**This is a corner of Staffordshire popular with those who commute to work in other areas of the West Midlands. It has remnants of both a rural and a mining tradition and includes the Chase itself - an area of rough and hilly woodland visited by nearby town dwellers. The boundaries were altered by redistribution necessary to allow the county an extra Westminster seat. For the past decade this seat has looked increasingly safe for Labour. Map 121**

# CANTERBURY

**C hold**

| Electorate | %Turnout | | 74,159 | 60.86% | 2001 | 74,548 | 72.58% | 1997 |
|---|---|---|---|---|---|---|---|---|
| **Brazier J** | **C** | | **18,711** | **41.46%** | **2.81%** | **20,913** | **38.65%** | **C** |
| Thornberry Ms E | Lab | | 16,642 | 36.87% | 5.55% | 16,949 | 31.32% | Lab |
| Wales P | LD | | 8,056 | 17.85% | -5.91% | 12,854 | 23.76% | LD |
| Dawe Ms H | Green | | 920 | 2.04% | 0.95% | 2,460 | 4.55% | Ref |
| Moore Ms L | UK Ind | | 803 | 1.78% | 1.26% | 588 | 1.09% | Green |
| | | | | | | 281 | 0.52% | UK Ind |
| | | | | | | 64 | 0.12% | NLP |
| **C to Lab swing** | **1.37%** | | **45,132** | **C maj 2,069** | | **54,109** | **C maj 3,964** | |
| | | | | 4.58% | | | 7.33% | |

**JULIAN BRAZIER,** b July 24, 1953. Elected 1987. PPS to Gillian Shephard, 1990-95. Member, Defence Select Cttee, 1997-2001. Vice-chairman, C backbench defence cttee, 1995-. Serving officer in TA for 13 years. Ex-project manager, HB Maynard, international management consultants; former sec, exec cttee, board of Charter Consolidated plc. Member, Bow Grp; Centre for Policy Studies. Ed Wellington Coll, Berkshire; Brasenose Coll, Oxford.

**This constituency is in the heart of Kent and might be considered a Conservative citadel. In fact, matters are more complicated. The cathedral city itself has some very staunch Labour areas. The surrounding countryside is much more friendly to the Tories, although the Liberal Democrats can win a fair proportion of the votes here too. The resort of Whitstable on the north Kent coast tends to back the Conservative candidate. Map 122**

# CARDIFF CENTRAL

**Lab hold**

| Electorate | %Turnout | | 59,785 | 58.28% | 2001 | 60,354 | 70.01% | 1997 |
|---|---|---|---|---|---|---|---|---|
| **Jones J** | **Lab Co-op** | | **13,451** | **38.61%** | **-5.09%** | **18,464** | **43.7%** | **Lab** |
| Willott Ms J | LD | | 12,792 | 36.71% | 11.76% | 10,541 | 24.95% | LD |
| Walker G | C | | 5,537 | 15.89% | -4.16% | 8,470 | 20.05% | C |
| Grigg R | PC | | 1,680 | 4.82% | 1.26% | 2,230 | 5.28% | Soc Lab |
| Bartley S | Green | | 661 | 1.9% | | 1,504 | 3.56% | PC |
| Goss J | Soc All | | 283 | 0.81% | | 760 | 1.8% | Ref |
| Hughes F | UK Ind | | 221 | 0.63% | | 204 | 0.48% | Loony |
| Jeremy Ms M | ProLife | | 217 | 0.62% | | 80 | 0.19% | NLP |
| **Lab Co-op to LD swing** | **8.43%** | | **34,842** | **Lab Co-op maj 659** | | **42,253** | **Lab Co-op maj 7,923** | |
| | | | | 1.89% | | | 18.75% | |

**JON OWEN JONES,** b April 19, 1954. Elected 1992. Member, Environmental Audit Select Cttee, 1997-2001. Under-Sec State, Welsh Office, 1998-99. Gvt whip, 1997-98; Lab whip, 1993-97. President, Mid-Glamorgan NUT, 1986. Teacher. Ed Ysgol Gyfun Rhydfelin; Univ of E Anglia; Univ Coll of Wales, Cardiff.
e-mail: jon-owen-jones@cardiff-central-clp.new.labour.org.uk
tel: 02920 635811 fax: 02920 635814

**This constituency is at the heart of the Welsh capital, with its castle and dominant civic buildings, and contains a large swath of the influential Cardiff University electorate. It is very diverse with much of the city's middle class and working class living in adjacent neighbourhoods. It was once a three-way marginal but had gravitated towards Labour; however, the Lib Dems made a strikingly powerful showing in 2001 to make it marginal again. Map 123**

## CARDIFF NORTH — Lab hold

| Electorate | %Turnout | | 62,634 | 69.04% | 2001 | 60,430 | 80.24% | 1997 |
|---|---|---|---|---|---|---|---|---|
| Morgan Ms J | Lab | | 19,845 | 45.9% | -4.55% | 24,460 | 50.45% | Lab |
| Watson A | C | | 13,680 | 31.64% | -2.05% | 16,334 | 33.69% | C |
| Dixon J | LD | | 6,631 | 15.34% | 4.42% | 5,294 | 10.92% | LD |
| Jobbins S | PC | | 2,471 | 5.71% | 3.23% | 1,201 | 2.48% | PC |
| Hulston D | UK Ind | | 613 | 1.42% | | 1,199 | 2.47% | Ref |
| Lab to C swing | 1.25% | | 43,240 | Lab maj 6,165 | | 48,488 | Lab maj 8,126 | |
| | | | | 14.26% | | | 16.76% | |

**JULIE MORGAN,** b Nov 2, 1944. Elected 1997. Member, Welsh Affairs Select Cttee, 1997-2001. Chairwoman, all-party grp, clinical depression. Former Cardiff and S Glamorgan cllr. Ex-principal social services officer, W Glamorgan. Member, management cttee, S Glamorgan women's workshop, computer training centre. Ed London, Manchester and Cardiff Univs. Married to Rhodri Morgan, Wales's First Sec, the former MP for Cardiff W.

This is plainly the most middle-class seat in Wales with more than 80 per cent of the electorate owning homes. If the same demographic conditions were repeated in England then a substantial Conservative majority might be expected. Although the Tories can still attract a powerful vote here, they were ousted by Labour in 1997 and failed to recapture the seat in 2001. Factors other than straightforward affluence are clearly at play in this region. Map 124

## CARDIFF SOUTH & PENARTH — Lab hold

| Electorate | %Turnout | | 62,125 | 57.55% | 2001 | 61,838 | 68.57% | 1997 |
|---|---|---|---|---|---|---|---|---|
| Michael A | Lab Co-op | | 20,094 | 56.21% | 2.81% | 22,647 | 53.41% | Lab |
| Kelly Owen Ms M | C | | 7,807 | 21.84% | 1.17% | 8,766 | 20.67% | C |
| Berman Dr R | LD | | 4,572 | 12.79% | 3.44% | 3,964 | 9.35% | LD |
| Haines Ms L | PC | | 1,983 | 5.55% | 2.35% | 3,942 | 9.3% | N Lab |
| Callan J | UK Ind | | 501 | 1.4% | | 1,356 | 3.2% | PC |
| Bartlett D | Soc All | | 427 | 1.19% | | 1,211 | 2.86% | Ref |
| Savoury Ms A | ProLife | | 367 | 1.03% | | 344 | 0.81% | Soc |
| | | | | | | 170 | 0.4% | NLP |
| C to Lab Co-op swing | 0.81% | | 35,751 | Lab Co-op maj 12,287 | | 42,400 | Lab Co-op maj 13,881 | |
| | | | | 34.37% | | | 32.74% | |

**ALUN MICHAEL,** b Aug 22, 1943. Elected 1987. Min of Rural Affairs, June, 2001-; First Sec, Nat Assembly for Wales, 1999, resigned, 2000. Home Office Min of State for Crime and Police, 1997. Lab Shadow, Home Affairs, 1992-97; Wales, 1988-92. Lab whip, 1987-88. Political co-ordinator for Vale of Glamorgan, 1989, Neath and Monmouth, 1991 by-elections. Cardiff City cllr, 1973-89. Member, nat exec, Co-op Party, 1988-92; parly cttee, Co-op Union, 1988-97. Ed Colwyn Bay GS; Keele Univ.

The former Prime Minister James Callaghan used to represent this essentially dockland constituency, which includes the Tiger Bay area of the city. The seat has been altered somewhat since his departure and elevation to the Upper House as Lord Callaghan of Cardiff, but is still extremely favourable territory for the Labour Party. The section around the seaside resort of Penarth, however, is rather more hospitable to the Tories. Map 125

## CARDIFF WEST — Lab hold

| Electorate | %Turnout | | 58,348 | 58.41% | 2001 | 58,198 | 69.21% | 1997 |
|---|---|---|---|---|---|---|---|---|
| Brennan K | Lab | | 18,594 | 54.56% | -5.76% | 24,297 | 60.32% | Lab |
| Davies A | C | | 7,273 | 21.34% | -0.18% | 8,669 | 21.52% | C |
| Gasson Ms J | LD | | 4,458 | 13.08% | 2.24% | 4,366 | 10.84% | LD |
| Bowen D | PC | | 3,296 | 9.67% | 4.83% | 1,949 | 4.84% | PC |
| Jenking Ms J | UK Ind | | 462 | 1.36% | | 996 | 2.47% | Ref |
| Lab to C swing | 2.79% | | 34,083 | Lab maj 11,321 | | 40,277 | Lab maj 15,628 | |
| | | | | 33.22% | | | 38.80% | |

**KEVIN BRENNAN,** b Oct 16, 1959. Elected 2001. Inherits seat from Rhodri Morgan, who stood down to focus on his role as First Sec of Wales. Research officer and special adviser to Mr Morgan, 1995-2000. Member, Cardiff City Council; vice-chairman, finance cttee, 1991-92; economic development, 1996-99, and chairman, economic scrutiny, 1999-2000. Head of economics, Radyr Comp Sch, 1985-94. Ed St Albans RC, Pontypool; Pembroke Coll, Oxford; Univ Coll Cardiff; Univ of Glamorgan.

This seat has proved unpredictable on occasions. It contains a number of troubled council estates offset by relatively few Conservative strongholds. It was represented by George Thomas, the former Speaker, for many years. When he retired, a split in the vote allowed the Tories to snatch the constituency for a four-year period. It now seems to be back safely inside the Labour Party's command. Map 126

## CARLISLE — Lab hold

| Electorate | %Turnout | | 58,811 | 59.36% | 2001 | 59,917 | 72.78% | 1997 |
|---|---|---|---|---|---|---|---|---|
| Martlew E | Lab | **17,856** | **51.15%** | **-6.25%** | | **25,031** | **57.4%** | **Lab** |
| Mitchelson M | C | 12,154 | 34.82% | 5.83% | | 12,641 | 28.99% | C |
| Guest J | LD | 4,076 | 11.68% | 1.19% | | 4,576 | 10.49% | LD |
| Paisley C | LCA | 554 | 1.59% | | | 1,233 | 2.83% | Ref |
| Wilcox P | Soc All | 269 | 0.77% | | | 126 | 0.29% | NLP |
| **Lab to C swing** | **6.04%** | **34,909** | | **Lab maj 5,702** | | **43,607** | **Lab maj 12,390** | |
| | | | | 16.33% | | | 28.41% | |

**ERIC MARTLEW,** b Jan 3, 1949. Elected 1987. PPS to David Clark, Chancellor of Duchy of Lancaster, 1997-98. Lab whip, 1995-97; spokesman on defence, 1992-95. Member, Agriculture Select Cttee, 1987-92. Chairman, Carlisle CLP, 1980-85; Cumbria county cllr, 1973-88 (chairman, 1983-85); Carlisle city cllr, 1972-74; member, E Cumbria HA, 1981-87. Ed Harraby Sec, Carlisle; Carlisle Tech Coll.

A distinctive seat wedged into the far north corner of Cumbria. Traditionally this is an industrial and textile constituency with a high proportion of council tenants. Historically it has been dominated by the town itself. This working-class bias means less in northwest England than elsewhere. In the past the seat has been competitive and, with the addition of a rural fringe, it could be again in the future. Map 127

## CARMARTHEN EAST & DINEFWR — PC gain

| Electorate | %Turnout | | 54,035 | 70.42% | 2001 | 53,079 | 78.62% | 1997 |
|---|---|---|---|---|---|---|---|---|
| Price A | PC | **16,130** | **42.39%** | **7.75%** | | **17,907** | **42.91%** | **Lab** |
| Williams A | Lab | 13,540 | 35.58% | -7.33% | | 14,457 | 34.64% | PC |
| Thomas D | C | 4,912 | 12.91% | 0.88% | | 5,022 | 12.03% | C |
| Evans D | LD | 2,815 | 7.4% | -0.15% | | 3,150 | 7.55% | LD |
| Squires M | UK Ind | 656 | 1.72% | | | 1,196 | 2.87% | Ref |
| **Lab to PC swing** | **7.54%** | **38,053** | | **PC maj 2,590** | | **41,732** | **Lab maj 3,450** | |
| | | | | 6.81% | | | 8.27% | |

**ADAM PRICE,** b Sept 23, 1968. Elected 2001. Takes seat from Alan Williams, Lab, who held it for the last 14 years. Managing dir, Newidiem Economic Development Consultancy. Speaks Welsh, English and German. Ed Cardiff Univ; Saarland Univ, Saarbrucken, Germany.
e-mail: adam@newidiem.co.uk

This West Wales seat is one of only five in the Principality where Welsh-speakers constitute a majority of the electorate. It is extremely rural, but also includes some of the old coalfields where Labour sentiment is strong. Agriculture now forms a significant part of the local economy. It is that relatively rare item, a well-established Labour/Plaid Cymru marginal; the Welsh Nationalists took the seat on a healthy swing in 2001. Map 128

## CARMARTHEN WEST & PEMBROKESHIRE SOUTH — Lab hold

| Electorate | %Turnout | | 56,518 | 65.32% | 2001 | 55,724 | 76.52% | 1997 |
|---|---|---|---|---|---|---|---|---|
| Ainger N | Lab | **15,349** | **41.58%** | **-7.57%** | | **20,956** | **49.15%** | **Lab** |
| Wilson R | C | 10,811 | 29.29% | 2.71% | | 11,335 | 26.58% | C |
| Hughes Griffiths L | PC | 6,893 | 18.67% | 6.0% | | 5,402 | 12.67% | PC |
| Jeremy W | LD | 3,248 | 8.8% | 0.55% | | 3,516 | 8.25% | LD |
| Phillips I | UK Ind | 537 | 1.45% | | | 1,432 | 3.36% | Ref |
| Turner N | Customer | 78 | 0.21% | | | | | |
| **Lab to C swing** | **5.14%** | **36,916** | | **Lab maj 4,538** | | **42,641** | **Lab maj 9,621** | |
| | | | | 12.29% | | | 22.57% | |

**NICK AINGER,** b Oct 24, 1949. Elected here 1997; MP, Pembroke 1992-97. Gvt whip, June, 2001. PPS to Paul Murphy, Sec of State, Wales, 1999-2001; to Alun Michael, Sec of State, Wales, 1998-99; and to Ron Davies, Sec of State, Wales, 1997-98. Ex-member, Welsh Affairs Select Cttee. Dyfed cllr, 1981-92. Rigger, Marine and Port Services Ltd, Pembroke Dock, 1977-92. Member, TGWU (branch sec, 1978-92). Ed Netherthorpe GS, Staveley.
e-mail: aingern@parliament.uk tel: 020-7219 2241fax: 020-7219 2690

This southwest Wales constituency, which includes industrial Pembroke Dock as well as the seaside resorts of Tenby and Saundersfoot, was created as a new seat for the 1997 election. Traditionally the Pembrokeshire part has been divided evenly between Labour and the Tories, while the Carmarthen section has seen competition between Labour and Plaid Cymru. The net effect has been to create a seat predisposed to Labour candidates. Map 129

## CARRICK, CUMNOCK & DOON VALLEY — Lab hold

| Electorate | %Turnout | 64,919 | 61.78% | 2001 | 65,593 | 74.96% | 1997 |
|---|---|---|---|---|---|---|---|
| Foulkes G | Lab Co-op | 22,174 | 55.29% | -4.5% | 29,398 | 59.79% | Lab |
| Miller G | C | 7,318 | 18.25% | 1.3% | 8,336 | 16.95% | C |
| Wilson T | SNP | 6,258 | 15.6% | -1.06% | 8,190 | 16.66% | SNP |
| Rogers Ms A | LD | 2,932 | 7.31% | 2.0% | 2,613 | 5.31% | LD |
| McFarlane Ms A | SSP | 1,058 | 2.64% | | 634 | 1.29% | Ref |
| McDaid J | Soc Lab | 367 | 0.92% | | | | |
| Lab Co-op to C swing | 2.9% | 40,107 | Lab Co-op maj 14,856 37.04% | | 49,171 | Lab Co-op maj 21,062 42.84% | |

**GEORGE FOULKES,** b Jan 21, 1942. Elected 1983. Min of State, Scotland Office, June, 2001-; Under Sec of State for International Development, 1997-2001. Lab spokesman, overseas development, 1994-97; defence, disarmament and arms control 1992-93; foreign and Commonwealth affairs, 1985-92; Euro and Community affairs, 1983-85. Joint chairman, all-party pensioners' grp, 1983-97; ex-chairman, all-party World Gvt grp. Rector's Assessor, Edinburgh Univ, 1972-75. Ed Keith GS, Banffshire; Haberdashers' Aske's; Edinburgh Univ.

This south Ayrshire seat is blessed with a poetic-sounding name. It is polarised politically between inland farms and coastal towns such as the resort of Girvan on the one hand, which lean towards the Conservatives, and the more industrial areas and former coalfields, which are solidly Labour. As these areas are larger in population, Labour can usually expect to win comfortably. Map 130

## CARSHALTON & WALLINGTON — LD hold

| Electorate | %Turnout | 67,337 | 60.31% | 2001 | 66,038 | 73.33% | 1997 |
|---|---|---|---|---|---|---|---|
| Brake T | LD | 18,289 | 45.03% | 6.85% | 18,490 | 38.18% | LD |
| Andrew K | C | 13,742 | 33.84% | 0.34% | 16,223 | 33.5% | C |
| Cooper Ms M | Lab | 7,466 | 18.38% | -5.5% | 11,565 | 23.88% | Lab |
| Dixon S | Green | 614 | 1.51% | 0.73% | 1,289 | 2.66% | Ref |
| Haley M | UK Ind | 501 | 1.23% | 0.78% | 377 | 0.78% | Green |
| | | | | | 261 | 0.54% | BNP |
| | | | | | 218 | 0.45% | UK Ind |
| C to LD swing | 3.26% | 40,612 | LD maj 4,547 11.20% | | 48,423 | LD maj 2,267 4.68% | |

**TOM BRAKE,** b May 6, 1962. Elected 1997; contested seat 1992. LD spokesman, natural resources and land use and transport in London, 1997-. Member, Environment, Transport and Reg Affairs Select Cttee and its Environment Sub-Cttee, 1997-2001. Joint chairman, all-party renewable and sustainable energy grp, 1997-; joint sec, Franco-British grp, 1997-. Hackney cllr, 1988-91; Sutton cllr, 1994-. Trustee, centre for environmental initiatives; governor, Carshalton HS for Girls. Ed Lycée International, France; Imperial Coll, London.

This is a South London seat with a strong flavour of Surrey. However, it is not as leafy a constituency as might be expected. There is a substantial minority of poor council tenants to provide Labour with a political base and the Liberal Democrats advanced steadily in the suburbs finally to overtake the Tories in 1997, holding the seat with an increased majority in 2001. This is likely to be a competitive constituency for many years. Map 131

## CASTLE POINT — C gain

| Electorate | %Turnout | 68,108 | 58.38% | 2001 | 67,146 | 72.34% | 1997 |
|---|---|---|---|---|---|---|---|
| Spink Dr R | C | 17,738 | 44.61% | 4.49% | 20,605 | 42.42% | Lab |
| Butler Ms C | Lab | 16,753 | 42.13% | -0.29% | 19,489 | 40.12% | C |
| Boulton B | LD | 3,116 | 7.84% | -1.38% | 4,477 | 9.22% | LD |
| Hurrell R | UK Ind | 1,273 | 3.2% | | 2,700 | 5.56% | Ref |
| Roberts D | Ind | 663 | 1.67% | | 1,301 | 2.68% | Consult |
| Searle N | Truth | 220 | 0.55% | | | | |
| Lab to C swing | 2.39% | 39,763 | C maj 985 2.48% | | 48,572 | Lab maj 1,116 2.30% | |

**ROBERT SPINK,** b Aug 4, 1948. Elected 2001. Previously held this seat, 1992-97, and regained it from Christine Butler, Lab MP, 1997-2001. PPS, Ann Widdecombe, 1994-97. Member, board Parly Office of Science and Tech. Chairman, all-party prisoners abroad grp, 1995-97; joint vice-chairman, Lomé grp. Dir, Bournemouth International Airport, 1989-93. Dorset cllr, 1985-93. Industrial engineer and management consultant. Ed Holycroft Sec Sch, Keighley; Manchester Univ; Cranfield Univ.

This very unusual constituency is set in southeast Essex with Canvey Island as a focal point. It has the second highest rate of owner-occupation - nine in ten voters - in the UK. But it is not overwhelmingly upper middle-class. These contradictions mean that while the Conservatives secured vast majorities throughout the 1980s, Labour was able to snatch the seat in 1997. It was only a temporary blip, however; the Tories regained it in 2001. Map 132

# CEREDIGION — PC hold

| Electorate %Turnout | | 56,118 | 61.67% | 2001 | 54,378 | 73.9% | 1997 |
|---|---|---|---|---|---|---|---|
| Thomas S | PC | 13,241 | 38.26% | -3.37% | 16,728. | 41.63% | PC |
| Williams M | LD | 9,297 | 26.87% | 10.41% | 9,767 | 24.3% | Lab |
| Davies P | C | 6,730 | 19.45% | 4.56% | 6,616 | 16.46% | LD |
| Grace D | Lab | 5,338 | 15.43% | -8.87% | 5,983 | 14.89% | C |
| | | | | | 1,092 | 2.72% | Ref |
| PC to LD swing | 6.89% | 34,606 | PC maj 3,944 11.40% | | 40,186 | PC maj 6,961 17.33% | |

**SIMON THOMAS,** b Dec 28, 1963. Elected 2000 by-election. PC spokesman, environment and the regions; transport; ed and employment; international development; culture; media and sport; energy. Member, Environmental Audit Select Cttee; vice-chairman, all-party environment grp. PC policy dir. Asst curator, Nat Library of Wales, Aberystwyth, 1986-92. Ed Aberdare Comp; Univ of Wales, Aberystwyth.

*Details of 2000 by-election on page 291*

A strongly Welsh-speaking constituency comprising dozens of villages and small farms. The English section of the seat is based on the university town of Aberystwyth and the holiday towns of southern Cardigan Bay. It produced one of the strangest results in Britain in 1992 when a well-established Liberal Democrat MP was unexpectedly ejected and Plaid Cymru leapt from fourth to first. Plaid entrenched itself in 1997 and again in 2001. Map 133

# CHARNWOOD — C hold

| Electorate %Turnout | | 74,836 | 64.49% | 2001 | 72,692 | 77.28% | 1997 |
|---|---|---|---|---|---|---|---|
| Dorrell S | C | 23,283 | 48.24% | 1.76% | 26,110 | 46.48% | C |
| Sheahan S | Lab | 15,544 | 32.21% | -3.77% | 20,210 | 35.98% | Lab |
| King Ms S | LD | 7,835 | 16.23% | 3.37% | 7,224 | 12.86% | LD |
| Bye J | UK Ind | 1,603 | 3.32% | | 2,104 | 3.75% | Ref |
| | | | | | 525 | 0.93% | BNP |
| Lab to C swing | 2.77% | 48,265 | C maj 7,739 16.03% | | 56,173 | C maj 5,900 10.50% | |

**STEPHEN DORRELL,** b March 25, 1952. Elected here 1997; MP, Loughborough 1979-97. Health Sec, 1995-97; Nat Heritage Sec, 1994-95; Financial Sec to Treasury, 1992-94; Under-Sec for Health, 1990-92; gvt whip, 1988-90; asst gvt whip, 1987-88; PPS to Energy Sec, 1983-87. Member, Transport Select Cttee, 1979-83. Contested leadership, 1997. Trustee, Uppingham Sch. Clothing co dir. Ed Uppingham; Brasenose Coll, Oxford.
e-mail: office@stephendorrell.org.uk www.stephendorrell.org.uk
tel: 020-7219 4472 fax: 020-7219 5838

Leicestershire acquired a new seat in 1997 as a result of population expansion and Charnwood was the result. It is an extremely attractive area with a high rate of owner-occupation and comprises a string of white (especially by the standards of Leicester itself) middle-class suburbs. The net result is territory highly favourable to the Conservative Party. Map 134

# CHATHAM & AYLESFORD — Lab hold

| Electorate %Turnout | | 69,759 | 56.96% | 2001 | 69,172 | 71.07% | 1997 |
|---|---|---|---|---|---|---|---|
| Shaw J | Lab | 19,180 | 48.27% | 5.16% | 21,191 | 43.11% | Lab |
| Holden S | C | 14,840 | 37.35% | -0.08% | 18,401 | 37.43% | C |
| Lettington D | LD | 4,705 | 11.84% | -3.19% | 7,389 | 15.03% | LD |
| Knopp G | UK Ind | 1,010 | 2.54% | 1.54% | 1,538 | 3.13% | Ref |
| | | | | | 493 | 1.0% | UK Ind |
| | | | | | 149 | 0.3% | NLP |
| C to Lab swing | 2.62% | 39,735 | Lab maj 4,340 10.92% | | 49,161 | Lab maj 2,790 5.68% | |

**JONATHAN SHAW,** b June 3, 1966. Elected 1997. Member, Environmental Audit Select Cttee; chairman, all-party paper grp. Rochester cllr. Ex-Unison steward. Social worker. Ed Vintners Boys Sch, Maidstone; West Kent Coll of FE; Bromley Coll of FHE.
e-mail: shawj@parliament.uk tel: 020-7219 6919 fax: 020-7219 0938

This constituency combines the relatively large north Kent town of Chatham with the village of Aylesford. The two components are rather different in political sentiment. Chatham has a long connection with the Royal Navy and has some strong Labour sections. Aylesford and the surrounding rural area are solidly Conservative. This makes for a competitive political contest with Labour currently in the driving seat. Map 135

# CHEADLE
LD gain

| Electorate | %Turnout | | 69,002 | 63.2% | 2001 | 67,627 | 77.58% | 1997 |
|---|---|---|---|---|---|---|---|---|
| Calton Ms P | | LD | 18,477 | 42.37% | 4.71% | 22,944 | 43.73% | C |
| Day S | | C | 18,444 | 42.3% | -1.43% | 19,755 | 37.66% | LD |
| Dawber H | | Lab | 6,086 | 13.96% | -1.77% | 8,253 | 15.73% | Lab |
| Cavanagh V | | UK Ind | 599 | 1.37% | | 1,511 | 2.88% | Ref |
| C to LD swing | 3.07% | | 43,606 | | LD maj 33 | 52,463 | | C maj 3,189 |
| | | | | | 0.08% | | | 6.07% |

**PATSY CALTON,** b Sept 19, 1948. Elected 2001. Takes seat, one of only two in Greater Manchester that in 1997 were still held by the Tories, from opposition whip Stephen Day. Contested seat, 1992 and 1997. Cllr, Stockport MBC, 1994-; deputy leader and chairwoman, social services cttee. Chemistry teacher. Member, Amnesty International and Stockport Cerebral Palsy Society. NASUWT. Ed Wymondham Coll, Norfolk; Univ of Manchester Inst of Science and Tech.

**Arguably the most socially desirable constituency in the Greater Manchester area, this seat enjoys an extremely high proportion of owner-occupiers and professional and managerial workers. It is overwhelmingly suburban in character. In other parts of England it would be a solidly Tory seat but the Lib Dems have steadily eclipsed Labour over the years to make a serious fight of it - and in 2001 scraped home with the smallest majority in the UK. Map 136**

# CHELMSFORD WEST
C hold

| Electorate | %Turnout | | 78,291 | 61.49% | 2001 | 76,086 | 76.99% | 1997 |
|---|---|---|---|---|---|---|---|---|
| Burns S | | C | 20,446 | 42.47% | 1.87% | 23,781 | 40.6% | C |
| Longden A | | Lab | 14,185 | 29.46% | 3.11% | 17,090 | 29.18% | LD |
| Robinson S | | LD | 11,197 | 23.26% | -5.92% | 15,436 | 26.35% | Lab |
| Burgess Mrs E | | Green | 837 | 1.74% | 1.04% | 1,536 | 2.62% | Ref |
| Wedon K | | UK Ind | 785 | 1.63% | 1.08% | 411 | 0.7% | Green |
| Philbin C | | LCA | 693 | 1.44% | | 323 | 0.55% | UK Ind |
| C to Lab swing | 0.62% | | 48,143 | | C maj 6,261 | 58,577 | | C maj 6,691 |
| | | | | | 13.01% | | | 11.42% |

**SIMON BURNS,** b Sept 6, 1952. Elected 1987. Member, Health Select Cttee, 1999-2001. Opposition spokesman, Social Security, 1997-98, Environment, 1998-99. Under-Sec of State for Health, 1996-97. Gvt whip, 1995-96; asst gvt whip, 1994-95. PPS to Min of Agriculture, 1993-94, and Min of State for Employment, Ed and Science and then Energy, 1989-93. Treas, 1922 Cttee, 1999-. Political adviser, Sally Oppenheim, 1975-81. Member, policy exec, Inst of Directors, 1983-87; dir, What to Buy Ltd, 1981-83. Ed Christ the King, Accra, Ghana; Stamford Sch, Lincs; Worcester Coll, Oxford.

**The greater part of this constituency is the town of Chelmsford itself, with some adjacent rural territory. It is predominantly middle-class and suburban with an element of the "Essex Man" skilled working class as well. This was a very competitive seat between the Conservatives and Liberal Democrats in the 1980s, but the Tories appear to have recaptured the initiative since then. Map 137**

# CHELTENHAM
LD hold

| Electorate | %Turnout | | 67,563 | 61.92% | 2001 | 67,950 | 74.03% | 1997 |
|---|---|---|---|---|---|---|---|---|
| Jones N | | LD | 19,970 | 47.74% | -1.71% | 24,877 | 49.45% | LD |
| Garnham R | | C | 14,715 | 35.17% | -1.07% | 18,232 | 36.24% | C |
| Erlam A | | Lab | 5,041 | 12.05% | 1.91% | 5,100 | 10.14% | Lab |
| Bessant K | | Green | 735 | 1.76% | | 1,065 | 2.12% | Ref |
| Hanks D | | Loony | 513 | 1.23% | 0.48% | 375 | 0.75% | Loony |
| Carver J | | UK Ind | 482 | 1.15% | 0.55% | 302 | 0.6% | UK Ind |
| Gates A | | ProLife | 272 | 0.65% | 0.16% | 245 | 0.49% | ProLife |
| Everest R | | Ind | 107 | 0.26% | | 107 | 0.21% | NLP |
| LD to C swing | 0.32% | | 41,835 | | LD maj 5,255 | 50,303 | | LD maj 6,645 |
| | | | | | 12.56% | | | 13.21% |

**NIGEL JONES,** b March 30, 1948. Elected 1992. Member, Select Cttees, Int Development, 2000-2001;Science and Tech, 1997-2000; Standards and Privileges, 1995-97; Broadcasting, 1992-97. LD spokesman, sport, science and tech, 1997-. Chairman, all-party beer grp, 1999-; exec cttee, Inter-Parly Union, Commonwealth Parly Assoc. Gloucestershire cllr, 1989-. Computer systems designer. Ed Prince Henry's GS, Evesham.
e-mail: nigeljonesmp@cix.co.uk www.nigeljones.org.uk
tel: 020-7219 4415 fax: 01242 256658

**An exceptionally elegant and appealing spa town surrounded by the Gloucestershire countryside. It has also enjoyed a booming economy in recent years. The Liberal Democrats captured the seat in controversial circumstances in 1992, apparently benefiting from a racist backlash against the black Conservative candidate, and have held it since. The local Lib Dem MP was injured in a sword attack in 1999 while conducting an advice surgery. Map 138**

## CHESHAM & AMERSHAM

**C hold**

| Electorate | %Turnout | | 70,021 | 64.67% | 2001 | 69,244 | 75.38% | 1997 |
|---|---|---|---|---|---|---|---|---|
| Gillan Mrs C | | C | 22,867 | 50.5% | 0.12% | 26,298 | 50.38% | C |
| Ford J | | LD | 10,985 | 24.26% | 0.43% | 12,439 | 23.83% | LD |
| Hulme K | | Lab | 8,497 | 18.76% | -0.86% | 10,240 | 19.62% | Lab |
| Harvey I | | UK Ind | 1,367 | 3.02% | 1.84% | 2,528 | 4.84% | Ref |
| Wilkins N | | Green | 1,114 | 2.46% | | 618 | 1.18% | UK Ind |
| Duval Ms G | | ProLife | 453 | 1.0% | | 74 | 0.14% | NLP |
| C to LD swing | | 0.16% | 45,283 | | C maj 11,882 | 52,197 | | C maj 13,859 |
| | | | | | 26.24% | | | 26.55% |

**CHERYL GILLAN,** b April 21, 1952. Elected 1992. C spokeswoman, Foreign and Commonwealth affairs, 1998-, and Trade and Industry, 1997-98. Under-Sec for Ed and Employment, 1995-97; PPS to Lord Cranborne, Leader of House of Lords, 1994-95. Member, Select Cttees on Science and Tech, 1992-95; Procedure, 1992-95. Chairwoman, Bow Grp, 1987-88. Hon pres, British Importers Assoc. Senior marketing consultant, Ernst and Young, 1986-91. Freeman, City of London, 1991. Ed Cheltenham Ladies Coll; Coll of Law.

Even by the standards of Buckinghamshire this is an extremely Conservative constituency. It consists of these two highly desirable towns and the intervening rural areas. It is one of the most middle-class seats in the entire country with a minimal stock of council housing. The Liberal Democrats can always pick up a reasonable minority of the vote but not enough to shake the Tory hegemony. Map 139

## CHESTER, CITY OF

**Lab hold**

| Electorate | %Turnout | | 70,382 | 63.76% | 2001 | 71,730 | 78.43% | 1997 |
|---|---|---|---|---|---|---|---|---|
| Russell Ms C | | Lab | 21,760 | 48.49% | -4.49% | 29,806 | 52.98% | Lab |
| Jones D | | C | 14,866 | 33.13% | -1.09% | 19,253 | 34.22% | C |
| Dawson T | | LD | 6,589 | 14.68% | 5.16% | 5,353 | 9.52% | LD |
| Weddell A | | UK Ind | 899 | 2.0% | | 1,487 | 2.64% | Ref |
| Rogers G | | Ind | 763 | 1.7% | | 204 | 0.36% | Loony |
| | | | | | | 154 | 0.27% | WCCC |
| Lab to C swing | | 1.70% | 44,877 | | Lab maj 6,894 | 56,257 | | Lab maj 10,553 |
| | | | | | 15.36% | | | 18.76% |

**CHRISTINE RUSSELL,** b March 25, 1945. Elected 1997. Member, Environmental Audit Select Cttee. Chester cllr, 1980-97; Sheriff of Chester, 1992-93. PA, Brian Simpson, MEP, 1992-94. Co-ordinator, Chester and Ellesmere Port advocacy project set up by MIND; member, Magistrates Assoc; founder, Chester economic forum; chairman, annual Chester Film Festival. Ex-librarian; Ed Spalding HS; NW London Poly.

The seat combines the historic walled city of Chester on the River Dee and the surrounding rural areas. The outsider would assume that this seat would be as affluent as many of the others in Cheshire and therefore safe for the Conservatives. But Chester has always contained a sizeable Labour vote and the Tories only scraped home in 1987 and 1992, before losing by a substantial margin in 1997 and again in 2001. Map 140

## CHESTERFIELD

**LD gain**

| Electorate | %Turnout | | 73,252 | 60.67% | 2001 | 72,472 | 70.91% | 1997 |
|---|---|---|---|---|---|---|---|---|
| Holmes P | | LD | 21,249 | 47.81% | 8.25% | 26,105 | 50.8% | Lab |
| Race R | | Lab | 18,663 | 42.0% | -8.8% | 20,330 | 39.56% | LD |
| Hitchcock S | | C | 3,613 | 8.13% | -1.12% | 4,752 | 9.25% | C |
| Robinson Ms J | | Soc All | 437 | 0.98% | | 202 | 0.39% | Ind OAP |
| Harrison B | | Soc Lab | 295 | 0.66% | | | | |
| Rawson C | | Ind | 184 | 0.41% | | | | |
| Lab to LD swing | | 8.53% | 44,441 | | LD maj 2,586 | 51,389 | | Lab maj 5,775 |
| | | | | | 5.82% | | | 11.24% |

**PAUL HOLMES,** b Jan 16, 1957. Elected 2001. Winner for the Lib Dems in a seat previously held by the veteran retiring Lab parliamentarian, Tony Benn. Chesterfield cllr for ten years. Teacher. Head of sixth form at Buxton Community Sch, Derbyshire. Ed Firth Park Sch, Sheffield; Sheffield and York Univs.

A traditional mining seat in the northeast corner of Derbyshire. Although coal is no longer king, steel and other heavy industry exercise a significant economic influence. It was represented by Tony Benn between 1984 and 2001. A controversial figure, Benn may have contributed to the strength of the Liberal Democrats locally, and when he stood down the Lib Dems finally took the seat. The Tories, meanwhile, are almost irrelevant here. Map 141

## CHICHESTER                C hold

| Electorate | %Turnout | | 77,703 | 63.72% | 2001 | 74,489 | 74.88% | 1997 |
|---|---|---|---|---|---|---|---|---|
| Tyrie A | | C | 23,320 | 47.1% | 0.68% | 25,895 | 46.42% | C |
| Ravenscroft Ms L | | LD | 11,965 | 24.17% | -4.8% | 16,161 | 28.97% | LD |
| Barlow Ms C | | Lab | 10,627 | 21.46% | 4.24% | 9,605 | 17.22% | Lab |
| Denny D | | UK Ind | 2,308 | 4.66% | 3.23% | 3,318 | 5.95% | Ref |
| Graham G | | Green | 1,292 | 2.61% | | 800 | 1.43% | UK Ind |
| LD to C swing | 2.74% | | 49,512 | | C maj 11,355 | 55,779 | | C maj 9,734 |
| | | | | | 22.93% | | | 17.45% |

**ANDREW TYRIE,** b Jan 15, 1957. Elected 1997. Member, Select Cttees: Public Administration, 1997-2001; Consolidation Bills, 1997-2001. Adviser, Prime Minister, 1990-92; special adviser, Chancellors (Nigel Lawson and John Major), 1986-90; head of economics team, C research dept, 1984-85. Ex-senior economist, Euro Bank for Reconstruction and Development. Ed Felsted Sch; Trinity Coll, Oxford; Wolfson Coll, Cambridge; Woodrow Wilson Scholar, Smithsonian Inst; Fellow, Nuffield Coll.
tel: 020-7219 6371 fax: 020-7219 0625

A strip of West Sussex adjacent to the Hampshire border. This is very desirable South Downs territory centred on the cathedral town at the head of Chichester Harbour and stretching from Selsey Bill to north of Midhurst and Petworth. It contains a large number of retired people and several stately homes, reinforcing the impression of a Tory stronghold. The Liberal Democrats can attract a reasonable vote but can scarcely be described as competitive. Map 142

## CHINGFORD & WOODFORD GREEN          C hold

| Electorate | %Turnout | | 63,252 | 58.47% | 2001 | 62,904 | 70.66% | 1997 |
|---|---|---|---|---|---|---|---|---|
| Duncan Smith I | | C | 17,834 | 48.22% | 0.73% | 21,109 | 47.49% | C |
| Webb Ms J | | Lab | 12,347 | 33.39% | -1.25% | 15,395 | 34.64% | Lab |
| Beanse J | | LD | 5,739 | 15.52% | 0.03% | 6,885 | 15.49% | LD |
| Griffin Ms J | | BNP | 1,062 | 2.87% | 0.49% | 1,059 | 2.38% | BNP |
| Lab to C swing | 0.99% | | 36,982 | | C maj 5,487 | 44,448 | | C maj 5,714 |
| | | | | | 14.84% | | | 12.85% |

**IAIN DUNCAN SMITH,** b April 9, 1954. Elected here 1997; MP for Chingford 1992-97. Challenger for the Conservative Party leadership, June 2001. Shadow Defence Sec, 1999-; Social Security Sec, 1997-99. Member, Select Cttees: Standards and Privileges, 1996-97; Health, 1994-95. Vice-chairman, Backbench European Affairs Cttee, 1996-97; sec, Backbench Foreign and Commonwealth Affairs Cttee, 1992-97. Scots Guards officer, 1975-81. Journalist, broadcaster and lecturer. Ed HMS Conway (cadet school), Anglesey; Universita di Perugia, Italy; RMA Sandhurst; Dunchurch Coll of Management.

The core of this seat on the London-Essex border is Chingford, the stronghold represented by Norman Tebbit for 22 years in the House of Commons. It is lower middle-class in flavour rather than aristocratic. The Woodford Green element has introduced additional affluence (and a few council estates as well), reinforcing the Tory bias. Map 143

## CHIPPING BARNET              C hold

| Electorate | %Turnout | | 70,217 | 60.46% | 2001 | 69,049 | 71.78% | 1997 |
|---|---|---|---|---|---|---|---|---|
| Chapman S | | C | 19,702 | 46.41% | 3.4% | 21,317 | 43.01% | C |
| Welfare D | | Lab | 17,001 | 40.04% | -0.88% | 20,282 | 40.92% | Lab |
| Hooker S | | LD | 5,753 | 13.55% | 1.2% | 6,121 | 12.35% | LD |
| | | | | | | 1,190 | 2.4% | Ref |
| | | | | | | 253 | 0.51% | Loony |
| | | | | | | 243 | 0.49% | ProLife |
| | | | | | | 159 | 0.32% | NLP |
| Lab to C swing | 2.14% | | 42,456 | | C maj 2,701 | 49,565 | | C maj 1,035 |
| | | | | | 6.36% | | | 2.09% |

**SIR SYDNEY CHAPMAN,** b Oct 17, 1935. Elected here 1979; MP for Birmingham Handsworth 1970 - Feb 1974. Chairman, Commons Accommodation and Works Cttee, 1997-; member, Exec, 1922 Cttee, 1997-; Ecclesiastical Cttee. Govt whip, 1992-95 and 1990-92; asst gvt whip, 1988-90. Memeber, Select Cttees: Public Service, 1995-97; Environment, 1983-87; Commons services, 1983-87. Member, Advisory Cttee, Commons works of art, 1988-89. FRSA. Originator, Nat Tree Planting Year, 1973. Pres, London Green Belt Council, 1985-89 Ed Rugby; Manchester Univ.

This seat contains the core of the North London Borough of Barnet. It is a mixture of very solidly middle-class commuterland and skilled working class. There is also a Jewish element in the constituency as well as more recent New Commonwealth immigration. A strong Labour vote in 1997 turned the constituency into marginal territory, although the Tory majority rose slightly in 2001. Map 144

## CHORLEY
Lab hold

| Electorate | %Turnout | | 77,036 | 62.25% | 2001 | 74,387 | 77.58% | 1997 |
|---|---|---|---|---|---|---|---|---|
| Hoyle L | | Lab | 25,088 | 52.32% | -0.72% | 30,607 | 53.04% | Lab |
| Booth P | | C | 16,644 | 34.71% | -1.23% | 20,737 | 35.94% | C |
| Fenn S | | LD | 5,372 | 11.2% | 2.71% | 4,900 | 8.49% | LD |
| Frost G | | UK Ind | 848 | 1.77% | | 1,319 | 2.29% | Ref |
| | | | | | | 143 | 0.25% | NLP |
| C to Lab swing | | 0.25% | 47,952 | Lab maj 8,444 | | 57,706 | Lab maj 9,870 | |
| | | | | 17.61% | | | 17.10% | |

**LINDSAY HOYLE,** b June 10, 1957. Elected 1997. Member, Trade and Industry Select Cttee, 1998-2001. Member, Commons Catering Cttee, 1997-. Chorley borough cllr (dep council leader). Founder/dir, 1988, and chairman, 1992-96, Chorley Rugby League Club. Former dir of printing co. Ed Bolton Sch; Horwich FE Coll.

A Lancashire seat that, like many others in this area, is polarised between an urban core and suburban and rural hinterland. The two sections vote in predictable patterns and the seat has been a critical swing marginal in numerous elections, although in 1997 and 2001 Labour has won quite comfortably. The constituency combines quite a high level of owner-occupation with a reasonably large number of non-manual workers. Map 145

## CHRISTCHURCH
C hold

| Electorate | %Turnout | | 73,503 | 67.44% | 2001 | 71,488 | 78.61% | 1997 |
|---|---|---|---|---|---|---|---|---|
| Chope C | | C | 27,306 | 55.09% | 8.66% | 26,095 | 46.43% | C |
| Webb Ms D | | LD | 13,762 | 27.76% | -14.82% | 23,930 | 42.58% | LD |
| Begg Ms J | | Lab | 7,506 | 15.14% | 8.23% | 3,884 | 6.91% | Lab |
| Strange Ms M | | UK Ind | 993 | 2.0% | 0.92% | 1,684 | 3.0% | Ref |
| | | | | | | 606 | 1.08% | UK Ind |
| LD to C swing | | 11.74% | 49,567 | C maj 13,544 | | 56,199 | C maj 2,165 | |
| | | | | 27.32% | | | 3.85% | |

**CHRISTOPHER CHOPE,** b May 19, 1947. Elected here 1997; MP for Southampton Itchen 1983-92. C spokesman, housing, construction, roads and transport, 1997. A vice-chairman, C Party with responsibility for local gvt. Min for Roads and Traffic, 1990-92; Under-Sec for Environment, 1986-90. PPS, Peter Brooke, Treasury Min, 1985-86. Member, Health and Safety Commission, 1993-; Local Gvt Commission for England, 1994-. Non-practising barrister. Ed St Andrew's Sch, Eastbourne; Marlborough Coll; St Andrews Univ.

This is an extremely affluent and attractive South Coast seat with an irregular recent political history. In theory, it should not only be one of the safest Conservative constituencies in Hampshire but the entire country. It has the highest proportion of detached houses in the United Kingdom. Yet the Liberal Democrats won a sensational by-election victory in 1993 and, although they lost four years later and again in 2001, they remain a local force. Map 146

## CITIES OF LONDON & WESTMINSTER
C hold

| Electorate | %Turnout | | 71,935 | 47.23% | 2001 | 69,047 | 58.16% | 1997 |
|---|---|---|---|---|---|---|---|---|
| Field M | | C | 15,737 | 46.32% | -0.95% | 18,981 | 47.27% | C |
| Katz M | | Lab | 11,238 | 33.08% | -2.03% | 14,100 | 35.11% | Lab |
| Horwood M | | LD | 5,218 | 15.36% | 3.08% | 4,933 | 12.28% | LD |
| Charlton H | | Green | 1,318 | 3.88% | | 1,161 | 2.89% | Ref |
| Merton C | | UK Ind | 464 | 1.37% | 0.83% | 266 | 0.66% | Barts |
| | | | | | | 215 | 0.54% | UK Ind |
| | | | | | | 176 | 0.44% | NLP |
| | | | | | | 138 | 0.34% | Loony |
| | | | | | | 112 | 0.28% | Hemp |
| | | | | | | 73 | 0.18% | Dream |
| Lab to C swing | | 0.54% | 33,975 | C maj 4,499 | | 40,155 | C maj 4,881 | |
| | | | | 13.24% | | | 12.16% | |

**MARK FIELD,** b Oct 6, 1964. Elected 2001. Inherits seat from Peter Brooke, who held it for 24 years. Contested Enfield N 1997. Kensington and Chelsea cllr, 1994-. Sec, Oxford Univ C assoc. Businessman. Ed Reading Sch; St Edmund Hall, Oxford.

This seat is at the very hub of what is generally considered to be Central London. Among the main tourist sites, it contains Buckingham Palace, the Houses of Parliament and Westminster Abbey. The constituency consists of some of the wealthiest territory in Britain, but also has, surprisingly, a few areas of abject poverty. Traditionally it has been solidly Conservative. Map 147

## CLEETHORPES — Lab hold

| Electorate | %Turnout | | 68,392 | 62.02% | 2001 | 68,763 | 73.4% | 1997 |
|---|---|---|---|---|---|---|---|---|
| McIsaac Ms S | Lab | | 21,032 | 49.58% | -2.05% | 26,058 | 51.63% | Lab |
| Howd S | C | | 15,412 | 36.33% | 2.88% | 16,882 | 33.45% | C |
| Smith G | LD | | 5,080 | 11.98% | 0.6% | 5,746 | 11.38% | LD |
| Hatton Ms J | UK Ind | | 894 | 2.11% | | 1,787 | 3.54% | Ref |
| Lab to C swing | 2.47% | | 42,418 | Lab maj 5,620 | | 50,473 | Lab maj 9,176 | |
| | | | | 13.25% | | | 18.18% | |

**SHONA McISAAC,** b April 3, 1960. Elected 1997. PPS to Adam Ingram, NI Min, 2001-. Member, Select Cttee on Standards and Privileges, 1997-2001. Wandsworth cllr, 1990-98 (dep Lab grp leader, 1992-95). Qualified lifeguard at Tooting pool in mid-1980s. Journalist. Ed SHAPE Sch, Belgium; Barne Barton Sec Mod, Plymouth; Stoke Damerel HS, Plymouth; Durham Univ.

The seaside town of Cleethorpes and its adjacent area used to be the Labour-leaning minority in a constituency that contained the neighbouring Lincolnshire town of Brigg and favoured the Conservatives. It is still allied with some rather different villages but the overall political complexion has changed and the seat now seems reliably Labour. There is heavy industry at the deep-sea port of Immingham and the seat also includes Barton-upon-Humber. Map 148

## CLWYD SOUTH — Lab hold

| Electorate | %Turnout | | 53,680 | 62.4% | 2001 | 53,495 | 73.62% | 1997 |
|---|---|---|---|---|---|---|---|---|
| Jones M | Lab | | 17,217 | 51.4% | -6.75% | 22,901 | 58.15% | Lab |
| Biggins T | C | | 8,319 | 24.84% | 1.76% | 9,091 | 23.08% | C |
| Edwards D | PC | | 3,982 | 11.89% | 5.54% | 3,684 | 9.35% | LD |
| Griffiths D | LD | | 3,426 | 10.23% | 0.88% | 2,500 | 6.35% | PC |
| Theunissen Mrs E | UK Ind | | 552 | 1.65% | | 1,207 | 3.06% | Ref |
| Lab to C swing | 4.25% | | 33,496 | Lab maj 8,898 | | 39,383 | Lab maj 13,810 | |
| | | | | 26.56% | | | 35.07% | |

**MARTYN JONES,** b March 1, 1947. Elected here 1997; MP for Clwyd SW 1987-97. Chairman, Welsh Affairs Select Cttee, 1997-2001; member, Agriculture Select Cttee, 1987-94 and 1995-97. Lab spokesman, agriculture, 1994-95; chairman, 1987-94 and vice-chairman, 1995-97, PLP Agriculture Cttee. Lab whip, 1988-92. Clwyd county cllr, 1981-89. Worked in brewing industry, 1968-87. Member, Inst of Biology. Ex-area rep, TGWU. Microbiologist. Ed Grove Park GS, Wrexham; Liverpool and Trent Polys.
e-mail: burgessjd@parliament.uk tel: 020-7219 3417 fax: 020-7219 6090

This is an extensive and essentially rural seat in North Wales, embracing the mountains around Llangollen and Corwen on the Dee. There is a fairly high proportion of Welsh-speakers and quite a strong nonconformist tradition. These offset demographic trends that, in other parts of the country, might be expected to assist the Conservatives. Labour also benefits from the legacy of coalmining and heavy industry around Wrexham. Map 149

## CLWYD WEST — Lab hold

| Electorate | %Turnout | | 53,960 | 64.12% | 2001 | 53,467 | 75.29% | 1997 |
|---|---|---|---|---|---|---|---|---|
| Thomas G | Lab | | 13,426 | 38.8% | 1.74% | 14,918 | 37.06% | Lab |
| James J | C | | 12,311 | 35.58% | 3.11% | 13,070 | 32.47% | C |
| Williams E | PC | | 4,453 | 12.87% | -0.6% | 5,421 | 13.47% | PC |
| Feeley Ms B | LD | | 3,934 | 11.37% | -1.43% | 5,151 | 12.8% | LD |
| Guest M | UK Ind | | 476 | 1.38% | | 1,114 | 2.77% | Ref |
| | | | | | | 583 | 1.45% | Cvty |
| Lab to C swing | 0.68% | | 34,600 | Lab maj 1,115 | | 40,257 | Lab maj 1,848 | |
| | | | | 3.22% | | | 4.59% | |

**GARETH THOMAS,** b Sept 25, 1954. Elected 1997. PPS to Paul Murphy, Sec of State for Wales, 2001-. Member, Select Cttees: Social Security, 1999-2001; Welsh Affairs, 1997-99. Flintshire county cllr, 1995-. Member, MSF; Fabian Soc. Barrister. Ed Rock Ferry HS, Birkenhead; Univ Coll of Wales, Aberystwyth.
e-mail: thomasg@parliament.uk tel: 020-7219 3516 fax: 020-7219 1263

This is an attractive area of the coast and countryside of North Wales that attracts many visitors from England every summer to resorts such as Colwyn Bay. Traditionally it had been the most Conservative seat in the Principality. It would certainly be a safe Tory seat if it was located in England. Labour won narrowly in 1997, creating a new battleground marginal that it just held in 2001. Map 150

## CLYDEBANK & MILNGAVIE — Lab hold

| Electorate | %Turnout | 52,534 | 61.85% | 2001 | 52,092 | 75.03% | 1997 |
|---|---|---|---|---|---|---|---|
| **Worthington T** | **Lab** | **17,249** | **53.09%** | **-2.13%** | **21,583** | **55.22%** | **Lab** |
| Yuill J | SNP | 6,525 | 20.08% | -1.06% | 8,263 | 21.14% | SNP |
| Ackland R | LD | 3,909 | 12.03% | 1.58% | 4,885 | 12.5% | C |
| Pickering Dr C | C | 3,514 | 10.82% | -1.68% | 4,086 | 10.45% | LD |
| Brennan Ms D | SSP | 1,294 | 3.98% | | | 269 | 0.69% | Ref |
| **Lab to SNP swing** | **0.54%** | **32,491** | **Lab maj 10,724** | | **39,086** | **Lab maj 13,320** | |
| | | | 33.01% | | | 34.08% | |

**TONY WORTHINGTON,** b Oct 11, 1941. Elected 1987. Member, International Development Select Cttee, 1999-2001. Under-Sec of State, NI Office, 1997-98. Lab spokesman on NI, 1995-97; foreign affairs, 1993-94; overseas development, 1992-93. Joint sec, all-party population, reproductive health and development grp, 1989-97. Chairman, Lab campaign for criminal justice, 1987-89. Strathclyde regional cllr, 1974-87. Social policy and sociology lecturer. Ed City Sch, Lincoln; LSE; York and Glasgow Univs.
e-mail: worthingtont@parliament.uk tel: 01389 873195 fax: 01389 873195

This western Central Scotland seat is, even by the standards of the Boundary Commission, an odd amalgamation. Clydebank is a very working-class town and solidly Labour. Milngavie, on the other hand, is affluent, residential, territory and willing to contemplate voting for an alternative. It divides, however, between the three non-Labour parties. It is also outnumbered decisively by Clydebank. Map 151

## CLYDESDALE — Lab hold

| Electorate | %Turnout | 64,423 | 59.33% | 2001 | 63,428 | 71.6% | 1997 |
|---|---|---|---|---|---|---|---|
| **Hood J** | **Lab** | **17,822** | **46.63%** | **-5.91%** | **23,859** | **52.54%** | **Lab** |
| Wright J | SNP | 10,028 | 26.24% | 4.11% | 10,050 | 22.13% | SNP |
| Newton K | C | 5,034 | 13.17% | -3.12% | 7,396 | 16.29% | C |
| Craig Ms M | LD | 4,111 | 10.76% | 2.4% | 3,796 | 8.36% | LD |
| Cockshott P | SSP | 974 | 2.55% | | 311 | 0.68% | BNP |
| MacKay D | UK Ind | 253 | 0.66% | | | | |
| **Lab to SNP swing** | **5.01%** | **38,222** | **Lab maj 7,794** | | **45,412** | **Lab maj 13,809** | |
| | | | 20.39% | | | 30.41% | |

**JIMMY HOOD,** b May 16, 1949. Elected 1987. Chairman, Select Cttee: European Scrutiny, 1992-2001 (member, 1987-2001) and its Sub Cttee on Road Safety, 1994-97; member, Defence Select Cttee, 1997-2001; Chairmen's Panel. Chairman, miners' grp, 1990-92. NUM official, 1973-85 and union nat exec, 1990-92. Miner/coalface engineer. Ed Lesmahagow Higher Grade Sch, Coatbridge; Motherwell Tech Coll; Nottingham Univ.
e-mail: hoodj@parliament.uk tel: 01555 673177 fax: 01555 673188

The name of this seat, southeast of Glasgow, suggests a heavily industrial area, working-class and likely to be dominated by the Labour Party. And there are plenty of constituencies in the Glasgow area with such characteristics. Clydesdale is, nonetheless, a shade more complicated. It has a lot more rural territory than one might suspect which means that, while Labour is always the most likely victor here, it is not without a challenge. Map 152

## COATBRIDGE & CHRYSTON — Lab hold

| Electorate | %Turnout | 52,178 | 58.09% | 2001 | 52,024 | 72.3% | 1997 |
|---|---|---|---|---|---|---|---|
| **Clarke T** | **Lab** | **19,807** | **65.35%** | **-2.97%** | **25,697** | **68.32%** | **Lab** |
| Kearney P | SNP | 4,493 | 14.82% | -2.2% | 6,402 | 17.02% | SNP |
| Tough A | LD | 2,293 | 7.56% | 2.11% | 3,216 | 8.55% | C |
| Ross-Taylor P | C | 2,171 | 7.16% | -1.39% | 2,048 | 5.45% | LD |
| Sheridan Ms L | SSP | 1,547 | 5.1% | | 249 | 0.66% | Ref |
| **Lab to SNP swing** | **0.39%** | **30,311** | **Lab maj 15,314** | | **37,612** | **Lab maj 19,295** | |
| | | | 50.52% | | | 51.30% | |

**TOM CLARKE,** b Jan 10, 1941. Elected here 1997. MP for Monklands W 1983-97; for Coatbridge and Airdrie 1982-83. Culture, Media and Sport Min, responsible for films and tourism, 1997-98. Lab spokesman, disabled people's rights, 1994-97; Shadow Cabinet, 1992-94 and 1995-97. Chief spokesman, overseas aid, 1993-94; Shadow Scottish Sec, 1992-93. Member, Lab frontbench health team, 1987-90 as spokesman on personal social services. Sponsored Disabled Persons Act, 1986. Ed Columba HS, Coatbridge; Scottish Coll of Commerce.

This east Strathclyde seat is located almost evenly between the Firth of Clyde and the Firth of Forth. It is not, however, in the middle of the political spectrum. Labour is by far the most popular political party. This area has, though, been at the centre of factional intrigue, with sectarian politics based on religion apparently as influential a factor as normal partisan colours. Map 153

## COLCHESTER — LD hold

| Electorate | %Turnout | | 78,955 | 55.39% | 2001 | 74,743 | 69.58% | 1997 |
|---|---|---|---|---|---|---|---|---|
| **Russell B** | **LD** | | **18,627** | **42.59%** | **8.2%** | **17,886** | **34.39%** | **LD** |
| Bentley K | C | | 13,074 | 29.89% | -1.46% | 16,305 | 31.35% | C |
| Fegan C | Lab | | 10,925 | 24.98% | -5.58% | 15,891 | 30.56% | Lab |
| Lord R | UK Ind | | 631 | 1.44% | | 1,776 | 3.41% | Ref |
| Overy-Owen L | Grey | | 479 | 1.1% | | 148 | 0.28% | NLP |
| **C to LD swing** | **4.83%** | | **43,736** | | **LD maj 5,553** | **52,006** | | **LD maj 1,581** |
| | | | | | 12.70% | | | 3.04% |

**BOB RUSSELL,** b March 31, 1946. Elected 1997; contested Sudbury and Woodbridge Oct 1974, and formerly Colchester 1979 for Lab. LD spokesman on sport. Colchester borough cllr, 1971- (leader 1987-91; ex-mayor). Ex-press officer, Essex Univ and British Telecommunications. Ed St Helena Sec, Colchester; NE Essex Tech Coll.

This Essex garrison town had, by 1997, evolved into one of those true rarities in British politics — a real three-way marginal. This is largely the result of decisions by the Boundary Commissioners. Colchester used to be split between two seats both allied with a rural fringe. It is now a single, compact, and more urban constituency offering a reasonable electoral base for all three main parties; the Lib Dems have been the leading force in 1997 and 2001. Map 154

## COLNE VALLEY — Lab hold

| Electorate | %Turnout | | 74,192 | 63.33% | 2001 | 73,338 | 76.92% | 1997 |
|---|---|---|---|---|---|---|---|---|
| **Mountford Ms K** | **Lab** | | **18,967** | **40.37%** | **-0.91%** | **23,285** | **41.28%** | **Lab** |
| Davies P | C | | 14,328 | 30.49% | -2.21% | 18,445 | 32.7% | C |
| Beever G | LD | | 11,694 | 24.89% | 2.28% | 12,755 | 22.61% | LD |
| Plunkett R | Green | | 1,081 | 2.3% | 1.43% | 759 | 1.35% | Soc Lab |
| Quarmby Dr A | UK Ind | | 917 | 1.95% | 1.1% | 493 | 0.87% | Green |
| | | | | | | 478 | 0.85% | UK Ind |
| | | | | | | 196 | 0.35% | Loony |
| **C to Lab swing** | **0.65%** | | **46,987** | | **Lab maj 4,639** | **56,411** | | **Lab maj 4,840** |
| | | | | | 9.87% | | | 8.58% |

**KALI MOUNTFORD,** b Jan 12, 1954. Elected 1997. Member, Finance Bill Standing Cttee, 1997, 1999 and 2000; Social Security Select Cttee, 1998-99; vice-chairman, Backbench Social Security Cttee, 1997-; all-party textile grp, 1999-; vice chairwoman, Huddersfield CAB; Huddersfield victim support; pres, Merhal-E-Niswan Pakistani ladies grp; ex-civil servant, Dept of Ed and Employment; ex-Sheffield city cllr.
e-mail: mountfordk@parliament.uk tel: 01484 319876 fax 01484 319878

A beautiful and prosperous West Yorkshire constituency, immortalised by *The Last of the Summer Wine* television series. It has a high rate of owner–occupation and professional/managerial employees but a significant poorer minority who back Labour. It has, at different times, been sympathetic to all three main parties and is likely to remain a fiercely fought marginal, though Labour currently holds the whiphand. Map 155

## CONGLETON — C hold

| Electorate | %Turnout | | 71,941 | 62.67% | 2001 | 68,873 | 77.56% | 1997 |
|---|---|---|---|---|---|---|---|---|
| **Winterton Mrs A** | **C** | | **20,872** | **46.3%** | **5.09%** | **22,012** | **41.21%** | **C** |
| Flanagan J | Lab | | 13,738 | 30.47% | 2.93% | 15,882 | 29.73% | LD |
| Lloyd-Griffiths D | LD | | 9,719 | 21.56% | -8.17% | 14,714 | 27.54% | Lab |
| Young B | UK Ind | | 754 | 1.67% | 0.15% | 811 | 1.52% | UK Ind |
| **Lab to C swing** | **1.08%** | | **45,083** | | **C maj 7,134** | **53,419** | | **C maj 6,130** |
| | | | | | 15.82% | | | 11.48% |

**ANN WINTERTON,** b March 6, 1941. Elected 1983. Member, Select Cttee, Agriculture, 1987-97; Chairmen's Panel, 1992; Unopposed Bills Panel. Opposition spokeswoman, national drug strategy, 1997-; chairwoman, all-party pro-life grp; vice-chairwoman, British Finnish grp; sec, St Helena grp and joint sec, Brit Danish grp; joint treas, Brit Taiwan grp. Joint chairwoman, breast cancer grp. Ed Erdington GS for Girls. Her husband, Nicholas Winterton, is MP for Macclesfield.
tel: 020-7219-3585 fax: 01260 271212

A Cheshire seat consisting of a patchwork of smaller towns and villages such as Sandbach, Alsager and Middlewich. It is dominated by high-wealth owner–occupiers, with a large slice of professionals and managers. The most urban elements of the constituency are favourable to Labour but almost everywhere else the Tories are dominant, with the Liberal Democrats providing the competition. That division of spoils suits the Conservatives. Map 156

## CONWY — Lab hold

| Electorate | %Turnout | | 54,751 | 62.77% | 2001 | 55,092 | 75.44% | 1997 |
|---|---|---|---|---|---|---|---|---|
| Williams Mrs B | Lab | | 14,366 | 41.8% | 6.76% | 14,561 | 35.04% | Lab |
| Logan D | C | | 8,147 | 23.71% | -0.56% | 12,965 | 31.2% | LD |
| Macdonald Ms V | LD | | 5,800 | 16.88% | -14.32% | 10,085 | 24.27% | C |
| Owen Ms A | PC | | 5,665 | 16.48% | 9.64% | 2,844 | 6.84% | PC |
| Barham A | UK Ind | | 388 | 1.13% | | 760 | 1.83% | Ref |
| | | | | | | 250 | 0.6% | Alt LD |
| | | | | | | 95 | 0.23% | NLP |
| C to Lab swing | 3.66% | | 34,366 | Lab maj 6,219 | | 41,560 | Lab maj 1,596 | |
| | | | | 18.10% | | | 3.84% | |

**BETTY WILLIAMS,** b July 31, 1944. Elected 1997; contested seat 1992 and 1987 and Caernarfon 1983. Member, Welsh Affairs Select Cttee, 1997-2001. Ex-Gwynedd county cllr; Arfon borough cllr, 1970-91 (mayor, 1990-91). Univ of Wales, 1995; Hon Fellow, Univ of Wales, Bangor. Freelance media researcher. Ed Ysgol Dyffryn Nantlle; Univ of Wales.

An intriguing North Wales constituency. It consists of such towns as Bangor (with its university), the seaside resort of Llandudno and the walled castle town of Conwy itself. More than four out of ten of the electorate speak Welsh but, unlike other areas in the Principality, this does not seem to have helped Plaid Cymru very much. The seat is instead, at least potentially, a three-way battle between Labour, Liberal Democrats and Tories. Map 157

## COPELAND — Lab hold

| Electorate | %Turnout | | 53,526 | 64.92% | 2001 | 54,263 | 76.19% | 1997 |
|---|---|---|---|---|---|---|---|---|
| Cunningham Dr J | Lab | | 17,991 | 51.77% | -6.34% | 24,025 | 58.11% | Lab |
| Graham M | C | | 13,027 | 37.49% | 8.27% | 12,081 | 29.22% | C |
| Gayler M | LD | | 3,732 | 10.74% | 1.52% | 3,814 | 9.22% | LD |
| | | | | | | 1,036 | 2.51% | Ref |
| | | | | | | 389 | 0.94% | ProLife |
| Lab to C swing | 7.30% | | 34,750 | Lab maj 4,964 | | 41,345 | Lab maj 11,944 | |
| | | | | 14.28% | | | 28.89% | |

**JACK CUNNINGHAM,** b Aug 4, 1939. Elected here 1983; MP for Whitehaven 1970-83. Min for Agriculture, Fisheries and Food, 1997-98; Chancellor of the Duchy of Lancaster, 1998-99. Shadow Heritage Sec, 1995-97. Shadow Trade and Industry Sec, 1994-95; chief spokesman, Foreign and Commonwealth Affairs, 1992-94; Shadow Leader of Commons and Lab campaigns co-ordinator, 1989-92; chief spokesman, environment, 1983-89; industry spokesman, 1979-83. Energy Under-Sec, 1976-79. PPS to James Callaghan, 1974-76. Ed Jarrow GS; Bede Coll, Durham.

A spectacular Cumbrian coastal constituency which contains the extremes of the modern world. On the one hand, the seat includes some of the most compelling Lake District scenery. On the other, the biggest single local employer is the Sellafield nuclear plant. Labour nearly lost the seat in the 1980s because of its perceived hostility to nuclear energy but has been much stronger since then. Map 158

## CORBY — Lab hold

| Electorate | %Turnout | | 72,304 | 65.31% | 2001 | 69,252 | 77.91% | 1997 |
|---|---|---|---|---|---|---|---|---|
| Hope P | Lab Co-op | | 23,283 | 49.31% | -6.08% | 29,888 | 55.39% | Lab |
| Griffith A | C | | 17,583 | 37.23% | 3.82% | 18,028 | 33.41% | C |
| Scudder K | LD | | 4,751 | 10.06% | 2.56% | 4,045 | 7.5% | LD |
| Gillman I | UK Ind | | 855 | 1.81% | 0.87% | 1,356 | 2.51% | Ref |
| Dickson A | Soc Lab | | 750 | 1.59% | | 507 | 0.94% | UK Ind |
| | | | | | | 133 | 0.25% | NLP |
| Lab Co-op to C swing | 4.95% | | 47,222 | Lab Co-op maj 5,700 | | 53,957 | Lab maj 11,860 | |
| | | | | 12.07% | | | 21.98% | |

**PHIL HOPE,** b April 19, 1955. Elected 1997; contested Kettering 1992. PPS to John Prescott, Deputy PM and First Sec of State, 2001-. Member, Public Accounts Cttee, 1997-2001. Joint vice-chairman, PLP Social Security Cttee, 1997-. Chairman, all-party charities and voluntary sector grp, 1997-. Member, Co-op Party; MSF. Enjoys tap dancing and juggling burning clubs. Teacher. Ed Wandsworth Comp; St Luke's Coll, Exeter.
e-mail: philhopemp@compuserve.com www.geocities.com/phil
hopemp tel: 01536 443325 fax: 01536 269462

This Northamptonshire constituency has enjoyed a rollercoaster economic history. It was initially based around the steel industry and was then designated a new town in 1950. The collapse of steel in the 1980s almost destroyed the town. It did not, though, damage the surrounding rural areas. The balance between these two traditions has made for a competitive constituency where Labour, at least for now, seems fairly well entrenched. Map 159

COR

## CORNWALL NORTH — LD hold

| Electorate | %Turnout | | 84,662 | 63.76% | 2001 | 80,076 | 73.16% | 1997 |
|---|---|---|---|---|---|---|---|---|
| Tyler P | | LD | 28,082 | 52.02% | -1.22% | 31,186 | 53.24% | LD |
| Weller J | | C | 18,250 | 33.81% | 4.36% | 17,253 | 29.45% | C |
| Goodman M | | Lab | 5,257 | 9.74% | 0.31% | 5,523 | 9.43% | Lab |
| Protz S | | UK Ind | 2,394 | 4.43% | | 3,636 | 6.21% | Ref |
| | | | | | | 645 | 1.1% | Meb Ker |
| | | | | | | 186 | 0.32% | Lib |
| | | | | | | 152 | 0.26% | NLP |
| LD to C swing | 2.79% | | 53,983 | | LD maj 9,832 | 58,581 | | LD maj 13,933 |
| | | | | | 18.21% | | | 23.79% |

**PAUL TYLER,** b Oct 29, 1941. Elected here 1992; Lib MP for Bodmin 1974. LD Leader of the House, 1997; confirmed June 2001. Member, Commons Selection Cttee, 1997-2001. Member; joint Parly Privilege Cttee, 1997-2001; Modernisation of Commons Cttee, 1997-2001; Procedure Cttee, 1992-97. Spokesman, agriculture and rural affairs, 1992-97. Chairman, all-party coastal grp, 1993-97; joint sec, water grp, 1993-97 ; treas, tourism cttee, 1993-97. Ex-PR consultant. Ed Sherborne Sch; Exeter Coll, Oxford. www.paultyler.libdem.org tel: 020-7219 6355

This constituency includes a sizeable chunk of the county. It is based on the town of Bodmin and the lively seaside resort of Newquay. but really consists of scores of small towns and villages which depend mostly on agriculture or tourism for their livelihood. There is no Labour vote of any magnitude and the seat has swung between the Conservatives and the Liberal Democrats, but both in 1997 and 2001 the Lib Dems have surged ahead. Map 160

## CORNWALL SOUTH EAST — LD hold

| Electorate | %Turnout | | 79,090 | 65.44% | 2001 | 75,825 | 75.74% | 1997 |
|---|---|---|---|---|---|---|---|---|
| Breed C | | LD | 23,756 | 45.9% | -1.19% | 27,044 | 47.09% | LD |
| Gray A | | C | 18,381 | 35.52% | -0.29% | 20,564 | 35.81% | C |
| Stevens B | | Lab | 6,429 | 12.42% | -0.39% | 7,358 | 12.81% | Lab |
| Palmer G | | UK Ind | 1,978 | 3.82% | 1.33% | 1,428 | 2.49% | UK Ind |
| George Dr K | | Meb Ker | 1,209 | 2.34% | 1.34% | 573 | 1.0% | Meb Ker |
| | | | | | | 268 | 0.47% | Lib |
| | | | | | | 197 | 0.34% | NLP |
| LD to C swing | 0.45% | | 51,753 | | LD maj 5,375 | 57,432 | | LD maj 6,480 |
| | | | | | 10.39% | | | 11.28% |

**COLIN BREED,** b May 4, 1947. Elected 1997. LD spokesman, agriculture, rural affairs and fisheries. Saltash cllr, 1982-97; mayor of Saltash, 1989-90 and 1995-96. Company dir. Ed Torquay GS. e-mail: colinbreedmp@compuserve.com www.colinbreed.org.uk tel: 020-7219 2588 fax: 020-7219 5905

This seat also represents a sizeable chunk of the county, stretching across from the Devon border. It contains no dominant single settlement but a number of notable towns such as Saltash and Liskeard and the charming fishing and tourist ports of Fowey and Looe. This is not much of a constituency for Labour. Intense competition between the Tories and Lib Dems can be expected for some time to come, but for now the latter hold sway. Map 161

## COTSWOLD — C hold

| Electorate | %Turnout | | 68,154 | 67.47% | 2001 | 67,333 | 75.92% | 1997 |
|---|---|---|---|---|---|---|---|---|
| Clifton-Brown G | | C | 23,133 | 50.31% | 3.95% | 23,698 | 46.36% | C |
| Lawrence Ms A | | LD | 11,150 | 24.25% | 1.3% | 11,733 | 22.95% | LD |
| Wilkins R | | Lab | 10,383 | 22.58% | -0.13% | 11,608 | 22.71% | Lab |
| Stopps Mrs J | | UK Ind | 1,315 | 2.86% | | 3,393 | 6.64% | Ref |
| | | | | | | 560 | 1.1% | Green |
| | | | | | | 129 | 0.25% | NLP |
| LD to C swing | 1.33% | | 45,981 | | C maj 11,983 | 51,121 | | C maj 11,965 |
| | | | | | 26.06% | | | 23.41% |

**GEOFFREY CLIFTON-BROWN,** b March 23, 1953. Elected here 1997; MP for Cirencester and Tewkesbury 1992-97. Opposition whip, 2001-. PPS to Douglas Hogg, Agriculture Min, 1995-97. Member, Public Accounts Cttee, 1997-2001; Environment Select Cttee, 1992-95. Public Accounts Commissioner, 1995-97. Chartered surveyor and farmer. Ed Tormore Sch, Kent; Eton; Royal Agricultural Coll, Cirencester. e-mail: gcb@gcbmp.demon.co.uk www.gcbmp.demon.uk tel: 01242 514551 fax: 01608 650033

Gloucestershire received an extra seat as part of the 1997 boundary review and, as a consequence, a new constituency called simply Cotswold was created. The vast majority of the voters here come from the Cirencester, Tewkesbury and Stroud areas. This is a predominantly rural and very scenic area that takes in the hugely popular Cotswold villages such as Bourton-on-the-Water, Moreton-in-Marsh and Chipping Campden. It is also solidly Conservative. Map 162

## COVENTRY NORTH EAST                                                      Lab hold

| Electorate | %Turnout | | 73,998 | 50.36% | 2001 | 74,274 | 64.74% | 1997 |
|---|---|---|---|---|---|---|---|---|
| **Ainsworth B** | **Lab** | | **22,739** | **61.02%** | **-5.23%** | **31,856** | **66.25%** | **Lab** |
| Bell G | C | | 6,988 | 18.75% | -0.56% | 9,287 | 19.31% | C |
| Sewards G | LD | | 4,163 | 11.17% | 3.13% | 3,866 | 8.04% | LD |
| Nellist D | Soc All | | 2,638 | 7.08% | | 1,181 | 2.46% | Lib |
| Sheppard E | BNP | | 737 | 1.98% | | 1,125 | 2.34% | Ref |
| | | | | | | 597 | 1.24% | Soc Lab |
| | | | | | | 173 | 0.36% | Dream |
| **Lab to C swing** | **2.34%** | | **37,265** | | **Lab maj 15,751** | **48,085** | | **Lab maj 22,569** |
| | | | | | 42.27% | | | 46.94% |

**BOB AINSWORTH,** b June 19, 1952. Elected 1992. Parly Sec, Home Office, June, 2001-; Parly Under-Sec at Environment Transport and Regions, 2001-. Govt whip, 1997-2001. Lab whip, 1995-97. Member, Environment Select Cttee, 1993-95. Joint vice-chairman, all-party Euro secure vehicle alliance grp. Ex-Jaguar worker and shop steward. Ed Foxford Comp, Coventry.

There are three parliamentary constituencies in the West Midlands heavy industrial and cathedral city of Coventry, and this is the most reliably Labour of the set. It is an overwhelmingly working-class constituency with a racial element providing the main sort of diversity in the population, although that does not extend to voting intentions. Map 163

## COVENTRY NORTH WEST                                                     Lab hold

| Electorate | %Turnout | | 76,652 | 55.51% | 2001 | 76,439 | 71.07% | 1997 |
|---|---|---|---|---|---|---|---|---|
| **Robinson G** | **Lab** | | **21,892** | **51.45%** | **-5.43%** | **30,901** | **56.88%** | **Lab** |
| Fairburn A | C | | 11,018 | 25.89% | -0.43% | 14,300 | 26.32% | C |
| Penlington N | LD | | 5,832 | 13.71% | 3.24% | 5,690 | 10.47% | LD |
| Oddy Ms C | Ind | | 3,159 | 7.42% | | 1,269 | 2.34% | Ref |
| Benson M | UK Ind | | 650 | 1.53% | | 940 | 1.73% | Soc Lab |
| | | | | | | 687 | 1.26% | Lib |
| | | | | | | 359 | 0.66% | ProLife |
| | | | | | | 176 | 0.32% | Dream |
| **Lab to C swing** | **2.50%** | | **42,551** | | **Lab maj 10,874** | **54,322** | | **Lab maj 16,601** |
| | | | | | 25.56% | | | 30.56% |

**GEOFFREY ROBINSON,** b May 25, 1938. Elected 1976 by-election. Paymaster General, 1997-98. Lab spokesman, trade and industry, 1983-87; science, 1982-83. Proprietor, *New Statesman*. Chairman, TransTec plc, 1986-97; ex-dir, Kleinwort Smaller Companies Investment Trust plc. Financial controller, British Leyland, 1971-72; managing dir, Leyland Innocenti, Italy, 1972-73; chief exec, Jaguar Cars, 1973-75; Triumph Motorcycles, 1977-80. dir, 1980-82. Ed Emanuel Sch, London; Clare Coll, Cambridge; Yale.

This is in some senses a curious seat. It has the highest proportion of owner-occupiers in Coventry. It has long been linked to the car industry but has endured decline under governments of both political stripes. It has a notable middle class to provide the Tories with some sort of political base. Yet it has consistently stuck with Labour even when other similar areas defected in the 1980s. Map 164

## COVENTRY SOUTH                                                          Lab hold

| Electorate | %Turnout | | 72,527 | 55.28% | 2001 | 71,826 | 69.79% | 1997 |
|---|---|---|---|---|---|---|---|---|
| **Cunningham J** | **Lab** | | **20,125** | **50.19%** | **-0.71%** | **25,511** | **50.9%** | **Lab** |
| Wheeler Ms H | C | | 11,846 | 29.54% | 0.5% | 14,558 | 29.04% | C |
| McKee V | LD | | 5,672 | 14.15% | 4.94% | 4,617 | 9.21% | LD |
| Windsor R | Soc All | | 1,475 | 3.68% | | 3,262 | 6.51% | Soc |
| Rogers Ms I | Ind | | 564 | 1.41% | | 943 | 1.88% | Ref |
| Logan T | Soc Lab | | 414 | 1.03% | | 725 | 1.45% | Lib |
| | | | | | | 328 | 0.65% | BNP |
| | | | | | | 180 | 0.36% | Dream |
| **Lab to C swing** | **0.61%** | | **40,096** | | **Lab maj 8,279** | **50,124** | | **Lab maj 10,953** |
| | | | | | 20.65% | | | 21.86% |

**JIM CUNNINGHAM,** b Feb 4, 1941. Elected here 1997; MP for Coventry SE 1992-97. Member, Select Cttees: Trade and Industry, 1997-2001; Home Affairs, 1992-97. Chairman, PLP Treasury Cttee, 1997- (sec, 1995-97, and former joint vice-chairman). Joint vice-chairman, all-party building societies grp, 1996-97. Coventry city cllr, 1972-92, leader, 1988-92. Member MSF. Engineer and ex-senior shop steward. Ed St Columbia HS, Coatbridge.
tel: 020-7219 6362 fax: 020-7219 6362

This seat, which includes Coventry city centre and the campus of Warwick University, is the by-product of the reduction in the city's parliamentary representation from four seats to three. It contains the old South East, which was solidly Labour, and much of the South West section, a marginal that had leant towards the Tories. The effect of this has been to create an electorate that is strongly inclined to back Labour but with a sizeable Tory minority. Map 165

## CRAWLEY — Lab hold

| Electorate | %Turnout | 71,626 | 55.18% | 2001 | 69,040 | 73.03% | 1997 |
|---|---|---|---|---|---|---|---|
| **Moffatt Ms L** | **Lab** | **19,488** | **49.31%** | **-5.73%** | **27,750** | **55.04%** | **Lab** |
| Smith H | C | 12,718 | 32.18% | 0.36% | 16,043 | 31.82% | C |
| Seekings Ms L | LD | 5,009 | 12.67% | 4.46% | 4,141 | 8.21% | LD |
| Galloway B | UK Ind | 1,137 | 2.88% | 2.24% | 1,931 | 3.83% | Ref |
| Staniford Ms C | Loony | 388 | 0.98% | | 322 | 0.64% | UK Ind |
| Khan A | JP | 271 | 0.69% | 0.23% | 230 | 0.46% | JP |
| Stewart K | Soc Lab | 260 | 0.66% | | | | |
| Hirsch Ms M | Soc All | 251 | 0.64% | | | | |
| **Lab to C swing** | **3.05%** | **39,522** | **Lab maj 6,770** | | **50,417** | **Lab maj 11,707** | |
| | | | 17.13% | | | 23.22% | |

**LAURA MOFFATT,** b April 9, 1954. Elected 1997; contested seat 1992. PPS to Lord Irvine of Lairg, the Lord Chancellor, 2001-. Member, Defence Select Cttee, 1997-2001. Vice-chairman, all-party drugs grp; financial officer, all-party grps on Aids. Crawley borough cllr, 1984-97, mayor, 1990-91. Hon vice-pres, Assoc of Port Health Authorities; pres, Crawley Access grp. Nurse. Ed Hazelwick Comp, Crawley; Crawley Coll.
e-mail: clewerd@parliament.uk fax: 01293 527610

This seat is defined by the new town itself which expanded rapidly in the 1960s and 1970s along with Gatwick Airport, a major local employer. A seat of this name in West Sussex was created in 1983 but it had an urban core surrounded by a highly Tory rural fringe. The next set of boundary revisions moved many of those rural voters elsewhere and left a constituency ripe for the Labour Party in 1997 and again in 2001. Map 166

## CREWE & NANTWICH — Lab hold

| Electorate | %Turnout | 69,040 | 60.18% | 2001 | 68,694 | 73.67% | 1997 |
|---|---|---|---|---|---|---|---|
| **Dunwoody Mrs G** | **Lab** | **22,556** | **54.29%** | **-3.93%** | **29,460** | **58.22%** | **Lab** |
| Potter D | C | 12,650 | 30.45% | 3.45% | 13,662 | 27.0% | C |
| Cannon D | LD | 5,595 | 13.47% | 1.73% | 5,940 | 11.74% | LD |
| Croston R | UK Ind | 746 | 1.8% | | 1,543 | 3.05% | Ref |
| **Lab to C swing** | **3.69%** | **41,547** | **Lab maj 9,906** | | **50,605** | **Lab maj 15,798** | |
| | | | 23.84% | | | 31.22% | |

**GWYNETH DUNWOODY,** b Dec 12 1930. Elected here 1983; MP for Crewe Feb 1974-83; Exeter 1966-70; MEP 1975-79. Member, Chairmen's Panel, 1992-2000. Joint chairwoman, Select Cttee: Environment, Transport and Reg Affairs, 1997-2001; chairwoman, Transport Sub-Cttee and member, Environment Sub-Cttee, 1997-2001; Transport, 1987-97. Chief Lab transport spokeswoman, 1984-85. Pres, Soc International Women, 1986-92. Ed Fulham County Sec; Convent of Notre Dame.
www.gwynethdunwoody.co.uk tel: 020-7219 3490 fax: 020-7219 6046

This Cheshire seat is a fascinating combination of two adjacent but extremely dissimilar settlements. The mixture made for a marginal seat which Labour managed to hang on to by a narrow margin in the 1980s. Crewe, the famed railway town, is essentially Labour while Nantwich, a prosperous market town, is equally Conservative. Boundary revisions for the 1997 election benefited Labour then, and once more in 2001. Map 167

## CROSBY — Lab hold

| Electorate | %Turnout | 57,375 | 64.25% | 2001 | 57,190 | 77.18% | 1997 |
|---|---|---|---|---|---|---|---|
| **Curtis-Thomas Ms C** | **Lab** | **20,327** | **55.14%** | **4.06%** | **22,549** | **51.08%** | **Lab** |
| Collinson R | C | 11,974 | 32.48% | -2.33% | 15,367 | 34.81% | C |
| Drake T | LD | 4,084 | 11.08% | -0.43% | 5,080 | 11.51% | LD |
| Holt M | Soc Lab | 481 | 1.3% | | 813 | 1.84% | Ref |
| | | | | | 233 | 0.53% | Lib |
| | | | | | 99 | 0.22% | NLP |
| **C to Lab swing** | **3.19%** | **36,866** | **Lab maj 8,353** | | **44,141** | **Lab maj 7,182** | |
| | | | 22.66% | | | 16.27% | |

**CLAIRE CURTIS-THOMAS,** b April 30, 1958. Elected 1997. Member, Select Cttee, Science and Tech, 1997-2001. Head of environmental affairs, Shell Chemicals; head of Distribution UK Ltd, Shell Chemicals. Fellow, Inst of Mechanical Engineers; senator, Engineering Council; corporate membership officer, Women's Engineering Soc (all unpaid). Member, TGWU; Co-op Party; Fabian Soc. Engineering consultant; chartered mechanical engineer. Ed Univ Coll of Wales, Cardiff; Aston Univ.
e-mail: curtisthomasc@parliament.uk tel: 020-7219 4193 fax: 020-7219 1540

An unusual seat with a distinctive political history. Crosby, on the northwest side of Liverpool towards Southport, has historically been the home of the Merseyside middle class, and was thus solidly Tory. Shirley Williams won the seat for the SDP in a by-election in 1981 but then lost it narrowly two years later back to the Tories. The gradual loss of the centre party influence and boundary alterations enabled Labour to win here in 1997 and 2001. Map 168

## CROYDON CENTRAL — Lab hold

| Electorate | %Turnout | | 77,567 | 59.12% | 2001 | 80,152 | 69.62% | 1997 |
|---|---|---|---|---|---|---|---|---|
| Davies G | Lab | | 21,643 | 47.19% | 1.61% | 25,432 | 45.58% | Lab |
| Congdon D | C | | 17,659 | 38.51% | -0.08% | 21,535 | 38.59% | C |
| Booth P | LD | | 5,156 | 11.24% | 0.38% | 6,061 | 10.86% | LD |
| Feisenberger J | UK Ind | | 545 | 1.19% | 0.67% | 1,886 | 3.38% | Ref |
| Miller Ms L | BNP | | 449 | 0.98% | | 595 | 1.07% | Green |
| Cartwright J | Loony | | 408 | 0.89% | | 290 | 0.52% | UK Ind |
| C to Lab swing | 0.85% | | 45,860 | | Lab maj 3,984 | 55,799 | | Lab maj 3,897 |
| | | | | | 8.69% | | | 6.99% |

**GERAINT DAVIES,** b May 3, 1960. Elected 1997; contested seat 1992 and Croydon S 1987. Member, Public Accounts Cttee, 1997-2001. Chairman, Backbench Finance and Industry Grp, 1998; Backbench Environment, Transport and Regions Cttee, 1997-. Croydon cllr, 1986-97. Previously marketing manager, Colgate Palmolive Ltd; grp product manager, Unilever. Member, MSF. Ed Llanishen Comp, Cardiff; Jesus Coll, Oxford.

Croydon, a vast, modern shopping, commercial and commuter centre south of the capital, is the largest borough in Greater London. But it nevertheless lost one of its four seats in the last boundary review. Croydon Central had traditionally been a Tory seat, albeit with an urban core. The seat now stretches down to include the Surrey borders. It also now contains a larger number of council estate electors to provide a real political base for Labour. Map 169

## CROYDON NORTH — Lab hold

| Electorate | %Turnout | | 76,600 | 54.68% | 2001 | 77,063 | 68.21% | 1997 |
|---|---|---|---|---|---|---|---|---|
| Wicks M | Lab | | 26,610 | 63.54% | 1.38% | 32,672 | 62.16% | Lab |
| Allison S | C | | 9,752 | 23.28% | -3.88% | 14,274 | 27.16% | C |
| Lawman Ms S | LD | | 4,375 | 10.45% | 2.71% | 4,066 | 7.74% | LD |
| Smith A | UK Ind | | 606 | 1.45% | 0.7% | 1,155 | 2.2% | Ref |
| Madgwick D | Soc All | | 539 | 1.29% | | 396 | 0.75% | UK Ind |
| C to Lab swing | 2.63% | | 41,882 | | Lab maj 16,858 | 52,563 | | Lab maj 18,398 |
| | | | | | 40.25% | | | 35.00% |

**MALCOLM WICKS,** b July 1, 1957. Elected here 1997; MP for Croydon NW 1992-97. Parly Sec, Dept for Work and Pensions, June 2001-; Parly Under-Sec, DfEE, 1999-2001. Lab spokesman, social security, 1995-97; member, Social Security Select Cttee, 1992-95 and 1997-99. Dir, family policy studies centre, 1983-92; member, family policy observatory, Euro Commission, 1987-92; chairman, winter action on cold homes, 1986-92; research dir and sec, study commission on the family, 1978-83. Member, TGWU. Ed Elizabeth Coll, Guernsey; NW London Poly; LSE.

An outstanding case of boundary revisions operating to the benefit of Labour. The core of this seat is the old Croydon North West which was a marginal won by Labour in 1992. The additional wards have been taken from the abolished Croydon North East seat and are much more favourable to Labour. There is also a rising ethnic minority which has altered the underlying political demographics here. Map 170

## CROYDON SOUTH — C hold

| Electorate | %Turnout | | 73,402 | 61.39% | 2001 | 73,787 | 73.45% | 1997 |
|---|---|---|---|---|---|---|---|---|
| Ottaway R | C | | 22,169 | 49.2% | 1.88% | 25,649 | 47.32% | C |
| Ryan G | Lab | | 13,472 | 29.9% | 4.59% | 13,719 | 25.31% | Lab |
| Gallop Ms A | LD | | 8,226 | 18.26% | -2.85% | 11,441 | 21.11% | LD |
| Garner Mrs K | UK Ind | | 998 | 2.21% | 1.64% | 2,631 | 4.85% | Ref |
| Samuel M | Choice | | 195 | 0.43% | 0.25% | 354 | 0.65% | BNP |
| | | | | | | 309 | 0.57% | UK Ind |
| | | | | | | 96 | 0.18% | Choice |
| C to Lab swing | 1.35% | | 45,060 | | C maj 8,697 | 54,199 | | C maj 11,930 |
| | | | | | 19.30% | | | 22.01% |

**RICHARD OTTAWAY,** b May 24, 1945. Elected here 1992; MP for Nottingham N 1983-87. C Treasury spokesman, 2000-, defence, 1999-2000; local govt and London, 1997-99. Govt whip, 1995-97; member, Procedure Select Cttee, 1996-97. PPS to Michael Heseltine, when Dep PM and Pres of Board of Trade, 1992-95. Served in RN, 1961-70; RNR, 1970-80. Chairman, population, dev and reproductive health grp, 1992-95. Unpaid member, parly panel, Harris Research Centre. Solicitor and arbitrator. Ed Backwell Sec Mod Sch, Somerset; RNC Dartmouth; Bristol Univ.

This is one of the safest Conservative seats in the whole of Greater London. It is solidly middle-class with a substantial commuter population. It consists of comfortable suburban towns such as Purley, Coulsdon, Sanderstead and Selsdon. While in other parts of the country the Liberal Democrats might be able to find a foothold among such affluent voters, they have not done so here. Map 171

## CUMBERNAULD & KILSYTH                                    Lab hold

| Electorate | %Turnout | | 49,739 | 59.71% | 2001 | 48,032 | 75.0% | 1997 |
|---|---|---|---|---|---|---|---|---|
| **McKenna Ms R** | Lab | **16,144** | **54.36%** | **-4.33%** | **21,141** | **58.69%** | **Lab** |
| McGlashan D | SNP | 8,624 | 29.04% | 1.24% | 10,013 | 27.8% | SNP |
| O'Donnell J | LD | 1,934 | 6.51% | 2.71% | 2,441 | 6.78% | C |
| Ross Ms A | C | 1,460 | 4.92% | -1.86% | 1,368 | 3.8% | LD |
| McEwan K | SSP | 1,287 | 4.33% | | 609 | 1.69% | ProLife |
| Taylor T | Scot Ref | 250 | 0.84% | | 345 | 0.96% | SSA |
| | | | | | 107 | 0.3% | Ref |
| **Lab to SNP swing** | **2.78%** | **29,699** | | **Lab maj 7,520** | **36,024** | | **Lab maj 11,128** |
| | | | | 25.32% | | | 30.89% |

**ROSEMARY McKENNA,** b May 8, 1941. Elected 1997. Member, Scottish Affairs Select Cttee, 1997-2001. PPS to Foreign Office team, 1999-. Cumbernauld & Kilsyth district cllr, 1984-96 (leader, 1984-88; provost, 1988-92); N Lanarkshire cllr, 1995-97. Pres, Cosla, 1994-96; exec member, Scottish Constitutional Convention. Chairman, Scotland Europa Brussels, 1995-; member, Cttee of the Regions of EU. Ed St Augustine's Comp, Glasgow; Notre Dame Coll of Ed.

This is the sort of seat which, if located in England, should be reasonably competitive. As a constituency set about 15 miles northeast of Glasgow, it is not. The seat consists of Cumbernauld, a new town, and the smaller and much older settlement of Kilsyth. A very substantial stock of council houses has been sold here over the past two decades, with apparently no impact on voting intentions. The constituency is safely Labour. Map 172

## CUNNINGHAME NORTH                                       Lab hold

| Electorate | %Turnout | | 54,993 | 61.49% | 2001 | 55,526 | 74.07% | 1997 |
|---|---|---|---|---|---|---|---|---|
| **Wilson B** | Lab | **15,571** | **46.05%** | **-4.25%** | **20,686** | **50.3%** | **Lab** |
| Martin C | SNP | 7,173 | 21.21% | 2.77% | 9,647 | 23.46% | C |
| Wilkinson R | C | 6,666 | 19.71% | -3.75% | 7,584 | 18.44% | SNP |
| Chmiel R | LD | 3,060 | 9.05% | 3.53% | 2,271 | 5.52% | LD |
| Scott S | SSP | 964 | 2.85% | | 501 | 1.22% | Soc Lab |
| McDaid Ms L | Soc Lab | 382 | 1.13% | -0.09% | 440 | 1.07% | Ref |
| **Lab to SNP swing** | **3.51%** | **33,816** | | **Lab maj 8,398** | **41,129** | | **Lab maj 11,039** |
| | | | | 24.83% | | | 26.84% |

**BRIAN WILSON,** b Dec 13, 1948. Elected 1987. Min, Industry and Energy, June 2001-; Min of State, FCO 2001; Min of State, Ed and Industry, Scotland Office, 1999-2001. Min of Trade, DTI, 1998-99. Member, Lab election team, 1996-97; spokesman, railways, 1995-96; trade and industry, 1994-95; transport, 1992-94; Scotland, 1988-92. Ex-joint sec, all-party Channel Tunnel grp. Journalist (first winner, Nicholas Tomalin Memorial Award, 1975). Ex-publisher and founding editor, *West Highland Free Press*, 1972. Former adviser, Scottish Professional FA. Ed Dunoon GS; Dundee Univ; Univ Coll of Wales.

An interesting, socially diverse, seat on the West Coast of Scotland. It consists of older, working-class towns such as Ardrossan and Saltcoats, as well as the remnants of a mining community vote. These are balanced against some Tory strongholds along the coast - including the resort of Largs and the Isle of Arran - and in the rural hinterland. These make for a degree of political competition but one firmly biased towards the Labour Party. Map 173

## CUNNINGHAME SOUTH                                       Lab hold

| Electorate | %Turnout | | 49,982 | 56.04% | 2001 | 49,543 | 71.54% | 1997 |
|---|---|---|---|---|---|---|---|---|
| **Donohoe B** | Lab | **16,424** | **58.64%** | **-4.09%** | **22,233** | **62.73%** | **Lab** |
| Kidd B | SNP | 5,194 | 18.54% | -2.24% | 7,364 | 20.78% | SNP |
| Paterson Mrs P | C | 2,682 | 9.58% | -0.5% | 3,571 | 10.08% | C |
| Boyd J | LD | 2,094 | 7.48% | 2.95% | 1,604 | 4.53% | LD |
| Byrne Ms R | SSP | 1,233 | 4.4% | | 494 | 1.39% | Soc Lab |
| Cochrane B | Soc Lab | 382 | 1.36% | -0.03% | 178 | 0.5% | Ref |
| **Lab to SNP swing** | **0.93%** | **28,009** | | **Lab maj 11,230** | **35,444** | | **Lab maj 14,869** |
| | | | | 40.09% | | | 41.95% |

**BRIAN DONOHOE,** b Sept 10, 1948. Elected 1992. Member, Select Cttes: Environment, Transport and Reg Affairs and its Environment and Transport Sub Cttees, 1997-2001; Transport 1993-97. Sec, all-party Scotch whisky grp, 1996-; sec/treas, all-party gardening and horticulture grp. Nalgo official, 1981-92. Ex-convener, Scottish political and educ cttee, AUEW (Tass); sec, Irvine and District Trades Council, 1973-81. Worked, Hunterston power station and ICI organic division as draughtsman, 1969-81. Ed Irvine Royal Acad; Kilmarnock Tech Coll.

This seat is based around the new town of Irvine, the only new town to be established next to the sea. It did not, however, achieve the population total that had been hoped for. This constituency is combined with a number of smaller, traditionally working-class, towns with a heavy stock of council housing. The result is a solidly Labour electorate. Map 174

# CYNON VALLEY
### Lab hold

| Electorate | %Turnout | | 48,591 | 55.48% | 2001 | 48,286 | 69.22% | 1997 |
|---|---|---|---|---|---|---|---|---|
| **Clwyd Ms A** | **Lab** | **17,685** | **65.6%** | **-4.13%** | **23,307** | **69.73%** | **Lab** |
| Cornelius S | PC | 4,687 | 17.39% | 6.76% | 3,552 | 10.63% | PC |
| Parry I | LD | 2,541 | 9.43% | -0.92% | 3,459 | 10.35% | LD |
| Waters J | C | 2,045 | 7.59% | 0.82% | 2,262 | 6.77% | C |
| | | | | | 844 | 2.53% | Ref |
| **Lab to PC swing** | **5.44%** | **26,958** | **Lab maj 12,998** 48.22% | | | **33,424** | **Lab maj 19,755** 59.10% |

**ANN CLWYD,** b March 21, 1937. Elected 1984 by-election. Contested deputy leadership of Lab Party, 1992. Member, Select Cttee, International Development, 1997-2001. Chairwoman, all-party human rights grp, 1997-; Vietnam grp, 1997-; vice-chairwoman, Cambodia grp, 1997-; joint vice-chairwoman, Portuguese grp 1997-. Lab spokeswoman, foreign affairs; asst to John Prescott, dep Lab leader, 1994-95. Broadcaster and journalist. Ed Holywell GS; Queen's, Chester; Univ Coll of Wales, Bangor.
e-mail: clwyda@parliament.uk tel: 020-7219 3437 fax: 01685 871394

This is the smallest of a set of South Wales Valleys constituencies, set between Merthyr Tydfil and the Rhondda at the heart of the old coalfield. It is based on Aberdare, but contains a series of rather similar industrial mining towns snaking up the valley. There is only a modest proportion of Welsh speakers. As a consequence, this is solid territory for the Labour Party. Map 175

# DAGENHAM
### Lab hold

| Electorate | %Turnout | | 59,340 | 46.48% | 2001 | 58,573 | 61.74% | 1997 |
|---|---|---|---|---|---|---|---|---|
| **Cruddas J** | **Lab** | **15,784** | **57.23%** | **-8.47%** | **23,759** | **65.7%** | **Lab** |
| White M | C | 7,091 | 25.71% | 7.17% | 6,705 | 18.54% | C |
| Gee-Turner A | LD | 2,820 | 10.22% | 2.74% | 2,704 | 7.48% | LD |
| Hill D | BNP | 1,378 | 5.0% | 2.51% | 1,411 | 3.9% | Ref |
| Hamilton B | Soc All | 262 | 0.95% | | 900 | 2.49% | BNP |
| Siggins R | Soc Lab | 245 | 0.89% | | 349 | 0.97% | Ind |
| | | | | | 183 | 0.51% | Nat Dem |
| | | | | | 152 | 0.42% | ProLife |
| **Lab to C swing** | **7.82%** | **27,580** | **Lab maj 8,693** 31.52% | | | **36,163** | **Lab maj 17,054** 47.16% |

**JON CRUDDAS,** b April 7, 1962. Elected 2001. Takes over from Judith Church in this solid Lab seat. Deputy political sec, PM, 1999-2001. Chief asst, gen sec Lab Party, 1994-97. Policy adviser, Lab Party, 1989-94. TGWU. Ed Oaklands RC Comp Sch, Portsmouth; Warwick Univ.

This seat neatly reflects a wider series of political events in outer East London. The constituency was once defined by a vast swath of council housing and the dominance of the Ford Motor Company. Much of the council housing has been sold off and the influence of Ford is rapidly waning. The seat edged very close to the Tories during the 1980s but has since swung back to Labour. Map 176

# DARLINGTON
### Lab hold

| Electorate | %Turnout | | 64,328 | 63.35% | 2001 | 65,140 | 73.95% | 1997 |
|---|---|---|---|---|---|---|---|---|
| **Milburn A** | **Lab** | **22,479** | **55.16%** | **-6.41%** | **29,658** | **61.57%** | **Lab** |
| Richmond T | C | 12,950 | 31.78% | 3.48% | 13,633 | 28.3% | C |
| Adamson R | LD | 4,358 | 10.69% | 3.46% | 3,483 | 7.23% | LD |
| Docherty A | Soc All | 469 | 1.15% | | 1,399 | 2.9% | Ref |
| Platt C | Ind | 269 | 0.66% | | | | |
| Rose Ms A | Soc Lab | 229 | 0.56% | | | | |
| **Lab to C swing** | **4.94%** | **40,754** | **Lab maj 9,529** 23.38% | | | **48,173** | **Lab maj 16,025** 33.27% |

**ALAN MILBURN,** b Jan 27, 1958. Elected 1992. Sec of State for Health, 1999-; confirmed, June 2001. Chief Sec, Treasury, 1998-99; Min of State for Health, 1997-98. Member, Lab Treasury team, 1996-97; health spokesman, 1995-96. Member, Public Accounts Cttee, 1992-95; ex-chairman all-party alcohol misuse grp. Senior business development officer, N Tyneside MBC, 1990-92; co-ordinator, trade union studies information unit, Newcastle, 1984-90. Former exec member, Northern region, Lab party; ex-chairman, Newcastle Central CLP. Ed Stokesley Comp; Lancaster Univ.

While most of Co Durham is Labour, this seat is a little more unpredictable. There is no mining legacy to inspire collective solidarity here - indeed, the seat was held by the Tories between 1983 and 1987. It consists of the town itself, by far the largest in the county, and a plusher suburban rural fringe. Despite Labour's apparently easy wins in 1997 and 2001, there will always be a tussle here except in very bad years for either of the main parties. Map177

# DARTFORD · Lab hold

| Electorate | %Turnout | | 72,258 | 61.92% | 2001 | 69,726 | 74.57% | 1997 |
|---|---|---|---|---|---|---|---|---|
| **Stoate H** | **Lab** | | **21,466** | **47.98%** | **-0.63%** | **25,278** | **48.61%** | **Lab** |
| Dunn B | C | | 18,160 | 40.59% | 0.3% | 20,950 | 40.29% | C |
| Morgan G | LD | | 3,781 | 8.45% | -0.83% | 4,827 | 9.28% | LD |
| Croucher M | UK Ind | | 989 | 2.21% | | 428 | 0.82% | BNP |
| Davenport K | FDP | | 344 | 0.77% | 0.22% | 287 | 0.55% | FDP |
| | | | | | | 228 | 0.44% | Ch D |
| **Lab to C swing** | **0.47%** | | **44,740** | **Lab maj 3,306** | | **51,998** | **Lab maj 4,328** | |
| | | | | 7.39% | | | 8.32% | |

**HOWARD STOATE,** b April 14, 1954. Elected 1997. Member, Health Select Cttee, 1997-2001. Co-chairman, all-party pharmacy grp and primary care and public health grp; treasurer, all-party regeneration grp; vice-chairman, all-party asthma grp. Dartford borough cllr, 1989-99. GP tutor at London Univ; former chairman, ethics cttee, Bexley Health Auth. Member, S Thames Reg Graduate Medical Board; Fellow and examiner, Royal Coll of GPs. General practitioner. Ed Kingston GS; King's Coll London.
e-mail: stoath@parliament.uk tel: 020-7219 4571 fax: 020-7219 6820

Dartford is, strictly speaking, in Kent rather than Greater London but it is adjacent to the capital. In political terms it is divided between those parts which are most socially similar to London (notably Dartford itself and Gravesend), which lean strongly towards Labour, and the more rural elements which regard themselves as very much part of Kent and are distinctly Tory. But Labour took the seat in 1997 and hung on in 2001. Map 178

# DAVENTRY · C hold

| Electorate | %Turnout | | 86,537 | 65.5% | 2001 | 80,151 | 77.04% | 1997 |
|---|---|---|---|---|---|---|---|---|
| **Boswell T** | **C** | | **27,911** | **49.24%** | **2.9%** | **28,615** | **46.34%** | **C** |
| Quigley K | Lab | | 18,262 | 32.22% | -2.17% | 21,237 | 34.39% | Lab |
| Calder J | LD | | 9,130 | 16.11% | 1.16% | 9,233 | 14.95% | LD |
| Baden P | UK Ind | | 1,381 | 2.44% | 1.72% | 2,018 | 3.27% | Ref |
| | | | | | | 443 | 0.72% | UK Ind |
| | | | | | | 204 | 0.33% | NLP |
| **Lab to C swing** | **2.54%** | | **56,684** | **C maj 9,649** | | **61,750** | **C maj 7,378** | |
| | | | | 17.02% | | | 11.95% | |

**TIM BOSWELL,** b Dec 2, 1942. Elected 1987. C spokesman, further and higher ed and disabilities, 1999-; Trade and Industry, 1997-99; Treasury matters, 1997. Parly Sec, Min of Agriculture, Fisheries and Food, 1995-97; Under Sec for Ed, 1992-95. Govt whip, 1992. PPS to Peter Lilley, Financial Sec to Treasury, 1989-90. Member, Agriculture Select Cttee, 1987-89; chairman, all-party charity law review panel, 1988-90. Farmer and self-employed partner. Ed Marlborough Coll; New Coll, Oxford.
tel: 020-7219 3520 fax: 020-7219 4919

This is by far the most rural seat in Northamptonshire and, unsurprisingly perhaps, also by far the best territory for the Tories. It consists of scores of villages and a number of smaller towns such as Daventry, Brackley and Towcester. The fact that the area retains some council housing has provided Labour with a core electorate. They are plainly outnumbered, however, by the Tories. Map 179

# DELYN · Lab hold

| Electorate | %Turnout | | 54,732 | 63.28% | 2001 | 53,693 | 74.02% | 1997 |
|---|---|---|---|---|---|---|---|---|
| **Hanson D** | **Lab** | | **17,825** | **51.46%** | **-4.65%** | **22,300** | **56.11%** | **Lab** |
| Brierley P | C | | 9,220 | 26.62% | -0.07% | 10,607 | 26.69% | C |
| Jones T | LD | | 5,329 | 15.39% | 4.92% | 4,160 | 10.47% | LD |
| Rowlinson P | PC | | 2,262 | 6.53% | 2.61% | 1,558 | 3.92% | PC |
| | | | | | | 1,117 | 2.81% | Ref |
| **Lab to C swing** | **2.29%** | | **34,636** | **Lab maj 8,605** | | **39,742** | **Lab maj 11,693** | |
| | | | | 24.84% | | | 29.42% | |

**DAVID HANSON,** b July 5, 1957. Elected 1992. PPS to Prime Minister, June 2001-; to Alistair Darling, Chief Sec to Treasury, 1997-98. Asst govt whip, 1998-99; Parly Under-Sec, Office of Sec State for Wales (formerly Welsh Office), 1999-2001. Member, Select Cttees, Welsh Affairs, 1992-95; Public Service, 1996-97. Ex-sec, all-party prevention of solvent abuse grp. Dir of nat charity, Soc for Prevention of Solvent Abuse, 1989-92; reg manager, Spastics Society, 1982-89. Ed Verdin Comp, Winsford, Cheshire; Hull Univ
e-mail: hansond@parliament.uk fax: 01352 730140

This seat is located in the most northeastern corner of Wales. It has traditionally been an evenly balanced constituency between the more urban aspects (such as Flint) and other coastal and rural regions that were more sympathetic to the Conservatives. The broader drift towards Labour in the 1990s, and a favourable set of boundary revisions for Labour, have made it less competitive. Map 180

## DENTON & REDDISH — Lab hold

| Electorate | %Turnout | | 69,236 | 48.52% | 2001 | 68,866 | 66.92% | 1997 |
|---|---|---|---|---|---|---|---|---|
| **Bennett A** | Lab | | **21,913** | 65.23% | -0.17% | 30,137 | 65.4% | Lab |
| Newman P | C | | 6,583 | 19.6% | -1.72% | 9,826 | 21.32% | C |
| Fletcher R | LD | | 4,152 | 12.36% | -0.92% | 6,121 | 13.28% | LD |
| Cadwallender A | UK Ind | | 945 | 2.81% | | | | |
| **C to Lab swing** | **0.78%** | | **33,593** | Lab maj 15,330 | | 46,084 | Lab maj 20,311 | |
| | | | | 45.63% | | | 44.08% | |

**ANDREW BENNETT,** b March 9, 1939. Elected here 1983; MP for Stockport N Feb 1974-83. Joint chairman, Environment, Transport and Reg Affairs Select Cttee, 1997-2001; chairman of its Environment Sub-Cttee, 1997-2001; chairman, Environment Select Cttee, 1992-97. Member, Select Cttees: Standing Orders, 1992-96; Commons Information Cttee, 1991-97; Statutory Instruments. Sec, backbench civil liberties grp, 1978-. Oldham borough cllr 1964-74. Teacher. Ed Hulme GS, Manchester; Birmingham Univ.
fax: 0161-320 1503

A seat in southern Greater Manchester which has endured a complicated set of boundary revisions over the past two decades. The effect has been to produce a seat with a strong Labour working-class core and a much smaller Tory fringe. That overall strength is perhaps surprising in view of a respectable number of owner-occupiers and a negligible ethnic minority vote. But Labour's majorities in both 1997 and 2001 have been huge. Map 181

## DERBY NORTH — Lab hold

| Electorate | %Turnout | | 76,489 | 57.6% | 2001 | 76,116 | 73.76% | 1997 |
|---|---|---|---|---|---|---|---|---|
| **Laxton B** | Lab | | **22,415** | 50.88% | -2.28% | 29,844 | 53.16% | Lab |
| Holden B | C | | 15,433 | 35.03% | 0.78% | 19,229 | 34.25% | C |
| Charlesworth R | LD | | 6,206 | 14.09% | 5.08% | 5,059 | 9.01% | LD |
| | | | | | | 1,816 | 3.23% | Ref |
| | | | | | | 195 | 0.35% | ProLife |
| **Lab to C swing** | **1.53%** | | **44,054** | Lab maj 6,982 | | 56,143 | Lab maj 10,615 | |
| | | | | 15.85% | | | 18.91% | |

**BOB LAXTON,** b Sept 7, 1944. Elected 1997; contested seat 1992. Member, Trade and Industry Select Cttee, 1997-2001. Derby city cllr, 1979-97 (council leader, 1986-88 and 1994-97). Chairman, NCU, E Midlands district council, 1984-87. Ex-BT telecommunications engineer. Ed Allestree Woodlands Sec; Derby Coll of Art & Tech.
e-mail: laxtonb@parliament.uk www.boblaxtonmp.org.uk
tel: 020-7219 4096 fax: 020-7219 2329

This is a socially mixed seat with a recent history of political competitiveness. It consists of a series of poorer inner-city sections in the north of Derby, which provide the core of the Labour vote, and some residential areas where the Tories have historically prospered. The Tories held the seat from 1983 to 1997 and it is the sort of constituency they would have to regain to form a government; but the past two elections have given them little joy. Map 182

## DERBY SOUTH — Lab hold

| Electorate | %Turnout | | 77,366 | 55.68% | 2001 | 76,386 | 67.84% | 1997 |
|---|---|---|---|---|---|---|---|---|
| **Beckett Mrs M** | Lab | | **24,310** | 56.44% | 0.18% | 29,154 | 56.26% | Lab |
| Spencer S | C | | 10,455 | 24.27% | -0.91% | 13,048 | 25.18% | C |
| Hanson A | LD | | 8,310 | 19.29% | 4.94% | 7,438 | 14.35% | LD |
| | | | | | | 1,862 | 3.59% | Ref |
| | | | | | | 317 | 0.61% | Nat Dem |
| **C to Lab swing** | **0.54%** | | **43,075** | Lab maj 13,855 | | 51,819 | Lab maj 16,106 | |
| | | | | 32.16% | | | 31.08% | |

**MARGARET BECKETT,** b Jan 15, 1943. Elected 1983. Sec of State, Environment, Food and Rural Affairs, June 2001-; Pres of Council and Leader of House, 1998-2001. Sec of State for Trade and Industry, 1997-98. Shadow Trade and Industry Sec, 1995-97; Shadow Health Sec, 1994-95. Dep leader of party, 1992-94, acting leader in 1994 following death of John Smith. Shadow Chief Sec to Treasury, 1989-92. Contested leadership of party, 1994. Ed Notre Dame HS, Manchester and Norwich; Manchester Coll of Science and Tech
tel: 020-7219 5135 fax: 020-7219 2088

This section of Derby has traditionally been the most sympathetic to Labour, although it nearly fell to the Tories in the 1980s. It consists of the core industries of the city - the railway works and Rolls-Royce aero-engines - with some middle-class suburban wards clustered around them. There has been some expansion of private housing but this now seems to be secure Labour territory. Map 183

## DERBYSHIRE NORTH EAST — Lab hold

| Electorate %Turnout | | 71,527 | 58.89% | 2001 | 71,653 | 72.54% | 1997 |
|---|---|---|---|---|---|---|---|
| **Barnes H** | **Lab** | **23,437** | **55.64%** | **-4.82%** | **31,425** | **60.46%** | **Lab** |
| Hollingsworth J | C | 11,179 | 26.54% | 1.33% | 13,104 | 25.21% | C |
| Higginbottom M | LD | 7,508 | 17.82% | 3.49% | 7,450 | 14.33% | LD |
| **Lab to C swing** | **3.08%** | **42,124** | **Lab maj 12,258** | 29.10% | **51,979** | **Lab maj 18,321** | 35.25% |

**HARRY BARNES**, b July 22, 1936. Elected 1987. Member, Select Cttees: NI, 1997-2001; Euro Legislation, 1989-97. Joint vice-chairman, PLP NI Cttee, 1997-. Chairman, all-party Malta grp, 1997-; ex-treas, Central region grp of Lab MPs, 1997-. Member, British-Irish inter-parly body. Joint pres, New Consensus (Britain), 1992- (chairman, 1990-92). Member, MSF. Politics and industrial relations lecturer at Sheffield Univ, 1966-87; previously lectured at North Notts FE Coll. Ex-railway clerk. Lecturer. Ed Easington Colliery Sec Mod; Ryhope GS; Ruskin Coll, Oxford; Hull Univ.

This seat curls around Chesterfield and shares many of the social aspects of that constituency. There are some very solid Labour areas rooted in the legacy of coalmining. These are combined with smaller pockets of Tory-inclined commuters on the edge of the Peak District. It is difficult to envisage the circumstances, however, that would allow Labour to be defeated here. Map 184

## DERBYSHIRE SOUTH — Lab hold

| Electorate %Turnout | | 81,010 | 64.12% | 2001 | 76,672 | 78.21% | 1997 |
|---|---|---|---|---|---|---|---|
| **Todd M** | **Lab** | **26,338** | **50.7%** | **-3.84%** | **32,709** | **54.54%** | **Lab** |
| Hakewill J | C | 18,487 | 35.59% | 4.34% | 18,742 | 31.25% | C |
| Eagling R | LD | 5,233 | 10.07% | 1.05% | 5,408 | 9.02% | LD |
| Blunt J | UK Ind | 1,074 | 2.07% | 1.04% | 2,491 | 4.15% | Ref |
| Liversuch P | Soc Lab | 564 | 1.09% | | 617 | 1.03% | UK Ind |
| Taylor J | Ind | 249 | 0.48% | | | | |
| **Lab to C swing** | **4.09%** | **51,945** | **Lab maj 7,851** | 15.11% | **59,967** | **Lab maj 13,967** | 23.29% |

**MARK TODD,** b Dec 29, 1954. Elected 1997. Member, Agriculture Select Cttee, 1997-2001. Treas, all-party pharmacy grp. Vice-chairman, rural grp of Lab MPs. Cambridge city cllr (leader, 1987-90). Member, Lab Campaign for Electoral Reform; Co-op Party; Greenpeace; MSF. Started Cambridge rock music competition. Businessman. Former UK operations dir of international publishers. Ed Cambridge Univ.
e-mail: mark@marktoddmp.freeserve.co.uk tel: 020-7219 3549 fax: 020-7219 2495

This seat is divided between towns that have a strong sense of their industrial history and remain aligned to the Labour Party, and suburban territory on the edge of Derby which became enthused by Margaret Thatcher in the 1980s. It was represented by Edwina Currie between 1983 and 1997 but a combination of boundary revisions and a strong regional swing ejected her from the Commons. Labour's 2001 majority was down, but still strong. Map 185

## DERBYSHIRE WEST — C hold

| Electorate %Turnout | | 75,067 | 67.39% | 2001 | 72,716 | 78.23% | 1997 |
|---|---|---|---|---|---|---|---|
| **McLoughlin P** | **C** | **24,280** | **47.99%** | **5.89%** | **23,945** | **42.1%** | **C** |
| Clamp S | Lab | 16,910 | 33.43% | -0.08% | 19,060 | 33.51% | Lab |
| Beckett J | LD | 7,922 | 15.66% | -1.81% | 9,940 | 17.47% | LD |
| Bavester S | UK Ind | 672 | 1.33% | 0.48% | 2,499 | 4.39% | Ref |
| Delves N | Loony | 472 | 0.93% | 0.44% | 593 | 1.04% | Ind Green |
| Goodall R | Ind | 333 | 0.66% | | 484 | 0.85% | UK Ind |
| | | | | | 281 | 0.49% | Loony |
| | | | | | 81 | 0.14% | Ind BB |
| **Lab to C swing** | **2.99%** | **50,589** | **C maj 7,370** | 14.57% | **56,883** | **C maj 4,885** | 8.59% |

**PATRICK McLOUGHLIN,** b Nov 30, 1957. Elected 1986 by-election. Opposition Deputy Chief Whip, 2001-; gvt whip, 1995-97. Member, Commons Selection Cttee, 1997-2001; Catering Cttee, 1997-2001. Member, Select Cttees: Procedure, 1995-96; Nat Heritage, 1994-95; Broadcasting, 1994-95. Under-Sec for Trade and Industry, 1993-94; Employment, 1992-93; Transport, 1989-92. PPS to Trade and Industry Sec, 1988-89, and to Min of State for Ed and Science, 1987-88. Ex-mineworker. Ed Cardinal Griffin RC Sch, Cannock; Staffordshire Coll of Agriculture.

This unusual, beautiful constituency has traditionally been regarded as by far the most rural of the Derbyshire seats and thus sympathetic territory for the Tories. It was represented by our own Matthew Parris between 1979 and 1986. It contains only two towns of any size, Matlock and Belper, and some smaller towns such as Ashbourne and Bakewell. The most distinctive features, however, are the scenic tourist attractions of the Peak District. Map 186

## DEVIZES — C hold

| Electorate | %Turnout | | 83,655 | 63.65% | 2001 | 80,383 | 74.69% | 1997 |
|---|---|---|---|---|---|---|---|---|
| **Ancram M** | C | | **25,159** | **47.25%** | **4.43%** | **25,710** | **42.82%** | C |
| Thorpe J | Lab | | 13,263 | 24.91% | 0.67% | 15,928 | 26.53% | LD |
| Frances Ms H | LD | | 11,756 | 22.08% | -4.45% | 14,551 | 24.24% | Lab |
| Wood A | UK Ind | | 1,521 | 2.86% | 1.82% | 3,021 | 5.03% | Ref |
| Kennedy L | Ind | | 1,078 | 2.02% | | 622 | 1.04% | UK Ind |
| Potter Ms V | Loony | | 472 | 0.89% | | 204 | 0.34% | NLP |
| **Lab to C swing** | **1.88%** | | **53,249** | | **C maj 11,896** | **60,036** | | **C maj 9,782** |
| | | | | | 22.34% | | | 16.29% |

**MICHAEL ANCRAM,** b July 7, 1945. Elected here 1992; MP for Edinburgh S 1979-87; Berwick and East Lothian, Feb to Oct 1974. Challenger for the Conservative Party leadership, June 2001. Chairman, C Party, 1998-; Shadow spokesman on the constitution, 1997-98; Min of State for NI, 1994-97; Under-Sec for NI, 1993-94; Under-Sec for Scotland, 1983-87. Privy Counsellor, 1995. Chairman, Scottish C and Unionist Party, 1980-83 and vice-chairman, 1975-80. Dir, Portzim Ltd, family estate co in Roxburghshire. Advocate. Ed Ampleforth; Christ Church, Oxford; Edinburgh Univ.

The creation of an additional seat in Wiltshire required an extensive revision of the boundaries of this constituency, none of which really altered its very solid Tory leanings. Although the market town of Devizes and the more industrial Melksham have manufacturing interests, the core of this constituency rests in smaller towns - such as Marlborough with its public school - and villages set amidst the undulating Wiltshire Downs. Map 187

## DEVON EAST — C hold

| Electorate | %Turnout | | 70,278 | 68.07% | 2001 | 69,094 | 76.06% | 1997 |
|---|---|---|---|---|---|---|---|---|
| **Swire H** | C | | **22,681** | **47.41%** | **4.03%** | **22,797** | **43.38%** | C |
| Dumper T | LD | | 14,486 | 30.28% | 1.15% | 15,308 | 29.13% | LD |
| Starr P | Lab | | 7,974 | 16.67% | -1.01% | 9,292 | 17.68% | Lab |
| Wilson D | UK Ind | | 2,696 | 5.64% | 4.77% | 3,200 | 6.09% | Ref |
| **LD to C swing** | **1.44%** | | **47,837** | | **C maj 8,195** | **52,550** | | **C maj 7,489** |
| | | | | | 17.13% | | | 14.25% |

**HUGO SWIRE,** b Nov 30, 1959. Elected 2001. Inherits seat from Sir Peter Emery. Contested Greenock and Inverclyde 1997. Kensington & Chelsea cllr, 1986 and member of the C fund raising cttee. Dir of Sotheby's; former head of development, Nat Gallery. Ex-Army. Fellow, Royal Soc of Arts. Financial consultant. Ed Eton; St Andrews Univ; Sandhurst.

This is a large constituency with distinct and diverse interests. The towns of Exmouth, Honiton and Tiverton provide many of the electors, but these are supplemented by a host of coastal resort towns, such as Sidmouth and Budleigh Salterton, and small villages. The appealing landscape has attracted many retired people. This in part explains the strength of the Conservative Party. Map 188

## DEVON NORTH — LD hold

| Electorate | %Turnout | | 72,100 | 68.31% | 2001 | 70,350 | 77.94% | 1997 |
|---|---|---|---|---|---|---|---|---|
| **Harvey N** | LD | | **21,784** | **44.23%** | **-6.51%** | **27,824** | **50.74%** | LD |
| Allen C | C | | 18,800 | 38.17% | -1.3% | 21,643 | 39.47% | C |
| Gale Ms V | Lab | | 4,995 | 10.14% | 0.35% | 5,367 | 9.79% | Lab |
| Knapman R | UK Ind | | 2,484 | 5.04% | | | | |
| Bown T | Green | | 1,191 | 2.42% | | | | |
| **LD to C swing** | **2.61%** | | **49,254** | | **LD maj 2,984** | **54,834** | | **LD maj 6,181** |
| | | | | | 6.06% | | | 11.27% |

**NICK HARVEY,** b Aug 3, 1961. Elected 1992; contested Enfield Southgate for L/All 1987. LD spokesman, culture, media and sport, June 2001-; health, 1999-; English regions, 1997-; trade and industry, 1994-97; transport, 1992-94. Chairman, LD Campaigns and Communications Cttee, 1994-99. Member, Trade and Industry Select Cttee, 1993-95. Ex-parly lobbyist. Member, Lib Party Council, 1981-82 and 1984-88; London Lib Party exec, 1984-86. Ed Queen's Coll, Taunton; Middlesex Poly.
tel: 020-7219 6232

This constituency has proved a bastion of West Country radicalism. It was once represented by Jeremy Thorpe, was then captured by the Tories after his arrest in 1978, but returned to the Liberal Democrats in 1992. Much of the electorate comes from the sizeable towns of Barnstaple and Ilfracombe but the bulk of it consists of villages scattered across Exmoor and to the south, where the personal touch is a crucial aspect of electoral politics. Map 189

## DEVON SOUTH WEST        C hold

| Electorate | %Turnout | | 70,922 | 66.13% | 2001 | 69,293 | 76.22% | 1997 |
|---|---|---|---|---|---|---|---|---|
| Streeter G | C | | 21,970 | 46.84% | 3.87% | 22,695 | 42.97% | C |
| Mavin C | Lab | | 14,826 | 31.61% | 2.71% | 15,262 | 28.9% | Lab |
| Hutty P | LD | | 8,616 | 18.37% | -5.38% | 12,542 | 23.75% | LD |
| Bullock R | UK Ind | | 1,492 | 3.18% | 2.25% | 1,668 | 3.16% | Ref |
| | | | | | | 491 | 0.93% | UK Ind |
| | | | | | | 159 | 0.3% | NLP |
| Lab to C swing | 0.58% | | 46,904 | | C maj 7,144 | 52,817 | | C maj 7,433 |
| | | | | | 15.23% | | | 14.07% |

**GARY STREETER,** b Oct 2, 1955. Elected here 1997; MP for Plymouth Sutton 1992-97. Shadow Sec of State, Int Development, 1998-; Shadow Min for Europe, 1997-98; PPS to John Major, 1997; C spokesman, Foreign Affairs, 1997. Parly Sec, Lord Chancellor's Dept, 1996-97. asst gvt whip 1995-96. PPS to Sir Nicholas Lyell, Attorney-General, 1994-95; Sir Derek Spencer, Solicitor General, 1993-95. Member, Environment Select Cttee, 1992-93. Plymouth city cllr, 1986-92. Solicitor. Ed Tiverton GS; Kings Coll, London.
fax: 01752 338401

This seat lying on the southern edge of Dartmoor is an uneasy amalgam of two very different components. The core of it is rural or suburban South Hams. But in 1997 the Boundary Commission added a large section of what locals would rightly regard as the city of Plymouth. These were largely middle-class and the resulting combination has been to entrench the Conservative Party. Map 190

## DEVON WEST & TORRIDGE        LD hold

| Electorate | %Turnout | | 78,976 | 70.51% | 2001 | 75,919 | 77.91% | 1997 |
|---|---|---|---|---|---|---|---|---|
| Burnett J | LD | | 23,474 | 42.16% | 0.32% | 24,744 | 41.84% | LD |
| Cox G | C | | 22,280 | 40.01% | 1.48% | 22,787 | 38.53% | C |
| Brenton D | Lab | | 5,959 | 10.7% | -1.67% | 7,319 | 12.37% | Lab |
| Edwards B | UK Ind | | 2,674 | 4.8% | 1.69% | 1,946 | 3.29% | Ref |
| Quinn M | Green | | 1,297 | 2.33% | | 1,841 | 3.11% | UK Ind |
| | | | | | | 508 | 0.86% | Lib |
| LD to C swing | 0.58% | | 55,684 | | LD maj 1,194 | 59,145 | | LD maj 1,957 |
| | | | | | 2.14% | | | 3.31% |

**JOHN BURNETT,** b Sept 19, 1945. Elected 1997; contested seat 1987. LD spokesman on legal affairs, 1997-. Member, council of Devon Cattle Breeders Soc. Ex-officer, Royal Marine Commandos. Served for 12 years on Law Soc's revenue law cttee. Solicitor; farmer and cattle breeder. Ed Ampleforth Coll; Coll of Law, London.

This is an extremely large seat by English standards, stretching from Clovelly on the North Devon coast, including market towns such as Okehampton and embracing much of Dartmoor. It relies heavily on agriculture, forestry and tourism. The seat has all the ingredients to make a classic South West marginal battleground between the Tories and the Liberal Democrats, with Labour a distant third. It is the Lib Dems who are just in control for now. Map 191

## DEWSBURY        Lab hold

| Electorate | %Turnout | | 62,344 | 58.79% | 2001 | 61,523 | 70.01% | 1997 |
|---|---|---|---|---|---|---|---|---|
| Taylor Mrs A | Lab | | 18,524 | 50.54% | 1.12% | 21,286 | 49.42% | Lab |
| Cole R | C | | 11,075 | 30.22% | 0.13% | 12,963 | 30.09% | C |
| Cuthbertson I | LD | | 4,382 | 11.96% | 1.69% | 4,422 | 10.27% | LD |
| Smith R | BNP | | 1,632 | 4.45% | -0.73% | 2,232 | 5.18% | BNP |
| Smithson Ms B | Green | | 560 | 1.53% | 0.64% | 1,019 | 2.37% | Ref |
| Peace D | UK Ind | | 478 | 1.3% | | 770 | 1.79% | Ind Lab |
| | | | | | | 383 | 0.89% | Green |
| C to Lab swing | 0.50% | | 36,651 | | Lab maj 7,449 | 43,075 | | Lab maj 8,323 |
| | | | | | 20.32% | | | 19.33% |

**ANN TAYLOR,** b July 2, 1947. Elected here 1987; MP for Bolton W Oct 1974-83. Leader of the Commons and Lord President of the Council, 1997-98. Gvt Chief Whip, 1998-2001; chairwoman, Select Cttee, Modernisation; member, Select Cttee, Standards and Privileges, 1995-97; joint Parly Privilege Cttee, 1997-98. Shadow Commons Leader, 1994-97; Shadow Ed Sec, 1992-94; spokeswoman, environmental protection, 1990-92 and education, 1979-81. Lab DoE team, 1981-83. Teacher. Ed Bolton Sch; Bradford and Sheffield Univs.

West Yorkshire did not prove easy territory for Labour in the 1980s. The social profile of this seat would not have indicated that the Tories captured it in 1983 and then held Labour's majority below 1,000 twice afterwards. This woollen town is, though, partly polarised along racial lines (the BNP held its deposit here in 1997). This is likely to prove a competitive constituency despite Labour's apparently firm control at present. Map 192

## DON VALLEY — Lab hold

| Electorate | %Turnout | | 66,244 | 55.3% | 2001 | 65,643 | 66.35% | 1997 |
|---|---|---|---|---|---|---|---|---|
| **Flint Ms C** | **Lab** | | **20,009** | **54.62%** | **-3.64%** | **25,376** | **58.26%** | Lab |
| Browne J | C | | 10,489 | 28.63% | 4.03% | 10,717 | 24.6% | C |
| Smith P | LD | | 4,089 | 11.16% | 1.43% | 4,238 | 9.73% | LD |
| Wilde T | Ind | | 800 | 2.18% | | 1,379 | 3.17% | Ref |
| Cooper D | UK Ind | | 777 | 2.12% | | 1,024 | 2.35% | Soc Lab |
| Ball N | Soc Lab | | 466 | 1.27% | -1.08% | 493 | 1.13% | Green |
| | | | | | | 330 | 0.76% | ProLife |
| **Lab to C swing** | **3.84%** | | **36,630** | | **Lab maj 9,520** | **43,557** | | **Lab maj 14,659** |
| | | | | | 25.99% | | | 33.66% |

**CAROLINE FLINT,** b Sept 20, 1961. Elected 1997. Member, Ed and Employment Select Cttee, 1997-99. PPS to Peter Hain, 1999-. Chairman, all-party childcare grp. Member, Fabian Soc. Editorial advisory board, *Renewal*. Ex-senior researcher/political officer, GMB. Ed Twickenham GS; Richmond Tertiary Coll; East Anglia Univ. e-mail: flintc@parliament.uk tel: 01302 366778 fax: 01302 328833

This South Yorkshire seat surrounds the town of Doncaster and was a significant regional centre for coalmining. It has some very strong Labour wards combined with two less overwhelmingly Conservative districts and a more marginal element. The net effect is to produce a seat which is solidly Labour but not as substantially so as others in urban northern England. Map 193

## DONCASTER CENTRAL — Lab hold

| Electorate | %Turnout | | 65,087 | 52.09% | 2001 | 67,965 | 63.92% | 1997 |
|---|---|---|---|---|---|---|---|---|
| **Winterton Ms R** | **Lab** | | **20,034** | **59.09%** | **-2.97%** | **26,961** | **62.06%** | Lab |
| Meggitt G | C | | 8,035 | 23.7% | 2.74% | 9,105 | 20.96% | C |
| Southcombe M | LD | | 4,390 | 12.95% | 3.53% | 4,091 | 9.42% | LD |
| Gordon D | UK Ind | | 926 | 2.73% | 1.67% | 1,273 | 2.93% | Ref |
| Terry Ms J | Soc All | | 517 | 1.52% | | 854 | 1.97% | Soc Lab |
| | | | | | | 697 | 1.6% | ProLife |
| | | | | | | 462 | 1.06% | UK Ind |
| **Lab to C swing** | **2.85%** | | **33,902** | | **Lab maj 11,999** | **43,443** | | **Lab maj 17,856** |
| | | | | | 35.39% | | | 41.10% |

**ROSIE WINTERTON,** b Aug 10, 1958. Elected 1997. Parly Sec, Lord Chancellor's Dept, June, 2001-. Member, Intelligence and Security Cttee, 1999-2001. Joint chairwoman, all-party lighting grp, 1997-2001. Constituency PA to John Prescott, MP, 1980-86; chief of staff, office of John Prescott, dep leader, Lab Party, 1994-97. Parly officer, Royal Coll of Nursing, 1988-90. Member, TGWU; NUJ; Co-op Party; Amnesty. Ed Doncaster GS; Hull Univ. tel: 020-7219 0925 fax: 020-7219 4581

This seat comprises, as the name implies, the majority of Doncaster's residents. The town has a coalmining heritage but in recent years has acquired a mixed and not unsuccessful economy. There is some Tory territory here but it is overwhelmed by the solidly Labour nature of the town. Map 194

## DONCASTER NORTH — Lab hold

| Electorate | %Turnout | | 62,124 | 50.48% | 2001 | 63,019 | 63.3% | 1997 |
|---|---|---|---|---|---|---|---|---|
| **Hughes K** | **Lab** | | **19,788** | **63.09%** | **-6.71%** | **27,843** | **69.8%** | Lab |
| Kapoor Mrs A | C | | 4,601 | 14.67% | -0.14% | 5,906 | 14.81% | C |
| Ross C | LD | | 3,323 | 10.6% | 2.15% | 3,369 | 8.45% | LD |
| Williams M | Ind | | 2,926 | 9.33% | | 1,589 | 3.98% | Ref |
| Wallis J | UK Ind | | 725 | 2.31% | | 1,181 | 2.96% | AS Lab |
| **Lab to C swing** | **3.28%** | | **31,363** | | **Lab maj 15,187** | **39,888** | | **Lab maj 21,937** |
| | | | | | 48.42% | | | 54.99% |

**KEVIN HUGHES,** b Dec 15, 1952. Elected 1992. Govt asst whip, 1997-2001; Lab whip, 1996-97. Member, European Legislation Select Cttee, 1992-96. Ex-joint vice-chairman, PLP Health and Personal Social Services Cttee until 1996; Ex-sec, all-party personal social services grp. Doncaster borough cllr, 1986-92 (chairman, social services, 1987-92); former sec/agent, Doncaster N CLP. Member, exec cttee, Yorkshire NUM, 1983-86. Miner, 1970-90. Ed local state schs; Sheffield Univ on day release.

This seat is even more powerfully shaped by the influence and legacy of coalmining than its southerly neighbour. The pits might have disappeared but the sense of community solidarity associated with them has not. This is powerful Labour territory. The reputation of the party has been affected locally, however, by a series of apparent scandals concerning the local council. Map 195

## DORSET MID & POOLE NORTH — LD gain

| Electorate | %Turnout | | 66,675 | 65.57% | 2001 | 67,049 | 75.67% | 1997 |
|---|---|---|---|---|---|---|---|---|
| **Brooke Ms A** | | **LD** | **18,358** | **41.99%** | **2.66%** | **20,632** | **40.67%** | **C** |
| Fraser C | | C | 17,974 | 41.11% | 0.44% | 19,951 | 39.33% | LD |
| Selby-Bennett J | | Lab | 6,765 | 15.47% | -0.33% | 8,014 | 15.8% | Lab |
| Mager J | | UK Ind | 621 | 1.42% | | 2,136 | 4.21% | Ref |
| **C to LD swing** | **1.11%** | | **43,718** | | **LD maj 384** | **50,733** | | **C maj 681** |
| | | | | | 0.88% | | | 1.34% |

**ANNETTE BROOKE,** b June 7, 1947. Elected 2001. Takes seat from Christopher Fraser, C, who won newly formed constituency in 1997. Local cllr and campaigner for people with special needs. Partner in small business, dealing in rocks and minerals. Taught economics at colleges and OU for more than 20 years. Ed Romford Tech Sch; LSE; Hughes Hall, Cambridge.

This seat is a slightly artificial amalgamation brought about by the population expansion in the county. It was carved out of four other constituencies although it is dominated by Poole, with its affluent and suburban residents, and the rural electors of middle Dorset. It has enough Conservative and Lib Dem supporters to make for a future of lively local contests; the Tories scraped home in 1997 but in 2001 it was the Lib Dems' turn. Map 196

## DORSET NORTH — C hold

| Electorate | %Turnout | | 72,140 | 66.29% | 2001 | 68,923 | 76.3% | 1997 |
|---|---|---|---|---|---|---|---|---|
| **Walter R** | | **C** | **22,314** | **46.66%** | **2.36%** | **23,294** | **44.3%** | **C** |
| Gasson Miss E | | LD | 18,517 | 38.72% | -0.35% | 20,548 | 39.07% | LD |
| Wareham M | | Lab | 5,334 | 11.15% | 0.92% | 5,380 | 10.23% | Lab |
| Jenkins P | | UK Ind | 1,019 | 2.13% | 0.61% | 2,564 | 4.88% | Ref |
| Duthie J | | Low Excise | 391 | 0.82% | | 801 | 1.52% | UK Ind |
| Bone Mrs C | | Ind | 246 | 0.51% | | | | |
| **LD to C swing** | **1.36%** | | **47,821** | | **C maj 3,797** | **52,587** | | **C maj 2,746** |
| | | | | | 7.94% | | | 5.23% |

**ROBERT WALTER,** b May 3, 1948. Elected 1997. Tory spokesman, Constitutional Affairs and Wales, 1999-2001; Member, Unopposed Bills Panel, 1997-2001; Health Select Cttee, 1997-99; Euro Scrutiny Cttee, 1998-99; vice-chairman, C Agriculture Cttee, 1997-99; sec, C European Affairs Cttee, 1997-99. Visiting lecturer in East-West trade, Westminster Univ. Freeman, City of London. Sheep farmer. Ed Lord Weymouth Sch, Warminster; Aston Univ.
e-mail: walterr@parliament.uk www.walter.tory.org.uk
tel: 020-7219 6981 fax: 020-7219 2608

This seat is predominantly rural but with a reasonable section of commuter electors. It is dominated by a set of small market towns, such as Shaftesbury, Gillingham and Blandford Forum, and open countryside. There is some pleasant scenery such as Cranborne Chase and the Blackmore Vale. The Conservative Party and Liberal Democrats are both competitive but Labour, even in its "new" form, does not have much of a foothold. Map 197

## DORSET SOUTH — Lab gain

| Electorate | %Turnout | | 69,233 | 65.5% | 2001 | 66,318 | 74.16% | 1997 |
|---|---|---|---|---|---|---|---|---|
| **Knight J** | | **Lab** | **19,027** | **41.96%** | **6.02%** | **17,755** | **36.1%** | **C** |
| Bruce I | | C | 18,874 | 41.62% | 5.52% | 17,678 | 35.94% | Lab |
| Canning A | | LD | 6,531 | 14.4% | -5.8% | 9,936 | 20.2% | LD |
| Moss L | | UK Ind | 913 | 2.01% | 0.26% | 2,791 | 5.67% | Ref |
| | | | | | | 861 | 1.75% | UK Ind |
| | | | | | | 161 | 0.33% | NLP |
| **C to Lab swing** | **0.25%** | | **45,345** | | **Lab maj 153** | **49,182** | | **C maj 77** |
| | | | | | 0.34% | | | 0.16% |

**JIM KNIGHT,** b March 6, 1965. Elected 2001. Takes seat from Ian Bruce, C, who held it for 14 years. Contested seat 1997. Stood for Euro Plmnt 1999. Mendip district cllr, 1997; leader, Lab grp, 1999–2000. Frome town cllr, 1995-. Managing dir, Central Studio, Basingstoke, 1988-90; dir, W Wilts Arts Centre, 1990-91 and dir, Dentons Directories, 1991-. Member, Co-op Party; Amnesty; MSF. Worked for touring theatre and in publishing. Ed Eltham Coll; Fitzwilliam Coll, Cambridge Univ.

This seat produced the smallest Tory majority of any in 1997. It consists predominantly of Weymouth, the Portland naval base and the Isle of Purbeck. There have always been pockets of Labour support here, unlike much of the rest of Dorset, but the party has done well to recover from the nadir of the 1980s and achieved its goal to win the seat by a tiny majority in 2001. There is also evidence of a strong Eurosceptic streak among the electorate. Map 198

## DORSET WEST — C hold

| Electorate | %Turnout | | 74,016 | 66.97% | 2001 | 70,369 | 76.1% | 1997 |
|---|---|---|---|---|---|---|---|---|
| **Letwin O** | **C** | | **22,126** | **44.63%** | **3.48%** | **22,036** | **41.15%** | **C** |
| Green S | LD | | 20,712 | 41.78% | 4.07% | 20,196 | 37.71% | LD |
| Hyde R | Lab | | 6,733 | 13.58% | -4.14% | 9,491 | 17.72% | Lab |
| **C to LD swing** | **0.29%** | | **49,571** | | **C maj 1,414** | **53,552** | | **C maj 1,840** |
| | | | | | 2.85% | | | 3.44% |

**OLIVER LETWIN,** b May 19, 1956. Elected 1997. Shadow Chief Sec to Treasury, 2001-. Special adviser to PM's policy unit, 1983-86; and to Sec of State for Ed and Science, 1982-88. Dir, head of utilities and privatisation team and previously manager and asst dir, corporate finance, N M Rothchilds Corporate Finance Ltd, investment banking subsidiary of Rothschild Grp. Editor, *Cambridge Review*, 1978-81. Merchant banker, Cambridge don, financial adviser and journalist. Ed Eton; Trinity Coll, Cambridge; London Business School.

Although most analysts do not consider Dorset to be part of the West Country, there would be a strong case for so describing this constituency. Its towns include Dorchester, Sherborne, Lyme Regis and Bridport, though the seat is the most rural in the county. Despite the presence of Tolpuddle, Dorset West usually sees a vigorous contest between traditional local Toryism and the type of Lib Dem radicalism more commonly associated with parts of Devon. Map 199

## DOVER — Lab hold

| Electorate | %Turnout | | 69,025 | 65.14% | 2001 | 68,669 | 78.93% | 1997 |
|---|---|---|---|---|---|---|---|---|
| **Prosser G** | **Lab** | | **21,943** | **48.81%** | **-5.68%** | **29,535** | **54.49%** | **Lab** |
| Watkins P | C | | 16,744 | 37.24% | 4.41% | 17,796 | 32.83% | C |
| Hook A | LD | | 5,131 | 11.41% | 3.47% | 4,302 | 7.94% | LD |
| Speakman L | UK Ind | | 1,142 | 2.54% | 1.72% | 2,124 | 3.92% | Ref |
| | | | | | | 443 | 0.82% | UK Ind |
| **Lab to C swing** | **5.05%** | | **44,960** | | **Lab maj 5,199** | **54,200** | | **Lab maj 11,739** |
| | | | | | 11.56% | | | 21.66% |

**GWYN PROSSER,** b April 27, 1943. Elected 1997. Member, East Kent Initiative. Trustee, Kent Enterprise Office; dir, Aylesham Community Workshop Trust; trustee, Roman Painted House Trust and Crabble Cornmill Trust. Served on exec cttee, Nat Union of Marine and Shipping Transport Officers; Numast liaison officer representing Sealink chief engineers at Dover. Local opposition grps against Channel Tunnel, 1985-87; parly agent for petitioners against Channel Tunnel Bill, 1986-87. Chartered marine engineer. Ed Swansea Coll of Tech.

This has been described as one of the most diverse seats in the country. It has a political tradition which includes the major Channel ferry port dominated by the White Cliffs, the seaside town of Walmer, a former coalmining area and some attractive surrounding countryside. The strong Labour presence in the centre of Dover made this Labour's best target seat in Kent well before the 1997 election and the party kept control in 2001. Map 200

## DOWN NORTH — UUP gain

| Electorate | %Turnout | | 63,212 | 58.83% | 2001 | 63,010 | 58.03% | 1997 |
|---|---|---|---|---|---|---|---|---|
| **Hermon Lady S** | **UUP** | | **20,833** | **56.02%** | **24.93%** | **12,817** | **35.05%** | **UKU** |
| McCartney R | UKU | | 13,509 | 36.33% | 1.28% | 11,368 | 31.09% | UUP |
| Farrell Ms M | SDLP | | 1,275 | 3.43% | -0.95% | 7,554 | 20.66% | Alliance |
| Robertson J | C | | 815 | 2.19% | -2.76% | 1,810 | 4.95% | C |
| Carter C | Ind | | 444 | 1.19% | | 1,602 | 4.38% | SDLP |
| McConvey E | SF | | 313 | 0.84% | | 1,240 | 3.39% | NI Women |
| | | | | | | 108 | 0.3% | NLP |
| | | | | | | 67 | 0.18% | NIP |
| **UKU to UUP swing** | **11.83%** | | **37,189** | | **UUP maj 7,324** | **36,566** | | **UKU maj 1,449** |
| | | | | | 19.69% | | | 3.96% |

**SYLVIA HERMON,** b Aug 11, 1955. Elected, 2001. Chairwoman N Down Ulster Unionist Assoc, 2001-. Governor, Bangor GS; chairwoman, Trinity nursery sch governors, Bangor, 1993-2001. Sec, Friends of Bangor community hospital; chairwoman, N Down Marie Curie cancer support grp. Law lecturer, Queen's Univ, Belfast, 1978-88. Wife of former RUC Chief Constable, Sir John Hermon. Ed Dungannon Girls' HS; Univ Coll of Wales; Coll of Law, Chester.

This is a very distinctive constituency. It is the most affluent seat in Northern Ireland and the one that most easily resembles a mainland seat, except for the very modest proportion of Roman Catholics. Although there are industrial areas, such as Bangor, the constituency is largely a refuge for Belfast commuters. It elects independent characters of high local standing; the winner in 2001, Sylvia Hermon, is a good example. Map 201

## DOWN SOUTH — SDLP hold

| Electorate | %Turnout | | 73,519 | 70.83% | 2001 | 69,855 | 70.84% | 1997 |
|---|---|---|---|---|---|---|---|---|
| McGrady E | SDLP | | 24,136 | 46.35% | -6.56% | 26,181 | 52.91% | SDLP |
| Murphy M | SF | | 10,278 | 19.74% | 9.38% | 16,248 | 32.83% | UUP |
| Nesbitt D | UUP | | 9,173 | 17.62% | -15.21% | 5,127 | 10.36% | SF |
| Wells J | DUP | | 7,802 | 14.98% | | 1,711 | 3.46% | Alliance |
| Campbell Ms B | Alliance | | 685 | 1.32% | -2.14% | 219 | 0.44% | NLP |
| SDLP to SF swing | 7.97% | | 52,074 | SDLP maj 13,858 | 26.61% | 49,486 | SDLP maj 9,933 | 20.08% |

**EDDIE McGRADY,** b June 3, 1935. Elected 1987, defeating Enoch Powell. Member, NI Assembly, 1998-. SDLP Chief Whip. Former member, NI Affairs Select Cttee. SDLP member for S Down, NI Assembly, 1973-75; Min in NI power-sharing exec, 1973-74; member, NI Constitutional Convention, 1975-76; NI Assembly, 1982-86. First chairman of SDLP, 1971-73, and first chairman of SDLP Assembly Party. Downpatrick cllr, 1961-89 (chairman, 1964-73). Chartered accountant. Ed St Patrick's HS, Downpatrick; Belfast Coll of Tech.

This is a predominantly rural Ulster seat which is better defined by sectarian affiliation than any other social characteristic. It was represented by Enoch Powell from 1974 to 1987 until the changing demographic balance, assisted by boundary revisions, made it impossible for a Unionist of whatever personality or persuasion to retain it. Down South now seems safe for the Social Democratic and Labour Party (SDLP). Map 202

## DUDLEY NORTH — Lab hold

| Electorate | %Turnout | | 68,964 | 55.92% | 2001 | 68,835 | 69.45% | 1997 |
|---|---|---|---|---|---|---|---|---|
| Cranston R | Lab | | 20,095 | 52.11% | 0.92% | 24,471 | 51.19% | Lab |
| Griffiths A | C | | 13,295 | 34.48% | 3.08% | 15,014 | 31.4% | C |
| Burt R | LD | | 3,352 | 8.69% | 0.45% | 3,939 | 8.24% | LD |
| Darby S | BNP | | 1,822 | 4.72% | | 2,155 | 4.51% | Soc Lab |
| | | | | | | 1,201 | 2.51% | Ref |
| | | | | | | 559 | 1.17% | NF |
| | | | | | | 469 | 0.98% | Nat Dem |
| Lab to C swing | 1.08% | | 38,564 | Lab maj 6,800 | 17.63% | 47,808 | Lab maj 9,457 | 19.79% |

**ROSS CRANSTON,** b July 23, 1948. Elected 1997; contested Richmond (Yorks) 1992. Solicitor-General, 1998-2001. Member, Home Affairs Select Cttee, 1997-98. Elected Master of the Bench of Gray's Inn, 1998. Ex-consultant overseas for UN, World Bank and Commonwealth Secretariat. Member, AUT. Visiting Professor, LSE, 1997-. Recorder and QC. Author. Ed Queensland Univ; Harvard; Oxford.
tel: 01384 233100 fax: 01384 233099

This West Midlands seat, centred on the town of Dudley with its castle and zoo and including Sedgley and Coseley, is a partial heir to the old Dudley West constituency. That seat had returned a Conservative to Westminster regularly but was still considered a Labour target. The new borders have since 1997 altered the constituency's dynamics. A relatively high level of council housing provides a solid Black Country base for the Labour Party. Map 203

## DUDLEY SOUTH — Lab hold

| Electorate | %Turnout | | 65,578 | 55.42% | 2001 | 66,731 | 71.78% | 1997 |
|---|---|---|---|---|---|---|---|---|
| Pearson I | Lab | | 18,109 | 49.83% | -6.79% | 27,124 | 56.62% | Lab |
| Sugarman J | C | | 11,292 | 31.07% | 1.64% | 14,097 | 29.43% | C |
| Burt Ms L | LD | | 5,421 | 14.92% | 4.04% | 5,214 | 10.88% | LD |
| Westwood J | UK Ind | | 859 | 2.36% | | 1,467 | 3.06% | Ref |
| Thompson Ms A | Soc All | | 663 | 1.82% | | | | |
| Lab to C swing | 4.22% | | 36,344 | Lab maj 6,817 | 18.76% | 47,902 | Lab maj 13,027 | 27.19% |

**IAN PEARSON,** b April 5, 1959. Elected here 1997; MP for Dudley West 1994-97. Asst govt whip, June 2001. Member, Educ and Employment Select Cttee, 1999-2001; Treasury Select Cttee, 1996-97; Deregulation, 1995-96. PPS to Geoffrey Robinson, Paymaster General, 1997-98. Joint chief exec, W Midlands Enterprise Board, 1991-94; dep dir, Urban Trust, 1987-88; Lab Party local gvt policy research officer, 1985-87. Ed Brierley Hill GS; Balliol Coll, Oxford; Warwick Univ. Visiting Fellow, Univ of Warwick.
e-mail: pearsoni@parliament.uk tel: 01384 482123 fax: 01384 482209

The remainder of the old Dudley West and Dudley East constituencies were fused to create this Black Country seat, which includes Brierley Hill and Kingswinford. It would appear to be slightly the stronger Labour of the two present constituencies, an outcome which is at first sight quite surprising. It holds a higher proportion of owner-occupiers than its neighbours. The Labour sections of the seat are, though, very Labour indeed. Map 204

# DULWICH & WEST NORWOOD

**Lab hold**

| Electorate | %Turnout | | 70,497 | 54.25% | 2001 | 69,655 | 65.49% | 1997 |
|---|---|---|---|---|---|---|---|---|
| **Jowell Ms T** | **Lab** | | **20,999** | **54.9%** | **-6.06%** | **27,807** | **60.96%** | **Lab** |
| Vineall N | C | | 8,689 | 22.72% | -1.48% | 11,038 | 24.2% | C |
| Pidgeon Ms C | LD | | 5,806 | 15.18% | 4.4% | 4,916 | 10.78% | LD |
| Jones Ms J | Green | | 1,914 | 5.0% | | 897 | 1.97% | Ref |
| Kelly B | Soc All | | 839 | 2.19% | | 587 | 1.29% | Lib |
| | | | | | | 173 | 0.38% | Dream |
| | | | | | | 159 | 0.35% | UK Ind |
| | | | | | | 38 | 0.08% | Rizz |
| **Lab to C swing** | **2.29%** | | **38,247** | **Lab maj 12,310** | | **45,615** | **Lab maj 16,769** | |
| | | | | 32.19% | | | 36.76% | |

**TESSA JOWELL,** b Sept 17, 1947. Elected here 1997. MP for Dulwich 1992. Sec of State, Culture, Media and Sport, June 2001-; Min for Employment, 1999-2001. Min for Public Health, 1997-99; deputy to Shadow Health Sec, 1996-97; chief Lab spokeswoman on women's issues, 1995-96. Lab whip, 1994-95. Ex-parly adviser, Royal Coll of Nursing. Dir, community care programme, Joseph Rowntree Foundation, and Visiting Fellow, King's Fund Inst, 1990-92. Ed St Margaret's, Aberdeen; Aberdeen and Edinburgh Univs.
e-mail: jowellt@parliament.uk tel: 020-7219 3409 fax: 020-7219 2702

This southeast London seat was carved out by the Boundary Commissioners as part of their efforts to reduce the capital's overall representation in Westminster. It is a study in contradictions, containing some of the most leafy and desirable districts of the capital along with a sizeable proportion of local authority housing and a substantial non-white population. But like the vast majority of London seats, it seems reliably Labour for the present. Map 205

# DUMBARTON

**Lab hold**

| Electorate | %Turnout | | 56,267 | 60.42% | 2001 | 56,229 | 73.39% | 1997 |
|---|---|---|---|---|---|---|---|---|
| **McFall J** | **Lab Co-op** | | **16,151** | **47.51%** | **-2.1%** | **20,470** | **49.61%** | **Lab** |
| Robertson I | SNP | | 6,576 | 19.34% | -3.89% | 9,587 | 23.23% | SNP |
| Thompson E | LD | | 5,265 | 15.49% | 7.87% | 7,283 | 17.65% | C |
| Ramsay P | C | | 4,648 | 13.67% | -3.98% | 3,144 | 7.62% | LD |
| Robertson L | SSP | | 1,354 | 3.98% | | 283 | 0.69% | SSA |
| | | | | | | 255 | 0.62% | Ref |
| | | | | | | 242 | 0.59% | UK Ind |
| **SNP to Lab Co-op swing 0.89%** | | | **33,994** | **Lab Co-op maj 9,575** | | **41,264** | **Lab maj 10,883** | |
| | | | | 28.17% | | | 26.38% | |

**JOHN McFALL,** b Oct 4, 1944. Elected 1987. Parly Under-Sec, NI Office, 1998-99. Gvt whip, 1997-98. Former opposition whip, responsible for foreign affairs, defence, trade and industry; resigned during Gulf War. Member Select Cttees, Defence, Sittings of the House and Information. Former dep Shadow Sec of State for Scotland; Lab spokesman, Scotland, 1992-97; Lab whip, 1989-91. Chairman, all-party Scotch whisky grp, 1997-; joint vice-capt, parly golfing soc. Ed St Patrick's Sec, Dumbarton; Paisley Coll; Strathclyde Univ; OU.

This is a more socially diverse constituency - on the north side of the Firth of Clyde - than might be expected. It has an industrial core, based on the old dominance of textiles and rooted in the Vale of Leven to the northwest of Glasgow. This influence has to be balanced against the coastal town of Helensburgh, which generally supports non-Labour candidates. The decisive votes are thus cast in Dumbarton itself which leans towards Labour. Map 206

# DUMFRIES

**Lab hold**

| Electorate | %Turnout | | 62,931 | 67.67% | 2001 | 62,759 | 78.92% | 1997 |
|---|---|---|---|---|---|---|---|---|
| **Brown R** | **Lab** | | **20,830** | **48.91%** | **1.4%** | **23,528** | **47.51%** | **Lab** |
| Charteris J | C | | 11,996 | 28.17% | 0.13% | 13,885 | 28.04% | C |
| Ross Scott J | LD | | 4,955 | 11.64% | 0.56% | 5,977 | 12.07% | SNP |
| Fisher G | SNP | | 4,103 | 9.63% | -2.44% | 5,487 | 11.08% | LD |
| Dennis J | SSP | | 702 | 1.65% | | 533 | 1.08% | Ref |
| | | | | | | 117 | 0.24% | NLP |
| **C to Lab swing** | **0.64%** | | **42,586** | **Lab maj 8,834** | | **49,527** | **Lab maj 9,643** | |
| | | | | 20.74% | | | 19.47% | |

**RUSSELL BROWN,** b Sept 17, 1951. Elected 1997. Member, Scottish Affairs Select Cttee and Deregulation Cttee. Galloway UA cllr, 1995- (leader, Lab grp); Dumfries and Galloway reg cllr, 1986-96. Production supervisor, ICI, 1974-97. Ed Annan Acad.
e-mail: russell@brownmp.new.labour.org.uk tel: 020-7219 4429 fax: 020-7219 0922

An often picturesque constituency which is set in the Scottish Lowlands on the north side of the Solway Firth. This has historically been Conservative territory but Labour seized the seat by a surprisingly wide margin in 1997 and kept its hold in 2001. It is divided between a small number of Labour-inclined towns and a large rural and Conservative element. The constituency was especially badly affected by the foot-and-mouth outbreak of 2001. Map 207

## DUNDEE EAST — Lab hold

| Electorate | %Turnout | | 56,535 | 57.24% | 2001 | 58,388 | 69.41% | 1997 |
|---|---|---|---|---|---|---|---|---|
| **Luke I** | **Lab** | **14,635** | **45.23%** | **-5.89%** | **20,718** | **51.12%** | **Lab** |
| Hosie S | SNP | 10,160 | 31.4% | 4.86% | 10,757 | 26.54% | SNP |
| Donnelly A | C | 3,900 | 12.05% | -3.73% | 6,397 | 15.78% | C |
| Lawrie R | LD | 2,784 | 8.6% | 4.46% | 1,677 | 4.14% | LD |
| Duke H | SSP | 879 | 2.72% | | 601 | 1.48% | Ref |
| | | | | | 232 | 0.57% | SSA |
| | | | | | 146 | 0.36% | NLP |
| **Lab to SNP swing** | **5.38%** | **32,358** | | **Lab maj 4,475** | **40,528** | | **Lab maj 9,961** |
| | | | | 13.83% | | | 24.58% |

**IAIN LUKE,** b Oct 8, 1951. Elected 2001. Inherits seat from John McAllion, who stood down to focus on the Scottish Parliament. Member, Scottish policy forum, 1998-2000. Dundee city cllr. Lecturer, Dundee Coll, 1983-. Ed Dundee Univ; Edinburgh Univ and Jordanhill Teacher Training Coll.

The Scottish city of Dundee on the Firth of Tay has long had a distinct political character. This seat was once the SNP's strongest bastion in industrial Scotland, the home of Gordon Wilson, party leader in Westminster from 1974 to 1987. His large personal vote disappeared with him, leaving Labour as the leading party in the 1990s and into the 21st century, with both the SNP and, to a lesser extent, the Tories, capable of making a showing. Map 208

## DUNDEE WEST — Lab hold

| Electorate | %Turnout | | 53,760 | 54.39% | 2001 | 57,346 | 67.67% | 1997 |
|---|---|---|---|---|---|---|---|---|
| **Ross E** | **Lab** | **14,787** | **50.57%** | **-3.22%** | **20,875** | **53.79%** | **Lab** |
| Archer G | SNP | 7,987 | 27.31% | 4.08% | 9,016 | 23.23% | SNP |
| Hail I | C | 2,656 | 9.08% | -4.07% | 5,105 | 13.15% | C |
| Dick Ms E | LD | 2,620 | 8.96% | 1.3% | 2,972 | 7.66% | LD |
| McFarlane J | SSP | 1,192 | 4.08% | | 428 | 1.1% | SSA |
| | | | | | 411 | 1.06% | Ref |
| **Lab to SNP swing** | **3.65%** | **29,242** | | **Lab maj 6,800** | **38,807** | | **Lab maj 11,859** |
| | | | | 23.25% | | | 30.56% |

**ERNIE ROSS,** b July 27, 1942. Elected 1979. Member, Select Cttees: Foreign Affairs, 1997 (resigned, 1999); Standards and Privileges, 1996-97; Ed and Employment, 1996-97; Employment, 1987-96; Standing Orders, 1981-97; Unopposed Bills Panel, 1981-97; Court of Referees, 1987-97. Chairman, PLP Foreign Affairs Cttee, 1987-; joint vice-chairman, PLP Trade and Industry Cttee, 1987-88. Chairman (1988-89) and vice-chairman (1987-88), Scottish grp of Lab MPs. Engineer. Ed St John's Junior Sec, Dundee.
tel: 020-7219 3480 fax: 020-7219 2359

Dundee is the fourth largest city in Scotland. Once the centre of the world's jute-mill industry, it has had to diversify into many smaller manufacturing industries and as a port for the oil industry. This left a legacy of a strongly working-class core in the city surrounded by some affluent, middle-class and traditionally Tory territory. The SNP now competes with the Conservatives for those votes but Labour remains the leading political player. Map 209

## DUNFERMLINE EAST — Lab hold

| Electorate | %Turnout | | 52,811 | 56.97% | 2001 | 52,072 | 70.25% | 1997 |
|---|---|---|---|---|---|---|---|---|
| **Brown G** | **Lab** | **19,487** | **64.77%** | **-2.04%** | **24,441** | **66.81%** | **Lab** |
| Mellon J | SNP | 4,424 | 14.7% | -0.85% | 5,690 | 15.55% | SNP |
| Randall S | C | 2,838 | 9.43% | -0.56% | 3,656 | 9.99% | C |
| Mainland J | LD | 2,281 | 7.58% | 1.66% | 2,164 | 5.92% | LD |
| Jackson A | SSP | 770 | 2.56% | | 632 | 1.73% | Ref |
| Dunsmore T | UK Ind | 286 | 0.95% | | | | |
| **Lab to SNP swing** | **0.60%** | **30,086** | | **Lab maj 15,063** | **36,583** | | **Lab maj 18,751** |
| | | | | 50.07% | | | 51.26% |

**GORDON BROWN,** b Feb 20, 1951. Elected 1983. Chancellor of the Exchequer, 1997-. Shadow Chancellor, 1992-97. Chief Lab trade and industry spokesman, 1989-92; elected to Shadow Cabinet, 1987; Shadow Chief Sec to Treasury, 1987-99; spokesman, reg affairs in Lab DTI frontbench team, 1985-87. Chairman, Scot Lab Party, 1983-84; member, Employment Select Cttee, 1983-85. Privy Counsellor, 1996. Journalist; editor, current affairs dept, Scottish TV, 1980-83; lecturer in politics, Glasgow Coll of Tech, 1976-80. Ed Kirkcaldy HS; Edinburgh Univ.

The Chancellor of the Exchequer represents one of the most solidly Labour seats in Britain. This eastern Scotland industrial seat on the north side of the Firth of Forth, and including Cowdenbeath, once even boasted a Communist tradition. The dominant industry in the seat is, or perhaps was, the Rosyth naval base. The fact that it was run down under the last Conservative Government will only have reinforced the tribal sentiments of the constituency. Map 210

## DUNFERMLINE WEST · Lab hold

| Electorate | %Turnout | | 54,293 | 57.05% | 2001 | 52,467 | 69.44% | 1997 |
|---|---|---|---|---|---|---|---|---|
| **Squire Ms R** | Lab | **16,370** | **52.85%** | -0.23% | **19,338** | **53.08%** | Lab |
| Goodall B | SNP | 5,390 | 17.4% | -1.77% | 6,984 | 19.17% | SNP |
| McPhate R | LD | 4,832 | 15.6% | 1.98% | 4,963 | 13.62% | LD |
| Mackie J | C | 3,166 | 10.22% | -2.42% | 4,606 | 12.64% | C |
| Stewart Ms K | SSP | 746 | 2.41% | | 543 | 1.49% | Ref |
| Harper A | UK Ind | 471 | 1.52% | | | | |
| **SNP to Lab swing** | **0.77%** | **30,975** | | Lab maj 10,980 | **36,434** | | Lab maj 12,354 |
| | | | | 35.45% | | | 33.91% |

**RACHEL SQUIRE,** b July 13, 1954. Elected 1992. Member, Select Cttees on Procedure, 1992-97; European Legislation, 1992-97. PPS to Minister of State for School Standards, 1997-. Chairwoman, PLP Defence Cttee; chairwoman Scottish Policy Forum, 1998-. Member, Nato Parly Assembly, 1997-. Full-time Nupe official, 1981-92, having joined union in 1975; ed officer with responsibility for Scotland, 1985-92. Served on Scottish exec of Lab Party; ex-chairwoman, Linlithgow CLP. Ed Godolphin and Latymer Girls' Sch; Durham and Birmingham Univs.

**This is a less monolithically Labour seat than its eastern neighbour. Encompassing the whole of the town of Dunfermline, it has a higher proportion of homeowners and professional/managerial workers. The local economy is also somewhat more diverse. The seat does, nonetheless, contain a very Labour core while the opposition has been divided fairly evenly over the years between the other three parties. Map 211**

## DURHAM NORTH · Lab hold

| Electorate | %Turnout | | 67,610 | 57.04% | 2001 | 67,891 | 69.48% | 1997 |
|---|---|---|---|---|---|---|---|---|
| **Jones K** | Lab | **25,920** | **67.21%** | -3.05% | **33,142** | **70.26%** | Lab |
| Palmer M | C | 7,237 | 18.76% | 4.25% | 6,843 | 14.51% | C |
| Field Ms C | LD | 5,411 | 14.03% | 2.95% | 5,225 | 11.08% | LD |
| | | | | | 1,958 | 4.15% | Ref |
| **Lab to C swing** | **3.65%** | **38,568** | | Lab maj 18,683 | **47,168** | | Lab maj 26,299 |
| | | | | 48.44% | | | 55.75% |

**KEVAN JONES,** b April 25, 1964 . Elected 2001. Inherits seat from retiring Giles Radice, MP since 1973. Chairman, Northern region, Lab party. Member, chief whip Newcastle upon Tyne City Council, 1990-2001. Senior organiser and political officer, GMB. Ed Portland Comp, Worksop; Newcastle upon Tyne Poly; Southern Maine Univ, US.

**This is an exceptionally strong Labour seat, even by the standards of the county of Durham, which is extremely loyal to the party. The core of this seat is Chester-le-Street and the surrounding working-class villages. The reasonably large number of owner-occupiers here seems to have made no difference to the prevailing partisan sentiment. Map 212**

## DURHAM NORTH WEST · Lab hold

| Electorate | %Turnout | | 67,062 | 58.49% | 2001 | 67,156 | 68.97% | 1997 |
|---|---|---|---|---|---|---|---|---|
| **Armstrong Ms H** | Lab | **24,526** | **62.52%** | -6.25% | **31,855** | **68.77%** | Lab |
| Clouston W | C | 8,193 | 20.89% | 5.56% | 7,101 | 15.33% | C |
| Ord A | LD | 5,846 | 14.9% | 4.12% | 4,991 | 10.78% | LD |
| Hartnell Ms J | Soc Lab | 661 | 1.69% | | 2,372 | 5.12% | Ref |
| **Lab to C swing** | **5.90%** | **39,226** | | Lab maj 16,333 | **46,319** | | Lab maj 24,754 |
| | | | | 41.64% | | | 53.44% |

**HILARY ARMSTRONG,** b Nov 30, 1945. Elected 1987. Gvt Chief Whip, June 2001-; Min for Local Gvt and Housing, 1997-2001. Dep chief spokeswoman on Environment, 1995-97; Treasury spokeswomen, 1994-95. PPS to John Smith, 1992-94; in Lab ed team, 1988-92; member, Select Cttee, Sittings of Commons, 1991-94. Chairwoman, PLP Ed, Science and Arts Cttee, 1987-88; member, NEC, Lab Party; Durham city cllr, 1985-87. Ed Monkwearmouth Comp; West Ham Coll of Tech; Birmingham Univ.
tel: 01388 767065 fax: 01388 767923

**The various sections of this constituency were either based on coalmining (such as Crook and Willington around the Upper Wear Valley) or steel (notably Consett). None of these industries has survived the enforced industrial changes of the 1980s and 1990s. The strong association with Labour, however, has continued without interruption. Map 213**

DUR

## DURHAM, CITY OF — Lab hold

| Electorate %Turnout | | 69,633 | 59.58% | 2001 | 69,340 | 70.86% | 1997 |
|---|---|---|---|---|---|---|---|
| **Steinberg G** | **Lab** | **23,254** | **56.05%** | **-7.25%** | **31,102** | **63.3%** | **Lab** |
| Woods Ms C | LD | 9,813 | 23.65% | 8.39% | 8,598 | 17.5% | C |
| Cartmell N | C | 7,167 | 17.28% | -0.22% | 7,499 | 15.26% | LD |
| Williamson Mrs C | UK Ind | 1,252 | 3.02% | | 1,723 | 3.51% | Ref |
| | | | | | 213 | 0.43% | NLP |
| **Lab to LD swing** | **7.82%** | **41,486** | **Lab maj 13,441** | | **49,135** | **Lab maj 22,504** | |
| | | | 32.40% | | | 45.80% | |

**GERRY STEINBERG,** b April 20, 1945. Elected 1987. Member, Catering Cttee, 1999-2001; Public Accounts Cttee, 1998-2001; Ed and Employment Select Cttee, 1987-98. Chairman, PLP Ed Cttee, 1990-96 (joint vice-chairman, 1988-90); vice-chairman, Northern grp of Lab MPs, 1997-. Adviser, Educational Psychologists Assoc, 1989-99. Headmaster, Whitworth House Special Sch, 1979-87. Durham city cllr, 1975-87. Ex-teacher. Ed Whinney Hill Sec Mod; Johnstone GS; Sheffield Coll of Ed; Newcastle Poly.
www.steinberg.pcrrn.co.uk tel: 0191-3860166 fax: 0191-3830047

Despite its name, the cathedral and university City of Durham's surprisingly small population provides only about half of the electorate in this constituency. The rest consists of working-class villages, often with historic links to coalmining, and a rural fringe. Although the seat flirted with the SDP in 1983, it has returned to previous form as a solid Labour fiefdom. **Map 214**

## EALING ACTON & SHEPHERD'S BUSH — Lab hold

| Electorate %Turnout | | 70,697 | 52.62% | 2001 | 72,078 | 66.68% | 1997 |
|---|---|---|---|---|---|---|---|
| **Soley C** | **Lab** | **20,144** | **54.15%** | **-4.21%** | **28,052** | **58.36%** | **Lab** |
| Greening Miss J | C | 9,355 | 25.15% | -0.66% | 12,405 | 25.81% | C |
| Tod M | LD | 6,171 | 16.59% | 5.85% | 5,163 | 10.74% | LD |
| Grant N | Soc All | 529 | 1.42% | | 637 | 1.33% | Ref |
| Lawrie A | UK Ind | 476 | 1.28% | 0.48% | 635 | 1.32% | Soc Lab |
| Rule C | Soc Lab | 301 | 0.81% | -0.51% | 385 | 0.8% | UK Ind |
| Ng Ms R | ProLife | 225 | 0.6% | 0.05% | 265 | 0.55% | ProLife |
| | | | | | 209 | 0.43% | Glow |
| | | | | | 163 | 0.34% | Ch P |
| | | | | | 150 | 0.31% | NLP |
| **Lab to C swing** | **1.77%** | **37,201** | **Lab maj 10,789** | | **48,064** | **Lab maj 15,647** | |
| | | | 29.00% | | | 32.55% | |

**CLIVE SOLEY,** b May 7, 1939. Elected here 1997; MP for Hammersmith 1983-97; Hammersmith N 1979-83. Chairman, PLP, 1997-; member, Select Cttees: Modernisation of Commons, 1997-2001; NI, 1995-97; Lab spokesman, housing, 1987-92; home affairs, 1984-87; and NI, 1981-84; chairman, all-party parenting grp, 1994-97; vice-chairman, all-party constitution and affairs grp, 1996-97. Chairman, Lab campaign for criminal justice, 1983-88. Ex-probation officer. Ed Downshall Sec Mod, Ilford; Newbattle Abbey Adult Ed Coll; Strathclyde and Southampton Univs.

This West London seat is, even by the standards of the Boundary Commission, an unfortunate amalgamation. The leafy suburbs of Ealing and Acton, which had proved sympathetic to the Conservatives over the years, were combined with the Labour-inclined wards of Hammersmith. The White City council estate as well as Shepherds Bush itself have a significant ethnic minority population. The net effect has been very positive to Labour. **Map 215**

## EALING NORTH — Lab hold

| Electorate %Turnout | | 77,524 | 57.99% | 2001 | 78,144 | 71.31% | 1997 |
|---|---|---|---|---|---|---|---|
| **Pound S** | **Lab** | **25,022** | **55.66%** | **2.0%** | **29,904** | **53.66%** | **Lab** |
| Walker C | C | 13,185 | 29.33% | -7.89% | 20,744 | 37.22% | C |
| Fruzza F | LD | 5,043 | 11.22% | 4.24% | 3,887 | 6.98% | LD |
| Seibe Ms A | Green | 1,039 | 2.31% | 1.41% | 689 | 1.24% | UK Ind |
| Moss D | UK Ind | 668 | 1.49% | 0.25% | 502 | 0.9% | Green |
| **C to Lab swing** | **4.94%** | **44,957** | **Lab maj 11,837** | | **55,726** | **Lab maj 9,160** | |
| | | | 26.33% | | | 16.44% | |

**STEPHEN POUND,** b July 3, 1948. Elected 1997. Member, NI Affairs Select Cttee, 1999-2001. Co-chairman, all-party Scout grp; vice-chairman, British/Polish parly grp. Ealing cllr. Member, Fabian Soc; Co-op Party. RC church lay reader. Ex-housing assoc manager. Interests include Fulham FC and collecting comics. Ed TUC postal studies course; LSE.
e-mail: stevepoundmp@parliament.uk www.stevepound.org.uk
tel: 020-7219 1140 fax: 020-7219 5982

This section of West London has an odd political tradition. It looks like a classic marginal with a social profile much like the theoretical average for the capital. On the other hand, it has witnessed some wild swings between the two major parties. The Tories appear to have benefited from a radical and unpopular Labour council in the 1980s, which to new Labour's relief disappeared in the 1990s; the party's majority actually increased in 2001. **Map 216**

140

## EALING SOUTHALL — Lab hold

| Electorate | %Turnout | | 82,373 | 56.85% | 2001 | 81,704 | 66.88% | 1997 |
|---|---|---|---|---|---|---|---|---|
| **Khabra P** | **Lab** | | **22,239** | **47.49%** | **-12.52%** | **32,791** | **60.01%** | **Lab** |
| Kawczynski D | C | | 8,556 | 18.27% | -2.53% | 11,368 | 20.8% | C |
| Lit A | Sunrise | | 5,764 | 12.31% | | 5,687 | 10.41% | LD |
| Sharma B | LD | | 4,680 | 9.99% | -0.42% | 2,107 | 3.86% | Soc Lab |
| Cook Ms J | Green | | 2,119 | 4.53% | 2.82% | 934 | 1.71% | Green |
| Dhillon S | Community | | 1,214 | 2.59% | | 854 | 1.56% | Ref |
| Choudhry M | Ind | | 1,166 | 2.49% | | 473 | 0.87% | ProLife |
| Brar H | Soc Lab | | 921 | 1.97% | -1.89% | 428 | 0.78% | UK Ind |
| Bhutta M | Qari | | 169 | 0.36% | | | | |
| **Lab to C swing** | **5.00%** | | **46,828** | **Lab maj 13,683** | | **54,642** | **Lab maj 21,423** | |
| | | | | 29.22% | | | 39.21% | |

**PIARA KHABRA,** b Nov 20, 1924. Elected 1992. Member, Select Cttees: International Development, 1997-2001; Members' Interests, 1992-95. Chairman, all-party advance directive grp, 1996-97; treas, Uganda grp. Ealing cllr, 1978-82. Chairman, Indian Workers' Assoc, Southall. Southall Community Law Centre, 1982-. Member, MSF. Social and welfare voluntary worker. Former teacher. Ed Punjab Univ; Whitelands Coll, London.
tel: 020-7219 5010 fax: 020-7219 5699

This is the southwestern part of the London Borough of Ealing. It has an extremely distinctive racial profile. Approximately half the electorate are of Asian descent, although divided between Sikhs and Hindus. The Northcote ward of Southall is approximately 90 per cent Asian, the highest in the country. The constituency remains strongly inclined to the Labour Party. Map 217

## EASINGTON — Lab hold

| Electorate | %Turnout | | 61,532 | 53.65% | 2001 | 62,518 | 67.01% | 1997 |
|---|---|---|---|---|---|---|---|---|
| **Cummings J** | **Lab** | | **25,360** | **76.83%** | **-3.37%** | **33,600** | **80.2%** | **Lab** |
| Lovel P | C | | 3,411 | 10.33% | 1.77% | 3,588 | 8.56% | C |
| Ord C | LD | | 3,408 | 10.32% | 3.1% | 3,025 | 7.22% | LD |
| Robinson D | Soc Lab | | 831 | 2.52% | | 1,179 | 2.81% | Ref |
| | | | | | | 503 | 1.2% | SPGB |
| **Lab to C swing** | **2.57%** | | **33,010** | **Lab maj 21,949** | | **41,895** | **Lab maj 30,012** | |
| | | | | 66.49% | | | 71.64% | |

**JOHN CUMMINGS,** b July 6, 1943. Elected 1987. Member, Select Cttee, Environment, Transport and Reg Affairs, 1997-2001. Lab whip, 1995-97; Northern region, 1994-95. Member, Council of Europe and WEU until 1997. Chairman, all-party Czech and Slovak grp, 1997-. Unpaid parly adviser, National Assoc of Licensed House Managers and Nat Assoc of Cllrs. Easington district cllr, 1973-87;rural cllr 1970-73. Vice-chairman, Coalfields Community Campaign, 1985-87. Mining electrician. Ed Murton Sch; Easington Tech Coll.

This east Durham seat is intensely loyal to the Labour Party. Characterised by large ex-mining villages near the North Sea coast, it was once represented here in 1935 by Ramsay MacDonald, but he was ejected here in 1935 after throwing in his lot with the Tories. He was replaced by Manny Shinwell, a legendary figure within the Labour Party. Political affiliations shaped by coalmining and the class struggle have not altered one iota. Map 218

## EAST HAM — Lab hold

| Electorate | %Turnout | | 71,255 | 52.31% | 2001 | 65,591 | 60.81% | 1997 |
|---|---|---|---|---|---|---|---|---|
| **Timms S** | **Lab** | | **27,241** | **73.08%** | **8.45%** | **25,779** | **64.63%** | **Lab** |
| Campbell P | C | | 6,209 | 16.66% | 0.56% | 6,421 | 16.1% | C |
| Fox Ms B | LD | | 2,600 | 6.97% | 0.45% | 2,697 | 6.76% | Soc Lab |
| Finlayson R | Soc Lab | | 783 | 2.1% | -4.66% | 2,599 | 6.52% | LD |
| Pandhal Ms J | UK Ind | | 444 | 1.19% | | 1,258 | 3.15% | BNP |
| | | | | | | 845 | 2.12% | Ref |
| | | | | | | 290 | 0.73% | Nat Dem |
| **C to Lab swing** | **3.95%** | | **37,277** | **Lab maj 21,032** | | **39,889** | **Lab maj 19,358** | |
| | | | | 56.42% | | | 48.53% | |

**STEPHEN TIMMS,** b July 29, 1955. Elected here 1997; won Newham NE in 1994 by-election. Min of Schools, Dept for Ed and Skills, June 2001-; Financial Sec to Treasury, 1999-2001; Min of State, DSS, 1999; Parly Under-Sec of State, DSS, 1998-99; Member, Treasury Select Cttee, 1995-97; joint Select Cttee on Consolidation Bills, 1994-97; joint vice-chairman, PLP Treasury Cttee, 1995-97. Ed Farnborough GS; Emmanuel Coll, Cambridge.
e-mail: stephen@stephentimmsmp.org.uk www.stephentimmsmp.org.uk tel: 020-7219 4000 fax: 020-7219 2949

This is a staunchly working-class part of the London Borough of Newham, on the northeast side of the capital. The overwhelming majority of the seat consists of terraced housing (the highest proportion of any London seat), but there is a more affluent minority in the southern section in the redeveloped Docklands around the old King George V and Royal Albert Docks and London City Airport. Map 219

141

## EAST KILBRIDE — Lab hold

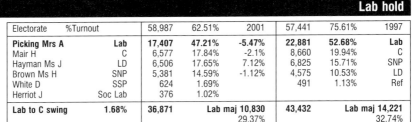

| Electorate | %Turnout | | 66,572 | 62.62% | 2001 | 65,229 | 74.81% | 1997 |
|---|---|---|---|---|---|---|---|---|
| **Ingram A** | **Lab** | | **22,205** | **53.26%** | **-3.27%** | 27,584 | 56.53% | Lab |
| Buchanan A | SNP | | 9,450 | 22.67% | 1.77% | 10,200 | 20.9% | SNP |
| Hawthorn E | LD | | 4,278 | 10.26% | 3.03% | 5,863 | 12.02% | C |
| McCulloch Mrs M | C | | 4,238 | 10.17% | -1.85% | 3,527 | 7.23% | LD |
| Stevenson D | SSP | | 1,519 | 3.64% | | 1,170 | 2.4% | ProLife |
| | | | | | | 306 | 0.63% | Ref |
| | | | | | | 146 | 0.3% | NLP |
| **Lab to SNP swing** | **2.52%** | | **41,690** | **Lab maj 12,755** | | **48,796** | **Lab maj 17,384** | |
| | | | | 30.59% | | | 35.63% | |

**ADAM INGRAM,** b Feb 1, 1947. Elected 1987. Min of State, Defence, June 2001-; Min for Security and Economic Development, NI Office, 1997-2001. Lab spokesman, trade and industry, 1995-97, responsible for science and tech; social security spokesman, 1993-95. PPS to Neil Kinnock, Lab leader, 1988-92. Member, Trade and Industry Select Cttee, 1992-93. Joint vice-chairman, Japanese grp, 1992-97; Lab whip, 1988. Ed Cranhill Sec.
e-mail: adam-ingram@compuserve.com tel: 01355 235343 fax: 01355 265252

As a Scottish new town with a substantial section of rural voters, a majority of owner-occupiers and relatively low unemployment, this seat situated south of Glasgow might be considered to be potentially competitive. And, by the standards of Glasgow, it is. But Labour remains the dominant actor here, with a solid base among council tenants, and the others scrambling for second place. Map 220

## EAST LOTHIAN — Lab hold

| Electorate | %Turnout | | 58,987 | 62.51% | 2001 | 57,441 | 75.61% | 1997 |
|---|---|---|---|---|---|---|---|---|
| **Picking Mrs A** | **Lab** | | **17,407** | **47.21%** | **-5.47%** | 22,881 | 52.68% | Lab |
| Mair H | C | | 6,577 | 17.84% | -2.1% | 8,660 | 19.94% | C |
| Hayman Ms J | LD | | 6,506 | 17.65% | 7.12% | 6,825 | 15.71% | SNP |
| Brown Ms H | SNP | | 5,381 | 14.59% | -1.12% | 4,575 | 10.53% | LD |
| White D | SSP | | 624 | 1.69% | | 491 | 1.13% | Ref |
| Herriot J | Soc Lab | | 376 | 1.02% | | | | |
| **Lab to C swing** | **1.68%** | | **36,871** | **Lab maj 10,830** | | **43,432** | **Lab maj 14,221** | |
| | | | | 29.37% | | | 32.74% | |

**ANNE PICKING,** b March 30, 1958. Elected 2001. Inherits seat from John Home Robertson, who represented East Lothian since winning 1978 by-election. Nat Pres, Unison. Lab NEC trade union member; former grp chairwoman, Ashford Lab Party, 1994-98. Nursing sister, Lynebank Hosp, 1985-2001. Ed Woodmill HS.

This seat, stretching east from Edinburgh with ex-mining communities nearer the city and farming and tourist areas nearer the North Sea, has been redesigned several times by the Boundary Commission. It has responded by producing some quirky election results. It now seems to have settled, however, into a more orthodox political pattern. Labour is the dominant force with the other three parties engaging in a lively contest for a distant second place. Map 221

## EASTBOURNE — C hold

| Electorate | %Turnout | | 73,784 | 60.68% | 2001 | 72,347 | 72.8% | 1997 |
|---|---|---|---|---|---|---|---|---|
| **Waterson N** | **C** | | **19,738** | **44.09%** | **1.97%** | 22,183 | 42.12% | C |
| Berry C | LD | | 17,584 | 39.28% | 0.95% | 20,189 | 38.33% | LD |
| Roles Ms G | Lab | | 5,967 | 13.33% | 0.84% | 6,576 | 12.49% | Lab |
| Jones B | UK Ind | | 907 | 2.03% | 1.55% | 2,724 | 5.17% | Ref |
| Williamson Ms T | Lib | | 574 | 1.28% | -0.13% | 741 | 1.41% | Lib |
| | | | | | | 254 | 0.48% | UK Ind |
| **LD to C swing** | **0.51%** | | **44,770** | **C maj 2,154** | | **52,667** | **C maj 1,994** | |
| | | | | 4.81% | | | 3.79% | |

**NIGEL WATERSON,** b Oct 12, 1950. Elected 1992; contested Islington S and Finsbury 1979. Shadow Min Housing and Local Gvt, 1999-. Opposition whip, 1997-. Member, Select Cttee, Nat Heritage, 1995-96; vice-chairman C Backbench Transport Cttee, 1992-97; sec, C Backbench Shipping and Shipbuilding Cttee, 1992-97. PPS to Deputy PM Michael Heseltine, 1996; and to Gerald Malone, Health Min, 1995. Chairman, Bow Grp, 1986-87 (hon patron, 1993-85). Cllr, London Borough of Hammersmith, 1974-78. Solicitor. Ed Leeds GS; Queen's Coll, Oxford (Pres, univ C Assoc).

This seat is an attractive East Sussex coastal resort, once utterly loyal to the Conservative Party but now somewhat more competitive. The constituency is one of the three in the country with the highest proportion of retired people, who are overwhelmingly Tory. But the Liberal Democrats won the seat in a sensational by-election result in 1990. They have managed to maintain a healthy presence since then despite the Tory dominance. Map 222

## EASTLEIGH — LD hold

| Electorate | %Turnout | | 74,603 | 63.77% | 2001 | 72,155 | 76.91% | 1997 |
|---|---|---|---|---|---|---|---|---|
| Chidgey D | | LD | 19,360 | 40.7% | 5.65% | 19,453 | 35.05% | LD |
| Burns C | | C | 16,302 | 34.27% | 0.57% | 18,699 | 33.7% | C |
| Jaffa S | | Lab | 10,426 | 21.92% | -4.9% | 14,883 | 26.82% | Lab |
| Challis S | | UK Ind | 849 | 1.78% | 0.98% | 2,013 | 3.63% | Ref |
| Lyn Ms M | | Green | 636 | 1.34% | | 446 | 0.8% | UK Ind |
| C to LD swing | 2.54% | | 47,573 | LD maj 3,058 | | 55,494 | LD maj 754 | |
| | | | | 6.43% | | | 1.35% | |

**DAVID CHIDGEY,** b July 9, 1942. Elected 1994 by-election. LD spokesman, trade and industry, 1997-99, transport, 1995-97; employment, 1994-95.Winchester city cllr, 1987-90; Alresford town cllr, 1975-83. Assoc partner, Brian Colquhoun and Partners, consulting engineers, responsible for Southern region, 1988-93; with Thorburn Colquhoun as assoc dir, southern England, and project dir, engineering facilities management, Hampshire, 1994. Non-practising consulting civil engineer. Ed Brune Park Cty HS, Gosport; RNC Portsmouth; Portsmouth Poly.

An industrial Hampshire town outside Southampton whose social profile has always been distinct from more rural sections of the county. There is a working-class base and there are large numbers of electors who commute into the nearby port city. The Tories were strong in the 1980s here, but not by crushing margins. The Lib Dems seized the seat in a 1994 by-election, were able to hang on - just - in 1997, and increased their lead in 2001. Map 223

## EASTWOOD — Lab hold

| Electorate | %Turnout | | 68,378 | 70.74% | 2001 | 66,697 | 78.32% | 1997 |
|---|---|---|---|---|---|---|---|---|
| Murphy J | | Lab | 23,036 | 47.63% | 7.88% | 20,766 | 39.75% | Lab |
| Robertson R | | C | 13,895 | 28.73% | -4.83% | 17,530 | 33.56% | C |
| Steele A | | LD | 6,239 | 12.9% | 1.2% | 6,826 | 13.07% | SNP |
| Maxwell S | | SNP | 4,137 | 8.55% | -4.52% | 6,110 | 11.7% | LD |
| Murray P | | SSP | 814 | 1.68% | | 497 | 0.95% | Ref |
| Tayan Dr M | | Ind | 247 | 0.51% | | 393 | 0.75% | ProLife |
| | | | | | | 113 | 0.22% | UK Ind |
| C to Lab swing | 6.35% | | 48,368 | Lab maj 9,141 | | 52,235 | Lab maj 3,236 | |
| | | | | 18.90% | | | 6.19% | |

**JIM MURPHY,** b Aug 23, 1967. Elected 1997. PPS to Helen Liddell, Sec of State for Scotland, 2001-. Member, Public Accounts Select Cttee. Pres, NUS, 1994-96; NUS (Scotland) 1992-94. Member, GMB; Co-op Party. Ex-projects manager, Scottish Lab Party, 1996-97. Dir, Endsleigh Investments, 1994-96. Ed Bellarmine Sec, Glasgow; Milnerton HS, Cape Town; Strathclyde Univ.
e-mail: murphyj@parliament.uk

This is a very middle-class Scottish constituency lying to the southwest of Glasgow. About four in five voters own their homes and there are a large number of commuters. If it were in England it would surely be securely Conservative and until 1997 it was the safest Tory seat in Scotland. It then fell to the Labour Party in what was, even by the standards of that year, an exceptional swing; and in 2001 Labour actually increased its lead. Map 224

## ECCLES — Lab hold

| Electorate | %Turnout | | 68,764 | 48.25% | 2001 | 69,645 | 65.6% | 1997 |
|---|---|---|---|---|---|---|---|---|
| Stewart I | | Lab | 21,395 | 64.48% | -2.2% | 30,468 | 66.68% | Lab |
| Caillard P | | C | 6,867 | 20.69% | 1.97% | 8,552 | 18.72% | C |
| Boyd B | | LD | 4,920 | 14.83% | 4.09% | 4,905 | 10.74% | LD |
| | | | | | | 1,765 | 3.86% | Ref |
| Lab to C swing | 2.09% | | 33,182 | Lab maj 14,528 | | 45,690 | Lab maj 21,916 | |
| | | | | 43.78% | | | 47.96% | |

**IAN STEWART,** b Aug 28, 1950. Elected 1997. Member, Select Cttees: Deregulation, 1997-2001; Information, 1998-2001. Chairman, parly grp, Vaccine Damaged Children, 1998-. Joint vice-chairman, all-party China grp, 1997-. TGWU reg officer, 1978-97. TUC dir for Salford Compact Partnership. Ed Calder Street Sec, Blantyre; Irlam HS, Manchester; Stretford Tech Coll; Manchester Metropolitan Univ.

Lying on the banks of the Manchester Ship Canal, this is the central of three seats in the Greater Manchester borough of Salford. It is an industrial and working-class community with a smaller middle class which commutes into Manchester. It is most famous for the eponymous cakes. It is not at all famous for electing candidates other than those who represent the Labour Party. Map 225

## EDDISBURY                                                                 C hold

| Electorate | %Turnout | | 69,181 | 64.16% | 2001 | 65,256 | 75.78% | 1997 |
|---|---|---|---|---|---|---|---|---|
| O'Brien S | C | | 20,556 | 46.31% | 3.79% | 21,027 | 42.52% | C |
| Eyres B | Lab | | 15,988 | 36.02% | -4.11% | 19,842 | 40.13% | Lab |
| Roberts P | LD | | 6,975 | 15.71% | 2.48% | 6,540 | 13.23% | LD |
| Carson D | UK Ind | | 868 | 1.96% | | 2,041 | 4.13% | Ref |
| Lab to C swing | 3.95% | | 44,387 | | C maj 4,568 | 49,450 | | C maj 1,185 |
| | | | | | 10.29% | | | 2.39% |

**STEPHEN O'BRIEN,** b April 1, 1957. Elected 1999 by-election. PPS to Michael Ancram, C Party chairman, 2001-. Member, Ed and Employment Select Cttee. Presented Private Member's Bill, Food Labelling, 1999-2000. Member, Shadow Foreign Affairs team. Solicitor. Ed Loretto Sch, Mombasa, Kenya; Handbridge Sch, Chester; Heronwater Sch, Abergele, N Wales; Sedbergh Sch, Cumbria; Emmanuel Coll, Cambridge; Coll of Law, Chester.
*Details of 1999 by-election on page 291*

This is the largest seat in Cheshire, with no single dominant settlement but a network of smaller towns and villages. The largest town is Winsford, formerly famous for rock-salt mines, which has traditionally been aligned with Labour. The rest of the seat is much more sympathetic to the Tories. The Conservatives, nonetheless, nearly managed to lose this seat in both 1997 and a 1999 by-election, though they reaffirmed their grip in 2001 . Map 226

## EDINBURGH CENTRAL                                                          Lab hold

| Electorate | %Turnout | | 66,089 | 52.04% | 2001 | 63,695 | 67.09% | 1997 |
|---|---|---|---|---|---|---|---|---|
| Darling A | Lab | | 14,495 | 42.15% | -4.94% | 20,125 | 47.09% | Lab |
| Myles A | LD | | 6,353 | 18.47% | 5.35% | 9,055 | 21.19% | C |
| Orr A | C | | 5,643 | 16.41% | -4.78% | 6,750 | 15.8% | SNP |
| McKee Dr I | SNP | | 4,832 | 14.05% | -1.75% | 5,605 | 13.12% | LD |
| Farmer G | Green | | 1,809 | 5.26% | 3.84% | 607 | 1.42% | Green |
| Williamson K | SSP | | 1,258 | 3.66% | | 495 | 1.16% | Ref |
| | | | | | | 98 | 0.23% | Ind Dem |
| Lab to LD swing | 5.15% | | 34,390 | | Lab maj 8,142 | 42,735 | | Lab maj 11,070 |
| | | | | | 23.68% | | | 25.90% |

**ALISTAIR DARLING,** b Nov 28, 1953. Elected 1987. Sec of State, Work and Pensions, June 2001-. Sec of State, Social Security, 1998-2001; Chief Sec to the Treasury, 1997-98; Shadow Chief Sec to Treasury, 1996-97;Treasury and economic affairs team, 1992-96, as spokesman on the City; spokesman on home affairs, 1988-92. Member, Lab working party on electoral systems, 1990. Lothian reg cllr, 1982-87; member, Lothian and Borders police board, 1982-86. Trustee (unpaid), Nat Library of Scotland. Non-practising advocate. Ed Loretto Sch; Aberdeen Univ.

The city of Edinburgh was obliged to lose one of its seats in the 1980s. As a consequence this seat, which includes most of the historic Old Town centre and the 18th-century terraces and squares of the New Town, was created. The latter provided a large slice of Tory voters. These were removed by boundary changes in the 1990s, making it somewhat safer for the Labour Party. It remains, however, a diverse and unpredictable electorate. Map 227

## EDINBURGH EAST & MUSSELBURGH                                               Lab hold

| Electorate | %Turnout | | 59,241 | 58.16% | 2001 | 59,648 | 70.61% | 1997 |
|---|---|---|---|---|---|---|---|---|
| Strang Dr G | Lab | | 18,124 | 52.6% | -0.97% | 22,564 | 53.57% | Lab |
| Munn R | SNP | | 5,956 | 17.29% | -1.78% | 8,034 | 19.07% | SNP |
| Peacock G | LD | | 4,981 | 14.46% | 3.75% | 6,483 | 15.39% | C |
| Finnie P | C | | 3,906 | 11.34% | -4.05% | 4,511 | 10.71% | LD |
| Durkin D | SSP | | 1,487 | 4.32% | | 526 | 1.25% | Ref |
| SNP to Lab swing | 0.41% | | 34,454 | | Lab maj 12,168 | 42,118 | | Lab maj 14,530 |
| | | | | | 35.32% | | | 34.50% |

**GAVIN STRANG,** b July 10, 1943. Elected here 1997; MP for Edinburgh E, 1970-79. Min for Transport, 1997-98. Joined Shadow Cabinet, 1994; chief Lab spokesman, agriculture and rural affairs, 1992-97; employment, 1987-89; agriculture, fisheries and food, 1979-82. Chairman, all-party grp for World Gvt, 2000-. Member, Agriculture Select Cttee, 1991-93 and 1984-87. Parly Sec, Min of Agriculture, Fisheries and Food, 1974-79.Officer, PLP CND grp, 1982-86. Agricultural scientist. Ed Morrison's Acad; Edinburgh Univ; Churchill Coll, Cambridge.

This is a diverse seat, as is true for a number of the Edinburgh constituencies. It comprises the south and east of the city proper, combined with a number of suburban areas. But as is so often true in Scottish politics this apparent variety disguises cruder political truths. Those parts of the city of Edinburgh represented here are very loyal to the Labour Party and that attitude is the most important aspect of local politics. Map 228

144

## EDINBURGH NORTH & LEITH
**Lab hold**

| Electorate | %Turnout | | 62,475 | 53.2% | 2001 | 61,617 | 66.45% | 1997 |
|---|---|---|---|---|---|---|---|---|
| **Lazarowicz M** | Lab | | 15,271 | 45.95% | -0.96% | 19,209 | 46.91% | Lab |
| Tombs S | LD | | 6,454 | 19.42% | 6.39% | 8,231 | 20.1% | SNP |
| Stewart Ms K | SNP | | 5,290 | 15.92% | -4.18% | 7,312 | 17.86% | C |
| Mitchell I | C | | 4,626 | 13.92% | -3.94% | 5,335 | 13.03% | LD |
| Grant Ms C | SSP | | 1,334 | 4.01% | | 441 | 1.08% | Ref |
| Jacobsen D | Soc Lab | | 259 | 0.78% | | 320 | 0.78% | SSA |
| | | | | | | 97 | 0.24% | NLP |
| **Lab to LD swing** | **3.67%** | | **33,234** | | **Lab maj 8,817** | **40,945** | | **Lab maj 10,978** |
| | | | | | 26.53% | | | 26.81% |

**MARK LAZAROWICZ,** b Aug 8, 1953. Elected 2001. Inherits seat from Malcolm Chisholm, who is concentrating on his role in the Scottish Parliament. Contested Edinburgh Pentlands 1987 and 1992. Former leader, Lab grp, Edinburgh City Council; member, Transport Cttee, 1999-. Ed St Andrews and Edinburgh Univs.

As in many other seats in this part of Scotland, a thoroughly diverse set of social groups are thrown together here but with the same end result, a Labour MP. Leith is the main port for Edinburgh and has been spruced up over recent years. The northern parts of Edinburgh consist partly of gentrified communities but also of distinctly grim council estates. Labour could be seriously challenged if a single alternative emerged, but so far none has. Map 229

## EDINBURGH PENTLANDS
**Lab hold**

| Electorate | %Turnout | | 59,841 | 65.06% | 2001 | 59,635 | 76.7% | 1997 |
|---|---|---|---|---|---|---|---|---|
| **Clark Dr L** | Lab | | 15,797 | 40.58% | -2.43% | 19,675 | 43.01% | Lab |
| Rifkind Sir M | C | | 14,055 | 36.1% | 3.72% | 14,813 | 32.38% | C |
| Walker D | LD | | 4,210 | 10.81% | 0.81% | 5,952 | 13.01% | SNP |
| Gibb S | SNP | | 4,210 | 10.81% | -2.2% | 4,575 | 10.0% | LD |
| Mearns J | SSP | | 555 | 1.43% | | 422 | 0.92% | Ref |
| McMurdo W | UK Ind | | 105 | 0.27% | 0.09% | 224 | 0.49% | Green |
| | | | | | | 81 | 0.18% | UK Ind |
| **Lab to C swing** | **3.08%** | | **38,932** | | **Lab maj 1,742** | **45,742** | | **Lab maj 4,862** |
| | | | | | 4.47% | | | 10.63% |

**LYNDA CLARK,** b Feb 26, 1949. Elected 1997; contested Fife NE, 1992. Advocate-General for Scotland, 1999-; confirmed June 2001. QC (Scot). Appointed QC, 1989; admitted advocate, Scottish Bar, 1977; called to English Bar, Inner Temple, 1988; law lecturer, Dundee Univ, 1973-76. Member, court, Edinburgh Univ until Sept 1997; Scottish Legal Aid Board, 1991-94. Ed Lawside Acad, Dundee; St Andrews and Edinburgh Univs.

This seat is one of the most socially polarised in Britain. It would appear, at first sight, to be a haven of the Edinburgh middle class and therefore natural territory for the Conservatives. These plush surroundings have to be balanced against a mass of solidly Labour council housing. Malcolm Rifkind, then Foreign Secretary, lost the seat in 1997 and only narrowly failed to regain it in 2001. Map 230

## EDINBURGH SOUTH
**Lab hold**

| Electorate | %Turnout | | 64,012 | 58.06% | 2001 | 62,467 | 71.78% | 1997 |
|---|---|---|---|---|---|---|---|---|
| **Griffiths N** | Lab | | 15,671 | 42.16% | -4.66% | 20,993 | 46.82% | Lab |
| MacLaren Ms M | LD | | 10,172 | 27.37% | 9.73% | 9,541 | 21.28% | C |
| Buchan G | C | | 6,172 | 16.61% | -4.67% | 7,911 | 17.64% | LD |
| Williams Ms H | SNP | | 3,683 | 9.91% | -3.01% | 5,791 | 12.92% | SNP |
| Fox C | SSP | | 933 | 2.51% | | 504 | 1.12% | Ref |
| Hendry Ms L | LCA | | 535 | 1.44% | | 98 | 0.22% | NLP |
| **Lab to LD swing** | **7.19%** | | **37,166** | | **Lab maj 5,499** | **44,838** | | **Lab maj 11,452** |
| | | | | | 14.80% | | | 25.54% |

**NIGEL GRIFFITHS,** b May 20, 1955. Elected 1987. Under-Sec of State, DTI, June 2001-; Min for Consumer Affairs, Trade and Industry Dept, 1997. Member, Public Accounts Cttee, 1998-2001; Procedures Cttee, 1998-2001; chairman, Scottish Charities Kosovo Appeal, 1999-; HEAT (Home Energy Action Team); the New Deal pilot project, 1999-. Lab spokesman, consumer affairs, 1989-97; Lab whip, 1987-89. Ex-joint chairman, all-party street children grp. Ed Hawick Comp; Edinburgh Univ; Moray Coll of Ed.
e-mail: ngriffithsmp@parliament.uk

This seat summarises many of the reasons why Scottish politics differs so much from what would be expected in England. This is comfortable residential territory - indeed the seat is often called the home of the Scottish Establishment. It was once a Conservative bastion. But as matters stand, it is Labour, or at least a branch of that party, which is the natural home of the local Establishment. This is reflected in voting patterns here. Map 231

## EDINBURGH WEST — LD hold

| Electorate | %Turnout | | 61,895 | 63.78% | 2001 | 61,133 | 77.91% | 1997 |
|---|---|---|---|---|---|---|---|---|
| **Barrett J** | | **LD** | **16,719** | **42.35%** | **-0.85%** | **20,578** | **43.2%** | **LD** |
| Alexandra Ms E | | Lab | 9,130 | 23.13% | 4.34% | 13,325 | 27.98% | C |
| Whyte I | | C | 8,894 | 22.53% | -5.45% | 8,948 | 18.79% | Lab |
| Smith A | | SNP | 4,047 | 10.25% | 1.41% | 4,210 | 8.84% | SNP |
| Scott B | | SSP | 688 | 1.74% | | 277 | 0.58% | Ref |
| | | | | | | 263 | 0.55% | Lib |
| | | | | | | 30 | 0.06% | AS |
| **LD to Lab swing** | | **2.59%** | **39,478** | | **LD maj 7,589** **19.22%** | **47,631** | | **LD maj 7,253** **15.22%** |

**JOHN BARRETT,** b Feb 11, 1954. Elected 2001. Takes over seat from Donald Gorrie, who stood down to concentrate on his role in the Scottish Parliament. Contested Linlithgow, Scottish Parliament 1999. Acted as Mr Gorrie's election agent, 1997. Edinburgh city cllr. Vice-president, Scottish Lib Club. Convener, Lothian reg LD Party, 1997-2000. Dir, Edinburgh International Film Festival, 1995-; Edinburgh and Lothian Screen Industries Office; the Edinburgh Filmhouse, 1997-2001. Company dir. Ed Telford Coll, Edinburgh; Napier Poly.

Another posh Edinburgh constituency which resolutely refuses to behave as an English seat with a similar social profile undoubtedly would. The difference here, however, is that the Liberal Democrats rather than Labour have become the preferred vehicle of anti-Conservative sentiment. This was a very marginal seat, held by the Conservatives for much of the Thatcher period. The Liberal Democrats now seem securely established. Map 232

## EDMONTON — Lab hold

| Electorate | %Turnout | | 62,294 | 55.82% | 2001 | 63,718 | 70.37% | 1997 |
|---|---|---|---|---|---|---|---|---|
| **Love A** | **Lab Co-op** | | **20,481** | **58.9%** | **-1.38%** | **27,029** | **60.28%** | **Lab** |
| Burrowes D | C | | 10,709 | 30.8% | 0.56% | 13,557 | 30.24% | C |
| Taylor D | LD | | 2,438 | 7.01% | 0.66% | 2,847 | 6.35% | LD |
| Rolph Miss G | UK Ind | | 406 | 1.17% | 0.59% | 708 | 1.58% | Ref |
| Basarik E | Reform | | 344 | 0.99% | | 437 | 0.97% | BNP |
| Medwell H | Soc All | | 296 | 0.85% | | 260 | 0.58% | UK Ind |
| Saxena Dr R | Ind | | 100 | 0.29% | | | | |
| **Lab Co-op to C swing** | **0.97%** | | **34,774** | | **Lab Co-op maj 9,772** **28.10%** | **44,838** | | **Lab Co-op maj 13,472** **30.04%** |

**ANDY LOVE,** b March 21, 1949. Elected 1997. Member, Public Accounts Cttee, 1997-2001. Sec, all-party small businesses grp, 1999-; co chairman, all-party grp, homelessness and housing need, 1998-; chairman, all-party building societies grp, 1997-; Ex-parly officer for Co-op Retail Soc. Haringey cllr, 1980-86. Ex-board member, Greater London Enterprise; ex-member, NE Thames RHA. Ex-chairman, Hornsey & Wood Green CLP. Ed state schools; Strathclyde Univ. e mail: lovea@parliament.uk tel 020-7219 6377 fax 020-7219 6623

This seat is located in the far north of the capital, close to Hertfordshire, within the London Borough of Enfield. The social profile of the seat is, however, closer to that of Tottenham than Hertfordshire. The Tories did very well to hold on to this constituency throughout the 1980s despite clearly unfavourable demographic trends. When the dam finally burst, however, Labour assumed a commanding political position. Map 233

## ELLESMERE PORT & NESTON — Lab hold

| Electorate | %Turnout | | 68,147 | 60.94% | 2001 | 67,573 | 77.79% | 1997 |
|---|---|---|---|---|---|---|---|---|
| **Miller A** | | **Lab** | **22,964** | **55.3%** | **-4.27%** | **31,310** | **59.57%** | **Lab** |
| Williams G | | C | 12,103 | 29.14% | 0.08% | 15,274 | 29.06% | C |
| Kelly S | | LD | 4,828 | 11.63% | 2.74% | 4,673 | 8.89% | LD |
| Crocker H | | UK Ind | 824 | 1.98% | | 1,305 | 2.48% | Ref |
| Nicholls G | | Green | 809 | 1.95% | | | | |
| **Lab to C swing** | | **2.18%** | **41,528** | | **Lab maj 10,861** **26.15%** | **52,562** | | **Lab maj 16,036** **30.51%** |

**ANDREW MILLER,** b March 23, 1949. Elected 1992. Member, Select Cttees: Information, 1992-2001; Science and Tech, 1992-97. Vice-chairman, Backbench IT and Science and Tech cttees, 1993-97; treas, parly and scientific grp, 1997. Vice-chairman, all-party tennis club grp. Trade union official, member ASTMS (now MSF) from 1967 and divisional officer, 1977-92. Ed Hayling Sec; LSE. e-mail millera@parliament.uk tel 020-7219 3580 fax 0151-356 8226

A classic mixed constituency on the edge of Merseyside. This is the sort of seat that can be easily, if slightly superficially, divided between an industrial heartland which is reliably Labour in sentiment and a group of small Wirral villages (plus Neston), whose voters prefer the Tories. The balance is, nonetheless, powerfully biased to Labour. Map 234

## ELMET
### Lab hold

| Electorate | %Turnout | | 70,041 | 65.59% | 2001 | 70,423 | 76.81% | 1997 |
|---|---|---|---|---|---|---|---|---|
| **Burgon C** | **Lab** | | **22,038** | **47.97%** | **-4.43%** | **28,348** | **52.4%** | **Lab** |
| Millard A | C | | 17,867 | 38.89% | 2.71% | 19,569 | 36.18% | C |
| Kirk Ms M | LD | | 5,001 | 10.89% | 2.22% | 4,691 | 8.67% | LD |
| Spence A | UK Ind | | 1,031 | 2.24% | | 1,487 | 2.75% | Ref |
| **Lab to C swing** | **3.57%** | | **45,937** | Lab maj 4,171 | 9.08% | **54,095** | Lab maj 8,779 | 16.22% |

**COLIN BURGON,** b April 22, 1948. Elected 1997. Member, NI Affairs and Procedure Select Cttees. Former chairman and sec, Elmet Lab Party; member, Yorks reg exec LP; ex-chairman, Leeds Euro party; election agent, Elmet, 1983 and Euro election, Leeds, 1989. Member, Nupe; MSF; NUT. Local gvt policy and research officer. Ex-teacher. Ed St Michael's Coll, Leeds; Carnegie Coll, Leeds; Huddersfield Poly.

This is one of those constituencies with names that outsiders could not recognise, let alone where it is. In fact it lies on the eastern edge of Leeds and stretches into the surrounding countryside. It is starkly divided between areas such as the Leeds ward of Whinmoor, with its solidly Labour council estates, and towns such as Wetherby, which are strikingly Conservative. The 1997 result disguised the extent to which this is really a marginal seat. Map 235

## ELTHAM
### Lab hold

| Electorate | %Turnout | | 57,519 | 58.75% | 2001 | 57,358 | 75.71% | 1997 |
|---|---|---|---|---|---|---|---|---|
| **Efford C** | **Lab** | | **17,855** | **52.84%** | **-1.76%** | **23,710** | **54.6%** | **Lab** |
| Massey Mrs S | C | | 10,859 | 32.13% | 0.98% | 13,528 | 31.15% | C |
| Morris M | LD | | 4,121 | 12.2% | 3.68% | 3,701 | 8.52% | LD |
| Jones T | UK Ind | | 706 | 2.09% | | 1,414 | 3.26% | Ref |
| Graham A | Ind | | 251 | 0.74% | | 584 | 1.34% | Lib |
| | | | | | | 491 | 1.13% | BNP |
| **Lab to C swing** | **1.37%** | | **33,792** | Lab maj 6,996 | 20.70% | **43,428** | Lab maj 10,182 | 23.45% |

**CLIVE EFFORD,** b July 10, 1958. Elected 1997. Greenwich cllr, 1986-98 (chief whip, 1990-91; grp sec, 1986-87). Unpaid member, London Taxi Board. Member, TGWU. London taxi driver. Ed Walworth Comp.

This is an unusual southeast London constituency located in the Borough of Greenwich. It is a mosaic of different neighbourhoods with distinctive voting patterns which, somewhat irritatingly, fail to conform with conventional generalisations about either London or politics more generally. It is not difficult to understand either why the Conservatives could hold the seat until 1997, or why Labour won so heartily then, and again in 2001. Map 236

## ENFIELD NORTH
### Lab hold

| Electorate | %Turnout | | 67,756 | 56.29% | 2001 | 67,680 | 70.43% | 1997 |
|---|---|---|---|---|---|---|---|---|
| **Ryan Ms J** | **Lab** | | **17,888** | **46.9%** | **-3.76%** | **24,148** | **50.66%** | **Lab** |
| De Bois N | C | | 15,597 | 40.89% | 4.54% | 17,326 | 36.35% | C |
| Leighter Ms H | LD | | 3,355 | 8.8% | -0.15% | 4,264 | 8.95% | LD |
| Johns R | BNP | | 605 | 1.59% | 0.35% | 857 | 1.8% | Ref |
| Hall B | UK Ind | | 247 | 0.65% | -0.37% | 590 | 1.24% | BNP |
| Akerman M | ProLife | | 241 | 0.63% | | 484 | 1.02% | UK Ind |
| Course R | Ind | | 210 | 0.55% | | | | |
| **Lab to C swing** | **4.15%** | | **38,143** | Lab maj 2,291 | 6.01% | **47,669** | Lab maj 6,822 | 14.31% |

**JOAN RYAN,** b Sept 8, 1955. Elected 1997. PPS to Andrew Smith, Chief Sec to Treasury, 1998-. Sec, London grp of Lab MPs and Women's PLP. Barnet cllr, 1990-97 (dep council leader, 1994-97). Member, NUT; MSF. Teacher and freelance researcher. Ed City of Liverpool Coll of Higher Ed; South Bank Poly.
e mail: joan-ryanmp@hotmail.com tel: 020-7219 6502 fax: 020-7219 2335

The Borough of Enfield on the northern edge of Greater London is hard-fought political territory. Although it seemed solidly Tory until 1997, the underlying demographics of Enfield North meant that Labour always had a chance of victory provided that it could shed its disastrous image in the capital. The social mixture here is quite representative of Britain more broadly. It is thus a classic bellwether constituency. Map 237

## ENFIELD SOUTHGATE
### Lab hold

| Electorate | %Turnout | | 66,418 | 63.1% | 2001 | 65,796 | 70.72% | 1997 |
|---|---|---|---|---|---|---|---|---|
| Twigg S | Lab | | 21,727 | 51.84% | 7.63% | 20,570 | 44.21% | Lab |
| Flack J | C | | 16,181 | 38.61% | -2.52% | 19,137 | 41.13% | C |
| Hoban W | LD | | 2,935 | 7.0% | -3.67% | 4,966 | 10.67% | LD |
| Graham-Leigh Ms E | Green | | 662 | 1.58% | | 1,342 | 2.88% | Ref |
| Freshwater R | UK Ind | | 298 | 0.71% | | 289 | 0.62% | Ch D |
| Malakouna A | Ind | | 105 | 0.25% | | 229 | 0.49% | Mal |
| C to Lab swing | 5.08% | | 41,908 | Lab maj 5,546 | 13.23% | 46,533 | Lab maj 1,433 | 3.08% |

**STEPHEN TWIGG,** b Dec 25, 1966. Elected 1997 (when he defeated Michael Portillo). Parly sec to Privy Council Office, June 2001-. Member, Ed and Employment Select Cttee; chairman, all-party grps on youth and epilepsy; Lab friends of Israel. Hon pres, British Youth Council. Islington cllr, 1992-97. General sec, Fabian Soc. Ex-pres, NUS, ex-research asst to Margaret Hodge. Member, Co-op Party; Amnesty. Ed Southgate Comp; Balliol Coll, Oxford.
e mail: twiggs@parliament.uk www.stephentwigg.com
tel: 020-7219 6554 fax: 020-7219 0948

This is the most overtly middle-class section of the London Borough of Enfield. It is dominated by owner-occupiers and commuters. There is, however, a significant non-white population and a notable number of Cypriot immigrants. The seat was represented by Michael Portillo until his high-profile defeat at the 1997 election, and Labour increased its lead in 2001. Map 238

## EPPING FOREST
### C hold

| Electorate | %Turnout | | 72,645 | 58.39% | 2001 | 72,795 | 72.82% | 1997 |
|---|---|---|---|---|---|---|---|---|
| Laing Mrs E | C | | 20,833 | 49.12% | 3.62% | 24,117 | 45.5% | C |
| Naylor C | Lab | | 12,407 | 29.25% | -6.34% | 18,865 | 35.59% | Lab |
| Heavens M | LD | | 7,884 | 18.59% | 5.24% | 7,074 | 13.35% | LD |
| Smith A | UK Ind | | 1,290 | 3.04% | | 2,208 | 4.17% | Ref |
| | | | | | | 743 | 1.4% | BNP |
| Lab to C swing | 4.98% | | 42,414 | C maj 8,426 | 19.87% | 53,007 | C maj 5,252 | 9.91% |

**ELEANOR LAING,** b Feb 1, 1958. Elected 1997; contested Paisley N 1987. Opposition whip, 1999-2000; Opposition spokesman, constitutional affairs, 2000-. Member, IoD policy unit, 1994-95. Solicitor in legal dept of construction firm, 1986-88. Solicitor; business and political consultant. Ed John Neilson Sch, Glasgow; St Columba's Sch, Kilmacolm; Edinburgh Univ (student union pres).

This constituency on the Essex side of the border with Greater London contains a range of prosperous, and in some cases extremely prosperous, suburban residents in towns such as Chigwell, Theydon Bois and Epping itself. They have been strongly inclined towards the Conservative Party, although this is "new" rather than "old" money territory. There are a set of council estates to provide a modest base for the Labour Party. Map 239

## EPSOM & EWELL
### C hold

| Electorate | %Turnout | | 74,266 | 62.81% | 2001 | 73,222 | 74.0% | 1997 |
|---|---|---|---|---|---|---|---|---|
| Grayling C | C | | 22,430 | 48.09% | 2.47% | 24,717 | 45.62% | C |
| Mansell C | Lab | | 12,350 | 26.48% | 2.13% | 13,192 | 24.35% | Lab |
| Vincent J | LD | | 10,316 | 22.12% | -0.73% | 12,380 | 22.85% | LD |
| Webster-Gardiner G | UK Ind | | 1,547 | 3.32% | 2.32% | 2,355 | 4.35% | Ref |
| | | | | | | 544 | 1.0% | UK Ind |
| | | | | | | 527 | 0.97% | Green |
| | | | | | | 466 | 0.86% | ProLife |
| Lab to C swing | 0.17% | | 46,643 | C maj 10,080 | 21.61% | 54,181 | C maj 11,525 | 21.27% |

**CHRIS GRAYLING,** b April 1, 1962. Elected 2001. Inherits seat from Sir Archibald Hamilton. Contested Warrington S 1997. Merton cllr. Nat council, Bow Grp. Journalist, BBC and Channel 4. Former programme editor, *Business Daily*, Ch 4, 1988-91. Business development manager, BBC Select, 1991-93. Author of several books, including a history of Bridgewater Canal. Ed RGS, High Wycombe; Sidney Sussex Coll, Cambridge.

This is an "inner Surrey" seat which hugs the southern border of Greater London. It consists of the two towns themselves and the intervening communities, all classic commuter country, plus the Downs and the famous Derby racecourse. In voting patterns, however, this is definitely a Surrey rather than a London constituency. There are some Labour votes to be found in Epsom but otherwise the Tories dominate in Westminster contests. Map 240

## EREWASH — Lab hold

| Electorate | %Turnout | | 78,484 | 61.92% | 2001 | 77,402 | 77.95% | 1997 |
|---|---|---|---|---|---|---|---|---|
| Blackman Ms L | | Lab | 23,915 | 49.21% | -2.49% | 31,196 | 51.7% | Lab |
| MacGregor G | | C | 16,983 | 34.95% | -1.61% | 22,061 | 36.56% | C |
| Garnett M | | LD | 5,586 | 11.49% | 2.9% | 5,181 | 8.59% | LD |
| Smith Ms L | | UK Ind | 692 | 1.42% | | 1,404 | 2.33% | Ref |
| Belshaw S | | BNP | 591 | 1.22% | | 496 | 0.82% | Soc Lab |
| Seerius R | | Loony | 428 | 0.88% | | | | |
| Waldock P | | Soc Lab | 401 | 0.83% | 0.01% | | | |
| Lab to C swing | 0.44% | | 48,596 | Lab maj 6,932 | 14.26% | 60,338 | Lab maj 9,135 | 15.14% |

**LIZ BLACKMAN,** b Sept 26, 1949. Elected 1997. PPS to Geoff Hoon, Sec of State for Defence, 2001-. Member, Treasury Select Cttee. Deputy leader, Broxtowe Borough Council. Member, Co-op Party; Fabian Soc; SEA; NASUWT. Head of upper sch, Bramcote Park comp, Nottingham. Ed Carlisle County HS; Prince Henry's GS, Otley; Clifton Coll, Nottingham.

This Derbyshire constituency, lying between Derby and Nottingham and centred on Ilkeston, has the makings of a benchmark seat. Lacking the mining industry influence that is so powerful in other parts of the county, it has a reasonably representative proportion of both owner-occupiers and council tenants. It swung decisively to the Conservatives during the 1980s but moved equally forcefully to Labour in 1997. Map 241

## ERITH & THAMESMEAD — Lab hold

| Electorate | %Turnout | | 66,371 | 50.25% | 2001 | 62,887 | 66.13% | 1997 |
|---|---|---|---|---|---|---|---|---|
| Austin J | | Lab | 19,769 | 59.28% | -2.79% | 25,812 | 62.07% | Lab |
| Brooks M | | C | 8,602 | 25.79% | 5.62% | 8,388 | 20.17% | C |
| Kempton J | | LD | 3,800 | 11.39% | -0.64% | 5,001 | 12.03% | LD |
| Dhillon H | | Soc Lab | 1,180 | 3.54% | | 1,394 | 3.35% | Ref |
| | | | | | | 718 | 1.73% | BNP |
| | | | | | | 274 | 0.66% | UK Ind |
| Lab to C swing | 4.21% | | 33,351 | Lab maj 11,167 | 33.48% | 41,587 | Lab maj 17,424 | 41.90% |

**JOHN AUSTIN,** b Aug 21, 1944. Elected here 1997; MP for Woolwich 1992-97. Former member, Health Select Cttee. Joint vice-chairman, London grp of Lab MPs, 1992-; chairman, campaign grp of Lab MPs, 1994-95; all-party osteoporosis grp, 1996-; treas, human rights grp, 1997-. Greenwich cllr, 1970-94 (mayor, 1987-88 and 1998-99; council leader, 1982-87). Dir, London Marathon Charitable Trust Ltd; Trustee, Greenwich Mind and Adolescent and Children's Trust. Ed Glyn GS, Epsom; Goldsmiths Coll, London; Bristol Univ. e mail: austinj@parliament.uk tel: 020-7219 5195 fax: 020-7219 2706

This should, in theory, be a marginal battleground. In practice, it is difficult to imagine any winner here other than Labour. The new seat, bordering the Thames on the east side of London and crossing the boroughs of Bexley and Greenwich, merged sections of the old Erith and Crayford seat (marginally Tory) with others from the old Woolwich seat (equally marginally Labour). The new seat is, though, dominated by the council estates of Thamesmead. Map 242

## ESHER & WALTON — C hold

| Electorate | %Turnout | | 73,541 | 61.91% | 2001 | 72,382 | 74.14% | 1997 |
|---|---|---|---|---|---|---|---|---|
| Taylor I | | C | 22,296 | 48.97% | -0.87% | 26,747 | 49.84% | C |
| McGowan J | | Lab | 10,758 | 23.63% | 0.86% | 12,219 | 22.77% | Lab |
| Marsh M | | LD | 10,241 | 22.49% | 2.11% | 10,937 | 20.38% | LD |
| Collignon B | | UK Ind | 2,236 | 4.91% | 3.87% | 2,904 | 5.41% | Ref |
| | | | | | | 558 | 1.04% | UK Ind |
| | | | | | | 302 | 0.56% | Dream |
| C to Lab swing | 0.86% | | 45,531 | C maj 11,538 | 25.34% | 53,667 | C maj 14,528 | 27.07% |

**IAN TAYLOR,** b April 18, 1945. Elected here 1997; MP for Esher 1987-97. C spokesman, NI, July-Oct, 1997, when he resigned over Shadow Cabinet policy on euro single currency. Min for Science and Tech at DTI, 1994-97; PPS, William Waldegrave in his ministerial posts, 1990-94. Member, Foreign Affairs Select Cttee, 1987-90. Chairman, Commonwealth Youth Exchange Council, 1980-84, and vice-pres since 1984. Ed Whitley Abbey Sch, Coventry; Keele Univ; LSE.
e mail: taylori@parliament.uk tel: 020-7219 5221 fax: 020-7219 5492

Surrey was the only county of any notable size to return a clean slate of Conservative MPs in 1997 - and this is one of the most solidly Tory seats in the county. While there is a poorer minority, their votes are swamped by the very high proportion of professional and managerial workers living in this leafy commuter belt. The sitting MP, Ian Taylor, ran into trouble with some Tory activists in the course of the last Parliament for his pro-European views. Map 243

## ESSEX NORTH — C hold

| Electorate | %Turnout | | 71,680 | 62.7% | 2001 | 68,008 | 75.3% | 1997 |
|---|---|---|---|---|---|---|---|---|
| **Jenkin B** | **C** | | **21,325** | **47.45%** | **3.55%** | **22,480** | **43.9%** | **C** |
| Hawkins P | Lab | | 14,139 | 31.46% | -1.75% | 17,004 | 33.21% | Lab |
| Ellis T | LD | | 7,867 | 17.5% | -2.08% | 10,028 | 19.58% | LD |
| Curtis G | UK Ind | | 1,613 | 3.59% | 1.24% | 1,202 | 2.35% | UK Ind |
| | | | | | | 495 | 0.97% | Green |
| **Lab to C swing** | **2.65%** | | **44,944** | | **C maj 7,186** | **51,209** | | **C maj 5,476** |
| | | | | | 15.99% | | | 10.69% |

**BERNARD JENKIN,** b April 9, 1959. Elected here 1997; MP for Colchester N 1992-97. Shadow Min. for Transport and for London, 1998-; C spokesman, constitutional affairs, 1997-98; PPS, Michael Forsyth, Scottish Sec, 1995-97. Member, Social Security Select Cttee, 1992-97. Vice-chairman, C Backbench Smaller Businesses Cttee, 1994-95. Ed Highgate Sch; William Ellis Sch; Corpus Christi Coll, Cambridge (Pres of Union, 1982). www.political.co.uk/bernardjenkin/ tel 020-7219 4029 fax: 020-7219 5963

This constituency was created as a consequence of the town of Colchester being awarded a single compact seat. The result - Essex North - is political territory that completely surrounds the town. This is a predominantly middle-class division, stretching from the Blackwater in the south up to Constable Country on the Suffolk border, with many small villages and gentle countryside. It leans firmly to the Conservatives. Map 244

## EXETER — Lab hold

| Electorate | %Turnout | | 81,942 | 64.21% | 2001 | 79,154 | 78.16% | 1997 |
|---|---|---|---|---|---|---|---|---|
| **Bradshaw B** | **Lab** | | **26,194** | **49.78%** | **2.26%** | **29,398** | **47.52%** | **Lab** |
| Jobson Mrs A | C | | 14,435 | 27.43% | -1.17% | 17,693 | 28.6% | C |
| Copus R | LD | | 6,512 | 12.38% | -5.64% | 11,148 | 18.02% | LD |
| Morrish D | Lib | | 2,596 | 4.93% | 1.6% | 2,062 | 3.33% | Lib |
| Edwards P | Green | | 1,240 | 2.36% | 1.32% | 643 | 1.04% | Green |
| Stuart J | UK Ind | | 1,109 | 2.11% | 1.08% | 638 | 1.03% | UK Ind |
| Choules F | Soc All | | 530 | 1.01% | | 282 | 0.46% | UKPP |
| **C to Lab swing** | **1.71%** | | **52,616** | | **Lab maj 11,759** | **61,864** | | **Lab maj 11,705** |
| | | | | | 22.35% | | | 18.92% |

**BEN BRADSHAW,** b Aug 30, 1960. Elected 1997. Parly Sec, FCO, June 2001-; member, European Scrutiny Cttee; Ecclesiastical Cttee. Ex-BBC journalist and newspaper reporter. Won journalism award for coverage of E German revolution and fall of Berlin Wall. Ed Thorpe St Andrew Sch, Norwich; Sussex Univ. e-mail: bradshawb@parliament.uk tel: 020-7219 6597 fax: 020-7219 0950

Exeter is the oldest city in Devon as well as its county town. Unlike other areas of the county it has not been unduly disturbed by revisions of boundaries. It is a relatively affluent city and would once have been thought more or less reliable for the Tories. In 1997, however, the openly gay Labour candidate, Ben Bradshaw, crushed Dr Adrian Rogers, head of the Conservative Family Campaign, in a bruising struggle, and held firm in 2001. Map 245

## FALKIRK EAST — Lab hold

| Electorate | %Turnout | | 57,633 | 58.48% | 2001 | 56,792 | 73.24% | 1997 |
|---|---|---|---|---|---|---|---|---|
| **Connarty M** | **Lab** | | **18,536** | **55.0%** | **-1.12%** | **23,344** | **56.12%** | **Lab** |
| Hutton Ms I | SNP | | 7,824 | 23.22% | -0.72% | 9,959 | 23.94% | SNP |
| Stevenson B | C | | 3,252 | 9.65% | -4.33% | 5,813 | 13.98% | C |
| Utting Ms K | LD | | 2,992 | 8.88% | 3.7% | 2,153 | 5.18% | LD |
| Weir T | SSP | | 725 | 2.15% | | 326 | 0.78% | Ref |
| Stead R | Soc Lab | | 373 | 1.11% | | | | |
| **Lab to SNP swing** | **0.20%** | | **33,702** | | **Lab maj 10,712** | **41,595** | | **Lab maj 13,385** |
| | | | | | 31.78% | | | 32.18% |

**MICHAEL CONNARTY,** b Sept 3, 1947. Elected 1992. Member, Select Cttees: Euro Scrutiny, 1998-2001, Information, 1997-2001. Sec, all-party offshore oil and gas grp; chairman, all-party jazz grp. Former PPS to Tom Clarke, Min for Film and Tourism. Chairman, Scottish PLP grp, 1998-99; all-party chemical industry grp, 1997-2000. Ed St Patrick's HS, Coatbridge; Stirling and Glasgow Univs; Jordanhill Coll of Ed. e mail: connartym@parliament.uk www.mconnartymp.org.uk tel: 020-7219 5071 fax: 020-7219 2541

This east Scotland seat consists of several towns along the inner end of the Firth of Forth - Stenhousemuir, and the oil-refinery communities of Grangemouth and Bo'ness. Labour has won all the elections fought here since 1983 quite comfortably. The seat does, though, have a high proportion of council tenants and it would not have been surprising had Labour's majorities been even bigger. The SNP has proved a lively opposition. Map 246

## FALKIRK WEST

Lab hold

| Electorate | %Turnout | | 53,583 | 57.65% | 2001 | 52,850 | 72.6% | 1997 |
|---|---|---|---|---|---|---|---|---|
| Joyce E | | Lab | 16,022 | 51.87% | -7.48% | 22,772 | 59.35% | Lab |
| Kerr D | | SNP | 7,490 | 24.25% | 0.82% | 8,989 | 23.43% | SNP |
| Murray S | | C | 2,321 | 7.51% | -4.58% | 4,639 | 12.09% | C |
| O'Donnell H | | LD | 2,203 | 7.13% | 2.0% | 1,970 | 5.13% | LD |
| Buchanan W | | Ind B | 1,464 | 4.74% | | | | |
| McAlpine Ms M | | SSP | 707 | 2.29% | | | | |
| Lynch H | | Ind | 490 | 1.59% | | | | |
| Forbes R | | Soc Lab | 194 | 0.63% | | | | |
| Lab to SNP swing | 4.15% | | 30,891 | | Lab maj 8,532 | 38,370 | | Lab maj 13,783 |
| | | | | | 27.62% | | | 35.92% |

**ERIC JOYCE,** b Oct 13, 1960. Elected 2000 by-election. Contested Central Scotland in 1999 Scottish Parliament elections. Member, Commission for Racial Equality, 1999-2000. Former Army officer who left the service after his controversial criticism of the Army. Sec, Tamfourhill Tenants and Residents Assoc. Ed Stirling Univ; RMA, Sandhurst.

*Details of 2000 by-election on page 291*

The whole town of Falkirk, with its traditions of iron-founding and more recent light engineering, distilling and heavy vehicle assembly, lies within this constituency. Recent political history here is turbulent. Its fiery left-wing MP Dennis Canavan, barred from fighting this seat for Labour in the Scottish Parliament, was duly elected as an Independent. He resigned his Commons seat, which Labour just held in a by-election; but it surged back in 2001. Map 247

## FALMOUTH & CAMBORNE

Lab hold

| Electorate | %Turnout | | 72,833 | 64.28% | 2001 | 71,383 | 75.13% | 1997 |
|---|---|---|---|---|---|---|---|---|
| Atherton Ms C | | Lab | 18,532 | 39.58% | 5.74% | 18,151 | 33.84% | Lab |
| Serpell N | | C | 14,005 | 29.91% | 1.08% | 15,463 | 28.83% | C |
| Brazil J | | LD | 11,453 | 24.46% | -0.73% | 13,512 | 25.19% | LD |
| Browne J | | UK Ind | 1,328 | 2.84% | 2.18% | 3,534 | 6.59% | Ref |
| Wasley Ms H | | Meb Ker | 853 | 1.82% | 1.38% | 1,691 | 3.15% | Ind Lab |
| Holmes P | | Lib | 649 | 1.39% | 0.41% | 527 | 0.98% | Lib |
| | | | | | | 355 | 0.66% | UK Ind |
| | | | | | | 238 | 0.44% | Meb Ker |
| | | | | | | 161 | 0.3% | Loony |
| C to Lab swing | 2.33% | | 46,820 | | Lab maj 4,527 | 53,632 | | Lab maj 2,688 |
| | | | | | 9.67% | | | 5.01% |

**CANDY ATHERTON,** b Sept 21, 1955. Elected 1997; contested Chesham and Amersham 1992. Member, Ed and Employment Select Cttee, 1997-2001. Islington cllr, 1986-91 (mayor, 1989-90). Journalist and co-founder of *Everywoman* magazine, 1985; former researcher for Jo Richardson, MP, and Judith Hart, MP. Ex-probation officer. Freeman, City of London, 1990. Ed Sutton HS; Midhurst GS, Sussex; N London Poly.

This very distinctive constituency, now more a tourist area than a port and tin-mining region, offers hope for all three of the main political parties. It has traditionally been Labour's best prospect in Cornwall, a fact confirmed by its capture in 1997 and retention in 2001. There has always been substantial support for the Tories, who held it from 1970 until 1997. The Lib Dems are also capable of a noteworthy showing in the right circumstances. Map 248

## FAREHAM

C hold

| Electorate | %Turnout | | 72,678 | 62.53% | 2001 | 68,787 | 75.85% | 1997 |
|---|---|---|---|---|---|---|---|---|
| Hoban M | | C | 21,389 | 47.06% | 0.23% | 24,436 | 46.83% | C |
| Carr J | | Lab | 14,380 | 31.64% | 4.66% | 14,078 | 26.98% | Lab |
| Pritchard H | | LD | 8,503 | 18.71% | -0.9% | 10,234 | 19.61% | LD |
| O'Brien W | | UK Ind | 1,175 | 2.59% | | 2,914 | 5.58% | Ref |
| | | | | | | 515 | 0.99% | Ind No |
| C to Lab swing | 2.21% | | 45,447 | | C maj 7,009 | 52,177 | | C maj 10,358 |
| | | | | | 15.42% | | | 19.85% |

**MARK HOBAN,** b March 31, 1964. Elected 2001. Takes over from Sir Peter Lloyd, who had held the seat since 1979. Contested South Shields, 1997. PA and campaign manager to Christopher Chope, 1987 and 1992. Senior manager, PricewaterhouseCoopers, specialising in the Internet, high-tech and media sectors. Chartered accountant. Ed St Leonards RC Comp, Durham; LSE.

This pleasant Hampshire seat, on the shores of Southampton Water and the northwestern side of Portsmouth Harbour, is centred on the market town and small port of Fareham and includes numerous affluent waterside communities and adjacent rural territory. It has a very high proportion of owner-occupiers and is almost exclusively white. It is also, unsurprisingly, a strongly Conservative seat. Map 249

## FAVERSHAM & KENT MID
## C hold

| Electorate | %Turnout | | 67,995 | 60.37% | 2001 | 67,490 | 73.5% | 1997 |
|---|---|---|---|---|---|---|---|---|
| **Robertson H** | | **C** | **18,739** | **45.65%** | **1.27%** | **22,016** | **44.38%** | **C** |
| Birchall G | | Lab | 14,556 | 35.46% | -0.51% | 17,843 | 35.97% | Lab |
| Sole M | | LD | 5,529 | 13.47% | 1.1% | 6,138 | 12.37% | LD |
| Gascoyne J | | UK Ind | 828 | 2.02% | 1.15% | 2,073 | 4.18% | Ref |
| Kemp Ms P | | Green | 799 | 1.95% | 1.18% | 511 | 1.03% | Loony |
| Davidson N | R & R Loony | | 600 | 1.46% | | 431 | 0.87% | UK Ind |
| | | | | | | 380 | 0.77% | Green |
| | | | | | | 115 | 0.23% | GRLNSP |
| | | | | | | 99 | 0.2% | NLP |
| **Lab to C swing** | **0.89%** | | **41,051** | | **C maj 4,183** | **49,606** | | **C maj 4,173** |
| | | | | | 10.19% | | | 8.41% |

**HUGH ROBERTSON,** b Oct 9, 1962. Elected 2001. Inherits seat from Andrew Rowe. Member, first Foreign Office/MoD team to visit Argentina since Falklands war. Member, Shadow Defence Secs policy grp; special adviser, security to Shadow NI spokesman. Commanded Household Cavalry for Queen's birthday and State Opening of Parliament, 1993. Candidate, GLC elections. Banker. Army officer, Life Guards, 1982-95. Ed King's Sch, Canterbury; RMA, Sandhurst; Reading Univ.

The expansion in the population of this part of Kent demanded a new parliamentary constituency. It was not easy to create one that reflected a natural community. This seat is an amalgamation of different parts of Faversham, mid-Kent, Maidstone and Tonbridge and Malling. The end result has been a seat where the Conservatives are clearly favoured to win but there are enough pockets of Labour support to make for a strong political presence. Map 250

## FELTHAM & HESTON
## Lab hold

| Electorate | %Turnout | | 73,229 | 49.4% | 2001 | 71,093 | 65.58% | 1997 |
|---|---|---|---|---|---|---|---|---|
| **Keen A** | **Lab Co-op** | | **21,406** | **59.17%** | **-0.54** | **27,836** | **59.71%** | **Lab** |
| Mammatt Mrs L | | C | 8,749 | 24.18% | -2.77% | 12,563 | 26.95% | C |
| Darley A | | LD | 4,998 | 13.82% | 4.67% | 4,264 | 9.15% | LD |
| Cheema S | | Soc Lab | 651 | 1.8% | | 1,099 | 2.36% | Ref |
| Prachar W | Ind Prachar | | 204 | 0.56% | | 682 | 1.46% | BNP |
| Khaira A | | Ind K | 169 | 0.47% | | 177 | 0.38% | NLP |
| **C to Lab Co-op swing** | **1.11%** | | **36,177** | **Lab Co-op maj 12,657** | | **46,621** | **Lab maj 15,273** | |
| | | | | | 34.99% | | | 32.76% |

**ALAN KEEN,** b Nov 25, 1937. Elected 1992. Member, Select Cttees: Culture, Media and Sport, 1997-2001; Ed, 1995-96; Deregulation, 1995-96. Vice-chairman, all-party sports grp; sec, Lords and Commons cricket club; chairman, Co-op grp of MPs, 1997-. Hounslow cllr, 1986-90. Former scout for Middlesbrough FC. Systems analyst, accountant and manager. Wife, Ann, is Lab MP for Brentford and Isleworth. Ed Sir William Turner's, Redcar.
tel: 020-7219 2819

Although the Tories snatched this seat on the western fringes of Greater London in the 1980s, it is not natural territory for them. This is the western half of the borough of Hounslow, located to the east of Heathrow Airport. It has a working-class base and a rising number of non-white electors. On current political trends this means some security for the Labour candidate for the foreseeable future. Map 251

## FERMANAGH & SOUTH TYRONE
## SF gain

| Electorate | %Turnout | | 66,640 | 77.99% | 2001 | 64,600 | 74.75% | 1997 |
|---|---|---|---|---|---|---|---|---|
| **Gildernew Ms M** | | **SF** | **17,739** | **34.13%** | **10.99%** | **24,862** | **51.48%** | **UUP** |
| Cooper J | | UUP | 17,686 | 34.03% | -17.45% | 11,174 | 23.14% | SF |
| Gallagher T | | SDLP | 9,706 | 18.67% | -4.23% | 11,060 | 22.9% | SDLP |
| Dixon J | | Ind UU | 6,843 | 13.17% | | 977 | 2.02% | Alliance |
| | | | | | | 217 | 0.45% | NLP |
| **UUP to SF swing** | **14.22%** | | **51,974** | | **SF maj 53** | **48,290** | | **UUP maj 13,688** |
| | | | | | 0.10% | | | 28.34% |

**MICHELLE GILDERNEW,** b Jan 1, 1970. Elected 2001. Won seat for Sinn Fein, following the retirement of Ken Maginnis, sitting UUP Member since 1983. Will not take her seat at Westminster. Member, NI Assembly, 1998-. Ex-head of Sinn Fein London office; member Sinn Fein delegation at London talks, 1997. Member, Sinn Fein Ard Comhairle, 1996-. Ed Ulster Univ, Coleraine.
The Fermanagh & South Tyrone result was immediately challenged in the Ulster courts.

This seat occupies a large slice of the Northern Ireland-Irish Republic border. It is primarily rural and agricultural. But the most notable feature is the narrow sectarian divide. It is always possible for a nationalist candidate to win if there is no split in the Catholic vote, as Bobby Sands did in a 1981 by-election, and as Sinn Fein did in capturing the seat in 2001. Otherwise, a Unionist, such as Ken Maginnis, the MP from 1983 to 1997, will prevail. Map 252

## FIFE CENTRAL — Lab hold

| Electorate | %Turnout | | 59,597 | 54.55% | 2001 | 58,315 | 69.9% | 1997 |
|---|---|---|---|---|---|---|---|---|
| MacDougall J | Lab | | 18,310 | 56.32% | -2.34% | 23,912 | 58.66% | Lab |
| Alexander D | SNP | | 8,235 | 25.33% | 0.31% | 10,199 | 25.02% | SNP |
| Riches Ms E | LD | | 2,775 | 8.54% | 2.14% | 3,669 | 9.0% | C |
| Balfour J | C | | 2,351 | 7.23% | -1.77% | 2,610 | 6.4% | LD |
| Balfour Ms M | SSP | | 841 | 2.59% | | | 375 | 0.92% | Ref |
| Lab to SNP swing | 1.33% | | 32,512 | Lab maj 10,075 | | 40,765 | Lab maj 13,713 | |
| | | | | 30.99% | | | 33.64% | |

**JOHN MacDOUGALL,** b Dec 8, 1947. Elected 2001. Inherits seat from Henry McLeish, the Scottish First Min, who stood down to concentrate on the Scottish Parliament. Convener, Fife council, 1996-2001. Cllr, Fife reg council for 18 years; developed Fife race equality grp; vice-pres and treas, Assembly of European regions, 1996-2000. Industrial manager, IoD. Boilermaker. Ed Templehall Sec Mod, Fife; Rosyth FE Coll (naval architecture); Glenrothes Technical Coll; Fife Coll (industrial studies)

Much of the most traditionally left-wing, even Communist, element of this seat was removed 20 years ago. But this area of eastern Scotland, centred on Glenrothes New Town, is still solidly working-class and equally reliably Labour — if not by the sort of overwhelming margins that can occur in Scotland. There is not much of a base for either the Tories or the Liberal Democrats. Map 253

## FIFE NORTH EAST — LD hold

| Electorate | %Turnout | | 61,900 | 56.05% | 2001 | 58,794 | 71.16% | 1997 |
|---|---|---|---|---|---|---|---|---|
| Campbell M | LD | | 17,926 | 51.67% | 0.45% | 21,432 | 51.22% | LD |
| Scott-Hayward M | C | | 8,190 | 23.61% | -2.86% | 11,076 | 26.47% | C |
| Brennan Ms C | Lab | | 3,950 | 11.39% | 1.11% | 4,545 | 10.86% | SNP |
| Murray-Browne Ms K | SNP | | 3,596 | 10.37% | -0.49% | 4,301 | 10.28% | Lab |
| White K | SSP | | 610 | 1.76% | | | 485 | 1.16% | Ref |
| Von Goetz Mrs L | LCA | | 420 | 1.21% | | | | | |
| C to LD swing | 1.66% | | 34,692 | LD maj 9,736 | | 41,839 | LD maj 10,356 | |
| | | | | 28.06% | | | 24.75% | |

**MENZIES CAMPBELL,** b May 22, 1941. Elected 1987. Chief LD spokesman, Foreign and Commonwealth Affairs, confirmed June 2001. Ex-defence spokesman. Member, Select Cttees: Defence, 1992-99; Trade and Industry, 1990-92; Members' Interests, 1987-90. Member, Advisory Cttee on Commons works of art, 1988-92; UK delegation, N Atlantic Assembly, 1989-. Broadcasting Council for Scotland, 1984-87. CBE, 1987 and Privy Counsellor, 1999. Former UK 100m record holder. Advocate, QC (Scot). Ed Hillhead HS, Glasgow; Glasgow Univ; Stanford Univ, California.

About half of the county of Fife is located in this seat and it is very different from its neighbours. They are working-class and industrial. This is a collection of small towns, relatively prosperous farming land, fishing villages, tourist havens and the University of St Andrews. There is a political base for the Liberal Democrats, who took the seat in 1987 and have held it ever since, and to some extent for the Tories, but for no other political party. Map 254

## FINCHLEY & GOLDERS GREEN — Lab hold

| Electorate | %Turnout | | 76,175 | 57.34% | 2001 | 72,225 | 69.65% | 1997 |
|---|---|---|---|---|---|---|---|---|
| Vis R | Lab | | 20,205 | 46.26% | 0.18% | 23,180 | 46.08% | Lab |
| Marshall J | C | | 16,489 | 37.75% | -1.99% | 19,991 | 39.74% | C |
| Teather Ms S | LD | | 5,266 | 12.06% | 0.79% | 5,670 | 11.27% | LD |
| Dunn Ms M | Green | | 1,385 | 3.17% | 2.03% | 684 | 1.36% | Ref |
| de Roeck J | UK Ind | | 330 | 0.76% | 0.35% | 576 | 1.14% | Green |
| | | | | | | 205 | 0.41% | UK Ind |
| C to Lab swing | 1.08% | | 43,675 | Lab maj 3,716 | | 50,306 | Lab maj 3,189 | |
| | | | | 8.51% | | | 6.34% | |

**RUDI VIS,** b April 4, 1941. Elected 1997. Member, Council of Europe, 1997- and WEU, 1997-. Head, board of governors, United International Coll. Barnet cllr, 1986-98. Treas, Finchley CLP, 1982-86. Member MSF; SEA. Hon PhD, Schiller International Univ, 1998. Economics lecturer. Ed HS in The Netherlands; Univ of Maryland; Brunel Univ.

This is a highly distinctive North London seat, with a notable Jewish flavour to its politics. Finchley itself was represented by Margaret Thatcher in the House of Commons from 1959 to 1992, although her backyard always contained a sizeable Labour minority. This new seat was supposed to be slightly more Tory than its predecessor, but in 1997 Labour seized it all the same and held on in 2001. Map 255

## FOLKESTONE & HYTHE                                    C hold

| Electorate | %Turnout | | 71,503 | 64.13% | 2001 | 71,153 | 73.15% | 1997 |
|---|---|---|---|---|---|---|---|---|
| **Howard M** | **C** | | **20,645** | **45.02%** | **5.99%** | **20,313** | **39.03%** | **C** |
| Carroll P | LD | | 14,738 | 32.14% | 5.28% | 13,981 | 26.86% | LD |
| Catterall A | Lab | | 9,260 | 20.19% | -4.67% | 12,939 | 24.86% | Lab |
| Baker J | UK Ind | | 1,212 | 2.64% | 1.91% | 4,188 | 8.05% | Ref |
| | | | | | | 378 | 0.73% | UK Ind |
| | | | | | | 182 | 0.35% | Soc |
| | | | | | | 69 | 0.13% | CFSS |
| **LD to C swing** | **0.36%** | | **45,855** | | **C maj 5,907** | **52,050** | | **C maj 6,332** |
| | | | | | 12.88% | | | 12.17% |

**MICHAEL HOWARD,** b July 7, 1941. Elected 1983; contested Liverpool Edge Hill 1966 and 1970. Shadow Foreign Sec, 1997-99; Home Sec, 1993-97; Environment Sec, 1992-93; Employment Sec, 1990-92; Housing and Planning Min, 1989-90; Planning and Water Min, 1988-89; Min of State, Dept of Environment, 1987-90; Corporate and Consumer Affairs Min, 1985-87. Privy Counsellor, 1990. Appointed Recorder, 1986. QC. Ed Llanelli GS; Peterhouse, Cambridge (Pres of Union 1962).

This is the southernmost section of the Kent coastline, including the ferry port of Folkestone, the Cinque Ports of Hythe and Romney and the bleak Romney Marsh. The local economy has been heavily influenced by the opening of the Channel Tunnel. Although this might appear solid Tory territory, there is a reasonable base for both Labour and Lib Dems.The Referendum Party performed well under the local celebrity John Aspinall in 1997. Map 256

## FOREST OF DEAN                                      Lab hold

| Electorate | %Turnout | | 66,240 | 67.34% | 2001 | 63,465 | 79.07% | 1997 |
|---|---|---|---|---|---|---|---|---|
| **Organ Ms D** | **Lab** | | **19,350** | **43.38%** | **-4.85%** | **24,203** | **48.23%** | **Lab** |
| Harper M | C | | 17,301 | 38.79% | 3.2% | 17,860 | 35.59% | C |
| Gayler D | LD | | 5,762 | 12.92% | 0.64% | 6,165 | 12.28% | LD |
| Pickering S | Green | | 1,254 | 2.81% | | 1,624 | 3.24% | Ref |
| Prout A | UK Ind | | 661 | 1.48% | | 218 | 0.43% | Ind Dean |
| Morgan G | Ind | | 279 | 0.63% | | 80 | 0.16% | 21st Cent |
| | | | | | | 34 | 0.07% | Ind F |
| **Lab to C swing** | **4.02%** | | **44,607** | | **Lab maj 2,049** | **50,184** | | **Lab maj 6,343** |
| | | | | | 4.59% | | | 12.64% |

**DIANA ORGAN,** b Feb 21, 1952. Elected 1997; contested Gloucestershire W 1992; Somerset and Dorset W 1989 Euro elections. Member, Culture, Media and Sport Select Cttee. Former asst sec, Somerset and Frome CLP; Somerset delegate, women's cttee; member, reg exec; board member, TV South West; member, Nupe. Special needs teacher. Ed Edgbaston C of E Coll for Girls; St Hugh's Coll, Oxford; Bath Univ Sch of Ed; Bristol Poly.
e-mail: lapingtona@parliament.uk tel: 01594 826835 fax: 01594 827892

This seat was the by-product of the need to create a new constituency in Gloucestershire west of the River Severn. The boundary revisions helped to create an opportunity for the Labour Party. The seat used to contain, improbably, an active coalmine, with strongly Labour mining communities. It is now quite evenly divided between suburban commuters and small, surprisingly industrial, towns such as Coleford and Cinderford. Map 257

## FOYLE                                              SDLP hold

| Electorate | %Turnout | | 70,943 | 68.9% | 2001 | 67,620 | 70.71% | 1997 |
|---|---|---|---|---|---|---|---|---|
| **Hume J** | **SDLP** | | **24,538** | **50.2%** | **-2.31%** | **25,109** | **52.51%** | **SDLP** |
| McLaughlin M | SF | | 12,988 | 26.57% | 2.63% | 11,445 | 23.94% | SF |
| Hay W | DUP | | 7,414 | 15.17% | -6.35% | 10,290 | 21.52% | DUP |
| Davidson A | UUP | | 3,360 | 6.87% | | 817 | 1.71% | Alliance |
| Cavanagh C | Alliance | | 579 | 1.18% | -0.53% | 154 | 0.32% | NLP |
| **SDLP to SF swing** | **2.47%** | | **48,879** | | **SDLP maj 11,550** | **47,815** | | **SDLP maj 13,664** |
| | | | | | 23.63% | | | 28.57% |

**JOHN HUME,** b Jan 18, 1937. Elected 1983; contested Londonderry Oct 1974. Leader, SDLP, 1979-; dep leader, 1970-79. Member, NI Assembly, 1998-2000. Member, Euro Parliament, 1979-. MP for Foyle, NI Parliament, 1969-73. Elected for Londonderry to NI Assembly, 1973-75; NI Constitutional Convention, 1975-76; NI Assembly, 1982-86; member, NI Forum, 1983-84. Min for Commerce in NI power-sharing exec, 1974. Associate Fellow, Centre for International Affairs, Harvard, 1976. Teacher. Ed St Columb's Coll, Londonderry; St Patrick's Coll, Maynooth.

The Boundary Commissioners clearly believe in tact when it comes to naming Northern Irish constituencies. Foyle is in fact Derry (for the majority of its residents) or Londonderry (for the minority Unionist population). Sectarian loyalties are a far more important factor here than any other social influence. It has been, and remains, the home of the SDLP and its long-serving champion, John Hume. Map 258

# FYLDE

**C hold**

| Electorate | %Turnout | | 72,207 | 61.96% | 2001 | 71,385 | 72.94% | 1997 |
|---|---|---|---|---|---|---|---|---|
| **Jack M** | C | | **23,383** | **52.27%** | **3.4%** | **25,443** | **48.87%** | C |
| Stockton J | Lab | | 13,773 | 30.79% | -0.86% | 16,480 | 31.65% | Lab |
| Begg J | LD | | 6,599 | 14.75% | 0.14% | 7,609 | 14.61% | LD |
| Brown Mrs L | UK Ind | | 982 | 2.2% | | 2,372 | 4.56% | Ref |
| | | | | | | 163 | 0.31% | NLP |
| **Lab to C swing** | **2.13%** | | **44,737** | | **C maj 9,610** | **52,067** | | **C maj 8,963** |
| | | | | | 21.48% | | | 17.22% |

**MICHAEL JACK,** b Sept 17, 1946. Elected 1987. Shadow Min of Agriculture, Fisheries and Food, 1997-99. Member, Select Cttee, Agriculture, 1999-2001; member, Public Accounts Cttee. 1922 Exec Cttee, 1999-2000. C health spokesman, 1997-98. Financial Sec to Treasury, 1995-97; Min of State for Agriculture, Fisheries and Food, 1993-95; Home Office, 1992-93. Under-Sec for Social Security, 1990-92. Privy Counsellor. PPS to John Gummer, 1988-90. Former sales dir. Ed Bradford GS; Bradford Tech Coll; Leicester Univ. tel: 020-7219 2473

Fylde is that peninsula of Lancashire which juts out into the Irish Sea south of Blackpool. It is based on the very affluent seaside resort of Lytham St Anne's. It has a large majority of owner-occupiers and a significant pensioner population. Although Labour did rather well here in 1997, the essential political characteristic of this seat is its Conservatism. Map 259

# GAINSBOROUGH

**C hold**

| Electorate | %Turnout | | 65,871 | 64.25% | 2001 | 64,106 | 74.56% | 1997 |
|---|---|---|---|---|---|---|---|---|
| **Leigh E** | C | | **19,555** | **46.21%** | **3.12%** | **20,593** | **43.09%** | C |
| Rhodes A | Lab | | 11,484 | 27.14% | -1.66% | 13,767 | 28.8% | Lab |
| Taylor S | LD | | 11,280 | 26.65% | -1.46% | 13,436 | 28.11% | LD |
| **Lab to C swing** | **2.39%** | | **42,319** | | **C maj 8,071** | **47,796** | | **C maj 6,826** |
| | | | | | 19.07% | | | 14.29% |

**EDWARD LEIGH,** b July 20, 1950. Elected here 1997; MP for Gainsborough and Horncastle 1983-97. Member, Public Accounts Cttee, 1999-2001; Select Cttees: Social Security, 1995-97; Defence, 1983-87. Under-Sec of State, Trade and Industry, 1990-93. Joint vice-chairman, Employment Cttee, 1987-88; sec, Defence Cttee, 1983-84; Agriculture Cttee, 1983-85. Member, Margaret Thatcher's private office, 1976-77. Arbitrator in newspaper trading disputes. Barrister. Ed St Philip's Sch, Kensington; Oratory Sch, Berkshire; French Lycée, London; Durham Univ (Pres of Union; chairman, univ C assoc).

This is a charming corner of Lincolnshire, bordering the east bank of the River Trent, and is something of an isolated, if perfectly content, community. It is overwhelmingly white and mostly consists of long-settled residents. The SDP made quite a strong showing here in the 1980s but could not sustain the effort. The Conservatives remain the dominant electoral force. Map 260

# GALLOWAY & UPPER NITHSDALE

**C gain**

| Electorate | %Turnout | | 52,756 | 68.08% | 2001 | 52,751 | 79.65% | 1997 |
|---|---|---|---|---|---|---|---|---|
| **Duncan P** | C | | **12,222** | **34.03%** | **3.51%** | **18,449** | **43.91%** | SNP |
| Fleming M | SNP | | 12,148 | 33.83% | -10.08% | 12,825 | 30.52% | C |
| Sloan T | Lab | | 7,258 | 20.21% | 3.88% | 6,861 | 16.33% | Lab |
| Wallace N | LD | | 3,698 | 10.3% | 3.87% | 2,700 | 6.43% | LD |
| Harvey A | SSP | | 588 | 1.64% | | 566 | 1.35% | Ind |
| | | | | | | 428 | 1.02% | Ref |
| | | | | | | 189 | 0.45% | UK Ind |
| **SNP to C swing** | **6.80%** | | **35,914** | | **C maj 74** | **42,018** | | **SNP maj 5,624** |
| | | | | | 0.21% | | | 13.39% |

**PETER DUNCAN,** b July 10, 1965. Elected 2001. Recaptures seat for C after the retirement of Alasdair Morgan, SNP MP, who won it from C Cabinet Min, Ian Lang, in 1997 - thus becoming the only Tory MP in Scotland. Chairman, Cunningham N constituency assoc. Project manager, Mackays Stores, 1985-88; dir, John Duncan and Sons, 1988-2000. Ed Ardrossan Acad; Birmingham Univ.

This seat is in the far southwestern corner of lowland Scotland. It has the highest proportion of residents engaged in fishing, forestry and farming of any constituency in the UK; tourism is centred on the ferry port of Stranraer. The constituency was badly hit by the foot-and-mouth outbreak in 2001. The recurring battle here is between the SNP and the Conservatives; the Tories' tiny win in 2001 makes it one of the UK's closest marginals. Map 261

## GATESHEAD EAST & WASHINGTON WEST

**Lab hold**

| Electorate | %Turnout | | 64,041 | 52.49% | 2001 | 64,114 | 67.19% | 1997 |
|---|---|---|---|---|---|---|---|---|
| Quin Ms J | | Lab | 22,903 | 68.13% | -3.94% | 31,047 | 72.07% | Lab |
| Beadle R | | LD | 4,999 | 14.87% | 4.14% | 6,097 | 14.15% | C |
| Campbell Ms E | | C | 4,970 | 14.79% | 0.64% | 4,622 | 10.73% | LD |
| Rouse M | | UK Ind | 743 | 2.21% | | 1,315 | 3.05% | Ref |
| Lab to LD swing | 4.04% | | 33,615 | Lab maj 17,904 | | 43,081 | Lab maj 24,950 | |
| | | | | 53.26% | | | 57.92% | |

**JOYCE QUIN,** b Nov 26, 1944. Elected here 1997; MP for Gateshead East 1987-97; MEP for Tyne and Wear 1979-89. Min of State and Deputy Min of Agriculture, Fisheries and Food, 1999-2001. Min of State, FCO, 1998-99. Lab European spokeswoman, 1993-97; spokeswoman, employment, 1992-93; trade and industry, 1989-92. Member, Treasury and Civil Service Select Cttee, 1987-89. Privy Counsellor. Chairwoman, Northern grp, Lab MPs, 1995-97; ex-joint vice-chairwoman, all-party social science and policy grp and Euro Atlantic grp. Ed Whitley Bay GS; Newcastle Univ; LSE.

This seat was obliged to endure substantial boundary revisions in the 1980s. It has previously been an inner-city Tyne and Wear seat based squarely on Gateshead. It was then obliged to subsume the western section of Washington New Town. It cannot be said that any of this manipulation has altered the political outlook of the constituency. This is a very safe Labour stronghold. Map 262

## GEDLING

**Lab hold**

| Electorate | %Turnout | | 68,540 | 63.93% | 2001 | 68,820 | 75.8% | 1997 |
|---|---|---|---|---|---|---|---|---|
| Coaker V | | Lab | 22,383 | 51.08% | 4.32% | 24,390 | 46.76% | Lab |
| Bullock J | | C | 16,785 | 38.31% | -1.16% | 20,588 | 39.47% | C |
| Gillam T | | LD | 4,648 | 10.61% | 0.68% | 5,180 | 9.93% | LD |
| | | | | | | 2,006 | 3.85% | Ref |
| C to Lab swing | 2.74% | | 43,816 | Lab maj 5,598 | | 52,164 | Lab maj 3,802 | |
| | | | | 12.78% | | | 7.29% | |

**VERNON COAKER,** b June 17, 1953. Elected 1997. Member, Social Security Select Cttee, 1998-99. PPS to Stephen Timms, Financial Sec to Treasury, 1999-2001, and at Dept Social Security, 1999. Rushcliffe Borough Council leader, 1987-. Member, League Against Cruel Sports; NUT; Friends of the Earth. Teacher. Ed Drayton Manor GS; Warwick Univ; Trent Poly.
e-mail: coakerv@parliament.uk www.vernon-coaker-mp.co.uk
tel: 020-7219 6627 fax: 0115-9204500

Gedling is essentially a suburban middle-class seat dominated by residents who work in and around the city of Nottingham. It is moderately affluent, but not as prosperous as other leafy constituencies in this county. It has a large number of owner-occupiers and has traditionally aligned itself with the Tories. The seat was captured by Labour in 1997, making it a critical marginal, but the Labour lead actually increased in 2001. Map 263

## GILLINGHAM

**Lab hold**

| Electorate | %Turnout | | 70,898 | 59.54% | 2001 | 70,389 | 72.0% | 1997 |
|---|---|---|---|---|---|---|---|---|
| Clark P | | Lab | 18,782 | 44.49% | 4.66% | 20,187 | 39.83% | Lab |
| Butcher T | | C | 16,510 | 39.11% | 3.19% | 18,207 | 35.92% | C |
| Hunt J | | LD | 5,755 | 13.63% | -5.41% | 9,649 | 19.04% | LD |
| Scholefield T | | UK Ind | 933 | 2.21% | 1.05% | 1,492 | 2.94% | Ref |
| Vaughan W | | Soc All | 232 | 0.55% | | 590 | 1.16% | UK Ind |
| | | | | | | 305 | 0.6% | Loony |
| | | | | | | 195 | 0.38% | BNP |
| | | | | | | 58 | 0.11% | NLP |
| C to Lab swing | 0.74% | | 42,212 | Lab maj 2,272 | | 50,683 | Lab maj 1,980 | |
| | | | | 5.38% | | | 3.91% | |

**PAUL CLARK,** b April 29, 1957. Elected 1997. PPS to Lord Chancellor's Dept, 1999-2001. Member, European Standing Cttee, 1997-2000. All-party grps: sec, Regeneration, 2000-, and Thames Gateway, 1997-; member, animal welfare, railways, rail freight. Member, Thames Gateway Kent Partnership Board, 2000-; Gillingham borough cllr, 1982-90 (Lab grp ldr, 1988-90). AEU. TUC administrator. Ed Gillingham GS; Keele Univ.
e-mail: clarkp@parliament.uk tel: 020-7219 5207 fax: 020-7219 2545

Gillingham is the largest of the Medway towns in Kent but is not especially industrial. It used to be associated with the Chatham naval dockyard (outside the seat but a source of employment for many residents) until it closed in the 1980s. Although there is a high rate of owner-occupation, this is not a prosperous seat like many others in Kent. It is solidly middle-class, however, and was a real surprise when Labour squeezed home in 1997. Map 264

## GLASGOW ANNIESLAND — Lab hold

| Electorate | %Turnout | | 53,290 | 50.14% | 2001 | 52,955 | 63.98% | 1997 |
|---|---|---|---|---|---|---|---|---|
| Robertson J | Lab | | 15,102 | 56.52% | -5.32% | 20,951 | 61.84% | Lab |
| Thoms G | SNP | | 4,048 | 15.15% | -1.96% | 5,797 | 17.11% | SNP |
| McGinty C | LD | | 3,244 | 12.14% | 4.9% | 3,881 | 11.46% | C |
| Connell S | C | | 2,651 | 9.92% | -1.54% | 2,453 | 7.24% | LD |
| McCarthy C | SSP | | 1,486 | 5.56% | | 374 | 1.1% | ProLife |
| McGavigan Ms K | Soc Lab | | 191 | 0.71% | | 229 | 0.68% | SSA |
| | | | | | | 86 | 0.25% | UK Ind |
| | | | | | | 84 | 0.25% | Ref |
| | | | | | | 24 | 0.07% | NLP |
| Lab to SNP swing | 1.68% | | 26,722 | Lab maj 11,054 | | 33,879 | Lab maj 15,154 | |
| | | | | 41.37% | | | 44.73% | |

**JOHN ROBERTSON,** b April 17, 1952. Elected 2000 by-election. Agent, Glasgow Garscadden CLP/Glasgow Anniesland CLP, 1994-2000; chairman, Glasgow Anniesland CLP. BT engineer and then manager. Ed Shawlands Acad, Glasgow; Stow Coll of Engineering, Glasgow.

*Details of 2000 by-election on page 291*

This seat grew out of the former Glasgow Garscadden but is now a little different in nature. On the northwestern edge of the city, it combines a tough, industrial, working-class core with a more genteel fringe. It was formerly part of Glasgow Hillhead, once represented by Roy Jenkins. This is, nonetheless, solid Labour territory; the MP elected in 1997 was Donald Dewar, subsequently First Minister of Scotland, until his untimely death in 2000. Map 265

## GLASGOW BAILLIESTON — Lab hold

| Electorate | %Turnout | | 49,268 | 47.21% | 2001 | 51,152 | 62.27% | 1997 |
|---|---|---|---|---|---|---|---|---|
| Wray J | Lab | | 14,200 | 61.05% | -4.64% | 20,925 | 65.69% | Lab |
| McNeill L | SNP | | 4,361 | 18.75% | -0.35% | 6,085 | 19.1% | SNP |
| Comrie D | C | | 1,580 | 6.79% | -0.96% | 2,468 | 7.75% | C |
| McVicar J | SSP | | 1,569 | 6.75% | 2.85% | 1,217 | 3.82% | LD |
| Dundas C | LD | | 1,551 | 6.67% | | 970 | 3.05% | SSA |
| | | | | | | 188 | 0.59% | Ref |
| Lab to SNP swing | 2.15% | | 23,261 | Lab maj 9,839 | | 31,853 | Lab maj 14,840 | |
| | | | | 42.30% | | | 46.59% | |

**JAMES WRAY,** b April 28, 1938. Elected here 1997; MP for Glasgow Provan 1987-97. Former vice-convener, Scottish grp of Lab MPs, and former vice-chairman, all-party Anti-Flouridation Cttee. Strathclyde reg cllr, 1976-. Led Gorbals rent strike and anti-dampness campaign. Pres, Scottish Fed of the Blind, 1987 (vice-pres, 1986); Gorbals Utd FC; St Enoch's Drug Centre; Scottish Ex-Boxers' Assoc. Ex-heavy goods vehicle driver. Ed St Bonaventures, Glasgow.

This northeast Glasgow seat has not experienced much of the prosperity that occurred nationally during the 1990s. It is dominated by a set of vast council estates, the highest proportion for any constituency in the United Kingdom. In so far as there is any opposition to Labour, it is provided by parties to the left of it. Map 266

## GLASGOW CATHCART — Lab hold

| Electorate | %Turnout | | 52,094 | 52.57% | 2001 | 49,312 | 69.17% | 1997 |
|---|---|---|---|---|---|---|---|---|
| Harris T | Lab | | 14,902 | 54.41% | -1.76% | 19,158 | 56.17% | Lab |
| Docherty Mrs J | SNP | | 4,086 | 14.92% | -5.35% | 6,913 | 20.27% | SNP |
| Cook R | C | | 3,662 | 13.37% | 0.92% | 4,248 | 12.45% | C |
| Henery T | LD | | 3,006 | 10.98% | 4.23% | 2,302 | 6.75% | LD |
| Stevenson R | SSP | | 1,730 | 6.32% | | 687 | 2.01% | ProLife |
| | | | | | | 458 | 1.34% | SSA |
| | | | | | | 344 | 1.01% | Ref |
| SNP to Lab swing | 1.80% | | 27,386 | Lab maj 10,816 | | 34,110 | Lab maj 12,245 | |
| | | | | 39.49% | | | 35.90% | |

**TOM HARRIS,** b Feb 20, 1964. Elected, 2001. Inherits seat from John Maxton, who won it from Sir Teddy Taylor, the C Eurosceptic, in 1979. Chief public relations and marketing officer, Strathclyde Passenger Exec, 1998-2001. PR manager, E Ayrshire Council, 1996-98. Senior media officer, Glasgow City Council, 1996. Press officer, Scottish Lab Party, 1990-92. Ex-reporter on *Paisley Daily Express*. Ed Garnock Acad, Ayrshire; Napier Coll, Edinburgh.

This was once the most Conservative division in Glasgow, lying in the south of the city. It is now increasingly secure for the Labour Party. The shift occurred because of changing demographics (more affluent electors moved elsewhere) and the decline of religious-inspired voting alignments in Scotland. It is difficult to see circumstances in which it would swap colours again in the near future. Map 267

## GLASGOW GOVAN — Lab hold

| Electorate | %Turnout | | 54,068 | 46.76% | 2001 | 49,836 | 64.7% | 1997 |
|---|---|---|---|---|---|---|---|---|
| **Sarwar M** | **Lab** | | **12,464** | **49.3%** | **5.21%** | **14,216** | **44.09%** | **Lab** |
| Neary Ms K | SNP | | 6,064 | 23.98% | -11.07% | 11,302 | 35.05% | SNP |
| Stewart B | LD | | 2,815 | 11.13% | 5.19% | 2,839 | 8.81% | C |
| Menzies M | C | | 2,167 | 8.57% | -0.24% | 1,915 | 5.94% | LD |
| McGartland W | SSP | | 1,531 | 6.06% | | 755 | 2.34% | SSA |
| Foster J | Comm | | 174 | 0.69% | | 325 | 1.01% | SLU |
| Mirza B | Ind | | 69 | 0.27% | | 319 | 0.99% | SLI |
| | | | | | | 221 | 0.69% | SCU |
| | | | | | | 201 | 0.62% | Ref |
| | | | | | | 149 | 0.46% | BNP |
| **SNP to Lab swing** | **8.14%** | | **25,284** | **Lab maj 6,400** | | **32,242** | **Lab maj 2,914** | |
| | | | | 25.31% | | | 9.04% | |

**MOHAMMED SARWAR,** b Aug 18, 1952. Elected 1997. Britain's first Muslim MP. Member, Scottish Affairs Select Cttee; all-party grps on shipbuilding and ship repairs, Punjabis, Kashmir. Chairman, Islamic centre and Glasgow Central Mosque, 1985-88. Glasgow city cllr, 1995-97. Member, GMB. Ed Faisalabad Univ, Pakistan.
e-mail: sarwar@sarwar.org.uk www.sarwar.org.uk
tel: 0141-427 5250 fax: 0141-427 5938

This has traditionally been the Glasgow constituency most associated with shipbuilding. It has also proved politically unpredictable, swinging wildly to the SNP in by-elections. Over the past five years it has been a hotbed of intrigue. Mohammed Sarwar became the first Asian MP in Scotland in 1997, survived a post-election trial on bribery charges and then more than doubled his majority in 2001. **Map 268**

## GLASGOW KELVIN — Lab hold

| Electorate | %Turnout | | 61,534 | 43.56% | 2001 | 57,438 | 56.85% | 1997 |
|---|---|---|---|---|---|---|---|---|
| **Galloway G** | **Lab** | | **12,014** | **44.83%** | **-6.14%** | **16,643** | **50.97%** | **Lab** |
| Mayberry Ms T | LD | | 4,754 | 17.74% | 3.56% | 6,978 | 21.37% | SNP |
| Rankin F | SNP | | 4,513 | 16.84% | -4.53% | 4,629 | 14.18% | LD |
| Rankin Miss D | C | | 2,388 | 8.91% | -1.93% | 3,539 | 10.84% | C |
| Ritchie Ms H | SSP | | 1,847 | 6.89% | | 386 | 1.18% | SSA |
| Shand T | Green | | 1,286 | 4.8% | | 282 | 0.86% | Ref |
| | | | | | | 102 | 0.31% | SPGB |
| | | | | | | 95 | 0.29% | NLP |
| **Lab to LD swing** | **4.85%** | | **26,802** | **Lab maj 7,260** | | **32,654** | **Lab maj 9,665** | |
| | | | | 27.09% | | | 29.60% | |

**GEORGE GALLOWAY,** b Aug 16, 1954. Elected here 1997; MP for Glasgow Hillhead 1987-97. Senior vice-chairman, PLP Foreign Affairs Cttee, 1987-90 and 1991-; sec, all-party British-Iranian grp. Ex-chairman, Scottish Lab Party. Gen sec, War on Want, 1983-87. Journalist. Ed Harris Acad, Dundee.
e-mail: gallowayg@parliament.uk tel: 020-7219 6940 fax: 020-7219 2879

This seat contains the overwhelming majority of the old Glasgow Hillhead combined with a segment of the former Glasgow Central. The net effect has been to create a seat where Labour is strongly favoured at present but future competition is perfectly plausible. **Map 269**

## GLASGOW MARYHILL — Lab hold

| Electorate | %Turnout | | 55,431 | 40.11% | 2001 | 52,523 | 56.59% | 1997 |
|---|---|---|---|---|---|---|---|---|
| **McKechin Ms A** | **Lab** | | **13,420** | **60.37%** | **-4.57%** | **19,301** | **64.94%** | **Lab** |
| Dingwall A | SNP | | 3,532 | 15.89% | -1.06% | 5,037 | 16.95% | SNP |
| Callison S | LD | | 2,372 | 10.67% | 3.54% | 2,119 | 7.13% | LD |
| Scott G | SSP | | 1,745 | 7.85% | | 1,747 | 5.88% | C |
| Towler G | C | | 1,162 | 5.23% | -0.65% | 651 | 2.19% | NLP |
| | | | | | | 409 | 1.38% | SSA |
| | | | | | | 344 | 1.16% | ProLife |
| | | | | | | 77 | 0.26% | Ref |
| | | | | | | 36 | 0.12% | SEP |
| **Lab to SNP swing** | **1.76%** | | **22,231** | **Lab maj 9,888** | | **29,721** | **Lab maj 14,264** | |
| | | | | 44.48% | | | 47.99% | |

**ANN McKECHIN,** b April 22, 1961. Elected 2001. Inherits seat from Maria Fyfe, who in 1997, consolidated Lab's hold on a constituency that has not left Lab's hands since 1945. Contested Scottish Parliament election, 1999. Women's officer, Glasgow Kelvin Lab Party and former constituency branch sec. Solicitor. Ed Sacred Heart HS Paisley; Paisley GS; Strathclyde Univ.

This is an overwhelmingly working-class seat in the north of the city. While there is a range of housing, council tenants remain the most important political block. There is also some racial diversity (including the largest number of Chinese-Britons in Scotland). There is not, as Labour can testify, much partisan diversity. **Map 270**

# GLASGOW POLLOK

**Lab hold**

| Electorate | %Turnout | | 49,201 | 51.37% | 2001 | 49,284 | 66.56% | 1997 |
|---|---|---|---|---|---|---|---|---|
| **Davidson I** | Lab Co-op | | **15,497** | **61.31%** | **1.4%** | **19,653** | **59.91%** | **Lab** |
| Ritchie D | SNP | | 4,229 | 16.73% | -1.14% | 5,862 | 17.87% | SNP |
| Baldassara K | SSP | | 2,522 | 9.98% | | 3,639 | 11.09% | SSA |
| Nelson Ms I | LD | | 1,612 | 6.38% | 2.91% | 1,979 | 6.03% | C |
| O'Brien R | C | | 1,417 | 5.61% | -0.42% | 1,137 | 3.47% | LD |
| | | | | | | 380 | 1.16% | ProLife |
| | | | | | | 152 | 0.46% | Ref |
| **SNP to Lab Co-op swing 1.27%** | | | **25,277** | **Lab Co-op maj 11,268** | | **32,802** | **Lab Co-op maj 13,791** | |
| | | | | 44.58% | | | 42.04% | |

**IAN DAVIDSON,** b Sept 8, 1950. Elected here 1997; MP for Glasgow Govan 1992-97. Member, Public Accounts Cttee, 1997-2001. Member, all-party warm homes grp; joint vice-chairman, PLP Defence Cttee. Strathclyde reg cllr, 1978-92; (chairman, ed cttee, 1986-92). Convener, Cosla ed cttee and negotiating cttee on teachers' salaries. With community service volunteers, 1985-92. PA to Janey Buchan, MEP, 1978-85. Ed Jedburgh GS; Galashiels Acad; Edinburgh Univ; Jordanhill Coll.

This seat comes close to the Englishman's popular image of Glasgow. It is a tough, working-class area with vast 1950s housing estates on the southwest side of the city that has suffered from difficult economic circumstances for decades. It is therefore strongly biased towards Labour. A degree of lively competition has arisen through the presence of the Scottish Socialist Alliance. Map 271

# GLASGOW RUTHERGLEN

**Lab hold**

| Electorate | %Turnout | | 51,855 | 56.34% | 2001 | 50,646 | 70.14% | 1997 |
|---|---|---|---|---|---|---|---|---|
| **McAvoy T** | Lab Co-op | | **16,760** | **57.37%** | **-0.15%** | **20,430** | **57.52%** | **Lab** |
| McLaughlin Ms A | SNP | | 4,135 | 14.15% | -1.12% | 5,423 | 15.27% | SNP |
| Jackson D | LD | | 3,689 | 12.63% | -1.92% | 5,167 | 14.55% | LD |
| Macaskill M | C | | 3,301 | 11.3% | 2.04% | 3,288 | 9.26% | C |
| Bonnar B | SSP | | 1,328 | 4.55% | | 812 | 2.29% | Ind Lab |
| | | | | | | 251 | 0.71% | SSA |
| | | | | | | 150 | 0.42% | Ref |
| **SNP to Lab Co-op swing 0.48%** | | | **29,213** | **Lab Co-op maj 12,625** | | **35,521** | **Lab maj 15,007** | |
| | | | | 43.22% | | | 42.25% | |

**THOMAS McAVOY,** b Dec 14, 1943. Elected 1987. Comptroller of HM Household, June 2001-. Gvt whip, 1997-2001; Lab whip, 1996-97 and 1990-93. Member, NI Affairs Select Cttee, 1994-97; Unopposed Bills Panel, 1992-97. Ex-joint vice-chairman, PLP NI cttee. Strathclyde reg cllr, 1982-87. Member, AEU. Engineering storeman. Ed St Columbkilles primary and junior sec schs.

This is a slightly more diverse constituency than others in Glasgow. The burgh of Rutherglen was an independent entity until swallowed up by the city in the 1970s. Lying on the southeast of Glasgow, the seat is working-class, but has a middle-class section. It is not as dominated by council tenants as its neighbours, but the Labour Party is always destined to be heavily favoured here. Map 272

# GLASGOW SHETTLESTON

**Lab hold**

| Electorate | %Turnout | | 51,557 | 39.69% | 2001 | 47,990 | 55.87% | 1997 |
|---|---|---|---|---|---|---|---|---|
| **Marshall D** | Lab | | **13,235** | **64.67%** | **-8.49%** | **19,616** | **73.16%** | **Lab** |
| Byrne J | SNP | | 3,417 | 16.7% | 2.72% | 3,748 | 13.98% | SNP |
| Kane Ms R | SSP | | 1,396 | 6.82% | | 1,484 | 5.53% | C |
| Hutton L | LD | | 1,105 | 5.4% | 1.44% | 1,061 | 3.96% | LD |
| Murdoch C | C | | 1,082 | 5.29% | -0.24% | 482 | 1.8% | SSA |
| Ritchie M | Soc Lab | | 230 | 1.12% | | 191 | 0.71% | BNP |
| | | | | | | 151 | 0.56% | Ref |
| | | | | | | 80 | 0.3% | WRP |
| **Lab to SNP swing** | **5.60%** | | **20,465** | **Lab maj 9,818** | | **26,813** | **Lab maj 15,868** | |
| | | | | 47.97% | | | 59.18% | |

**DAVID MARSHALL,** b May 7, 1941. Elected 1979. Chairman, Select Cttee, Scottish Affairs, 1997-2001; member, Liaison Select Cttee and Unopposed Bills Panel, 1992-2001; Transport, 1985-92 (chairman, 1987-92). Vice-chairman and chairman of IPU British grp between 1994 and 2000. Sec and treas, Scottish grp of Lab MPs, 1981- (chairman, 1987-), and joint vice-chairman, PLP Transport Cttee, 1983-87. Piloted the Solvent Abuse (Scotland) Bill through Parliament. Ex-transport worker and shop steward. Ed Larbert HS, Denny HS, Falkirk HS; Woodside Senior Sec.

This is a very working-class district which covers virtually all of the southern and eastern sections of the inner city. These are tough areas with a high proportion of local authority accommodation and a distinct shortage of professionals and managers. The Labour Party has traditionally dominated local politics. There are no signs that this is about to change. Map 273

## GLASGOW SPRINGBURN — Speaker

| Electorate | %Turnout | | 55,192 | 43.67% | 2001 | 53,473 | 59.05% | 1997 |
|---|---|---|---|---|---|---|---|---|
| Martin M | Speaker | | 16,053 | 66.6% | | 22,534 | 71.36% | Lab |
| Bain S | SNP | | 4,675 | 19.4% | 2.91% | 5,208 | 16.49% | SNP |
| Leckie Ms C | SSP | | 1,879 | 7.8% | | 1,893 | 5.99% | C |
| Houston D | Scot U | | 1,289 | 5.35% | | 1,349 | 4.27% | LD |
| Silvester R | Ind | | 208 | 0.86% | | 407 | 1.29% | SSA |
| | | | | | | 186 | 0.59% | Ref |
| No swing | | | 24,104 | Speaker maj 11,378 47.20% | | 31,577 | Lab maj 17,326 54.87% | |

**MICHAEL MARTIN,** b July 3, 1945. Elected 1979. Elected Speaker, October 2000. Dep Speaker and First Deputy Chairman, Ways and Means, 1997-2000. Chairman, Commons Admin Cttee, 1992-97; Finance and Services Cttee, 1992-97; member, Commons Chairmen's Panel, 1987-97. PPS to Denis Healey, Dep Leader of Lab Party, 1981-83. Member, Glasgow Corp, 1973-74; Glasgow district cllr, 1974-79. Shop steward and sheet metal worker. Ed St Patrick's Sch, Glasgow.

Another very working-class and Labour-leaning Glasgow constituency with a high proportion of council tenants. It is dominated by some extremely stark tower blocks. This is the northern section of the city and it has historically been associated with the railway industry. Poverty and unemployment persist to a disturbing degree in this part of the city. The seat is currently held by the Speaker. Map 274

## GLOUCESTER — Lab hold

| Electorate | %Turnout | | 81,144 | 59.43% | 2001 | 78,682 | 73.61% | 1997 |
|---|---|---|---|---|---|---|---|---|
| Dhanda P | Lab | | 22,067 | 45.76% | -4.22% | 28,943 | 49.98% | Lab |
| James P | C | | 18,187 | 37.71% | 1.99% | 20,684 | 35.72% | C |
| Bullamore T | LD | | 6,875 | 14.26% | 3.78% | 6,069 | 10.48% | LD |
| Lines T | UK Ind | | 822 | 1.7% | 0.91% | 1,482 | 2.56% | Ref |
| Smyth S | Soc All | | 272 | 0.56% | | 455 | 0.79% | UK Ind |
| | | | | | | 281 | 0.49% | NLP |
| Lab to C swing | 3.11% | | 48,223 | Lab maj 3,880 8.05% | | 57,914 | Lab maj 8,259 14.26% | |

**PARMJIT DHANDA,** b Sept 17, 1971. Elected 2001. Takes over from Tess Kingham, who was heralded as the archetypal "Blair Babe" but stood down in protest at the nature of the House of Commons proceedings. Contested Euro elections, 1999. Worked for three years as a Lab Party organiser, 1996-98, and as asst nat organiser, Connect 1998-2001. Ed Mellow Lane Comp; Nottingham Univ.

This seat fits the city of Gloucester local boundaries exactly. Gloucester is a bustling and broadly prosperous commercial and cathedral city. It has a reasonable pool of working-class voters on whom Labour can base a campaign, but until the 1997 election it had been dominated by the Tories. The newly elected MP, Tess Kingham, stood down after one term and was less than flattering about parliamentary life, but Labour hung on in 2001. Map 275

## GORDON — LD hold

| Electorate | %Turnout | | 59,996 | 58.34% | 2001 | 58,767 | 71.89% | 1997 |
|---|---|---|---|---|---|---|---|---|
| Bruce M | LD | | 15,928 | 45.51% | 2.9% | 17,999 | 42.61% | LD |
| Milne Mrs N | C | | 8,049 | 23.0% | -3.04% | 11,002 | 26.04% | C |
| Kemp Mrs R | SNP | | 5,760 | 16.46% | -3.51% | 8,435 | 19.97% | SNP |
| Thorpe E | Lab | | 4,730 | 13.51% | 3.21% | 4,350 | 10.3% | Lab |
| Sangster J | SSA | | 534 | 1.53% | | 459 | 1.09% | Ref |
| C to LD swing | 2.97% | | 35,001 | LD maj 7,879 22.51% | | 42,245 | LD maj 6,997 16.57% | |

**MALCOLM BRUCE,** b Nov 17, 1944. Elected for L/All 1983, becoming LD MP 1988. LD chief spokesman, Environment, Food and Rural Affairs, June 2001. Spokesman, Treasury and Civil Service, 1993-2001. Leader, Scottish LDs, 1988-92; chief spokesman, Scotland, 1990-93. Lib, and then LD spokesman, trade and industry, 1987-88; Lib spokesman, energy, 1985-87. Member, Select Cttees: Treasury and Civil Service, 1994-97; Trade and Industry, 1992-94. Joint vice-chairman, all-party Scottish housing grp. Barrister. Ed Wrekin Coll, Shropshire; St Andrews and Strathclyde Univs.

This seat on the outskirts of Aberdeen has experienced an extraordinary boom in population over the past two decades. This is largely because those who work in the oil industry prefer to live in more rural and suburban territory. Many of its social characteristics are Conservative, but this does not mean that it elects Tory MPs. The Liberal Democrats have been the dominant force for the better part of the past 20 years. Map 276

## GOSPORT — C hold

| Electorate | %Turnout | | 69,626 | 57.15% | 2001 | 68,830 | 70.25% | 1997 |
|---|---|---|---|---|---|---|---|---|
| **Viggers P** | | C | **17,364** | **43.64%** | **0.04%** | 21,085 | 43.6% | C |
| Williams R | | Lab | 14,743 | 37.05% | 6.39% | 14,827 | 30.66% | Lab |
| Roberts R | | LD | 6,011 | 15.11% | -4.49% | 9,479 | 19.6% | LD |
| Bowles J | | UK Ind | 1,162 | 2.92% | | 2,538 | 5.25% | Ref |
| Chetwynd K | | Soc Lab | 509 | 1.28% | | 426 | 0.88% | Ind |
| **C to Lab swing** | **3.18%** | | **39,789** | | C maj 2,621 | 48,355 | | C maj 6,258 |
| | | | | | 6.59% | | | 12.94% |

**PETER VIGGERS,** b March 13, 1938. Elected 1974. Vice-chairman, Defence Select Cttee, 2000-01; Members' Interests, 1991-93. Chairman, all-party Japanese grp, 1992-; joint sec, C Backbench Defence Cttee, 1991-97; junior NI Min, 1986-89; delegate, N Atlantic Assembly, 1992- and 1980-86; chairman, Central and Eastern Europe subcttee, 1998-. Dir, Warrior Preservation Trust; member, management cttee, Royal Nat Lifeboat Inst (both unpaid). Solicitor and Lloyd's underwriter. Ed Portsmouth GS; Trinity Hall, Camb.

Although Gosport has a high proportion of owner-occupiers, the number of professionals and managers is relatively low, especially for a seat that appears to be comfortably Tory. The town, just across the harbour from Portsmouth, has long been associated with the Royal Navy. This not only produces a strong Services vote for the Tories, but has also created a local working class which, despite recent trends, still doubts Labour's credibility on defence. Map 277

## GOWER — Lab hold

| Electorate | %Turnout | | 58,943 | 63.37% | 2001 | 57,691 | 75.12% | 1997 |
|---|---|---|---|---|---|---|---|---|
| **Caton M** | | Lab | **17,676** | **47.32%** | **-6.48%** | 23,313 | 53.8% | Lab |
| Bushell J | | C | 10,281 | 27.52% | 3.74% | 10,306 | 23.78% | C |
| Waye Ms S | | LD | 4,507 | 12.07% | -0.91% | 5,624 | 12.98% | LD |
| Caiach Ms S | | PC | 3,865 | 10.35% | 5.21% | 2,226 | 5.14% | PC |
| Shrewsbury Ms T | | Green | 607 | 1.63% | | 1,745 | 4.03% | Ref |
| Hickery D | | Soc Lab | 417 | 1.12% | | 122 | 0.28% | FP |
| **Lab to C swing** | **5.11%** | | **37,353** | | Lab maj 7,395 | 43,336 | | Lab maj 13,007 |
| | | | | | 19.80% | | | 30.02% |

**MARTIN CATON,** b June 15, 1951. Elected 1997. Member, Welsh Affairs Select Cttee, 1997-2001. Ex-political asst/researcher to David Morris, MEP for S Wales W, 1984-97. Former scientific officer, Welsh Plant Breeding Station, 1972-84. Ex-Swansea city cllr and Swansea UA cllr. Ed Newport GS, Essex; Norfolk Sch of Agriculture; Aberystwyth Coll of FE.

This is a constituency of two rather different sections. The Gower Peninsula has attractive holiday beaches such as Mumbles and is home to Swansea's more affluent commuters. The other side of the seat is, however, rather more like classic South Wales mining territory. The end result, as is often true in Wales, is a seat with the sort of social characteristics which imply a degree of partisan competition but solid Labour loyalty in practice. Map 278

## GRANTHAM & STAMFORD — C hold

| Electorate | %Turnout | | 74,459 | 62.17% | 2001 | 72,310 | 73.25% | 1997 |
|---|---|---|---|---|---|---|---|---|
| **Davies Q** | | C | **21,329** | **46.08%** | **3.28%** | 22,672 | 42.8% | C |
| Robinson J | | Lab | 16,811 | 36.32% | -1.4% | 19,980 | 37.72% | Lab |
| Carr Ms J | | LD | 6,665 | 14.4% | 1.92% | 6,612 | 12.48% | LD |
| Swain Miss M | | UK Ind | 1,484 | 3.21% | 2.16% | 2,721 | 5.14% | Ref |
| | | | | | | 556 | 1.05% | UK Ind |
| | | | | | | 314 | 0.59% | ProLife |
| | | | | | | 115 | 0.22% | NLP |
| **Lab to C swing** | **2.34%** | | **46,289** | | C maj 4,518 | 52,970 | | C maj 2,692 |
| | | | | | 9.76% | | | 5.08% |

**QUENTIN DAVIES,** b May 29, 1944. Elected here 1997. MP for Stamford and Spalding 1987-97. Opposition defence spokesman, 2000-. Shadow Paymaster General, 1999-2000 and Shadow Min of Pensions, 1998-99. Member, Select Cttees: Standards and Privileges, 1995-98; Treasury, 1992-98. Joint sec, Backbench Finance Cttee, 1991-; sec, Trade and Industry Cttee, 1991-; joint vice-chairman, Trade and Industry Deregulation Sub-Cttee, 1994-. Liveryman, Goldsmiths' Co; Freeman, City of London. Ed Leighton Park; Gonville and Caius Coll, Cambridge; Harvard.

Lincolnshire has witnessed an increase in population over recent years, a process that has led the Boundary Commission to set about its parliamentary borders with vigour. The end result here is the amalgamation of Grantham, well known as the home town of Margaret Thatcher, which contains a lot of both Tory and Labour supporters, and the beautiful old town of Stamford, which leans more forcefully towards the Tories. Map 279

## GRAVESHAM — Lab hold

| Electorate | %Turnout | | 69,590 | 62.71% | 2001 | 69,234 | 76.92% | 1997 |
|---|---|---|---|---|---|---|---|---|
| **Pond C** | **Lab** | | **21,773** | **49.89%** | 0.2% | **26,460** | **49.69%** | Lab |
| Arnold J | C | | 16,911 | 38.75% | -0.09% | 20,681 | 38.84% | C |
| Parmenter B | LD | | 4,031 | 9.24% | 1.49% | 4,128 | 7.75% | LD |
| Jenner W | UK Ind | | 924 | 2.12% | | 1,441 | 2.71% | Ref |
| | | | | | | 414 | 0.78% | Ind |
| | | | | | | 129 | 0.24% | NLP |
| **C to Lab swing** | **0.15%** | | **43,639** | Lab maj 4,862 | | **53,253** | Lab maj 5,779 | |
| | | | | 11.14% | | | 10.85% | |

**CHRIS POND,** b Sept 25, 1952. Elected 1997; contested Welwyn Hatfield 1987. PPS to Dawn Primarolo, Paymaster-General, 1999-. Expert, social policy directorate, Euro Commission, 1996. Visiting Professor, Middlesex Univ; consultant, OU, 1987-88 and 1991-92. Visiting Professor/research fellow, Univ of Surrey, 1984-86, visiting lecturer, economics, Univ of Kent, 1981-82; lecturer (economics), Civil Service Coll, 1979-80. Dir, Low Pay Unit, 1980-97. Research asst (economics) Birkbeck Coll, London, 1974-75. Marathon runner. Ed Michenden Sch, Southgate; Sussex Univ.

A socially polarised Kent constituency - it used to be named Gravesend and is based on the town - which makes for a classic marginal battleground. There is a strong Labour vote in the towns along the south bank of the River Thames and an equally robust Tory heartland in the more rural areas and villages such as Meopham. There is also a notable Indian community in Gravesend, large by the standards of Kent. This will always be a hard-fought contest. Map 280

## GREAT GRIMSBY — Lab hold

| Electorate | %Turnout | | 63,157 | 52.28% | 2001 | 65,043 | 66.26% | 1997 |
|---|---|---|---|---|---|---|---|---|
| **Mitchell A** | **Lab** | | **19,118** | **57.9%** | -1.89% | **25,765** | **59.79%** | Lab |
| Cousins J | C | | 7,634 | 23.12% | 1.03% | 9,521 | 22.09% | C |
| de Freitas A | LD | | 6,265 | 18.98% | 0.86% | 7,810 | 18.12% | LD |
| **Lab to C swing** | **1.46%** | | **33,017** | Lab maj 11,484 | | **43,096** | Lab maj 16,244 | |
| | | | | 34.78% | | | 37.70% | |

**AUSTIN MITCHELL,** b Sept 19, 1934. Elected here 1983; represented Grimsby 1977-83. Member, Select Cttee, Agriculture, 1997-2001. Former opposition whip. Chairman: fisheries, trans-Pennine, media, consumer affairs and trading standards, advertising and photography all-party grps.Joint sec, Esperanto parly grp. Journalist/TV presenter. Fellow, Industry and Parliament Trust. Ed Woodbottom Council Sch; Bingley GS; Manchester Univ; Nuffield Coll, Oxford.

This Humberside seat has long been known as a fishing and container port and many are also employed in the petrochemical complexes on the estuary. It suffered some difficult economic times in the 1980s and 1990s but has staged something of a recovery. The heart of the town is solidly Labour and stuck with the party even during its most unpopular years. This is only a little offset by Conservative support to the south and east of the constituency. Map 281

## GREAT YARMOUTH — Lab hold

| Electorate | %Turnout | | 69,131 | 58.39% | 2001 | 68,625 | 71.23% | 1997 |
|---|---|---|---|---|---|---|---|---|
| **Wright T** | **Lab** | | **20,344** | **50.4%** | -2.96% | **26,084** | **53.36%** | Lab |
| Reynolds C | C | | 15,780 | 39.09% | 3.46% | 17,416 | 35.63% | C |
| Leeke M | LD | | 3,392 | 8.4% | -2.61% | 5,381 | 11.01% | LD |
| Poole B | UK Ind | | 850 | 2.11% | | | | |
| **Lab to C swing** | **3.21%** | | **40,366** | Lab maj 4,564 | | **48,881** | Lab maj 8,668 | |
| | | | | 11.31% | | | 17.73% | |

**TONY WRIGHT,** b Aug 12, 1954. Elected 1997. Member, Select Cttee on Public Admin. Chairman, all-party grp on ME. Chaired Euro transport project, which established a private port authority. Leader, Great Yarmouth borough council, 1995-97. Former dir, Great Yarmouth tourist authority; district cllr. Engineer. Lab Party organiser and agent, 1983-97. Ed Hospital Sec Mod, Great Yarmouth.
e-mail: wrighta@parliament.uk tel: 01493 332291 fax: 01493 332189

This is the premier holiday resort and the largest working port in Norfolk. The town itself has usually provided a reasonably solid vote for Labour but this has traditionally been more than offset by the staunchly Conservative coastal villages, such as Gorleston-on-Sea, and rural areas. Labour won the seat, nonetheless, in 1997, creating a marginal battleground which it held in 2001. Map 282

# GREENOCK & INVERCLYDE

**Lab hold**

| Electorate | %Turnout | | 47,884 | 59.35% | 2001 | 48,818 | 71.05% | 1997 |
|---|---|---|---|---|---|---|---|---|
| **Cairns D** | | **Lab** | **14,929** | **52.53%** | **-3.63%** | **19,480** | **56.16%** | **Lab** |
| Brodie C | | LD | 5,039 | 17.73% | 3.92% | 6,440 | 18.57% | SNP |
| Murie A | | SNP | 4,248 | 14.95% | -3.62% | 4,791 | 13.81% | LD |
| Haw A | | C | 3,000 | 10.56% | -0.9% | 3,976 | 11.46% | C |
| Landels D | | SSP | 1,203 | 4.23% | | | | |
| **Lab to LD swing** | | **3.77%** | **28,419** | **Lab maj 9,890** | | **34,687** | **Lab maj 13,040** | |
| | | | | 34.80% | | | 37.59% | |

**DAVID CAIRNS,** b Aug 7, 1966. Elected 2001. Inherits seat from retiring Norman Godman. A former Roman Catholic priest, he became eligible to stand as an MP after a law barring clergy from sitting in the Commons was changed in May 2001. Dir, Soc Christian Movement, 1994-97. Ed Notre Dame High; Gregnor Univ, Rome.

Greenock, sandwiched between the hills and the Clyde, is a town formerly associated with heavy industry and seafaring but now diversifying into electronics and computing. The most recent boundary changes included the coastal towns of Gourock and Wemyss Bay in the constituency. This was once quite competitive political territory with the Liberals, especially, making a decent showing. It is now dominated by Labour. Map 283

# GREENWICH & WOOLWICH

**Lab hold**

| Electorate | %Turnout | | 62,530 | 52.03% | 2001 | 61,352 | 65.85% | 1997 |
|---|---|---|---|---|---|---|---|---|
| **Raynsford N** | | **Lab** | **19,691** | **60.52%** | **-2.92%** | **25,630** | **63.44%** | **Lab** |
| Forsdyke R | | C | 6,258 | 19.23% | 0.66% | 7,502 | 18.57% | C |
| Pyne R | | LD | 5,082 | 15.62% | 3.12% | 5,049 | 12.5% | LD |
| Gain S | | UK Ind | 672 | 2.07% | | 1,670 | 4.13% | Ref |
| Paton Miss K | | Soc All | 481 | 1.48% | | 428 | 1.06% | Fellowship |
| Sharkey Ms M | | Soc Lab | 352 | 1.08% | | 124 | 0.31% | Constit |
| **Lab to C swing** | | **1.79%** | **32,536** | **Lab maj 13,433** | | **40,403** | **Lab maj 18,128** | |
| | | | | 41.29% | | | 44.87% | |

**NICK RAYNSFORD,** b Jan 28, 1945. Elected here 1997; MP for Fulham 1986-87; Greenwich 1992-97. Min for Local Govt, June 2001-; Min for Housing and Planning, 1999-2001 (for London, 1999). Lab housing spokesman, 1994-97. Hammersmith and Fulham cllr, 1971-75. Consultant, Housing Assoc Consultancy and Advisory Service, 1993-97. Dir, SHAC, the London Housing Aid Centre, 1976-86. Housing consultant. Ed Repton Sch; Sidney Sussex Coll, Cambridge; Chelsea Sch of Art.
e-mail: seabeckaj@parliament.uk tel: 020-7219 2773

This southeast London seat consists of all the former Greenwich seat and part of the old Woolwich constituency. It has a large proportion of council tenants but also a sizeable professional minority. Attractions such as the Royal Observatory and the *Cutty Sark* bring in substantial tourist revenue, though the Millennium Dome failed to live up to expectations. At one stage the SDP held both Greenwich and Woolwich, but this is solidly Labour now. Map 284

# GUILDFORD

**LD gain**

| Electorate | %Turnout | | 76,046 | 62.91% | 2001 | 75,541 | 75.4% | 1997 |
|---|---|---|---|---|---|---|---|---|
| **Doughty Ms S** | | **LD** | **20,358** | **42.55%** | **8.42%** | **24,230** | **42.54%** | **C** |
| St Aubyn N | | C | 19,820 | 41.43% | -1.11% | 19,439 | 34.13% | LD |
| Still Ms J | | Lab | 6,558 | 13.71% | -3.75% | 9,945 | 17.46% | Lab |
| Porter Ms S | | UK Ind | 736 | 1.54% | 0.84% | 2,650 | 4.65% | Ref |
| Morris J | | Pacifist | 370 | 0.77% | 0.25% | 400 | 0.7% | UK Ind |
| | | | | | | 294 | 0.52% | Pacifist |
| **C to LD swing** | | **4.77%** | **47,842** | **LD maj 538** | | **56,958** | **C maj 4,791** | |
| | | | | 1.12% | | | 8.41% | |

**SUE DOUGHTY,** b April 13, 1948. Elected 2001. Won seat from Nick St Aubyn, C. Contested London in Euro elections, 1999. Former constituency chairwoman, Reading E; deputy reg chairwoman, Chilterns region. Consultant project manager, Norwich Union, 2000-01. Former manager, Thames Water. Ed Millmount GS, York; Northumberland Coll.

Although Surrey is an extremely Tory county, the cathedral and university town of Guildford has increasingly appeared to be one of the less safe Conservative seats within it. And so it transpired in 2001, when the Liberal Democrats sprang one of the surprises of the election by snatching the seat, albeit with a tiny majority. There are council estates here as well as highly affluent suburbs and villages such as Bramley, Cranleigh and Ewhurst. Map 285

## HACKNEY NORTH & STOKE NEWINGTON

**Lab hold**

| Electorate | %Turnout | | 60,444 | 49.01% | 2001 | 62,045 | 52.95% | 1997 |
|---|---|---|---|---|---|---|---|---|
| **Abbott Ms D** | | **Lab** | **18,081** | **61.04%** | **-3.22%** | **21,110** | **64.26%** | **Lab** |
| Dye Mrs P | | C | 4,430 | 14.96% | -1.73% | 5,483 | 16.69% | C |
| Ece Ms M | | LD | 4,170 | 14.08% | 2.49% | 3,806 | 11.59% | LD |
| Chong C | | Green | 2,184 | 7.37% | 3.12% | 1,395 | 4.25% | Green |
| Chandan S | | Soc Lab | 756 | 2.55% | | 544 | 1.66% | Ref |
| | | | | | | 368 | 1.12% | None |
| | | | | | | 146 | 0.44% | Rain Ref |
| **Lab to C swing** | | **0.74%** | **29,621** | Lab maj **13,651** | | **32,852** | Lab maj **15,627** | |
| | | | | 46.09% | | | 47.57% | |

**DIANE ABBOTT,** b Sept 27, 1953. Elected 1987. Member, Select Cttees: Foreign Affairs, 1997-2001; Treasury, 1989-97. Member, Lab Party NEC. Joint vice-chairwoman, all-party race and community grp, 1997-; sec, Ghana grp, 1997-. Former press officer, Lambeth Borough Council; ex-civil servant and former employee of NCCL, Thames TV, Breakfast TV and ACTT. Westminster cllr, 1982-86. Ed Harrow County Girls' GS; Newnham Coll, Cambridge.

Hackney is arguably the most deprived of the London boroughs. It has suffered from striking crime and drugs problems and is racially polarised between Anglo-Saxon white, Jewish, Afro-Caribbean and some Asian electors. It is, nonetheless, a very safe Labour seat but in a part of the capital that is definitely suffering from population flight. Map 286

## HACKNEY SOUTH & SHOREDITCH

**Lab hold**

| Electorate | %Turnout | | 63,990 | 47.42% | 2001 | 61,728 | 54.67% | 1997 |
|---|---|---|---|---|---|---|---|---|
| **Sedgemore B** | | **Lab** | **19,471** | **64.16%** | **4.75%** | **20,048** | **59.41%** | **Lab** |
| Vickers T | | LD | 4,422 | 14.57% | -0.45% | 5,068 | 15.02% | LD |
| White P | | C | 4,180 | 13.77% | 0.45% | 4,494 | 13.32% | C |
| Prosper Ms C | | Soc All | 1,401 | 4.62% | | 2,436 | 7.22% | N Lab |
| Kokshal S | | Reform | 471 | 1.55% | | 613 | 1.82% | Ref |
| Beavis I | | Comm | 259 | 0.85% | | 531 | 1.57% | BNP |
| Rogers W | | WRP | 143 | 0.47% | 0.14% | 298 | 0.88% | Comm Brit |
| | | | | | | 145 | 0.43% | NLP |
| | | | | | | 113 | 0.33% | WRP |
| **LD to Lab swing** | | **2.60%** | **30,347** | Lab maj **15,049** | | **33,746** | Lab maj **14,980** | |
| | | | | 49.59% | | | 44.39% | |

**BRIAN SEDGEMORE,** b March 17, 1937. Elected here 1983; MP, Luton W Feb 1974-79. Former member, Treasury Select Cttee. PPS to Tony Benn, 1977-78. Wandsworth cllr, 1971-74. Researcher, Granada Television, 1979-83. Barrister, freelance journalist, writer. Ed Newtown Primary; Heles Sch, Exeter; Corpus Christi Coll, Oxford.

This section of Hackney has much in common with its Inner London neighbour. The non-white population is slightly smaller but the proportion of council tenants is even larger. Similar problems of persistent poverty and high unemployment continue despite several efforts at regeneration. In the past two elections the Liberal Democrats have advanced into second place, but the Labour vote remains powerful all the same. Map 287

## HALESOWEN & ROWLEY REGIS

**Lab hold**

| Electorate | %Turnout | | 65,683 | 59.79% | 2001 | 66,245 | 73.61% | 1997 |
|---|---|---|---|---|---|---|---|---|
| **Heal Ms S** | | **Lab** | **20,804** | **52.97%** | **-1.1%** | **26,366** | **54.07%** | **Lab** |
| Jones L | | C | 13,445 | 34.23% | 1.36% | 16,029 | 32.87% | C |
| Harley P | | LD | 4,089 | 10.41% | 1.86% | 4,169 | 8.55% | LD |
| Sheath A | | UK Ind | 936 | 2.38% | | 1,244 | 2.55% | Ref |
| | | | | | | 592 | 1.21% | Nat Dem |
| | | | | | | 361 | 0.74% | Green |
| **Lab to C swing** | | **1.23%** | **39,274** | Lab maj **7,359** | | **48,761** | Lab maj **10,337** | |
| | | | | 18.74% | | | 21.20% | |

**SYLVIA HEAL,** b July 20, 1942. Elected here 1997; MP, Staffs Mid 1990-92. First deputy chairwoman, Ways and Means. Former PPS to George Robertson, Defence Sec. Lab spokeswoman, health and women's issues, 1991-92. Member, Select Cttee, ed, science and arts, 1990-92. Nat young carers officer, Carers Nat Assoc, 1992-97. Advertising Standards Authority, 1992-97; exec council, SSAFA, 1990-91. Social worker, health service and Dept of Employment, 1968-70 and 1980-90. Ed Elfred Sec Mod, Buckley, N Wales; Coleg Harlech; Univ Coll of Wales, Swansea.

This is a cross-borough seat which stretches across Dudley and Sandwell in the West Midlands. In theory, it has all the makings of a marginal. There is a fair proportion of council tenants, who provide a Labour base in the Black Country towns such as Cradley Heath and Rowley Regis. There are also plenty of Tories in prosperous Halesowen and the areas which share the flavour of neighbouring Worcestershire. But Labour now wins here quite easily. Map 288

# HALIFAX

**Lab hold**

| Electorate | %Turnout | | 69,870 | 57.81% | 2001 | 71,701 | 70.51% | 1997 |
|---|---|---|---|---|---|---|---|---|
| **Mahon Ms A** | | **Lab** | **19,800** | **49.02%** | **-5.31%** | **27,465** | **54.33%** | **Lab** |
| Walsh J | | C | 13,671 | 33.85% | 1.7% | 16,253 | 32.15% | C |
| Durkin J | | LD | 5,878 | 14.55% | 2.57% | 6,059 | 11.98% | LD |
| Martinek Mrs H | | UK Ind | 1,041 | 2.58% | 1.04% | 779 | 1.54% | UK Ind |
| **Lab to C swing** | **3.50%** | | **40,390** | **Lab maj 6,129** | | **50,556** | **Lab maj 11,212** | |
| | | | | 15.17% | | | 22.18% | |

**ALICE MAHON,** b Sept 28, 1937. Elected 1987. Joint chairwoman, all-party breast cancer grp; Member, Lab nat policy forum, 1998-. PPS to Chris Smith, Culture Sec, until Dec 1997 when dismissed over her opposition to proposed cut in lone parents' benefit. Member, Health Select Cttee, 1991-97. Worked as nursing auxiliary for ten years. Taught trade union studies, Bradford Coll, 1980-87. Lecturer. Ed local GS; Bradford Univ.

West Yorkshire offers a misleading social profile. Halifax is a tough industrial Pennine town which certainly offers the impression of being solidly Labour. Its political loyalties are, in fact, more evenly divided. There are surrounding middle-class sections which also offer the Tories some hope and there is also a sizeable Asian population. Labour narrowly hung on in 1987 and 1992 but it won more easily in 1997 and 2001. Map 289

# HALTEMPRICE & HOWDEN

**C hold**

| Electorate | %Turnout | | 67,055 | 65.51% | 2001 | 65,602 | 75.53% | 1997 |
|---|---|---|---|---|---|---|---|---|
| **Davis D** | | **C** | **18,994** | **43.24%** | **-0.77%** | **21,809** | **44.01%** | **C** |
| Neal J | | LD | 17,091 | 38.91% | 10.06% | 14,295 | 28.85% | LD |
| Howell L | | Lab | 6,898 | 15.7% | -7.91% | 11,701 | 23.61% | Lab |
| Robinson Ms J | | UK Ind | 945 | 2.15% | 1.54% | 1,370 | 2.76% | Ref |
| | | | | | | 301 | 0.61% | UK Ind |
| | | | | | | 74 | 0.15% | NLP |
| **C to LD swing** | **5.41%** | | **43,928** | **C maj 1,903** | | **49,550** | **C maj 7,514** | |
| | | | | 4.33% | | | 15.16% | |

**DAVID DAVIS,** b Dec 23, 1948. Elected here 1997; MP for Boothferry 1987-97. Challenger for the Conservative Party leadership, June 2001. Chairman, Public Accounts Cttee, 1997-2001. Foreign Office Min, 1994-97. Parly sec, Office of Public Service and Science, 1993-94. Former PPS to Francis Maude. Ex-dir, Tate and Lyle. Exec member, Industrial Soc, 1985-87. Author. Ed Bec GS; Warwick Univ; London Business Sch; Harvard.

This is a very middle-class slice of East Yorkshire on the north bank of the Humber and the Ouse. There are both high rates of owner-occupation and a strikingly large section of professional and managerial employees. Both Haltemprice, a suburb of Hull, and Howden, a small rural town on the flat lands to the west, are areas that have traditionally backed the Conservatives. Map 290

# HALTON

**Lab hold**

| Electorate | %Turnout | | 63,673 | 54.14% | 2001 | 64,987 | 68.38% | 1997 |
|---|---|---|---|---|---|---|---|---|
| **Twigg D** | | **Lab** | **23,841** | **69.16%** | **-1.72%** | **31,497** | **70.88%** | **Lab** |
| Davenport C | | C | 6,413 | 18.6% | 0.94% | 7,847 | 17.66% | C |
| Walker P | | LD | 4,216 | 12.23% | 4.89% | 3,263 | 7.34% | LD |
| | | | | | | 1,036 | 2.33% | Ref |
| | | | | | | 600 | 1.35% | Lib |
| | | | | | | 196 | 0.44% | Rep GB |
| **Lab to C swing** | **1.33%** | | **34,470** | **Lab maj 17,428** | | **44,439** | **Lab maj 23,650** | |
| | | | | 50.56% | | | 53.22% | |

**DEREK TWIGG,** b July 9, 1959. Elected 1997. PPS to Stephen Byers, Sec of State for Transport, Local Gvt and the Regions, 2001-; previous PPS to Helen Liddell, Min of State for Energy, DTI. Former member of Public Accounts Cttee. Member, Lab NW reg exec cttee, 1988-92. Chairman, Halton CLP, 1985-96; Halton Borough Cllr, 1983-97; Cheshire cllr, 1981-85. Political consultant; previously civil servant, Dept for Ed and Employment. Ed Bankfield HS; Halton Coll of FE, Widnes.
e-mail: derek.twigg@virgin.net tel: 0151-424 7030 fax: 0151-495 3800

A slightly confusing name as this Cheshire seat is really the amalgamation of Widnes on the north bank of the Mersey and Runcorn on the south. The two towns are both industrial and specialise in chemical production. Runcorn was designated a new town in 1964. This has long been Labour's stronghold in Cheshire. It shares the political affiliations of Merseyside seats rather than the sort of loyalties more conventionally associated with this county. Map 291

## HAMILTON NORTH & BELLSHILL · Lab hold

| Electorate | %Turnout | | 53,539 | 56.79% | 2001 | 53,607 | 70.88% | 1997 |
|---|---|---|---|---|---|---|---|---|
| **Reid Dr J** | **Lab** | **18,786** | **61.79%** | **-2.22%** | **24,322** | **64.01%** | **Lab** |
| Stephens C | SNP | 5,225 | 17.19% | -1.9% | 7,255 | 19.09% | SNP |
| Frain Bell B | C | 2,649 | 8.71% | -1.67% | 3,944 | 10.38% | C |
| Legg K | LD | 2,360 | 7.76% | 2.7% | 1,924 | 5.06% | LD |
| Blackall Ms S | SSP | 1,189 | 3.91% | | | 554 | 1.46% | Ref |
| Mayes S | Soc Lab | 195 | 0.64% | | | | | |
| **Lab to SNP swing** | **0.16%** | **30,404** | **Lab maj 13,561** | | **37,999** | **Lab maj 17,067** | |
| | | | | 44.60% | | | 44.92% | |

**JOHN REID,** b May 8, 1947. Elected here 1997; MP for Motherwell N 1987-97. Sec of State, NI, 2001-; Scotland Office, 1999-2001; Min for Transport, 1998-99; Min for Armed Forces, 1997-98. Lab spokesman, defence, 1990-97. Adviser to Neil Kinnock, when Leader of Opposition, 1983-85. Member, Armed Forces parly scheme; spokesman, children, 1989-90. Member, Public Accounts Cttee, 1988-90; joint vice-chairman, PLP Transport Cttee, 1987-89. Scottish organiser, Trade Unionists for Lab, 1986-87. Ed St Patrick's Senior Sec Sch; Coatbridge; Stirling Univ.

This seat contains the northern part of Motherwell, southeast of Glasgow. It takes in a set of largely working-class communities, including the small town of Bellshill, with the legacy of coal and the economic influence of the Ravenscraig steelworks. There are some middle-class enclaves but otherwise, like many seats near the Clyde, this is staunchly Labour territory. Map 292

## HAMILTON SOUTH · Lab hold

| Electorate | %Turnout | | 46,665 | 57.32% | 2001 | 46,562 | 71.07% | 1997 |
|---|---|---|---|---|---|---|---|---|
| **Tynan B** | **Lab** | **15,965** | **59.68%** | **-5.92%** | **21,709** | **65.6%** | **Lab** |
| Wilson J | SNP | 5,190 | 19.4% | 1.78% | 5,831 | 17.62% | SNP |
| Oswald J | LD | 2,381 | 8.9% | 3.78% | 2,858 | 8.64% | C |
| Richardson N | C | 1,876 | 7.01% | -1.63% | 1,693 | 5.12% | LD |
| Mitchell Ms G | SSP | 1,187 | 4.44% | | 684 | 2.07% | ProLife |
| Murdoch Ms J | UK Ind | 151 | 0.56% | | 316 | 0.95% | Ref |
| **Lab to SNP swing** | **3.85%** | **26,750** | **Lab maj 10,775** | | **33,091** | **Lab maj 15,878** | |
| | | | | 40.28% | | | 47.98% | |

**BILL TYNAN,** b Aug 18, 1940. Elected 1999 by-election caused by elevation of George Robertson to House of Lords. Member, Scottish Affairs Select Cttee, 1999-2001; Backbench Cttees on: Trade and Industry; Health and Social Services. Member, Scottish Lab Policy Forum, 1998; Scottish Exec, 1982-88; chairman, Hamilton S CLP, 1987. Joined Lab Party, 1969. Member, AEEU. Press toolmaker; full-time union official. Ed St Joseph's Sch; St Mungo's Acad; Stow Coll. tel: 020-7219 6285

*Details of 1999 by-election on page 291*

This seat is broadly typical of the "Red Belt" which is Central Scotland. Containing most of the town of Hamilton itself, it is heavily working-class, industrial in character and instinctively loyal to Labour. The only plausible alternative here is the SNP, a fact reinforced by its performance in the 1999 by-election caused by George Robertson's quitting Westminster for Nato; Labour just held the seat by 556 votes, but reasserted its powerful hold in 2001. Map 293

## HAMMERSMITH & FULHAM · Lab hold

| Electorate | %Turnout | | 79,302 | 56.37% | 2001 | 78,637 | 68.7% | 1997 |
|---|---|---|---|---|---|---|---|---|
| **Coleman I** | **Lab** | **19,801** | **44.3%** | **-2.46%** | **25,262** | **46.76%** | **Lab** |
| Carrington M | C | 17,786 | 39.79% | 0.14% | 21,420 | 39.65% | C |
| Burden J | LD | 5,294 | 11.84% | 3.09% | 4,728 | 8.75% | LD |
| Dias D | Green | 1,444 | 3.23% | 2.19% | 1,023 | 1.89% | Ref |
| Roberts G | UK Ind | 375 | 0.84% | 0.5% | 695 | 1.29% | N Lab |
| | | | | | | 562 | 1.04% | Green |
| | | | | | | 183 | 0.34% | UK Ind |
| | | | | | | 79 | 0.15% | NLP |
| | | | | | | 74 | 0.14% | Care |
| **Lab to C swing** | **1.30%** | **44,700** | **Lab maj 2,015** | | **54,026** | **Lab maj 3,842** | |
| | | | | 4.51% | | | 7.11% | |

**IAIN COLEMAN,** b Jan 18, 1958. Elected 1997. Hammersmith and Fulham borough cllr (leader, 1991). Vice-chairman, Assoc of London Authorities, 1992. Senior administrative officer, London Borough of Islington. Ed Tonbridge Sch.

This is an interesting seat which says much about the recent political and demographic history of the capital. The West London borough once contained two seats, but Fulham needed to merge with another to create a viable constituency. The Tories did well here during the 1980s through a combination of gentrification and a deep suspicion of Labour. The former factor is still at work but the professionals have become less concerned about Tony Blair. Map 294

## HAMPSHIRE EAST — C hold

| Electorate | %Turnout | | 78,802 | 63.82% | 2001 | 76,604 | 75.88% | 1997 |
|---|---|---|---|---|---|---|---|---|
| **Mates M** | **C** | | **23,950** | **47.62%** | **-0.42%** | **27,927** | **48.04%** | **C** |
| Booker R | LD | | 15,060 | 29.95% | 1.84% | 16,337 | 28.11% | LD |
| Burfoot Ms B | Lab | | 9,866 | 19.62% | 2.51% | 9,945 | 17.11% | Lab |
| Coles S | UK Ind | | 1,413 | 2.81% | 1.93% | 2,757 | 4.74% | Ref |
| | | | | | | 649 | 1.12% | Green |
| | | | | | | 513 | 0.88% | UK Ind |
| **C to LD swing** | **1.13%** | | **50,289** | | C maj 8,890 | **58,128** | | C maj 11,590 |
| | | | | | 17.68% | | | 19.93% |

**MICHAEL MATES,** b June 9, 1934. Elected here 1983; MP for Petersfield 1974-83. Member, Intelligence and Security Select Cttee. Min of State, NI, 1992-93. Chairman, Defence Select Cttee, 1987-92. Joint vice-chairman, all-party arts and heritage grp; treas, cricket grp, 1997-. Sec, 1922 Cttee. Member, British-Irish inter-parly body; chairman, all-party Anglo-Irish grp, 1979-92. Adviser, defence matters (no parliament involvement) to ABS Aircraft AG. Master, Farriers' Co, 1986-87. Army officer. Ed Blundell's; King's Coll, Cambridge.

This seat was formed by the amalgamation of parts of three constituencies: the old East Hampshire, a slice of Havant and a section of the Winchester seat. The main centres are now the country towns of Alton and Petersfield, plus Horndean, which is essentially a suburb adjoining the built-up area of Havant. The net result is a more compact constituency, although not necessarily a more cohesive community, with a strong Conservative bias. Map 295

## HAMPSHIRE NORTH EAST — C hold

| Electorate | %Turnout | | 71,323 | 61.62% | 2001 | 69,111 | 73.95% | 1997 |
|---|---|---|---|---|---|---|---|---|
| **Arbuthnot J** | **C** | | **23,379** | **53.2%** | **2.3%** | **26,017** | **50.9%** | **C** |
| Plummer M | LD | | 10,122 | 23.03% | 0.3% | 11,619 | 22.73% | LD |
| Jones B | Lab | | 8,744 | 19.9% | 3.85% | 8,203 | 16.05% | Lab |
| Mellstrom G | UK Ind | | 1,702 | 3.87% | 2.99% | 2,420 | 4.73% | Ref |
| | | | | | | 2,400 | 4.7% | Ind |
| | | | | | | 452 | 0.88% | UK Ind |
| **LD to C swing** | **1.00%** | | **43,947** | | C maj 13,257 | **51,111** | | C maj 14,398 |
| | | | | | 30.17% | | | 28.17% |

**JAMES ARBUTHNOT,** b Aug 4, 1952. Elected here 1997; MP for Wanstead and Woodford 1987-97; contested Cynon Valley 1983 and 1984 by-election. Tory Chief Whip, 1997-. Defence Procurement Min, 1995-97; Under-Sec, Social Security, 1994-95; asst gvt whip, 1992-94. PPS to Peter Lilley, Trade and Industry Sec, 1990-92; and to Archie Hamilton, Armed Forces Min, 1988-90. Privy Counsellor. Kensington and Chelsea cllr, 1978-87. Non-practising barrister. Member of Lloyd's. Ed Wellesley House, Broadstairs; Eton; Trinity Coll, Cambridge.

This comprises the northern half of east Hampshire. It consists of fast-growing towns close to the M3, such as Fleet, Liss, Liphook and Hook, a collection of rural villages, and some rolling countryside; a different collection of electors but with a shared sympathy for the Conservative Party. It is a very safe Tory seat. Map 296

## HAMPSHIRE NORTH WEST — C hold

| Electorate | %Turnout | | 76,359 | 63.69% | 2001 | 73,222 | 74.66% | 1997 |
|---|---|---|---|---|---|---|---|---|
| **Young Sir G** | **C** | | **24,374** | **50.12%** | **4.88%** | **24,730** | **45.24%** | **C** |
| Mumford M | Lab | | 12,365 | 25.43% | 1.83% | 13,179 | 24.11% | LD |
| Bentley A | LD | | 10,329 | 21.24% | -2.87% | 12,900 | 23.6% | Lab |
| Oram S | UK Ind | | 1,563 | 3.21% | 0.68% | 1,533 | 2.8% | Ref |
| | | | | | | 1,383 | 2.53% | UK Ind |
| | | | | | | 486 | 0.89% | Green |
| | | | | | | 231 | 0.42% | Bypass |
| | | | | | | 225 | 0.41% | Ind |
| **Lab to C swing** | **1.53%** | | **48,631** | | C maj 12,009 | **54,667** | | C maj 11,551 |
| | | | | | 24.69% | | | 21.13% |

**SIR GEORGE YOUNG,** b July 16, 1941. Elected here 1997. MP for Ealing Acton 1974-97. Shadow Leader of House, 1998-2000. Opposition spokesman, Constitutional Affairs, 1999-2000. Shadow Defence Sec, 1997-98. C Spokesman, Modernisation Select Cttee, 1998-2000. Transport Sec, 1995-97; Financial Sec to Treasury, 1994-95; Min for Housing and Planning at DoE, 1990-94. Pres, friends of cycling grp. Economist. Ed Eton; Christ Church, Oxford.
e-mail: sir-george-young@nwh-tories.org.uk tel: 020-7219 6665 fax: 020-7219 2566

This constituency includes the rural parts of the western half of the Basingstoke and Deane borough. The core of the constituency is the town of Andover, which is supplemented by a set of surrounding villages. There is a Labour vote of sorts in Andover and the Liberal Democrats make a spirited effort elsewhere. But this is, in essence, very reliable terrain for the Conservatives. Map 297

## HAMPSTEAD & HIGHGATE — Lab hold

| Electorate | %Turnout | | 65,309 | 54.21% | 2001 | 64,889 | 67.86% | 1997 |
|---|---|---|---|---|---|---|---|---|
| Jackson Ms G | Lab | | 16,601 | 46.89% | -10.51% | 25,275 | 57.4% | Lab |
| Mennear A | C | | 8,725 | 24.64% | -2.59% | 11,991 | 27.23% | C |
| Simpson J | LD | | 7,273 | 20.54% | 8.09% | 5,481 | 12.45% | LD |
| Cornwell A | Green | | 1,654 | 4.67% | | 667 | 1.51% | Ref |
| Cooper Ms H | Soc All | | 559 | 1.58% | | 147 | 0.33% | NLP |
| McDermott T | UK Ind | | 316 | 0.89% | 0.61% | 141 | 0.32% | Dream |
| XNunoftheabove Ms S | Ind X | | 144 | 0.41% | | 123 | 0.28% | UK Ind |
| Teale Ms M | ProLife | | 92 | 0.26% | | 105 | 0.24% | Hum |
| Klein A | Ind Kl | | 43 | 0.12% | | 101 | 0.23% | Rizz |
| Lab to C swing | 3.96% | | 35,407 | Lab maj 7,876 | 22.24% | 44,031 | Lab maj 13,284 | 30.17% |

**GLENDA JACKSON,** b May 9, 1936. Elected 1992. Under-Sec for Environment and Transport, responsible for transport in London, 1997-99. Pres, Play Matters, 1976-. Repertory company actress, 1957-63; joined Royal Shakespeare Co, 1963. Awarded Oscars in 1971 and 1974 for performances in *Women in Love* and *A Touch of Class*; best film actress awards from Variety Club of Gt Britain, New York Film Critics, and US Nat Soc of Film Critics. Actress. Ed West Kirby County GS for Girls; RADA.

This is an extremely distinctive North London seat. It is a very mixed community including the leafy and affluent suburb of Hampstead itself (with a strong middle-class radical streak), Kilburn, with its Irish and Afro-Caribbean flavours, and Highgate, which is slightly more conventional, but not much more so. It was a very marginal seat in 1987 and 1992 but Labour now seems to be entrenched. Map 298

## HARBOROUGH — C hold

| Electorate | %Turnout | | 73,300 | 63.34% | 2001 | 70,424 | 75.27% | 1997 |
|---|---|---|---|---|---|---|---|---|
| Garnier E | C | | 20,748 | 44.69% | 2.87% | 22,170 | 41.82% | C |
| Hope Ms J | LD | | 15,496 | 33.38% | 3.86% | 15,646 | 29.52% | LD |
| Jethwa R | Lab | | 9,271 | 19.97% | -5.18% | 13,332 | 25.15% | Lab |
| Knight D | UK Ind | | 912 | 1.96% | | 1,859 | 3.51% | Ref |
| C to LD swing | 0.49% | | 46,427 | C maj 5,252 | 11.31% | 53,007 | C maj 6,524 | 12.30% |

**EDWARD GARNIER,** b Oct 26, 1952. Elected 1992. Shadow Attorney-General,1999-. Opposition spokesman, Legal Affairs and Shadow Min, Lord Chancellor's Dept, 1997-99. PPS to Attorney-General and Solicitor-General, and to Chancellor of the Duchy of Lancaster, 1995-97. Member, Home Affairs Select Cttee, 1992-95. Member, Soc of C Lawyers. Crown Court Recorder, 2000. Visiting parly fellow, St Antony's, Oxford, 1996-97. QC. Ed Wellington Coll; Jesus Coll, Oxford; Coll of Law, London.
e-mail: garniere@parliament.uk tel: 020-7219 4034 fax: 020-7219 2875

This is a very middle-class section of southeast Leicestershire. It includes prosperous suburbs of Leicester, the market town of Market Harborough, numerous villages and some open countryside. Although both Labour and the Liberal Democrats have managed to secure a respectable share of the vote, it remains a safe Conservative constituency. Map 299

## HARLOW — Lab hold

| Electorate | %Turnout | | 67,074 | 59.81% | 2001 | 64,072 | 74.62% | 1997 |
|---|---|---|---|---|---|---|---|---|
| Rammell B | Lab | | 19,169 | 47.79% | -6.3% | 25,861 | 54.09% | Lab |
| Halfon R | C | | 13,941 | 34.75% | 2.65% | 15,347 | 32.1% | C |
| Spenceley Ms L | LD | | 5,381 | 13.41% | 3.95% | 4,523 | 9.46% | LD |
| Bennett T | UK Ind | | 1,223 | 3.05% | 2.34% | 1,422 | 2.97% | Ref |
| Hobbs J | Soc All | | 401 | 1.0% | | 340 | 0.71% | UK Ind |
| | | | | | | 319 | 0.67% | BNP |
| Lab to C swing | 4.48% | | 40,115 | Lab maj 5,228 | 13.03% | 47,812 | Lab maj 10,514 | 21.99% |

**BILL RAMMELL,** b Oct 10, 1959. Elected 1997. PPS to Tessa Jowell, Sec of State for Culture, Media & Sport, 2001-. Member, European Legislation and European Scrutiny Select Cttees, 1997-2001. Reg officer, NUS, 1984-87. Head of youth, Basildon council, 1987-89. Former general manager, King's Coll London Students Union, and former senior univ business manager, London Univ, 1980-97. Harlow cllr, 1985-. Member, MSF; Lab campaign for electoral reform. Ed Burnt Hill Comp, Harlow; Univ Coll of Wales, Cardiff (Pres, Students' Union, 1982-83).

An Essex new town, situated in a previously rural corner in the northwest of the county, which the Tories did well to capture and then control until the 1997 election. The rate of owner-occupation is relatively low, as is the proportion of professionals and managers. This seat is dominated by the skilled working class and the lower middle class, slightly offset by two more conventionally Conservative wards. Labour now looks fairly comfortable here. Map 300

## HARROGATE & KNARESBOROUGH — LD hold

| Electorate | %Turnout | | 65,185 | 64.71% | 2001 | 65,155 | 73.14% | 1997 |
|---|---|---|---|---|---|---|---|---|
| Willis P | LD | | 23,445 | 55.58% | 4.04% | 24,558 | 51.54% | LD |
| Jones A | C | | 14,600 | 34.61% | -3.84% | 18,322 | 38.45% | C |
| MacDonald A | Lab | | 3,101 | 7.35% | -1.38% | 4,159 | 8.73% | Lab |
| Brown B | UK Ind | | 761 | 1.8% | | 614 | 1.29% | LC |
| Cornforth J | ProLife | | 272 | 0.64% | | | | |
| C to LD swing | 3.94% | | 42,179 | LD maj 8,845 | | 47,653 | LD maj 6,236 | |
| | | | | 20.97% | | | 13.09% | |

**PHIL WILLIS,** b Nov 30, 1941. Elected 1997. LD chief spokesman on Ed and Employment, 1999-; confirmed June 2001; member, Select Cttee on Ed and Employment, 1999-2001. Vice-chairman, all-party univ grp, 1999-. Leader, Harrogate Borough Council, 1990-97. Chairman, Harrogate International Centre, 1992-2001. Head teacher. Ed Burnley GS; City of Leeds and Carnegie Coll; Birmingham Univ.
tel: 020-7219 5709 fax: 020-7219 0971

Harrogate is, after Bath, perhaps the most famous spa town in England, and certainly the largest in the North. Knaresborough is a prosperous town set on a bend of the River Nidd. The combination should, in theory, produce a Conservative victory. That is certainly what Norman Lamont, the former Chancellor, thought when he chose to fight here in 1997. He did not consider the strength of the local Lib Dems - who even increased their lead in 2001. Map 301

## HARROW EAST — Lab hold

| Electorate | %Turnout | | 81,575 | 58.94% | 2001 | 79,846 | 71.37% | 1997 |
|---|---|---|---|---|---|---|---|---|
| McNulty T | Lab | | 26,590 | 55.31% | 2.79% | 29,927 | 52.52% | Lab |
| Wilding P | C | | 15,466 | 32.17% | -3.26% | 20,189 | 35.43% | C |
| Kershaw G | LD | | 6,021 | 12.52% | 4.28% | 4,697 | 8.24% | LD |
| | | | | | | 1,537 | 2.7% | Ref |
| | | | | | | 464 | 0.81% | UK Ind |
| | | | | | | 171 | 0.3% | NLP |
| C to Lab swing | 3.02% | | 48,077 | Lab maj 11,124 | | 56,985 | Lab maj 9,738 | |
| | | | | 23.14% | | | 17.09% | |

**TONY McNULTY,** b Nov 3, 1958. Elected 1997; contested seat 1992. Gvt whip, 2001-; asst gvt whip, 1999-2001. PPS at DfEE, 1997-99. Harrow borough cllr, 1986- (dep leader, Lab grp). Sec, Greater London Lab Exec, 1987-90. Member, NATFHE; Fabians; Lab friends of Israel; founding sec, Lab friends of India. Ex-senior poly lecturer. Ed Salvatorian Coll, Harrow; Stanmore Sixth Form Coll; Liverpool Univ; Virginia Poly Inst and State Univ, US.

This is the less prosperous and less leafy section of the London Borough of Harrow, to the northwest of the capital. It also contains a substantial Asian minority. It used to be polarised between Tory suburbia and more urban Labour areas, with the Conservative section dominating proceedings. A huge swing, reinforced by underlying demographic change, produced a surprisingly comfortable Labour win in 1997 and an even bigger one in 2001. Map 302

## HARROW WEST — Lab hold

| Electorate | %Turnout | | 73,505 | 63.46% | 2001 | 72,005 | 72.92% | 1997 |
|---|---|---|---|---|---|---|---|---|
| Thomas G | Lab | | 23,142 | 49.61% | 8.07% | 21,811 | 41.54% | Lab |
| Finkelstein D | C | | 16,986 | 36.41% | -2.77% | 20,571 | 39.18% | C |
| Noyce C | LD | | 5,995 | 12.85% | -2.63% | 8,127 | 15.48% | LD |
| Kefford P | UK Ind | | 525 | 1.13% | | 1,997 | 3.8% | Ref |
| C to Lab swing | 5.42% | | 46,648 | Lab maj 6,156 | | 52,506 | Lab maj 1,240 | |
| | | | | 13.20% | | | 2.36% | |

**GARETH R. THOMAS,** b July 15, 1967. Elected 1997. PPS to Charles Clarke, Min without Portfolio & party chairman, 2001-, also when Min of State, Home Office, 1999-2001. Environmental Audit Select Cttee, 1997-99. All-party grps: chairman, renewable and sustainable energy, 1999-; joint vice-chairman, personal social services, 1997-. Chairman, Co-op Party, 2000-. Harrow cllr, 1990-97; vice-chairman, assoc of local gvt social services cttee. Teacher. Ed Univ Coll of Wales, Aberystwyth; King's Coll London.
tel: 020-7219 4243

This is middle-class Metroland. There is a lot of very desirable residential housing here as well as the famous public school in Harrow-on-the-Hill. There is also a substantial Indian minority, although it is often affluent and more Conservative than is the norm. Labour overturned a Conservative majority of almost 18,000 to win the seat in 1997 and held it with an increased majority in 2001. Map 303

## HARTLEPOOL · Lab hold

| Electorate | %Turnout | | 67,652 | 56.25% | 2001 | 67,712 | 65.65% | 1997 |
|---|---|---|---|---|---|---|---|---|
| **Mandelson P** | Lab | | **22,506** | **59.15%** | **-1.58%** | **26,997** | **60.73%** | Lab |
| Robinson G | C | | 7,935 | 20.85% | -0.5% | 9,489 | 21.35% | C |
| Boddy N | LD | | 5,717 | 15.02% | 0.96% | 6,248 | 14.06% | LD |
| Scargill A | Soc Lab | | 912 | 2.4% | | 1,718 | 3.86% | Ref |
| Cameron I | Ind Cam | | 557 | 1.46% | | | | |
| Booth J | Ind Booth | | 424 | 1.11% | | | | |
| **Lab to C swing** | **0.54%** | | **38,051** | Lab maj 14,571 | | **44,452** | Lab maj 17,508 | |
| | | | | 38.29% | | | 39.38% | |

**PETER MANDELSON,** b Oct 21, 1953. Elected 1992. Sec of State for NI, 1999-2001 (resigned, Jan 2001). Min without Portfolio in Cabinet Office, 1997-98; Sec of State for Trade and Industry, 1998 (resigned, Dec 1998). Member. John Prescott's team, 1995, shadowing Dep PM, Chancellor of the Duchy of Lancaster and Public Services Min. Lab whip, 1994-95. Lab Party dir of campaigns and communications, 1985-90. Producer, London Weekend Television, 1982-85. Chairman, British Youth Council. 1978-80. Lambeth cllr, 1979-82. Ed Hendon Senior HS; St Catherine's Coll, Oxford.

This is a typical northeastern industrial town a few miles north of Teesside, one that used to depend on the steel industry and the docks for employment but has been forced to make painful adjustments. The town itself is solidly Labour although there are some Conservative edges. The main interest for 2001 was the degree to which Peter Mandelson's personality would become a defining local issue; in the event, it seemed to change little. Map 304

## HARWICH · Lab hold

| Electorate | %Turnout | | 77,539 | 62.05% | 2001 | 75,775 | 70.62% | 1997 |
|---|---|---|---|---|---|---|---|---|
| **Henderson I** | Lab | | **21,951** | **45.62%** | **6.86%** | **20,740** | **38.76%** | Lab |
| Sproat I | C | | 19,355 | 40.23% | 3.75% | 19,524 | 36.48% | C |
| Wilcock P | LD | | 4,099 | 8.52% | -4.63% | 7,037 | 13.15% | LD |
| Finnegan-Butler T | UK Ind | | 2,463 | 5.12% | | 4,923 | 9.2% | Ref |
| Lawrance C | Ind | | 247 | 0.51% | | 1,290 | 2.41% | CRP |
| **C to Lab swing** | **1.56%** | | **48,115** | Lab maj 2,596 | | **53,514** | Lab maj 1,216 | |
| | | | | 5.40% | | | 2.28% | |

**IVAN HENDERSON,** b June 7, 1958. Elected 1997.National parly campaign team, responsible for Eastern region; member, all-party cancer grp, maritime grp, drug abuse grp, animal welfare grp, child abduction grp, parly football team, sailing club, curry club, beer club. Exec officer, NUR/RMT, 1991-94. Member, RNLI. Harwich district cllr, 1986-97. Union organiser. Stevedore/Harwich dock operative. Ed Sir Anthony Deane Comp.
e-mail: ivanhenderson@houseofcommons.fsnet.co.uk tel/fax: 020-7219 3434

This constituency covers the northeastern corner of Essex. It is centred on the North Sea ferry port of Harwich, the seaside resort of Clacton and the more genteel towns of Frinton-on-Sea and Walton-on-the-Naze. Although there has always been a Labour vote here, this has been regarded historically as Tory territory. Labour pulled off an unexpected triumph here in 1997, helped by a strong vote for the now defunct Referendum Party, and held on in 2001. Map 305

## HASTINGS & RYE · Lab hold

| Electorate | %Turnout | | 70,632 | 58.36% | 2001 | 70,388 | 69.71% | 1997 |
|---|---|---|---|---|---|---|---|---|
| **Foster M** | Lab | | **19,402** | **47.07%** | **12.7%** | **16,867** | **34.37%** | Lab |
| Coote M | C | | 15,094 | 36.62% | 7.46% | 14,307 | 29.16% | C |
| Peters G | LD | | 4,266 | 10.35% | -17.6% | 13,717 | 27.95% | LD |
| Coomber A | UK Ind | | 911 | 2.21% | 1.25% | 2,511 | 5.12% | Ref |
| Phillips Ms S | Green | | 721 | 1.75% | | 1,046 | 2.13% | Lib |
| Bargery Mrs G | Ind | | 486 | 1.18% | | 472 | 0.96% | UK Ind |
| Ord-Clarke J | Loony | | 198 | 0.48% | 0.18% | 149 | 0.3% | Loony |
| McLean B | R & R Loony | | 140 | 0.34% | | | | |
| **C to Lab swing** | **2.62%** | | **41,218** | Lab maj 4,308 | | **49,069** | Lab maj 2,560 | |
| | | | | 10.45% | | | 5.21% | |

**MICHAEL (JABEZ) FOSTER,** b Feb 26, 1946. Elected 1997. PPS to Attorney-General and Solicitor-General, 1999-. Member, Select Cttee, Standards and Privileges, 1997-2001. Member, all-party grps, consumer affairs (sec); animal welfare; older people; fishing. Sec, trading standards grp, 1997-. Dep Lieutenant of E Sussex, 1993. Member, Fabian Soc; Christian Socialist Movement; Methodist Church; Soc of Lab Lawyers. Qualified FA referee. Solicitor. Ed Hastings Sec; Hastings GS; Leicester Univ.
e-mail: mp@1066.net tel: 01424 460070 fax 020-7219 1393

This constituency, based on the South Coast resort town of Hastings, also includes the Ancient Towns of Rye and Winchelsea and the beach resort of Camber Sands. It is at the easternmost end of East Sussex stretching towards Kent. Labour won here in 1997 with a huge swing, having previously been marooned in a poor third place. All three main parties have notable pockets of support, but for now Labour is top of the pile. Map 306

## HAVANT · C hold

| Electorate | %Turnout | | 70,246 | 57.56% | 2001 | 68,420 | 70.63% | 1997 |
|---|---|---|---|---|---|---|---|---|
| Willetts D | C | | 17,769 | 43.94% | 4.2% | 19,204 | 39.74% | C |
| Guthrie P | Lab | | 13,562 | 33.54% | 1.52% | 15,475 | 32.02% | Lab |
| Cole Ms H | LD | | 7,508 | 18.57% | -3.79% | 10,806 | 22.36% | LD |
| Jacks K | Green | | 793 | 1.96% | | | | |
| Cuell T | UK Ind | | 561 | 1.39% | | 2,395 | 4.96% | Ref |
| Stanley R | Ind | | 244 | 0.6% | | 442 | 0.91% | BIPF |
| Lab to C swing | 1.34% | | 40,437 | | C maj 4,207 | 48,322 | | C maj 3,729 |
| | | | | | 10.40% | | | 7.72% |

**DAVID WILLETTS,** b March 9, 1956. Elected 1992. Shadow Social Security Sec, 2001-. C Employment spokesman, 1997-. Chairman, C Research Dept, 1997; Paymaster General, 1996. Public Service and Science Min, 1995-96. Gvt whip, 1994-95. PPS, Chairman of C Party, 1993-94. Member, PM's Downing St policy unit, 1984-86. Dir of Studies, Centre for Policy Studies, 1987-92; member, Social Security Advisory Cttee, 1989-92. Economic adviser to Dresdner Kleinwort Benson, merchant bank. Author. Ed King Edward's Sch, Birmingham; Christ Church, Oxford.

This is the part of Hampshire which is located just north of Portsmouth. While there are some urban council estates which resemble the adjacent city more than the surrounding countryside, they are more than offset by the villages where the Tories are strong and the Liberal Democrats are competitive. Tactical voting on a sizeable scale would be needed to oust the Conservatives. Map 307

## HAYES & HARLINGTON · Lab hold

| Electorate | %Turnout | | 57,561 | 56.29% | 2001 | 56,829 | 72.31% | 1997 |
|---|---|---|---|---|---|---|---|---|
| McDonnell J | Lab | | 21,279 | 65.67% | 3.71% | 25,458 | 61.96% | Lab |
| McLean R | C | | 7,813 | 24.11% | -3.07% | 11,167 | 27.18% | C |
| Boethe Ms N | LD | | 1,958 | 6.04% | -1.38% | 3,049 | 7.42% | LD |
| Burch G | BNP | | 705 | 2.18% | | 778 | 1.89% | Ref |
| Kennedy W | Soc Alt | | 648 | 2.0% | | 504 | 1.23% | NF |
| | | | | | | 135 | 0.33% | ANP |
| C to Lab swing | 3.39% | | 32,403 | | Lab maj 13,466 | 41,091 | | Lab maj 14,291 |
| | | | | | 41.56% | | | 34.78% |

**JOHN McDONNELL,** b Sept 8, 1951. Elected 1997; contested seat 1992. Member Deregulation Select Cttee and Unopposed Bills Panel. Editor, *Labour Herald*, 1985-88. Sec, Assoc of London Authorities, 1987-95. GLC cllr, 1981-86 (dep leader, Lab grp). Principal policy adviser, Camden council, 1985-87. TUC researcher, 1978-82; asst head, social insurance dept, NUM, 1977-78. Ed Great Yarmouth GS; Burnley Tech Coll; Brunel Univ; Birkbeck Coll, London.

This seat rests in the southeast section of the London Borough of Hillingdon, on the far west of Greater London. Although it would have made many of the locals furious, the constituency legitimately could have been called Heathrow Airport. There has been a substantial increase in the non-white population in recent decades. This may explain why, having been very marginal during the 1980s, it swung decisively to Labour in 1997. Map 308

## HAZEL GROVE · LD hold

| Electorate | %Turnout | | 65,107 | 59.1% | 2001 | 63,694 | 77.46% | 1997 |
|---|---|---|---|---|---|---|---|---|
| Stunell A | LD | | 20,020 | 52.03% | -2.46% | 26,883 | 54.49% | LD |
| Bargery Ms N | C | | 11,585 | 30.11% | -0.43% | 15,069 | 30.54% | C |
| Miller M | Lab | | 6,230 | 16.19% | 4.27% | 5,882 | 11.92% | Lab |
| Price G | UK Ind | | 643 | 1.67% | 1.13% | 1,055 | 2.14% | Ref |
| | | | | | | 268 | 0.54% | UK Ind |
| | | | | | | 183 | 0.37% | Ind Hum |
| LD to C swing | 1.01% | | 38,478 | | LD maj 8,435 | 49,340 | | LD maj 11,814 |
| | | | | | 21.92% | | | 23.95% |

**ANDREW STUNELL,** b Nov 24, 1942. Elected 1997; contested seat 1992. LD acting Chief Whip, June 2001; dep whip, 1997-; spokesman, energy and deputy spokesman, transport, 1997-. Member, Select Cttees: Broadcasting, 1997-2001; Modernisation of Commons, 1997-2001; Unopposed Bills Panel, 1997-2001. Member, Nalgo, 1967-81; staff side member, Whitley Council for New Towns, 1977-80. Former Baptist lay preacher. Ed Surbiton GS; Manchester Univ; Liverpool Poly.
www.stunell.co.uk tel: 0161-406 7070

This seat in the Metropolitan Borough of Stockport and including the commuter town of Cheadle has distinct political characteristics. On the southeastern edge of Greater Manchester, it is predominantly suburban but with a few working-class wards and a semi-rural fringe. It has been a Conservative/Liberal Democrat battleground for decades. The Lib Dems broke through by a surprisingly large margin in 1997 and held on easily four years later. Map 309

## HEMEL HEMPSTEAD — Lab hold

| Electorate | %Turnout | 72,086 | 63.58% | 2001 | 71,468 | 77.09% | 1997 |
|---|---|---|---|---|---|---|---|
| **McWalter T** | **Lab Co-op** | **21,389** | **46.67%** | **0.97%** | **25,175** | **45.7%** | **Lab** |
| Ivey P | C | 17,647 | 38.5% | -0.6% | 21,539 | 39.1% | C |
| Stuart N | LD | 5,877 | 12.82% | 0.5% | 6,789 | 12.32% | LD |
| Newton B | UK Ind | 920 | 2.01% | | 1,327 | 2.41% | Ref |
| | | | | | 262 | 0.48% | NLP |
| **C to Lab Co-op swing** | **0.78%** | **45,833** | **Lab Co-op maj 3,742** | | **55,092** | **Lab Co-op maj 3,636** | |
| | | | 8.16% | | | 6.60% | |

**TONY McWALTER,** b March 20, 1945. Elected 1997; contested Luton N 1992; St Albans 1987; Bedfordshire S 1989 Euro elections and Hertfordshire 1984 Euro elections. Member, Select Cttee, NI Affairs, 1997-2001. N Hertfordshire district cllr, 1979-83. Lecturer, philosophy and computing. Ed Univ Coll of Wales, Aberystwyth; McMaster Univ, Canada; Univ Coll, Oxford.
tel: 01442 251251 fax: 01442 241268;

This seat, based in west Hertfordshire, has steadily become more urban over the years as a result of population expansion. Like many new towns, it fell out of love in a drastic fashion with Labour from 1979 onwards. This enabled the Conservatives, buoyed by votes from the rural areas of the constituency, to maintain control. Labour did well to win the seat in 1997 and again in 2001. Map 310

## HEMSWORTH — Lab hold

| Electorate | %Turnout | 67,948 | 51.84% | 2001 | 66,964 | 67.91% | 1997 |
|---|---|---|---|---|---|---|---|
| **Trickett J** | **Lab** | **23,036** | **65.39%** | **-5.17%** | **32,088** | **70.56%** | **Lab** |
| Truss Mrs E | C | 7,400 | 21.01% | 3.21% | 8,096 | 17.8% | C |
| Waller E | LD | 3,990 | 11.33% | 2.46% | 4,033 | 8.87% | LD |
| Turek P | Soc Lab | 801 | 2.27% | | 1,260 | 2.77% | Ref |
| **Lab to C swing** | **4.19%** | **35,227** | **Lab maj 15,636** | | **45,477** | **Lab maj 23,992** | |
| | | | 44.39% | | | 52.76% | |

**JON TRICKETT,** b July 2, 1950. Elected 1996 by-election. PPS to Peter Mandelson, Min without Portfolio, 1997-98. Member, Unopposed Bills Panel, 1996-. Former chairman, Leeds City Development Co; board member, Leeds Development Corp. Member, W Yorks Passenger Transport Authority. Dir, Leeds/Bradford Airport; Leeds Playhouse; Leeds Theatre Co, all 1988-. Ex-builder and plumber. Ed Roundhay HS; Hull and Leeds Univs.
e-mail: trickettj@parliament.uk tel: 020-7219 5074

This West Yorkshire seat involves an unusual and not entirely comfortable combination. The vast majority of it is working-class, strongly influenced by the coalmining tradition and by habit strongly Labour. However, there is a small section — the Wakefield South ward — that is much more Conservative. It can only dent slightly the massive margins by which Labour wins in this area. Map 311

## HENDON — Lab hold

| Electorate | %Turnout | 78,212 | 52.23% | 2001 | 76,195 | 65.67% | 1997 |
|---|---|---|---|---|---|---|---|
| **Dismore A** | **Lab** | **21,432** | **52.46%** | **3.13%** | **24,683** | **49.33%** | **Lab** |
| Evans R | C | 14,015 | 34.31% | -2.72% | 18,528 | 37.03% | C |
| Casey W | LD | 4,724 | 11.56% | 0.71% | 5,427 | 10.85% | LD |
| Crosbie C | UK Ind | 409 | 1.0% | 0.47% | 978 | 1.95% | Ref |
| Taylor Ms S | WRP | 164 | 0.4% | 0.09% | 267 | 0.53% | UK Ind |
| Stewart M | Prog Dem | 107 | 0.26% | | 153 | 0.31% | WRP |
| **C to Lab swing** | **2.93%** | **40,851** | **Lab maj 7,417** | | **50,036** | **Lab maj 6,155** | |
| | | | 18.16% | | | 12.30% | |

**ANDREW DISMORE,** b Sept 2, 1954. Elected 1997. Member, Social Security, 1998-2001. Sec, all-party war crimes grp; member, Lab friends of Israel, Cyprus and India. Member, Backbench Legal Affairs, Home Affairs and Social Security Sub Cttees. Vice-chairman, inter-parly council against racism and anti-Semitism; member, exec cttee, Assoc of Personal Injuries Lawyers (unpaid). Solicitor. Ed Bridlington GS; Warwick Univ; LSE; Guildhall Coll of Law.
e-mail: andrewdismoremp@parliament.uk tel: 020-7219 4026 fax: 020-7219 1279

This Outer London seat in the northwest of the capital features some stark social divisions. It includes the middle-class suburbs of Edgware and Mill Hill as well as vast council estates in the south of the constituency. It was Tory territory, but demographic change, notably a rising non-white population, had been undermining the party before Labour romped home on a huge swing in 1997. With a bigger majority in 2001, it now looks quite safe here. Map 312

## HENLEY
**C hold**

| Electorate | %Turnout | | 69,081 | 64.27% | 2001 | 66,424 | 77.6% | 1997 |
|---|---|---|---|---|---|---|---|---|
| Johnson B | C | 20,466 | 46.09% | -0.29% | 23,908 | 46.38% | C |
| Bearder Ms C | LD | 12,008 | 27.04% | 2.32% | 12,741 | 24.72% | LD |
| Mathews Ms J | Lab | 9,367 | 21.1% | -1.6% | 11,700 | 22.7% | Lab |
| Collings P | UK Ind | 1,413 | 3.18% | | 2,299 | 4.46% | Ref |
| Tickell O | Green | 1,147 | 2.58% | 1.58% | 514 | 1.0% | Green |
| | | | | | | 221 | 0.43% | NLP |
| | | | | | | 160 | 0.31% | Whig |
| C to LD swing | 1.31% | 44,401 | | C maj 8,458 | 51,543 | | C maj 11,167 |
| | | | | 19.05% | | | 21.66% |

**BORIS JOHNSON,** b June 19, 1964. Elected 2001. Inherits seat from Michael Heseltine, who has retired from the seat he held since Feb 1974. Contested Clwyd S 1997. Broadcaster and writer. Trainee reporter *The Times* and Wolverhampton *Express and Star.* Leader and feature writer, *The Daily Telegraph.* Editor, *The Spectator,* 1999-. Ed Eton; Balliol Coll, Oxford (Pres of the Union).

This seat covers a large area of southern and eastern Oxfordshire and is based on the affluent and elegant town on the Thames. For many years it was represented by its now retired MP, Michael Heseltine. It is very secure Conservative territory. Labour has some support in the far west of the constituency which borders urban Oxford. Elsewhere the Liberal Democrats are the main opposition. Both are distant rivals to the Tories. Map 313

## HEREFORD
**LD hold**

| Electorate | %Turnout | | 70,305 | 63.47% | 2001 | 69,864 | 75.22% | 1997 |
|---|---|---|---|---|---|---|---|---|
| Keetch P | LD | 18,244 | 40.88% | -7.07% | 25,198 | 47.95% | LD |
| Taylor Mrs V | C | 17,276 | 38.71% | 3.41% | 18,550 | 35.3% | C |
| Hallam D | Lab | 6,739 | 15.1% | 2.55% | 6,596 | 12.55% | Lab |
| Easton C | UK Ind | 1,184 | 2.65% | | 2,209 | 4.2% | Ref |
| Gillett D | Green | 1,181 | 2.65% | | | | |
| LD to C swing | 5.24% | 44,624 | | LD maj 968 | 52,553 | | LD maj 6,648 |
| | | | | 2.17% | | | 12.65% |

**PAUL KEETCH,** b May 21, 1961. Elected 1997. LD defence spokesman, June 2001; Employment and Training, 1997-2001. Sec, all-party electoral reform grp, 1997-; Albania grp, 1997-. Member, Hereford City Council, 1983. Assisted Simon Hughes, MP, in 1987 and 1992 elections. Election observer, Albania, Lithuania and Ireland. Political consultant, specialising in Eastern Europe matters. Worked in banking and water hygiene industry. Ed Hereford Boys HS; Hereford Sixth-Form Coll.
tel: 020-7219 2419 fax: 020-7219 1184

The cathedral city of Hereford has light industry and an unexpectedly high number of council tenants. The beautiful surrounding area, which includes the Wye Valley and Ross, the Golden Valley and the Black Mountains, is much more rural and agricultural. The seat extends westwards to the border with Wales. It has become a Liberal Democrat-Conservative battleground with Labour being marginalised; for now, the Lib Dems hold sway. Map 314

## HERTFORD & STORTFORD
**C hold**

| Electorate | %Turnout | | 75,141 | 62.78% | 2001 | 71,759 | 76.03% | 1997 |
|---|---|---|---|---|---|---|---|---|
| Prisk M | C | 21,074 | 44.67% | 0.63% | 24,027 | 44.04% | C |
| Speller S | Lab | 15,471 | 32.79% | 1.37% | 17,142 | 31.42% | Lab |
| Goldspink Ms M | LD | 9,388 | 19.9% | 2.16% | 9,679 | 17.74% | LD |
| Rising S | UK Ind | 1,243 | 2.63% | 0.39% | 2,105 | 3.86% | Ref |
| | | | | | 1,223 | 2.24% | UK Ind |
| | | | | | 259 | 0.47% | ProLife |
| | | | | | 126 | 0.23% | Logic |
| C to Lab swing | 0.37% | 47,176 | | C maj 5,603 | 54,561 | | C maj 6,885 |
| | | | | 11.88% | | | 12.62% |

**MARK PRISK,** b June 12, 1962. Elected 2001. Inherits seat from Bowen Wells, MP since 1979. Contested Newham NW 1992. Principal, Mark Prisk Connection, 1991-96. Previously marketing dir, Derrick Wade and Waters. Ed Truro Sch, Cornwall; Reading Univ.

This section of east Hertfordshire, which shares a border with Essex, is based on a number of prosperous market towns and their rural surroundings. The towns include Bishop's Stortford, Ware and Sawbridgeworth. They all have enough of an urban element to allow the Labour Party to make a showing. But this cannot compensate for the powerfully Conservative inclinations of the seat as a whole. Map 315

## HERTFORDSHIRE NORTH EAST — C hold

| Electorate | %Turnout | | 68,790 | 64.9% | 2001 | 67,161 | 77.42% | 1997 |
|---|---|---|---|---|---|---|---|---|
| **Heald O** | | C | **19,695** | **44.11%** | **2.35%** | **21,712** | **41.76%** | **C** |
| Gibbons I | | Lab | 16,251 | 36.4% | 0.58% | 18,624 | 35.82% | Lab |
| Kingman Ms A | | LD | 7,686 | 17.22% | -1.04% | 9,493 | 18.26% | LD |
| Virgo M | | UK Ind | 1,013 | 2.27% | | 2,166 | 4.17% | Ref |
| **Lab to C swing** | **0.89%** | | **44,645** | | **C maj 3,444** | **51,995** | | **C maj 3,088** |
| | | | | | 7.71% | | | 5.94% |

**OLIVER HEALD,** b Dec 15, 1954. Elected here 1997; MP for Hertfordshire N 1992-97. Shadow Home Affairs spokesman, 2000-; C whip, 1997-2000. Member Admin Cttee, 1998-2000. Social Security Under-Sec, 1995-97. PPS to Min of Agriculture, Fisheries and Food, 1994-95. Member, Employment Select Cttee, 1992-94. Vice-chairman, Backbench Employment Cttee, 1992-94. Barrister. Ed Reading Sch; Pembroke Coll, Cambridge.
e-mail: healdo@parliament.uk www.oliverhealdmp.com
tel: 01763 247640 fax: 01763 247640

This is a new seat based on the former Hertfordshire North plus some additional villages. The largest town is Letchworth, the first garden city in Britain, and other towns are Baldock and Royston, but no single settlement dominates the area. It is not exceptionally affluent, which explains, in part, why the Labour vote is greater than might be expected. Nonetheless, this is solid Conservative country. Map 316

## HERTFORDSHIRE SOUTH WEST — C hold

| Electorate | %Turnout | | 73,367 | 64.43% | 2001 | 71,671 | 77.31% | 1997 |
|---|---|---|---|---|---|---|---|---|
| **Page R** | | C | **20,933** | **44.28%** | **-1.67%** | **25,462** | **45.95%** | **C** |
| Dale G | | Lab | 12,752 | 26.98% | -0.89% | 15,441 | 27.87% | Lab |
| Featherstone E | | LD | 12,431 | 26.3% | 3.96% | 12,381 | 22.34% | LD |
| Dale-Mills C | | UK Ind | 847 | 1.79% | | 1,853 | 3.34% | Ref |
| Goffin Ms J | | ProLife | 306 | 0.65% | | 274 | 0.49% | NLP |
| **C to Lab swing** | **0.39%** | | **47,269** | | **C maj 8,181** | **55,411** | | **C maj 10,021** |
| | | | | | 17.31% | | | 18.08% |

**RICHARD PAGE,** b Feb 22, 1941. Elected here 1979 by-election; MP, Workington 1976-79. Opposition spokesman, DTI, 2000-; Under-Sec, Industry and Energy, 1995-97. Member, Public Accounts Cttee, 1997-2000 and 1987-95. Joint chairman, all-party Racing and Bloodstock Industries Cttee, 1997-. PPS to John Biffen, Leader of the House, 1982-87. Joint vice-chairman, C Backbench Trade and Industry Cttee, 1988-95. Hon treas, Leukaemia Research Fund, 1987-95. Company dir. Ed Hurstpierpoint Coll; Luton Tech Coll. fax: 020-7219 2775

This area of the county is known as the Three Rivers district - the rivers being the Chess, the Colne and the Grade. It includes some very affluent middle-class territory, such as Rickmansworth and Chorleywood, that produces overwhelming backing for the Conservatives. Tring and Berkhamsted are the other main towns. There are Labour areas, such as the ex-GLC overspill estate at South Oxhey, but the end result is a very secure Tory seat. Map 317

## HERTSMERE — C hold

| Electorate | %Turnout | | 68,780 | 60.34% | 2001 | 68,011 | 74.03% | 1997 |
|---|---|---|---|---|---|---|---|---|
| **Clappison J** | | C | **19,855** | **47.84%** | **3.54%** | **22,305** | **44.3%** | **C** |
| Broderick Ms H | | Lab | 14,953 | 36.03% | -2.16% | 19,230 | 38.19% | Lab |
| Thompson P | | LD | 6,300 | 15.18% | 2.34% | 6,466 | 12.84% | LD |
| Dry J | | Soc Lab | 397 | 0.96% | | 1,703 | 3.38% | Ref |
| | | | | | | 453 | 0.9% | UK Ind |
| | | | | | | 191 | 0.38% | NLP |
| **Lab to C swing** | **2.85%** | | **41,505** | | **C maj 4,902** | **50,348** | | **C maj 3,075** |
| | | | | | 11.81% | | | 6.11% |

**JAMES CLAPPISON,** b Sept 14, 1956. Elected 1992. Frontbench Treasury spokesman, 2001-. Frontbench spokesman on ed, 1999-2001; home affairs, 1997-99. Junior Environment Min, 1995-97; ex-PPS to Lady Blatch, Home Office Min. Member, Select Cttee, Members' Interests, 1992-95. Joint sec, all-party rugby league grp, 1997-. Barrister and farmer. Ed St Peter's Sch, York; Queen's Coll, Oxford; Central London Poly; Gray's Inn.
e-mail: clappisonj@parliament.uk tel: 020-7219 4152 fax: 020-7219 0514

This constituency contains the Hertfordshire towns of Potters Bar, Borehamwood, Elstree, Bushey and Radlett, on the fringes of Greater London. It was once represented by Cecil Parkinson, a former chairman of the Conservative Party. It was then a very safe Tory seat, but boundary changes and the increasing independence of the commuting classes have made it more competitive. However, it is still inclined firmly towards the Tories. Map 318

## HEXHAM — C hold

| Electorate | %Turnout | | 59,807 | 70.92% | 2001 | 58,914 | 77.52% | 1997 |
|---|---|---|---|---|---|---|---|---|
| **Atkinson P** | **C** | | **18,917** | **44.6%** | **5.84%** | **17,701** | **38.76%** | **C** |
| Brannen P | Lab | | 16,388 | 38.64% | 0.37% | 17,479 | 38.27% | Lab |
| Latham P | LD | | 6,380 | 15.04% | -2.39% | 7,959 | 17.43% | LD |
| Patterson A | UK Ind | | 728 | 1.72% | -0.84% | 1,362 | 2.98% | Ref |
| | | | | | | 1,170 | 2.56% | UK Ind |
| **Lab to C swing** | **2.74%** | | **42,413** | | **C maj 2,529** | **45,671** | | **C maj 222** |
| | | | | | 5.96% | | | 0.49% |

**PETER ATKINSON,** b Jan 19, 1943. Elected 1992. Opposition whip, 1999-; Member, Chairmen's Panel, 1997-; Select Cttees: Deregulation, 1995-97, Euro Legislation, 1992-97; Scottish Affairs, 1992-2001. PPS to Foreign Office Mins, 1995-96. Joint vice-chairman, 1994-95 and previously sec, Backbench Agriculture, Fisheries and Food Cttee. Joint sec, all-party forestry grp. Dep dir, British Field Sports Soc, 1987-92. Journalist with London *Evening Standard*, 1961-81. Ed Cheltenham Coll.
e-mail: atkinsonp@parliament.uk tel: 020-7219 6547 fax: 020-7219 2775

This vast Northumberland seat, based on the prosperous market town of Hexham, is the second largest constituency in England. It takes in much of Hadrian's Wall, Kielder Forest and other unspoilt countryside. Much of the area is agricultural, but there are also many professionals and managers, especially in Newcastle commuter districts such as Ponteland. The Tories almost lost this seat in 1997 despite their many local advantages. Map 319

## HEYWOOD & MIDDLETON — Lab hold

| Electorate | %Turnout | | 73,005 | 53.12% | 2001 | 73,898 | 68.41% | 1997 |
|---|---|---|---|---|---|---|---|---|
| **Dobbin J** | **Lab Co-op** | | **22,377** | **57.7%** | **-0.02%** | **29,179** | **57.72%** | **Lab** |
| Hopkins Mrs M | C | | 10,707 | 27.61% | 4.59% | 11,637 | 23.02% | C |
| Greenhalgh I | LD | | 4,329 | 11.16% | -4.48% | 7,908 | 15.64% | LD |
| Burke P | Lib | | 1,021 | 2.63% | 1.15% | 1,076 | 2.13% | Ref |
| West Ms C | Ch D | | 345 | 0.89% | | | 750 | 1.48% | Lib |
| **Lab Co-op to C swing** | **2.30%** | | **38,779** | | **Lab Co-op maj 11,670** | **50,550** | | **Lab Co-op maj 17,542** |
| | | | | | 30.09% | | | 34.70% |

**JIM DOBBIN,** b May 26, 1941. Elected 1997. Member, European Scrutiny Cttee. Backbench Cttees: Health, NI, and Environment. Leader, Rochdale council, 1996-97; member, Rochdale HA. Chairman, Rochdale credit union. Fellow, Inst of Medical Laboratory Sciences. Member, MSF. Medical microbiogist. Ed St Columbus HS, Cowdenbeath; and St Andrews HS, Kirkcaldy.

This seat is located within the Metropolitan Borough of Rochdale in northern Greater Manchester. It contains an interesting mix of political instincts. While the core of the constituency supports Labour habitually, the area closest to Rochdale has a number of Liberal Democrat supporters and there are some staunchly Conservative wards in the south. Nonetheless, Labour remains the dominant force. Map 320

## HIGH PEAK — Lab hold

| Electorate | %Turnout | | 73,774 | 65.22% | 2001 | 72,315 | 79.03% | 1997 |
|---|---|---|---|---|---|---|---|---|
| **Levitt T** | **Lab** | | **22,430** | **46.62%** | **-4.21%** | **29,052** | **50.83%** | **Lab** |
| Chapman S | C | | 17,941 | 37.29% | 1.84% | 20,261 | 35.45% | C |
| Ashenden P | LD | | 7,743 | 16.09% | 4.86% | 6,420 | 11.23% | LD |
| | | | | | | 1,420 | 2.48% | Ref |
| **Lab to C swing** | **3.03%** | | **48,114** | | **Lab maj 4,489** | **57,153** | | **Lab maj 8,791** |
| | | | | | 9.33% | | | 15.38% |

**TOM LEVITT,** b April 10, 1954. Elected 1997. Member Standards and Privileges Select Cttee, 1997-2001. PPS to Barbara Roche, Home Office Min, 1999-. Co-chairman, all-party minerals grp; joint vice-chairman, all-party charities and voluntary sector grp, 1997-; sec, Future of Europe grp, 1997-. Derbyshire county cllr, 1993-97; Stroud district cllr, 1989-97. Ex-research consultant, teacher and author. Ed Westwood HS, Leek, Staffordshire; Lancaster and Oxford Univs.
e-mail:tomlevittmp@parliament.uk www.cel.co.uk/labour/tom
tel: 01298 71111 fax: 01298 71522

This northwest Derbyshire seat includes the Peak District National Park with its dramatic scenery. But around 80 per cent of the residents live in five small towns - Glossop, New Mills, Chapel-en-le-Frith, Whaley Bridge and the spa town of Buxton. These always saw lively competition between Conservatives and Labour even during the Tory domination at Westminster. The strong swing to Labour in 1997, and its follow-up in 2001, were reflected here. Map 321

## HITCHIN & HARPENDEN — C hold

| Electorate | %Turnout | | 67,196 | 66.86% | 2001 | 67,219 | 77.99% | 1997 |
|---|---|---|---|---|---|---|---|---|
| Lilley P | | C | 21,271 | 47.35% | 1.5% | 24,038 | 45.85% | C |
| Amos A | | Lab | 14,608 | 32.52% | -0.61% | 17,367 | 33.13% | Lab |
| Murphy J | | LD | 8,076 | 17.98% | -2.08% | 10,515 | 20.06% | LD |
| Saunders J | | UK Ind | 606 | 1.35% | | 290 | 0.55% | NLP |
| Rigby P | | Ind | 363 | 0.81% | | 217 | 0.41% | Soc |
| Lab to C swing | 1.06% | | 44,924 | C maj 6,663 | | 52,427 | C maj 6,671 | |
| | | | | 14.83% | | | 12.72% | |

**PETER LILLEY,** b Aug 23, 1943. Elected here 1997; MP for St Albans 1983-97. Shadow Chancellor, 1997, responsible for development of party policy. Social Security Sec, 1992-97; Trade and Industry Sec, 1990-92; Financial Sec to the Treasury, 1989-90; Economic Sec, 1987-89. Investment adviser on N Sea oil and other energy industries, 1972-84; chairman, London Oil Analysts grp, 1979-80; economic consultant in underdeveloped countries, 1966-72. Fellow, Inst of Petroleum, since, 1978. Ed Dulwich Coll; Clare Coll, Cambridge.

This seat was created by the need for Hertfordshire to have additional representation in the House of Commons. Harpenden, with its solid London commuter element, is affluent and decisively Conservative. Hitchin is a mixed bag, with a spread of working-class and middle-class residents as well as a notable Asian minority. The Tories are, nonetheless, well entrenched. Map 322

## HOLBORN & ST PANCRAS — Lab hold

| Electorate | %Turnout | | 62,813 | 49.56% | 2001 | 63,037 | 60.28% | 1997 |
|---|---|---|---|---|---|---|---|---|
| Dobson F | | Lab | 16,770 | 53.87% | -11.15% | 24,707 | 65.02% | Lab |
| Green N | | LD | 5,595 | 17.97% | -1.02% | 6,804 | 17.91% | C |
| Serelli Mrs R | | C | 5,258 | 16.89% | 5.47% | 4,750 | 12.5% | LD |
| Whitley R | | Green | 1,875 | 6.02% | | 790 | 2.08% | Ref |
| Udwin Ms C | | Soc All | 971 | 3.12% | | 191 | 0.5% | NLP |
| Brar J | | Soc Lab | 359 | 1.15% | | 173 | 0.46% | JP |
| Nielsen M | | UK Ind | 301 | 0.97% | | 171 | 0.45% | WRP |
| | | | | | | 157 | 0.41% | Dream |
| | | | | | | 140 | 0.37% | EUP |
| | | | | | | 114 | 0.3% | ProLife |
| Lab to LD swing | 8.31% | | 31,129 | Lab maj 11,175 | | 37,997 | Lab maj 17,903 | |
| | | | | 35.90% | | | 47.11% | |

**FRANK DOBSON,** b March 15, 1940. Elected here 1983; MP for Holborn and St Pancras S 1979-83. Sec of State for Health, 1997-99, when he resigned to stand for Mayor of London, but was beaten by Ken Livingstone. Chief Lab spokesman, environment and London, 1994-97; transport and London, 1993-94; employment, 1992-93; energy, 1989-92. Shadow Leader of Commons and Lab campaigns co-ordinator, 1987-89. Elected to Shadow Cabinet, 1987. Health spokesman, 1985-87; ed, 1981-83. Governor, Inst of Child Health, 1987-. Ed Archbishop Holgate GS, York; LSE (a governor since 1986).

This Central London seat covers the southern half of the London Borough of Camden. It includes King's Cross and St Pancras, Camden Town, Kentish Town, Primrose Hill, Holborn and Bloomsbury. Thus the electorate appears to be divided between a solidly Labour working-class core and a middle-class fringe which contains a fair degree of chic radicalism. This probably explains why Labour is such a crushing political presence here. Map 323

## HORNCHURH — Lab hold

| Electorate | %Turnout | | 61,008 | 58.28% | 2001 | 60,775 | 72.3% | 1997 |
|---|---|---|---|---|---|---|---|---|
| Cryer J | | Lab | 16,514 | 46.44% | -3.78% | 22,066 | 50.22% | Lab |
| Squire R | | C | 15,032 | 42.28% | 4.99% | 16,386 | 37.29% | C |
| Lea Ms S | | LD | 2,928 | 8.23% | 0.39% | 3,446 | 7.84% | LD |
| Webb L | | UK Ind | 893 | 2.51% | | 1,595 | 3.63% | Ref |
| Durant D | | Third | 190 | 0.53% | -0.06% | 259 | 0.59% | Third |
| | | | | | | 189 | 0.43% | ProLife |
| Lab to C swing | 4.38% | | 35,557 | Lab maj 1,482 | | 43,941 | Lab maj 5,680 | |
| | | | | 4.17% | | | 12.93% | |

**JOHN CRYER,** b April 11, 1964. Elected 1997. Member, Deregulation Select Cttee, 1997-2001; European Safeguards Cttee. Son of the late Bob Cryer, Lab MP for Bradford South, and Ann Cryer, Lab MP for Keighley. Journalist, *Tribune*, 1992-96; *Morning Star*, 1989-92; freelance, *Labour Briefing, The Guardian, GMPU Journal* and Lloyd's of London Publications. Member, Amnesty International. Ed Oakbank Sch, Keighley; Hatfield Poly; London Coll of Printing.
e-mail: brunel@parliament.uk tel: 020-7219 1134 fax: 020-7219 1183

This seat is located in the Borough of Havering, on London's northeast fringe. There is some heavy industry, including the Ford motor works, in the south of the constituency. The area is, however, more similar socially to Essex than to the rest of Greater London. There is a high percentage of owner-occupiers and, while many residents are not that affluent, this seemed to be enough to return a Tory MP. However, Labour broke this pattern in 1997. Map 324

# HORNSEY & WOOD GREEN

**Lab hold**

| Electorate | %Turnout | | 75,967 | 58.0% | 2001 | 74,537 | 69.08% | 1997 |
|---|---|---|---|---|---|---|---|---|
| **Roche Ms B** | | **Lab** | **21,967** | **49.85%** | **-11.9%** | **31,792** | **61.75%** | **Lab** |
| Featherstone Ms L | | LD | 11,353 | 25.77% | 14.52% | 11,293 | 21.93% | C |
| Hollands J | | C | 6,921 | 15.71% | -6.22% | 5,794 | 11.25% | LD |
| Forbes Ms J | | Green | 2,228 | 5.06% | 2.7% | 1,214 | 2.36% | Green |
| Christian Ms L | | Soc All | 1,106 | 2.51% | | 808 | 1.57% | Ref |
| Rule Ms E | | Soc Lab | 294 | 0.67% | -0.47% | 586 | 1.14% | Soc Lab |
| Ataman E | | Reform | 194 | 0.44% | | | | |
| **Lab to LD swing** | **13.21%** | | **44,063** | | **Lab maj 10,614** | **51,487** | | **Lab maj 20,499** |
| | | | | | 24.09% | | | 39.82% |

**BARBARA ROCHE,** b April 13, 1954. Elected 1992. Min of State, Cabinet Office, June 2001-; Min of State, Home office, responsible for immigration and asylum, nationality, Passport Agency and EU matters, 1999-2001. Financial Sec to the Treasury, 1999; Under-Sec of State, Trade and Industry, 1997-99. Lab spokeswoman, trade and industry, 1995-97; Lab whip, 1994-95. PPS to Margaret Beckett, party deputy leader, 1993-94. Member, Soc of Lab Lawyers. Non-practising barrister. Ed Jewish Free Sch Comp, Camden; Lady Margaret Hall, Oxford. tel: 020-8348 8668 fax: 020-8342 8088

This North London seat is part of the London Borough of Haringey. It has become increasingly reliable for Labour. Even the most overtly middle-class areas - such as Muswell Hill - contain strong pockets of middle-class radicalism. This has been helped by the emergence of a very cosmopolitan population with sizeable minorities of Asians, Afro-Caribbeans and Cypriot immigrants. Map 325

# HORSHAM

**C hold**

| Electorate | %Turnout | | 79,604 | 63.78% | 2001 | 75,432 | 75.78% | 1997 |
|---|---|---|---|---|---|---|---|---|
| **Maude F** | | **C** | **26,134** | **51.48%** | **0.72%** | **29,015** | **50.76%** | **C** |
| Carr H | | LD | 12,468 | 24.56% | -0.2% | 14,153 | 24.76% | LD |
| Sully Ms J | | Lab | 10,267 | 20.22% | 1.52% | 10,691 | 18.7% | Lab |
| Miller H | | UK Ind | 1,472 | 2.9% | 1.47% | 2,281 | 3.99% | Ref |
| Duggan J | | Ind | 429 | 0.84% | | 819 | 1.43% | UK Ind |
| | | | | | | 206 | 0.36% | FEP |
| **LD to C swing** | **0.46%** | | **50,770** | | **C maj 13,666** | **57,165** | | **C maj 14,862** |
| | | | | | 26.92% | | | 26.00% |

**FRANCIS MAUDE,** b July 4, 1953. Elected here 1997; MP for Warwickshire N 1983-92. Campaign manager for Michael Portillo in the C Party leadership contest, 2001. Shadow Foreign Sec, 2000-; Shadow Chancellor, 1998-2000; Shadow Culture, Media and Sport Sec, 1997. Financial Sec to Treasury, 1990-92; Foreign Office Min for European Matters, 1989-90; Corporate Affairs Min, 1987-89; asst gvt whip, 1985-87. Member, Public Accounts Cttee, 1990-92. Barrister. Ed Abingdon Sch, Corpus Christi Coll, Cambridge.

This seat is, even by the standards of West Sussex, lucrative territory for the Tories. The constituency is based around the market and commuter town of Horsham, supplemented by numerous small towns such as Billingshurst, quaint villages and open countryside. The Liberal Democrats will always be lively actors but even in local government elections they find it difficult to escape the Conservative electoral steamroller. Map 326

# HOUGHTON & WASHINGTON EAST

**Lab hold**

| Electorate | %Turnout | | 67,946 | 49.51% | 2001 | 67,343 | 62.1% | 1997 |
|---|---|---|---|---|---|---|---|---|
| **Kemp F** | | **Lab** | **24,628** | **73.21%** | **-3.17%** | **31,946** | **76.38%** | **Lab** |
| Devenish T | | C | 4,810 | 14.3% | 1.41% | 5,391 | 12.89% | C |
| Ormerod R | | LD | 4,203 | 12.49% | 4.82% | 3,209 | 7.67% | LD |
| | | | | | | 1,277 | 3.05% | Ref |
| **Lab to C swing** | **2.29%** | | **33,641** | | **Lab maj 19,818** | **41,823** | | **Lab maj 26,555** |
| | | | | | 58.91% | | | 63.49% |

**FRASER KEMP,** b Sept 1, 1958. Elected 1997. Asst gvt whip, June 2001-. Member, Public Administration Select Cttee, 1997-2001; chairman, PLP Cabinet Office Cttee, 1997-. Private Member's Bill on Gas Safety; former member, Public Admin Select Cttee, and member, Selection Cttee. Full-time Lab Party official, 1981-96, being reg sec, W Midlands, 1986-94; sec, conference arrangements cttee, 1993-96; nat general election co-ordinator, 1994-96. Ex-civil servant. Ed Washington Comp. tel: 0191-584 9266 fax: 0191-584 8329

Tyne and Wear has traditionally backed the Labour Party and with some vigour. This seat is, to put it mildly, no exception. The bulk of the constituency is essentially outer Sunderland. Much of the remainder comes from the new town of Washington. The legacy of mining community politics in the former Durham coalfield remains very powerful in what is a staunchly Labour area. Map 327

# HOVE
**Lab hold**

| Electorate | %Turnout | | 70,889 | 59.23% | 2001 | 69,016 | 69.72% | 1997 |
|---|---|---|---|---|---|---|---|---|
| **Caplin I** | Lab | | **19,253** | **45.85%** | **1.26%** | **21,458** | **44.59%** | **Lab** |
| Langston Mrs J | C | | 16,082 | 38.3% | 1.94% | 17,499 | 36.36% | C |
| de Souza H | LD | | 3,823 | 9.1% | -0.55% | 4,645 | 9.65% | LD |
| Ballam Ms A | Green | | 1,369 | 3.26% | 1.92% | 1,931 | 4.01% | Ref |
| Richards A | Soc All | | 531 | 1.26% | | 1,735 | 3.61% | Ind C |
| Franklin R | UK Ind | | 358 | 0.85% | 0.42% | 644 | 1.34% | Green |
| Donovan N | Lib | | 316 | 0.75% | | 209 | 0.43% | UK Ind |
| Dobbshead S | Free | | 196 | 0.47% | | | | |
| Major T | Ind | | 60 | 0.14% | | | | |
| **Lab to C swing** | **0.34%** | | **41,988** | Lab maj 3,171 | | **48,121** | Lab maj 3,959 | |
| | | | | 7.55% | | | 8.23% | |

**IVOR CAPLIN,** b Nov 8, 1958. Elected 1997. Asst gvt whip, June 2001. Member, Broadcasting Select Cttee, 1997-2001; treas, all-party animal welfare grp, 1997-. Hove borough cllr, 1991-97 (leader, 1995-97); Brighton and Hove UA cllr. Trustee (unpaid), Old Market Trust, Brunswick, Hove. Chairman, Hove CLP, 1986-92. Member, MSF; Co-op Party. Sales and marketing quality manager. Ed King Edward's Sch, Witley; Brighton Coll of Tech.

This constituency is almost entirely residential, taking in the whole of Hove - stretching back from the elegant Regency squares near the seafront adjoining Brighton - as well as smaller towns and villages on the South Downs. It presents the impression of being solidly Tory. With a spectacular 20 per cent increase in its vote, Labour snatched the seat in 1997, a bounty drawn almost equally from the Tories and Lib Dems, and held on in 2001. Map 328

# HUDDERSFIELD
**Lab hold**

| Electorate | %Turnout | | 64,349 | 54.99% | 2001 | 65,824 | 67.69% | 1997 |
|---|---|---|---|---|---|---|---|---|
| **Sheerman B** | Lab Co-op | | **18,840** | **53.25%** | **-3.25%** | **25,171** | **56.5%** | **Lab** |
| Baverstock P | C | | 8,794 | 24.85% | 3.92% | 9,323 | 20.93% | C |
| Bentley N | LD | | 5,300 | 14.98% | -2.17% | 7,642 | 17.15% | LD |
| Phillips J | Green | | 1,254 | 3.54% | 1.43% | 1,480 | 3.32% | Ref |
| Longman Mrs J | UK Ind | | 613 | 1.73% | | 938 | 2.11% | Green |
| Hellawell G | Soc All | | 374 | 1.06% | | | | |
| Randall G | Soc Lab | | 208 | 0.59% | | | | |
| **Lab Co-op to C swing** | **3.59%** | | **35,383** | Lab Co-op maj 10,046 | | **44,554** | Lab Co-op maj 15,848 | |
| | | | | 28.39% | | | 35.57% | |

**BARRY SHEERMAN,** b Aug 17, 1940. Elected here 1983; MP for Huddersfield E 1979-83. Chairman, Ed Select Cttee; Cross-Party Cttee on Preparation for the euro; member, trade and industry task force on manufacturing; joint chairman, all-party manufacturing industry grp; joint vice-chairman, univ grp; sec, sustainable waste management grp. Lecturer. Ed Hampton GS; Kingston Tech Coll; LSE; London Univ.
e-mail: sheermanb@parliament.uk www.epolitix.com/barry.sheerman.htm tel: 020-7219 5037 fax: 020-7219 2404

A number of West Yorkshire textile towns swung sharply towards the Conservatives in the 1980s before returning to Labour in 1997. Huddersfield was an exception. Labour control here was never under threat, but not because it is more working-class than its neighbours. Tories perform well in the western area of the town, but are swamped by the Labour loyalists in the east. Map 329

# HULL EAST
**Lab hold**

| Electorate | %Turnout | | 66,473 | 46.45% | 2001 | 68,733 | 58.9% | 1997 |
|---|---|---|---|---|---|---|---|---|
| **Prescott J** | Lab | | **19,938** | **64.58%** | **-6.73%** | **28,870** | **71.31%** | **Lab** |
| Swinson Ms J | LD | | 4,613 | 14.94% | 0.14% | 5,552 | 13.71% | C |
| Verma Ms S | C | | 4,276 | 13.85% | 5.15% | 3,965 | 9.79% | LD |
| Jenkinson Ms J | UK Ind | | 1,218 | 3.94% | | 1,788 | 4.42% | Ref |
| Muir Ms L | Soc Lab | | 830 | 2.69% | | 190 | 0.47% | ProLife |
| | | | | | | 121 | 0.3% | NLP |
| **Lab to LD swing** | **5.94%** | | **30,875** | Lab maj 15,325 | | **40,486** | Lab maj 23,318 | |
| | | | | 49.64% | | | 57.60% | |

**JOHN PRESCOTT,** b May 31, 1938. Elected 1970. Deputy PM and First Sec of State, June 2001-. Deputy PM and Sec of State for Environment, Transport and the Regions, 1997-2001. Dep leader of Lab Party, 1994-. Joined Shadow Cabinet, 1983. Chief Lab spokesman on employment, 1984-87, 1993-94; transport, 1979-81, 1983-84, 1988-93; energy, 1987-88; reg affairs, 1981-83. MEP, 1975-79. Member, Council of Europe, 1972-75. Official, Nat Union of Seamen, 1968-70. Merchant Navy steward and trainee chef. Ed Grange Sec Mod, Ellesmere Port; Ruskin Coll, Oxford; Hull Univ.

This seat is at the heart of Hull's principal industrial areas. It is the safest Labour part of the city with a high proportion of council tenants and with the legacy of the docks remaining powerful. Even in a good year for the Tories, there is not much hope for the Conservative candidate standing against Labour's deputy leader, John Prescott. It has, however, tended to have spectacularly low turnouts at local elections. Map 330

# HULL NORTH

**Lab hold**

| Electorate | %Turnout | | 63,022 | 45.43% | 2001 | 68,106 | 56.96% | 1997 |
|---|---|---|---|---|---|---|---|---|
| **McNamara K** | **Lab** | | **16,364** | **57.15%** | **-8.69%** | **25,542.** | **65.84%** | **Lab** |
| Butterworth Ms S | LD | | 5,643 | 19.71% | 5.1% | 5,837 | 15.05% | C |
| Charlson P | C | | 4,902 | 17.12% | 2.07% | 5,667 | 14.61% | LD |
| Robinson Ms T | UK Ind | | 655 | 2.29% | | 1,533 | 3.95% | Ref |
| Smith R | Soc All | | 490 | 1.71% | | 215 | 0.55% | NLP |
| Wagner C | LCA | | 478 | 1.67% | | | | |
| Veasey C | Ind | | 101 | 0.35% | | | | |
| **Lab to LD swing** | **6.89%** | | **28,633** | **Lab maj 10,721** | | **38,794** | **Lab maj 19,705** | |
| | | | | 37.44% | | | 50.79% | |

**KEVIN McNAMARA,** b Sept 5, 1934. Elected here 1983; MP for Hull Central Feb 1974-83, and for Hull N 1966-74. Lab spokesman, Civil Service, 1994-95; NI, 1987-94; defence and disarmament, 1982-87. Member, British-Irish inter-parly body; Foreign Affairs Select Cttee, 1977-82. Ex-chairman, Overseas Development Select Cttee. Sec, all-party Anglo-Irish grp; TGWU parly grp. Lecturer in law. Ed St Mary's Coll, Crosby; Hull Univ.

This part of Hull does, at least, have a middle-class enclave to provide the Conservative and Liberal Democrat candidates with a little cause for optimism. These electors are, nonetheless, completely swamped by the voters from council estates elsewhere who, provided they bother to vote, can invariably produce a rich electoral harvest for the Labour Party. Map 331

# HULL WEST & HESSLE

**Lab hold**

| Electorate | %Turnout | | 63,077 | 45.84% | 2001 | 65,840 | 58.25% | 1997 |
|---|---|---|---|---|---|---|---|---|
| **Johnson A** | **Lab** | | **16,880** | **58.38%** | **-0.34%** | **22,520** | **58.72%** | **Lab** |
| Sharp J | C | | 5,929 | 20.5% | 2.42% | 6,995 | 18.24% | LD |
| Wastling Ms A | LD | | 4,364 | 15.09% | -3.15% | 6,933 | 18.08% | C |
| Cornforth J | UK Ind | | 878 | 3.04% | | 1,596 | 4.16% | Ref |
| Harris D | Ind | | 512 | 1.77% | | 310 | 0.81% | NLP |
| Skinner D | Soc Lab | | 353 | 1.22% | | | | |
| **Lab to C swing** | **1.38%** | | **28,916** | **Lab maj 10,951** | | **38,354** | **Lab maj 15,525** | |
| | | | | 37.87% | | | 40.48% | |

**ALAN JOHNSON,** b May 17, 1950. Elected 1997. Min of Employment and Regions, June 2001-; Min for Competitiveness, DTI, 1999-2001; PPS to Dawn Primarolo, Financial Sec to Treasury, 1997-99, and Paymaster General, 1999. Member, Trade and Industry Select Cttee, 1997-99. Joint general sec, CWU, 1992-97; member, TUC General Council. Governor, Ruskin Coll, Oxford. Ex-postman and union official. Ed Sloane GS, Chelsea.
tel: 020-7219 6637 fax: 020-7219 5856

This seat combines most of the city centre, the western section of Hull - which has similar political sentiments to the rest of the city - and Hessle, at the northern end of the Humber Bridge. This latter slice of the constituency is somewhat more middle-class and Conservative. The net result remains a solidly Labour seat, but one that is usually a little more pluralist than its city neighbours. Map 332

# HUNTINGDON

**C hold**

| Electorate | %Turnout | | 78,604 | 62.45% | 2001 | 76,094 | 74.86% | 1997 |
|---|---|---|---|---|---|---|---|---|
| **Djanogly J** | **C** | | **24,507** | **49.92%** | **-5.38%** | **31,501** | **55.3%** | **C** |
| Pope M | LD | | 11,715 | 23.86% | 9.13% | 13,361 | 23.46% | Lab |
| Sulaiman T | Lab | | 11,211 | 22.84% | -0.62% | 8,390 | 14.73% | LD |
| Norman D | UK Ind | | 1,656 | 3.37% | 2.79% | 3,114 | 5.47% | Ref |
| | | | | | | 331 | 0.58% | UK Ind |
| | | | | | | 177 | 0.31% | Ch D |
| | | | | | | 89 | 0.16% | Ind |
| **C to LD swing** | **7.26%** | | **49,089** | **C maj 12,792** | | **56,963** | **C maj 18,140** | |
| | | | | 26.06% | | | 31.84% | |

**JONATHAN DJANOGLY,** b June 3, 1965. Elected 2001. Inherits the safe seat of the former Prime Minister, John Major. Contested Oxford E 1997. Member, C Party, 1985-. Westminster cllr, 1994 and 1998. Solicitor for 13 years and partner in a commercial law firm specialising in advertising. Ed Univ Coll Sch, Oxford; Oxford Poly; Guildford Coll of Law.

It was perhaps appropriate that the seat represented by the former Prime Minister John Major should stick with him in 1997 while so many others deserted the Tories. This is one of the largest and safest of any Conservative majorities. The seat is centred on Huntingdon itself and takes in a large section of Cambridgeshire countryside. It has a surprisingly low relative proportion of owner-occupation, but cultural conservatism is deeply rooted. Map 333

## HYNDBURN — Lab hold

| Electorate | %Turnout | | 66,445 | 57.56% | 2001 | 66,806 | 72.26% | 1997 |
|---|---|---|---|---|---|---|---|---|
| Pope G | Lab | | 20,900 | 54.65% | -0.93% | 26,831 | 55.58% | Lab |
| Britcliffe P | C | | 12,681 | 33.16% | 1.29% | 15,383 | 31.87% | C |
| Greene B | LD | | 3,680 | 9.62% | 1.04% | 4,141 | 8.58% | LD |
| Tomlin J | UK Ind | | 982 | 2.57% | | 1,627 | 3.37% | Ref |
| | | | | | | 290 | 0.6% | IAC |
| Lab to C swing | 1.11% | | 38,243 | Lab maj 8,219 | | 48,272 | Lab maj 11,448 | |
| | | | | 21.49% | | | 23.71% | |

**GREG POPE,** b Aug 29, 1960. Elected 1992. Gvt asst whip, 1997; Lab whip, 1995-97. Member, Ed Select Cttee, 1992-95; Local gvt officer, 1987-92. Hyndburn borough cllr, 1984-88; Blackburn borough cllr, 1989-91. Member, Nalgo/Nupe. Ed St Mary's Coll, Blackburn; Hull Univ.

This seat, comprising several small east Lancashire former textile towns such as Accrington, was once described accurately as a classic Lancashire marginal. It pits a Labour-inclined urban core - now including a significant non-white population - against the aspirational middle classes surrounding it. Labour won the seat in 1992 and since then has appeared well entrenched. Nevertheless, potentially it remains a highly competitive constituency. Map 334

## ILFORD NORTH — Lab hold

| Electorate | %Turnout | | 68,893 | 58.4% | 2001 | 68,218 | 71.6% | 1997 |
|---|---|---|---|---|---|---|---|---|
| Perham Ms L | Lab | | 18,428 | 45.8% | -1.56% | 23,135 | 47.36% | Lab |
| Bendall V | C | | 16,313 | 40.55% | -0.21% | 19,911 | 40.76% | C |
| Stollar G | LD | | 4,717 | 11.72% | 1.38% | 5,049 | 10.34% | LD |
| Levin M | UK Ind | | 776 | 1.93% | | 750 | 1.54% | BNP |
| Lab to C swing | 0.67% | | 40,234 | Lab maj 2,115 | | 48,845 | Lab maj 3,224 | |
| | | | | 5.26% | | | 6.60% | |

**LINDA PERHAM,** b June 29, 1947. Elected 1997. Member, Select Cttee, Trade and Industry, 1998-2001. Chairman, all-party libraries grp, 1998-; vice-chairman, mole cancers grp, 1998-; hon sec, British Israeli grp, 1997-; sec, all-party grp on ageing and older people. Member, Commons Accommodation and Works Cttee, 1997-. Member, Unison; Co-op Party; SEA. Librarian. Ed Mary Datchelor GS, Camberwell; Leicester Univ; Ealing Tech Coll.
e-mail: lindaperhammp@parliament.uk tel: 020-7219 5853 fax: 020-7219 1161

This seat, which forms part of the Outer London Borough of Redbridge, sits on the border with Essex and shares some of the characteristics more normally associated with that county. There is a high rate of owner-occupation, but not conspicuous affluence. This is lower middle-class territory. The northern parts of Ilford are very urban and pretty solidly Labour. The rest of the constituency is more Conservative. A marginal battleground. Map 335

## ILFORD SOUTH — Lab hold

| Electorate | %Turnout | | 76,025 | 54.32% | 2001 | 72,104 | 69.37% | 1997 |
|---|---|---|---|---|---|---|---|---|
| Gapes M | Lab Co-op | | 24,619 | 59.62% | 1.1% | 29,273 | 58.52% | Lab |
| Kuma S | C | | 10,622 | 25.72% | -4.41% | 15,073 | 30.13% | C |
| Scott R | LD | | 4,647 | 11.25% | 4.95% | 3,152 | 6.3% | LD |
| Khan H | UK Ind | | 1,407 | 3.41% | | 1,073 | 2.15% | Ref |
| | | | | | | 868 | 1.74% | Soc Lab |
| | | | | | | 580 | 1.16% | BNP |
| C to Lab Co-op swing | 2.75% | | 41,295 | Lab Co-op maj 13,997 | | 50,019 | Lab Co-op maj 14,200 | |
| | | | | 33.90% | | | 28.39% | |

**MIKE GAPES,** b Sept 4, 1952. Elected 1992. PPS to Min of State for NI, 1997-99, Member, Select Cttees: Defence, 1999-2001; Foreign Affairs, 1992-97. Joint vice-chairman; parly council against anti-Semitism, 1992-; all-party Netherlands and Spain grps, 1997-. Pres, Redbridge Utd Chinese Assoc; vice-chairman, Ilford FC. Member, Co-op Party; TGWU. Ed Buckhurst Hill HS, Essex; Fitzwilliam Coll, Cambridge; Middlesex Poly.
e-mail: gapesm@parliament.uk www.mikegapes.org.uk
tel: 020-7219 6485/4172 fax: 020-7219 0978

This is, in some senses, a curious constituency in northeast London. It embraces the major shopping and commercial centre of Ilford and has a slightly higher rate of owner-occupation than its northern neighbour but a similar number of professionals. Labour is, however, much stronger in this section of Redbridge borough. This is partly because it is more of a London than an Essex seat and also because of a substantial non-white population. Map 336

## INVERNESS EAST, NAIRN & LOCHABER

**Lab hold**

| Electorate | %Turnout | | 67,139 | 63.24% | 2001 | 65,701 | 72.71% | 1997 |
|---|---|---|---|---|---|---|---|---|
| **Stewart D** | Lab | | **15,605** | **36.75%** | **2.86%** | **16,187** | **33.89%** | **Lab** |
| MacNeil A | SNP | | 10,889 | 25.64% | -3.35% | 13,848 | 28.99% | SNP |
| Kenton Ms P | LD | | 9,420 | 22.19% | 4.68% | 8,364 | 17.51% | LD |
| Jenkins R | C | | 5,653 | 13.31% | -4.18% | 8,355 | 17.49% | C |
| Arnott S | SSP | | 894 | 2.11% | | 436 | 0.91% | Ref |
| | | | | | | 354 | 0.74% | Green |
| | | | | | | 224 | 0.47% | Ch U |
| **SNP to Lab swing** | **3.10%** | | **42,461** | | **Lab maj 4,716** | **47,768** | | **Lab maj 2,339** |
| | | | | | 11.11% | | | 4.90% |

**DAVID STEWART,** b May 5, 1956. Elected 1997. Member, Scottish Affairs Select Cttee, 1997-99. Sec, all-party diabetic grp; member, all-party offshore oil and gas grp; all-party British/American grp. Dumfries district cllr, 1984-86; Inverness district cllr, 1988-97 (dep leader, Lab grp, 1988-96). Member, Unison, Tribune, Scottish Council for Single Homeless. Ex-social work area manager, Highland Council. Ed Paisley Coll; Stirling Univ; OU Business Sch.
e-mail: stewartd@parliament.uk www.davidstewartmp.co.uk
tel: 01463 237441 fax: 01463 237661

Personal campaigning appears to matter much more in the Scottish Highlands than in the rest of the UK. This vast and beautiful seat, stretching from the newly designated city of Inverness down Loch Ness to Mallaig, Fort William and Glencoe, and including Speyside and part of the Cairngorms, was a four-way marginal in 1992 when it was won by the Lib Dems. In 1997 it went narrowly to Labour, whose lead over the SNP rose in 2001. Map 337

## IPSWICH

**Lab hold**

| Electorate | %Turnout | | 68,198 | 57.0% | 2001 | 66,947 | 72.24% | 1997 |
|---|---|---|---|---|---|---|---|---|
| **Cann J** | Lab | | **19,952** | **51.33%** | **-1.36%** | **25,484** | **52.69%** | **Lab** |
| Wild E | C | | 11,871 | 30.54% | -0.57% | 15,045 | 31.11% | C |
| Gilbert T | LD | | 5,904 | 15.19% | 3.03% | 5,881 | 12.16% | LD |
| Vinyard W | UK Ind | | 624 | 1.61% | 1.18% | 1,637 | 3.38% | Ref |
| Leach P | Soc All | | 305 | 0.78% | | 208 | 0.43% | UK Ind |
| Gratton S | Soc Lab | | 217 | 0.56% | | 107 | 0.22% | NLP |
| **Lab to C swing** | **0.40%** | | **38,873** | | **Lab maj 8,081** | **48,362** | | **Lab maj 10,439** |
| | | | | | 20.79% | | | 21.58% |

**JAMIE CANN,** b June 28, 1946. Elected 1992. Member, Defence Select Cttee, 1997-2001. Treas, all-party Northern Cyprus grp, 1996-97. Ipswich borough cllr, 1973-91; leader, Lab grp, 1976-91; council leader, 1979-91. Deputy head, Handford Hall Primary Sch, Ipswich, 1981-92. Ex-member, Ipswich Port Authority. Teacher. Ed Barton on Humber GS; Kesteven Coll of Ed.

This county town and port on the River Orwell is the largest town in Suffolk. It is socially polarised and has often been marginal territory. There are areas with a surprisingly high number of council tenants where Labour does well and other suburbs where the Conservatives are better placed. The Tories captured the seat against the national trend in 1987, lost it by a narrow margin in 1992 and then Labour romped home in 1997 and again in 2001. Map 338

## ISLE OF WIGHT

**C gain**

| Electorate | %Turnout | | 106,305 | 59.72% | 2001 | 101,680 | 71.95% | 1997 |
|---|---|---|---|---|---|---|---|---|
| **Turner A** | C | | **25,223** | **39.73%** | **5.74%** | **31,274** | **42.75%** | **LD** |
| Brand Dr P | LD | | 22,397 | 35.28% | -7.47% | 24,868 | 33.99% | C |
| Gardiner Ms D | Lab | | 9,676 | 15.24% | 2.06% | 9,646 | 13.18% | Lab |
| Lott D | UK Ind | | 2,106 | 3.32% | 1.85% | 4,734 | 6.47% | Ref |
| Holmes D | Ind | | 1,423 | 2.24% | | 1,072 | 1.47% | UK Ind |
| Scivier P | Green | | 1,279 | 2.01% | 1.27% | 848 | 1.16% | Ind Isl |
| Murray P | IOW | | 1,164 | 1.83% | | 544 | 0.74% | Green |
| Spensley J | Soc Lab | | 214 | 0.34% | | 87 | 0.12% | NLP |
| | | | | | | 86 | 0.12% | Rain Isl |
| **LD to C swing** | **6.61%** | | **63,482** | | **C maj 2,826** | **73,159** | | **LD maj 6,406** |
| | | | | | 4.45% | | | 8.76% |

**ANDREW TURNER,** b Oct 24, 1953. Elected 2001. Takes the seat from Peter Brand, LD, having contested it in 1997; also contested Hackney S and Shoreditch 1992 and Birmingham E, Euro elections, 1994. Special adviser to DHSS Mins. Member, education manifesto grps, 1987 and 1992. Oxford city cllr. Teacher and ed consultant. Set up and ran the Grant-Maintained Schools Foundation. Ed Rugby Sch; Keble Coll, Oxford; Birmingham Univ.

This is a huge constituency in terms of the number of electors, of whom there are around 100,000. It should, logically, be divided into two with the smaller portion allied to a section of Hampshire across the Solent. This notion, though, is opposed bitterly by the islanders, whose livelihoods depend largely on tourism and farming. This has been a Tory-Lib Dem battleground for decades, and in 2001 provided one of the few Conservative gains. Map 339

## ISLINGTON NORTH                                             Lab hold

| Electorate | %Turnout | 61,970 | 48.76% | 2001 | 57,385 | 62.49% | 1997 |
|---|---|---|---|---|---|---|---|
| Corbyn J | Lab | 18,699 | 61.88% | -7.37% | 24,834 | 69.25% | Lab |
| Willoughby Ms L | LD | 5,741 | 19.0% | 5.39% | 4,879 | 13.61% | LD |
| Rands N | C | 3,249 | 10.75% | -2.16% | 4,631 | 12.91% | C |
| Ashby C | Green | 1,876 | 6.21% | 1.98% | 1,516 | 4.23% | Green |
| Cook S | Soc Lab | 512 | 1.69% | | | | |
| Hassan E | Reform | 139 | 0.46% | | | | |
| **Lab to LD swing** | **6.38%** | **30,216** | **Lab maj 12,958** | | **35,860** | **Lab maj 19,955** | |
| | | | 42.88% | | | 55.64% | |

**JEREMY CORBYN,** b May 26, 1949. Elected 1983. Member, Social Security Select Cttee, 1990-97. Chairman, London grp of Lab MPs, 1993-95, vice-chairman, 1985-93; chairman, campaign for non-alignment. Vice-chairman, PLP Health Cttee, 1989-90, and PLP Health and Social Security Cttee, 1985-89. Vice-chairman, all-party human rights grp, 1997-; treas, Vietnam grp. Haringey cllr, 1974-83. Unpaid dir, Red Rose Lab and Socialist Club. Member, National Trust; Unison; Cuba Solidarity. Former union official. Ed Adams GS, Newport, Shropshire.

The rise of Tony Blair has made Islington, the site of his former London home, a term of virtual abuse for many Conservatives. This section of Islington is, however, old rather than new Labour. It is a relatively poor area of Inner London with a sizeable ethnic minority and a distinct Irish flavour. It remains extremely loyal to Labour. Map 340

## ISLINGTON SOUTH & FINSBURY                              Lab hold

| Electorate | %Turnout | 59,515 | 47.39% | 2001 | 55,468 | 63.67% | 1997 |
|---|---|---|---|---|---|---|---|
| Smith C | Lab | 15,217 | 53.95% | -8.57% | 22,079 | 62.52% | Lab |
| Sharp K | LD | 7,937 | 28.14% | 6.86% | 7,516 | 21.28% | LD |
| Morgan Mrs N | C | 3,860 | 13.69% | 0.7% | 4,587 | 12.99% | C |
| Booth Ms J | Soc All | 817 | 2.9% | | 741 | 2.1% | Ref |
| McCarthy T | Ind | 267 | 0.95% | 0.66% | 171 | 0.48% | ACA |
| Thomson C | Stuck | 108 | 0.38% | | 121 | 0.34% | NLP |
| | | | | | 101 | 0.29% | Ind |
| **Lab to LD swing** | **7.71%** | **28,206** | **Lab maj 7,280** | | **35,316** | **Lab maj 14,563** | |
| | | | 25.81% | | | 41.24% | |

**CHRIS SMITH,** b July 24, 1951. Elected 1983. Sec of State, Culture, Media and Sport, 1997-2001. Shadow Health Sec, 1996-97; Shadow Social Security Sec, 1995-96; spokesman, nat heritage, 1994-95; environmental protection, 1992-94; Treasury, 1987-92. Member, exec cttee, Fabian Soc, 1990-97; ex-governor, Sadler's Wells Theatre; exdir, Grand Union orchestra. Completed ascent of all Scottish "Munro" mountains, 1989. Author, *Creative Britain 1998.* Ed George Watson's Coll, Edinburgh; Pembroke Coll, Cambridge, Harvard. tel: 020-7219 5119 fax: 0207-219 5820

This section of Islington, despite the myths, is more than a haven for affluent Hampstead-style middle-class London radicals. Such voters do, indeed, exist in some of the smarter parts, but they are atypical of the seat as a whole. There are large numbers of council tenants and a substantial number of ethnic minority electors. Labour is established securely, having fought off a determined drive by the SDP in the 1980s. Map 341

## ISLWYN                                                    Lab hold

| Electorate | %Turnout | 51,230 | 61.86% | 2001 | 50,540 | 72.03% | 1997 |
|---|---|---|---|---|---|---|---|
| Touhig D | Lab Co-op | 19,505 | 61.55% | -12.6% | 26,995 | 74.15% | Lab |
| Etheridge K | LD | 4,196 | 13.24% | 4.82% | 3,064 | 8.42% | LD |
| Thomas L | PC | 3,767 | 11.89% | 5.65% | 2,864 | 7.87% | C |
| Howells P | C | 2,543 | 8.02% | 0.15% | 2,272 | 6.24% | PC |
| Taylor P | Ind | 1,263 | 3.99% | | 1,209 | 3.32% | Ref |
| Millington Ms M | Soc Lab | 417 | 1.32% | | | | |
| **Lab Co-op to LD swing** | **8.71%** | **31,691** | **Lab Co-op maj 15,309** | | **36,404** | **Lab Co-op maj 23,931** | |
| | | | 48.31% | | | 65.73% | |

**DON TOUHIG,** b Dec 5, 1947. Elected 1995 by-election following resignation of Neil Kinnock to become Euro Commissioner. Under Sec, Wales Office, June 2001-; gvt whip, 1999-2001; PPS to Chancellor of Exchequer, 1997-99. Member, Select Cttee on Welsh Affairs, 1995-97; sec, Welsh grp of Lab MPs, 1995-99; chairman, all-party alcohol misuse grp, 1996-99; vice-chairman, penal affairs grp, 1997-. Gen manager, Free Press Grp, 1988-92; with Bailey Print, 1993-95. Editor, Free Press of Monmouthshire, 1976-88. Journalist. Ed St Francis Sch, Aberyschan; E Monmouth Coll.

This seat is set in the heart of the Welsh Valleys. It is, in essence, a collection of broadly similar former mining communities on the Rivers Ebbw and Sirhowy above Newport. There are only a small number of Welsh speakers. It was represented by Neil Kinnock for many years and is as safe a Labour seat as can be imagined. Plaid Cymru did, however, cause a minor sensation by winning this division in the 1999 elections for the Welsh Assembly. Map 342

## JARROW
### Lab hold

| Electorate | %Turnout | | 63,172 | 54.58% | 2001 | 63,828 | 68.84% | 1997 |
|---|---|---|---|---|---|---|---|---|
| **Hepburn S** | **Lab** | | **22,777** | **66.06%** | **1.21%** | **28,497** | **64.85%** | **Lab** |
| Selby J | LD | | 5,182 | 15.03% | 3.96% | 6,564 | 14.94% | C |
| Wood D | C | | 5,056 | 14.66% | -0.28% | 4,865 | 11.07% | LD |
| Badger A | UK Ind | | 716 | 2.08% | | 2,538 | 5.78% | Ind Lab |
| Le Blond A | Ind | | 391 | 1.13% | | 1,034 | 2.35% | Ref |
| Bissett J | Soc | | 357 | 1.04% | | 444 | 1.01% | SPGB |
| **Lab to LD swing** | **1.37%** | | **34,479** | **Lab maj 17,595** | | **43,942** | **Lab maj 21,933** | |
| | | | | 51.03% | | | 49.91% | |

**STEPHEN HEPBURN,** b Dec 6, 1959. Elected 1997. Member, Defence Select Cttee, 1997-2001. South Tyneside cllr, 1985- (dep council ldr). Chairman, Tyne and Wear pensions, 1989-97. Member, Assoc of Lab Cllrs; Co-op Party. Former research asst to Don Dixon, ex-Lab MP for Jarrow. Ed Springfield Comp; Newcastle Univ.

This seat on the south bank of the Tyne is synonymous with the 1936 hunger march to London, and the collapse of Tyneside shipbuilding meant an economic catastrophe for the area. It suffered another battering in the 1980s, but has shown signs of recovery. Labour is plainly the dominant force here, but sometimes not by the huge margins found in other seats in this region where the economic legacy is one of coal or steel, not ships. Map 343

## KEIGHLEY
### Lab hold

| Electorate | %Turnout | | 68,349 | 63.4% | 2001 | 67,231 | 76.57% | 1997 |
|---|---|---|---|---|---|---|---|---|
| **Cryer Ms A** | **Lab** | | **20,888** | **48.2%** | **-2.38%** | **26,039** | **50.58%** | **Lab** |
| Cooke S | C | | 16,883 | 38.96% | 2.23% | 18,907 | 36.73% | C |
| Doyle M | LD | | 4,722 | 10.9% | 1.06% | 5,064 | 9.84% | LD |
| Cassidy M | UK Ind | | 840 | 1.94% | | 1,470 | 2.86% | Ref |
| **Lab to C swing** | **2.30%** | | **43,333** | **Lab maj 4,005** | | **51,480** | **Lab maj 7,132** | |
| | | | | 9.24% | | | 13.85% | |

**ANN CRYER,** b Dec 13, 1939. Elected 1997. Member, social security appeals tribunal; all-party film industry grp, arts and heritage grp, domestic violence grp. Vice-pres, Keighley and Worth Valley Railway Preservation Soc. Former researcher and PA to her late husband, Bob Cryer, former Lab MP for Bradford S and MEP. Mother of John Cryer, Lab MP for Hornchurch. Researcher, oral history project, Essex Univ. Ed technical coll.
e-mail: lowingc@parliament.uk www.epolitix.com/webminster/ann-cryer tel: 01535 210083 fax: 01535 210085

This semi-rural West Yorkshire seat in the Pennines is, like many of its neighbours, not nearly as Labour-inclined as might be assumed. Keighley itself is largely Labour, with a number of ethnic minority voters. Areas such as the spa town of Ilkley are very Conservative, while a string of small towns like the Brontës' Haworth tend to be similarly inclined. Labour took the seat from the Tories in 1997 and held it in 2001, but this will always be marginal. Map 344

## KENSINGTON & CHELSEA
### C hold

| Electorate | %Turnout | | 62,007 | 45.22% | 2001 | 67,786 | 54.71% | 1997 |
|---|---|---|---|---|---|---|---|---|
| **Portillo M** | **C** | | **15,270** | **54.46%** | **0.84%** | **19,887** | **53.62%** | **C** |
| Stanley S | Lab | | 6,499 | 23.18% | -4.78% | 10,368 | 27.96% | Lab |
| Falkner Ms K | LD | | 4,416 | 15.75% | 0.47% | 5,668 | 15.28% | LD |
| Stephenson Ms J | Green | | 1,158 | 4.13% | | 540 | 1.46% | UK Ind |
| Hockney N | UK Ind | | 416 | 1.48% | 0.02% | 218 | 0.59% | Teddy |
| Quintavalle Ms J | ProLife | | 179 | 0.64% | | 176 | 0.47% | UKPP |
| Crab G | Wrestling | | 100 | 0.36% | | 122 | 0.33% | NLP |
| | | | | | | 65 | 0.18% | Dream |
| | | | | | | 44 | 0.12% | Heart |
| **Lab to C swing** | **2.81%** | | **28,038** | **C maj 8,771** | | **37,088** | **C maj 9,519** | |
| | | | | 31.28% | | | 25.66% | |

**MICHAEL PORTILLO,** b May 26, 1953. Elected here 1999 by-election. MP, Enfield Southgate 1984-97. Challenger for the Conservative Party leadership, June 2001. Shadow Chancellor, 2000-. Sec of State for Defence, 1995-97; Employment, 1994-95; Chief Sec to Treasury, 1992-94. Special adviser to Nigel Lawson, Chancellor of the Exchequer. Former oil industry consultant; TV political researcher. Ed Harrow County Sch for Boys; Peterhouse, Cambridge.
www.michaelportillo.co.uk
*Details of 1999 by-election on page 291*

This is the strongest Conservative seat in London and one of the most reliable in the country. It is associated with fashionable affluence, which obscures the fact that the poor in this borough are very poor indeed. The local Tories clearly like to have lively personalities as candidates. Alan Clark became the MP in 1997 and after his unexpected death the seat provided a way back to the Commons for Michael Portillo in a by-election in late 1999. Map 345

## KETTERING — Lab hold

| Electorate | %Turnout | | 79,697 | 67.45% | 2001 | 75,153 | 75.79% | 1997 |
|---|---|---|---|---|---|---|---|---|
| **Sawford P** | **Lab** | | **24,034** | **44.71%** | **1.43%** | **24,650** | **43.28%** | **Lab** |
| Hollobone P | C | | 23,369 | 43.48% | 0.53% | 24,461 | 42.95% | C |
| Aron R | LD | | 5,469 | 10.17% | -0.54% | 6,098 | 10.71% | LD |
| Mahoney B | UK Ind | | 880 | 1.64% | | 1,551 | 2.72% | Ref |
| | | | | | | 197 | 0.35% | NLP |
| **C to Lab swing** | **0.45%** | | **53,752** | **Lab maj 665** | | **56,957** | **Lab maj 189** | |
| | | | | 1.24% | | | 0.33% | |

**PHIL SAWFORD,** b June 26, 1950. Elected 1997. Member, Information and Environmental Audit Select Cttees. Desborough town cllr, 1977-97; Kettering borough cllr, 1979-83 and 1986-97. Ex-manager of training partnership, Wellingborough, 1985-97. Wellingborough Community Relations Council, 1985. Ed Kettering GS; Ruskin Coll, Oxford; Leicester Univ.

This Northamptonshire town was simply destined to receive more than its fair share of attention during the 2001 election. In 1997 it produced the smallest Labour majority in percentage terms of any constituency in Britain. The fact that it has marginal status, reaffirmed once more in 2001, is logical since the seat consists of the town, which is supported by a range of light industry, some smaller conurbations and rural villages. Map 346

## KILMARNOCK & LOUDOUN — Lab hold

| Electorate | %Turnout | | 61,049 | 61.7% | 2001 | 61,376 | 77.24% | 1997 |
|---|---|---|---|---|---|---|---|---|
| **Browne D** | **Lab** | | **19,926** | **52.9%** | **3.08%** | **23,621** | **49.82%** | **Lab** |
| Brady J | SNP | | 9,592 | 25.47% | -9.05% | 16,365 | 34.52% | SNP |
| Reece D | C | | 3,943 | 10.47% | -0.34% | 5,125 | 10.81% | C |
| Stewart J | LD | | 3,177 | 8.43% | 4.44% | 1,891 | 3.99% | LD |
| Muir J | SSP | | 1,027 | 2.73% | | 284 | 0.6% | Ref |
| | | | | | | 123 | 0.26% | NLP |
| **SNP to Lab swing** | **6.07%** | | **37,665** | **Lab maj 10,334** | | **47,409** | **Lab maj 7,256** | |
| | | | | 27.44% | | | 15.30% | |

**DESMOND BROWNE,** b March 22, 1952. Elected 1997. Under Sec, NI Office, June 2001-; member, Select Cttees: Public Administration, 1999-2000; NI, 1997-99. PPS to Adam Ingram, Min of State for NI, 2000-2001 and the late Donald Dewar, Sec of State for Scotland, 1998-99. Treas, all-party Scotch whisky grp, 1997-; sec, Backbench Cttee on Social Security; member, PLP civil liberties grp; all-party grps on Great Lakes; Rwanda; prevention of genocide, and diabetes. Advocate, family law. Ed St Michael's Acad, Kilwinning; Glasgow Univ.

This Scottish seat is based around the town of Kilmarnock itself, some 20 miles southwest of Glasgow, and a set of surrounding towns, including many with a textile industry heritage. It is most famous for the production and bottling of whisky. It has an independent streak and still suffers from relatively high unemployment. Labour receives a healthy challenge from the SNP but not much from any other contenders. Map 347

## KINGSTON & SURBITON — LD hold

| Electorate | %Turnout | | 72,687 | 67.54% | 2001 | 73,879 | 75.35% | 1997 |
|---|---|---|---|---|---|---|---|---|
| **Davey E** | **LD** | | **29,542** | **60.18%** | **23.51%** | **20,411** | **36.67%** | **LD** |
| Shaw D | C | | 13,866 | 28.24% | -8.33% | 20,355 | 36.57% | C |
| Woodford P | Lab | | 4,302 | 8.76% | -14.25% | 12,811 | 23.01% | Lab |
| Spruce C | Green | | 572 | 1.17% | | 1,470 | 2.64% | Ref |
| Burns Miss A | UK Ind | | 438 | 0.89% | 0.14% | 418 | 0.75% | UK Ind |
| Hayball J | Soc Lab | | 319 | 0.65% | | 100 | 0.18% | NLP |
| Middleton J | Unrep | | 54 | 0.11% | | 100 | 0.18% | Dream |
| **C to LD swing** | **15.92%** | | **49,093** | **LD maj 15,676** | | **55,665** | **LD maj 56** | |
| | | | | 31.93% | | | 0.10% | |

**EDWARD DAVEY,** b Dec 25, 1965. Elected 1997. LD Treasury spokesman, June, 2001. Spokesman, economic affairs, public spending and taxation, 1997-2000. Spokesman on London, 2000-. Member, Treasury Select Cttee, 1999-2001. Member, Standing Cttees on the Finance, Gvt Resources and Accounts, Bank of England and Gvt for London Bills. Bravery awards from Royal Humane Soc and British Transport Police, 1994, for rescuing woman from railway line. Ed Nottingham HS; Jesus Coll, Oxford; Birkbeck Coll, London. www.edwarddavey.co.uk

This southwest Outer London seat provided one of the biggest surprises of the 1997 election. Although the Liberal Democrats did well in neighbouring affluent suburban seats along the Thames, the national HQ had not even seriously targeted this one; but by 2001 the Lib Dems had stretched their lead to more than 15,000. It has a very high number of professionals and managers, is a thriving shopping centre, and will remain a middle-class bellwether. Map 348

## KINGSWOOD — Lab hold

| Electorate | %Turnout | | 80,531 | 65.41% | 2001 | 77,026 | 77.75% | 1997 |
|---|---|---|---|---|---|---|---|---|
| **Berry Dr R** | **Lab** | | **28,903** | **54.87%** | **1.13%** | **32,181** | **53.74%** | **Lab** |
| Marven R | C | | 14,941 | 28.36% | -1.58% | 17,928 | 29.94% | C |
| Greenfield C | LD | | 7,747 | 14.71% | 1.9% | 7,672 | 12.81% | LD |
| Smith D | UK Ind | | 1,085 | 2.06% | | 1,463 | 2.44% | Ref |
| | | | | | | 290 | 0.48% | BNP |
| | | | | | | 238 | 0.4% | NLP |
| | | | | | | 115 | 0.19% | Scrapit |
| **C to Lab swing** | **1.35%** | | **52,676** | Lab maj 13,962 | 26.51% | **59,887** | Lab maj 14,253 | 23.80% |

**ROGER BERRY,** b July 4, 1948. Elected 1992. Member, Select Cttees: Trade and Industry, 1995-2001; Deregulation, 1995-97. Sec, all-party disablement grp, 1994-. Avon county cllr, 1981-93 (leader, Lab grp, 1986-92). Chairman, SW grp of Lab MPs, 1997-. Dir. Tribune Publications Ltd, 1997-. Lecturer. Ed Huddersfield New Coll; Bristol and Sussex Univs.
e-mail: berryr@parliament.uk  www.bristol.digitalcity.org/members/rberry tel: 0117-956 1837 fax: 0117-970 1363

This is an urban seat and very much a part of the Bristol conurbation, lying to the east of the city. It has quite a high rate of owner-occupation but not an especially large number of professionals and managers. This suggests a combination of lower middle-class and skilled working-class electors. That assumption chimes with its partisan patterns. This was a very marginal seat at one stage but since 1997 has swung very firmly to Labour. Map 349

## KIRKCALDY — Lab hold

| Electorate | %Turnout | | 51,559 | 54.61% | 2001 | 52,186 | 67.02% | 1997 |
|---|---|---|---|---|---|---|---|---|
| **Moonie Dr L** | **Lab Co-op** | | **15,227** | **54.08%** | **0.52%** | **18,730** | **53.56%** | **Lab** |
| Somerville Ms S | SNP | | 6,264 | 22.25% | -0.68% | 8,020 | 22.93% | SNP |
| Campbell S | C | | 3,013 | 10.7% | -2.96% | 4,779 | 13.66% | C |
| Weston A | LD | | 2,849 | 10.12% | 1.45% | 3,031 | 8.67% | LD |
| Kinnear D | SSP | | 804 | 2.86% | | 413 | 1.18% | Ref |
| **SNP to Lab Co-op swing 0.60%** | | | **28,157** | Lab Co-op maj 8,963 | 31.83% | **34,973** | Lab Co-op maj 10,710 | 30.63% |

**LEWIS MOONIE,** b Feb 25, 1947. Elected 1987. Under-Sec of State for Defence, 2000-; confirmed, June 2001. Member, Treasury Select Cttee, 1997-99; chairman, Financial Services Cttee, House of Commons, 1997-2000; spokesman, nat heritage, 1995-97; science, tech and industry, 1989-95. Consultant in Public Health Medicine with Fife Health Board; research adviser and clinical pharmacologist in Switzerland and The Netherlands. Member, ASTMS; TGWU. Ed Grove Acad, Dundee; St Andrews and Edinburgh Univs. tel: 01592 564115

The town of Kirkcaldy has a long esplanade on the north shore of the Firth of Forth and is the birthplace of Adam Smith. If one assumes that he would be a Conservative voter today then he would be disappointed with the attitudes of his fellow residents. This is an industrial and working-class town, once primarily a port for the coal industry but now more varied in economic profile. The SNP is the only realistic, if distant, challenger to Labour. Map 350

## KNOWSLEY NORTH & SEFTON EAST — Lab hold

| Electorate | %Turnout | | 70,781 | 53.0% | 2001 | 70,918 | 70.09% | 1997 |
|---|---|---|---|---|---|---|---|---|
| **Howarth G** | **Lab** | | **25,035** | **66.73%** | **-3.18%** | **34,747** | **69.91%** | **Lab** |
| Chapman K | C | | 6,108 | 16.28% | -1.02% | 8,600 | 17.3% | C |
| Roberts R | LD | | 5,173 | 13.79% | 2.73% | 5,499 | 11.06% | LD |
| Waugh R | Soc Lab | | 574 | 1.53% | -0.19% | 857 | 1.72% | Soc Lab |
| Rossiter T | Ind R | | 356 | 0.95% | | | | |
| Jones D | Ind J | | 271 | 0.72% | | | | |
| **Lab to C swing** | **1.08%** | | **37,517** | Lab maj 18,927 | 50.45% | **49,703** | Lab maj 26,147 | 52.61% |

**GEORGE HOWARTH,** b June 29, 1949. Elected here 1997; MP for Knowsley N 1986-97. Under-Sec, NI Office, 1999-; Under-Sec for Deregulation and Drugs (Home Office), 1997-99. Lab spokesman, home affairs, 1994-97; environmental protection, 1993-94; environment, 1990-92. Member, Select Cttees: Parly Commissioner for Administration, 1987-90; Environment, 1989-90. Ex-joint vice-chairman, all-party Mersey Barrage grp. Knowsley borough cllr, 1975-86. Chief exec. Wales co-op centre, 1984-86. Ed Huyton Hey Sec; Kirkby CFE; Liverpool Poly.

The political gurus Robert Waller and Byron Criddle have described this seat on the northern edge of Merseyside as a "social and political monstrosity". It certainly represents the triumph of mathematics over community. Before the 1997 election, the Boundary Commission combined some very poor parts of Knowsley and Kirkby, solidly Labour, with some very middle-class areas of Crosby, leaving a Tory island in a sea of unreconstructed socialism. Map 351

## KNOWSLEY SOUTH — Lab hold

| Electorate | %Turnout | | 70,681 | 51.77% | 2001 | 70,532 | 67.47% | 1997 |
|---|---|---|---|---|---|---|---|---|
| O'Hara E | | Lab | 26,071 | 71.25% | -5.86% | 36,695 | 77.11% | Lab |
| Smithson D | | LD | 4,755 | 13.0% | 4.69% | 5,987 | 12.58% | C |
| Jemetta P | | C | 4,250 | 11.62% | -0.96% | 3,954 | 8.31% | LD |
| Fogg A | | Soc Lab | 1,068 | 2.92% | | 954 | 2.0% | Ref |
| McNee Ms M | | Ind | 446 | 1.22% | | | | |
| Lab to LD swing | 5.27% | | 36,590 | Lab maj 21,316 | | 47,590 | Lab maj 30,708 | |
| | | | | 58.26% | | | 64.53% | |

**EDWARD O'HARA,** b Oct 1, 1937. Elected 1990 by-election. Member, Select Cttees: Ed and Employment, 1996-97; Education, 1991-96. Member, Chairmen's Panel. Joint chairman, all-party older people grp, 1997-; chairman, Greek grp, 1997-. Member, management board, Royal Liverpool Philharmonic Soc, 1987-90. Chairman, trustees, Community Development Foundation; governor, Knowsley Community Coll; vice-chairman, nat wild flower centre (all unpaid). Ed Liverpool Collegiate Sch; Magdalen Coll, Oxford; London Univ.

This Merseyside seat contains the majority of the Knowsley area. It was once called Huyton and was represented for many years by Harold Wilson. Although owner-occupation is not strikingly low by inner-city standards, Labour is utterly dominant in the large council estates fringing the Liverpool conurbation. The Ford motor plant at Halewood is situated here. In 1997 Knowsley South produced the largest numerical majority for any party in the UK. Map 352

## LAGAN VALLEY — UUP hold

| Electorate | %Turnout | | 72,671 | 63.22% | 2001 | 71,225 | 62.21% | 1997 |
|---|---|---|---|---|---|---|---|---|
| Donaldson J | | UUP | 25,966 | 56.52% | 1.09% | 24,560 | 55.43% | UUP |
| Close S | | Alliance | 7,624 | 16.6% | -0.63% | 7,635 | 17.23% | Alliance |
| Poots E | | DUP | 6,164 | 13.42% | -0.13% | 6,005 | 13.55% | DUP |
| Lewsley Ms P | | SDLP | 3,462 | 7.54% | -0.21% | 3,436 | 7.75% | SDLP |
| Butler P | | SF | 2,725 | 5.93% | 3.42% | 1,212 | 2.74% | C |
| | | | | | | 1,110 | 2.51% | SF |
| | | | | | | 203 | 0.46% | WP |
| | | | | | | 149 | 0.34% | NLP |
| Alliance to UUP swing | 0.86% | | 45,941 | UUP maj 18,342 | | 44,310 | UUP maj 16,925 | |
| | | | | 39.93% | | | 38.20% | |

**JEFFREY DONALDSON,** b Dec 7, 1962. Elected 1997. UUP spokesman, trade and industry. Member, Select Cttees: NI Affairs, 1997-2000; Environment, Transport and Regions, 2000-01. Member, UU team in constitutional talks on future of Province. Elected at 22 to NI Assembly, 1985 (its youngest member). Former asst to Sir James Molyneaux; former agent to Enoch Powell. Estate agent/fin adviser. Ed Kilkeel HS, Co Down and Castlereagh Coll. Belfast. e-mail: laganvalley@uup.org www.uup.org tel: 02892 668001 fax: 02892 671845

This seat is centred on the boundaries of the Lisburn District Council, southwest of Belfast. It is, even by Ulster's standards, an overwhelmingly Protestant seat and strongly Unionist in sentiment. It was represented for many years by James Molyneaux, the former UUP leader. The main issue in recent years has been which strand of Unionism would triumph here, though the UUP does seem well established for the present. Map 353

## LANCASHIRE WEST — Lab hold

| Electorate | %Turnout | | 72,858 | 58.98% | 2001 | 73,175 | 74.79% | 1997 |
|---|---|---|---|---|---|---|---|---|
| Pickthall C | | Lab | 23,404 | 54.46% | -5.88% | 33,022 | 60.34% | Lab |
| Myers J | | C | 13,761 | 32.02% | 2.96% | 15,903 | 29.06% | C |
| Thornton J | | LD | 4,966 | 11.56% | 4.36% | 3,938 | 7.2% | LD |
| Hill D | | Ind Hill | 523 | 1.22% | | 1,025 | 1.87% | Ref |
| Braid D | | Indep Braid | 317 | 0.74% | | 449 | 0.82% | NLP |
| | | | | | | 392 | 0.72% | Home Rule |
| Lab to C swing | 4.42% | | 42,971 | Lab maj 9,643 | | 54,729 | Lab maj 17,119 | |
| | | | | 22.44% | | | 31.28% | |

**COLIN PICKTHALL,** b Sept 13, 1944. Elected 1992. PPS to Jack Straw, Foreign Sec, 2001-; and as Home Sec, 1998-2001; and to Alun Michael, 1997-98. Member, Agriculture Select Cttee, 1992-97. Chairman, MPs' Usdaw grp; all-party grp, church and allied colleges, 1997-; sec, all-party diabetes grp; Canada grp, 1997-. Lancs county cllr, 1989-93. Senior posts, Edge Hill Coll of Higher Ed, 1970-92; ex-member, NW reg advisory cttee and Lancs higher ed consultative cttee;ex-chairman, governors, Skelmersdale CFE. Higher ed teacher. Ed Ulverston GS; Wales and Lancaster Univs.

Lying on the northern edge of Merseyside and stretching over the fertile west Lancashire plain, this is a much more diverse and interesting constituency than outsiders might expect. It was very marginal until 1997. The Tory vote is centred on the prosperous town of Ormskirk; indeed, some of the wards here rival Surrey for their loyalty to Conservatism. However, the bleak new town of Skelmersdale is just as strongly sympathetic to Labour. Map 354

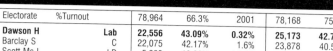

# LANCASTER & WYRE
**Lab hold**

| Electorate | %Turnout | | 78,964 | 66.3% | 2001 | 78,168 | 75.3% | 1997 |
|---|---|---|---|---|---|---|---|---|
| Dawson H | Lab | | **22,556** | **43.09%** | **0.32%** | 25,173 | 42.77% | Lab |
| Barclay S | C | | 22,075 | 42.17% | 1.6% | 23,878 | 40.57% | C |
| Scott Ms L | LD | | 5,383 | 10.28% | -1.28% | 6,802 | 11.56% | LD |
| Whitelegg Prof J | Green | | 1,595 | 3.05% | 1.7% | 1,516 | 2.58% | Ref |
| Whittaker Dr J | UK Ind | | 741 | 1.42% | 0.23% | 795 | 1.35% | Green |
| | | | | | | 698 | 1.19% | UK Ind |
| Lab to C swing | 0.64% | | 52,350 | | Lab maj 481 | 58,862 | | Lab maj 1,295 |
| | | | | | 0.92% | | | 2.20% |

**(THOMAS) HILTON DAWSON,** b Sept 30, 1953. Elected 1997. Member, Administration Select Cttee, 1997-2001. Joint vice-chairman, all-party welfare of park homeowners grp, 1997-. Lancaster city cllr, 1987-. Member, Unison. Social work manager, 1983-97; manager of foster and adoption day care centre. Ed Ashington GS, Northumberland; Warwick and Lancaster Univs.

This has become a very marginal constituency, partly because the Boundary Commission assisted the Conservatives. The seat, lying to the northeast of Blackpool, had historically been divided between Lancaster, inclined towards Labour, and the surrounding rural areas which backed the Tories. The addition of part of the old Wyre seat meant a reinforcement of the Tory base. Labour snatched the seat in 1997 and only just held on in 2001. Map 355

# LEEDS CENTRAL
**Lab hold**

| Electorate | %Turnout | | 65,497 | 41.69% | 2001 | 67,664 | 54.7% | 1997 |
|---|---|---|---|---|---|---|---|---|
| Benn H | Lab | | **18,277** | **66.93%** | **-2.69%** | 25,766 | 69.62% | Lab |
| Richmond Miss V | C | | 3,896 | 14.27% | 0.55% | 5,077 | 13.72% | C |
| Arnold S | LD | | 3,607 | 13.21% | 1.96% | 4,164 | 11.25% | LD |
| Burgess D | UK Ind | | 775 | 2.84% | | 1,042 | 2.82% | Ref |
| Johnson S | Soc All | | 751 | 2.75% | | 656 | 1.77% | Soc Lab |
| | | | | | | 304 | 0.82% | Soc |
| Lab to C swing | 1.62% | | 27,306 | | Lab maj 14,381 | 37,009 | | Lab maj 20,689 |
| | | | | | 52.67% | | | 55.90% |

**HILARY BENN,** b Nov 26, 1953. Elected 1999 by-election. Under Sec of State, Dept for International Development, June 2001-; former special adviser to Sec of State for Ed and Employment, 1997-99. Member, Environment Select Cttee, 1999-2001. Vice-chairman, PLP Ed and Employment Cttee, 2000-. Ealing borough cllr, 1979-99. Son of Tony Benn, veteran parliamentarian who retired in 2001. Ed Holland Park Comp Sch and Sussex Univ.
e-mail: bennh@parliament.uk tel: 020-7219 5770 fax: 020-8994 3976
*Details of 1999 by-election on page 291*

The centre of Leeds, like many conurbations, has been depopulated over the decades. The result is that this seat now covers much of Leeds city proper. It includes the buildings once associated with the woollen industry, imposing civic buildings, the university and a small ethnic minority community. This is a very solid Labour seat which returned Hilary Benn to Parliament in a 1999 by-election marked by an astonishingly low turnout. Map 356

# LEEDS EAST
**Lab hold**

| Electorate | %Turnout | | 56,400 | 51.52% | 2001 | 56,963 | 62.83% | 1997 |
|---|---|---|---|---|---|---|---|---|
| Mudie G | Lab | | **18,290** | **62.95%** | **-4.53%** | 24,151 | 67.48% | Lab |
| Anderson B | C | | 5,647 | 19.44% | 0.76% | 6,685 | 18.68% | C |
| Jennings B | LD | | 3,923 | 13.5% | 3.19% | 3,689 | 10.31% | LD |
| Northgreaves R | UK Ind | | 634 | 2.18% | | 1,267 | 3.54% | Ref |
| King M | Soc Lab | | 419 | 1.44% | | | | |
| Socrates P | Ind | | 142 | 0.49% | | | | |
| Lab to C swing | 2.64% | | 29,055 | | Lab maj 12,643 | 35,792 | | Lab maj 17,466 |
| | | | | | 43.51% | | | 48.80% |

**GEORGE MUDIE,** b Feb 6, 1945. Elected 1992. Under-Sec of State for Ed and Employment, 1998-99. Deputy chief whip, 1997-98; Lab pairing whip, 1995-97. Former member, Selection Cttee; Commons Accommodation and Works Cttee, 1997-2001. Joined Nupe, 1968; formerly AEU. Ex-leader, Leeds City Council. Ex-union official. Ed local state schools.

This seat is divided between four wards, roughly equal in size but different in social complexion. One of them (Seacroft) is dominated by predominantly white council estate tenants. The second (Halton) is very middle-class. The third (Burmantofts) is broadly working-class, benefiting from new housing. The final one (Harehills) has a large immigrant population living in traditional terraced housing. The net effect of this mixture is a safe Labour seat. Map 357

## LEEDS NORTH EAST                                     Lab hold

| Electorate | %Turnout | 64,123 | 62.03% | 2001 | 63,185 | 72.03% | 1997 |
|---|---|---|---|---|---|---|---|
| **Hamilton F** | **Lab** | **19,540** | **49.13%** | -0.02% | **22,368** | **49.15%** | **Lab** |
| Rhys O | C | 12,451 | 31.31% | -2.55% | 15,409 | 33.86% | C |
| Brown J | LD | 6,325 | 15.9% | 2.02% | 6,318 | 13.88% | LD |
| Foote Ms C | Left All | 770 | 1.94% | | 946 | 2.08% | Ref |
| Miles J | UK Ind | 382 | 0.96% | | 468 | 1.03% | Soc Lab |
| Muir C | Soc Lab | 173 | 0.43% | -0.6% | | | |
| Zaman M | Ind | 132 | 0.33% | | | | |
| **C to Lab swing** | **1.27%** | **39,773** | Lab maj **7,089** | | **45,509** | Lab maj **6,959** | |
| | | | 17.82% | | | 15.29% | |

**FABIAN HAMILTON,** b April 4, 1955. Elected 1997. Member, Administration Select Cttee, 1997-2001. Sec, all-party motor club grp, 1997-. Vice-chairman, hospices and business services grps. Trustee, Nat Heart Research Fund. Leeds cllr, 1987-98. Chairman, Leeds W CLP, 1987-88. Governor, Northern school of Contemporary Dance. Graphic designer; systems consultant; ex-company dir; ex-taxi driver. Ed Brentwood Sch, Essex; York Univ.
e-mail: fabian@leedsne.co.uk www.leedsne.co.uk
tel: 020-7219 3493 fax: 020-7219 4945

This was once considered the most reliable Tory patch in the city - it includes the older residential district of Roundhay - and was represented in the Commons by Sir Keith Joseph. Social change, notably the influx of students and other multi-occupiers, has altered its political character. The seat has a strong Jewish influence as well as an expanding Asian community in Chapeltown. Labour finally captured the constituency in 1997. Map 358

## LEEDS NORTH WEST                                     Lab hold

| Electorate | %Turnout | 72,945 | 58.2% | 2001 | 69,972 | 70.57% | 1997 |
|---|---|---|---|---|---|---|---|
| **Best H** | **Lab** | **17,794** | **41.92%** | 2.03% | **19,694** | **39.89%** | **Lab** |
| Pritchard A | C | 12,558 | 29.58% | -2.52% | 15,850 | 32.1% | C |
| Hall-Matthews D | LD | 11,431 | 26.93% | 3.26% | 11,689 | 23.67% | LD |
| Jones S | UK Ind | 668 | 1.57% | | 1,325 | 2.68% | Ref |
| | | | | | 335 | 0.68% | Soc Lab |
| | | | | | 251 | 0.51% | ProLife |
| | | | | | 232 | 0.47% | Ronnie |
| **C to Lab swing** | **2.27%** | **42,451** | Lab maj **5,236** | | **49,376** | Lab maj **3,844** | |
| | | | 12.33% | | | 7.79% | |

**HAROLD BEST,** b Dec 18, 1939. Elected 1997. Member, Nupe; Unison; TGWU; Liberty; Amnesty. Principal electrical technician, Leeds ed authority, 1997. Ed Meanwood County Sec Sch.

This has traditionally been a seat populated by the Leeds middle class. It has a large proportion of professionals and managers, many of whom are associated with the city's booming university sector - though many have moved further out from the leafy inner-city suburb of Headingley. It would appear more like a Tory-Lib Dem battleground, but in 1997 the Labour candidate surged from third position to win, and he increased his majority in 2001. Map 359

## LEEDS WEST                                           Lab hold

| Electorate | %Turnout | 64,218 | 49.98% | 2001 | 63,965 | 62.88% | 1997 |
|---|---|---|---|---|---|---|---|
| **Battle J** | **Lab** | **19,943** | **62.14%** | -4.54% | **26,819** | **66.68%** | **Lab** |
| Hopkins K | C | 5,008 | 15.6% | -1.92% | 7,048 | 17.52% | C |
| Finlay D | LD | 3,350 | 10.44% | 1.43% | 3,622 | 9.01% | LD |
| Blackburn D | Green | 2,573 | 8.02% | 5.79% | 1,210 | 3.01% | Ref |
| Finley W | UK Ind | 758 | 2.36% | | 896 | 2.23% | Green |
| Nowosielski N | Lib | 462 | 1.44% | -0.11% | 625 | 1.55% | Lib |
| **Lab to C swing** | **1.31%** | **32,094** | Lab maj **14,935** | | **40,220** | Lab maj **19,771** | |
| | | | 46.54% | | | 49.16% | |

**JOHN BATTLE,** b April 26, 1951. Elected 1987. Min of State, FCO, 1999-2001; Industry, Energy and Science, 1997-99. Energy spokesman, 1995-97; Commons affairs and citizen's charter, 1994-95; local gvt, 1992-94. Lab whip, 1988-90. Member, Select Cttees: Environment, 1991-92; Broadcasting, 1992-97. Chairman, PLP Treasury and Civil Service Cttee, 1991-92. Ex-chairman, all-party epilepsy grp. Ed St Michael's Coll, Kirkby Lonsdale; Leeds Univ. MSF.
e-mail: johnbattle@leedswest.co.uk tel: 0113-231 0258 fax: 0113-279 5850

This essentially urban and working-class patch of Leeds consisting of four wards near the River Aire has had a quixotic electoral history. On paper it would seem safe Labour territory and the most recent results confirm this. The constituency was, however, captured by Michael Meadowcroft, the radical Liberal in 1983 and he lost only narrowly four years later. It has taken some time for his influence to disappear. Map 360

# LEICESTER EAST

**Lab hold**

| Electorate | %Turnout | | 65,527 | 62.05% | 2001 | 64,012 | 69.37% | 1997 |
|---|---|---|---|---|---|---|---|---|
| **Vaz K** | **Lab** | | **23,402** | **57.55%** | **-7.95%** | **29,083** | **65.5%** | **Lab** |
| Mugglestone J | C | | 9,960 | 24.5% | 0.49% | 10,661 | 24.01% | C |
| Athwal Ms H | LD | | 4,989 | 12.27% | 5.28% | 3,105 | 6.99% | LD |
| Roberts D | Soc Lab | | 837 | 2.06% | 1.08% | 1,015 | 2.29% | Ref |
| Potter C | BNP | | 772 | 1.9% | | 436 | 0.98% | Soc Lab |
| Bennett S | Ind | | 701 | 1.72% | | 102 | 0.23% | Glow |
| **Lab to C swing** | **4.22%** | | **40,661** | | **Lab maj 13,442** | **44,402** | | **Lab maj 18,422** |
| | | | | | 33.06% | | | 41.49% |

**KEITH VAZ,** b Nov 26, 1956. Elected 1987. Min of State for Europe, FCO, 1999-2001. Min, Lord Chancellor's Dept, 1999. PPS to John Morris, Attorney-General, 1997-99. Member, Home Affairs Select Cttee, 1987-92. Chairman, all-party Indo-British grp, 1997-; Yemen grp, 1997-; member, all-party footwear and leather industries grp, 1990-. Barrister. Ed St Joseph's Convent, Aden; Latymer HS, Hammersmith; Gonville and Caius, Cambridge; Coll of Law, Lancaster Gate.
tel: 0116-212 2020 fax: 0116-212 2121

This seat has been transformed by social change over the past two decades. It is now strongly Asian, one of the most Asian in the UK. This factor has added a certain tension to internal Labour politics in the city of Leicester, as Keith Vaz discovered in the later stages of the last Parliament. There is considerable variety in the wealth of the new immigrants but less so in their voting habits. Map 361

# LEICESTER SOUTH

**Lab hold**

| Electorate | %Turnout | | 72,671 | 57.99% | 2001 | 71,750 | 67.06% | 1997 |
|---|---|---|---|---|---|---|---|---|
| **Marshall J** | **Lab** | | **22,958** | **54.48%** | **-3.54%** | **27,914** | **58.02%** | **Lab** |
| Hoile R | C | | 9,715 | 23.05% | -0.69% | 11,421 | 23.74% | C |
| Singh Gill P | LD | | 7,243 | 17.19% | 3.36% | 6,654 | 13.83% | LD |
| Layton Ms M | Green | | 1,217 | 2.89% | | 1,184 | 2.46% | Ref |
| Gardner A | Soc Lab | | 676 | 1.6% | 0.28% | 634 | 1.32% | Soc Lab |
| Ladwa K | UK Ind | | 333 | 0.79% | | 307 | 0.64% | Nat Dem |
| **Lab to C swing** | **1.43%** | | **42,142** | | **Lab maj 13,243** | **48,114** | | **Lab maj 16,493** |
| | | | | | 31.42% | | | 34.28% |

**JIM MARSHALL,** b March 13, 1941. Elected here 1987 (being its MP, Oct 1974-83); contested seat, Feb 1974. Member, European Legislation Select Cttee, 1997-2001. Spokesman, NI, 1987-92; home affairs, 1982-83. Asst gvt whip, 1977-79. Member, British-Irish interparly body. Leeds city cllr, 1965-68; Leicester city cllr, 1971-76 (leader, 1974). Lecturer. Ed Sheffield City GS; Leeds Univ.

This is easily the most polarised seat in Leicester and arguably the entire East Midlands. Besides covering most of the city centre, the constituency includes some of the city's most desirable sections of residential territory but also white working-class council tenants and many Asian immigrants. There is a sizeable Afro-Caribbean section as well. The seat is solid Labour as a consequence. Map 362

# LEICESTER WEST

**Lab hold**

| Electorate | %Turnout | | 65,267 | 50.9% | 2001 | 64,570 | 63.36% | 1997 |
|---|---|---|---|---|---|---|---|---|
| **Hewitt Ms P** | **Lab** | | **18,014** | **54.23%** | **-0.96%** | **22,580** | **55.19%** | **Lab** |
| Shaw C | C | | 8,375 | 25.21% | 1.46% | 9,716 | 23.75% | C |
| Vincent A | LD | | 5,085 | 15.31% | 1.15% | 5,795 | 14.16% | LD |
| Gough M | Green | | 1,074 | 3.23% | 1.8% | 970 | 2.37% | Ref |
| Kirkpatrick S | Soc Lab | | 350 | 1.05% | -0.05% | 586 | 1.43% | Green |
| Score S | Soc All | | 321 | 0.97% | | 452 | 1.1% | Soc Lab |
| | | | | | | 327 | 0.8% | Soc |
| | | | | | | 302 | 0.74% | BNP |
| | | | | | | 186 | 0.45% | Nat Dem |
| **Lab to C swing** | **1.21%** | | **33,219** | | **Lab maj 9,639** | **40,914** | | **Lab maj 12,864** |
| | | | | | 29.02% | | | 31.44% |

**PATRICIA HEWITT,** b Dec 2, 1948. Elected 1997. Sec of State for Trade and Industry, June 2001-; Min of State, DTI, 1999-2001. Member, Social Security Select Cttee, 1997-99. Policy co-ordinator to Neil Kinnock, 1988-89. Dep dir, Inst for Public Policy Research, 1989-94. Head of research, Andersen Consulting, 1994-97. FRSA, 1992. Trustee, Inst for Public Policy Research; member, council, Inst for Fiscal Studies (both unpaid). Associate, Newnham Coll, Cambridge. Ed C of E Girls' GS, Canberra; Australian Nat Univ; Newnham Coll, Cambridge.

Although this seat is scarcely less favourable to Labour than its neighbours, it is very different in character. The proportion of non-white residents is much smaller and the number of council tenants much larger. The seat was held by, and associated with, Greville Janner, the prominent Jewish MP, for many years. Map 363

## LEICESTERSHIRE NORTH WEST                     Lab hold

| Electorate | %Turnout | | 68,414 | 65.79% | 2001 | 65,069 | 79.95% | 1997 |
|---|---|---|---|---|---|---|---|---|
| **Taylor D** | Lab Co-op | | **23,431** | **52.06%** | **-4.32%** | **29,332** | **56.38%** | **Lab** |
| Weston N | C | | 15,274 | 33.94% | 2.97% | 16,113 | 30.97% | C |
| Fraser-Fleming C | LD | | 4,651 | 10.33% | 1.7% | 4,492 | 8.63% | LD |
| Nattrass W | UK Ind | | 1,021 | 2.27% | | 2,088 | 4.01% | Ref |
| Nettleton R | Ind | | 632 | 1.4% | | | | |
| **Lab Co-op to C swing** | **3.64%** | | **45,009** | **Lab Co-op maj 8,157** | | **52,025** | **Lab Co-op maj 13,219** | |
| | | | | | 18.12% | | | 25.41% |

**DAVID TAYLOR,** b Aug 22, 1946. Elected 1997. Leicestershire district cllr, 1981-87. Founder and chairman, Leics NW safer communities forum. Accountant and computer manager, Leicestershire County Council, 1977-97. Ed Ashby de la Zouch Boys GS; Leicester Poly; Coventry Poly; OU.

This seat is set in a large slice of relatively rural Leicestershire. This might imply a Conservative bias and it was reasonably solid for the Tories through the 1980s and only became a hyper-marginal in 1992. It then swung firmly in Labour's direction in the past two elections. The core of the seat is the town of Coalville, named after the industry, but this is partially offset politically by the market town of Ashby de la Zouch. Map 364

## LEIGH                                          Lab hold

| Electorate | %Turnout | | 71,054 | 49.68% | 2001 | 69,908 | 65.69% | 1997 |
|---|---|---|---|---|---|---|---|---|
| **Burnham A** | Lab | | **22,783** | **64.54%** | **-4.39%** | **31,652** | **68.93%** | **Lab** |
| Oxley A | C | | 6,421 | 18.19% | 2.61% | 7,156 | 15.58% | C |
| Atkins R | LD | | 4,524 | 12.82% | 1.58% | 5,163 | 11.24% | LD |
| Kelly W | Soc Lab | | 820 | 2.32% | | 1,949 | 4.24% | Ref |
| Best C | UK Ind | | 750 | 2.12% | | | | |
| **Lab to C swing** | **3.50%** | | **35,298** | **Lab maj 16,362** | | **45,920** | **Lab maj 24,496** | |
| | | | | | 46.35% | | | 53.35% |

**ANDY BURNHAM,** b Jan 7, 1970. Elected 2001. Takes over from Lawrence Cunliffe, MP since 1979. Parly officer, NHS Confed, 1997. Administrator, football task force, 1997-98. Adviser to Chris Smith, 1998-2001; researcher to Tessa Jowell, 1994-97. Member, Co-op Party. Ed St Aelred's RC HS, Merseyside; Fitzwilliam Coll, Cambridge.

This seat is located in the Metropolitan Borough of Wigan, due west of Manchester. It was, at one stage, the heart of the Lancashire coalfield, although light industry now predominates. It is very much a white working-class constituency, though with a large number of skilled workers who are homeowners. There is a very strong cultural loyalty to the Labour Party. Map 365

## LEOMINSTER                                     C hold

| Electorate | %Turnout | | 68,695 | 68.02% | 2001 | 65,993 | 76.6% | 1997 |
|---|---|---|---|---|---|---|---|---|
| **Wiggin B** | C | | **22,879** | **48.96%** | **3.68%** | **22,888** | **45.28%** | **C** |
| Downie Ms C | LD | | 12,512 | 26.78% | -1.02% | 14,053 | 27.8% | LD |
| Hart S | Lab | | 7,872 | 16.85% | -0.62% | 8,831 | 17.47% | Lab |
| Bennett Ms P | Green | | 1,690 | 3.62% | 1.47% | 2,815 | 5.57% | Ref |
| Kingsley C | UK Ind | | 1,590 | 3.4% | 2.24% | 1,086 | 2.15% | Green |
| Haycock J | Ind | | 186 | 0.4% | | 588 | 1.16% | UK Ind |
| | | | | | | 292 | 0.58% | BNP |
| **LD to C swing** | **2.35%** | | **46,729** | **C maj 10,367** | | **50,553** | **C maj 8,835** | |
| | | | | | 22.19% | | | 17.48% |

**BILL WIGGIN,** b June 4, 1966. Elected 2001. Regained seat for Tories after Peter Temple-Morris, who held it in 1997, crossed the floor and joined the Lab Party. Contested Burnley 1997. Former vice-chairman, Hammersmith and Fulham Conservatives Assoc; governor Hammersmith and W London FE Coll. TA officer. Banker, former foreign trader and investment manager. Ed Eton; Univ Coll of N Wales.
www.billwiggin.co.uk

This is the northern half of Herefordshire lying between the Malvern Hills and the Welsh borders. It is rural and agricultural with a number of small market towns such as Leominster itself, Kington in the west and Bromyard and Ledbury in the east. It has historically been strongly Conservative. However, in 1998 its MP, Peter Temple-Morris, defected to Labour. This is probably the only circumstance in which Leominster would produce a Labour Member. Map 366

# LEWES

**LD hold**

| Electorate | %Turnout | | 66,332 | 68.49% | 2001 | 64,340 | 76.42% | 1997 |
|---|---|---|---|---|---|---|---|---|
| **Baker N** | | **LD** | **25,588** | **56.32%** | **13.1%** | **21,250** | **43.22%** | **LD** |
| Sinnatt S | | C | 15,878 | 34.95% | -5.62% | 19,950 | 40.57% | C |
| Richards P | | Lab | 3,317 | 7.3% | -3.34% | 5,232 | 10.64% | Lab |
| Harvey J | | UK Ind | 650 | 1.43% | 0.91% | 2,481 | 5.05% | Ref |
| | | | | | | 256 | 0.52% | UK Ind |
| **C to LD swing** | | **9.36%** | **45,433** | | **LD maj 9,710** | **49,169** | | **LD maj 1,300** |
| | | | | | 21.37% | | | 2.65% |

**NORMAN BAKER,** b July 26, 1957. Elected 1997. LD spokesman, consumer affairs and waste, 1997-. Member, European Legislation Select Cttee, 1997-2001. Joint vice-chairman, all-party consumer affairs and trading standards grp, 1997-; energy studies grp, 1997-. Lewes district cllr, 1987-99 (council leader, 1991-97); E Sussex county cllr, 1989-97; Beddingham parish cllr, 1987-. Dir, Newhaven Economic Partnership. Member, Greenpeace; Amnesty. Teacher. Ed Royal Liberty, Gidea Park; Royal Holloway Coll, London.
e-mail: baker@parliament.uk tel: 020-7219 2864 fax: 020-7219 0445

East Sussex has been reasonably encouraging territory for the Liberal Democrats over the past two decades. This seat was, however, the only one in the county to fall to them in 1997. It includes the county town of Lewes, the resort of Seaford, the former ferry port of Newhaven, and villages on the South Downs. It is not as prosperous as other parts of Sussex, which may explain both the Tories' problems here and the Lib Dems' growing strength. Map 367

# LEWISHAM DEPTFORD

**Lab hold**

| Electorate | %Turnout | | 62,869 | 46.3% | 2001 | 58,141 | 57.87% | 1997 |
|---|---|---|---|---|---|---|---|---|
| **Ruddock Mrs J** | | **Lab** | **18,915** | **64.98%** | **-5.84%** | **23,827** | **70.82%** | **Lab** |
| McCartney Ms C | | C | 3,622 | 12.44% | -2.27% | 4,949 | 14.71% | C |
| Wiseman A | | LD | 3,409 | 11.71% | 2.78% | 3,004 | 8.93% | LD |
| Johnson D | | Green | 1,901 | 6.53% | | 996 | 2.96% | Soc Lab |
| Page I | | Soc All | 1,260 | 4.33% | | 868 | 2.58% | Ref |
| **Lab to C swing** | | **1.78%** | **29,107** | | **Lab maj 15,293** | **33,644** | | **Lab maj 18,878** |
| | | | | | 52.54% | | | 56.11% |

**JOAN RUDDOCK,** b Dec 28, 1943. Elected 1987. Under-Sec for Women (Dept of Social Security), 1997-98; spokeswoman, environmental protection, 1994-97; home affairs, 1992-94; transport, 1989-92. Member, Select Cttee on Televising Commons 1988-91. Chairwoman, CND, 1981-85, vice-chairwoman 1985-86. Chairwoman, Globe UK; sec, all-party grp on breast cancer; dir, Oxford housing aid centre, 1973-77; Shelter, 1968-73. Ed Pontypool GS for Girls; Imperial Coll, London Univ.
www.joanruddock.org.uk

This is a socially diverse section of inner-city South London. It contains both a middle-class electorate which commutes into Central London and a notable Afro-Caribbean community. The north of the seat is staunchly Labour while the southern wards are more competitive. There is not a great deal of competition for Labour overall, however. Map 368

# LEWISHAM EAST

**Lab hold**

| Electorate | %Turnout | | 58,302 | 51.52% | 2001 | 56,333 | 66.41% | 1997 |
|---|---|---|---|---|---|---|---|---|
| **Prentice Ms B** | | **Lab** | **16,116** | **53.65%** | **-4.68%** | **21,821** | **58.33%** | **Lab** |
| McInnes D | | C | 7,157 | 23.82% | -2.09% | 9,694 | 25.91% | C |
| Buxton D | | LD | 4,937 | 16.43% | 5.26% | 4,178 | 11.17% | LD |
| Roberts B | | BNP | 1,005 | 3.35% | | 910 | 2.43% | Ref |
| Kysow Ms J | | Soc All | 464 | 1.54% | | 431 | 1.15% | NF |
| Link M | | UK Ind | 361 | 1.2% | | 277 | 0.74% | Lib |
| | | | | | | 97 | 0.26% | Dream |
| **Lab to C swing** | | **1.30%** | **30,040** | | **Lab maj 8,959** | **37,408** | | **Lab maj 12,127** |
| | | | | | 29.82% | | | 32.42% |

**BRIDGET PRENTICE,** b Dec 28, 1952. Elected 1992. PPS to Lord Chancellor, Lord Irvine of Lairg, 1999-, and to Min for Trade, Brian Wilson, 1998-99. Asst gvt whip, 1997-98; Lab whip, 1995-97. Member, Select Cttee, Parly Commissioner for Administration, 1992-95. Hammersmith and Fulham cllr, 1986-92; chairman, Fulham Lab Party, 1982-85. Teacher. Ed Our Lady and St Francis Sch, Glasgow; Glasgow and London Univs; South Bank Poly.
e-mail: prenticeb@parliament.uk fax: 020-7219 5581

This southeast London seat was won by the Tories in 1983 and 1987, lost narrowly by them in 1992 and heavily in 1997 and 2001. Despite part of affluent Blackheath falling in the constituency, the largest political mystery is why it was ever held by the Tories. Owner-occupation is low and there are many council tenants. On the other hand, the proportion of non-manual workers is quite high. Lewisham East now looks solidly Labour. Map 369

## LEWISHAM WEST — Lab hold

| Electorate | %Turnout | | 60,947 | 50.56% | 2001 | 58,659 | 64.0% | 1997 |
|---|---|---|---|---|---|---|---|---|
| Dowd J | | Lab | 18,816 | 61.06% | -0.93% | 23,273 | 61.99% | Lab |
| Johnson G | | C | 6,896 | 22.38% | -1.42% | 8,936 | 23.8% | C |
| Thomas R | | LD | 4,146 | 13.45% | 3.67% | 3,672 | 9.78% | LD |
| Pearson F | | UK Ind | 485 | 1.57% | | 1,098 | 2.92% | Ref |
| Long N | | Ind | 472 | 1.53% | | 398 | 1.06% | Soc Lab |
| | | | | | | 167 | 0.44% | Lib |
| C to Lab swing | 0.25% | | 30,815 | Lab maj 11,920 | | 37,544 | Lab maj 14,337 | |
| | | | | 38.68% | | | 38.19% | |

**JIM DOWD,** b March 5, 1951. Elected 1992; contested seat 1987 and Beckenham 1983. Lab spokesman, NI, 1995-97; Gvt whip, 1997-2001; Lab whip, 1993-95. Lewisham cllr, 1974-94 (mayor, 1992). With Plessey Co, later GPT, 1973-92; senior negotiator, ASTMS and then MSF. Telecoms systems engineer. Ed Sedgehill Comp, London; London Nautical Sch.

In terms of simple demographics, this seat - stretching from inner-city Deptford to the edge of suburban Bromley and Beckenham - resembles the average for London across a range of social indicators. For many postwar years it was thus a marginal, but sizeable Labour majorities in 1997 and 2001 now contradict that status. It is quite polarised between Labour terrain (including Bellingham) and Tory territory (such as suburban parts of Catford). Map 370

## LEYTON & WANSTEAD — Lab hold

| Electorate | %Turnout | | 61,549 | 54.78% | 2001 | 62,176 | 63.24% | 1997 |
|---|---|---|---|---|---|---|---|---|
| Cohen H | | Lab | 19,558 | 58.0% | -2.84% | 23,922 | 60.84% | Lab |
| Heckels E | | C | 6,654 | 19.73% | -2.49% | 8,736 | 22.22% | C |
| Wilcock A | | LD | 5,389 | 15.98% | 0.92% | 5,920 | 15.06% | LD |
| Gunstock A | | Green | 1,030 | 3.05% | | 488 | 1.24% | ProLife |
| Labern Ms S | | Soc All | 709 | 2.1% | | 256 | 0.65% | Ind |
| Skaife D'Ingerthorp M | | UK Ind | 378 | 1.12% | | | | |
| Lab to C swing | 0.17% | | 33,718 | Lab maj 12,904 | | 39,322 | Lab maj 15,186 | |
| | | | | 38.27% | | | 38.62% | |

**HARRY COHEN,** b Dec 10, 1949. Elected here 1997; MP, Leyton 1983-97. Member, Defence Select Cttee, 1997-2001. Chairman, Lab friends of Palestine, 1987-90. Sec, all-party race and community grp, 1997-. Member, Nato Parly Assembly. Vice-pres, Royal Coll of Midwives; member, Nalgo. Accountant and local gvt employee. Ed George Gascoigne Sec Mod; East Ham Further Ed Coll; Birkbeck Coll, London.
e-mail: cohenh@parliament.uk www.callnetuk.com/home/harrycohen tel: 020-7219 6376 fax: 020-7219 0438

This seat was the outcome of a somewhat brutal decision taken by the Boundary Commission. The old Wanstead and Woodford seat, a Tory stronghold in northeast London once represented by Sir Winston Churchill, was ripped asunder. The Wanstead segment was merged with the very different East End seat of Leyton. The net result is a very safe Labour seat but one with an isolated Conservative enclave. Map 371

## LICHFIELD — C hold

| Electorate | %Turnout | | 63,794 | 65.34% | 2001 | 62,720 | 77.48% | 1997 |
|---|---|---|---|---|---|---|---|---|
| Fabricant M | | C | 20,480 | 49.14% | 6.23% | 20,853 | 42.91% | C |
| Machray M | | Lab | 16,054 | 38.52% | -3.9% | 20,615 | 42.42% | Lab |
| Bennion P | | LD | 4,462 | 10.71% | -0.55% | 5,473 | 11.26% | LD |
| Phazey J | | UK Ind | 684 | 1.64% | | 1,652 | 3.4% | Ref |
| Lab to C swing | 5.06% | | 41,680 | C maj 4,426 | | 48,593 | C maj 238 | |
| | | | | 10.62% | | | 0.49% | |

**MICHAEL FABRICANT,** b June 12, 1950. Elected here 1997; MP for Staffordshire Mid 1992-97. Member, Select Cttees: Home Affairs, 1999-2001; Culture, Media and Sport, 1997-99; Nat Heritage, 1992-96. Joint vice-chairman, C Backbench Media Cttee, 1992-97; sec, C Ed and Employment Cttee, 1995-97. Joint chairman, all-party Internet grp, 1997-. Ex-BBC current affairs broadcaster; chartered engineer. Ed Brighton and Hove GS; Loughborough, Sussex and London Univs; Univ of Southern California, Los Angeles. tel: 020-7219 5022

Staffordshire acquired an additional seat in 1997. The pattern of population expansion did not make that an easy task. This seat was created out of four previous constituencies. It is centred on the prosperous cathedral city of Lichfield, 15 miles due north of Birmingham, with several nearby villages and a section of the old Cannock and Burntwood seat. In 1997 it produced a surprisingly close win for the Tories, who increased their lead in 2001. Map 372

# LINCOLN

**Lab hold**

| Electorate | %Turnout | | 66,299 | 56.0% | 2001 | 65,485 | 71.08% | 1997 |
|---|---|---|---|---|---|---|---|---|
| **Merron Ms G** | | Lab | **20,003** | 53.88% | -1.04% | 25,563 | 54.92% | Lab |
| Talbot Mrs C | | C | 11,583 | 31.2% | 0.19% | 14,433 | 31.01% | C |
| Gabriel Ms L | | LD | 4,703 | 12.67% | 1.83% | 5,048 | 10.84% | LD |
| Doughty R | | UK Ind | 836 | 2.25% | | 1,329 | 2.86% | Ref |
| | | | | | | 175 | 0.38% | NLP |
| **Lab to C swing** | | **0.61%** | **37,125** | Lab maj 8,420 | | 46,548 | Lab maj 11,130 | |
| | | | | 22.68% | | | 23.91% | |

**GILLIAN MERRON,** b April 12, 1959. Elected 1997. PPS to John Reid, 1998-. Member, Trade and Industry Select Cttee, 1997-98. Member, all-party grps on engineering, football, adult ed, community health councils, FE, town centre management and groundwork. Member, Amnesty. Graduate, Armed Forces parly scheme (RAF), 1997-98. Ex-business development adviser. Ed Lancaster Univ. e-mail: merrong@parliament.uk tel: 020-7219 6942 fax: 020-7219 0489

The county of Lincolnshire is distinctive political territory. The core of this seat is the cathedral city itself, which is reliably Labour with some manufacturing industry and council estates. Tourism also boosts the local economy. Most of the suburbs and the surrounding rural fringe are more Conservative. The Tories staged a recovery here in the 1980s but the Labour Party has since become the dominant force again. Map 373

# LINLITHGOW

**Lab hold**

| Electorate | %Turnout | | 54,599 | 57.98% | 2001 | 53,706 | 73.84% | 1997 |
|---|---|---|---|---|---|---|---|---|
| **Dalyell T** | | Lab | **17,207** | 54.36% | 0.22% | 21,469 | 54.14% | Lab |
| Sibbald J | | SNP | 8,078 | 25.52% | -1.29% | 10,631 | 26.81% | SNP |
| Lindhurst G | | C | 2,836 | 8.96% | -3.56% | 4,964 | 12.52% | C |
| Oliver M | | LD | 2,628 | 8.3% | 2.42% | 2,331 | 5.88% | LD |
| Cornoch E | | SSP | 695 | 2.2% | | 259 | 0.65% | Ref |
| Cronin Ms H | | R & R Loony | 211 | 0.67% | | | | |
| **SNP to Lab swing** | | **0.75%** | **31,655** | Lab maj 9,129 | | 39,654 | Lab maj 10,838 | |
| | | | | 28.84% | | | 27.33% | |

**TAM DALYELL,** b Aug 9, 1932. Elected here 1983; MP, W Lothian 1962-83; MEP 1975-79. Father of the House, June 2001, after 39 years' continuous service. Chairman, all-party Latin America grp, 1998-. Lab spokesman, Science, 1980-82. PPS to Richard Crossman, 1964-70. Hon doctorate, City Univ, London and hon Doctor of Science, Univ of Edinburgh. Council member, National Trust for Scotland, 1976-81. Political columnist, New Scientist since 1967. Author and former teacher. Ed Edinburgh Acad; Eton; King's Coll, Cambridge; Moray House Teachers' Training Coll, Edinburgh.

The infamous West Lothian question may be more relevant than ever now that a Scottish Parliament has been established. The seat of Linlithgow, based on the ancient town just south of the Forth and represented by Tam Dalyell (now Father of the House), has long since been reshaped and renamed. It is the successor seat to West Lothian, to the west of Edinburgh in the old county of Lothian. A solid Labour seat but with SNP competition. Map 374

# LIVERPOOL GARSTON

**Lab hold**

| Electorate | %Turnout | | 65,094 | 50.16% | 2001 | 66,755 | 65.14% | 1997 |
|---|---|---|---|---|---|---|---|---|
| **Eagle Ms M** | | Lab | **20,043** | 61.39% | 0.06% | 26,667 | 61.33% | Lab |
| Keaveney Ms P | | LD | 7,549 | 23.12% | 4.15% | 8,250 | 18.97% | LD |
| Sutton Miss H | | C | 5,059 | 15.49% | -0.19% | 6,819 | 15.68% | C |
| | | | | | | 833 | 1.92% | Ref |
| | | | | | | 666 | 1.53% | Lib |
| | | | | | | 127 | 0.29% | NLP |
| | | | | | | 120 | 0.28% | SEP |
| **Lab to LD swing** | | **2.05%** | **32,651** | Lab maj 12,494 | | 43,482 | Lab maj 18,417 | |
| | | | | 38.27% | | | 42.36% | |

**MARIA EAGLE,** b Feb 17, 1961. Elected 1997. Parly Sec, Dept for Work and Pensions, June 2001-; Member, Public Accounts Cttee, 1997-2001. Represented Lancs and England in chess competitions. Solicitor, specialising in housing and employment law. Twin sister is Angela Eagle, Lab MP for Wallasey. Ed Formby HS; Pembroke Coll, Oxford; Lancaster Gate Coll of Law.

This seat, on the southeast of Liverpool with some of its most attractive suburbs but also containing the vast council estate of Speke and much urban deprivation, neatly captures social and political change on Merseyside. Three decades ago it was strikingly Conservative, largely because many of the city's electors voted along religious lines and this was a staunchly Protestant area. It has steadily swung to Labour as class and economic interests prevailed. Map 375

## LIVERPOOL RIVERSIDE — Lab hold

| Electorate | %Turnout | 74,827 | 34.08% | 2001 | 73,429 | 51.93% | 1997 |
|---|---|---|---|---|---|---|---|
| **Ellman Ms L** | **Lab Co-op** | **18,201** | **71.37%** | **0.94%** | **26,858** | **70.43%** | **Lab** |
| Marbrow R | LD | 4,251 | 16.67% | 3.4% | 5,059 | 13.27% | LD |
| Edwards Miss J | C | 2,142 | 8.4% | -1.13% | 3,635 | 9.53% | C |
| Wilson Ms C | Soc All | 909 | 3.56% | | 776 | 2.03% | Soc |
| | | | | | 594 | 1.56% | Lib |
| | | | | | 586 | 1.54% | Ref |
| | | | | | 277 | 0.73% | ProLife |
| | | | | | 179 | 0.47% | MRAC |
| | | | | | 171 | 0.45% | NLP |
| **Lab Co-op to LD swing** | **1.23%** | **25,503** | **Lab Co-op maj 13,950** | | **38,135** | **Lab Co-op maj 21,799** | |
| | | | 54.70% | | | 57.16% | |

**LOUISE ELLMAN,** b Nov 14, 1945. Elected 1997. Member, Select Cttee, Environment, Transport and the Regions, 1997-2001. Chairwoman, all-party Israel grp, 1997-. Leader, Lancs County Council, 1981-97 (chairwoman, 1981-85; leader, Lab grp, 1977-97; member, 1970-97). Established Lancs Enterprises as county's economic development agency, 1982 and vice-chairwoman since. W Lancs district cllr, 1974-87. Member, Lab NEC local gvt advisory cttee, 1977-. Founder member, Co-op Enterprises NW, 1979-. OU counsellor. Ed Manchester HS for Girls; Hull and York Univs.

The Riverside seat is at the heart of Liverpool's imposing city centre, stretches along the waterfront and docks and has felt much of the economic pain endured here for two decades. It is quite polarised between very white wards and those with a notable immigrant population. There is a modest middle-class section which leans towards the Liberal Democrats. But this is one of the most deprived urban areas in the UK - and is solidly Labour. Map 376

## LIVERPOOL WALTON — Lab hold

| Electorate | %Turnout | 66,237 | 42.96% | 2001 | 67,527 | 59.54% | 1997 |
|---|---|---|---|---|---|---|---|
| **Kilfoyle P** | **Lab** | **22,143** | **77.81%** | **-0.57%** | **31,516** | **78.38%** | **Lab** |
| Reid K | LD | 4,147 | 14.57% | 3.43% | 4,478 | 11.14% | LD |
| Horgan S | C | 1,726 | 6.07% | -0.27% | 2,551 | 6.34% | C |
| Forrest P | UK Ind | 442 | 1.55% | | 620 | 1.54% | Ref |
| | | | | | 444 | 1.1% | Soc |
| | | | | | 352 | 0.88% | Lib |
| | | | | | 246 | 0.61% | ProLife |
| **Lab to LD swing** | **2.00%** | **28,458** | **Lab maj 17,996** | | **40,207** | **Lab maj 27,038** | |
| | | | 63.24% | | | 67.24% | |

**PETER KILFOYLE,** b June 9, 1946. Elected 1991 by-election. Parly Under-Sec for Defence, 1999-2000. Under-Sec of State for Public Service, 1997-99. Spokesman, education, 1994-97; employment, 1995-97. Previously Lab whip. Party reg organiser in NW, 1985-91. Member, MSF; TGWU; Co-op Party. Ex-building labourer, teacher, youth worker. Ed St Edwards Coll, Liverpool; Durham Univ; Christ's Coll, Liverpool.

This is the most northerly of the Liverpool constituencies and contains the football stadiums of both Liverpool and Everton. It is solidly working-class with a very low number of professional and managerial workers. It was represented by Eric Heffer for many years at a time when the Labour Party was deeply divided as to how to deal with the Militant Tendency. It is overwhelmingly Labour in sentiment. Map 377

## LIVERPOOL WAVERTREE — Lab hold

| Electorate | %Turnout | 72,555 | 44.29% | 2001 | 73,063 | 62.85% | 1997 |
|---|---|---|---|---|---|---|---|
| **Kennedy Ms J** | **Lab** | **20,155** | **62.71%** | **-1.74%** | **29,592** | **64.45%** | **Lab** |
| Newby C | LD | 7,836 | 24.38% | 2.84% | 9,891 | 21.54% | LD |
| Allen G | C | 3,091 | 9.62% | -1.15% | 4,944 | 10.77% | C |
| Lane M | Soc Lab | 359 | 1.12% | | 576 | 1.25% | Ref |
| O'Brien M | Soc All | 349 | 1.09% | | 391 | 0.85% | Lib |
| Miney N | UK Ind | 348 | 1.08% | | 346 | 0.75% | ProLife |
| | | | | | 178 | 0.39% | WRP |
| **Lab to LD swing** | **2.29%** | **32,138** | **Lab maj 12,319** | | **45,918** | **Lab maj 19,701** | |
| | | | 38.33% | | | 42.91% | |

**JANE KENNEDY**, b May 4, 1958. Elected here 1997; MP for Liverpool Broadgreen 1992-97. Min of State, NI Office, June 2001-; Min in Lord Chancellor's Dept, 1999-2001. Member, Select Cttees: Administration, 1997-99; Social Security, 1992-94. Gvt whip, 1997-99; Lab whip, 1995-97. Chairwoman, 1995-97, and former vice-chairwoman, NW grp of Lab MPs. Nupe area organiser, 1988-92. Care asst, 1984-88, and child care residential worker, 1979-84, Liverpool social services. Ed Haughton Comp; Queen Elizabeth Sixth Form Coll; Liverpool Univ.

The Boundary Commission was obliged to reduce Liverpool's parliamentary representation and the seat of Mossley Hill, held by the Liberal Democrat David Alton, was the primary victim. This new seat emerged from the amalgamation of his old patch with Liverpool Broadgreen. That seat was solidly Labour and, since Alton's retirement, the Liberal Democrats have found it impossible to mount a really serious challenge. Map 378

# LIVERPOOL WEST DERBY
**Lab hold**

| Electorate | %Turnout | | 67,921 | 45.5% | 2001 | 68,682 | 61.38% | 1997 |
|---|---|---|---|---|---|---|---|---|
| **Wareing R** | Lab | | **20,454** | **66.18%** | **-4.99%** | **30,002** | **71.17%** | Lab |
| Radford S | Lib | | 4,601 | 14.89% | 5.31% | 4,037 | 9.58% | Lib |
| Moloney P | LD | | 3,366 | 10.89% | 1.86% | 3,805 | 9.03% | LD |
| Clare B | C | | 2,486 | 8.04% | -0.63% | 3,656 | 8.67% | C |
| | | | | | | 657 | 1.56% | Ref |
| **Lab to Lib swing** | **5.15%** | | **30,907** | Lab maj 15,853 | | 42,157 | Lab maj 25,965 | |
| | | | | 51.29% | | | 61.59% | |

**BOB WAREING,** b Aug 20, 1930. Elected 1983. Member, Foreign Affairs Select Cttee, 1992-97. Lab whip, 1987-92. Chairman, 1994-97, vice-chairman, 1985-94, Yugoslavia grp; joint vice-chairman, 1992-97, sec, 1997-, Russian grp. Merseyside county cllr, 1981-86 (Lab grp chief whip, 1981-83). Vice-pres, AMA, 1984-. Chairman, Merseyside Economic Development Co, 1981-86. Ex-lecturer. Ed Ranworth Square Sch, Liverpool; Alsop HS, Liverpool; Bolton Coll of Ed; London Univ (external student).

This seat sits on the northeast edge of the city and is dominated by a set of large council estates. The electorate is almost entirely white, and has a strong working-class culture. But there are a few middle-class residential areas too, of the type where the TV soap opera *Brookside* is set. Overall, the seat is overwhelmingly aligned to Labour and in both 1997 and 2001 placed the renegade Liberal Party in second place ahead of the Liberal Democrats. Map 379

# LIVINGSTON
**Lab hold**

| Electorate | %Turnout | | 64,850 | 55.56% | 2001 | 60,296 | 71.04% | 1997 |
|---|---|---|---|---|---|---|---|---|
| **Cook R** | Lab | | **19,108** | **53.03%** | **-1.86%** | **23,510** | **54.89%** | Lab |
| Sutherland G | SNP | | 8,492 | 23.57% | -3.89% | 11,763 | 27.46% | SNP |
| Mackenzie G | LD | | 3,969 | 11.01% | 4.3% | 4,028 | 9.4% | C |
| Mowat I | C | | 2,995 | 8.31% | -1.09% | 2,876 | 6.71% | LD |
| Milne Ms W | SSP | | 1,110 | 3.08% | | 444 | 1.04% | Ref |
| Kingdon R | UK Ind | | 359 | 1.0% | | 213 | 0.5% | SPGB |
| **SNP to Lab swing** | **1.02%** | | **36,033** | Lab maj 10,616 | | 42,834 | Lab maj 11,747 | |
| | | | | 29.46% | | | 27.43% | |

**ROBIN COOK,** b Feb 28, 1946. Elected here 1983; MP for Edinburgh Central Feb 1974-83. President of the Council and Leader of the House of Commons, June 2001-. Foreign Sec, 1997-2001; Shadow Foreign Sec, 1994-97. Chief spokesman, trade and industry, 1992-94; health, 1989-92; health and social security, 1987-89; spokesman, Euro and Community affairs, 1983-85; campaigns co-ordinator, 1985-86; trade and industry spokesman, 1986-87; economic affairs, 1980-83. Chairman, Lab NEC, 1996-97. Ex-tutor and organiser in adult ed. Ed Aberdeen GS; Royal HS, Edinburgh; Edinburgh Univ.

This is the only new town in the Lothian region of Central Scotland and took its inhabitants from both Edinburgh and Glasgow. It contains a fair section where the legacy of coalmining still influences voting behaviour. Labour is clearly the leading party in this seat, but not by the sort of crushing margin that can be seen elsewhere in Scotland. The SNP has proved to be a lively political presence. Map 380

# LLANELLI
**Lab hold**

| Electorate | %Turnout | | 58,148 | 62.25% | 2001 | 58,323 | 70.66% | 1997 |
|---|---|---|---|---|---|---|---|---|
| **Davies D** | Lab | | **17,586** | **48.58%** | **-9.3%** | **23,851** | **57.88%** | Lab |
| Jones D | PC | | 11,183 | 30.89% | 11.93% | 7,812 | 18.96% | PC |
| Hayes S | C | | 3,442 | 9.51% | -2.63% | 5,003 | 12.14% | C |
| Rees K | LD | | 3,065 | 8.47% | -0.72% | 3,788 | 9.19% | LD |
| Cliff Ms J | Green | | 515 | 1.42% | | 757 | 1.84% | Soc Lab |
| Willock J | Soc Lab | | 407 | 1.12% | -0.72% | | | |
| **Lab to PC swing** | **10.62%** | | **36,198** | Lab maj 6,403 | | 41,211 | Lab maj 16,039 | |
| | | | | 17.69% | | | 38.92% | |

**DENZIL DAVIES,** b Oct 9, 1938. Elected 1970. Member, Public Accounts Cttee, 1991-97. Member, Shadow Cabinet, 1985-88; chief spokesman, defence and disarmament, 1983-88 (resigned in disagreement over policy); chief spokesman, Wales, 1983; spokesman, defence, 1982-83; foreign affairs, 1981-82; Treasury and economic affairs, 1979-81. Min of State, Treasury, 1975-79. Member, Select Cttees: Euro Legislation, 1974-75; Wealth Tax, 1974-75. Privy Counsellor, 1978. Lectured at Chicago and Leeds Univs. Barrister. Ed Carmarthen GS; Pembroke Coll, Oxford.

This constituency is the most industrial area of that large slice of southwest Wales that used to constitute the county of Dyfed. It is not a rural West Wales seat but rather an outpost of the South Wales Valley constituencies. It has the heritage of coal and tin. There are a large number of Welsh speakers but this has not unduly altered the pattern of local politics. This seat is solidly Labour, though Plaid Cymru has made steady progress in the past decade. Map 381

## LONDONDERRY EAST
### DUP gain

| Electorate | %Turnout | | 60,276 | 66.14% | 2001 | 58,831 | 64.77% | 1997 |
|---|---|---|---|---|---|---|---|---|
| **Campbell G** | **DUP** | | **12,813** | **32.14%** | **6.51%** | **13,558** | **35.58%** | **UUP** |
| Ross W | UUP | | 10,912 | 27.37% | -8.21% | 9,764 | 25.63% | DUP |
| Dallat J | SDLP | | 8,298 | 20.81% | -0.9% | 8,273 | 21.71% | SDLP |
| Brolly F | SF | | 6,221 | 15.6% | 6.51% | 3,463 | 9.09% | SF |
| Boyle Mrs Y | Alliance | | 1,625 | 4.08% | -2.29% | 2,427 | 6.37% | Alliance |
| | | | | | | 436 | 1.14% | C |
| | | | | | | 100 | 0.26% | NLP |
| | | | | | | 81 | 0.21% | Nat Dem |
| **UUP to DUP swing** | **7.36%** | | **39,869** | **DUP maj 1,901** | | **38,102** | **UUP maj 3,794** | |
| | | | | 4.77% | | | 9.95% | |

**GREGORY CAMPBELL,** b Feb 15, 1953. Elected 2001. Member, NI Assembly, 1998-, and 1982-86; forum for political dialogue, 1996-98. Londonderry city cllr, 1981-. Self-employed publisher. Publications:*Discrimination - the Truth; Discrimination - Where Now?; Ulster Verdict on the Joint Declaration; Working toward 2000.*Ed Ebrington Primary Sch; Londonderry Tech Coll.

This is one of the more strangely named constituencies. It contains none of the city of Londonderry itself but is instead a mainly rural seat, stretching up to Lough Foyle and the Atlantic coast, with very urban wards bordering the city. The other main centres are Coleraine and Limavady. It is predominantly Protestant and Unionist and has been fiercely fought between the UUP and DUP from 1992 onwards. The SDLP also has a firm presence. Map 382

## LOUGHBOROUGH
### Lab hold

| Electorate | %Turnout | | 70,077 | 63.15% | 2001 | 68,945 | 75.95% | 1997 |
|---|---|---|---|---|---|---|---|---|
| **Reed A** | **Lab Co-op** | | **22,016** | **49.75%** | **1.15%** | **25,448** | **48.6%** | **Lab** |
| Lyon N | C | | 15,638 | 35.34% | -2.35% | 19,736 | 37.69% | C |
| Simons Ms J | LD | | 5,667 | 12.81% | 0.99% | 6,190 | 11.82% | LD |
| Bigger J | UK Ind | | 933 | 2.11% | | | 991 | 1.89% | Ref |
| **C to Lab Co-op swing** | **1.75%** | | **44,254** | **Lab Co-op maj 6,378** | | **52,365** | **Lab Co-op maj 5,712** | |
| | | | | 14.41% | | | 10.91% | |

**ANDREW REED,** b Sept 17, 1964. Elected 1997. PPS to Margaret Beckett, Sec of State, Environment, Food & Rural Affairs, 2001-. Member, John Smith's leadership campaign team, 1992. Member, Lab Party reg exec cttee, 1992-93. Former European affairs adviser, Leicester County Council and employment initiatives officer. Member, Leicester City Council, 1988-90. Party asst, Keith Vaz, 1987-88. Charnwood borough cllr, 1995-. Member, Nalgo. Ed Stonehill HS, Birstall, Leicestershire; Longsade Community Coll; Leicester Poly. e-mail: reeda@parliament.uk www.andyreedmp.org.uk

The town of Loughborough in Leicestershire, notable for industrial engineering and the sporting reputation of its university, has witnessed several boundary revisions in recent decades. In its latest incarnation a number of solidly Tory wards have been moved elsewhere. What remains is still distinctly middle-class but the seat is now plainly competitive. Labour proved the point by snatching it in 1997 then holding it quite comfortably in 2001. Map 383

## LOUTH & HORNCASTLE
### C hold

| Electorate | %Turnout | | 71,556 | 62.13% | 2001 | 68,824 | 72.58% | 1997 |
|---|---|---|---|---|---|---|---|---|
| **Tapsell Sir P** | **C** | | **21,543** | **48.45%** | **5.01%** | **21,699** | **43.44%** | **C** |
| Bolland D | Lab | | 13,989 | 31.46% | 1.83% | 14,799 | 29.63% | Lab |
| Martin Ms F | LD | | 8,928 | 20.08% | -4.36% | 12,207 | 24.44% | LD |
| | | | | | | 1,248 | 2.5% | Green |
| **Lab to C swing** | **1.59%** | | **44,460** | **C maj 7,554** | | **49,953** | **C maj 6,900** | |
| | | | | 16.99% | | | 13.81% | |

**SIR PETER TAPSELL,** b Feb 1, 1930. Elected here 1997; MP for Lindsey E 1983-97; Horncastle 1966-83; Nottingham W 1959-64. C spokesman, Treasury and economic affairs, 1977-78; foreign and Commonwealth affairs, 1976-77. PA to Anthony Eden, 1955 election. Adviser, Japanese trading and stockbroking firms and banks. Vice-chairman, Mitsubishi Trust Oxford Foundation, 1988-. Vice-pres, Tennyson Soc. Trustee, Oxford Union, 1985-. Ed Tonbridge Sch; Merton Coll, Oxford. fax: 020-7219 4484

This constituency covers the northeast section of Lincolnshire. Louth itself is affluent and attractive. It is surrounded by hillside farming and a number of seaside towns such as Mablethorpe, and villages in the Wolds. The market town of Horncastle and the constituency of the same name have been added but without altering the overall political character of the seat. The Tories are strong here and the opposition to them is evenly divided. Map 384

# LUDLOW

**LD gain**

| Electorate | %Turnout | | 63,053 | 68.39% | 2001 | 61,267 | 75.55% | 1997 |
|---|---|---|---|---|---|---|---|---|
| **Green M** | | **LD** | **18,620** | **43.18%** | **13.53%** | **19,633** | **42.42%** | **C** |
| Taylor-Smith M | | C | 16,990 | 39.4% | -3.02% | 13,724 | 29.65% | LD |
| Knowles N | | Lab | 5,785 | 13.41% | -11.97% | 11,745 | 25.38% | Lab |
| Gaffney J | | Green | 871 | 2.02% | 0.3% | 798 | 1.72% | Green |
| Gutteridge P | | UK Ind | 858 | 1.99% | 1.16% | 385 | 0.83% | UK Ind |
| **C to LD swing** | **8.27%** | | **43,124** | | **LD maj 1,630** | **46,285** | | **C maj 5,909** |
| | | | | | 3.78% | | | 12.77% |

**MATTHEW GREEN,** b April 12, 1970. Elected 2001. Won seat from C after retirement of Christopher Gill, the sitting MP: contested Wolverhampton SW 1997. Member, LD's national exec, parly candidate assoc; LD W Midlands exec; treasurer, region's youth and student grp. Former managing dir, W Midlands media relations and training consultancy. Previously sales and marketing manager, timber industry. Ed: Priory Sch, Shrewsbury; Birmingham Univ.

This constituency, based on the attractive castle town of Ludlow, stretches over southern Shropshire with its small towns and villages in rolling countryside around Wenlock Edge and the Long Mynd. However, near Bridgnorth there is another element that feels more aligned to the urban West Midlands. This has traditionally been a strongly Tory seat, although increasing Lib Dem support over the past decade finally bore fruit in 2001. Map 385

# LUTON NORTH

**Lab hold**

| Electorate | %Turnout | | 65,998 | 59.28% | 2001 | 64,618 | 73.25% | 1997 |
|---|---|---|---|---|---|---|---|---|
| **Hopkins K** | | **Lab** | **22,187** | **56.71%** | **2.07%** | **25,860** | **54.64%** | **Lab** |
| Sater Mrs A | | C | 12,210 | 31.21% | -3.09% | 16,234 | 34.3% | C |
| Hoyle Dr B | | LD | 3,795 | 9.7% | 0.62% | 4,299 | 9.08% | LD |
| Brown C | | UK Ind | 934 | 2.39% | 0.93% | 689 | 1.46% | UK Ind |
| | | | | | | 250 | 0.53% | NLP |
| **C to Lab swing** | **2.58%** | | **39,126** | | **Lab maj 9,977** | **47,332** | | **Lab maj 9,626** |
| | | | | | 25.50% | | | 20.34% |

**KELVIN HOPKINS,** b Aug 22, 1941. Elected 1997. Hon fellow, Luton Univ; former lecturer in higher ed. TUC economic department,1969-70; 1973-77. Policy and research officer, Nalgo/Unison, 1977-94. Economist and statistician. Ed Queen Elizabeth GS, High Barnet; Nottingham Univ.

The latest series of boundary changes have made both Luton seats more urban and removed the influence of the more rural Bedfordshire hinterland. This is the more Conservative portion of the town, although that did not impede Labour in 1997 or 2001. The striking majority recorded in 1997 was unexpected. There are social bases here on which both major parties can build. Map 386

# LUTON SOUTH

**Lab hold**

| Electorate | %Turnout | | 68,985 | 57.04% | 2001 | 68,395 | 70.45% | 1997 |
|---|---|---|---|---|---|---|---|---|
| **Moran Ms M** | | **Lab** | **21,719** | **55.19%** | **0.34%** | **26,428** | **54.85%** | **Lab** |
| Henderson G | | C | 11,586 | 29.44% | -1.92% | 15,109 | 31.36% | C |
| Martins R | | LD | 4,292 | 10.91% | 1.34% | 4,610 | 9.57% | LD |
| Scheimann M | | Green | 798 | 2.03% | 1.29% | 1,205 | 2.5% | Ref |
| Lawman C | | UK Ind | 578 | 1.47% | 0.66% | 390 | 0.81% | UK Ind |
| Hearne J | | Soc All | 271 | 0.69% | | 356 | 0.74% | Green |
| Bolton R | | WRP | 107 | 0.27% | | 86 | 0.18% | NLP |
| **C to Lab swing** | **1.13%** | | **39,351** | | **Lab maj 10,133** | **48,184** | | **Lab maj 11,319** |
| | | | | | 25.75% | | | 23.49% |

**MARGARET MORAN,** b April 24, 1955. Elected 1997. PPS to Mo Mowlam, 2000-; and to Transport Min, 1997-2000; Member, NI Affairs Select Cttee, 1997. Chairwoman, all-party grp on domestic violence; member, all-party grps on small business, IT, Kashmir and children. Chairwoman, Backbench Housing and Parly Affairs Cttee, 2000-. Lewisham cllr, 1984- (first woman council leader, 1993-95). Ed St Ursula's Convent Sch, Greenwich; St Mary's Coll of Ed, Twickenham; Birmingham Univ; Hackney Coll. e-mail: moranm@parliament.uk tel: 020-7219 5049 fax: 020-7219 5094

This seat contains most of the core of the town including the Vauxhall Motors plant and Luton Airport. It had long been marginal political territory, although it swung heavily to Labour in the 1990s and now shows every sign of staying that way. Most wards are urban and skilled working-class or middle-class. There is also a sizeable non-white population that may become politically decisive. Map 387

## MACCLESFIELD — C hold

| Electorate | %Turnout | | 73,123 | 62.34% | 2001 | 72,049 | 75.22% | 1997 |
|---|---|---|---|---|---|---|---|---|
| Winterton N | | C | 22,284 | 48.88% | -0.73% | 26,888 | 49.61% | C |
| Carter S | | Lab | 15,084 | 33.09% | -0.55% | 18,234 | 33.64% | Lab |
| Flynn M | | LD | 8,217 | 18.03% | 1.29% | 9,075 | 16.74% | LD |
| C to Lab swing | 0.09% | | 45,585 | | C maj 7,200 | 54,197 | | C maj 8,654 |
| | | | | | 15.79% | | | 15.97% |

**NICHOLAS WINTERTON,** b March 31, 1938. Elected 1971 by-election. Chairman, Health Select Cttee, 1991-92; member, Select Cttees: Modernisation of Commons, 1997-2001; Social Services, 1979-90; Standing Orders, 1981-97, Member, Chairmen's Panel. Vice-chairman, clothing and textiles grp, 1997-; joint vice-chairman, road transport study grp, 1997-. Member, exec cttee, UK branch, CPA, 1997-. Freeman, City of London. His wife, Ann, is C MP for Congleton. Ed Rugby.
tel: 020-7219 6434

The east Cheshire town of Macclesfield, sandwiched between Greater Manchester and the northern edge of the Peak District, is responsible for only about half of the votes in the constituency. The rest is essentially an affluent commuter belt. While Macclesfield is fairly evenly divided between the two main parties, the prosperous suburbanites of this section of the North West are very loyal to the Tories and determine election outcomes. Map 388

## MAIDENHEAD — C hold

| Electorate | %Turnout | | 68,130 | 63.58% | 2001 | 67,302 | 75.61% | 1997 |
|---|---|---|---|---|---|---|---|---|
| May Mrs T | | C | 19,506 | 45.03% | -4.77% | 25,344 | 49.8% | C |
| Newbound Ms K | | LD | 16,222 | 37.45% | 11.19% | 13,363 | 26.26% | LD |
| O'Farrell J | | Lab | 6,577 | 15.18% | -2.91% | 9,205 | 18.09% | Lab |
| Cooper Dr D | | UK Ind | 741 | 1.71% | 1.17% | 1,638 | 3.22% | Ref |
| Clarke L | | Loony | 272 | 0.63% | | 896 | 1.76% | Lib |
| | | | | | | 277 | 0.54% | UK Ind |
| | | | | | | 166 | 0.33% | Glow |
| C to LD swing | 7.98% | | 43,318 | | C maj 3,284 | 50,889 | | C maj 11,981 |
| | | | | | 7.58% | | | 23.54% |

**THERESA MAY,** b Oct 1, 1956. Elected 1997; contested Durham NW 1992 and Barking by-election 1994. Shadow Ed spokeswoman, 2001-. Member, Ed and Employment Select Cttee and its Ed Sub-Cttee, 1997-2001. Merton cllr, 1986-94 (dep leader, C grp, 1992-94; chairwoman, ed cttee, 1988-90). Member, Surrey CCC. Fellow, Royal Geographical Soc. Ex-head, European affairs unit, Assoc for Payment Clearing Services; previously worked at Bank of England. Ed Wheatley Park Comp, Oxfordshire; St Hugh's Coll, Oxford.

The expansion of Berkshire - still known thus despite local government boundary changes - over the past two decades rendered an extra seat inevitable. The solution was to separate the old Windsor and Maidenhead seat and make both Thames-side towns the centres of new constituencies. Maidenhead, which takes in small riverside towns such as Cookham and Sonning, is a very safe Tory area and - despite Lib Dem inroads - is likely to remain so. Map 389

## MAIDSTONE & THE WEALD — C hold

| Electorate | %Turnout | | 74,002 | 61.59% | 2001 | 72,466 | 73.98% | 1997 |
|---|---|---|---|---|---|---|---|---|
| Widdecombe Miss A | | C | 22,621 | 49.63% | 5.5% | 23,657 | 44.13% | C |
| Davis M | | Lab | 12,303 | 26.99% | 0.77% | 14,054 | 26.22% | Lab |
| Wainman Ms A | | LD | 9,064 | 19.89% | -2.47% | 11,986 | 22.36% | LD |
| Botting J | | UK Ind | 978 | 2.15% | 1.52% | 1,998 | 3.73% | Ref |
| Hunt N | | Ind | 611 | 1.34% | | 979 | 1.83% | Soc Lab |
| | | | | | | 480 | 0.9% | Green |
| | | | | | | 339 | 0.63% | UK Ind |
| | | | | | | 115 | 0.21% | NLP |
| Lab to C swing | 2.36% | | 45,577 | | C maj 10,318 | 53,608 | | C maj 9,603 |
| | | | | | 22.64% | | | 17.91% |

**ANN WIDDECOMBE,** b Oct 4, 1947. Elected here 1997; MP for Maidstone 1987-97, Shadow Home Sec, 1999-; Shadow Health Sec, 1998-99; Home Office Min for Prisons, 1995-97; Employment Min, 1994-95; Employment Under-Sec, 1993-94; Social Security Under-Sec, 1990-93. Privy Counsellor, 1997. Member, Select Cttee, Standards and Privileges, 1997. Joint sec, all-party pro-life grp, 1997-. Senior administrator at London Univ, 1975-87; in marketing with Unilever, 1973-75. Ed La Sainte Union Convent, Bath; Birmingham Univ; Lady Margaret Hall, Oxford.

Kent has been obliged to endure a series of boundary changes and Maidstone has been at the centre of many of them. The new version of the seat includes most, but not all, of Maidstone combined with most, but not all, of the Weald down towards the Sussex border. The Tories are strong right across this constituency, with the other two parties struggling to secure second place. Map 390

## MAKERFIELD — Lab hold

| Electorate | %Turnout | 68,457 | 50.92% | 2001 | 67,358 | 66.83% | 1997 |
|---|---|---|---|---|---|---|---|
| McCartney I | Lab | 23,879 | 68.51% | -5.06% | 33,119 | 73.57% | Lab |
| Brooks Mrs J | C | 6,129 | 17.58% | 2.16% | 6,942 | 15.42% | C |
| Crowther D | LD | 3,990 | 11.45% | 3.13% | 3,743 | 8.32% | LD |
| Jones M | Soc All | 858 | 2.46% | | 1,210 | 2.69% | Ref |
| Lab to C swing | 3.61% | 34,856 | Lab maj 17,750 | | 45,014 | Lab maj 26,177 | |
| | | | 50.92% | | | 58.15% | |

**IAN McCARTNEY,** b April 25, 1951. Elected 1987. Min for Pensions, June 2001-; Min of State, Cabinet Office, 1999-2001; Min of State, Trade and Industry, 1997-99. Chief spokesman, employment, 1996-97; health spokesman, 1992-94. Member, Select Cttees: Social Security, 1991-92; Social Services, 1989-91. Chairman, all-party rugby league grp, 1989-91. *Spectator's* Minister to Watch, 1999. Former seaman, local gvt manual worker and chef. Ed Lenzie Acad; Langside Coll, Glasgow; Merchant Navy Sea Training Coll, Gravesend.

This seat is based in the old Lancashire coalfield around Wigan in the Greater Manchester conurbation. The largest single town is Ashton-in-Makerfield and other small industrial settlements include Ince-in-Makerfield and Abram. With the exception of the small town of Orrell, which is sympathetic to the Tories, this is a working-class and industrial constituency. It is staunchly Labour. Map 391

## MALDON & CHELMSFORD EAST — C hold

| Electorate | %Turnout | 69,201 | 63.73% | 2001 | 66,184 | 76.13% | 1997 |
|---|---|---|---|---|---|---|---|
| Whittingdale J | C | 21,719 | 49.25% | 0.58% | 24,524 | 48.67% | C |
| Kennedy R | Lab | 13,257 | 30.06% | 1.31% | 14,485 | 28.75% | Lab |
| Jackson Ms J | LD | 7,002 | 15.88% | -3.49% | 9,758 | 19.37% | LD |
| Harris G | UK Ind | 1,135 | 2.57% | 0.71% | 935 | 1.86% | UK Ind |
| Schwarz W | Green | 987 | 2.24% | 0.88% | 685 | 1.36% | Green |
| C to Lab swing | 0.37% | 44,100 | C maj 8,462 | | 50,387 | C maj 10,039 | |
| | | | 19.19% | | | 19.92% | |

**JOHN WHITTINGDALE,** b Oct 16, 1959. Elected here 1997; MP for Colchester S and Maldon 1992-97. Frontbench Treasury spokesman, 1997-98. PPS to William Hague, 1999-, and to Mins of State for Ed and Employment, 1994-96. Opposition whip, 1997-98. Joint sec, all-party film industry grp. Political sec to Mrs Margaret Thatcher when she was PM, 1988-90, then manager of her private office, 1990-92. Ed Winchester; University Coll London.
e-mail: jwhittingdale.mp@tory.org.uk tel: 020-7219 3557 fax: 020-7219 2522

The Maldon district in eastern Essex, between the Rivers Blackwater and Crouch, was until the last boundary revisions associated with the southern parts of Colchester. The seat has been turned around and is now linked to the eastern sections of Chelmsford instead. The other main settlement is Burnham-on-Crouch. In political terms the boundary realignments are less than consequential. It is a very safe Conservative constituency. Map 392

## MANCHESTER BLACKLEY — Lab hold

| Electorate | %Turnout | 59,111 | 44.87% | 2001 | 62,227 | 57.46% | 1997 |
|---|---|---|---|---|---|---|---|
| Stringer G | Lab | 18,285 | 68.94% | -1.1% | 25,042 | 70.04% | Lab |
| Stanbury L | C | 3,821 | 14.41% | -0.84% | 5,454 | 15.25% | C |
| Riding G | LD | 3,015 | 11.37% | 0.36% | 3,937 | 11.01% | LD |
| Barr K | Soc Lab | 485 | 1.83% | | 1,323 | 3.7% | Ref |
| Reissmann Ms K | Soc All | 461 | 1.74% | | | | |
| Bhatti A | Anti-Corrupt | 456 | 1.72% | | | | |
| Lab to C swing | 0.13% | 26,523 | Lab maj 14,464 | | 35,756 | Lab maj 19,588 | |
| | | | 54.53% | | | 54.79% | |

**GRAHAM STRINGER,** b Feb 17, 1950. Elected 1997. Lord Commissioner (Gvt whip) June 2001. Parly Sec, Cabinet Office, 1999-2001; member, Select Cttee, Environment, Transport and Reg Affairs and its Transport Sub-Cttee, 1997-99. Vice-chairman, all-party aviation grp, 1997-. Manchester city cllr (leader, 1984-96). Chairman, Manchester Airport plc, 1996-97; Dir, Commonwealth Games organising cttee; Campus Ventures plc; trustee, Nat Museum of Lab History (all unpaid). Analytical chemist in plastics industry. Ed Sheffield Univ.

This seat contains the northern sections of the city of Manchester. It is a fairly mixed bag. There are some quite strong Tory wards but in the main this is a working-class constituency with a high proportion of council tenants and many mainly Asian immigrants. Labour now seems extremely well established in this gritty northern city seat. Map 393

## MANCHESTER CENTRAL — Lab hold

| Electorate | %Turnout | | 66,268 | 39.13% | 2001 | 63,815 | 52.55% | 1997 |
|---|---|---|---|---|---|---|---|---|
| Lloyd T | Lab | 17,812 | 68.7% | -2.28% | 23,803 | 70.98% | Lab |
| Hobson P | LD | 4,070 | 15.7% | 3.41% | 4,121 | 12.29% | LD |
| Powell A | C | 2,328 | 8.98% | -2.84% | 3,964 | 11.82% | C |
| Hall Ms V | Green | 1,018 | 3.93% | | 810 | 2.42% | Soc Lab |
| Sinclair R | Soc Lab | 484 | 1.87% | -0.55% | 742 | 2.21% | Ref |
| Brosnan Ms T | ProLife | 216 | 0.83% | | 97 | 0.29% | Comm Lge |
| Lab to LD swing | 2.84% | 25,928 | Lab maj 13,742 | | 33,537 | Lab maj 19,682 | |
| | | | 53.00% | | | 58.69% | |

**TONY LLOYD,** b Feb 25, 1950. Elected here 1997; MP for Stretford 1983-97. Min of State, Foreign Office, 1997-99. Spokesman, foreign affairs, 1995-97; environment, 1994-95; ed, 1992-94; employment, 1988-92; transport, 1987-88. Previously Lab whip. Joint vice-chairman, all-party Trans-Pennine grp; sec, British-Japanese grp. Member, Select Cttees: Home Affairs, 1985-87; Social Services, 1983-85. Trafford district cllr, 1979-84. Lecturer, dept of business and admin, Salford Univ, 1979-83. Ed Stretford GS; Nottingham Univ; Manchester Business Sch.

This seat contains many of Manchester's finest civic buildings. These striking monuments are, however, surrounded by inner-city blight, poor council estates with stark social problems and doggedly high rates of unemployment. One of the worst districts is the notorious Moss Side. A mere quarter of the electors are homeowners, an astonishingly low number. This is overwhelmingly Labour territory. Map 394

## MANCHESTER GORTON — Lab hold

| Electorate | %Turnout | | 63,834 | 42.66% | 2001 | 64,349 | 56.43% | 1997 |
|---|---|---|---|---|---|---|---|---|
| Kaufman G | Lab | 17,099 | 62.8% | -2.48% | 23,704 | 65.28% | Lab |
| Pearcey Ms J | LD | 5,795 | 21.28% | 3.76% | 6,362 | 17.52% | LD |
| Causer C | C | 2,705 | 9.93% | -1.77% | 4,249 | 11.7% | C |
| Bingham B | Green | 835 | 3.07% | 1.19% | 812 | 2.24% | Ref |
| Bhatti R | UK Ind | 462 | 1.7% | | 683 | 1.88% | Green |
| Muir Ms K | Soc Lab | 333 | 1.22% | -0.16% | 501 | 1.38% | Soc Lab |
| Lab to LD swing | 3.12% | 27,229 | Lab maj 11,304 | | 36,311 | Lab maj 17,342 | |
| | | | 41.51% | | | 47.76% | |

**GERALD KAUFMAN,** b June 21, 1930. Elected here 1983; MP for Manchester Ardwick 1970-83. Member, Royal Commission on the Reform of House of Lords, 1999-. Chairman, Culture, Media and Sport Select Cttee, 1997-2001; Nat Heritage, 1992-97. Chief spokesman, foreign and Commonwealth affairs, 1987-92; home affairs, 1983-87; environment, 1980-83. Shadow Cabinet, 1980-92. Privy Counsellor, 1978. Member, Lab NEC, 1991-92. Political correspondent, New Statesman, 1964-65; political staff, Daily Mirror, 1955-64. Ed Leeds GS; Queen's Coll, Oxford.

This constituency is essentially the southeastern section of the city. It includes Belle Vue zoological park and funfair and also Manchester Grammar School. It is quite diverse in the sense that neither owner-occupiers nor council tenants are dominant and there are middle-class enclaves. There is also a growing non-white electorate. There is not much diversity, however, in partisan loyalty. Gorton is another solid Labour seat. Map 395

## MANCHESTER WITHINGTON — Lab hold

| Electorate | %Turnout | | 67,480 | 51.94% | 2001 | 66,116 | 66.59% | 1997 |
|---|---|---|---|---|---|---|---|---|
| Bradley K | Lab | 19,239 | 54.89% | -6.67% | 27,103 | 61.56% | Lab |
| Zalzala Ms Y | LD | 7,715 | 22.01% | 8.38% | 8,522 | 19.36% | C |
| Samways J | C | 5,349 | 15.26% | -4.1% | 6,000 | 13.63% | LD |
| Valentine Ms M | Green | 1,539 | 4.39% | | 1,079 | 2.45% | Ref |
| Clegg J | Soc All | 1,208 | 3.45% | | 614 | 1.39% | ProLife |
| | | | | | 376 | 0.85% | Soc |
| | | | | | 181 | 0.41% | Dream |
| | | | | | 152 | 0.35% | NLP |
| Lab to LD swing | 7.53% | 35,050 | Lab maj 11,524 | | 44,027 | Lab maj 18,581 | |
| | | | 32.88% | | | 42.20% | |

**KEITH BRADLEY,** b May 17, 1950. Elected 1987. Min of State, Home Office, June 2001-; Parly Under-Sec for Social Security, 1997-98. Govt dep chief whip, 1998-2001. Lab road and rail spokesman, 1996-97; social security, 1991-96. Member, Agriculture Select Cttee, 1989-91. Manchester city cllr, 1983-88. Dir (unpaid), Parrs Wood Rural Trust. Ex-city council dir of Manchester Ship Canal and Manchester Airport plc. Ed Manchester Poly; York Univ. e-mail: keithbradleymp@parliament.uk www.keithbradleymp.free-online.co.uk tel: 0161-446 2047 fax: 0161-445 5543

This was once considered the most middle-class seat in Manchester and a plausible political prospect for the Conservatives. It could not be described in such terms today. The middle classes have essentially fled this southern part of the city for the suburbs and for Cheshire, leaving their large homes to multi-occupation. There are professionals and managers here but they tend to be associated with the university and other public services. Map 396

## MANSFIELD
### Lab hold

| Electorate | %Turnout | | 66,748 | 55.21% | 2001 | 67,057 | 70.72% | 1997 |
|---|---|---|---|---|---|---|---|---|
| **Meale A** | Lab | | **21,050** | 57.12% | -7.31% | **30,556** | 64.43% | Lab |
| Wellesley W | C | | 10,012 | 27.17% | 6.0% | 10,038 | 21.17% | C |
| Hill T | LD | | 5,790 | 15.71% | 4.65% | 5,244 | 11.06% | LD |
| | | | | | | 1,588 | 3.35% | Ref |
| **Lab to C swing** | **6.65%** | | **36,852** | | Lab maj 11,038 | **47,426** | | Lab maj 20,518 |
| | | | | | 29.95% | | | 43.26% |

**ALAN MEALE,** b July 31, 1949. Elected 1987. Former PPS to John Prescott, Deputy PM. Lab whip, 1992-97; member, Select Cttees: Home Affairs, 1989-92; Euro Legislation, 1988-89. Chairman, all-party beer grp, 1993-; treas, football grp, 1989-; Cyprus grp, 1997-. Unpaid dir, Mansfield 2010; unpaid parly spokesman and consultant to Stand By Me Club, devoted to promoting the song *Stand By Me.* Member, exec board, SSAFA; exec cttee on war pensions. Engineering worker, 1968-75; Merchant Navy seaman, 1964-68. Ed St Joseph's RC Sch; Ruskin Coll, Oxford.

The Mansfield constituency has traditionally been associated with the Nottinghamshire coalfield. This one fact largely explains its political behaviour in recent years. It was the home of the Union of Democratic Mineworkers who broke away from the National Union of Mineworkers during the 1984-85 strike. Labour almost lost an otherwise safe seat in 1987 because of that split, but recovered substantially in 1992 and fully in the subsequent polls. Map 397

## MEDWAY
### Lab hold

| Electorate | %Turnout | | 64,930 | 59.46% | 2001 | 61,736 | 72.47% | 1997 |
|---|---|---|---|---|---|---|---|---|
| **Marshall-Andrews R** | Lab | | **18,914** | 49.9% | 1.05% | **21,858** | 48.85% | Lab |
| Reckless M | C | | 15,134 | 39.2% | 2.31% | 16,504 | 36.89% | C |
| Juby G | LD | | 3,604 | 9.33% | -0.85% | 4,555 | 10.18% | LD |
| Sinclaire Ms N | UK Ind | | 958 | 2.48% | 1.57% | 1,420 | 3.17% | Ref |
| | | | | | | 405 | 0.91% | UK Ind |
| **Lab to C swing** | **1.08%** | | **38,610** | | Lab maj 3,780 | **44,742** | | Lab maj 5,354 |
| | | | | | 9.79% | | | 11.96% |

**BOB MARSHALL-ANDREWS,** b April 10, 1944. Elected 1997; contested this seat 1992; Richmond-upon-Thames Oct 1974. Ex-chairman, Richmond CLP. Member, Consolidation Bills Select Cttee, 1997-2001. Member, Soc of Lab Lawyers. Bencher, 1996; Recorder, Crown Court, 1982. Trustee, Adamson Wildlife Trust and Geffrye Museum. QC and novelist. Ed Mill Hill Sch; Bristol Univ.

This Kent seat consists of Rochester and Strood along with a further 20,000 voters on the north bank of the River Medway. The local economy is essentially light industry, boosted by tourism attracted by Rochester's castle, cathedral and Dickensian associations. Rochester has invariably leant towards Labour while the more rural parts of the constituency have tended to back the Tories. This is, therefore, a classic marginal battleground. Map 398

## MEIRIONNYDD NANT CONWY
### PC hold

| Electorate | %Turnout | | 33,175 | 63.51% | 2001 | 32,345 | 75.98% | 1997 |
|---|---|---|---|---|---|---|---|---|
| **Llwyd E** | PC | | **10,459** | 49.64% | -1.08% | **12,465** | 50.72% | PC |
| Jones Ms D | Lab | | 4,775 | 22.66% | -0.37% | 5,660 | 23.03% | Lab |
| Francis Ms L | C | | 3,962 | 18.81% | 2.85% | 3,922 | 15.96% | C |
| Raw-Rees D | LD | | 1,872 | 8.89% | 1.9% | 1,719 | 6.99% | LD |
| | | | | | | 809 | 3.29% | Ref |
| **PC to Lab swing** | **0.36%** | | **21,068** | | PC maj 5,684 | **24,575** | | PC maj 6,805 |
| | | | | | 26.98% | | | 27.69% |

**ELFYN LLWYD,** b Sept 26, 1951. Elected 1992. Plaid Cymru spokesman, Treasury and economy, trade and industry and other responsibilities. Member, Welsh Affairs Select Cttee, 1992-95. Joint vice-chairman, all-party head injuries grp. Solicitor. Partner in Guthrie Jones and Jones, solicitors of Dolgellau and Bala, Gwynedd. Pigeon breeder. Ed Ysgol Duffryn Conwy, Llanrwst; Univ Coll of Wales, Aberystwyth; Christleton Coll of Law, Chester.

This seat has a small population which is dominated by Welsh speakers. It covers a large slice of scenically spectacular northwest Wales, notably the mountains of Snowdonia and the pretty coastal towns of Harlech and Barmouth. The most significant settlement is Blaenau Ffestiniog, a slate-mining hill town where, historically, Labour and Plaid Cymru engage in a reasonably close competition. The rest of this seat is, however, reliably nationalist. Map 399

## MERIDEN — C hold

| Electorate | %Turnout | | 74,439 | 59.86% | 2001 | 76,287 | 71.73% | 1997 |
|---|---|---|---|---|---|---|---|---|
| Spelman Mrs C | | C | 21,246 | 47.68% | 5.65% | 22,997 | 42.03% | C |
| Shawcroft Ms C | | Lab | 17,462 | 39.19% | -1.77% | 22,415 | 40.96% | Lab |
| Hicks N | | LD | 4,941 | 11.09% | -1.88% | 7,098 | 12.97% | LD |
| Adams R | | UK Ind | 910 | 2.04% | | 2,208 | 4.04% | Ref |
| Lab to C swing | 3.71% | | 44,559 | | C maj 3,784 | 54,718 | | C maj 582 |
| | | | | | 8.49% | | | 1.07% |

**CAROLINE SPELMAN,** b May 4, 1958. Elected 1997. Opposition health spokeswoman, 1999-. Opposition whip, 1998-99. Member, Science and Tech Select Cttee, 1997-2001. Joint vice-chairman, all-party poverty grp, 1997-. Ex-commercial negotiator, specialising in purchase contracts for food and pharmaceutical industries. Research fellow, Wye Coll, London. Ed Herts and Essex Girls' GS; Queen Mary Coll, London.
e-mail: spelmanc@parliament.uk www.carolinespelman.com
tel: 020-7219 4189 fax: 020-7219 0378

This West Midlands marginal is an unusual amalgam. It curves around Solihull and contains some wards which are essentially Birmingham outer suburbs such as Chelmsley Wood, strongly Labour. The National Exhibition Centre is located here too. There are also affluent dormitory towns such as Knowle, Dorridge, Hampton in Arden and Meriden itself, plus some rural villages. The balance leans to the Tories, narrow winners in 1997 and again in 2001. Map 400

## MERTHYR TYDFIL & RHYMNEY — Lab hold

| Electorate | %Turnout | | 55,368 | 57.22% | 2001 | 56,507 | 69.27% | 1997 |
|---|---|---|---|---|---|---|---|---|
| Havard D | | Lab | 19,574 | 61.78% | -14.9% | 30,012 | 76.68% | Lab |
| Hughes R | | PC | 4,651 | 14.68% | 8.69% | 2,926 | 7.48% | LD |
| Rogers K | | LD | 2,385 | 7.53% | 0.05% | 2,508 | 6.41% | C |
| Cuming R | | C | 2,272 | 7.17% | 0.76% | 2,344 | 5.99% | PC |
| Edwards J | | Ind | 1,936 | 6.11% | | 691 | 1.77% | O Lab |
| Evans K | | Soc Lab | 692 | 2.18% | | 660 | 1.69% | Ref |
| Lewis A | | ProLife | 174 | 0.55% | | | | |
| Lab to PC swing | 11.80% | | 31,684 | | Lab maj 14,923 | 39,141 | | Lab maj 27,086 |
| | | | | | 47.10% | | | 69.20% |

**DAI HAVARD,** b Aug 7, 1950. Elected 2001. Inherits seat from Ted Rowlands, who held it for 29 years. Wales sec, MSF, 1998-; member, Co-op Party. Union official, 1982-97, researcher, 1975-76; TUC tutor in FE, 1976-82. Maintenance engineer. Ed Quakers Yard GS; Afon Taf Comp; St Peters Coll, Birmingham; Warwick Univ.

This constituency, at the head of the Taf and Rhymney Valleys, is the heart of South Wales, and its fortunes have fluctuated with the fates of the local industries, coal and iron, which arrived in the late 18th century. In recent years, with the closure of the pits and steelworks, it has had to overcome much economic hardship. It is astonishingly loyal to the Labour Party, whose first leader, Keir Hardie, sat for Merthyr from 1900 to 1915. Map 401

## MIDDLESBROUGH — Lab hold

| Electorate | %Turnout | | 67,659 | 49.83% | 2001 | 70,931 | 64.99% | 1997 |
|---|---|---|---|---|---|---|---|---|
| Bell S | | Lab | 22,783 | 67.57% | -3.86% | 32,925 | 71.43% | Lab |
| Finn A | | C | 6,453 | 19.14% | 1.99% | 7,907 | 17.15% | C |
| Miller K | | LD | 3,512 | 10.42% | 1.89% | 3,934 | 8.53% | LD |
| Kerr-Morgan G | | Soc All | 577 | 1.71% | | 1,331 | 2.89% | Ref |
| Andersen K | | Soc Lab | 392 | 1.16% | | | | |
| Lab to C swing | 2.92% | | 33,717 | | Lab maj 16,330 | 46,097 | | Lab maj 25,018 |
| | | | | | 48.43% | | | 54.28% |

**STUART BELL,** b May 16, 1938. Elected 1983. Second Church Estates Commissioner, 1997-. Chairman, Financial Services Cttee, 1999-. Chairman, First Past the Post grp; all-party Jordanian grp, 1997-; all-party Saudi Arabia grp, 1997-; sec, all-party Israel grp, 1990-. Member, House of Commons Commission. Lab spokesman, trade and industry, 1992-97; NI, 1984-87. Joint vice-chairman, PLP Treasury and Civil Service Cttee, 1990-92 . Newcastle city cllr, 1980-83. Barrister and writer. Ed Hookergate GS, Durham, Pitman's Coll; Council of Legal Ed, Gray's Inn.

This Teesside steel and chemicals town is not quite large enough for two parliamentary seats but is too big for one. This seat consists of much of Middlesbrough proper but also some wards to the west of the town which are solidly middle-class. These districts are, however, swamped by the political sympathies of most of the urban population. It all makes for extremely reliable Labour territory. Map 402

## MIDDLESBROUGH SOUTH & CLEVELAND EAST — Lab hold

| Electorate | %Turnout | | 71,485 | 61.54% | 2001 | 70,481 | 76.03% | 1997 |
|---|---|---|---|---|---|---|---|---|
| Kumar Dr A | Lab | | 24,321 | 55.29% | 0.58% | 29,319 | 54.71% | Lab |
| Harpham Mrs B | C | | 14,970 | 34.03% | -0.89% | 18,712 | 34.92% | C |
| Parrish Ms L | LD | | 4,700 | 10.68% | 3.21% | 4,004 | 7.47% | LD |
| | | | | | | 1,552 | 2.9% | Ref |
| C to Lab swing | 0.73% | | 43,991 | Lab maj 9,351 | | 53,587 | Lab maj 10,607 | |
| | | | | 21.26% | | | 19.79% | |

**ASHOK KUMAR,** b May 28, 1956. Elected here 1997; gained Langbaurgh for Lab at 1991 by-election, but was defeated in 1992 general election. Member, Science and Tech Select Cttee, Parly Scientific Cttee, PLP Trade and Ind Cttee, PLP Treasury Cttee, PLP Ed and Employment Cttee and PLP job creation grp. Chairman, all-party grp for energy studies. Sec, all-party grp for chemical industry. Middlesborough borough cllr, 1987-97. Ed Rykneld Boys Sch, Derby; Aston Univ.
tel: 01287 610878 fax: 01287 631894

This mouthful of a constituency, part urban Middlesbrough, part rural Cleveland Hills, and including the seaside resort of Saltburn, disguises the fact that it is similar to the old Cleveland constituency of Langbaurgh. That was very marginal territory; the addition of south Middlesbrough wards has made it slightly less competitive. But this is the sort of seat where the Tories need to compete seriously if they are to win a Commons majority. Map 403

## MIDLOTHIAN — Lab hold

| Electorate | %Turnout | | 48,625 | 59.07% | 2001 | 47,552 | 74.13% | 1997 |
|---|---|---|---|---|---|---|---|---|
| Hamilton D | Lab | | 15,145 | 52.73% | -0.78% | 18,861 | 53.51% | Lab |
| Goldie I | SNP | | 6,131 | 21.34% | -4.17% | 8,991 | 25.51% | SNP |
| Bell Ms J | LD | | 3,686 | 12.83% | 3.65% | 3,842 | 10.9% | C |
| Traquair R | C | | 2,748 | 9.57% | -1.33% | 3,235 | 9.18% | LD |
| Goupillot B | SSP | | 837 | 2.91% | | 320 | 0.91% | Ref |
| Holden T | ProLife | | 177 | 0.62% | | | | |
| SNP to Lab swing | 1.69% | | 28,724 | Lab maj 9,014 | | 35,249 | Lab maj 9,870 | |
| | | | | 31.38% | | | 28.00% | |

**DAVID HAMILTON,** b Oct 24, 1950. Elected 2001. Takes over seat from Eric Clarke. Both are former miners. Employment and training scheme supervisor, Midlothian council, 1987-89; placement and training officer, Craigmillar Festival Soc, 1989-92; chief exec, Craigmillar Opportunities, 1992-2000. Ed Dalkeith HS

This constituency achieved its moment in the sun in the 19th century. William Gladstone virtually invented political campaigning with his famous effort here. This county south of Edinburgh is predominantly working-class, dominated by small towns with a background in mining. It should be solidly Labour, which to some extent it is, but the SNP is a lively force too. Map 404

## MILTON KEYNES NORTH EAST — Lab hold

| Electorate | %Turnout | | 75,526 | 62.35% | 2001 | 70,395 | 72.78% | 1997 |
|---|---|---|---|---|---|---|---|---|
| White B | Lab | | 19,761 | 41.96% | 2.53% | 20,201 | 39.43% | Lab |
| Rix Mrs M | C | | 17,932 | 38.08% | -0.88% | 19,961 | 38.96% | C |
| Yeoward D | LD | | 8,375 | 17.78% | 0.4% | 8,907 | 17.38% | LD |
| Phillips M | UK Ind | | 1,026 | 2.18% | | 1,492 | 2.91% | Ref |
| | | | | | | 576 | 1.12% | Green |
| | | | | | | 99 | 0.19% | NLP |
| C to Lab swing | 1.71% | | 47,094 | Lab maj 1,829 | | 51,236 | Lab maj 240 | |
| | | | | 3.88% | | | 0.47% | |

**BRIAN WHITE,** b May 5, 1957. Elected 1997. Member, Select Cttees: Consolidation Bills, Deregulation, Statutory Instruments, Public Administration. Milton Keynes cllr (dep leader). Chairman, local gvt assoc planning cttee; sec, local gvt assoc Lab grp. Ex-systems analyst for Abbey National plc; previously civil servant, HM Customs & Excise. Ed Methodist Coll, Belfast.

The Buckinghamshire new city of Milton Keynes expanded so much in the 1980s that a new seat had to be introduced here for the 1992 election. This is definitely the more Conservative of them although Labour produced a spectacular result to capture it in 1997, making it a tight marginal again in 2001. It consists of a section of the new city and some prosperous rural and commuting areas such as Olney, Newport Pagnell and Woburn Sands. Map 405

## MILTON KEYNES SOUTH WEST — Lab hold

| Electorate | %Turnout | 76,607 | 59.24% | 2001 | 71,070 | 71.42% | 1997 |
|---|---|---|---|---|---|---|---|
| **Starkey Dr P** | **Lab** | **22,484** | **49.54%** | **-4.24%** | **27,298** | **53.78%** | **Lab** |
| Stewart I | C | 15,506 | 34.17% | 0.67% | 17,006 | 33.5% | C |
| Mohammad N | LD | 4,828 | 10.64% | -1.31% | 6,065 | 11.95% | LD |
| Francis A | Green | 957 | 2.11% | | 389 | 0.77% | NLP |
| Davies C | UK Ind | 848 | 1.87% | | | | |
| Denning P | LCA | 500 | 1.1% | | | | |
| Bradbury D | Soc All | 261 | 0.58% | | | | |
| **Lab to C swing** | **2.45%** | **45,384** | Lab maj **6,978** | | **50,758** | Lab maj **10,292** | |
| | | | 15.38% | | | 20.28% | |

**PHYLLIS STARKEY,** b Jan 4, 1947. Elected 1997. Member, Select Cttees: Foreign Affairs 1999-2001; Modernisation of Commons, 1997-99. Chairwoman, all-party British-Palestine grp. Oxford city cllr, 1983-97 (leader 1990-93). Member, parly panel, Royal Coll of Nursing. Science policy administrator; ex-lecturer in obstetrics, Oxford Univ. Ed Perse Sch for Girls, Cambridge; Lady Margaret Hall, Oxford; Clare Hall, Cambridge.
e mail: starkeyp@miltonkeynes-sw.demon.co.uk tel: 020-7219 0456 fax: 020-7219 6865

Milton Keynes has been a spectacular success, now a new city rather than a new town. The bulk of the ultra-modern city, with its spruce housing and shopping centres, dual carriageways and countless roundabouts, is in this constituency, although there are also some more rural wards. Neither the Tories nor Labour have achieved dominance here and it is likely to remain a bellwether of wider sentiment. Map 406

## MITCHAM & MORDEN — Lab hold

| Electorate | %Turnout | 65,671 | 57.8% | 2001 | 65,385 | 73.33% | 1997 |
|---|---|---|---|---|---|---|---|
| **McDonagh Ms S** | **Lab** | **22,936** | **60.42%** | **2.05%** | **27,984** | **58.37%** | **Lab** |
| Stokes H | C | 9,151 | 24.11% | -5.6% | 14,243 | 29.71% | C |
| Harris N | LD | 3,820 | 10.06% | 2.48% | 3,632 | 7.58% | LD |
| Walsh T | Green | 926 | 2.44% | 1.57% | 810 | 1.69% | Ref |
| Tyndall J | BNP | 642 | 1.69% | 0.6% | 521 | 1.09% | BNP |
| Roberts A | UK Ind | 486 | 1.28% | 1.04% | 415 | 0.87% | Green |
| | | | | | 144 | 0.3% | Ind |
| | | | | | 117 | 0.24% | UK Ind |
| | | | | | 80 | 0.17% | ACC |
| **C to Lab swing** | **3.83%** | **37,961** | Lab maj **13,785** | | **47,946** | Lab maj **13,741** | |
| | | | 36.31% | | | 28.66% | |

**SIOBHAIN McDONAGH,** b Feb 20, 1960. Elected 1997. Development co-ordinator, Battersea churches housing trust, 1988-97. Housing adviser, 1986-87; voluntary adviser, Catholic housing advice service, Wandsworth; ex-member, Merton voluntary service council. Merton cllr, 1982-97. Ed Holy Cross Convent, New Malden; Essex Univ.

This seat, comprising dense housing and some light industry, is situated in the South London Borough of Merton. Mitcham and Morden is set in the southern part and has long been more competitive than other seats in this area. It was represented by a Labour MP who defected to the SDP in 1982 only to discover that the by-election he nobly called coincided with the Falklands conflict. The Tories held the seat until 1997 but then lost by a hefty margin. Map 407

## MOLE VALLEY — C hold

| Electorate | %Turnout | 67,770 | 69.46% | 2001 | 69,140 | 78.86% | 1997 |
|---|---|---|---|---|---|---|---|
| **Beresford Sir P** | **C** | **23,790** | **50.54%** | **2.53%** | **26,178** | **48.01%** | **C** |
| Savage Ms C | LD | 13,637 | 28.97% | -0.3% | 15,957 | 29.27% | LD |
| Redford D | Lab | 7,837 | 16.65% | 1.87% | 8,057 | 14.78% | Lab |
| Walters R | UK Ind | 1,333 | 2.83% | 2.03% | 2,424 | 4.45% | Ref |
| Newton W | ProLife | 475 | 1.01% | | 1,276 | 2.34% | Ind CRP |
| | | | | | 435 | 0.8% | UK Ind |
| | | | | | 197 | 0.36% | NLP |
| **LD to C swing** | **1.41%** | **47,072** | C maj **10,153** | | **54,524** | C maj **10,221** | |
| | | | 21.57% | | | 18.74% | |

**SIR PAUL BERESFORD,** b April 6, 1946. Elected here 1997; MP for Croydon Central 1992-97. Environment Under-Sec, 1994-97. Former vice-chairman, C backbench housing improvement subcttee. Member, Audit Commission, 1991-92. Wandsworth cllr, 1978-94 (leader, 1983-92). Dental surgeon. Ed Richmond Primary and Waimea Coll, Nelson, New Zealand; Otago Univ, Dunedin, New Zealand; Eastman Dental Hospital, London .

This quaintly named seat is centred on the Surrey Hills and includes two population centres, Dorking and Leatherhead. There are also small towns and pretty villages reaching as far west as the Guildford border, as well as Leith Hill and Box Hill. It is solid Conservative country and was represented from 1983 to 1997 by Kenneth Baker, the former Home Secretary. The Lib Dems make a spirited effort locally but have little chance of winning. Map 408

# MONMOUTH — Lab hold

| Electorate | %Turnout | | 62,202 | 71.48% | 2001 | 60,703 | 80.76% | 1997 |
|---|---|---|---|---|---|---|---|---|
| Edwards H | Lab | | 19,021 | 42.78% | -4.96% | 23,404 | 47.74% | Lab |
| Evans R | C | | 18,637 | 41.92% | 2.7% | 19,226 | 39.22% | C |
| Parker N | LD | | 5,080 | 11.43% | 1.87% | 4,689 | 9.56% | LD |
| Hubbard M | PC | | 1,068 | 2.4% | 1.35% | 1,190 | 2.43% | Ref |
| Rowlands D | UK Ind | | 656 | 1.48% | | 516 | 1.05% | PC |
| Lab to C swing | 3.83% | | 44,462 | Lab maj 384 | | 49,025 | Lab maj 4,178 | |
| | | | | 0.86% | | | 8.52% | |

**HUW EDWARDS,** b April 12, 1953. Elected here 1997; also MP for Monmouth from 1991 by-election to 1992 general election. Member, Welsh Affairs Select Cttee; chairman, Welsh grp of Lab MPs; member, Parliament for Wales campaign; Lab campaign for electoral reform. Research associate, Low Pay Unit, 1985-1997. Member, exec, Shelter Cymru, 1988-91. Lecturer. Ed Eastfields HS, Mitcham, Surrey; Manchester Poly; York Univ.
e mail: edwardsh@parliament.uk fax: 020-7219 3949

This borders seat is an unusual hybrid of Welsh and English influence. It has proved the most sympathetic constituency in Wales, of late, to the Conservatives, who won here in the Welsh Assembly elections of 1999. The main towns include Monmouth and Chepstow on the River Wye, and Abergavenny, near the Black Mountains. There are only a tiny number of Welsh speakers. This is one of those rare Labour-Tory marginals in the Principality. Map 409

# MONTGOMERYSHIRE — LD hold

| Electorate | %Turnout | | 44,243 | 65.51% | 2001 | 42,618 | 74.91% | 1997 |
|---|---|---|---|---|---|---|---|---|
| Opik L | LD | | 14,319 | 49.4% | 3.52% | 14,647 | 45.88% | LD |
| Jones D | C | | 8,085 | 27.9% | 1.76% | 8,344 | 26.14% | C |
| Davies P | Lab | | 3,443 | 11.88% | -7.26% | 6,109 | 19.14% | Lab |
| Senior D | PC | | 1,969 | 6.79% | 1.75% | 1,608 | 5.04% | PC |
| Rowlands D | UK Ind | | 786 | 2.71% | | 879 | 2.75% | Ref |
| Davies Miss R | ProLife | | 210 | 0.72% | | 338 | 1.06% | Green |
| Taylor R | Ind | | 171 | 0.59% | | | | |
| C to LD swing | 0.88% | | 28,983 | LD maj 6,234 | | 31,925 | LD maj 6,303 | |
| | | | | 21.51% | | | 19.74% | |

**LEMBIT OPIK,** b March 2, 1965. Elected 1997; contested Newcastle upon Tyne Central 1992; Northumbria 1994 Euro elections. LD spokesman, Wales, NI and youth affairs. Member, Agriculture Select Cttee, 1999-2001; member, all-party BBC grp; all-party friends of the Bahai. Newcastle upon Tyne city cllr, 1992-. Member, Greenpeace; Charter 88. Training and development manager, Procter & Gamble. Ed Royal Belfast Academical Inst; Bristol Univ.
e mail: opikl@parliament.uk tel: 020-7219 1144 fax: 020-7219 2210

This is an extremely rural seat set in the heart of the Mid Wales countryside. The only towns of any size are Newtown and Welshpool. It has an exceptionally large proportion of its population engaged in farming. It is also extraordinarily loyal to the Liberal Democrats. With the single exception of 1979, the Liberal Party (in various forms) has held the seat for more than a century. Map 410

# MORAY — SNP hold

| Electorate | %Turnout | | 58,008 | 57.27% | 2001 | 58,302 | 68.21% | 1997 |
|---|---|---|---|---|---|---|---|---|
| Robertson A | SNP | | 10,076 | 30.33% | -11.24% | 16,529 | 41.57% | SNP |
| Munro Mrs C | Lab | | 8,332 | 25.08% | 5.25% | 10,963 | 27.57% | C |
| Spencer-Nairn F | C | | 7,677 | 23.11% | -4.46% | 7,886 | 19.83% | Lab |
| Gorn Ms L | LD | | 5,224 | 15.72% | 6.8% | 3,548 | 8.92% | LD |
| Anderson Ms N | SSP | | 821 | 2.47% | | 840 | 2.11% | Ref |
| Jappy B | Ind | | 802 | 2.41% | | | | |
| Kenyon N | UK Ind | | 291 | 0.88% | | | | |
| SNP to Lab swing | 8.25% | | 33,223 | SNP maj 1,744 | | 39,766 | SNP maj 5,566 | |
| | | | | 5.25% | | | 14.00% | |

**ANGUS ROBERTSON,** b Sept 28, 1969. Elected 2001. Inherits seat from Margaret Ewing who stood down after 14 years to concentrate on work at the Scottish Parliament. Contested Midlothian in the Scottish Parliament election, 1999. Euro policy adviser to SNP at Scottish Parliament, 1999-2001. SNP international press officer, 1997 and 1999 Scottish elections. Journalist, based in Austria for eight years. Ed Broughton HS; Edinburgh and Aberdeen Univs.

This northeast rural Scottish seat has developed a distinctive political culture. The largest centre is the cathedral town of Elgin, the only patch where Labour performs with any vitality. The rolling Speyside countryside, with its whisky distilleries, and the Moray Firth fishing ports of Lossiemouth and Buckie, are also situated here. This has been a Tory-SNP battleground, with the SNP latterly on top; in 2001 Labour pitched in to make it a three-way marginal. Map 411

## MORECAMBE & LUNESDALE — Lab hold

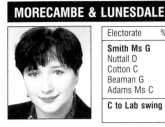

| Electorate | %Turnout | 68,607 | 60.72% | 2001 | 68,013 | 72.41% | 1997 |
|---|---|---|---|---|---|---|---|
| Smith Ms G | Lab | 20,646 | 49.56% | 0.7% | 24,061 | 48.86% | Lab |
| Nuttall D | C | 15,554 | 37.34% | 0.6% | 18,096 | 36.74% | C |
| Cotton C | LD | 3,817 | 9.16% | -2.24% | 5,614 | 11.4% | LD |
| Beaman G | UK Ind | 935 | 2.24% | | 1,313 | 2.67% | Ref |
| Adams Ms C | Green | 703 | 1.69% | | 165 | 0.34% | NLP |
| C to Lab swing | 0.05% | 41,655 | Lab maj 5,092 | | 49,249 | Lab maj 5,965 | |
| | | | 12.22% | | | 12.12% | |

**GERALDINE SMITH,** b Aug 29, 1961. Elected 1997. Member, UK delegation to Council of Europe. Chairwoman, economic development and tourism policy and coastal protection, Lancaster City Council. CWU local and area rep. Ex-Royal Mail clerical employee, 1980-97. Ed Morecambe HS; Lancaster and Morecambe Coll. e-mail: smithg@parliament.uk tel: 020-7219 5816 fax: 020-7219 0977

This Lancashire seat is based on the seaside resort itself, some elegant suburbs and industrial territory associated with the ferry port of Heysham and its surroundings. It has traditionally been dominated by the Tories, especially in the villages between the Lune and Morecambe Bay, though there has always been a sizeable Labour minority, including the railway town of Carnforth. It switched spectacularly in 1997 and Labour kept control in 2001. Map 412

## MORLEY & ROTHWELL — Lab hold

| Electorate | %Turnout | 71,815 | 53.53% | 2001 | 68,385 | 67.12% | 1997 |
|---|---|---|---|---|---|---|---|
| Challen C | Lab | 21,919 | 57.02% | -1.45% | 26,836 | 58.47% | Lab |
| Schofield D | C | 9,829 | 25.57% | -0.76% | 12,086 | 26.33% | C |
| Golton S | LD | 5,446 | 14.17% | 3.09% | 5,087 | 11.08% | LD |
| Bardsley J | UK Ind | 1,248 | 3.25% | | 1,359 | 2.96% | Ref |
| | | | | | 381 | 0.83% | BNP |
| | | | | | 148 | 0.32% | ProLife |
| Lab to C swing | 0.35% | 38,442 | Lab maj 12,090 | | 45,897 | Lab maj 14,750 | |
| | | | 31.45% | | | 32.14% | |

**COLIN CHALLEN,** b June 12, 1953. Elected 2001. This seat includes the area formerly represented by Hugh Gaitskell and Merlyn Rees. The current MP was a supplier accountant, RAF, 1971-74; postman, 1974-78; printer, 1982-94. Marketing development worker, Humberside Co-op Development Agency, 1991-93. Member, Hull City Council; Lab grp sec, 1986-94. Lab organiser, 1994-2000. Ed Norton Sec Sch; Malton GS; Hull Univ.

This West Yorkshire seat consists of the district broadly to the south of Leeds and one ward, Middleton - with two vast council estates - which could be considered part of the city itself. The patch has a long association with the Labour Party with some eminent representatives in the House of Commons. It was solidly but not overwhelmingly Labour in the 1980s but moved more decisively towards the party in the 1997 election. Map 413

## MOTHERWELL & WISHAW — Lab hold

| Electorate | %Turnout | 52,418 | 56.61% | 2001 | 52,252 | 70.08% | 1997 |
|---|---|---|---|---|---|---|---|
| Roy F | Lab | 16,681 | 56.22% | -1.18% | 21,020 | 57.4% | Lab |
| McGuigan J | SNP | 5,725 | 19.29% | -3.18% | 8,229 | 22.47% | SNP |
| Nolan M | C | 3,155 | 10.63% | -0.36% | 4,024 | 10.99% | C |
| Brown I | LD | 2,791 | 9.41% | 3.04% | 2,331 | 6.37% | LD |
| Smellie S | SSP | 1,260 | 4.25% | | 797 | 2.18% | Soc Lab |
| Watt Ms C | Soc Lab | 61 | 0.21% | -1.97% | 218 | 0.6% | Ref |
| SNP to Lab swing | 1.00% | 29,673 | Lab maj 10,956 | | 36,619 | Lab maj 12,791 | |
| | | | 36.92% | | | 34.93% | |

**FRANK ROY,** b Aug 29, 1958. Elected 1997. Member, Social Security Select Cttee, 1997-98. PPS to John Reid, 1999-; and PPS to Helen Liddell, Dep Sec of State for Scotland, 1998-99. Ex-steelworker, Ravenscraig, and election agent. Ed Our Lady's HS, Motherwell; Glasgow Caledonian Univ. e-mail: royf@parliament.uk

Much of this seat in the built-up Clyde Valley southeast of Glasgow used to be known as Motherwell South. The inclusion of two wards from the old Motherwell North led to its being renamed. Like much of the Central Belt of Scotland it is industrial in character, with the steelworks at Ravenscraig dominating the area. There are a huge number of council tenants. In the circumstances it is surprising only that the Labour majority is not even larger. Map 414

# NEATH

**Lab hold**

| Electorate | %Turnout | | 56,107 | 62.42% | 2001 | 55,525 | 74.28% | 1997 |
|---|---|---|---|---|---|---|---|---|
| **Hain P** | **Lab** | | **21,253** | **60.69%** | **-12.84%** | **30,324** | **73.53%** | **Lab** |
| Llywelyn A | PC | | 6,437 | 18.38% | 10.27% | 3,583 | 8.69% | C |
| Davies D | LD | | 3,335 | 9.52% | 3.22% | 3,344 | 8.11% | PC |
| Devine D | C | | 3,310 | 9.45% | 0.76% | 2,597 | 6.3% | LD |
| Pudner H | Soc All | | 483 | 1.38% | | | 975 | 2.36% | Ref |
| Brienza G | ProLife | | 202 | 0.58% | | | 420 | 1.02% | LCP |
| **Lab to PC swing** | **11.56%** | | **35,020** | | **Lab maj 14,816** | **41,243** | | **Lab maj 26,741** |
| | | | | | 42.31% | | | 64.84% |

**PETER HAIN,** b Feb 16, 1950. Elected 1991 by-election. Min for Europe, June 2001-; Min of State, DTI, 2001; Min of State, FCO, 1999-2001; Under-Sec of State, Welsh Office 1997-99. Lab spokesman, employment, 1996-97. Lab whip, 1995-96. Sec, Tribune grp of Lab MPs until 1993. Nat chairman, Young Libs, 1971-3.Civil rights and anti-apartheid campaigner, and author. Chairman, Stop the 70 (South African) tour campaign, 1969-70. Ed Pretoria Boys HS; Emanuel Sch, Wandsworth; Queen Mary's Coll, London Univ; Sussex Univ.

This seat, stretching inland above Swansea and Port Talbot, is typical of many Welsh Valley seats, except that its MP was born in Kenya, brought up in South Africa and then became a resident of England. Coal and timber have been influential industries here, while aluminium and engineering are now more prominent. The Labour Party is entirely dominant in this seat; the rest engage in a contest for a pathetically distant second place. Map 415

# NEW FOREST EAST

**C hold**

| Electorate | %Turnout | | 66,767 | 63.17% | 2001 | 65,717 | 74.64% | 1997 |
|---|---|---|---|---|---|---|---|---|
| **Lewis Dr J** | **C** | | **17,902** | **42.44%** | **-0.48%** | **21,053** | **42.92%** | **C** |
| Dash B | LD | | 14,073 | 33.37% | 1.08% | 15,838 | 32.29% | LD |
| Goodfellow A | Lab | | 9,141 | 21.67% | -3.12% | 12,161 | 24.79% | Lab |
| Howe W | UK Ind | | 1,062 | 2.52% | | | | |
| **C to LD swing** | **0.78%** | | **42,178** | | **C maj 3,829** | **49,052** | | **C maj 5,215** |
| | | | | | 9.08% | | | 10.63% |

**JULIAN LEWIS,** b Sept 26, 1951. Elected 1997. Member, Select Cttees: Defence, 2000-01; Welsh Affairs, 1998-2001. Vice-chairman, C Foreign Affairs and Euro Affairs Cttees, 2000-; sec, C Defence Cttee, 1997-. Dep dir, C Research Dept, 1990-96; dir, Coalition for Peace through Security, 1981-85. Former parly aide to MPs and peers. Military historian. Research consultant. Ed Dynevor GS, Swansea; Balliol Coll, Oxford. St Antony's Coll. Oxford. www.julianlewis.net

As the name implies, this seat includes a large section of the New Forest, including the towns of Brockenhurst and Lyndhurst. The bulk of the population is, though, drawn from the suburbs on the western shore of Southampton Water. While some of these areas are quite industrial, such as the oil refinery town of Fawley, most voters are relatively affluent, including those in the beauty spots of Bucklers Hard and Beaulieu. A fairly secure Tory seat. Map 416

# NEW FOREST WEST

**C hold**

| Electorate | %Turnout | | 67,806 | 65.02% | 2001 | 66,522 | 74.79% | 1997 |
|---|---|---|---|---|---|---|---|---|
| **Swayne D** | **C** | | **24,575** | **55.74%** | **5.19%** | **25,149** | **50.55%** | **C** |
| Bignell M | LD | | 11,384 | 25.82% | -1.95% | 13,817 | 27.77% | LD |
| Onuegbu Ms C | Lab | | 6,481 | 14.7% | 0.44% | 7,092 | 14.26% | Lab |
| Clark M | UK Ind | | 1,647 | 3.74% | 0.64% | 2,150 | 4.32% | Ref |
| | | | | | | 1,542 | 3.1% | UK Ind |
| **LD to C swing** | **3.57%** | | **44,087** | | **C maj 13,191** | **49,750** | | **C maj 11,332** |
| | | | | | 29.92% | | | 22.78% |

**DESMOND SWAYNE,** b Aug 20, 1956. Elected 1997. C frontbench health spokesman, 2001-. Ex-schoolmaster; taught economics at Charterhouse and Wrekin Coll. TA officer, Warwickshire and Worcestershire Yeomanry Sqn. Former prison visitor, Wormwood Scrubs and Wandsworth Prison. Member, Bow Grp. Ex-manager, Royal Bank of Scotland. Ed Bedford Sch; St Andrews Univ.

This seat includes most of the old New Forest constituency which was divided in two in 1997, and is centred on Ringwood, the undeclared capital of the forest. It is very much rural Hampshire, consisting of attractive towns, such as the Isle of Wight ferry port of Lymington in the south and Fordingbridge in the north, and small villages, but there are some Bournemouth commuters in New Milton. It is one of the safest Tory seats in the South of England. Map 417

## NEWARK — C gain

| Electorate | %Turnout | | 71,089 | 63.51% | 2001 | 69,763 | 74.5% | 1997 |
|---|---|---|---|---|---|---|---|---|
| **Mercer P** | | **C** | **20,983** | **46.48%** | **7.07%** | **23,496** | **45.21%** | **Lab** |
| Jones Ms F | | Lab | 16,910 | 37.46% | -7.75% | 20,480 | 39.41% | C |
| Harding-Price D | | LD | 5,970 | 13.22% | 1.75% | 5,960 | 11.47% | LD |
| Haxby D | | Ind | 822 | 1.82% | | 2,035 | 3.92% | Ref |
| Thomson I | | Soc All | 462 | 1.02% | | | | |
| **Lab to C swing** | **7.41%** | | **45,147** | | **C maj 4,073** | **51,971** | | **Lab maj 3,016** |
| | | | | | 9.02% | | | 5.80% |

**PATRICK MERCER,** b June 26, 1956. Elected 2001. Takes seat from Fiona Jones, Lab, who won it 1997, and had conviction for election expenses fraud quashed in 1999. Army officer for 25 years; served as a colonel in Bosnia; also served in Ulster; established British presence in Uganda post-1985 civil war. Freelance journalist since 1999. Lecturer, Cranfield Univ. Oxford boxing Blue. Ed King's Sch, Chester; Oxford Univ.

From 1979 to 1992 this Nottinghamshire marginal was Tory territory, embracing the market towns of Newark-on-Trent and East Retford and small villages on either side of the A1. As well as its historic centre and fine town houses, Newark does have some council estates, but the tiny cathedral city of Southwell is solidly Tory. Although Fiona Jones took the seat for Labour in 1997, the Tories overthrew her again in 2001 following her post-election troubles. Map 418

## NEWBURY — LD hold

| Electorate | %Turnout | | 75,490 | 67.3% | 2001 | 73,680 | 76.65% | 1997 |
|---|---|---|---|---|---|---|---|---|
| **Rendel D** | | **LD** | **24,507** | **48.24%** | **-4.68%** | **29,887** | **52.92%** | **LD** |
| Benyon R | | C | 22,092 | 43.48% | 5.64% | 21,370 | 37.84% | C |
| Billcliffe S | | Lab | 3,523 | 6.93% | 1.43% | 3,107 | 5.5% | Lab |
| Gray-Fisk Ms D | | UK Ind | 685 | 1.35% | 0.82% | 992 | 1.76% | Ref |
| | | | | | | 644 | 1.14% | Green |
| | | | | | | 302 | 0.53% | UK Ind |
| | | | | | | 174 | 0.31% | Soc Lab |
| **LD to C swing** | **5.16%** | | **50,807** | | **LD maj 2,415** | **56,476** | | **LD maj 8,517** |
| | | | | | 4.75% | | | 15.08% |

**DAVID RENDEL,** b April 15, 1949. Elected 1993 by-election. Member, Public Accounts Cttee, 1999-. Chief LD spokesman, social security and welfare, 1997-99; spokesman, local gvt, 1993-97 (also housing, 1993). Member, all-party grps: welfare of park homeowners; cycling, housing and homelessness, paper ind and parenting. Newbury district cllr, 1987-95. Ex-management consultant and financial analyst. Ed Eton; Magdalen Coll, Oxford (rowing Blue, 1974); St Cross Coll, Oxford.
e-mail: drendel@cix.co.uk www.davidrendel.org.uk

This stretch of prosperous country, west of Reading across the rolling Downs, was once regarded as Tory as any similar seat in the Home Counties. It is mostly rural but has a scattering of small towns such as Newbury itself and Hungerford, a dynamic local economy including the mobile phone industry, and the racehorse stables of Lambourn. The Lib Dems captured the seat with a spectacular swing at a 1993 by-election and have retained it since then. Map 419

## NEWCASTLE-UNDER-LYME — Lab hold

| Electorate | %Turnout | | 65,739 | 58.83% | 2001 | 66,686 | 73.67% | 1997 |
|---|---|---|---|---|---|---|---|---|
| **Farrelly P** | | **Lab** | **20,650** | **53.4%** | **-3.07%** | **27,743** | **56.47%** | **Lab** |
| Flynn M | | C | 10,664 | 27.57% | 6.12% | 10,537 | 21.45% | C |
| Roodhouse J | | LD | 5,993 | 15.5% | 1.54% | 6,858 | 13.96% | LD |
| Fyson R | | Ind | 773 | 2.0% | | 1,510 | 3.07% | Ref |
| Godfrey P | | UK Ind | 594 | 1.54% | | 1,399 | 2.85% | Lib |
| | | | | | | 1,082 | 2.2% | Soc Lab |
| **Lab to C swing** | **4.60%** | | **38,674** | | **Lab maj 9,986** | **49,129** | | **Lab maj 17,206** |
| | | | | | 25.82% | | | 35.02% |

**PAUL FARRELLY,** b March 2, 1962. Elected 2001. Inherits seat from Llin Golding, who took over as MP from her husband John Golding in 1986. Contested Chesham and Amersham 1997. Business journalist, who has worked for Reuters, *Independent on Sunday* and, more recently, as City editor of *The Observer*. Ed Wolstanton GS; Marshlands Comp, Newcastle-under-Lyme; St Edmund Hall, Oxford.

This Staffordshire seat, west of Stoke-on-Trent on the edge of the Potteries, is a collection of rather varied districts. There are communities still strongly influenced by coalmining, a substantial population associated with Keele University, and some rural areas. In political terms, nonetheless, it is far less competitive: Labour continues to hold the seat by a solid margin. Map 420

## NEWCASTLE UPON TYNE CENTRAL — Lab hold

| Electorate | %Turnout | | 67,970 | 51.3% | 2001 | 69,781 | 66.05% | 1997 |
|---|---|---|---|---|---|---|---|---|
| Cousins J | | Lab | 19,169 | 54.97% | -4.2% | 27,272 | 59.17% | Lab |
| Psallidas S | | LD | 7,564 | 21.69% | 6.69% | 10,792 | 23.42% | C |
| Ruff A | | C | 7,414 | 21.26% | -2.16% | 6,911 | 15.0% | LD |
| Potts G | | Soc Lab | 723 | 2.07% | | 1,113 | 2.41% | Ref |
| Lab to LD swing | 5.44% | | 34,870 | Lab maj 11,605 | | 46,088 | Lab maj 16,480 | |
| | | | | 33.28% | | | 35.75% | |

**JIM COUSINS,** b Feb 21, 1944. Elected 1987. Member, Select Cttees: Treasury, 1997-2001; Public Service, 1995-97; Trade and Industry, 1989-92. Sec, all-party finance grp, 1999-. Lab spokesman, foreign affairs, 1994-95; trade and industry, 1992-94. Former contract researcher and lecturer in steel, shipbuilding and inner city job markets for trade unions, Commission on Industrial Relations and Depts of Employment and Environment. Tyne and Wear county cllr, 1973-86 (dep leader, 1981-86). Ed New College, Oxford; LSE. e-mail: jcousins@globalnet.co.uk tel: 0191-281 9888 fax: 0191-281 3383

The term "central" here is somewhat misleading in that it implies the inner city. In fact, more of what Americans might call "downtown" Newcastle is in the Tyne Bridge constituency. Central consists mostly of the northern sector above the city centre, and adjacent suburbs; both of Newcastle's universities are here. There was a respectable Tory vote in the seat but it was badly eroded in 1997. Labour is still clearly the dominant political force. Map 421

## NEWCASTLE UPON TYNE EAST & WALLSEND — Lab hold

| Electorate | %Turnout | | 61,494 | 53.17% | 2001 | 63,272 | 65.73% | 1997 |
|---|---|---|---|---|---|---|---|---|
| Brown N | | Lab | 20,642 | 63.14% | -8.05% | 29,607 | 71.19% | Lab |
| Ord D | | LD | 6,419 | 19.63% | 9.01% | 5,796 | 13.94% | C |
| Troman T | | C | 3,873 | 11.85% | -2.09% | 4,415 | 10.62% | LD |
| Gray A | | Green | 651 | 1.99% | | 966 | 2.32% | Ref |
| Narang Dr H | | Ind | 563 | 1.72% | | 642 | 1.54% | Soc Lab |
| Carpenter Ms B | | Soc Lab | 420 | 1.28% | -0.26% | 163 | 0.39% | Comm Brit |
| Levy M | | Comm | 126 | 0.39% | | | | |
| Lab to LD swing | 8.53% | | 32,694 | Lab maj 14,223 | | 41,589 | Lab maj 23,811 | |
| | | | | 43.50% | | | 57.25% | |

**NICK BROWN,** b June 13, 1950. Elected here 1997; MP for Newcastle E 1983-97. Min for Work, June, 2001-; Min of Agriculture, 1998-2001. Gvt Chief Whip, 1997; dep chief whip, 1996-97; senior whip in charge of organisation, 1995-96. Shadow Dep Leader of House and campaign co-ordinator, 1992-94. Spokesman, health, 1994-95; Treasury and economic affairs, 1988-92; legal affairs, 1985-87. Newcastle upon Tyne city cllr, 1980-84. Ed Swattenden Sec Mod; Tunbridge Wells Tech HS; Manchester Univ. tel: 020-7219 6814

The title of this seat is something of a mouthful. It does at least accurately describe this mostly working-class constituency on the north bank of the Tyne. It is a combination of the eastern sectors of Newcastle with Wallsend from the Borough of North Tyneside. In political terms, however, there is not much difference between the two components of this territory. It is Labour to the core. Map 422

## NEWCASTLE UPON TYNE NORTH — Lab hold

| Electorate | %Turnout | | 63,208 | 57.54% | 2001 | 65,357 | 69.2% | 1997 |
|---|---|---|---|---|---|---|---|---|
| Henderson D | | Lab | 21,874 | 60.15% | -2.03% | 28,125 | 62.18% | Lab |
| Smith P | | C | 7,424 | 20.41% | 0.97% | 8,793 | 19.44% | C |
| Soult G | | LD | 7,070 | 19.44% | 4.9% | 6,578 | 14.54% | LD |
| | | | | | | 1,733 | 3.83% | Ref |
| Lab to C swing | 1.50% | | 36,368 | Lab maj 14,450 | | 45,229 | Lab maj 19,332 | |
| | | | | 39.73% | | | 42.74% | |

**DOUG HENDERSON,** b June 9 1949. Elected 1987. Min for Armed Forces, 1998-99; Min for Europe, 1997-98. Lab spokesman, home affairs, 1995-97; public services, 1994-95; local gvt, 1992-94; trade and industry, 1988-92. Sec, GMB parly grp, 1987-97; British-Russian grp, 1994-97. Dir, Smart People First; adviser to BIC Systems Ltd. Full-time reg organiser, GMWU and then GMB, 1975-87; research officer, GMWU, 1973-75; clerk, British Rail, 1969; apprentice, Rolls-Royce, 1966-68. Ed Waid Acad, Anstruther, Fife; Central Coll, Glasgow; Strathclyde Univ. tel: 0191-286 2024

This is quite a mixed section of the city with a suburban element which is prosperous and council estates which are definitely not. Despite the name, the seat sweeps around the northwestern edge of the city, including Newcastle Airport. It is, like all the other constituencies in this part of the North East, very solid for Labour. Map 423

## NEWPORT EAST — Lab hold

| Electorate | %Turnout | 56,118 | 55.74% | 2001 | 50,997 | 73.06% | 1997 |
|---|---|---|---|---|---|---|---|
| Howarth A | Lab | 17,120 | 54.73% | -2.92% | 21,481 | 57.65% | Lab |
| Oakley I | C | 7,246 | 23.16% | 1.8% | 7,958 | 21.36% | C |
| Cameron A | LD | 4,394 | 14.05% | 3.64% | 3,880 | 10.41% | LD |
| Batcup M | PC | 1,519 | 4.86% | 2.92% | 1,951 | 5.24% | Soc Lab |
| Screen Ms L | Soc Lab | 420 | 1.34% | -3.9% | 1,267 | 3.4% | Ref |
| Reynolds N | UK Ind | 410 | 1.31% | | 721 | 1.94% | PC |
| Griffiths R | Comm | 173 | 0.55% | | | | |
| Lab to C swing | 2.36% | 31,282 | Lab maj 9,874 | 31.56% | 37,258 | Lab maj 13,523 | 36.29% |

**ALAN HOWARTH,** b June 11, 1944. Elected here 1997; C MP for Stratford-on-Avon 1983 to Oct 1995 when he became first Tory MP to defect to Lab Party, being Lab MP until 1997. Min for Arts, 1998-2001; Min for Employment and Disabled People, 1997-98; Min, Higher Ed and Science, 1990-92; Schools Min, 1989-90. Gvt whip, 1988-89; asst gvt whip, 1987-88. Member, Select Cttees: Social Security, 1995-97; Nat Heritage, 1992-93. Chairman, all-party panel on charities and voluntary sector, 1992-97. Teacher. Ed Rugby; King's Coll, Cambridge. tel: 020-7219 6421

This South Wales port and industrial centre is the third largest town in Wales after Cardiff and Swansea. Steel - and especially the vast Llanwern steelworks - has been at the economic heart of Newport, but this relationship remains under threat. Nevertheless, it is a solid Labour seat represented now by Alan Howarth, the former Tory minister; a small local backlash against him in 1997 does not seem to have caused long-term damage. Map 424

## NEWPORT WEST — Lab hold

| Electorate | %Turnout | 59,742 | 58.69% | 2001 | 53,914 | 74.57% | 1997 |
|---|---|---|---|---|---|---|---|
| Flynn P | Lab | 18,489 | 52.73% | -7.79% | 24,331 | 60.52% | Lab |
| Morgan Dr W | C | 9,185 | 26.2% | 1.84% | 9,794 | 24.36% | C |
| Watkins Ms V | LD | 4,095 | 11.68% | 1.96% | 3,907 | 9.72% | LD |
| Salkeld A | PC | 2,510 | 7.16% | 5.55% | 1,199 | 2.98% | Ref |
| Moelwyn-Hughes H | UK Ind | 506 | 1.44% | 0.64% | 648 | 1.61% | PC |
| Cavill T | BNP | 278 | 0.79% | | 323 | 0.8% | UK Ind |
| Lab to C swing | 4.81% | 35,063 | Lab maj 9,304 | 26.54% | 40,202 | Lab maj 14,537 | 36.16% |

**PAUL FLYNN,** b Feb 9, 1935. Elected 1987. Member, Council of Europe and WEU. Lab spokesman, social security, 1988-90; Wales, 1987. Member, Transport Select Cttee, 1992-97. Columnist for *South Wales Echo* and *Golweg*, Welsh language magazine. Research officer for Llewellyn Smith, Labour MEP for SE Wales, 1984-87. Ex-chairman, Broadcasting Council for Wales. Gwent county cllr, 1974-82. Ex-steelworker. Author. Ed St Illtyd's; Univ Coll of Wales, Cardiff.
e-mail: paul flynnmp@talk21.com tel: 020-7219 3478

It is difficult to conceive now but the Conservatives actually won Newport West in 1983. There are some middle-class wards but they are heavily outnumbered now by voters in the more industrial parts, including the docks and the town centre, and a small but not insignificant ethnic minority electorate. This now looks a very safe Labour seat. Map 425

## NEWRY & ARMAGH — SDLP hold

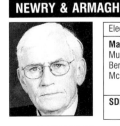

| Electorate | %Turnout | 72,466 | 76.75% | 2001 | 70,652 | 75.4% | 1997 |
|---|---|---|---|---|---|---|---|
| Mallon S | SDLP | 20,784 | 37.37% | -5.62% | 22,904 | 42.99% | SDLP |
| Murphy C | SF | 17,209 | 30.94% | 9.88% | 18,015 | 33.82% | UUP |
| Berry P | DUP | 10,795 | 19.41% | | 11,218 | 21.06% | SF |
| McRoberts Mrs S | UUP | 6,833 | 12.28% | -21.54% | 1,015 | 1.91% | Alliance |
| | | | | | 123 | 0.23% | NLP |
| SDLP to SF swing | 7.75% | 55,621 | SDLP maj 3,575 | 6.43% | 53,275 | SDLP maj 4,889 | 9.17% |

**SEAMUS MALLON,** b Aug 17, 1936. Elected 1986 by-election. Deputy First Min, NI Assembly, 2000-2001 (designate, 1998-99). Dep leader, SDLP, 1978-. Member, Agriculture Select Cttee, 1987-97. Member, British-Irish Inter-Parly Body, 1990-; NI Assembly, 1973-74 and 1982; NI Convention, 1975-76; Irish Senate, 1981-82. Armagh district cllr, 1973-86. Ed St Mary's Coll of Ed, Belfast.
tel: 02830 267933 fax: 02830 267828

This is a scenic, rural, nationalist Northern Ireland seat which has been represented by the SDLP since 1986. Roman Catholics constitute slightly more than 60 per cent of the electorate so a Unionist victory is not inconceivable if the nationalist vote were ever to split badly. This area includes the South Armagh "bandit country" and the town of Newry, where the British Army is also less than welcome. Map 426

## NORFOLK MID

C hold

| Electorate | %Turnout | | 74,911 | 70.15% | 2001 | 75,311 | 76.29% | 1997 |
|---|---|---|---|---|---|---|---|---|
| Simpson K | | C | 23,519 | 44.76% | 5.18% | 22,739 | 39.58% | C |
| Zeichner D | | Lab | 18,957 | 36.08% | -1.17% | 21,403 | 37.25% | Lab |
| Clifford-Jackson Ms V | | LD | 7,621 | 14.5% | -0.5% | 8,617 | 15.0% | LD |
| Agnew J | | UK Ind | 1,333 | 2.54% | | 3,229 | 5.62% | Ref |
| Reeve P | | Green | 1,118 | 2.13% | -0.05% | 1,254 | 2.18% | Green |
| | | | | | | 215 | 0.37% | NLP |
| Lab to C swing | 3.18% | | 52,548 | | C maj 4,562 | 57,457 | | C maj 1,336 |
| | | | | | 8.68% | | | 2.33% |

**KEITH SIMPSON,** b March 29, 1949. Elected 1997. Opposition Defence spokesman, 1998-99; opposition whip, 1999-; sec, C Backbench Defence Cttee, 1997-98. Member, Catering Select Cttee, 1998-2001. Political adviser to Tom King, Defence Sec, 1988-91. Exdir, Cranfield Security Studies Inst, Cranfield Univ; senior lecturer in war studies and international affairs, RMA Sandhurst, 1973-86. Ed Thorpe GS; Hull Univ; postgrad research, King's Coll London. e-mail: keithsimpsonmp@parliament.uk tel: 020-7219 4053 fax: 020-7219 0975

This attractive and broadly affluent East Anglia seat is an interesting amalgamation. It almost surrounds Norwich and includes parts of the Norfolk Broads, some very rural territory and more suburban constituents. On the face of it, this should be a comfortable seat for the Conservative contender. A sharp swing meant that the Tories came within a whisker of losing it in 1997, but they managed to strengthen their hold again in 2001. Map 427

## NORFOLK NORTH

LD gain

| Electorate | %Turnout | | 80,061 | 70.22% | 2001 | 77,113 | 76.27% | 1997 |
|---|---|---|---|---|---|---|---|---|
| Lamb N | | LD | 23,978 | 42.65% | 8.37% | 21,456 | 36.48% | C |
| Prior D | | C | 23,495 | 41.79% | 5.31% | 20,163 | 34.28% | LD |
| Gates M | | Lab | 7,490 | 13.32% | -11.74% | 14,736 | 25.06% | Lab |
| Sheridan M | | Green | 649 | 1.15% | | 2,458 | 4.18% | Ref |
| Simison P | | UK Ind | 608 | 1.08% | | | | |
| C to LD swing | 1.53% | | 56,220 | | LD maj 483 | 58,813 | | C maj 1,293 |
| | | | | | 0.86% | | | 2.20% |

**NORMAN LAMB,** b Sept 16, 1957. Elected 2001. Gained seat from senior C MP, David Prior. Contested seat 1992 and 1997. Member, Norwich City Council, 1987-91, leading the LDs, 1989-91. Employment lawyer. Ed Wymondham Coll, Norfolk; Leicester Univ; City of London Poly.

This marginal seat contains a sweep of the Norfolk coast including resorts such as Sheringham, Cromer and Wells-next-the-Sea, plus the greater part of the Broads and inland towns such as Holt and Fakenham. It might seem solidly Tory but owner-occupation is not especially high and there is a tradition of rural radicalism backing Labour. The outcome is usually decided by the degree of tactical voting; in 2001 the Lib Dems became the beneficiaries. Map 428

## NORFOLK NORTH WEST

C gain

| Electorate | %Turnout | | 77,387 | 66.16% | 2001 | 77,083 | 74.72% | 1997 |
|---|---|---|---|---|---|---|---|---|
| Bellingham H | | C | 24,846 | 48.52% | 7.01% | 25,250 | 43.84% | Lab |
| Turner Dr G | | Lab | 21,361 | 41.72% | -2.12% | 23,911 | 41.51% | C |
| Mack Dr I | | LD | 4,292 | 8.38% | -1.19% | 5,513 | 9.57% | LD |
| Durrant I | | UK Ind | 704 | 1.37% | | 2,923 | 5.07% | Ref |
| Lab to C swing | 4.57% | | 51,203 | | C maj 3,485 | 57,597 | | Lab maj 1,339 |
| | | | | | 6.81% | | | 2.33% |

**HENRY BELLINGHAM,** b Sept 29, 1955. Elected 2001. Wins seat back from George Turner, Lab MP for this seat 1983-97. PPS to Malcolm Rifkind, Foreign, Defence and Transport Sec, 1990-97. Former chairman, C council on Eastern Europe. Investment consultant. Barrister. Ed Eton; Magdalene Coll, Cambridge; Inns of Court Sch of Law.

This, another marginal Norfolk seat, is based on the ancient port town of King's Lynn, now with substantial farming-related industry, and the surrounding flatness of the Fens. The seat also contains the seaside resort of Hunstanton and the royal estate at Sandringham. King's Lynn has always been sympathetic to Labour but has invariably been trumped by solid Tory voting elsewhere. Labour won in 1997 but the Tories took over again four years later. Map 429

## NORFOLK SOUTH — C hold

| Electorate    %Turnout | | 82,710 | 67.62% | 2001 | 79,239 | 78.37% | 1997 |
|---|---|---|---|---|---|---|---|
| **Bacon R** | **C** | **23,589** | **42.18%** | **2.03%** | **24,935** | **40.15%** | **C** |
| Lee Dr A | LD | 16,696 | 29.85% | 1.58% | 17,557 | 28.27% | LD |
| Wells M | Lab | 13,719 | 24.53% | -1.54% | 16,188 | 26.07% | Lab |
| Ross-Wagenknecht Ms S | Green | 1,069 | 1.91% | 1.13% | 2,533 | 4.08% | Ref |
| Neal J | UK Ind | 856 | 1.53% | 0.89% | 484 | 0.78% | Green |
| | | | | | 400 | 0.64% | UK Ind |
| **LD to C swing** | **0.22%** | **55,929** | | **C maj 6,893** | **62,097** | | **C maj 7,378** |
| | | | | 12.32% | | | 11.88% |

**RICHARD BACON,** b Dec 3, 1962. Elected 2001. Inherits the safest Norfolk seat from John MacGregor, who held it from Feb 1974. Financial journalist. Deputy dir, Management Consultancies Assoc, 1994-96. Brunswick Public Relations, 1996-99; MD, English Word Factory, 1999-. Ed King's Sch, Worcester; LSE.

This seat, lying to the south of Norwich, is based on small towns such as Diss, Wymondham, Harleston and Loddon and dozens of villages extending towards the Suffolk border. It lacks any dominant settlement and this may explain why the Conservatives retained a decent majority here in 1997 while being badly attacked by Labour in other parts of the county, and also why they repeated the feat in 2001. Map 430

## NORFOLK SOUTH WEST — C hold

| Electorate    %Turnout | | 83,903 | 63.11% | 2001 | 80,236 | 73.28% | 1997 |
|---|---|---|---|---|---|---|---|
| **Shephard Mrs G** | **C** | **27,633** | **52.19%** | **10.19%** | **24,694** | **42.0%** | **C** |
| Hanson Ms A | Lab | 18,267 | 34.5% | -3.31% | 22,230 | 37.81% | Lab |
| Dean G | LD | 5,681 | 10.73% | -3.18% | 8,178 | 13.91% | LD |
| Smith I | UK Ind | 1,368 | 2.58% | | 3,694 | 6.28% | Ref |
| **Lab to C swing** | **6.75%** | **52,949** | | **C maj 9,366** | **58,796** | | **C maj 2,464** |
| | | | | 17.69% | | | 4.19% |

**GILLIAN SHEPHARD,** b Jan 22, 1940. Elected 1987. Former Shadow Leader of Commons and Shadow Chancellor of Duchy of Lancaster. Ed and Employment Sec, 1995-97; Ed Sec, 1994-95; Agriculture, Fisheries and Food Min, 1993-94; joined Cabinet, 1992 as Employment Sec. Min of State, Treasury, 1990-92; Social Security Under-Sec, 1989-90. A dep chairwoman, C Party, 1991-92. Privy Counsellor, 1992. Norfolk county cllr, 1977-89. Ex-schools inspector and Mental Health Act commissioner. Ed N Walsham Girls' HS, Norfolk; St Hilda's Coll, Oxford (hon fellow, 1991).

A seat bearing this name was once the most distinctive marginal anywhere in Britain. However, boundary changes in the 1980s made it somewhat more representative of the rest of Norfolk. This is a predominantly agricultural area with strong links to the military and including big airfields; the main towns are Thetford, Swaffham and Downham Market. It has been solidly Tory from the late 1970s despite a very strong Labour showing in 1997. Map 431

## NORMANTON — Lab hold

| Electorate    %Turnout | | 65,392 | 52.23% | 2001 | 62,980 | 68.28% | 1997 |
|---|---|---|---|---|---|---|---|
| **O'Brien W** | **Lab** | **19,152** | **56.07%** | **-4.5%** | **26,046** | **60.57%** | **Lab** |
| Smith G | C | 9,215 | 26.98% | 3.37% | 10,153 | 23.61% | C |
| Pearson S | LD | 4,990 | 14.61% | 2.18% | 5,347 | 12.43% | LD |
| Appleyard M | Soc Lab | 798 | 2.34% | | 1,458 | 3.39% | Ref |
| **Lab to C swing** | **3.93%** | **34,155** | | **Lab maj 9,937** | **43,004** | | **Lab maj 15,893** |
| | | | | 29.09% | | | 36.96% |

**BILL O'BRIEN,** b Jan 25, 1929. Elected 1983. Member, Environment Select Cttee; member, Chairmen's Panel; Public Accounts Cttee, 1983-88. Lab spokesman, NI, 1992-94; local gvt, 1987-92. Chairman, all-party grps: inland waterways; sustainable waste. Ex-chairman, PLP Home Affairs Cttee; chairman, Urban, county and metropolitan district cllr, 1951-83, serving on Wakefield District Council, 1973-83. Miner, 1945-83. Ed St Joseph's Sch, Castleford; Leeds Univ (day release).

This constituency is set in West Yorkshire. It might be most accurately described as the area surrounding Wakefield but it does have a sense of shared identity. There are some very safe Labour areas, where the political influence of coalmining remains strong, partially offset by more middle-class territory. Labour would not, however, have any reason to feel threatened. Map 432

## NORTHAMPTON NORTH
**Lab hold**

| Electorate | %Turnout | | 74,124 | 55.98% | 2001 | 73,664 | 70.18% | 1997 |
|---|---|---|---|---|---|---|---|---|
| **Keeble Ms S** | Lab | | 20,507 | 49.42% | -3.28% | 27,247 | 52.7% | Lab |
| Whelan J | C | | 12,614 | 30.4% | -2.96% | 17,247 | 33.36% | C |
| Church R | LD | | 7,363 | 17.74% | 5.01% | 6,579 | 12.73% | LD |
| Torbica D | UK Ind | | 596 | 1.44% | 0.54% | 464 | 0.9% | UK Ind |
| White G | Soc All | | 414 | 1.0% | | 161 | 0.31% | NLP |
| **Lab to C swing** | 0.16% | | 41,494 | | Lab maj 7,893 | 51,698 | | Lab maj 10,000 |
| | | | | | 19.02% | | | 19.34% |

**SALLY KEEBLE,** b Oct 13, 1951. Elected 1997. Under Sec, Dept of Transport, Local Govt and Regions, June, 2001-. Head, GMB communications, 1986-90. Southwark cllr (leader, 1990-93). Asst dir, external relations, ILEA, 1984-86. Public affairs consultant. Journalist on *Daily News*, Durban, 1974-79, and *The Birmingham Post*, 1979-83. Member, Fabian Soc; Anti-Racist Alliance. Journalist and author. Ed Cheltenham Ladies' Coll; Oxford Univ; Univ of South Africa.

Northampton was one of the last places in the UK to be designated a new town and even then this was an uneasy exercise as a large traditional county town was already in existence. This constituency contains most of the new town influence as it spreads towards Wellingborough. The Conservatives hung on here through the 1980s despite less than favourable social conditions. Labour finally broke through in 1997. Map 433

## NORTHAMPTON SOUTH
**Lab hold**

| Electorate | %Turnout | | 85,271 | 59.84% | 2001 | 79,384 | 71.94% | 1997 |
|---|---|---|---|---|---|---|---|---|
| **Clarke T** | Lab | | 21,882 | 42.88% | 0.48% | 24,214 | 42.4% | Lab |
| Vara S | C | | 20,997 | 41.15% | 0.05% | 23,470 | 41.1% | C |
| Simpson A | LD | | 6,355 | 12.45% | 1.39% | 6,316 | 11.06% | LD |
| Clark D | UK Ind | | 1,237 | 2.42% | 0.39% | 1,405 | 2.46% | Ref |
| Harvey Miss T | LP | | 362 | 0.71% | | 1,159 | 2.03% | UK Ind |
| Johnson Ms C | ProLife | | 196 | 0.38% | | 541 | 0.95% | NLP |
| **C to Lab swing** | 0.22% | | 51,029 | | Lab maj 885 | 57,105 | | Lab maj 744 |
| | | | | | 1.73% | | | 1.30% |

**TONY CLARKE,** b Sept 6, 1963. Elected 1997. Member, NI Select Cttee. Northampton borough cllr, 1991-. Dir, Northampton Town Football Club (non-pecuniary); vice-chairman, Northampton Town Supporters Trust. Member, CWU. Social work trainer, Northants County Council. Ed Lings Upper, Northampton; Inst of Training and Development; Inst of Safety and Health.
e-mail: tonyclarkemp@hotmail.com tel: 01604 250044 fax: 01604 250055

This part of Northampton contains most of the traditional county town, the Nene Valley ward, and some distinctly rural territory with affluent villages. The urban centre has invariably leant towards Labour but historically it has been swamped by the rest of the constituency. A huge swing delivered the Labour Party an unexpected victory in 1997 and it hung on with another tiny majority four years later. This is now firmly a marginal. Map 434

## NORTHAVON
**LD hold**

| Electorate | %Turnout | | 78,841 | 70.72% | 2001 | 78,943 | 79.21% | 1997 |
|---|---|---|---|---|---|---|---|---|
| **Webb S** | LD | | 29,217 | 52.4% | 10.02% | 26,500 | 42.38% | LD |
| Ruxton Dr C | C | | 19,340 | 34.69% | -4.27% | 24,363 | 38.96% | C |
| Hall R | Lab | | 6,450 | 11.57% | -4.05% | 9,767 | 15.62% | Lab |
| Carver Mrs C | UK Ind | | 751 | 1.35% | | 1,900 | 3.04% | Ref |
| **C to LD swing** | 7.15% | | 55,758 | | LD maj 9,877 | 62,530 | | LD maj 2,137 |
| | | | | | 17.71% | | | 3.42% |

**STEVE WEBB,** b July 18, 1965. Elected 1997. Chief LD spokesman, work and pensions, June 2001; spokesman, social security, 1999-. Visiting professor, social policy, Bath Univ, 1997-. Member, Amnesty; World Development Movement; formerly worked for Inst of Fiscal Studies. Ed Dartmouth HS; Hertford Coll, Oxford.
e-mail: stevewebb@cix.co.uk www.stevewebb.org.uk
tel: 01454 322100 fax: 01454 866515

This seat includes much of South Gloucestershire. It has no dominant town but a number of significant settlements to the northeast of Bristol including Chipping Sodbury, Yate and Thornbury. It is otherwise quite rural with scores of small villages. It looks like Tory territory, so it was quite a surprise when, in 1997, the Liberal Democrats snatched the seat, and strongly consolidated their lead in 2001. Map 435

## NORWICH NORTH — Lab hold

| Electorate | %Turnout | | 74,911 | 60.89% | 2001 | 72,521 | 75.92% | 1997 |
|---|---|---|---|---|---|---|---|---|
| Gibson Dr I | Lab | | 21,624 | 47.41% | -2.26% | 27,346 | 49.67% | Lab |
| Mason Ms K | C | | 15,761 | 34.55% | 2.08% | 17,876 | 32.47% | C |
| Toye Ms M | LD | | 6,750 | 14.8% | 2.17% | 6,951 | 12.63% | LD |
| Tinch R | Green | | 797 | 1.75% | | 1,777 | 3.23% | Ref |
| Cheyney G | UK Ind | | 471 | 1.03% | | 512 | 0.93% | LCP |
| Betts M | Ind | | 211 | 0.46% | | 495 | 0.9% | Soc Lab |
| | | | | | | 100 | 0.18% | NLP |
| Lab to C swing | 2.17% | | 45,614 | Lab maj 5,863 | | 55,057 | Lab maj 9,470 | |
| | | | | 12.85% | | | 17.20% | |

**IAN GIBSON,** b Sept 26, 1938. Elected 1997. Member, Select Cttee, Science and Tech, 1997-2001. Chairman, Parly Office of Science and Tech (POST); all-party cancer grp; MSF Parly Cttee. Co-manager, parly football team. Member, Medical Research Council and cancer research campaign grants cttees. Governor, John Innes biotechnology centre. Former exec cttee member, ASTMS/MSF. Founder and coach, Red Rose FC for 8 to 11-year-old children. Ex-Dean of biological sciences, East Anglia Univ. Ed Dumfries local state schs; Edinburgh Univ.

The cathedral and university city of Norwich, county town, regional centre and famous for its mustard and footwear, was historically the strongest section of Norfolk for Labour, a tradition that faltered in the 1980s. This section is, however, the more affluent half and largely consists of suburban electors. The Labour Party fought back to come within a whisker of victory in 1992 and then romped home five years later and again in 2001. Map 436

## NORWICH SOUTH — Lab hold

| Electorate | %Turnout | | 65,792 | 64.74% | 2001 | 70,009 | 72.56% | 1997 |
|---|---|---|---|---|---|---|---|---|
| Clarke C | Lab | | 19,367 | 45.47% | -6.24% | 26,267 | 51.71% | Lab |
| French A | C | | 10,551 | 24.77% | 1.09% | 12,028 | 23.68% | C |
| Aalders-Dunthorne A | LD | | 9,640 | 22.63% | 4.01% | 9,457 | 18.62% | LD |
| Holmes A | Green | | 1,434 | 3.37% | 1.92% | 1,464 | 2.88% | Ref |
| Buffrey A | LCA | | 620 | 1.46% | | 765 | 1.51% | LCP |
| Manningham E | Soc All | | 507 | 1.19% | | 736 | 1.45% | Green |
| Mills T | UK Ind | | 473 | 1.11% | | 84 | 0.17% | NLP |
| Lab to C swing | 3.67% | | 42,592 | Lab maj 8,816 | | 50,801 | Lab maj 14,239 | |
| | | | | 20.70% | | | 28.03% | |

**CHARLES CLARKE,** b Sept 21, 1950. Elected 1997. Party chairman and Min without Portfolio, June 2001-; Min of State, Home Office, 1999-2001. Parly Under-Sec, Department for Ed and Employment, 1998-99. Lab nat policy forum, 1998-2001. Ex-head, Neil Kinnock's private office. Ex-pres, NUS. Public affairs management consultant. Ed King's Coll, Cambridge (Pres of Union 1971-72).

This seat contains the city centre, the cathedral and much of the University of East Anglia. It has a much higher proportion of council house tenants than its neighbour in the north of the city and the combination of this vote with the middle-class radicalism often associated with university towns has helped to entrench Labour in this area. Map 437

## NOTTINGHAM EAST — Lab hold

| Electorate | %Turnout | | 65,339 | 45.5% | 2001 | 65,581 | 60.6% | 1997 |
|---|---|---|---|---|---|---|---|---|
| Heppell J | Lab | | 17,530 | 58.96% | -3.33% | 24,755 | 62.29% | Lab |
| Allan R | C | | 7,210 | 24.25% | 0.76% | 9,336 | 23.49% | C |
| Ball T | LD | | 3,874 | 13.03% | 2.95% | 4,008 | 10.08% | LD |
| Radcliff P | Soc All | | 1,117 | 3.76% | | 1,645 | 4.14% | Ref |
| Lab to C swing | 2.04% | | 29,731 | Lab maj 10,320 | | 39,744 | Lab maj 15,419 | |
| | | | | 34.71% | | | 38.80% | |

**JOHN HEPPELL,** b Nov 3, 1948. Elected 1992. Gvt whip, 2001-. PPS to John Prescott and to Lord Richard, Leader of House of Lords, 1997-98. Ex-joint vice-chairman, PLP transport cttee; ex-chairman, all-party home safety grp; head injuries grp; ex-treas, breast cancer grp. Nottinghamshire county cllr, 1981-93. Formerly workshop supervisor, British Rail. Member, Co-op Party; Nottingham Anti-Apartheid. Ed Rutherford GS; SE Northumberland Tech Coll; Ashington Tech Coll.

This seat consists of a long strip of wards right on the edge of the city. They are quite diverse in terms of economic interest, affluence and race. There are some middle-class districts here but the overall owner-occupation rate is distinctly modest. The Tories held the constituency while Labour was out of favour nationally in the 1980s. It is difficult to envisage how they would recapture it now. Map 438

## NOTTINGHAM NORTH — Lab hold

| Electorate | %Turnout | | 64,281 | 46.74% | 2001 | 65,698 | 63.02% | 1997 |
|---|---|---|---|---|---|---|---|---|
| Allen G | | Lab | 19,392 | 64.55% | -1.16% | 27,203 | 65.71% | Lab |
| Wright M | | C | 7,152 | 23.81% | 3.52% | 8,402 | 20.29% | C |
| Lee R | | LD | 3,177 | 10.58% | 2.61% | 3,301 | 7.97% | LD |
| Botham A | | Soc Lab | 321 | 1.07% | | 1,858 | 4.49% | Ref |
| | | | | | | 637 | 1.54% | Soc |
| Lab to C swing | 2.34% | | 30,042 | Lab maj 12,240 | | 41,401 | Lab maj 18,801 | |
| | | | | 40.74% | | | 45.42% | |

**GRAHAM ALLEN,** b Jan 11, 1953. Elected 1987. Former Gvt whip. Lab spokesman: transport, 1995-97; nat heritage, 1994-95; media, 1994; home affairs, 1992-94; social security, 1991-92. Member, Select Cttees: Procedure, 1990-91; Members' Interests, 1987-90; Public Accounts Cttee, 1988-91. Chairman, PLP Treasury and Civil Service Cttee, 1990-91. Ex-joint vice-chairman, all-party cricket grp. Reg research and ed officer, GMB, 1986-87; nat co-ordinator, political funds campaign for trades union coordinating cttee, 1984-86. Ed Forest Fields GS; City of London Poly; Leeds Univ.

This is probably the most traditionally working-class of the three Nottingham constituencies. There are a large number of council tenants and the seat is distinctly industrial in flavour. It should always be considered safe for Labour and it has been in all elections since the party's 1983 debacle. Map 439

## NOTTINGHAM SOUTH — Lab hold

| Electorate | %Turnout | | 73,049 | 50.11% | 2001 | 72,418 | 67.0% | 1997 |
|---|---|---|---|---|---|---|---|---|
| Simpson A | | Lab | 19,949 | 54.5% | -0.79% | 26,825 | 55.29% | Lab |
| Manning Mrs W | | C | 9,960 | 27.21% | -0.53% | 13,461 | 27.74% | C |
| Mulloy K | | LD | 6,064 | 16.57% | 3.66% | 6,265 | 12.91% | LD |
| Bartrop D | | UK Ind | 632 | 1.73% | | 1,523 | 3.14% | Ref |
| | | | | | | 446 | 0.92% | Nat Dem |
| Lab to C swing | 0.13% | | 36,605 | Lab maj 9,989 | | 48,520 | Lab maj 13,364 | |
| | | | | 27.29% | | | 27.55% | |

**ALAN SIMPSON,** b Sept 20, 1948. Elected 1992. Chairman, all-party grps: social services; warm homes. Sec, Socialist Campaign Grp of Lab MPs. Notts county cllr, 1985-93. Ex-chairman, WasteNotts Ltd, a Notts County Council waste disposal co. Research and info officer with Nottingham Racial Equality Council, 1979-92. Author of books and articles on housing, racism, Europe, globalisations, economics and GM foods. Member, Unison. Ed Bootle GS; Nottingham Trent Poly.
e-mail: simpsona@parliament.uk tel: 0115-956 0460 fax: 0115-956 0445

This is potentially the most unpredictable constituency in Nottingham, although it may appear solidly Labour at present. It is polarised between industrial areas, based around the city centre, which have historically supported Labour, and an ad hoc coalition of more affluent middle-class electors and the university area. The lecturers had abandoned the Tories by 1992, however, and the odds are now stacked against the party. Map 440

## NUNEATON — Lab hold

| Electorate | %Turnout | | 72,101 | 60.07% | 2001 | 72,032 | 74.29% | 1997 |
|---|---|---|---|---|---|---|---|---|
| Olner B | | Lab | 22,577 | 52.13% | -4.08% | 30,080 | 56.21% | Lab |
| Lancaster M | | C | 15,042 | 34.73% | 3.82% | 16,540 | 30.91% | C |
| Ferguson T | | LD | 4,820 | 11.13% | 2.29% | 4,732 | 8.84% | LD |
| James B | | UK Ind | 873 | 2.02% | 1.58% | 1,533 | 2.86% | Ref |
| | | | | | | 390 | 0.73% | Loc Ind |
| | | | | | | 238 | 0.44% | UK Ind |
| Lab to C swing | 3.95% | | 43,312 | Lab maj 7,535 | | 53,513 | Lab maj 13,540 | |
| | | | | 17.40% | | | 25.30% | |

**BILL OLNER,** b May 9, 1942. Elected 1992. Member, Select Cttees: Environment, Transport and Regions, 1997-2001; Environment, 1995-97. Chairman, all-party child abduction grp, 1994-; cable and satellite TV grp; engineering development grp. Member, exec cttee, CPA, 1995-. Nuneaton and Bedworth borough cllr, 1972-92 (leader, 1982-87); Mayor of Nuneaton and Bedford, 1986-87. Co-founder, Mary Ann Evans Hospice, Nuneaton, and chairman, hospice trustees. Engineer with Rolls-Royce and ex-shop steward. Ed Atherstone Sec Mod; N Warwickshire Tech Coll.

This is a working-class and industrial town and a former centre for the old Warwickshire coalfield, situated on the eastern edge of the West Midlands conurbation. It has therefore historically been linked with the Labour Party. That tradition is partially offset by a quite high rate of owner-occupation. The Conservatives won here in 1983 and 1987. Labour has again been the dominant political force since then. Map 441

## OCHIL Lab hold

| Electorate | %Turnout | | 57,554 | 61.34% | 2001 | 56,572 | 77.4% | 1997 |
|---|---|---|---|---|---|---|---|---|
| O'Neill M | Lab | | 16,004 | 45.33% | 0.32% | 19,707 | 45.01% | Lab |
| Brown K | SNP | | 10,655 | 30.18% | -4.2% | 15,055 | 34.38% | SNP |
| Campbell A | C | | 4,235 | 12.0% | -2.58% | 6,383 | 14.58% | C |
| Edie P | LD | | 3,253 | 9.21% | 4.04% | 2,262 | 5.17% | LD |
| Thompson Ms P | SSP | | 751 | 2.13% | | 210 | 0.48% | Ref |
| Approaching F | Loony | | 405 | 1.15% | | 104 | 0.24% | D Nat |
| | | | | | | 65 | 0.15% | NLP |
| SNP to Lab swing | 2.26% | | 35,303 | Lab maj 5,349 | | 43,786 | Lab maj 4,652 | |
| | | | | 15.15% | | | 10.63% | |

**MARTIN O'NEILL** b Jan 6, 1945. Elected here 1997; MP for Clackmannan 1983-97, and for Stirlingshire E and Clackmannan 1979-83. Chairman, Trade and Industry Select Cttee, 1995-2001; member, Scottish Affairs Select Cttee, 1979-80. Lab spokesman, energy, 1992-95; defence and disarmament, 1984-92; Scotland, 1980-84. Ex-teacher. Ed Trinity Acad; Heriot-Watt Univ; Moray House Coll of Ed, Edinburgh.

The rolling Ochil Hills run across the eastern central band of Scotland, between Stirling and Perth. The dominant district in this seat is Clackmannan, an industrial working-class town, and a number of smaller but similar settlements such as Alloa, Dollar and Kinross. There are only two viable political parties here, Labour and the SNP. The former has been dominant in recent years but the nationalists are strong enough to make for a spirited contest. Map 442

## OGMORE Lab hold

| Electorate | %Turnout | | 52,185 | 58.16% | 2001 | 52,078 | 73.1% | 1997 |
|---|---|---|---|---|---|---|---|---|
| Powell Sir Raymond | Lab | | 18,833 | 62.05% | -11.93% | 28,163 | 73.98% | Lab |
| Pulman Ms A | PC | | 4,259 | 14.03% | 6.99% | 3,716 | 9.76% | C |
| Lewis I | LD | | 3,878 | 12.78% | 3.56% | 3,510 | 9.22% | LD |
| Hill R | C | | 3,383 | 11.15% | 1.39% | 2,679 | 7.04% | PC |
| Lab to PC swing | 9.46% | | 30,353 | Lab maj 14,574 | | 38,068 | Lab maj 24,447 | |
| | | | | 48.02% | | | 64.22% | |

**SIR RAYMOND POWELL,** b June 19, 1928. Elected 1979. Chairman, Accommodation and Works Cttee, 1991-97; member, Finance and Services Cttee, 1992-97; Selection Cttee, 1992-95; Services Cttee, 1987-91 (chairman of New Parly Building Sub-Cttee, 1987-91); Select Cttees: Employment, 1979-82; Welsh Affairs, 1982-85. Chairman, all-party showman's guild, 1987-96. Chairman, Welsh Lab Party, 1977-78. Ex-British Rail employee; shop manager; admin officer, Welsh Water Authority. Ed Pentre GS; Nat Council of Labour Colls; LSE.

This is an industrial seat situated in the heart of the South Wales Valleys, taking its name from Ogmore Vale and Ogmore Forest between Maesteg and Pontypridd, an area that boomed with coal then slumped with its demise. It consists of small towns dominated by terraced housing, close communities and the chapel. It has a decent rate of owner-occupation but this, in Wales, is often politically irrelevant. A very strong Labour area. Map 443

## OLD BEXLEY & SIDCUP C hold

| Electorate | %Turnout | | 67,841 | 62.11% | 2001 | 68,044 | 75.53% | 1997 |
|---|---|---|---|---|---|---|---|---|
| Conway D | C | | 19,130 | 45.4% | 3.35% | 21,608 | 42.05% | C |
| Dickson J | Lab | | 15,785 | 37.46% | 2.36% | 18,039 | 35.1% | Lab |
| Ford Ms B | LD | | 5,792 | 13.75% | -2.37% | 8,284 | 16.12% | LD |
| Cronin Mrs J | UK Ind | | 1,426 | 3.38% | 2.43% | 2,457 | 4.78% | Ref |
| | | | | | | 489 | 0.95% | UK Ind |
| | | | | | | 415 | 0.81% | BNP |
| | | | | | | 99 | 0.19% | NLP |
| Lab to C swing | 0.49% | | 42,133 | C maj 3,345 | | 51,391 | C maj 3,569 | |
| | | | | 7.94% | | | 6.95% | |

**DEREK CONWAY,** b Feb 15, 1953. Elected here 2001. MP for Shrewsbury & Atcham 1983-97. Takes over seat from former Prime Minister, Sir Edward Heath. Gvt whip, 1994-97; member, several Select Cttees. Former leader, Tyne and Wear Metropolitan Council, 1979-82. Vice-chairman, Young Conservatives, 1973-75. Chief executive, Cats Protection League. Ed Beacon Hill Boys' Sch; Gateshead Tech Coll; Newcastle Poly.

Sir Edward Heath, the former Tory Prime Minister, retired as Father of the House of Commons in 2001, having represented sections of this seat for half a century. This section of suburban southeast London has long been solidly Tory and enjoys a very high rate of owner-occupation (the highest in Greater London). Labour did well to come reasonably close in 1997 and similarly in 2001. Map 444

## OLDHAM EAST & SADDLEWORTH — Lab hold

| Electorate | %Turnout | | 74,511 | 60.96% | 2001 | 73,189 | 73.92% | 1997 |
|---|---|---|---|---|---|---|---|---|
| **Woolas P** | | **Lab** | **17,537** | **38.61%** | **-3.06%** | **22,546** | **41.67%** | **Lab** |
| Sykes H | | LD | 14,811 | 32.61% | -2.8% | 19,157 | 35.41% | LD |
| Heeley C | | C | 7,304 | 16.08% | -3.63% | 10,666 | 19.71% | C |
| Treacy M | | BNP | 5,091 | 11.21% | | 1,116 | 2.06% | Ref |
| Little Ms B | | UK Ind | 677 | 1.49% | | 470 | 0.87% | Soc Lab |
| | | | | | | 146 | 0.27% | NLP |
| **Lab to LD swing** | **0.13%** | | **45,420** | Lab maj 2,726 | | **54,101** | Lab maj 3,389 | |
| | | | | 6.00% | | | 6.26% | |

**PHIL WOOLAS,** b Dec 11, 1959. Elected 1997; contested Littleborough and Saddleworth by-election 1995. Asst chief whip, June 2001. PPS to Transport Min, Lord Macdonald of Tradeston, 1999-2001. Dir of communications, GMB; ex-TV producer. Adviser, Friends of John McCarthy campaign. Organised "Fat Cats" campaign against high pay in privatised industries, 1995. Member, Lancs CCC. Ed Nelson GS; Nelson and Colne Coll; Manchester Univ.

This is an unusual seat on the northeast of Greater Manchester in both social and political terms. It is sharply polarised between the tough urban politics of Oldham itself and the rather affluent and desirable housing to be found in Saddleworth's valleys. There are enough commuters to provide the Conservatives with a reasonable political base but they have been badly eclipsed recently. This is now a Labour-Liberal Democrat marginal. Map 445

## OLDHAM WEST & ROYTON — Lab hold

| Electorate | %Turnout | | 69,409 | 57.57% | 2001 | 69,203 | 66.09% | 1997 |
|---|---|---|---|---|---|---|---|---|
| **Meacher M** | | **Lab** | **20,441** | **51.15%** | **-7.65%** | **26,894** | **58.8%** | **Lab** |
| Reed D | | C | 7,076 | 17.71% | -5.67% | 10,693 | 23.38% | C |
| Griffin N | | BNP | 6,552 | 16.4% | | 5,434 | 11.88% | LD |
| Ramsbottom M | | LD | 4,975 | 12.45% | 0.57% | 1,311 | 2.87% | Soc Lab |
| Roney D | | Green | 918 | 2.3% | | 1,157 | 2.53% | Ref |
| | | | | | | 249 | 0.54% | NLP |
| **Lab to C swing** | **0.99%** | | **39,962** | Lab maj 13,365 | | **45,738** | Lab maj 16,201 | |
| | | | | 33.44% | | | 35.42% | |

**MICHAEL MEACHER,** b Nov 4, 1939. Elected here 1997; MP, Oldham W 1970-97. Min for Environment, 1997-2001 and from June 2001. Member, Shadow Cabinet, 1983-97. Lab spokesman, environmental protection, 1996-97; employment, 1995-96; transport, 1994-95; Citizen's Charter, 1993-94; overseas development and co-operation, 1992-93; social security, 1989-92. Contested dep leadership after 1983 election. Member, Lab NEC, 1983-88. Visiting Professor, dept of sociology, Surrey Univ, 1980-87. Ed Berkhamsted Sch; New Coll, Oxford; LSE.

This seat contains the bulk of the former cotton mill town of Oldham, including the centre, plus some additional territory, such as the towns of Royton and Chadderton. Much of it consists of traditional working-class electors, plus an expanding Asian population. Racial tensions exploded into street rioting during the 2001 campaign and more than 6,500 subsequently voted for the British National Party. But this remains a strong Labour seat. Map 446

## ORKNEY & SHETLAND — LD hold

| Electorate | %Turnout | | 31,909 | 52.44% | 2001 | 32,291 | 64.0% | 1997 |
|---|---|---|---|---|---|---|---|---|
| **Carmichael A** | | **LD** | **6,919** | **41.35%** | **-10.64%** | **10,743** | **51.99%** | **LD** |
| Mochrie R | | Lab | 3,444 | 20.58% | 2.31% | 3,775 | 18.27% | Lab |
| Firth J | | C | 3,121 | 18.65% | 6.42% | 2,624 | 12.7% | SNP |
| Mowat J | | SNP | 2,473 | 14.78% | 2.08% | 2,527 | 12.23% | C |
| Andrews P | | SSP | 776 | 4.64% | | 820 | 3.97% | Ref |
| | | | | | | 116 | 0.56% | NLP |
| | | | | | | 60 | 0.29% | Ind |
| **LD to Lab swing** | **6.48%** | | **16,733** | LD maj 3,475 | | **20,665** | LD maj 6,968 | |
| | | | | 20.77% | | | 33.72% | |

**ALISTAIR CARMICHAEL,** b July 15, 1965. Inherits seat from Jim Wallace, leader of the Scottish LDs and Deputy First Min of the Scottish Parliament. Contested Paisley S in 1987. Former hotel manager and solicitor. Procurator Fiscal Depute, 1993-96. Ed Islay HS, Argyll; Aberdeen Univ (Scottish Law).

This is the farthest-flung constituency in the UK and a highly distinctive one as well. Lerwick, the capital of Shetland, is almost as close to Bergen in Norway as it is to Aberdeen. North Sea oil brought a population boom in the 1970s but there are still only some 31,000 electors scattered across the many islands. The seat was held for many years by Jo Grimond, leader of the Liberal Party, and then by Jim Wallace, leader of the Scottish Liberal Democrats. Map 447

## ORPINGTON — C hold

| Electorate | %Turnout | | 74,423 | 68.41% | 2001 | 78,749 | 76.4% | 1997 |
|---|---|---|---|---|---|---|---|---|
| **Horam J** | | **C** | **22,334** | **43.87%** | **3.28%** | **24,417** | **40.59%** | **C** |
| Maines C | | LD | 22,065 | 43.34% | 7.66% | 21,465 | 35.68% | LD |
| Purnell C | | Lab | 5,517 | 10.84% | -7.03% | 10,753 | 17.87% | Lab |
| Youles J | | UK Ind | 996 | 1.96% | 1.09% | 2,316 | 3.85% | Ref |
| | | | | | | 526 | 0.87% | UK Ind |
| | | | | | | 494 | 0.82% | Lib |
| | | | | | | 191 | 0.32% | ProLife |
| **C to LD swing** | **2.19%** | | **50,912** | | **C maj 269** | **60,162** | | **C maj 2,952** |
| | | | | | 0.53% | | | 4.91% |

**JOHN HORAM,** b March 7, 1939. Elected as C 1992; previously Lab MP for Gateshead W 1970-81; SDP MP for that seat 1981-83. Chairman, Environmental Audit Select Cttee, 1997-2001. Under-Sec for Health, 1995-97; Public Services, 1995. Parly sec for Transport, 1976-79 (in Lab Gvt); Lab spokesman, economic affairs, 1979-81; SDP spokesman, economic affairs, 1981-83. Economist. Ed Silcoates Sch, Wakefield; St Catharine's Coll, Cambridge.
e-mail: bowdenp@parliament.uk www.epolitix.com/webminster/john-horam; tel: 020-7219 4462 fax: 020-7219 3806

This seat, set on the fringe of rural Kent but part of the vast commuter belt of the London Borough of Bromley, is still more famous for a political contest held four decades ago than any result subsequently. The Liberal victory in a by-election in 1962 (when massive swings on such occasions were rare) was little short of sensational. The Tories have held it since 1970 but the Lib Dems are again a powerful force here, coming very close in 2001. Map 448

## OXFORD EAST — Lab hold

| Electorate | %Turnout | | 74,421 | 53.54% | 2001 | 69,339 | 69.05% | 1997 |
|---|---|---|---|---|---|---|---|---|
| **Smith A** | | **Lab** | **19,681** | **49.39%** | **-7.43%** | **27,205** | **56.82%** | **Lab** |
| Goddard S | | LD | 9,337 | 23.43% | 8.73% | 10,540 | 22.01% | C |
| Potter Ms C | | C | 7,446 | 18.69% | -3.32% | 7,038 | 14.7% | LD |
| Singh P | | Green | 1,501 | 3.77% | 1.73% | 1,391 | 2.91% | Ref |
| Lister J | | Soc All | 708 | 1.78% | | 975 | 2.04% | Green |
| Gardner P | | UK Ind | 570 | 1.43% | 0.94% | 318 | 0.66% | Embryo |
| Ahmed F | | Soc Lab | 274 | 0.69% | | 234 | 0.49% | UK Ind |
| Hodge Ms L | | ProLife | 254 | 0.64% | | 108 | 0.23% | NLP |
| Mylvaganan P | | Ind | 77 | 0.19% | | 68 | 0.14% | Anti-maj |
| **Lab to LD swing** | **8.08%** | | **39,848** | | **Lab maj 10,344** | **47,877** | | **Lab maj 16,665** |
| | | | | | 25.96% | | | 34.81% |

**ANDREW SMITH,** b Feb 1, 1951. Elected 1987. Chief Sec to Treasury, 1999-; confirmed June 2001. Min for Employment and Welfare to Work and Equal Opportunities, 1997-99. Shadow Transport Sec, 1996-97; Shadow Treasury Chief Sec, 1994-96; spokesman, Treasury and economic affairs, 1992-94; higher and continuing educ, 1988-92. Privy Counsellor, 1997. Oxford city cllr, 1976-87. Chairman, board of governors, Oxford Brookes Univ, 1987-93. Ed Reading GS; St John's Coll, Oxford. Tel: 01865 772893 fax: 01865 715990

This is the industrial section of Oxford. It is a combination of working-class electors, many still employed in the motor works at Cowley, many living in vast council estates such as Blackbird Leys, and public sector workers linked to Oxford Brookes University and the John Radcliffe Hospital. It was very marginal in 1983 and 1987 but has since become solidly Labour. Map 449

## OXFORD WEST & ABINGDON — LD hold

| Electorate | %Turnout | | 79,915 | 64.53% | 2001 | 79,329 | 77.14% | 1997 |
|---|---|---|---|---|---|---|---|---|
| **Harris Dr E** | | **LD** | **24,670** | **47.84%** | **4.92%** | **26,268** | **42.92%** | **LD** |
| Matts E | | C | 15,485 | 30.03% | -2.62% | 19,983 | 32.65% | C |
| Kirk Ms G | | Lab | 9,114 | 17.67% | -2.53% | 12,361 | 20.2% | Lab |
| Woodin M | | Green | 1,423 | 2.76% | 1.63% | 1,258 | 2.06% | Ref |
| Watney M | | UK Ind | 451 | 0.87% | 0.45% | 691 | 1.13% | Green |
| Shreeve Ms S | | Ind | 332 | 0.64% | | 258 | 0.42% | UK Ind |
| Twigger R | | Ext Club | 93 | 0.18% | | 238 | 0.39% | ProLife |
| | | | | | | 91 | 0.15% | NLP |
| | | | | | | 48 | 0.08% | LGR |
| **C to LD swing** | **3.77%** | | **51,568** | | **LD maj 9,185** | **61,196** | | **LD maj 6,285** |
| | | | | | 17.81% | | | 10.27% |

**EVAN HARRIS,** b Oct 21, 1965. Elected 1997. LD chief spokesman, health and women's issues, June 2001; spokesman on NHS, 1997-99; higher ed, science and women's issues, 1999-. Member, Ed and Employment Select Cttee and its Ed sub-cttee, 1999-2001. Member, Green Democrats; President Della, 2000-; BMA medical ethics cttee, 1999-; central Oxford research ethics cttee, 1996-98. Ed Blue Coat Sch, Liverpool; Harvard HS, Los Angeles; Wadham Coll, Oxford; Oxford Univ Medical Sch.
e-mail: harrise@parliament.uk tel: 01865 245584 fax: 01865 245589

This seat contains the University itself and the shopping and commercial centre of Oxford, the rather affluent town of Abingdon and a series of smaller towns and villages in between. The Conservatives held the seat under John Patten from 1983 to 1997 but were gradually squeezed out as Labour sympathisers chose to support the Liberal Democrats for tactical reasons. This model was repeated in 2001. Map 450

## PAISLEY NORTH — Lab hold

| Electorate | %Turnout | | 47,994 | 56.58% | 2001 | 49,725 | 68.65% | 1997 |
|---|---|---|---|---|---|---|---|---|
| Adams Ms I | | Lab | 15,058 | 55.46% | -4.0% | 20,295 | 59.46% | Lab |
| Adam G | | SNP | 5,737 | 21.13% | -0.79% | 7,481 | 21.92% | SNP |
| Hook Ms J | | LD | 2,709 | 9.98% | 3.05% | 3,267 | 9.57% | C |
| Stevenson C | | C | 2,404 | 8.85% | -0.72% | 2,365 | 6.93% | LD |
| Halfpenny J | | SSP | 982 | 3.62% | | 531 | 1.56% | ProLife |
| Graham R | | ProLife | 263 | 0.97% | -0.59% | 196 | 0.57% | Ref |
| Lab to SNP swing | 1.61% | | 27,153 | Lab maj 9,321 34.33% | | 34,135 | Lab maj 12,814 37.54% | |

**IRENE ADAMS,** b Dec 27, 1947. Elected 1990 by-election, succeeding late husband, Allen Adams. Member, Scottish Affairs Select Cttee, 1997-2001; member, Commons Catering Cttee, 1991-95. Former vice-chairwoman, Children and Family Backbench Cttee. Ex-sec, all-party Scottish housing and sports grps. Strathclyde reg cllr, 1979-84; Renfrew dist cllr, 1974-78. Member, GMB. Ed Stanely Green HS, Paisley.
e-mail:contact@ireneadams-mp.newlabour.org.uk

Paisley, due west of Glasgow, is - surprisingly for the outsider - the fifth largest town in Scotland. The northern section has been combined with the towns of Renfrew and Linwood, home of the car plant, to create this constituency. It is evenly divided between owner-occupiers and council tenants. It is also a safe Labour seat with only the SNP, among the other parties, capable of making an impression. Map 451

## PAISLEY SOUTH — Lab hold

| Electorate | %Turnout | | 53,351 | 57.24% | 2001 | 54,040 | 69.12% | 1997 |
|---|---|---|---|---|---|---|---|---|
| Alexander D | | Lab | 17,830 | 58.39% | 0.88% | 21,482 | 57.51% | Lab |
| Lawson B | | SNP | 5,920 | 19.39% | -3.99% | 8,732 | 23.38% | SNP |
| O'Malley B | | LD | 3,178 | 10.41% | 1.04% | 3,500 | 9.37% | LD |
| Cossar A | | C | 2,301 | 7.54% | -1.13% | 3,237 | 8.67% | C |
| Curran Ms F | | SSP | 835 | 2.73% | | 254 | 0.68% | Ref |
| Graham Ms P | | ProLife | 346 | 1.13% | | 146 | 0.39% | SSA |
| O'Donnell T | | Ind | 126 | 0.41% | | | | |
| SNP to Lab swing | 2.44% | | 30,536 | Lab maj 11,910 39.00% | | 37,351 | Lab maj 12,750 34.13% | |

**DOUGLAS ALEXANDER,** b Oct 26, 1967. Elected 1997 by-election, following the death of sitting member, Gordon McMaster. Min for E-Commerce and Competitiveness, June 2001-. General election campaign co-ordinator. Former researcher to Gordon Brown, MP, 1990-91. Lawyer. Ed Park Manor HS Erskine; Lester B Pearson Coll, Vancouver; Edinburgh Univ; Pennsylvania Univ.
*Details of 1997 by-election on page 291*

This part of Paisley has been allied with the town of Johnstone for parliamentary elections. It is heavily industrial and broadly similar in political inclinations to its neighbour. The Liberals were once strong here (indeed Herbert Asquith was the MP) but it is firm Labour country now. The party fought off a challenge from the SNP to retain it in a by-election in November 1997 after the suicide of the newly re-elected MP, Gordon McMaster. Map 452

## PENDLE — Lab hold

| Electorate | %Turnout | | 62,870 | 63.2% | 2001 | 63,049 | 74.6% | 1997 |
|---|---|---|---|---|---|---|---|---|
| Prentice G | | Lab | 17,729 | 44.62% | -8.66% | 25,059 | 53.28% | Lab |
| Skinner R | | C | 13,454 | 33.86% | 3.6% | 14,235 | 30.26% | C |
| Whipp D | | LD | 5,479 | 13.79% | 2.18% | 5,460 | 11.61% | LD |
| Jackson C | | BNP | 1,976 | 4.97% | | 2,281 | 4.85% | Ref |
| Cannon G | | UK Ind | 1,094 | 2.75% | | | | |
| Lab to C swing | 6.13% | | 39,732 | Lab maj 4,275 10.76% | | 47,035 | Lab maj 10,824 23.02% | |

**GORDON PRENTICE,** b Jan 28, 1951. Elected 1992. PPS to Gavin Strang, Transport Min, until Dec 1997 when he resigned over proposed cut in benefit for lone parents. Member, Select Cttees: Modernisation of House of Commons; Agriculture, 1996-97; Deregulation 1995-97; Statutory Instruments. Sec, treas, all-party China grp, 1997-. vice-chairman, NW grp of Lab MPs, 1995-. Lab Party's local gvt officer in policy directorate, 1982-92. Hammersmith and Fulham cllr, 1986-92. Member, TGWU. Ed George Heriot's Sch, Edinburgh; Glasgow Univ

This diverse seat stretches across northeast Lancashire on the edge of the Pennines. Incorporating the old Nelson and Colne seat and the former Yorkshire towns of Barnoldswick and Earby, it includes some very urban as well as rural territory and has a significant number of ethnic minority voters in Nelson. The Tories held it until 1992, were swamped by Labour in 1997, but substantially cut the majority in 2001. It may well become very competitive again. Map 453

## PENRITH & THE BORDER — C hold

| Electorate | %Turnout | | 67,776 | 65.29% | 2001 | 66,496 | 73.63% | 1997 |
|---|---|---|---|---|---|---|---|---|
| **Maclean D** | **C** | | **24,302** | **54.92%** | **7.33%** | **23,300** | **47.59%** | **C** |
| Walker K | LD | | 9,625 | 21.75% | -4.94% | 13,067 | 26.69% | LD |
| Boaden M | Lab | | 8,177 | 18.48% | -3.12% | 10,576 | 21.6% | Lab |
| Lowther T | UK Ind | | 938 | 2.12% | | 2,018 | 4.12% | Ref |
| Gibson M | LCA | | 870 | 1.97% | | | | |
| Moffat J | Ind | | 337 | 0.76% | | | | |
| **LD to C swing** | **6.13%** | | **44,249** | **C maj 14,677** | | **48,961** | **C maj 10,233** | |
| | | | | 33.17% | | | 20.90% | |

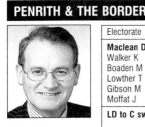

**DAVID MACLEAN,** b May 16, 1953. Elected 1983 by-election, caused by elevation to House of Lords of William Whitelaw. Home Office Min, 1993-97, responsibile for police and criminal justice policy. Environment Min, 1992-93; parly sec, Min of Agriculture, Fisheries and Food, 1989-92; gvt whip, 1988-89; asst gvt whip, 1987-88. Member, Agriculture Select Cttee, 1983-86. Privy Counsellor. Ed Fortrose Acad; Aberdeen Univ.

This is a huge seat encompassing much of Cumbria and is the largest in England by some margin. It extends from the Solway Firth to the Yorkshire Dales, from Gretna Green to the heart of the Lakes; the only towns of any size are Penrith, Wigton and Appleby. Most of the area, however, consists of agricultural land and small villages. This countryside was badly affected by the 2001 foot-and-mouth outbreak. It is staunch Conservative territory. Map 454

## PERTH — SNP hold

| Electorate | %Turnout | | 61,497 | 61.49% | 2001 | 60,313 | 73.87% | 1997 |
|---|---|---|---|---|---|---|---|---|
| **Ewing Ms A** | **SNP** | | **11,237** | **29.71%** | **-6.67%** | **16,209** | **36.38%** | **SNP** |
| Smith Miss E | C | | 11,189 | 29.59% | 0.26% | 13,068 | 29.33% | C |
| Dingwall Ms M | Lab | | 9,638 | 25.49% | 0.72% | 11,036 | 24.77% | Lab |
| Harris Ms V | LD | | 4,853 | 12.83% | 4.79% | 3,583 | 8.04% | LD |
| Byrne F | SSP | | 899 | 2.38% | | 366 | 0.82% | Ref |
| | | | | | | 289 | 0.65% | UK Ind |
| **SNP to C swing** | **3.46%** | | **37,816** | **SNP maj 48** | | **44,551** | **SNP maj 3,141** | |
| | | | | 0.13% | | | 7.05% | |

**ANNABELLE EWING,** b Jan 1, 1960. Elected 2001. Inherits seat from Roseanna Cunningham, SNP deputy leader, who stood down to concentrate on the Scottish Parliament. Contested Stirling (Scottish Parliament) and Hamilton S (by-election) in 1999. Campaign spokeswoman on Europe. Daughter of Winnie Ewing, SNP President and MSP for Highlands & Islands. Lawyer. Ed Craigholme Sch and Glasgow Univ (Law).

The Perth seats consists of the town itself and some charming and fertile surrounding countryside. Perth is predominantly prosperous although it contains some council estates which share the social problems common to other parts of urban Scotland. It has been a Conservative-SNP battleground, but the nationalists triumphed in 1997 and just held on with a double-figure majority in 2001, while Labour too has now begun to make more of a showing. Map 455

## PETERBOROUGH — Lab hold

| Electorate | %Turnout | | 64,918 | 61.33% | 2001 | 65,926 | 73.46% | 1997 |
|---|---|---|---|---|---|---|---|---|
| **Brinton Mrs H** | **Lab** | | **17,975** | **45.15%** | **-5.16%** | **24,365** | **50.31%** | **Lab** |
| Jackson S | C | | 15,121 | 37.98% | 2.79% | 17,042 | 35.19% | C |
| Sandford N | LD | | 5,761 | 14.47% | 3.79% | 5,170 | 10.68% | LD |
| Fairweather J | UK Ind | | 955 | 2.4% | 1.75% | 924 | 1.91% | Ref |
| | | | | | | 334 | 0.69% | NLP |
| | | | | | | 317 | 0.65% | UK Ind |
| | | | | | | 275 | 0.57% | ProLife |
| **Lab to C swing** | **3.98%** | | **39,812** | **Lab maj 2,854** | | **48,427** | **Lab maj 7,323** | |
| | | | | 7.17% | | | 15.12% | |

**HELEN BRINTON,** b Dec 23, 1954. Elected 1997. Member, Environmental Audit Select Cttee, 1997-2001. Joint vice-chairwoman, PLP Environment, Transport and Regions Cttee, 1997-. Chairwoman, all-party wildlife protection grp; vice-chairwoman, all-party child abduction grp. Presented three 10-minute rule Bills: Home Zones, Country Lanes and Villages, Marine Conservation. Member, Lab full employment forum. Teacher; examiner/moderator. Ed Bristol Univ.
tel: 020-7219 4469 fax: 020-7219 0951

This Cambridgeshire constituency, although affected by recent boundary revisions, remains a political marker. The Conservatives won here by clear but not crushing margins when they were strong nationally, a trick repeated by Labour in 1997 and 2001. The combination of historic cathedral and market town with new town status, as well as high-tech industries and high-speed rail links to London, has produced the scenario for a tight marginal. Map 456

## PLYMOUTH DEVONPORT — Lab hold

| Electorate | %Turnout | | 73,666 | 56.63% | 2001 | 74,483 | 69.76% | 1997 |
|---|---|---|---|---|---|---|---|---|
| Jamieson D | Lab | | 24,322 | 58.3% | -2.57% | 31,629 | 60.87% | Lab |
| Glen J | C | | 11,289 | 27.06% | 2.89% | 12,562 | 24.17% | C |
| Baldry K | LD | | 4,513 | 10.82% | 0.1% | 5,570 | 10.72% | LD |
| Parker M | UK Ind | | 958 | 2.3% | 1.38% | 1,486 | 2.86% | Ref |
| Staunton T | Soc All | | 334 | 0.8% | | 478 | 0.92% | UK Ind |
| Hawkins R | Soc Lab | | 303 | 0.73% | | 238 | 0.46% | Nat Dem |
| Lab to C swing | 2.73% | | 41,719 | Lab maj 13,033 | | 51,963 | Lab maj 19,067 | |
| | | | | 31.24% | | | 36.70% | |

**DAVID JAMIESON,** b May 18, 1947. Elected 1992. Under Sec for Transport, Local Gvt and Regions, June 2001-; Gvt whip, 1998-2001; asst whip, 1997-98. Member, Select Cttees: Ed and Employment, 1996-97; Education, 1992-96. Sec, PLP Defence Cttee, 1995-97; joint vice-chairman, PLP Ed Cttee, 1995-97. Ex-parly consultant, Natural Gas Vehicles Assoc. Vice-principal, John Kitto Community Coll, Plymouth, 1981-92. Solihull borough cllr, 1970-74. Teacher, Riland Bedford Sch, 1970-76. Ed Tudor Grange GS, Solihull; St Peter's Coll, Birmingham; OU.

This is one of those seats whose affiliations have clearly been affected by the fortunes of the sitting MP. It is an essentially urban seat with strong links to the naval base and dockyards, and with large council estates built on the hills of the city's northern edge. It was a Labour-Tory marginal until David Owen defected to the SDP and took his constituency with him. Now that the "Owen effect" has evaporated, Labour has restored a healthy majority. Map 457

## PLYMOUTH SUTTON — Lab hold

| Electorate | %Turnout | | 68,438 | 57.09% | 2001 | 70,666 | 67.43% | 1997 |
|---|---|---|---|---|---|---|---|---|
| Gilroy Mrs L | Lab Co-op | | 19,827 | 50.74% | 0.62% | 23,881 | 50.12% | Lab |
| Colvile O | C | | 12,310 | 31.51% | 1.2% | 14,441 | 30.31% | C |
| Connett A | LD | | 5,605 | 14.34% | 0.46% | 6,613 | 13.88% | LD |
| Whitton A | UK Ind | | 970 | 2.48% | 1.43% | 1,654 | 3.47% | Ref |
| Leary H | Soc Lab | | 361 | 0.92% | | 499 | 1.05% | UK Ind |
| | | | | | | 396 | 0.83% | Plymouth |
| | | | | | | 168 | 0.35% | NLP |
| Lab Co-op to C swing | 0.29% | | 39,073 | Lab Co-op maj 7,517 | | 47,652 | Lab Co-op maj 9,440 | |
| | | | | 19.24% | | | 19.81% | |

**LINDA GILROY,** b July 19, 1949. Elected 1997. Member, European Scrutiny Select Cttee, 1997-98. Joint vice-chairwoman, all-party older people grp, 1997-; treas, all-party grp on kidneys. Chairwoman, Cornwall Lab Party, 1990-94; sec, Plymouth Drake CLP, 1987-88. Head of SW Office, Gas Consumers' Council, 1979-96. Dep dir, Age Concern Scotland, 1972-79. Member, Inst of Trading Standards; Nalgo; Co-op Party. Ed Edinburgh and Strathclyde Univs. fax: 020-7219 0987 tel: 020-7219 4746

This seat consists of the more middle-class section of the city and includes the shopping and commercial centre and Plymouth Hoe. It has only a slightly higher rate of owner-occupation but far fewer council tenants than the rest of Plymouth and a much larger number of professionals and managers. This should be very competitive territory but Labour won by a wide margin in both 1997 and 2001. Map 458

## PONTEFRACT & CASTLEFORD — Lab hold

| Electorate | %Turnout | | 63,181 | 49.68% | 2001 | 62,350 | 66.39% | 1997 |
|---|---|---|---|---|---|---|---|---|
| Cooper Ms Y | Lab | | 21,890 | 69.73% | -5.98% | 31,339 | 75.71% | Lab |
| Singleton Ms P | C | | 5,512 | 17.56% | 4.0% | 5,614 | 13.56% | C |
| Paxton W | LD | | 2,315 | 7.37% | 0.02% | 3,042 | 7.35% | LD |
| Burdon J | UK Ind | | 739 | 2.35% | | 1,401 | 3.38% | Ref |
| Bolderson T | Soc Lab | | 605 | 1.93% | | | | |
| Gill J | Soc All | | 330 | 1.05% | | | | |
| Lab to C swing | 4.99% | | 31,391 | Lab maj 16,378 | | 41,396 | Lab maj 25,725 | |
| | | | | 52.17% | | | 62.15% | |

**YVETTE COOPER,** b March 20, 1969. Elected 1997. Under-Sec of State for Public Health, 1999-; confirmed, June 2001. Ed and Employment Select Cttee and its Employment Sub-Cttee, 1997-99; member, Parly Intelligence and Security Cttee, 1997-99. Former economics correspondent for *The Independent*. Aide to Gordon Brown and the late John Smith. Member, NUJ; GMB. Journalist. Ed Eggars Comp, Alton; Alton Sixth-Form Coll; Balliol Coll, Oxford; Harvard (Kennedy Scholar); LSE.
e-mail: coopery@parliament.uk tel: 020-7219 6617 fax: 020-7219 0912

This part of West Yorkshire, southeast of Leeds, is solid industrial territory. The enormous Ferrybridge power station towers by the A1 near Knottingley, the third main town in the constituency after Pontefract and Castleford. This area was once the heart of the Yorkshire coalmining industry and although the employment linked with the pits has disappeared, the political tradition associated with it has not. It is an extremely safe Labour seat. Map 459

## PONTYPRIDD — Lab hold

| Electorate | %Turnout | | 66,105 | 57.95% | 2001 | 64,185 | 71.44% | 1997 |
|---|---|---|---|---|---|---|---|---|
| Howells Dr K | | Lab | 22,963 | 59.94% | -3.94% | 29,290 | 63.88% | Lab |
| Hancock B | | PC | 5,279 | 13.78% | 7.29% | 6,161 | 13.44% | LD |
| Dailey Ms P | | C | 5,096 | 13.3% | 0.41% | 5,910 | 12.89% | C |
| Brooke E | | LD | 4,152 | 10.84% | -2.6% | 2,977 | 6.49% | PC |
| Warry Ms S | | UK Ind | 603 | 1.57% | | 874 | 1.91% | Ref |
| Biddulph J | | ProLife | 216 | 0.56% | | 380 | 0.83% | Soc Lab |
| | | | | | | 178 | 0.39% | Comm Brit |
| | | | | | | 85 | 0.19% | NLP |
| Lab to PC swing | 5.61% | | 38,309 | Lab maj 17,684 | | 45,855 | Lab maj 23,129 | |
| | | | | 46.16% | | | 50.44% | |

**KIM HOWELLS,** b Nov 27, 1946. Elected 1989 by-election. Min for Tourism, Film and Broadcasting, June 2001; Under-Sec, Consumers and Corporate Affairs, DTI, 1998-2001; Under-Sec, Ed, 1997-98. Lab spokesman, trade and industry, 1995-97; home affairs, 1994-95; overseas development, 1993-94. Former coalminer and steelworker. Ed Mountain Ash GS; Hornsey Coll of Art; Cambridge Coll of Advanced Tech; Warwick Univ. e-mail: kimhowells@khowells4b.fsnet.co.uk tel: 01443 402551 fax: 01443 408314

This seat is set in the heart of the Mid-Glamorgan Valleys — a part of Wales that is on the fringe of coal-mining country rather than at the centre of it. It lies northwest of Cardiff to embrace the Taff and Ely Valleys between Rhondda and Caerphilly. It has quite a high rate of owner-occupation and only a modest number of Welsh speakers. If it were located in West Yorkshire it could easily be marginal. In this region, however, it is rock-solid Labour. Map 460

## POOLE — C hold

| Electorate | %Turnout | | 64,644 | 60.69% | 2001 | 66,078 | 70.84% | 1997 |
|---|---|---|---|---|---|---|---|---|
| Syms R | | C | 17,710 | 45.14% | 3.0% | 19,726 | 42.14% | C |
| Watt D | | Lab | 10,544 | 26.88% | 5.3% | 14,428 | 30.82% | LD |
| Westbrook N | | LD | 10,011 | 25.52% | -5.3% | 10,100 | 21.58% | Lab |
| Bass J | | UK Ind | 968 | 2.47% | 1.43% | 1,932 | 4.13% | Ref |
| | | | | | | 487 | 1.04% | UK Ind |
| | | | | | | 137 | 0.29% | NLP |
| C to Lab swing | 1.15% | | 39,233 | C maj 7,166 | | 46,810 | C maj 5,298 | |
| | | | | 18.27% | | | 11.32% | |

**ROBERT SYMS,** b Aug 15, 1956. Elected 1997. Frontbench DETR spokesman, 1999-. Former member, Health Select Cttee. Joint vice-chairman, C Backbench Constitutional Cttee, 1997-. PPS to chairman C Party, 1999. Wilts city cllr, 1985-. Member, C Way Forward. Founder dir, N Wilts Enterprise Agency, 1986-90. Officer, N Wilts C Assoc, 1982-88; member, Wessex area provincial council, 1982-90. Member, Freedom Assoc. Dir, family building, property and plant hire businesses. Ed Colston's, Bristol. fax: 020-7219 6867

Although understandably associated with the larger neighbouring South Coast resort of Bournemouth, the yachting centre and holiday town of Poole is a very distinctive political entity and not a mere satellite. It has enjoyed a population boom over the past two decades and is quietly affluent. The Conservatives are clearly the strongest party in Westminster elections but Labour and the Liberal Democrats can both mount a respectable showing. Map 461

## POPLAR & CANNING TOWN — Lab hold

| Electorate | %Turnout | | 75,173 | 45.37% | 2001 | 67,172 | 58.46% | 1997 |
|---|---|---|---|---|---|---|---|---|
| Fitzpatrick J | | Lab | 20,862 | 61.16% | -2.01% | 24,807 | 63.17% | Lab |
| Marr R | | C | 6,758 | 19.81% | 4.81% | 5,892 | 15.0% | C |
| Sugden Ms A | | LD | 3,795 | 11.13% | 0.76% | 4,072 | 10.37% | LD |
| Borg P | | BNP | 1,743 | 5.11% | -2.15% | 2,849 | 7.26% | BNP |
| Boomla Dr K | | Soc All | 950 | 2.79% | | 1,091 | 2.78% | Ref |
| | | | | | | 557 | 1.42% | Soc Lab |
| Lab to C swing | 3.41% | | 34,108 | Lab maj 14,104 | | 39,268 | Lab maj 18,915 | |
| | | | | 41.35% | | | 48.17% | |

**JIM FITZPATRICK,** b April 4, 1952. Elected 1997. Asst chief whip, June 2001. Previously PPS to Alan Milburn, Health Sec. Chairman, Greater London Lab Party, 1991-. Member, executive cttee, FBU, 1988-97. Fire brigade long service and good conduct medal, 1994. London rep, FBU. Member, Amnesty, Greenpeace. Firefighter. Ed Holyrood Senior Sch, Glasgow.

This East London seat nearly swung to the Conservatives in 1987. It is hard to imagine Labour losing it now. The constituency is an uneasy combination of the traditional white working-class East End, a substantial immigrant population and the affluent middle-class City workers attracted by Docklands redevelopment and London City Airport. These tensions are manifested in the continuing presence at the polls of the British National Party. Map 462

## PORTSMOUTH NORTH

Lab hold

| Electorate | %Turnout | | 64,256 | 57.37% | 2001 | 64,539 | 70.14% | 1997 |
|---|---|---|---|---|---|---|---|---|
| Rapson S | | Lab | 18,676 | 50.66% | 3.52% | 21,339 | 47.14% | Lab |
| Day C | | C | 13,542 | 36.73% | -0.86% | 17,016 | 37.59% | C |
| Sanders D | | LD | 3,795 | 10.29% | -0.29% | 4,788 | 10.58% | LD |
| McCabe W | | UK Ind | 559 | 1.52% | 0.86% | 1,757 | 3.88% | Ref |
| Bundy B | | Ind | 294 | 0.8% | | 298 | 0.66% | UK Ind |
| | | | | | | 72 | 0.16% | WessexReg |
| C to Lab swing | 2.19% | | 36,866 | | Lab maj 5,134 | 45,270 | | Lab maj 4,323 |
| | | | | | 13.93% | | | 9.55% |

**SYD RAPSON,** b April 17, 1942. Elected 1997; contested Portsmouth S 1992. Sec, PLP Defence Cttee; Commons Accommodation and Works Cttee, 1997-. Member, Council of Europe; WEU; Lord Mayor, Portsmouth, 1990-91; Portsmouth city cllr, 1971-78; Hampshire county cllr, 1973-77. Shop steward, AEU convener. Appointed MBE, 1984. Ex-aircraft fitter. Ed Southsea Mod; Paulsgrove Mod. e-mail: syd.rapson.mp@amserve tel: 020-7219 6351/6248 fax: 020-7219 0915.

This is a socially polarised constituency which delivered a surprisingly large swing to Labour in 1997. This part of Britain's principal naval port has a high rate of owner-occupation and strong links to the Royal Navy. Those Conservative traits are partly offset by council estates which have traditionally produced a solid vote for Labour. This is likely to continue as a tough marginal battleground, despite Labour's current ascendancy. Map 463

## PORTSMOUTH SOUTH

LD hold

| Electorate | %Turnout | | 77,095 | 50.87% | 2001 | 80,514 | 64.21% | 1997 |
|---|---|---|---|---|---|---|---|---|
| Hancock M | | LD | 17,490 | 44.6% | 5.1% | 20,421 | 39.5% | LD |
| Warr P | | C | 11,396 | 29.06% | -2.07% | 16,094 | 31.13% | C |
| Heaney G | | Lab | 9,361 | 23.87% | -1.44% | 13,086 | 25.31% | Lab |
| Molyneux J | | Soc All | 647 | 1.65% | | 1,629 | 3.15% | Ref |
| Tarrant M | | UK Ind | 321 | 0.82% | 0.55% | 184 | 0.36% | Lib |
| | | | | | | 141 | 0.27% | UK Ind |
| | | | | | | 140 | 0.27% | NLP |
| C to LD swing | 3.58% | | 39,215 | | LD maj 6,094 | 51,695 | | LD maj 4,327 |
| | | | | | 15.54% | | | 8.37% |

**MIKE HANCOCK,** b April 9, 1946. Elected 1997; contested seat 1992; SDP/All MP here, 1984 by-election to 1987; contested it for SDP, 1983 and SDP/All, 1987. Member, Defence Select Cttee; Chairmen's Panel; UK Parly delegation to Council of Europe and WEU. Dep leader, LD grp, WEU; UK rep, North Atlantic Assembly. Vice-chairman, all-party grp on football; joint vice-chairman, Russian parly grp, 1997-; treas, Romanian grp, 1997-. Hants city cllr, 1973-97, leader, 1993-97. Ed Copner and Portsea Sch. www.mikehancock.co.uk tel: 020-7219 5180 fax: 023-9283 0530

This seat consists of most of densely populated Portsea Island, including Portsmouth city centre, the harbour areas and the resort of Southsea. It has swung between the Tories and the SDP/Liberal Democrats with Labour a close third; captured by the SDP in a by-election in 1984, it was very narrowly regained by the Tories twice, then won by the Lib Dems in 1997 and 2001. Who wins depends on fortune, the flavour of the times and tactical voting. Map 464

## PRESELI PEMBROKESHIRE

Lab hold

| Electorate | %Turnout | | 54,283 | 67.75% | 2001 | 54,088 | 78.4% | 1997 |
|---|---|---|---|---|---|---|---|---|
| Lawrence Ms J | | Lab | 15,206 | 41.35% | -6.94% | 20,477 | 48.29% | Lab |
| Crabb S | | C | 12,260 | 33.34% | 5.65% | 11,741 | 27.69% | C |
| Sinnet R | | PC | 4,658 | 12.67% | 6.34% | 5,527 | 13.03% | LD |
| Dauncey A | | LD | 3,882 | 10.56% | -2.47% | 2,683 | 6.33% | PC |
| Bowen Ms T | | Soc Lab | 452 | 1.23% | | 1,574 | 3.71% | Ref |
| Jones H | | UK Ind | 319 | 0.87% | | 401 | 0.95% | Green |
| Lab to C swing | 6.29% | | 36,777 | | Lab maj 2,946 | 42,403 | | Lab maj 8,736 |
| | | | | | 8.01% | | | 20.60% |

**JACKIE LAWRENCE,** b Aug 9, 1948. Elected 1997. Member, Welsh Affairs Select Cttee, 1997-2001. Lab election agent when party gained Pembroke, 1992. Pembrokeshire county cllr; leader, Lab grp; member, Dyfed Powys police authority. Member, Christian Socialist Movement. Ex-political adviser. Ed Upperthorpe Sch and Coll, Darlington.

Pembrokeshire, on the southwest Wales coast, has been more affected than most by boundary changes in the Principality. This seat is essentially the northern part of the county, named after the Preseli Hills which run east of the ferry port of Fishguard. Other centres include Haverfordwest, the oil port of Milford Haven and the tiny cathedral city of St David's. It was expected to be marginal in 1997 but Labour romped home easily - less so in 2001. Map 465

## PRESTON
**Lab hold**

| Electorate | %Turnout | | 72,077 | 50.0% | 2001 | 72,933 | 65.92% | 1997 |
|---|---|---|---|---|---|---|---|---|
| **Hendrick M** | Lab Co-op | | **20,540** | **56.99%** | **-3.79** | **29,220** | **60.78%** | **Lab** |
| O'Hare G | C | | 8,272 | 22.95% | 1.03% | 10,540 | 21.92% | C |
| Chadwick B | LD | | 4,746 | 13.17% | -1.48% | 7,045 | 14.65% | LD |
| Patel B | Ind P | | 1,241 | 3.44% | | 924 | 1.92% | Ref |
| Merrick R | Green | | 1,019 | 2.83% | | 345 | 0.72% | NLP |
| Braid The Rev D | Ind Br | | 223 | 0.62% | | | | |
| **Lab Co-op to C swing** | **2.41%** | | **36,041** | **Lab Co-op maj 12,268** | | **48,074** | **Lab maj 18,680** | |
| | | | | 34.04% | | | 38.86% | |

**MARK HENDRICK,** b Nov 2, 1958. Elected 2000 by-election, following death of sitting MP, Audrey Wise. MEP, Lancs Central 1994-99. Member, EU Economic and Monetary Affairs and Industrial Policy Cttee, 1994-99l; Foreign Affairs, Security and Defence Policy Cttee, 1994-97; Environment, Public Health and Consumer Protection Cttee, 1997-99. Member, Japan delegation, 1994-99. Former lecturer, electronics and software design, Stockport Coll. Ed Salford GS; Liverpool Poly; Manchester Univ.
*Details of 2000 by-election on page 291*

The town of Preston in Lancashire is now contained in a single parliamentary constituency. Preston originally made its money from cotton but now supports a wide range of industry. There is an expanding Asian population which is becoming more important politically. This is strong Labour terrain, although the solid majority in 1997 was heavily eroded in a by-election in 2000. Normal service, however, was resumed just over six months later. Map 466

## PUDSEY
**Lab hold**

| Electorate | %Turnout | | 71,405 | 63.27% | 2001 | 70,922 | 74.35% | 1997 |
|---|---|---|---|---|---|---|---|---|
| **Truswell P** | Lab | | **21,717** | **48.07%** | **-0.04%** | **25,370** | **48.11%** | **Lab** |
| Procter J | C | | 16,091 | 35.62% | -0.72% | 19,163 | 36.34% | C |
| Boddy S | LD | | 6,423 | 14.22% | 0.23% | 7,375 | 13.99% | LD |
| Sewards D | UK Ind | | 944 | 2.09% | | 823 | 1.56% | Ref |
| **C to Lab swing** | **0.34%** | | **45,175** | **Lab maj 5,626** | | **52,731** | **Lab maj 6,207** | |
| | | | | 12.45% | | | 11.77% | |

**PAUL TRUSWELL,** b Nov 17, 1955. Elected 1997. Member, Leeds family health services authority, 1992-96; Leeds HA, 1982-90. Ex-chairman, Leeds green strategy grp. Yorks reg press officer, 1992 general election. Leeds city cllr, 1982-; local govt officer, Wakefield MDC; member, Unison; NUJ; Co-op Party; SHA; Liberty; SERA. Ed Leeds Univ.

This constituency lies betwen the two largest cities in West Yorkshire, Leeds and Bradford. It divides into three sections: Pudsey, Horsforth (essentially a Leeds suburb), and the Aireborough ward which includes Guiseley, Yeadon and Rawdon. It is a middle-class seat with some working-class sections. Pudsey also claims to be the home of Yorkshire cricket. Labour snatched it in 1997 largely because of mass defections from the Liberal Democrats. Map 467

## PUTNEY
**Lab hold**

| Electorate | %Turnout | | 60,643 | 56.48% | 2001 | 60,176 | 73.11% | 1997 |
|---|---|---|---|---|---|---|---|---|
| **Colman T** | Lab | | **15,911** | **46.45%** | **0.8%** | **20,084** | **45.65%** | **Lab** |
| Simpson M | C | | 13,140 | 38.36% | -0.53% | 17,108 | 38.89% | C |
| Burrett T | LD | | 4,671 | 13.64% | 2.87% | 4,739 | 10.77% | LD |
| Wild Ms P | UK Ind | | 347 | 1.01% | | 1,518 | 3.45% | Ref |
| Windsor Ms Y | ProLife | | 185 | 0.54% | 0.48% | 233 | 0.53% | UK Ind |
| | | | | | | 101 | 0.23% | Stan |
| | | | | | | 90 | 0.2% | Spts All |
| | | | | | | 66 | 0.15% | NLP |
| | | | | | | 49 | 0.11% | Ind Beaut |
| | | | | | | 7 | 0.02% | Ren Dem |
| **C to Lab swing** | **0.66%** | | **34,254** | **Lab maj 2,771** | | **43,995** | **Lab maj 2,976** | |
| | | | | 8.09% | | | 6.76% | |

**TONY COLMAN,** b July 24, 1943. Elected 1997. Member, Select Cttees: International Development, 2000-01; Treasury, 1997-98. Chairman, PLP Trade and Ind Cttee, 1997-99. PPS to Adam Ingram, 1998-99. Former Merton borough cllr. Dir, Church, Charity and Local Authority Investment Management Ltd, 1995- (investment management for C of E, charities and local authorities). Ex-dir, Burton Grp plc. Ed Paston GS, N Walsham; Magdalene Coll, Cambridge. tel: 020-7219 2843 fax: 020- 7219 1137

This southwest London seat on the south side of the Thames has proved socially and politically distinctive. It has both very affluent and some rather poor pockets. The Conservatives dug in during the 1980s, benefiting from the popularity of Wandsworth Council. Labour snatched the seat in 1997 while the searchlight of publicity was on the sitting Tory MP, David Mellor, and Sir James Goldsmith, of the Referendum Party - and held on in 2001. Map 468

## RAYLEIGH — C hold

| Electorate | %Turnout | | 70,073 | 61.04% | 2001 | 68,737 | 74.65% | 1997 |
|---|---|---|---|---|---|---|---|---|
| **Francois M** | C | | **21,434** | **50.11%** | **0.38%** | 25,516 | 49.73% | C |
| Clark P | Lab | | 13,144 | 30.73% | 1.83% | 14,832 | 28.9% | Lab |
| Williams G | LD | | 6,614 | 15.46% | -4.29% | 10,137 | 19.75% | LD |
| Morgan C | UK Ind | | 1,581 | 3.7% | | 829 | 1.62% | Lib |
| **C to Lab swing** | **0.72%** | | **42,773** | | **C maj 8,290** | **51,314** | | **C maj 10,684** |
| | | | | | 19.38% | | | 20.83% |

**MARK FRANCOIS,** b Aug 14, 1965. Elected 2001. Inherits seat from retiring Michael Clark. Contested Brent E 1997. Basildon district cllr, 1991-95. Chairman, Bristol Univ C Assoc, 1984. Public affairs consultant, Francois Associates, since 1996. Ed Nicholas Comp, Basildon; Bristol Univ and London Univs.

This Essex seat comprises a number of affluent suburban communities northwest of Southend. As well as the town of Rayleigh itself these include Hockley and Hawkwell, plus the rapidly expanding South Woodham Ferrers on the north bank of the Crouch. Though not upper middle-class, the area is certainly comfortable. Almost nine in ten properties are owned by their occupiers. The Conservatives are very strong here. Map 469

## READING EAST — Lab hold

| Electorate | %Turnout | | 74,637 | 58.44% | 2001 | 71,586 | 70.15% | 1997 |
|---|---|---|---|---|---|---|---|---|
| **Griffiths Ms J** | Lab | | **19,531** | **44.78%** | **2.05%** | 21,461 | 42.73% | Lab |
| Tanswell B | C | | 13,943 | 31.97% | -3.21% | 17,666 | 35.18% | C |
| Dobrashian T | LD | | 8,078 | 18.52% | -0.01% | 9,307 | 18.53% | LD |
| Kennett Ms M | Green | | 1,053 | 2.41% | | 1,042 | 2.07% | Ref |
| Thornton Miss A | UK Ind | | 525 | 1.2% | 0.7% | 254 | 0.51% | NLP |
| Williams D | Soc All | | 394 | 0.9% | | 252 | 0.5% | UK Ind |
| Hammerson P | Ind | | 94 | 0.22% | | 238 | 0.47% | BNP |
| **C to Lab swing** | **2.63%** | | **43,618** | | **Lab maj 5,588** | **50,220** | | **Lab maj 3,795** |
| | | | | | 12.81% | | | 7.55% |

**JANE GRIFFITHS,** b April 17, 1954. Elected 1997. Reading's first woman MP. Member, Public Accounts Cttee, 1997-99. Joint chairwoman, all-party grps; male cancers, Estonia, Mongolia and earth sciences. Sec, Japanese and Far East prisoner of war grps. Member, PLP Cttees: Environment, Transport and the Regions; Culture, and Foreign Affairs. Reading borough cllr, 1989-99 . Ex-BBC editor. NUJ. Ed Cedars GS, Leighton Buzzard; Durham Univ.
e-mail: griffithsj@parliament.uk www.janegriffithsmp.org
tel: 020-7219 4122 fax: 020-7219 0719

The two seats in Reading have traditionally divided the town between them, with each seat then being supplemented by a swath of more rural territory. This has historically operated to the detriment of Labour. An urban minority has been swamped by the alliance of suburbia and countryside. Labour overcame that disadvantage to win here in 1997 and again four years later, but this remains marginal terrain. Map 470

## READING WEST — Lab hold

| Electorate | %Turnout | | 71,688 | 58.57% | 2001 | 69,073 | 70.05% | 1997 |
|---|---|---|---|---|---|---|---|---|
| **Salter M** | Lab | | **22,300** | **53.11%** | **7.97%** | 21,841 | 45.14% | Lab |
| Reid S | C | | 13,451 | 32.04% | -6.9% | 18,844 | 38.94% | C |
| Martin Ms P | LD | | 5,387 | 12.83% | 0.11% | 6,153 | 12.72% | LD |
| Black D | UK Ind | | 848 | 2.02% | 1.49% | 976 | 2.02% | Ref |
| | | | | | | 320 | 0.66% | BNP |
| | | | | | | 255 | 0.53% | UK Ind |
| **C to Lab swing** | **7.44%** | | **41,986** | | **Lab maj 8,849** | **48,389** | | **Lab maj 2,997** |
| | | | | | 21.08% | | | 6.20% |

**MARTIN SALTER,** b April 19, 1954. Elected 1997. Member, NI Affairs Grand Select Cttee, 1997-2001; NI Affairs Select Cttee, 1997-99. Member, Backbench Cttees: Environment, Transport and Regions, 1997-, NI, 1997-, Parly Affairs, 1997-. All-party grps: chairman, community banking; sec, Punjabi; member, human rights, media, MS, leasehold reform, Rwanda and genocide, football, environment. Dep leader, Reading Borough Council, 1987-96. Member, Greenpeace. Ed Hampton GS; Sussex Univ.
e-mail: salterm@parliament.uk tel: 020-7219 2416 fax: 020-7219 2749

This seat contains most of urban Reading, a thriving industrial centre, university town and important rail junction. It also extends westwards to very prosperous small towns such as Theale, and Pangbourne on the Thames. In the highly favourable circumstances of 1997 Labour was able to supplement its council tenant base to capture the seat, and to widen its lead in 2001. However, this is the sort of seat in which the Tories should, in theory, prosper. Map 471

## REDCAR — Lab hold

| Electorate | %Turnout | | 66,179 | 57.72% | 2001 | 68,965 | 70.99% | 1997 |
|---|---|---|---|---|---|---|---|---|
| **Baird Ms V** | **Lab** | | **23,026** | **60.28%** | **-7.07%** | **32,972** | **67.35%** | **Lab** |
| Main C | C | | 9,583 | 25.09% | 1.99% | 11,308 | 23.1% | C |
| Wilson S | LD | | 4,817 | 12.61% | 3.05% | 4,679 | 9.56% | LD |
| Taylor J | Soc Lab | | 772 | 2.02% | | | | |
| **Lab to C swing** | **4.53%** | | **38,198** | Lab maj 13,443 | | **48,959** | Lab maj 21,664 | |
| | | | | 35.19% | | | 44.25% | |

**VERA BAIRD,** b Feb 13, 1951. Elected 2001. Inherits seat from former Cabinet Min, Mo Mowlam, who won in 1987. Specialist criminal and civil liberties barrister; deputy head of Michael Mansfield's law chambers. Vice-chairwoman, Society of Lab Lawyers. Member, Fabian Soc, Greenpeace, RSPCA. Ed Univ of Northumbria; OU; London Univ.

By the standards of the North East this constituency on south Teesside is not entirely hostile to the Conservatives. While Labour invariably romps home in general elections it is possible for the Tories to win some wards in local contests. Redcar, despite being a North Sea resort, is dominated by heavy industry, such as chemicals and steelmaking, and is strongly working-class in culture. Mo Mowlam has handed on a very safe Labour seat to her successor. Map 472

## REDDITCH — Lab hold

| Electorate | %Turnout | | 62,543 | 59.21% | 2001 | 60,841 | 73.55% | 1997 |
|---|---|---|---|---|---|---|---|---|
| **Smith Ms J** | **Lab** | | **16,899** | **45.63%** | **-4.16%** | **22,280** | **49.79%** | **Lab** |
| Lumley Mrs K | C | | 14,415 | 38.93% | 2.83% | 16,155 | 36.1% | C |
| Ashall M | LD | | 3,808 | 10.28% | -0.75% | 4,935 | 11.03% | LD |
| Flynn G | UK Ind | | 1,259 | 3.4% | | 1,151 | 2.57% | Ref |
| Armstrong R | Green | | 651 | 1.76% | | 227 | 0.51% | NLP |
| **Lab to C swing** | **3.49%** | | **37,032** | Lab maj 2,484 | | **44,748** | Lab maj 6,125 | |
| | | | | 6.71% | | | 13.69% | |

**JACQUI SMITH,** b Nov 3, 1962. Elected 1997. Min of State, Health, June 2001-; Parly Under-Sec for Sch Standards, 1999-2001; Redditch borough cllr, 1991-97. Head of economics and business studies at local comp. Dir, Redditch and Bromsgrove Business Link; chairwoman, Redditch Ed Forum. Member, NUT; SEA; Anti-Apartheid Movement. Teacher. Ed Dyson Perrins HS, Malvern; Hertford Coll, Oxford; Worcester Coll of HE.
e-mail: smithjj@parliament.uk tel: 020-7219 5190 fax: 020-7219 4815

This seat is located in Worcestershire, due south of Birmingham. Redditch itself was designated a new town in the 1960s and has expanded steadily since then. The residents have rather more in common with the urban West Midlands than other parts of their county, though rural villages such as Inkberrow belie that trend. Both of the main parties are strong here and the seat is likely to be carried by whichever holds the Commons. Map 473

## REGENT'S PARK & KENSINGTON NORTH — Lab hold

| Electorate | %Turnout | | 75,886 | 48.83% | 2001 | 73,752 | 64.19% | 1997 |
|---|---|---|---|---|---|---|---|---|
| **Buck Ms K** | **Lab** | | **20,247** | **54.64%** | **-5.28%** | **28,367** | **59.92%** | **Lab** |
| Wilson P | C | | 9,981 | 26.94% | -2.02% | 13,710 | 28.96% | C |
| Boyle D | LD | | 4,669 | 12.6% | 4.06% | 4,041 | 8.54% | LD |
| Miller Dr P | Green | | 1,268 | 3.42% | | 867 | 1.83% | Ref |
| Mieville C | Soc All | | 459 | 1.24% | | 192 | 0.41% | NLP |
| Crisp A | UK Ind | | 354 | 0.96% | | 167 | 0.35% | Dream |
| Regan Ms C | Ind | | 74 | 0.2% | | | | |
| **Lab to C swing** | **1.63%** | | **37,052** | Lab maj 10,266 | | **47,344** | Lab maj 14,657 | |
| | | | | 27.71% | | | 30.96% | |

**KAREN BUCK,** b Aug 30, 1958. Elected 1997. Member, Social Security Select Cttee, 1997-2001; member, Selection Cttee, 1997-2001. Lab Party campaign strategy co-ordinator, Millbank media centre, and acting Lab dir of communications, 1995. Westminster city cllr, 1990-. Ex-chairwoman, Westminster Objectors Trust. Ex-board member, inner city regeneration project and EC urban funding project. Chairwoman, Westminster N CLP, 1988-90. Member, TGWU. Ed Chelmsford County HS; LSE.

The rather grand title of this Central London seat might suggest a political complexion not dissimilar to that of Kensington and Chelsea. It is, in fact, very different. There are some extremely plush pockets but this is effectively the poorer half of West London, with a sizeable Afro-Caribbean community in Notting Hill, home of the massive annual carnival. It is a very reliable prospect for Labour. Map 474

## REIGATE

**C hold**

| Electorate | %Turnout | | 65,023 | 60.71% | 2001 | 64,750 | 74.4% | 1997 |
|---|---|---|---|---|---|---|---|---|
| **Blunt C** | | **C** | **18,875** | **47.82%** | **3.97%** | **21,123** | **43.85%** | **C** |
| Charleton S | | Lab | 10,850 | 27.49% | -0.29% | 13,382 | 27.78% | Lab |
| Kulka Ms J | | LD | 8,330 | 21.1% | 1.14% | 9,615 | 19.96% | LD |
| Smith S | | UK Ind | 1,062 | 2.69% | 2.09% | 3,352 | 6.96% | Ref |
| Green H | | Ref UK | 357 | 0.9% | | 412 | 0.86% | Ind |
| | | | | | | 290 | 0.6% | UK Ind |
| **Lab to C swing** | **2.13%** | | **39,474** | | **C maj 8,025** | **48,174** | | **C maj 7,741** |
| | | | | | 20.33% | | | 16.07% |

**CRISPIN BLUNT,** b July 15, 1960. Elected 1997. Member, Environment, Transport and Reg Affairs Select Cttee and Environment Sub-Cttee, 1997-2001. Ex-adviser to Foreign Sec; special adviser to Defence Sec, 1993-97. Sec, C Backbench Foreign and Commonwealth Affairs Cttee, 1997-. Former army officer. Ed Wellington Coll, Berkshire; Sandhurst; Durham Univ; Cranfield Sch of Management.
e- mail: crispinbluntmp@parliament.uk www.crispinbluntmp.com
tel: 020-7219 2254/1539 fax: 020-7219 3373

This seat might conjure up images of comfortable, suburban Surrey but it is rather more complicated. The Tories are strong here but there are working-class voters as well as many middle-class commuters. Sandwiched between the North Downs and the approaches to Gatwick Airport, the seat is dominated by Reigate itself and Redhill, its bustling, commercial neighbour. It is Tory territory but with room for progress by both the other main parties. Map 475

## RENFREWSHIRE WEST

**Lab hold**

| Electorate | %Turnout | | 52,889 | 63.33% | 2001 | 52,348 | 76.0% | 1997 |
|---|---|---|---|---|---|---|---|---|
| **Sheridan J** | | **Lab** | **15,720** | **46.93%** | **0.37%** | **18,525** | **46.56%** | **Lab** |
| Puthucheary Ms C | | SNP | 7,145 | 21.33% | -5.18% | 10,546 | 26.51% | SNP |
| Sharpe D | | C | 5,522 | 16.49% | -2.08% | 7,387 | 18.57% | C |
| Hamblen Ms C | | LD | 4,185 | 12.49% | 4.84% | 3,045 | 7.65% | LD |
| Nunnery Ms A | | SSP | 925 | 2.76% | | 283 | 0.71% | Ref |
| **SNP to Lab swing** | **2.77%** | | **33,497** | | **Lab maj 8,575** | **39,786** | | **Lab maj 7,979** |
| | | | | | 25.60% | | | 20.05% |

**JAMES SHERIDAN,** b Nov 24, 1952. Elected 2001. Seat previously held by Tommy Graham, who was expelled from the Lab party. T&G member. Renfrewshire cllr, 1999-. Member, council's children's panel advisory cttee. Set up local bus users' forum to improve transport for the elderly. Chairman, youth audit team campaigning for better youth leisure facilities. Ed Sixtus Primary Sch and St Pius Comp Schs, Glasgow.

This seat is the heir to a part of Scotland in which Labour and the Tories were highly competitive. The Boundary Commissioners have largely removed that competition. This part of Clydeside consists of the old shipbuilding and engineering town of Port Glasgow and pleasant inland countryside away from the Firth. It is solid terrain for Labour with only the SNP capable of mounting any sort of challenge. Map 476

## RHONDDA

**Lab hold**

| Electorate | %Turnout | | 56,059 | 60.65% | 2001 | 57,105 | 71.46% | 1997 |
|---|---|---|---|---|---|---|---|---|
| **Bryant C** | | **Lab** | **23,230** | **68.32%** | **-6.13%** | **30,381** | **74.45%** | **Lab** |
| Wood Ms L | | PC | 7,183 | 21.13% | 7.77% | 5,450 | 13.36% | PC |
| Hobbins P | | C | 1,557 | 4.58% | 0.78% | 2,307 | 5.65% | LD |
| Cox G | | LD | 1,525 | 4.49% | -1.16% | 1,551 | 3.8% | C |
| Summers G | | Ind | 507 | 1.49% | | 658 | 1.61% | Ref |
| | | | | | | 460 | 1.13% | Green |
| **Lab to PC swing** | **6.95%** | | **34,002** | | **Lab maj 16,047** | **40,807** | | **Lab maj 24,931** |
| | | | | | 47.19% | | | 61.09% |

**CHRIS BRYANT,** b Jan 11, 1962. Elected, 2001. Takes over seat from Allan Rogers, who held it for 18 years. Curate (All Saints, High Wycombe; Diocese of Peterborough). Ordained, 1987. Head of European affairs at the BBC, 1998-2000. Author of *Stafford Cripps: the first modern Chancellor* (1997). Former Hackney cllr and local gvt development officer. Christian Socialist. Ed Cheltenham Coll; Mansfield Coll, Oxford (English); Ripon Coll, Cuddesdon (theology).

This is one of those parts of the South Wales Valleys where they don't count the Labour vote but weigh it. The Communists were at times the second party in this mining seat; but more recently Plaid Cymru pulled off a huge upset in the 1999 Welsh Assembly elections. Rhondda consists of a string of small towns with evocative names - Tonpentre, Tonypandy, Treorchy and so on - based on the heritage of coal, the chapel, rugby and male voice choirs. Map 477

## RIBBLE SOUTH (SOUTH RIBBLE) — Lab hold

| Electorate | %Turnout | | 73,794 | 62.51% | 2001 | 71,670 | 77.06% | 1997 |
|---|---|---|---|---|---|---|---|---|
| **Borrow D** | | **Lab** | **21,386** | **46.36%** | **-0.45%** | **25,856** | **46.81%** | **Lab** |
| Owens A | | C | 17,594 | 38.14% | 0.53% | 20,772 | 37.61% | C |
| Alcock M | | LD | 7,150 | 15.5% | 4.86% | 5,879 | 10.64% | LD |
| | | | | | | 1,475 | 2.67% | Ref |
| | | | | | | 1,127 | 2.04% | Lib |
| | | | | | | 122 | 0.22% | NLP |
| **Lab to C swing** | | **0.49%** | **46,130** | Lab maj **3,792** | | **55,231** | Lab maj **5,084** | |
| | | | | 8.22% | | | 9.20% | |

**DAVID BORROW,** b Aug 2, 1952. Elected 1997. Member, Agriculture Select Cttee, 1997-2001. Chairman, PLP Trade and Industry Cttee, 1997-. Preston borough cllr, leader, 1992-94 and 1995-97. Member, Co-op Party; Fabian Soc; Lab campaign for electoral reform. Tribunal clerk. Ed Mirfield GS; Lanchester Poly, Coventry. e-mail; david-borrow.labour@virgin.net tel/fax: 020-7219 4126

This seat hugs the south bank of the River Ribble, across the water from Preston. It contains the industrial town of Leyland and the parishes of Penwortham and Longton. It is a mixed area socially with a surprisingly high rate of owner-occupation. The Conservatives dominated here until 1997 when Labour won to create a crucial marginal; the vote in 2001 confirmed this trend. **Map 478**

## RIBBLE VALLEY — C hold

| Electorate | %Turnout | | 74,319 | 66.16% | 2001 | 72,664 | 78.75% | 1997 |
|---|---|---|---|---|---|---|---|---|
| **Evans N** | | **C** | **25,308** | **51.47%** | **4.81%** | **26,702** | **46.66%** | **C** |
| Carr M | | LD | 14,070 | 28.61% | -6.45% | 20,062 | 35.06% | LD |
| Johnstone M | | Lab | 9,793 | 19.92% | 4.17% | 9,013 | 15.75% | Lab |
| | | | | | | 1,297 | 2.27% | Ref |
| | | | | | | 147 | 0.26% | NLP |
| **LD to C swing** | | **5.63%** | **49,171** | C maj **11,238** | | **57,221** | C maj **6,640** | |
| | | | | 22.85% | | | 11.60% | |

**NIGEL EVANS,** b Nov 10, 1957. Elected 1992. Vice-chairman, C Party, 1999-. Frontbench spokesman, Constitutional Affairs and Wales, 1997-. PPS to Welsh Sec, 1996-97. Joint vice-chairman, all-party grps: Euro secure vehicle alliance; retail industry, 1997-; joint treas, space cttee, 1997-; sec and treas, occupational safety and health grp, 1997-. Owner, convenience store. Ed Dynevor Sch; Univ Coll, Swansea. e-mail: nigelmp@hotmail.com www.nigelmp.com fax: 0870-131 3711

This is affluent and attractive rural north Lancashire, inland and further north than the similarly named Ribble South. It extends from the Preston suburb of Fulwood up to the Bowland Forest, and to Clitheroe in the east. Owner-occupation is very high and council tenants and non-white faces very few. The Liberal Democrats captured the seat in a 1991 by-election and continue to be a force here; but this is instinctively Conservative territory. **Map 479**

## RICHMOND (YORKS) — C hold

| Electorate | %Turnout | | 65,360 | 67.37% | 2001 | 65,058 | 73.38% | 1997 |
|---|---|---|---|---|---|---|---|---|
| **Hague W** | | **C** | **25,951** | **58.93%** | **10.07%** | **23,326** | **48.86%** | **C** |
| Tinnion Ms F | | Lab | 9,632 | 21.87% | -5.94% | 13,275 | 27.81% | Lab |
| Forth E | | LD | 7,890 | 17.92% | -0.46% | 8,773 | 18.38% | LD |
| Staniforth Mrs M | | Loony | 561 | 1.27% | | 2,367 | 4.96% | Ref |
| **Lab to C swing** | | **8.00%** | **44,034** | C maj **16,319** | | **47,741** | C maj **10,051** | |
| | | | | 37.06% | | | 21.05% | |

**WILLIAM HAGUE,** b March 26, 1961. Elected 1989 by-election; contested Wentworth 1987. Opposition Leader, July 1997-2001. Welsh Sec, 1995-97. Min for Social Security and the Disabled, 1994-95; Under-Sec for Social Security, 1993-94; PPS, Norman Lamont, Chancellor, 1990-93. Management consultant, McKinsey and Co Ltd, 1983-88. Political adviser, Treasury, 1983. Ed Wath-upon-Dearne Comp; Magdalen Coll, Oxford (Pres of Union); Institut Européen d'Administration des Affaires.

William Hague, who led the Tories to defeat in the 2001 election and then quit as leader, represents one of the largest constituencies in England. This vast swath of North Yorkshire includes Swaledale and Wensleydale, the towns of Richmond and Northallerton, and many remote hill villages. There is also a military influence through the Army at Catterick. Despite Mr Hague's personal political misfortune, his majority here remains rock-solid. **Map 480**

## RICHMOND PARK

**LD hold**

| Electorate | %Turnout | | 72,663 | 67.64% | 2001 | 71,572 | 79.43% | 1997 |
|---|---|---|---|---|---|---|---|---|
| **Tonge Dr J** | | LD | **23,444** | **47.7%** | **3.04%** | **25,393** | **44.66%** | **LD** |
| Harris T | | C | 18,480 | 37.6% | -1.87% | 22,442 | 39.47% | C |
| Langford B | | Lab | 5,541 | 11.27% | -1.34% | 7,172 | 12.61% | Lab |
| Page J | | Green | 1,223 | 2.49% | | 1,467 | 2.58% | Ref |
| St John Howe P | | UK Ind | 348 | 0.71% | | 204 | 0.36% | Loony |
| Perrin R | | Ind | 115 | 0.23% | | 102 | 0.18% | NLP |
| | | | | | | 73 | 0.13% | Dream |
| **C to LD swing** | **2.45%** | | **49,151** | | **LD maj 4,964** | **56,853** | | **LD maj 2,951** |
| | | | | | 10.10% | | | 5.19% |

**JENNY TONGE,** b Feb 19, 1941. Elected 1997. LD spokeswoman, International Development, 1997-; confirmed June 2001. Member, International Development Select Cttee, 1997-99. Joint chairwoman, all-party breast cancer grp; joint vice-chairwoman, all-party grps on Aids, doctor-assisted dying, pro-choice and Rwanda prevention of genocide. Doctor; ex-NHS manager. Ed Dudley Girls' HS; Univ Coll and Univ Coll Hosp, London.
e-mail: tonge@cix.co.uk www.jennytonge.org.uk tel: 020-7219 5563 fax: 020-7219 4596

This seat is a highly distinctive southwest London constituency, merging Richmond and Barnes with the northern part of Kingston upon Thames. It has a very high number of professionals and managers, many living in large houses near the park. About a third of the voters have higher education qualifications. It has long been a battleground between the Tories and the Lib Dems, a struggle won by the latter in 1997 and again in 2001. Map 481

## ROCHDALE

**Lab hold**

| Electorate | %Turnout | | 69,506 | 56.7% | 2001 | 68,529 | 70.16% | 1997 |
|---|---|---|---|---|---|---|---|---|
| **Fitzsimons Ms L** | | Lab | **19,406** | **49.24%** | **-0.17%** | **23,758** | **49.41%** | **Lab** |
| Rowen P | | LD | 13,751 | 34.89% | -5.07% | 19,213 | 39.96% | LD |
| Cohen Ms E | | C | 5,274 | 13.38% | 4.57% | 4,237 | 8.81% | C |
| Harvey N | | Green | 728 | 1.85% | | 653 | 1.36% | BNP |
| Salim M | | Ind | 253 | 0.64% | | 221 | 0.46% | IZB |
| **LD to Lab swing** | **2.45%** | | **39,412** | | **Lab maj 5,655** | **48,082** | | **Lab maj 4,545** |
| | | | | | 14.35% | | | 9.45% |

**LORNA FITZSIMONS,** b Aug 6, 1967. Elected 1997. PPS to Robin Cook, Leader of the House of Commons, June 2001-. Member, Modernisation of the Commons Procedures Select Cttee, 1997-2001; chairwoman, PLP Women's Cttee. Sec, all-party Kashmir grp, 1997-; treas, all-party textile, footwear and clothing grp. Co-parly chairwoman, Commonwealth ed council; member, Lab campaign for electoral reform. Parly vice-pres, British Dyslexia Assoc; member, Fabian Soc; Co-op Party. Ed Wardle HS, Wardle; Rochdale Coll of Art and Design; Loughborough Coll of Art and Design.

This industrial and textile town on the northeastern edge of Greater Manchester has been a marginal constituency for three decades. Cyril Smith won it for the Liberal Party in a 1972 by-election. Although he stood down 20 years later, and had little time for the merger of the Liberal and Social Democratic parties, his influence has continued. But in 1997 Labour at last won back a seat that has an Asian population of some 15 per cent. Map 482

## ROCHFORD & SOUTHEND EAST

**C hold**

| Electorate | %Turnout | | 69,991 | 53.51% | 2001 | 72,848 | 63.97% | 1997 |
|---|---|---|---|---|---|---|---|---|
| **Taylor Sir Teddy** | | C | **20,058** | **53.56%** | **4.88%** | **22,683** | **48.68%** | **C** |
| Dandridge C | | Lab | 13,024 | 34.78% | -4.83% | 18,458 | 39.61% | Lab |
| Newton S | | LD | 2,780 | 7.42% | -1.99% | 4,387 | 9.41% | LD |
| Hedges A | | Green | 990 | 2.64% | | 1,070 | 2.3% | Lib |
| Lynch B | | Lib | 600 | 1.6% | -0.7% | | | |
| **Lab to C swing** | **4.86%** | | **37,452** | | **C maj 7,034** | **46,598** | | **C maj 4,225** |
| | | | | | 18.78% | | | 9.07% |

**SIR TEDDY TAYLOR,** b April 18, 1937. Elected here 1997; MP for Southend E 1980-97; Glasgow Cathcart 1964-79. Member, Treasury Select Cttee, 1997-2001. Joint vice-chairman, all-party consumer affairs and trading standards grp, 1997-. Under-Sec for Scotland, 1974, and, 1970-71, when he resigned over govt policy on Europe. C whip withdrawn, 1994-95. Vice-chairman, 1992-94 and joint sec, 1983-92, C Backbench Home Affairs Cttee. Sec, C Europe reform grp, 1980-. Parly adviser to the Port of London Police Fed, 1972-. Consultant/director. Ed Glasgow HS; Glasgow Univ.

The eastern part of Southend is the less affluent part of this Essex seaside resort town. It is quite competitive between the Conservatives and Labour. The rest of the seat - notably Rochford, Great Wakering and Foulness Island (once proposed as the site of the third London airport at Maplin Sands) - is, however, more inclined towards the Tories. It would take a devastating result nationally for them to lose here. Map 483

## ROMFORD — C gain

| Electorate | %Turnout | | 59,893 | 59.61% | 2001 | 59,611 | 70.66% | 1997 |
|---|---|---|---|---|---|---|---|---|
| **Rosindell A** | **C** | | **18,931** | **53.03%** | **11.39%** | **18,187** | **43.18%** | **Lab** |
| Gordon Ms E | Lab | | 12,954 | 36.28% | -6.9% | 17,538 | 41.64% | C |
| Meyer N | LD | | 2,869 | 8.04% | 0.11% | 3,341 | 7.93% | LD |
| Ward S | UK Ind | | 533 | 1.49% | | 1,431 | 3.4% | Ref |
| McAllister F | BNP | | 414 | 1.16% | -0.08% | 1,100 | 2.61% | Lib |
| | | | | | | 522 | 1.24% | BNP |
| **Lab to C swing** | **9.14%** | | **35,701** | | **C maj 5,977** | **42,119** | | **Lab maj 649** |
| | | | | | 16.74% | | | 1.54% |

**ANDREW ROSINDELL,** b March 17, 1966. Elected 2001; contested Thurrock 1997 and Glasgow Provan 1992. Member, nat union exec cttee of C Party, 1992-94 and 1986-88. Chairman, Romford C assoc, 1998-. Member, Romford council. Dir, The European Foundation, 1997-. Chairman European Young Conservatives, 1993-97; National Young Conservatives, 1993-94. Freelance journalist. Ed Marshalls Park Sec Sch, Romford.
e mail andrew@andrew1.tory.org.uk

This constituency covers the northwestern section of the London Borough of Havering, on the northeast edge of Greater London. Like many of these Outer London seats, however, it has the flavour of Essex about it. Romford is a big regional shopping centre, while the vast majority of residents are white owner-occupiers but not especially affluent. Labour secured a huge swing to win by a tiny majority in 1997 but failed to hold on in 2001. Map 484

## ROMSEY — LD gain

| Electorate | %Turnout | | 70,584 | 68.65% | 2001 | 67,306 | 76.99% | 1997 |
|---|---|---|---|---|---|---|---|---|
| **Gidley Mrs S** | **LD** | | **22,756** | **46.96%** | **17.53%** | **23,834** | **45.99%** | **C** |
| Raynes P | C | | 20,386 | 42.07% | -3.92% | 15,249 | 29.43% | LD |
| Roberts S | Lab | | 3,986 | 8.23% | -10.34% | 9,623 | 18.57% | Lab |
| McCabe A | UK Ind | | 730 | 1.51% | -2.01% | 1,824 | 3.52% | UK Ind |
| Large D | LCA | | 601 | 1.24% | 0.16% | 1,291 | 2.49% | Ref |
| **C to LD swing** | **10.73%** | | **48,459** | | **LD maj 2,370** | **51,821** | | **C maj 8,585** |
| | | | | | 4.89% | | | 16.56% |

**SANDRA GIDLEY,** b March 26, 1957. Elected 2000 by-election. Member, all-party grps, drugs misuse; breast cancer, aids; alternative medicine; cancer; community health councils; male cancers; maternity; mental health; pharmacy; post offices; primary care and public health. Mayor of Romsey, 1997-98. Pharmacist. Ed Eggars GS, Alton, Hants; Afcent Int Brunssum, Netherlands; Windsor GS, Hamm, W Germany; Bath Univ.
e-mail: sgidley@cix.co.uk www.sandragidley.org tel: 01794 511900 fax: 01794 512538. *Details of 2000 by-election on page 291*

The politics of this largely rural Hampshire seat, extending from the Southampton suburbs to the pretty villages of the Test Valley towards Stockbridge, were transformed by a by-election in 2000. On paper Romsey should be as solidly Tory as many of its Hampshire neighbours. This was indeed the case in 1997 but the Lib Dems usurped the Tories in the 2000 contest - and kept control a year later. For a while at least Romsey looks a close call. Map 485

## ROSS, SKYE & INVERNESS WEST — LD hold

| Electorate | %Turnout | | 56,522 | 61.59% | 2001 | 55,639 | 71.81% | 1997 |
|---|---|---|---|---|---|---|---|---|
| **Kennedy C** | **LD** | | **18,832** | **54.1%** | **15.38%** | **15,472** | **38.72%** | **LD** |
| Crichton D | Lab | | 5,880 | 16.89% | -11.77% | 11,453 | 28.66% | Lab |
| Urquhart Ms J | SNP | | 4,901 | 14.08% | -5.49% | 7,821 | 19.57% | SNP |
| Laing A | C | | 3,096 | 8.89% | -2.04% | 4,368 | 10.93% | C |
| Scott Dr E | Green | | 699 | 2.01% | 1.24% | 535 | 1.34% | Ref |
| Topp S | SSP | | 683 | 1.96% | | 306 | 0.77% | Green |
| Anderson P | UK Ind | | 456 | 1.31% | | | | |
| Crawford J | Country | | 265 | 0.76% | | | | |
| **Lab to LD swing** | **13.57%** | | **34,812** | | **LD maj 12,952** | **39,955** | | **LD maj 4,019** |
| | | | | | 37.21% | | | 10.06% |

**CHARLES KENNEDY,** b Nov 25, 1959. Elected here 1997. Leader, Liberal Democrats, 1999-; won Ross, Cromarty and Skye 1983 for SDP/All. Became LD MP, 1988. Pres, LD, 1990-94. Member, Standards and Privileges Select Cttee, 1997-99. LD spokesman: agriculture and rural affairs, 1997-99; EU, 1992-97; health, 1989-92; trade and industry, 1988-89. Assoc editor, *The House Magazine*. Ed Lochaber HS, Fort William; Glasgow Univ; Indiana Univ.
e-mail: rossldp@cix.co.uk www.charleskennedy.org.uk
tel: 020-7219 6226 fax: 020-7219 4881

This spectacular Highlands and Islands constituency is the largest in the UK. It extends from the lochs and mountains of Skye and the West Coast eastwards to the Cromarty Firth, including parts of Inverness west of the Caledonian Canal. The almost two million acres contain a relatively small number of electors. The personal vote is as important here as partisan allegiance; Charles Kennedy appears to have secured a huge personal loyalty. Map 486

# ROSSENDALE & DARWEN
**Lab hold**

| Electorate | %Turnout | | 70,280 | 58.85% | 2001 | 69,749 | 73.42% | 1997 |
|---|---|---|---|---|---|---|---|---|
| **Anderson Ms J** | | **Lab** | **20,251** | **48.97%** | **-4.67%** | 27,470 | 53.64% | Lab |
| Lee G | | C | 15,028 | 36.34% | 4.08% | 16,521 | 32.26% | C |
| Dunning B | | LD | 6,079 | 14.7% | 4.09% | 5,435 | 10.61% | LD |
| | | | | | | 1,108 | 2.16% | Ref |
| | | | | | | 674 | 1.32% | BNP |
| **Lab to C swing** | **4.38%** | | **41,358** | Lab maj 5,223 | | **51,208** | Lab maj 10,949 | |
| | | | | 12.63% | | | 21.38% | |

**JANET ANDERSON,** b Dec 6, 1949. Elected 1997. Min for Tourism, Film and Broadcasting, 1998-2001. Gvt Whip, 1997-98. Lab spokeswoman, women's issues, 1996-97; Lab whip, 1995-96. Member,Home Affairs Select Cttee, 1992-95. PPS to Margaret Beckett, Lab dep leader, 1992-93. Sec, Tribune Grp of Lab MPs, 1993-97. PA to Barbara Castle, 1974-81, and Jack Straw, 1981-87. Ed Kingsfield Comp, Bristol; Central London Poly; Nantes Univ.
e-mail: andersonj@parliament.uk fax: 020-7219 2148

Labour's recent successes in this constituency are deceptive. This is, in essence, a classic Lancashire marginal, situated in the Bolton-Blackburn-Burnley triangle up the Pennine valleys. One half of the seat, Rossendale, named from the valley of the Irwell west of Bacup, has a powerful industrial heritage and tends to support Labour. Further west, Darwen, now a favoured residential area, and other smaller communities are more Conservative territory. Map 487

# ROTHER VALLEY
**Lab hold**

| Electorate | %Turnout | | 69,174 | 53.2% | 2001 | 68,622 | 67.26% | 1997 |
|---|---|---|---|---|---|---|---|---|
| **Barron K** | | **Lab** | **22,851** | **62.09%** | **-5.47%** | 31,184 | 67.56% | Lab |
| Duddridge J | | C | 7,969 | 21.65% | 4.97% | 7,699 | 16.68% | C |
| Knight Ms W | | LD | 4,603 | 12.51% | 0.94% | 5,342 | 11.57% | LD |
| Cutts D | | UK Ind | 1,380 | 3.75% | | 1,932 | 4.19% | Ref |
| **Lab to C swing** | **5.22%** | | **36,803** | Lab maj 14,882 | | **46,157** | Lab maj 23,485 | |
| | | | | 40.44% | | | 50.88% | |

**KEVIN BARRON,** b Oct 26, 1946. Elected 1983. Member, Parly Intelligence and Security Cttee, 1997-2001. Chairman, PLP Health Cttee, 1997-. Chairman, all-party grps: smoking and health and pharmaceutical industry, 1997-. Member, Select Cttees: Environment, 1992-93; Energy, 1983-85. Lab spokesman, health, 1995-97; employment, 1993-95; energy, particularly coal, 1988-92. PPS to Neil Kinnock, Opposition Leader, 1985-88. Chairman, Yorkshire grp of Lab MPs. Miner, 1962-83; NUM delegate for Maltby colliery. Ed Maltby Hall Sec Mod; Ruskin Coll, Oxford.

This South Yorkshire constituency is bordered by the Sheffield seats to the west, Rotherham to the northwest and Don Valley to the north. It has a number of small towns where the social and political legacy of coalmining remain dominant. These are supplemented by more rural territory which is less hostile to the Conservatives. This is, nonetheless, an extremely solid Labour constituency. Map 488

# ROTHERHAM
**Lab hold**

| Electorate | %Turnout | | 57,931 | 50.67% | 2001 | 59,895 | 62.86% | 1997 |
|---|---|---|---|---|---|---|---|---|
| **MacShane D** | | **Lab** | **18,759** | **63.91%** | **-7.41%** | 26,852 | 71.32% | Lab |
| Powell R | | C | 5,682 | 19.36% | 5.06% | 5,383 | 14.3% | C |
| Hall C | | LD | 3,117 | 10.62% | 0.21% | 3,919 | 10.41% | LD |
| Griffith P | | UK Ind | 730 | 2.49% | | 1,132 | 3.01% | Ref |
| Penycate D | | Green | 577 | 1.97% | | 364 | 0.97% | ProLife |
| Smith Ms F | | Soc All | 352 | 1.2% | | | | |
| Bartholomew G | | JLDP | 137 | 0.47% | | | | |
| **Lab to C swing** | **6.24%** | | **29,354** | Lab maj 13,077 | | **37,650** | Lab maj 21,469 | |
| | | | | 44.55% | | | 57.02% | |

**DENIS MacSHANE,** b May 21, 1948. Elected 1994 by-election. Parly Sec, FCO, June, 2001-; PPS to Min of State for Foreign Affairs, 1997-2001. Member, Council, Royal Inst of International Affairs, 1999-; member, Deregulation Select Cttee, 1996-97. Ex-joint vice-chairman, all-party future of Europe grp. Dir, European policy inst, 1992-94. Editorial board member, *Critical Quarterly*; policy dir, International Metalworkers Fed, 1980-92. Pres, NUJ, 1978-9. Journalist. Ed Merton Coll, Oxford; Birkbeck Coll, London.

Another heavily industrial South Yorkshire seat, Rotherham once relied on coal and steel as its main sources of employment and as the centre of community activity. The old industries have all but disappeared and the economic transition has been painful. The vast Meadowhall shopping centre, just in neighbouring Sheffield but right on the Rotherham border, helps to alleviate the urban blight. But this remains a completely secure Labour seat. Map 489

## ROXBURGH & BERWICKSHIRE — LD hold

| Electorate | %Turnout | 47,059 | 61.19% | 2001 | 47,259 | 73.91% | 1997 |
|---|---|---|---|---|---|---|---|
| Kirkwood A | LD | 14,044 | 48.77% | 2.27% | 16,243 | 46.5% | LD |
| Turnbull G | C | 6,533 | 22.69% | -1.18% | 8,337 | 23.87% | C |
| Maxwell-Stuart Ms C | Lab | 4,498 | 15.62% | 0.66% | 5,226 | 14.96% | Lab |
| Campbell R | SNP | 2,806 | 9.74% | -1.59% | 3,959 | 11.33% | SNP |
| Millar Ms A | SSP | 463 | 1.61% | | 922 | 2.64% | Ref |
| Neilson P | UK Ind | 453 | 1.57% | 0.99% | 202 | 0.58% | UK Ind |
| | | | | | 42 | 0.12% | NLP |
| C to LD swing | 1.73% | 28,797 | LD maj 7,511 | | 34,931 | LD maj 7,906 | |
| | | 26.08% | | | | 22.63% | |

**ARCHY KIRKWOOD,** b April 22, 1946. Elected 1983, becoming LD MP 1988. Member, LD frontbench team, confirmed June 2001. Chairman, Social Security Select Cttee, 1997-2001, and member, Liaison Select Cttee. Vice-chairman, all-party sub-post offices grp, 2000-. LD Chief Whip, 1992-97. Spokesman, community care, 1994-97; social security, 1992-94; welfare, 1988-92. Chairman, Joseph Rowntree Reform Trust. Ed Cranhill Sec, Glasgow; Heriot-Watt Univ (Union Pres).
e-mail: kirkwooda@parliament.uk tel: 020-7219 6523 fax: 020-7219 6437

This Scottish Borders seat was created by the Boundary Commissioners in the 1980s by reorganising David Steel's old constituency. It now contains towns such as Hawick, Jedburgh and Kelso, strongly associated with the tweed and knitwear industry and now tourist attractions as well. This is also big farming country, stretching up the North Sea coast above Berwick. The Liberal Democrats now seem well dug in, with the opposition badly splintered. Map 490

## RUGBY & KENILWORTH — Lab hold

| Electorate | %Turnout | 79,764 | 67.44% | 2001 | 79,384 | 77.1% | 1997 |
|---|---|---|---|---|---|---|---|
| King A | Lab | 24,221 | 45.02% | 1.96% | 26,356 | 43.06% | Lab |
| Martin D | C | 21,344 | 39.68% | -2.57% | 25,861 | 42.25% | C |
| Fairweather Ms G | LD | 7,444 | 13.84% | -0.43% | 8,737 | 14.27% | LD |
| Garratt P | UK Ind | 787 | 1.46% | | 251 | 0.41% | NLP |
| C to Lab swing | 2.27% | 53,796 | Lab maj 2,877 | | 61,205 | Lab maj 495 | |
| | | | 5.35% | | | 0.81% | |

**ANDY KING,** b Sept 14, 1948. Elected 1997. Member, Deregulation and Social Security Select Cttees, 1999-2001. Former social work manager, Northants County Council. Member, Warwickshire County Council, 1989-; chairman social services, 1993-96. Labourer. Postal officer. Apprentice motor vehicle mechanic. Ed Coatbridge Tech Coll; Missionary Inst, London; Hatfield Poly.

This Warwickshire marginal south of Coventry is an odd and not uncontroversial amalgamation. Rugby, in spite of the image of its famous public school, is an urban and largely working-class town seriously inclined to support Labour. Kenilworth, by contrast, is distinctly affluent commuter territory and, in alliance with the leafy Warwickshire villages, is rather Conservative. The combination worked in favour of the Tories until their 1997 meltdown. Map 491

## RUISLIP-NORTHWOOD — C hold

| Electorate | %Turnout | 60,788 | 61.1% | 2001 | 60,393 | 74.24% | 1997 |
|---|---|---|---|---|---|---|---|
| Wilkinson J | C | 18,115 | 48.77% | -1.47% | 22,526 | 50.24% | C |
| Travis Ms G | Lab | 10,578 | 28.48% | -4.38% | 14,732 | 32.86% | Lab |
| Cox M | LD | 7,177 | 19.32% | 3.08% | 7,279 | 16.24% | LD |
| Lee G | Green | 724 | 1.95% | | 296 | 0.66% | NLP |
| Edward I | BNP | 547 | 1.47% | | | | |
| Lab to C swing | 1.46% | 37,141 | C maj 7,537 | | 44,833 | C maj 7,794 | |
| | | | 20.29% | | | 17.38% | |

**JOHN WILKINSON,** b Sept 23, 1940. Elected here 1979; MP for Bradford W 1970-74. Had C whip withdrawn, 1994-95, over failure to support Govt's EU policy. Chairman, federated grp of Christian Democrat and C MPs; Assembly of WEU, 2000-. Chairman, Manx and Philippines all-party grps; joint vice-chairman, Chile, Estonia and Iceland grps; sec, Latin America grp. Pres, London green belt council, 1997-. Commonwealth War Graves Commissioner, 1997-. RAF pilot. Ed Eton; RAF Coll, Cranwell; Churchill Coll, Cambridge. fax: 0207-219 7850

This constituency is located on the far northwestern tip of Greater London. With its many wealthy and middle-class residential areas, it has a social composition closer to neighbouring Hertfordshire than to the capital city. There is a large commuter population who travel into London via the Metropolitan Underground line. This is extremely solid territory for the Conservative Party. Map 492

## RUNNYMEDE & WEYBRIDGE

**C hold**

| Electorate | %Turnout | | 75,569 | 56.14% | 2001 | 72,177 | 71.44% | 1997 |
|---|---|---|---|---|---|---|---|---|
| **Hammond P** | **C** | **20,646** | **48.66%** | **0.07%** | **25,051** | **48.59%** | **C** |
| Briginshaw Ms J | Lab | 12,286 | 28.96% | -0.47% | 15,176 | 29.43% | Lab |
| Bushill C | LD | 6,924 | 16.32% | 0.03% | 8,397 | 16.29% | LD |
| Browne C | UK Ind | 1,332 | 3.14% | 1.93% | 2,150 | 4.17% | Ref |
| Gilman C | Green | 1,238 | 2.92% | | 625 | 1.21% | UK Ind |
| | | | | | 162 | 0.31% | NLP |
| **Lab to C swing** | **0.27%** | **42,426** | | **C maj 8,360** | **51,561** | | **C maj 9,875** |
| | | | | 19.70% | | | 19.16% |

**PHILIP HAMMOND,** b Dec 4, 1955. Elected 1997. Opposition spokesman, Health and Social Services, 1998-. Member, Unopposed Bills Panel, 1997; Environment, Transport and Regions Select Cttee, 1997-98; sec, C Backbench Health Cttee, 1997. Ex-chairman, E Lewisham C assoc. Former dir, medical equipment manufacturing co. Co-founder and ex-managing dir, business development consultancy. Ed Shenfield Sch, Brentwood; Univ Coll, Oxford. e-mail: hammondp@parliament.uk fax: 020-7219 5851

Set in northwest Surrey, this seat is a slightly artificial creation assembled by the Boundary Commissioners. Taking part of its name from the Magna Carta Thames-side meadows near Staines, it contains some of the most exclusive private estates in Britain (St George's Hill, Weybridge, and the Wentworth Estate near Virginia Water), as well as towns such as Addlestone that are no more than comfortably affluent. It is very reliably Conservative. Map 493

## RUSHCLIFFE

**C hold**

| Electorate | %Turnout | | 81,839 | 66.53% | 2001 | 78,735 | 78.89% | 1997 |
|---|---|---|---|---|---|---|---|---|
| **Clarke K** | **C** | **25,869** | **47.51%** | **3.14%** | **27,558** | **44.37%** | **C** |
| Fallon P | Lab | 18,512 | 34.0% | -2.23% | 22,503 | 36.23% | Lab |
| Hargreaves J | LD | 7,395 | 13.58% | -0.67% | 8,851 | 14.25% | LD |
| Browne K | UK Ind | 1,434 | 2.63% | 1.98% | 2,682 | 4.32% | Ref |
| Baxter A | Green | 1,236 | 2.27% | | 403 | 0.65% | UK Ind |
| | | | | | 115 | 0.19% | NLP |
| **Lab to C swing** | **2.69%** | **54,446** | | **C maj 7,357** | **62,112** | | **C maj 5,055** |
| | | | | 13.51% | | | 8.14% |

**KENNETH CLARKE,** b July 2, 1940. Elected 1970. Challenger for the Conservative Party leadership, June 2001. Chancellor of the Exchequer, 1993-97; Home Sec, 1992-93; Ed and Science Sec, 1990-92; Health Sec, 1988-90; Trade and Industry Min, 1987-88. Joined Cabinet, 1985 as Paymaster General; Employment Min, 1985-87; Health Min 1982-85; Parly Sec (1979-81) and Under-Sec (1981-82) for Transport. Privy Counsellor. QC. Non-exec chairman, Unichem and then Alliance Unichem, 1997. Ed Nottingham HS; Gonville and Caius Coll, Cambridge (Pres of Union 1963).

This is the southernmost section of Nottinghamshire with a high rate of owner-occupation and many professionals and managers. Rushcliffe is the name of a local authority district rather than a town, and the largest community is West Bridgford, a middle-class commuter suburb on the southeast of Nottingham. The rest of the seat consists of smaller towns such as Bingham and Radcliffe-on-Trent, and tiny villages. It is the Tories' best seat in this county. Map 494

## RUTLAND & MELTON

**C hold**

| Electorate | %Turnout | | 72,448 | 64.95% | 2001 | 70,150 | 75.02% | 1997 |
|---|---|---|---|---|---|---|---|---|
| **Duncan A** | **C** | **22,621** | **48.07%** | **2.27%** | **24,107** | **45.8%** | **C** |
| O'Callaghan M | Lab | 14,009 | 29.77% | 0.75% | 15,271 | 29.02% | Lab |
| Lee K | LD | 8,386 | 17.82% | -1.39% | 10,112 | 19.21% | LD |
| Baker P | UK Ind | 1,223 | 2.6% | 1.04% | 2,317 | 4.4% | Ref |
| Davies C | Green | 817 | 1.74% | | 823 | 1.56% | UK Ind |
| **Lab to C swing** | **0.76%** | **47,056** | | **C maj 8,612** | **52,630** | | **C maj 8,836** |
| | | | | 18.30% | | | 16.78% |

**ALAN DUNCAN,** b March 31, 1957. Elected 1992. Opposition spokesman, Trade and Industry. Party vice-chairman, 1997-98. PPS to Brian Mawhinney, party chairman, 1995-97. Member, Social Security Select Cttee, 1992-95; chairman, C Backbench Constitutional Affairs Cttee, 1994-95. Freeman, City of London; liveryman, Merchant Taylors' Co. Oil trader. Ed Beechwood Park Sch, St Albans; Merchant Taylors' Sch, Northwood; St John's Coll, Oxford (Pres of Union, 1979); Harvard Univ (Kennedy Scholar). e-mail: duncana@parliament.uk tel: 020-7219 5204

Rutland was once England's smallest county and, although a unitary authority once more, is still part of Leicestershire. This is attractive and prosperous East Midland territory. It is an overwhelmingly rural constituency dotted with small towns centred around Melton Mowbray, and Rutland Water. Often described as an area of foxhunting, pork pies and Stilton cheese, it is equally well associated with voting Conservative. Map 495

## RYEDALE — C hold

| Electorate | %Turnout | | 66,543 | 65.97% | 2001 | 65,215 | 74.8% | 1997 |
|---|---|---|---|---|---|---|---|---|
| **Greenway J** | | **C** | **20,711** | **47.18%** | **3.41%** | **21,351** | **43.77%** | **C** |
| Orrell K | | LD | 15,836 | 36.07% | 2.67% | 16,293 | 33.4% | LD |
| Ellis D | | Lab | 6,470 | 14.74% | -3.22% | 8,762 | 17.96% | Lab |
| Feaster S | | UK Ind | 882 | 2.01% | 0.13% | 1,460 | 2.99% | Ref |
| | | | | | | 917 | 1.88% | UK Ind |
| **LD to C swing** | **0.37%** | | **43,899** | | **C maj 4,875** | **48,783** | | **C maj 5,058** |
| | | | | | 11.11% | | | 10.37% |

**JOHN GREENWAY,** b Feb 15, 1946. Elected 1987. C spokesman, sport and tourism. Member, Home Affairs Select Cttee, 1987-97; vice-chairman, C Backbench Agriculture, Fisheries and Food Cttee, 1989-97. Chairman, all-party insurance and financial services grp, 1992-; opera grp, 1994-; joint vice-chairman, football grp, 1990-. Insurance broker, policeman and financial journalist. Ed Sir John Deane's GS, Northwich; Hendon Police Coll.
e-mail: greenwayj@parliament.uk www.ryedaleconservatives.org. uk tel: 020-7219 5483 fax: 020-7219 6059

This large, mostly agricultural North Yorkshire constituency has a high rate of owner-occupation for such a rural seat and virtually no council tenants or non-white electors. The main towns are Malton, Helmsley, Pickering and the North Sea coastal resort of Filey. The Liberal Democrats snatched this seat in a 1986 by-election, the only occasion when they have seriously threatened the Conservative hegemony of this area. Map 496

## SAFFRON WALDEN — C hold

| Electorate | %Turnout | | 76,724 | 65.22% | 2001 | 74,097 | 76.99% | 1997 |
|---|---|---|---|---|---|---|---|---|
| **Haselhurst Sir A** | | **C** | **24,485** | **48.93%** | **3.58%** | **25,871** | **45.35%** | **C** |
| Tealby-Watson Mrs E | | LD | 12,481 | 24.94% | -1.88% | 15,298 | 26.82% | LD |
| Rogers Ms T | | Lab | 11,305 | 22.59% | 1.07% | 12,275 | 21.52% | Lab |
| Glover R | | UK Ind | 1,769 | 3.54% | 2.39% | 2,308 | 4.05% | Ref |
| | | | | | | 658 | 1.15% | UK Ind |
| | | | | | | 486 | 0.85% | Ind |
| | | | | | | 154 | 0.27% | NLP |
| **LD to C swing** | **2.73%** | | **50,040** | | **C maj 12,004** | **57,050** | | **C maj 10,573** |
| | | | | | 23.99% | | | 18.53% |

**SIR ALAN HASELHURST,** b June 23, 1937. Elected here 1977 by-election; MP for Middleton and Prestwich 1970 - Feb 74. Deputy Speaker and Chairman, Ways and Means, 1997-. Member, Select Cttees: European Legislation, 1982-97; Transport 1992-97. Commons Catering Cttee, 1991-97. Privy Counsellor. Sec, all-party cricket grp, 1993-. Ex-sec, all-party aerospace grp. Chairman, Rights of Way Review Cttee, 1983-93. Ed King Edward VI Sch, Birmingham; Cheltenham Coll; Oriel Coll, Oxford.
e-mail:haselhursta@parliament.uk tel: 020-7219 5214 fax: 020-7219 5600

This seat covers the northwest section of Essex. It consists of appealing small towns such as Saffron Walden, Halstead and Great Dunmow, along with a series of rural villages. Stansted Airport has become an expanding source of local employment. The Conservatives are very strong here with the opposition vote often fragmented between the two other main parties. Map 497

## ST ALBANS — Lab hold

| Electorate | %Turnout | | 66,040 | 66.26% | 2001 | 65,560 | 77.49% | 1997 |
|---|---|---|---|---|---|---|---|---|
| **Pollard K** | | **Lab** | **19,889** | **45.45%** | **3.45%** | **21,338** | **42.0%** | **Lab** |
| Elphicke C | | C | 15,423 | 35.24% | 2.02% | 16,879 | 33.22% | C |
| Rijke N | | LD | 7,847 | 17.93% | -3.12% | 10,692 | 21.05% | LD |
| Sherwin C | | UK Ind | 602 | 1.38% | | 1,619 | 3.19% | Ref |
| | | | | | | 166 | 0.33% | Dream |
| | | | | | | 111 | 0.22% | NLP |
| **C to Lab swing** | **0.71%** | | **43,761** | | **Lab maj 4,466** | **50,805** | | **Lab maj 4,459** |
| | | | | | 10.21% | | | 8.78% |

**KERRY POLLARD,** b April 27, 1944. Elected 1997. Member, Ed and Employment Select Cttee. Chairman, all-party small business grp; vice-chairman, PLP Eastern grp; sec, Lab housing grp. St Albans district cllr, 1982-. Herts cty cllr, 1989-. Member Nalgo, MSF. Engineer. Ed Thornleigh College, Bolton.
e-mail: pollardk@talk21.com www.kerrypollardmp.co.uk
tel 01727 761031 fax 01727 761032

This Hertfordshire seat is based on the historic cathedral city of St Albans itself, where all three main parties can draw on reasonable sources of support, and the area immediately to the south which used to be part of the Watford constituency. The net result is a fairly competitive seat which, with a surprisingly large swing, fell to Labour in 1997. The party held on with an almost identical majority on a smaller turnout in 2001. Map 498

# ST HELENS NORTH
## Lab hold

| Electorate | %Turnout | | 70,545 | 53.3% | 2001 | 71,380 | 68.97% | 1997 |
|---|---|---|---|---|---|---|---|---|
| **Watts D** | Lab | | **22,977** | **61.11%** | -3.8% | **31,953** | **64.91%** | Lab |
| Pearce S | C | | 7,076 | 18.82% | 1.48% | 8,536 | 17.34% | C |
| Beirne J | LD | | 6,609 | 17.58% | 4.84% | 6,270 | 12.74% | LD |
| Whatham S | Soc Lab | | 939 | 2.5% | 0.81% | 1,276 | 2.59% | Ref |
| | | | | | | 832 | 1.69% | Soc Lab |
| | | | | | | 363 | 0.74% | UK Ind |
| **Lab to C swing** | **2.64%** | | **37,601** | Lab maj **15,901** | | **49,230** | Lab maj **23,417** | |
| | | | | 42.29% | | | 47.57% | |

**DAVE WATTS,** b Aug 26, 1951. Elected 1997. PPS to John Spellar, Min of State for the Armed Forces and Transport Min. Former member, Finance and Services Select Cttee. Leader, St Helens Borough Council. NW reg organiser, 1992 election. Research asst to John Evans, former Lab MP for this seat. Ed Seel Street Sec Mod.

Although the borough of St Helens was part of the old Merseyside metropolitan area, this seat is an independent entity and not a mere suburb of Liverpool, 11 miles to the west. This is a moderately industrial, former mining and now commuting area, with small towns such as Newton-le-Willows, with strong links to the railway industry, Haydock, with its racecourse, and Rainford, with its new private estates. Overall, it is very strongly Labour. Map 499

# ST HELENS SOUTH
## Lab hold

| Electorate | %Turnout | | 65,122 | 51.91% | 2001 | 66,526 | 66.53% | 1997 |
|---|---|---|---|---|---|---|---|---|
| **Woodward S** | Lab | | **16,799** | **49.7%** | -18.91% | **30,367** | **68.61%** | Lab |
| Spencer B | LD | | 7,814 | 23.12% | 9.75% | 6,628 | 14.98% | C |
| Rotherham Dr L | C | | 4,675 | 13.83% | -1.15% | 5,919 | 13.37% | LD |
| Thompson N | Soc All | | 2,325 | 6.88% | | 1,165 | 2.63% | Ref |
| Perry M | Soc Lab | | 1,504 | 4.45% | | 179 | 0.4% | NLP |
| Slater B | UK Ind | | 336 | 0.99% | | | | |
| Murphy M | Ind | | 271 | 0.8% | | | | |
| Braid D | Ind Braid | | 80 | 0.24% | | | | |
| **Lab to LD swing** | **14.33%** | | **33,804** | Lab maj **8,985** | | **44,258** | Lab maj **23,739** | |
| | | | | 26.58% | | | 53.63% | |

**SHAUN WOODWARD,** b Oct 26, 1958. Elected for Witney 1997 as C. Joined Lab, Dec 1999. C spokesman, DETR, 1999. Member, Euro Legislation, and Broadcasting Select Cttees, 1997-2001. Dir, Communications, C Central Office, 1990-92. Professor, Fellow of Politics, Queen Mary and Westfield Coll, London. Ex-producer, *Panorama* and *Newsnight*. Dir, English National Opera; Childline. Broadcaster and univ lecturer. Ed Bristol GS; Jesus Coll, Cambridge; Kennedy Sch, Harvard.
tel: 020-7219 2680 fax: 020-7219 0979

The north and south seats of St Helens on Merseyside are not dissimilar, although the latter contains a larger share of the heavily industrial town itself. It is dominated by the factories of Pilkingtons, the glassmaker, and has a legacy of coalmining. Though Labour is usually even stronger here than in St Helens North, its selection of the ex-Tory defector Shaun Woodward as its candidate in 2001 drastically cut the party's majority. Map 500

# ST IVES
## LD hold

| Electorate | %Turnout | | 74,256 | 66.35% | 2001 | 71,680 | 75.2% | 1997 |
|---|---|---|---|---|---|---|---|---|
| **George A** | LD | | **25,413** | **51.58%** | 7.12% | **23,966** | **44.46%** | LD |
| Richardson Miss J | C | | 15,360 | 31.18% | 0.02% | 16,796 | 31.16% | C |
| Morris W | Lab | | 6,567 | 13.33% | -1.85% | 8,184 | 15.18% | Lab |
| Faulkner M | UK Ind | | 1,926 | 3.91% | 2.86% | 3,714 | 6.89% | Ref |
| | | | | | | 567 | 1.05% | UK Ind |
| | | | | | | 425 | 0.79% | Lib |
| | | | | | | 178 | 0.33% | R Alt |
| | | | | | | 71 | 0.13% | BHMBCM |
| **C to LD swing** | **3.55%** | | **49,266** | LD maj **10,053** | | **53,901** | LD maj **7,170** | |
| | | | | 20.41% | | | 13.30% | |

**ANDREW GEORGE,** b Dec 2, 1958. Elected 1997. PPS to Charles Kennedy, June 2001. Spokesman, fisheries, 1997-; disability, 1999-. Member, Agriculture Select Cttee, 1997-2000. Vice-chairman, family farms, fisheries all-pty grps; member, domestic violence, disability, international development, asylum and immigration, sustainable energy, rail freight, housing and homelessness grps. Pres, council for Racial Equality in Cornwall, W Cornwall Reliant owners' club. Charity worker. Ed Helston Sch; Sussex Univ; Univ Coll, Oxford.
e-mail coopern@parliament.uk tel 0207-219 4588 fax 0207-219 5572

Cornwall has a political culture of its own and St Ives, which consists of the southwestern tip of England - Land's End and Lizard Point - and the Isles of Scilly, is proof of that. The primary industries for the towns of St Ives, with its strong artistic community, Penzance with its ferry port for the Scillies, Helston and St Just, are fishing and tourism. The decline of fishing may explain the strength of Euroscepticism in a seat which is strong for the Lib Dems. Map 501

## SALFORD — Lab hold

| Electorate | %Turnout | | 54,152 | 41.58% | 2001 | 58,610 | 56.51% | 1997 |
|---|---|---|---|---|---|---|---|---|
| Blears Ms H | | Lab | 14,649 | 65.07% | -3.91% | 22,848 | 68.98% | Lab |
| Owen N | | LD | 3,637 | 16.15% | 5.86% | 5,779 | 17.45% | C |
| King C | | C | 3,446 | 15.31% | -2.14% | 3,407 | 10.29% | LD |
| Grant P | | Soc All | 414 | 1.84% | | 926 | 2.8% | Ref |
| Wallace Ms H | | Ind | 216 | 0.96% | | 162 | 0.49% | NLP |
| Masterson R | | Ind Masters | 152 | 0.68% | | | | |
| Lab to LD swing | | 4.89% | 22,514 | Lab maj 11,012 | | 33,122 | Lab maj 17,069 | |
| | | | | 48.91% | | | 51.53% | |

**HAZEL BLEARS,** b May 14, 1956. Elected 1997. Under Sec, Dept of Health, June, 2001-; vice-chairwoman, PLP Home Affairs Cttee. Lab party development co-ordinator. Vice-chairwoman, NW grp of Lab MPs, 1997-. Salford city cllr, 1984-92. Trustee, Imperial Soc of Teachers of Dancing, and Working Class Museum and Library. Ex-chairman, Bury and Radcliffe CLP. Solicitor. Ed Wardley GS; Eccles Sixth Form Coll; Trent Poly; Chester Coll of Law.
e-mail: blearsh@parliament.uk tel: 0161-925 0705 fax: 0161-743 9173

The city of Salford, which penetrates almost into the centre of adjoining Manchester behind Deansgate, has suffered heavy depopulation over recent decades. This is a very urban and working-class seat with bleak tower blocks dominating the skyline. Granada TV's studios, home of *Coronation Street*, are located here and regeneration is bearing fruit with the likes of the splendid new Lowry Gallery at Salford Quays. It is all very safe for Labour. Map 502

## SALISBURY — C hold

| Electorate | %Turnout | | 80,538 | 65.31% | 2001 | 78,973 | 73.75% | 1997 |
|---|---|---|---|---|---|---|---|---|
| Key R | | C | 24,527 | 46.63% | 3.68% | 25,012 | 42.95% | C |
| Emmerson-Peirce Ms Y | | LD | 15,824 | 30.08% | -2.09% | 18,736 | 32.17% | LD |
| Mallory Ms S | | Lab | 9,199 | 17.49% | -0.1% | 10,242 | 17.59% | Lab |
| Wood M | | UK Ind | 1,958 | 3.72% | -2.0% | 3,332 | 5.72% | UK Ind |
| Soutar H | | Green | 1,095 | 2.08% | 1.01% | 623 | 1.07% | Green |
| | | | | | | 184 | 0.32% | Ind |
| | | | | | | 110 | 0.19% | NLP |
| LD to C swing | | 2.88% | 52,603 | C maj 8,703 | | 58,239 | C maj 6,276 | |
| | | | | 16.54% | | | 10.78% | |

**ROBERT KEY,** b April 22, 1945. Elected 1983. Shadow Defence Min, 1997-; Under-Sec, Transport, 1993-94; Nat Heritage, 1992-93; Environment, 1990-92. Member, Select Cttees: Defence, 1995-97; Health, 1994-95. Political sec to Sir Edward Heath, 1984-85. Chairman, all-party Aids grp, 1996-97; joint vice-chairman, 1988-90. Asst master, Harrow, 1969-83. Member, chorus of Academy of St Martin-in-the-Fields, 1975-89. Ed Sherborne Sch; Clare Coll, Cambridge.
e-mail: rob@robertkey.com www.robertkey.com
tel: 01722 782703 fax: 01722 782793

This ancient cathedral city in south Wiltshire is too small to have a seat of its own and so the constituency extends over a wide range of rural territory. The military element is strong on Salisbury Plain and there are dozens of attractive small towns and villages such as Amesbury and Tisbury. Stonehenge brings tourist revenue to the area. The Tories have historically been able to beat off the challenge from the vigorous local Liberal Democrats. Map 503

## SCARBOROUGH & WHITBY — Lab hold

| Electorate | %Turnout | | 75,213 | 63.18% | 2001 | 75,862 | 71.61% | 1997 |
|---|---|---|---|---|---|---|---|---|
| Quinn L | | Lab | 22,426 | 47.19% | 1.55% | 24,791 | 45.64% | Lab |
| Sykes J | | C | 18,841 | 39.65% | 3.44% | 19,667 | 36.21% | C |
| Pearce T | | LD | 3,977 | 8.37% | -5.75% | 7,672 | 14.12% | LD |
| Dixon J | | Green | 1,049 | 2.21% | | 2,191 | 4.03% | Ref |
| Jacob J | | UK Ind | 970 | 2.04% | | | | |
| Murray Ms T | | ProLife | 260 | 0.55% | | | | |
| Lab to C swing | | 0.94% | 47,523 | Lab maj 3,585 | | 54,321 | Lab maj 5,124 | |
| | | | | 7.54% | | | 9.43% | |

**LAWRIE QUINN,** b Dec 25, 1956. Elected 1997. Sec, PLP Agriculture Cttee, 1997-. Joint chairman, all-party rail freight grp, 1997-. Member, Lab Electoral Reform Soc; Fabian Soc; Institute of Civil Engineers; Transport 2000. Planning and development chartered engineer, Railtrack. Ed Harraby Sch, Carlisle; Hatfield Poly.

This section of North Yorkshire might be considered natural territory for the Conservatives. Scarborough is a thriving seaside resort and Whitby is a traditional fishing port also much favoured by tourists. Much of the remaining territory consists of the wild and bleak North York Moors but farming is also strong. Labour nonetheless romped home in 1997 on a huge swing to create a bellwether marginal, and the pattern was similar four years later. Map 504

# SCUNTHORPE · Lab hold

| Electorate | %Turnout | | 59,689 | 56.33% | 2001 | 60,393 | 68.84% | 1997 |
|---|---|---|---|---|---|---|---|---|
| **Morley E** | **Lab** | | **20,096** | **59.77%** | **-0.62%** | **25,107** | **60.39%** | **Lab** |
| Theobald B | C | | 9,724 | 28.92% | 2.62% | 10,934 | 26.3% | C |
| Tress B | LD | | 3,156 | 9.39% | 0.98% | 3,497 | 8.41% | LD |
| Cliff J | UK Ind | | 347 | 1.03% | | 1,637 | 3.94% | Ref |
| Patterson D | Ind | | 302 | 0.9% | | 399 | 0.96% | Soc Lab |
| **Lab to C swing** | **1.62%** | | **33,625** | Lab maj 10,372 | | **41,574** | Lab maj 14,173 | |
| | | | | 30.85% | | | 34.09% | |

**ELLIOT MORLEY,** b July 6, 1952. Elected here 1997; MP for Glanford and Scunthorpe 1987-97. Parly Sec, Dept Environment, Food and Rural Affairs, June 2001-; Min for Fisheries and Countryside, 1997-2001. Lab spokesman, Agriculture, Food and Rural Affairs, 1989-97. Member, Agriculture Select Cttee, 1987-89; vice-chairman, PLP Ed, Science and Arts Cttee, 1987-89. Vice-pres, Wildlife and Countryside Link, 1990-. Remedial teacher. Ed St Margaret's CE HS, Liverpool; Hull Coll of Ed.
e-mail: emorleymp@aol.com tel: 01724 842000

This is a North Lincolnshire industrial constituency set on a bluff overlooking the River Trent to the west, and south of the River Humber. The town was historically dominated by iron and steel and that inheritance still shapes political attitudes. Most of Scunthorpe is therefore solidly Labour and it can more than outvote the relatively small pro-Tory middle-class enclaves. The seat is therefore safe for Labour in all but extreme circumstances. **Map 505**

# SEDGEFIELD · Lab hold

| Electorate | %Turnout | | 64,925 | 62.01% | 2001 | 64,923 | 72.57% | 1997 |
|---|---|---|---|---|---|---|---|---|
| **Blair T** | **Lab** | | **26,110** | **64.86%** | **-6.3%** | **33,526** | **71.16%** | **Lab** |
| Carswell D | C | | 8,397 | 20.86% | 3.07% | 8,383 | 17.79% | C |
| Duffield A | LD | | 3,624 | 9.0% | 2.53% | 3,050 | 6.47% | LD |
| Spence A | UK Ind | | 974 | 2.42% | | 1,683 | 3.57% | Ref |
| Gibson B | Soc Lab | | 518 | 1.29% | 0.28% | 474 | 1.01% | Soc Lab |
| Driver C | R & R Loony | | 375 | 0.93% | | | | |
| John Ms H | WFLOE | | 260 | 0.65% | | | | |
| **Lab to C swing** | **4.69%** | | **40,258** | Lab maj 17,713 | | **47,116** | Lab maj 25,143 | |
| | | | | 44.00% | | | 53.37% | |

**TONY BLAIR,** b May 6, 1953. Elected 1983. Became Prime Minister, May 2, 1997, having been elected Leader of Lab Party, 1994. Entered his second term, June 2001. Joined Shadow Cabinet, 1988, being chief spokesman, home affairs, 1992-94; employment, 1989-92; energy, 1988-89; spokesman, trade and industry, 1987-88; Treasury and economic affairs, 1984-87. Privy Counsellor. Chairman, all-party America grp, 1997-. Barrister (non-practising); called to Bar (Lincoln's Inn) 1976; hon Bencher, 1994. Ed Durham Choristers Sch; Fettes Coll, Edinburgh; St John's Coll, Oxford.

Tony Blair represents an extremely safe Labour constituency. It is in southeastern Co Durham, surrounding but not including the town of Darlington, though incorporating the borough's rural wards. The new town at Newton Aycliffe was brought in under the last boundary changes, and with it some light industry. There is still a powerful legacy of coalmining shaping community attitudes, if not the local economy in recent decades. **Map 506**

# SELBY · Lab hold

| Electorate | %Turnout | | 77,924 | 64.51% | 2001 | 75,141 | 74.95% | 1997 |
|---|---|---|---|---|---|---|---|---|
| **Grogan J** | **Lab** | | **22,652** | **45.06%** | **-0.82%** | **25,838** | **45.88%** | **Lab** |
| Mitchell M | C | | 20,514 | 40.81% | 1.74% | 22,002 | 39.07% | C |
| Wilcock J | LD | | 5,569 | 11.08% | -0.96% | 6,778 | 12.04% | LD |
| Kenwright Ms H | Green | | 902 | 1.79% | | 1,162 | 2.06% | Ref |
| Lewis B | UK Ind | | 635 | 1.26% | 0.31% | 536 | 0.95% | UK Ind |
| **Lab to C swing** | **1.28%** | | **50,272** | Lab maj 2,138 | | **56,316** | Lab maj 3,836 | |
| | | | | 4.25% | | | 6.81% | |

**JOHN GROGAN,** b Feb 24, 1961. Elected 1997. Member, NI Affairs Select Cttee, 1997-2001. Former asst to Dr Barry Seal, MEP, Yorkshire W and ex-leader, Lab grp in Euro Parliament. Ex-PA, leader, Leeds City council. Member, Nupe. Ed St Michael's Coll, Leeds; St John's Coll, Oxford (Pres of Union, 1982-83).

The very flat countryside south of York, including the towns of Selby and Tadcaster, contains diverse economic and political interests. Employment has come from mining, farming and brewing. Now marginal, this was a reasonably safe Conservative seat for years, although the Tory majority was not crushing and Labour probably benefits from the presence of York University in the constituency. Labour won unexpectedly in 1997 and held on in 2001. **Map 507**

## SEVENOAKS — C hold

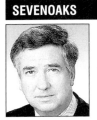

| Electorate | %Turnout | | 66,648 | 63.94% | 2001 | 66,474 | 75.44% | 1997 |
|---|---|---|---|---|---|---|---|---|
| **Fallon M** | **C** | | **21,052** | **49.4%** | **3.98%** | **22,776** | **45.42%** | **C** |
| Humphreys Ms C | Lab | | 10,898 | 25.57% | 1.01% | 12,315 | 24.56% | Lab |
| Gray C | LD | | 9,214 | 21.62% | -2.48% | 12,086 | 24.1% | LD |
| Hawkins Mrs L | UK Ind | | 1,155 | 2.71% | | 2,138 | 4.26% | Ref |
| Ellis M | PF | | 295 | 0.69% | 0.2% | 443 | 0.88% | Green |
| | | | | | | 244 | 0.49% | PF |
| | | | | | | 147 | 0.29% | NLP |
| **Lab to C swing** | **1.48%** | | **42,614** | **C maj 10,154** | | **50,149** | **C maj 10,461** | |
| | | | | 23.83% | | | 20.86% | |

**MICHAEL FALLON,** b May 14, 1952. Elected here 1997; MP for Darlington 1983-92. Member, Treasury Select Cttee, 1999-2001. C spokesman, Treasury, 1997-98; trade and industry, 1997. Ed and Science Under-Sec, 1990-92; govt whip, 1990; asst govt whip, 1988-90. PPS to Cecil Parkinson, 1987-88; asst to Lady Elles, MEP, 1979-83; and to Lord Carrington, 1974-77. Member, advisory council, Social Market Foundation, 1994-. Co dir. Ed Craigflower Sch, Fife; Epsom Coll; St Andrews Univ. e-mail: fallonm@parliament.uk tel: 020-7219 6482 fax: 020-7219 6791

This part of west Kent is adjacent to Surrey and political sentiment is similar to that in the neighbouring county. The seat has the highest proportion of professional and managerial workers in Kent, the largest number of detached properties and the fewest council tenants. There is some Labour support in Swanley, but the very affluent suburban commuter territory of Sevenoaks itself and pretty villages such as Westerham make it solidly Tory. Map 508

## SHEFFIELD ATTERCLIFFE — Lab hold

| Electorate | %Turnout | | 68,386 | 52.38% | 2001 | 68,548 | 64.65% | 1997 |
|---|---|---|---|---|---|---|---|---|
| **Betts C** | **Lab** | | **24,287** | **67.8%** | **2.51%** | **28,937** | **65.29%** | **Lab** |
| Perry J | C | | 5,443 | 15.19% | -0.87% | 7,119 | 16.06% | C |
| Smith Ms G | LD | | 5,092 | 14.21% | -1.52% | 6,973 | 15.73% | LD |
| Arnott Ms P | UK Ind | | 1,002 | 2.8% | | 1,289 | 2.91% | Ref |
| **C to Lab swing** | **1.69%** | | **35,824** | **Lab maj 18,844** | | **44,318** | **Lab maj 21,818** | |
| | | | | 52.60% | | | 49.23% | |

**CLIVE BETTS,** b Jan 13, 1950. Elected 1992. Member, Selection Cttee, 1997-2001; Treasury Select Cttee, 1995-97. Chairman, 1995-97, and sec, 1994-95, PLP Treasury Cttee. Govt whip, 1998-; asst whip, 1997-98, Lab whip, 1996-97. Sec, Lab leader's campaign team, 1995-97. Sheffield city cllr, 1976-92. Chairman, S Yorks pension authority, 1989-92. Principal economist, S Yorks County Council. Member, TGWU. Ed King Edward VII Sch, Sheffield; Pembroke Coll, Cambridge. e-mail: bettsc@parliament.uk tel: 020-7219 5114 fax: 020-7219 2289

This is one of those interesting seats where social or demographic information cannot properly explain voting patterns. The South Yorkshire constituency falls in southeast Sheffield and was once dominated by the steel industry in the Don Valley. But this is not an industrial wasteland. There is now a high proportion of owner-occupiers but a relatively large number of ethnic minority electors. It is an extremely solid Labour seat. Map 509

## SHEFFIELD BRIGHTSIDE — Lab hold

| Electorate | %Turnout | | 54,711 | 46.7% | 2001 | 58,930 | 57.47% | 1997 |
|---|---|---|---|---|---|---|---|---|
| **Blunkett D** | **Lab** | | **19,650** | **76.9%** | **3.37%** | **24,901** | **73.53%** | **Lab** |
| Wilson M | C | | 2,601 | 10.18% | 1.76% | 4,947 | 14.61% | LD |
| Firth Ms A | LD | | 2,238 | 8.76% | -5.85% | 2,850 | 8.42% | C |
| Wilson B | Soc All | | 361 | 1.41% | | 624 | 1.84% | Ref |
| Morris R | Soc Lab | | 354 | 1.39% | -0.03% | 482 | 1.42% | Soc Lab |
| Suter M | UK Ind | | 348 | 1.36% | | 61 | 0.18% | NLP |
| **C to Lab swing** | **0.81%** | | **25,552** | **Lab maj 17,049** | | **33,865** | **Lab maj 19,954** | |
| | | | | 66.72% | | | 58.92% | |

**DAVID BLUNKETT,** b June 6, 1947. Elected 1987. Home Sec, June, 2001-. Sec for Ed and Employment, 1997-2001. Shadow Ed and Employment Sec, 1994-97; Health, 1992-94. Elected Shadow Cabinet, 1992. Member, Lab Party, NEC, 1983-99; Lab Party chairman, 1993-94. Lab leader, Sheffield City Council (city cllr, 1970-88); S Yorks county cllr, 1973-77. Dep chairman, AMA, 1984-87. Industrial relations tutor. Ed Royal Nat Coll for the Blind, Shrewsbury; Richmond CFE, Sheffield; Sheffield Univ; Huddersfield Coll of Ed (Tech). tel: 020-7219 4043 fax: 020-7219 5903

This section of northeast Sheffield conforms more comfortably with the stereotype of a deprived industrial constituency. It is the most working-class of the seats in this city with a strikingly high number of council houses sprawling over the Sheffield hills. Labour utterly dominates the seat, with neither the Conservatives nor the Liberal Democrats apparently capable of more than token resistance. Map 510

## SHEFFIELD CENTRAL — Lab hold

| Electorate | %Turnout | | 62,018 | 48.48% | 2001 | 68,667 | 53.04% | 1997 |
|---|---|---|---|---|---|---|---|---|
| Caborn R | Lab | | 18,477 | 61.45% | -2.2% | 23,179 | 63.65% | Lab |
| Qadar A | LD | | 5,933 | 19.73% | 2.51% | 6,273 | 17.22% | LD |
| Brelsford Miss N | C | | 3,289 | 10.94% | -0.98% | 4,341 | 11.92% | C |
| Little B | Green | | 1,008 | 3.35% | 0.73% | 954 | 2.62% | Green |
| Riley N | Soc All | | 754 | 2.51% | | 863 | 2.37% | Ref |
| Hadfield D | Soc Lab | | 289 | 0.96% | | 466 | 1.28% | Soc |
| Schofield Ms C | UK Ind | | 257 | 0.85% | | 280 | 0.77% | ProLife |
| Driver M | WRP | | 62 | 0.21% | 0.04% | 63 | 0.17% | WRP |
| Lab to LD swing | 2.36% | | 30,069 | Lab maj 12,544 | | 36,419 | Lab maj 16,906 | |
| | | | | 41.72% | | | 46.43% | |

**RICHARD CABORN** b Oct 6, 1943. Elected 1983; MEP, Sheffield 1979-84. Min of Sport, June 2001-; Min for Trade, DTI, 1999-2001; Environment and Transport Min, responsible for regions, regeneration and planning, 1997-99. Chairman, Trade and Industry Select Cttee, 1992-95; member, Select Cttee, Euro Legislation, 1983-88. Vice-chairman, Tribune Grp, 1986-87. Fitter; convener, shop stewards, Firth Brown Ltd, 1967-79; vice-president, Sheffield Trades Council, 1968-79. Member, BBC Advisory Council, 1975-78. Ed Hurlfield Comp, Sheffield; Granville CFE; Sheffield Poly.

Much of this seat consists of high-rise buildings or sprawling council estates, surrounding the bustling city centre with its ultra-modern tram system. But even in times of national prosperity, poverty and unemployment remain persistent features of local life. There is a significant ethnic minority population here. The city centre also contains the university and most of the notable civic buildings. This is solid Labour terrain. **Map 511**

## SHEFFIELD HALLAM — LD hold

| Electorate | %Turnout | | 60,288 | 63.44% | 2001 | 62,834 | 72.38% | 1997 |
|---|---|---|---|---|---|---|---|---|
| Allan R | LD | | 21,203 | 55.44% | 4.11% | 23,345 | 51.33% | LD |
| Harthman J | C | | 11,856 | 31.0% | -2.14% | 15,074 | 33.14% | C |
| Furniss Ms G | Lab | | 4,758 | 12.44% | -1.08% | 6,147 | 13.52% | Lab |
| Arnott L | UK Ind | | 429 | 1.12% | | 788 | 1.73% | Ref |
| | | | | | | 125 | 0.27% | SIP |
| C to LD swing | 3.12% | | 38,246 | LD maj 9,347 | | 45,479 | LD maj 8,271 | |
| | | | | 24.44% | | | 18.19% | |

**RICHARD ALLAN,** b Feb 11, 1966. Elected 1997. LD spokesman, community relations and urban affairs, 1997-. Member, Select Cttees: Home Affairs, 1997-2001; Information, 1997-2001. Avon county cllr, 1993-; Bath City cllr, 1994-. Member, World Development Movement; voting reform grp; CPRE. NHS computer manager. Ed Oundle; Pembroke Coll, Cambridge; Bristol Poly.

This is an extremely interesting constituency. Situated on the leafy residential southwest side of the city on the edge of the Peak District, it is essentially the home of Sheffield's middle classes and many of those associated with the university. It has a very high percentage of professionals and managers. Hallam was held by the Tories for many years before the Lib Dems turned them out in spectacular fashion in 1997 and held on convincingly in 2001. **Map 512**

## SHEFFIELD HEELEY — Lab hold

| Electorate | %Turnout | | 62,758 | 54.4% | 2001 | 66,599 | 64.96% | 1997 |
|---|---|---|---|---|---|---|---|---|
| Munn Ms M | Lab | | 19,452 | 56.98% | -3.75% | 26,274 | 60.73% | Lab |
| Willis D | LD | | 7,748 | 22.7% | 1.45% | 9,196 | 21.25% | LD |
| Abbott Ms C | C | | 4,864 | 14.25% | -1.39% | 6,767 | 15.64% | C |
| Unwin R | Green | | 774 | 2.27% | | 1,029 | 2.38% | Ref |
| Fischer B | Soc Lab | | 667 | 1.95% | | | | |
| Dunn D | UK Ind | | 634 | 1.86% | | | | |
| Lab to LD swing | 2.60% | | 34,139 | Lab maj 11,704 | | 43,266 | Lab maj 17,078 | |
| | | | | 34.28% | | | 39.48% | |

**MEG MUNN,** b Aug 24, 1959. Elected 2001. Inherits seat from Bill Michie, a left winger, who held it for 18 years. Child services manager, Wakefield Metropolitan Council; district manager, Barnsley council and asst dir, City of York Council, 1999-2000. Social worker. Ed Rowlinson Comp Sch, Sheffield; York and Nottingham Univs.

This constituency covers much of south Sheffield. It is predominantly working-class with a large number of council tenants housed in more tower blocks and estates clinging to the hills. There is one middle-class enclave towards Hallam. As is broadly true in Sheffield these days, therefore, Labour is the dominant political force and only the Liberal Democrats can put up a spirited struggle. **Map 513**

## SHEFFIELD HILLSBOROUGH — Lab hold

| Electorate | %Turnout | | 75,097 | 56.64% | 2001 | 74,642 | 71.04% | 1997 |
|---|---|---|---|---|---|---|---|---|
| Jackson Ms H | Lab | | 24,170 | 56.82% | -0.04% | 30,150 | 56.86% | Lab |
| Commons J | LD | | 9,601 | 22.57% | -3.27% | 13,699 | 25.84% | LD |
| King G | C | | 7,801 | 18.34% | 3.81% | 7,707 | 14.53% | C |
| Webb P | UK Ind | | 964 | 2.27% | | 1,468 | 2.77% | Ref |
| LD to Lab swing | 1.62% | | 42,536 | Lab maj 14,569 | | 53,024 | Lab maj 16,451 | |
| | | | | 34.25% | | | 31.02% | |

**HELEN JACKSON,** b May 19, 1939. Elected 1992. Member, Select Cttees: Modernisation of Commons, 1997-2001; Environment, 1992-97. PPS to NI Sec, John Reid, 2001-; to Peter Mandelson, 1999-2001; and to Mo Mowlam, 1997-99. Member, Lab Party NEC, 1999-. Chairwoman, all-party environment grp, 1997-; joint chairwoman, PLP women's grp, 1992-97. Sheffield city cllr, 1980-91; Huyton UD cllr, 1972-74; member TGWU. Teacher. Ed Berkhamsted GS; St Hilda's Coll, Oxford.
tel: 020-7219 4587 fax: 020-7219 2442

This section of northwest Sheffield may become increasingly competitive in years to come. Labour has traditionally dominated here but this is not an inner-city seat as such. There are many owner-occupiers and the Liberal Democrats have become a seriously active force in local elections. Surprisingly, this seat does not include the Hillsborough stadium of Sheffield Wednesday FC, which is in neighbouring Brightside. Map 514

## SHERWOOD — Lab hold

| Electorate | %Turnout | | 75,670 | 60.66% | 2001 | 74,788 | 75.59% | 1997 |
|---|---|---|---|---|---|---|---|---|
| Tipping P | Lab | | 24,900 | 54.25% | -4.25% | 33,071 | 58.5% | Lab |
| Lewis B | C | | 15,527 | 33.83% | 5.07% | 16,259 | 28.76% | C |
| Harris P | LD | | 5,473 | 11.92% | 3.27% | 4,889 | 8.65% | LD |
| | | | | | | 1,882 | 3.33% | Ref |
| | | | | | | 432 | 0.76% | BNP |
| Lab to C swing | 4.66% | | 45,900 | Lab maj 9,373 | | 56,533 | Lab maj 16,812 | |
| | | | | 20.42% | | | 29.74% | |

**PADDY TIPPING,** b Oct 24, 1949. Elected 1992. Parly Sec, Privy Council Office, 1998-2001. PPS to Jack Straw, Home Sec, 1996-98. Member, Select Cttee, Parly Commissioner for Administration, 1996-97. Joint chairman, all-party minerals grp, 1996-98 ; energy studies grp, 1996-98; joint sec, forestry grp 1997-. Chairman, central reg grp, Lab MPs, 1997-. Notts county cllr, 1981-93. Project leader, C of E Children's Soc, Nottingham, 1979-83. Member, Co-op Party; Unison. Ex- social worker. Ed Hipperholme GS; Nottingham Univ.
tel: 0115-9640314 fax: 0115-9681639

This Nottinghamshire seat, based roughly on the area of the ancient Sherwood Forest, is rather an amalgamation. It includes a number of towns traditionally associated with the mining industry, and especially the Dukeries coalfield between Worksop and Mansfield. This is combined with agricultural villages and some affluent residential suburbs. The Tories managed to win here in the 1980s but Labour now appears seriously dominant. Map 515

## SHIPLEY — Lab hold

| Electorate | %Turnout | | 69,577 | 66.14% | 2001 | 69,281 | 76.32% | 1997 |
|---|---|---|---|---|---|---|---|---|
| Leslie C | Lab | | 20,243 | 43.99% | 0.56% | 22,962 | 43.43% | Lab |
| Senior D | C | | 18,815 | 40.88% | 3.12% | 19,966 | 37.76% | C |
| Wright Ms H | LD | | 4,996 | 10.86% | -4.24% | 7,984 | 15.1% | LD |
| Love M | Green | | 1,386 | 3.01% | | 1,960 | 3.71% | Ref |
| Whitacker W | UK Ind | | 580 | 1.26% | | | | |
| Lab to C swing | 1.28% | | 46,020 | Lab maj 1,428 | | 52,872 | Lab maj 2,996 | |
| | | | | 3.10% | | | 5.67% | |

**CHRISTOPHER LESLIE,** b June 28, 1972. Elected 1997. Parly Sec, Cabinet Office, June 2001-; PPS to Min of State, Cabinet Office, 1998-2001. Member, Public Accounts Cttee, 1997-98. Researcher for Barry Seal, MEP, 1997. Bradford City cllr, 1994-. Political research asst/office administrator. Member, TGWU; GMB. Ed Bingley GS; Leeds Univ.
e-mail: lesliec@parliament.uk

This is a largely prosperous section of West Yorkshire to the northwest of Bradford that has recently become a marginal. It consists of towns such as Shipley itself, Bingley and Baildon. To these are added a large slice of the moors and a salient into lower Wharfedale. There are industrial parts here which have always backed Labour. The Tories held the seat for many years but Labour won with a huge swing in 1997 and just held on in 2001. Map 516

## SHREWSBURY & ATCHAM — Lab hold

| Electorate | %Turnout | 74,964 | 66.58% | 2001 | 73,542 | 75.25% | 1997 |
|---|---|---|---|---|---|---|---|
| **Marsden P** | **Lab** | **22,253** | **44.59%** | **7.58%** | 20,484 | 37.01% | Lab |
| McIntyre Miss A | C | 18,674 | 37.42% | 3.43% | 18,814 | 33.99% | C |
| Rule J | LD | 6,173 | 12.37% | -12.63% | 13,838 | 25.0% | LD |
| Curteis H | UK Ind | 1,620 | 3.25% | 2.39% | 1,346 | 2.43% | Ref |
| Bullard Ms E | Green | 931 | 1.87% | | 477 | 0.86% | UK Ind |
| Gollins J | Ind | 258 | 0.52% | | 257 | 0.46% | CFSS |
| | | | | | 128 | 0.23% | The PPP |
| **C to Lab swing** | **2.08%** | **49,909** | Lab maj 3,579 | | **55,344** | Lab maj 1,670 | |
| | | | 7.17% | | | 3.02% | |

**PAUL MARSDEN,** b March 18, 1968. Elected 1997. Member, Agriculture Select Cttee, 1997-2001. Member, Inst of Management; American soc of quality control; CWU; nat exec, Young Fabians, 1990. Chairman, Nesscliffe branch, Shrewsbury CLP, 1995-. Quality assurance manager. Ed Helsby HS; Mid-Cheshire Coll; Teesside Poly; OU.

This constituency is dominated by Shrewsbury, the historic county town of Shropshire built on a bend of the River Severn. The seat runs all the way to the Welsh border. Atcham is a small village southeast of the town and the seat is named after the local government borough. It appears straightforward Tory territory but there has always been support for both Labour and the Lib Dems. It was still a shock when the Tories were ejected in 1997. Map 517

## SHROPSHIRE NORTH — C hold

| Electorate | %Turnout | 73,716 | 63.11% | 2001 | 70,852 | 72.71% | 1997 |
|---|---|---|---|---|---|---|---|
| **Paterson O** | **C** | **22,631** | **48.65%** | **8.41%** | 20,730 | 40.24% | C |
| Ion M | Lab | 16,390 | 35.23% | -0.75% | 18,535 | 35.98% | Lab |
| Jephcott B | LD | 5,945 | 12.78% | -7.58% | 10,489 | 20.36% | LD |
| Trevanion D | UK Ind | 1,165 | 2.5% | | 1,764 | 3.42% | Ref |
| Maxfield R | Ind | 389 | 0.84% | | | | |
| **Lab to C swing** | **4.58%** | **46,520** | C maj 6,241 | | **51,518** | C maj 2,195 | |
| | | | 13.42% | | | 4.26% | |

**OWEN PATERSON,** b June 24, 1956. Elected 1997. Opposition whip, 2000-. Member, Select Cttees: Agriculture, 2000-01; Welsh Affairs, 1997-2001. Member, Inst Standing Cttee; 1922 Exec Cttee, 2000-. Managing dir, British Leather Co, 1993-99. Pres, Cotance, the Euro Tanners' Confed, 1997-98. Member, Ellesmere community care centre trust, 1990-97. Tanner. Ed Radley; Corpus Christi Coll, Cambridge.
e-mail: owenpatersonmp@parliament.uk tel: 020-7219 5185 fax: 020-7219 3955

This Shropshire seat is set along the Welsh borders north of the Shrewsbury constituency and has a definite Welsh flavour about it. There are wards with names that sound far more Welsh than English. The population is divided between a dozen towns, the biggest of which are Oswestry, Market Drayton, Whitchurch, Wem and Ellesmere, and many villages. The Tories are well established here and were able to survive the meltdowns of 1997 and 2001. Map 518

## SITTINGBOURNE & SHEPPEY — Lab hold

| Electorate | %Turnout | 65,825 | 57.51% | 2001 | 63,850 | 72.3% | 1997 |
|---|---|---|---|---|---|---|---|
| **Wyatt D** | **Lab** | **17,340** | **45.8%** | **5.24%** | 18,723 | 40.56% | Lab |
| Lee A | C | 13,831 | 36.53% | 0.15% | 16,794 | 36.38% | C |
| Lowe Ms E | LD | 5,353 | 14.14% | -4.16% | 8,447 | 18.3% | LD |
| Young M | R & R Loony | 673 | 1.78% | | 1,082 | 2.34% | Ref |
| Oakley R | UK Ind | 661 | 1.75% | 0.73% | 644 | 1.4% | Loony |
| | | | | | 472 | 1.02% | UK Ind |
| **C to Lab swing** | **2.54%** | **37,858** | Lab maj 3,509 | | **46,162** | Lab maj 1,929 | |
| | | | 9.27% | | | 4.18% | |

**DEREK WYATT,** b Dec 4, 1949. Elected 1997. Member, Select Cttee, Culture, Media and Sport, 1997-2001. Founder and chairman, all party Internet and British Council grps; chairman, rugby union grp; founder, library grp. Haringey cllr. Awarded UN commendation for sport and apartheid, 1987. Played rugby for Oxford Univ, Barbarians and England. FRSA. Worked, corporate dept, BSkyB. Ed OU; St Catherine's Coll, Oxford.
e-mail: wyattd@parliament.uk www.derekwyattmp.co.uk
tel: 020-7219 5807 fax: 020-7219 5520

This is one of the most industrial sections of north Kent. The largest element in the constituency is Sittingbourne itself, a substantially and politically competitive town. The Isle of Sheppey and its ferry port of Sheerness are more working-class and have a bias towards Labour in Westminster elections. The villages, some lying among fruit orchards, are much more Tory. The result is a fiercely fought marginal, won by Labour in 1997 and 2001. Map 519

## SKIPTON & RIPON      C hold

| Electorate | %Turnout | | 75,201 | 65.33% | 2001 | 72,042 | 75.44% | 1997 |
|---|---|---|---|---|---|---|---|---|
| **Curry D** | | **C** | **25,736** | **52.39%** | **5.85%** | 25,294 | 46.54% | C |
| Bateman B | | LD | 12,806 | 26.07% | 0.91% | 13,674 | 25.16% | LD |
| Dugher M | | Lab | 8,543 | 17.39% | -5.0% | 12,171 | 22.39% | Lab |
| Holdsworth Mrs N | | UK Ind | 2,041 | 4.15% | | 3,212 | 5.91% | Ref |
| **LD to C swing** | | **2.47%** | **49,126** | | **C maj 12,930** | **54,351** | | **C maj 11,620** |
| | | | | | 26.32% | | | 21.38% |

**DAVID CURRY,** b June 13, 1944. Elected 1987; MEP, Essex NE 1979-89. Chairman, Agriculture Select Cttee, 2000-01. Shadow Agriculture Min, July-Nov, 1997, when he resigned over Shadow Cabinet policy on the single currency. Min of Local Govt, Housing and Urban Regeneration, 1993-97; Min for W Country, 1996; Min of State for Agriculture, Fisheries and Food, 1992-93; Parly Sec, Min of Agriculture, Fisheries and Food, 1989-92. Privy Counsellor. Former *Financial Times* foreign news editor. Ed Ripon GS; Corpus Christi Coll, Oxford; Kennedy Inst of Gvt, Harvard.

This large Pennine constituency consists of much of the Yorkshire Dales. It includes towns such as Settle, Skipton and Ripon and also takes in most of Wharfedale. There are many smaller villages in the dales and on the moors. The dominant industries here are agriculture and tourism. This is a very solid Conservative seat, a factor assisted by the fairly even division of the opposition vote. Map 520

## SLEAFORD & NORTH HYKEHAM      C hold

| Electorate | %Turnout | | 74,561 | 65.34% | 2001 | 71,486 | 74.39% | 1997 |
|---|---|---|---|---|---|---|---|---|
| **Hogg D** | | **C** | **24,190** | **49.65%** | **5.72%** | 23,358 | 43.93% | C |
| Donnelly Ms E | | Lab | 15,568 | 31.95% | -2.34% | 18,235 | 34.29% | Lab |
| Arbon R | | LD | 7,894 | 16.2% | 1.04% | 8,063 | 15.16% | LD |
| Ward-Barrow M | | UK Ind | 1,067 | 2.19% | | 2,942 | 5.53% | Ref |
| | | | | | | 578 | 1.09% | Ind |
| **Lab to C swing** | | **4.03%** | **48,719** | | **C maj 8,622** | **53,176** | | **C maj 5,123** |
| | | | | | 17.70% | | | 9.64% |

**DOUGLAS HOGG,** b Feb 5, 1945. Elected here 1997; MP, Grantham 1979-97. Member, Select Cttees: Home Affairs, 1997-2001; Agriculture, 1979-82. Joined Cabinet 1995 as Min of Agriculture, Fisheries and Food. Min for Foreign and Commonwealth Affairs, 1990-95; Min for Industry, with rank of Min of State, DTI, 1989-90; Under-Sec, Home Office, 1986-89; asst govt whip, 1983-84. PPS to Chief Sec to Treasury, 1982-83. Chairman, exec cttee, Soc of C Lawyers. QC. Ed Eton; Christ Church, Oxford (Pres of Union); Lincoln's Inn.

The best, if imperfect, description of this seat would be middle Lincolnshire. Sleaford is an old market town in the Fens that has long served as a hub for numerous small farming villages. North Hykeham, on the other hand, is really a suburb to the south of Lincoln. The Conservatives are the dominant force here but Labour is certainly capable of making its presence felt. Map 521

## SLOUGH      Lab hold

| Electorate | %Turnout | | 72,429 | 53.84% | 2001 | 70,283 | 67.91% | 1997 |
|---|---|---|---|---|---|---|---|---|
| **Mactaggart Ms F** | | **Lab** | **22,718** | **58.25%** | **1.62%** | 27,029 | 56.63% | Lab |
| Coad Mrs D | | C | 10,210 | 26.18% | -3.06% | 13,958 | 29.24% | C |
| Kerr K | | LD | 4,109 | 10.54% | 3.19% | 3,509 | 7.35% | LD |
| Haines M | | Ind Haines | 859 | 2.2% | | 1,835 | 3.84% | Lib |
| Lane J | | UK Ind | 738 | 1.89% | | 1,124 | 2.35% | Ref |
| Nazir C | | Ind Nazir | 364 | 0.93% | | 277 | 0.58% | Slough |
| **C to Lab swing** | | **2.34%** | **38,998** | | **Lab maj 12,508** | **47,732** | | **Lab maj 13,071** |
| | | | | | 32.07% | | | 27.39% |

**FIONA MACTAGGART,** b Sept 12, 1953. Elected 1997. PPS to Chris Smith, Culture, Media and Sport Sec, 1997-2001. Member, Public Administration Select Cttee, 1997. Sec, PLP Home Affairs Cttee, 1997-. Chairwoman, all-party voice charity grp, 1997-. Founder, board member and assoc editor, *Renewal*, discussion journal. Dir, Fabian ed sch, 1995. Founder, David Hodge Memorial Trust/ Young Photojournalist of the Year award. Ed Cheltenham Ladies' Coll; King's Coll London.
e-mail: fionamac@slough.clp.new.labour.org.uk fax: 020-7219 0989

This seat, based on the town itself and its sprawling industrial estates along the A4 due west of Central London, was long regarded as crucial marginal territory, a fact overshadowed by the wide margin of Labour's 1997 and 2001 wins. There is a sizeable Asian community and some big council estates, but also middle-class areas such as Burnham and Langley. It is the sort of seat the Tories can hold when they have a reasonable Commons majority. Map 522

## SOLIHULL

**C hold**

| Electorate | %Turnout | | 77,094 | 62.61% | 2001 | 78,898 | 74.66% | 1997 |
|---|---|---|---|---|---|---|---|---|
| Taylor J | C | | 21,935 | 45.44% | 0.79% | 26,299 | 44.65% | C |
| Byron Ms J | LD | | 12,528 | 25.95% | 0.65% | 14,902 | 25.3% | LD |
| O'Brien B | Lab | | 12,373 | 25.63% | 1.3% | 14,334 | 24.33% | Lab |
| Moore A | UK Ind | | 1,061 | 2.2% | | 2,748 | 4.67% | Ref |
| Pyne Ms S | ProLife | | 374 | 0.77% | -0.29% | 623 | 1.06% | ProLife |
| LD to C swing | 0.07% | | 48,271 | | C maj 9,407 | 58,906 | | C maj 11,397 |
| | | | | | 19.49% | | | 19.35% |

**JOHN TAYLOR,** b Aug 19, 1941. Elected 1983. Opposition spokesman, NI, 1999-; opposition whip, 1997-99. Under-Sec of State, Dept of Trade and Industry, 1995-97; Parly Sec, Lord Chancellor's Dept, 1992-95. Vice-chairman, C Backbench Cttee, Trade and Industry, 1997 and Legal Affairs, 1997. Gvt whip, 1988-92. PPS to Chancellor of Duchy of Lancaster and Min for Trade and Industry, 1987-88. Member, Parly Assembly, Council of Europe and WEU, 1997; member, Euro Parliament 1979-84. Solicitor. Ed: Bromsgrove Sch.

This West Midlands town is the home of large numbers of affluent middle-class Birmingham commuters. Lying to the southeast of the city, it has an owner-occupation rate of more than 85 per cent and a very big proportion of non-manual workers. It is also strikingly white for a region of considerable racial diversity. It is extremely solid Conservative territory with the Liberal Democrats and Labour vying closely for second place. Map 523

## SOMERTON & FROME

**LD hold**

| Electorate | %Turnout | | 74,991 | 70.25% | 2001 | 73,988 | 77.58% | 1997 |
|---|---|---|---|---|---|---|---|---|
| Heath D | LD | | 22,983 | 43.62% | 4.1% | 22,684 | 39.52% | LD |
| Marland J | C | | 22,315 | 42.36% | 3.07% | 22,554 | 39.29% | C |
| Perkins A | Lab | | 6,113 | 11.6% | -4.75% | 9,385 | 16.35% | Lab |
| Bridgwood P | UK Ind | | 919 | 1.74% | 1.16% | 2,449 | 4.27% | Ref |
| Pollock Ms J | Lib | | 354 | 0.67% | | 331 | 0.58% | UK Ind |
| C to LD swing | 0.52% | | 52,684 | | LD maj 668 | 57,403 | | LD maj 130 |
| | | | | | 1.27% | | | 0.23% |

**DAVID HEATH,** b March 16, 1954. Elected 1997. Spokesman, agricultureand rural affairs, 1999-; foreign affairs, 1999; Europe, 1997-98. Parly consultant, World Wide Fund for Nature and Age Concern, 1991. Somerset county cllr, 1985-97 (leader, 1985-89, opposition leader, 1989-91). Chairman, Avon and Somerset police authority, 1993-96. Member, Lib Party nat exec, 1986-89. Consultant/non-practising optician. Ed Millfield; St John's Coll, Oxford; City Univ. e-mail: davidheath@davidheath.co.uk www.davidheath.co.uk tel: 07373 473618 fax: 07373 455152

This Somerset seat is not entirely typical of the county. It consists of several small, semi-industrial towns - Frome, Castle Cary, Langport, Wincanton and Somerton - as well as the more typical rural and agricultural fare. The Liberal Democrats chipped away for years at the Conservative majority here before finally edging home in 1997, and again in 2001, in what is now an ultra-marginal battleground. Map 524

## SOUTH HOLLAND & THE DEEPINGS

**C hold**

| Electorate | %Turnout | | 73,880 | 62.54% | 2001 | 69,642 | 71.98% | 1997 |
|---|---|---|---|---|---|---|---|---|
| Hayes J | C | | 25,611 | 55.43% | 6.18% | 24,691 | 49.25% | C |
| Walker G | Lab | | 14,512 | 31.41% | -1.9% | 16,700 | 33.31% | Lab |
| Hill Ms G | LD | | 4,761 | 10.3% | -5.33% | 7,836 | 15.63% | LD |
| Charlesworth M | UK Ind | | 1,318 | 2.85% | | 902 | 1.8% | NPC |
| Lab to C swing | 4.04% | | 46,202 | | C maj 11,099 | 50,129 | | C maj 7,991 |
| | | | | | 24.02% | | | 15.94% |

**JOHN HAYES,** b June 23, 1958. Elected 1997. Frontbench spokesman, ed and employment. Member, Agriculture Select Cttee, 1997-2001. Joint vice-chairman, C Ed and Employment Cttee, 1997-. Notts county cllr, 1985. Member, nat cttee, Fed of C Students, 1982-84; chairman, Aspley ward, Nottingham C, 1980-83. Sales dir. Ed Colfe's GS, London; Nottingham Univ.

This seat, created in 1997, consists of the flat agricultural countryside of the Fens in southeast Lincolnshire. Spalding, surrounded by its famed bulb fields, is the only sizeable town but there are many small villages in this rural constituency that extends west from the shores of the Wash as far as the cluster of the Deeping villages just north of Peterborough. The Conservatives, strong in much of Lincolnshire, are extremely well entrenched. Map 525

## SOUTH SHIELDS — Lab hold

| Electorate | %Turnout | 61,802 | 49.27% | 2001 | 62,261 | 62.6% | 1997 |
|---|---|---|---|---|---|---|---|
| **Miliband D** | **Lab** | **19,230** | **63.16%** | **-8.25%** | **27,834** | **71.41%** | **Lab** |
| Gardner Miss J | C | 5,140 | 16.88% | 2.31% | 5,681 | 14.57% | C |
| Grainger M | LD | 5,127 | 16.84% | 8.04% | 3,429 | 8.8% | LD |
| Hardy A | UK Ind | 689 | 2.26% | | 1,660 | 4.26% | Ref |
| Nettleship R | Ind | 262 | 0.86% | | 374 | 0.96% | Shields |
| **Lab to C swing** | **5.28%** | **30,448** | **Lab maj 14,090** | | **38,978** | **Lab maj 22,153** | |
| | | | 46.28% | | | 56.84% | |

**DAVID MILIBAND,** b July 15, 1965. Elected 2001. Won seat following sudden retirement of former Cabinet Min, David Clark. Head of Tony Blair's policy unit, 1994-2001. Sec, Commission on Social Justice, 1992-94. Resident Fellow with the Institute of Public Policy Research, 1989-94. Ed Haverstock Comp Sch; Corpus Christi, Oxford.

This town was once a shipbuilding metropolis on the south bank of the mouth of the Tyne. It has also been an active coalmining community and a moderately successful North Sea holiday resort at one stage. Now it is fighting back from years of decline to diversify into light industry and again some tourism. The politics are, however, somewhat less diverse, consisting of a staunch tribal loyalty to the Labour Party. Map 526

## SOUTHAMPTON ITCHEN — Lab hold

| Electorate | %Turnout | 76,603 | 54.01% | 2001 | 76,869 | 70.06% | 1997 |
|---|---|---|---|---|---|---|---|
| **Denham J** | **Lab** | **22,553** | **54.51%** | **-0.26%** | **29,498** | **54.77%** | **Lab** |
| Nokes Mrs C | C | 11,330 | 27.39% | -1.0% | 15,289 | 28.39% | C |
| Cooper M | LD | 6,195 | 14.97% | 3.29% | 6,289 | 11.68% | LD |
| Rose K | UK Ind | 829 | 2.0% | | 1,660 | 3.08% | Ref |
| Marsh G | Soc All | 241 | 0.58% | 1.68% | 628 | 1.17% | Soc Lab |
| Holmes M | Soc Lab | 225 | 0.54% | -0.63% | 172 | 0.32% | UK Ind |
| | | | | | 113 | 0.21% | Soc |
| | | | | | 110 | 0.2% | NLP |
| | | | | | 99 | 0.18% | ProLife |
| **C to Lab swing** | **0.37%** | **41,373** | **Lab maj 11,223** | | **53,858** | **Lab maj 14,209** | |
| | | | 27.13% | | | 26.38% | |

**JOHN DENHAM,** b July 15, 1953. Elected 1992. Min of State, Home Office, June 2001-; Min of State, Dept of Health, 1998-2001; Under-Sec, Social Security, 1997-98. Lab spokesman, social security, 1995-97. Member, Environment Select Cttee, 1992-95. Ex-joint sec, all-party overseas development, insurance and financial services grps. Hants county cllr, 1981-89; Southampton city cllr, 1989-93. Consultant, voluntary organisations, 1988-92. Nat campaigns officer, War on Want, 1984-88. Head of youth affairs, British Youth Council, 1979-82; Ed Woodroffe Comp, Lyme Regis; Southampton Univ.

This has traditionally been the more working-class of the Southampton seats and one of Labour's best prospects in the South of England. It is basically eastern Southampton but also contains much of the city centre. Labour regained this seat from the Conservatives in 1992 and now appears to be very firmly entrenched. Map 527

## SOUTHAMPTON TEST — Lab hold

| Electorate | %Turnout | 73,893 | 56.26% | 2001 | 72,983 | 71.85% | 1997 |
|---|---|---|---|---|---|---|---|
| **Whitehead A** | **Lab** | **21,824** | **52.49%** | **-1.66%** | **28,396** | **54.15%** | **Lab** |
| Gueterbock R | C | 10,617 | 25.54% | -2.51% | 14,712 | 28.05% | C |
| Shaw J | LD | 7,522 | 18.09% | 4.42% | 7,171 | 13.67% | LD |
| Rankin-Moore G | UK Ind | 792 | 1.9% | 1.48% | 1,397 | 2.66% | Ref |
| Abel M | Soc All | 442 | 1.06% | | 388 | 0.74% | LCP |
| Bahia P | Soc Lab | 378 | 0.91% | | 219 | 0.42% | UK Ind |
| | | | | | 81 | 0.15% | Glow |
| | | | | | 77 | 0.15% | NLP |
| **C to Lab swing** | **0.43%** | **41,575** | **Lab maj 11,207** | | **52,441** | **Lab maj 13,684** | |
| | | | 26.96% | | | 26.10% | |

**ALAN WHITEHEAD,** b Sept 15, 1950. Elected 1997. Under Sec, Dept Transport, Local Govt and Regions, June 2001-. Member, Select Cttee, Environment, Transport and Reg Affairs and its Environment Sub-Cttee, 1997-2001. Formerly PPS to Baroness Blackstone, Min for Ed and Employment. Chairman, all-party ports grp, 1998-. Professor, public policy, Southampton Inst. Ex-dir, British Inst of Industrial Therapy. Ed Isleworth GS; Southampton Univ. e-mail: post@alan-whitehead.org.uk www.alan-whitehead,org.uk-tel: 02380 231942 fax: 02380 231943

This seat, based on western Southampton, had long appeared to be classic marginal territory. The rate of owner-occupation is low for southern England but much of the seat has links to the sea through the Merchant Navy or the ferry port. The critical voters are probably the skilled working-class. Labour romped home in 1997 and repeated the feat in 2001 but would face a real fight if the national contest were more even. Map 528

## SOUTHEND WEST — C hold

| Electorate | %Turnout | | 64,116 | 58.29% | 2001 | 66,493 | 69.95% | 1997 |
|---|---|---|---|---|---|---|---|---|
| **Amess D** | | **C** | **17,313** | **46.32%** | **7.56%** | **18,029** | **38.76%** | **C** |
| Fisher P | | Lab | 9,372 | 25.08% | -8.21% | 15,414 | 33.14% | LD |
| de Ste Croix R | | LD | 9,319 | 24.93% | 2.29% | 10,600 | 22.79% | Lab |
| Lee B | | UK Ind | 1,371 | 3.67% | 2.3% | 1,734 | 3.73% | Ref |
| | | | | | | 636 | 1.37% | UK Ind |
| | | | | | | 101 | 0.22% | NLP |
| **Lab to C swing** | | **2.64%** | **37,375** | | **C maj 7,941** | **46,514** | | **C maj 2,615** |
| | | | | | 21.25% | | | 5.62% |

**DAVID AMESS,** b March 26, 1952. Elected here 1997; MP for Basildon 1983-97. Member, Health Select Cttee, 1997-2001. Former member, Broadcasting Select Cttee. PPS to Michael Portillo, Defence Sec and previous posts, 1989-97. Chairman, 1912 Club; all-party fire safety grp and Scout Assoc grp; joint chairman, all-party Scout grp, 1997-; treas, Hungary grp, 1997-. Redbridge cllr, 1982-86. Senior partner, 1981-87, employment agency (accountancy aids). Ed St Bonaventure GS; Bournemouth Coll of Tech.

Southend, at the mouth of the Thames Estuary, is a large and busy seaside resort and the western section of it is considered the more desirable. This constituency consists of the middle-class section of the town (many of whose residents commute into London) and some very appealing Essex villages. It is, in theory, very comfortable territory for the Conservatives, while the opposition is now split fairly evenly between the Lib Dems and Labour. Map 529

## SOUTHPORT — LD hold

| Electorate | %Turnout | | 70,785 | 58.14% | 2001 | 70,194 | 72.08% | 1997 |
|---|---|---|---|---|---|---|---|---|
| **Pugh J** | | **LD** | **18,011** | **43.77%** | **-4.35%** | **24,346** | **48.12%** | **LD** |
| Jones L | | C | 15,004 | 36.46% | 0.52% | 18,186 | 35.94% | C |
| Brant P | | Lab | 6,816 | 16.56% | 4.45% | 6,125 | 12.11% | Lab |
| Green D | | Lib | 767 | 1.86% | 1.1% | 1,368 | 2.7% | Ref |
| Kelley G | | UK Ind | 555 | 1.35% | | 386 | 0.76% | Lib |
| | | | | | | 93 | 0.18% | NLP |
| | | | | | | 92 | 0.18% | Nat Dem |
| **LD to C swing** | | **2.44%** | **41,153** | | **LD maj 3,007** | **50,596** | | **LD maj 6,160** |
| | | | | | 7.31% | | | 12.18% |

**JOHN PUGH,** b June 28, 1948. Elected 2001. Inherits seat from Ronnie Fearn. Birkdale cllr, 1987-; leader, LDs, 1992- and leader, Sefton Borough Council, 2000. Head of philosophy, Merchant Taylor's Sch, Crosby. Doctorate in logic. Describes himself as philosopher turned politician. Ed Prescot GS, Lancs; Maidstone GS, Kent; Durham, Manchester, Nottingham and Liverpool Univs.

This is an upmarket Lancashire seaside town, rather different in character from Blackpool, which is farther up the coast. Some 16 miles north of Liverpool, this genteel resort is home to a large number of Merseyside commuters. There is a very high rate of owner-occupation. It would appear to be solid Tory territory, but they and the Liberal Democrats have fought it out in a series of close polls over 15 years; the latter have come out on top recently. Map 530

## SOUTHWARK NORTH & BERMONDSEY — LD hold

| Electorate | %Turnout | | 73,527 | 50.13% | 2001 | 65,598 | 62.19% | 1997 |
|---|---|---|---|---|---|---|---|---|
| **Hughes S** | | **LD** | **20,991** | **56.94%** | **8.33%** | **19,831** | **48.61%** | **LD** |
| Abrams K | | Lab | 11,359 | 30.81% | -9.5% | 16,444 | 40.31% | Lab |
| Wallace E | | C | 2,800 | 7.6% | 0.65% | 2,835 | 6.95% | C |
| Jenkins Ms R | | Green | 752 | 2.04% | | 713 | 1.75% | BNP |
| Shore Ms L | | NF | 612 | 1.66% | | 545 | 1.34% | Ref |
| McWhirter R | | UK Ind | 271 | 0.74% | | 175 | 0.43% | Comm Lge |
| Davies J | | Ind | 77 | 0.21% | | 157 | 0.38% | Lib |
| | | | | | | 95 | 0.23% | Nat Dem |
| **Lab to LD swing** | | **8.91%** | **36,862** | | **LD maj 9,632** | **40,795** | | **LD maj 3,387** |
| | | | | | 26.13% | | | 8.30% |

**SIMON HUGHES,** b May 17, 1951. Elected here 1997; won Southwark and Bermondsey for L/All 1983 by-election; became LD MP 1988. Chief LD spokeman, home and legal affairs, 1999-; previously, spokesman, health and future of NHS, also ed, community relations, urban policy, young people, environment and natural resources. Non-practising barrister. Ed Westgate Sch, Cowbridge; Llandaff Cathedral Sch; Christ Coll, Brecon; Selwyn Coll, Cambridge; Inns of Court Sch of Law; Coll of Europe, Bruges. www.simonhughesmp.org.uk

This is one of the few seats intimately linked with an elected MP. It is one of the poorest parts of inner-city London - including the Elephant and Castle, Borough and Rotherhithe - although an element of gentrification has arrived in the past decade. On every conventional social indicator it should be extremely safe for Labour. But the Liberal Democrat Simon Hughes has managed to build a strong personal vote to overcome that partisan disadvantage. Map 531

## SPELTHORNE — C hold

| Electorate | %Turnout | | 68,731 | 60.81% | 2001 | 70,562 | 73.58% | 1997 |
|---|---|---|---|---|---|---|---|---|
| **Wilshire D** | | C | **18,851** | **45.1%** | **0.21%** | **23,306** | **44.89%** | C |
| Shaw A | | Lab | 15,589 | 37.3% | -0.9% | 19,833 | 38.2% | Lab |
| Rimmer M | | LD | 6,156 | 14.73% | 1.59% | 6,821 | 13.14% | LD |
| Squire R | | UK Ind | 1,198 | 2.87% | 1.98% | 1,495 | 2.88% | Ref |
| | | | | | | 462 | 0.89% | UK Ind |
| **Lab to C swing** | **0.56%** | | **41,794** | | **C maj 3,262** | **51,917** | | **C maj 3,473** |
| | | | | | 7.80% | | | 6.69% |

**DAVID WILSHIRE,** b Sept 16, 1943. Elected 1987. Member, Select Cttees: Foreign Affairs, 1997-2000; NI, 1994-97. PPS to Home Office and Defence Mins, 1992-94. Member, British-Irish Inter-Parly Body. Joint chairman, all-party Gulf region grp, 1997-; sec, aviation grp, 1997-; joint vice-chairman, photography grp, 1997-; member, exec cttee, British grp, IPU, 1994- (treas, 1997-). Wansdyke district cllr, Avon, 1976-87 (leader, 1981-87); Avon county cllr, 1977-81. Political consultant; personnel officer; teacher. Ed Kingswood Sch, Bath; Fitzwilliam Coll, Cambridge.

This is a busy and bustling part of Surrey. It includes Staines, Sunbury-on-Thames, Shepperton and Ashford. Although not as leafy and affluent as other parts of the county, this is still a reasonably prosperous part of the heavily residential commuter belt near Heathrow Airport. It enjoys a high rate of owner-occupation. Political sentiment is Conservative but not by the sorts of margins witnessed elsewhere in Surrey. Map 532

## STAFFORD — Lab hold

| Electorate | %Turnout | | 67,934 | 65.31% | 2001 | 67,555 | 76.64% | 1997 |
|---|---|---|---|---|---|---|---|---|
| **Kidney D** | | Lab | **21,285** | **47.98%** | **0.45%** | **24,606** | **47.53%** | Lab |
| Cochrane P | | C | 16,253 | 36.63% | -2.56% | 20,292 | 39.19% | C |
| Pinkerton Ms J | | LD | 4,205 | 9.48% | -1.1% | 5,480 | 10.58% | LD |
| Bradford Earl of | | UK Ind | 2,315 | 5.22% | | 1,146 | 2.21% | Ref |
| Hames M | | R & R Loony | 308 | 0.69% | | 248 | 0.48% | Loony |
| **C to Lab swing** | **1.50%** | | **44,366** | | **Lab maj 5,032** | **51,772** | | **Lab maj 4,314** |
| | | | | | 11.34% | | | 8.34% |

**DAVID KIDNEY,** b March 21, 1955. Elected 1997. Member, Treasury Select Cttee, 1997-2001. Stafford borough cllr, 1987-97. Member, MSF; Soc of Lab Lawyers. Solicitor, equity partner in practice. Ed Longdon HS, Stoke-on-Trent; Stoke-on-Trent Sixth-Form Coll; Bristol Univ.
e-mail: kidneyd@parliament.uk tel: 020-219 6472 fax: 01785 250357

This is a mixed town with a light industrial and railway flavour and is destined to be hard fought in future elections. Stafford is not a large enough urban area to stand on its own and the constituency is supplemented by more rural surroundings, mostly drawn from south Staffordshire near Penkridge. The more urban areas lean towards Labour and have given it the edge recently, while the rural aspects are still quite strongly Conservative. Map 533

## STAFFORDSHIRE MOORLANDS — Lab hold

| Electorate | %Turnout | | 66,760 | 63.9% | 2001 | 66,095 | 77.34% | 1997 |
|---|---|---|---|---|---|---|---|---|
| **Atkins Ms C** | | Lab | **20,904** | **49.0%** | **-3.21%** | **26,686** | **52.21%** | Lab |
| Hayes M | | C | 15,066 | 35.32% | 2.77% | 16,637 | 32.55% | C |
| Redfern J | | LD | 5,928 | 13.9% | 1.79% | 6,191 | 12.11% | LD |
| Gilbert P | | UK Ind | 760 | 1.78% | | 1,603 | 3.14% | Ref |
| **Lab to C swing** | **2.99%** | | **42,658** | | **Lab maj 5,838** | **51,117** | | **Lab maj 10,049** |
| | | | | | 13.69% | | | 19.66% |

**CHARLOTTE ATKINS,** b Sept 24, 1950. Elected 1997. Member, Ed and Employment Select Cttee and its Ed Sub-Ctee, 1997-2001; Selection Cttee, 1997-2001. Former parly officer, Unison. Member, Lab nat policy forum and nat exec women's cttee. Wandsworth cllr, 1982-88 (dep leader). Ed Colchester County HS for Girls; LSE; Sch of American Studies, London.

This is the most northern seat in Staffordshire, bordering Cheshire and Derbyshire's Peak District. Based on the textile town of Leek, it contains some of the most attractive countryside in the North Midlands, including Dovedale and the Manifold Valley and the moors near Buxton. It might be Conservative territory were it not for Kidsgrove, on the edge of the Potteries, the largest single element of the constituency, which is solidly for Labour. Map 534

## STAFFORDSHIRE SOUTH — C hold

| Electorate | %Turnout | | 69,925 | 60.32% | 2001 | 68,896 | 74.19% | 1997 |
|---|---|---|---|---|---|---|---|---|
| **Cormack Sir Patrick** | C | | **21,295** | **50.49%** | 0.47% | 25,568 | 50.02% | C |
| Kalinauckas P | Lab | | 14,414 | 34.17% | -0.55% | 17,747 | 34.72% | Lab |
| Harrison Ms J | LD | | 4,891 | 11.6% | 0.26% | 5,797 | 11.34% | LD |
| Lynch M | UK Ind | | 1,580 | 3.75% | | 2,002 | 3.92% | Ref |
| **Lab to C swing** | **0.51%** | | **42,180** | | **C maj 6,881** | **51,114** | | **C maj 7,821** |
| | | | | | 16.31% | | | 15.30% |

**SIR PATRICK CORMACK,** b May 18, 1939. Elected here 1974; MP for Cannock 1970-74. Dep Shadow Leader of House and spokesman on constitutional affairs, 1997-2000. Contested Speakership of House, 2000. Member, Joint Parly Privilege Cttee, 1997-; Chairmen's Panel. Chairman, Advisory Cttee, Commons Works of Art, 1988-2000. Chairman, all-party grps, Bosnia, 1992; Croatia, 1992. Chairman, C Advisory Cttee, Arts and Heritage, 1998-; Governor, English Speaking Union, 1999-. Freeman, City of London. Journalist. Ed St James's Choir and Havelock Schs, Grimsby; Hull Univ

This is a seat, north and west of Wolverhampton, in which no large town dominates. It consists instead of small towns, such as Wombourne and Great Wyrley, and rural villages. It is certainly a booming part of the West Midlands which - with many young voters - is likely to witness further expansion. The Conservative Party is very well entrenched locally. Map 535

## STALYBRIDGE & HYDE — Lab hold

| Electorate | %Turnout | | 66,265 | 48.36% | 2001 | 65,468 | 65.8% | 1997 |
|---|---|---|---|---|---|---|---|---|
| **Purnell J** | Lab | | **17,781** | **55.49%** | -3.38% | 25,363 | 58.87% | Lab |
| Reid A | C | | 8,922 | 27.84% | 3.33% | 10,557 | 24.51% | C |
| Jones B | LD | | 4,327 | 13.5% | 1.5% | 5,169 | 12.0% | LD |
| Bennett F | UK Ind | | 1,016 | 3.17% | | 1,992 | 4.62% | Ref |
| **Lab to C swing** | **3.36%** | | **32,046** | | **Lab maj 8,859** | **43,081** | | **Lab maj 14,806** |
| | | | | | 27.64% | | | 34.36% |

**JAMES PURNELL,** b Feb 3, 1970. Elected 2001. Inherits seat from Tom Pendry, who held it for 31 years. Special adviser, broadcasting; member, PM's policy unit; researcher for Tony Blair, 1989-1992. Former Islington cllr. Head, corporate planning, BBC, 1995-97. Ed Oxford Univ.

This seat is essentially the southeast part of the Metropolitan Borough of Tameside, on the eastern edge of Greater Manchester. It is a predominantly working-class seat with a high percentage of skilled manual workers. Most of it consists of reliably Labour towns, such as Mossley, and Manchester overspill housing at Hattersley in Hyde, partially offset by Tory wards in the more rural corners. A solid Labour seat overall. Map 536

## STEVENAGE — Lab hold

| Electorate | %Turnout | | 69,203 | 61.35% | 2001 | 66,889 | 76.82% | 1997 |
|---|---|---|---|---|---|---|---|---|
| **Follett Ms B** | Lab | | **22,025** | **51.88%** | -3.47% | 28,440 | 55.35% | Lab |
| Quar G | C | | 13,459 | 31.7% | -1.11% | 16,858 | 32.81% | C |
| Davies H | LD | | 6,027 | 14.2% | 5.27% | 4,588 | 8.93% | LD |
| Glennon S | Soc All | | 449 | 1.06% | | 1,194 | 2.32% | Ref |
| Losonczi A | Ind | | 320 | 0.75% | | 196 | 0.38% | ProLife |
| Bell Ms S | ProLife | | 173 | 0.41% | 0.03% | 110 | 0.21% | NLP |
| **Lab to C swing** | **1.18%** | | **42,453** | | **Lab maj 8,566** | **51,386** | | **Lab maj 11,582** |
| | | | | | 20.18% | | | 22.54% |

**BARBARA FOLLETT,** b Dec 25, 1942. Elected 1997. Member, International Development Select Cttee. Chairwoman, all-party retail industry grp. Joint vice-chairwoman, PLP Trade and Industry Cttee, 1997-. Lecturer, Inst of Public Policy and Research. Ed Sandford Sch, Addis Ababa, Ethiopia; Ellerslie Girls' HS, Cape Town; Cape Town Univ; LSE; OU. Married to Ken Follett, the novelist. e-mail: barbara@barbara-follett.org.uk www.poptel.org.uk/barbara.follett tel: 020-7219 2649 fax: 020-7219 1158

This part of Hertfordshire has produced some dramatic swings over the past three decades. That is not especially surprising. Stevenage, the oldest new town (1946), is the sort of area likely to attract a large proportion of youthful workers who then move on. At one stage in the 1980s it had the appearance of a Conservative-SDP marginal. Labour has staged a striking recovery since then. Map 537

STI

## STIRLING · Lab hold

| Electorate | %Turnout | | 53,097 | 67.67% | 2001 | 52,491 | 81.84% | 1997 |
|---|---|---|---|---|---|---|---|---|
| **McGuire Ms A** | **Lab** | | **15,175** | **42.23%** | **-5.22%** | **20,382** | **47.45%** | **Lab** |
| Mawdsley G | C | | 8,901 | 24.77% | -7.75% | 13,971 | 32.52% | C |
| Macaulay Ms F | SNP | | 5,877 | 16.36% | 2.97% | 5,752 | 13.39% | SNP |
| Freeman C | LD | | 4,208 | 11.71% | 5.48% | 2,675 | 6.23% | LD |
| Mullen Dr C | SSP | | 1,012 | 2.82% | | 154 | 0.36% | UK Ind |
| Ruskell M | Green | | 757 | 2.11% | | 24 | 0.06% | Value |
| **C to Lab swing** | **1.27%** | | **35,930** | | **Lab maj 6,274** | **42,958** | | **Lab maj 6,411** |
| | | | | | 17.46% | | | 14.93% |

**ANNE McGUIRE,** b May 26, 1949. Elected 1997. Gvt whip, June 2001-; asst gvt whip, 1998-2001. PPS to Donald Dewar, 1997-98. Chairman, all-party ports grp, 1998-. Chairwoman, Lab Party, Scotland, 1992-93; member, Scottish exec, 1984-; Scottish council GMB; Co-op Party. Parly agent to Norman Hogg, 1979-92. Dep dir, Scottish Council for Voluntary Organisations. Ed. Our Lady and St Francis Sec, Glasgow; Glasgow Univ.
e-mail mcguirea@parliament.uk tel 01786 446515 fax 01786 446513

While this seat is based on the town of Stirling in Central Scotland it is certainly not an urban monolith. Had it been then it could not have been held by the Conservatives until 1997. It spreads northwards past Dunblane into the lochs and hills of the Trossachs, and includes the small towns of Callander, and Killin on Loch Tay; this rural area leans towards the Tories. Labour won solidly in 1997 and 2001 but this will never be totally safe for any party. Map 538

## STOCKPORT · Lab hold

| Electorate | %Turnout | | 66,397 | 53.29% | 2001 | 65,232 | 71.54% | 1997 |
|---|---|---|---|---|---|---|---|---|
| **Coffey Ms A** | **Lab** | | **20,731** | **58.59%** | **-4.27%** | **29,338** | **62.86%** | **Lab** |
| Allen J | C | | 9,162 | 25.89% | 3.55% | 10,426 | 22.34% | C |
| Hunter M | LD | | 5,490 | 15.52% | 4.91% | 4,951 | 10.61% | LD |
| | | | | | | 1,280 | 2.74% | Ref |
| | | | | | | 255 | 0.55% | Soc Lab |
| | | | | | | 213 | 0.46% | Loony |
| | | | | | | 206 | 0.44% | Ind |
| **Lab to C swing** | **3.91%** | | **35,383** | | **Lab maj 11,569** | **46,669** | | **Lab maj 18,912** |
| | | | | | 32.70% | | | 40.52% |

**ANN COFFEY,** b Aug 31, 1946. Elected 1992. Member, Select Cttees: Modernisation of House of Commons, 1997-2001; Trade and Industry, 1992-95. PPS to Alistair Darling, 1998- and to Tony Blair, 1997. Lab whip, 1995-97. Joint vice-chairwoman, PLP Trade and Industry Cttee, 1993-95. Ex-sec, NW grp Lab MPs. Stockport borough cllr, 1984-92 (Lab grp ldr, 1988-92). Social worker. Ed Nairn Acad; Bushey GS; South Bank Poly; Manchester Univ.
tel: 0161-491 0615 fax: 0161-491 0338

This seat in the south of Greater Manchester had been surprisingly competitive until the 1997 election. The Conservatives held it through the 1980s, helped by the opposition vote being split between Labour and the SDP. Their hegemony ended in 1992 and boundary revisions transferred Brinnington, a large hilltop council estate, into the constituency. Labour now looks very strong indeed. Map 539

## STOCKTON NORTH · Lab hold

| Electorate | %Turnout | | 65,192 | 54.34% | 2001 | 64,380 | 69.08% | 1997 |
|---|---|---|---|---|---|---|---|---|
| **Cook F** | **Lab** | | **22,470** | **63.43%** | **-3.41%** | **29,726** | **66.84%** | **Lab** |
| Vigar Ms A | C | | 7,823 | 22.08% | 3.26% | 8,369 | 18.82% | C |
| Wallace Ms M | LD | | 4,208 | 11.88% | 1.05% | 4,816 | 10.83% | LD |
| Wennington B | Green | | 926 | 2.61% | | 1,563 | 3.51% | Ref |
| **Lab to C swing** | **3.34%** | | **35,427** | | **Lab maj 14,647** | **44,474** | | **Lab maj 21,357** |
| | | | | | 41.34% | | | 48.02% |

**FRANK COOK,** b Nov 3, 1935. Elected 1983. Dep Speaker, Westminster Hall, 1999-. Member, Chairmen's Panel; Defence Select Cttee, 1992-97. Chairman, UK Eurosolar all-party grp; vice-chairman, skin grp. Vice-president, Nato Parly Assembly, 1998-. Construction project manager, teacher, transport manager, gravedigger and Butlins redcoat. Ed Corby Sch, Sunderland; De La Salle Coll, Manchester; Inst of Ed, Leeds.
e-mail: cookf@parliament.uk tel: 01642 643288 fax: 020-7219 4303

This North East seat further up the River Tees from Middlesbrough looks like a Labour stronghold; and since the former MP and SDP founder William Rodgers stopped contesting it, Stockton has indeed returned to the fold. The town centre and the council estates to the northwest are staunchly Labour, as is Billingham, dominated by its towering chemical plants. These are slightly offset by middle-class pockets in the smaller villages. Map 540

248

## STOCKTON SOUTH — Lab hold

| Electorate | %Turnout | | 71,026 | 62.24% | 2001 | 68,470 | 76.12% | 1997 |
|---|---|---|---|---|---|---|---|---|
| Taylor Ms D | Lab | | 23,414 | 52.96% | -2.28% | 28,790 | 55.24% | Lab |
| Devlin T | C | | 14,328 | 32.41% | -0.6% | 17,205 | 33.01% | C |
| Fletcher Mrs S | LD | | 6,012 | 13.6% | 4.54% | 4,721 | 9.06% | LD |
| Coombes L | Soc All | | 455 | 1.03% | | 1,400 | 2.69% | Ref |
| Lab to C swing | 0.84% | | 44,209 | Lab maj 9,086 | | 52,116 | Lab maj 11,585 | |
| | | | | 20.55% | | | 22.23% | |

**DARI TAYLOR,** b Dec 13, 1944. Elected 1997. Member, Defence Select Cttee, 1997-2001. Standing Cttee, Finance Bill, 1999-. Member, all-party grps: chemical industries and opera, 1997, cancer grp, 1998, hospice and palliative care, 1999-. Sunderland city cllr, 1986-97. Ex-regional ed officer, GMB. Chairwoman, trade union studies and info unit, 1991-95. Member, SEA; Northern Arts Board; Wearside Women in Need. Ed Ynyshir GS; Nottingham and Durham Univs. e-mail: contact@dari-taylor-mp42.new.labour.org.uk www.epolitix. com/webminster/dari-taylor tel: 020-7219 4608

This is one of a handful of seats transformed by a Labour MP defecting to the SDP in the early 1980s. Ian Wrigglesworth was re-elected by a tiny margin in 1983 and only narrowly lost in 1987 in a tight three-way contest. When he left, the centre vote collapsed, initially to benefit the Tories but more recently Labour. The seat is far more rural and middle-class than Stockton North and includes Yarm, the scene of spectacular expansion since the 1980s. Map 541

## STOKE-ON-TRENT CENTRAL — Lab hold

| Electorate | %Turnout | | 59,750 | 47.36% | 2001 | 64,113 | 62.77% | 1997 |
|---|---|---|---|---|---|---|---|---|
| Fisher M | Lab | | 17,170 | 60.67% | -5.58% | 26,662 | 66.25% | Lab |
| Clark Ms J | C | | 5,325 | 18.82% | 2.08% | 6,738 | 16.74% | C |
| Webb G | LD | | 4,148 | 14.66% | 2.71% | 4,809 | 11.95% | LD |
| Wise R | Ind | | 1,657 | 5.86% | | 1,071 | 2.66% | Ref |
| | | | | | | 606 | 1.51% | BNP |
| | | | | | | 359 | 0.89% | Lib |
| Lab to C swing | 3.83% | | 28,300 | Lab maj 11,845 | | 40,245 | Lab maj 19,924 | |
| | | | | 41.86% | | | 49.51% | |

**MARK FISHER,** b Oct 29, 1944. Elected 1983. Min for Arts, 1997-98. Lab spokesman, nat heritage and the arts, 1993-97; Citizen's Charter, 1992-93; arts, 1987-92. Lab whip, 1985-87. Member, Treasury and Civil Service Select Cttee, 1983-86. Joint chairman, all-party Central Asia grp. Chairman, PLP Ed, Science and Arts Cttee, 1984-86; vice-chairman, PLP Treasury Cttee, 1983-84. Staffs county cllr, 1981-85. Documentary film producer and scriptwriter, 1966-75. Principal, Tattershall Ed Centre, 1975-83. Ed Eton; Trinity Coll, Cambridge.

The Potteries city of Stoke has elected Labour MPs to its three seats in every postwar election - an unrivalled record of partisan loyalty. This seat consists of the administrative and commercial centre of Stoke, the shopping centre of Hanley (one of the Potteries' Five Towns), and some of the poorer districts. This is still a major industrial area, with the scars of pottery and coal very evident. It has remained solidly for the Labour Party. Map 542

## STOKE-ON-TRENT NORTH — Lab hold

| Electorate | %Turnout | | 57,998 | 51.92% | 2001 | 59,030 | 65.5% | 1997 |
|---|---|---|---|---|---|---|---|---|
| Walley Ms J | Lab | | 17,460 | 57.98% | -7.17% | 25,190 | 65.15% | Lab |
| Browning B | C | | 5,676 | 18.85% | -1.32% | 7,798 | 20.17% | C |
| Jebb H | LD | | 3,580 | 11.89% | 1.18% | 4,141 | 10.71% | LD |
| Wanger L | Ind | | 3,399 | 11.29% | | 1,537 | 3.98% | Ref |
| Lab to C swing | 2.92% | | 30,115 | Lab maj 11,784 | | 38,666 | Lab maj 17,392 | |
| | | | | 39.13% | | | 44.98% | |

**JOAN WALLEY,** b Jan 23, 1949. Elected 1987. Member Select Cttees: Environmental Audit 1997-2001; Trade and Industry, 1995-2001. Lab spokesman, transport, 1990-95; environmental protection and conservation, 1988-90. Member, Commons Services Cttee, 1987-91. Vice-chairwoman, all-party football grp. Lambeth cllr, 1982-86; Wandsworth cllr, 1978-79; Swansea city cllr, 1974-78. Vice-pres, Inst of Environmental Health Officers, 1987-; pres, W Midlands home and water safety council, 1990-. Ed Biddulph GS; Hull Univ; Univ Coll of Wales, Swansea.

This seat, somewhat reconfigured by the Boundary Commission and covering two more of the Five Towns, Burslem and Tunstall, consists of two rather contrasting sections. The bulk of the seat is urban, industrial and working-class, similar to the rest of the city. It is supplemented by two somewhat different wards, Brown Edge, and Endon and Stanley, that are (highly unusually in this seat) middle-class suburbs sympathetic to the Tories. Map 543

## STOKE-ON-TRENT SOUTH — Lab hold

| Electorate | %Turnout | | 70,032 | 51.45% | 2001 | 69,968 | 66.08% | 1997 |
|---|---|---|---|---|---|---|---|---|
| Stevenson G | Lab | | 19,366 | 53.75% | -8.2% | 28,645 | 61.95% | Lab |
| Bastiman P | C | | 8,877 | 24.64% | 2.27% | 10,342 | 22.37% | C |
| Coleman C | LD | | 4,724 | 13.11% | 2.92% | 4,710 | 10.19% | LD |
| Knapper A | Ind | | 1,703 | 4.73% | | 1,103 | 2.39% | Ref |
| Batkin S | BNP | | 1,358 | 3.77% | 2.54% | 580 | 1.25% | Lib |
| | | | | | | 568 | 1.23% | BNP |
| | | | | | | 288 | 0.62% | Nat Dem |
| Lab to C swing | 5.23% | | 36,028 | Lab maj 10,489 | | 46,236 | Lab maj 18,303 | |
| | | | | 29.11% | | | 39.58% | |

GEORGE STEVENSON, b Aug 30, 1938. Elected 1992; MEP, Staffs E 1984-94. Member Select Cttees: Transport, Environment and Regions; Euro Legislation, 1995-97; Agriculture, 1992-95. Member, Chairmen's Panel. Chairman, all-party Tibet grp. Chairman, Euro parly delegation, S Asia, 1989-92. Stoke-on-Trent city cllr, 1972-86; Staffs county cllr, 1981-85. Transport driver/miner/pottery caster. Ed Queensberry Rd Sec, Stoke-on-Trent.
e-mail: stevensonp@parliament.uk/psteven745@aol.com
fax: 020-7219 2688

By the standards of Stoke this is not a monolithically safe Labour seat, although by almost any other standard it probably is. There is a consistently Tory ward here, Trentham Park, and some middle-class enclaves. The southernmost of the Potteries' Five Towns, Longton and Fenton, also display a degree of partisan independence. On the whole, however, Labour is entrenched in all but the most exceptional circumstances. Map 544

## STONE — C hold

| Electorate | %Turnout | | 68,847 | 66.29% | 2001 | 68,242 | 77.77% | 1997 |
|---|---|---|---|---|---|---|---|---|
| Cash W | C | | 22,395 | 49.07% | 2.23% | 24,859 | 46.84% | C |
| Palfreyman J | Lab | | 16,359 | 35.84% | -3.8% | 21,041 | 39.64% | Lab |
| McKeown B | LD | | 6,888 | 15.09% | 3.05% | 6,392 | 12.04% | LD |
| | | | | | | 545 | 1.03% | Lib |
| | | | | | | 237 | 0.45% | NLP |
| Lab to C swing | 3.01% | | 45,642 | C maj 6,036 | | 53,074 | C maj 3,818 | |
| | | | | 13.22% | | | 7.20% | |

BILL CASH, b May 10, 1940. Elected here 1997; MP for Stafford, 1984-97. Member, Euro Scrutiny Select Cttee, 1997-2001. Founder and chairman, European Foundation, 1993-. Joint vice-chairman, C Backbench Euro Affairs Cttee, 1997-; vice-chairman, all-party Kenya grp; chairman, alternative and complementary medicine grp, 1989-97. Member, Select Cttees: Employment, 1989-90; Statutory Instruments, 1986-90; Consolidation Bills, 1987-90. Joint vice-chairman, 1988-89, and joint sec, 1985-88, C Small Businesses Cttee. Solicitor. Ed Stonyhurst Coll; Lincoln Coll, Oxford.

Staffordshire obtained additional parliamentary representation after the most recent boundary review and this seat is created from three existing constituencies. Much more rural than the nearby Stoke seats, Stone also includes Britain's most popular theme park, Alton Towers, in the Churnet Valley near Cheadle. There is a strong rate of owner-occupation and virtually no non-white electors. The Tories are a very strong local political force. Map 545

## STOURBRIDGE — Lab hold

| Electorate | %Turnout | | 64,610 | 61.79% | 2001 | 64,966 | 76.5% | 1997 |
|---|---|---|---|---|---|---|---|---|
| Shipley Ms D | Lab | | 18,823 | 47.15% | -0.04% | 23,452 | 47.19% | Lab |
| Eyre S | C | | 15,011 | 37.6% | 1.77% | 17,807 | 35.83% | C |
| Bramall C | LD | | 4,833 | 12.11% | -2.22% | 7,123 | 14.33% | LD |
| Knotts J | UK Ind | | 763 | 1.91% | | 1,319 | 2.65% | Ref |
| Atherton M | Soc Lab | | 494 | 1.24% | | | | |
| Lab to C swing | 0.91% | | 39,924 | Lab maj 3,812 | | 49,701 | Lab maj 5,645 | |
| | | | | 9.55% | | | 11.36% | |

DEBRA SHIPLEY, b June 22, 1957. Elected 1997. Member, Standing Cttee, Protection of Children Act, 1999. Member, Social Security Select Cttee, 1998-99. Delegate, Council of Europe, 1997-98, and WEU, 1997-98. Vice-chairwoman, community health councils and domestic violence all-pty grps; treas, all-party adult ed grp, 1997-99; member, nat policy forum; nat exec, SERA; trustee and management cttee, Nat Alliance of Women's Organisations; GMB. Author, lecturer. Ed Kidderminster HS; Oxford Poly; London Univ.
fax: 020-7219 1185

This is a prosperous and independent town within the borough of Dudley. It has aspects of both the West Midlands - or specifically fringe Black Country (Quarry Bank, Lye and Cradley) - and rural Worcestershire about it. There has been a rapid expansion of private homes in Amblecote. Labour won in 1997 and again in 2001, but if the Conservatives are at all competitive nationally then they should be capable of capturing this constituency. Map 546

# STRANGFORD

## DUP gain

| Electorate | %Turnout | | 72,192 | 59.92% | 2001 | 69,980 | 59.47% | 1997 |
|---|---|---|---|---|---|---|---|---|
| Robinson Mrs I | DUP | | 18,532 | 42.84% | -12.62% | 18,431 | 44.29% | UUP |
| McNarry D | UUP | | 17,422 | 40.28% | 4.01% | 12,579 | 30.22% | DUP |
| McCarthy K | Alliance | | 2,902 | 6.71% | -6.43% | 5,467 | 13.14% | Alliance |
| McCarthy D | SDLP | | 2,646 | 6.12% | -0.55% | 2,775 | 6.67% | SDLP |
| Johnstone L | SF | | 930 | 2.15% | 0.94% | 1,743 | 4.19% | C |
| Wilson C | NI Unionist | | 822 | 1.9% | | 503 | 1.21% | SF |
| | | | | | | 121 | 0.29% | NLP |
| UUP to DUP swing | 8.32% | | 43,254 | DUP maj 1,110 | | 41,619 | UUP maj 5,852 | |
| | | | | 2.57% | | | 14.07% | |

**IRIS ROBINSON,** b Sept 6, 1949. Elected 2001. Takes seat from UUPs John Taylor, who was elected here in 1983. NI Assembly member, 1998-. Castlereagh cllr; mayor, 1992, 1998 and 2000. Elected, NI Forum for political dialogue. Married to Peter Robinson, MP for E Belfast. Ed Cregagh Primary Sch; Knockbreda Intermediate Sch; Cregagh Tech Coll.

The core of this Ulster constituency is the Ards peninsula and Strangford Lough. It is a combination of very rural territory with affluent towns such as Newtownards and Comber which house many Belfast commuters. The seat is overwhelmingly Unionist but not traditionally associated with the most strident forms of loyalism. John Taylor's standing down in 2001 made this a crucial test of Unionist sentiment; in the event it went to the DUP. Map 547

# STRATFORD-ON-AVON

## C hold

| Electorate | %Turnout | | 85,241 | 64.42% | 2001 | 81,434 | 76.26% | 1997 |
|---|---|---|---|---|---|---|---|---|
| Maples J | C | | 27,606 | 50.27% | 2.01% | 29,967 | 48.26% | C |
| Juned Dr S | LD | | 15,804 | 28.78% | 3.24% | 15,861 | 25.54% | LD |
| Hussain M | Lab | | 9,164 | 16.69% | -3.85% | 12,754 | 20.54% | Lab |
| Mole R | UK Ind | | 1,184 | 2.16% | 1.26% | 2,064 | 3.32% | Ref |
| Davies M | Green | | 1,156 | 2.11% | | 556 | 0.9% | UK Ind |
| | | | | | | 307 | 0.49% | NLP |
| | | | | | | 306 | 0.49% | SFDC |
| | | | | | | 284 | 0.46% | ProLife |
| C to LD swing | 0.61% | | 54,914 | C maj 11,802 | | 62,099 | C maj 14,106 | |
| | | | | 21.49% | | | 22.72% | |

**JOHN MAPLES,** b April 22, 1943. Elected here 1997; MP for Lewisham W 1983-92. Shadow Foreign Sec, 1999-2000; Defence, 1998-99; Health, 1997-98. Economic Sec to the Treasury, 1990-92. PPS to Norman Lamont when Treasury Min, 1987-90. Joint deputy chairman, C Party, 1994-95. Chief exec, Saatchi & Saatchi govt communications, 1992-96. Barrister. Ed Marlborough Coll, Wiltshire; Downing Coll, Cambridge; Harvard Business Sch.

This is a desirable stretch of south Warwickshire, stretching from the Birmingham commuter village of Wootton Wawen south as far as the Cotswolds, and centred on the historic town of Shakespeare's birthplace. Other small towns include Bidford-on-Avon and Alcester, and there are many picturesque villages. It is easily the most rural of the Warwickshire constituencies, thrives economically through massive tourism, and is solidly Tory. Map 548

# STRATHKELVIN & BEARSDEN

## Lab hold

| Electorate | %Turnout | | 62,729 | 66.14% | 2001 | 62,974 | 78.94% | 1997 |
|---|---|---|---|---|---|---|---|---|
| Lyons J | Lab | | 19,250 | 46.4% | -6.46% | 26,278 | 52.86% | Lab |
| Macdonald G | LD | | 7,533 | 18.16% | 8.42% | 9,986 | 20.09% | C |
| Smith C | SNP | | 6,675 | 16.09% | -0.23% | 8,111 | 16.32% | SNP |
| Roxburgh M | C | | 6,635 | 15.99% | -4.1% | 4,843 | 9.74% | LD |
| Telfer W | SSP | | 1,393 | 3.36% | | 339 | 0.68% | Ref |
| | | | | | | 155 | 0.31% | NLP |
| Lab to LD swing | 7.44% | | 41,486 | Lab maj 11,717 | | 49,712 | Lab maj 16,292 | |
| | | | | 28.24% | | | 32.77% | |

**JOHN LYONS,** b July 11, 1949. Elected 2001. Inherits seat from Sam Galbraith, former Ed Min in Scottish Parliament. British Airways pilot, flying 747s. Former RAF officer, serving in Ethiopian famine relief operation. Reg officer, Scotland, for Unison. Ed Aberdeen and Stirling Univs.

This constituency, on the northern edge of Greater Glasgow, epitomises the diffences between Scottish and English politics. Bearsden is an extremely affluent Glasgow suburb which in southern England would be resolutely Tory. The administrative district of Strathkelvin (including the towns of Bishopbriggs and Kirkintilloch), while more working-class, is hardly poverty-stricken either. But Labour retains a commanding advantage. Map 549

## STREATHAM — Lab hold

| Electorate | %Turnout | | 76,021 | 48.67% | 2001 | 74,509 | 60.24% | 1997 |
|---|---|---|---|---|---|---|---|---|
| **Hill K** | **Lab** | | **21,041** | **56.87%** | **-5.91%** | **28,181** | **62.78%** | **Lab** |
| O'Brien R | LD | | 6,771 | 18.3% | 4.75% | 9,758 | 21.74% | C |
| Hocking S | C | | 6,639 | 17.94% | -3.8% | 6,082 | 13.55% | LD |
| Sajid M | Green | | 1,641 | 4.44% | | 864 | 1.92% | Ref |
| Tucker G | Soc All | | 906 | 2.45% | | | | |
| **Lab to LD swing** | **5.33%** | | **36,998** | **Lab maj 14,270** | | **44,885** | **Lab maj 18,423** | |
| | | | | 38.57% | | | 41.04% | |

**KEITH HILL,** b July 28, 1943. Elected 1992. Deputy chief whip, June 2001-; Under-Sec, DETR, 1999-2001. Gvt asst whip, 1998-99. PPS to Hilary Armstrong, Local Gvt and Housing Min, 1997-98. Member, Transport Select Cttee, 1992-97. Sec/joint vice-chairman, 1995-97, London grp Lab MPs; joint vice-chairman, S Africa all-party grp, 1997-. Political liaison officer, RMT (formerly NUR), 1976-92. Politics lecturer, Strathclyde Univ, 1969-73. Ed City of Leicester Boys' GS; Corpus Christi Coll, Oxford; Univ Coll of Wales, Aberystwyth.

This was once a conventional suburban seat in South London, probably the most middle-class part of Lambeth borough. It is now a much more cosmopolitan place with a large non-white population in central Lambeth, plus pockets of gentrification. The impact of this demographic change has been to move securely into the Labour orbit a seat that the Tories held for many years until 1992. Map 550

## STRETFORD & URMSTON — Lab hold

| Electorate | %Turnout | | 70,924 | 54.95% | 2001 | 69,913 | 69.65% | 1997 |
|---|---|---|---|---|---|---|---|---|
| **Hughes Ms B** | **Lab** | | **23,804** | **61.08%** | **2.59%** | **28,480** | **58.49%** | **Lab** |
| Mackie J | C | | 10,565 | 27.11% | -3.37% | 14,840 | 30.48% | C |
| Bridges J | LD | | 3,891 | 9.98% | 1.81% | 3,978 | 8.17% | LD |
| Price Ms K | Ind | | 713 | 1.83% | | 1,397 | 2.87% | Ref |
| **C to Lab swing** | **2.98%** | | **38,973** | **Lab maj 13,239** | | **48,695** | **Lab maj 13,640** | |
| | | | | 33.97% | | | 28.01% | |

**BEVERLEY HUGHES,** b March 30, 1950. Elected 1997. Parly Sec, Home Office, June 2001-. Under-Sec of State, Dept of Environment, Transport and Regions, 1999-2001; PPS to Min of State, Dept of Environment, Transport and Regions, 1998-99. Member, Home Affairs Select Cttee, 1997-98. Trafford MBC, 1986-97 (leader, 1995-97; Lab grp leader, 1992-97). Manchester Univ lecturer on social policy, and former probation officer. Ed Ellesmere Port GS; Manchester and Liverpool Univs.

This Greater Manchester seat consists of the north-western element of those former parts of Cheshire that adjoined the southwest of the city. A large proportion of residents commute into the city and there is a high rate of owner-occupation in these areas, Urmston, Flixton and Davyhulme. Stretford itself, is, though, solidly Labour, while most of the rest of the seat is more evenly divided. Labour now appears to be very well entrenched. Map 551

## STROUD — Lab hold

| Electorate | %Turnout | | 78,878 | 69.95% | 2001 | 77,494 | 80.45% | 1997 |
|---|---|---|---|---|---|---|---|---|
| **Drew D** | **Lab Co-op** | | **25,685** | **46.55%** | **4.58%** | **26,170** | **41.97%** | **Lab** |
| Carmichael N | C | | 20,646 | 37.42% | 0.11% | 23,260 | 37.31% | C |
| Beasley Ms J | LD | | 6,036 | 10.94% | -4.3% | 9,502 | 15.24% | LD |
| Cranston K | Green | | 1,913 | 3.47% | -2.01% | 3,415 | 5.48% | Green |
| Blake A | UK Ind | | 895 | 1.62% | | | | |
| **C to Lab Co-op swing** | **2.24%** | | **55,175** | **Lab Co-op maj 5,039** | | **62,347** | **Lab Co-op maj 2,910** | |
| | | | | 9.13% | | | 4.66% | |

**DAVID DREW,** b April 13, 1952. Elected 1997. Chairman, PLP Agriculture Cttee, 1997-; Member, Agriculture Procedures Select Cttee. Member, all-party grps: poverty, housing, meningitis, Globe; vice-chairman, rural affairs grp, 1997-. Gloucs county cllr, 1993-97; Stonehouse town cllr, 1987-; Stroud district cllr 1987-93. Member, NATFHE; Nupe. Ex-senior lecturer, Bristol Poly. Ed Kingsfield Sch, Kingswood, Bristol; Nottingham and Birmingham Univs; Bristol Poly.
e-mail: drewd@parliament.uk tel: 020-7219 6479 fax: 020-7219 0910

This constituency, based on the hilly town of Stroud, lies on the edge of the Cotswolds, south of Gloucester and extending to the Severn Estuary. It is a mixture of light industry and agricultural interests. It is not a bad microcosm of English constituencies as a whole, although more white than average. The Conservatives used to be the dominant political force. Labour did well to win here in 1997 and even increased its majority four years later. Map 552

## SUFFOLK CENTRAL & IPSWICH NORTH — C hold

| Electorate | %Turnout | | 74,200 | 63.48% | 2001 | 70,222 | 75.22% | 1997 |
|---|---|---|---|---|---|---|---|---|
| Lord M | | C | 20,924 | 44.42% | 1.84% | 22,493 | 42.58% | C |
| Jones Ms C | | Lab | 17,455 | 37.06% | 1.18% | 18,955 | 35.88% | Lab |
| Elvin Mrs A | | LD | 7,593 | 16.12% | -4.49% | 10,886 | 20.61% | LD |
| Wright J | | UK Ind | 1,132 | 2.4% | | | 489 | 0.93% | Ind |
| Lab to C swing | | 0.33% | 47,104 | | C maj 3,469 | 52,823 | | C maj 3,538 |
| | | | | | 7.36% | | | 6.70% |

**MICHAEL LORD,** b Oct 17, 1938. Elected here 1997; MP for Suffolk Central 1983-97. Dep Speaker and dep chairman, Ways and Means, 1997. Member, Select Cttees: Parly Commissioner for Administration, 1990-97; Agriculture, 1983-84. PPS to John MacGregor, Min of Agriculture and then Chief Sec to Treasury, 1984-87. Sec, all-party forestry grp. Member, Council of Europe and WEU, 1987-91. Dir, Palmer Family Trust, 1988-, family property co. Arboricultural consultant. Ed William Hulme's GS, Manchester; Christ's Coll, Cambridge (rugby Blue).

This Suffolk seat was substantially affected by the last wave of boundary revisions. A set of Ipswich suburbs, two of which are quite affluent, while the other two are not, have been combined with a large section of richly agricultural East Anglia. Framlingham and Eye are two of the small towns here. The overall combination is one that benefits the Conservatives. Map 553

## SUFFOLK COASTAL — C hold

| Electorate | %Turnout | | 75,963 | 66.36% | 2001 | 74,219 | 75.8% | 1997 |
|---|---|---|---|---|---|---|---|---|
| Gummer J | | C | 21,847 | 43.34% | 4.77% | 21,696 | 38.57% | C |
| Gardner N | | Lab | 17,521 | 34.76% | 1.98% | 18,442 | 32.78% | Lab |
| Schur T | | LD | 9,192 | 18.24% | -3.16% | 12,036 | 21.4% | LD |
| Burn M | | UK Ind | 1,847 | 3.66% | | 3,416 | 6.07% | Ref |
| | | | | | | 514 | 0.91% | Green |
| | | | | | | 152 | 0.27% | NLP |
| Lab to C swing | | 1.40% | 50,407 | | C maj 4,326 | 56,256 | | C maj 3,254 |
| | | | | | 8.58% | | | 5.79% |

**JOHN GUMMER,** b Nov 26, 1939. Elected here 1983; MP for Eye 1979-83; Lewisham W 1970 - Feb 1974. Environment Sec, 1993-98; joined Cabinet, 1989 as Min of Agriculture, Fisheries and Food. Chairman, C Party, 1983-85. Privy Counsellor, 1985. Member, joint Parly Ecclesiastical Cttee; General Synod, C of E, 1979-92. Dir, Walsingham Coll (Affiliated Schs) Ltd; guardian, Shrine of Our Lady of Walsingham; trustee, Theodore Trust, Open Churches Trust, Catholic Central Library (all unpaid). Writer and broadcaster. Ed King's Sch, Rochester; Selwyn Coll, Cambridge (Pres of Union, 1962).

This seat includes almost the whole of the Suffolk coast. The largest town is Felixstowe, a bustling container port and resort. Other centres are Woodbridge, east of Ipswich up the River Deben, and the picturesque Aldeburgh (with its music festival and Snape Maltings) and elegantly traditional Southwold (with its brewery). Here too is the Sizewell nuclear plant. The Tories have traditionally been dominant here, although Labour has made inroads. Map 554

## SUFFOLK SOUTH — C hold

| Electorate | %Turnout | | 68,408 | 66.21% | 2001 | 67,323 | 77.2% | 1997 |
|---|---|---|---|---|---|---|---|---|
| Yeo T | | C | 18,748 | 41.39% | 4.06% | 19,402 | 37.33% | C |
| Young M | | Lab | 13,667 | 30.17% | 0.87% | 15,227 | 29.3% | Lab |
| Munt Mrs T | | LD | 11,296 | 24.94% | -2.76% | 14,395 | 27.7% | LD |
| Allen D | | UK Ind | 1,582 | 3.49% | | 2,740 | 5.27% | Ref |
| | | | | | | 211 | 0.41% | NLP |
| Lab to C swing | | 1.59% | 45,293 | | C maj 5,081 | 51,975 | | C maj 4,175 |
| | | | | | 11.22% | | | 8.03% |

**TIM YEO,** b March 20, 1945. Elected 1983. Shadow Min, Agriculture and member Shadow Cabinet, 1998-; C spokesman, Environment and Local Gvt, 1997-98; Min of State for Environment, 1993-94; Under-Sec for Environment, 1990-92; Health, 1992-93. Member, Select Cttees: Treasury 1996-97; Employment, 1994-97. PPS to Douglas Hurd, Home Sec, and then Foreign Sec, 1988-90. Capt, parly golfing soc, 1991-95. Freelance journalist. Ed Charterhouse; Emmanuel Coll, Cambridge. tel: 020-7219 6353 fax: 020-7219 4857

Much of this section of Suffolk consists of what is often described as Constable Country, which lies on the Stour near East Bergholt. There are former wool towns, such as Lavenham and Long Melford, along with scores of picturesque villages. Other main centres are Hadleigh and Sudbury and there are also a fair number of long-distance London commuters. The Tories remain the leading party here, helped by an often badly divided opposition. Map 555

## SUFFOLK WEST                                                          C hold

| Electorate | %Turnout | | 71,220 | 59.6% | 2001 | 68,638 | 71.51% | 1997 |
|---|---|---|---|---|---|---|---|---|
| **Spring R** | **C** | | **20,201** | **47.59%** | **6.68%** | **20,081** | **40.91%** | **C** |
| Jeffreys M | Lab | | 15,906 | 37.47% | 0.36% | 18,214 | 37.11% | Lab |
| Martlew R | LD | | 5,017 | 11.82% | -2.22% | 6,892 | 14.04% | LD |
| Burrows W | UK Ind | | 1,321 | 3.11% | | 3,724 | 7.59% | Ref |
| | | | | | | 171 | 0.35% | NLP |
| **Lab to C swing** | | **3.16%** | **42,445** | | **C maj 4,295** | **49,082** | | **C maj 1,867** |
| | | | | | 10.12% | | | 3.80% |

**RICHARD SPRING,** b Sept 24, 1946. Elected here 1997; MP, Bury St Edmunds 1992-97. Frontbench spokesman, Foreign & Commonwealth affairs, 2000-; spokesman, culture, media and sport, 1997-2000. PPS to Defence Min of State, 1996-97, DTI, 1995-96; NI Sec until 1995. Member, Select Cttees: Deregulation, 1997-2001; Health, 1995-97; NI, 1994-97. Joint treas, all-party Spain grp, 1997-. Ed Rondebosch, Cape Town; Cape Town Univ; Magdalene Coll, Cambridge.
www.richardspringmp.com tel: 020-7219 5192

**The last boundary changes created the impression that this was a new seat, which it is not. A large part of it is essentially the Bury St Edmunds constituency without the town itself. The rest consists of western Suffolk, notably the racing town of Newmarket, and the more working-class and Labour Haverhill. The air force bases at Mildenhall and Lakenheath are in the northwest. Labour ran the Tories a close second in 1997 but fell back relatively in 2001. Map 556**

## SUNDERLAND NORTH                                                     Lab hold

| Electorate | %Turnout | | 60,846 | 49.01% | 2001 | 64,711 | 59.05% | 1997 |
|---|---|---|---|---|---|---|---|---|
| **Etherington B** | **Lab** | | **18,685** | **62.66%** | **-5.56%** | **26,067** | **68.22%** | **Lab** |
| Harris M | C | | 5,331 | 17.88% | 1.21% | 6,370 | 16.67% | C |
| Lennox J | LD | | 3,599 | 12.07% | 1.67% | 3,973 | 10.4% | LD |
| Herron N | Ind | | 1,518 | 5.09% | | 1,394 | 3.65% | Ref |
| Guynan D | BNP | | 687 | 2.3% | | 409 | 1.07% | Loony |
| **Lab to C swing** | | **3.38%** | **29,820** | | **Lab maj 13,354** | **38,213** | | **Lab maj 19,697** |
| | | | | | 44.78% | | | 51.55% |

**BILL ETHERINGTON,** b July 17, 1941. Elected 1992. Member, Select Cttees: Parly Commissioner for Administration, 1996-97; Members' Interests, 1992-95. Member, Commons Catering Cttee, 1995-97. Member, Council of Europe and WEU, 1996-. Member, NUM, 1963-: vice-pres, NE area 1988-92; full-time NUM official, 1983-93. Fitter, Dawdon Colliery, 1963-83; branch delegate, Durham mechanics branch, 1973-83; also chairman and later sec of branch. Ed Monkwearmouth GS; Durham Univ.

**The city of Sunderland has been obliged to cope with severe economic depression in the past 20 years. But new employers have now arrived on Wearside to offset the decline of heavy industry, especially coal and shipbuilding. This constituency includes the city's central terraces and massive housing estates to the northwest, as well as a new leisure complex on the coast at Seaburn. It is staunchly working-class with a strong loyalty to Labour. Map 557**

## SUNDERLAND SOUTH                                                     Lab hold

| Electorate | %Turnout | | 64,577 | 48.29% | 2001 | 67,937 | 58.77% | 1997 |
|---|---|---|---|---|---|---|---|---|
| **Mullin C** | **Lab** | | **19,921** | **63.88%** | **-4.18%** | **27,174** | **68.06%** | **Lab** |
| Boyd J | C | | 6,254 | 20.05% | 1.17% | 7,536 | 18.88% | C |
| Greenfield M | LD | | 3,675 | 11.78% | 0.24% | 4,606 | 11.54% | LD |
| Dobbie J | BNP | | 576 | 1.85% | | 609 | 1.53% | UK Ind |
| Moore J | UK Ind | | 470 | 1.51% | -0.02% | | | |
| Warner Ms R | Loony | | 291 | 0.93% | | | | |
| **Lab to C swing** | | **2.68%** | **31,187** | | **Lab maj 13,667** | **39,925** | | **Lab maj 19,638** |
| | | | | | 43.82% | | | 49.18% |

**CHRIS MULLIN,** b Dec 12, 1947. Elected 1987. Under-Sec of State, DETR, 1999-2001; International Development, 2001 (resigned). Member, Home Affairs Select Cttee, 1992-99 (chairman, 1997-99). Member, all-party grps: Cambodia, Vietnam, Tibet, animal welfare. Private Member's Bills include Secret Societies (Declaration) and Welfare of Calves (Export). Member, Greenpeace; CND. Author of *A Very British Coup*, *Error of Judgment*. Ed St Philips' Priory, Chelmsford; St Joseph's Coll, Birkfield, Ipswich; Hull Univ. e-mail chrismullin@lineone.net tel: 0191-567 2848 fax: 0191-510 1063

**Traditionally this Tyne and Wear seat had incorporated the more middle-class sections of Sunderland, but it is now almost identical in social and political composition to its northern neighbour. This is very strong working-class territory, trying to recover from the demise of coal and shipbuilding, and deeply loyal to Labour. The seat's strongest claim to fame is its ability to produce one of the fastest counts on election night. Map 558**

## SURREY EAST — C hold

| Electorate | %Turnout | | 75,049 | 62.69% | 2001 | 72,852 | 75.02% | 1997 |
|---|---|---|---|---|---|---|---|---|
| Ainsworth P | | C | 24,706 | 52.51% | 2.4% | 27,389 | 50.11% | C |
| Pursehouse J | | LD | 11,503 | 24.45% | 1.95% | 12,296 | 22.5% | LD |
| Tanner Ms J | | Lab | 8,994 | 19.12% | -2.05% | 11,573 | 21.17% | Lab |
| Stone A | | UK Ind | 1,846 | 3.92% | 2.88% | 2,656 | 4.86% | Ref |
| | | | | | | 569 | 1.04% | UK Ind |
| | | | | | | 173 | 0.32% | NLP |
| LD to C swing | 0.23% | | 47,049 | | C maj 13,203 | 54,656 | | C maj 15,093 |
| | | | | | 28.06% | | | 27.61% |

**PETER AINSWORTH,** b Nov 16, 1956. Elected 1992. Shadow Sec of State for Culture, Media and Sport, 1998-; opposition deputy chief whip, 1997-98; asst gvt whip 1996-97. Member, Public Service Select Cttee, 1995-96. PPS to Virginia Bottomley, Nat Heritage Sec, 1995-96, and to Jonathan Aitken, Chief Sec to Treasury, 1994-95. Ex-joint sec, C Backbench Arts and Heritage Cttee. Wandsworth cllr, 1986-94. Ed Bradfield Coll, Berkshire; Lincoln Coll, Oxford.

As the name implies, this is the eastern section of Surrey extending to the Kent border and Greater London in the north. It includes towns such as Caterham, Horley (near Gatwick Airport) and Warlingham, as well as a set of smaller, affluent villages such as Godstone and Lingfield. The Conservatives have been dominant here for many years regardless of their fortunes at national level. Map 559

## SURREY HEATH — C hold

| Electorate | %Turnout | | 75,858 | 59.46% | 2001 | 73,813 | 74.14% | 1997 |
|---|---|---|---|---|---|---|---|---|
| Hawkins N | | C | 22,401 | 49.67% | -1.92% | 28,231 | 51.59% | C |
| Lelliott M | | LD | 11,582 | 25.68% | 3.85% | 11,944 | 21.83% | LD |
| Norman J | | Lab | 9,640 | 21.37% | 0.34% | 11,511 | 21.03% | Lab |
| Hunt N | | UK Ind | 1,479 | 3.28% | 2.09% | 2,385 | 4.36% | Ref |
| | | | | | | 653 | 1.19% | UK Ind |
| C to LD swing | 2.89% | | 45,102 | | C maj 10,819 | 54,724 | | C maj 16,287 |
| | | | | | 23.99% | | | 29.76% |

**NICK HAWKINS,** b March 27, 1957. Elected here 1997; MP, Blackpool S 1992-97. Shadow Min, Home Office, 2000-; Lord Chancellor's Dept, 1999. PPS to Sec of State, Nat Heritage, 1996-97; and to Defence Mins, 1995-97. Member, Transport Select Cttee, 1992-95. Joint vice-chairman,C Home Affairs Cttee, 1997-99; co-chairman, all-party railways grp, 1997-; joint vice-chairman, all-party insurance and financial services grp. Member, Bar Council, 1988-95. Barrister. Ed Bedford Modern Sch; Lincoln Coll, Oxford; Middle Temple (Harmsworth Scholar); Inns of Court Sch of Law.

This is a very suburban commuter belt seat located amidst sandy heathland in the northwest of the county. It is based on towns such as Camberley, Frimley and Bagshot as well as smaller, prosperous villages like Windlesham. There is also a strong military presence around Bisley and Camberley. All of these factors make it one of the safest Conservative seats in the country. Map 560

## SURREY SOUTH WEST — C hold

| Electorate | %Turnout | | 74,127 | 66.9% | 2001 | 72,350 | 78.03% | 1997 |
|---|---|---|---|---|---|---|---|---|
| Bottomley Mrs V | | C | 22,462 | 45.29% | 0.72% | 25,165 | 44.57% | C |
| Cordon S | | LD | 21,601 | 43.56% | 3.76% | 22,471 | 39.8% | LD |
| Whelton M | | Lab | 4,321 | 8.71% | -0.74% | 5,333 | 9.45% | Lab |
| Clark T | | UK Ind | 1,208 | 2.44% | 1.73% | 2,830 | 5.01% | Ref |
| | | | | | | 401 | 0.71% | UK Ind |
| | | | | | | 258 | 0.46% | ProLife |
| C to LD swing | 1.52% | | 49,592 | | C maj 861 | 56,458 | | C maj 2,694 |
| | | | | | 1.74% | | | 4.77% |

**VIRGINIA BOTTOMLEY,** b March 12, 1948. Elected 1984 by-election. Joined Cabinet, 1992, as Health Sec; Health Min, 1989-92; Nat Heritage Sec, 1995-97. Member, Foreign Affairs Select Cttee, 1997-98. Privy Counsellor, 1992. Joint vice-chairman, all-party tourism grp, 1997-; vice-chairman, pharmaceutical industry grp, 1997-. Member, court of governors, LSE, 1985-; governor, Ditchley Foundation, 1991-. Psychiatric social worker, 1973-84. Ed Putney HS; Essex Univ; LSE. Her husband is Peter Bottomley, MP for Worthing W. e-mail: bottomleyv@parliament.uk tel: 020-7219 6499 fax: 020-7219 6279

This section of Surrey stretches towards the Sussex and Hampshire borders. It includes the affluent towns of Godalming, Haslemere and Farnham, and scenic features such as the Devil's Punchbowl at Hindhead. Whereas most Surrey seats are basically suburban this one can claim to be part of the rural Home Counties. The Conservatives just remain the dominant political force, but the Liberal Democrats are now pushing them very hard indeed. Map 561

## SUSSEX MID — C hold

| Electorate | %Turnout | | 70,632 | 64.87% | 2001 | 68,784 | 77.73% | 1997 |
|---|---|---|---|---|---|---|---|---|
| **Soames N** | C | **21,150** | **46.16%** | **2.71%** | 23,231 | 43.45% | C |
| Wilkins Ms L | LD | 14,252 | 31.1% | 0.47% | 16,377 | 30.63% | LD |
| Mitchell P | Lab | 8,693 | 18.97% | 0.32% | 9,969 | 18.65% | Lab |
| Holdsworth Miss P | UK Ind | 1,126 | 2.46% | 1.33% | 3,146 | 5.88% | Ref |
| Berry P | Loony | 601 | 1.31% | | 606 | 1.13% | UK Ind |
| | | | | | 134 | 0.25% | Ind JRP |
| **LD to C swing** | **1.12%** | **45,822** | | **C maj 6,898** | **53,463** | | **C maj 6,854** |
| | | | | 15.05% | | | 12.82% |

**NICHOLAS SOAMES,** b Feb 12, 1948. Elected here 1997; MP, Crawley 1983-97; Armed Forces Min, 1994-97; junior MAFF Min, 1992-94. PPS to Nicholas Ridley, Environment Sec and Trade and Industry Sec, 1987-90, and to John Gummer, Employment Min and C Party chairman. Equerry, Prince of Wales, 1970-72. Member, advisory board, GSG Foundation. Son of the late Lord Soames and grandson of Sir Winston Churchill. Ed St Aubyns, Sussex; Eton.

This seat covers a substantial strip of West Sussex but the population is based almost exclusively on four settlements. These are the old market towns of East Grinstead and Cuckfield and the commuter towns of Haywards Heath and Burgess Hill. The electorate is mostly affluent with very little council housing. Conservatives win here by a decent margin regardless of their national performance. Map 562

## SUTTON & CHEAM — LD hold

| Electorate | %Turnout | | 63,648 | 62.41% | 2001 | 62,785 | 75.01% | 1997 |
|---|---|---|---|---|---|---|---|---|
| **Burstow P** | LD | **19,382** | **48.79%** | **6.49%** | 19,919 | 42.3% | LD |
| Maitland Lady O | C | 15,078 | 37.96% | 0.11% | 17,822 | 37.85% | C |
| Homan Ms L | Lab | 5,263 | 13.25% | -2.21% | 7,280 | 15.46% | Lab |
| | | | | | 1,784 | 3.79% | Ref |
| | | | | | 191 | 0.41% | UK Ind |
| | | | | | 96 | 0.2% | NLP |
| **C to LD swing** | **3.19%** | **39,723** | | **LD maj 4,304** | **47,092** | | **LD maj 2,097** |
| | | | | 10.84% | | | 4.45% |

**PAUL BURSTOW,** b May 13, 1962. Elected 1997. LD chief spokesman, older people, including long-term personal care, June 2001. Spokesman, local gvt (social services and community care) and disabled people, 1997-. Joint chairman, all-party older people grp, 1997-; joint vice-chairman, personal social services grp, 1997-. Acting political sec, assoc of LD cllrs. Member, London reg LD exec; fed policy cttee, 1988-90. Sutton cllr, 1986- (dep leader). Non-exec dir, Business Ecologic and Business Link London South (both unpaid). Ed Glastonbury HS, Carshalton; South Bank Univ.

This heavily built-up South London suburban constituency is one of a band of seats in the area that have been fought over fiercely for years by the Conservatives and Liberal Democrats. There is a high level of owner-occupation and a strikingly large proportion of non-manual employees. The Lib Dems took the seat in 1997 and held it with a bigger majority in 2001, but the spirited political competition is likely to continue. Map 563

## SUTTON COLDFIELD — C hold

| Electorate | %Turnout | | 71,856 | 60.47% | 2001 | 71,864 | 72.92% | 1997 |
|---|---|---|---|---|---|---|---|---|
| **Mitchell A** | C | **21,909** | **50.42%** | **-1.82%** | 27,373 | 52.24% | C |
| Pocock R | Lab | 11,805 | 27.17% | 3.34% | 12,488 | 23.83% | Lab |
| Turner M | LD | 8,268 | 19.03% | -0.32% | 10,139 | 19.35% | LD |
| Nattrass M | UK Ind | 1,186 | 2.73% | | 2,401 | 4.58% | Ref |
| Robinson I | Ind | 284 | 0.65% | | | | |
| **C to Lab swing** | **2.58%** | **43,452** | | **C maj 10,104** | **52,401** | | **C maj 14,885** |
| | | | | 23.25% | | | 28.41% |

**ANDREW MITCHELL,** b March 23, 1956. Elected here 2001; MP, Gedling 1987-97; contested Sunderland S, 1983. Inherits seat, which has been C since 1945, from Sir Norman Fowler. Former PPS to William Waldegrave and to John Wakeham. Under-Sec of State, DSS, 1995-97; govt whip, 1992-95. Dir, commer grp. Ex-Army. Ed Rugby Sch; Jesus Coll, Cambridge.

This seat has long been an ultra-middle-class suburb on the northeast of Birmingham. It has a very high level of owner-occupation and commuters and is overwhelmingly white despite the racial diversity of the West Midlands as a whole. This is leafy, affluent, territory that includes the impressively large Sutton Park. Like Solihull to the southeast of the city, it is one of the safest Tory areas in the UK. Map 564

## SWANSEA EAST — Lab hold

| Electorate | %Turnout | | 57,273 | 52.51% | 2001 | 57,373 | 67.41% | 1997 |
|---|---|---|---|---|---|---|---|---|
| Anderson D | | Lab | 19,612 | 65.22% | -10.16% | 29,151 | 75.38% | Lab |
| Ball J | | PC | 3,464 | 11.52% | 8.14% | 3,582 | 9.26% | C |
| Speht R | | LD | 3,064 | 10.19% | 1.3% | 3,440 | 8.89% | LD |
| Morris P | | C | 3,026 | 10.06% | 0.8% | 1,308 | 3.38% | PC |
| Young T | | Green | 463 | 1.54% | | 904 | 2.34% | Ref |
| Jenkins T | | UK Ind | 443 | 1.47% | | 289 | 0.75% | Soc |
| Lab to PC swing | 9.15% | | 30,072 | Lab maj 16,148 | | 38,674 | Lab maj 25,569 | |
| | | | | 53.70% | | | 66.12% | |

**DONALD ANDERSON,** b June 17, 1939. Elected here 1974; MP, Monmouth 1966-70. Chairman, Foreign Affairs Select Cttee, 1997-2001; member, Joint Parly Ecclesiastical Cttee. Chairman, all-party South Africa grp, 1997-; Franco-British grp, 1997-; joint chairman, Norwegian grp, German grp; vice-chairman, Methodist grp; joint vice-chairman, Council of Christians and Jews grp; sec, Christian Fellowship grp; joint sec, Europe grp. Methodist preacher. Ed Swansea GS; Univ Coll of Wales, Swansea (Hon Fellow). e-mail: trotmang@parliament.uk tel: 020-7219 3425 fax: 020-7219 4801

The north and east sides of Swansea, the second city of Wales, constitute its industrial and working-class heartland. The docks and an assortment of heavy and light industry are contained within its borders. Only about one in ten of the local population speaks Welsh, rendering Plaid Cymru almost as much of an irrelevance here as the Lib Dems and the Tories. Even by South Wales standards, this is extraordinarily solid Labour territory. Map 565

## SWANSEA WEST — Lab hold

| Electorate | %Turnout | | 57,074 | 56.24% | 2001 | 58,703 | 68.94% | 1997 |
|---|---|---|---|---|---|---|---|---|
| Williams A | | Lab | 15,644 | 48.74% | -7.47% | 22,748 | 56.21% | Lab |
| Harper Ms M | | C | 6,094 | 18.98% | -1.5% | 8,289 | 20.48% | C |
| Day M | | LD | 5,313 | 16.55% | 2.04% | 5,872 | 14.51% | LD |
| Titherington I | | PC | 3,404 | 10.6% | 3.99% | 2,675 | 6.61% | PC |
| Lewis R | | UK Ind | 653 | 2.03% | | 885 | 2.19% | Soc Lab |
| Shrewsbury M | | Green | 626 | 1.95% | | | | |
| Thraves A | | Soc All | 366 | 1.14% | | | | |
| Lab to C swing | 2.99% | | 32,100 | Lab maj 9,550 | | 40,469 | Lab maj 14,459 | |
| | | | | 29.75% | | | 35.73% | |

**ALAN WILLIAMS,** b Oct 14, 1930. Elected 1964. Member, Select Cttee, Standards and Privileges, 1997-2001; former member, joint Parly Privilege Cttee and Public Accounts Ctte; Lab spokesman, Commons affairs, 1988-89 and 1984-87; chief spokesman, Wales, 1987-88; trade and industry, 1983-84; Civil Service, 1980-83. Joint treas, all-party America grp. Former Min at Trade and Industry and MinTech, 1974-79. Under-Sec for Economic Affairs, 1967-69. Privy Counsellor, 1977. Economics lecturer. Ed Cardiff HS; Cardiff Coll of Tech; London and Oxford Univs.

Historically this has been the more affluent section of the city. It contains a bustling university as well as the neatly designed postwar city centre. Therefore there are Conservative sections, such as the suburbs out towards the Mumbles (the resort of Mumbles itself is in the Gower constituency), though they are more than matched by traditional Labour neighbourhoods. In England this might be a competitive seat, but in Wales it is solidly Labour. Map 566

## SWINDON NORTH — Lab hold

| Electorate | %Turnout | | 69,335 | 61.05% | 2001 | 65,535 | 73.66% | 1997 |
|---|---|---|---|---|---|---|---|---|
| Wills M | | Lab | 22,371 | 52.85% | 3.07% | 24,029 | 49.78% | Lab |
| Martin N | | C | 14,266 | 33.7% | -0.15% | 16,341 | 33.85% | C |
| Nation D | | LD | 4,891 | 11.55% | -1.37% | 6,237 | 12.92% | LD |
| Lloyd B | | UK Ind | 800 | 1.89% | | 1,533 | 3.18% | Ref |
| | | | | | | 130 | 0.27% | NLP |
| C to Lab swing | 1.61% | | 42,328 | Lab maj 8,105 | | 48,270 | Lab maj 7,688 | |
| | | | | 19.15% | | | 15.93% | |

**MICHAEL WILLS,** b May 20, 1952. Elected 1997. Under Sec, Lord Chancellor's Dept, June 2001-; Dept of Ed and Employment, 1999-2001; Dept of Trade and Industry, 1999. Policy adviser to Lab opposition Treasury team over VAT on fuel and "fat cats". Formed Juniper Communications Ltd, TV co, 1985-97, producers of economic and current affairs, documentaries and period drama for BBC and Channel 4; now consultant. Ed Glastonbury HS, Carshalton; South Bank Univ. www.michael-wills-mp.co.uk

The railway town of Swindon has expanded rapidly over recent decades and now has much modern industry. This seat includes most of the areas at the heart of this postwar growth, as well as the small Wiltshire town of Cricklade on the upper reaches of the Thames, and some rural territory. There is a large enough political base for both major parties to be very competitive. However, this is the more Labour-inclined of the two Swindon seats. Map 567

## SWINDON SOUTH — Lab hold

| Electorate | %Turnout | | 71,080 | 61.04% | 2001 | 70,207 | 72.87% | 1997 |
|---|---|---|---|---|---|---|---|---|
| **Drown Ms J** | **Lab** | | **22,260** | **51.31%** | **4.51%** | **23,943** | **46.8%** | **Lab** |
| Coombs S | C | | 14,919 | 34.39% | -1.37% | 18,298 | 35.76% | C |
| Brewer G | LD | | 5,165 | 11.91% | -2.5% | 7,371 | 14.41% | LD |
| Sharp Mrs V | UK Ind | | 713 | 1.64% | | 1,273 | 2.49% | Ref |
| Gillard R | R & R Loony | | 327 | 0.75% | | 181 | 0.35% | Route 66 |
| | | | | | | 96 | 0.19% | NLP |
| **C to Lab swing** | **2.94%** | | **43,384** | Lab maj 7,341 | | **51,162** | Lab maj 5,645 | |
| | | | | 16.92% | | | 11.04% | |

**JULIA DROWN,** b Aug 23, 1962. Elected 1997. Member, Health Select Cttee, 1997-99. Chairwoman, all-party maternity grp, 2000-; member, Rwanda and prevention of genocide grp, 1999-; further ed grp, 1998-99; hon sec, osteoporosis grp. Vice-chairwoman, Jubilee 2000 grp, 1999-. Oxfordshire county cllr, 1989-96. Member, Unison, Friends of the Earth, TGWU, Amnesty, Greenpeace; Co-op Party. Ex-NHS accountant. Ed Hampstead Comp; Univ Coll, Oxford.
e-mail:juliadrownmp@parliament.uk tel: 020-7219 2392 fax: 020-7219 0266

This part of Swindon contains much of the old marginal Swindon seat plus a small amount of territory formerly with Devizes. These latter sections are quite Conservative, as are a number of the wards in the town itself. The Labour vote is based on council estates near the railway station and town centre. As new industry spreads along the M4 corridor west from London, this has the makings of becoming a marginal seat again at some stage. Map 568

## TAMWORTH — Lab hold

| Electorate | %Turnout | | 69,596 | 57.83% | 2001 | 67,205 | 74.18% | 1997 |
|---|---|---|---|---|---|---|---|---|
| **Jenkins B** | **Lab** | | **19,722** | **49.0%** | **-2.77%** | **25,808** | **51.77%** | **Lab** |
| Gunter Ms L | C | | 15,124 | 37.58% | 0.85% | 18,312 | 36.73% | C |
| Pinkett Ms J | LD | | 4,721 | 11.73% | 3.66% | 4,025 | 8.07% | LD |
| Sootheran P | UK Ind | | 683 | 1.7% | 0.96% | 1,163 | 2.33% | Ref |
| | | | | | | 369 | 0.74% | UK Ind |
| | | | | | | 177 | 0.36% | Lib |
| **Lab to C swing** | **1.81%** | | **40,250** | Lab maj 4,598 | | **49,854** | Lab maj 7,496 | |
| | | | | 11.42% | | | 15.04% | |

**BRIAN JENKINS,** b Sept 19, 1942. Elected here 1997; MP, Staffordshire SE 1996-97. PPS to Joyce Quin, Min of State, MAFF. Member, Unopposed Bills Panel, 1997-2001. Tamworth borough cllr (ex-leader). Member, NATFHE. Previously industrial engineer, instrument mechanic and labourer. Lecturer. Ed Aston and Coventry Tech Colls; Coleg Harlech; LSE; Wolverhampton Poly.
e-mail: cleanc@parliament.uk; tel: 01827 311957; fax: 01827 311958

This Staffordshire town on the northeast edge of the West Midlands conurbation has been among the fastest growing in Britain during the postwar era. Before 1997 it did not have a parliamentary constituency named after it. Expanding Tamworth has a large number of council estates and some private housing. The Conservatives were very strong here, but with the assistance of a 1996 by-election Labour has become the dominant party. Map 569

## TATTON — C gain

| Electorate | %Turnout | | 64,954 | 63.55% | 2001 | 63,822 | 76.45% | 1997 |
|---|---|---|---|---|---|---|---|---|
| **Osborne G** | **C** | | **19,860** | **48.11%** | **10.65%** | **29,354** | **60.16%** | **Ind Bell** |
| Conquest S | Lab | | 11,249 | 27.25% | | 18,277 | 37.46% | C |
| Ash M | LD | | 7,685 | 18.62% | | 295 | 0.6% | Ind |
| Sheppard M | UK Ind | | 769 | 1.86% | | 187 | 0.38% | Ind |
| Sharratt P | Ind Sh | | 734 | 1.78% | | 128 | 0.26% | Miss M |
| Allinson Mrs V | Tatton | | 505 | 1.22% | | 126 | 0.26% | Albion |
| Batchelor J | Ind Batch | | 322 | 0.78% | | 123 | 0.25% | NLP |
| Boyd Hunt J | Ind Hunt | | 154 | 0.37% | | 116 | 0.24% | Byro |
| | | | | | | 113 | 0.23% | Ind |
| | | | | | | 73 | 0.15% | Juice |
| **No swing applicable** | | | **41,278** | C maj 8,611 | | **48,792** | Ind Bell maj 11,077 | |
| | | | | 20.86% | | | 22.70% | |

**GEORGE OSBORNE,** b May 23, 1971. Elected 2001. Won seat back after 4 years in the hands of Independent MP Martin Bell, former BBC journalist, 1965-96. Political sec to Leader of the Opposition and sec, Shadow Cabinet, 1997-. Special adviser, MAFF, 1995-97; head, political section, C research dept, 1994-95. Ed Davidson Coll, North Carolina, US; St Paul's Sch, London; Magdalen Coll, Oxford.

This slice of mostly rural Cheshire to the south of Greater Manchester got more than its 15 minutes of fame during the 1997 election. It was the scene of Martin Bell's improbable triumph over Neil Hamilton after the "cash for questions" scandal. The result was exceptional, because this is strong Conservative territory. Now it is difficult to envisage the towns of Knutsford, Alderley Edge or Wilmslow being again represented by anyone other than a Tory. Map 570

## TAUNTON — C gain

| Electorate | %Turnout | | 81,651 | 67.64% | 2001 | 79,783 | 76.47% | 1997 |
|---|---|---|---|---|---|---|---|---|
| **Flook A** | C | | **23,033** | **41.71%** | **2.99%** | **26,064** | **42.72%** | LD |
| Ballard Mrs J | LD | | 22,798 | 41.28% | -1.44% | 23,621 | 38.72% | C |
| Govier A | Lab | | 8,254 | 14.95% | 1.43% | 8,248 | 13.52% | Lab |
| Canton M | UK Ind | | 1,140 | 2.06% | | 2,760 | 4.52% | Ref |
| | | | | | | 318 | 0.52% | BNP |
| **LD to C swing** | **2.21%** | | **55,225** | | **C maj 235** | **61,011** | | **LD maj 2,443** |
| | | | | | 0.43% | | | 4.00% |

**ADRIAN FLOOK,** b July 9, 1963. Elected 2001. Gained by C from anti-hunting MP Jackie Ballard, who won it for Lib Dems in 1997. Contested Pontefract and Castleford 1997. Financial consultant, previously working as a stockbroker. Vice-chairman, Somerset CCC and member of Taunton Rugby Club. Ed King Edward's Sch, Bath; Mansfield Coll, Oxford.

This West Country seat combines the borough of Taunton Deane, which takes in the county town itself as well as Wellington, with the four wards of the West Somerset district across Exmoor to the Devon border. There is light industry in Taunton, but this is also cider country. Like most of rural Somerset, it is a Conservative-Lib Dem marginal. The Tories did well to resist the yellow tide until they were beaten in 1997, but they just crept back in 2001. Map 571

## TAYSIDE NORTH — SNP hold

| Electorate | %Turnout | | 61,645 | 62.48% | 2001 | 61,398 | 74.25% | 1997 |
|---|---|---|---|---|---|---|---|---|
| **Wishart P** | SNP | | **15,441** | **40.09%** | **-4.76%** | **20,447** | **44.85%** | SNP |
| Fraser M | C | | 12,158 | 31.57% | -4.15% | 16,287 | 35.72% | C |
| Docherty T | Lab | | 5,715 | 14.84% | 3.56% | 5,141 | 11.28% | Lab |
| Robertson Ms J | LD | | 4,363 | 11.33% | 3.18% | 3,716 | 8.15% | LD |
| Adams Ms R | SSP | | 620 | 1.61% | | | | |
| MacDonald Ms T | Ind | | 220 | 0.57% | | | | |
| **SNP to C swing** | **0.30%** | | **38,517** | | **SNP maj 3,283** | **45,591** | | **SNP maj 4,160** |
| | | | | | 8.52% | | | 9.13% |

**PETER WISHART,** b March 9, 1962. Elected 2001. Inherits seat from John Swinney, SNP leader who stood down to concentrate on the Scottish Parliament. Vice-convener, SNP, and campaign spokesman on ed. Musician with Scottish rock band, Runrig; anti-drugs campaigner; dir of healthy lifestyles charity. Ed Queen Anne HS, Dunfermline; Moray House Coll of Ed.

This is a large and predominantly rural constituency stretching across the northern parts of the old counties of Perthshire and Angus. The biggest towns in the east are Forfar and Brechin, while smaller centres such as Glamis, Coupar Angus, Blairgowrie, Pitlochry and the castle at Blair Atholl are strung along the southern fringes of the Highlands. The Tories hung on here for years but the SNP finally took the seat in 1997 and held on in 2001. Map 572

## TEIGNBRIDGE — LD gain

| Electorate | %Turnout | | 85,533 | 69.34% | 2001 | 81,667 | 77.08% | 1997 |
|---|---|---|---|---|---|---|---|---|
| **Younger-Ross R** | LD | | **26,343** | **44.42%** | **5.66%** | **24,679** | **39.21%** | C |
| Nicholls P | C | | 23,332 | 39.34% | 1.33% | 24,398 | 38.76% | LD |
| Bain C | Lab | | 7,366 | 12.42% | -5.55% | 11,311 | 17.97% | Lab |
| Viscount Exmouth P | UK Ind | | 2,269 | 3.83% | 1.29% | 1,601 | 2.54% | UK Ind |
| | | | | | | 817 | 1.3% | Green |
| | | | | | | 139 | 0.22% | Dream |
| **C to LD swing** | **2.76%** | | **59,310** | | **LD maj 3,011** | **62,945** | | **C maj 281** |
| | | | | | 5.08% | | | 0.45% |

**RICHARD YOUNGER-ROSS,** b Jan 29, 1953. Elected 2001. Gained seat from Patrick Nicholls, C, who held it from 1983. Contested Teignbridge 1992 and 1997 and Chislehurst 1987. Organising vice-chairman, 1979-80, Nat League Young Libs; member, Lib Party Council, 1979-84. Exec member, British Kurdish Friendship Soc; member, Howard League and Anti-Slavery International. Design consultant. Ed Walton-on-Thames Sec Mod; Ewell Tech Coll; Oxford Poly.

This South Devon constituency covers the coastal area between Torbay and Exmouth plus the hinterland to the eastern edge of Dartmoor. The largest town is Newton Abbot. It also includes the seaside retirement community of Dawlish and the resort of Teignmouth. It is a prosperous area with a high rate of owner-occupation by the standards of the region. Since 1992 it has become a very close Tory-Lib Dem marginal that the latter just took in 2001. Map 573

## TELFORD · Lab hold

| Electorate | %Turnout | | 59,486 | 51.9% | 2001 | 56,558 | 65.62% | 1997 |
|---|---|---|---|---|---|---|---|---|
| **Wright D** | **Lab** | | **16,854** | **54.59%** | **-3.22%** | **21,456** | **57.81%** | **Lab** |
| Henderson A | C | | 8,471 | 27.44% | 0.05% | 10,166 | 27.39% | C |
| Wiggin Ms S | LD | | 3,983 | 12.9% | 1.12% | 4,371 | 11.78% | LD |
| Brookes Ms N | UK Ind | | 1,098 | 3.56% | | 1,119 | 3.02% | Ref |
| Jeffries M | Soc All | | 469 | 1.52% | | | | |
| **Lab to C swing** | **1.63%** | | **30,875** | | **Lab maj 8,383** | **37,112** | | **Lab maj 11,290** |
| | | | | | 27.15% | | | 30.42% |

**DAVID WRIGHT,** b Dec 22, 1966. Elected 2001. Inherits seat from Bruce Grocott, Tony Blair's former PPS, now elevated to House of Lords. . Wrekin district cllr, 1989-97. Member, Chartered Institute of Housing. Worked for 13 years on development of housing and regeneration for local communities in Sandwell. Local gvt officer. Former instructor, Boy's Brigade. Ed Wrockwardine Comp; Wolverhampton Poly.

Telford has been one of the more successful of Britain's new towns. It is also historic. It was the site of the first stirrings of the Industrial Revolution, exemplified by the forge at Coalbrookdale and Thomas Telford's 1779 iron bridge over the Severn at Ironbridge. It was also a mining region; now this is a predominantly built-up slice of Shropshire with a sizeable number of council tenants. There are some Tory wards, but Labour is well entrenched. Map 574

## TEWKESBURY · C hold

| Electorate | %Turnout | | 70,276 | 64.31% | 2001 | 68,208 | 76.46% | 1997 |
|---|---|---|---|---|---|---|---|---|
| **Robertson L** | **C** | | **20,830** | **46.09%** | **0.34%** | **23,859** | **45.75%** | **C** |
| Dhillon K | Lab | | 12,167 | 26.92% | 0.72% | 14,625 | 28.04% | LD |
| Martin S | LD | | 11,863 | 26.25% | -1.79% | 13,665 | 26.2% | Lab |
| Vernall C | Ind | | 335 | 0.74% | | | | |
| **C to Lab swing** | **0.19%** | | **45,195** | | **C maj 8,663** | **52,149** | | **C maj 9,234** |
| | | | | | 19.17% | | | 17.71% |

**LAURENCE ROBERTSON,** b March 29, 1958. Elected 1997; contested Ashfield 1992 and Makerfield 1987. Member, Consolidation Bills Select Cttee, 1997-2001. Joint sec, C Backbench Constitutional Affairs, Scotland and Wales Cttee, 1997-; C Finance Cttee, 1997-. Vice-chairman, Assoc of C Clubs Ltd. Former consultant, Church Army, Portman House Trust. Proprietor, charity fundraiser co, now run by his wife. Ed Farnworth GS.

Much of this seat, on the edge of the Cotswolds, consists of Gloucester and Cheltenham suburbs rather than the rural villages that dominate other areas of Gloucestershire. Despite this, there are pretty spots such as Winchcombe and Cleeve Hill. The largest single section is not the abbey town of Tewkesbury itself, but Churchdown, an affluent Gloucester suburb. This is very strong Tory territory, especially as the opposition vote is often splintered. Map 575

## THANET NORTH · C hold

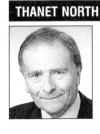

| Electorate | %Turnout | | 70,581 | 59.32% | 2001 | 71,112 | 68.84% | 1997 |
|---|---|---|---|---|---|---|---|---|
| **Gale R** | **C** | | **21,050** | **50.28%** | **6.19%** | **21,586** | **44.09%** | **C** |
| Stewart Laing J | Lab | | 14,400 | 34.39% | -4.05% | 18,820 | 38.44% | Lab |
| Proctor S | LD | | 4,603 | 10.99% | -0.4% | 5,576 | 11.39% | LD |
| Moore J | UK Ind | | 980 | 2.34% | 1.45% | 2,535 | 5.18% | Ref |
| Shortt D | Ind | | 440 | 1.05% | | 438 | 0.89% | UK Ind |
| Holmes T | NF | | 395 | 0.94% | | | | |
| **Lab to C swing** | **5.12%** | | **41,868** | | **C maj 6,650** | **48,955** | | **C maj 2,766** |
| | | | | | 15.88% | | | 5.65% |

**ROGER GALE,** b Aug 20, 1943. Elected 1983. Member, Chairmen's Panel. Member, Select Cttees; Broadcasting, 1997-2001; Home Affairs, 1990-92. Vice-chairman, C Media Cttee, 1997-. PPS to Armed Forces Min, 1992-94. Chairman, all-party animal welfare grp; sec, Cyprus grp, 1997-; joint sec, Esperanto grp. Member, advisory panel, Magellan Medical Communications Ltd. Producer, Thames TV, 1979-83; dir, BBC Children's TV, 1976-79; producer, BBC radio current affairs, 1973-76. Member, Equity, NUJ, ACTT. Ed Hardye's Sch, Dorchester; Guildhall Sch of Music and Drama.

This section of the northeastern Kent coast is the more Conservative of the two Thanet seats. It includes Herne Bay and Reculver and a strip of resorts including Cliftonville, Margate and Westgate-on-Sea. Some of these are quite working-class in flavour with a strong sense of displaced London. However, the more Tory territory and the large numbers of pensioners are the most crucial aspects of constituency politics. Map 576

## THANET SOUTH — Lab hold

| Electorate | %Turnout | | 61,462 | 64.16% | 2001 | 62,792 | 71.65% | 1997 |
|---|---|---|---|---|---|---|---|---|
| **Ladyman Dr S** | Lab | | **18,002** | **45.65%** | -0.53% | 20,777 | 46.18% | Lab |
| Macgregor M | C | | 16,210 | 41.11% | 1.32% | 17,899 | 39.79% | C |
| Voizey G | LD | | 3,706 | 9.4% | -2.3% | 5,263 | 11.7% | LD |
| Baldwin W | Ind | | 770 | 1.95% | | 631 | 1.4% | UK Ind |
| Eccott T | UK Ind | | 501 | 1.27% | -0.13% | 418 | 0.93% | Green |
| Franklin B | NF | | 242 | 0.61% | | | | |
| **Lab to C swing** | **0.92%** | | **39,431** | | **Lab maj 1,792** | **44,988** | | **Lab maj 2,878** |
| | | | | | 4.54% | | | 6.39% |

**STEPHEN LADYMAN,** b Nov 6, 1952. Elected 1997. Member, Environment, Transport and Regions Select Cttee and Transport Sub-Cttee, 1999-2001. Member, Euro Standing Cttee B, 1997-99 and C, 1999-. Treas all-party joint industry grp, 2000-; chairman, all-party grp on autism, 2000-. Thanet district cllr, 1995-99. Member, Fabian Soc, GMB. Computer scientist; ex-computing manager, Pfizer central research. Ed Liverpool Poly; Strathclyde Univ.
e-mail: steveladyman@souththanetlp.freeserve.co.uk  www.south thanetlp.freeserve.co.uk tel: 01843 852696 fax: 01843 852689

This part of the Isle of Thanet consists of the resorts of Broadstairs, Ramsgate, with its ferry port, and Sandwich, with its top-grade golf course, as well as the largely cargo airport at Manston. There are the council estate wards of Newington and Northwood and the constituency is not quite as affluent as its neighbour, while the number of pensioners is not quite so large. This explains how Labour was able to win in 1997 and to hold on in 2001. Map 577

## THURROCK — Lab hold

| Electorate | %Turnout | | 76,524 | 48.82% | 2001 | 71,600 | 65.94% | 1997 |
|---|---|---|---|---|---|---|---|---|
| **Mackinlay A** | Lab | | **21,121** | **56.53%** | -6.79% | 29,896 | 63.32% | Lab |
| Penning M | C | | 11,124 | 29.77% | 3.0% | 12,640 | 26.77% | C |
| Lathan J | LD | | 3,846 | 10.29% | 2.15% | 3,843 | 8.14% | LD |
| Sheppard C | UK Ind | | 1,271 | 3.4% | 1.64% | 833 | 1.76% | UK Ind |
| **Lab to C swing** | **4.90%** | | **37,362** | | **Lab maj 9,997** | **47,212** | | **Lab maj 17,256** |
| | | | | | 26.76% | | | 36.55% |

**ANDREW MACKINLAY,** b April 24, 1949. Elected 1992. Member, Select Cttees: Foreign Affairs, 1997-2001; Transport, 1992-97. Backbench rep, Lab Parliamentary Cttee. Vice-chairman, S and E grp of Lab MPs, 1997-. Kingston upon Thames cllr, 1971-78. Nalgo official, 1972-92. Admin clerk, Surrey County Council, 1965-75. Member, Chartered Inst of Secretaries and Administrators. Ed Salesian Coll, Chertsey.

The Borough of Thurrock in Essex stretches along the northern bank of the Thames, east of London from Purfleet and the Dartford Tunnel through Grays to Tilbury, the capital's outermost docks and now the main container port. A recent addition is the vast Lakeside shopping centre. This is skilled working-class territory - very Essex man - which allowed the Tories to capture the seat in 1987. Since then it has swung remorselessly back to Labour. Map 578

## TIVERTON & HONITON — C hold

| Electorate | %Turnout | | 80,646 | 69.17% | 2001 | 75,744 | 78.06% | 1997 |
|---|---|---|---|---|---|---|---|---|
| **Browning Mrs A** | C | | **26,258** | **47.07%** | 5.74% | 24,438 | 41.33% | C |
| Barnard J | LD | | 19,974 | 35.81% | -2.72% | 22,785 | 38.53% | LD |
| Owen Ms I | Lab | | 6,647 | 11.92% | -0.93% | 7,598 | 12.85% | Lab |
| Langmaid A | UK Ind | | 1,281 | 2.3% | | 2,952 | 4.99% | Ref |
| Burgess M | Green | | 1,030 | 1.85% | 1.03% | 635 | 1.07% | Lib |
| Roach Mrs J | Lib | | 594 | 1.06% | -0.01% | 485 | 0.82% | Green |
| | | | | | | 236 | 0.4% | Nat Dem |
| **LD to C swing** | **4.23%** | | **55,784** | | **C maj 6,284** | **59,129** | | **C maj 1,653** |
| | | | | | 11.26% | | | 2.80% |

**ANGELA BROWNING,** b Dec 4, 1946. Elected here 1997; MP, Tiverton 1992-97. Shadow Sec, Trade and Industry, 1999-2000; Shadow Leader of House, 2000-. Spokeswoman, Ed and Disability, 1997-98. Parly Sec, Min of Agriculture, Fisheries and Food, 1994-97. Former self-employed management consultant, specialising in training, communications and finance; former dir of the Small Business Bureau. Member, Nat Autistic Soc; Thomas Hardy Soc. Ed Westwood Girls' GS; Reading and Bournemouth Colls of Tech.
www.abrowning.demon.co.uk tel: 020-7219 5067 fax: 020-7219 2557

There are two elements to this inland Devon seat, summed up by its name. The rolling farmland of the Tiverton section is dotted with market towns such as Cullompton and Crediton, while the Honiton element has a large number of residents who came to Devon to retire. The Conservatives and Liberal Democrats engage in a lively fight in all parts of the seat, but the Honiton area tips the balance in favour of the Tories, who stretched their lead in 2001. Map 579

## TONBRIDGE & MALLING — C hold

| Electorate | %Turnout | | 65,939 | 64.36% | 2001 | 64,798 | 75.97% | 1997 |
|---|---|---|---|---|---|---|---|---|
| **Stanley Sir J** | **C** | | **20,956** | **49.38%** | **1.36%** | **23,640** | **48.02%** | **C** |
| Hayman Ms V | Lab | | 12,706 | 29.94% | 2.7% | 13,410 | 27.24% | Lab |
| Canet Ms M | LD | | 7,605 | 17.92% | -1.31% | 9,467 | 19.23% | LD |
| Croucher Ms L | UK Ind | | 1,169 | 2.75% | | 2,005 | 4.07% | Ref |
| | | | | | 1.73% | 502 | 1.02% | UK Ind |
| | | | | | | 205 | 0.42% | NLP |
| **C to Lab swing** | **0.67%** | | **42,436** | | **C maj 8,250** | **49,229** | | **C maj 10,230** |
| | | | | | 19.44% | | | 20.78% |

**SIR JOHN STANLEY,** b Jan 19, 1942. Elected Feb 1974. Former member, Foreign Affairs Select Cttee. NI Min, 1987-88; Armed Forces Min, 1983-87; Housing Min, 1979-83. PPS to Margaret Thatcher, 1976-79. Exec cttee, UK branch, CPA, 1997-. Privy Counsellor, 1984. Joint vice-chairman, Japanese grp, 1997-; all-party child abduction grp, 1994-; vice-chairman, overseas development grp, 1997-; chairman, Korean Republic grp; Nepal grp, 1997-. Ed Repton; Lincoln Coll, Oxford.

This seat consists of some very attractive parts of the Kent countryside that fully live up to the epithet "Garden of England". It includes the town of Edenbridge and the rich farming areas around Hever Castle and Penshurst Place. The majority of local residents are plainly more prosperous than the national average. This is a very solid Conservative constituency. Map 580

## TOOTING — Lab hold

| Electorate | %Turnout | | 68,447 | 54.92% | 2001 | 66,653 | 69.17% | 1997 |
|---|---|---|---|---|---|---|---|---|
| **Cox T** | **Lab** | | **20,332** | **54.09%** | **-5.59%** | **27,516** | **59.68%** | **Lab** |
| Nicoll A | C | | 9,932 | 26.42% | -0.7% | 12,505 | 27.12% | C |
| James S | LD | | 5,583 | 14.85% | 5.48% | 4,320 | 9.37% | LD |
| Ledbury M | Green | | 1,744 | 4.64% | 3.5% | 829 | 1.8% | Ref |
| | | | | | | 527 | 1.14% | Green |
| | | | | | | 161 | 0.35% | BFAIR |
| | | | | | | 94 | 0.2% | Rights |
| | | | | | | 83 | 0.18% | Dream |
| | | | | | | 70 | 0.15% | NLP |
| **Lab to C swing** | **2.45%** | | **37,591** | | **Lab maj 10,400** | **46,105** | | **Lab maj 15,011** |
| | | | | | 27.67% | | | 32.56% |

**TOM COX,** b Dec 9, 1930. Elected here 1974; MP, Wandsworth Central 1970-74. Chairman, all-party construction grp, 1997-. Member and ex-officer, exec cttee, British grp, IPU; joint vice-chairman (1994-95) and member, exec cttee, UK branch, CPA. Member and office holder, all-party grps: Argentina, Cyprus, Hungary, Kenya, Pakistan, Portugal, Austria, Nepal, Philippines, Sudan, Argentina, Sri Lanka, Franco-British, Greek. Electrician. Ed state schools and LSE.

This seat is the political exception within the South London Borough of Wandsworth. Its neighbours Battersea and Putney swung wildly to the Tories in the 1980s and early 1990s while bustling, cosmopolitan Tooting remained loyal to Labour. This is a predominantly working-class constituency with a high number of ethnic minority voters. Some recent gentrification seems unlikely to change the prevailing political balance. Map 581

## TORBAY — LD hold

| Electorate | %Turnout | | 72,409 | 65.69% | 2001 | 72,258 | 73.79% | 1997 |
|---|---|---|---|---|---|---|---|---|
| **Sanders A** | **LD** | | **24,015** | **50.48%** | **10.92%** | **21,094** | **39.56%** | **LD** |
| Sweeting C | C | | 17,307 | 36.38% | -3.16% | 21,082 | 39.54% | C |
| McKay J | Lab | | 4,484 | 9.43% | -5.43% | 7,923 | 14.86% | Lab |
| Booth G | UK Ind | | 1,512 | 3.18% | -0.5% | 1,962 | 3.68% | UK Ind |
| Neale Ms P | Ind | | 251 | 0.53% | | 1,161 | 2.18% | Lib |
| | | | | | | 100 | 0.19% | Dream |
| **C to LD swing** | **7.04%** | | **47,569** | | **LD maj 6,708** | **53,322** | | **LD maj 12** |
| | | | | | 14.10% | | | 0.02% |

**ADRIAN SANDERS,** b April 25, 1959. Elected 1997. LD spokesman, Housing and Local Govt, 1997-. Member, Consolidation Bills Select Cttee, 1997-2001. Chairman, all-party diabetes grp; vice-chairman, housing and homelessness, charities and voluntary sector grps. Joint vice-chairman, building societies grp, 1997-. Worked in Paddy Ashdown's office, 1992-93. Torbay borough cllr, 1984-86. Member, Diabetes UK. Policy officer, Nat Council for Voluntary Organisations, 1993-94. Ex-funding adviser. Ed Torquay Boys' GS. e-mail: asanders@cix.co.uk tel: 020-7219 6304 fax: 020-7219 3963

This is a bustling part of the South Devon coastline, popularly known as the Devon Riviera. There is a huge amount of hotel, guesthouse and bed-and-breakfast accommodation. The seat is based on the resorts of Torquay and Paignton. Traditionally the Conservatives have been strong here but the Liberal Democrats chipped away to seize an improbable 12-vote victory in 1997 - which they stretched to an impressive 6,700-vote lead in 2001. Map 582

# TORFAEN

**Lab hold**

| Electorate | %Turnout | | 61,110 | 57.67% | 2001 | 60,343 | 71.67% | 1997 |
|---|---|---|---|---|---|---|---|---|
| **Murphy P** | **Lab** | | **21,883** | **62.09%** | **-6.97%** | **29,863** | **69.06%** | **Lab** |
| Evans J | C | | 5,603 | 15.9% | 3.58% | 5,327 | 12.32% | C |
| Masters A | LD | | 3,936 | 11.17% | -0.97% | 5,249 | 12.14% | LD |
| Smith S | PC | | 2,720 | 7.72% | 5.31% | 1,245 | 2.88% | Ref |
| Vipass Mrs B | UK Ind | | 657 | 1.86% | | 1,042 | 2.41% | PC |
| Bell S | Soc All | | 443 | 1.26% | | 519 | 1.2% | Green |
| **Lab to C swing** | **5.27%** | | **35,242** | Lab maj 16,280 | | **43,245** | Lab maj 24,536 | |
| | | | | 46.19% | | | 56.74% | |

**PAUL MURPHY,** b Nov 25, 1948. Elected 1987. Sec of State for Wales, 1999-; confirmed June 2001. Min of State, NI Office, 1997-99; Lab spokesman, defence, 1995-97; NI, 1994-9; Wales, 1988-94. Member, Welsh Affairs Select Cttee, 1987-89. Chairman, 1997-, and vice-chairman, 1995-97, Welsh grp of Lab MPs. Ex-joint sec, all-party Franco-British Parly Relations Cttee. Ex-parly consultant, NATFHE. Torfaen borough cllr, 1973-87. Lecturer, history and gvt, Ebbw Vale Coll of FE, 1971-87. Torfaen CLP sec, 1972-87. Ed West Monmouth Sch, Pontypool; Oriel Coll, Oxford.

This constituency is the furthest east of the classic South Wales Valleys, running north from Newport. The two most significant settlements are Pontypool and Cwmbran, the only new town in South Wales. With the demise of coal, the local economy has been obliged to change drastically, but that has not fed through to electoral patterns. This is utterly reliable territory for Labour. Map 583

# TOTNES

**C hold**

| Electorate | %Turnout | | 72,548 | 67.88% | 2001 | 70,473 | 76.3% | 1997 |
|---|---|---|---|---|---|---|---|---|
| **Steen A** | **C** | | **21,914** | **44.5%** | **7.98%** | **19,637** | **36.52%** | **C** |
| Oliver Ms R | LD | | 18,317 | 37.19% | 2.3% | 18,760 | 34.89% | LD |
| Wildy T | Lab | | 6,005 | 12.19% | -4.17% | 8,796 | 16.36% | Lab |
| Mackinlay C | UK Ind | | 3,010 | 6.11% | 4.25% | 2,552 | 4.75% | Ref |
| | | | | | | 2,369 | 4.41% | Loc C |
| | | | | | | 999 | 1.86% | UK Ind |
| | | | | | | 548 | 1.02% | Green |
| | | | | | | 108 | 0.2% | Dream |
| **LD to C swing** | **2.84%** | | **49,246** | C maj 3,597 | | **53,769** | C maj 877 | |
| | | | | 7.30% | | | 1.63% | |

**ANTHONY STEEN,** b July 22, 1939. Elected here 1997; MP, South Hams 1983-97; Liverpool Wavertree 1974-83. Member, Select Cttees: Deregulation, 1997-2001; Euro Legislation, 1997-2001; Environment, 1991-92. PPS to Nat Heritage Sec, 1992-94. Chairman, all-party Cambodia grp; vice-chairman, Vietnam grp; joint vice-chairman, S Africa grp, 1997-; treas, Greek grp. Member, exec council, Nat Playing Fields Assoc; chairman, Outlandos Trust, 1981-; vice-pres, International Centre of Child Studies. Barrister. Lloyd's underwriter. Youth leader; social worker. Ed Westminster; Gray's Inn.

This South Devon seat, based on the town of Totnes on the River Dart, includes several small seaside towns and fishing ports such as Brixham, Salcombe and Dartmouth (with its Royal Naval College) that attract hordes of summer tourists. Inland the seat extends to the southern edge of Dartmoor. There is fishing and a significant farming sector. Despite a typical Devon battle between Tories and Lib Dems, the Tories continue to hold on here. Map 584

# TOTTENHAM

**Lab hold**

| Electorate | %Turnout | | 65,567 | 48.2% | 2001 | 66,173 | 56.98% | 1997 |
|---|---|---|---|---|---|---|---|---|
| **Lammy D** | **Lab** | | **21,317** | **67.46%** | **-1.82%** | **26,121** | **69.28%** | **Lab** |
| Fernandes Ms U | C | | 4,401 | 13.93% | -1.77% | 5,921 | 15.7% | C |
| Khan Ms M | LD | | 3,008 | 9.52% | -1.26% | 4,064 | 10.78% | LD |
| Budge P | Green | | 1,443 | 4.57% | 1.76% | 1,059 | 2.81% | Green |
| Bennett W | Soc All | | 1,162 | 3.68% | | 210 | 0.56% | ProLife |
| Shefki U | Reform | | 270 | 0.85% | | 181 | 0.48% | WRP |
| | | | | | | 148 | 0.39% | SEP |
| **Lab to C swing** | **0.03%** | | **31,601** | Lab maj 16,916 | | **37,704** | Lab maj 20,200 | |
| | | | | 53.53% | | | 53.58% | |

**DAVID LAMMY,** b June 19, 1972. Elected 2000 by-election, following the death of sitting MP Bernie Grant. PPS to Estelle Morris, Sec of State for Ed and Skills, 2001-. Member, Procedure and Public Administration Select Cttees. Member, GLA, 2000; Archbishops' council/dir of the C of E board of finance; Soc of Lab Lawyers; MSF; Fabian Soc. Barrister. Ed King's Sch, Peterborough; Sch of Oriental and African Studies, London Univ; Inns of Court; Harvard Law Sch.

*Details of 2000 by-election on page 291*

Tottenham is set in the North London Borough of Haringey. It is an extremely diverse, cosmopolitan seat, stretching from the edge of fashionable Hampstead Heath to the industrial Lea Valley. Around 40 per cent of the electorate is non-white, mostly Afro-Caribbean. There is also a significant Cypriot community. This is strong territory for Labour, a fact reinforced by its wins here in a by-election in 2000 and in the general election a year later. Map 585

## TRURO & ST AUSTELL  LD hold

| Electorate | %Turnout | | 79,219 | 63.49% | 2001 | 76,824 | 73.87% | 1997 |
|---|---|---|---|---|---|---|---|---|
| **Taylor M** | **LD** | | **24,296** | **48.31%** | **-0.15%** | **27,502** | **48.46%** | **LD** |
| Bonner T | C | | 16,231 | 32.27% | 5.84% | 15,001 | 26.43% | C |
| Phillips D | Lab | | 6,889 | 13.7% | -1.63% | 8,697 | 15.33% | Lab |
| Wonnacott J | UK Ind | | 1,664 | 3.31% | 2.29% | 3,682 | 6.49% | Ref |
| Jenkin C | Meb Ker | | 1,137 | 2.26% | 1.47% | 576 | 1.02% | UK Ind |
| Lee J | Ind | | 78 | 0.16% | | 482 | 0.85% | Green |
| | | | | | | 450 | 0.79% | Meb Ker |
| | | | | | | 240 | 0.42% | PP |
| | | | | | | 117 | 0.21% | NLP |
| **LD to C swing** | **3.00%** | | **50,295** | LD maj 8,065 | | **56,747** | LD maj 12,501 | |
| | | | | 16.04% | | | 22.03% | |

**MATTHEW TAYLOR,** b Jan 3, 1963. Elected here 1997; MP, Truro 1987-97. Chief Treasury spokesman, 1999-; confirmed June 2001; spokesman, environment and transport, 1997-99; environment, 1994-99; Citizen's Charter and chairman of campaigns and communications, 1992-94; ed, 1990-92; trade and industry, 1989-90. Member, Environment Select Cttee, 1995-2001. Research asst to late David Penhaligon, MP for Truro, 1974-86. Ed St Paul's, Truro; Trel-iske Sch, Truro; Univ Coll Sch, London; Lady Margaret Hall, Oxford. tel: 020-7219 6686

The Boundary Commission did virtually nothing in Cornwall last time except to add St Austell to this constituency's title. It was appropriate as St Austell is not merely larger than Truro but is the biggest town in the county. This is the old china-clay mining belt; in one former clay pit near St Austell is the David Eden Project, a series of ecological/horticultural domes that promises to become a top tourist draw. This is now a very secure Lib Dem seat. Map 586

## TUNBRIDGE WELLS C hold

| Electorate | %Turnout | | 64,534 | 62.29% | 2001 | 65,259 | 74.1% | 1997 |
|---|---|---|---|---|---|---|---|---|
| **Norman A** | **C** | | **19,643** | **48.86%** | **3.67%** | **21,853** | **45.19%** | **C** |
| Brown K | LD | | 9,913 | 24.66% | -5.01% | 14,347 | 29.67% | LD |
| Carvell I | Lab | | 9,332 | 23.21% | 2.78% | 9,879 | 20.43% | Lab |
| Webb V | UK Ind | | 1,313 | 3.27% | 2.72% | 1,858 | 3.84% | Ref |
| | | | | | | 264 | 0.55% | UK Ind |
| | | | | | | 153 | 0.32% | NLP |
| **LD to C swing** | **4.34%** | | **40,201** | C maj 9,730 | | **48,354** | C maj 7,506 | |
| | | | | 24.20% | | | 15.52% | |

**ARCHIE NORMAN,** b May 1, 1954. Elected 1997. Shadow Sec of State, Dept of Environment and Regions, 2000-; Shadow Min for Europe, 1999-2000; chief exec, C Party, 1998-99; vice-chairman, C Party, responsible for party reform, 1997-98. Chairman, Asda Supermarkets, 1996-99; chief exec, 1991-96. Member, British Railways Board, 1992-94; consultative cttee, Dulwich Picture Gallery, 1990-. Member of Lloyd's. Variously with Citibank, McKinsey, Woolworth, Kingfisher and Chartwell Land. Ed Minnesota Univ; Emmanuel Coll, Cambridge; Harvard Business Sch.

This seat is based on the elegant and affluent spa town of Royal Tunbridge Wells itself and includes a swath of small towns and villages such as Lamberhurst. It is the part of rural Kent that stretches along the East Sussex border, including part of The Weald. The Liberal Democrats became quite a force here in local government in the mid-1990s. At parliamentary level, however, the Conservatives are extremely well-entrenched. Map 587

## TWEEDDALE, ETTRICK & LAUDERDALE LD hold

| Electorate | %Turnout | | 51,966 | 63.92% | 2001 | 50,891 | 76.64% | 1997 |
|---|---|---|---|---|---|---|---|---|
| **Moore M** | **LD** | | **14,035** | **42.25%** | **11.03%** | **12,178** | **31.22%** | **LD** |
| Geddes K | Lab | | 8,878 | 26.73% | -0.68% | 10,689 | 27.41% | Lab |
| Brocklehurst A | C | | 5,118 | 15.41% | -6.7% | 8,623 | 22.11% | C |
| Thomson R | SNP | | 4,108 | 12.37% | -4.73% | 6,671 | 17.1% | SNP |
| Lockhart N | SSP | | 695 | 2.09% | | 406 | 1.04% | Ref |
| Hein J | Lib | | 383 | 1.15% | 0.16% | 387 | 0.99% | Lib |
| | | | | | | 47 | 0.12% | NLP |
| **Lab to LD swing** | **5.86%** | | **33,217** | LD maj 5,157 | | **39,001** | LD maj 1,489 | |
| | | | | 15.53% | | | 3.81% | |

**MICHAEL MOORE,** b June 3, 1965. Elected 1997. LD spokesman, Scotland, June 2001; UK transport, 1999-. LD spokesman, health and economy, 1996-99; small business and employment. Member, Scottish Affairs Select Cttee, 1997-99. Sec, all-party textiles grp, 2000-; research asst to Archy Kirkwood, MP, 1987-88. Member, Amnesty. Chartered accountant. Ed Strathallan Sch; Jedburgh GS; Edinburgh Univ.
e-mail: michaelmoore@cix.co.uk www.libdem.org
tel: 01896 831011 fax: 01896 831437

A version of this seat was represented by David Steel for many years and the Liberal Democrats remain strong in this part of the Scottish Borders. The seat consists of textile and market towns such as Galashiels, Selkirk, Lauder and Peebles (north of the almost treeless Ettrick Forest), as well as substantial farms and dozens of villages. This is in many ways conservative country but the Tories have not been able to exploit that fact for decades. Map 588

## TWICKENHAM — LD hold

| Electorate | %Turnout | | 74,135 | 67.36% | 2001 | 73,281 | 79.34% | 1997 |
|---|---|---|---|---|---|---|---|---|
| **Cable Dr V** | | **LD** | **24,344** | **48.75%** | **3.63%** | **26,237** | **45.12%** | **LD** |
| Longworth N | | C | 16,689 | 33.42% | -4.34% | 21,956 | 37.76% | C |
| Rogers D | | Lab | 6,903 | 13.82% | -1.77% | 9,065 | 15.59% | Lab |
| Maciejowska Ms J | | Green | 1,423 | 2.85% | | 589 | 1.01% | Ind ECR |
| Hollebone R | | UK Ind | 579 | 1.16% | | 155 | 0.27% | Dream |
| | | | | | | 142 | 0.24% | NLP |
| **C to LD swing** | **3.98%** | | **49,938** | | **LD maj 7,655** | **58,144** | | **LD maj 4,281** |
| | | | | | 15.33% | | | 7.36% |

**VINCENT CABLE,** b May 9, 1943. Elected 1997. LD spokesman, trade and industry, 1999-; confirmed June 2001; Member, Treasury Select Cttee, 1998-99. Chairman, all-party police grp. Ex-adviser, Commonwealth Sec-Gen; dep dir, Overseas Development Inst. Special adviser to John Smith when Trade Sec. Glasgow city cllr, 1971-74. Ex-chief economist, Shell International Oil; occasional economic adviser to Shell, 1997-98. Ed Nunthorpe GS, York; Fitzwilliam Coll, Cambridge (Pres of Union).

This is a highly distinctive suburb of West London. It includes Twickenham itself, home of English rugby union, and other populous suburbs such as Teddington and Whitton and the more attractive Hamptons. Although the rate of owner-occupation is not exceptionally high, the proportion of professional and non-manual workers is striking. This may explain why the Liberal Democrats have become such a force here and are keeping the Conservatives at bay. **Map 589**

## TYNE BRIDGE — Lab hold

| Electorate | %Turnout | | 58,900 | 44.2% | 2001 | 61,058 | 57.08% | 1997 |
|---|---|---|---|---|---|---|---|---|
| **Clelland D** | | **Lab** | **18,345** | **70.47%** | **-6.34%** | **26,767** | **76.81%** | **Lab** |
| Cook J | | C | 3,456 | 13.28% | 2.2% | 3,861 | 11.08% | C |
| Wallace J | | LD | 3,213 | 12.34% | 4.35% | 2,785 | 7.99% | LD |
| Fitzpatrick J | | Soc Lab | 533 | 2.05% | | 919 | 2.64% | Ref |
| Robson S | | Soc All | 485 | 1.86% | | 518 | 1.49% | Soc |
| **Lab to C swing** | **4.27%** | | **26,032** | | **Lab maj 14,889** | **34,850** | | **Lab maj 22,906** |
| | | | | | 57.19% | | | 65.73% |

**DAVID CLELLAND,** b June 27, 1943. Elected 1985. Gvt asst whip, 1997-2001; Lab whip, 1995-97. Member, Select Cttees: Energy, 1989-90; Home Affairs, 1985-89; Parly Commissioner for Administration, 1985-87. Chairman, 1990-97, joint vice-chairman, 1988-90, PLP Environment Cttee; chairman, PLP reg gvt grp, 1992-93; sec and treas, Northern grp, Lab MPs, 1990-. Exec officer, all-party non-profitmaking members' clubs grp, 1997-. Gateshead borough cllr, 1972-86. Electrical tester, 1964-81. Ed Kelvin Grove Boys' Sch, Gateshead; Gateshead and Hebburn Tech Colls.

This seat manages to combine inner-city Newcastle, including the thriving city centre, with the central area of Gateshead across the Tyne. Socially it is tough territory with uncompromising tower blocks of flats, and the residents of Tyne Bridge have not seen much of any national prosperity. The rate of owner-occupation is low and the number of council tenants is striking. It is, perhaps unsurprisingly, a very safe seat for the Labour Party. **Map 590**

## TYNEMOUTH — Lab hold

| Electorate | %Turnout | | 65,184 | 67.35% | 2001 | 66,341 | 77.11% | 1997 |
|---|---|---|---|---|---|---|---|---|
| **Campbell A** | | **Lab** | **23,364** | **53.22%** | **-2.14%** | **28,318** | **55.36%** | **Lab** |
| Poulsen K | | C | 14,686 | 33.45% | 0.13% | 17,045 | 33.32% | C |
| Reid Ms P | | LD | 5,108 | 11.63% | 2.82% | 4,509 | 8.81% | LD |
| Rollings M | | UK Ind | 745 | 1.7% | 0.8% | 819 | 1.6% | Ref |
| | | | | | | 462 | 0.9% | UK Ind |
| **Lab to C swing** | **1.14%** | | **43,903** | | **Lab maj 8,678** | **51,153** | | **Lab maj 11,273** |
| | | | | | 19.77% | | | 22.04% |

**ALAN CAMPBELL,** b July 8, 1957. Elected 1997. Member, Public Accounts Select Cttee, 1997-2001. Sec, campaign co-ordinator, Tynemouth CLP. Teacher, Whitley Bay High Sch, 1980-89; Hirst HS, Ashington, 1989-97, where he was head, sixth form and history. Ed Blackfyne Sec Sch, Consett; Lancaster Univ; Leeds Univ and Newcastle upon Tyne Polytechnic.

Until 1997 this was the only Tory constituency in Tyne and Wear. The seat rests in the southeast corner of the old Northumberland between the Tyne and the North Sea. It is polarised between a heavy industrial area based on declining shipbuilding and with strong loyalties to Labour, and a set of seaside resorts and middle-class residential areas, notably Whitley Bay and Tynemouth, which are much better territory for the Conservatives. **Map 591**

## TYNESIDE NORTH  Lab hold

| Electorate | %Turnout | | 64,914 | 57.88% | 2001 | 66,449 | 67.9% | 1997 |
|---|---|---|---|---|---|---|---|---|
| **Byers S** | **Lab** | | **26,127** | **69.54%** | **-3.18%** | **32,810** | **72.72%** | **Lab** |
| Ruffell M | C | | 5,459 | 14.53% | 0.86% | 6,167 | 13.67% | C |
| Reed S | LD | | 4,649 | 12.37% | 1.82% | 4,762 | 10.55% | LD |
| Taylor A | UK Ind | | 770 | 2.05% | | 1,382 | 3.06% | Ref |
| Burnett P | Soc All | | 324 | 0.86% | | | | |
| Capstick K | Soc Lab | | 240 | 0.64% | | | | |
| **Lab to C swing** | **2.02%** | | **37,569** | **Lab maj 20,668** | | **45,121** | **Lab maj 26,643** | |
| | | | | 55.01% | | | 59.05% | |

**STEPHEN BYERS,** b April 13, 1953. Elected here 1997; MP, Wallsend 1992-97. Sec of State, Transport, Local Gvt and Regions, June 2001-; Trade and Industry, 1998-2001. Chief Sec to Treasury, 1998. Min, DfEE, responsible for sch standards, 1997-98. Spokesman, ed and employment, 1995-97. Lab whip, 1994-95. Member, Home Affairs Select Cttee, 1994; ex-joint chairman, all-party police grp. North Tyneside cllr, 1980-92 (dep leader, 1985-92). Senior lecturer in law, Newcastle Poly, 1977-92. Ed Chester City GS; Chester Coll of FE; Liverpool Poly.

Much of this Tyneside seat is based on Wallsend, the eastern extremity of Hadrian's Wall, on the north side of the river. It includes part of North Shields and some very tough neighbourhoods associated with persistent poverty, but there are also a few more affluent villages. This is not an area noted for much partisan competition. It is, like the whole of this region, very safe for Labour. Map 592

## TYRONE WEST SF gain

| Electorate | %Turnout | | 60,739 | 79.9% | 2001 | 58,168 | 79.55% | 1997 |
|---|---|---|---|---|---|---|---|---|
| **Doherty P** | **SF** | | **19,814** | **40.83%** | **9.97%** | **16,003** | **34.58%** | **UUP** |
| Thompson W | UUP | | 14,774 | 30.44% | -3.34% | 14,842 | 32.07% | SDLP |
| Rodgers Ms B | SDLP | | 13,942 | 28.73% | 4.14% | 14,280 | 30.86% | SF |
| | | | | | | 829 | 1.79% | Alliance |
| | | | | | | 230 | 0.5% | WP |
| | | | | | | 91 | 0.2% | NLP |
| **UUP to SF swing** | **7.05%** | | **48,530** | **SF maj 5,040** | | **46,275** | **UUP maj 1,161** | |
| | | | | 10.39% | | | 2.51% | |

**PAT DOHERTY,** b July 18, 1945. Elected 2001. Has not taken seat at Westminster. Vice-president, Sinn Fein since 1988. Member, Sinn Fein talks team. Member NI Assembly, 1998-. Headed delegation to the Forum for Peace and Reconciliation. Former director of elections and national organiser. Contested this seat, 1997. Site engineer. Ed St Joseph's Coll, Lockwinnock, Scotland.
e-mail: patdoherty@ireland.com tel: 02871 886464 fax: 02871 886466

This is an unusual Northern Ireland constituency even by the standards of Ulster politics. The predominantly rural seat in the northwest of the Province is based on the local government districts of Omagh and Strabane. The clear majority of residents are Roman Catholic, but they have been represented by Protestant Unionists who have exploited a divided nationalist vote. Not so in 2001, however, when Sinn Fein surged through to win. Map 593

## ULSTER MID SF hold

| Electorate | %Turnout | | 61,390 | 81.34% | 2001 | 58,836 | 86.12% | 1997 |
|---|---|---|---|---|---|---|---|---|
| **McGuinness M** | **SF** | | **25,502** | **51.07%** | **11.02%** | **20,294** | **40.05%** | **SF** |
| McCrea I | DUP | | 15,549 | 31.14% | -5.2% | 18,411 | 36.34% | DUP |
| Haughey Ms E | SDLP | | 8,376 | 16.77% | -5.34% | 11,205 | 22.11% | SDLP |
| Donnelly F | WP | | 509 | 1.02% | 0.55% | 460 | 0.91% | Alliance |
| | | | | | | 238 | 0.47% | WP |
| | | | | | | 61 | 0.12% | NLP |
| **DUP to SF swing** | **8.11%** | | **49,936** | **SF maj 9,953** | | **50,669** | **SF maj 1,883** | |
| | | | | 19.93% | | | 3.71% | |

**MARTIN McGUINNESS,** b May 23, 1950. Elected 1997. Has not taken seat at Westminster. Elected, NI Assembly, 1998. Assembly Min of Ed, 1999-. Chief negotiator, Sinn Fein. Sinn Fein NI Assembly member, 1982-86. Ed Christian Brothers Tech Coll.
tel: 028-8676 5850; fax: 028-8676 6734

This is a very rural Northern Ireland seat, set to the west of Lough Neagh. Although the majority of residents are Catholic, the Unionists could win in theory provided they were united and the nationalist vote was split. However, Martin McGuinness captured the seat for Sinn Fein in 1997 and - with a vastly increased majority in 2001 on a turnout of 81.34 per cent, the highest anywhere in the general election - the party now seems well-entrenched here. Map 594

# UPMINSTER
**C gain**

| Electorate | %Turnout | | 56,829 | 59.57% | 2001 | 57,149 | 72.3% | 1997 |
|---|---|---|---|---|---|---|---|---|
| **Watkinson Mrs A** | **C** | | **15,410** | **45.52%** | **6.03%** | **19,085** | **46.19%** | **Lab** |
| Darvill K | Lab | | 14,169 | 41.86% | -4.33% | 16,315 | 39.49% | C |
| Truesdale P | LD | | 3,183 | 9.4% | -0.08% | 3,919 | 9.48% | LD |
| Murray T | UK Ind | | 1,089 | 3.22% | | 2,000 | 4.84% | Ref |
| **Lab to C swing** | **5.18%** | | **33,851** | | **C maj 1,241** | **41,319** | | **Lab maj 2,770** |
| | | | | | 3.67% | | | 6.70% |

**ANGELA WATKINSON,** b Nov 18, 1941. Elected 2001. Wins seat back for C from Keith Darvill, Lab, who won in 1997. Chairwoman, Emerson Park branch, Upminster C Assoc. Local gvt officer for 12 years. Banker. Charity worker. Sch governor. Ed Wanstead County HS; Anglia Univ.

This seat, located in the London Borough of Havering, is at the very eastern edge of the capital. In character, however, it is more of an Essex constituency. It has the smallest proportion of non-white residents in London. It is divided between a northern half dominated by council estates and a much more affluent southern sector. This is, therefore, crucial marginal territory and it provided the Tories with one of their few gains in 2001. Map 595

# UPPER BANN
**UUP hold**

| Electorate | %Turnout | | 72,574 | 70.32% | 2001 | 70,398 | 67.88% | 1997 |
|---|---|---|---|---|---|---|---|---|
| **Trimble D** | **UUP** | | **17,095** | **33.5%** | **-10.1%** | **20,836** | **43.6%** | **UUP** |
| Simpson D | DUP | | 15,037 | 29.46% | 17.99% | 11,584 | 24.24% | SDLP |
| O'Hagan Dr D | SF | | 10,770 | 21.1% | 9.02% | 5,773 | 12.08% | SF |
| Kelly Ms D | SDLP | | 7,607 | 14.91% | -9.33% | 5,482 | 11.47% | DUP |
| French T | WP | | 527 | 1.03% | -0.13% | 3,017 | 6.31% | Alliance |
| | | | | | | 554 | 1.16% | WP |
| | | | | | | 433 | 0.91% | C |
| | | | | | | 108 | 0.23% | NLP |
| **UUP to DUP swing** | **14.05%** | | **51,036** | | **UUP maj 2,058** | **47,787** | | **UUP maj 9,252** |
| | | | | | 4.03% | | | 19.36% |

**DAVID TRIMBLE,** b Oct 15, 1944. Elected 1990 by-election. First Min of NI from 1998 until his resignation on July 1, 2001 over IRA failure to decommission arms. Member, NI Assembly, 1998-; UUP leader, 1995-. Spokesman, constitutional affairs. Privy Counsellor, 1998. Nobel Peace Prize, 1998. Member, NI Constitutional Convention, 1975-76. Non-practising barrister. Lecturer from 1968, senior lecturer, 1977, Queen's Univ, Belfast, Faculty of Law. Ed Bangor GS; Queen's Univ, Belfast.
tel: 028-9052 1645; fax: 020-7219 0575

Upper Bann is located in the very heart of Northern Ireland to the south of Lough Neagh. It is based on the towns of Lurgan, Craigavon and Portadown, and it also includes Banbridge, an important market town. This is a popular tourist area, with first-class fishing on the River Bann. The majority of residents are Unionists, but the sizeable Roman Catholic minority has become increasingly significant to David Trimble's vote. Map 596

# UXBRIDGE
**C hold**

| Electorate | %Turnout | | 58,066 | 57.55% | 2001 | 57,497 | 72.26% | 1997 |
|---|---|---|---|---|---|---|---|---|
| **Randall J** | **C** | | **15,751** | **47.13%** | **3.57%** | **18,095** | **43.56%** | **C** |
| Salisbury-Jones D | Lab | | 13,653 | 40.86% | -0.95% | 17,371 | 41.81% | Lab |
| Royce Ms C | LD | | 3,426 | 10.25% | -0.65% | 4,528 | 10.9% | LD |
| Cannons P | UK Ind | | 588 | 1.76% | | 1,153 | 2.78% | Ref |
| | | | | | | 398 | 0.96% | Soc |
| **Lab to C swing** | **2.26%** | | **33,418** | | **C maj 2,098** | **41,545** | | **C maj 724** |
| | | | | | 6.28% | | 1.75% | |

**JOHN RANDALL,** b Aug 5, 1955. Elected 1997 by-election. Opposition whip, 2000. Member, Deregulation Select Cttee. Chairman, Uxbridge C assoc; Uxbridge Retailers Assoc; Cowley Residents' Assoc. Member, Uxbridge town centre steering cttee. Dir, Randalls of Uxbridge Ltd, family-owned retail store (managing dir, 1986-97). Ed Rutland House Sch, Hillingdon; Merchant Taylors' Sch, Herts; London Univ.

*Details of 1997 by-election on page 291*

Uxbridge is set in the outer West London Borough of Hillingdon. It is very much a suburban and commuter seat and has few non-white residents by London standards. The Tories clung on here in 1997 and also in the by-election that occurred a mere two months later, and once again in 2001 . They are strongest in the West Drayton section of the constituency near Heathrow Airport, a significant employer in the area. Map 597

VAL

## VALE OF CLWYD — Lab hold

| Electorate | %Turnout | | 51,247 | 63.12% | 2001 | 52,418 | 74.65% | 1997 |
|---|---|---|---|---|---|---|---|---|
| Ruane C | | Lab | 16,179 | 50.02% | -2.67% | 20,617 | 52.69% | Lab |
| Murphy B | | C | 10,418 | 32.21% | 2.41% | 11,662 | 29.8% | C |
| Rees G | | LD | 3,058 | 9.45% | 0.7% | 3,425 | 8.75% | LD |
| Williams J | | PC | 2,300 | 7.11% | 1.23% | 2,301 | 5.88% | PC |
| Campbell W | | UK Ind | 391 | 1.21% | 0.46% | 834 | 2.13% | Ref |
| | | | | | | 293 | 0.75% | UK Ind |
| Lab to C swing | | 2.54% | 32,346 | Lab maj 5,761 | | 39,132 | Lab maj 8,955 | |
| | | | | 17.81% | | | 22.89% | |

**CHRIS RUANE,** b July 8, 1958. Elected 1997. Lab Party campaign team, 1997 and 1999-, responsible for Welsh Affairs. Member, Welsh Affairs Select Cttee. Treas, all-party Objective One grp; Lab grp, seaside MPs. Rhyl town cllr, 1988-97. Founder, Rhyl environment assoc; member, Vale of Clwyd trades council. Chairman and founder, Rhyl anti-apartheid movement. Ed Blessed Edward Jones Comp, Rhyl; Univ Coll of Wales, Aberystwyth; Liverpool Univ. e-mail: ruanec@parliament.uk www.chrisruane-co.uk tel: 01745 354626 fax: 01745 334827

This North Wales seat is situated, as the name suggests, in the low-lying farming area around the River Clwyd. It includes the seaside resorts of Rhyl and Prestatyn, small inland towns such as Denbigh, and the tiny cathedral village of St Asaph. It has a reasonably large number of owner-occupiers and only about one fifth of residents are Welsh-speaking. The Tories should really be in a position here to mount a much stronger challenge to Labour. Map 598

## VALE OF GLAMORGAN — Lab hold

| Electorate | %Turnout | | 67,071 | 67.37% | 2001 | 67,213 | 80.21% | 1997 |
|---|---|---|---|---|---|---|---|---|
| Smith J | | Lab | 20,524 | 45.42% | -8.47% | 29,054 | 53.89% | Lab |
| Inkin Lady S | | C | 15,824 | 35.02% | 0.67% | 18,522 | 34.35% | C |
| Smith D | | LD | 5,521 | 12.22% | 3.05% | 4,945 | 9.17% | LD |
| Franks C | | PC | 2,867 | 6.35% | 3.77% | 1,393 | 2.58% | PC |
| Warry N | | UK Ind | 448 | 0.99% | | | | |
| Lab to C swing | | 4.57% | 45,184 | Lab maj 4,700 | | 53,914 | Lab maj 10,532 | |
| | | | | 10.40% | | | 19.54% | |

**JOHN SMITH,** b March 17, 1951. Elected 1997; first won seat 1989 by-election, but defeated 1992 election. PPS to John Reid, Min for Transport and Armed Forces, 1997-99. Member, N Atlantic Assembly, 1999-. Member, Select Cttees: Broadcasting, 1991-92; Welsh Affairs, 1990-92. PPS to dep Lab leader, 1989-92. Ex-Vale of Glamorgan borough cllr (ex-leader, Lab grp). Chief exec, Gwent Image Partnership, 1992-97. Ed Penarth GS; Gwent Coll of Higher Ed; Univ Coll of Wales, Cardiff. e-mail: smithj@parliament.uk; tel: 01446 743769 fax: 01446 743769

The Vale of Glamorgan is much more politically competitive than other parts of South Wales. It is divided between an urban core, the port of Barry, and a large swath of farming country together with middle-class Cardiff commuting villages and the market town of Cowbridge. This division will always make for a reasonable contest. The Conservatives held on to the seat until 1992 but have struggled in the more recent elections. Map 599

## VALE OF YORK — C hold

| Electorate | %Turnout | | 73,335 | 66.12% | 2001 | 70,077 | 76.01% | 1997 |
|---|---|---|---|---|---|---|---|---|
| McIntosh Miss A | | C | 25,033 | 51.63% | 6.92% | 23,815 | 44.71% | C |
| Jukes C | | Lab | 12,516 | 25.81% | -0.65% | 14,094 | 26.46% | Lab |
| Stone G | | LD | 9,799 | 20.21% | -3.55% | 12,656 | 23.76% | LD |
| Thornber P | | UK Ind | 1,142 | 2.36% | | 2,503 | 4.7% | Ref |
| | | | | | | 197 | 0.37% | Soc Dem |
| Lab to C swing | | 3.78% | 48,490 | C maj 12,517 | | 53,265 | C maj 9,721 | |
| | | | | 25.81% | | | 18.25% | |

**ANNE McINTOSH,** b Sept 20, 1954. Elected 1997; MEP, Essex N and Suffolk S, 1994-99. Member, Environment, Transport and Reg Affairs Select Cttee and Transport Sub-Cttee, 1999-2001. Sec, all-party S Africa grp, 1997. Former member, EU Parly Transport and Tourism Cttee; former, chairwoman, all-party trans-Euro and transport infrastructure grp; co-chairwoman, Euro transport safety council. Non-practising advocate; practised Euro law in Community Law Office, Brussels, 1982-83. Ed Harrogate Coll; Edinburgh Univ; Aarhus Univ, Denmark.

Population expansion in North Yorkshire meant the Boundary Commissioners had to create a new seat for the area. The Vale of York is fertile farmland, an amalgamation of territory formerly within the constituencies of Ryedale, Richmond, Harrogate, Skipton and Ripon. This leaves the market and racing town of Thirsk as the main centre. From the outset it seemed that this would be an extremely strong seat for the Conservatives and so it has proved. Map 600

# VAUXHALL
## Lab hold

| Electorate | %Turnout | | 74,474 | 44.84% | 2001 | 70,402 | 55.49% | 1997 |
|---|---|---|---|---|---|---|---|---|
| **Hoey Ms K** | **Lab** | **19,738** | **59.11%** | **-4.68%** | **24,920** | **63.79%** | **Lab** |
| Bottrall A | LD | 6,720 | 20.12% | 4.1% | 6,260 | 16.02% | LD |
| Compton G | C | 4,489 | 13.44% | -1.77% | 5,942 | 15.21% | C |
| Collins S | Green | 1,485 | 4.45% | 2.24% | 983 | 2.52% | Soc Lab |
| Bennett Ms T | Soc All | 853 | 2.55% | | 864 | 2.21% | Green |
| Boyd M | Ind | 107 | 0.32% | | 97 | 0.25% | SPGB |
| **Lab to LD swing** | **4.39%** | **33,392** | **Lab maj 13,018** | | **39,066** | **Lab maj 18,660** | |
| | | | | 38.99% | | | 47.77% |

**KATE HOEY,** b June 21, 1948. Elected 1989 by-election. Min for Sport, 1999-2001; Under-Sec of State, Home Office, 1998-99. PPS to Frank Field, Min for Welfare Reforms, 1997-98. Member, Select Cttees: Broadcasting, 1991-97; Social Security, 1992-97. Spokeswoman, Citizen's Charter and women, 1992-93. Chairwoman, all-party Scout grp, 1997-; sec, child abduction grp, 1991-. Former NI athlete; ed adviser, London's first division football clubs, 1985-89. Senior lecturer, Kingsway Coll, 1976-85. Ed Belfast Royal Acad; Ulster Coll of Physical Ed; City of London Coll.

This Inner London seat in the north end of the borough of Lambeth is diverse even by the standards of the capital. Large council estates sit alongside pockets of serious gentrification. together with the South Bank arts complex at Waterloo, County Hall and the Oval cricket ground. More than a third of residents are non-white, primarily Afro-Caribbean. The seat has the highest percentage of single mothers in the country. It is totally safe Labour terrain. Map 601

# WAKEFIELD
## Lab hold

| Electorate | %Turnout | | 75,750 | 54.46% | 2001 | 73,210 | 68.96% | 1997 |
|---|---|---|---|---|---|---|---|---|
| **Hinchliffe D** | **Lab** | **20,592** | **49.92%** | **-7.48%** | **28,977** | **57.4%** | **Lab** |
| Karran Mrs T | C | 12,638 | 30.63% | 2.16% | 14,373 | 28.47% | C |
| Dale D | LD | 5,097 | 12.36% | 1.16% | 5,656 | 11.2% | LD |
| Greenwood Ms S | Green | 1,075 | 2.61% | | 1,480 | 2.93% | Ref |
| Cannon Ms J | UK Ind | 677 | 1.64% | | | | |
| Aziz A | Soc Lab | 634 | 1.54% | | | | |
| Griffiths M | Soc All | 541 | 1.31% | | | | |
| **Lab to C swing** | **4.82%** | **41,254** | **Lab maj 7,954** | | **50,486** | **Lab maj 14,604** | |
| | | | | 19.28% | | | 28.93% |

**DAVID HINCHLIFFE,** b Oct 14, 1948. Elected 1987. Chairman, Health Select Cttee, 1997-2001 (member, 1991-92). Spokesman, social services and community care, 1992-95; joint vice-chairman, PLP Social Security Cttee, 1990-91; vice-chairman, PLP Health and Personal Social Services Cttee, 1990-92. Sec, all-party rugby league grp, 1987-; personal social services grp, 1997-. Social work tutor, Kirklees, 1980-87. Principal social worker, Leeds, 1968-79. Member, Unison. Ed Cathedral C of E Sec Mod, Wakefield; Leeds Poly; Bradford Univ; Huddersfield Poly.

Wakefield, eight miles south of Leeds on the River Calder, was once the capital of the old West Riding of Yorkshire. It is a cathedral city and also an historic market town. It has been influenced by its industrial heritage and the communities that were once based around the coalfields. The seat is solidly Labour, held by the party since 1932, but it does have a respectable minority of Tory voters. Map 602

# WALLASEY
## Lab hold

| Electorate | %Turnout | | 64,889 | 57.55% | 2001 | 63,714 | 73.52% | 1997 |
|---|---|---|---|---|---|---|---|---|
| **Eagle Ms A** | **Lab** | **22,718** | **60.83%** | **-3.78%** | **30,264** | **64.61%** | **Lab** |
| Rennie Mrs L | C | 10,442 | 27.96% | 4.07% | 11,190 | 23.89% | C |
| Reisdorf P | LD | 4,186 | 11.21% | 2.89% | 3,899 | 8.32% | LD |
| | | | | | 1,490 | 3.18% | Ref |
| **Lab to C swing** | **3.92%** | **37,346** | **Lab maj 12,276** | | **46,843** | **Lab maj 19,074** | |
| | | | | 32.87% | | | 40.72% |

**ANGELA EAGLE,** b Feb 17, 1961. Elected 1992. Under Sec of State, Home Office, June 2001-; Under-Sec for Environment and Transport, 1995-96; Member, Select Cttees: Employment, 1992-96; Members' Interests, 1992-95. Joint sec, all-party film industry grp. Parly liaison officer, Cohse (now Unison), 1987-92. Chaired nat conference, Lab women, 1991. Ed Formby HS; St John's Coll, Oxford. Her twin sister, Maria, is MP for Liverpool Garston.

This Merseyside seat is located in the northeast Wirral across the Mersey from Liverpool. It was once a Tory stronghold but this part of the North West has moved sharply to the left in recent decades. It is a fairly diverse constituency, including industrial areas that have suffered from the decline of shipbuilding, and New Brighton, a rather faded seaside resort at the tip of the Wirral peninsula. It appears to be a reliable Labour area now. Map 603

## WALSALL NORTH — Lab hold

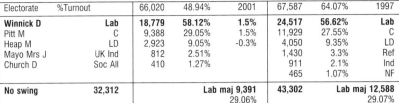

| Electorate | %Turnout | | 66,020 | 48.94% | 2001 | 67,587 | 64.07% | 1997 |
|---|---|---|---|---|---|---|---|---|
| **Winnick D** | **Lab** | | **18,779** | **58.12%** | **1.5%** | **24,517** | **56.62%** | **Lab** |
| Pitt M | C | | 9,388 | 29.05% | 1.5% | 11,929 | 27.55% | C |
| Heap M | LD | | 2,923 | 9.05% | -0.3% | 4,050 | 9.35% | LD |
| Mayo Mrs J | UK Ind | | 812 | 2.51% | | 1,430 | 3.3% | Ref |
| Church D | Soc All | | 410 | 1.27% | | 911 | 2.1% | Ind |
| | | | | | | 465 | 1.07% | NF |
| **No swing** | **32,312** | | | **Lab maj 9,391** | | **43,302** | **Lab maj 12,588** | |
| | | | | 29.06% | | | 29.07% | |

**DAVID WINNICK,** b June 26, 1933. Elected here 1979; MP, Croydon S 1966-70. Member, Select Cttees: Home Affairs, 1997-2001, and 1983-87; Procedure, 1989-92; Treasury and Civil Service, 1987-89; Environment, 1979-83; Race Relations and Immigration, 1969-70. Chairman, 1997-, vice-chairman, 1993-97, British-Irish inter-parly body; chairman, UK immigrants advisory service, 1984-90. Brent cllr, 1964-66; Willesden cllr, 1959-64; Vice-pres, Apex, 1983-88 and exec council member, 1978-88. Ed state sec schs; LSE. tel: 020-7219 5003 fax: 020-7219 0257

This is a predominantly working-class seat in the north of the West Midlands conurbation. Walsall is an industrial and engineering town with a tradition of leather manufacturing. There are a large number of council tenants who provide the base for the Labour vote. The number of professional and managerial employees is low by the standards of the region. This is solid Labour territory. Map 604

## WALSALL SOUTH — Lab hold

| Electorate | %Turnout | | 62,657 | 55.7% | 2001 | 64,221 | 67.33% | 1997 |
|---|---|---|---|---|---|---|---|---|
| **George B** | **Lab** | | **20,574** | **58.95%** | **1.08%** | **25,024** | **57.87%** | **Lab** |
| Bird M | C | | 10,643 | 30.5% | -1.21% | 13,712 | 31.71% | C |
| Tomlinson B | LD | | 2,365 | 6.78% | 0.54% | 2,698 | 6.24% | LD |
| Bennett D | UK Ind | | 974 | 2.79% | | 1,662 | 3.84% | Ref |
| Smith P | Soc All | | 343 | 0.98% | | 144 | 0.33% | NLP |
| **C to Lab swing** | **1.15%** | | **34,899** | **Lab maj 9,931** | | **43,240** | **Lab maj 11,312** | |
| | | | | 28.46% | | | 26.16% | |

**BRUCE GEORGE,** b June 1, 1942. Elected Feb 1974. Chairman, Defence Select Cttee, 1997-2001. Vice-pres, OSCE parly assembly. Parly advisor, Royal British Legion. Co-founder, sec and captain, House of Commons football club. Patron, Nat Assoc of Widows. Pres, Walsall and District Gilbert and Sullivan Soc. Visiting lecturer, Essex Univ, 1985-86. Author, eight books on defence; co-author, *Private Security*. Ed Mountain Ash GS; Univ Coll of Wales, Swansea; Warwick Univ. e-mail: georgeb@parliament.uk tel: 020-7219 4049 fax: 020-7219 3823

In terms of crude electoral statistics, Walsall South would appear to be a very similar seat to its northern neighbour. Labour usually wins by approximately the same margin in the two seats. But this constituency, which has several inner-city wards, does contain a much larger number of non-white residents and fewer council tenants. There are also some very Conservative pockets, notably near the main road south into Birmingham. Map 605

## WALTHAMSTOW — Lab hold

| Electorate | %Turnout | | 64,403 | 53.46% | 2001 | 63,818 | 62.76% | 1997 |
|---|---|---|---|---|---|---|---|---|
| **Gerrard N** | **Lab** | | **21,402** | **62.16%** | **-0.97%** | **25,287** | **63.13%** | **Lab** |
| Boys Smith N | C | | 6,221 | 18.07% | -2.25% | 8,138 | 20.32% | C |
| Dunphy P | LD | | 5,024 | 14.59% | 0.88% | 5,491 | 13.71% | LD |
| Donovan S | Soc Alt | | 806 | 2.34% | | 1,139 | 2.84% | Ref |
| Phillips W | BNP | | 389 | 1.13% | | | | |
| Mayer Ms G | UK Ind | | 298 | 0.87% | | | | |
| Duffy Ms B | ProLife | | 289 | 0.84% | | | | |
| **C to Lab swing** | **0.64%** | | **34,429** | **Lab maj 15,181** | | **40,055** | **Lab maj 17,149** | |
| | | | | 44.09% | | | 42.81% | |

**NEIL GERRARD,** b July 3, 1942. Elected 1992. Member, Select Cttees: Environmental Audit, 1999-2001; Information, 1997-2001. PPS to Dawn Primarolo, Treasury Financial Sec, to Dec, 1997, when resigned over cut in lone parents' benefit. Chairman, all-party Aids grp, 1997-; refugees grp, 1997-; sec, greyhound grp, 1997-. Board member, Theatre Royal, Stratford, E London. Ed Manchester GS; Wadham Coll, Oxford; Chelsea Coll, London. e-mail: gerrardn@parliament.uk www.neilgerrard.co.uk tel: 020-7219 6368 fax: 020-7219 4899

Situated in the London Borough of Waltham Forest in the northern part of the capital, this constituency has proved a distinctive political entity. Its social characteristics would indicate that it should be an extremely safe Labour seat — a relatively low rate of owner-occupation and a high number of non-white residents. This has indeed been the case since 1997. But the Conservatives won here in 1987 and were within 3,000 votes five years later. Map 606

# WANSBECK

**Lab hold**

| Electorate | %Turnout | | 62,989 | 59.41% | 2001 | 62,998 | 71.7% | 1997 |
|---|---|---|---|---|---|---|---|---|
| **Murphy D** | **Lab** | | **21,617** | **57.77%** | **-7.69%** | **29,569** | **65.46%** | **Lab** |
| Thompson A | LD | | 8,516 | 22.76% | 6.82% | 7,202 | 15.94% | LD |
| Lake Mrs R | C | | 4,774 | 12.76% | -1.18% | 6,299 | 13.94% | C |
| Kirkup M | Ind | | 1,076 | 2.88% | | 1,146 | 2.54% | Ref |
| Best Dr N | Green | | 954 | 2.55% | 0.43% | 956 | 2.12% | Green |
| Attwell G | UK Ind | | 482 | 1.29% | | | | |
| **Lab to LD swing** | **7.25%** | | **37,419** | Lab maj 13,101 | | **45,172** | Lab maj 22,367 | |
| | | | | 35.01% | | | 49.52% | |

**DENIS MURPHY,** b Nov 2, 1948. Elected 1997. Member, Deregulation Select Cttee, 1997-2001. Joint treas, all-party energy studies grp, 1997-. Wansbeck district cllr; ex-union official. Underground electrician. Ellington Colliery, Northumberland, 1969-94. Ed St Cuthbert's GS, Newcastle upon Tyne; Northumberland Coll.
tel: 01670 523100 fax: 01670 813208

This seat, named after the River Wansbeck and consisting largely of the old seat of Morpeth, is based in one of the more desirable areas of the old county of Northumberland. There is a mining tradition here, centred around Ashington, but there are also large numbers of affluent commuters into Newcastle. In this part of the North East, however, traditional partisan loyalties count for more than social characteristics. This is a very solid Labour area. Map 607

# WANSDYKE

**Lab hold**

| Electorate | %Turnout | | 70,728 | 70.05% | 2001 | 69,032 | 79.27% | 1997 |
|---|---|---|---|---|---|---|---|---|
| **Norris D** | **Lab** | | **23,206** | **46.84%** | **2.74%** | **24,117** | **44.07%** | **Lab** |
| Watt C | C | | 17,593 | 35.50% | 0.20% | 19,318 | 35.3% | C |
| Coleshill Ms G | LD | | 7,135 | 14.40% | -2.42% | 9,205 | 16.82% | LD |
| Hayden F | Green | | 958 | 1.93% | | 1,327 | 2.42% | Ref |
| Sandell P | UK Ind | | 655 | 1.32% | 0.52% | 438 | 0.8% | UK Ind |
| | | | | | | 225 | 0.41% | Loony |
| | | | | | | 92 | 0.17% | NLP |
| **C to Lab swing** | **1.30%** | | **49,547** | Lab maj 5,613 | | **54,722** | Lab maj 4,799 | |
| | | | | 11.32% | | | 8.77% | |

**DAN NORRIS,** b Jan 28, 1960. Elected 1997. Asst gvt whip, June 2001-. Member, parly campaign team, 2000-; leadership campaign team, 1998-2000. Bristol UA cllr, 1995-97; Avon county cllr, 1994-96; Bristol city cllr, 1989-92. Member, GMB, Nupe. Child protection social worker, lecturer. Ed Avon Comp; Sussex Univ (Fellow).
e-mail: norrisd@parliament.uk www.freespace.virgin.net/norris.wansdyke

This part of North Somerset would not appear to be natural territory for Labour. Yet it captured the seat from the Tories in 1997 and held on comfortably in 2001. It is, though, a more mixed area than the high rate of owner-occupation would imply. It is based on Keynsham and takes in Midsomer Norton and Radstock, centres of the now worked-out Somerset coalfield. There are affluent Bristol and Bath commuters here but also skilled working-class voters. Map 608

# WANTAGE

**C hold**

| Electorate | %Turnout | | 76,129 | 64.53% | 2001 | 71,657 | 78.23% | 1997 |
|---|---|---|---|---|---|---|---|---|
| **Jackson R** | **C** | | **19,475** | **39.64%** | **-0.16%** | **22,311** | **39.8%** | **C** |
| Beer S | Lab | | 13,875 | 28.24% | -0.79% | 16,272 | 29.03% | Lab |
| Fawcett N | LD | | 13,776 | 28.04% | 1.6% | 14,822 | 26.44% | LD |
| Brooks-Saxl D | Green | | 1,062 | 2.16% | 1.02% | 1,549 | 2.76% | Ref |
| Tolstoy Count N | UK Ind | | 941 | 1.92% | 1.09% | 640 | 1.14% | Green |
| | | | | | | 465 | 0.83% | UK Ind |
| **Lab to C swing** | **0.31%** | | **49,129** | C maj 5,600 | | **56,059** | C maj 6,039 | |
| | | | | 11.40% | | | 10.77% | |

**ROBERT JACKSON,** b Sept 24, 1946. Elected 1983. Member, Science and Tech Select Cttee, 1999-2001. Civil Service Min, 1992-93; Under-Sec for Employment, 1990-92; Under-Sec, Ed and Science, 1987-90. Member, British-Irish inter-party body. Political adviser to Lord Soames, Governor of Rhodesia, 1980 (served in his private office when he was Euro Commission Vice-Pres, 1974-76). Oxford city cllr, 1969-71. Ed Falcon Coll, Bulawayo; St Edmund Hall (Pres of Union, 1967) and All Souls Coll, Oxford (Fellow, 1968-86).
e-mail: jackson@parliament.uk tel: 020-7219 6350 fax: 020-7219 2718

This seat covers the southwestern quarter of Oxfordshire. It is based on the old railway centre and now commuting town of Didcot (which has boomed in recent years), Faringdon, Wallingford on the Thames and Wantage itself. The rest of the seat consists of attractive villages and farmland. The Tories have traditionally been the dominant party here, not least because Labour and the Liberal Democrats have divided the remaining votes quite evenly. Map 609

## WARLEY — Lab hold

| Electorate | %Turnout | | 58,071 | 54.1% | 2001 | 59,758 | 65.08% | 1997 |
|---|---|---|---|---|---|---|---|---|
| Spellar J | Lab | | 19,007 | 60.5% | -3.3% | 24,813 | 63.8% | Lab |
| Pritchard M | C | | 7,157 | 22.78% | -1.29% | 9,362 | 24.07% | C |
| Cockings R | LD | | 3,315 | 10.55% | 0.84% | 3,777 | 9.71% | LD |
| Dardi H | Soc Lab | | 1,936 | 6.16% | | 941 | 2.42% | Ref |
| Lab to C swing | 1.00% | | 31,415 | Lab maj 11,850 | | 38,893 | Lab maj 15,451 | |
| | | | | 37.72% | | | 39.73% | |

**JOHN SPELLAR,** b Aug 5, 1947. Elected here 1997; MP, Warley W 1992-97; Birmingham Northfield 1982-83. Min for Transport, June 2001-; Min of State for Defence (Armed Forces), 1999-2001. Under Sec for Defence, 1997-99. Spokesman, defence, 1995-97; NI, 1994-95. Ex-sec, all-party construction grp; former joint treas, British-Finland grp. Bromley cllr, 1970-74. EETPU nat official, 1976-92; research officer, 1969-76. Ed Dulwich Coll; St Edmund Hall, Oxford.
e-mail: spellarj@parliament.uk

This seat is situated in the borough of Sandwell in the West Midlands, between Birmingham and the Black Country. It includes Warley itself, Smethwick, and Langley to the west. This is a polarisised constituency in many respects. The main division runs on racial lines: about a quarter of the electorate is non-white, but there is also a stark split in income levels among the white voters. The result is strong Labour territory, but with a notable Tory minority. Map 610

## WARRINGTON NORTH — Lab hold

| Electorate | %Turnout | | 72,445 | 53.71% | 2001 | 72,694 | 70.5% | 1997 |
|---|---|---|---|---|---|---|---|---|
| Jones Ms H | Lab | | 24,026 | 61.75% | -0.35% | 31,827 | 62.1% | Lab |
| Usher J | C | | 8,870 | 22.8% | -1.2% | 12,300 | 24.0% | C |
| Smith R | LD | | 5,232 | 13.45% | 3.09% | 5,308 | 10.36% | LD |
| Kirkham J | UK Ind | | 782 | 2.01% | | 1,816 | 3.54% | Ref |
| C to Lab swing | 0.43% | | 38,910 | Lab maj 15,156 | | 51,251 | Lab maj 19,527 | |
| | | | | 38.95% | | | 38.10% | |

**HELEN JONES,** b Dec 24, 1954. Elected 1997; contested Ellesmere Port and Neston 1987; Shropshire N 1983; Lancashire Central 1984 Euro elections. Member, Select Cttees: Ed and Employment, 1997-2001; Unopposed Bills Panel, 1997-2001. Ex-Chester city cllr. Development officer, MIND. Solicitor. Ed Ursuline Convent, Chester; Chester Coll; Univ Coll London; Liverpool and Manchester Metroplitan Univs.
e-mail: jonesh@parliament.uk tel: 01925 232480 fax: 01925 232239

Warrington is a heavily industrial town on the Mersey halfway between Liverpool and Manchester. It has a new town element to it but, along with its factories, it has inner-city qualities which might be more commonly associated with the neighbouring Merseyside. Labour is the dominant political force in this area, even more in Warrington North than in Warrington South. Map 611

## WARRINGTON SOUTH — Lab hold

| Electorate | %Turnout | | 74,283 | 61.23% | 2001 | 72,262 | 76.23% | 1997 |
|---|---|---|---|---|---|---|---|---|
| Southworth Ms H | Lab | | 22,409 | 49.26% | -2.88% | 28,721 | 52.14% | Lab |
| Mosley Ms C | C | | 15,022 | 33.02% | 0.5% | 17,914 | 32.52% | C |
| Barlow R | LD | | 7,419 | 16.31% | 3.24% | 7,199 | 13.07% | LD |
| Kelley Mrs J | UK Ind | | 637 | 1.4% | | 1,082 | 1.96% | Ref |
| | | | | | | 166 | 0.3% | NLP |
| Lab to C swing | 1.69% | | 45,487 | Lab maj 7,387 | | 55,082 | Lab maj 10,807 | |
| | | | | 16.24% | | | 19.62% | |

**HELEN SOUTHWORTH,** b Nov 13, 1956. Elected 1997. St Helens borough cllr, 1994-97. Ex-dir, Age Concern, St Helens; ex-governor, Age Concern, England; ex-dir, Grosvenor housing assoc; non-exec dir, St Helens and Knowsley HA. Member, MSF; Co-op Party; Fabian Soc. Ed Larkhill Convent Sch; Lancaster Univ.

This is by far the more middle-class of the two Warrington seats. Around 80 per cent of residents are owner-occupiers and there are substantial numbers of professional and managerial employees in suburbs south of the Manchester Ship Canal. This enabled the Tories to hold the seat in the 1980s and only lose by a very narrow margin in 1992. Labour has become entrenched since then but this is not irreversible. Map 612

## WARWICK & LEAMINGTON · Lab hold

| Electorate | %Turnout | | 81,405 | 65.77% | 2001 | 79,374 | 75.71% | 1997 |
|---|---|---|---|---|---|---|---|---|
| **Plaskitt J** | **Lab** | | **26,108** | **48.76%** | **4.25%** | **26,747** | **44.51%** | **Lab** |
| Campbell Bannerman D | C | | 20,155 | 37.65% | -1.21% | 23,349 | 38.86% | C |
| Forbes Ms L | LD | | 5,964 | 11.14% | -0.73% | 7,133 | 11.87% | LD |
| Kime Ms C | Soc All | | 664 | 1.24% | 0.7% | 1,484 | 2.47% | Ref |
| Warwick G | UK Ind | | 648 | 1.21% | | 764 | 1.27% | Green |
| | | | | | | 306 | 0.51% | UK Ind |
| | | | | | | 183 | 0.3% | EDP |
| | | | | | | 125 | 0.21% | NLP |
| **C to Lab swing** | **2.73%** | | **53,539** | **Lab maj 5,953** 11.12% | | **60,091** | **Lab maj 3,398** 5.65% | |

**JAMES PLASKITT,** b June 23, 1954. Elected 1997; contested Witney 1992. Member, Select Cttees: Treasury, 1999-2001; Consolidation Bills, 1997-2001. Vice-chairman, Backbench Treasury Cttee. Oxfordshire county cllr, 1985-97 (leader, Lab grp, 1990-96). Member, MSF; Co-op Party; Charter 88. Ex-business consultant. Ed Pilgrim Sch, Bedford; Univ Coll, Oxford.
e-mail: plaskittj@parliament.uk www.jamesplaskitt.com

Labour did well to capture this seat on the southern edge of the West Midlands in 1997 and it will always be competitive political territory. Historic Warwick and the old spa town of Leamington attract substantial tourist revenue, but there is also industry here and the towns have long had many Labour voters. In the past, however, they were always outpolled by voters in the affluent commuter villages such as Henley-in-Arden and Tanworth-in-Arden. Map 613

## WARWICKSHIRE NORTH · Lab hold

| Electorate | %Turnout | | 73,828 | 60.15% | 2001 | 72,602 | 74.71% | 1997 |
|---|---|---|---|---|---|---|---|---|
| **O'Brien M** | **Lab** | | **24,023** | **54.09%** | **-4.3%** | **31,669** | **58.39%** | **Lab** |
| Parsons G | C | | 14,384 | 32.39% | 1.23% | 16,902 | 31.16% | C |
| Powell W | LD | | 5,052 | 11.38% | 3.93% | 4,040 | 7.45% | LD |
| Flynn J | UK Ind | | 950 | 2.14% | 1.16% | 917 | 1.69% | Ref |
| | | | | | | 533 | 0.98% | UK Ind |
| | | | | | | 178 | 0.33% | Bert |
| **Lab to C swing** | **2.76%** | | **44,409** | **Lab maj 9,639** 21.71% | | **54,239** | **Lab maj 14,767** 27.23% | |

**MIKE O'BRIEN,** b June 19, 1954. Elected 1992. Under-Sec of State, Home Office, responsible for Immigration and Community Relations, 1997-. Spokesman, Treasury and City affairs, 1995-97. Member, Treasury Select Cttee, 1993-95. Ex-chairman, PLP Home Affairs Cttee; ex-joint sec, all-party police grp. Ex-chairman, Worcester CLP. Lecturer in law, Colchester Inst, 1981-87. Non-practising solicitor. Ed Worcester Tech Coll; North Staffs Poly.

Although this seat was represented by Francis Maude until 1992 it would now seem solidly Labour. The constituency, on the eastern edge of the West Midlands, has traditionally divided between industrial communities such as Atherstone and the former coalfield villages outside Nuneaton, plus pro-Labour Bedworth, near Coventry; and on the other hand, Tory-inclined villages and Birmingham commuter towns such as Coleshill and Water Orton. Map 614

## WATFORD · Lab hold

| Electorate | %Turnout | | 75,724 | 61.24% | 2001 | 74,015 | 74.63% | 1997 |
|---|---|---|---|---|---|---|---|---|
| **Ward Ms C** | **Lab** | | **20,992** | **45.27%** | **-0.02%** | **25,019** | **45.29%** | **Lab** |
| McManus M | C | | 15,437 | 33.29% | -1.52% | 19,227 | 34.81% | C |
| Hames D | LD | | 8,088 | 17.44% | 0.65% | 9,272 | 16.79% | LD |
| Kingsley Ms D | Green | | 900 | 1.94% | | 1,484 | 2.69% | Ref |
| Stewart-Mole E | UK Ind | | 535 | 1.15% | | 234 | 0.42% | NLP |
| Berry J | Soc All | | 420 | 0.91% | | | | |
| **C to Lab swing** | **0.75%** | | **46,372** | **Lab maj 5,555** 11.98% | | **55,236** | **Lab maj 5,792** 10.48% | |

**CLAIRE WARD,** b May 9, 1972. Elected 1997. Member, Culture, Media and Sport Select Cttee, 1997-2001. Member, board of Howard League for Penal Reform; Council of Britain in Europe; sec, all-party film industry grp; youth affairs grp. Elstree and Boreham Wood cllr, 1994-98 (mayor, 1996-97). Member, London reg Co-op Retail Soc cttee, 1993-2000; Fabian Soc; Soc of Lab Lawyers; TGWU; Co-op Party. Solicitor. Ed Loretto Coll, St Albans; Hertfordshire and Brunel Univs; Coll of Law, London.
e-mail: wardc@parliament.uk tel: 020-7219 4910 fax: 020-7219 0468

Watford was traditionally Labour's best prospect in Hertfordshire. The fact that it was held by the Tories between 1979 and 1997 indicates just how badly Labour was performing then in this section of the Home Counties northwest of London. Watford is a distinctly mixed town with a fairly large number of council tenants and some very affluent suburbs. Although Labour is now in control, this is likely to prove a hard-fought seat for some time. Map 615

## WAVENEY — Lab hold

| Electorate | %Turnout | | 76,585 | 61.59% | 2001 | 75,266 | 75.21% | 1997 |
|---|---|---|---|---|---|---|---|---|
| **Blizzard B** | **Lab** | | **23,914** | **50.7%** | **-5.55%** | **31,846** | **56.25%** | **Lab** |
| Scott L | C | | 15,361 | 32.57% | -1.69% | 19,393 | 34.26% | C |
| Young D | LD | | 5,370 | 11.39% | 2.46% | 5,054 | 8.93% | LD |
| Aylett B | UK Ind | | 1,097 | 2.33% | | 318 | 0.56% | Ind |
| Elliot G | Green | | 983 | 2.08% | | | | |
| Mallin R | Soc All | | 442 | 0.94% | | | | |
| **Lab to C swing** | **1.93%** | | **47,167** | Lab maj 8,553 | | **56,611** | Lab maj 12,453 | |
| | | | | 18.13% | | | 21.99% | |

**BOB BLIZZARD,** b May 31, 1950. Elected 1997. PPS to Baroness Hayman, 1999-; chairman, all-party British offshore oil and gas industry grp; British Brazilian grp, 1997-; treas, pensions grp, 1997-. Waveney district cllr, 1987-97 (council leader, 1991-97). Set up Lowestoft 2000 partnership with town businesses to increase investment and tourism. Member, NUT. Teacher. Ed Culford Sch, Bury St Edmunds; Birmingham Univ.
tel: 01502 514913 fax: 020-7219 4088

This is the northernmost section of the county of Suffolk. It is based predominantly on the fishing and cargo port of Lowestoft, the county's second largest town which is also quite industrial, along with the smaller settlements of Beccles and Bungay, which also have some light industry. The Conservatives held the largely rural constituency for many years but Labour stormed home in 1997 and kept control comfortably in 2001. Map 616

## WEALDEN — C hold

| Electorate | %Turnout | | 83,066 | 63.51% | 2001 | 79,519 | 74.32% | 1997 |
|---|---|---|---|---|---|---|---|---|
| **Hendry C** | **C** | | **26,279** | **49.81%** | **0.03%** | **29,417** | **49.78%** | **C** |
| Murphy S | LD | | 12,507 | 23.71% | -2.03% | 15,213 | 25.74% | LD |
| Fordham Ms K | Lab | | 10,705 | 20.29% | 3.06% | 10,185 | 17.23% | Lab |
| Riddle K | UK Ind | | 1,539 | 2.92% | 1.96% | 3,527 | 5.97% | Ref |
| Salmon J | Green | | 1,273 | 2.41% | | 569 | 0.96% | UK Ind |
| Thornton C | Pensioner | | 453 | 0.86% | | 188 | 0.32% | NLP |
| **LD to C swing** | **1.03%** | | **52,756** | C maj 13,772 | | **59,099** | C maj 14,204 | |
| | | | | 26.11% | | | 24.04% | |

**CHARLES HENDRY,** b May 6, 1959. Elected here 2001. Inherits seat from Sir Geoffrey Johnson Smith, who represented the area since 1965. MP, High Peak 1992-97. Former PPS to William Hague. Member, NI Affairs Select Cttee, 1994-97. Pres, British Youth Council, 1992-97. Trustee, drive for youth, 1989-99. Assoc dir, public relations, Burston-Marsteller. Ed Rugby Sch; Edinburgh Univ.

This seat is set in the most agricultural part of East Sussex. There are no really large towns here, but Crowborough, Hailsham and Uckfield are quite prominent. Ashdown Forest is also situated in this part of the Sussex Weald. There is a very high rate of owner-occupation and a large number of professional and managerial employees. As might be expected, this is comfortable Conservative territory. Map 617

## WEAVER VALE — Lab hold

| Electorate | %Turnout | | 68,236 | 57.55% | 2001 | 66,011 | 73.17% | 1997 |
|---|---|---|---|---|---|---|---|---|
| **Hall M** | **Lab** | | **20,611** | **52.48%** | **-3.92%** | **27,244** | **56.4%** | **Lab** |
| Cross C | C | | 10,974 | 27.94% | -0.62% | 13,796 | 28.56% | C |
| Griffiths N | LD | | 5,643 | 14.37% | 2.05% | 5,949 | 12.32% | LD |
| Cooksley M | Ind | | 1,484 | 3.78% | | 1,312 | 2.72% | Ref |
| Bradshaw J | UK Ind | | 559 | 1.42% | | | | |
| **Lab to C swing** | **1.65%** | | **39,271** | Lab maj 9,637 | | **48,301** | Lab maj 13,448 | |
| | | | | 24.54% | | | 27.84% | |

**MIKE HALL,** b Sept 20, 1952. Elected here 1997; MP, Warrington S 1992-97. PPS to Alan Milburn, Sec of State for Health, 2001-, and previously to Ann Taylor, 1997-2001. Member, Select Cttees: Modernisation, 1997-98; Public Accounts Cttee, 1992-97. Chairman, PLP Ed Cttee, 1995-97. Chairman, Warrington N CLP, 1983-85. Warrington cllr, 1979-93 (leader, 1985-92). Ed St Damian's Sec, Ashton-under-Lyne; Ashton-under-Lyne CFE; Stretford Tech Coll; Padgate Coll of higher ed; N Cheshire Coll; Manchester Univ; Bangor Univ.

This seat was created by the 1997 boundary revisions out of four Cheshire divisions - Eddisbury, Warrington South, Tatton and Halton. It might appear at first sight to be a potential marginal. But in practice, there are two predominantly urban and strongly Labour sections, the eastern spread of Runcorn New Town and Northwich, only partly offset by a rural Tory section in the centre. Map 618

## WELLINGBOROUGH — Lab hold

| Electorate | %Turnout | | 77,389 | 65.91% | 2001 | 74,955 | 75.1% | 1997 |
|---|---|---|---|---|---|---|---|---|
| Stinchcombe P | | Lab | 23,867 | 46.79% | 2.64% | 24,854 | 44.15% | Lab |
| Bone P | | C | 21,512 | 42.18% | -1.64% | 24,667 | 43.82% | C |
| Gaskell P | | LD | 4,763 | 9.34% | -0.04% | 5,279 | 9.38% | LD |
| Ellwood A | | UK Ind | 864 | 1.69% | -0.43% | 1,192 | 2.12% | UK Ind |
| | | | | | | 297 | 0.53% | NLP |
| C to Lab swing | | 2.14% | 51,006 | | Lab maj 2,355 | 56,289 | | Lab maj 187 |
| | | | | | 4.62% | | | 0.33% |

**PAUL STINCHCOMBE,** b April 25, 1962. Elected 1997. Member, Select Cttees: Home Affairs, 1998-2001; Procedure, 1997-98. Camden cllr, 1990-94 (chairman, Lab grp). Member, MSF; Friends of the Earth; Christian Socialist Movement. Barrister, specialising in environmental law and judicial review. Ed Royal GS, High Wycombe; Trinity Coll, Cambridge; Harvard Law Sch, Inns of Court Sch of Law.
tel: 020-7219 4066 fax: 020-7219 0923

This eastern section of Northamptonshire is based on the towns of Wellingborough itself, Rushden and Higham Ferrers. There is a range of light industry in this area, to add to the traditional trades of shoe-making, tanning and iron foundries, and many quite affluent voters. That factor was enough to sustain the Tories in the seat until 1997 when they fell, very narrowly, on a swing close to the national average; in 2001 they failed to reverse the trend. **Map 619**

## WELLS — C hold

| Electorate | %Turnout | | 74,189 | 69.17% | 2001 | 72,178 | 78.11% | 1997 |
|---|---|---|---|---|---|---|---|---|
| Heathcoat-Amory D | | C | 22,462 | 43.77% | 4.38% | 22,208 | 39.39% | C |
| Oakes G | | LD | 19,666 | 38.32% | -0.13% | 21,680 | 38.45% | LD |
| Merryfield A | | Lab | 7,915 | 15.42% | -2.68% | 10,204 | 18.1% | Lab |
| Reed S | | UK Ind | 1,104 | 2.15% | | 2,196 | 3.89% | Ref |
| Bex C | | Wessex Reg | 167 | 0.33% | | 92 | 0.16% | NLP |
| LD to C swing | | 2.25% | 51,314 | | C maj 2,796 | 56,380 | | C maj 528 |
| | | | | | 5.45% | | | 0.94% |

**DAVID HEATHCOAT-AMORY,** b March 21, 1949. Elected 1983. Shadow Sec of State, Trade and Industry, 2000-; Shadow Chief Sec, Treasury, 1997-2000; Paymaster General, 1994-96; Foreign Office Min of State, 1993-94; dep gvt chief whip, 1992-93; Under-Sec, Energy, 1990-92, Environment, 1989-90; gvt whip, 1988-89. Privy Counsellor, 1995. PPS to Douglas Hurd when Home Sec, 1987-88, and to Financial Sec to Treasury, 1985-87. Chartered accountant. Ed Eton; Oxford Univ.
fax: 020-7219 6270

The centres of this Somerset seat are the fine cathedral city of Wells, nestling below the Mendip Hills, and Glastonbury, famous for its abbey, the ancient Tor and the outdoor pop festival. There are significant industrial pockets as well as tourism and rolling countryside. The Tories used to be dominant here but more recently the Lib Dems have become serious rivals. They came very close in 1997 but the Tories pulled slightly ahead again in 2001. **Map 620**

## WELWYN HATFIELD — Lab hold

| Electorate | %Turnout | | 67,004 | 63.91% | 2001 | 67,395 | 78.59% | 1997 |
|---|---|---|---|---|---|---|---|---|
| Johnson Ms M | | Lab | 18,484 | 43.17% | -3.91% | 24,936 | 47.08% | Lab |
| Shapps G | | C | 17,288 | 40.37% | 3.86% | 19,341 | 36.51% | C |
| Cooke D | | LD | 6,021 | 14.06% | 0.54% | 7,161 | 13.52% | LD |
| Biggs M | | UK Ind | 798 | 1.86% | | 1,263 | 2.38% | RA |
| Pinto Ms F | | ProLife | 230 | 0.54% | 0.04% | 267 | 0.5% | ProLife |
| Lab to C swing | | 3.89% | 42,821 | | Lab maj 1,196 | 52,968 | | Lab maj 5,595 |
| | | | | | 2.79% | | | 10.57% |

**MELANIE JOHNSON,** b Feb 5, 1955. Elected 1997. Under Sec, DTI, June 2001-; Economic Sec, Treasury, 1999-2001; PPS to Barbara Roche, Financial Sec, Treasury, 1999. Member, Select Cttees: Home Affairs, 1998-99; Public Administration, 1997-98. Chairman, all-party parenting grp, 1998-. Cambridgeshire county cllr, 1981. JP. Ex-senior manager, family health services authority. Schools inspector. Member, Unison. Ed Clifton HS, Bristol; Univ Coll London; King's Coll, Cambridge.
tel: 01707 262920 fax: 01707 262834

This Hertfordshire seat contains not one but two new towns - Hatfield and Welwyn Garden City. There is some light industry but commercial and residential areas dominate. Such areas traditionally have quite high turnout and are thus prone to be volatile and competitive. This is very true here as Labour took the constituency from the Tories in 1997 and held on in 2001 - but not by the sorts of margins likely to make it secure in future contests. **Map 621**

## WENTWORTH — Lab hold

| Electorate | %Turnout | | 64,033 | 52.75% | 2001 | 63,951 | 65.33% | 1997 |
|---|---|---|---|---|---|---|---|---|
| Healey J | Lab | | 22,798 | 67.49% | -4.85% | 30,225 | 72.34% | Lab |
| Roberts M | C | | 6,349 | 18.8% | 3.8% | 6,266 | 15.0% | C |
| Wildgoose D | LD | | 3,652 | 10.81% | 1.55% | 3,867 | 9.26% | LD |
| Wilkinson J | UK Ind | | 979 | 2.9% | | 1,423 | 3.41% | Ref |
| **Lab to C swing** | **4.32%** | | **33,778** | **Lab maj 16,449** | | **41,781** | **Lab maj 23,959** | |
| | | | | 48.70% | | | 57.34% | |

**JOHN HEALEY,** b Feb 13, 1960. Elected 1997. Under Sec, Min for Ed and Skills, June 2001-; PPS to Chancellor of Exchequer, 1999-2001; member, Ed and Employment Select Ctte and its Employment Sub-Cttee, 1997-99. Associate editor, *House Magazine.* Member, Child Poverty Action Grp; Liberty; Amnesty; World Development Movement. Ex-TUC campaigns dir. Former part-time tutor, OU business sch. Ed Lady Lumley's Comp, Pickering; St Peter's Sch, York; Christ's Coll, Cambridge.
e-mail: healeyj@parliament.uk tel: 020-7219 5170 fax: 020-7219 2451

This constituency covers the northern and eastern sections of the borough of Rotherham in South Yorkshire, but not the town itself. Named after the village of Wentworth and its 18th-century mansion and park, the seat is predominantly industrial and working-class with a strong tradition based on the legacy of coalmining. It is, even by the standards of socialist South Yorkshire, a very strong seat for Labour. Map 622

## WEST BROMWICH EAST — Lab hold

| Electorate | %Turnout | | 61,198 | 53.37% | 2001 | 63,401 | 65.44% | 1997 |
|---|---|---|---|---|---|---|---|---|
| Watson T | Lab | | 18,250 | 55.87% | -1.28% | 23,710 | 57.15% | Lab |
| MacFarlane D | C | | 8,487 | 25.98% | 1.57% | 10,126 | 24.41% | C |
| Garrett I | LD | | 4,507 | 13.8% | -1.09% | 6,179 | 14.89% | LD |
| Grey S | UK Ind | | 835 | 2.56% | | 1,472 | 3.55% | Ref |
| Johal S | Soc Lab | | 585 | 1.79% | | | | |
| **Lab to C swing** | **1.43%** | | **32,664** | **Lab maj 9,763** | | **41,487** | **Lab maj 13,584** | |
| | | | | 29.89% | | | 32.74% | |

**TOM WATSON,** b Jan 8, 1967. Elected 2001. Seat formerly held by Peter Snape for Lab, 1974-2001. AEEU trade union official, 1997. Campaigned to save Rover's Longbridge plant from closure in 2000. Nat co-ordinator of the First Past the Post campaign. Former fundraising exec, Save the Children. Ed King Charles I Sch, Kidderminster.

This has historically been the more marginal of the two West Bromwich seats set in the heart of the heavily industrial West Midlands on the Birmingham-Black Country borders. The constituency is polarised between council tenants and a notable number of ethnic minorities on the one hand and a substantial block of affluent middle-class voters on the other. In recent contests the demographic shifts have worked to the advantage of Labour. Map 623

## WEST BROMWICH WEST — Lab win from Speaker

| Electorate | %Turnout | | 66,777 | 47.68% | 2001 | 67,496 | 54.37% | 1997 |
|---|---|---|---|---|---|---|---|---|
| Bailey A | Lab Co-op | | 19,352 | 60.78% | | 23,969 | 65.32% | Speaker |
| Bissell Mrs K | C | | 7,997 | 25.12% | | 8,546 | 23.29% | Lab Change |
| Smith Mrs S | LD | | 2,168 | 6.81% | | 4,181 | 11.39% | Nat Dem |
| Salvage J | BNP | | 1,428 | 4.48% | | | | |
| Walker K | UK Ind | | 499 | 1.57% | | | | |
| Singh B | Soc Lab | | 396 | 1.24% | | | | |
| **No swing applicable** | | | **31,840** | **Lab Co-op maj 11,355** | | **36,696** | **Speaker maj 15,423** | |
| | | | | 35.66% | | | 42.03% | |

**ADRIAN BAILEY,** b Dec 11, 1945. Elected 2000 by-election. The seat was held by Betty Boothroyd from 1974 to 2000 (as Speaker, 1992-2000). Sec, West Bromwich W CLP; Co-op Party conference arrangements cttee. Ed Cheltenham GS; Exeter Univ; Loughborough Coll of Librarianship.
*Details of 2000 by-election on page 291*

This West Midlands seat consists of a string of Black Country towns such as Wednesbury, Tipton and Oldbury, mostly industrial and solidly Labour, together with a few Tory pockets. It was represented by Betty Boothroyd until her retirement, both as the Speaker of the Commons and as an MP, in 2000. The fact that Labour was able to retain the seat comfortably in the subsequent by-election, and again in 2001, indicates its local strength. Map 624

## WEST HAM — Lab hold

| Electorate | %Turnout | | 59,828 | 48.93% | 2001 | 57,058 | 58.99% | 1997 |
|---|---|---|---|---|---|---|---|---|
| **Banks T** | | **Lab** | **20,449** | **69.86%** | **-3.02%** | **24,531** | **72.88%** | **Lab** |
| Kamall S | | C | 4,804 | 16.41% | 1.45% | 5,037 | 14.96% | C |
| Fox P | | LD | 2,166 | 7.4% | 0.04% | 2,479 | 7.36% | LD |
| Chandler Oatts Ms J | | Green | 1,197 | 4.09% | | 1,198 | 3.56% | BNP |
| Batten G | | UK Ind | 657 | 2.24% | | 300 | 0.89% | Loony |
| | | | | | | 116 | 0.34% | Dream |
| **Lab to C swing** | | **2.24%** | **29,273** | | **Lab maj 15,645** | **33,661** | | **Lab maj 19,494** |
| | | | | | 53.45% | | | 57.92% |

**TONY BANKS,** b April 8, 1945. Elected here 1997; MP, Newham NW 1983-97. Chairman, Commons Works of Art Cttee. Min for Sport (Under-Sec, Nat Heritage Dept renamed Culture, Media and Sport) 1997-99. Spokesman, London and transport, 1992-93; social security, 1990-91. Member, Select Cttee on Procedure, 1987-97. GLC chairman, 1985-86. Ex-parly adviser, musicians' union; London beekeepers' assoc (received 12 jars of honey a year). Board member, Nat Theatre, 1981-85; English Nat Opera, 1981-83; London Festival Ballet, 1981-83. Ed Archbishop Tenisons, Kennington; York Univ; LSE.

This East London seat is located in the borough of Newham, an area that has experienced a sharp decline in population over the past three decades. There are a large number of council tenants and an expanding ethnic minority population, both Afro–Caribbean and Asian in origin. The seat is overwhelmingly aligned with the Labour Party. Map 625

## WESTBURY — C hold

| Electorate | %Turnout | | 75,911 | 66.69% | 2001 | 74,301 | 76.38% | 1997 |
|---|---|---|---|---|---|---|---|---|
| **Murrison Dr A** | | **C** | **21,299** | **42.07%** | **1.48%** | **23,037** | **40.59%** | **C** |
| Vigar D | | LD | 16,005 | 31.61% | 1.71% | 16,969 | 29.9% | LD |
| Cardy Ms S | | Lab | 10,847 | 21.42% | 0.33% | 11,969 | 21.09% | Lab |
| Booth-Jones C | | UK Ind | 1,261 | 2.49% | 1.13% | 1,956 | 3.45% | Lib |
| Gledhill B | | Green | 1,216 | 2.4% | | 1,909 | 3.36% | Ref |
| | | | | | | 771 | 1.36% | UK Ind |
| | | | | | | 140 | 0.25% | NLP |
| **C to LD swing** | | **0.12%** | **50,628** | | **C maj 5,294** | **56,751** | | **C maj 6,068** |
| | | | | | 10.46% | | | 10.69% |

**ANDREW MURRISON,** b April 24, 1961. Elected 2001. Inherits seat from Harold Wilson's grandson, David Faber. Sch governor; prison visitor and author of a Bow Grp pamphlet on community investment. GP and consultant, formerly RN surgeon. Ed Harwich Sch; Bristol and Cambridge Univs.

This pleasant section of west Wiltshire consists of four main towns on the edge of Salisbury Plain — Bradford-on-Avon, Trowbridge, Westbury and Warminster — and surrounding countryside. There are some industrial sections as well as a military influence. The Tories, sustained by rural voters and also in hilly Bradford-on-Avon by its Bath and Bristol commuters, are the strongest force but both the other main parties can perform respectably. Map 626

## WESTERN ISLES — Lab hold

| Electorate | %Turnout | | 21,807 | 60.34% | 2001 | 22,983 | 70.08% | 1997 |
|---|---|---|---|---|---|---|---|---|
| **MacDonald C** | | **Lab** | **5,924** | **45.02%** | **-10.58%** | **8,955** | **55.6%** | **Lab** |
| Nicholson A | | SNP | 4,850 | 36.86% | 3.46% | 5,379 | 33.4% | SNP |
| Taylor D | | C | 1,250 | 9.5% | 2.85% | 1,071 | 6.65% | C |
| Horne J | | LD | 849 | 6.45% | 3.38% | 495 | 3.07% | LD |
| Telfer Ms J | | SSP | 286 | 2.17% | | 206 | 1.28% | Ref |
| **Lab to SNP swing** | | **7.02%** | **13,159** | | **Lab maj 1,074** | **16,106** | | **Lab maj 3,576** |
| | | | | | 8.16% | | | 22.20% |

**CALUM MacDONALD,** b May 7, 1956. Elected 1987. Min for Housing, Transport and Euro Affairs, Scottish Office, 1997-99. PPS to Donald Dewar, Scottish Sec, June-Dec 1997. Former member, Agriculture Select Cttee; ex-joint chairman, all-party future of Europe grp; ex-joint vice-chairman, all-party coastal grp; Bosnian and world gvt grps. Chairman, Fabian Soc, 1999-2000; unpaid dir, Future of Europe Trust. Member, TGWU; crofters union. Ed Bayble Sch; Nicolson Inst, Stornoway; Edinburgh Univ; Univ Coll of Los Angeles.

This seat, which stretches for 130 miles down the Outer Hebrides, has by far the smallest electorate in the UK, mostly Gaelic speakers, and the highest total of detached houses, mostly crofts or small farms. The economy on the windswept islands of Lewis, Harris, North and South Uist and Barra, depends on fishing, farming, whisky and tourism. Votes are cast largely for personal, not partisan, reasons; Labour currently just holds sway over the SNP. Map 627

## WESTMORLAND & LONSDALE — C hold

| Electorate | %Turnout | | 70,637 | 67.82% | 2001 | 68,389 | 74.29% | 1997 |
|---|---|---|---|---|---|---|---|---|
| **Collins T** | **C** | | **22,486** | **46.94%** | **4.68%** | **21,470** | **42.26%** | **C** |
| Farron T | LD | | 19,339 | 40.37% | 7.01% | 16,949 | 33.36% | LD |
| Bateson J | Lab | | 5,234 | 10.93% | -9.65% | 10,459 | 20.58% | Lab |
| Gibson R | UK Ind | | 552 | 1.15% | | 1,931 | 3.8% | Ref |
| Bell T | Ind | | 292 | 0.61% | | | | |
| **C to LD swing** | **1.17%** | | **47,903** | | **C maj 3,147** | **50,809** | | **C maj 4,521** |
| | | | | | 6.57% | | | 8.90% |

**TIM COLLINS,** b May 7, 1964. Elected 1997. Senior vice-chairman, C Party, 1999-; opposition whip, 1998-99. Member, Downing Street policy unit, 1995. Press sec to PM, 1992 and 1995. Special adviser to Cabinet Mins, David Hunt and Michael Howard. Strategy consultant, WCT Communications Ltd (now part of Caribiner (Europe) Ltd), 1995-97. Ed Chigwell Sch; LSE; King's Coll London.
e-mail: listening@timcollins.co.uk www.timcollins.co.uk
tel: 01539 721010 fax: 01539 733039

This large Cumbrian seat is largely dependent on farming and the tourist industry, incorporating Windermere, Coniston Water and Grasmere in the southern Lake District. It stretches east to Kendal, the main town in the constituency, and Kirkby Lonsdale. It was particularly badly hit by the foot-and-mouth outbreak in the spring of 2001. It has historically been relatively affluent and Tory, but both Labour and Lib Dems made inroads in the 1990s. Map 628

## WESTON-SUPER-MARE — LD hold

| Electorate | %Turnout | | 74,343 | 62.79% | 2001 | 72,445 | 73.68% | 1997 |
|---|---|---|---|---|---|---|---|---|
| **Cotter B** | **LD** | | **18,424** | **39.47%** | **-0.64%** | **21,407** | **40.11%** | **LD** |
| Penrose J | C | | 18,086 | 38.74% | 1.02% | 20,133 | 37.72% | C |
| Kraft D | Lab | | 9,235 | 19.78% | 1.88% | 9,557 | 17.9% | Lab |
| Lukins B | UK Ind | | 650 | 1.39% | | 2,280 | 4.27% | Ref |
| Peverelle J | Ind Pev | | 206 | 0.44% | | | | |
| Sibley R | Ind Sib | | 79 | 0.17% | | | | |
| **LD to C swing** | **0.83%** | | **46,680** | | **LD maj 338** | **53,377** | | **LD maj 1,274** |
| | | | | | 0.72% | | | 2.39% |

**BRIAN COTTER,** b Aug 24, 1936. Elected 1997. LD spokesman, small businesses, 1997-. Member, Deregulation Select Cttee, 1997-2001. Vice-chairman, all-party small business grp; retail industry grp, 1997-; treas, autism grp. Woking district cllr, 1986-90. Member, Charter 88; Amnesty; Green LDs. Chairman, plastics co. Ed St Benedict's, Ealing; Downside Sch, Somerset.
e-mail: brian@briancotter.org tel: 01934 419200 fax: 01934 419300

This Somerset seaside resort, where the Bristol Channel meets the Severn Estuary, has a population of around 60,000 and thus forms the overwhelming majority of the constituency. With its many hotels and guesthouses, it has long been associated with the tourist industry. The Tory hegemony in this area was steadily eroded by the Liberal Democrats, who finally captured the seat in 1997 and just scraped home again in 2001. Map 629

## WIGAN — Lab hold

| Electorate | %Turnout | | 64,040 | 52.45% | 2001 | 64,689 | 67.74% | 1997 |
|---|---|---|---|---|---|---|---|---|
| **Turner N** | **Lab** | | **20,739** | **61.74%** | **-6.82%** | **30,043** | **68.56%** | **Lab** |
| Page M | C | | 6,996 | 20.83% | 3.94% | 7,400 | 16.89% | C |
| Beswick T | LD | | 4,970 | 14.8% | 4.78% | 4,390 | 10.02% | LD |
| Lowe D | Soc All | | 886 | 2.64% | | 1,450 | 3.31% | Ref |
| | | | | | | 442 | 1.01% | Green |
| | | | | | | 94 | 0.21% | NLP |
| **Lab to C swing** | **5.38%** | | **33,591** | | **Lab maj 13,743** | **43,819** | | **Lab maj 22,643** |
| | | | | | 40.91% | | | 51.67% |

**NEIL TURNER,** b Sept 16, 1945. Elected 1999 by-election; contested Oswestry 1970. Member, Public Administration Select Cttee, 2000-01. Member, Wigan MBC, 1975-2000; chairman, highways and works cttee, 1980-97. Member, quality panel, LGA. Quantity surveyor; operations manager, North Shropshire District Council, 1995-97. Ed Carlisle GS.
e mail gerrard@labour.u-net.com
*Details of 1999 by-election on page 291*

This Greater Manchester constituency consists of a variety of industry and a modern town centre. Wigan is nowadays widely regarded as an attractive part of Lancashire and even draws tourists. It has a higher white population than many other urban seats in the region. Although the town no longer relies economically on coalmining, the legacy of mining still exercises a very powerful influence on local politics. This is again staunch Labour territory. Map 630

# WILTSHIRE NORTH

**C hold**

| Electorate | %Turnout | | 79,524 | 66.58% | 2001 | 77,237 | 75.11% | 1997 |
|---|---|---|---|---|---|---|---|---|
| **Gray J** | | C | **24,090** | 45.5% | 1.73% | 25,390 | 43.77% | C |
| Pym H | | LD | 20,212 | 38.17% | 0.39% | 21,915 | 37.78% | LD |
| Garton Ms J | | Lab | 7,556 | 14.27% | 0.03% | 8,261 | 14.24% | Lab |
| Dowdney N | | UK Ind | 1,090 | 2.06% | 1.35% | 1,774 | 3.06% | Ref |
| | | | | | | 410 | 0.71% | UK Ind |
| | | | | | | 263 | 0.45% | NLP |
| **LD to C swing** | **0.67%** | | **52,948** | | **C maj 3,878** | | **58,013** | **C maj 3,475** |
| | | | | | 7.32% | | | 5.99% |

**JAMES GRAY,** b Nov 7, 1954. Elected 1997. Member, Environment, Transport and Regions Select Cttee and its Environment and Transport Sub-Cttees, 1997-2001. Treas, all-party grp, genetic modification, 1999-; sec, family farms grp, 1999-; co-chairman, minerals grp, 1997-. Special adviser to John Gummer and Michael Howard, Environment Secs, 1992-95. Dir, public affairs consultants, 1995-99; member, Baltic Exchange. Freeman, City of London, 1978. Ed Glasgow HS; Glasgow Univ; Christ Church, Oxford.
e-mail: jamesgraymp@parliament.uk

This seat is based around the town of Chippenham. It also includes the settlements of Corsham, Wootton Bassett, Lyneham (with its big RAF base) and the historic and attractive Malmesbury. Most residents are relatively affluent. The Conservatives have historically been the dominant force here but the Liberal Democrats are more than capable of providing some powerful competition. Map 631

# WIMBLEDON

**Lab hold**

| Electorate | %Turnout | | 63,930 | 64.3% | 2001 | 64,070 | 75.47% | 1997 |
|---|---|---|---|---|---|---|---|---|
| **Casale R** | | Lab | **18,806** | 45.75% | 2.99% | 20,674 | 42.76% | Lab |
| Hammond S | | C | 15,062 | 36.64% | 0.05% | 17,694 | 36.59% | C |
| Pierce M | | LD | 5,341 | 12.99% | -3.58% | 8,014 | 16.57% | LD |
| Thacker R | | Green | 1,007 | 2.45% | 1.47% | 993 | 2.05% | Ref |
| Glencross R | | CPA | 479 | 1.17% | | 474 | 0.98% | Green |
| Bell Ms M | | UK Ind | 414 | 1.01% | | 346 | 0.72% | ProLife |
| | | | | | | 112 | 0.23% | Mongolian |
| | | | | | | 47 | 0.1% | Dream |
| **C to Lab swing** | **1.47%** | | **41,109** | | **Lab maj 3,744** | **48,354** | | **Lab maj 2,980** |
| | | | | | 9.11% | | | 6.17% |

**ROGER CASALE,** b May 22, 1960. Elected 1997. Member, European Scrutiny Select Cttee. Sec, Backbench Foreign Affairs Cttee. Chairman, British-Italian grp. Ex-policy adviser to Tony Blair and John Prescott. Founder and sole dir, European Socialist Initiative, a network promoting convergence of European Left. Member, Fabian Soc. Founder and pres, Wimbledon civic forum and London and SE direct aid to Kosovo. Univ lecturer. Ed Brasenose Coll, Oxford; Johns Hopkins (Bologna); LSE.

This is an attractive and affluent residentiai corner of southwest London, centred on its own "urban village". Despite an overwhelmingly middle-class image, not to mention its fame as the home of lawn tennis, it does contain sections with a significant working-class population and a steadily increasing number of ethnic minority voters. These factors helped Labour to pull off a rather improbable victory in 1997 and to strengthen its grip in 2001. Map 632

# WINCHESTER

**LD hold**

| Electorate | %Turnout | | 81,852 | 72.27% | 2001 | 78,884 | 78.66% | 1997 |
|---|---|---|---|---|---|---|---|---|
| **Oaten M** | | LD | **32,282** | 54.57% | 12.51% | 26,100 | 42.06% | LD |
| Hayes A | | C | 22,648 | 38.28% | -3.78% | 26,098 | 42.06% | C |
| Wyeth S | | Lab | 3,498 | 5.91% | -4.61% | 6,528 | 10.52% | Lab |
| Martin Ms J | | UK Ind | 664 | 1.12% | 0.35% | 1,598 | 2.58% | Ref |
| Rouse Ms H | | Wessex Reg | 66 | 0.11% | | 640 | 1.03% | Top |
| | | | | | | 476 | 0.77% | UK Ind |
| | | | | | | 307 | 0.49% | Ind AFE |
| | | | | | | 307 | 0.49% | Loony |
| **C to LD swing** | **8.14%** | | **59,158** | | **LD maj 9,634** | **62,054** | | **LD maj 2** |
| | | | | | 16.29% | | | 0.00% |

**MARK OATEN,** b March 8, 1964. Elected May 1997 but result declared invalid by High Court; re-elected Nov 1997 by-election. LD Cabinet Office spokesman June 2001. Spokesman, social security and welfare, 1997-2001. Managing dir, public relations consultancy. Elected first SDP cllr in Watford, 1986 and became LD cllr when party was formed and then grp leader (cllr, 1986-94). Dir, Westminster Communications Ltd and Oasis Radio. Ed Queens Sec Mod, Watford; Hertfordshire Poly.

Details of 1997 by-election on page 291

This affluent Hampshire cathedral city was the scene of much political turbulence in the last Parliament. The Liberal Democrats won by a mere two votes in 1997 but a court challenge by the Tories forced a by-election to be held six months later. The Lib Dems promptly stormed that contest by more than 21,000 votes, and easily held on in 2001. The villages that surround the city have proved a surprising reservoir of middle-class radicalism. Map 633

## WINDSOR

| | | | | | | C hold | | |
|---|---|---|---|---|---|---|---|---|

| Electorate | %Turnout | | 69,136 | 60.91% | 2001 | 69,132 | 73.46% | 1997 |
|---|---|---|---|---|---|---|---|---|
| **Trend M** | | C | **19,900** | **47.26%** | **-0.94%** | 24,476 | 48.2% | C |
| Pinfield N | | LD | 11,011 | 26.15% | -2.52% | 14,559 | 28.67% | LD |
| Muller M | | Lab | 10,137 | 24.07% | 5.78% | 9,287 | 18.29% | Lab |
| Fagan J | | UK Ind | 1,062 | 2.52% | 1.93% | 1,676 | 3.3% | Ref |
| | | | | | | 388 | 0.76% | Lib |
| | | | | | | 302 | 0.59% | UK Ind |
| | | | | | | 93 | 0.18% | Dynamic |
| **LD to C swing** | | **0.79%** | **42,110** | | **C maj 8,889** | **50,781** | | **C maj 9,917** |
| | | | | | 21.11% | | | 19.53% |

**MICHAEL TREND,** b April 19, 1952. Elected here 1997; MP for Windsor and Maidenhead 1992-97. PPS to Brian Mawhinney, Transport Sec, 1994-95 and Health Min, 1993-94. Member, Speaker's Advisory Cttee, Works of Art, 1993-97. Chairman, C party, International Office, 2000-; asst chairman, International Democratic Union, 2000-. Consultant (Euro external affairs), International Distillers and Vintners Ltd, London. Board member, Victoria County History, 1992-. Journalist, editor and broadcaster. Ed Tormore Sch, Upper Deal, Kent; Westminster; Oriel Coll, Oxford.

This seat emerged from the break-up of the Windsor and Maidenhead constituency in the pre-1997 boundary review. With Windsor Castle at the centre of the town, it has strong royal associations - and thus attracts large numbers of tourists - and institutions such as Eton College. It also includes Ascot and its racecourse, Sunningdale, Old Windsor, and the Thames-side village of Bray. This is a seriously affluent and ultra-strong Tory area. Map 634

## WIRRAL SOUTH

| | | | | | | Lab hold | | |
|---|---|---|---|---|---|---|---|---|

| Electorate | %Turnout | | 60,653 | 65.65% | 2001 | 59,372 | 81.01% | 1997 |
|---|---|---|---|---|---|---|---|---|
| **Chapman B** | | Lab | **18,890** | **47.44%** | **-3.5%** | 24,499 | 50.94% | Lab |
| Millard A | | C | 13,841 | 34.76% | -1.62% | 17,495 | 36.38% | C |
| Gilchrist P | | LD | 7,087 | 17.8% | 7.37% | 5,018 | 10.43% | LD |
| | | | | | | 768 | 1.6% | Ref |
| | | | | | | 264 | 0.55% | ProLife |
| | | | | | | 51 | 0.11% | NLP |
| **Lab to C swing** | | **0.94%** | **39,818** | | **Lab maj 5,049** | **48,095** | | **Lab maj 7,004** |
| | | | | | 12.68% | | | 14.56% |

**BEN CHAPMAN,** b July 8, 1940. Elected 1997. PPS to Richard Caborn, Min for Regions, Regeneration and Planning, 1997-2001. Chairman, all-party China grp, 1997-. Former reg dir, Dept of Trade and Industry, and commercial counsellor, Beijing Embassy. Fellow, Inst of Management. Ex-pilot officer, RAFVR. Ex-consultant and dir of own co. Ed Appleby GS, Westmorland.

This part of the Wirral Peninsula on Merseyside has traditionally been the most affluent and middle-class. Labour has a political base at Bromborough and Port Sunlight but until 1997 this mattered less than the Conservative strength inland and especially at Heswall on the Dee Estuary. It is a mark of Labour's hold on this part of the country that it can win a seat where more than four in five adults are homeowners. Map 635

## WIRRAL WEST

| | | | | | | Lab hold | | |
|---|---|---|---|---|---|---|---|---|

| Electorate | %Turnout | | 62,294 | 64.97% | 2001 | 60,908 | 76.98% | 1997 |
|---|---|---|---|---|---|---|---|---|
| **Hesford S** | | Lab | **19,105** | **47.2%** | **2.34%** | 21,035 | 44.86% | Lab |
| Lynch C | | C | 15,070 | 37.23% | -1.79% | 18,297 | 39.02% | C |
| Holbrook S | | LD | 6,300 | 15.57% | 2.89% | 5,945 | 12.68% | LD |
| | | | | | | 1,613 | 3.44% | Ref |
| **C to Lab swing** | | **2.06%** | **40,475** | | **Lab maj 4,035** | **46,890** | | **Lab maj 2,738** |
| | | | | | 9.97% | | | 5.84% |

**STEPHEN HESFORD,** b May 27, 1957. Elected 1997. Member, Select Cttees: Health, 1999-; Deregulation, 1997-. Sec, all-party primary care and public health grp; vice-chairman, autism grp; joint sec, maritime grp, 1997-. Non-exec dir, Arch Initiatives, (drug abuse charity); Village Aid, (West Africa aid charity), both unpaid. Member, Greenpeace; Fabians; Liberty; Amnesty; Child Poverty Action Grp. Non-practising barrister. Ed Urmston GS; Bradford and Westminster Univs; Inns of Court Sch of Law.
e-mail: hesfords@parliament.uk tel: 0151-522 0531 fax: 0151-522 0558

This northwest corner of the Wirral consists predominantly of middle-class districts. The seaside towns of West Kirby and Hoylake are more Liverpool and Birkenhead commuter districts than tourist resorts. The Woodchurch area, which is far less affluent, has provided Labour with votes even when it was doing badly nationally. This was an unexpected Labour win in 1997 and the political demographics of the region meant it consolidated its hold in 2001. Map 636

## WITNEY — C hold

| Electorate | %Turnout | | 74,624 | 65.93% | 2001 | 73,520 | 76.72% | 1997 |
|---|---|---|---|---|---|---|---|---|
| **Cameron D** | | **C** | **22,153** | **45.02%** | **1.97%** | **24,282** | **43.05%** | **C** |
| Bartlet M | | Lab | 14,180 | 28.82% | -1.77% | 17,254 | 30.59% | Lab |
| Epps G | | LD | 10,000 | 20.32% | 0.46% | 11,202 | 19.86% | LD |
| Stevenson M | | Green | 1,100 | 2.24% | 1.11% | 2,262 | 4.01% | Ref |
| Beadle B | | Ind | 1,003 | 2.04% | | | 765 | 1.36% | UK Ind |
| Dukes K | | UK Ind | 767 | 1.56% | 0.2% | 636 | 1.13% | Green |
| **Lab to C swing** | | **1.87%** | **49,203** | | **C maj 7,973** | **56,401** | | **C maj 7,028** |
| | | | | | 16.20% | | | 12.46% |

**DAVID CAMERON,** b Oct 9, 1966. Elected 2001. Seat previously held by Shaun Woodward, who defected to Lab in 1999. Contested Stafford 1997. Former special adviser to Home Sec and Treasury Min, 1992-94. Member, 1992 general election team. Dir, corporate affairs, Carlton Communications plc, 1994-. Ed Eton; Brasenose Coll, Oxford Univ.

This is an improbable seat to have found itself, albeit in unusual circumstances, with a Labour MP in the last Parliament. It is a predominantly rural, solidly middle-class and mostly affluent section of west Oxfordshire, based on expanding Witney and including Chipping Norton, Charlbury and Woodstock. Shaun Woodward's defection to Labour in 1999 must have stunned some local residents. Normal service was restored at the 2001 election. Map 637

## WOKING — C hold

| Electorate | %Turnout | | 71,163 | 60.3% | 2001 | 70,053 | 72.68% | 1997 |
|---|---|---|---|---|---|---|---|---|
| **Malins H** | | **C** | **19,747** | **46.02%** | **7.62%** | **19,553** | **38.4%** | **C** |
| Hilliar A | | LD | 12,988 | 30.27% | 3.02% | 13,875 | 27.25% | LD |
| Hussain S | | Lab | 8,714 | 20.31% | -0.7% | 10,695 | 21.01% | Lab |
| Harvey M | | UK Ind | 1,461 | 3.4% | 2.39% | 3,933 | 7.72% | Ind C |
| | | | | | | 2,209 | 4.34% | Ref |
| | | | | | | 512 | 1.01% | UK Ind |
| | | | | | | 137 | 0.27% | NLP |
| **LD to C swing** | | **2.30%** | **42,910** | | **C maj 6,759** | **50,914** | | **C maj 5,678** |
| | | | | | 15.75% | | | 11.15% |

**HUMFREY MALINS,** b July 31, 1945. Elected 1997; MP, Croydon NW 1983-92. Member, Select Cttees: Home Affairs, 1997-2001; Broadcasting, 1991-92; Statutory Instruments, 1991-92; Chairmen's Panel; Consolidation Bills, 1983-87. PPS to Virginia Bottomley, Min of State for Health, 1989-92; to Timothy Renton, Home Office Min, and to Douglas Hogg, Home Office Under-Sec, 1987-89. Chairman, Immigration Advisory Service, 1993-. Mole Valley district cllr, 1973-82. Recorder, Crown Court, 1996-. Ed St John's, Leatherhead; Brasenose Coll, Oxford; Coll of Law, Guildford.

This is the largest town in Surrey - a major shopping centre - and until the 1997 election was also among the most Conservative of the county's heavily residential and commuter-belt Tory seats. The results then, however, were rather misleading. An independent Conservative and the Eurosceptic fringe parties secured some 13 per cent of the vote between them. This is, in reality, very Tory territory, though the Lib Dems do mount a decent challenge. Map 638

## WOKINGHAM — C hold

| Electorate | %Turnout | | 68,430 | 64.08% | 2001 | 66,161 | 75.74% | 1997 |
|---|---|---|---|---|---|---|---|---|
| **Redwood J** | | **C** | **20,216** | **46.1%** | **-3.96%** | **25,086** | **50.06%** | **C** |
| Longton Dr R | | LD | 14,222 | 32.43% | 1.06% | 15,721 | 31.37% | LD |
| Syed M | | Lab | 7,633 | 17.41% | 0.6% | 8,424 | 16.81% | Lab |
| Carstairs F | | UK Ind | 897 | 2.05% | | | 877 | 1.75% | Loony |
| Owen P | | Loony | 880 | 2.01% | 0.26% | | | |
| **C to LD swing** | | **2.51%** | **43,848** | | **C maj 5,994** | **50,108** | | **C maj 9,365** |
| | | | | | 13.67% | | | 18.69% |

**JOHN REDWOOD,** b June 15, 1951. Elected 1987. Contested party leadership for the second time, 1997. Shadow Environment Sec, 1999-2000; Trade and Industry Sec, 1997-99. Joined Cabinet, 1993 as Welsh Sec, resigning 1995 to contest party leadership against John Major. Local Gvt Min, 1992-93; Trade and Industry Min, 1990-92. Visiting professor, Middlesex Univ Business Sch, 2000-. Ed Kent Coll, Canterbury; Magdalen and St Antony's Colls, Oxford. Fellow of All Souls, Oxford, 1972.
e-mail: redwoodj@parliament.uk tel: 07711-486555 fax: 01189 733979

The work of the Boundary Commission meant that while the name of this (formerly) Berkshire seat remained the same, it was reshaped considerably. It is still based on Wokingham itself but now includes much of the countryside south of Reading. The reorganisation has not made much difference to the constituency's partisan profile. Despite a regularly strong showing from the Lib Dems, this is a very residential, booming, Conservative seat. Map 639

## WOLVERHAMPTON NORTH EAST — Lab hold

| Electorate | %Turnout | | 60,486 | 52.07% | 2001 | 61,642 | 67.17% | 1997 |
|---|---|---|---|---|---|---|---|---|
| Purchase K | Lab Co-op | | 18,984 | 60.28% | 1.027% | 24,534 | 59.26% | Lab |
| Miller Ms M | C | | 9,019 | 28.64% | 0.75% | 11,547 | 27.89% | C |
| Bourne S | LD | | 2,494 | 7.92% | 2.57% | 2,214 | 5.35% | LD |
| McCartney T | UK Ind | | 997 | 3.17% | | 1,560 | 3.77% | Lib |
| | | | | | | 1,192 | 2.88% | Ref |
| | | | | | | 356 | 0.86% | Nat Dem |
| C to Lab Co-op swing | 0.14% | | 31,494 | Lab Co-op maj 9,965 | 31.64% | 41,403 | Lab maj 12,987 | 31.37% |

**KEN PURCHASE,** b Jan 8, 1939. Elected 1992. PPS to Robin Cook, Leader of the House, 2001-; also as Foreign Sec, 1997-2001. Member, Trade and Industry Select Cttee, 1992-97; chairman, PLP Trade and Industry Cttee, 1992-97. Joint chairman, all-party exports grp; sec, jazz appreciation grp, 1997-. Wolverhampton cllr, 1970-90. Business development adviser and co sec, Black Country CDA Ltd, 1982-92. Member, Co-op Party; Fabian Soc. Ex- toolmaker and housing manager. Ed Springfield Sec Mod; Wolverhampton Poly.
e-mail: ken.purchase@cwcom.net tel: 020-7219 3602 fax: 020-7219 2110

This part of Wolverhampton - which was recently awarded city status - now seems safe for Labour, but it has been competitive until quite recently. At the northwest end of the West Midlands conurbation, the constituency is predominantly white, with a sizeable number of skilled working-class electors. There are also pockets of middle-class affluence. The Tories won here in 1987 and lost narrowly five years later. They are a long way behind now. Map 640

## WOLVERHAMPTON SOUTH EAST — Lab hold

| Electorate | %Turnout | | 53,931 | 50.61% | 2001 | 54,291 | 64.15% | 1997 |
|---|---|---|---|---|---|---|---|---|
| Turner D | Lab Co-op | | 18,409 | 67.44% | 3.7% | 22,202 | 63.74% | Lab |
| Pepper A | C | | 5,945 | 21.78% | 1.62% | 7,020 | 20.16% | C |
| Wild P | LD | | 2,389 | 8.75% | -0.7% | 3,292 | 9.45% | LD |
| Barry J | NF | | 554 | 2.03% | | 980 | 2.81% | Ref |
| | | | | | | 689 | 1.98% | Soc Lab |
| | | | | | | 647 | 1.86% | Lib |
| C to Lab Co-op swing | 1.04% | | 27,297 | Lab Co-op maj 12,464 | 45.66% | 34,830 | Lab maj 15,182 | 43.58 |

**DENNIS TURNER,** b Aug 26, 1942. Elected 1987. PPS to Clare Short, International Development Sec, 1997-. Chairman, Commons Catering Cttee, 1997-2001. Member, Select Cttees: Science and Tech, 1997-2001; Ed, Science and Arts, 1989-94. Lab whip, 1993-97. Member, Unopposed Bills Panel, 1992-97. Joint vice-chairman and treas, non-profitmaking members' clubs grp. Dir, Springvale Co-op Ltd, sports and social club; Springvale Enterprise Ltd, sports, leisure and ed activities (both unpaid). Ed Stonefield Sec Mod Sch, Bilston; Bilston CFE.

This seat includes a slice of Wolverhampton, the town of Bilston and the wards of Ettingshall and Blakenhall. Set among some of the most scarred industrial landscapes in Britain, it has traditionally been the safest Labour part of the newly designated city. There are a large number of council tenants and a sizeable ethnic minority community. Labour now seems to be very well entrenched here. Map 641

## WOLVERHAMPTON SOUTH WEST — Lab hold

| Electorate | %Turnout | | 67,171 | 60.88% | 2001 | 67,482 | 72.49% | 1997 |
|---|---|---|---|---|---|---|---|---|
| Marris R | Lab | | 19,735 | 48.26% | -2.14% | 24,657 | 50.4% | Lab |
| Chambers D | C | | 16,248 | 39.73% | -0.21% | 19,539 | 39.94% | C |
| Dixon M | LD | | 3,425 | 8.37% | 0.17% | 4,012 | 8.2% | LD |
| Walker Ms W | Green | | 805 | 1.97% | | 713 | 1.46% | Lib |
| Hope D | UK Ind | | 684 | 1.67% | | | | |
| Lab to C swing | 0.97% | | 40,897 | Lab maj 3,487 | 8.53% | 48,921 | Lab maj 5,118 | 10.46% |

**ROB MARRIS,** b April 8, 1955. Elected 2001. Inherits seat from Jenny Jones, who stood down after 20 years in politics. Former firefighter, labourer, trucker and bus driver. Solicitor since 1987. Ed St Edward's, Oxford; Univ of British Columbia; Birmingham Poly.

This seat was represented by Enoch Powell and then by Nicholas Budgen before being taken by Labour in 1997. It has by far the highest number of owner–occupiers in the city and many non-manual workers in pleasant suburbs such as Tettenhall and Penn, while Merry Hill contains the West Midlands' biggest out-of-town shopping mall. An expanding immigrant community near the centre of Wolverhampton has clearly boosted Labour here. Map 642

## WOODSPRING — C hold

| Electorate | %Turnout | | 71,023 | 68.65% | 2001 | 69,964 | 78.51% | 1997 |
|---|---|---|---|---|---|---|---|---|
| **Fox Dr L** | **C** | | **21,297** | **43.68%** | **-0.79%** | **24,425** | **44.47%** | **C** |
| Stevens C | Lab | | 12,499 | 25.63% | 4.92% | 16,691 | 30.39% | LD |
| Eldridge C | LD | | 11,816 | 24.23% | -6.16% | 11,377 | 20.71% | Lab |
| Shopland D | Ind | | 1,412 | 2.9% | 2.72% | 1,614 | 2.94% | Ref |
| Lawson Dr R | Green | | 1,282 | 2.63% | 1.42% | 667 | 1.21% | Green |
| Crean F | UK Ind | | 452 | 0.93% | | 101 | 0.18% | Ind |
| | | | | | | 52 | 0.09% | NLP |
| **C to Lab swing** | **2.86%** | | **48,758** | | **C maj 8,798** | **54,927** | | **C maj 7,734** |
| | | | | | 18.04% | | | 14.08% |

**LIAM FOX,** b Sept 22, 1961. Elected 1992. Shadow Health Sec, 1999-; spokesman, constitutional affairs, 1997-99; Under-Sec, FCO, 1996-97; gvt whip, 1994-96. PPS to Home Sec, 1993-94. Former, member, Scottish Affairs Select Cttee, 1992. Nat vice-chairman, Scottish YCs, 1983-84. Member, Central Cttee, Families for Defence, 1987-89. Army civilian medical officer, 1981-91; divisional surgeon, St John Ambulance, 1987-91. Doctor. Beaconsfield GP, 1987-91. Ed St Bride's HS, East Kilbride; Glasgow Univ.

This is the safest Conservative seat in Somerset, taking its name from a now defunct and unloved local government district. It consists of towns such as Clevedon and Portishead on the Severn Estuary, and nearby Nailsea, and the upmarket outer suburbs of southwest Bristol. There is a high rate of owner-occupation and a number of affluent commuters. The Lib Dems have so far failed to make the progress they have achieved in other parts of this region. Map 643

## WORCESTER — Lab hold

| Electorate | %Turnout | | 71,255 | 62.04% | 2001 | 69,234 | 74.56% | 1997 |
|---|---|---|---|---|---|---|---|---|
| **Foster M** | **Lab** | | **21,478** | **48.58%** | **-1.49%** | **25,848** | **50.07%** | **Lab** |
| Adams R | C | | 15,712 | 35.54% | -0.15% | 18,423 | 35.69% | C |
| Chandler P | LD | | 5,578 | 12.62% | 0.1% | 6,462 | 12.52% | LD |
| Chamings R | UK Ind | | 1,442 | 3.26% | 1.54% | 886 | 1.72% | UK Ind |
| **Lab to C swing** | **0.67%** | | **44,210** | | **Lab maj 5,766** | **51,619** | | **Lab maj 7,425** |
| | | | | | 13.04% | | | 14.38% |

**MICHAEL FOSTER,** b March 14, 1963. Elected 1997. Former member, Ed Select Cttee. Introduced Wild Mammals (Hunting With Dogs) Bill, 1997. Amended Transport Bill (2000) to improve role of school crossing patrols. Ex-management accountant, Jaguar Cars; trained head teachers in accountancy at Jaguar as part of industry/education compact. Member, Chartered Inst of Management Accountants. Lecturer in accountancy and finance. Ed Great Wyrley HS, Cannock; Wolverhampton Univ.
e-mail: fosterm@parliament.uk

A parliamentary constituency of this name has existed for centuries but the character of the seat changed in 1997. The cathedral city and county town of Worcester on the River Severn had traditionally been supplemented by surrounding countryside - an arrangement that benefited the Tories. The seat is now more tightly based on Worcester itself, where Labour has always had a strong presence. This helped it to win in both 1997 and 2001. Map 644

## WORCESTERSHIRE MID — C hold

| Electorate | %Turnout | | 71,985 | 62.37% | 2001 | 68,381 | 74.32% | 1997 |
|---|---|---|---|---|---|---|---|---|
| **Luff P** | **C** | | **22,937** | **51.09%** | **3.68%** | **24,092** | **47.41%** | **C** |
| Bannister D | Lab | | 12,310 | 27.42% | -1.47% | 14,680 | 28.89% | Lab |
| Woodthorpe-Browne R | LD | | 8,420 | 18.75% | 0.14% | 9,458 | 18.61% | LD |
| Eaves T | UK Ind | | 1,230 | 2.74% | 1.47% | 1,780 | 3.5% | Ref |
| | | | | | | 646 | 1.27% | UK Ind |
| | | | | | | 163 | 0.32% | NLP |
| **Lab to C swing** | **2.57%** | | **44,897** | | **C maj 10,627** | **50,819** | | **C maj 9,412** |
| | | | | | 23.67% | | | 18.52% |

**PETER LUFF,** b Feb 18, 1955. Elected here 1997; MP, Worcester 1992-97. Opposition whip, 2000-. Chairman, Agriculture Select Cttee, 1997-2000; member, Select Cttee, Welsh Affairs, 1992-97. Prison Min, 1995-97. PPS to Lord Mackay, Lord Chancellor; to Ann Widdecombe, 1996-97, and to Tim Eggar, Energy and Industry Min. Joint sec, all-party overseas development grp; vice-chairman, Yemen grp, 1997-; treas, Ghana grp, 1997-. Head, Edward Heath's office, 1980-82. Ed Windsor GS; Corpus Christi Coll, Cambridge.
www.peterluff.co.uk tel: 01905 763952

The ever-expanding population of Worcestershire ensured that a new seat would need to be created in the heart of this largely rural county. This constituency includes the spa town of Droitwich, Evesham - famed for its fruit-growing orchards in the Vale of Evesham - and a cluster of villages in the gentle surrounding countryside down towards the fringe Cotswold town of Broadway. It is strongly disposed to support the Conservatives. Map 645

## WORCESTERSHIRE WEST — C hold

| Electorate | %Turnout | | 66,769 | 67.11% | 2001 | 64,712 | 76.25% | 1997 |
|---|---|---|---|---|---|---|---|---|
| Spicer Sir Michael | | C | 20,597 | 45.97% | 0.93% | 22,223 | 45.04% | C |
| Hadley M | | LD | 15,223 | 33.97% | -3.27% | 18,377 | 37.24% | LD |
| Azmi W | | Lab | 6,275 | 14.0% | -1.68% | 7,738 | 15.68% | Lab |
| Morris I | | UK Ind | 1,574 | 3.51% | | 1,006 | 2.04% | Green |
| Victory M | | Green | 1,138 | 2.54% | 0.5% | | | |
| LD to C swing | 2.10% | | 44,807 | | C maj 5,374 | 49,344 | | C maj 3,846 |
| | | | | | 11.99% | | | 7.80% |

**SIR MICHAEL SPICER,** b Jan 22, 1943. Elected here 1997; MP, Worcestershire S Feb 1974-97. Chairman, 1922 Cttee, June 2001- (member, 1997-2001). Member, Treasury Select Cttee, 1997-2001; Min for Housing and Planning (DoE), 1990; Under-Sec for Energy, 1987-90. PPS to Mins of State for Trade, 1979-81. Chairman, all-party scientific grp, 1996-99; joint sec, energy studies grp, 1997-. Chairman and capt, Commons and Lords tennis club. Author, economic consultant and journalist. Ed Sacré Coeur, Vienna; Wellington Coll; Emmanuel Coll, Cambridge.

This seat is basically rural with a strong fruit-growing emphasis. The largest centre is the spa town of Great Malvern at the foot of the Malvern Hills, which - along with Bredon Hill to the southeast - form a gentle scenic backdrop. The area is a patchwork of small towns such as Pershore and many attractive villages. This is Elgar country, quintessentially English, and should be strong Tory territory. It is, but the Lib Dems have proved highly competitive. Map 646

## WORKINGTON — Lab hold

| Electorate | %Turnout | | 65,965 | 63.4% | 2001 | 65,766 | 75.08% | 1997 |
|---|---|---|---|---|---|---|---|---|
| Cunningham T | | Lab | 23,209 | 55.49% | -8.75% | 31,717 | 64.24% | Lab |
| Stoddart T | | C | 12,359 | 29.55% | 5.12% | 12,061 | 24.43% | C |
| Francis I | | LD | 5,214 | 12.47% | 4.44% | 3,967 | 8.03% | LD |
| Peacock J | | LCA | 1,040 | 2.49% | | 1,412 | 2.86% | Ref |
| | | | | | | 217 | 0.44% | UA |
| Lab to C swing | 6.93% | | 41,822 | | Lab maj 10,850 | 49,374 | | Lab maj 19,656 |
| | | | | | 25.94% | | | 39.81% |

**TONY CUNNINGHAM,** b Sept 16, 1952. Elected 2001. Inherits seat, which has been held by Lab since 1918, from Dale Campbell-Savours, MP since 1979. MEP, Cumbria and Lancashire N 1994-99; MEP, NW Region 1999. Leader, Allerdale District Council, 1992-94; member, 1987-92. Mayor of Workington, 1990-91. Teacher. Ed Workington GS; Liverpool Univ.

This west Cumbrian seat consists of two very different sections. There is an urban, coastal industrial strip, allied with a much more rural hinterland that stretches through Cockermouth into the Lake District, including Keswick and Derwentwater, and also Buttermere. But Workington, with its depressed estates and steelworks, plus Maryport with its defunct docks, have long been the dominant influence, making it Labour's safest seat in Cumbria. Map 647

## WORSLEY — Lab hold

| Electorate | %Turnout | | 69,300 | 51.03% | 2001 | 68,978 | 67.82% | 1997 |
|---|---|---|---|---|---|---|---|---|
| Lewis T | | Lab | 20,193 | 57.1% | -5.07% | 29,083 | 62.17% | Lab |
| Ellwood T | | C | 8,406 | 23.77% | -0.47% | 11,342 | 24.24% | C |
| Bleakley R | | LD | 6,188 | 17.5% | 3.91% | 6,356 | 13.59% | LD |
| Entwistle Ms D | | Soc Lab | 576 | 1.63% | | | | |
| Lab to C swing | 2.30% | | 35,363 | | Lab maj 11,787 | 46,781 | | Lab maj 17,741 |
| | | | | | 33.33% | | | 37.93% |

**TERRY LEWIS,** b Dec 29, 1935. Elected 1983. Member, Select Cttees: Standards and Privileges, 1997-2001; Consolidation Bills, 1993-97; Members' Interests, 1992-95; Environment, 1991-92. Former joint vice-chairman, all-party animal welfare grp. Bolton borough cllr, 1975-83; Kearsley urban district cllr, 1971-74. Former personnel officer. Ed Mount Carmel Sch, Salford. e-mail: terry.lewismp@btinternet.com tel: 0161-703 8017; fax: 0161-703 8346

This constituency on the northwest side of Greater Manchester is an unusual amalgamation of two very different areas. The vast majority of the seat is urban, staunchly working-class and very strongly disposed to support Labour. The exception is the town of Worsley itself and its immediate surroundings, which are extremely affluent and - unusually for this region - more or less solidly Conservative. But for the Tories, it is not enough. Map 648

## WORTHING EAST & SHOREHAM | C hold

| Electorate | %Turnout | | 71,890 | 59.91% | 2001 | 70,771 | 72.87% | 1997 |
|---|---|---|---|---|---|---|---|---|
| **Loughton T** | **C** | **18,608** | **43.21%** | **2.75%** | **20,864** | **40.46%** | **C** |
| Yates D | Lab | 12,469 | 28.95% | 5.03% | 15,766 | 30.57% | LD |
| Elgood P | LD | 9,876 | 22.93% | -7.64% | 12,335 | 23.92% | Lab |
| McCulloch J | UK Ind | 1,195 | 2.77% | 0.98% | 1,683 | 3.26% | Ref |
| Baldwin C | LCA | 920 | 2.14% | | | 921 | 1.79% | UK Ind |
| **C to Lab swing** | **1.14%** | **43,068** | | **C maj 6,139** | **51,569** | | **C maj 5,098** |
| | | | | 14.25% | | | 9.89% |

**TIM LOUGHTON,** b May 30, 1962. Elected 1997. Frontbench spokesman, environment, regions, urban regeneration, housing and poverty, 2000-; treas, all-party maritime grp, 1997-. Carlton Club political cttee, 1994-. Chairman, Battersea Business Forum, 1994-96. Member, Sussex Archaeological Soc; dir, Fleming Private Asset Management, 1992-99. English wine and Stock Exchange lecturer. Ed Priory Sch, Lewes; Warwick Univ; Clare Coll, Cambridge. e-mail: loughtont@parliament.uk www.timloughton.com tel: 020-7219 4471 fax: 020-7219 0461

This South Coast seat emerged from a set of quite radical changes made in West Sussex. Worthing is a seaside retirement resort, the eastern section of which is now amalgamated with Shoreham, a working port. It is predominantly an attractive, affluent area where the Liberal Democrats often do well in local elections. They have not yet made any breakthrough in Westminster polls, however. Map 649

## WORTHING WEST | C hold

| Electorate | %Turnout | | 72,419 | 59.67% | 2001 | 71,329 | 72.12% | 1997 |
|---|---|---|---|---|---|---|---|---|
| **Bottomley P** | **C** | **20,508** | **47.46%** | **1.32%** | **23,733** | **46.14%** | **C** |
| Walsh J | LD | 11,471 | 26.55% | -4.59% | 16,020 | 31.14% | LD |
| Butcher A | Lab | 9,270 | 21.45% | 5.22% | 8,347 | 16.23% | Lab |
| Cross T | UK Ind | 1,960 | 4.54% | 2.54% | 2,313 | 4.5% | Ref |
| | | | | | 1,029 | 2.0% | UK Ind |
| **LD to C swing** | **2.96%** | **43,209** | | **C maj 9,037** | **51,442** | | **C maj 7,713** |
| | | | | 20.91% | | | 15.00% |

**PETER BOTTOMLEY,** b July 30, 1944. Elected here 1997; MP, Eltham 1983-97; Woolwich W 1975-83. Member, Select Cttees: Standards and Privileges, 1997-2001; Unnoposed Bills Panel. Sec, all-party parenting grp; treas, race and community grp. Min for Agriculture and Environment, NI, 1989-90. Under-Sec, Roads and Traffic, 1986-89. Hon pres, Water Companies Assoc. Economist. Ed Comp sch, Washington DC; Westminster Sch; Trinity Coll, Cambridge. His wife, Virginia, is MP for Surrey SW. e-mail: herbertl@parliament.uk fax: 020-7219 1212

The vast majority of the old Worthing seat is now in this part of West Sussex. The more industrial areas of the town were moved out of the seat, leaving a constituency dominated to an extraordinary extent by the elderly, who have retired in droves to the bracing air of the South Coast. The area has the highest number of pensioners of any parliamentary district in Britain. This helps to explain its strong attachment to the Conservatives. Map 650

## WREKIN, THE | Lab hold

| Electorate | %Turnout | | 65,837 | 63.02% | 2001 | 59,126 | 76.56% | 1997 |
|---|---|---|---|---|---|---|---|---|
| **Bradley P** | **Lab** | **19,532** | **47.08%** | **0.15%** | **21,243** | **46.93%** | **Lab** |
| Rees-Mogg J | C | 15,945 | 38.43% | -1.81% | 18,218 | 40.24% | C |
| Jenkins I | LD | 4,738 | 11.42% | -1.41% | 5,807 | 12.83% | LD |
| Brookes D | UK Ind | 1,275 | 3.07% | | | | | |
| **C to Lab swing** | **0.98%** | **41,490** | | **Lab maj 3,587** | **45,268** | | **Lab maj 3,025** |
| | | | | 8.65% | | | 6.69% |

**PETER BRADLEY,** b April 12, 1953. Elected 1997. Member, Public Administration Select Cttee, 1997-99. Chairman, Lab grp of rural MPs, 1997-. Member, Backbench Cttees: Environment, Transport and Regions Cttee; Home Affairs Cttee; Trade and Industry Cttee. Member, all-party cricket grp; GMB, 1998-; MSF, 1979-. Vice-pres, Local Gvt Assoc. Central TV MP of the Year, 1999. Dir, Millbank Consultants Ltd, public relations, until Sept, 1997. Ed Abingdon Sch; Sussex Univ; Occidental Coll, Los Angeles. tel: 020-7219 4112

Shropshire was awarded an extra seat as part of the last boundary review. This had an impact on this constituency, which is dominated by the craggy slopes of The Wrekin, south of the small industrial town of Wellington. It is now mostly rural, as around Shifnal and Newport, but with some new town elements from Telford and older industrial areas near Donnington. It might be expected to be Tory, but Labour defied the odds in 1997 and again in 2001. Map 651

## WREXHAM — Lab hold

| Electorate | %Turnout | | 50,465 | 59.54% | 2001 | 50,741 | 71.78% | 1997 |
|---|---|---|---|---|---|---|---|---|
| Lucas I | Lab | | 15,934 | 53.03% | -3.12% | 20,450 | 56.15% | Lab |
| Elphick Ms F | C | | 6,746 | 22.45% | -1.4% | 8,688 | 23.85% | C |
| Davies R | LD | | 5,153 | 17.15% | 3.88% | 4,833 | 13.27% | LD |
| Evans M | PC | | 1,783 | 5.93% | 2.72% | 1,195 | 3.28% | Ref |
| Brookes Mrs J | UK Ind | | 432 | 1.44% | | 1,170 | 3.21% | PC |
| | | | | | | 86 | 0.24% | NLP |
| Lab to C swing | 0.86% | | 30,048 | Lab maj 9,188 | | 36,422 | Lab maj 11,762 | |
| | | | | 30.58% | | | 32.30% | |

**IAN LUCAS,** b Sept 18, 1960. Elected 2001. Takes over seat from John Marek, who stood down to focus on role as member of the Welsh Assembly. Vice-chairman, N Shropshire Lab Party, 1993-2000; chairman, Wrexham Lab Party, 1992-93. Member, Gresford Community Council, Wrexham, 1987-91. Principal, Crawford Lucas, Oswestry, 1997-2000; partner, Stevens Lucas, 2000-. Solicitor. Ed Greenwell Comp Sch, Gateshead; Royal GS, Newcastle upon Tyne; New Coll, Oxford.

Traditionally Wrexham has been the unofficial capital of North Wales. It once relied almost entirely on coalmining and mineral extraction for jobs. The local economy had to diversify and a big drive to encourage investment has created a huge industrial estate on the outskirts. But there are still no real signs of affluence. This helps to explain why Labour, though clearly dominant, cannot command the crushing majorities associated with South Wales. Map 652

## WYCOMBE — C hold

| Electorate | %Turnout | | 74,647 | 60.25% | 2001 | 73,589 | 71.1% | 1997 |
|---|---|---|---|---|---|---|---|---|
| Goodman P | C | | 19,064 | 42.39% | 2.46% | 20,890 | 39.93% | C |
| Shafique C | Lab | | 15,896 | 35.34% | -0.06% | 18,520 | 35.4% | Lab |
| Tomlin Ms D | LD | | 7,658 | 17.03% | -1.47% | 9,678 | 18.5% | LD |
| Cooke C | UK Ind | | 1,059 | 2.35% | | 2,394 | 4.58% | Ref |
| Laker J | Green | | 1,057 | 2.35% | 0.98% | 716 | 1.37% | Green |
| Fitton D | Ind | | 240 | 0.53% | | 121 | 0.23% | NLP |
| Lab to C swing | 1.26% | | 44,974 | C maj 3,168 | | 52,319 | C maj 2,370 | |
| | | | | 7.04% | | | 4.53% | |

**PAUL GOODMAN,** b Nov 17, 1959. Elected 2001. Inherits seat from pro-European Ray Whitney, sitting MP since 1978. Research asst to Tom King, MP. Novice monk, Quarr Abbey, 1988-90; journalist, *Catholic Herald*; comment editor, *The Daily Telegraph*, 1995-2001. Chairman, Nat Fed of C Students, 1983-83. Ed Cranleigh Sch, Surrey; York Univ

Set in affluent Buckinghamshire to the northwest of London, this seat has a rather different political character from others in the county. This is partly because High Wycombe, set in a bowl of the Chilterns, is quite industrial with many working-class voters and a substantial Asian community. Although this offers Labour some hope, it is offset by the very prosperous Tory territory at Marlow on the Thames and in the surrounding Chiltern villages. Map 653

## WYRE FOREST — KHHC gain

| Electorate | %Turnout | | 72,152 | 68.0% | 2001 | 73,063 | 75.35% | 1997 |
|---|---|---|---|---|---|---|---|---|
| Taylor Dr R | KHHC | | 28,487 | 58.06% | | 26,843 | 48.76% | Lab |
| Lock D | Lab | | 10,857 | 22.13% | -26.63% | 19,897 | 36.14% | C |
| Simpson M | C | | 9,350 | 19.06% | -17.08% | 4,377 | 7.95% | LD |
| Millington J | UK Ind | | 368 | 0.75% | 0.18% | 1,956 | 3.55% | Ref |
| | | | | | | 1,670 | 3.03% | Lib |
| | | | | | | 312 | 0.57% | UK Ind |
| No swing applicable | | | 49,062 | KHHC maj 17,630 | | 55,055 | Lab maj 6,946 | |
| | | | | 35.93% | | | 12.62% | |

**RICHARD TAYLOR,** b July 7, 1934. Elected 2001. Takes seat from David Lock, Parly Sec, Lord Chancellor's Dept. Retired consultant who stood as an Independent, campaigning against the downgrading of local health facilities. Chairman, Save Kidderminster Hospital Campaign Cttee, 1997-2001, and of the hospital's medical staff cttee, 1986-90. Consultant physician, Kidderminster General Hospital, 1972-95. Ed Leys Sch, Cambridge; Clare Coll, Cambridge; Westminster Medical Sch.

This usually marginal seat in the northwest corner of Worcestershire contains three notable settlements - Kidderminster, Stourport-on-Severn, and Bewdley lying just east of the Wyre Forest itself. It is a fairly prosperous, semi-rural and overwhelmingly white area, with some Birmingham and Black Country commuters. The spectacular triumph of the single-issue "Save Kidderminster Hospital" candidate was one of the surprises of the 2001 election. Map 654

## WYTHENSHAWE & SALE EAST — Lab hold

| Electorate | %Turnout | | 72,127 | 48.6% | 2001 | 71,986 | 63.25% | 1997 |
|---|---|---|---|---|---|---|---|---|
| **Goggins P** | **Lab** | | **21,032** | **60.0%** | **1.91%** | **26,448** | **58.09%** | **Lab** |
| Fildes Mrs S | C | | 8,424 | 24.03% | -1.07% | 11,429 | 25.1% | C |
| Tucker Ms V | LD | | 4,320 | 12.32% | -0.06% | 5,639 | 12.38% | LD |
| Crookes L | Green | | 869 | 2.48% | | 1,060 | 2.33% | Ref |
| Shaw F | Soc Lab | | 410 | 1.17% | -0.93% | 957 | 2.1% | Soc Lab |
| **C to Lab swing** | **1.49%** | | **35,055** | Lab maj 12,608 | | **45,533** | Lab maj 15,019 | |
| | | | | 35.97% | | | 32.99% | |

**PAUL GOGGINS,** b June 16, 1953. Elected 1997. PPS to David Blunkett, 2001-; and to John Denham, Min for Health, 1998-2001. Member, Social Security Select Cttee, 1997-98. Sec, all-party poverty grp, 1997-. Salford MDC, 1990-98. Nat dir, Church Action on Poverty, 1989-97; Project dir, NCH Action for Children, Salford, 1984-89. Officer in charge, local authority children's home, Wigan, 1976-84. Ed St Bede's, Manchester; Manchester Poly.
tel: 0161-499 7900 fax: 0161-499 7911

This seat in southern Greater Manchester was created as part of a series of moves necessitated by a decline in the city's population. The shrinking seat of Manchester Wythenshawe was salvaged by the addition of three wards from Sale. These areas were strong territory for the Tories, but the rest of the seat is so dominated by the council-estate vote that Labour is extremely well placed here. Map 655

## YEOVIL — LD hold

| Electorate | %Turnout | | 75,977 | 63.35% | 2001 | 74,165 | 72.88% | 1997 |
|---|---|---|---|---|---|---|---|---|
| **Laws D** | **LD** | | **21,266** | **44.18%** | **-4.57%** | **26,349** | **48.75%** | **LD** |
| Forgione M | C | | 17,338 | 36.02% | 8.37% | 14,946 | 27.65% | C |
| Conway J | Lab | | 7,077 | 14.7% | -0.2% | 8,053 | 14.9% | Lab |
| Boxall N | UK Ind | | 1,131 | 2.35% | | 3,574 | 6.61% | Ref |
| Begg A | Green | | 786 | 1.63% | 0.28% | 728 | 1.35% | Green |
| Prior T | Lib | | 534 | 1.11% | | 306 | 0.57% | Musician |
| | | | | | | 97 | 0.18% | Dream |
| **LD to C swing** | **6.47%** | | **48,132** | LD maj 3,928 | | **54,053** | LD maj 11,403 | |
| | | | | 8.16% | | | 21.10% | |

**DAVID LAWS,** b Nov 30, 1965. Elected 2001. Inherits seat from Paddy Ashdown, who won in 1983. LD parly economic adviser; author, 1994 and 1995, of LD alternative budgets. Member, Inst of Fiscal Studies. Won Observer Mace nat schools debating competition, 1984. Vice-pres, JP Morgan, 1987-92; managing dir, Barclays de Zoete Wedd, 1992-94. Investment banker. Ed St George's Coll, Weybridge; King's Coll, Cambridge.

Yeovil in south Somerset was represented from 1983 to 2001 by Paddy Ashdown, ex-leader of the Liberal Democrats. It is a manufacturing town dominated by Westland Helicopters, and is joined in this seat by other towns near the Dorset border such as Ilminster, Chard and Crewkerne. The test for the Lib Dems in 2001 was whether they could hold on without the personal vote Ashdown had inspired. They did, but with a much reduced majority. Map 656

## YNYS MON — Lab gain

| Electorate | %Turnout | | 53,117 | 64.04% | 2001 | 52,952 | 75.41% | 1997 |
|---|---|---|---|---|---|---|---|---|
| **Owen A** | **Lab** | | **11,906** | **35.0%** | **1.75%** | **15,756** | **39.46%** | **PC** |
| Williams E | PC | | 11,106 | 32.65% | -6.81% | 13,275 | 33.25% | Lab |
| Fox A | C | | 7,653 | 22.5% | 1.04% | 8,569 | 21.46% | C |
| Bennett N | LD | | 2,772 | 8.15% | 4.3% | 1,537 | 3.85% | LD |
| Wykes F | UK Ind | | 359 | 1.06% | | 793 | 1.99% | Ref |
| Donald Ms N | Ind | | 222 | 0.65% | | | | |
| **PC to Lab swing** | **4.28%** | | **34,018** | Lab maj 800 | | **39,930** | PC maj 2,481 | |
| | | | | 2.35% | | | 6.21% | |

**ALBERT OWEN,** b Aug 10, 1959. Elected 2001. Takes this predominantly Welsh-speaking seat for Lab from Plaid Cymru's Ieuan Wyn Jones. Elected, Welsh Assembly, 1999. Dir, homelessness forum and chairman, regeneration partnership. Welfare rights and employment adviser, CAB, 1995-97. Centre manager, Isle of Anglesey County Council, 1997-2001. Merchant seaman, 1976-92. Ed Holyhead County Comp; York Univ.

This is a highly distinctive seat based on the island of Anglesey, whose Welsh name is Ynys Mon and whose only sizeable town is the ferry port of Holyhead. Farming and tourism are important here, and it is a big retirement area. It has been held by four different parties since the war. Plaid Cymru had held the whiphand for some time, not least because more than 60 per cent of the population speak Welsh, but Labour slipped in to win in 2001. Map 657

## YORK, CITY OF — Lab hold

| Electorate | %Turnout | | 80,431 | 59.65% | 2001 | 79,383 | 73.5% | 1997 |
|---|---|---|---|---|---|---|---|---|
| **Bayley H** | **Lab** | | **25,072** | **52.26%** | **-7.65%** | **34,956** | **59.91%** | **Lab** |
| McIntyre M | C | | 11,293 | 23.54% | -1.2% | 14,433 | 24.74% | C |
| Waller A | LD | | 8,519 | 17.76% | 6.56% | 6,537 | 11.2% | LD |
| Shaw B | Green | | 1,465 | 3.05% | 1.54% | 1,083 | 1.86% | Ref |
| Ormston F | Soc All | | 674 | 1.4% | | 880 | 1.51% | Green |
| Bate R | UK Ind | | 576 | 1.2% | 0.65% | 319 | 0.55% | UK Ind |
| Cambridge G | Loony | | 381 | 0.79% | | 137 | 0.23% | Ch Nat |
| **Lab to C swing** | **3.23%** | | **47,980** | **Lab maj 13,779** | | **58,345** | **Lab maj 20,523** | |
| | | | | 28.72% | | | 35.17% | |

**HUGH BAYLEY,** b Jan 9, 1952. Elected 1992. Under-Sec of State Social Security, 1999-. PPS to Frank Dobson, Health Sec, 1997-99. Member, Health Select Cttee, 1992-97. Chairman, all-party overseas development grp, 1997-. UK delegate, N Atlantic Assembly, 1997-99. Research fellow, York Univ, 1987-92; member, York HA, 1988-90; chairman, Yorks region, Fabian Soc, 1988-; founder and general sec, International Broadcasting Trust, 1982-86. Former TV producer. Ed Haileybury Sch; Bristol and York Univs.
tel: 01904 623713 fax: 01904 623260

The city of York used to be a marginal that the Conservatives could win in a good year, but it now looks increasingly secure for the Labour Party. It is a mix of an elegant and historic city centre with the magnificent Minster, combined with engineering and light industry, such as the famous chocolate factories, as well as being an important railway centre. The rate of owner-occupation is perhaps surprisingly modest for a reasonably affluent area. Map 658

## YORKSHIRE EAST — C hold

| Electorate | %Turnout | | 72,342 | 59.87% | 2001 | 69,409 | 70.55% | 1997 |
|---|---|---|---|---|---|---|---|---|
| **Knight G** | **C** | | **19,861** | **45.85%** | **3.16%** | **20,904** | **42.69%** | **C** |
| Simpson-Laing Ms T | Lab | | 15,179 | 35.04% | -0.83% | 17,567 | 35.87% | Lab |
| Hardy Ms M | LD | | 6,300 | 14.54% | -3.98% | 9,070 | 18.52% | LD |
| Pearson T | UK Ind | | 1,661 | 3.83% | | 1,049 | 2.14% | Soc Dem |
| Dessoy P | Ind | | 313 | 0.72% | | 381 | 0.78% | Nat Dem |
| **Lab to C swing** | **1.99%** | | **43,314** | **C maj 4,682** | | **48,971** | **C maj 3,337** | |
| | | | | 10.81% | | | 6.82% | |

**GREG KNIGHT,** b April 4, 1949. Elected 2001; MP, Derby N 1983-97. Inherits seat from controversial C John Townend. Min for Industry, 1996-97. Deputy chief whip, 1993-96; govt whip, 1990-93. PPS to Min of State, Home Office, 1987. Privy Counsellor. Vice-chairman, Conservatives Candidates Assoc, 1998-. Member, Leicestershire County Council, 1977-83. Author, *Honourable Insults* and *Parliamentary Sauce*. Employment lawyer. Ed Alderman Newton GS, Leicester; Coll of Law, Guildford.

This seat earned a few minutes of fame (or infamy) before the 2001 election when the retiring MP, John Townend, made some controversial remarks on race. It is centred around the East Coast resort of Bridlington, just below Flamborough Head, along with rolling coastal terrain and inland market towns such as Driffield. It is mostly prosperous, overwhelmingly white and inclined to back the Tories despite recent spirited challenges from Labour. Map 659

# ABBREVIATIONS

The following abbreviations have been used in the biographies of MPs:

| | |
|---|---|
| ABA | Amateur Boxing Association |
| Acad | Academy |
| ACC | Association of County Councils |
| ACTS | Administrative, Clerical and Technical Staff (section of TGWU) |
| ACTT | Association of Cinematograph, Television and Allied Technicians |
| AEEU | Amalgamated Engineering and Electrical Union |
| AHA | Area Health Authority |
| ALC | Association of Liberal Councillors |
| ALDC | Association of LD Councillors |
| AMA | Association of Metropolitan Authorities |
| AMMA | Assistant Masters and Mistresses Association |
| Apex | Association of Professional Executive Clerical and Computer Staff |
| APCT | Association of Polytechnic and College Teachers |
| APT | Association of Polytechnic Teachers |
| ASH | Action on Smoking and Health |
| ASLDC | Association of Social and Liberal Democratic Councillors |
| Aslef | Associated Society of Locomotive Engineers and Firemen |
| Assoc | Association |
| Asst | Assistant |
| ASTMS | Association of Scientific, Technical and Managerial Staffs (now part of MSF) |
| ATL | Association of Teachers and Lecturers |
| ATTI | Association of Teachers in Technical Institutions |
| AUEW/TASS | Amalgamated Union of Engineering Workers (Technical Administrative and Supervisory Section) |
| AUT | Association of University Teachers |
| B | Born |
| BACM | British Association of Colliery Management |
| BEC | Building Employers' Confederation |
| Bifu | Banking Insurance and Finance Union |
| BMA | British Medical Association |
| BR | British Rail |
| C | Conservative |
| CAB | Citizens' Advice Bureau |
| Camra | Campaign for Real Ale |
| CBI | Confederation of British Industry |
| CCC | County Cricket Club |
| CFE | College of Further Education |
| CHC | Community Health Council |
| CLA | Country Landowners' Association |
| Cllr | Councillor |
| CLP | Constituency Labour Party |
| CND | Campaign for Nuclear Disarmament |
| Co | Company |
| Cohse | Confederation of Health Service Employees |
| Coll | College |
| Coll of FE | College of Further Education |
| Comp | Comprehensive school |
| Confed | Confederation |
| Co-op | Co-operative Party |
| Corp | Corporation |
| Cosla | Convention of Scottish local authorities |
| CPA | Commonwealth Parliamentary Association |
| CPC | Conservative Political Centre |
| CPRE | Council for the Protection of Rural England |
| CPSA | Civil and Public Service Association |
| CSD | Council for Social Democracy |
| Cttee | Committee |
| CWU | Communications Workers' Union |
| Dept | Department |
| DETR | Department of Transport & Regions |
| DfEE | Department for Education and Employment |
| DHA | District Health Authority |
| DHSS | Department of Health and Social Security |
| Dir | Director |
| Div | Division |
| DLP | Divisional Labour Party |
| DSS | Department of Social Security |
| DTI | Department of Trade and Industry |
| E | East |
| EC | European Community |
| Ed | Education/educated |
| EEC | European Economic Community |
| EETPU | Electrical, Electronic, Telecommunication and Plumbing Union |
| EIS | Educational Institute of Scotland |
| EPEA | Electrical Power Engineers Association |
| EU | European Union |
| Euro | European |
| Exec | Executive |
| FBU | Fire Brigades Union |
| FCO | Foreign and Commonwealth Office |
| FE | Further Education |
| Fed | Federation |
| FEFC | Further Education Funding Council |
| FIMechE | Fellow, Institute of Mechanical Engineers |
| FoC | Father (chairman) of Chapel (branch) NUJ |
| FRS | Fellow of the Royal Society |
| FRSA | Fellow of the Royal Society of Arts |
| FRSC | Fellow of the Royal Society of Chemistry |
| GLA | Greater London Authority |
| GLC | Greater London Council |
| Gloucs | Gloucestershire |
| GMB | General, Municipal, Boilermakers and Allied Trades Union |
| GMC | General management committee |
| Gvt | Government |
| GPMU | Graphical, Paper and Media Union |
| GS | Grammar School |
| HA | Health Authority |
| Hosp | Hospital |
| HS | High School |
| ILEA | Inner London Education Authority |
| Info | Information |
| Inst | Institute |
| IoD | Institute of Directors |
| IoJ | Institute of Journalists |
| IPCS | Institute of Professional Civil Servants |
| IPU | Interparliamentary Union |
| IRSF | Inland Revenue Staff Federation |
| ISTC | Iron and Steel Trades Confederation |
| IT | Information Technology |
| JP | Justice of the Peace |
| LGA | Local Government Association |
| Lib | Liberal |
| L/All | Liberal Alliance |

| | |
|---|---|
| **Lab** | Labour |
| **Lancs** | Lancashire |
| **LBC** | London Broadcasting Company |
| **Lincs** | Lincolnshire |
| **LD** | Liberal Democrat |
| **LSE** | London School of Economics |
| **MAFF** | Ministry of Agriculture, Fisheries and Food |
| **MATSA** | Managerial Administrative Technical Staff Association |
| **MBC** | Metropolitan Borough Council |
| **MDC** | Metropolitan District Council |
| **ME** | Myalgic encephalomyelitis |
| **Mencap** | Royal Society for Mentally Handicapped Children and Adults |
| **MEP** | Member of the European Parliament |
| **Min** | Minister, ministry |
| **MS** | Multiple sclerosis |
| **MSF** | Manufacturing, Science and Finance Union |
| **N** | North |
| **Nacods** | National Association of Colliery Overmen, Deputies and Shotfirers |
| **NAHT** | National Association of Head Teachers |
| **Nalgo** | National and Local Government Officers' Association |
| **NASUWT** | National Association of Schoolmasters and Union of Women Teachers |
| **Nat** | National |
| **NATFHE** | National Association of Teachers in Further and Higher Education |
| **Nato** | North Atlantic Treaty Organisation |
| **NCB** | National Coal Board |
| **NCER** | National Council for Electoral Reform |
| **NCH** | National Children's Homes |
| **NCU** | National Communications Union |
| **NE** | North East |
| **NEC** | National Executive |
| **NFBTE** | National Federation of Building Trades Employers |
| **NFU** | National Farmers' Union |
| **NHS** | National Health Service |
| **NI** | Northern Ireland |
| **NLVA** | National Licensed Victuallers' Association |
| **NLYL** | National League of Young Liberals |
| **Notts** | Nottinghamshire |
| **NSPCC** | National Society for the Prevention of Cruelty to Children |
| **NUJ** | National Union of Journalists |
| **NUM** | National Union of Mineworkers |
| **Numast** | National Union of Marine, Aviation and Shipping Transport Officers |
| **Nupe** | National Union of Public Employees |
| **NUR** | National Union of Railwaymen (now RMT) |
| **NUS** | National Union of Seamen/ National Union of Students |
| **NUT** | National Union of Teachers |
| **NW** | North West |
| **OSCE** | Organisation for Security and Co-operation in Europe |
| **OU** | Open University |
| **PAC** | Public Accounts Committee |
| **Parly** | Parliamentary |
| **Plmnt** | Parliament |
| **PAT** | Professional Association of Teachers |
| **PLP** | Parliamentary Labour Party |
| **Poly** | Polytechnic |
| **PPS** | Parliamentary Private Secretary |
| **Pres** | President |
| **RCN** | Royal College of Nursing |
| **RCVS** | Royal College of Veterinary Surgeons |
| **RDC** | Rural District Council |
| **Reg** | Regional |
| **Rep** | Representative |
| **Res** | Reserve |
| **RHA** | Regional Health Authority |
| **RIBA** | Royal Institute of British Architects |
| **RMA** | Royal Military Academy |
| **RMT** | Rail, Maritime and Transport Union |
| **RNC** | Royal Naval College |
| **RNLI** | Royal National Lifeboat Institution |
| **RNR** | Royal Naval Reserve |
| **RSPB** | Royal Society for the Protection of Birds |
| **RSPCA** | Royal Society for the Prevention of Cruelty to Animals |
| **S** | South |
| **SD** | Social Democrat |
| **SDLP** | Social Democratic and Labour Party |
| **SDP** | Social Democratic Party |
| **SE** | South East |
| **SEA** | Socialist Education Association |
| **Sec** | Secondary/ Secondary school |
| **Sec Mod** | Secondary modern school |
| **SERA** | Socialist Environment and Resources Association |
| **SFHEA** | Scottish Further and Higher Education Association |
| **SHA** | Secondary Heads Association/ Special Health Authority |
| **SLDP** | Social and Liberal Democratic Party |
| **SLP** | Scottish Liberal Party |
| **Soc** | Society/Socialist |
| **SSAFA** | Soldiers', Sailors', and Airmen's Families Association |
| **SSTA** | Scottish Secondary Teachers Association |
| **Staffs** | Staffordshire |
| **SW** | South West |
| **TA** | Territorial Army |
| **Tech** | Technical/Technology |
| **TGWU** | Transport and General Workers' Union |
| **Treas** | Treasurer |
| **TSSA** | Transport Salaried Staffs Association |
| **TV** | Television |
| **UA** | Unitary Authority |
| **Ucatt** | Union of Construction, Allied Trades and Technicians |
| **UCW** | Union of Communication Workers |
| **UDC** | Urban District Council/Urban Development Corporation |
| **UMIST** | University of Manchester Institute of Science and Technology |
| **UN** | United Nations |
| **UNA** | United Nations Association |
| **Univ** | University |
| **Usdaw** | Union of Shop, Distributive and Allied Workers |
| **W** | West |
| **WEA** | Workers' Educational Association |
| **WEU** | Western European Union |
| **Worcs** | Worcestershire |
| **WRVS** | Women's Royal Voluntary Service |
| **WWF** | World Wide Fund for Nature |
| **YCs** | Young Conservatives |
| **YHA** | Youth Hostels Association |
| **YLs** | Young Liberals |
| **Yorks** | Yorkshire |

# RULING PARTY STAYS INTACT

*by* **Tim Austin**

*of The Times*

The two most memorable of the 17 by-elections in the 1997-2001 Parliament involved a crushing humiliation for the Conservative Party at the hands of the Liberal Democrats in **Romsey** and a return to the front line of one of the Tories' leading heavyweights in **Kensington and Chelsea**. There was a flurry of activity in the months after the general election of May 1997, with the first by-election coming at the end of July following the death of Sir Michael Shersby, Conservative MP for **Uxbridge**, only a week into the new Parliament. The Tories duly increased their majority there with a victory for John Randall.

This "no change" set the pattern for all but two of the contests that followed — the **Romsey** result on May 4, 2000, and **Antrim South** on September 21 of the same year (and that reverted to the Ulster Unionist Party in June 2001). Technically the result at **West Bromwich West** in November 2000 was a Labour gain from the Speaker, the much-respected Betty Boothroyd who decided to step down before the end of the Parliament, but otherwise this was a predictable series of results. In fact, Labour did not lose a single seat at a by-election during this whole period, a feat unmatched since the 1951-55 Parliament.

Another remarkable facet was that there were no by-elections at all in 1998, the first year entirely without such contests since 1832. The four years of this Parliament were not without their excitements, however. The first real drama came in **Winchester** on November 20, 1997. After an extraordinary result in May when the Liberal Democrats crept in with the tiniest majority of just two votes, the Tories contested the result in court. A rerun was ordered, Labour made but a token effort, and the Lib Dems' Mark Oaten surged back with a majority this time of 21,556 over his hapless Tory opponent.

The second contest to capture serious national attention came in November 1999, after the death of the maverick historian and diarist Alan Clark as Member for the safe Tory seat of **Kensington and Chelsea**. The local Conservative association, clearly favouring "big name" candidates after the deselection before the 1997 election of Sir Nicholas Scott, went this time for Michael Portillo, himself sensationally defeated in 1997 at Enfield Southgate and now reinvented as a more liberal, compassionate Conservative. On a turnout of under 30 per cent, Portillo duly romped home comfortably.

Scandals, resignations and unexpected deaths were other triggers for this Parliament's by-elections. In **Paisley South**, unsavoury accusations in the local Labour Party were linked to the suicide of Gordon McMaster in the autumn of 1997; his replacement, Douglas Alexander, much more a new Labour man, saw off the challenge of the SNP with a narrow majority that returned to more normal levels in 2001.

Another scandal, this time with sexual and extramarital overtones involving the Tory MP for **Beckenham**, Piers Merchant, brought his resignation and the subsequent by-election victory in November 1997 of Jacqui Lait, who had recently lost Hastings and Rye for the Conservatives. She too looked much better established after 2001.

The highest-profile deaths besides Alan Clark's were Donald Dewar, MP for **Glasgow Anniesland**, and, more importantly, First Minister of the new Scottish Assembly by the time of his fatal brain haemorrhage in October 2000; and perhaps to a slightly lesser extent, the exuberant figure of Bernie Grant, one of Britain's first black MPs and a booming voice of anti-racism in his North London constituency of **Tottenham**, who died in April 2000 aged only 56. Anniesland and Tottenham, both solid Labour seats, duly returned Labour successors. In **Preston**, too, Labour lost one of its longest-serving and toughest leftwingers in the veteran Audrey Wise, who first entered Parliament in 1974 for Coventry South West. She died in September 2000 aged 65.

One of the most shocking events precipitating a by-election was a devastating early-morning fire at the country manor house near Andover, Hampshire, of the Tory MP for **Romsey,** Michael Colvin. He and his wife perished in the blaze that swept their home on February 24, 2000. The subsequent Romsey by-election produced the most spectacular win of this Parliament, the Liberal Democrats' Sandra Gidley overturning Colvin's 8,585 general election majority to romp home by 3,311.

Three resignations caused ripples but failed to dent Labour's vast majority. At **Hamilton South** in September 1999 George Robertson, Defence Secretary, resigned to go to the House of Lords and to be the new Secretary-General of Nato. His successor, Bill Tynan, just held the seat with a tiny majority of 556 after a 22 per cent swing to the SNP. At **Falkirk West,** the sparky leftwinger Dennis Canavan resigned in November 2000 after being barred from fighting the seat for Labour in the Scottish Parliament, standing as an Independent and winning. He quit his Commons seat, where Labour just held off the SNP challenge with a majority of only 705. The third was **Eddisbury** in July 1999, where Sir Alastair Goodlad resigned to become High Commissioner to Australia — a predictable Conservative hold, predictably strengthened again in 2001. Two other "holds", for Labour and Plaid Cymru respectively, were at **Wigan** in September 1999 — caused by the death of Roger Stott after 26 years in the House — and at **Ceredigion** in February 2000, caused by the resignation of the Welsh Nationalist Cynog Dafis.

Of the winning newcomers, perhaps the highest-profile is Hilary Benn, son of the veteran Labour leftwinger Tony Benn, who won a by-election in **Leeds Central** in June 1999, giving father and son two years together in the House before father stepped down in June 2001. The Benn name carries on — but there will never be, as most of the British public agree, another Betty Boothroyd.

## 1997

### July 31: UXBRIDGE
*Caused by the death of Sir Michael Shersby, May 8,1997:*
**Total vote:31,867 (55%)**
**J Randall (C) 16,288 (51.1%)** ;
A Slaughter (Lab) 12,522 (39.3%);
K Kerr (LD)1,792 (5,6%);
D Sutch (Loony) 396 (1.2%);
J Leonard (Soc )259 (0.8%);
F Taylor (BNP) 205 (0.6%);
I Anderson (Nat Dem) 157 (0.5%);
J McAuley (NF)110 ().3%);
H Middleton (Original Lib) 69 (0.2%);
J Feisenberger (UKIP) 39 (0.1%);
R Carroll (Emerald Rainbow Islands Dream Ticket) 30 (0.1%)
C maj 3,766.
*No change*

### November 6: PAISLEY SOUTH
*Caused by the death of Gordon McMaster, July 28, 1997:*
**Total vote: 23,435 (42.9%)**
**D Alexander (Lab) 10,346 (44.1%);**
I Blackford (SNP) 7,615 (32.5%);
E McCartin (LD) 2,582 (11.0%);
S Laidlaw (C) 1,643 (7.0%);
J Deighan (Pro Life All) 578 (2.5%);
F Curran (Scot Soc All) 306 (1.3%);
C McLauchlan (Scot Ind Lab) 155 (0.7%);
C Herriot (Soc Lab) 153 (0.7%);
K Blair (NLP) 57 (0.2%).
Lab maj 2,731.
*No change.*

### November 20: BECKENHAM
*Caused by the resignation of Piers*

*Merchant, Oct 21, 1997:*
**Total vote: 31,908 (43.7%)**
**J Lait (C) 13,162 (41.2%);**
R Hughes (Lab) 11,935 (37.4%);
R Vetterlein (LD) 5,864 (18.4%);
P Rimmer (Lib) 330 (1.0%);
J McAuley (NF) 267 ().8%);
L Mead (New Britn Ref) 237 (0.7%);
T Campion (Soc Found) 69 (0.2%);
J Small (NLP) 44 (0.1%).
C maj 1,227.
*No change.*

### November 20: WINCHESTER
*Caused by the Conservatives' legal challenge to general election result:*
**Total vote: 54,384 (68.7%).**
**M Oaten (LD) 37,006 (68.0%);**
G Malone (C) 15,450 (28.4%);
P Davies (Lab) 944 (1.7%);
R Page (Ref/UK Ind All) 521 (1.0%);
D Sutch (Loony) 316 (0.6%);
R Huggett (Literal Dem) 59 (0.1%);
R Barry (NLP) 48 (0.1%);
R Everest (Euro C) 40 (0.1%).
LD maj 21,556.
*No change.*

## 1999

### June 10: LEEDS CENTRAL
*Caused by the death of Derek Fatchett, May 9, 1999:*
**Total vote: 13,187 (19.6%)**
**H Benn (Lab) 6,361 (48.2%);**
P Wild (LD) 4,068 (30.8%);
W E Wild (C) 1,618 (12.3%);

D Blackburn (Green) 478 (3.6%);
R Northgreaves (UK Ind) 353 (2.7%);
C Hill (Left All) 258 (2.0%);
J Fitzgerald (Parenting) 51 (0.4%).
Lab maj 2,293.
*No change.*

### July 22: EDDISBURY
*Caused by the resignation of Sir Alastair Goodlad, June 28, 1999:*
**Total vote: 34,497 (51.4%)**
**S O'Brien (C) 15,465 (44.8%);**
M Hanson (Lab) 13,859 (40.2%);
P Roberts (LD) 4,757 (13.8%);
A Hope (Loony) 238 (0.7%);
R Everest (Ind Euro C) 98 (0.3%);
D Grice (NLP) 80 (0.2%).
C maj 1,606.
*No change.*

### September 23: HAMILTON SOUTH
*Caused by the elevation to the peerage of George Robertson, Aug 24, 1999:*
**Total vote: 19,454 (41.3%)**
**B Tynan (Lab) 7,172 (36.9%);**
A Ewing (SNP) 6,616 (34.0%);
S Blackall (SSP) 1,847 (9.5%);
C Ferguson (C) 1,406 (7.2%);
S Mungall (Accies) 1,075 (5.5%);
M MacLaren (LD) 634 (3.3%);
M Burns (Pro Life) 257 (1.3%);
T Dewar (Soc Lab) 238 (1.2%);
J Reid (SUP) 113 (0.6%)
A McConnachie (UK Ind) 61 (0.3%);
G Stidolph (NLP) 18 (0.1%);
J Drummond Moray (Status Quo) 17 (0.1%).
Lab maj 556.
*No change.*

### September 23: WIGAN

*Caused by the death of Roger Stott, Aug 8, 1999:*
**Total vote: 16,187 (25%)**
**N Turner (Lab) 9,641 (59.6%)**;
T Peet (C) 2,912 (18%);
J Rule (LD) 2,148 (13.3%);
J Whittaker (UK Ind) 834 (5.2%);
W Kelly (Soc Lab) 240 (1.5%);
C Maile (Ind Green) 190 (1.2%)
S Ebbs (Nat Democratic Resistance) 100 (0.6%);
P Davis (NLP) 64 (0.4%);
D Braid (Ind) 58 (0.4%).
Lab maj 6,729.
*No change.*

### November 25: KENSINGTON AND CHELSEA

*Caused by the death of Alan Clark, Sept 4, 1999:*
**Total vote: 19,513 (29.68 %).**
**M Portillo (C) 11,004 (56.4%)**;
R Atkinson (Lab) 4,298 (22.0%);
R Woodthorpe Browne (LD) 1,831 (9.4%);
J Stevens (Pro Euro C) 740 (3.8%);
D Hockney (UK Ind) 450 (2.3%);
H Charlton (Green) 446 (2.3%);
C de Vere Beauclerk (Democratic) 182 (0.9%);
C Paisley (Legalise Cannabis All) 141 (0.7%);
M Irwin (Campaign Living Will Legislation) 97 (0.5%);
G Oliver (UK Pensioners) 75 (0.4%);
S Scott-Fawcett (Referendum) 57 (0.3%);
L Hodges (Daily and Sunday Sport) 48 (0.2%);
G Valente (Natural Law) 35 (0.2%);
L Lovebuckett (People's Net Dream Ticket) 26 (0.1%);
J Davies (Independent Environmentalist) 24 (0.1%);
P May (Equal Parenting) 24 (0.1%);
A Hope (Loony) 20 (0.1%);
T Samuelson (Stop Tobacco Companies Farming Our Children) 15 (0.1%).
C maj 6,706.
*No change.*

## 2000

### February 3: CEREDIGION

*Caused by the resignation of Cynog Dafis, Jan 10, 2000:*
**Total vote: 25,065 (45.6%)**
**S Thomas (Plaid Cymru) 10,716 (42.8%)**;

M Williams (LD) 5,768 (23.0%);
P Davies (C) 4,138 (16.5%);
M Battle (Lab) 3,612 (14.4%);
J Bufton (UK Ind) 487 (1.9%);
J Berkeley Davies (Ind Green) 289 (1.2%);
M Shipton (Wales on Sunday Match Funding Now) 55 (0.2%).
PC maj 4,948.
*No change.*

### May 4: ROMSEY

*Caused by the death in a fire of Michael Colvin, Feb 24, 2000:*
**Total vote: 38,709 (55.5%)**
**S Gidley (LD) 19,571 (50.6%)**;
T Palmer (C) 16,260 (42.0%);
A Howard (Lab) 1,451 (3.7%);
G Rankin-Moore (UK Ind) 901 (2.3%);
D Large (Legalise Cannabis All) 417 (1.1%);
T Lamont (Ind) 109 (0.3%);
LD maj 3,311.
*Lib Dem gain.*

### June 22: TOTTENHAM

*Caused by the death of Bernie Grant, April 8, 2000:*
**Total vote: 16,417 (25.43%).**
**D Lammy (Lab) 8,785 (53.5%)**;
D Hames (LD) 3,139 (19.1%);
J Ellison (C) 2,634 (16.0%);
W Bennett (London Soc All) 885 (5.4%);
P Budge (Green) 606 (3.7%);
E Basarik (Reform 2000 Anti-VAT) 177 (1.1%);
A Tanna (UK Ind) 136 (0.8%);
D De Braam (Ind C) 55 (0.3%).
Lab maj 5,646.
*No change.*

### September 21: ANTRIM SOUTH

*Caused by the death of Clifford Forsythe, April 27, 2000:*
**Total vote: 30,567 (43.02%)**
**W McCrea (DUP) 11,601 (38.0%)**;
D Burnside (UUP) 10,779 (35.3%);
D McClelland (SDLP) 3,496 (11.4%);
M Meehan (Sinn Fein) 2,611 (8.5%);
D Ford (Alliance) 2,031 (6.6%);
D Collins (Natural Law) 49. (0.2%).
DUP maj 822.
*Democratic Unionist Party gain.*

### November 23: WEST BROMWICH WEST

*The seat was previously held by the Speaker, Betty Boothroyd, who resigned on Oct 23, 2000:*
**Total vote: 18,879 (27.60%)**
**A Bailey (Lab) 9,640 (51.1%)**;

K Bissell (C) 6,408 (33.9%);
S Smith (LD) 1,791 (9.5%);
N Griffin (BNP) 794 (4.2%);
J Oakton (UK Ind) 246 (1.3%).
Lab maj 3,232.
*Labour win from Speaker.*

### November 23: PRESTON

*Caused by the death of Audrey Wise, Sept 2, 2000:*
**Total vote: 21,363 (29.6%).**
**M Hendrick (Lab) 9,765 (45.7%)**;
G O'Hare (C) 5,339 (25.0%);
B Chadwick (LD) 3,454 (16.2%);
T Cartwright (Lancs Soc All) 1,210 (5.7%);
G Beaman (UK Ind) 458 (2.1%);
R Merrick (Green) 441 (2.1%);
P Garrett (Preston Alliance) 416 (1.9%);
C Jackson (BNP) 229 (1.1%);
D Franklin-Braid (Battle of Britain Christian All) 51 (0.2%).
Lab maj 4,426.
*No change.*

### November 23: GLASGOW ANNIESLAND

*Caused by the death of Donald Dewar, Oct 11, 2000:*
**Total vote: 20,212 (38.4%).**
**J Robertson (Lab) 10,539 (52.1%)**;
G Thoms (SNP) 4,202 (20.8%);
D Luckhurst (C) 2,188 (10.8%);
C McGinty (LD) 1,630 (8.1%);
C McCarthy (SSP) 1,441 (7.1%);
W Lyden (Family) 212 (1.0%).
Lab maj 6,337.
*No change*

### December 21: FALKIRK WEST

*Caused by the resignation of Dennis Canavan, Nov 11, 2000:*
**Total vote: 19,504 (36.2%).**
**E Joyce (Lab) 8,492 (43.54%)**;
D Kerr (SNP) 7,787 (39.93%);
C Stevenson (C) 1,621 (8.31%);
I Hunter (SSP) 989 (5.1%);
H O' Donnell (LD) 615 (3.2%).
Lab maj 705.
*No change.*

# BRITISH POLITICS ONLINE

THE following websites, compiled by EDWARD HARDMAN, and their various links should keep even the most devoted political enthusiast satisfied.

## PARLIAMENTS

**www.parliament.uk**   The House of Commons and House of Lords
**www.scottish.parliament.uk**   The Scottish Parliament
**www.wales.gov.uk**   The Welsh Assembly
**www.ni-assembly.gov.uk**   The Northern Ireland Assembly
**www.europarl.eu.int**   The European Parliament

## THE UK EXECUTIVE

**www.royal.gov.uk**   The Monarchy website
**www.cabinet-office.gov.uk**   The Cabinet Office
**www.coi.gov.uk**   Central Office of Information
**www.culture.gov.uk**   Dept for Culture, Media and Sport
**www.mod.uk**   Ministry of Defence
**www.dfes.gov.uk**   Dept for Education and Skills
**www.defra.gov.uk**   Dept for Environment, Food and Rural Affairs
**www.doh.gov.uk**   Dept of Health
**www.fco.gov.uk**   Foreign Office
**www.homeoffice.gov.uk**   Home Office
**www.dfid.gov.uk**   Dept for International Development
**www.lcd.gov.uk**   Lord Chancellor's Department
**www.nio.gov.uk**   Northern Ireland Office
**www.pmo.gov.uk**   No 10 Downing Street
**www.privy-council.org.uk**   Privy Council
**www.scottishsecretary.gov.uk**   Scottish Office
**www.dti.gov.uk**   Dept of Trade and Industry
**www.dtlr.gov.uk**   Dept for Transport, Local Government and Regions
**www.hmso.gov.uk**   Her Majesty's Stationery Office
**www.hm-treasury.gov.uk**   The Treasury
**www.walesoffice.gov.uk**   Welsh Office
**www.dwp.gov.uk**   Dept for Work and Pensions

## POLITICAL PARTIES

**www.conservatives.com**   Conservative Party
**www.labour.org.uk**   Labour Party
**www.libdems.org.uk**   Liberal Democrats
**www.snp.org.uk**   Scottish National Party
**www.plaidcymru2001.com**   Plaid Cymru
**www.uup.org**   Ulster Unionist Party
**www.dup.org.uk**   Democratic Unionist Party
**www.sinnfein.org**   Sinn Fein
**www.sdlp.ie**   Social Democratic and Labour Party

## POLLING ORGANISATIONS

**www.mori.com**   MORI
**www.nop.co.uk**   NOP Research
**www.gallup.co.uk**   Gallup Organisation
**www.icmresearch.co.uk**   ICM Research

# STATISTICS

# HOW THE NATION VOTED

## JUNE 2001

| | | Lab | C | LD | Nat | Other | Total |
|---|---|---|---|---|---|---|---|
| **ENGLAND** | | | | | | | |
| Electorate 36,976,985 | Votes | 9,056,466 | 7,705,589 | 4,246,849 | 0 | 861,225 | 21,870,129 |
| Lab to C swing % 1.8 | % of vote/Turnout | 41.4 | 35.2 | 19.4 | 0.0 | 4.0 | 59.1 |
| | MPs | 323 | 165 | 40 | 0 | 1 | 529 |
| | Candidates | 529 | 529 | 528 | 0 | 1,002 | 2,588 |
| **SCOTLAND** | | | | | | | |
| Electorate 3,980,974 | Votes | 1,017,226 | 360,658 | 380,034 | 464,314 | 93,471 | 2,315,703 |
| C to Lab swing % 0.1 | % of vote/Turnout | 43.9 | 15.6 | 16.4 | 20.1 | 4.0 | 58.2 |
| | MPs | 55 | 1 | 10 | 5 | 1* | 72 |
| | Candidates | 71 | 71 | 71 | 72 | 48 | 333 |
| **WALES** | | | | | | | |
| Electorate 2,228,723 | Votes | 666,956 | 288,623 | 189,254 | 195,893 | 31,598 | 1,372,324 |
| Lab to C swing % 3.75 | % of vote/Turnout | 48.6 | 21 | 13.8 | 14.3 | 2.3 | 61.6 |
| | MPs | 34 | 0 | 2 | 4 | 0 | 40 |
| | Candidates | 40 | 40 | 40 | 40 | 64 | 224 |
| **NORTHERN IRELAND** | | | | | | | |
| Electorate 1,191,070 | Votes | 0 | 2,422 | 0 | 0 | 807,952 | 810,374 |
| | % of vote/Turnout | 0.0 | 0.2 | 0.0 | 0.0 | 99.8 | 68.0 |
| | MPs | 0 | 0 | 0 | 0 | 18 | 18 |
| | Candidates | 0 | 3 | 0 | 0 | 97 | 100 |
| **UNITED KINGDOM** | | | | | | | |
| Electorate 44,377,752 | Votes | 10,740,648 | 8,357,292 | 4,816,137 | 660,207 | 1,794,246 | 26,368,530 |
| Lab to C swing % 1.8 | % of vote/Turnout | 40.7 | 31.7 | 18.3 | 2.5 | 6.8 | 59.4 |
| | MPs | 412 | 166 | 52 | 9 | 20* | 659 |
| | Candidates | 640 | 643 | 639 | 112 | 1,211 | 3,133 |

## MAY 1997

| | | Lab | C | LD | Nat | Other | Total |
|---|---|---|---|---|---|---|---|
| **ENGLAND** | | | | | | | |
| Electorate 36,462,327 | Votes | 11,348,623 | 8,780,896 | 4,678,061 | 0 | 1,253,361 | 26,060,941 |
| C to Lab swing % 10.7 | % of vote/Turnout | 43.5 | 33.7 | 18.0 | 0.0 | 4.8 | 71.5 |
| | MPs | 328 | 165 | 34 | 0 | 2* | 529 |
| | Candidates | 527 | 528 | 527 | 0 | 1,363 | 2,945 |
| **SCOTLAND** | | | | | | | |
| Electorate 3,946,113 | Votes | 1,283,353 | 493,059 | 365,359 | 622,260 | 53,408 | 2,817,439 |
| C to Lab swing % 7.4 | % of vote/Turnout | 45.6 | 17.5 | 13.0 | 22.1 | 1.9 | 71.4 |
| | MPs | 56 | 0 | 10 | 6 | 0 | 72 |
| | Candidates | 72 | 72 | 72 | 72 | 143 | 431 |
| **WALES** | | | | | | | |
| Electorate 2,200,611 | Votes | 885,935 | 317,127 | 200,020 | 161,030 | 54,932 | 1,619,044 |
| C to Lab swing % 7.1 | % of vote/Turnout | 54.7 | 19.6 | 12.4 | 9.9 | 3.4 | 73.6 |
| | MPs | 34 | 0 | 2 | 4 | 0 | 40 |
| | Candidates | 40 | 40 | 40 | 40 | 63 | 223 |
| **NORTHERN IRELAND** | | | | | | | |
| Electorate 1,175,508 | Votes | 0 | 9,858 | 0 | 0 | 780,920 | 790,778 |
| | % of vote/Turnout | 0.0 | 1.2 | 0.0 | 0.0 | 98.8 | 67.3 |
| | MPs | 0 | 0 | 0 | 0 | 18 | 18 |
| | Candidates | 0 | 8 | 0 | 0 | 117 | 125 |
| **UNITED KINGDOM** | | | | | | | |
| Electorate 43,784,559 | Votes | 13,517,911 | 9,600,940 | 5,243,440 | 783,290 | 2,142,621 | 31,288,202 |
| C to Lab swing % 10.0 | % of vote/Turnout | 43.2 | 30.7 | 16.8 | 2.5 | 6.8 | 71.5 |
| | MPs | 418 | 165 | 46 | 10 | 20* | 659 |
| | Candidates | 639 | 648 | 639 | 112 | 1,686 | 3,724 |

* includes the Speaker

# METROPOLITAN AND COUNTY VOTING

## *by Tim Hames*

T HERE was once a time, from 1945 to 1979 in fact, when electoral trends at the metropolitan and county level were almost irrelevant. There was a national swing to one party and that swing would be almost uniform in its distribution across the entirety of Great Britain. The 2001 election represented both a continuation and an escalation of a shift in a completely different direction.

The results across regions and counties and even between adjacent and seemingly similar seats are now so distinct from one another that to aggregrate them all and produce an allegedly "national" result is almost a pointless exercise. This fact explains why the Conservatives could enjoy a national swing of 1.8 per cent in their favour in this general election but end up with precisely one extra MP for their efforts. Despite these highly individual outcomes some broad conclusions can be drawn from the metropolitan and county information. In most cities turnout fell to very low levels indeed and Labour suffered disproportionately in terms of votes as a consequence. It made virtually no difference to their parliamentary representation.

As a rule, the counties followed certain regional lines. Those in the South and South East of England produced the smallest shifts away from Labour while others further north tended, but by no means uniformly, to do the opposite. Labour did, though, remain entrenched in Scotland and Wales while the Liberal Democrats dug themselves in more deeply in the South West of England.

The individual county results will have proved perplexing to senior Conservative strategists. They had invested an enormous amount of energy in Northamptonshire, home to a set of ultra-marginal seats, but received virtually no positive swing at all. There were similar expectations made of Kent, where the issue of asylum-seekers appeared to be especially salient, but although a notable swing occurred, it was concentrated in those seats which the Tories already held. There were several counties in southern England where the Conservatives made striking advances in the county council elections on June 7 but absolutely no progress in the same places at the parliamentary level. This implies that some instinctive Conservatives could not bring themselves to back William Hague. Seats making up metropolitan counties and the voting in them was as follows:

| GREATER MANCHESTER | | | Lab | C | LD | Other | Total |
|---|---|---|---|---|---|---|---|
| 2001 | Electorate | 1,904,660 | Votes | 540,950 | 245,361 | 184,334 | 37,573 | 1,008,218 |
| | Turnout % | 52.9 | Votes % | 53.7 | 24.3 | 18.3 | 3.7 | 100.0 |
| | Swing % | 1.4 | Seats | 25 | 1 | 2 | 0 | 28 |
| | Lab to C | | Candidates | 28 | 28 | 28 | 40 | 124 |
| 1997 | Electorate | 1,891,138 | Votes | 724,905 | 310,635 | 206,469 | 44,461 | 1,286,470 |
| | Turnout % | 68 | Votes % | 56.3 | 24.1 | 16 | 3.5 | 100.0 |
| | | | Seats | 25 | 2 | 1 | 0 | 28 |
| | | | Candidates | 28 | 28 | 28 | 56 | 140 |
| | | | Change 01-97 | -2.6 | 0.2 | 2.3 | 0.2 | |

Altrincham & Sale West, Ashton-under-Lyne, Bolton North East, Bolton South East, Bolton West, Bury North, Bury South, Cheadle, Denton & Reddish, Eccles, Hazel Grove, Heywood & Middleton, Leigh, Makerfield, Manchester Blackley, Manchester Central, Manchester Gorton, Manchester Withington, Oldham East & Saddleworth, Oldham West & Royton, Rochdale, Salford, Stalybridge & Hyde, Stockport, Stretford & Urmston, Wigan, Worsley, Wythenshawe & Sale East.

| INNER LONDON | | | Lab | C | LD | Other | Total |
|---|---|---|---|---|---|---|---|
| 2001 | Electorate | 1,664,501 | Votes | 439,610 | 201,223 | 144,513 | 51,465 | 836,811 |
| | Turnout % | 50.3 | Votes % | 52.5 | 24 | 17.3 | 6.2 | 100.0 |
| | Swing % | 1.35 | Seats | 22 | 2 | 1 | 0 | 25 |
| | Lab to C | | Candidates | 25 | 25 | 25 | 70 | 145 |
| 1997 | Electorate | 1,609,932 | Votes | 568,648 | 253,157 | 132,735 | 56,584 | 1,011,124 |
| | Turnout % | 62.8 | Votes % | 56.2 | 25 | 13.1 | 5.6 | 100.0 |
| | | | Seats | 22 | 2 | 1 | 0 | 25 |
| | | | Candidates | 25 | 25 | 25 | 109 | 184 |
| | | | Change 01-97 | -3.7 | -1.0 | 4.2 | 0.6 | |

Battersea, Bethnal Green & Bow, Camberwell & Peckham, Cities of London & Westminster, Dulwich & West Norwood, Eltham, Greenwich & Woolwich, Hackney North & Stoke Newington, Hackney South & Shoreditch, Hammersmith & Fulham, Hampstead & Highgate, Holborn & St Pancras, Islington North, Islington South & Finsbury, Kensington & Chelsea, Lewisham Deptford, Lewisham East, Lewisham West, Poplar & Canning Town, Putney, Regent's Park & Kensington North, Southwark North & Bermondsey, Streatham, Tooting, Vauxhall.

## METROPOLITAN TABLES

| MERSEYSIDE | | | | | Lab | C | LD | Other | Total |
|---|---|---|---|---|---|---|---|---|---|
| 2001 | Electorate | 1,056,805 | Votes | | 321,552 | 109,965 | 97,247 | 18,624 | 547,388 |
| | Turnout % | 51.8 | Votes % | | 58.7 | 20.1 | 17.8 | 3.4 | 100.0 |
| | Swing % | 1.8 | Seats | | 15 | 0 | 1 | 0 | 16 |
| | Lab to C | | Candidates | | 16 | 16 | 16 | 22 | 70 |
| 1997 | Electorate | 1,057,256 | Votes | | 442,362 | 141,120 | 103,152 | 28,157 | 714,791 |
| | Turnout % | 67.6 | Votes % | | 61.9 | 19.7 | 14.4 | 3.9 | 100.0 |
| | | | Seats | | 15 | 0 | 1 | 0 | 16 |
| | | | Candidates | | 16 | 16 | 16 | 44 | 92 |
| | | | Change 01-97 | | -3.2 | 0.4 | 3.4 | -0.5 | |

Birkenhead, Bootle, Crosby, Knowsley North & Sefton East, Knowsley South, Liverpool Garston, Liverpool Riverside, Liverpool Walton. Liverpool Wavertree, Liverpool West Derby, St Helens North, St Helens South, Southport, Wallasey, Wirral South, Wirral West.

| OUTER LONDON | | | | | Lab | C | LD | Other | Total |
|---|---|---|---|---|---|---|---|---|---|
| 2001 | Electorate | 3,333,111 | Votes | | 867,211 | 640,528 | 338,376 | 77,267 | 1,923,382 |
| | Turnout % | 57.7 | Votes % | | 45.1 | 33.3 | 17.6 | 4 | 100.0 |
| | Swing % | 4 | Seats | | 33 | 11 | 5 | 0 | 49 |
| | Lab to C | | Candidates | | 49 | 49 | 49 | 110 | 257 |
| 1997 | Electorate | 3,291,818 | Votes | | 1,074,685 | 783,018 | 353,278 | 99,483 | 2,310,464 |
| | Turnout % | 70.2 | Votes % | | 46.5 | 33.9 | 15.3 | 4.3 | 100.0 |
| | | | Seats | | 35 | 9 | 5 | 0 | 49 |
| | | | Candidates | | 49 | 49 | 49 | 156 | 303 |
| | | | Change 01-97 | | -1.4 | -0.6 | 2.3 | -0.3 | |

Barking, Beckenham, Bexleyheath & Crayford, Brent East, Brent North, Brent South, Brentford & Isleworth, Bromley & Chislehurst, Carshalton & Wallington, Chingford & Woodford Green, Chipping Barnet, Croydon Central, Croydon North, Croydon South, Dagenham, Ealing Acton & Shepherd's Bush, Ealing North, Ealing Southall, East Ham, Edmonton, Enfield North, Enfield Southgate, Erith & Thamesmead, Feltham & Hes-ton, Finchley & Golders Green, Harrow East, Harrow West, Hayes & Harlington, Hendon, Hornchurch, Hornsey & Wood Green, Ilford North, Ilford South, Kingston & Surbiton, Leyton & Wanstead, Mitcham & Morden, Old Bexley & Sidcup, Orpington, Richmond Park, Romford, Ruislip Northwood, Sutton & Cheam, Tottenham, Twickenham, Upminster, Uxbridge, Walthamstow, West Ham, Wimbledon.

| SOUTH YORKSHIRE | | | | | Lab | C | LD | Other | Total |
|---|---|---|---|---|---|---|---|---|---|
| 2001 | Electorate | 958,883 | Votes | | 296,403 | 94,503 | 90,624 | 21,282 | 502,812 |
| | Turnout % | 52.4 | Votes % | | 58.9 | 18.8 | 18 | 4.2 | 100.0 |
| | Swing % | 2.75 | Seats | | 14 | 0 | 1 | 0 | 15 |
| | Lab to C | | Candidates | | 15 | 15 | 15 | 30 | 75 |
| 1997 | Electorate | 983,182 | Votes | | 392,835 | 105,209 | 104,842 | 27,989 | 630,875 |
| | Turnout % | 64.2 | Votes % | | 62.3 | 16.7 | 16.6 | 4.4 | 100.0 |
| | | | Seats | | 14 | 0 | 1 | 0 | 15 |
| | | | Candidates | | 15 | 15 | 15 | 32 | 77 |
| | | | Change 01-97 | | -3.4 | 2.1 | 1.4 | -0.2 | |

Barnsley Central, Barnsley East & Mexborough, Barnsley West & Penistone, Don Valley, Doncaster Central, Doncaster North, Rother Valley, Rotherham, Sheffield Attercliffe, Sheffield Brightside, Sheffield Central, Sheffield Hallam, Sheffield Heeley, Sheffield Hillsborough, Wentworth.

| TYNE AND WEAR | | | | Lab | C | LD | Other | Total |
|---|---|---|---|---|---|---|---|---|
| 2001 | Electorate | 828,628 | Votes | 278,005 | 78,088 | 73,339 | 12,280 | 441,712 |
| | Turnout % | 53.3 | Votes % | 62.9 | 17.7 | 16.6 | 2.8 | 100.0 |
| | Swing % | 2.3 | Seats | 13 | 0 | 0 | 0 | 13 |
| | Lab to C | | Candidates | 13 | 13 | 13 | 22 | 61 |
| 1997 | Electorate | 847,151 | Votes | 372,999 | 96,141 | 65,594 | 21,183 | 555,917 |
| | Turnout % | 65.6 | Votes % | 67.1 | 17.3 | 11.8 | 3.8 | 100.0 |
| | | | Seats | 13 | 0 | 0 | 0 | 13 |
| | | | Candidates | 13 | 13 | 13 | 21 | 60 |
| | | | Change 01-97 | -4.2 | 0.4 | 4.8 | -1.0 | |

Blaydon, Gateshead East & Washington West, Houghton & Washington East, Jarrow, Newcastle upon Tyne Central, Newcastle upon Tyne East & Wallsend, Newcastle upon Tyne North, South Shields, Sunderland North, Sunderland South, Tyne Bridge, Tynemouth, Tyneside North.

| WEST MIDLANDS | | | | Lab | C | LD | Other | Total |
|---|---|---|---|---|---|---|---|---|
| 2001 | Electorate | 1,912,185 | Votes | 535,189 | 319,267 | 136,493 | 53,085 | 1,044,034 |
| | Turnout % | 54.6 | Votes % | 51.3 | 30.6 | 13.1 | 5.1 | 100.0 |
| | Swing % | 4 | Seats | 25 | 4 | 0 | 0 | 29 |
| | Lab to C | | Candidates | 29 | 29 | 29 | 68 | 155 |
| 1997 | Electorate | 2,065,425 | Votes | 715,916 | 435,011 | 156,752 | 99,662 | 1,407,341 |
| | Turnout % | 68.1 | Votes % | 50.9 | 30.9 | 11.1 | 7.1 | 100.0 |
| | | | Seats | 24 | 6 | 0 | 1 | 31 |
| | | | Candidates | 30 | 30 | 30 | 74 | 164 |
| | | | Change 01-97 | -0.8 | 0.0 | 1.4 | -2.3 | |

Aldridge-Brownhills, Birmingham Edgbaston, Birmingham Erdington, Birmingham Hall Green, Birmingham Hodge Hill, Birmingham Ladywood, Birmingham Northfield, Birmingham Perry Bar, Birmingham Selly Oak, Birmingham Sparkbrook & Small Heath, Birmingham Yardley, Coventry North East, Coventry North West, Coventry South, Dudley North, Dudley South, Halesowen & Rowley Regis, Meriden, Solihull, Stourbridge, Sutton Coldfield, Walsall North, Walsall South, Warley, West Bromwich East, West Bromwich West, Wolverhampton North East, Wolverhampton South East, Wolverhampton South West.

| WEST YORKSHIRE | | | | Lab | C | LD | Other | Total |
|---|---|---|---|---|---|---|---|---|
| 2001 | Electorate | 1,562,883 | Votes | 456,341 | 265,615 | 123,533 | 40,026 | 885,515 |
| | Turnout % | 56.7 | Votes % | 51.5 | 30 | 14 | 4.5 | 100.0 |
| | Swing % | 1.85 | Seats | 23 | 0 | 0 | 0 | 23 |
| | Lab to C | | Candidates | 23 | 23 | 23 | 52 | 121 |
| 1997 | Electorate | 1,551,571 | Votes | 581,256 | 310,247 | 139,007 | 45,382 | 1,075,892 |
| | Turnout % | 69.3 | Votes % | 54 | 28.8 | 12.9 | 4.2 | 100.0 |
| | | | Seats | 23 | 0 | 0 | 0 | 23 |
| | | | Candidates | 23 | 23 | 23 | 49 | 118 |
| | | | Change 01-97 | -2.5 | 1.2 | 1.1 | 0.3 | |

Batley & Spen, Bradford North, Bradford South, Bradford West, Calder Valley, Colne Valley, Dewsbury, Elmet, Halifax, Hemsworth, Huddersfield, Keighley, Leeds Central, Leeds East, Leeds North East, Leeds North West, Leeds West, Morley & Rothwell, Normanton, Pontefract & Castleford, Pudsey, Shipley, Wakefield.

# NON-METROPOLITAN COUNTIES

B Y the standards of the past two decades, local government in England did not endure too much turbulence during the 1997-2001 Parliament. Labour resisted the temptation to revisit the question of whether one tier of councils would be preferable to two and if so whether counties or districts should be the preferred unit. This means that the results below can easily be compared to those recorded four years ago. That statistical blessing might not, however, be a permanent feature of politics. If the Government proceeds with plans for elected regional assemblies, then the boundaries and fate of the old counties could once again become contentious.

The Isle of Wight is still one seat; its detailed analysis is in the election results.

| AVON | | | | Lab | C | LD | Other | Total |
|------|------|------|------|------|------|------|------|------|
| 2001 | Electorate | 751,184 | Votes | 177,982 | 152,030 | 134,170 | 19,194 | 483,376 |
| | Turnout % | 64.3 | Votes % | 36.8 | 31.5 | 27.8 | 4 | 100.0 |
| | Swing % | -.75 | Seats | 6 | 1 | 3 | 0 | 10 |
| | Lab to C | | Candidates | 10 | 10 | 10 | 25 | 55 |
| 1997 | Electorate | 739,487 | Votes | 202,778 | 181,606 | 146,270 | 24,724 | 555,378 |
| | Turnout % | 75.1 | Votes % | 36.5 | 32.7 | 26.3 | 4.5 | 100.0 |
| | | | Seats | 6 | 1 | 3 | 0 | 10 |
| | | | Candidates | 10 | 10 | 10 | 34 | 64 |
| | | | Change 01-97 | 0.3 | -1.2 | 1.5 | -0.5 | |

Bath, Bristol East, Bristol North West, Bristol South, Bristol West, Kingswood, Northavon, Wansdyke, Weston-super-Mare, Woodspring.

| BEDFORDSHIRE | | | | Lab | C | LD | Other | Total |
|------|------|------|------|------|------|------|------|------|
| 2001 | Electorate | 414,917 | Votes | 109,113 | 100,265 | 37,599 | 7,817 | 254,794 |
| | Turnout % | 61.4 | Votes % | 42.8 | 39.4 | 14.8 | 3.1 | 100.0 |
| | Swing % | 1 | Seats | 3 | 3 | 0 | 0 | 6 |
| | Lab to C | | Candidates | 6 | 6 | 6 | 10 | 28 |
| 1997 | Electorate | 401,076 | Votes | 131,978 | 115,838 | 38,514 | 13,898 | 300,228 |
| | Turnout % | 74.9 | Votes % | 44 | 38.6 | 12.8 | 4.6 | 100.0 |
| | | | Seats | 3 | 3 | 0 | 0 | 6 |
| | | | Candidates | 6 | 6 | 6 | 16 | 34 |
| | | | Change 01-97 | -1.2 | 0.8 | 2.0 | -1.5 | |

Bedford, Bedfordshire Mid, Bedfordshire North East, Bedfordshire South West, Luton North, Luton South.

| BERKSHIRE | | | | Lab | C | LD | Other | Total |
|------|------|------|------|------|------|------|------|------|
| 2001 | Electorate | 581,058 | Votes | 108,668 | 142,280 | 91,960 | 11,002 | 353,910 |
| | Turnout % | 60.9 | Votes % | 30.7 | 40.2 | 26 | 3.1 | 100.0 |
| | Swing % | -2.1 | Seats | 3 | 4 | 1 | 0 | 8 |
| | Lab to C | | Candidates | 8 | 8 | 8 | 16 | 40 |
| 1997 | Electorate | 566,509 | Votes | 117,950 | 174,727 | 101,621 | 19,388 | 413,686 |
| | Turnout % | 73 | Votes % | 28.5 | 42.2 | 24.6 | 4.7 | 100.0 |
| | | | Seats | 3 | 4 | 1 | 0 | 8 |
| | | | Candidates | 8 | 8 | 8 | 27 | 51 |
| | | | Change 01-97 | 2.2 | -2.0 | 1.4 | -1.6 | |

Bracknell, Maidenhead, Newbury, Reading East, Reading West, Slough, Windsor, Wokingham.

| BUCKINGHAMSHIRE | | | Lab | C | LD | Other | Total |
|---|---|---|---|---|---|---|---|
| 2001 | Electorate | 510,451 | Votes | 98,165 | 145,128 | 63,121 | 12,724 | 319,138 |
| | Turnout % | 62.5 | Votes % | 30.8 | 45.5 | 19.8 | 4 | 100.0 |
| | Swing % | 8 | Seats | 2 | 5 | 0 | 0 | 7 |
| | Lab to C | | Candidates | 7 | 7 | 7 | 14 | 35 |
| 1997 | Electorate | 495,249 | Votes | 111,289 | 158,884 | 76,993 | 16,497 | 363,663 |
| | Turnout % | 73.4 | Votes % | 30.6 | 43.7 | 21.2 | 4.5 | 100.0 |
| | | | Seats | 2 | 5 | 0 | 0 | 7 |
| | | | Candidates | 7 | 7 | 7 | 19 | 40 |
| | | | Change 01-97 | 0.2 | 1.8 | -1.4 | -0.5 | |

Aylesbury, Beaconsfield, Buckingham, Chesham & Amersham, Milton Keynes North East, Milton Keynes South West, Wycombe.

| CAMBRIDGESHIRE | | | Lab | C | LD | Other | Total |
|---|---|---|---|---|---|---|---|
| 2001 | Electorate | 518,403 | Votes | 104,506 | 138,798 | 68,824 | 11,843 | 323,971 |
| | Turnout % | 62.5 | Votes % | 32.3 | 42.8 | 21.2 | 3.7 | 100.0 |
| | Swing % | 1.5 | Seats | 2 | 5 | 0 | 0 | 7 |
| | Lab to C | | Candidates | 7 | 7 | 7 | 15 | 36 |
| 1997 | Electorate | 501,052 | Votes | 128,183 | 156,154 | 66,411 | 20,714 | 371,462 |
| | Turnout % | 74.1 | Votes % | 34.5 | 42 | 17.9 | 5.6 | 100.0 |
| | | | Seats | 2 | 5 | 0 | 0 | 7 |
| | | | Candidates | 7 | 7 | 7 | 24 | 45 |
| | | | Change 01-97 | -2.2 | 0.8 | 3.3 | -1.9 | |

Cambridge, Cambridgeshire North East, Cambridgeshire North West, Cambridgeshire South, Cambridgeshire South East, Huntingdon, Peterborough.

| CHESHIRE | | | Lab | C | LD | Other | Total |
|---|---|---|---|---|---|---|---|
| 2001 | Electorate | 765,405 | Votes | 214,226 | 164,470 | 72,118 | 11,609 | 462,423 |
| | Turnout % | 60.4 | Votes % | 46.3 | 35.6 | 15.6 | 2.5 | 100.0 |
| | Swing % | 3.4 | Seats | 7 | 4 | 0 | 0 | 11 |
| | Lab to C | | Candidates | 11 | 11 | 11 | 16 | 49 |
| 1997 | Electorate | 753,951 | Votes | 262,655 | 188,250 | 69,182 | 44,268 | 564,355 |
| | Turnout % | 74.9 | Votes % | 46.5 | 33.4 | 12.3 | 7.8 | 100.0 |
| | | | Seats | 7 | 3 | 0 | 1 | 11 |
| | | | Candidates | 10 | 11 | 10 | 23 | 52 |
| | | | Change 01-97 | 0.2 | 2.2 | 3.3 | -5.3 | |

Chester City of, Congleton, Crewe & Nantwich, Eddisbury, Ellesmere Port & Neston, Halton, Macclesfield, Tatton, Warrington North, Warrington South, Weaver Vale.

| CLEVELAND | | | Lab | C | LD | Other | Total |
|---|---|---|---|---|---|---|---|
| 2001 | Electorate | 409,193 | Votes | 138,520 | 61,092 | 28,966 | 5,015 | 233,593 |
| | Turnout % | 57.1 | Votes % | 59.3 | 26.2 | 12.4 | 2.1 | 100.0 |
| | Swing % | 2.05 | Seats | 6 | 0 | 0 | 0 | 6 |
| | Lab to C | | Candidates | 6 | 6 | 6 | 8 | 26 |
| 1997 | Electorate | 410,939 | Votes | 180,729 | 72,990 | 28,402 | 7,564 | 289,685 |
| | Turnout % | 70.5 | Votes % | 62.4 | 25.2 | 9.8 | 2.6 | 100.0 |
| | | | Seats | 6 | 0 | 0 | 0 | 6 |
| | | | Candidates | 6 | 6 | 6 | 5 | 23 |
| | | | Change 01-97 | -3.1 | 1.0 | 2.6 | -0.5 | |

Hartlepool, Middlesbrough, Middlesbrough South & Cleveland East, Redcar, Stockton North, Stockton South.

## NON-METROPOLITAN TABLES

| CORNWALL | | | | Lab | C | LD | Other | Total |
|----------|--|--|--|-----|---|----|-------|-------|
| 2001 | Electorate | 390,060 | Votes | 43,674 | 82,227 | 113,000 | 13,216 | 252,117 |
| | Turnout % | 64.6 | Votes % | 17.3 | 32.6 | 44.8 | 5.2 | 100.0 |
| | Swing % | 1 | Seats | 1 | 0 | 4 | 0 | 5 |
| | Lab to C | | Candidates | 5 | 5 | 5 | 10 | 25 |
| 1997 | Electorate | 375,788 | Votes | 47,913 | 85,077 | 123,210 | 24,093 | 280,293 |
| | Turnout % | 74.6 | Votes % | 17.1 | 30.4 | 44 | 8.6 | 100.0 |
| | | | Seats | 1 | 0 | 4 | 0 | 5 |
| | | | Candidates | 5 | 5 | 5 | 25 | 40 |
| | | | Change 01-97 | 0.2 | 2.2 | 0.8 | -3.4 | |

Cornwall North, Cornwall South East, Falmouth & Camborne, St Ives, Truro & St Austell.

| CUMBRIA | | | | Lab | C | LD | Other | Total |
|---------|--|--|--|-----|---|----|-------|-------|
| 2001 | Electorate | 381,461 | Votes | 94,191 | 96,163 | 46,736 | 5,563 | 242,653 |
| | Turnout % | 63.6 | Votes % | 38.8 | 39.6 | 19.3 | 2.3 | 100.0 |
| | Swing % | 6.55 | Seats | 4 | 2 | 0 | 0 | 6 |
| | Lab to C | | Candidates | 6 | 6 | 6 | 9 | 27 |
| 1997 | Electorate | 381,791 | Votes | 129,438 | 94,686 | 46,637 | 11,565 | 282,326 |
| | Turnout % | 73.9 | Votes % | 45.8 | 33.5 | 16.5 | 4.1 | 100.0 |
| | | | Seats | 4 | 2 | 0 | 0 | 6 |
| | | | Candidates | 6 | 6 | 6 | 10 | 28 |
| | | | Change 01-97 | -7.0 | 6.1 | 2.8 | -1.8 | |

Barrow & Furness, Carlisle, Copeland, Penrith & The Border, Westmorland & Lonsdale, Workington.

| DERBYSHIRE | | | | Lab | C | LD | Other | Total |
|------------|--|--|--|-----|---|----|-------|-------|
| 2001 | Electorate | 748,304 | Votes | 227,768 | 141,717 | 79,845 | 6,392 | 455,722 |
| | Turnout % | 60.9 | Votes % | 50 | 31.1 | 17.5 | 1.4 | 100.0 |
| | Swing % | 2.6 | Seats | 8 | 1 | 1 | 0 | 10 |
| | Lab to C | | Candidates | 10 | 10 | 10 | 13 | 43 |
| 1997 | Electorate | 734,213 | Votes | 293,561 | 161,396 | 75,862 | 17,041 | 547,860 |
| | Turnout % | 74.6 | Votes % | 53.6 | 29.5 | 13.8 | 3.1 | 100.0 |
| | | | Seats | 9 | 1 | 0 | 0 | 10 |
| | | | Candidates | 10 | 10 | 10 | 16 | 46 |
| | | | Change 01-97 | -3.6 | 1.6 | 3.7 | -1.7 | |

Amber Valley, Bolsover, Chesterfield, Derby North, Derby South, Derbyshire North East, Derbyshire South, Derbyshire West, Erewash, High Peak.

| DEVON | | | | Lab | C | LD | Other | Total |
|-------|--|--|--|-----|---|----|-------|-------|
| 2001 | Electorate | 827,458 | Votes | 128,599 | 212,576 | 173,639 | 30,182 | 544,996 |
| | Turnout % | 65.9 | Votes % | 23.6 | 39 | 31.9 | 5.5 | 100.0 |
| | Swing % | 2.25 | Seats | 3 | 4 | 4 | 0 | 11 |
| | Lab to C | | Candidates | 11 | 11 | 11 | 22 | 55 |
| 1997 | Electorate | 809,101 | Votes | 157,776 | 224,454 | 190,786 | 36,974 | 609,990 |
| | Turnout % | 75.4 | Votes % | 25.9 | 36.8 | 31.3 | 6.1 | 100.0 |
| | | | Seats | 3 | 5 | 3 | 0 | 11 |
| | | | Candidates | 11 | 11 | 11 | 36 | 69 |
| | | | Change 01-97 | -2.3 | 2.2 | 0.6 | -0.6 | |

Devon East, Devon North, Devon South West, Devon West & Torridge, Exeter, Plymouth Devonport, Plymouth Sutton, Teignbridge, Tiverton & Honiton, Torbay, Totnes.

| DORSET | | | | Lab | C | LD | Other | Total |
|--------|------|--------|-----------|--------|---------|---------|--------|---------|
| 2001 | Electorate | 542,703 | Votes | 72,715 | 156,222 | 108,426 | 7,339 | 344,702 |
| | Turnout % | 63.5 | Votes % | 21.1 | 45.3 | 31.5 | 2.1 | 100.0 |
| | Swing % | 6 | Seats | 1 | 6 | 1 | 0 | 8 |
| | Lab to C | | Candidates | 8 | 8 | 8 | 9 | 33 |
| 1997 | Electorate | 534,115 | Votes | 73,821 | 164,650 | 134,045 | 21,047 | 393,563 |
| | Turnout % | 73.7 | Votes % | 18.8 | 41.8 | 34.1 | 5.3 | 100.0 |
| | | | Seats | 0 | 8 | 0 | 0 | 8 |
| | | | Candidates | 8 | 8 | 8 | 19 | 43 |
| | | | Change 01-97 | 2.3 | 3.5 | -2.6 | -3.2 | |

Bournemouth East, Bournemouth West, Christchurch, Dorset Mid & Poole North, Dorset North, Dorset South, Dorset West, Poole.

| DURHAM | | | | Lab | C | LD | Other | Total |
|--------|------|--------|-----------|--------|---------|---------|--------|---------|
| 2001 | Electorate | 462,467 | Votes | 170,329 | 56,109 | 38,533 | 6,890 | 271,861 |
| | Turnout % | 58.8 | Votes % | 62.7 | 20.6 | 14.2 | 2.5 | 100.0 |
| | Swing % | 4.4 | Seats | 7 | 0 | 0 | 0 | 7 |
| | Lab to C | | Candidates | 7 | 7 | 7 | 11 | 32 |
| 1997 | Electorate | 463,722 | Votes | 223,242 | 57,441 | 31,496 | 13,608 | 325,787 |
| | Turnout % | 70.3 | Votes % | 68.5 | 17.6 | 9.7 | 4.2 | 100.0 |
| | | | Seats | 7 | 0 | 0 | 0 | 7 |
| | | | Candidates | 7 | 7 | 7 | 10 | 31 |
| | | | Change 01-97 | -5.8 | 3.0 | 4.5 | -1.7 | |

Bishop Auckland, Darlington, Durham North, Durham North West, Durham, City of, Easington, Sedgefield.

| ESSEX | | | | Lab | C | LD | Other | Total |
|-------|------|--------|-----------|--------|---------|---------|--------|---------|
| 2001 | Electorate | 1,237,422 | Votes | 255,526 | 315,589 | 122,663 | 42,884 | 736,662 |
| | Turnout % | 59.5 | Votes % | 34.7 | 42.8 | 16.7 | 5.8 | 100.0 |
| | Swing % | 2.1 | Seats | 5 | 11 | 1 | 0 | 17 |
| | Lab to C | | Candidates | 17 | 17 | 17 | 33 | 84 |
| 1997 | Electorate | 1,207,900 | Votes | 320,231 | 354,014 | 160,082 | 44,249 | 878,576 |
| | Turnout % | 72.7 | Votes % | 36.4 | 40.3 | 18.2 | 5 | 100.0 |
| | | | Seats | 6 | 10 | 1 | 0 | 17 |
| | | | Candidates | 17 | 17 | 17 | 36 | 87 |
| | | | Change 01-97 | -1.7 | 2.5 | -1.5 | 0.8 | |

Basildon, Billericay, Braintree, Brentwood & Ongar, Castle Point, Chelmsford West, Colchester, Epping Forest, Essex North, Harlow, Harwich, Maldon & Chelmsford East, Rayleigh, Rochford & Southend East, Saffron Walden, Southend West, Thurrock.

303

## NON-METROPOLITAN TABLES

| GLOUCESTERSHIRE | | | Lab | C | LD | Other | Total |
|---|---|---|---|---|---|---|---|
| 2001 | Electorate | 432,255 | Votes | 94,693 | 114,812 | 61,656 | 9,855 | 281,016 |
| | Turnout % | 65 | Votes % | 33.7 | 40.9 | 21.9 | 3.5 | 100.0 |
| | Swing % | 85 | Seats | 3 | 2 | 1 | 0 | 6 |
| | Lab to C | | Candidates | 6 | 6 | 6 | 14 | 32 |
| 1997 | Electorate | 423,132 | Votes | 109,689 | 127,593 | 72,971 | 13,765 | 324,018 |
| | Turnout % | 76.6 | Votes % | 33.9 | 39.4 | 22.5 | 4.2 | 100.0 |
| | | | Seats | 3 | 2 | 1 | 0 | 6 |
| | | | Candidates | 6 | 6 | 6 | 16 | 34 |
| | | | Change 01-97 | -0.2 | 1.5 | -0.6 | -0.7 | |

Cheltenham, Cotswold, Forest of Dean, Gloucester, Stroud, Tewkesbury.

| HAMPSHIRE | | | Lab | C | LD | Other | Total |
|---|---|---|---|---|---|---|---|
| 2001 | Electorate | 1,249,865 | Votes | 210,607 | 316,519 | 211,625 | 23,583 | 762,334 |
| | Turnout % | 61 | Votes % | 27.6 | 41.5 | 27.8 | 3.1 | 100.0 |
| | Swing % | 5 | Seats | 3 | 10 | 4 | 0 | 17 |
| | Lab to C | | Candidates | 17 | 17 | 17 | 32 | 83 |
| 1997 | Electorate | 1,223,687 | Votes | 253,445 | 369,213 | 226,992 | 45,825 | 895,475 |
| | Turnout % | 73.2 | Votes % | 28.3 | 41.2 | 25.3 | 5.1 | 100.0 |
| | | | Seats | 3 | 11 | 3 | 0 | 17 |
| | | | Candidates | 17 | 17 | 17 | 50 | 101 |
| | | | Change 01-97 | -0.7 | 0.3 | 2.5 | -2.0 | |

Aldershot, Basingstoke, Eastleigh, Fareham, Gosport, Hampshire East, Hampshire North East, Hampshire North West, Havant, New Forest East, New Forest West, Portsmouth North, Portsmouth South, Romsey, Southampton Itchen, Southampton Test, Winchester.

| HEREFORD AND WORCESTER | | | Lab | C | LD | Other | Total |
|---|---|---|---|---|---|---|---|
| 2001 | Electorate | 551,819 | Votes | 97,932 | 146,806 | 69,215 | 43,092 | 357,045 |
| | Turnout % | 64.7 | Votes % | 27.4 | 41.1 | 22.5 | 12.1 | 100.0 |
| | Swing % | 2.65 | Seats | 2 | 4 | 1 | 1 | 8 |
| | Lab to C | | Candidates | 8 | 8 | 7 | 14 | 37 |
| 1997 | Electorate | 539,832 | Votes | 132,541 | 166,848 | 89,060 | 18,449 | 406,898 |
| | Turnout % | 75.4 | Votes % | 32.6 | 41 | 21.9 | 4.5 | 100.0 |
| | | | Seats | 3 | 4 | 1 | 0 | 8 |
| | | | Candidates | 8 | 8 | 8 | 17 | 41 |
| | | | Change 01-97 | -5.2 | 0.1 | 0.6 | 7.6 | |

Bromsgrove, Hereford, Leominster, Redditch, Worcester, Worcestershire Mid, Worcestershire West, Wyre Forest.
* Herefordshire and Worcestershire are now separate counties but have been combined here for statistical purposes.

| HERTFORDSHIRE | | | Lab | C | LD | Other | Total |
|---|---|---|---|---|---|---|---|
| 2001 | Electorate | 772,313 | Votes | 188,308 | 202,569 | 81,899 | 11,828 | 484,604 |
| | Turnout % | 62.7 | Votes % | 38.9 | 41.8 | 16.9 | 2.4 | 100.0 |
| | Swing % | 1 | Seats | 5 | 6 | 0 | 0 | 11 |
| | Lab to C | | Candidates | 11 | 11 | 11 | 19 | 52 |
| 1997 | Electorate | 757,868 | Votes | 229,011 | 234,340 | 92,346 | 21,508 | 577,205 |
| | Turnout % | 76.2 | Votes % | 39.7 | 40.6 | 16 | 3.7 | 100.0 |
| | | | Seats | 5 | 6 | 0 | 0 | 11 |
| | | | Candidates | 11 | 11 | 11 | 27 | 60 |
| | | | Change 01-97 | -0.8 | 1.2 | 0.9 | -1.3 | |

Broxbourne, Hemel Hempstead, Hertford & Stortford, Hertfordshire North East, Hertfordshire South West, Hertsmere, Hitchin & Harpenden, St Albans, Stevenage, Watford, Welwyn Hatfield.

| HUMBERSIDE | | | Lab | C | LD | Other | Total |
|---|---|---|---|---|---|---|---|
| 2001 | Electorate | 661,889 | Votes | 173,958 | 122,005 | 63,664 | 12,528 | 372,155 |
| | Turnout % | 56.2 | Votes % | 46.7 | 32.8 | 17.1 | 3.4 | 100.0 |
| | Swing % | 3.05 | Seats | 7 | 3 | 0 | 0 | 10 |
| | Lab to C | | Candidates | 10 | 10 | 10 | 18 | 48 |
| 1997 | Electorate | 667,453 | Votes | 227,441 | 137,105 | 71,426 | 15,070 | 451,042 |
| | Turnout % | 67.6 | Votes % | 50.4 | 30.4 | 15.8 | 3.3 | 100.0 |
| | | | Seats | 7 | 3 | 0 | 0 | 10 |
| | | | Candidates | 10 | 10 | 10 | 18 | 48 |
| | | | Change 01-97 | -3.7 | 2.4 | 1.3 | 0.1 | |

Beverley & Holderness, Brigg & Goole, Cleethorpes, Great Grimsby, Haltemprice & Howden, Hull East, Hull North, Hull West & Hessle, Scunthorpe, Yorkshire East.

| KENT | | | Lab | C | LD | Other | Total |
|---|---|---|---|---|---|---|---|
| 2001 | Electorate | 1,172,536 | Votes | 261,458 | 301,364 | 109,216 | 24,317 | 715,269 |
| | Turnout % | 61 | Votes % | 36.6 | 42.1 | 15.3 | 3.4 | 100.0 |
| | Swing % | 2.7 | Seats | 9 | 8 | 0 | 0 | 17 |
| | Lab to C | | Candidates | 17 | 17 | 17 | 31 | 82 |
| 1997 | Electorate | 1,161,137 | Votes | 317,762 | 346,885 | 145,896 | 45,998 | 856,541 |
| | Turnout % | 73.4 | Votes % | 37.1 | 40.5 | 17.0 | 5.4 | 100.0 |
| | | | Seats | 8 | 9 | 0 | 0 | 17 |
| | | | Candidates | 17 | 17 | 17 | 57 | 108 |
| | | | Change 01-97 | -0.5 | 1.6 | -1.7 | -2.0 | |

Ashford, Canterbury, Chatham & Aylesford, Dartford, Dover, Faversham & Kent Mid, Folkestone & Hythe, Gillingham, Gravesham, Maidstone & The Weald, Medway, Sevenoaks, Sittingbourne & Sheppey, Thanet North, Thanet South, Tonbridge & Malling, Tunbridge Wells.

| LANCASHIRE | | | Lab | C | LD | Other | Total |
|---|---|---|---|---|---|---|---|
| 2001 | Electorate | 1,077,238 | Votes | 298,739 | 232,697 | 84,827 | 22,818 | 639,081 |
| | Turnout % | 59.3 | Votes % | 46.7 | 36.4 | 13.3 | 3.6 | 100.0 |
| | Swing % | 2.2 | Seats | 13 | 2 | 0 | 0 | 15 |
| | Lab to C | | Candidates | 15 | 15 | 15 | 22 | 67 |
| 1997 | Electorate | 1,073,348 | Votes | 382,476 | 265,819 | 98,744 | 30,445 | 777,484 |
| | Turnout % | 72.4 | Votes % | 49.2 | 34.2 | 12.7 | 3.9 | 100.0 |
| | | | Seats | 13 | 2 | 0 | 0 | 15 |
| | | | Candidates | 15 | 15 | 15 | 33 | 78 |
| | | | Change 01-97 | -2.5 | 2.2 | 0.6 | -0.3 | |

Blackburn, Blackpool North & Fleetwood, Blackpool South, Burnley, Chorley, Fylde, Hyndburn, Lancashire West, Lancaster & Wyre, Morecambe & Lunesdale, Pendle, Preston, Ribble South, Ribble Valley, Rossendale & Darwen.

| LEICESTERSHIRE | | | Lab | C | LD | Other | Total |
|---|---|---|---|---|---|---|---|
| 2001 | Electorate | 706,439 | Votes | 182,290 | 167,748 | 74,964 | 14,779 | 439,781 |
| | Turnout % | 62.3 | Votes % | 41.5 | 38.1 | 17 | 3.4 | 100.0 |
| | Swing % | 1.8 | Seats | 5 | 5 | 0 | 0 | 10 |
| | Lab to C | | Candidates | 10 | 10 | 10 | 17 | 47 |
| 1997 | Electorate | 686,196 | Votes | 221,422 | 185,787 | 76,500 | 21,667 | 505,376 |
| | Turnout % | 73.6 | Votes % | 43.8 | 36.8 | 15.1 | 4.3 | 100.0 |
| | | | Seats | 5 | 5 | 0 | 0 | 10 |
| | | | Candidates | 10 | 10 | 10 | 23 | 53 |
| | | | Change 01-97 | -2.3 | 1.3 | 1.9 | -0.9 | |

Blaby, Bosworth, Charnwood, Harborough, Leicester East, Leicester South, Leicester West, Leicestershire North West, Loughborough, Rutland & Melton.

## NON-METROPOLITAN TABLES

| LINCOLNSHIRE | | | | Lab | C | LD | Other | Total |
|---|---|---|---|---|---|---|---|---|
| 2001 | Electorate | 495,636 | Votes | 109,150 | 141,109 | 49,225 | 5,943 | 305,427 |
| | Turnout % | 61.6 | Votes % | 35.7 | 46.2 | 16.1 | 1.9 | 100.0 |
| | Swing % | 2.5 | Seats | 1 | 6 | 0 | 0 | 7 |
| | Lab to C | | Candidates | 7 | 7 | 7 | 6 | 27 |
| 1997 | Electorate | 479,476 | Votes | 128,147 | 147,196 | 60,923 | 10,880 | 347,146 |
| | Turnout % | 72.4 | Votes % | 36.9 | 42.4 | 17.5 | 3.1 | 100.0 |
| | | | Seats | 1 | 6 | 0 | 0 | 7 |
| | | | Candidates | 7 | 7 | 7 | 10 | 31 |
| | | | Change 01-97 | -1.2 | 3.8 | -1.4 | -1.2 | |

Boston & Skegness, Gainsborough, Grantham & Stamford, Lincoln, Louth & Horncastle, Sleaford & North Hykeham, South Holland & The Deepings.

| NORFOLK | | | | Lab | C | LD | Other | Total |
|---|---|---|---|---|---|---|---|---|
| 2001 | Electorate | 608,806 | Votes | 141,129 | 165,174 | 78,050 | 13,068 | 397,421 |
| | Turnout % | 65.3 | Votes % | 35.5 | 41.6 | 19.6 | 3.3 | 100.0 |
| | Swing % | 4.65 | Seats | 3 | 4 | 1 | 0 | 8 |
| | Lab to C | | Candidates | 8 | 8 | 8 | 16 | 40 |
| 1997 | Electorate | 600,137 | Votes | 179,504 | 165,055 | 81,817 | 23,123 | 449,499 |
| | Turnout % | 74.9 | Votes % | 39.9 | 36.7 | 18.2 | 5.1 | 100.0 |
| | | | Seats | 4 | 4 | 0 | 0 | 8 |
| | | | Candidates | 8 | 8 | 8 | 17 | 41 |
| | | | Change 01-97 | -4.4 | 4.9 | 1.4 | -1.8 | |

Great Yarmouth, Norfolk Mid, Norfolk North, Norfolk North West, Norfolk South, Norfolk South West, Norwich North, Norwich South.

| NORTHAMPTONSHIRE | | | | Lab | C | LD | Other | Total |
|---|---|---|---|---|---|---|---|---|
| 2001 | Electorate | 475,322 | Votes | 131,835 | 123,986 | 37,831 | 7,535 | 301,187 |
| | Turnout % | 63.4 | Votes % | 43.8 | 41.2 | 12.6 | 2.5 | 100.0 |
| | Swing % | 1 | Seats | 5 | 1 | 0 | 0 | 6 |
| | Lab to C | | Candidates | 6 | 6 | 6 | 10 | 28 |
| 1997 | Electorate | 452,559 | Votes | 152,090 | 136,488 | 37,550 | 11,628 | 337,756 |
| | Turnout % | 74.6 | Votes % | 45 | 40.4 | 11.1 | 3.4 | 100.0 |
| | | | Seats | 5 | 1 | 0 | 0 | 6 |
| | | | Candidates | 6 | 6 | 6 | 15 | 33 |
| | | | Change 01-97 | -1.2 | 0.8 | 1.5 | -0.9 | |

Corby, Daventry, Kettering, Northampton North, Northampton South, Wellingborough.

| NORTHUMBERLAND | | | | Lab | C | LD | Other | Total |
|---|---|---|---|---|---|---|---|---|
| 2001 | Electorate | 242,988 | Votes | 65,067 | 39,368 | 41,986 | 4,269 | 150,690 |
| | Turnout % | 62 | Votes % | 43.2 | 26.1 | 27.9 | 2.8 | 100.0 |
| | Swing % | 4.45 | Seats | 2 | 1 | 1 | 0 | 4 |
| | Lab to C | | Candidates | 4 | 4 | 4 | 5 | 17 |
| 1997 | Electorate | 240,101 | Votes | 85,289 | 39,722 | 43,708 | 6,409 | 175,128 |
| | Turnout % | 72.9 | Votes % | 48.7 | 22.7 | 25 | 3.7 | 100.0 |
| | | | Seats | 2 | 1 | 1 | 0 | 4 |
| | | | Candidates | 4 | 4 | 4 | 6 | 18 |
| | | | Change 01-97 | -5.5 | 3.4 | 2.9 | -0.9 | |

Berwick-upon-Tweed, Blyth Valley, Hexham, Wansbeck.

| NOTTINGHAMSHIRE | | | Lab | C | LD | Other | Total |
|---|---|---|---|---|---|---|---|
| 2001 | Electorate | 785,231 | Votes | 221,348 | 165,958 | 61,774 | 9,295 | 458,375 |
| | Turnout % | 58.4 | Votes % | 48.3 | 36.2 | 13.5 | 2 | 100.0 |
| | Swing % | 3.25 | Seats | 8 | 3 | 0 | 0 | 11 |
| | Lab to C | | Candidates | 11 | 11 | 11 | 10 | 43 |
| 1997 | Electorate | 779,254 | Votes | 302,419 | 169,979 | 60,464 | 23,673 | 556,535 |
| | Turnout % | 72 | Votes % | 54.3 | 30.5 | 10.9 | 4.3 | 100.0 |
| | | | Seats | 10 | 1 | 0 | 0 | 11 |
| | | | Candidates | 11 | 11 | 11 | 17 | 50 |
| | | | Change 01-97 | -6.0 | 5.7 | 2.6 | -2.3 | |

Ashfield, Bassetlaw, Broxtowe, Gedling, Mansfield, Newark, Nottingham East, Nottingham North, Nottingham South, Rushcliffe, Sherwood.

| OXFORDSHIRE | | | Lab | C | LD | Other | Total |
|---|---|---|---|---|---|---|---|
| 2001 | Electorate | 457,562 | Votes | 84,269 | 108,296 | 78,007 | 15,092 | 285,664 |
| | Turnout % | 62.4 | Votes % | 29.5 | 37.9 | 27.3 | 5.3 | 100.0 |
| | Swing % | 1.05 | Seats | 1 | 4 | 1 | 0 | 6 |
| | Lab to C | | Candidates | 6 | 6 | 6 | 19 | 37 |
| 1997 | Electorate | 437,725 | Votes | 105,131 | 126,100 | 81,832 | 18,459 | 331,522 |
| | Turnout % | 75.7 | Votes % | 31.7 | 38 | 24.7 | 5.6 | 100.0 |
| | | | Seats | 1 | 4 | 1 | 0 | 6 |
| | | | Candidates | 6 | 6 | 6 | 26 | 44 |
| | | | Change 01-97 | -2.2 | -0.1 | 2.6 | -0.3 | |

Banbury, Henley, Oxford East, Oxford West & Abingdon, Wantage, Witney.

| SHROPSHIRE | | | Lab | C | LD | Other | Total |
|---|---|---|---|---|---|---|---|
| 2001 | Electorate | 337,056 | Votes | 80,814 | 82,711 | 39,459 | 8,934 | 211,918 |
| | Turnout % | 62.9 | Votes % | 38.1 | 39 | 18.6 | 4.2 | 100.0 |
| | Swing % | 1.7 | Seats | 3 | 1 | 1 | 0 | 5 |
| | Lab to C | | Candidates | 5 | 5 | 5 | 10 | 25 |
| 1997 | Electorate | 321,345 | Votes | 93,463 | 87,561 | 48,229 | 6,274 | 235,527 |
| | Turnout % | 73.3 | Votes % | 39.7 | 37.2 | 20.5 | 2.7 | 100.0 |
| | | | Seats | 3 | 2 | 0 | 0 | 5 |
| | | | Candidates | 5 | 5 | 5 | 8 | 23 |
| | | | Change 01-97 | -1.6 | 1.8 | -1.9 | 1.5 | |

Ludlow, Shrewsbury & Atcham, Shropshire North, Telford, Wrekin The.

| SOMERSET | | | Lab | C | LD | Other | Total |
|---|---|---|---|---|---|---|---|
| 2001 | Electorate | 380,887 | Votes | 42,162 | 104,502 | 101,080 | 7,458 | 255,202 |
| | Turnout % | 67 | Votes % | 16.5 | 40.9 | 39.6 | 2.9 | 100.0 |
| | Swing % | 2.65 | Seats | 0 | 3 | 2 | 0 | 5 |
| | Lab to C | | Candidates | 5 | 5 | 5 | 9 | 24 |
| 1997 | Electorate | 373,152 | Votes | 49,409 | 103,503 | 115,155 | 15,402 | 283,469 |
| | Turnout % | 76 | Votes % | 17.4 | 36.5 | 40.6 | 5.4 | 100.0 |
| | | | Seats | 0 | 2 | 3 | 0 | 5 |
| | | | Candidates | 5 | 5 | 5 | 11 | 26 |
| | | | Change 01-97 | -0.9 | 4.4 | -1.0 | -2.5 | |

Bridgwater, Somerton & Frome, Taunton, Wells, Yeovil.

## NON-METROPOLITAN TABLES

| STAFFORDSHIRE | | | | Lab | C | LD | Other | Total |
|---|---|---|---|---|---|---|---|---|
| 2001 | Electorate | 808,992 | Votes | 229,216 | 171,434 | 59,678 | 17,086 | 477,414 |
| | Turnout % | 59 | Votes % | 48 | 35.9 | 12.5 | 3.6 | 100.0 |
| | Swing % | 2.75 | Seats | 9 | 3 | 0 | 0 | 12 |
| | Lab to C | | Candidates | 12 | 12 | 12 | 14 | 50 |
| 1997 | Electorate | 805,473 | Votes | 301,258 | 197,643 | 63,030 | 24,746 | 586,677 |
| | Turnout % | 72.8 | Votes % | 51.3 | 33.7 | 10.7 | 4.2 | 100.0 |
| | | | Seats | 9 | 3 | 0 | 0 | 12 |
| | | | Candidates | 12 | 12 | 12 | 26 | 62 |
| | | | Change 01-97 | -3.3 | 2.2 | 1.8 | -0.6 | |

Burton, Cannock Chase, Lichfield, Newcastle-under-Lyme, Stafford, Staffordshire Moorlands, Staffordshire South, Stoke-on-Trent Central, Stoke-on-Trent North, Stoke-on-Trent South, Stone, Tamworth.

| SUFFOLK | | | | Lab | C | LD | Other | Total |
|---|---|---|---|---|---|---|---|---|
| 2001 | Electorate | 510,720 | Votes | 127,762 | 130,802 | 51,370 | 11,612 | 321,546 |
| | Turnout % | 63 | Votes % | 39.7 | 40.7 | 16 | 3.6 | 100.0 |
| | Swing % | 1.8 | Seats | 2 | 5 | 0 | 0 | 7 |
| | Lab to C | | Candidates | 7 | 7 | 7 | 13 | 34 |
| 1997 | Electorate | 496,632 | Votes | 149,090 | 139,400 | 65,246 | 16,898 | 370,634 |
| | Turnout % | 74.6 | Votes % | 40.2 | 37.6 | 17.6 | 4.6 | 100.0 |
| | | | Seats | 2 | 5 | 0 | 0 | 7 |
| | | | Candidates | 7 | 7 | 7 | 14 | 35 |
| | | | Change 01-97 | -0.5 | 3.1 | -1.6 | -1.0 | |

Bury St Edmunds, Ipswich, Suffolk Central & Ipswich North, Suffolk Coastal, Suffolk South, Suffolk West, Waveney.

| SURREY | | | | Lab | C | LD | Other | Total |
|---|---|---|---|---|---|---|---|---|
| 2001 | Electorate | 797,143 | Votes | 107,897 | 236,024 | 133,636 | 17,878 | 495,435 |
| | Turnout % | 62.2 | Votes % | 21.8 | 47.6 | 27 | 3.6 | 100.0 |
| | Swing % | 5 | Seats | 0 | 10 | 1 | 0 | 11 |
| | Lab to C | | Candidates | 11 | 11 | 11 | 15 | 48 |
| 1997 | Electorate | 786,842 | Votes | 130,916 | 271,690 | 144,132 | 40,996 | 587,734 |
| | Turnout % | 74.7 | Votes % | 22.3 | 46.2 | 24.5 | 7 | 100.0 |
| | | | Seats | 0 | 11 | 0 | 0 | 11 |
| | | | Candidates | 11 | 11 | 11 | 34 | 67 |
| | | | Change 01-97 | -0.5 | 1.4 | 2.5 | -3.4 | |

Epsom & Ewell, Esher & Walton, Guildford, Mole Valley, Reigate, Runnymede & Weybridge, Spelthorne, Surrey East, Surrey Heath, Surrey South West, Woking.

| SUSSEX EAST | | | | Lab | C | LD | Other | Total |
|---|---|---|---|---|---|---|---|---|
| 2001 | Electorate | 570,534 | Votes | 105,937 | 138,652 | 84,232 | 22,053 | 350,874 |
| | Turnout % | 61.5 | Votes % | 30.2 | 39.5 | 24 | 6.3 | 100.0 |
| | Swing % | -.45 | Seats | 4 | 3 | 1 | 0 | 8 |
| | Lab to C | | Candidates | 8 | 8 | 8 | 28 | 52 |
| 1997 | Electorate | 552,772 | Votes | 117,400 | 158,427 | 96,606 | 29,769 | 402,202 |
| | Turnout % | 72.8 | Votes % | 29.2 | 39.4 | 24 | 7.4 | 100.0 |
| | | | Seats | 4 | 3 | 1 | 0 | 8 |
| | | | Candidates | 8 | 8 | 8 | 29 | 53 |
| | | | Change 01-97 | 1.0 | 0.1 | 0.0 | -1.1 | |

Bexhill & Battle, Brighton Kemptown, Brighton Pavilion, Eastbourne, Hastings & Rye, Hove, Lewes, Wealden.

| SUSSEX WEST | | | Lab | C | LD | Other | Total |
|---|---|---|---|---|---|---|---|
| 2001 | Electorate | 581,733 | Votes | 92,261 | 164,009 | 82,152 | 18,338 | 356,760 |
| | Turnout % | 61.3 | Votes % | 25.9 | 46 | 23 | 5.1 | 100.0 |
| | Swing % | -.15 | Seats | 1 | 7 | 0 | 0 | 8 |
| | Lab to C | | Candidates | 8 | 8 | 8 | 17 | 41 |
| 1997 | Electorate | 563,966 | Votes | 101,289 | 186,569 | 106,987 | 22,770 | 417,615 |
| | Turnout % | 74 | Votes % | 24.3 | 44.7 | 25.6 | 5.5 | 100.0 |
| | | | Seats | 1 | 7 | 0 | 0 | 8 |
| | | | Candidates | 8 | 8 | 8 | 17 | 41 |
| | | | Change 01-97 | 1.6 | 1.3 | -2.6 | -0.4 | |

Arundel & South Downs, Bognor Regis & Littlehampton, Chichester, Crawley, Horsham, Sussex Mid, Worthing East & Shoreham, Worthing West.

| WARWICKSHIRE | | | Lab | C | LD | Other | Total |
|---|---|---|---|---|---|---|---|
| 2001 | Electorate | 392,339 | Votes | 106,093 | 98,531 | 39,084 | 6,262 | 249,970 |
| | Turnout % | 63.7 | Votes % | 42.4 | 39.4 | 15.6 | 2.5 | 100.0 |
| | Swing % | 1.05 | Seats | 4 | 1 | 0 | 0 | 5 |
| | Lab to C | | Candidates | 5 | 5 | 5 | 7 | 22 |
| 1997 | Electorate | 384,826 | Votes | 127,606 | 112,619 | 40,503 | 10,419 | 291,147 |
| | Turnout % | 75.7 | Votes % | 43.8 | 38.7 | 13.9 | 3.6 | 100.0 |
| | | | Seats | 4 | 1 | 0 | 0 | 5 |
| | | | Candidates | 5 | 5 | 5 | 17 | 32 |
| | | | Change 01-97 | -1.4 | 0.7 | 1.7 | -1.1 | |

Nuneaton, Rugby & Kenilworth, Stratford-on-Avon, Warwick & Leamington, Warwickshire North.

| WILTSHIRE | | | Lab | C | LD | Other | Total |
|---|---|---|---|---|---|---|---|
| 2001 | Electorate | 460,043 | Votes | 85,496 | 124,260 | 73,853 | 11,531 | 295,140 |
| | Turnout % | 64.2 | Votes % | 29 | 42.1 | 25 | 3.9 | 100.0 |
| | Swing % | 45 | Seats | 2 | 4 | 0 | 0 | 6 |
| | Lab to C | | Candidates | 6 | 6 | 6 | 11 | 29 |
| 1997 | Electorate | 446,636 | Votes | 92,995 | 133,788 | 87,156 | 18,532 | 332,471 |
| | Turnout % | 74.4 | Votes % | 28 | 40.2 | 26.2 | 5.6 | 100.0 |
| | | | Seats | 2 | 4 | 0 | 0 | 6 |
| | | | Candidates | 6 | 6 | 6 | 19 | 37 |
| | | | Change 01-97 | 1.0 | 1.9 | -1.2 | -1.7 | |

Devizes, Salisbury, Swindon North, Swindon South, Westbury, Wiltshire North.

| YORKSHIRE NORTH | | | Lab | C | LD | Other | Total |
|---|---|---|---|---|---|---|---|
| 2001 | Electorate | 579,192 | Votes | 110,412 | 162,679 | 87,841 | 12,571 | 373,503 |
| | Turnout % | 64.5 | Votes % | 29.6 | 43.6 | 23.5 | 3.4 | 100.0 |
| | Swing % | 3.4 | Seats | 3 | 4 | 1 | 0 | 8 |
| | Lab to C | | Candidates | 8 | 8 | 8 | 15 | 39 |
| 1997 | Electorate | 567,933 | Votes | 138,046 | 168,210 | 96,941 | 17,578 | 420,775 |
| | Turnout % | 74.1 | Votes % | 32.8 | 40 | 23 | 4.2 | 100.0 |
| | | | Seats | 3 | 4 | 1 | 0 | 8 |
| | | | Candidates | 8 | 8 | 8 | 14 | 38 |
| | | | Change 01-97 | -3.2 | 3.6 | 0.5 | -0.8 | |

Harrogate & Knaresborough, Richmond (Yorks), Ryedale, Scarborough & Whitby, Selby, Skipton & Ripon, Vale of York, York City of.

# SCOTLAND

T HE most recent Conservative Government undertook a major review of Scottish local government. Labour has placed a Scottish Parliament on top of these authorities. Scotland still has 72 parliamentary constituencies; it should have between 56 and 60 if the same population rules applying to England or the United Kingdom as a whole were followed. At some point, a sharp reduction in the number of Scottish Members will be the unavoidable consequence of devolution. That moment is not expected to arrive, however, until after the next general election.

This analysis compares results in the seven major Scottish regions with those recorded four years ago. The statistics for Orkney and Shetland and the Western Isles (the two minor regions) are presented in the constituency section.

| BORDERS AND LOTHIAN | | | | Lab | C | LD | Nat | Other | Total |
|---|---|---|---|---|---|---|---|---|---|
| 2001 | Electorate | 699,639 | Votes | 170,731 | 70,103 | 93,757 | 73,693 | 4,667 | 412,951 |
| | Turnout % | 59 | Votes % | 41.3 | 17 | 22.7 | 8.9 | 1.1 | 100.0 |
| | Swing % | -.6 | Seats | 9 | 0 | 3 | 0 | 0 | 12 |
| | Lab to C | | Candidates | 12 | 12 | 12 | 24 | 10 | 70 |
| 1997 | Electorate | 685,340 | Votes | 214,150 | 98,983 | 89,953 | 87,808 | 8,216 | 499,110 |
| | Turnout % | 72.8 | Votes % | 42.9 | 19.8 | 18 | 17.6 | 1.6 | 100.0 |
| | | | Seats | 9 | 0 | 3 | 0 | 0 | 12 |
| | | | Candidates | 12 | 12 | 12 | 12 | 26 | 74 |
| | | | Change 01-97 | -1.6 | -2.8 | 4.7 | -8.7 | -0.5 | |

East Lothian, Edinburgh Central, Edinburgh East & Musselburgh, Edinburgh North & Leith, Edinburgh Pentlands, Edinburgh South, Edinburgh West, Linlithgow, Livingston, Midlothian, Roxburgh & Berwickshire, Tweeddale Ettrick & Lauderdale.

| CENTRAL AND TAYSIDE | | | | Lab | C | LD | Nat | Other | Total |
|---|---|---|---|---|---|---|---|---|---|
| 2001 | Electorate | 514,308 | Votes | 118,695 | 57,348 | 32,291 | 96,535 | 3,903 | 308,772 |
| | Turnout % | 60 | Votes % | 38.4 | 18.6 | 10.5 | 15.6 | 1.3 | 100.0 |
| | Swing % | -.9 | Seats | 6 | 0 | 0 | 3 | 0 | 6 |
| | Lab to C | | Candidates | 9 | 9 | 9 | 18 | 7 | 52 |
| 1997 | Electorate | 515,858 | Votes | 150,708 | 82,266 | 25,073 | 116,976 | 4,239 | 379,262 |
| | Turnout % | 73.5 | Votes % | 39.7 | 21.7 | 6.6 | 30.8 | 1.1 | 100.0 |
| | | | Seats | 6 | 0 | 0 | 3 | 0 | 6 |
| | | | Candidates | 9 | 9 | 9 | 9 | 14 | 50 |
| | | | Change 01-97 | -1.3 | -3.1 | 3.9 | -15.2 | 0.2 | |

Angus, Dundee East, Dundee West, Falkirk East, Falkirk West, Ochil, Perth, Stirling, Tayside North.

| DUMFRIES AND GALLOWAY | | | | Lab | C | LD | Nat | Other | Total |
|---|---|---|---|---|---|---|---|---|---|
| 2001 | Electorate | 115,687 | Votes | 28,088 | 24,218 | 8,653 | 17,541 | 3,903 | 78,500 |
| | Turnout % | 67.9 | Votes % | 35.8 | 30.9 | 11 | 11.2 | 1.3 | 100.0 |
| | Swing % | -.45 | Seats | 1 | 1 | 0 | 0 | 0 | 2 |
| | Lab to C | | Candidates | 2 | 2 | 2 | 4 | 7 | 10 |
| 1997 | Electorate | 115,510 | Votes | 30,389 | 26,710 | 8,187 | 24,426 | 1,833 | 91,545 |
| | Turnout % | 79.3 | Votes % | 33.2 | 29.2 | 8.9 | 26.7 | 2 | 100.0 |
| | | | Seats | 1 | 0 | 0 | 1 | 0 | 2 |
| | | | Candidates | 2 | 2 | 2 | 2 | 5 | 13 |
| | | | Change 01-97 | 2.6 | 1.7 | 2.1 | -15.5 | -0.7 | |

Dumfries, Galloway & Upper Nithsdale.

| FIFE | | | Lab | C | LD | Nat | Other | Total |
|------|------|------|------|------|------|------|------|------|
| 2001 | Electorate | 280,160 | Votes | 73,344 | 19,558 | 30,663 | 31,680 | 1,177 | 156,422 |
| | Turnout % | 55.8 | Votes % | 46.9 | 12.5 | 19.6 | 10.1 | .8 | 100.0 |
| | Swing % | -.7 | Seats | 4 | 0 | 1 | 0 | 0 | 5 |
| | Lab to C | | Candidates | 5 | 5 | 5 | 10 | 3 | 28 |
| 1997 | Electorate | 273,834 | Votes | 90,722 | 27,786 | 34,200 | 35,438 | 2,448 | 190,594 |
| | Turnout % | 69.6 | Votes % | 47.6 | 14.6 | 17.9 | 18.6 | 1.3 | 100.0 |
| | | | Seats | 4 | 0 | 1 | 0 | 0 | 5 |
| | | | Candidates | 5 | 5 | 5 | 5 | 5 | 25 |
| | | | Change 01-97 | -0.7 | -2.1 | 1.7 | -8.5 | -0.5 | |

Dunfermline East, Dunfermline West, Fife Central, Fife North East, Kirkcaldy.

| GRAMPIAN | | | Lab | C | LD | Nat | Other | Total |
|------|------|------|------|------|------|------|------|------|
| 2001 | Electorate | 397,431 | Votes | 61,972 | 47,525 | 60,274 | 59,446 | 1,403 | 230,620 |
| | Turnout % | 58 | Votes % | 26.9 | 20.6 | 26.1 | 12.9 | .6 | 100.0 |
| | Swing % | -2.85 | Seats | 3 | 0 | 2 | 2 | 0 | 5 |
| | Lab to C | | Candidates | 7 | 7 | 7 | 14 | 3 | 38 |
| 1997 | Electorate | 403,734 | Votes | 72,581 | 70,937 | 63,998 | 71,457 | 4,498 | 283,471 |
| | Turnout % | 70.2 | Votes % | 25.6 | 25 | 22.6 | 25.2 | 1.6 | 100.0 |
| | | | Seats | 3 | 0 | 2 | 2 | 0 | 5 |
| | | | Candidates | 7 | 7 | 7 | 7 | 7 | 35 |
| | | | Change 01-97 | 1.3 | -4.4 | 3.5 | -12.3 | -1.0 | |

Aberdeen Central, Aberdeen North, Aberdeen South, Aberdeenshire West & Kincardine, Banff & Buchan, Gordon, Moray.

| HIGHLAND | | | Lab | C | LD | Nat | Other | Total |
|------|------|------|------|------|------|------|------|------|
| 2001 | Electorate | 218,602 | Votes | 37,150 | 16,633 | 45,061 | 31,569 | 1,619 | 132,032 |
| | Turnout % | 60.4 | Votes % | 28.1 | 12.6 | 34.1 | 12 | 1.2 | 100.0 |
| | Swing % | 1.7 | Seats | 2 | 0 | 3 | 0 | 0 | 5 |
| | Lab to C | | Candidates | 5 | 5 | 5 | 10 | 4 | 29 |
| 1997 | Electorate | 218,180 | Votes | 48,492 | 19,469 | 45,455 | 36,382 | 3,868 | 153,666 |
| | Turnout % | 70.4 | Votes % | 31.6 | 12.7 | 29.6 | 23.7 | 2.5 | 100.0 |
| | | | Seats | 2 | 0 | 3 | 0 | 0 | 5 |
| | | | Candidates | 5 | 5 | 5 | 5 | 12 | 32 |
| | | | Change 01-97 | -3.5 | -0.1 | 4.5 | -11.7 | -1.3 | |

Caithness Sutherland & Easter Ross, Inverness East Nairn & Lochaber, Orkney & Shetland, Ross Skye & Inverness West, Western Isles.

| STRATHCLYDE | | | Lab | C | LD | Nat | Other | Total |
|------|------|------|------|------|------|------|------|------|
| 2001 | Electorate | 1,755,147 | Votes | 511,193 | 125,173 | 107,326 | 229,337 | 21,259 | 994,288 |
| | Turnout % | 56.6 | Votes % | 52.7 | 12.9 | 11.1 | 11.1 | 2.1 | 100.0 |
| | Swing % | 5 | Seats | 30 | 0 | 1 | 0 | 1 | 32 |
| | Lab to C | | Candidates | 31 | 31 | 31 | 67 | 20 | 180 |
| 1997 | Electorate | 1,733,657 | Votes | 676,311 | 166,908 | 98,493 | 249,773 | 28,306 | 1,219,791 |
| | Turnout % | 70.4 | Votes % | 55.4 | 13.7 | 8.1 | 20.5 | 2.3 | 100.0 |
| | | | Seats | 31 | 0 | 1 | 0 | 0 | 32 |
| | | | Candidates | 32 | 32 | 32 | 32 | 74 | 202 |
| | | | Change 01-97 | -2.7 | -0.8 | 3.0 | -9.4 | -0.2 | |

Airdrie & Shotts, Argyll & Bute, Ayr, Carrick Cumnock & Doon Valley, Clydebank & Milngavie, Clydesdale, Coatbridge & Chryston, Cumbernauld & Kilsyth, Cunninghame North, Cunninghame South, Dumbarton, East Kilbride, Eastwood, Glasgow Anniesland, Glasgow Baillieston, Glasgow Cathcart, Glasgow Govan, Glasgow Kelvin, Glasgow Maryhill, Glasgow Pollock, Glasgow Rutherglen, Glasgow Shettleston, Glasgow Springburn, Greenock & Inverclyde, Hamilton North & Bellshill, Hamilton South, Kilmarnock & Loudoun, Motherwell & Wishaw, Paisley North, Paisley South, Renfrewshire West, Strathkelvin & Bearsden.

311

# WALES

T HE introduction of a National Assembly for Wales completed a fundamental reform of local government in the Principality. There are 22 unitary authorities in Wales which can be collected together under eight different counties for administrative and analytical purposes.

The Welsh Labour Party endured a tortured period during the first three years of the previous Parliament. The referendum on devolution was carried by a mere whisper, Ron Davies, Secretary of State for Wales and Labour's candidate for leader of the Assembly, was obliged to resign in embarrassing circumstances. Alun Michael then became First Minister only after a bitter and controversial contest with Rhodri Morgan. Labour performed poorly in the 1999 Assembly elections and Mr Michael was driven from office nine months later. In the circumstances, therefore, Labour will be relieved that the results for 2001 and 1997, outlined below, were ultimately very similar.

| CLWYD | | | Lab | C | LD | Nat | Other | Total |
|---|---|---|---|---|---|---|---|---|
| 2001 | Electorate | 324,562 | Votes | 99,106 | 56,317 | 25,485 | 15,962 | 3,677 | 200,547 |
| | Turnout % | 61.8 | Votes % | 49.4 | 28.1 | 12.7 | 8 | 1.8 | 100.0 |
| | Swing % | 2.95 | Seats | 6 | 0 | 0 | 0 | 0 | 6 |
| | Lab to C | | Candidates | 6 | 6 | 6 | 6 | 8 | 32 |
| 1997 | Electorate | 321,905 | Votes | 127,141 | 62,670 | 25,329 | 13,688 | 8,056 | 236,884 |
| | Turnout % | 73.6 | Votes % | 53.7 | 26.5 | 10.7 | 5.8 | 3.4 | 100.0 |
| | | | Seats | 6 | 0 | 0 | 0 | 0 | 6 |
| | | | Candidates | 6 | 6 | 6 | 6 | 9 | 33 |
| | | | Change 01-97 | -4.3 | 1.6 | 2.0 | 2.2 | -1.6 | |

Alyn & Deeside, Clwyd South, Clwyd West, Delyn, Vale of Clwyd, Wrexham.

| DYFED | | | Lab | C | LD | Nat | Other | Total |
|---|---|---|---|---|---|---|---|---|
| 2001 | Electorate | 279,102 | Votes | 67,019 | 38,155 | 22,307 | 52,105 | 2,964 | 182,550 |
| | Turnout % | 65.4 | Votes % | 36.7 | 20.9 | 12.2 | 28.5 | 1.6 | 100.0 |
| | Swing % | 5.05 | Seats | 3 | 0 | 0 | 2 | 0 | 3 |
| | Lab to C | | Candidates | 5 | 5 | 5 | 5 | 7 | 27 |
| 1997 | Electorate | 275,592 | Votes | 92,958 | 39,084 | 22,597 | 47,082 | 6,452 | 208,173 |
| | Turnout % | 75.5 | Votes % | 44.7 | 18.8 | 10.9 | 22.6 | 3.1 | 100.0 |
| | | | Seats | 4 | 0 | 0 | 1 | 0 | 4 |
| | | | Candidates | 5 | 5 | 5 | 5 | 6 | 26 |
| | | | Change 01-97 | -8.0 | 2.1 | 1.3 | 5.9 | -1.5 | |

Carmarthen East & Dinefwr, Carmarthen West & Pembrokeshire South, Ceredigion, Llanelli, Preseli Pembrokeshire.

| GLAMORGAN MID | | | Lab | C | LD | Nat | Other | Total |
|---|---|---|---|---|---|---|---|---|
| 2001 | Electorate | 407,397 | Votes | 144,304 | 28,143 | 23,460 | 36,883 | 4,351 | 237,141 |
| | Turnout % | 58.2 | Votes % | 60.9 | 11.9 | 9.9 | 15.6 | 1.8 | 100.0 |
| | Swing % | 4.6 | Seats | 7 | 0 | 0 | 0 | 0 | 7 |
| | Lab to C | | Candidates | 7 | 7 | 7 | 7 | 7 | 35 |
| 1997 | Electorate | 402,503 | Votes | 196,965 | 30,672 | 27,055 | 23,034 | 8,099 | 285,825 |
| | Turnout % | 71 | Votes % | 68.9 | 10.7 | 9.5 | 8.1 | 2.8 | 100.0 |
| | | | Seats | 7 | 0 | 0 | 0 | 0 | 7 |
| | | | Candidates | 7 | 7 | 7 | 7 | 12 | 40 |
| | | | Change 01-97 | -8.0 | 1.2 | 0.4 | 7.5 | -1.0 | |

Bridgend, Caerphilly, Cynon Valley, Merthyr Tydfil & Rhymney, Ogmore, Pontypridd, Rhondda.

| GLAMORGAN SOUTH | | | Lab | C | LD | Nat | Other | Total |
|---|---|---|---|---|---|---|---|---|
| 2001 | Electorate | 309,963 | Votes | 92,508 | 50,121 | 33,974 | 12,297 | 4,200 | 193,100 |
| | Turnout % | 62.3 | Votes % | 47.9 | 26 | 17.6 | 6.4 | 2.2 | 100.0 |
| | Swing % | 1.85 | Seats | 5 | 0 | 0 | 0 | 0 | 5 |
| | Lab to C | | Candidates | 5 | 5 | 5 | 5 | 10 | 30 |
| 1997 | Electorate | 308,033 | Votes | 118,922 | 60,761 | 29,110 | 7,403 | 11,136 | 227,332 |
| | Turnout % | 73.8 | Votes % | 52.3 | 26.7 | 12.8 | 3.3 | 4.9 | 100.0 |
| | | | Seats | 5 | 0 | 0 | 0 | 0 | 5 |
| | | | Candidates | 5 | 5 | 5 | 5 | 10 | 30 |
| | | | Change 01-97 | -4.4 | -0.7 | 4.8 | 3.1 | -2.7 | |

Cardiff Central, Cardiff North, Cardiff South & Penarth, Cardiff West, Vale of Glamorgan.

| GLAMORGAN WEST | | | Lab | C | LD | Nat | Other | Total |
|---|---|---|---|---|---|---|---|---|
| 2001 | Electorate | 279,057 | Votes | 93,248 | 25,007 | 19,152 | 20,125 | 7,203 | 164,735 |
| | Turnout % | 59 | Votes % | 56.6 | 15.2 | 11.6 | 12.2 | 4.4 | 100.0 |
| | Swing % | 5 | Seats | 5 | 0 | 0 | 0 | 0 | 5 |
| | Lab to C | | Candidates | 5 | 5 | 5 | 5 | 12 | 32 |
| 1997 | Electorate | 279,317 | Votes | 131,186 | 28,595 | 21,612 | 11,641 | 6,651 | 199,685 |
| | Turnout % | 71.5 | Votes % | 65.7 | 14.3 | 10.8 | 5.8 | 3.3 | 100.0 |
| | | | Seats | 5 | 0 | 0 | 0 | 0 | 5 |
| | | | Candidates | 5 | 5 | 5 | 5 | 9 | 29 |
| | | | Change 01-97 | -9.1 | 0.9 | 0.8 | 6.4 | 1.1 | |

Aberavon, Gower, Neath, Swansea East, Swansea West.

| GWENT | | | Lab | C | LD | Nat | Other | Total |
|---|---|---|---|---|---|---|---|---|
| 2001 | Electorate | 343,755 | Votes | 118,873 | 45,597 | 24,646 | 15,126 | 5,223 | 209,465 |
| | Turnout % | 60.9 | Votes % | 56.8 | 21.8 | 11.8 | 7.2 | 2.5 | 100.0 |
| | Swing % | 4.85 | Seats | 6 | 0 | 0 | 0 | 0 | 6 |
| | Lab to C | | Candidates | 6 | 6 | 6 | 6 | 10 | 34 |
| 1997 | Electorate | 331,297 | Votes | 157,567 | 47,776 | 24,247 | 7,271 | 8,903 | 245,764 |
| | Turnout % | 74.2 | Votes % | 64.1 | 19.4 | 9.9 | 3 | 3.6 | 100.0 |
| | | | Seats | 6 | 0 | 0 | 0 | 0 | 6 |
| | | | Candidates | 6 | 6 | 6 | 6 | 8 | 32 |
| | | | Change 01-97 | -7.3 | 2.4 | 1.9 | 4.2 | -1.1 | |

Blaenau Gwent, Islwyn, Monmouth, Newport East, Newport West, Torfaen.

## WELSH TABLES

| GWYNEDD | | | Lab | C | LD | Nat | Other | Total |
|---|---|---|---|---|---|---|---|---|
| **2001** | **Electorate** | **188,397** | Votes | 40,430 | 24,165 | 12,267 | 40,124 | 1,519 | 118,505 |
| | **Turnout %** | **62.9** | Votes % | 34.1 | 20.4 | 10.4 | 33.9 | 1.3 | 100.0 |
| | **Swing %** | **-.85** | Seats | 2 | 0 | 0 | 2 | 0 | 4 |
| | **Lab to C** | | Candidates | 4 | 4 | 4 | 4 | 4 | 20 |
| **1997** | **Electorate** | **187,204** | Votes | 43,163 | 26,806 | 17,907 | 48,681 | 3,518 | 140,075 |
| | **Turnout %** | **75.1** | Votes % | 30.8 | 19.1 | 12.8 | 34.8 | 2.5 | 100.0 |
| | | | Seats | 1 | 0 | 0 | 3 | 0 | 4 |
| | | | Candidates | 4 | 4 | 4 | 4 | 6 | 22 |
| | | | Change 01-97 | 3.3 | 1.3 | -2.4 | -0.9 | -1.2 | |

Caernarfon, Conwy, Meirionnydd Nant Conwy, Ynys Mon.

| POWYS | | | Lab | C | LD | Nat | Other | Total |
|---|---|---|---|---|---|---|---|---|
| **2001** | **Electorate** | **96,490** | Votes | 11,467 | 21,158 | 28,143 | 3,270 | 2,461 | 66,499 |
| | **Turnout %** | **68.9** | Votes % | 17.2 | 31.8 | 42.3 | 4.9 | 3.7 | 100.0 |
| | **Swing %** | **5.1** | Seats | 0 | 0 | 2 | 0 | 0 | 2 |
| | **Lab to C** | | Candidates | 2 | 2 | 2 | 2 | 6 | 14 |
| **1997** | **Electorate** | **94,760** | Votes | 17,533 | 20,763 | 32,163 | 2,230 | 2,117 | 74,806 |
| | **Turnout %** | **78.9** | Votes % | 23.4 | 27.8 | 43 | 3 | 2.8 | 100.0 |
| | | | Seats | 0 | 0 | 2 | 0 | 0 | 2 |
| | | | Candidates | 2 | 2 | 2 | 2 | 3 | 11 |
| | | | Change 01-97 | -6.2 | 4.0 | -0.7 | 1.9 | 0.9 | |

Brecon & Radnorshire, Montgomeryshire.

# MANIFESTOS

 **LABOUR MANIFESTO**

## AMBITIONS FOR BRITAIN

Five pledges for the next five years

**Economic pledge**

1. Mortgages as low as possible, low inflation and sound public finances As we deliver economic stability **not** return the economy to Tory boom and bust

**Schools pledge**

2. 10,000 extra teachers and higher standards in secondary schools. As we invest in our schools **not** make reckless tax cuts

**Health pledge**

3. 20,000 extra nurses and 10,000 extra doctors in a reformed NHS. As we improve NHS care for all **not** push patients into paying for operations.

**Crime pledge**

4. 6,000 extra recruits to raise police numbers to their highest ever level. As we tackle drugs and crime **not** cut police funding

**Families pledge**

5. Pensioners' winter fuel payment retained, minimum wage rising to £4.20. As we help hard-working families **not** the privileged few

**Built on five achievements since 1997**

● Typical mortgage £1,200 less than under the Tories, inflation lowest for 30 years
● The best ever results in primary schools
● 17,000 extra nurses now in the NHS
● Crime down ten per cent
● One million more people in work and a new Children's Tax Credit

## FULFILLING BRITAIN'S GREAT POTENTIAL

This general election is in many ways even more important than the last. Since May 1997 we have laid the foundations of a Britain whose economy is stronger, where investment is now pouring into public services, where social division is being slowly healed and where influence abroad is being regained.

But these are only the foundations of larger change. Now is the chance to build the future properly, to make the second term the basis for a radical programme of British renewal: to keep a firm grip on inflation, with low interest rates and the public finances sound, and then build the dynamic and productive economy of the future; to keep investment coming into public services and then making the reforms so we use the money well; to re-fashion the welfare state on the basis of rights and responsibilities, with people helped to help themselves, not just given handouts; to ensure all families are safe in their communities by tackling crime and its causes; and to give Britain back its leadership role in the world. We need the second term to do all this. That is the choice: to make progress or to dismantle the foundations laid. And with the state of today's Conservatives, the choice is stark.

This choice will decide whether more people will be able to realise their aspirations for themselves and their children - to be able to rely on a stable economy where hard work is rewarded by rising living standards, to receive world-class education and healthcare, to enjoy a dignified old age, to feel safe and secure in a strong community, and to be proud to be British. Or whether we will be held back by the traditional British malaise of restricting life's great opportunities and blessings to a minority.

There is much still to be done, but we have come a long way in four years. Britain stands more prosperous, more equal, more respected. Our country is on a new course.

My passion is to continue the modernisation of Britain in favour of hard-working families, so that all our children, wherever they live, whatever their background, have an equal chance to benefit from the opportunities our country has to offer and to share in its wealth.

### The challenge for Britain

I am honoured to be Prime Minister. And I have a confident belief in our country.

We are not boastful. But we have real strengths. Great people. Strong values. A proud history.

The British people achieved magnificent things in the 20th century. But for too long, our strengths have been undermined by weaknesses of elitism and snobbery, vested interests and social division, complacency bred by harking back to the past.

We achieved spurts of economic growth, but inflation would then get out of control. Our welfare state was founded to offer security, but its progress was stalled. We reached out to Europe, then drew back to become semi-detached.

It is as if a glass ceiling has stopped us fulfilling our potential. In the 21st century, we have the opportunity to break through that glass ceiling, because our historic strengths match the demands of the modern world.

We can use our openness and entrepreneurial flair to become a global centre in the knowledge economy. We can use our sense of fair play and mutual responsibility to be a strong, dynamic, multiracial society held together by strong values. We can use our historic and geographical position to link Europe and America, and help the developing world.

The key to tapping our strengths, to breaking through this glass ceiling, is contained in a simple but hard-to-achieve idea, set out at the heart of our party's constitution: the determination to put power, wealth and opportunity in the hands of the many, not the few.

I know as well as anyone that we have just begun; millions of hard-working families want, need and deserve more. That means more change in a second term, not less - to extend opportunity for all. We reject the quiet life. We must secure a mandate for change.

### Ten goals for 2010

- Long-term economic stability
- Rising living standards for all
- Expanded higher education as we raise standards in secondary schools
- A healthier nation with fast treatment, free at the point of use
- Full employment in every region
- Opportunity for all children, security for all pensioners
- A modern criminal justice system
- Strong and accountable local government
- British ideas leading a reformed and enlarged Europe
- Global poverty and climate change tackled

### Shifting the odds for hard-working families

In 1997 we promised a start, not a revolution. We made five specific five-year pledges. Three have been completed early; all will be completed within five years, as we promised.

Each pledge is matched by further achievement: the lowest inflation and unemployment for a generation; one million new jobs; over 17,000 extra nurses, the best primary school test results ever and, as the British Crime Survey shows, crime is down by ten per cent.

We also offered a ten-point contract to the British people. The results are at the back of this manifesto. Not everything has gone right - it never does. But we are getting there, easing burdens and extending opportunities, by choice not chance.

Economic instability wrecks the lives of hard-working families. So we chose to put the public finances right. It meant tough decisions that were opposed by the Conservatives. But today the economy is stable and growing, and interest rates are nearly half the level they averaged under the Conservatives.

Unemployment steals dignity. So we chose to introduce a windfall tax on the excess profits of the privatised utilities and to use the money to help unemployed people back to work. That was opposed by the Conservatives, who are now pledged to abolish the New Deal. But today, youth unemployment is at its lowest level since 1975 and long-term unemployment at its lowest level since 1978.

Poor education is a cruel injustice. So we chose to introduce a new system for teaching the basics in primary schools. We met opposition, and the Conservatives want to roll back our programmes. But today, primary schools are achieving their best results ever.

A run-down health service causes insecurity. So we chose to reform the NHS, and inject new money. Waiting lists and times are now down and falling, and the number of nurses and doctors is now rising.

Poverty denies basic rights. So we chose to reform the NHS, and inject extra money to the poorest pensioners and poorest children. Today, single pensioners can look forward to a minimum income of £100 a week and pensioner couples £154, and over one million children have been taken out of poverty.

The centralisation of power only helps the powerful. So we chose to break the suffocating centralisation of British government. The UK has been strengthened. Today, it is the Conservatives who threaten the stability of the UK with their proposals for two classes of MP. Our Scottish and Welsh manifestos, alongside this one, set out our vision for continued partnership.

Isolation from Europe does not help anyone. So we chose to engage constructively in Europe, not to shout abuse from the sidelines. Today, Europe is moving in a direction that is good for Britain and good for Europe. In policy for aid, development and international debt relief, we have led the way.

Of course, there are still big problems, but we are better off, better educated, better governed, better respected abroad. There has been another change too - a change of priorities and values.

We learnt in the 1980s that looking after number one was not enough; that without opportunity, responsibility was weak; that an unfair society was a less prosperous one. The philosophy was wrong - it hurt millions of families and left our country with lasting problems.

We have shown we are a reformed party, competent to govern. Now we offer more. More change, and more rewards for Britain's hard-working families: more prosperity, more opportunities, more security.

### Ambitions for Britain

Stretching the family budget, finding time for children as well as work, holding on to mutual respect, staying healthy when there can be danger even in the air we breathe. These are daily worries that people face.

They are my concerns too. But, while there is always a market for people who say we are doomed, that all new ideas are bad ideas even as things improve, that we might as well curl up with our prejudices and shut the door on the world, I am an optimist. New Labour is ambitious for Britain's future and is ready to lead.

First, we will sustain economic stability and build deeper prosperity that reaches every region of the country. Skills, infrastructure, the technological revolution - all are vital to raise British living standards faster. We will put as much energy into helping the seven million adults without basic skills as we did when tackling long-term unemployment through the New Deal.

Second, we seek to achieve a renaissance of status and quality for public services and their staff. We will build on our success in primary schools to overhaul secondary schools; we will invest new resources and empower doctors and nurses to transform health services; and we will seek to extend the very best in culture and sport to all.

Third, we seek to modernise the welfare state. The benefits system will be restructured around work; support for children and families through the tax and benefits system will be transformed; cash and services for pensioners will be radically improved.

Fourth, we will strengthen our communities. We will reform the criminal justice system at every level so that criminals are caught, punished and rehabilitated. And because we know that without tackling the causes of crime we will never tackle crime, we will empower local communities by combining resources with responsibility.

Fifth, we will turn our inner confidence to strength abroad, in Europe and beyond, to tackle global problems - above all, environmental degradation and the shame of global poverty. We will engage fully in Europe, help enlarge the European Union and make it more effective, and insist that the British people have the final say on any proposal to join the Euro.

These ambitions are summarised in ten goals for 2010. They will never be achieved by government alone. We know it is people who ultimately change the country. Our partnership with the voluntary sector has steadily strengthened since 1997, as we learn from its diversity. We work with the private sector, drawing on its vitality. Countries only prosper on the basis of partnership - between government, employers and their employees, and the voluntary sector. What Britain needs is an active, enabling state, not a nanny state, doing things with people not to them.

So, while the Conservatives will spend most of this election telling you what their government cannot do, this manifesto sets out what our government can do. We know the power and value of markets, but we also know their limits. Now is the time to renew our civic and social institutions to deliver improvements in education, health, safety, transport and the environment.

### Fighting for values, not just for election victory

The Conservatives always look back.

In economic policy they promise to repeat the mistakes of the 1980s - unaffordable tax cuts and spending cuts, followed by ballooning deficits, rising interest rates and the old cycle of boom and bust.

In social policy their renewed commitment to cuts and privatisation and to withdrawing the support helping to heal social division, is just a throwback to the 1980s.

In foreign policy they risk not just isolation but exit from the EU. Jobs, trade, investment depend on our membership of the European Union. The Conservative policy of opposing the enlargement of Europe in the Nice Treaty and their pledge to renegotiate the terms of Britain's EU membership is dangerous and ill thought-out. Standing up for Britain means fighting for Britain's interests in Europe, not leaving Europe - which threatens our national interest.

So the choice Britain faces today is starker than in 1997. The Conservatives have swung further to the right. And, in government, Labour's agenda has become increasingly bold and ambitious.

For many years, the Conservatives claimed to offer economic strength while Labour dominated social issues. Many people found their head telling them to vote Tory, and their heart telling them to vote Labour.

Today, head and heart are coming together. New Labour is proving that it is only by using the talents of all that we get a healthy economy, and that it is only by giving a stake to all that we are a healthy society.

We have made our choice: stability not boom and bust; investment not cuts; engagement not isolationism; the many, not the few.

A lot done and a lot more to do with new Labour - or a lot for you to lose under the Conservatives.

I deeply believe that, for Britain, the best is still to come. So I ask you to continue on this journey with us. Together we can achieve so much more. — **Tony Blair, Prime Minister and Leader of the Labour Party**

### INVESTMENT AND REFORM

Public services; investment and reform. Renewal of our public services is at the centre of new Labour's manifesto.

A single aim drives our policy programme: to liberate people's potential, by spreading power, wealth and opportunity more widely, breaking down the barriers that hold people back.

But this is only possible on the continued foundation of economic stability: mortgages as low as possible, low inflation and sound public finances.

The manifesto is comprehensive. Here we set out some of the key measures for investment and reform that we believe give us a historic opportunity to modernise our schools, NHS, criminal justice system and welfare state.

### Economic stability: the foundation

New Labour believes that a stable economy is the platform for rising living standards and opportunity for all
Our ten-year goals are for long-term economic stability and faster productivity growth than our main competitors.

We will now:

- deliver economic stability with mortgages as low as possible, low inflation and sound public finances
- reform further education, and help 750,000 adults achieve basic skills
- expand the Children's Tax Credit to offer up to £1,000 per year for parents of newborn children
- create a new Child Trust Fund for every child at birth
- increase the minimum wage to £4.20
- not raise the basic or top rate of income tax and extend the 10p band
- strengthen regional economies with venture capital funds and new powers for reformed Regional Development Agencies
- develop the Small Business Service and cut red tape
- give British people the final say in any referendum on the single currency

### Renewing public services: substantial investment

New Labour believes that Britain needs investment in schools and hospitals, not reckless tax cuts
Before 1997 we promised and kept to two tough years on spending to get the public finances in shape. Now, consistent with meeting our fiscal rules, we promise substantial rises for key public services. To help deliver our plans, our ten-year goal is the renewal of local government.

We will now:

- increase education spending by more than five per cent in real terms each year for the next three years as we increase the share of national income for education in the next Parliament
- increase health spending by an average of six per cent in real terms each year for the next three years
- increase spending on our police - an extra £1.6 billion a year by 2003/04
- increase spending on transport by 20 per cent for the next three years, on our way to a £180 billion investment of public and private money for transport over the next ten years
- use a £400 million reward fund for local government in return for signing up to clear targets to improve local services

### Renewing public services: more frontline staff

New Labour believes in renewing a public service ethic by giving frontline staff new freedoms to respond to public needs
For public services to be renewed, we will need more staff, properly rewarded. It is these frontline staff, operating in new ways, who will drive up standards in our key public services. We will decentralise power to make that possible.

We will now deliver:

- 20,000 more nurses who will be given new enhanced roles and more power for matrons and ward sisters with control over budgets
- 10,000 more doctors, and access to a £500 million Performance Fund to spend on new patient services
- 10,000 more teachers. Invest in further rapid promotion and rewards for classroom excellence, more classroom assistants and help with housing costs in high-cost areas
- 6,000 extra police recruits, raising police numbers to their highest ever level, with strong local leadership and proper rewards for those on the frontline.

### Renewing public services: education reform

New Labour believes that schools need a step change in reform to make quality education open to all
We plan a radical improvement in secondary schools, building on our success in primary schools. Our aim is to develop fully the talents of each child. Our ten-year goal is 50 per cent of young adults entering higher education.

We will now:

- ensure every secondary school develops a distinctive mission including the expansion of specialist schools
- diversify state schools with new City Academies and more church schools
- direct more money to headteachers, more freedom for successful schools
- reform provision for 11- to 14-year-olds to ensure higher standards in English, maths, science and information technology
- introduce new vocational options from 14 onwards, with expanded apprenticeship opportunities
- ensure primary schools offer more chance to learn languages, music and sport, as well as higher standards in the basics
- provide a good-quality nursery place for every three-year-old

### Renewing public services: NHS reform

New Labour believes that the NHS needs radical reform to fulfil its founding principle of quality treatment based on need, not ability to pay

## LABOUR MANIFESTO

The NHS needs radical reform if it is to be designed around the needs of patients. Investment is vital but not enough. Labour's ten-year goal is a maximum waiting time of three months as we become a healthier nation with fast, high-quality treatment, free at the point of use.

We will now:

- decentralise power to give local Primary Care Trusts control of 75 per cent of NHS funding, and cut by two thirds the number of health authorities
- reform the appointments system so that by the end of 2005 every hospital appointment is booked for the convenience of the patient
- cut maximum waiting times by the end of 2005 for outpatient appointments from six months to three months and inpatients, from 18 to six months
- work with the private sector to use spare capacity, where it makes sense, for NHS patients
- create a new type of hospital - specially built surgical units, managed by the NHS or the private sector - to guarantee shorter waiting times
- allow successful NHS hospitals to take over failing ones.

### Renewing public services: welfare reform

New Labour believes that rights and responsibilities should be at the centre of reform of the welfare state - to lift children and pensioners out of poverty, and help parents balance work and family
We will continue to reform the tax and benefit system to reward work, not irresponsibility. Our ten-year goals are to achieve full employment in every region, to halve child poverty and tackle pensioner poverty.

We will now:

- create an integrated Child Credit of cash support for children, built on the foundation of universal child benefit
- establish a new Pension Credit for lower- and middle-income pensioners
- establish a new 'Employment First' interview for people entering the welfare system, and integrate the Benefits Agency and Employment Service through major reform
- extend and increase paid maternity leave to £100 each week for six months
- introduce paid paternity leave
- expand childcare places to provide for 1.6 million children

### Renewing public services: criminal justice reform

New Labour believes that crime can only be cut by dealing with the causes of crime as well as being tough on criminals
We plan the most comprehensive reform of the criminal justice system since the war - to catch, convict, punish and rehabilitate more of the 100,000 persistent offenders. Our ten-year goal is a modernised criminal justice system with the burglary rate halved.

We will now:

- overhaul sentencing so that persistent offending results in more severe punishment
- reform custodial sentences so that every offender gets punishment and rehabilitation designed to minimise reoffending
- reform rules of evidence to simplify trials and bring the guilty to justice
- introduce specialist, late-sitting and review courts to reflect crime patterns and properly monitor offenders
- establish a new Criminal Assets Recovery Agency to seize assets of crime barons and a register of dealers to tackle drugs
- introduce a victims bill of rights providing legal rights to compensation, support and information

## 1. PROSPERITY FOR ALL

### Our ten-year goals

Fiscal rules consistently met, low inflation, and interest rates as low as possible, as we deliver long-term economic stability.
Faster productivity growth than our main competitors, as we achieve rising living standards for all.

Our next steps

- Basic skills for 750,000 people
- Venture capital funds in every region
- £180 billion investment in transport, with 25 local rail and tram schemes
- Raise the minimum wage to £4.20
- £1,000 tax cut - the Children's Tax Credit - for parents of newborn children

Labour's purpose is to help every family, not just a few, to raise their living standards and plan ahead with security. We have a ten-year vision: higher living standards, affordable mortgages and fairer taxes combined with much greater investment in vital public services.

Economic stability is the foundation. We know the price of boom and bust - it was paid in the 1980s and 1990s by millions of hard-working families.

Our reforms since 1997 have helped cut interest rates to nearly half the average under the Conservatives, saving mortgage payers on average £1,200 a year. By 2010, we want Britain to break away from the decades of boom and bust, as we stick to clear rules for spending and borrowing. We will take no risks with economic policy, make no compromise on fiscal responsibility.

Stability comes first. But stability is not enough. We need to produce more, better and to a higher value to raise our earning power and to meet our ten-year goal of faster productivity growth than our main competitors.

We must make Britain the best place to do business in Europe - a dynamic economy, founded on skills and knowledge, developing the talent of all our people, and contributing to sustainable development. That means investment by private and public sectors in infrastructure and skills, and the right competitive framework to support enterprise, small and large, manufacturing and services.

Every extra trained, employed worker contributes to a fairer society, as well as a more prosperous one. With social failure, from school drop-outs to crime, comes economic failure. Fairness and enterprise go together. It is up to government to do everything it can to help ensure that no individual and no community is left behind.

## The fundamentals
### Better off with Labour

The foundation of opportunity and prosperity is economic stability. We know the risks of promises that cannot be paid for: the Conservatives led Britain into two deep recessions, double-digit inflation, record unemployment, 15 per cent interest rates and a doubling of the national debt.

Choice, not chance, has turned things round. Independence for the Bank of England and long-term fiscal rules have given the UK the most stable and transparent economic framework in Europe. Britain now has the best combination of low interest rates, low inflation and low unemployment since the 1960s.

We are saving nearly £9 billion this year from debt and unemployment, so 84p of every extra pound of public spending goes on national priorities, compared to 58p under the Conservatives.

So we will pursue a balanced approach on the economy with stability the foundation, more investment not less and, as affordable, targeted tax cuts on our priorities.

Our aim is to put more wealth in the hands of more people. That is why we will keep mortgage rates as low as possible, ensure competition keeps down household bills, support savings and share ownership, and create a new Child Trust Fund for every child at birth to invest for when they reach adulthood.

There are no guarantees in an integrated world economy. But we showed during the Asian economic crisis how to steer a course of stability in turbulent times. We will continue to work at international level to minimise global economic turbulence, and to protect Britain if it occurs.

## Tax and spending

Fiscal responsibility and monetary stability are the foundation of our future plans. New Labour's inflation target is 2.5 per cent. We will continue to meet our fiscal rules: over the economic cycle we will borrow only to invest, and keep net debt at a stable and prudent level.

We are pledged to raise health and education spending for the next three years at twice the rate of the Conservative years. Labour will double net public investment. And we are on track to save £1 billion in the costs of government purchasing by 2003.

Tax policy will be governed by the health of the public finances, the requirement for public investment, and the needs of families, business and the environment.

We have rewarded work through the new 10p starting rate of tax and the Working Families Tax Credit. The basic rate of tax has been cut to 22p. We will support families through the new Children's Tax Credit, set at up to £1,000 a year for new parents - the first recognition of the costs of children in the tax system for 20 years. On average, UK households have benefited by £590 a year from personal tax and benefit measures introduced since 1997. During this Parliament, living standards have risen by ten per cent for a single earner family on average earnings. To help those who work and save, we will extend the 10p tax band. We will continue to tackle tax avoidance.

We will not raise the basic or top rates of income tax in the next Parliament. We renew our pledge not to extend VAT to food, children's clothes, books, newspapers and public transport fares.

### Labour rewards work

Labour believes that if you work hard you should be able to support a family. We will guarantee a minimum family income of £225 for a 35-hour week; in the next Parliament, an Employment Tax Credit will reward the work of people on low incomes, whether or not they have children (see 'A modern welfare state').

The first-ever National Minimum Wage for Britain, bitterly opposed at every stage by the Conservatives, has been a success in our first term. It fulfils, after 100 years, a founding ambition of the Labour Party. Up to 1.5 million people, the majority of them women, have been helped; jobs have not been lost. The Low Pay Commission, which we will make permanent, has made clear recommendations for the future. New Labour will raise the minimum wage to £4.10 this October, and is committed, subject to economic conditions, to raising it to £4.20 in October 2002.

### Labour rewards saving

Nine million people invested in ISAs in their first year. To encourage more saving, we will maintain the £7,000 contribution limit for the next Parliament. We will help pensioners: the Pension Credit will match private saving with government funds, and pensioners will no longer be penalised because of their thrift (see 'A modern welfare state'). To boost the savings habit, we will create a new Savings Gateway for people on lower incomes where their savings will be matched by the government.

## The productivity challenge
### Staying better off

To raise living standards, our ambition is to raise our productivity faster than our competitors and to ensure our goods and services are competitive in world markets. Labour has four priorities:

### Investment in skills and innovation
### Skills

We are passionate about giving every child the chance of a decent education. But we are equally determined to offer learning opportunities to adults. Our ambition is for everyone to have the opportunity to train, in a partnership of employers, employees and government, each giving time and/or money to raise standards of skills in the UK. Our first priority is to help the estimated seven million adults who lack basic literacy and numeracy skills, with 750,000 people achieving basic skill levels by 2004.

We will:

● ensure that job seekers get the benefit of a basic skills test, as well as incentives and obligations to take courses to tackle literacy and/or numeracy problems
● set up a network of 6,000 IT learning centres around the country
● extend Individual Learning Accounts, which have already been opened by over a million people
● dramatically improve the quality and quantity of prison education
● tackle the financial barriers that prevent adults studying in further education.

Basic skills are the start; updating skills is relevant for all of us. We have created the Learning and Skills Council for all post-school learning outside higher education. Further education colleges have a critical role to play in the future. We will encourage dedicated colleges for under-19s and specialist adult provision to meet local skills needs, with half of all colleges to be recognised as centres of vocational excellence by 2003-04. The world's first University for Industry now offers over 400 skills courses. For skill shortages in information technology, we will open two Technology Institutes in every region to meet the rising demand for high-level technical skills.

We need a step-change in workplace learning - particularly in small and medium-sized firms. We are determined to develop a three-way partnership to bring this about. Current arrangements have secured increased participation, but not enough. Unions and employers have a key role - but we also need to motivate individual employees. Where both sides of industry in a sector agree, we will help set up a statutory framework for training. We will boost the efforts of trade unions to raise skill levels by giving statutory backing to union learning representatives and supporting the Union Learning Fund. Government has a wide-ranging role to play and is seeking to develop a training tax credit. We will look to business and unions to come forward with proposals on how they can contribute to meeting the nation's training goals. Everyone has a responsibility to help deliver a high-skill, high-productivity economy.

### Innovation

Science and technology are the basis of new products and industries, both vital to productivity growth. Since 1997 extra investment of £1.5 billion over three years has given science a fresh start, and a new stream of university funding has helped create new links between scientific breakthroughs and new products.

But we need to invest more to be at the cutting edge of science - in biotechnology and genome research. We propose an R&D tax credit to promote business investment in research. We will work for a European patent system by the end of this year to simplify the process of bringing ideas to market. The £235 billion a year, and growing, global market for green technology gives real opportunity to British industry to benefit from a shift to low carbon technologies. We will continue to encourage the best scientists to work in the UK, as well as making the most of our science base in universities (see 'World-class public services').

### Supporting British business

Government cannot make a business successful. But government must create the right framework to help business achieve healthy long-term growth.

Since 1997, corporation tax rates have been cut to their lowest levels ever. Companies no longer face a perverse incentive to pay out dividends rather than invest for the future. Reform of capital gains tax has given the entrepreneur or investor new incentives for investment. We support vital investment through the tax system - with allowances for high tech as well as small business investment. The Myners report has identified weaknesses in our venture capital market, undermining long-term investment and economic dynamism. We will act on its recommendations, including the abolition of the minimum funding requirement and reforms to pension fund management, and review progress in two years.

When people have worked hard, they want their money to go as far as possible. Competition policy has already helped cut cash-machine charges and new car prices. We will extend our fair and robust competition regime by giving more independence to the competition authorities. We will toughen the laws on rogue traders, unfair terms in contracts, and loan sharks.

In the labour market, minimum standards for people at work offer dignity and self-esteem. Regulation should be introduced, where it is necessary, in a light-touch way. We will cut back the red tape associated with regulation, examine opportunities to put time limits on regulations, deregulate by secondary legislation, and offer help to small firms.

Over 150,000 small businesses have been set up since 1997. We will develop the Small Business Service as an advocate for small business in government and a servant of small businesses around the country. We are committed to reforming the tax treatment of small business, including VAT, and to seeking a reduction in payroll burdens. Small business will also benefit from extending the 10p tax band. We will reform the bankruptcy laws to ensure second chances for people who go bankrupt through no fault of their own, and provide funds for new start-ups. We will also promote the development of entrepreneurship in the school curriculum.

We will modernise company law to promote transparency, reduce burdens on small business and promote long-term economic success. We welcome the recommendations of the Co-operative Commission, which also covered the significant mutual sector, and will examine them with a view to strengthening these important parts of our economy.

### Modernising our infrastructure for the information age
### Digital nation

The infrastructure of the future includes fast, efficient and affordable communication - telecommunications, the internet and broadcasting. That requires the best competitive environment, effective regulation and continued public and private investment in the technologies of the future.

A 'digital divide' would hurt business as well as individuals: universal access is vital to effective markets. We will put all government services on-line by 2005, to improve access to services and spur business on-line. We will work to ensure that broadband, which allows fast internet access, is accessible in all parts of the country.

English is the language of the internet. We have the best TV in the world. The next challenge is to open up the learning opportunities and enjoyment offered by digital TV and the internet to every household. We are committed to making the switchover from analogue to digital signals as soon as conditions for access and cost have been met.

The governance of this fast-changing industry is out of date. We will merge the five separate regulators into one, to create the world's most competitive and advanced regulatory system. We believe in the value and necessity of public service broadcasting and have committed to major funding increases for the BBC and to supporting a publicly owned Channel 4 and S4C. Ofcom will ensure a level playing field, benefiting consumers in terms of choice, price and quality, in particular through promoting competition.

### Transport

A strong economy needs good transport. Yet our inheritance was massive under-investment, with British Rail broken into over a hundred privatised pieces, and bus services in decline.

Labour's priority is to improve and expand railway and road travel. Our ten-year Transport Plan, supported by all the key players, matches large resources with major reform. £180 billion of investment, split between railways, roads and local transport and delivered in partnership with the private sector, offers real hope to motorists and passengers alike.

● Rail: Passenger numbers have risen by 17 per cent since 1997, and freight increased by 22 per cent. But recent crises have proved the need for urgent investment and strong regulation. With Labour, £60 billion will be spent on upgrading the rail network, with the majority of rolling stock replaced. Five hundred new carriages are already in use, another 3,000 ordered. We plan to expand capacity to boost passenger levels by 50 per cent, and freight by more. Safer train protection systems are now being installed and will be extended following Lord Cullen's report into rail safety.

The Strategic Rail Authority (SRA) has been set up to provide strong, strategic direction. Train companies will get longer franchises in return for higher investment and improved services. The SRA will lead the expansion of the network, using public-private partnerships (PPPs). Railtrack is being reformed to focus on the operation of existing track and signalling. The Rail Regulator, with strengthened powers, will ensure the delivery of higher standards, increased safety and increased investment by the company.

London will benefit from new trains and reduced overcrowding on its commuter services. We support plans to build a new East-West Cross-rail tunnel and to extend the East London Line. We have pledged increased, long-term investment in the Tube to underpin a public-private partnership to upgrade Tube infrastructure, with operations remaining in the public sector. Our agreement with the London Mayor and Transport Commissioner offers the best chance in a generation to upgrade the Tube.

Supertrams will transform transport in our big cities, with 25 new light rail or tram schemes. Services have been introduced or expanded in Manchester, Birmingham, Croydon, Sheffield, Nottingham, Tyne and Wear with plans under way for supertrams in Leeds, Portsmouth and Bristol.

● Roads: The Transport Plan allocates £60 billion to road improvement. Motorways will be upgraded: a hundred new bypasses will reduce accidents and pollution. But environmentally damaging road schemes have been scrapped: all new roads must now be strictly appraised for maximum benefits and minimum environmental damage. Our trunk roads are the safest in Europe and we aim to reduce serious road casualties by a further 40 per cent over ten years. £8.4 billion is now being invested in local authority schemes in England. We have given local authorities the freedom to choose to use charges to reduce traffic - but we insist they put the money into better transport services. New road safety schemes will mean more school bus services and traffic-free Home Zones where people can walk safely, and children play without danger, to help cut the number of child road deaths and serious injuries by 50 per cent by 2010.

Road tax is being cut on smaller, cleaner cars and duty reduced on greener fuels. Tax incentives are creating a cleaner lorry fleet while the road haulage industry will benefit from steep reductions in Vehicle Excise Duty to among the lowest in Europe. We will also ensure that hauliers from overseas pay their fair share towards the cost of our roads. Smarter driving will be encouraged by new highway communications technology. We are also working with the motor industry on safer, more fuel-efficient vehicles.

● Buses: are vital to local journeys. With Labour, 25,000 new buses are already in operation. By 2006, almost the whole national bus fleet will be renewed. Lower concessionary fares have been introduced for over five million older and disabled travellers. Park and ride schemes are increasing, and over 100 towns now have bus services linked to train stations, with cut-price fares. Bus partnerships between local authorities and private bus companies will improve passenger numbers and service quality. Nationally we will work to improve inter-city coach services.

### Integrated transport

Good transport systems offer choice across transport modes. Transport Direct - a phone and internet system designed to plan journeys and sell tickets - will put transport services at people's fingertips. Walking and cycling will be encouraged in thousands of local transport schemes. Inland waterways are being revitalised and we will take forward the recommendations of the enquiry into the *Marchioness* disaster.

International links are also vital. Plans for aviation and airports over the next 30 years will be produced next year. Merchant ships are returning to the British flag. We will complete the high-speed Channel Tunnel Rail Link.

Major national infrastructure projects, such as Heathrow Terminal 5, raise vital issues. We will continue to modernise the planning system and introduce new fast-track procedures for major projects of national significance.

### The Post Office and postal services

We are committed to high-quality, universal postal services, and a dynamic Post Office which can thrive in a world of technological change and increased competitive pressure. Labour is working with the banks to offer a new universal banking service. This will allow all benefit and pension recipients to receive their payments, at no charge, in full at the post office after the switch to Automated Credit Transfer in 2003. We also intend the local post office to become an invaluable resource for access to government information. There will be increased incentives for people to take over and modernise post offices. Business customers, representing by far the majority of the Post Office's turnover, want a full range of express, parcels and logistics services. We have given the Post Office greater commercial freedom in the public sector. It needs to be able to gain an advantage in the new postal market and become a leading force in domestic and international postal services through alliances and joint ventures. We want to help the Post Office keep up with the best in a fast-changing market.

### Energy

Labour is committed to a secure, diverse and sustainable supply of energy at competitive prices. We have brought full competition to the gas and electricity markets. Coal and nuclear energy currently play important roles in ensuring diversity in our sources of electricity generation.

We are putting an obligation on electricity companies to deliver ten per cent of the UK's electricity from renewable sources by 2010, with a doubling of combined heat and power. We will consider setting further targets for renewables, with particular focus on offshore wind, solar and biomass technologies, supported by a £100 million fund. It will back up the Climate Change Levy, which includes agreements to improve efficiency in energy-intensive sectors, and the new Carbon Trust, which will recycle £100 million to accelerate the take-up of cost-effective, low-carbon technologies. We will support research into clean coal technology and investigate its commercial possibilities. We will double the expenditure on energy efficiency. Fuel poverty blights lives: our aim is that by 2010 no vulnerable household in the UK need risk ill-health due to a cold home.

BNFL is an important employer and major exporter. The government insists it maintains the highest health, safety and environmental standards. We are examining the scope for turning the company into a public-private partnership.

### Europe and the wider world

Labour will be engaged and influential, fighting for the British national interest, as we set out in 'Britain strong in the world'. We will support British Trade International, which gives business direct access to UK posts abroad, and maintain the UK's position as the location of choice within Europe for multinational business.

Labour's position on the single currency was set out by the Chancellor in October 1997 and reiterated by the Prime Minister in February 1999. We have made it clear that, provided the economic conditions are met, membership of a successful Euro would bring benefits to Britain in terms of jobs, investment and trade. So, in principle, we are in favour of joining a successful single currency. But, in practice, the five economic tests we have set out must be met before the government would recommend entry to the single currency. An assessment of the tests will be carried out early in the next Parliament. If the government and Parliament recommend entry, the British people will have the final say in a referendum.

So the choice is between a Conservative Party which will deny the people of Britain the chance to join, even if it is in our national interest to do so - and the Labour Party which says that, if it is in our national economic interest, the decision should be made by the British people in a referendum.

**No one left behind**
**Helping everyone become better off**
Britain is better off than in 1997 - but our ambition is to widen the winners' circle so more people share in the benefits of economic growth. In 'A modern welfare state' we set out the route to full employment.

**Fair and flexible work**
We are proud of our commitment to combine a dynamic economy with fair standards in the workplace. Labour has put right historic wrongs. Every employee now has the right to four weeks' paid holiday; trade unions have the right to recognition where a majority of the workforce want it; part-time workers have proper rights. Our objective has been to promote fairness consistent with the competitive position of British business. That will continue to be our position.

We have reformed the labour market to build a durable and fair basis for constructive employee relations. As we learn from the reforms, we will keep their effectiveness under review. We want to strengthen partnership at work, which can foster employee commitment and help at a time of industrial change. We have established the Partnership Fund and want to expand it.

Information and consultation need to be appropriate to national traditions, with timely discussion of problems. When large-scale redundancies are being considered, there is an especially strong case for consultation. The government is reviewing the effectiveness of the UK's current arrangements for information and consultation - works councils in larger firms operating across Europe as well as consultation on large-scale redundancies. We will implement the findings of our review in this area. We support conciliation in the workplace to avoid resort to litigation. We will examine reforms that promote efficiency and fairness.

Women still suffer an 18 per cent pay gap compared to men. We are committed to tackling the causes of this inequality. We will work with employers and employees to develop effective proposals, building on good practice and the sound business case, in both the private and public sectors.

We will develop career services for all. We aim for a ten per cent cut in death and major injuries at work by 2010 and will clarify responsibility, improve enforcement and toughen penalties for offences. We are also committed to working with managers and employees to reduce the problems of bullying and violence in the workplace. As a major employer, our ambition is to improve the quality of work for our employees - helping recruitment and retention.

**Prosperity for every region**
**Regions**
Balanced and sustainable growth depends on every region developing its capacity to the full. Sitting back and leaving regional problems to the market is not acceptable. The causes of disparities within and between regions must be addressed. The new regional economic policy must be based on boosting regional capacity for innovation, enterprise and skill development, modernising regional infrastructure and improving university/industry links.
This is why Regional Development Agencies (RDAs) have been set up and why they now have extra money and new freedoms.

We will work in partnership with local people to ensure that all regions and communities build on their own strengths. Our task is to anticipate change, handle restructuring and enable businesses to move into high-skill, high value-added product markets. Labour's Job Transition Service will provide an intensive and personalised response to large-scale redundancies, helping people secure work or acquire new skills. The JTS will focus its work on new Employment Action Plans drawn up by local economic partners.

Our commitment is to use the £1.2 billion rising to £1.7 billion a year now pledged to RDAs to promote business start-ups, strengthen links between business and universities, for example through university innovation centres and the establishment of a Centre for Manufacturing Excellence in every region to help firms develop. They will develop venture capital funds to boost wealth-creating capacity.

The Conservatives are so obsessed with the market and so out of touch with what goes on beyond Westminster that they even want to scrap RDAs - and with them the vital jobs, inward investment and prosperity that they bring.

**Urban renewal**
Eighty per cent of people live in urban and inner-city Britain. We are ambitious for Britain's urban areas: we want to make them better places to live and better places to set up a business. The New Deal for Communities, worth £1.9 billion over three years, and the £900 million Neighbourhood Renewal Fund (see 'A modern welfare state'), as well as our reforms to local governance (see 'Strong and safe communities') will drive forward progress.

Labour offers £1 billion of tax cuts over the next five years to increase capital investment in urban areas, for new businesses and for new housing. Labour will reform the planning system to speed up decision-making, promote the most efficient use of land, and strike the right balance of environmental protection, safer communities and economic growth.

We have put urban renewal at the heart of the planning system and set a target of 60 per cent of new house building to be on brownfield land or provided through the conversion of existing buildings. Two Millennium Villages have set high standards in design. We will designate more in other parts of the country and continue to raise standards of urban design, with a quality mark to tackle cowboy builders.

## LABOUR MANIFESTO

### Housing
Lower interest rates enable more people to own their own homes. Labour will make it easier for people buying and selling homes through a new sellers' pack, through grants for low-income homeowners, and help for key workers in high-cost areas. We will honour our commitment to tackle homelessness. We will continue to promote housing choice, with reforms to leasehold and commonhold law, a licensing scheme for houses in multiple occupation, and new powers for council tenants. We will develop a modern basis for land registration to make conveyancing faster and cheaper. We will also examine the ways in which tenants can be helped to gain an equity stake in the value of their home.

Labour is committed to reducing by one third the backlog of sub-standard housing by 2004, with all social housing brought up to a decent standard by 2010. We will seek to reduce the use of costly bed-and-breakfast accommodation. We propose additional investment of £1.8 billion over the next three years. Some local authorities will continue to provide high-quality council housing. We are supporting the transfer of 200,000 dwellings per year, where tenants agree, to social landlords like housing associations, and new arms-length council housing companies. We will also help 10,000 key workers buy their own homes in high-cost areas to tackle recruitment problems.

### Rural Britain
The recent outbreak of foot and mouth disease has caused strain and distress in rural areas. Labour's priorities have been clear: to eradicate the disease as quickly and effectively as possible, to compensate those directly affected, and to protect the wider economy. As the number of new cases falls significantly, and the clean-up of infected areas gathers pace, we are committed to help the most affected regions with a recovery plan including advice on sustainable restocking, organic conversion, and early retirement and outgoer schemes. We will conduct a scientific review of how to prevent animal disease outbreaks from occurring in the future, and will introduce tough rules to back this up. But we must also learn some of the wider lessons.

### Agriculture and fishing
Since the Second World War the economy of rural areas has undergone massive change. About two per cent of the national workforce are now employed in agriculture. But the industry is particularly important because of the links with food production, our landscape and our environment. Labour's aim is to promote economic renewal with a sustainable future for farming, strengthened communities and sustainable land use.

Short-term pressures need to be met. Since the early 1990s, sectors of farming have been hard hit by BSE, the weakness of the Euro and falling world commodity prices. Labour has provided £1.35 billion in short-term relief for farmers, including aid for diversification, farm business advice, better marketing, small slaughterhouses and restructuring of the industry. We have minimised many regulatory burdens and improved the way food safety, environmental and animal health regulations are implemented.

But British agriculture will only thrive in the longer term through a further, radical reorientation of the Common Agricultural Policy (CAP), away from distorting Europe-wide production subsidies towards more national responsibility for domestic farming, environmental and rural development priorities. CAP reform is now more possible; Labour's engagement with the EU gives us the best chance of making it happen.

We have begun the process of change with our farming strategy and our seven-year, £3 billion Rural Development Plans for England, Scotland, Wales and Northern Ireland. Labour will expand this programme so farming can become more diverse and responsive to consumers, and produce in a way that sustains and improves the environment. We have already increased payments for organic conversion from £0.5 million to £18 million, and will increase them further.

We have set up an independent, open and consumer-focused Food Standards Agency to ensure that all food meets the highest standards. We will argue for the extension of food labelling, to give consumers more choice. Genetically modified (GM) foods and crops have caused concern despite stringent safety checks. There should be high standards of safety - regulation must be strict, to protect the environment and promote public health and consumer choice - but we must use science to establish the facts, the opportunities and the risks before taking final decisions in an open way.

It is also important to reform the Common Fisheries Policy to preserve fish stocks for the future. In the short term, Labour is providing more than £60 million in structural funds over the next three years to help the industry, including a new decommissioning scheme while also tackling the problem of 'quota-hoppers'.

### Economic renewal
The economic hub of a rural area is often a thriving market town. That is why Labour is committing an extra £100 million of public and private funding over the next three years for the renewal of market towns. RDAs will be charged with renewal of rural as well as urban areas. We will support village life with rate relief for pubs, garages and shops, as well as farmers who diversify part of their activity into other enterprises.

Tourism is a vital, growing industry for Britain, with 1.8 million employees, and links to the museums, arts and heritage that people want to enjoy. Quality is our platform - which is why we now have a unified grading scheme for hotels and guest houses in England, and new training and New Deal opportunities. We will support well-targeted promotion, regional programmes linked to RDAs, and high-quality information via the internet. Traditional tourist resorts face special problems, so we have extended the assisted area map to include many seaside resorts and have negotiated an extension to the European Union regeneration funding so that seaside towns throughout the country can start rebuilding their economy.

## Rural life

Labour is pledged to a rural services standard to set out specifically what rural people can expect from 21 public service providers - with annual auditing and commitments to service improvement. The rural school closure programme has been ended; 3,000 new, affordable homes a year are on the way; a £30 million police programme will help cut rural crime; £239 million over three years has been set aside for rural transport services; and the Post Office is now obliged to prevent closure of rural post offices except in unavoidable circumstances, with £270 million to help achieve this and recruit sub-postmasters.

Labour is determined to protect Britain's landscapes and wildlife. Planning, transport and energy policy all make a difference. We have also designated the first new national parks since 1948 and brought consensus to a large increase in access to open countryside. We will press ahead with an £8 billion programme for water companies to clean up rivers and minimise damage from waste. The dangers of coastal and inland flooding are now widely appreciated, and we are committed to investment in preventative solutions, including more sensitive use of agricultural land. We have increased the number of protected nature sites. We have also initiated important steps to improve animal welfare in Britain, and argued successfully for higher welfare standards for battery hens and pigs across the EU.

## Leadership for the future

Labour is committed to support our countryside and the people who live and work in it. We are committed to create a new department to lead renewal in rural areas - a Department for Rural Affairs.

Independent and wide-ranging views are essential to the development of strategic and long-term policy. We will set up an independent commission to advise on how we create a sustainable, competitive and diverse farming and food sector within a thriving rural economy which advances environmental, health and animal welfare goals.

## Coalfield communities

Labour is committed to a ring-fenced £400 million package of help for Britain's ex-mining communities. This will support local regeneration, including support for new businesses. We will ensure that compensation due is paid quickly. We will also honour our commitment to ex-miners, suffering industrial diseases. We have set aside £4 billion to compensate those men who suffered from lung disease and vibration white finger after working in Britain's mining industry and the widows who nursed them.

Britain led the first industrial revolution. Other countries got ahead in the second industrial revolution. Now our ambition is for Britain to succeed in the third industrial revolution - enhancing knowledge, speeding up communication and developing the talents of all the British people.

## How Labour makes you better off:

● by saving money on your mortgage, through economic stability and low interest rates
● by targeted tax cuts for families and pensioners
● by improving living standards through action to tackle Britain's productivity gap
● by extending jobs and opportunity to every part of Britain, through regional support and a revitalised infrastructure
● by offering a minimum wage of £4.20 and an Employment Tax Credit.

## 2. WORLD-CLASS PUBLIC SERVICES

### Our ten-year goals

50 per cent of young people entering higher education, as we raise standards in secondary schools.
Maximum waiting time of three months for any stage of treatment, as we become a healthier nation with fast, high-quality treatment free at the point of use.

### Our next steps

● Every secondary school with a distinct ethos, mission and centre of excellence
● Recruit an extra 10,000 teachers
● More power to frontline staff with budgets for ward sisters and consultants and 75 per cent of NHS spending controlled by Primary Care Trusts
● More health service workers - 20,000 more nurses, and at least 10,000 more GPs and consultants
● Free access to national museums and galleries

The whole country depends on high-quality public services. We have a ten-year vision for Britain's public services: record improvement to match record investment, so they deliver high standards to all the people, all the time, wherever they live.

Since 1997 there has been investment with reform. Thanks to committed public servants, we have shown that rapid progress is possible and have begun to break the fatalism that says public services are always second class. Now is the time to move forward. Economic stability makes more investment possible. Labour will put education and healthcare first. We promise reform to match. We will decentralise power within a clear framework of national standards to increase the quality and diversity of public services and meet the challenge of rising expectations.

In education, we offer step-change in secondary schools to match the vast improvements in primary schools already achieved. Every school will have a clear mission, with more teachers, new types of school, new opportunities for children and education tailored to fulfil their potential. By 2010, we want a majority of Britain's young people entering higher education.

In health, we will recruit 20,000 extra nurses and at least 10,000 extra doctors. Our ten-year goal is a healthier nation, with fast, high-quality treatment meeting rising expectations and demographic and technological challenges. Doctors and nurses will be in the driving seat of reform.

The job of government is also about ensuring that the enjoyment, excitement and inspiration of arts and sport come alive for everyone. In all our public services, the key is to devolve and decentralise power to give freedom to frontline staff who perform well, and to change things where there are problems. Services need to be highly responsive to the demands of users. Where the quality is not improving quickly enough, alternative providers should be brought in. Where private-sector providers can support public endeavour, we should use them. A 'spirit of enterprise' should apply as much to public service as to business.

Labour's ambition for public services is simple: we want excellent services for all. Our challenge is to reverse decades of denigration and under-investment. The citizen - the patient, the pupil, their needs and aspirations - must be central. We will work with frontline staff to deliver a revival of our public services that is every bit as profound as the changes to the private sector in the 1980s.

In our first term, national action was vital to tackle crises of funding and quality. Government must take national responsibility for investment and for setting a clear national framework. Now we need to move on, empowering frontline staff. Each service needs the right structure and incentives at local level - decentralisation of power with strong incentives for high performance. Frontline staff are advocates for citizens, and ambassadors for their services. Motivated by an ethos of service, they must be supported to carry through change. (The proposals and statistics in this chapter refer to England; reform programmes for Scotland and Wales are detailed in the Scottish and Welsh manifestos.)

## Education
### Labour's number one priority
Education remains Labour's top priority. Excellence for the many, not just the few is our driving passion. Our goal is to develop education to harness the individual talents of every pupil.

Since 1997 rising standards have been achieved through major new investment and significant reforms: 17,000 schools have had vital repairs or refurbishment; 20,000 schools are now connected to the internet; there are nearly half a million fewer primary pupils in classes of more than 30; over 150,000 teachers are set to receive a £2,000 pay rise above the usual annual increase; every school is getting additional grants of up to £110,000 paid direct; and there are 11,000 more teachers and over 44,000 more support staff and classroom assistants.

Our partnership with teachers has achieved what OfSTED calls a 'transformation' in primary school standards, thanks to smaller infant class sizes and major reform in the teaching of literacy and numeracy skills. Our task now is to achieve a similar transformation in secondary education, liberating the particular talent of every child. Our pledge to parents is clear: children should be on track to achieve their best, or receiving extra expert help to catch up.

### Investment
Money alone cannot guarantee a good education, but extra investment is indispensable to achieving our ambitions. We pledge a further step-change in investment in return for a further step-change in standards.

In 1997 Labour promised to increase the share of national income devoted to education. Over this Parliament, we have increased it from 4.7 per cent to 5 per cent - £540 extra per pupil in real terms - and we are pledged to raise it to 5.3 per cent by 2003-04. Investment in buildings and equipment has trebled. During the next Parliament, we will again increase the share of national income for education.

### Under-fives
The early years of a child's life are vital. That is why we are doubling investment in early years education. There is now a free nursery place available for every four-year-old. Our new Foundation Stage provides a distinct phase of learning appropriate for the early years.

By 2004 every three-year-old will be entitled to a free nursery place in the private, voluntary or statutory sector. OfSTED will help drive up standards. Children with special educational needs will have those needs identified earlier. We will continue to provide services which integrate early years education with childcare.

By 2004 we will have 100 Early Excellence Centres as beacons of good practice providing care and education for children from 0-5; we will set up 500 Sure Start Centres in disadvantaged areas to support children's early development; and we will provide an extra 100,000 places offering wraparound care linked to early education.

### Primary schools
Primary school teachers have achieved excellent results. In 1997 barely half of 11-year-olds were up to standard in English and maths tests. The figures are now 75 per cent and 72 per cent respectively, well on the way to meeting our targets of 80 per cent in English and 75 per cent in maths by 2002. The lowest-scoring Local Education Authorities (LEAs) are now achieving better results than the national average in 1996.

But Labour will not be satisfied until every child leaves primary school with the basic skills they need. We are setting targets for an 85 per cent success rate for 11-year-olds in English and maths, and will provide further intensive support for teachers to meet them. Primary education without the basics is a betrayal; but every parent rightly wants far more. We will provide primary pupils with wider opportunities to learn sports, musical instruments and a foreign language.

### Secondary schools

Transforming secondary education is the critical challenge of the next decade. We reject a return to the 11-plus. The principles of inclusion and equality of opportunity remain central to our commitment to liberate the potential of every child. But, on their own, they are not enough to guarantee high standards.

Standards have risen in the past four years, particularly among pupils in less advantaged areas. Strong school leadership and better teaching have turned around 700 failing schools. But the challenge ahead is immense. Too many pupils fall back and become disillusioned in the first two years of secondary school. Just half of 16-year-olds currently gain good school-leaving qualifications, and levels of drop-out remain too high.

The dramatic advances at primary level mean pupils will increasingly arrive at secondary school demanding the best. We will radically modernise comprehensive schools.

In future every school must have:

### The right leadership

Headteachers must have the freedom and resources necessary to run their schools effectively. We have improved pay and training for headteachers and delegated more funding to schools. Where they demonstrate success, we will further extend their freedom to manage their schools effectively. We will reduce the regulatory burden on all schools.

### High standards in the core curriculum

We will modernise the secondary curriculum to promote higher standards and better progression from school and college to university or work-based training. All pupils should reach the age of 14 fully competent in a broad range of subjects. Effective teaching is the key. We will develop the literacy and numeracy strategies in secondary schools with the right balance of targets and flexibility, particularly for pupils not up to standard in the basics. We will set demanding targets for high achievement by the large majority of 14-year-old pupils in English, maths, science and IT tests - the passport to future success. We will promote more effective pathways beyond 14, including high-quality vocational routes that build on the new vocational GCSEs and A-levels. We will ensure there is an apprenticeship place for every young person who reaches the required standard.

### A mission to achieve

We want every secondary school to develop a distinct ethos, mission and centre of excellence. Specialist schools offer the full national curriculum to the whole ability range while developing a centre of excellence - and their rates of improvement outstrip the national average. Having trebled their number since 1997, we have pledged to expand their numbers to at least 1,500 by 2006, on the way to making specialist status available to all schools ready for it. We will encourage more church and other faith-sponsored schools, where parents wish it, We will establish more City Academies, and promote greater innovation in the supply of new schools with local consultation. We will allow greater involvement in schools by outside organisations with a serious contribution to make to raising standards. We will extend provision for gifted children as we nurture children's special talents. As part of our reform of the vital further education sector, we will encourage the development of free-standing sixth-form colleges. Schools with sixth forms will be guaranteed their funding for pupils in real terms, provided numbers are maintained. We are committed to expand Educational Maintenance Allowances so they cover 30 per cent of the country, and build upon them on the basis of the experience. Pupils will be given greater opportunities through the promotion of partnerships between schools. We will build on the partnerships established between the state and private sectors.

### Better infrastructure

We will invest nearly £8 billion in school buildings and equipment over the next three years, including the construction of 650 new or completely refurbished schools. IT has enormous potential to raise standards, and it is vital that every child leaves school able to make use of the new technologies. Today, nearly all schools are connected to the internet. Labour is committed to spend £1.8 billion over six years on equipping our schools for the information age. We will pioneer Curriculum Online to ensure materials are available to pupils in school and at home. We are committed to continue to extend access to IT for pupils and teachers, including the possibility of a national leasing scheme to make top-quality hardware available at very low prices.

### The right support

Good schools also depend on parents and the local community, We will continue to ensure that headteachers have the powers they need to tackle disruption and unacceptable behaviour in schools. Local education authorities will focus on supporting school improvement, especially weak and failing schools, and delivering services that cannot be provided by individual schools. We will ensure better training and support for school governors.

Schools should be used more effectively as assets for the whole community, including for childcare and community learning, We will pilot 'extended hours schools' to develop this resource. We will build on the success of more than 40 study centres based in leading football clubs by extending community involvement to other sports. Over time we want to develop safe places for children to play outside school hours and every pupil to have access to a summer school programme. An Academy for Talented Youth will be established in partnership with a leading university to pioneer summer and other dedicated provision for those with special talents.

We have significantly improved support and provision for children with special needs or disabilities. They should have access to the best possible education, with appropriate support, whether mainstream or special schooling most suits their needs.

Schools in the toughest areas, and the teachers who work in them, need special support. We will expand the Excellence in Cities programme for urban secondary schools, with extra help for the weakest schools, learning mentors and in-school units to help manage pupil behaviour. Where LEAs cannot effectively support school improvement, alternative provision will be made. For schools facing exceptional pressures, for example very high pupil turnover, we will provide additional support, including significant reductions in the size of teaching groups where appropriate.

### Teachers

Nothing in education is more important than having good teachers. We have made teaching a far more attractive career, through better pay, better incentives to train including training salaries and loan write-offs, more recognition and improved support. The General Teaching Council and National College for School Leadership are both now up and running.

We want teaching to be a career of choice for the best graduates and attractive to people making career changes. We will continue to invest more in the profession and improve conditions for teachers. High status, better salaries and proper professional support are all essential. We are conducting a strategic review of teacher workload and the right balance between teaching and administration, central direction and local discretion. We will build on its findings significantly to improve support for teachers in the classroom and in administrative tasks, so they can concentrate on their job. We will:

- recruit 10,000 extra teachers and improve the adult: pupil ratio
- support teachers in the classroom by employing more adults to help them
- invest in rapid promotion and rewards for classroom excellence
- boost recruitment and retention packages for teachers, particularly in high-cost areas and schools facing exceptional challenges
- create new routes into teaching, including 'train-to-teach' courses accredited as part of undergraduate degrees and a stronger training mission for outstanding schools
- further improve in-service training opportunities for teachers
- develop school achievement awards that reward staff in 7,000 fast-improving schools a year
- subsidise new PCs for teachers so that they have direct access to the latest technology.

### Higher education - a world leader

Higher education brings on average 20 per cent higher earnings and a 50 per cent lower chance of unemployment. It is time for an historic commitment to open higher education to half of all young people before they are 30, combined with increased investment to maintain academic standards.

In 1997 we inherited a system where the number of qualified people able to go to university was capped. Today, the numbers are rising and universities have the funds to expand, with new two-year foundation degrees to offer students the option of a vocationally relevant, high-quality qualification as a way into skilled work or further study. Over the next three years, we will continue to expand student numbers, taking us towards our 50 per cent target.

We will maintain university entry standards while intensifying efforts to extend the huge advantages that a university education confers to able young people from all backgrounds. University summer schools, master classes and mentoring support will be offered to potential students from disadvantaged areas through a new Excellence Challenge programme, backed up by £190 million of funding.

We will not introduce 'top-up' fees and have legislated to prevent them. Since 1997 we have increased university funding by more than a billion pounds a year over the Parliament - and invested considerably more in research. Our new system of university finance ensures that 50 per cent of students pay no tuition fees at all, that no parents pay more than under the old system, and that students pay back loans progressively when they are earning. We will ensure that the funding system continues to promote access and excellence.

We will strengthen research and teaching excellence. It is vital that our world-leading universities are able to compete with the best internationally. We will also support world-class research and the development of public-private partnerships. We are determined to ensure that our universities have the freedom and incentives to meet our ambitions for them. Reforms to the inspection system for teaching will slash red tape for higher performing departments.

### Health
### Quality services from a growing NHS

For over 50 years the NHS has been part and parcel of what it means to be British. If you fall ill, the NHS is there. Its foundations - tax-based funding and care according to need - remain as valid today as ever.

The NHS employs one million dedicated people. But it needs far-reaching reform to redesign its services around the needs of patients. Labour's ten-year NHS Plan is our strategy for ensuring fast, convenient, high-quality care in all parts of the country. We will implement it through the next Parliament and, if elected, beyond. Reform will be driven through primary care trusts (PCTs) as power and resources are decentralised to frontline staff.

In 1997, waiting lists were at record levels and rising, hospital building had ground to a halt, and the number of nurses working in the NHS had fallen. Today, waiting lists are down by over 100,000 and waiting times are falling. There are 17,000 more nurses, over 6,500 more doctors, and over 9,000 more therapists, scientists and technicians working for patients. The biggest-ever hospital building programme is under way. NHS Direct, the 24-hour nurse helpline, is available across the country. Eye tests for people who are 60 and over are now free.

But there is a lot more to do. We are committed to investment and reform.

With Labour, in just four years the NHS will have grown by a third. Spending on the health service is now rising by an average of over six per cent a year in real terms - the biggest sustained increase in its history and double that under the Conservatives. Provided that as a country we maintain economic stability, we will, if elected, be able to sustain significant funding increases throughout the next Parliament. So over time we will bring UK health spending up to the EU average.

### The fundamentals of care

That money will help us get the basics right. By 2005 there will be 10,000 more doctors and 20,000 more nurses, with ward sisters in charge of ward budgets. Matrons will make sure that hospital food is good and wards are clean. with power to stop payments to contractors who fail to keep hospitals up to scratch.

'Nightingale' wards for older people and mixed sex wards will be abolished, and mental health wards will be modernised. There will be 7,000 extra beds in hospitals and in intermediate care. And we will build 100 new hospital developments by 2010 and 500 one-stop primary care centres, with over 3,000 GP premises modernised by 2004. We are investing an extra £7 billion of capital investment into the health service. We have said that Private Finance Initiative (PFI) should not be delivered at the expense of the pay and conditions of the staff employed in these schemes. We will seek ways in which, within the framework of PFI management, support staff could remain part of the NHS team.

### Improving health

Our job is not just to improve the nation's health service. It is to improve the nation's health. Deaths from cancer and heart disease are too high. There has been a growing health gap between rich and poor. Beyond other commitments to combat child poverty and poor housing, we will tackle the long-standing causes of ill-health and health inequality by:
- making the fight against cancer, heart disease and stroke the top priority for investment and reform, with earmarked extra funding of £1 billion by 2004. The number of cardiologists will increase by around half and cancer specialists by nearly a third by 2005 compared to 1999-2000. Waiting times for cancer treatment will be cut. Our ambition is to prevent 300,000 avoidable deaths over the next decade
- tough targets to close the health gap to cut deaths in poorer communities and among poorer children, improving mental health services, and a new emphasis on prevention, with more screening services including for conditions like sickle cell disease, cystic fibrosis and newborn hearing problems
- offering the world's best smoking cessation services to help the seven in ten smokers who say they want to give up
- giving children aged four to six in nursery and primary schools a free piece of fruit every school day - the biggest boost to child nutrition since free school milk was introduced in 1946.

We remain committed to our bill - blocked by the Tories - to ban tobacco advertising and sponsorship.

### Reforming the NHS

The NHS has to earn the confidence of each new generation. It has to change the way it works if it is to meet today's challenges and provide fast and modern services. With Labour, by 2004 patients will be able to see a GP within 48 hours. By the end of 2005 we will cut maximum waiting times for outpatient appointments from six months to three months, and for inpatients from 18 months to six months by expanding staff numbers and reforming how care is delivered. Major conditions like cancer and heart disease will have priority, with all patients treated according to clinical urgency.

We will give patients more choice. We have restored the right of family doctors to refer patients to the hospital that is right for them. Now we will redesign the system around the needs of patients. Same day tests and diagnosis will become the norm. By extending the use of NHS Direct and increasing the numbers of dentists, patients will get easier access to NHS dentistry wherever they live. Specially built surgical units - managed by the NHS or the private sector - will guarantee shorter waiting times. We will use spare capacity in private-sector hospitals, treating NHS patients free of charge, where high standards and value for money are guaranteed. It would be wrong to push people into paying for their operations. That is why we reject the approach of the Conservatives, which would lead to this outcome.

By the end of 2005 every hospital appointment will be booked for the convenience of the patient, making it easier for patients and their GP to choose the hospital and consultant that best suits their needs. From next year, if an operation is cancelled on the day of surgery for non-clinical reasons, the hospital will have to offer another binding date within 28 days, or fund the patient's treatment at the time and hospital of the patient's choice. By modernising all maternity units, increasing the number of midwives and giving women greater choice over childbirth, we will ensure that women receive the highest quality maternity care. There will be tough new standards for care of children, the elderly and people with conditions like diabetes, kidney failure, multiple sclerosis, Parkinson's disease and epilepsy.

We will further tackle the 'lottery of care' as we direct local health authorities and trusts to fund drugs and treatments recommended by the National Institute for Clinical Excellence (NICE). Genetic services will be extended in the NHS so that more patients enjoy the benefit of the latest advances in testing and treatment; but we will ban by law human cloning, and implement a moratorium on the use of genetic tests for insurance, following a recommendation of the Human Genetics Commission. We will continue to examine demographic and technological challenges as they affect the NHS.

Patients will have more say, as in the NHS Plan. We will give every citizen a personal smartcard containing key medical data giving access to their medical records. Older people, people with disabilities and their carers will be able to decide which services they want, with the choice of having cash given to them directly by local councils. Patients will be represented on trust boards and have more information on local services' quality.

## Power devolved

To achieve this vision there will be clear national standards but greater decentralisation to frontline services and to the staff who run them. Locally agreed personal medical services schemes will be extended. By 2004 all local healthcare will be organised by primary care trusts (PCTs) run by frontline doctors and nurses. Together with the new care trusts, combining health and social services, PCTs will control 75 per cent of NHS funding. With more power for PCTs we will cut the number of health authorities by two-thirds and devolve to the remainder the functions of NHS Regional Offices. We will use the savings of £100 million a year for investment in frontline services. Hospitals and other local services will have greater control over their own affairs and access to a £500 million performance fund, while consistently failing NHS hospitals will be taken over by successful NHS hospitals. Appointments to trust boards will no longer be made by ministers but by an independent panel.

## NHS staff

None of these ambitions will be possible without major investment in the skill, working conditions and working practices of all NHS staff. There will be extra pay too in high-cost areas, with pressure relieved through expanded staff numbers, reformed working practices and investment in training.

Every NHS employer will offer more flexible working hours for staff and especially nurses. Childcare provision will be improved and we will offer targeted subsidies for childcare for NHS staff. The pay system will be reformed to make it fairer. As set out in the NHS Plan, there will be new contracts for GPs and hospital consultants, coupled to extra money. We will examine the case for a public-private partnership with a commercial mortgage lender to make home ownership more affordable for nurses and other staff.

We will set up a University of the NHS to guarantee to staff at all levels opportunities for training and career development. Healthcare assistants, porters, cooks and cleaners will be offered an individual learning account worth £300 a year to develop their careers. We will examine the potential for sabbaticals to help GPs, consultant nurses and consultants keep their skills up to date.

There will be new systems to learn from when things go wrong, a core education curriculum for all health professionals and reforms to modernise the way health professions are regulated. We will take action to protect NHS staff from violence and abuse, and reform the clinical negligence system.

This is a vision worth fighting for. It will take time to achieve, but this is the most comprehensive plan ever put before the British people to improve the state of the nation's health and our health service. It will deliver an NHS to be proud of.

## Culture and sport

The arts and sports are key to our quality of life. They matter for their own sake. Millions make their living out of their creativity. Government can and must make sure the opportunities are there. But, for the last 20 years, under-investment, misplaced priorities, and lack of organisation held back access and excellence.

Since 1997 this has begun to change. We have started to invest and to reform the system. Investment in theatre develops the film and television stars of tomorrow; investment in sport will produce the Olympic and Paralympic medal winners of 2012.

Culture and sport should not be seen as peripheral issues - they are vital to our identity and enjoyment as a country. We are pledged to the investment necessary to expand access and excellence together in culture and sport, building on excellence in film and broadcasting.

## Sport

The performance of British athletes at the Sydney Olympics and Paralympics thrilled everyone. Labour is committed to a radical extension of sporting opportunities and facilities. Sport is a good health policy, a good crime reduction policy, a good way of building communities.

We pledge a sports entitlement for all children, giving them access to at least two hours a week of sport in or after school. Thanks to our ban on the enforced sale of playing fields and a commitment of nearly £1 billion to new sports facilities and 1,000 school sports co-ordinators, all children will be offered coaching and competitive games. Children with talent need more investment: we have pledged to fund 200 specialist sports colleges. We will maintain the elite funding we put in place for individual athletics, with a first-class athletics stadium for the World Athletics Championships in 2005 and a new stadium in Manchester for next year's Commonwealth Games.

We are committed to sell the Tote to a racing trust to allow it to compete commercially, with all long-term profits invested in the sport. We are committed to finding ways to support the amateur sports clubs to which 5.6 million people now belong.

The House of Commons elected in 1997 made clear its wish to ban fox-hunting. The House of Lords took a different view (and reform has been blocked). Such issues are rightly a matter for a free vote and we will give the new House of Commons an early opportunity to express its view.

We will then enable Parliament to reach a conclusion on this issue. If the issue continues to be blocked we will look at how the disagreement can be resolved. We have no intention whatsoever of placing restrictions on the sports of angling and shooting.

## Arts

Thirty million people enjoy arts activities each year. The arts are crucial to national life, with a huge importance for the creative and tourist industries. Yet the Conservatives introduced charges for our national museums and galleries, cut the arts budget, and reduced support for arts education.

Since 1997 that has changed. National museums are already free for children and pensioners. Labour is committed to reform the VAT system to ensure they will be made free for everyone from December. By 2004, arts funding will be 60 per cent above its 1997 level in real terms.

An extra £25 million a year will go to regional theatre, increasing the number and quality of productions for audiences in England. We have invested in our orchestras, and put an extra £10 million a year into developing our regional museums and galleries. We have maintained our commitment to the nation's heritage and to its historic buildings, and we will continue our drive to put architectural quality at the heart of the design of new public buildings.

Education is the bedrock of an artistic society. We are once again giving children the opportunity to learn music, and we will ensure the opportunity is available to all. New creative partnerships - linking schools with artists and arts organisations particularly in disadvantaged areas - will offer children the chance to develop artistic and creative talents. We will build on the pilot projects.

We have made the largest-ever investment in computerising libraries; all will be on-line by 2002, with guaranteed standards to meet users' needs.

From 2002, Culture On-line will offer children and adults alike tailored access to our national collections and cultural activity over the internet. We will create new specialist arts schools and city academies to offer specialist education to the most talented young people.

Public money devoted to the arts should be spent on excellent art, not bureaucracy. The Arts Council is undergoing substantial reform - creating a simpler structure which gives more power to the regions, cuts bureaucratic costs further, and which can deliver a better service to individual artists and arts organisations. We will ensure that our arts funding system backs excellence, giving artists and arts organisations the long-term stability they need to become world leaders.

## Creative industries

The creative industries are a vital engine of our economy, providing jobs for over one million people. The National Endowment for Science, Technology and the Arts (NESTA) has been set up to back our most talented young people.

Creative entrepreneurs need seed funding, cheap accommodation near other similar companies, and advice on how to develop their talent into a business. To meet those needs, we now plan to provide start-up advice, services and funding for new businesses. Venture capital will be available through RDAs, and a creative industries champion will be appointed in every Business Link.

## Lottery

Under the Conservatives, many communities missed out on their fair share of lottery money. The number of grants to community groups has trebled with Labour, yet there are still communities which have received a disproportionately small share of lottery funding. We will ensure a fairer deal for them.

Labour has reshaped the lottery to match people's priorities. Money goes for revenue as well as capital. The New Opportunities Fund (NOF) directs help to education, health and the environment - after-school clubs, vital cancer-beating equipment, local green spaces.

We backed going ahead with the Dome as an opportunity to showcase British talent and give people a good day out in millennium year.

Despite being enjoyed by more than six million visitors, the Dome did not fulfil expectations and we have learned the lessons, good and bad, from it. But the development of the Dome has been the catalyst for unlocking the value of the North Greenwich peninsula and regenerating local communities.

We need a revolution in the status, standards and focus of our public services. Labour is prepared to make the investment in staff and services and we are ready to match investment with reform.

### How Labour helps young people

- by raising standards and investing more in education, from nursery schools to adult learning
- by giving the majority of young adults the opportunity to study in higher education
- by tackling youth unemployment with the New Deal made permanent
- by opportunities to train as you work, through modern apprenticeships and the right to time off to study
- by expanding sports facilities in schools and in the community
- by cleaning up the environment, with support for green technologies and global action to tackle climate change

## 3. A MODERN WELFARE STATE

### Our ten-year goals

Sustain a higher percentage of people in work than ever before, as we seek full employment in every region. Child poverty halved and pensioner poverty tackled, as we extend opportunity for all children and security for all pensioners.

### Our next steps

- An 'Employment First' interview for everyone coming on to benefits
- Expanded support for children through tax and benefit reform
- Extend and increase paid maternity leave and introduce paid paternity leave
- New pension credit for lower- and middle-income pensioners, and the Winter Fuel Payment retained
- £900 million Neighbourhood Renewal Fund for jobs, education and crime prevention

As society changes, so the welfare state must change. We have a ten-year vision for an active welfare state: to promote work for those who can, security for those who cannot, and rewards for those who save, volunteer, learn or train. Since 1997, we have cut the costs of unemployment, saving £4 billion last year. As a result, we have been able to spend more on tackling poverty and raising family support within a social security budget that has grown, in Labour's first term, at the lowest rate since 1948.

Employment is not just the foundation of affordable welfare, it is the best anti-poverty, anti-crime and pro-family policy yet invented. After years of mass unemployment, full employment is now on the agenda. Our ten-year goal is to sustain a higher percentage of people in work than ever before. With more than one million more people in work than in 1997, and a million vacancies in the economy, we need to extend the New Deal, not abolish it as the Conservatives propose.

We judge our society by how we treat the young and old. In this Parliament, over one million children have been taken out of poverty; our ten-year goal is to halve child poverty, ending it in a generation. We will transform support for children to achieve it.

For those in retirement, security depends on partnership between state and funded provision. We promise that, within two years, no pensioner need live on less than £100 per week, increased annually in line with earnings growth. On top of that, we will reward pensioners who save.

Government cannot achieve social inclusion for people, but it can help them achieve it for themselves, by transferring power and opportunity to local communities. That is our promise.

### Full employment

#### Labour's goal

With Labour, the welfare state helps people into work, makes work pay, supports them at work, and demands responsibilities in return. Our ambition is full employment in every region - good for the economy and good for social justice.

The New Deal has already helped to cut long-term youth unemployment by 75 per cent - 280,000 young people have been helped into work. Long-term unemployment is down by over 60 per cent. The claimant count is the lowest for 25 years.

But too many people are still denied the opportunity to work. A million people remain unemployed; 100,000 lone parents have come off income support since 1997, but our target is to raise the current 50 per cent employment rate to 70 per cent. Many people with disabilities out of work say they would like to work. Older people, with a wealth of talent and experience, are a resource we cannot afford to waste.

Labour has ended the days of low-grade job schemes. The New Deal leads to real jobs, a lower benefits bill and higher tax receipts. We now need to build on its success, extending it to more people across the country.

We also need to ensure that the barriers to work are pulled down by delivering on our obligation to tackle discrimination so that all people can make the most of their talents.

### Making the New Deal a permanent deal

The benefits system we inherited was fragmented, complex and contradictory. We are putting in place clear, consistent rules: those who can work should be in work or in contact with the labour market. As unemployment falls, we need further reform to help people into work. Labour will introduce a new principle of 'employment first', with rights and responsibilities balanced at every stage. The contract is simple: quality opportunities for real responsibility. 'Something for something' is the foundation.

Labour is pledged to create a new Working Age Agency, JobCentre Plus, merging the old Employment Service and Benefits Agency, and focusing on the key skill needs of areas of the country and sectors of the economy. Whoever you are, wherever you live, you will get the opportunities suited to your needs - from one office, one adviser, one system.

The New Deals for young people and older workers will focus on numeracy, literacy, IT skills and presentation. Where people are homeless or suffer drug or mental health problems we will offer specialist support. More than 140,000 adults aged over 25 have been unemployed for over 18 months. Labour will deliver more intensive and flexible help, with increased responsibilities for claimants.

We will offer greater flexibility to personal advisers and encourage greater engagement of employers, with IT training for all New Dealers. Employment Zones include funding geared to results and public-private partnership. On the basis of the evidence we will consider their extension to new areas and new claimant groups. We will build on the Action Teams for Jobs model, which is targeting 40 of the most severely disadvantaged areas, to tackle the employment gap for ethnic minorities, and devote £45 million to provide stepping stones into employment for the hardest to employ.

All lone parents will be invited to employment interviews to help them seek employment opportunities. We will build on the lessons of the Choices programme, which offers help with learning, work and childcare. Partners of unemployed people with children, like those without children, will also be asked to interviews to discuss their options.

Parents need good-quality and affordable childcare if they are to have real choice about work. For the first time, Britain has a National Childcare Strategy - covering cost, provision and quality. We have already created 300,000 extra childcare places. By 2004 our target is to have childcare places for 1.6 million children. Our vision is ambitious: safe and reliable childcare nationwide, allowing all parents to combine home and work, confident in the childcare they have chosen. We will help with the costs of childcare through the Childcare Tax Credit - and will look to extend it to people looking after children with disabilities, and shift workers. We will support the commitment of community and voluntary groups to build up a diverse range of childcare - from Early Excellence Centres to neighbourhood nurseries and informal care (see 'World-class public services').

Many older workers now want to continue in work full- or part-time. Yet one in three people between 50 and state pension age is not working. To help them we will build on the New Deal 50+. To help bridge the divide between work and retirement, we will examine ways to ensure that people will be able to draw on their occupational pension and continue to work part-time for the same employer, phasing their retirement without compromising their pension. We are exploring how to facilitate the transition from work to positive voluntary activity.

Our ambition of full employment is part of a deal: if you put in a fair day's work, the government will ensure you are able to support yourself and your family. The minimum wage is the foundation. But we offer a guarantee of take-home pay too. For people with families, we promise to match your effort with support through the tax system. For those on low incomes without children we will create an Employment Tax Credit to boost their earnings, tackle poverty and improve work incentives.

### People with disabilities

Our ambition is to enable people with disabilities to play a full part in the community. The Disability Rights Commission now ensures full civil rights for people with disabilities; we have legislated so those with special needs or disabilities have equal access to education. We are now committed to extending basic rights and opportunities, as indicated in our response to the Disability Rights Taskforce.

We are requiring different kinds of public transport to be made accessible, and introducing concessionary bus fares for the first time, for people with disabilities.

The New Deal for Disabled People pioneers new ways of helping people with disabilities into jobs. The opportunity to work is vital to civil rights; we are testing how best to offer help with rehabilitation and job retention. We will invest an additional £40 million to help people with disabilities into work, ensure that it is worthwhile to try out a job and stay in work if they have high care costs, and improve assessment for equipment and services as people move in and out of work.

We will not use disability benefits to disguise unemployment - the Tory approach in the 1980s. The number of people getting Incapacity Benefit (IB) has fallen by 11 per cent since 1997; but too many people are written off when in fact they could, with support, work.

We will help break down the barriers that keep people with disabilities out of work. We will continue to modernise the operation of the benefits system so that, if people can work, we help them to do so, and stop them slipping from lack of work to inability to work. Around 18 million working days are lost each year due to work-related illness - at a cost of over £17 billion. Many people on Industrial Injuries Benefit are helped into work by combining support with effective services, and we want to help as many of the rest as possible. But if people cannot work society has a duty to provide security for them.

For people unable to take up paid work, we are committed to offer security. We have increased support for children with parents on income support by 80 per cent in real terms since 1997. There is now a minimum income guarantee of £142 per week for people with disabilities under 60. Incapacity Benefit has been extended to people disabled from a young age. Disability Living Allowance has been extended to three- and four-year-olds. We will continue to keep the system under review.

### Housing benefit

Although the number of people claiming housing benefit is currently falling, it remains the main way in which accommodation is made affordable. Our first priority has been to work with local authorities to drive up administrative standards and tackle fraud and error. But we must continue to reform it. So we will simplify housing benefit and its administration, distinguishing between people of working age and pensioners, reforming provision for private tenants, and examining the case for longer awards. We will spread best practice in administration. In the longer term, we will build on our restructuring of rents to ensure that for people of working age, housing benefit as well as the Working Families Tax Credit strengthen work incentives.

### Children and families

Strong and stable family life offers the best possible start to children. And marriage provides a strong foundation for stable relationships. The government supports marriage. But it has to do more than that. It must support families, above all families with children. Our vision of the tax and benefits system for families with children is to provide help for all families; to give most help at the time families need it most; and to give more help to those families most in need. The Conservatives stacked the tax system against families: over four million children lived in poverty; one in five children were growing up in households without work; the average income of households with children had fallen to 30 per cent below the level for those without children.

Labour has started to turn this round. We have raised child benefit for the first child by over a quarter. The Working Families Tax Credit has meant a tax cut averaging £31 per week for 1.1 million families. In 2001-02, an average of nearly £500 above 1997-98 levels will be invested in every child in Britain. Personal tax and benefit changes have made families with children an average of £1,000 a year better off.

We are pledged to go further - to eradicate child poverty in a generation and halve it by 2010. In the next Parliament we will make major changes. The Children's Tax Credit - the family tax cut - is worth up to £520 a year for five million families, with half a million families removed from paying tax altogether. It is paid until one parent earns more than £40,000 per year.

From 2003, the Integrated Child Credit will bring together all existing income-related payments for children, providing most help to the neediest children, building on the foundation of universal child benefit. With the new system of child support, every family will receive at least £15 per week, and those most in need £50 per week - over £2,500 per year. For the first time, Britain will have a seamless system of child support, whether parents are in or out of work, paid to the main carer.

Our aim is to make the goal of ending child poverty in Britain a political litmus test for any political party running for office. The task for the next Parliament is to help another million children out of poverty.

## Assets

Our active welfare state has so far been based on work, finance and services. It is now time to add a fourth pillar to the welfare state - a programme to extend to all children the advantages that come from reaching adulthood backed by a financial nest-egg.

Nearly a third of individuals have no financial savings or assets at all. People without assets are much more likely to have lower earnings and higher unemployment, and are less likely to start a business or enter higher education.

The government already encourages people to save for a rainy day and save for a pension. We are determined to extend the savings habit to more people. But we are pledged also to use saving to promote opportunity for the next generation.

All newly born children will have an interest-bearing Child Trust Fund set up in their name with an initial endowment from the government, with more for poorer children. The endowment will be locked until the child reaches adulthood. We will provide incentives for extended family and friends as well as parents to contribute to the fund. All the next generation will have the backing of a real financial asset to invest in learning, buying a home or setting up a business.

## Caring for children

A safe childhood is not just about financial security. It is also about care for children, especially the 58,000 children in care. Society is failing these children: 70 per cent leave school without any GCSEs and too many have been abused while in care.

Labour supports a national children's rights director to act as a champion for children in need and we will consult on whether to develop and extend the director's role. The Criminal Records Bureau will help stop paedophiles and others who are a danger to children from working with them. From next year, all children's homes will, for the first time, be subject to independent spot checks. The level of educational attainment of children in care will be significantly increased. Every child leaving care will be guaranteed access to a job, training or education.

For many children in care, adoption offers the best chance of success in life. We will make adoption faster and fairer. Children who need new families will be placed within 12 months by 2004. We aim to ensure that at least 1,000 more children a year are adopted, with improved post-adoption support for parents.

## Family-friendly working

For the majority of parents, time is precious. Many employers offer excellent schemes for family-friendly working. But we want to go further - with government funding to help parents devote more time to their children early in life. We want government to promote choice because, without our help, many people are denied the choices that should be theirs. A flexible labour market must work to the benefit of both employers and employees.

Statutory maternity leave is currently 18 weeks; we propose to increase it to six months. Statutory maternity pay is paid at a flat rate of £60 a week; we propose to increase it to £100 per week, as big an increase in the next two years as in the past 40 years. Fathers currently have no legal right to paid time off on the birth of a child; we propose to introduce it for two weeks, also paid at £100 per week. We need to do more to help parents balance work and family. Many parents, especially mothers, want to work reduced hours when they do go back to work. We will work with business and employees to combine flexible working with the needs of business.

## Child Support Agency

Some families break up. Government's role is to ensure that both parents retain responsibility for the financial support of their children where they are able to do so. We have always supported the principle underlying the work of the Child Support Agency (CSA), but the Conservatives bungled its introduction. That is why we have already legislated to reform the CSA and these improvements will come on stream from 2002. A simple system will ensure a better deal for children, that fathers pay a fair share, that mothers benefit from their doing so, and that tougher action is taken against parents who do not comply.

### Pensions and pensioners
In 1997 Labour made a clear commitment to ensure pensioners share fairly in the rising prosperity of the nation. At this election, we repeat our commitment to pensioners - we honour your lifetime of work by ensuring that you share fairly in the nation's rising prosperity, and are committed to tackling pensioner poverty. We will build a secure system on the foundation of the basic state pension.

As a result of Labour's policies, in this Parliament spending on pensioners will be £4.5 billion a year more in real terms than in 1997. Of this, £2 billion is going to the poorest third of pensioners.

Our first priority was to help those on lowest incomes: we have lifted the incomes of the 1.7 million poorest pensioners by at least £800 a year, and for some couples by up to £1,400. Pensioner households are on average £11 per week better off than they were in 1997; and over three million pensioner households benefit from free TV licences for those over-75s.

The pensioners tax allowance means six out of ten pensioners pay no tax. We have halved the rate of tax they pay on savings income. We have pledged to extend tax allowances further so that by 2003 no pensioner pays tax until their income reaches £127 per week.

We now need to go further. With Labour, the basic state pension will rise by 2003 to £77 a week for a single pensioner and £123 a week for a pensioner couple. We guarantee that the Minimum Income Guarantee will be uprated each year in line with earnings, throughout the next Parliament. In 2003, this will mean no single pensioner will have an income below £100 per week and no pensioner couple an income below £154 per week.

Labour introduced the Winter Fuel Payment. Its level is set each year. Last winter it was raised to £200. For next winter it will also be £200.

We will also do more to reward pensioners who have saved. Pensioners who work and save will find, for the first time ever, the government rewarding their saving.

Pensioner couples with an income up to £200 per week and single pensioners with income up to £135 per week will be rewarded for saving - the government adding up to 60p for each £1 of savings income up to a maximum of £23. In the process, we will abolish the weekly means test for pensioners, along with removing the unfair test of savings, which penalises pensioners who have modest savings and whose thrift should be recognised.

It is also vital to have in place long-term pension reform. We support a fair balance of public and private provision. Occupational and personal pensions, properly regulated, will continue to offer security for middle and high earners.

We will continue discussions on annuity reform to ensure tax rules do not unnecessarily restrict the development of annuity products and markets. For low- to middle-income earners, stakeholder pensions cap costs, guarantee value for money, offer flexibility, and drive down fees across the board.

And for the lowest paid and carers, full-time parents and people with disabilities, the state second pension will top up their pension contributions to give a decent pension in retirement to 18 million people.

Today's pensioners have much to give to society. Labour's NHS Plan offers £1.4 billion of investment for older people to promote better health and support independence. Pensioners also need simple, accessible services that treat them with dignity and promote independence.

We will build on Care Direct to provide a better integration of health, housing, benefits and social care for older people. This will be an integrated 'third age service' to help older people and those who care for them.

### Carers
Not only are the large majority of people who require care older, but also the majority of carers are older people. Labour will tackle the problems faced by people requiring care and the problems of carers themselves.

The national carers strategy is the first step, with information, support and care for carers: Labour will spend £500 million over the next three years providing financial support for 300,000 carers through the benefits system, and £255 million for social care services for carers.

More is being done for carers through income support; carers will be better able to combine work and care; and 75,000 more carers each year are now able to take a break from their caring responsibilities. We are proud that, with Labour, care by qualified nurses will be made free to all, wherever it is received.

One hundred and fifty thousand more older people will receive rehabilitation and convalescence through growing investment in the NHS and social services that the Tories refuse to match. We want to see carers given access to the cash and services appropriate to their service to their relatives and the community.

The Carers and Disabled Children's Act gives carers a right to an independent assessment of their needs. We will examine the development of a fund to help local authorities produce tailored care packages to back up the results of these assessments.

### Social inclusion
Social exclusion, affecting around ten per cent of the population, living in fewer than 1,000 of the most deprived wards in Britain, damages lives and wrecks communities. Before 1997, social exclusion was ignored. Now we have a new approach - improving the quality of mainstream services, preventing people falling between the cracks, and reintegrating them into society if things go wrong. We have targeted five priorities:

**Homelessness**
The number of people living on the streets is down by one third since 1997. Labour's target is to cut rough sleeping to two-thirds of its 1998 level by 2002. Beyond then, we will maintain the drive to keep the number as low as possible.

**Teenage pregnancy rates are falling**
Yet Britain has the highest rates in Europe. Labour's strategy tackles the causes of teenage pregnancy, provides mothers under 18 with access to supervised housing if they cannot live at home, and ensures that, if they do have children, teenagers get access to training, education or work. By 2004 we are pledged to reduce teenage pregnancy by 15 per cent.

**Truancy and exclusion**
Labour has a target of reducing truancy and exclusion by a third by 2002. The police are conducting truancy sweeps; parents are now subject to fines of up to £2,500; funds are being targeted towards pupils at risk.

**16- to 18-year-olds**
Nearly ten per cent of 16- to 18-year-olds are not in education, training or work. The new Connexions service will bridge the gap, providing a single adviser to ensure all young people receive clear advice on the transition to work.

**Neighbourhood renewal**
Over the next three years Labour is pledged to back reform, with £900 million of investment in deprived neighbourhoods. We want local people to lead renewal - a coalition of public, private and voluntary organisations specifying priorities, engaging local effort. Local Strategic Partnerships, which we have introduced to help co-ordinate public service improvement, will be properly inclusive of local people, involving them in decision-making. They will be backed by specific funds to engage the local community. Nearly £100 million has been set aside for business start-ups, and we will create a new tax credit for community investment to create £1 billion of investment in disadvantaged areas.

**A popular welfare state**
Labour's objective is to get the right benefit to the right people at the right time. We want those entitled to benefits to take up their rights to claim them. Fraud undermines confidence in the welfare system, so we are committed to reduce it.

We have been prepared to be tough - preventing fraud by tightening gateways, sharpening sanctions on fraudsters, and now with 'two-strikes-and-you're-out'. We have saved £1 billion in fraud and error over the course of the Parliament by tightening up the way we administer income support. The introduction of Automated Credit Transfer will save a further £100 million per year.

Labour is committed to clear targets for fraud reduction for each benefit, including a commitment to halve the rate of fraud and error in income support and Job Seeker's Allowance by 2006, and to incorporate fraud prevention into the design of new policies on benefits and tax credits. We are also committed to data sharing between government agencies and action to reduce to a minimum the number of 'spare' national insurance numbers that are a gateway to fraud.

Our welfare state is underpinned by clear values - we help you to help yourself, we invest in children, we support our pensioners, we insist that no community be written off, and we minimise fraud and error. Our reforms will build a strong and inclusive society.

**How Labour helps pensioners:**
● by boosting the basic state pension for a single pensioner to £77 each week in 2003, £123 for couples
● by retaining the Winter Fuel Payment and free TV licences for over-75s
● by rewarding those who save with the Pension Credit
● by raising the Minimum Income Guarantee to £100 each week (£154 for couples) in 2003
● by tackling discrimination against over-50s in health care and in the workplace
● by boosting police numbers and cutting overall crime, and crimes like burglary that affect senior citizens the most.

## 4. STRONG AND SAFE COMMUNITIES

**Our ten-year goals**
Halve the burglary rate and double the chance of a persistent offender being caught and punished, as we modernise the criminal justice system.
Reformed local government with higher-quality services, as we decentralise power.

**Our next steps**
● An extra 6,000 police recruits raising police numbers to their highest ever level
● Double the amount of assets seized from drug traffickers and other major criminals
● Increased sentences plus education and drug treatment for persistent offenders
● A bill of rights for victims
● New freedoms with new targets for local government

We all know the sort of Britain we want to live in - a Britain where we can walk the streets safely and know our children are safe. We have a ten-year vision: a new social contract where everyone has a stake based on equal rights, where they pay their dues by exercising responsibility in return, and where local communities shape their own futures.

Overall crime is down ten per cent in Labour Britain, recorded crime down seven per cent, and police numbers are now rising. Our strategy is clear and consistent - tough on crime and tough on the causes of crime.

Our ten-year goal of reducing crime depends on reform of the criminal justice system at every level, from police to courts to prison - to put crime reduction centre stage. And, because crime is changing, crime fighting has to change too - to tackle repeat offending, drug-related crime and organised crime. We are investing to raise police numbers to their highest level ever. Offenders must know they will be supervised in or out of prison until they can prove they have gone straight.

Safe communities reclaim their streets; then they can shape their own affairs. In the 19th century, local politics was the motor for economic and social change. Our purpose is simple: to create a Britain that is democratic, decentralised and diverse, with decisions always taken as close to the people as is consistent with efficiency and equity. Our ten-year goal is a new settlement with local government - over finance, structures and services.

## Responsibility from all
### Winning the battle against crime
Recorded crime doubled under the Conservatives: burglary went up 105 per cent, car crime 110 per cent, violent crime 182 per cent. The number of offenders caught, convicted and punished fell. The criminal justice system, especially for young offenders, was in disarray. Anti-social behaviour was unchecked. And investment was falling.

The British Crime Survey shows crime down ten per cent in Labour's first two and a half years, including a four per cent drop in violent crime. Recorded crime is down seven per cent from 1997, domestic burglary down 28 per cent, car crime down 20 per cent. Investment in crime fighting is up. We have reversed the declining trend in police numbers, reformed youth justice, and supported every community to prevent crime and anti-social behaviour. We have reduced by seven weeks the time from arrest to sentence for persistent young offenders, and are on track to meet our pledge to halve the time by May 2002.

But we are not satisfied. Drug-related crime is a menace. Recorded violent crime has risen, partly because more domestic and racial violence is being reported. And new crimes are being committed - fraud through the internet, human trafficking.

The only way to reduce crime is by being tough on crime and tough on its causes. Government can help families and communities prevent crime. But when people do commit crimes, we need an effective criminal justice system able to catch, punish and rehabilitate people. (The proposals on crime relate to England and Wales. See our Scottish manifesto for crime policy in Scotland.)

### Supporting the police
The foundation is our police force. Police numbers started falling in 1993. Our investment in 2000-01 increased the number of recruits by an extra 3,000, boosting the number of officers in training by 77 per cent over the previous year. Now Labour pledges a further 6,000 extra recruits. Labour's pledge is that over the next three years annual funding for the police will rise by £1.6 billion, to £9.3 billion.

We also need to create a more effective police service. Basic command units are the heart of modern policing, and local commanders and senior detectives should be properly trained and rewarded. Strong leadership, modern equipment and specialist training and expertise are all essential. We will bring in new arrangements for the development and appointment of chief officers. We will introduce a new national core curriculum for officers at every level. We will ensure that specialist detective expertise is built up using outside experts where necessary.

Labour will ensure more people see more police in the community. We will discuss with the police how those on the frontline might be rewarded for their skills, experience and commitment. We will promote co-operation across force boundaries for common services like training. We are also committed to a new independent police complaints commission.

### Persistent offending
About 100,000 persistent offenders, mostly young men, commit about half of all serious crimes. We need a new approach to catch, convict, punish and rehabilitate more of them:
- Youth offending teams will track up to 2,500 of the most persistent young offenders 24 hours a day, seven days a week
- Every active offender will be on the DNA database by 2004
- Persistent offending should lead to increased punishment. We will end the failed policy of repeat financial penalties; where offending continues, firmer measures will be taken. We will invest over £200 million over three years to reduce reoffending by those in custody. Sentences will combine time in prison and in the community, with proper supervision after release for ex-prisoners. In time, all offenders will have their own plan for return to lawful life, starting in custody with drug treatment or literacy training
- New Review Courts will ensure that offenders who breach the conditions of their sentence will get extra community service, more intensive supervision or custody. Those who break their bail can expect to go straight into custody for the remainder of their remand period
- To deal with the most dangerous offenders of all - those with a dangerous severe personality disorder - we will pass new legislation and create over 300 more high-security prison and hospital places

## LABOUR MANIFESTO

Our proposals are based on a simple principle: stay straight or you will stay supervised or go back inside. The continued modernisation of the probation, parole and prison services, so every offender gets punishment designed to minimise reoffending, will carry this forward. We will build on our youth justice reforms to improve the standard of custodial accommodation and offending programmes for 18- to 20-year-old offenders.

### Crime in the community

Broken windows, graffiti and litter all send a signal about lawlessness. Labour supports fines for anti-social behaviour and new powers to tackle unruly behaviour and kerb crawlers. Every local authority should have an anti-social behaviour unit. We will tackle alcohol-related disorder, with an overhaul of licensing laws, greater flexibility over opening times, and tougher controls on rogue landlords. We will also streamline the system for removal of untaxed and abandoned cars.

Crime fighting now starts in every community thanks to new statutory Crime and Disorder Partnerships. Our Safe Communities Fund will target hundreds of neighbourhoods with the highest crime rates with extra crime-fighting investment. Domestic violence accounts for at least a quarter of all violent crime, so Labour is committed to expanding the safe hostel network.

Crime prevention requires that those most at risk of falling into a life of crime - children excluded from school, teenagers leaving care - are given real help and opportunity. That includes drugs education for every child at primary and secondary school, and youth inclusion schemes in high-crime areas. We will also take measures to tackle the problem of child pornography on the internet.

### Drugs

One of the biggest contemporary drivers of crime is drugs. Access to effective treatment is essential. Prisoners are already subject to compulsory testing and offered treatment where necessary, which has led to a 50 per cent cut in the number testing positive. Drug Testing and Treatment Orders ensure people punished in the community stay drug-free.

We are pledged to raise spending on drug treatment by 70 per cent by 2004. We will roll out drug testing to cover offenders at every stage of the system. People in prison for drug-related offences will have to kick the habit before they are free from supervision on the outside. Drug dealers will be required to register with the police after leaving prison.

We will simplify the law on extradition to target organised crime including drug traffickers. The Criminal Assets Recovery Agency will target their ill-gotten gains. We will follow the money trail, through bureaux de change to offshore accounts, to convict them, and remove their money and passports.

Our ambition is to mobilise every neighbourhood against drugs. We will therefore ensure that crime-fighting partnerships, covering every locality, get over £200 million over the next three years to fight crime and drugs.

### A modern criminal justice system

The UK's legal traditions are precious. But too much of our criminal law and the organisation of the courts are stuck in the past. Our ambition is to re-equip the criminal justice system to deliver justice for all - the victims, the public and the defendant, with a short-term target of 100,000 more crimes ending in a criminal brought to justice. Our White Paper *Criminal Justice: The Way Ahead* set out our initial views on reform. The Auld enquiry will also make major recommendations.

### Prosecution

Despite an increase of 25 per cent since 1997, we have too few prosecutors. By 2004, Labour pledges 300 new prosecutors, including specialists in areas like serious and organised crime, paid on a level playing field with the defence. We will modernise and consolidate the whole criminal law system to promote public confidence and to speed up criminal proceedings. Law reform is necessary to make provisions against corporate manslaughter.

### Courts

The current system, split between magistrates and crown courts, needs reform. A unified system, including lower or intermediate tiers of court, offers simplicity and flexibility. Lay magistrates as well as professional judges have their place in the system. We will remove the widely abused right of defendants alone to dictate whether or not they should be tried in crown court. For specialist cases such as those involving domestic violence or fraud, there is a strong case for specialist courts and specialist judges. We will also develop late sitting, seven-day-a-week courts in high-crime areas to ensure there is no delay in getting people through the criminal justice system. We have established a Judicial Commissioner to scrutinise the appointments process, and will take forward reform on the basis of experience.

### Rules of evidence

Our rules of evidence fail to trust the good sense of judges and jurors. Recent case law has extended the admissibility of evidence of previous conduct. If there is any remaining doubt, we will consider legislation to reinforce the judgement. Pending the findings of the Auld report, we see a strong case for a new presumption that would allow evidence of previous convictions where relevant. Currently only the prosecution must disclose all expert evidence and names of all witnesses. In the light of the Auld report, we will consider whether the defence should do so too. In addition, witnesses should be able to refer to their original statements in the witness box, as well as offer evidence by video-link.

## Representation

We have created the Community Legal Service and will extend it to 90 per cent of the population by April 2002. We will continue to pursue the principle of best value for the benefit of the taxpayer and criminal defendants in the Criminal Defence Service. We will examine reforms of the tribunal system in the light of the Leggatt Review. We will subject restrictive practices in the legal professions to the closest scrutiny to ensure both the professions and the courts serve the wider public interest.

## Victims have rights

In 1997, victims were the forgotten people in legal battles. That has begun to change. We have more than doubled the funding for Victim Support, taken powers to protect vulnerable witnesses in court, and prevented personal cross-examination by the defendant of rape victims. We now propose further action. First, victims will be given the legal right to present their views on the impact of the crime to the court and other criminal justice agencies before sentencing decisions. Second, prosecutors will be able to challenge defence pleas in mitigation of the crime. Third, we will legislate for a Victims' Bill of Rights to give support, protection, and rights to information and compensation to victims.

## Our diverse nation

Labour believes that Britain can be a model of a multicultural, multi-racial society. We have made major legal change; now is the time to build the inclusive society in tune with British values.

Our commitment to protection for every citizen is expressed in the 1998 Human Rights Act. It ensures that British citizens are able to enforce rights in our own courts. Other legal change was necessary too. The Race Relations (Amendment) Act learns the legal lessons from the shocking death of Stephen Lawrence and places a positive duty on all public bodies to promote equal opportunity. We abhor racism and shall continue to implement the recommendations of the Macpherson report, including the reform of the 'double jeopardy' law for murder. The repeal of Section 28 of the 1988 Local Government Act was grossly misrepresented as an attempt to use teaching to promote particular lifestyles. We will ensure that such teaching continues to be prohibited, based on the provisions of the Learning and Skills Act, while removing discrimination on grounds of sexual orientation.

The UK now has the most comprehensive anti-discrimination legislation in Europe. But an inclusive, tolerant, open society, where people rise on their merits, depends on culture and action as well as law.

We now need to reduce the barriers - to services, opportunities, institutions - that still hold people back. This applies in the public and private sectors. There are too few black and Asian staff in key public services and, in almost all organisations, far too few in middle and senior grades. This is why we now have targets for the diversity of central government and other public services.

Voluntary and community organisations are key to Labour's vision for Britain. From large national charities to local community groups and faith-based institutions, these sectors are a vital and diverse part of national life. We have changed the tax rules to encourage individuals and businesses to give to charity, supported initiatives to increase volunteering, involved voluntary and community groups in the design and delivery of key government programmes like Sure Start, and helped charities build up their capacity to do their job even better. Labour will build on its Compact with the voluntary sector, as we develop more far-reaching partnerships for the delivery of services and the renewal of our communities. We will also build on our financial incentives for volunteering, by developing an effective infrastructure to support voluntary work in every community in Britain. We welcome the contribution of churches and other faith-based organisations as partners of local and central government in community renewal. We will use a successor to the Lambeth Group to look at government's interface with faith communities.

## Immigration

People from abroad make a positive contribution to British society. As our economy changes and expands, so our rules on immigration need to reflect the need to meet skills shortages. The primary purpose rule, which split families and did nothing to stop abuse, has been ended. A right of appeal for family visitors has been introduced. Immigration rules will remain clear, firm and fair, and help ensure that those who come and work here continue to make a major contribution to our economic and social life.

## Asylum

It is right that people fleeing persecution are able to make a new life as hard-working citizens in a new country. Britain has a long record of providing a home for such people, and it is important that we maintain this position. But asylum should not be an alternative route to immigration.

The UK is ninth per head of population among European nations for asylum applications. The key is to hear cases swiftly as well as fairly. By cutting the decision time and increasing the processing of claims to over 10,000 a month, Labour has reduced the backlog we inherited. We have tightened controls against traffickers, and introduced a civil penalty for lorry drivers who bring in illegal immigrants. A national support system has been introduced to relieve pressure on local authorities. Asylum seekers and their dependants whose claims are rejected will be removed from Britain with the aim of more than 30,000 in 2003-04. We will also help those granted refugee status to integrate into the local community, supporting them so they can come off benefits and into work. We support tough penalties for those who engage in the barbaric trade of human trafficking. We will bring forward proposals to ensure a common interpretation of the 1951 Convention across the EU and to improve the international response to regional crises.

## LABOUR MANIFESTO

### Political renewal

Change comes from the bottom up as much as the top down. For the last 50 years, governments have failed to respect this basic truth.

Local authorities are responsible for the effective delivery of over £90 billion of public services a year. The staff and councillors who work for the community often have the hardest jobs and their expertise is a real resource when it comes to achieving reform. The best of local government is an inspiring example of what government can achieve.

Labour's ambition is a partnership of mutual respect and mutual responsibility. We want to combine additional rights and resources with responsibility and reform, working with councillors and officers to develop the structures, services and finance to help local communities.

The job of local government is to provide the leadership to improve quality of life, and offer the citizen a seamless, one-stop service. We have worked with local government to establish clear targets for standards of service; and to offer incentives for service improvement and innovation. Partnership with the voluntary and private sectors is key.

The foundation of effective service delivery is best value in every service. Year on year, local authorities and their staff will now work to achieve improvement in services, matching themselves against the best. Citizens need a voice - we will work with local government to ensure that citizens' needs are the driving force in the procurement and delivery of local services. Electronic service delivery offers the prospect of greater convenience, access and quality, and we have set demanding targets for its use.

When public services are delivered in partnership with the private and voluntary sectors, this should be on the basis of best value not worst labour standards. The TUPE regulations protect the rights of any transferred employees. Newly hired workers are protected by minimum standards at work. We will use a wide-ranging review of TUPE regulations to consider whether unfair disparities are being created between these two groups of workers.

We want to give successful local councils more leeway to meet local needs using a £400 million reward fund. We have piloted local public service agreements to offer new investment and greater financial flexibility in return for higher performance. We will extend this reform to all upper-tier councils. We will offer further flexibility for high-performance authorities, with reformed inspections and more local discretion to encourage civic renewal. We consulted last year on a range of reforms aimed at enabling councils to deliver key local services on the basis of transparent, stable and adequate funding. These remain our aims. We will give new freedoms to local authorities to enable them to invest in local capital projects.

Labour believes that local quality of life issues - from litter to parks - are vital issues, not peripheral. We will pilot home zones, redesigning local areas to enhance safety and the quality of the local neighbourhood. Local authorities should have the incentive and means to improve the local environment by recycling local fines into a local environment fund.

Our ambition is the development of active, in-touch local government, serving the people. We support the introduction of elected mayors for our cities, which is why every local council now has the power to ballot citizens for a mayor.

### Regional government

Some functions are best tackled at the regional level. Economic development is the core of regional policy today. In our first term, we have created RDAs to drive regional economic development. Regional chambers have been set up to provide some accountability for regional economic decision-making.

We are committed, as RDAs take on more power, to enhance the scrutiny functions of regional chambers. For some regions this degree of political representation will be sufficient. However, in other parts of the country there may be a stronger sense of regional identity and a desire for a regional political voice.

In 1997 we said that provision should be made for directly elected regional government to go ahead in regions where people decided in a referendum to support it and where predominantly unitary local government is established. This remains our commitment.

### The nations of the UK

Devolution has strengthened the UK, preserving the union on the basis of a fairer partnership. The nationalist lie has also been exposed: the UK is strong enough and flexible enough to devolve power while retaining the benefits of staying together.

The Scottish Parliament and the Welsh Assembly have put power in the hands of local people. In Scotland the Parliament has power over primary legislation. In Wales we will build on the already successful legislative partnership with the Assembly, and continue to enact specific legislation for Wales, where appropriate.

The UK Parliament makes the essential financial allocations to all devolved bodies. English MPs make up 85 per cent of the UK Parliament so there is no case for threatening the unity of the UK with an English Parliament or the denial of voting rights to Scottish, Welsh and Northern Ireland's MPs at Westminster.

### Northern Ireland

We have made working for peace in Northern Ireland a priority. The Good Friday Agreement was overwhelmingly supported by the people of Northern Ireland and in the Republic of Ireland. While it has not brought a perfect peace, and while the peace process has not been smooth, it has made life immeasurably better.

Northern Ireland now has its own Assembly and Executive. They have produced their first programme for government and first budget on a cross-community basis. The security situation has been transformed. People can walk again on the streets of Belfast free from fear. Troops no longer patrol in most of the province. And the number of murders has been drastically reduced.

We will build on these foundations to ensure that the Good Friday Agreement is implemented in full and the new institutions take root. We will establish a modern, responsive and fully accountable police service properly representative of the two main traditions in Northern Ireland and enjoying their trust and support. And we will bring about the key reforms in the civil and criminal justice system which secure the respect and trust of both traditions.

### Parliamentary reform

The House of Commons is now more representative than ever before, yet only one in five MPs is a woman. Labour increased women's representation five-fold in the 1997 Parliament through all-women shortlists. We are committed, through legislation, to allow each party to make positive moves to increase the representation of women. Labour will continue to modernise the procedures of the House of Commons so it can effectively fulfil its functions of representation and scrutiny.

The government has introduced major innovations in the electoral systems used in the UK - for the devolved administrations, the European Parliament, and the London Assembly. The Independent Commission on the Voting System made proposals for electoral reform at Westminster. We will review the experience of the new systems and the Jenkins report to assess whether changes might be made to the electoral system for the House of Commons. A referendum remains the right way to agree any change for Westminster.

We are committed to completing House of Lords reform, including removal of the remaining hereditary peers, to make it more representative and democratic, while maintaining the House of Commons' traditional primacy. We have given our support to the report and conclusions of the Wakeham Commission, and will seek to implement them in the most effective way possible. Labour supports modernisation of the House of Lords' procedures to improve its effectiveness. We will put the independent Appointments Commission on a statutory footing.

### Whitehall

Our civil service is world-renowned for its independence. Labour is committed to maintaining the political impartiality of the civil service. But it needs reform to make it more effective and more entrepreneurial. There have been important reforms already. We want to take further radical steps to ensure the civil service has the skills base necessary to meet the challenges set out in this manifesto.

Equal rights for all, proper enforcement of the law, and reformed structures of self-government: these are the foundations of a strong civic society. Labour offers opportunity with responsibility - the right combination for Britain in the 21st century.

### How Labour is tackling crime:

- by increasing police funding by 20 per cent over the next three years and taking police numbers to record levels
- by targeting investment on fighting crime in the highest-risk areas and tough targets to reduce car crimes, burglaries and robberies
- by cracking down on local disorder and anti-social behaviour through local partnerships and measures to deal with the 'yob culture'
- by implementing our ten-year strategy to tackle drugs, including tougher punishments for dealers
- by reforming the criminal justice system to deal with persistent offenders and ensuring the victims of crime have a greater say
- by tackling the causes of crime through measures like the New Deal and action on truancy

## 5. BRITAIN STRONG IN THE WORLD

### Our ten-year goals

Europe to have the most competitive knowledge-based economies in the world, as British ideas lead a reformed and enlarged Europe.

Delivering Kyoto and international development targets, as we help tackle climate change and global poverty.

### Our next steps

- Lead economic reform in Europe
- Work for the re-start of world trade talks
- Strong, effective and responsive armed forces
- Raise international aid towards the UN target
- Be the first country to introduce greenhouse gas trading to cut pollution

Britain needs a government ready to stand up for our interests and values. We have a ten-year vision for British foreign policy: a leading player in Europe, our alliance with the USA strengthened, using our global connections to help Britain and tackle global problems.

Unlike the Conservatives, we see Europe as an opportunity not a threat. Because we participate fully, we are able to work with our partners to shape an EU agenda that advances our national interests. We will put democratically elected national governments in the driving seat of EU policy. Our ten-year goal is to work with our partners for Europe to have the most competitive knowledge-based economies in the world. We hold to our promise: no membership of the single currency without the consent of the British people in a referendum.

Britain has some of the best armed forces in the world. With Labour, they are being developed to meet the challenges of the post-Cold War world.

Labour is committed to lead the development of a comprehensive agenda for poverty reduction and sustainable development. We want to mobilise the international community to deliver the International Development Targets, generate growth and equity in developing countries, and help them benefit from global economic integration.

We are convinced of the science of global warming. We pledge to meet tough national targets for environmental protection, and we will work at international level to halt and reverse climate change.

We face a choice between an inward-looking chauvinism that leads to isolation and a modern patriotism where the British national interest is pursued through international engagement.

### Reform in Europe

Europe is changing. Economic reform is under way in the European Union, with over two million new jobs created last year. Many new members are going to join the EU. Co-operation is being extended in defence and security policy. A new way of conducting EU business has been born - comparing best practice to share the benefits of diversity in order to reduce over-reliance on centralised regulation.

We face a very simple question. Do we want to be part of the change, influencing its direction? Or do we want to opt out? We have spent 50 years on the margins; it is time to make the most of our membership.

We have seen the alternative. By 1997 Britain had retreated into itself: business was global, people travelled and worked around the world, our culture was open to new ideas, yet our government was closing itself off. And Britain got a worse deal. Because they were backward looking and divided on Europe, the Conservatives were weak and ineffective in Europe. And because of their weakness in Europe, Britain lost influence around the world. We lost our say over decisions that affected our lives.

In the last four years we have seen the benefits of engagement. Our rebate has been protected and our contributions are falling to similar levels as France and Italy. The Labour model of defence co-operation - giving Europe the option to act where NATO chooses not to - has won through. Economic reform is now helping the European economy. The veto on crucial issues of national sovereignty, such as tax, is safe. All this happened only because Labour had the strength to get involved, argue for its ideas, and persuade others to follow us.

Labour believes that Europe brings benefits for Britain, and a Europe reformed by British ideas, working with our MEPs, will be even better for Britain. Together with virtually all other European countries we do not support a United States of Europe. But we do believe a Europe made up of nation states and offering a unique blend of inter-governmental co-operation where possible and integration where necessary, can be a major force for good - for its own members and in the wider world.

We want to take Europe forward, to meet British needs.

### A Europe of prosperity

Europe is a crucial market, accounting for more than half of our trade. Britain has secured a shift in economic policy in Europe - away from harmonisation of rules and towards a system based on dynamic markets allied to comparison and promotion of best practice.

The key priorities are: to deliver more choice and lower prices through liberalisation of financial services and utilities; to promote business development with a common EU patent and cuts in red tape; to develop our common research effort in frontier technologies like bioscience; to cut delays and fares by establishing an integrated Air Traffic Control system for Europe; and to develop effective labour market policy to tackle unemployment in dialogue with the social partners.

We support efforts being made across the EU to reform welfare states, modernise social partnership and advance social inclusion. EU state aid policy should bear down on aids that distort the single market while supporting economic modernisation. We will keep the veto on vital matters of national sovereignty, such as tax and border controls.

Trade has been a vital source of prosperity for Europe's citizens. Our vision is of an open European economy. That requires a genuine single market, in an open world trading system.

### A wider Europe

New countries joining the EU will give Britain a bigger market and Europe a bigger voice. Membership will help guarantee the freedoms of the new democracies in central and eastern Europe. Labour is pledged to do all it can to enable the first group of applicant countries to join in time to take part in the next European Parliamentary elections in 2004.

It is vital we ratify the Treaty of Nice which is essential to enlargement; Labour in government will do so. The Conservatives have said they will insist on trying to renegotiate Europe's treaties at the first summit after the election. No other country agrees with this. That means that a Conservative government would either have to back down in the face of opposition, or take Britain out of Europe altogether with disastrous consequences for Britain.

Our argument is that if Britain is stronger in Europe, it will be stronger in the rest of the world. We reject the view of those who say we must choose between Europe and the USA. We shall remain the USA's firm ally and friend; but we are not going to turn our backs on Europe. The USA and Europe account for ten per cent of world population but 60 per cent of global GDP; working together we can tackle many problems and spread the benefits of freedom, peace and prosperity.

## A Europe of the future

The main sources of popular legitimacy in Europe remain national governments and parliaments. So national governments should be seen to be setting the agenda of the EU, with the European Council setting the EU's priorities, a strong independent Commission ensuring that the European interest is heard and enforced, and an effective European Parliament improving draft legislation and holding the Commission to account.

Labour wants the next Inter-governmental Conference in 2004 to address public concerns about the way the EU works, spelling out in a clear statement of principles what should and should not be done at European level.

Labour supports a stronger role for national parliaments in European affairs, for example in a second chamber of the European Parliament, with a particular remit to oversee the division of competences. We will also insist that the Commission completes its internal reform programme.

## Defence

Britain's national security is based on the mutual support that comes from membership of NATO. That will not change. And although Britain has rarely been more secure from foreign invasion, there are new threats to our people from crime and terrorism.

Instability around the world can affect us directly and we have a global responsibility to play our part in reducing international conflict, controlling the spread of weapons of mass destruction, and contributing to international peace-keeping and peace-making operations.

To enable the European Union to act where NATO chooses not to, the EU should improve its military capabilities for humanitarian, peace-keeping and crisis management tasks.

Our armed forces are the best in the world at fighting if they have to, and keeping the peace where they can. Labour is committed to investing more in real terms in our armed services over the next three years, the first year-on-year real increase in funds for over a decade. An important part of that investment will be in better service accommodation. We are determined to recruit and retain the best people, from all walks of life and all backgrounds.

We will look after the interests of Britain's veterans. We have doubled funding for research on Gulf War illnesses, and will continue this important work.

In 1997 Labour promised a strategic defence review. Today, that review is admired around the world for its clarity, efficiency and foresight.

We need more mobile and more flexible armed forces, with the ability to project force at distance and speed, to work closely with other nations and international bodies, and to fight and keep the peace. We have shown what this means in practice in Kosovo and Sierra Leone, and our servicemen and women have responded magnificently.

We are determined to maximise resources for frontline use by disposing of surplus spares and promoting smart procurement and efficiency savings.

The European Defence Initiative is an important part of our defence policy. Europe spends two-thirds as much as the US on defence, but gets only a fraction of its effectiveness. European nations need to modernise their armed forces for rapid and flexible deployment. Improved EU military capabilities will not be separate from NATO structures and would only be deployed where NATO as a whole chooses not to engage. The launch of an EU operation will follow a unanimous decision, with each member state free to decide whether to take part.

We support Trident, Britain's minimum nuclear deterrent. The Nuclear Non-Proliferation Treaty commits us to work for the global elimination of nuclear weapons. We are enthusiastic signatories to the Comprehensive Test Ban Treaty, whose coming into force will impede nuclear proliferation, and we want to see the USA and Russia continue to reduce their nuclear stockpiles.

We recognise the new dangers posed by the proliferation of nuclear, chemical and biological weapons, and the need to combat them. Nuclear arms reductions and proliferation controls remain an important part of defence and security policy. We will seek effective inspections against the development of chemical and biological weapons. We will encourage the US to consult closely with NATO allies on its ideas for missile defence, and to pursue dialogue with Russia on a new framework for strategic arms control that will encourage further cuts in nuclear weapons.

The British defence industry is a vital part of our economy, sustaining some 350,000 high-technology jobs. We will continue to work closely with our best companies to get the best equipment for our armed forces - a good deal for the taxpayer as well as a secure future for high-technology jobs.

The UK has introduced the most open report on arms exports of any European nation and has led the EU to adopt a code of conduct on arms sales. Labour will lead efforts to control the trade in small arms, and work for a comprehensive action plan at this year's UN conference on small arms, including an international arms surrender fund to provide development aid in exchange for firearms. We will legislate to modernise the regulation of arms exports, with a licensing system to control the activities of arms brokers and traffickers wherever they are located. We will work with EU applicant countries to strengthen their capacity to control legal and illicit arms transfers.

## LABOUR MANIFESTO

### The modern world
Britain belongs to a unique range of influential global organisations, giving us responsibilities and opportunities. Labour will stand up for Britain.
- At the UN, where we support a more modern and representative Security Council, with more effective peace-keeping.
- At the Group of 7 leading industrialised countries, where we will stay at the forefront of efforts to promote development.
- In the Commonwealth, where we will work to promote human rights and bridge the digital divide.

We will argue for an early, comprehensive world trade round, to the benefit of industrialised and developing countries alike. The World Trade Organisation must be reformed, not rejected. We will support fairer terms of trade for developing countries, and a reduction in protectionism in the developed world in areas such as agriculture. We will continue to help developing countries exercise their rights within the WTO.

We support the promotion of higher labour standards around the world, as well as respect for the environment, as we expand world trade. The International Labour Organisation (ILO) is the place to set labour standards, but we believe there should be closer co-operation between the ILO and WTO through the creation of a joint standing forum of the two organisations.

We are committed to encouraging universal observance of human rights. Governments that are democratically elected will be firmer allies for peace; open societies that respect individual freedom will be more reliable trade partners. Labour will be a friend of those denied human rights and a supporter of steps to strengthen them.

Labour has played a leading role in bringing war criminals, notably from former Yugoslavia, to justice, and in establishing a permanent court to try war crimes. We will work to make the International Criminal Court a reality, with Britain as one of its first members.

### International development
In 1997 Labour pledged to give new priority to tackling global poverty. Four years on, there have been real achievements - a cabinet minister heads an internationally respected department, the aid budget has been substantially raised, and tied aid abolished. Britain is playing a leading world role on debt relief, education, HIV/AIDS, and in responding to humanitarian disasters. With strong UK leadership, the international development effort is now increasingly focused on poverty reduction.

This is morally right, but also in our interest. Many of the world's biggest challenges - from violent conflict to rapid population growth to environmental threat - are caused or exacerbated by global poverty and inequality. There can be no secure future for any of us unless we promote greater global social justice.

Labour will continue to focus Britain's development effort on the achievement of the international development targets by 2015 - including halving the proportion of the world's population living in extreme poverty, reducing child and infant mortality by two-thirds, primary education for all children, and sustainable development plans in every country.

With Labour the aid budget will rise to 0.33 per cent of GNP by 2003-04, reaching £3.6 billion - a 45 per cent increase in real terms since 1997 level. We remain committed to the UN target of 0.7 per cent of national income devoted to development and will make further substantial increases over the next Parliament. We remain committed to our bill, blocked by the Tories, to consolidate our poverty-focused approach to development.

We are using this aid to support political and economic reform in developing countries. Our aid is an investment to help countries put in place policies to raise the growth rate with greater equity, crack down on corruption, promote human rights, including for women and girls, and develop effective governance and democracy. We will legislate to toughen controls over UK nationals who commit offences of corruption abroad.

Labour will champion increased effectiveness and a stronger focus on poverty reduction within international institutions - particularly the EU, but also the World Bank, IMF, UN and Commonwealth - with full support for poverty reduction strategies where they genuinely prioritise poverty reduction. We are committed to international action to put the needs of children at the centre of these strategies. By 2006 we want to raise to 70 per cent the proportion of EU aid going to low income countries, and work with the Commission, Parliament and other governments to strengthen the EU's development effort.

Labour has led internationally on debt relief, providing 100 per cent relief for countries committed to spending the proceeds on poverty reduction. We will work to help more of the heavily indebted poor countries qualify for debt relief where this benefits the poor. And we will work to prevent new debt burdens through international agreement not to give export credits for excessive military spending or prestige projects.

Education has a special place for Labour. We will increase further our support for quality primary education for all, particularly for girls. Our Imfundo project, part of an £800 million education programme, will bring together public and private sector commitment to use IT to ensure effective teacher training and education management. We will give top priority to combating the spread of HIV/AIDS, which is inflicting massive human and economic costs across the developing world. We will work for the creation of a global health fund to make essential drugs and commodities more accessible to the poor, focusing on TB, malaria and HIV/AIDS. This will complement our existing support for the development of basic healthcare systems, and our new tax credits to incentivise research by the drug companies into the diseases of poverty.

Development goes much wider than aid and debt relief. It is also about how we manage the global economy. Our aim is to shape globalisation so that it works better for the world's poor.

Trade is key but so is private investment. We will promote socially responsible business practice through advisory services on codes of social responsibility, the ethical trading initiative, the Export Credits Guarantee Department's new code of business principles, the Commonwealth Development Corporation's partnership with the private sector, and our initiatives to encourage private investment in infrastructure.

Nowhere will our resolve be more tested than in Africa. Labour is committed to strengthening our partnership for development with Africa.

We will work with reforming governments, international institutions, the private sector and civil society in support of nationally owned development strategies.

We will also redouble our efforts to prevent and resolve violent conflicts in Africa, using our new Africa conflict fund to provide help for security sector reform, demilitarisation programmes and tighter controls over small arms.

### The environmental challenge

The poor make the smallest per capita contribution to climate change, but are often most affected when it happens. We are convinced by the scientific evidence of climate change — and convinced that now is the time to act.

We need action at local, national and international level if we are to preserve the stability of our natural environment over the next 50 years. The principle of mutual responsibility that governs our approach to social problems also applies to environmental issues.

The healthy future of our environment is one of the world's great challenges. We must make substantial changes in the way we work and live to safeguard all our futures. The UK played a leading role in the Kyoto conference. The targets for reducing greenhouse gas emissions agreed at that conference are a vital first step in the battle against global warming.

It is critical that the whole international community plays its part in making a reality of sustainable development. We are determined to play a constructive role at the 'Rio plus 10' meeting in South Africa next year.

We are one of the few countries to have met our 1992 obligations to hold greenhouse gases in 2000 below their 1990 levels.

In 1997 we set a target of reducing $CO_2$ emissions by 20 per cent by 2010. We will meet our obligations arising from the Kyoto protocol and have set out a detailed strategy to achieve more — a 23 per cent cut in greenhouse gases by 2010.

The Royal Commission on Environmental Pollution has said the UK will need to cut $CO_2$ production by 60 per cent by 2050, so we need to press ahead with a radical agenda for the development of low carbon economic growth, embodied in our £700 million commitment to renewable energy.

In addition to our proposals for environmental technology and renewable energy described in 'Prosperity for all', we must also make progress in the following areas:

- We must make the market work for the environment. Britain is developing the first national $CO_2$ emissions trading system in the world. It will help companies find the most efficient way of reducing emissions - and reward them for doing so. Once the system is established here we will seek to extend it around the world.
- We will support hybrid and fuel cell vehicles, which already offer a halving of fuel consumption and $CO_2$ emissions, with cheaper motoring to match - and for cleaner fuels and biofuels. By increasing demand for new technologies we can boost innovation and the vitality of the UK car industry.
- It is imperative that we use natural resources more efficiently and recycle more. We will continue to tax pollution and reward clean production. We will develop environmental productivity indicators. We have set a target for the recycling of 35 per cent of household waste by 2015, and will work with all local authorities to introduce kerbside recycling schemes wherever appropriate.
- Water management is a vital challenge for the future — for the environment and for the growing world population. We will continue to make our contribution at home: leakage is down by almost 30 per cent since 1997, bills have been cut by 12 per cent and disconnections have been ended.
- Environmental protection and sustainable development go hand in hand. We cannot protect the environment without addressing the development needs of the poor, and poverty reduction depends on safeguarding natural resources on which poor people depend.
- We will continue to provide leadership abroad, working for international agreement on climate change, improved integration of the environment in European policies and a strong global environment agency built around the current UN environment programme. We will work to improve marine and forest conservation overseas and in the UK.

Britain can be pivotal to world affairs, using our alliances to advance our interests and values. The key is to use our strengths of history and geography to engage with other countries, not retreat. That is Labour's promise.

### How Labour is strengthening your voice in the world:

- by taking a lead in Europe, standing up for Britain's rights and reforming Europe to promote jobs and deepen democracy
- by supporting our armed forces, making sure our troops are always available and effective in times of crisis
- by working to tackle global climate change, meeting our own tough targets and pushing other countries to meet theirs
- by leading the fight against global poverty, with increased aid, better spent

## LABOUR MANIFESTO

### THE CHOICES FOR BRITAIN

These are our ambitions for Britain — and how they can be achieved. Clear in our values, confident in our policies, we seek a new mandate from the British people.

We are proud of our record in government. But we are not yet satisfied. Labour is the party of reform and we fight this election as agents of change for Britain. Change to our economy, so more people share the benefits of growth. Change in our public services, so that they better advance equality of opportunity.

Change in our welfare system, so that we extend security, responsibility and independence. Change to tackle crime and its causes. Change to deepen our democracy. Change to Britain's role in the world.

The Conservatives were rejected in 1997 because they had failed. The national debt had doubled; crime had doubled; we were 42nd in the world education league; one in five households was on benefit; and we were marginalised in Europe.

Yet instead of learning, the Conservatives have become more dogmatic, more extreme, more divided. They are worse than ever.

The British people now face a choice. New Labour stands in the political mainstream, rooted in the best values of the British people. The Conservatives have veered to extreme positions.

This election will decide whether we continue the policies that have brought us economic stability, steady growth, investment in public services and targeted tax cuts for children and families, or whether we lurch back to boom and bust.

It will decide whether we put our schools, hospitals and police officers first, or put them second after unaffordable tax cuts. It will decide whether we modernise the criminal justice system. It will decide whether we stand for a positive engagement with Europe and the wider world, or retreat to the sidelines.

We want everyone to vote in this election. But before you do, think of your job; think of your mortgage; think of your school and hospital; think of your children and your parents; think of police and crime prevention, think of the choice of leadership.

Think of who you want to succeed in Britain — the many or the few.

There is still much to do with new Labour — and a lot for you to lose under the Conservatives.

The choice is clear: for an ambitious and confident Britain, the choice is Labour.

### 25 STEPS TO A BETTER BRITAIN

1. Basic skills for 750,000 people

2. Venture capital funds in every region

3. £180 billion investment in transport, with 25 local rail and tram schemes

4. Raise the minimum wage to £4.20

5. £1,000 tax cut — the Children's Tax Credit — for parents of newborn children

6. Every secondary school with a distinct ethos, mission or centre of excellence

7. Recruit an extra 10,000 teachers

8. More power to frontline staff

9. More health service workers — 20,000 more nurses, and at least 10,000 more doctors

10. Free access to national museums and galleries

11. An 'Employment First' interview for everyone coming on to benefits

12. Expanded support for children through tax and benefit reform

13. Extend and increase paid maternity leave and introduce paid paternity leave

14. New pension credit for lower- and middle-income pensioners and the Winter Fuel Payment retained

15. £900 million Neighbourhood Renewal Fund for jobs, education and crime prevention

16. An extra 6,000 police recruits raising police numbers to their highest-ever level

17. Double the amount of assets seized from drug traffickers and other major criminals

18. Increased sentences plus education and drug treatment for persistent offenders

19. A bill of rights for victims

20. New freedoms with new targets for local government

21. Lead economic reform in Europe

22. Work for the re-start of world trade talks

23. Strong, effective and responsive armed forces

24. Raise international aid towards the UN target

25. Be the first country to introduce greenhouse gas trading to cut pollution

## THE CONTRACT DELIVERED

In the 1997 Labour manifesto Tony Blair said: 'We set out in the manifesto that follows ten commitments, commitments that form our bond of trust with the people. Judge us on them. Have trust in us and we will repay that trust. This is our contract with the people.' This is a summary of Labour's record since 1997. For more information on Labour's policies, please visit our website at www.labour.org.uk, or contact your local Labour campaign team.

**1.   Education will be our number one priority, and we will increase the share of national income spent on education as we decrease it on the bills of economic and social failure**

The record: Key Stage 2 results for literacy and numeracy reached 75 per cent (up 12 per cent since 1997) and 72 per cent (up 10 per cent since 1997) in 2001. GCSE and A-level results have also improved. This September there will be no five-, six- and seven-year-olds in class sizes over 30. We have cut the costs of debt and unemployment by nearly £9 billion per year. Education spending has risen from 4.7 per cent of national income to 5 per cent this year.

**2.   There will be no increase in the basic or top rates of income tax**

The record: We cut the basic rate of income tax to 22p in April 2000 and introduced the 10p band in April 1999. There has been no increase in the top rate of income tax. The direct tax burden on a single earner family on average earnings with two children is the lowest since 1972.

**3.   We will provide stable economic growth with low inflation and promote dynamic and competitive business and industry at home and abroad**

The record: Net borrowing in every year from 1997 to 2003-04 is forecast to be lower than in any Tory year from 1992-93 to 1996-97. Inflation has been consistently under control and on target. Economic growth has been steady, averaging 2.75 per cent a year since 1997. Living standards are on average about 10 per cent higher in real terms than in 1997.

**4.   We will get 250,000 young unemployed off benefit and into work**

The record: Over 280,000 unemployed young people have been helped into work by Labour's New Deal. There are over one million more jobs in the economy than in 1997. Youth unemployment now stands at its lowest level since 1975, long-term unemployment among under-25s is down 75 per cent. Unemployment is at its lowest level for 25 years.

**5.   We will rebuild the NHS, reducing spending on administration and increasing spending on patient care**

The record: The next four years will see the biggest-ever sustained increase in NHS spending. Over £1 billion will have been released from administration by next year. The NHS is treating 620,000 more in-patients and is seeing over 650,000 more outpatients than in 1996-97. There are 17,100 more nurses and 6,700 more doctors than in 1997. There are 124,000 fewer people on waiting lists.

**6.   We will be tough on crime and tough on the causes of crime, and halve the time it takes persistent juvenile offenders to come to court**

The record: The British Crime Survey shows that overall crime fell by 10 per cent from 1997 to 1999. Investment is now rising. The time from arrest to sentence for persistent young offenders is down from 142 days to 89 days - on track to halve the time within the five years promised in 1997.

**7.   We will help build strong families and strong communities, and lay the foundations of a modern welfare state in pensions and community care**

The record: Child benefit has been raised by over 25 per cent for the first child. The Children's Tax Credit is worth up to £520 a year. We have introduced parental leave and rights to holidays. We have extended maternity leave. £4.5 billion extra in real terms is being spent this year on pensioners. The basic state pension will rise to £75.50 for single pensioners and £120.70 for pensioner couples next year, while the minimum income guarantee is helping over 1.6 million of the poorest pensioners. TV licence fees have been abolished for the over-75s, with free access to national museums and galleries for children and pensioners.

**8.   We will safeguard our environment, and develop an integrated transport policy to fight congestion and pollution**

The record: With the private sector, we will invest a record £180 billion in transport infrastructure over the next ten years. We will achieve a 23 per cent cut in greenhouse gas emissions. We have legislated to promote protection for and access to the countryside. A £1.6 billion strategy for farming and rural enterprise will redirect subsidies to promote growth and the environment.

**9.   We will clean up politics, decentralise political power throughout the United Kingdom and put the funding of political parties on a proper and accountable basis**

The record: The funding of political parties, campaign expenditure and conduct of referendums is now regulated. For the first time the UK has a Freedom of Information Act. The Scottish Parliament, Welsh Assembly and Northern Ireland Assembly are now up and running, while local democracy has been returned to the people of London. The first stage of reform of the House of Lords has reduced the number of hereditary peers to fewer than 100.

**10.We will give Britain the leadership in Europe which Britain and Europe need**

The record: Labour has negotiated successfully for Britain in Europe. Our rebate is protected, enlargement is being taken forward. We have led the debate on European economic reform and on the development of a European defence capacity rooted in NATO structures. In Kosovo, our armed forces played a leading role in standing up against ethnic cleansing.

# CONSERVATIVE MANIFESTO

## TIME FOR COMMON SENSE

We present here the most ambitious Conservative programme for a generation.

Its aim is to release the wisdom, decency and enterprise of British citizens.

We can achieve that by handing back to individuals and families the ability to shape their own lives and communities.

We will free entrepreneurs to build businesses and to create prosperity, free those who use public services to choose what is best for them and free those who work in our schools and hospitals and police service from endless political interference.

We want to set people free so that they have greater power over their own lives. That is what I have always believed.

But there is something else too. I value those aspects of our national life which are bigger than individuals and families.

That is why we will nurture our towns and cities, our countryside, our local institutions, our charities, our democracy - for they make us who we are as a nation.

Our programme is rooted in the instincts of millions of people whose beliefs are mocked by Labour. It is rooted, in other words, in common sense.

It shouldn't be necessary to make an appeal to common sense. Yet the common sense wisdom of the mainstream majority, on crime, or on taxes, or the family, or on Europe, is under threat as never before.

Labour does not understand our country and cannot value what it cannot understand.

This meddling and interfering Government is eroding our freedoms as well as weakening the institutions that give us a sense of common purpose.

At this Election Britain has a choice between a Labour Party that trusts government instead of people and a Conservative Party that trusts people instead of government.

I trust the British people.

I trust their common sense.

It's time for common sense. — **William Hague**

## *THROUGH OUR LIVES*

### RAISING A FAMILY

Common sense means strengthening the family

- Less tax for families
- Support for marriage
- Freedom for headteachers and governors to run their own schools
- Power for parents to change management of failing schools
- Endowed universities and less onerous student loan repayments

Families feel more than ever that they are struggling to bring up their children in an environment that is hostile.

They feel it is getting harder to make ends meet, especially when their children are very young. They feel the Government only values childcare if someone else is paid to provide it, and that it doesn't value marriage at all. They feel that they are paying a fortune in tax, but they aren't getting the education they want for their children.

They also worry that, however hard they try to bring up their children well, the dangers of being drawn into crime and drug use are growing. And they fear that passing our values on from one generation to the next is harder than ever.

It's time for common sense.

Conservatives will help families bringing up children. We will let families keep more of what they earn. We will support marriage. We will provide choice and high standards in schools. And we will help parents who feel they aren't getting enough help at the time they need it the most.

### Cutting tax for families

The task of bringing up children is made much harder when families keep less of what they earn, because the Government is taking more.

Labour have increased taxes on hardworking families. After four years of Labour, a typical family was paying £670 more tax per year than when the Government took office.

Despite all the evidence that marriage provides the best environment for bringing up children, married couples do not fit into Labour's politically correct agenda.

That is why they have penalised millions of families by abolishing the Married Couple's Tax Allowance. Conservatives will give families a break.

We will cut taxes on families with children under 5 by increasing the Children's Tax Credit by £200 a year. This means an extra £4 a week will be taken off the tax bill of most families with young children, in addition to what they receive in Child Benefit.

The arrival of children often puts a family under particular pressure. One parent may give up work for a while, reducing the couple's income just when their expenses are greatest.

A Conservative government will support families coping with these pressures.

We will introduce a new Married Couple's Allowance which will give a tax cut worth £1,000 to many families when they need help most. If someone is not using all or part of their personal tax allowance they will be able to transfer it to a working spouse if they have children under 11 or receive Invalid Care Allowance in respect of a relative.

Mothers or fathers who stop working to care for children can sometimes find it difficult to get back into paid work afterwards. This is where our Family Scholarships scheme will help. Parents who have taken time out from their careers in order to care for their children will be able to apply for a scholarship to help them undertake vocational or professional training.

Widows and widowers find supporting children particularly difficult. Conservatives will give extra help to all widows and widowers with dependent children by removing tax on the Widowed Mother's Allowance and the new Widowed Parent's Allowance. This will provide a valuable increase of up to £20 per week in widowed parents'income.

It is right to boost the incomes of families with modest earnings. We will reform the Working Families Tax Credit so it is once more paid as a benefit direct to the caring parent. Up to 400,000 mothers will gain from this reform.

### More choice and higher standards in schools

The least parents should expect from all the taxes they pay is a decent school for their children.

Labour promised much on education, but after four years in power they have failed to deliver. That failure is no accident. It is because Labour have tried to run the nation's schools from Whitehall.

Conservatives will pursue a very different policy.

Our objective is to give parents choice, and headteachers freedom. These reforms will lead to schools of the sort parents want — schools with high standards, schools which have their own traditions, a distinct ethos and which wear their school uniform with pride.

Headteachers and their staff cannot command respect in their own schools if they are treated as mere branch managers on the receiving end of instructions from the council or from Whitehall. And teachers are leaving the profession in droves because of all the pointless paperwork.

That is why it's time for common sense.

Conservatives will introduce "Free Schools". We will free every school in the country from bureaucratic control and allow them to shape their own character.

Heads and Governors will have complete responsibility for running their schools. They will be able to choose how to reward excellence amongst their teachers. And they will be able to use, as a criterion for admission, the willingness of a pupil or parent to subscribe to a home-school agreement which sets out the responsibilities of students and their school to each other.

We will abolish the nonsensical rules that make it difficult for Heads to exclude disruptive pupils - we will not allow a few unruly pupils to damage the education of everyone else.

Instead, we will set up Progress Centres outside the schools. These Centres will make sure disruptive pupils get specialist help to overcome their problems so that where possible they may return to mainstream schools.

We plan to spend what the Government has planned. But with us more of the money will actually get to the schools. We will save money currently wasted on government and council bureaucracy, giving this money directly to schools according to the number of pupils. By doing that each school would have received, on average, an extra £540 per pupil in 1999/2000 to spend on its own priorities.

Britain has some excellent schools. Often they are next door to mediocre ones. Nothing is more frustrating for parents than to be told that they cannot send their child to the school of their choice because its numbers are artificially restricted in order to keep up numbers at a weaker school. So we will abolish the rule that stops successful schools from expanding to take more pupils. More parents will get their first choice of school for their children.

Letting our best schools expand isn't enough. We want to see good new schools springing up. We will allow churches and other faith communities, groups of parents, charitable foundations and companies to set up new schools. They will be entitled to per-pupil funding in the same way as existing schools, and will be subject to the same standards and inspections.

The people who are most likely to realise that a school has problems are not officials in a distant bureaucracy but the parents of children at the school.

Conservatives will give parents the right to call for a special Ofsted inspection if they fear that their child's school is failing. If the inspectors confirm their view, the school's management will have to be changed. This is our Parent's Guarantee.

### Reducing barriers for students

Students feel particularly aggrieved because Labour broke the promises they made to them at the last election.

Good students are put off going to college because they will be burdened by loans that must be repaid even when their income is relatively low.

Some are deterred from taking vital jobs, in teaching or in the health service, because of the cost of their student loans.

Under Labour, student loans must be repaid as soon as a graduate's income reaches £10,000 per year. With us, graduates will not have to pay anything unless and until their income tops £20,000 per year. And we will not introduce top-up fees.

### Freeing our universities

Our universities used to be the best in the world. Many of them still have a formidable reputation, but they are under threat from interference by politicians and uncertainty over their funding.

Conservatives want our universities to be free to shape their own character and specialisms, competing with the world's best for students and research funding.

To achieve their independence they need to have their own resources. We will therefore create permanent endowment funds for Britain's universities.

### LIVING SAFELY

Common sense means having enough police to keep our streets safe and a criminal justice system that reflects our values rather than undermines them

- Increase police numbers
- Free police from bureaucracy so that they can get on with policing
- Take persistent young offenders off our streets
- Criminals to serve the sentence given by the court
- More rights for victims

We may have grown more prosperous as a nation, but the quality of our life is still impoverished by crime.

Decent people, who work hard and who obey the law, are outraged that criminals seem free to make their lives a misery.

Labour have talked tough on law and order but they have failed to deliver. Police numbers have fallen, and violent crime is on the rise.

It's time for common sense.

Conservatives will trust the instincts of the mainstream majority on law and order. That means more police and less bureaucracy holding them back. It also means tougher sentences for some crimes and more honest sentencing for all crimes.

### More police, tougher sentences

Conservatives will increase the number of police officers on our streets by reversing the cuts in police numbers that Labour have made.

We will free the police to get on with policing rather than paperwork. Weighed down by regulations and under heavy political attack, police morale has fallen to its lowest point for many years. We must raise police morale. We will work with police forces to cut out bureaucracy, and to devolve work that doesn't have to be carried out by the police to other bodies.

People feel safer if they see police officers around.

So we will implement our "cops in shops" initiative - getting paperwork done in visible places on the beat and not back in the station. And we will encourage parish and town councils to create an additional new role, that of the parish constable.

Under the Conservatives, the police will be encouraged to combat loutish behaviour, graffiti, and vandalism which destroy the quality of every day life for millions of people.

A hard core of persistent young offenders commit a disproportionate number of crimes. They offend again and again, laughing at the law and making their neighbours' lives a misery.

It's time to stop turning a blind eye to crimes committed by young offenders and ensure instead that they are put back on the right track.

We will increase tenfold the number of places in Secure Training Centres - taking persistent young menaces off our streets for at least 6 months.

We will link their release date to the attainment of objectives such as a recognised qualification or standard of behaviour.

Drugs are now blighting even our rural communities, ruining lives and causing a wave of other crimes like burglary and mugging. Conservatives will give the police new powers to crack down on drug dealers.

Most evil of all are the drug dealers who try to lure children into addiction. We will give a mandatory prison sentence to dealers convicted of selling drugs to under-16s.

And, in sentencing drug-pushers, judges will be allowed to take into account, as an aggravating factor, any dealing done in the vicinity of schools.

Conservatives will end the nonsense whereby criminals know full well they will serve only a fraction of the prison sentence handed down by a judge.

We will introduce honesty in sentencing so that the sentence handed down in court is the one served by the criminal. We will abolish Labour's special early release scheme as well as automatic early release and ensure that any discounts from the sentence are transparent, have to be earned and are neither automatic nor substantial.

Prison life should not be a life of idleness. Under the Conservatives, prisoners will be required to perform a proper day's work.

The proceeds will contribute to reparations for their victims and to the upkeep of their own families. And prisoners will learn the habit of working, just as everyone else has to do each day.

Sex offenders who have been released can now only be supervised for a maximum of 10 years. Courts should be able to place sex offenders under supervision for life.

We will also introduce new laws to protect children from paedophiles who use internet chat rooms.

### Victims first

Too often criminals seem to enjoy more rights than their victims. Conservatives will make sure that the justice system treats victims fairly.

A named police officer who is working on their case will be identified to each victim, and they will have a similar continuous point of contact in the Crown Prosecution Service. Both the police and the CPS will be required to keep the victim informed as the investigation and prosecution progress and written reasons must be given where charges are dropped or reduced.

We will also overhaul the law so that it is on the side of the victim not the criminal. This will include the law on self defence and the double jeopardy rule.

Average sentences, and average time served on Labour's special early release scheme 1999-2001:

### Robbery:
- average sentence: 2 years 2 months
- average time served: 11 months

### Inflicting Grievous Bodily Harm:
- average sentence: 1 year 7 months
- average time served: 8 months

### Assault on a police officer:
- average sentence: 5 months
- average time served: 6 weeks

Since 1997-98 violent crime has risen by 15 per cent.

"We could all make a list of the additional paperwork that creates a bureaucratic nightmare for officers who want to spend more time actually delivering the goods . . . The situation is far more frustrating nowadays than at any time in my 28 years' service. The public is getting a raw deal" — A Chief Inspector of Police.

## EARNING A LIVING

Common sense means less tax and regulation for people and businesses
- Lower taxes for businesses, families, savers, pensioners and motorists
- Public spending not to outstrip the growth of the economy
- No more stealth taxes - transparent economic policy
- Cut the cost of regulation on business every year
- Keep the pound

It is getting harder for people and businesses in Britain to earn a living.

It should be getting easier. The tough decisions and hard choices made by the British people and Conservative Governments in the 1980s and 1990s transformed our economic prospects, and made Britain's businesses competitive.

But instead of advancing further we are slipping back. People who have to watch every penny, see more and more of their money taken by the Government.

Businesses are spending too much time dealing with new regulations, with too little time to focus on their customers.

It would be disastrous to re-elect a Government whose central economic policy is to increase tax and regulation by stealth.

It's time for common sense.

We will cut taxes on people and businesses and cut government interference and regulation in order to match the competition in the global marketplace.

### Lower taxes

All over the world, governments of all political persuasions are cutting taxes on people and businesses.

Yet Britain is going in the opposite direction. Labour promised not to raise taxes. They have broken that promise. Experts have catalogued forty-five separate tax increases since 1997.

Labour have said that, if they were re-elected, they would increase spending each year faster than the growth of our national income. That inevitably means even higher taxes.

Higher taxes come naturally to Labour, because they don't trust people to spend their own money.

Conservatives do trust people to spend their own money, and we will therefore pursue a very different policy.

We will be a tax-cutting government.

## CONSERVATIVE MANIFESTO

Each year, as the economy grows, we can spend more on vital public services, but also allow people to keep more of their own money. We will improve the performance of government and make policy changes so that after two years we will be able to save £8 billion a year compared to Labour's plans. These changes do not affect schools, the NHS, police or defence.

We will return this £8 billion to people in tax cuts - set out throughout this manifesto - targeted to help those who have been hit hardest by Labour's tax increases.

Conservatives understand that our circumstances change through our lives - most of us face financial pressures when we have young children, for example, or find ourselves living on a fixed income in old age. So we will carefully target tax cuts to help people at times in their lives when they need it most, when they are struggling hard with difficult responsibilities.

This is not the end of our tax cutting ambitions. With proper control of government spending in the second half of the next Parliament we can cut taxes further. Among our priorities will be to raise the Inheritance Tax threshold and to raise the threshold at which people begin to pay higher rate income tax, because it currently catches people who are not, by any definition, rich.

### Conservative tax cuts
● Abolish taxes on savings and dividends £3 billion
● Raise Personal Allowance for pensioners by £2,000 £0.8 billion
● Increase Children's Tax Credit by £200 a year for families with children under the age of 5 £0.3 billion
● Abolish tax on Widowed Mother's Allowance and Widowed Parent's Allowance £0.1 billion
● Introduce a new Married Couple's Allowance £1 billion
● Cut petrol tax by 6p per litre £2.2 billion
● Tax relief on Approved Share Options £0.1 billion
● Regeneration Tax Breaks £0.2 billion
● Business Rates reductions £0.2 billion
● Abolish IR35 £0.1 billion

The tax burden has risen under Labour by 3 per cent of GDP from 35.2 per cent in 1996/97 to 38.2 per cent in 2000/01 - that is the equivalent of 10p on the basic rate of income tax.

### Clearer and simpler taxes

Labour have tried to disguise their tax increases by introducing new stealth taxes and making the tax system more complex. We want people to be able to see how much they pay in tax, and to see it come down. We will run the economy with discipline, and discipline requires transparency. So we will send every taxpayer a clear statement of how the Government raises money and then spends it.

We will create a National Accounts Commission to set standards of transparency for the public accounts and stop politicians from meddling with them for their own ends.

We need simpler taxes, too. Capital Gains Tax, for example, is exactly what a tax ought not to be - at a high rate with lots of complicated exemptions. Capital Gains Tax should be simplified, allowances removed and the rate cut.

The experience of the US and Ireland is that this stimulates enterprise and tax revenues rise.

Conservatives will repeal the tax on IT consultants, the notorious IR35, which has driven away from Britain some of our most productive workers. We will replace it with targeted anti-avoidance measures.

### Less regulation

Regulation is the new way Labour politicians control the economy. Businesses they wouldn't dream of nationalising, they regulate.

It has the same consequences: the judgment of politicians and civil servants is substituted for that of owners and entrepreneurs.

So a Conservative Government will cut the burden of regulation and free businesses to serve their customers rather than serving their regulators.Governments are held to account for the taxpayers' money they spend. We think they should be similarly held responsible for the other costs they impose on businesses. All new regulations will have to be scrutinised by a new Deregulation Commission, which will have the power to send them to Parliament for full debate. And the Commission will calculate, through an independent audit, the cost of government regulations for business. It will then set regulatory budgets for each government department alongside their financial budgets. We will bring these regulatory budgets down, year after year. The burden of regulation has ratcheted up for far too long. We will reverse it.

Small businesses will be exempt from some regulations altogether.

Britain has been ahead of the field in the information economy because we created an environment of low taxes and light regulation. But now we are losing that advantage fast. We don't need more regulations, we need more competition. The utility regulators must focus on competition and address the market dominance of incumbents which stand in the way of competition.

We will abolish Labour's Climate Change Levy package. The necessary carbon dioxide reduction can be achieved far more efficiently by other means. We will also review the future of nuclear energy and its role in contributing to reductions in $CO_2$ emissions.

### £8 billion of Conservative savings
● Social Security £2.5 billion

We will reform welfare to reduce dependency and create a national anti-benefit fraud squad with new powers.
- Dept of Environment, Transport & The Regions £1 billion
We will abolish regional bureaucracy, cut local government red tape and renovate council housing by transferring it to the voluntary sector.
- Dept of Trade & Industry £0.3 billion
We will slim down the DTI and improve its effectiveness for business.
- Reversing the growth in government bureaucracy £1.8 billion
We will return the cost of government to the level at which we maintained it during the last Conservative Government.
- Britain Works £0.6 billion
We will replace the failing New Deal with Britain Works and contract out the job-finding work of the Employment Service.
- Creation of a Community Legal Aid Fund £0.3 billion
We will reform legal aid by creating a new Community Legal Aid Fund. In return for financing civil cases, the Fund will receive a portion of the damages when its clients win.
- Endowing Universities £1.3 billion
We will free universities from reliance on state funding and provide endowments paid for by future asset sales and the reform of student loans.
- Endowing Britain's culture £0.2 billion
We will privatise Channel 4 and give the money to cultural institutions like museums and galleries so they are more independent of the state.
Total - £8 billion

### Five disciplines for a sound economy

The next Conservative Government will operate within a sound and stable financial framework based on five disciplines.
- We will keep the pound. Labour's plan for early entry into the euro is the single biggest threat to our economic stability. By keeping the pound we will keep control of our economic policy, including the ability to set interest rates to suit British economic conditions.
- We will enhance the independence of the Bank of England's Monetary Policy Committee.
- We will set up a Council of Economic Advisers, which will comment publicly on whether the balance between spending and taxes represents a prudent approach to the national finances, and is helping secure low inflation and low interest rates.
- We will appoint a National Accounts Commission to draw up proper national accounts, including a proper presentation of the Government's long term liabilities.
- We will plot a course away from the direction in which the Chancellor is leading us, and towards real annual increases in spending which are within the trend rate of growth of the economy.

### STAYING HEALTHY

Common sense means ending political interference in medical judgments and giving choice to patients
- Increase funding for the NHS
- Trust doctors and nurses, not politicians, to make medical decisions
- Give patients and GPs the right to choose in which hospital to be treated
- Remove tax penalty on private medical insurance
- Guaranteed limits on waiting times for patients
The National Health Service is in a state of almost permanent crisis.
Too many of us experience a second-class system.
People are waiting too long to be treated; they are suffering shabby and unhygenic conditions in hospitals; they have no choice in how, when or where they are looked after.
As people become used to choice and quality in other areas of their life, the service they get from the NHS is increasingly unacceptable.
It's not just about money.
Ask anyone who works in the health service and they will tell you that the NHS is now creaking under the strain of bureaucracy and Government gimmicks.
All the Government has done in four years is to substitute its own political priorities and the pursuit of headlines for the clinical judgment of doctors and nurses.
Labour said they would cut waiting lists - so hospitals have been forced to bring in waiting lists to get on the waiting list, and to give priority to non-urgent operations over those in genuine medical need.
It's time for common sense.
The next Conservative Government will match the Government's plans for spending on the NHS but ensure the money goes further.
We will take politicians out of the day-to-day management of the NHS, putting in their place respect for clinical decisions and accountability to patients.
We will also build a new partnership between the state and independent sectors.

## CONSERVATIVE MANIFESTO

### The Patient's Guarantee

The NHS cannot succeed if those who work within it are not allowed to succeed. Our National Health Service used to be an example to the world. We still have first class doctors and nurses, and many of our hospitals have international reputations for excellence. The clinical judgment of professionals in the NHS is still among the best anywhere.

Yet, immediately on taking office, Labour introduced their Waiting List Initiative which replaced clinical judgment with bogus political priorities.

Immediately on our taking office we will abolish the Waiting List Initiative. We will introduce a Patient's Guarantee instead.

The Patient's Guarantee will give patients a maximum waiting time in defined clinical areas, starting with cardiac and cancer services, based on their medical need as assessed by the patient's own consultant. The health authority will be obliged either to treat the patient within that maximum waiting time, or to arrange for the patient to have the choice of being treated in another health authority or in a private hospital.

We will stop politicians interfering in clinical decisions and in the running of hospitals.

The role of the Secretary of State will be to agree funding, and to regulate standards of quality, not to micro-manage hospitals. We will create a properly independent appointments body, and ensure that ministers cannot interfere in its workings, so that people who work in the NHS are chosen because of their expertise, not their politics.

The quality of the care people receive in hospital is determined as much by standards on the ward as by their surgical procedures. Yet while Ward Sisters are held responsible for the well-being of their patients, they do not have authority over many of the activities, such as feeding and cleaning, that determine the quality of the care they provide.

We will require hospitals to give back authority to Ward Sisters, so that they can make sure that their patients get the care they demand. And we want to bring back Matron so that someone is responsible for overseeing and supporting the nursing staff.

### Choice for GPs and patients

One of the best ways of improving the performance of the NHS is to give patients choice.

When Labour were elected they limited GPs' freedom to refer patients to the hospital of their choice.

We will give back to patients and their doctors the power to choose.

Patients will be able to be treated in the hospital which they and their GPs choose, and will have full access to information on hospitals' waiting lists and success rates to enable them to make that choice.

Hospitals will be rewarded for the operations they carry out, so that good hospitals can attract more patients and more funding, and patients will be able to choose to be treated in hospitals with world-class expertise in their illness.

We will allow alternative and complementary therapies to be made available through the NHS, provided they are of proven clinical effectiveness.

We will give doctors the right to decide how they organise themselves to deliver the best care to their patients.

GPs have told us that they don't want a new upheaval in primary care: we will follow their advice. Instead, we will give GPs the choice of whether to operate as Primary Care Trusts if they think that is right for themselves and their patients. And we will encourage GPs to specialise, so that GP teams will be increasingly able to offer expert diagnosis and treatment to their patients. That way, many patients will get expert opinions and care by doctors they know, without the need to go to hospital.

Choice for patients extends to private healthcare.

Because of the problems in the health service many people with modest incomes spend their hard-earned savings on paying privately for operations or for medical insurance for themselves and their families. In doing so, they free resources in the NHS and help reduce waiting times, but often at considerable personal cost.

The Conservative Party is committed to a comprehensive NHS free to all its users. There is no question of anyone being forced to take out private insurance. But if people do choose to insure themselves privately they should not be penalised for making this choice.

Labour imposes a tax penalty on employers who offer their employees private medical insurance, and then taxes again any employee who has this benefit. It doesn't make sense and, when affordable, we will abolish both taxes.

We will ensure hospices are properly funded by increasing the state's contribution from 32% to 40% for adult hospices and from 4% to 40% for children's hospices.

### More patients treated, more quickly

Conservatives will unblock the bottlenecks that slow down treatment in the NHS.

We will, for example, encourage the development of stand-alone surgical units specialising in a particular type of standard operation, such as cataract surgery or hip replacements. These units would be funded by the NHS and be free of charge for patients, but could be operated by either NHS or private providers. They would enable us to make rapid reductions in the waiting times required for these procedures.

It doesn't take a doctor to take a patient's blood pressure. We will encourage an expansion in the role of practice nurses to take on some of the tasks carried out by GPs, allowing them more time to see more patients.

Some health authorities allow doctors to prescribe certain new drugs, and some do not. Conservatives will end this lottery whereby the postcode you live in determines the treatment you receive by introducing an

Exceptional Medicines Fund. Expensive new medicines - such as Beta Interferon for multiple sclerosis - will be funded direct to doctors from a budget set by the Secretary of State. Access to the funding will be decided by criteria laid down by a panel of senior clinicians and academics.

Conservatives will ensure that important issues of medical ethics are properly debated in Parliament.

## GROWING OLDER

Common sense means respect and independence for older people
- Cut taxes for pensioners
- Increase the basic state pension
- Abolish compulsory annuities at age 75
- Allow younger workers to opt for properly funded private pensions
- Protect the savings and homes of those needing long term care

Older people are among our most responsible citizens and give a great deal to their communities, but they have been demeaned and patronised by this Government. They resent being seen as a burden. And they fear they do not have a place in Blair's Cool Britannia.

To be able to have the standard of living to which they are entitled, Britain's pensioners now have to apply to the State for special favours.

When Labour came into office, 37 per cent of pensioners had to take the means test in order to get their benefit entitlement. On Labour's current plans, within two years most pensioners - 57 per cent - will have to apply to the State for help in this undignified and intrusive way.

Pensioners are proud of being able to take responsibility for themselves, but Labour has denied them this dignity. Instead they have taxed pensioners more heavily and driven them on to means-tested benefits.

It's time for common sense.

Conservatives will give pensioners greater independence from the State, by cutting taxes, removing a million pensioners from income tax altogether, and by increasing the basic state pension - with no strings attached.

### Freeing pensioners from tax

It is wrong that pensioners with modest incomes find themselves paying income tax. It is particularly unfair that pensioners who have saved for their retirement - from their salaries on which they have already paid tax - are then taxed again on the interest their savings earn. We will abolish taxes on savings for most savers - which will be of particular benefit to pensioners.

A Conservative Government will also raise the special age tax allowance for pensioners by £2,000, from around £6,000 to over £8,000 per year. This will take one million pensioners out of income tax altogether and many other pensioners will pay £8.50 less tax per week.

### A higher pension

Conservatives want to provide support to pensioners when they need it most. This should not entail more and more pensioners facing the indignity and bureaucracy of means tests.

So we will offer pensioners a substantial increase in the basic state pension.

At our first opportunity to uprate pensions, in April 2002, we will match the Government's plans for an increase of £3 a week for a single pensioner under 75 and £4.80 for a married couple under 75.

But we will go further in helping older pensioners, who tend to be poorer. Over-75s will have a bigger uprating of £4 for a single pensioner and £6.80 for a married couple. We will be helping poorer pensioners without more means-testing.

Pensioners can carry on receiving the free TV licence, the Winter Fuel Payment, and the Christmas bonus exactly as at present. But, if they prefer it, we will give every pensioner the choice to opt for a higher basic pension, which consolidates these individual payments, tax-free.

This option will be available to all pensioners who get their pension uprated, including groups that Labour forgot - the 200,000 in nursing homes and residential accommodation who do not receive the winter fuel payment and 360,000 pensioners living abroad.

### Funded pensions

The best way to make sure that people have decent incomes in their retirement is for them to invest during their lives in assets that will grow. But the state takes people's national insurance contributions and then fails to invest them, leaving pensioners with miserly pensions.

We need to make it easier for people to provide for a prosperous retirement.

But Labour have hit private and occupational pensions with higher taxes. And many of the current generation of working people have expectations of the pension they are likely to receive which are unfortunately way ahead of the likely reality.

The best way to achieve higher pensions in the future is by more genuine funding of pensions. We wish to enable young people to build up a funded alternative to the basic pension for the future. No one would be forced to change.

The basic state pension would continue to be paid as now, not merely to current pensioners but to people of working age and new entrants who want it in the future. We will consult on how best to offer this new option of funded pensions for young people.

We will also abolish the rule which currently forces pensioners to buy an annuity when they reach 75.

People with personal pensions will only need to ensure that they have sufficient income to keep free of

CONSERVATIVE MANIFESTO

means-tested benefits.

The remaining capital in the pension fund will be theirs to keep and — if they wish — to pass on to their children.

**Long term care**

We also want to tackle another problem which preys on the minds of many people as they become older - meeting the costs of long-term care.

Our proposed funding of the NHS matches Labour's plans and includes a commitment that all nursing care will be free at the point of use. But we need to go further to get at the source of the problem.

We will consider how people who have made prudent provision in advance for the cost of long term care can be protected from having their assets taken by the state if their actual care costs are more than could reasonably be foreseen.

**Your pension with the Conservatives**

| | Basic state pension 2001/02 | Basic state pension 2002/03 (Conservative plans) | Value of pension with optional consolidated special payments |
|---|---|---|---|
| Single pensioner | £72.50 | £75.50 | £78.60 |
| Married pensioner couple | £115.90 | £120.70 | £124.00 |
| Single pensioner over 75 | £72.50 | £76.50 | £81.75 |
| Married couple over 75 | £115.90 | £122.70 | £128.20 |

## KNOWING WHO WE ARE

**A WORLD LEADER**

Common sense means valuing what makes us distinctive as a nation

● A more flexible European Union
● Veto further transfers of power from Westminster to Brussels
● No European army outside NATO
● Global free trade by 2020
● A safe haven, not a soft touch, on asylum

Britain is one of the world's most respected democracies, one of its most influential leaders, one of its most prosperous nations and one of its greatest military powers.

Our possession of all of these qualities, which we rightly value, depends upon our ability to govern ourselves. And all of them are put at risk by the threat that is now posed to our independence.

Labour have lost confidence in our ability to govern ourselves.

It's time for common sense.

The next Conservative Government will secure our independence and use Britain's great strengths to help create a flexible Europe of nations, to maintain the Atlantic Alliance and to develop the role of the Commonwealth.

**In Europe, not run by Europe**

The guiding principle of Conservative policy towards the European Union is to be in Europe, but not run by Europe.

We will lead a debate in Europe about its future, promoting our own clear and positive vision.

The European Union has, with the prospect of enlargement, reached a fork in the road. Down one route lies a fully integrated superstate with nation states and the national veto disappearing. The Government is taking us down this route.

The alternative is a Europe of nations coming together in different combinations for different purposes and to differing extents. In other words, a network Europe. If Britain leads the debate, we can make this alternative a reality.

We will insist on a Treaty 'flexibility' provision, so that outside the areas of the single market and core elements of an open, free-trading and competitive EU, countries need only participate in new legislative actions at a European level if they see this as in their national interest.

At the same time, we are willing to support the principle of 'reinforced co-operation' in Europe, under which small groups of countries can become more closely integrated if they wish to do so, providing it does not damage Britain's national interest.

The next Conservative Government will keep the pound. We will maintain our national veto on European legislation.

Giving up either would put our ability to govern ourselves at risk. We will not ratify the Nice Treaty but will renegotiate it so that Britain does not lose its veto.

We also propose to amend our domestic law to include 'reserved powers'.

This will prevent EU law from overriding the will of Parliament in areas which Parliament never intended to transfer to the EU.

This policy will be reinforced with a determination to veto further transfers of power from Westminster to

Brussels. Should any future Government wish to surrender any more of Parliament's rights and power to Brussels they should be required to secure approval for such a transfer in a referendum.

We intend to press for the single market to be completed and for competition laws to be stronger so that British businesses which play by the rules are not undercut by other companies that do not.

We want early enlargement of the European Union - the first wave, including Cyprus, should be admitted by 2004.

We will also press for Europe to tackle fraud and maladministration as a matter of priority. If the EU reduced waste and abandoned ill-considered programmes, it could make significant reductions in the overall size of the European budget.

### A military power and a staunch ally

One of the reasons that Britain is respected around the world is that it remains a first-class military power.

The British way of life and freedom and democracy around the world are made more secure by the professionalism of our armed forces and the success of our long term military alliances.

Yet now all this is under threat.

The last four years have seen our armed forces come under increased pressure. Overstretched and undermanned, they have also come under attack from those more interested in political correctness than operational effectiveness. At the same time, our primary alliance, NATO, is being weakened by a concerted drive to create an independent military structure in the EU. And for the first time, a British government is leading this attempt.

A Conservative Government would pursue a very different policy.

We think it is common sense to support institutions that work. Our armed forces and NATO work very well.

So we will support our armed forces by setting out to match commitments to capabilities, by making it a priority to achieve the armed forces' full manning levels and by opposing political correctness. We will exempt the armed forces from the European Convention on Human Rights, just as France, Spain, Portugal and others have done.

We will seek greater flexibility to deal with unplanned commitments and to reduce overstretch. We will reform the Territorial Army and enhance the role of the Royal Auxiliary Air Force and our other Reserve Forces.

Conservatives have always supported stronger European defence co-operation, but always inside NATO. We will not participate in a structure outside NATO, but will insist instead that any European initiative is under the NATO umbrella.

We will also end this Government's equivocation over the development by the US of ballistic missile defences. We believe our close ally deserves our support in countering new threats from rogue states and terrorists equipped with weapons of mass destruction. We will take a lead in building support for ballistic missile defence against threats to Europe and America.

We remain fully committed to Britain's independent nuclear deterrent.

### Coming to the aid of others

Playing our part in world leadership means playing our part in helping the development of other countries.

We will work towards the UN aid target of 0.7% of GNP.

We will do what we can to encourage responsible behaviour by aid recipients, by focusing on good governance, and by strengthening civil society, free markets, the rule of law and anti-corruption measures.

We will increase the involvement of charities and the voluntary sector. We will double the proportion of our aid budget spent through aid charities, as they are often better placed than governments to relieve suffering. We will also establish a central information service, 'Aid Direct', that will build strong direct links between aid donors and recipients.

Multilateral aid and development institutions are crying out for reform. In particular, we are calling for the EU to set its house in order. Unless the Commission reforms its management, we will propose a treaty amendment allowing member states to deliver aid bilaterally instead.

We will press for more effective debt relief, action on HIV/AIDS and conflict prevention and resolution.

We will appoint an Envoy for Religious Freedom.

### Taking a lead in the world

The world is changing. The old power blocs are declining in importance. Nations, and networks between nations, are taking centre stage.

Conservatives will build on Britain's strengths, so Britain can be a force for good. Britain has prospered when trade has been free. We will lead the campaign for a trans-Atlantic free trade area, encompassing the EU and NAFTA. This is a step towards our vision of global free trade by 2020. Britain has an unrivalled diplomatic service. We will strengthen it further by creating a new Foreign, Commonwealth and Trade Office to bring diplomacy and free trade together, giving renewed impetus to trade and commerce.

The Commonwealth has huge potential - as a force for stability, for promoting the rule of law, democracy and the open economy, and potentially as a means of focusing UK aid. We will consult with our partners on implementing many of the recommendations of the Commonwealth Commission.

We will use Britain's influence in the world for peace and stability, whether in Kashmir or Cyprus or the Middle East.

Britain has vast global reach. In a world where geography matters less, Britain is not on the periphery of anything. Uniquely, we have a central place in the EU, NATO, the Commonwealth and the UN. A Conservative government will be outward-looking, using our influence to the full.

### A safe haven, not a soft touch, on asylum

Over the centuries Britain has welcomed people who have been persecuted by oppressive regimes overseas.

But now our ability to be a safe haven for the genuinely oppressed is severely hampered by the virtual collapse of our asylum system. This chaos encourages unfounded asylum claims.

Britain has gained a reputation as a soft touch for bogus asylum seekers.

This Government has allowed a crisis to develop which has encouraged an illegal trade in human misery, blighting many lives.

The problem here is worse than anywhere else in Europe because of Labour's mismanagement. The Government has presided over massive delays in processing applications and admits that thousands of those whose cases are rejected simply disappear and never leave.

In four years, Labour has seen the cost of the asylum system double and put a great strain on many communities.

Our policy will be that all new asylum applicants are housed in secure reception centres until their cases are determined. This will speed up the process of establishing which claims are well-founded. Asylum applications from safe countries will not normally be accepted.

We will ensure that those whose claims are rejected are quickly deported by a new Removals Agency.

Conservatives will restore common sense to Britain's asylum procedures.

## A STRONGER SOCIETY

Common sense means responsible citizens and a smaller state
● Create an Office of Civil Society to champion families, voluntary organisations and faith communities
● Reform taxation for charities
● Pay independent groups to get people back to work and find them lasting jobs
● Protect the savings of disabled people and help them find work
● Tackle welfare fraud

A strong society rests on responsible individuals and families. They need to be able to turn to straightforward, reliable help when times are bad. But that should not become dependence on the state when times are good.

Labour promised to reform the welfare state, but they shirked the challenge.

It's time for common sense.

The next Conservative Government will help build a stronger society. We will provide support for individuals and families when they need it. And we will encourage people to take responsibility for themselves and their families.

Tolerance is one of Britain's historic virtues. A strong society is built on respect for all people - whatever their race, religion, gender or sexual orientation. Britain is made up of many ethnic communities. Conservatives believe that we are richer and stronger for it.

### Welfare without the state

Many of our poorest people are forced to struggle with a mess of complicated and ill thought out government schemes. And at the same time, the Government is squeezing out genuine voluntary groups, who are best able to help people in real need.

Conservative policy will be very different.

A Conservative Government will tackle the problems of poverty and disadvantage with the same vigour and inventiveness with which we tackle Britain's economic problems. Central government will not try to do everything by itself. Instead we will work with volunteers, charities and local institutions to bring new life to our communities.

We will establish a new Office of Civil Society to give families, faith communities and voluntary groups a voice at the heart of Government. The Office will cut through the bureaucracy that stops the good neighbours of Britain from helping those in need.

We hope to help charities by abolishing their irrecoverable VAT liabilities. The Government refuses to be frank about the money that Whitehall departments have set aside for preparations for converting to the euro, but we believe they are substantial. We will divert this money to fund this major reform of taxation for charities.

### Effective help for unemployed people

It is a cruel trick on unemployed people to place them on training schemes which often do little or nothing to improve their long-term employment prospects.

Labour's New Deal raised people's hopes but has failed to deliver. Unemployment has fallen more slowly under this Government than under the last one.

The next Conservative Government will help unemployed people back into work more effectively than ever before.

We will replace the New Deal with 'Britain Works'. Independent contractors will be rewarded not just for their success in helping the unemployed to find jobs but also for enabling them to keep those jobs.

This will address one of the worst failures of this Government's employment policies - the revolving door which takes people through a cycle of benefits, training schemes, and temporary work, only to end up back on benefits.

The best way of helping unemployed people is to get them back into work as quickly as possible. That is the basis of our Can Work, Must Work Guarantee. Those who can work must do so or they will lose their unemployment benefits.

### Helping people into the labour market

There is evidence that it is in the best interests of children of a lone parent for that parent to be working when the child is of secondary school age. It increases the chances that the child will get good qualifications and go on successfully to hold down a job.

We will therefore expect lone parents on income support with children over 11 to be actively seeking the sort of jobs which they can combine with their family responsibilities.

Labour have treated people with disabilities appallingly - means-testing their benefits and eroding their supported employment. It is time for them to have a better deal.

The Government is treating the savings of disabled people on Income Support less generously than pensioners in the same circumstances. This is an indefensible and unprecedented discrimination against disabled people. We will tackle it head-on. We will increase the amount of savings which a disabled person can have before losing benefit, matching the entitlement of pensioners.

Disabled people who have lost their jobs can become trapped on Incapacity Benefit.

We will address this problem by creating a new agency which will pay Incapacity Benefit on the basis of current entitlements.

But it will also have the funds to obtain the physiotherapy or the physical aids which can help disabled people back to work as quickly as possible.

### An effective attack on fraud

Instead of reforming welfare, Labour have made it even more complex. Instead of encouraging self-reliance they have spread dependence on means tests. Complicated means-tested benefits are not just demeaning, they are also wide open to fraud and abuse. The Government itself has admitted that there could be £7 billion of fraud. In 1998/99 there were 160,000 established cases of Housing Benefit and Council Tax benefit fraud, but just 800 successful prosecutions - 99.5% of fraudsters are not successfully prosecuted. We will introduce a tough anti-fraud package, including a single integrated task force to tackle fraud nationwide. There are 80 million National Insurance numbers which is rather more than the entire UK population. Some of these numbers are fraudulent and we will clean them up.

## TOWN AND COUNTRY
### Common sense means valuing the distinctiveness of both town and country

● Implement a Strategy for Recovery from Foot and Mouth for farms and rural businesses
● Establish Regeneration Companies to revitalise inner cities and housing estates
● Abolish housebuilding targets which threaten our green fields
● Cut business rates for rural shops, pubs, garages and village post offices
● Cut fuel tax to help motorists

Local communities are life's essential harbours. They provide us with a strong sense of local identity. But too many are under enormous pressure. Our countryside, ignored by the Government, has been devastated by the Foot and Mouth crisis. There are too many urban and rural communities that are not sharing in our country's prosperity and where deprivation passes from generation to generation. There are other neighbourhoods where many young people cannot afford to live, despite having grown up there.

It's time for common sense.

Conservatives will restore to communities a sense that they can shape their neighbourhoods, influence local architecture and improve the quality of their surroundings. And we will take effective action to help our rural communities and businesses recover from the effects of Foot and Mouth.

Farming and the countryside are in crisis. Foot and Mouth disease is but the latest in a series of blows inflicted on our farmers.

### Recovering from Foot and Mouth

The Foot and Mouth crisis has been a disaster for our countryside. Farmers have seen years of hard work destroyed in weeks. Rural businesses have seen their turnover collapse. Animals have suffered welfare problems of a kind we never expected to see in Britain. The tragedy is that the crisis need not have been as widespread or so prolonged if the Government had acted urgently and decisively from the beginning.

The priority now must to be help the countryside recover. Immediately upon taking office, we will implement our Strategy for Recovery - practical steps to stamp out Foot and Mouth once and for all; help for struggling tourism and other rural business and firm action to prevent infection entering Britain again.

### Farming and the countryside

Foot and Mouth disease is but the latest in a series of blows inflicted on our farmers.

The Common Agricultural Policy has damaged consumers, farmers, the taxpayer and the environment.

## CONSERVATIVE MANIFESTO

It must be reformed to cut the bill for taxpayers and consumers, provide sustainable long term support for farming, and protect the environment and the countryside. We will renegotiate the CAP so that many decisions currently taken at EU level would be taken by the governments of individual member states.

Farmers and other rural businesses spend too much time on form-filling and red tape. The next Conservative Government will not enforce European regulations any sooner or more zealously than other countries.

We will also fight for a fair deal for consumers, by introducing honesty in labelling and requiring the country of origin and method of production of the main ingredients to be stated on the label of all food products.

We will also renegotiate the Common Fisheries Policy. We will insist on national or local controls being established over our own waters, whether through zonal management, or coastal management, or in some other way.

We will improve animal protection and welfare by building on the successes of the last Conservative Government to raise animal welfare standards in Europe.

The Foot and Mouth crisis has not only badly damaged farming but has also damaged the general rural economy and all that depends on it. Alongside the farming crisis, rural communities are losing their post offices, pubs and police stations at alarming rates.

Labour neither understands the needs of the countryside nor even cares about its survival.

We need a new approach.

The next Conservative government will protect the liberty and livelihood of rural communities. Our policies on transport, crime, planning and Europe will all benefit the countryside.

We will cut business rates for rural shops, pubs, garages and village post offices and change the rules so that they can provide new, much-needed local services. We will encourage more passenger-friendly rural transport services and give community transport schemes a tax rebate on their fuel cost.

Post offices round the country are closing in record numbers because the Government has announced the ending of cash payment of pensions and benefits at post offices. We recognise the essential part played by post offices as a focus of community life.

We will remove Labour's threat and instead introduce a benefit card which will cut fraud and bring large efficiency gains while continuing to bring business into post offices.

We will abolish centrally-driven national or regional housebuilding targets. Local councils accountable to local people should be responsible for meeting local housing needs. Where there is rapid population growth, central government should work in partnership with local councils to invest in additional infrastructure.

As well as our Green Belts, we will take action to protect our rivers, wetlands, lakes, canals and coastline from development by establishing "Blue Belt" areas.

The Conservatives will establish a new Select Committee on Rural Affairs to monitor the impact on rural communities of all aspects of government policy.

### Foot and Mouth: A Strategy for Recovery

Conservatives have played a constructive role throughout the Foot and Mouth crisis. We have put forward practical policies to speed up the eradication of the disease, given real help to businesses hit by the crisis and to ease the suffering of animals.

Immediately upon taking office we will implement a Strategy for Recovery including action to:
- speed up disposal of slaughtered animals
- unblock delays in compensation for affected farms
- offer interest-free loans for affected businesses
- properly fund campaigns to promote the tourist industry
- block high risk food imports to prevent Foot and Mouth recurring

### The regeneration of urban Britain

The future of the countryside is bound up with the future of our inner cities. As long as people leave the cities to occupy new houses built on green fields there can be no prospect of an urban revival.

We must start by making our cities places where families want to live and put down roots. That means tackling the problems that drive many familes to leave. First and foremost this means education and crime. In too many of our inner cities families with young children feel they have to get out to get educated. And until there is effective policing and the streets are safe, money spent improving houses or encouraging enterprise will have little impact.

The next Conservative Government will establish new local Regeneration Companies to drive the campaign to revitalise our inner cities and outer urban estates.

Working with local councils, businesses and people they will be able to buy extra policing strength, help set up Partner Schools, and tear down the worst tower blocks. They will have statutory powers to accelerate the planning and development of rundown areas.

We will support radical solutions to the long term decline of coastal towns - bringing in new measures to help them support and market their heritage, protect their coastline, improve transport links, and tackle the problems they face in housing asylum-seekers.

We will also tackle the problem of 'neighbours from hell'. We will enable the eviction of residents who break tenancy agreements, fail to pay their rent and desecrate the neighbourhood. We will tackle the problems which undermine the quality of life in these areas such as litter, graffiti, and dumped cars. We will also tackle insensitive siting of mobile phone masts without adequate consultation.

We will streamline planning procedures to make it easier for new houses to be built on brownfield sites. We will give local councils power to declare extra areas of local Green Belt.

And we will make Britain a nation of homeowners. We will increase the right-to-buy discounts on council homes and introduce a new rent-to-mortgage scheme. Homesteading grants will allow people to first repair, and then own empty council housing.

Conservatives will give housing associations more freedom to compete in the housing market. We will encourage greater involvement of tenants in running their estates.

### Transport

Labour promised 'immediate benefits' in transport. But public transport has become worse, while our roads are more congested than ever. Britain has the highest road user taxes in Europe and the worst traffic jams.

Labour want to force car drivers off the roads, without offering an alternative. They will tax drivers who come into town centres, and tax those who need to park at work.

Last year, Labour took £36 billion from road users but they spent less than £8 billion on transport. Conservatives are not anti-car, but we are anti-pollution, and so we will cut taxes on cleaner fuels and cleaner vehicles.

We will set out long term investment plans for roads and public transport, meeting the needs of commuters, cyclists, pedestrians, and elderly and disabled people. We will establish a new Roads Standards Unit to champion the interests of road users. It will aim to take through traffic out of towns and villages and minimise the environmental effects of roads. It will set sensible speed limits for each stretch of road, and make roads safer.

Unlike Labour, we will not ban people from driving if they marginally exceed the 70mph limit on motorways. Instead we will look to improve the traffic flow on motorways by increasing the speed limit to 80 mph where it is safe to do so, and enforcing this speed limit rigorously. We will target the hard core of bad drivers who are the main cause of accidents.

We will restore the competitiveness of the British haulage, shipping, and aviation industries. We will charge foreign lorries for the use of British roads with our Brit Disc scheme.

We will cut tax on petrol and diesel by 6p per litre. It is technology, not taxation, that cuts pollution from vehicles.

We will revive the railway industry so it achieves airline standards of service and safety. We will stop Labour's policy of blame and shame. We will implement the Cullen Inquiry recommendations. Subject to a 'no strike' deal we will work with Bob Kiley - who transformed the New York subway - and support his ambitions to create a world class London Underground.

### The wider environment

Conservatives believe that each of us should act as a steward preserving and enhancing the natural world and the built environment for future generations.

The biggest global environmental challenge is to prevent climate change causing long-term damage through extreme weather conditions. We will meet the commitments made by successive British governments by a comprehensive package of emission permit trading, energy conservation measures, tax incentives, greater encouragement of renewable energy and cleaner energy generation.

### A CIVILISED COUNTRY

Common sense means supporting the people that create a thriving culture
● Free arts organisations from dependence on the state by giving them endowments
● Back the tourism industry
● Privatise the commercially successful Channel Four
● Simplify regulation of British broadcasting and communications
● Support youth, grass roots and elite sport

Government policy towards the arts, sports and broadcasting has stumbled from fiasco to disaster in the last four years.

The Government wasted millions of pounds on bailing out the Dome, botched the development of Wembley stadium, dithered over the new UK Sports Institute, and supervised a bizarre competition to run the National Lottery only to end up handing it back to the existing firm.

This incompetence has been accompanied by a disdain for British traditions and a modish contempt for our heritage. Labour even promoted a bogus new culture - 'Cool Britannia' - in an attempt to supplant the culture and identity which has shaped us.

It's time for common sense.

A Conservative Government will be optimistic about Britain's future because we are comfortable with Britain's past.

Tony Blair said that the Dome would be a vivid symbol of Labour's Britain. That is exactly what it was. Step inside and you could be anywhere - it was banal, anonymous and rootless. It lacked a sense of Britain's history or culture.

### Freeing our culture from political interference

The last Conservative Government transformed the funding of sport, the arts and our historic environment by creating the National Lottery. We ensured that money from this source was additional to Government spending, and administered independently.

Labour have increasingly taken control of Lottery funds. The rules which govern applications for Lottery funds are excessively complex. We will reform them, so that they are more accessible to small community groups.

We will set about freeing the arts from Government interference. Using the proceeds from the sale of Channel 4 and undistributed surpluses from the Lottery, we will create a £3 billion endowment fund for cultural organisations. This will dramatically extend freedom from State dependency and political control.

Conservatives recognise the role of the arts in developing the creative skills which are essential to Britain's future prosperity.

We will undertake a radical review of the Arts Council of England and the Regional Arts Boards.

We want to create a less bureaucratic funding structure which delivers more for the arts and for artists.

Britain's £65 billion tourist industry is a powerful force for urban and rural regeneration.

Under Labour, Britain's trade deficit in tourism has doubled, and tourist businesses have been hit by a tide of new regulations. We will back Britain around the world by increasing support for the British Tourist Authority and restoring a voice for English Tourism.

This will be all the more important in the light of the disastrous impact of Foot and Mouth disease on the whole sector.

## Championing sport

The success of our athletes in the Sydney Olympics showed how important sport can be in creating a sense of national pride.

The dedication and skill of our Olympic team was supported by funds from the National Lottery, established by the last Conservative Government. We will ensure that our elite athletes get the funding they need to achieve excellence in the future.

But our future success is threatened because too few young people get the chance to take part in sport at school.

Conservatives will give back to headteachers and governors the right to offer adequate time for sport. We will also give further protection to playing fields.

We will reform the law to enable local voluntary sports clubs to apply for charitable status, strengthening their financial base and encouraging private investment in grassroots sport, and helping to safeguard their assets for future generations.

We will look to streamline the over-complex funding structures for sport, reducing the number of quangoes and devolving more funds to a more rationalised network of governing bodies.

## Freeing the media and communications industries

Our best media companies lead the world in quality and innovation.

Conservatives deregulated the telecommunications market and Britain was well placed to benefit from the convergence of media and communications technologies.

But we are throwing away our head start. Labour have stalled over liberalising telecommunications. The numerous overlapping regulatory authorities in the communications industries urgently need rationalising.

The next Conservative Government will make Britain once again a beacon of competition in the communications industries.

We will privatise Channel 4, while maintaining its public service remit. The State has no business owning a commercial TV company.

We will introduce early legislation to create a single regulator for the media and communications industries charged with speeding up the introduction of competition. We will liberate media companies from outdated ownership rules and ensure that regulation is minimised, while protecting the vulnerable from offensive material.

Our policy will deliver fair and independent regulation of the BBC. The regulator will require the BBC to make the most of its assets for the benefit of the licence fee payer but to rein in any expansion plans which are hostile to competition.

We will ensure that religious broadcasters have fair and equal access to future competitions for local, national, digital and programme service licences.

## A PROUD DEMOCRACY

Common sense means fewer politicians and more local decision-making
● Transfer power from central government to effective local councils
● Local referendums before large increases in Council Tax
● Abolish artificial regional tiers of administration in England
● Reform Parliament so that only English and Welsh MPs vote on exclusively English and Welsh matters
● Strengthen parliamentary scrutiny of the Government

Britain's democracy has always been one of our greatest strengths. It has made our country what it is, and has embodied and defended our freedoms.

But after four years of Labour, the way we govern ourselves has been abused. We have an arrogant and complacent Government which ignores Parliament and people.

We have the anomaly of MPs from Scotland and Northern Ireland voting on laws that apply only to England and Wales. The House of Lords, historically a source of balance and independence, has suffered a botched reform.

People identify with their local communities. But under this Government they are being marginalised by alien new regional bureaucracies that are costly, unaccountable and unnecessary.

Our constitution is being perverted, and faith in politics and politicians is at an all time low.

It's time for common sense.

A Conservative Government will revitalise our democracy by giving more power to local people, and once more placing Parliament at the centre of our national life.

### Revitalising local government

People feel at home in their local communities, be they counties, towns, villages or parishes.

But real communities are being weakened by too much government from Whitehall, and by the imposition of artificial new layers of government with which people don't identify. The next Conservative Government will revolutionise the attitude of central government to local government.

The best councils offer excellent value for money and serve their communities well. Conservatives believe that councils that have such a track record of success should be trusted with more power. They will be able to become 'free councils'. We will devolve financial and administrative power from central government to them, and establish a stronger link between the money they raise and the money they spend.

We believe that local citizens should decide how much their council will spend. The next Conservative Government will not use its powers to cap local council budgets.

We will abolish many of the national targets and plans that local councils are forced to follow by Whitehall.

Alongside this policy of granting greater freedom to the best councils must come some protection from abuses by the worst. So we will look at ways in which local councils proposing increases in their budgets significantly above the rate of inflation can be obliged to hold a local referendum on the increase in the Council Tax which this would entail. We will also retain Section 28 of the Local Government Act.

Labour have introduced a new tier of regional bureaucracy. But almost no one identifies with the arbitrary regions into which the country has been carved up - they owe nothing to where people feel they actually belong.

We will abolish the Regional Development Agencies that the Government has introduced and scrap Labour's plans for new Regional Assemblies. We will give responsibility for enterprise and development back to county councils, and to unitary authorities where appropriate, and save the £70 million a year that the RDAs are spending in administration.

### Restoring balance in the constitution

Britain's constitution has never been set in stone, but has evolved and adapted to cope with the changing circumstances of different centuries. Because Labour do not understand how the history and stability of our democratic structures have underpinned our national life, they have altered them in a crude, unthinking way, often for narrow party advantage.

As Conservatives have demonstrated in our constructive participation in the Scottish Parliament and Welsh Assembly, we will work to ensure devolution is a success.

But we will restore balance to our vandalised democracy.

When Parliament is discussing something that affects the whole of the United Kingdom, all MPs should vote. But only English and Welsh MPs will be entitled to vote on Government Bills relating to England and Wales. And English MPs alone will vote on the remaining laws which apply exclusively to England.

In changing the way Parliament works our overriding objective will be to strengthen the ability of the House of Lords and the House of Commons to hold the Government to account. We will strengthen the independence of the House of Lords as an effective revising chamber by requiring new members to be approved by an independent appointments commission. We will set up a Joint Committee of both Houses of Parliament in order to seek consensus on lasting reform in the House of Lords. We would like to see a stronger House of Lords in the future, including a substantial elected element.

Conservatives will support reforms of the House of Commons to make ministers more accountable. As a first step we will once again require the Prime Minister to appear before the House of Commons twice a week, and make sure that Select Committees are independent of party managers.

We reaffirm our commitment to keeping Britain's voting system for general elections.

### Northern Ireland

As a Unionist party, we value the contribution that Northern Ireland makes to the United Kingdom. Conservatives have always upheld the principle that the future of Northern Ireland will be determined solely by democracy and consent and never by violence. The next Conservative Government will resolutely maintain Northern Ireland's position within the United Kingdom, in accordance with the democratically expressed wishes of the greater number of its people.

Conservatives continue to believe that the Belfast Agreement offers the best chance for lasting peace and political stability. The key to progress is maintaining confidence on all sides. So the next Conservative Government will work tirelessly and constructively to bring about the full implementation of all aspects of the Agreement, including the decommissioning of illegally-held terrorist arms and explosives.

We remain unstinting in our praise for the work of the Royal Ulster Constabulary and the armed forces in fighting terrorism. Improvements to the overall security situation will inevitably bring about changes, but reductions in security will only be made on the basis of the prevailing terrorist threat. Conservatives will not countenance any measure that weakens the ability of the police and army to uphold the rule of law and protect the people of Northern Ireland against terrorism.

## CONSERVATIVE MANIFESTO

### Restoring faith in politics

At a time when the Government has interfered as never before in everyone's lives, they have abandoned any pretence of accountability. No wonder the British people have become disillusioned with politicians.

We want to return to people responsibility for their lives by reducing the level of political interference and regulation. And that involves reducing the number of politicians.

We will abandon the Government's plans for a new tier of regional politicians in England. We will cut the number of government ministers and, once we have strengthened parliamentary scrutiny, we will reduce the size of the House of Commons.

And we will cut the number of political advisers and spin doctors employed, at the taxpayer's expense, to serve government ministers.

### Time to deliver

Conservatives have a vision of what our country can be when it is true to its own character.

We want strong families and enterprising business. We want a free and responsible society. We want to govern ourselves, confident in a stable and trusted constitution. This manifesto sets out the vision that will inspire the next Conservative Government.

It's time for a Government that will deliver.

It's time to support marriage and the family; time for a war on crime; time to cut taxes and regulation; time for our schools and hospitals to benefit from choice and freedom; time to show respect to our pensioners; time for real savings not welfare dependency; time to endow our universities; time to rebuild our inner cities; time to end the crisis in the countryside; time to be in Europe, but not run by it.

It's time for common sense. — **William Hague**

# LIBERAL DEMOCRAT MANIFESTO

## FREEDOM
## JUSTICE
## HONESTY

Three simple words. Freedom, justice, honesty. These sum up what the Liberal Democrats stand for. Freedom - because everybody should have the opportunity to make the most of their life. Justice - because freedom depends on fairness. Honesty - because where fairness has a cost, like investing in schools, hospitals and pensions, we explain how it will be paid for.

This manifesto sets out our priorities: investing in schools and hospitals to cut class sizes and waiting times; extra police to prevent crime and catch criminals; increasing the basic state pension; and providing free personal care.

In Scotland, where Liberal Democrats are part of the government, we have already guaranteed free personal care. We have also abolished tuition fees, and we want to do this for the rest of the United Kingdom.

We will also recognise the professionalism of teachers, doctors, nurses and the police, valuing their contribution to the community. We believe that they must be given the freedom to exercise their professional judgement.

All our policies have a green dimension. So there is an environmental section in every chapter, a green thread binding together all our thinking. Without steps to preserve our planet for future generations, none of our other policies would have much purpose.

### A Real Chance for Real Change

The United Kingdom has huge potential. Unlock the energies, skills and talents of its people, and its rich ethnic and cultural diversity, and there is nothing that cannot be achieved.

But we do not want government always telling people how to develop those assets. So in this manifesto every section explains how we want government to stop interfering.

Government works best as an enabler. Its task is not to curb but to stimulate. To enjoy true freedom, people must have good education, decent healthcare, reliable public transport, safety on the streets and a secure income in old age. The state must provide these basic public services to allow all its citizens to achieve their full potential.

Under eighteen years of Conservative government, these freedoms steadily diminished. The sick waited longer for operations. Children were taught in larger and larger classes. Rail passengers suffered the consequences of a disastrous privatisation. Crime rose. Pensioners' incomes fell behind. But Labour has been disappointing, sticking quite unnecessarily for two years to Tory spending limits.

Our programme for government will deliver more. For schools, hospitals, pensioners, the police and the environment, we offer Britain a real chance for real change.

### Applicability and Costings

This document contains Federal Liberal Democrat policy, except in areas where policy of the Scottish and Welsh Liberal Democrats applies. Separate manifestos set out our agenda for Scotland and Wales. Guarantees represent our minimum commitment over a five-year Parliament. This manifesto also sets out policies to be implemented as economic growth allows. Our ambitions are not limited to these, and are set out in other policy documents. A full costing of our programme has been published with this manifesto. Figures included in both are changes to existing Government revenue and spending plans due to our manifesto commitments. Except for specified items, all Departments will work within current spending plans, unless economic growth allows more. Figures presented are calculated on a UK-wide basis to make comparisons with UK-wide figures from central government and other parties. Different priorities in Scotland, Wales and Northern Ireland may result in different priorities in practice in the budgetary areas they control.

### Freedom, Justice, Honesty:

### HEALTH

Health is a fundamental freedom. No one can fulfil their potential without the best possible health. We will prioritise investment to cut waiting times. But we also believe that it is best to improve health by preventing illness, tackling pollution and reducing poverty.

### Liberal Democrats will:

- Cut waiting times by recruiting 27,500 more nurses, 4,600 more doctors, and 10,250 more professionals allied to medicine.
- Cut waiting times by retaining more staff through increasing pay for the worst paid NHS staff by an average of £1,000 each per year.

- Cut waiting times by providing an additional 10,000 beds.
- Keep people healthy by investing in scanning equipment and abolishing charges for dental and eye checks.
- End the scandal of elderly and long-term patients having to pay for long-term personal care costs.

The NHS has suffered for decades from under-investment, most notably during the eighteen years of the Thatcher and Major Governments. Labour promised to save the NHS. Instead, they spent three years unnecessarily locked into the Conservative spending plans which caused the problem in the first place. The new NHS plan falls far short of Tony Blair's declared aim of bringing health spending in Britain up to the levels of our European neighbours.

The NHS still lacks the capacity to give patients the first-class treatment which they deserve. It is short of staff, beds, hospitals and residential homes. Liberal Democrats offer something different based on clear and distinct priorities. Our starting point is that prevention is better than cure.

It is also important to give professionals greater freedom to do their jobs. Labour has tried to control far too much of the NHS from the centre. The Conservatives' attempt to apply market principles produced inefficiency and inequity. Liberal Democrats will cut the role of Whitehall back and give doctors and managers the freedom to get on and run the NHS without political interference.

## Cutting Waiting Times

Lengthy waiting times are one of the worst aspects of the NHS. The best way to cut waiting times is to increase the number of doctors, nurses and professionals allied to medicine. They are the greatest asset of the NHS and increasing their numbers is the best way of increasing the capacity of the NHS. Under the Conservatives, too many left and too few were trained and recruited. Four years on, the service is just as overstretched. There is also now a severe year-round lack of acute and intermediate care beds and the staff to support them. To cut waiting times, we will:

- Provide training places for an extra 4,600 doctors and 27,500 nurses and midwives over five years. This means an extra 2,500 training places for doctors and 7,500 for nurses on top of the measures that the government has proposed in the NHS National Plan. We would also provide 10,250 extra professionals allied to medicine such as occupational therapists, podiatrists, physiotherapists and speech therapists. This means an extra 3,750 training places on top of the measures that the government has proposed.
- Reward low-paid nurses, midwives and other low-paid professionals by paying them an additional £1,000 on average every year. We will also boost staff retention by making additional funds available for pay increases for other NHS staff. After taking these immediate steps to help retain dedicated staff, we would set up a Commission to examine terms and working conditions throughout the health service, and to establish a single pay review system to ensure fairness for all staff.
- Provide an extra 10,000 hospital beds over five years. This means providing 3,000 extra beds on top of the government's current plans. We also will review the criteria by which PFI contracts are judged, creating a level playing field between different financial options and so ensure there are enough new beds to meet local health needs.
- Guarantee booked dates for appointments with consultants and for surgery after the GP first refers a patient.
- Give priority to the most needy. We will introduce a scorecard system that takes account not just of clinical need but also of the needs of the patient. This would give doctors objective guidelines to help them (but not bind them) in determining priorities.

## Keeping People Healthy

To support good health it is vital to tackle poverty and to have a clean environment. But it is also important that the National Health Service delivers high quality preventive care. The NHS should not just be a National Sickness Service. We will invest more in early detection and prevention, and in improving the environment. This will not only achieve better levels of health, but also save money in the long run. Liberal Democrats will:

- Inject an extra £500 million over five years into dental services. The money will be used to guarantee access for everyone to an NHS dentist. We will do so by rewarding dentists for working in the NHS and offering them incentives to invest in new equipment and buildings, to encourage practitioners to return to NHS work. The British Dental Association estimates that this would bring back the equivalent of 1,000 full-time dentists to NHS work.
- Double the Government's commitment to invest more in the latest scanning and diagnostic equipment. We will provide extra advanced equipment in hospitals across the country.
- Restore free NHS dental check-ups for all to promote oral health and prevent disease.
- Provide free eye checks for all to ensure that problems are spotted earlier.
- Appoint a Minister of Public Health based in the Cabinet Office rather than the Department of Health to co-ordinate all aspects of public health policy across government departments.
- Make more tests available in GP surgeries and pharmacies for diabetes, cholesterol, anaemia, HIV/AIDS, TB, prostate and colorectal diseases.
- Promote a wider availability of complementary medicines and healthcare through the NHS to take maximum advantage of different approaches to health.

## Caring for Patients

All too often, the NHS fails to provide the care that patients need. Except in Scotland, people in long-term care have to pay for someone to bath or feed them. Drugs available on the NHS in one part of the country are not available in another - the 'postcode lottery'. Liberal Democrats will:

● Pay for all long-term personal care costs. The Royal Commission on Long Term Care, set up by Labour, recommended that these costs should be met by the state. The Westminster Government ignored this key finding, though Liberal Democrats in Scotland are using their influence in the Scottish Executive to implement it.

● Tackle the postcode lottery which means that some medicines are only available in some parts of the country. We will scrap the present secretive system for buying medicines. In its place we will create a Pharmaceutical Agency to use the purchasing power of the NHS to drive down the price of established drugs and secure the more sophisticated medicines and technologies at affordable prices. The money saved would be used to end the postcode lottery and make advanced and expensive drugs more available within the NHS. Over time, we will use further savings to reduce and eventually scrap prescription charges for all.

In the long term we will aim to:

● Increase funding for mental health services. All people in need of care and support should be assessed individually to ensure that they receive the treatment they need. Our proposals for ending the postcode lottery will ensure that mental health care offers the best treatment with the fewest side effects. This will encourage them to comply with treatment and diminish the risk to themselves and to the community.

● Increase local authority social services budgets. This would provide more community care places, improve preventive and rehabilitation services, give further support and respite to carers, and provide more social workers to support elderly people, those with learning difficulties and others.

## Improving Quality

Patients should have a right to a high-quality NHS. They should know how well the NHS is performing and who is responsible when things go wrong. They should also have access to proper information about their own cases. Vulnerable people need someone to champion them if they are not receiving adequate treatment. The private sector should complement, not compete with, the NHS, which we are committed to making world class, comprehensive and accessible to everyone. Labour have not addressed these questions adequately. When they abolished Community Health Councils, they failed to set up an adequate alternative. Liberal Democrats will:

● Develop Patient Care Guarantees, to provide patients with minimum standards of treatment, to which the NHS will be held accountable. We will start by building on existing National Service Frameworks (NSFs), for example on cancer, heart disease and mental health, and ensure that future NSFs incorporate Patient Care Guarantees. We will develop new NSFs on children in care, prosthetic limbs, hepatitis C, HIV and AIDS, palliative care, nutrition, adoption, neurological services, diabetes, maternity services and dentistry among others.

● Make the NHS more accountable by increasing local democracy on Trust and Primary Care Trust boards, giving the Commons Health Select Committee more resources and increasing the powers of the Health Ombudsman to examine policies and initiate inquiries. We will also transfer local responsibility for public health from health authorities to local councils.

● Give patients access to independent advocates. Children, frail elderly people and those with learning difficulties would particularly benefit. There would be a Children's Rights Commissioner to represent children.

● Introduce no-fault compensation. At the moment, compensation for medical negligence is a lottery. While some are awarded excessive multi-million pound payouts, the length and cost of the process of going to court leaves others with nothing. Our system would be far simpler, with fair compensation for patients and their families, and an end to burdensome legal costs.

● Promote better access to services. If local NHS services do not offer patients the treatment they need, we will enable the patient to use an alternative facility. Choice will extend into use of the private sector - but at NHS cost price.

● End the use of mixed wards so that patients have more dignity when they are in hospital.

● Legislate against discrimination on the grounds of age in health and social care. Clinical need, not preconceived judgments about age, should be the criterion for deciding who receives treatment and when.

## Setting You Free

● Stop government wasting doctors' and nurses' time by scrapping meaningless bureaucratic targets. National targets for waiting lists serve no purpose. Doctors, not government, should decide priorities for treatment, using guidelines which allow them to assess patients' needs fairly and openly.

## Green Action

### Healthy Homes

We will improve health by requiring an energy efficiency audit to be completed on all homes before sale to promote high energy efficiency standards throughout the housing market. Coupled with our comprehensive strategy to tackle fuel poverty this will mean that everyone can have a warm home. This will tackle the damp and cold which affect the health of millions of people, and reduce winter deaths caused by fuel poverty. With less energy needed to heat homes, $CO_2$ emissions will also be reduced.

## Clean Air

We will tackle the air pollution responsible for respiratory problems like asthma by introducing incentives for people to switch to less polluting vehicles, reducing reliance on cars by increasing the use of public transport, and tackling industrial pollution. We will also provide better quality information, increasing the number of air monitoring sites for key pollutants in all areas.

### Freedom, Justice, Honesty:

## EDUCATION AND EMPLOYMENT

High quality education is the key to personal freedom. We believe that every child matters. Education provides the freedom to choose a fulfilling job, the freedom to exploit one's talents to the full, and the freedom to contribute fully to society. Education is also the key to Britain's future prosperity.

Liberal Democrats will:

● Cut class sizes to 25 on average for 5-11 year-olds
● Recruit 5,000 extra secondary school teachers to reduce class sizes for 11-16 year-olds
● Increase funding for books and equipment in schools
● Cut bureaucracy in schools and interfere less in the professional judgements of teachers
● Abolish university tuition fees

Britain has been held back by under-investment in education. Children from poorer families have been particularly ill-served. The Conservatives failed to fund schools and colleges adequately. Labour have done far too little to put things right. In schools, they have invested in paperwork rather than people, demoralising teachers and wasting resources by creating a mountain of extra bureaucracy. In the Higher Education sector, they have made matters worse by introducing university tuition fees.

We are clear about our goals and determined to reach them. Our plans will cost around £3 billion extra each year. We guarantee to introduce the extra funding needed at the beginning of the next Parliament, irrespective of short-term economic growth. We will put an extra penny on the basic rate of income tax to meet this commitment. Growth in the future may allow us to be more ambitious still.

We believe that most day-to-day decision-making in education is best done by teachers, schools and local authorities, not by central government.

### Every Child Matters:
### Class Sizes and Teachers

Under the Conservatives, class sizes were far too high. Even the most dedicated teachers cannot give the attention which pupils need when there are more than thirty to a class. Labour pledged to do better, but their reduction of class sizes for 5-7 year olds came at the price of larger classes for 8-11 year olds. The parents whose children were five in 1997 now see their nine year-olds suffering the consequences of this sleight of hand. In secondary schools, classes are larger than they have been for twenty years.

To make a real difference to class sizes and improve standards achieved by all children, more teachers are needed in schools. The Conservatives under-valued and demoralised the profession. Many of Labour's efforts to make amends have misfired. Performance-related pay is a crude and unfair approach to rewarding teachers. Teachers are also burdened with more and more unnecessary bureaucracy. Small wonder that there is now a grave shortage of teachers. Liberal Democrats will spend over £1 billion extra each year to:

● Cut class sizes to 25 for all 5-11 year olds. We will do this by establishing a maximum average class size of 25 in each local authority's primary schools.
● Fund 5,000 additional secondary teacher places. This will bring pupil:teacher ratios back to around 1997 levels and start to improve on them. We will put particular emphasis on recruiting teachers in shortage subjects.
● Guarantee a classroom assistant for every 25 pupils in the 5-7 age bracket (Key Stage 1) to improve the ratio of adults to children in infant school classrooms. We will provide 40,000 extra classroom assistants, including 25,000 for 5-7 year olds, compared to the government's plan to spread 20,000 across all age groups.
● Introduce paid preparation hours for primary teachers. By funding extra posts, we will be able to allow all primary teachers two paid hours a week to prepare and plan lessons.
● Pay trainee teachers a full training salary replacing the current training grants to improve teacher recruitment.
● Improve Information and Communications Technology (ICT) support for teachers. At the moment, teachers have to spend too much time out of the classroom maintaining computer equipment and so have less time to devote to their pupils. Drawing on the experience of the recently established e-learning foundations, we will establish educational charitable trusts to arrange the lease of computer equipment and services. We will also invest in training related to the use of new science equipment.
● Scrap Performance Related Pay. Instead we will link teachers' pay with professional development to boost morale in the teaching profession and improve retention of experienced teachers. Teachers will have the opportunity to take a series of in-service training courses. Each time they pass, they will gain a significant salary increase.

In the long term, our goal is:

● A maximum average class size of 18 for all secondary classes with a practical element such as science and modern languages

**Every Child Matters: Books and Equipment**

There are still too many schools having to make do with dog-eared and outdated textbooks shared between several pupils. Schools also lack the computer equipment needed to prepare children for the digital age in which they live and will have to work. Liberal Democrats will:

● Increase funding for books and equipment in schools over and above existing spending levels. We would provide an average of £1,250 per primary school and £4,250 per secondary school per year. Schools could choose to spend this money on books Information Communications Technology (ICT) software such as CD-ROMs.
● Increase funding for ICT and science equipment and purchase and maintenance, and ICT training for teachers within schools, over and above existing spending levels.

**Widening Choice, Cutting Bureaucracy**

Under the Conservatives and Labour, schools have been deluged with bureaucracy absorbing far too much of teachers' time to the detriment of their pupils. Whitehall has enclosed the school system in a straitjacket which stifles professional creativity and confines teachers to a curriculum which is too narrow and cannot adapt to local circumstances. We will:

● Replace the National Curriculum with a less rigid Minimum Curriculum Entitlement. We will provide for a broad and balanced curriculum including languages, science, maths, the humanities, physical development (including sports instruction and advice on healthy eating), religious education, parenting, citizenship and creative arts. We will increase funding for free musical tuition to encourage more children to learn an instrument.
● Replace all national school targets with a statutory requirement for schools to develop individual education plans for pupils, with clear individual targets and criteria for improvement. The quality of the plans would be guaranteed through national value-added criteria.
● Maintain the key role of Local Education Authorities in providing education and guaranteeing standards and in co-ordinating vital services such as the provision of Special Educational Needs.
● Annually review all Whitehall directives. This would result in an annual cull of all irrelevant instructions to LEAs, schools and governing bodies.
● Issue annual reports to all parents on their children's school's performance. Unlike the current crude league tables, these reports would measure the value added each year by a school, using the test results from a child's start at the school as the baseline. This will result in league tables that genuinely show how schools are performing. We will also promote school councils to give pupils a greater say in how their school is run.
● Reduce testing of the youngest school children. We will scrap testing ('SATs') at age 7, while keeping it for older pupils.
● Reform the school inspection system. Tough, independent inspection is essential, but the current approach of Ofsted often intimidates schools instead of helping them. We will require inspectors to offer advice on improvement, not merely criticism, and require Ofsted to take account of a school's self-evaluation. We will also establish Departments within Ofsted for each of the various areas which it inspects (such as Early Years and Schools), and ensure each is headed up by someone with technical expertise in the subject.

**In the long term, our goal is to:**

● Reduce the disparity in per-pupil funding through a minimum education funding entitlement based on the current median level.
● Promote co-operation between state and private schools. We will encourage independent schools to share their facilities with state schools to spread opportunity for all. We will require independent schools to offer the Minimum Curriculum Entitlement. We will extend charitable status to all schools and maintain the VAT exemption on school fees.

**Early Years Education**

Under both Labour and Conservative governments the inequalities in British society have been increased by the lack of proper early years education. Better-off children, with greater stimulus from the home, pre-school playgroups or from nursery schools, have had a flying start at primary school over those who have not had these advantages. Often children deprived in these early years never catch up. Too much early years provision is still not of a sufficient standard. We will guarantee quality nursery education, which makes a real contribution to intellectual, emotional and social development at this all-important stage in life. We will:

● Fund 1,000 early years specialists to work with early years development partnerships to ensure that children receive proper stimulus in the early years either at nursery school, pre-school playgroups or at home.
● Establish a budget to give additional training to nursery teachers. This would fund courses and extra supply teachers to cover for those undertaking training.
● Increase funding for outdoor facilities for nurseries. Ultimately, all nurseries should have a place for children to play out of doors.
● Strengthen links between home and school recognising that children's early development depends critically on the relationship between school and family.
● Ensure that the early years curriculum has sufficient quality and breadth to facilitate intellectual, emotional and social development and ensure that play is recognised as a key component of this process.

# LIBERAL DEMOCRAT MANIFESTO

## Higher Education

Britain's universities have traditionally had a high international reputation. During the eighteen years of Conservative rule, that reputation was threatened by an ever tighter squeeze on resources. Labour has attempted to address the problem of underfunding by the counterproductive method of introducing tuition fees, which deter many students from going to university. Tuition fees also impose great hardship on many who take up university places, and their parents. We are also opposed to the levying of top-up fees. Liberal Democrats will:

- Abolish university tuition fees throughout the United Kingdom. Liberal Democrats have already achieved this in Scotland by making it a priority issue and have set abolition in train in Wales.
- Reform student maintenance. We would restore grants for poor students and access to benefits for all during the summer holidays, and raise the salary threshold at which student loans are repaid, in the first instance from £10,000 to £13,000 per year.
- Improve access for under-represented groups by tripling the incentive payments for recruitment and retention of under-represented, mature and part-time students. We would pay colleges one third on admission and two thirds on completion of a course.
- Improve salaries to attract and retain high-quality staff. Our first steps will be to end the unacceptable gap between pay for men and women at universities and to tackle similar inequalities faced by casual and part-time staff.
- Ensure that universities are properly resourced by opposing any reduction in the 'unit of resource' - the money that a university receives per student. In the long term, our goal is to increase the unit of resource.

## Further Education and Lifelong Learning

Few jobs these days are for life. To succeed as a nation, we need a flexible workforce which is used to acquiring new skills. Access to good quality further education is equally important to individuals as a means of fulfilling their aspirations. For too long, this sector has been at the bottom of the educational pile. Liberal Democrats see further education as an important priority. We will:

- Give every adult an entitlement to publicly funded tuition. We will provide the funding to allow any adult the chance to acquire a Level 2 qualification (the equivalent of 5 GCSEs at grades A to C, an intermediate GNVQ or a Foundation Modern Apprenticeship). We will fund those aged 16 to 24 up to Level 3 (equivalent to 2 A-Levels at grades A to E, an Advanced GNVQ or an Advanced Modern Apprenticeship). In the long term, our goal is to extend this further entitlement to every adult. All those on these courses would be entitled to a student loan to cover maintenance, depending on their income.
- Simplify the funding and qualification systems. We will merge the Learning and Skills Council and the Higher Education Funding Council for England into a single Learning Council for England. We will also reform the National Vocational Qualification system to cut bureaucracy and allow students to accumulate credits from different courses and transfer them.

In the long term, our goal is to:

- Give every citizen an Individual Learning Account. Ultimately this approach to life-long learning would provide the flexibility to access each person's entitlement to post-sixteen education throughout a person's life, rather than at times imposed by the state. Tuition would be paid for and student loans would be available for maintenance. This would help, for example, women with children who have to study part-time.

## Employment and Training

Britain is still held back by a lack of skills in the workforce. Without placing unnecessary burdens on individual firms, Liberal Democrats are committed to training programmes which would bring enormous benefits to the economy as a whole.

The recent relative health of the economy has concealed hotspots of unemployment and deprivation in many parts of the country. Labour's efforts to combat unemployment have not always been directed where they are most needed. We will:

- Introduce tax incentives for small and medium-sized enterprises to improve training. Companies eligible would include those working with Investors in People, those introducing a company training plan under the Skills for Small Businesses programme, and those training an employee to master training level. We will also require all registered companies to report on staff training and development in their Annual Reports and Accounts.
- Empower National Training Organisations to conduct ballots of member employers. This will enable them to introduce a training levy if support is demonstrated.
- Entitle every 16-24 year-old to study leave with pay. Employers will be obliged to release their staff for courses which are relevant to their work. The scheme will be implemented in consultation with small businesses.
- Replace the New Deal with a Flexible Guarantee of help for all jobseekers, administered through a combined Benefits and Jobs Agency. This will be a world-class job search and placement service. It will be equally open to those not on the unemployment register who would like work.
- Tackle unemployment hotspots by transferring budgets to the nations and regions of the UK. A proportion of the Government's Employment Opportunities Fund should be administered by the nations and regions which are best placed to spend the money effectively alongside their economic regeneration budgets.

### Setting You Free

● Abolish the excessive benefit sanctions brought in under the New Deal. These have done little to encourage people back to work and have made the families of those penalised suffer. We will not impose further sanctions until the effects of existing penalties have been evaluated.

● Stop government wasting teachers' time by scrapping directives and targets in education which undermine the professional judgement and expertise of teachers. We will also return the main responsibilities for standards to universities themselves.

### Green Action

### Learning for a Green Future

We will increase environmental awareness amongst young people, by encouraging local environmental projects and by teaching sustainability in schools. Children's influence on their parents' involvement in 'green' activities will relate directly to the aims of our National Recycling Programme.

### Healthy and Safe Journeys to School

We will promote the development of Safe Routes to School, to encourage parents to allow their children to walk or cycle to school in safety rather than driving them. Children will gain benefits for their physical health from the increased exercise. At the same time, this will assist in reducing congestion and pollution during peak times of the day by reducing car use.

### Greener School Buildings

We will fund a 'Schools 2010' programme to tackle the backlog of school building repairs. The programme would include environmental assessment of buildings and would promote the use of better insulation, double-glazing and solar panels where possible. We will work in partnership with the Further and Higher Education sectors to develop a similar scheme that covers all educational establishments.

### Freedom, Justice, Honesty

### PENSIONS, WAGES AND BENEFITS

Poverty restricts freedom because people without a decent income do not have the opportunities enjoyed by others. More needs to be done for pensioners and those with low incomes to ensure that all in Britain have a better quality of life.

Liberal Democrats will:

● Boost the basic state pension, particularly for the over-75s
● Support disabled people by extending winter fuel allowance payments to the severely disabled
● Help the lower paid by aiming to reduce taxation for poorer taxpayers
● Protect workers on low incomes by reviewing the minimum wage annually
● Tackle child poverty with extra money for families on long-term income support

It is a great indictment of the Governments of Margaret Thatcher, John Major and Tony Blair that all of them allowed the gap between rich and poor people in Britain to become wider than before. The Blair Government has taken a disappointingly mean-spirited approach towards pensioners and lone parents in particular.

We recognise that there are many theatres in the war against poverty. Our success in tackling poverty in Britain would be measured by a Quality of Life Index. This would include a statement of the standards which a citizen of the UK might reasonably expect to enjoy in order to participate fully in society and have a decent quality of life.

### Pensions

Britain's pensioners have not forgotten the miserliness of the 75p increase they were allowed last year. Under first the Conservatives and now Labour, the real value of state pensions has fallen further and further. Elderly people require both an immediate substantial boost to their incomes and a guarantee that their interests will always be considered not just in the run-up to General Elections.

Under Labour, there has been a big increase in means-testing for pensioners. Many elderly people are too proud to claim money which is due to them. It is quite possible to target the poorest people in society without resorting to means tests.

Liberal Democrats will:

● Increase the basic state pension by £5 a week for each single pensioner, £10 for the over-75s and £15 for the over-80s. Couples will receive £8, £18 and £28 respectively. We will give the most to older pensioners because they are amongst the poorest and neediest people in the country. For the past thirty years, they have received a derisory 25p a week at 80 over and above the basic pension. We will also reward pensioners who have saved throughout their lives by scrapping the rules which deny help to people with savings above £12,000.
● Fund our big increases in pensions by setting a new top tax rate of 50p on income over £100,000 a year. To put this measure into perspective, for most of the Thatcher years, the top rate was 60p starting on substantially lower incomes.

- Establish an Independent Pensions Authority. To guarantee that pensioners do not fall behind the rest of the population, the Authority will report annually to the Government on an appropriate uprating for the state pension. It will take into account levels of pensioner poverty, the growth in earnings and national income and affordability. We will also establish a more stable environment for pension planning by seeking to secure all-party consensus before making future pension reforms.
- Strengthen the position of people with private pensions by ensuring that members of company pension schemes, including retired members, have a greater say over the use of their pension fund. We will also relax current rules which require people with personal pensions to buy an annuity on or before their 75th birthday.

In the long term, our goal is to:

- Introduce a new Owned Second Pension Account. We believe that the best way to prevent poverty among future generations is to ensure that all people have a second pension of their own to top up the state pension. Over time we would ensure that a growing proportion of the workforce were members either of a company pension scheme or had an Owned Second Pension Account, with the government making contributions for those who because of ill health, unemployment or caring responsibilities are too poor to do so.
- Extend the entitlement to the basic state pension to all citizens. People would no longer have to show a history of contributions in order to claim their basic pension. This would eventually help around 3.4 million people, mainly women, carers and long-term disabled people.

### Low Pay and Benefits

There is a great deal of talk about scroungers on the welfare state. Liberal Democrats will be vigilant against those who seek to cheat the system. Equally, there are many people in Britain who are in need who have to depend on the state. Among them are low-paid workers with families, lone parents and children. We will:

- Protect workers on low incomes by reviewing the national minimum wage annually on the basis of recommendations from the Low Pay Commission. The minimum wage has proved an effective way of protecting workers on low incomes, without causing damage to business. We believe it is wrong to set a lower rate minimum wage for workers under 21. We will set the same rate for all people aged 16 and over.
- Alleviate child poverty by paying an additional £200 per year to all families with children who have been on income support for more than a year. Such children suffer from the poverty their parents find themselves in. We will also abolish the Child Support Agency, which has caused unjustifiable hardship to so many people, and replace it with a system of family courts. Their maintenance assessments will be strongly enforced and will supplant the rough justice of the current crude and simplistic formula.
- Support young people and reduce homelessness by restoring 16 and 17 year-olds' entitlements to benefits and by increasing housing benefit for the under-25s by ending the Single Room Rent Restriction which effectively requires them to share accommodation.
- Provide more support for disabled people. We will support severely disabled people by bringing them within the scope of the Winter Fuel Payment system. We also believe that the benefits system should recognise what disabled people can do rather than requiring them to prove what they cannot. In particular, we will investigate the feasibility of introducing a Partial Capacity Benefit for those able to do some work.
- Simplify Housing Benefit administration and reduce the scope for benefit fraud by requiring all local authorities to adopt effective anti-fraud strategies.
- End discrimination in gas, water and electricity charges encouraging the regulator to offer a wider tariff choice which helps the poorest people in society. At the moment, for instance, households which use pre-payment meters end up paying higher rates than other users. We will also seek to have standing charges replaced with a banded system of charging to protect poor households and encourage high users to conserve energy.
- Make cold weather payments to people receiving income support more effective by ensuring that they take account of 'wind chill' which is currently overlooked. We will also seek to take proper account of local weather conditions.

In the long term, our goal is to:

- Remove taxation for the lowest paid. We believe that people start paying tax at too low a level and will work to reduce the burden of taxation on the low paid. Over time, we will cut the 10p tax rate to zero so nobody pays any tax on their earnings up to £6,500. At present, this would take 1.4 million people on low incomes (1.1 million of whom are women) out of tax altogether. Anyone earning less than £21,000 would pay less tax - even allowing for our 1p for education.
- Establish a minimum income standard after carrying out research to establish the appropriate amount.
- Make the Social Fund more effective by shifting the balance from discretionary loans to grants.

### Setting You Free

- Abolish the benefit sanctions which were brought in under the New Deal. These have placed harsh burdens on poor people and in many cases, the children of those penalised are the ones who suffer the most. We will not impose further penalties until the effects of penalties have been evaluated.

### Green Action

### Eradicating Fuel Poverty

Our homes insulation programme, to provide decent levels of home insulation within 15 years by speeding up the current 30-year programme funded by the energy utilities, will also cut fuel bills. This will be achieved through a targeted programme of investment funded by the Energy Savings Trust and the energy supply companies. We will work with colleagues in Europe to agree zero-rating of VAT on all energy conservation materials within the EU. We will cut fuel bills and reduce pollution by requiring all new housing to meet improved energy and water efficiency standards through the use of environmentally friendly building materials and techniques.

### Freedom, Justice, Honesty

### LAW AND ORDER

We all want freedom from crime. Fear of crime blights the lives of many people, particularly the most vulnerable in society. The state should offer all its citizens equal and adequate protection. Our approach is rooted in the belief that the best way to beat crime in the medium and long term is to have effective policies to tackle its causes.

Liberal Democrats will:

- Recruit 6,000 extra police officers
- Fund 2,000 part-time community officers
- Reinforce front-line police with a new Community Safety Constabulary and by retaining retired officers in a back-up role
- Cut reoffending by preparing prisoners adequately for a law-abiding life on their release
- Give victims greater rights to be heard in court

During their eighteen years in office, the Conservatives pursued a policy on crime which was superficially populist yet highly ineffective. They filled the prisons to overflowing, at a huge cost to the taxpayer. Crime doubled, violent crime rose year after year, and the number of convictions fell. Meanwhile, contrary to repeated promises, police numbers fell during the last Conservative government.

Labour has been trying to sound as tough or tougher than the Conservatives, but it is no more effective. Police numbers have fallen further over the past four years. Labour too often proposes simplistic solutions. Many are impractical or irrelevant. Some actually undermine civil liberties.

### Police

Our priority is to increase police numbers to prevent crime, to catch criminals when offences do take place, and to increase the current deplorably low clear-up rate. To make policing across the country more effective, we will:

- Fund the police for 6,000 more police officers than March 2000 levels. We will fund 2,000 recruits on top of the government's plans to ensure there is real increase in police strength, not just replacing cuts under Labour and the Conservatives. We will also ensure that the police spend more time on front-line policing and provide extra resources to boost retention of police officers.
- Fund 2,000 part-time community officers by creating a new category of part time retained police officers. This would give the police more flexibility. Suitable members of the public and police officers near retirement wishing to continue in work will be recruited, given proper training and equipped for the duties of a police constable. The scheme will build on the current role of unpaid special constables, and free existing police to use their time and resources more effectively. Retained officers will supplement the work of regular police and provide a more adequate presence in areas where resources have not permitted. This scheme will help to meet our aim of creating a network of named local police officers for every community.
- Establish a Community Safety Force to work with the police by co-ordinating the public safety work of traffic wardens, estate and neighbourhood wardens, park superintendents and other public officials who deal with nuisance crimes like littering, vandalism and graffiti. They will receive special training. This will free the police to concentrate on more serious offences.
- Make local Crime and Disorder Partnerships focus on real improvements for local residents. We will give local crime partnerships the responsibility for managing and directing Community Safety Forces. We will also fund the involvement of local police forces in community activities designed to involve ethnic minorities and increase public confidence in all sections of society.
- Make the police more accountable. Public confidence in the police has declined. As well as seeking to improve the visibility of the police and improving police relations with the community, we will create a genuinely independent police complaints system to deal with complaints speedily, efficiently and impartially. We will encourage police forces to be more representative of the communities they serve, and ensure that 'stop and search' is based on intelligence and attaches no relevance to the race or colour of those stopped by the police.
- Commission an independent report on the police resources the country needs in the long term. We will establish a Standing Conference on Policing comprising representatives of all police ranks, the public and experts in policing issues. This will regularly report to government and parliament, advising on the resources required to provide an effective police presence in every community, and the management of police stations

and technology. It will also review the use of police time, in particular that devoted to paperwork and court procedures.

● Support the work of Europol, the EU police agency, and the establishment of a European police college, subject to proper democratic oversight. We wish to see police forces working together in the fight against crime, particularly international crimes such as drug trafficking, terrorism, customs fraud, money laundering and the trade in human beings for slave labour or sexual exploitation.

## Prisons

The last Conservative Home Secretary Michael Howard famously said "prison works". But half of the people who have served time in Britain's jails go on to reoffend on release. Many prisons are colleges of crime. People incarcerated for minor offences learn how to commit much more serious ones.

Liberal Democrats reject the knee-jerk Conservative approach and Labour's attempts to echo it. We will not be any less tough on crime, but we will be more effective. We will:

● Focus resources on crime prevention rather than prison building. Prisons are very expensive. There are many more cost-effective ways of reducing crime than ever-longer sentences. We believe that people should be sent to prison if the public need to be protected from them or if this is the only way to punish them effectively. But to release resources for crime prevention and to cut reoffending, we believe there is more scope for the use of community sentences which are proven to work, such as electronic tagging, reparation to victims, fines, drug treatment, and probation orders.

● Cut reoffending by ex-prisoners. Previous governments have concentrated a great deal on sending people to prison, but not nearly enough on what goes on once they are there. We believe that prisoners should put in a full working day in jail. They should also have access to skill training and courses in literacy to equip them for work after release, and be given more support and rehabilitation once they have completed their sentences. We will also use weekend and evening custody to permit some offenders during sentence to enter paid work prior to release.

● Make prisons more effective. We will make minimum levels of education and work, and rehabilitation programmes, central to prison regimes, and set standards expected through Service Delivery Agreements. We will increase the amount of commercial activity undertaken by prison industries. We will also boost the powers of the prison inspectorate so that it can force change, not just report on failure.

In the long term, our goal is to:

● Improve the successful resettlement of released prisoners. There should be more use of pre-release assessments of the resettlement needs of prisoners, in particular for the majority who have served sentences, and for whom current arrangements are totally inadequate. The focus of resettlement should be on housing needs, employment and training schemes, and preventing substance misuse.

## The Criminal Justice System

Conservative and Labour Governments in turn have attempted to erode the criminal justice system. Labour have been intent on curtailing the right to the fundamental freedom of jury trial, as first proposed by the Conservatives. The Conservatives increased the use of mandatory sentences, taking away judicial discretion to make decisions based appropriately on the facts of an individual case. Liberal Democrats wish to enhance the powers of the courts. We also want to see a greater recognition of the rights of victims of crime. We will:

● Give victims or their families greater rights to be heard in court. We will give victims the right to be kept fully informed about the progress of the cases with which they are involved. We will also provide opportunities for them to make statements in court about the effect that the crime has had on them after the jury has delivered its verdict and before the judge passes sentence. We will offer victims greater support during the progress of a case. Criminal injury compensation is often inadequate or unavailable and so we will improve the scheme to ensure that the most serious cases receive adequate compensation. We will strengthen support for victims of domestic violence by offering more training in this area to the relevant professionals.

● Tackle hate crimes. We will establish police hate crime investigation units to co-ordinate information and action against racist, homophobic and other hate crimes. We will also legislate against hate crimes by widening current legislation to include all hate crimes on the same basis as that existing for racially motivated crime.

● End mandatory sentencing except for minor offences (such as fixed penalty motoring offences), so that judges and not politicians set sentences.

● Retain jury trials for middle-ranking cases threatened by the Mode of Trial Bill and restore the right to silence.

● Ensure that fostering and adoption law and practice are based on the suitability of individual fosterers and the needs of the child.

In the long term, we will also:

● Propose a new way of sentencing for the most serious offenders. We will consult on introducing indefinite sentences for the most serious sex and violent offenders, so that they would only be released following an assessment by the court of the risk which they pose to society.

● Create a Department of Justice. This will ensure a separation of powers between the legal system and law enforcement agencies, reform the powers of the Lord Chancellor, and help to provide a fairer system of justice for all. We will establish a review of the legal aid system, to ensure genuine access to justice.

● Overhaul the youth justice system. We will expand reform of the youth justice system to ensure a greater focus on the root causes of misbehaviour, and on education and rehabilitation. We want a greater role for the principles of restorative justice, with offenders meeting their victims, discovering the consequences of their actions and planning to improve their behaviour in the future. Reform would respond not only to the problems caused by child offenders but also to the problems they face. We also favour smaller youth custody units rather than large Young Offender Institutions and would ensure that those young people who must be held are sent to specialised units.

### Tackling the Causes of Crime

We recognise that many of the most effective measures against crime are not the responsibility of the police, the prison system or the courts. Our policies in many other areas will have a significant impact on the causes of crime. We will:

● Invest in education to offer young people more opportunities.
● Encourage young people into constructive activity by increasing support for sport, recreation and the youth service.
● Encourage the use of Acceptable Behaviour Contracts (ABCs). These will help reduce anti-social behaviour in communities by young people, without resorting to blanket curfews or immediate use of heavy-handed court action through Anti-Social Behaviour Orders.
● Expand facilities to help drug and alcohol abusers. We will prioritise funds to aim for a maximum four-week waiting time after an abuser is referred for treatment.
● Replace the New Deal with a Flexible Guarantee of help for all jobseekers, administered through a combined Benefits and Jobs Agency.
● Help ensure that care leavers do not drift into crime by offering them support with housing, education and training.
● Establish a National Crime Reduction Agency to oversee and advise on the work of local Crime Reduction Partnerships and other crime reduction work undertaken by central government. This will ensure that those partnerships are effective at finding local solutions to local crime problems.
● Establish a Standing Royal Commission to tackle the range of problems currently associated with drugs. The approach of successive governments has demonstrably failed. An independent Royal Commission will take a fresh look at the issue of illegal drugs and ways to tackle problems in such areas as health and the huge profits of organised crime. The Commission will also be charged with recommending strategies to address misuse of legal drugs such as alcohol and tobacco, and other legal substances such as solvents.

### Setting You Free

● Liberalise licensing laws. We will replace mandatory closing times for pubs with locally determined opening times.
● Make non-payment of TV Licences a civil matter rather than a criminal offence.
● Abandon plans to introduce a Public Defender Scheme which would limit the independence of defence advocates.

### Green Action

### Preventing Pollution

We will improve enforcement of pollution controls through an expanded inspectorate for the Environment Agency, to support full implementation of the statutory pollution control regime. This will be reinforced by increasing the level of penalties which polluters have to pay and the introduction of legislation on corporate environmental liability. We will also use these same powers to ensure that biotech companies are liable for any harm caused by GM crops and food.

### Freedom, Justice, Honesty

### TRANSPORT

A decent transport system is fundamental to an equitable and environmentally sustainable society. We will work to build an integrated transport system throughout the country that is safe, reliable and affordable. Our policies place special emphasis on reducing problems from pollution and congestion.
Liberal Democrats will:

● Provide free off-peak local travel on buses for pensioners and disabled people, and aim for half-price travel at all times for under-19s in full time education
● Abolish car tax for those who drive less-polluting vehicles
● Establish stronger public control over the railways

While progress in other public services in Britain has been disappointingly slow over the past four years, in transport the country has clearly gone backwards. Roads are more congested. Buses are less reliable. Railways are in chaos.

Privatisation of the railways by the Conservatives has been a disaster. Regulation is too lax. Companies do not have the right incentives for long-term investment. The system is fragmented. It is all too easy, when things go wrong, for one firm to pass the buck to another. Safety can be compromised.

Labour has failed to win the case for increased investment in public transport. When the price of petrol went up and revenues from petrol tax consequently soared, the Labour Government should have earmarked the extra revenue specifically for improving public transport. It failed to do so.

### Reducing Congestion and Pollution

Many people rely on their car. But it is in everyone's interests to reduce pollution to protect the environment and to provide a viable alternative to the car wherever possible. We will:

● Reward motorists who drive less-polluting vehicles by reducing car tax (Vehicle Excise Duty) on more environmentally friendly cars and motorcycles - abolishing it altogether for the greenest vehicles. We will fund this by increasing the amount of VED charged on the most polluting vehicles.

● Guarantee not to increase the tax per litre of fuel taken by the government, in real terms, in the next Parliament. Should the government receive extra revenue from VAT due to increases in fuel prices, we will use it to ease burdens on the travelling public. Our policies for improving public transport and encouraging less polluting vehicles means that we do not need to increase petrol taxes further in order to meet our environmental objectives.

● Introduce environmental incentives for bus operators. We will reform fuel duty rebates for bus operators so that these are tied more closely to those running more efficient vehicles, particularly those using alternative fuels.

● Reduce road traffic. As part of our policies for reducing pollution and congestion we will introduce legislation to ensure that there are stronger targets for local authorities to reduce road traffic. We will also enable local authorities to raise bonds and establish congestion charging and private non-residential parking taxes to promote use of public transport.

● Reduce freight on the roads through increased use of railways and waterways. We will explore partnership options for developing Britain's waterways (which are vastly under-utilised at present). We also plan to double the amount of freight carried on Britain's railways by 2010.

### Improving Public Transport

Britain's public transport system could be the envy of the world. At the moment, however, it is expensive, out of date and decaying. We will:

● Extend free off-peak local travel on buses to pensioners and people with disabilities. This would extend across the UK the scheme currently operating in London and those being developed in Wales. In addition we aim to introduce a scheme of half-fares at all times for under 19s in full-time education.

● Increase investment in public transport. We will enable local authorities to raise bonds and establish congestion charging and private non-residential parking taxes (including out-of-town retail and workplace parking) to fund improved public transport. Priorities for investment include: reopening disused railway lines and stations; developing bus routes, cycle paths, trams, light rail systems, and walkways; better information for passengers through a National Public Transport Information System; Local Authority sponsored car-pooling schemes; and improving the ease with which passengers are able to transfer between different modes of transport.

● Create a Rural Transport Regeneration Fund to improve community transport schemes and public transport in rural areas.

● Support community transport, particularly in rural areas, including dial-a-ride, taxi buses, post buses and school buses, by widening eligibility for the existing fuel duty rebate tied into the emission standards of the vehicle. This will be funded in part by reducing eligibility for fuel duty rebate for commercial tour buses.

### Improving Transport Regulation and Performance

Much of the public transport system is run by private companies. This provides valuable competition, investment and innovation in the sector. But if it is to deliver everything that passengers deserve, it must be properly regulated. We will:

● Reform the regulatory system for public transport. We will establish a Sustainable Transport Authority (STA) which will take over the functions of the Strategic Rail Authority and the existing Rail Regulator and also have responsibility for oversight of bus and coach operators, trams, ferries, coastal shipping and inland waterways. The STA will work to: upgrade safety, access and quality; enhance the rail network; tackle monopolies, particularly taking immediate and effective action against predatory behaviour in the bus industry; develop through-ticketing and timetable integration; improve the safety and quality of rail and bus stations by introducing a Safer Stations Charter Mark scheme; and ensure refunds for failure to fulfil adequate standards of service, including punctuality.

### Railways and the London Underground

Britain's railways are in chaos. They are a major casualty of many years of neglect and underinvestment by successive governments. We will work to see Railtrack become a not-for-profit, public interest company, and develop the railway system as the backbone of a modern transport system. In addition, we will:

● Secure increased public control over public investment in the railways by ensuring the Sustainable Transport Authority (STA) takes responsibility for the allocation of public funds intended for new developments (as distinct from repair and renewal). As part of this we will prioritise modernisation and development of the

East and West Coast mainlines, and a new high-speed East Coast mainline between Aberdeen, London and the new Channel Tunnel Rail Link.

● Seek to restructure Railtrack. We will ask the Competition Commission to review Railtrack's activities under a public interest reference so that a suitable restructuring can be imposed on the company. We believe that any changes must simplify the structure of our railway system by using the STA to reduce the number of franchises, and by encouraging Railtrack to pass responsibility for track renewal and repair to the major train operating companies.

● Simplify regulation. We will bring together the role of the Rail Regulator and SRA within the STA. We will also seek to alter the current bureaucratic penalty system into a simpler scheme of incentives. In addition, the range of fares that can only be altered with agreement from the fares regulator (at present the SRA) will be widened. We will create a new independent body within the STA with responsibility for timetabling.

● Improve railway safety. We will implement the recommendations made by Lord Cullen's inquiry into Railway Safety. We will create a new Railway Safety body within the STA to take regulation of railway safety. We will also create an accident investigation body modelled on the Air Accidents Investigation Branch.

● Modernise the London Underground. We believe that the best way to modernise the Underground, without compromising safety, is through a not-for-profit, public interest company funded through bonds.

### Roads

For many people, roads are the backbone of the country's transport. But there has been too much focus on building new ones and not enough attention paid to the roads that already exist. We will:

● Boost the repair and maintenance of roads. We are committed to improving the quality of the existing network, with the safety benefits that this would bring. We will undertake road widening and by-pass schemes only where there are clear safety benefits and where, on balance, there is an environmental benefit.

● Establish fair competition for British freight companies. We will cut significantly freight vehicle excise duty, funding this by introducing a daily charge which includes overseas hauliers who currently escape VED.

● Improve road safety. We will work towards a target of at least a 40% reduction in those killed and seriously injured on the roads by 2010. We will implement a National Programme of Home Zones for residential areas, and Quiet Lanes in rural areas. This will reduce vehicle speeds and make communities safer by giving greater priority to pedestrians and cyclists. We will also strengthen the enforcement of weights and safety standards on the road haulage industry.

### Aviation

Travel by air is growing, raising environmental and safety issues. We will:

● Reject privatisation of National Air Traffic Services creating instead a not-for-profit, public body to protect safety in the air.

● Work to reform aviation fuel taxation. We will work at the European level to ensure that the whole system of aviation fuel taxation is reformed internationally, as part of a longer-term strategy for reducing energy use and pollution through cleaner fuels and more efficient aircraft. We will also press the EU Commission to allow removal of remaining air passenger duty on flights to peripheral and less accessible parts of the UK which rely on air transport.

● Restrict noisy night flights and airport expansion. We will ensure that restrictions are imposed on the expansion of night flights where these will have a negative impact upon residential areas. In addition, we will ensure that there are clear rules governing future expansion of airports, strengthening consideration of environmental impacts and safety implications.

### Setting You Free

● Cut restrictions on local government which prevent councils from raising funds to improve public transport and the environment.

### Green Action

### Planning for Public Transport

Our policies are designed to reduce the need to travel through better use of the planning system, and investment in improving public transport so that people are no longer forced to use their car unnecessarily. We will introduce Regional Transport Plans and strengthen Local Transport Plans to set effective strategies for reducing congestion, pollution and traffic growth.

### Less Road Building

We will reverse plans for new road building in environmentally sensitive areas.

### Cleaner and More Efficient Vehicles

We will promote technologies which improve vehicle efficiency and the use of alternative fuel systems such as Liquefied Petroleum Gas, and, in the longer term, biofuels and zero emission vehicles. In addition, we will improve testing of vehicle emissions and strictly enforce freight vehicle weight limits and other safety standards by increasing resources devoted to roadside testing as well as strengthening the MOT test. We will oppose further increases in weight limits for freight vehicles.

## LIBERAL DEMOCRAT MANIFESTO

### Freedom, Justice, Honesty
### BRITAIN'S ECONOMY

No Government can deliver freedom without creating a sound and sustainable economy, in which business can thrive, the environment is safeguarded and employees are properly protected, nationally and internationally.

Liberal Democrats will:

● Create a competitive and sound economy to deliver prosperity for all
● Enable British euro entry, subject to the decision of the British people in a referendum
● Make taxation and spending policies clearer and more accountable
● Strengthen the independence of the Bank of England

The Conservatives were incompetent stewards of the British economy. The Thatcher and Major years went from boom to bust to boom and bust again. While some made their fortunes, sectors of the economy such as manufacturing and farming suffered a steady decline. The Conservatives failed to make the public investment needed for the long term, starving schools, training and the transport system.

Labour has done too little to redress the mistakes of the Conservatives. They were too timid in their first three years in power, failing to recognise the very poor state of the public sector.

### A Competitive and Sound Economy

Labour have been timid over the euro, leaving manufacturing, farming and tourism to suffer the effects of an uncompetitively high value of the pound. We will:

● Create a competitive and sound economy, enabling British euro entry subject to the decision of the British people in a referendum. Membership of the euro at a competitive and sustainable rate would offer Britain considerable benefits. It would end the exchange rate instability which has destroyed many thousands of jobs, safeguard the investment in hundreds of thousands of further jobs by overseas firms, and reduce the costs of trade with the rest of the EU. Unlike the Conservatives, we believe the British people deserve the opportunity to have their say in a referendum.
● Encourage sustainable economic development. We will give local authorities greater powers to borrow and invest for local development, encourage the use of local exchange and trading systems, and promote volunteering.
● Improve the infrastructure of the nations and regions of the UK. We would allow the Scottish Parliament, the National Assembly for Wales, the Northern Ireland Assembly, the English regions and local authorities to borrow for investment directly from the market, subject to rules similar to those already established for central government.

### Open and Honest Taxes

Schools, hospitals, pensions and the police desperately need further investment, and this is our priority.

We will be honest about the cost of the investment we wish to make and clear about the benefits this will bring. We will:

● Provide improvements in education costing more than £3 billion a year, funded by putting one penny on the basic rate of income tax.
● Provide substantial immediate increases in pensions and raise investment in the NHS, funded by setting a new top tax rate of 50% on income over £100,000 a year and by closing loopholes in Capital Gains Tax. To put this measure into perspective, for most of the Thatcher years the top rate was 60%, starting on substantially lower incomes.
● Invest in the police and public transport by closing loopholes in Capital Gains Tax (CGT). We will abolish the CGT exemption on capital gains held at death (but maintain the present exemptions for transfers between spouses, and reintroduce indexation and retirement relief) and abolish the complex CGT taper introduced by Gordon Brown.
● Send each household an annual Citizen's Tax Contract. This would show in simple terms how much tax is being raised, what services are being delivered and why changes have been made. It would oblige central government to provide the kind of information about expenditure and taxation which local government already sends out with Council Tax bills. People will have a right to know how their taxes are being used and why.
● Make taxation and spending policies clearer and more accountable. We will require an annual Fiscal Assessment to be published sixty days before every budget by the Monetary Policy Committee of the Bank of England. It would set out the current effect of tax policy on interest rates, and the anticipated impact in the year ahead of existing plans and likely alternatives. This would make fiscal policy more transparent and open.
● Promote better value for money. Too many government programmes have been introduced in the past without proper analysis of pilot projects. We will use evidence-based policy making to give the taxpayer better value for money.

As resources allow, we plan to:

● Give taxpayers greater choice over how taxes are spent. Taxpayers in each of the nations of the UK will be given a series of specific investment options and will be able to express their choice by returning a tear-off slip from their annual P60 forms. They would be given the opportunity, say, to choose to give 1% of income tax (currently around £1 billion) money to hospitals or schools. This measure will be introduced when revenues allow following consultation between the UK government and the nations and regions of the UK.

● Remove taxation for the lowest paid. We believe that people start paying tax at too low a level and will work to reduce the burden of taxation on the low paid. Over time, we will cut the 10p tax rate to zero so nobody pays any tax on their earnings up to £6,500. At present, this would take 1.4 million people on low incomes (1.1 million of whom are women) out of tax altogether. Anyone earning less than £21,000 would pay less tax - even allowing for our 1p on education.

### Setting You Free
● Strengthen the independence of the Bank of England. The Liberal Democrats were the only party to propose independence for the Bank at the last election. Labour adopted our proposal, but we would go further. We will make members of the Monetary Policy Committee more independent by giving them non-renewable terms and making them more representative of the UK as a whole. We will also make the appointments system more open and transparent.

### Green Action
### Greening the Budget
We will publish a full 'Green Budget' assessment of every budget. This will ensure that environmental priorities are at the heart of government spending plans, and that the Chancellor is held to account for making economic policy more sustainable.

### Making the Polluter Pay
We regard it as essential to make a major shift in taxation from 'goods' like wealth creation which benefit Britain to 'bads' which are harmful like pollution. We also want to support green technology and new environmental industries. We will establish a Green Tax Commission to make clear recommendations on reforming the tax system, guaranteeing that increases in environmental taxes will be matched by tax cuts elsewhere. Green taxation will involve taxing differently, not taxing more.

### Freedom, Justice, Honesty
### BUSINESS, CONSUMERS AND INNOVATION
Liberal Democrats are committed to a free market economy in which enterprise thrives. Competition and open markets are by far the best guarantee of wealth creation. It is the Government's role to ensure the conditions under which innovation and competition can flourish and benefit the greatest number of people.

Liberal Democrats will:

● Ease the burdens on business
● Defend consumers against the power of monopolies
● Promote innovation and training in new technology

The UK now operates in a global market in which international competition is intense. Liberal Democrats' social objectives cannot be achieved without the creation of wealth and the promotion of enterprise. The Conservatives have always posed as the champions of enterprise. But too often they have in fact defended vested interests and monopoly power. Labour has over-regulated in some areas and under-regulated in others. Neither party has really backed new enterprise and new ideas. Small businesses have to deal with an avalanche of red tape, while the utility and railway companies have been allowed to get away with far too much.

Liberal Democrats seek to encourage innovation and risk-taking, protect the rights of consumers and workers, and safeguard the environment. We also want to maintain the City of London's pre-eminence as an international financial centre.

### Business
Business people want to get on with running their companies, creating wealth and providing more opportunities for their staff. They should not have to spend large amounts of their time acting as agents for the Government, coping with interminable regulations and filling in endless forms. We will:

● Scrap unnecessary business regulations. We have published a list of 25 specific major regulations which we will scrap. We believe any new regulations should be subject to a "sunset clause", setting a deadline after which they would automatically lapse. We will also consult business before introducing any new measures.
● Cut business rates on small businesses by introducing a Business Rates Allowance, similar to personal tax allowances. This tax-free allowance would be set at £1,500 and apply to all small businesses. With larger businesses paying a little more to cover the cost of the scheme, smaller businesses will pay less.
● Promote diversity of ownership. We will initiate a review of policy governing mutual ownership of building societies, insurance companies and credit unions to encourage and develop them. We will also review legislation in order to stimulate employee share ownership and co-operatives.
● Invest in a knowledge-based economy through research. Scientific research is the cornerstone to a successful knowledge-based economy. We welcome the extra resources the sector has already seen as a result of partnership with charities and will further this by increasing government investment in scientific research, paid for by stopping taxpayers' money being used to help finance arms exports. We would give priority to research

on climate change mitigation and cleaner production and consumption techniques, and set up an Academy of British Invention. This will be funded by stopping the Export Credits Guarantee Department using tax-payers' money to support arms exports.

● Encourage ethical business practice. We want the UK to play a leading role in seeing the OECD Anti-Bribery Convention implemented world-wide. We will encourage ethical shareholding by reforming corporate governance to enhance stakeholders' rights. We will require the largest companies to report on their social and environmental performance.

● Encourage innovation by measures including promoting links between academic and industrial research and strengthening the roles of local and regional authorities to stimulate development and implementation.

## Consumers

Consumers should have as much choice as possible, but more and more ownership is concentrated in the hands of fewer and fewer companies. This has been particularly true in fields like banking, telecommunications, broadcasting and civil aviation. Elsewhere, large concerns have been driving small businesses to the wall. We intend to level the playing field to support competition and smaller businesses, and give consumers more protection against poor service and faulty goods. We will:

● Introduce tough legislation to control monopolies and cartels with a presumption against a high concentration of ownership. Even in apparently competitive markets, anti-competitive behaviour is creating localised monopolies where, for example, supermarkets, large newsagents and oil companies have an unfair advantage over small shops and independents. We will strengthen the powers of the competition authorities to tackle localised monopolies.

● Strengthen consumer protection. We will introduce new safeguards for people taking out mortgages and require 'workmanship guarantees' in respect of 'Cowboy builders' and garages. We will also introduce tougher penalties against counterfeiters to protect the public from dangerous and shoddy goods.

● Tighten controls on banks. We will make it a legal requirement for banks to look after the interests of vulnerable customers, particularly elderly and disabled people, those on low incomes and those who live in remote communities. We will apply full competition law to banks, refer bank mergers to the Competition Commission, prohibit anti-competitive cash machine charges and regulate the clearance system.

● Review regulation of the life insurance sector in the light of recent events at Equitable Life and elsewhere, to protect the savings and pensions of millions of people.

● Establish a universal service obligation for the Post Office branch network. Post Offices are a vital part of all communities, particularly the more isolated ones. We will ensure that sub-post offices continue to offer the services which their customers need.

## Employees' Rights

Most employers have no objection to good health, safety and anti-discrimination rules. But the law needs to be tightened to clamp down on the small minority of companies who exploit their workforce. We will promote a business culture which embraces equal opportunity as essential to a committed and motivated workforce. We will:

● Give the Health and Safety Executive new powers to investigate breaches of its rules. We will make businesses which flagrantly flout the rules criminally liable for the consequences. However, we will train inspectors to carry out a range of inspections on one visit where possible, rather than having several separate inspections from different bodies.

● Fight age discrimination by banning compulsory retirement ages. Instead, we will provide for individuals aged 60 and over who wish to work to have an assessment of their ability to continue their job as part of an annual appraisal process.

● Review the minimum wage annually. The review will follow the recommendations of the Low Pay Commission. Equal work deserves equal pay, so we will also extend the full Minimum Wage to all those aged 16 and over, abolishing the lower rate paid to people under 21.

● Promote consultation of employees. We believe that workers should have a statutory right to consultation over key business decisions affecting their future, such as factory closures.

## Setting You Free

● End unnecessary regulation. We will relieve businesses of tasks which they unnecessarily perform on behalf of the government, like administering Working Families Tax Credit, and collecting student loans.

● Liberalise Sunday trading laws. We will make Sunday opening hours a matter for local councils rather than for national government, within a national framework to guarantee extra pay for Sunday work and protect conscientious objection to Sunday working.

## Green Action

### Cutting Pollution from Energy Use

The burning of fossil fuels - coal, oil and gas - is a major contributor to climate change, and also causes acid rain and local air pollution. Our top priorities are to reduce energy consumption overall, by improving the efficiency with which it is used, and to switch from polluting forms to clean energy sources.

### Reducing the Demand for Energy

Half the energy currently used in the UK is wasted, and could be saved by using it more efficiently, in homes, businesses and transport. Our homes insulation programme will improve household energy efficiency standards, help to eradicate fuel poverty and provide substantial new employment opportunities. Mandatory standards and labels for buildings, machinery, vehicles and appliances, together with lower VAT on energy conservation materials, will encourage householders and businesses to cut energy use. We will encourage Combined Heat and Power schemes to reduce the energy wasted in power generation.

### Boosting Renewable Energy

We will require a minimum of 10% of the UK's energy to be generated from UK-based renewable energy sources by 2010, increasing by 1% a year thereafter. As well as benefiting the environment, this will create thousands of new jobs in the green energy sector. Waste incineration will no longer be classed as renewable energy.

### Phasing out Nuclear Power

We will decommission and not replace nuclear power stations as they reach the end of their safe operating lives. We will maintain BNFL in wholly public ownership. We will establish an International Centre of Excellence at Dounreay to lead and spread good practice on decommissioning.

### Taxing Energy Fairly

The Climate Change Levy is overcomplicated and bureaucratic. We will gradually replace it with a carbon tax falling on all energy use according to its carbon content. We will invest in more energy conservation and efficiency grants. We will introduce a properly monitored emissions trading scheme to allow businesses to cut greenhouse gas emissions in the most cost-effective way, and argue for an EU-wide scheme as soon as feasible.

### Reduce Pollution from Chemicals

We will end UK production and use of POPs (persistent bio-accumulative chemicals). We will also ban the use of the most toxic chemicals.

### Preserve Scarce Water Resources

We will set tough requirements for water companies to reduce leaks. We will encourage the use of water meters for domestic households in areas with scarce supplies, with effective measures to provide security for disadvantaged people.

### Freedom, Justice, Honesty
## INNOVATION IN CULTURE, ARTS AND SPORT

Everyone should have a freedom to explore their talents and experience the talents of others. The arts and sport make a huge contribution to our society. They play an important role in both education and the economy and are a means of promoting social inclusion.

Liberal Democrats will:

- Place the arts at the heart of school education
- Support community sports plans
- Promote diversity in culture, the arts and sport

### Arts and Culture

Recent Governments have not given the arts and sport the priority which they deserve. Our goal is to make a substantial increase in investment in the arts to enhance public access, performance opportunities and artistic innovation. We will:

- Give all pupils an entitlement to arts education throughout their school careers. We will recruit and train more specialist art teachers and ensure that all primary teachers are well trained in the arts. We will restore funding for free instrumental tuition to at least 1990 levels, giving many more pupils the chance to learn an instrument once again.
- Protect our cultural heritage by lowering the cost of maintaining listed buildings. We will do this by cutting VAT on renovation and repairs, paid for by introducing VAT, at the same low level, on new building.
- Encourage artists and artistic diversity. We will support artists by maintaining the support provided by schedule D taxation. We will establish a fund to bring artists to schools, hospitals and prisons.
- Increase the powers of Regional Arts Boards. We will devolve all funding decisions, except those involving national companies, from the Department for Culture, Media and Sport to the Regional Arts Boards.
- Develop the use of libraries by making them centres for free internet access.
- Invest in local libraries, arts and museums by replacing the Millennium Commission with a Local Initiatives Fund which would give grants to support libraries, museums and galleries in communities across Britain. We will restore the principle that Lottery cash should not fund services more properly provided through taxation, and ensure that all Lottery money goes to the arts, charity, sport, heritage and local cultural institutions.

### Broadcasting

High-quality television and radio are essential components of a modern democracy and of a modern civilised society. But as media outlets multiply, the current system of regulation is increasingly ineffective. This is exacerbated by the complicated and often overlapping roles of many different regulators. We will:

- Create a single Office of Communications (OFCOM) with the flexibility to regulate emerging communications technologies and ensure service provision across the country.
- Redefine public service broadcasting including breadth and quality of output, distinct regional output and free-to-air status. OFCOM would ensure that these standards are maintained into the future. Channels could apply to be designated public service broadcasters, regulated by OFCOM, which would then guarantee them the right to be carried on all platforms on a profit-free basis.
- Guarantee the editorial independence of the BBC, abolishing the government appointed Board of Governors, and requiring OFCOM to recommend a new structure for running the BBC, but requiring financial accountability through the National Audit Office.
- Create an additional TV watershed at 11pm so that programmes highly unsuitable for children could not be broadcast until at least two hours after the existing 9pm watershed.
- Simplify but tighten rules governing cross-media ownership to ensure it is not concentrated in the hands of too few.

### Sport

Sport plays an important role in our aim of raising the overall quality of life of all the country's citizens. Participation in sport raises levels of fitness and health, and helps to foster local and national pride. We will:

- Promote Community Sports Plans. These will stimulate local authorities, schools and sports clubs to share facilities, which they lack due to school fields being sold off, and include provisions to support so-called minority sports.
- Develop sport in schools. Our simpler minimum curriculum entitlement replacing the national curriculum will allow greater provision of sport and physical education in schools.

### Setting You Free

- Streamline government involvement in the arts by abolishing QUEST (Quality, Efficiency and Standards Team).
- Reduce interference by central government in culture and arts by decentralising decision-making powers and funding in England in order to promote community involvement in the arts. We will also protect the independence of trustees of museums and galleries.
- Remove the anomaly of Home Office regulation of film and video. We will pass this responsibility to the Department for Culture, Media and Sport, which oversees all creative industries.

### Green Action

### Bring Art and Sport to the Centre of Communities

Our Community Arts and Sports Fund, alongside our plans to cut VAT on renovation and redevelopment will help with the cost of restoring and developing sustainable arts and sports facilities within local communities where they are easily accessible.

### Freedom, Justice, Honesty

## REFORMING POLITICS AND THE CONSTITUTION

Democracy is the guarantee of all our freedoms, but the state of British democracy still leaves much to be desired. Liberal Democrats want to make government the true servant of the people, and we will develop a political process in which all voices can be heard.
Liberal Democrats will:

- Reform the voting system for Westminster so that every vote counts
- Give Parliament more power to hold the government to account
- Devolve more power to the nations and regions of Britain and to local authorities

Britain's political system has changed for the better since 1997. We have championed devolution for over a century, so we welcomed the opportunity to play our part in the creation of the Scottish Parliament, the National Assembly for Wales and the Northern Ireland Assembly. We welcome too the introduction of fairer votes for these bodies.

But the gap between government and the governed is still too great. Public bodies are not sufficiently accountable. Voters do not have a strong enough voice or enough choice. No wonder that more and more people feel alienated from politics.

### Voting

We need a voting system which accurately reflects the wishes of voters and fosters a more constructive approach to politics. Liberal Democrats will:

- Secure fair votes for all national and local elections. For Westminster, we support the system of AV+ as proposed by the Jenkins Commission as a first step. We will therefore put the Jenkins Commission's recommendations before the British people in a referendum at the earliest possible opportunity. Ultimately, we wish to see the Single Transferable Vote (STV) used for Westminster elections. We will introduce STV immediately for local government and European elections.

- Introduce voting at sixteen. We will also allow people to stand for elected office at this age, the stage in life at which they are able to begin full-time work and pay taxes. We will promote the action and habit of participation earlier in life through citizenship education and school councils.
- Introduce new methods of voting. We will extend the right to vote by post and investigate internet voting, while ensuring that votes remain secure. We will also promote public involvement in decision-making, through Citizens' Juries, Citizens' Initiative Referenda and electronic consultation.

### Westminster

The Westminster Parliament is not sufficiently accountable to the voters, and the Government is not sufficiently accountable to Parliament. We will strengthen the House of Commons and democratise the House of Lords. We will:

- Replace the House of Lords with a smaller directly elected Senate with representatives from the nations and regions of the UK. The Senate will be given new powers to improve legislation. We will transfer the judicial functions currently undertaken by the House of Lords to a new Supreme Court.
- Streamline and strengthen the House of Commons. We will increase the powers of Select Committees and allow more pre-legislative scrutiny of bills. We will give MPs more say over the budget by allowing them to propose spending amendments. We will introduce a new annual Tax Bill, separate from the Finance Bill, to allow for greater consultation on tax matters. A new parliamentary commission will support Parliament by providing expert analysis of expenditure proposals.
- Introduce more family friendly and efficient working practices for Parliament to bring a wider range of people, particularly women, into Parliament.
- Carry out a Social Justice Audit of all bills to ensure that government legislation tackles inequality as a priority.
- Introduce a Civil Service Act to maintain the independence of the civil service. We will ensure that governments are not able to use the civil service for party political purposes by setting clear rules on the use of public money and government facilities.

In the long term, we will:

- Develop a written constitution for the United Kingdom in order to define and protect the constitutional freedoms our policies are designed to achieve.
- Separate Church and State. We will support the disestablishment of the Church of England to end political interference in the Church. The Head of State will be able to be a member of any faith or none.

### The Nations and Regions and Local Government

Despite the progress made in Scotland, Wales and Northern Ireland, the United Kingdom is still too centralised. We will take steps towards the creation of a federal United Kingdom where services are delivered at the lowest level possible. This will build a stronger democracy within the UK as a whole. We will:

- Give greater powers to the nations and regions. As we move to a more federal United Kingdom, we will build on the present devolution settlement and strengthen the powers of the Scottish Parliament. We will allow the Welsh Assembly the right to pass primary legislation and to vary taxes. We will extend tax-varying powers to the Northern Ireland Assembly for both income tax and corporation tax, should the Assembly wish to have those powers.
- Give the regions of England more democratic power. We will legislate for referenda on elected regional assemblies. If local people vote for a regional assembly, the assembly would take on a set of core powers from Westminster and from current undemocratic regional quangos. Regions will normally be based on existing Regional Development Agency boundaries, but with scope for smaller areas where local identity, geography and preferences make that appropriate. We would allow further devolution of powers and boundary changes in subsequent referenda.
- Build on the work of the Northern Ireland peace process. We will develop co-operation within the British Isles through the Council of the Isles, and we welcome the establishment of North-South bodies in the island of Ireland within this overall framework. To support the work of the Council we will work to establish its own permanent secretariat, based in a central location such as Cardiff. We will also seek to establish meetings of a 'Council of the Irish Sea' within this framework to promote understanding between representatives of Cardiff, Dublin, Belfast, Edinburgh, the Isle of Man and appropriate regions of England on areas such as fishing, transport and pollution.
- Allocate funding according to need through a Finance Commission for the Nations and Regions. Its Revenue Distribution Formula will allocate funds from central government to the nations and regions on the basis of need. To secure stability, there will be no cuts in current funding. Any changes, which will happen in the medium-term, will be funded from growth in the economy. Over time, we will give the nations and regions more power to raise their own money.
- Give local people more power. We will replace the Council Tax with local income tax, so that people pay according to their ability, and we will give local authorities more discretion over their spending. We will ensure that where local government acquires new duties from central government, they have the means to fund them, and introduce a constitutional power of general competence that will give local government wider

scope for action. We will also define a minimum standard of service for local councils across the country. Fair votes for local elections will prevent local domination by one party, which damages local government.

### Setting You Free

- Cut the size and cost of central government. We will reduce the number of ministers and (as part of voting reform) cut the membership of both the House of Commons and the Upper House, while not reducing the current size of the Scottish Parliament, National Assembly for Wales and the Northern Ireland Assembly. This will include replacing separate UK ministers for the devolved nations of the UK with one Secretary of State for the Nations and Regions.

### Green Action
### Strengthening National Environment Policy

Strengthen government environment policy by transferring the Department of Trade and Industry's water and energy roles to the Department of the Environment, Transport and the Regions, renamed the Department of the Environment, Energy and Transport. Meanwhile, housing, regional issues and local government will move from the DETR to a new Department of Local Government and the Regions.

### Improving Environmental Accountability

An Environmental Responsibility Act will set out reporting requirements and environmental standards for government and businesses, and introduce environmental audits across all government departments and local authorities where this is not already done.

### Freedom, Justice, Honesty
### CIVIL LIBERTIES

Civil liberties are the basis of a genuinely free society. They are essential to a liberal society in which people are enabled to fulfil their potential and make informed choices about their lives.
Liberal Democrats will:

- Pass an Equality Act to outlaw all forms of discrimination
- Reform the asylum system so that applicants are dealt with fairly and quickly
- Extend Freedom of Information legislation to provide genuinely open administration at all levels of government

Civil liberties are at the core of our critique of the other parties. Asylum seekers, in particular, have been treated in a disgraceful manner by both Labour and the Conservatives. The BSE scandal demonstrated the dangers of resistance to freedom of information legislation. Labour has made a start but has fallen short of building the truly open society we want to see.
We will establish a strong framework of individual rights, extending the protection already afforded by European law, so that the rights of the individual outweigh the interests of the government.

### Discrimination

We will combat discrimination on the grounds of race and in all its other forms. We will:

- Strengthen the fight against discrimination with an Equality Act. This will fight unfair discrimination on whatever grounds, including race, sex, religion, sexual orientation, disability, age or gender identity. A new Equality Commission will be able to investigate potential breaches of the Act and take action in its own name. The Commission will also have responsibility for Children's Rights, through a Children's Rights Commissioner. We will also create a separate Human Rights Commission to safeguard human rights.
- Support recent European anti-discrimination legislation. We will back measures under Article 13 of the Treaty of Amsterdam on anti-discrimination. This includes race and employment legislation and action.
- Establish a scheme for the civil registration of partnerships. This will give two unrelated adults who wish to register a settled personal relationship legal rights, such as next-of-kin arrangements, which are at present only available to married couples.

### Immigration and Asylum

Immigrants are too often labelled as a problem for British society. Britain has benefited hugely from immigration, in the same way that many Britons who have emigrated have benefited from their experience. There are practical as well as humanitarian reasons for treating immigrants decently.
The shortage of skilled workers in many fields means they have an important contribution to make to British society. We will:

- Protect people fleeing from persecution by dealing with asylum applications fairly and more quickly, which will also minimise any opportunities for anyone to exploit either the system or asylum seekers. We will introduce fair benefits for asylum seekers to replace the demeaning voucher system. We will review the failing dispersal system, end any unnecessary restrictions on asylum seekers undertaking voluntary work and review restrictions on paid work by asylum seekers in their first six months. Recognising pressures on host communities, we will ensure that local services are adequately compensated for the cost of supporting asylum seekers. We will work with other countries to ensure that responsibilities are sensibly shared, and to seek a system which discourages illegal trafficking in people.

- Free immigration laws from discrimination. We will ensure that immigration policy is non-discriminatory in its application. We will reform current immigration laws so that families are not divided. We will also regularly review immigration policy, separate from our asylum obligations, including an assessment of skills needs of the country in an increasingly global economy.

### The Right to Know and the Right to Privacy

While individuals should have the right to know as much as possible about decisions taken by government, there should be limits to the information which government can obtain about individuals. We will:

- Strengthen Freedom of Information legislation. This will break open the excessive secrecy of government and develop open and accountable administration. In particular, it will increase access to facts and figures underlying government policy decisions and reduce ministers' powers to block the release of information.
- Protect privacy. Privacy is protected by the European Convention on Human Rights which is now incorporated into UK law. We are opposed to further privacy laws which could threaten free speech, except for a civil offence of physical intrusion to prevent harassment of individuals by the media. We will not introduce compulsory national identity cards.
- Bring the security services under parliamentary control. At the moment, the security services are overseen by a committee reporting to the Prime Minister. We will make them accountable to a Parliamentary Select Committee.

### Setting You Free

- Improve safeguards against the misuse of surveillance and interception powers by law enforcement agencies including interception and tracking of electronic communications. We will replace the system of warrants approved by Ministers with a system of approval by judges to remove any conflicts of interest and to increase accountability. We believe that there should be a presumption in favour of an individual's freedom from intrusion into their private life and that it should be up to the Government to prove the need for it. We would ensure adequate safeguards against unnecessary monitoring and access to private electronic communications and review the impact on the electronic commerce industry of Labour's Regulation of Investigatory Powers Act.

- Repeal Section 28 of the 1988 Local Government Act. This gives legal sanction to discrimination, preventing schools taking effective measures against bullying and hampering responsible sex education.

### Green Action
### Improving Environmental Knowledge

A 'Right to Environmental Information', as part of Freedom of Information legislation, will cover issues such as local air quality, emissions from factories, and the potential environmental risks from Genetically Modified Organisms (GMOs). We will also introduce a duty to electronic publication of environmental information.

### Protecting Protest

We will protect the right to legal and peaceful protest on all issues, including environmental matters.

### Protecting Animals

Although we support firm action against violent protests by animal rights activists, we are committed to strengthening animal welfare. We will establish an Animal Protection Commission to strengthen animal welfare protection. We will extend the size and powers of the Home Office Inspectorate and encourage more unannounced inspections. We will end the use of animals in the development and testing of weapons and household goods, and end unnecessary repetitive tests. We will fund research into alternatives to animal testing. We believe that farm animals should be entitled to high welfare standards. We will provide more customs officers with Convention on International Trade in Endangered Species training so that the law can be enforced more effectively. We believe that the issue of hunting with hounds should be settled by MPs on a free vote.

### Freedom, Justice, Honesty
### RURAL, URBAN AND SUBURBAN LIFE

Outside their family, most people's immediate concerns involve the local community where they live, work, shop and spend their leisure time. We wish to build sustainable communities which provide for the needs of their citizens, enhance their lives, and preserve the environment.

Liberal Democrats will:

- Boost local economies by protecting local services and promoting local innovation
- Support rural employers, farming and fishing
- Revive depressed areas by introducing a one-stop regeneration grant system to distribute funds more effectively
- Create incentives for developers to build on brownfield rather than greenfield sites

Margaret Thatcher notoriously remarked "there is no such thing as society". It was an attitude which weakened communities all over Britain during the Conservative years. Now, in many communities in Britain, there is growing dissatisfaction with Labour too. In rural areas, people feel that the Labour Party does not understand their needs. In much of urban Britain, arrogant and complacent Labour councils are out of touch with local people.

Our opponents want to control from the centre. We will allow communities to make decisions for themselves, while providing high-quality services and protecting the environment.

## Building Strong Local Communities

The strongest local communities are built on the actions of individuals within them. Government should not interfere and hamper their efforts. It can nonetheless play a role in stimulating and supporting communities. We will:

- Regenerate deprived communities wherever they are through a one-stop regeneration grant systems. This would streamline existing regeneration measures, including Regional Selective Assistance, English Partnerships and the New Deal for Communities. The new single scheme will help match-funding applications and simplify the application and appeal process. We will ensure that all regeneration schemes are truly in line with the aspirations of the communities they are designed to help by strengthening local democratic input into decision-making.
- Boost rural local services by directing more money to provide high-quality services, such as schools and post offices, to the rural population. We will do this by reforming funding formulae to ensure that resources are allocated fairly throughout the UK, and by giving local authorities greater financial freedoms. We will tackle rural social exclusion by providing employment opportunities in new industries and in farming for the young.
- Help everyone feel safe in their homes. People living in inner city housing blocks across the country suffer unacceptable levels of crime on their own doorsteps because there is no secure front door on the building in which they live. We will give a high priority to tackling the security of these buildings through our "Safe Front Doors for All" initiative, organised as part of our wider crime prevention programme.

## Supporting Farming and Fisheries

Many communities are highly dependent on a single local industry. In many areas, this means fishing or agriculture. Government could be doing much more to support both. We will:

- Reform the Common Agricultural Policy. Reform is long overdue. We will promote the sustainability of agriculture and redirect support so that small and family farms are more effectively supported. We will seek to refocus payments on achieving public environmental and social goals rather than encouraging unnecessary production while maintaining the current overall level of support for farmers and rural areas. We will work within Europe to limit bureaucracy by administering CAP payments through a single Countryside Management Contract which would include stewardship and agri-environment schemes as well as support for diversification, organic farming and farmers' co-operatives.
- Protect tenant farmers by funding a targeted early retirement and new entrant scheme and by reassessing diversification schemes to allow tenants more scope to diversify.
- Encourage organic farming by better support for transition from current methods of farming.
- Reform the present Common Fisheries Policy. The main objective of fisheries policy must be to integrate the long-term conservation of the marine environment with the socio-economic interests of local communities. We want to establish Regional Management Committees through which fishermen would work with scientists and government to agree sustainable and fairly enforced 'zonal management' for their local fisheries. We will make the case for establishing the 6-12 mile fishing limit as a permanent feature of policy, and work with other fishing nations to agree to extend the national protection zones out to 24 miles. We will strengthen and update the regulatory framework for Seas Fisheries Committees and take low impact fishing methods out of the quota system altogether.
- Establish an Agricultural Ombudsman to monitor the work of the Ministry of Agriculture, Fisheries and Food and tackle maladministration.

## Supporting Local Economies

Local economies operate most effectively when there is local innovation and money circulates locally in a diverse range of small businesses providing for local needs. Strong voluntary and non-governmental bodies also enrich and strengthen these communities. We will:

- Support local markets including farmers markets by providing funds from Single Regeneration Grants to regenerate local shopping areas, preserving a diverse range of retail outlets and encouraging flexibility in planning regulations for smaller outlets.
- Tackle financial exclusion by promoting community banking, Local Exchange and Trading Schemes (LETS), and credit unions. We will also support initiatives such as the Community Loan Fund in Wales.
- Encourage volunteering by setting up a network of mutual volunteering exchanges or 'time banks' through which people could exchange time spent volunteering, registered through the local time bank, with help for themselves or discounts on public transport and sports facilities.
- Protect village pubs and local breweries by extending the 50% mandatory rate relief currently enjoyed by some village shops and post offices to sole village pubs and encourage wider use of local authority powers to grant additional discretionary relief for services and businesses.
- Promote tourism. We will bring together the marketing and infrastructure work of government, local councils and tourist boards. We will ensure that local communities are involved in the planning of tourism from the earliest stages.

## A Decent Living Environment

The quality of life for all people depends very much on their surroundings - the quality and cost of their housing, the fabric of nearby buildings, and their natural surroundings. To promote a clean and healthy living environment we will:

- Promote decent and more affordable housing. We will open up conveyancing to greater competition, take action to tackle gazumping, strengthen leaseholders' legal rights, involve tenants in the management of housing estates, and protect tenants against misuse of rent deposits. We will allow local authorities to specify the percentage of social housing for all new developments. We will aim to provide lifetime homes and make sure that building regulations provide for flexibility to undertake low-cost conversion for wheelchair access, fittings, showers and stair lifts. We will give local councils the power to end the 50% rebate on council tax for second homes.
- Combat homelessness by giving local authorities greater freedom to invest in housing, and by making health authorities responsible for ensuring that patients discharged into the community have somewhere to live. We will increase the availability of affordable housing by taking action to require public and private landlords to bring empty homes back into use. We will make renovation a more affordable option by equalising VAT at a lower level to be charged equally on new build and refurbishment costs.
- Protect greenfield sites and encourage urban regeneration through partnership between local authorities and private enterprise, and our reform of the VAT system. In addition to an immediate cut in business rates through a Business Rate Allowance, we will also allow local councils to replace the Uniform Business Rate with a system based on the value of each site (Site Value Rating). This would encourage rather than penalise those who develop inner-city sites. We will also clean up brownfield and damaged wildlife sites using revenue from a greenfield development levy set by local authorities.
- Require mobile phone companies to obtain local planning permission for all new mobile phone mast installations.
- Establish effective measurement of living costs throughout the country. We want to ensure that public service workers like teachers and nurses are properly supported when they live in expensive areas. We will therefore collect data on price variations between regions so that measures can be effectively targeted.

## Setting You Free

- Lessen central controls on fishing by reforming the Common Fisheries Policy to promote local management of fisheries.
- Reduce red tape for farmers through single Countryside Management Contracts to manage farm payments, and an Agricultural Ombudsman to tackle maladministration.
- Put local priorities first in planning regeneration schemes so that communities develop according to the aspirations of those that live there.

## Green Action

### Guard Against Possible Dangers of GM Crops

We will seek to introduce a moratorium at an EU level, on commercial growing of genetically modified crops until 2004, to allow research into their safety and environmental impact to be completed.

### Protect our Seas

We will develop a national oceans and coasts policy in consultation with scientists and the fishing industry to provide sustainable livelihoods and prosperity for coastal communities, improved health of the seas for wildlife and a safer environment for marine activities. This will include a network of Marine Protected Areas covering 10 per cent of our seas and piloting Fishing-Free Zones to help the recovery of fish stocks. We will underpin this by introducing consolidated marine legislation in collaboration with the devolved institutions of the UK. We will also implement pollution reduction and prevention programmes to meet targets under the OSPAR convention by 2020.

### Boost Conservation Schemes

We will protect the environment and create 'green jobs' in urban, rural and marine habitats, for example, through more organic farming, increasing green spaces in urban areas, and woodland management. Such schemes will form part of our Wildlife Guarantee to protect endangered species. We will also aim to preserve and increase the area of greenfield sites in the UK.

### Reform Planning

We will ensure that local authority structure plans incorporate targets for $CO_2$ emission reductions to encourage the development of renewable energy facilities and account for the climate change consequences of their policies, including transport.

### Protect Green Spaces

We will create a new designation of Protected Site, with equivalent protection to Sites of Specific Scientific Interest, for green areas of particular importance or value to the community. We will manage SSSIs to enhance their environmental value and impose a binding 'duty of care' on owners and tenants to avoid further significant damage or fragmentation.

## LIBERAL DEMOCRAT MANIFESTO

### Reducing Waste and Promoting Recycling
Our National Recycling Programme will provide a doorstep recycling collection for every household by the end of the next Parliament. We will seek to recycle 60% of household waste within 10 years. We will also gradually increase the landfill tax to encourage alternative methods of disposal, backed up by an eventual ban on all but certain types of waste. We will not build incinerators unless results of research on their impact show that they are safe and the best environmental option.

### Floods and Flooding
We will immediately set up a National Task Force to review arrangements for flood defence management and response. We will also use planning measures to reduce future developments taking place on floodplains and improve standards of drainage from both urban and rural (particularly agricultural) land use. In the long term, flooding will continue to become more severe unless climate change is tackled effectively - which our energy and transport policies are designed to do.

### Freedom, Justice, Honesty
### BRITAIN'S ROLE IN THE EUROPEAN UNION
The European Union has a fundamental role in guaranteeing peace and freedom in Europe. By promoting enterprise, protecting the environment and fighting discrimination, the EU brings enormous benefits to Britain. Yet neither Conservative nor Labour governments have made the most of Britain's potential as a core member of the EU.
Our priorities in Europe are:

● Enlargement of the EU to include the emerging democracies of central and eastern Europe
● Reform of the EU's institutions to make them more open, democratic and effective
● Reaching agreement on a constitutional settlement for Europe to define and limit the powers of the EU
● Co-operation with our European Liberal Democrat partners to achieve our aims in these areas

Liberal Democrats are firm supporters of the European Union, but as critical members of the European family, we are also firm on its failings. We believe that the EU offers the best means of promoting Britain's interests in Europe and in the wider world. Nations acting together can achieve more.
   The EU must have the resources and powers to act in areas where problems cannot be solved at a national level. But it should stay clear when European action is not necessary.
   Europe needs a new agenda for reform. Liberal Democrats are determined that Britain should lead this reform. We want a Europe where the interests of people, not bureaucrats, come first; a Europe that seeks to empower people, not impose upon them; and where European institutions concentrate on what they do best. We will work to:

● Establish a Constitution for the European Union to define and limit the powers of the EU ensuring that decisions are made at the most appropriate level. It would set out the roles, responsibilities and powers of EU institutions in relation to member states. It would provide a stable and legitimate framework to reinforce democracy and restore public confidence in the EU. The Charter of Fundamental Rights should be at the heart of a Constitution for Europe.
● Focus the scope of European Union action. We need to improve the quality of EU governance. The EU should focus its policy-making only on those areas for which EU-wide action is indispensable. This means ensuring that the principle of subsidiarity is fully respected. A standing scrutiny committee in the European Parliament should be established to ensure that EU proposals meet the criteria of subsidiarity and proportionality.
● Make the European Commission more democratically accountable. The Commission President's 'State of the Union' speech should be accompanied by a detailed list of proposals, individually justified and explained. Each new EU legislative proposal should include a justification of why EU action is necessary. The work programme should be put to a substantive vote by the European Parliament in plenary session. The committees of the European Parliament should be able to cross-examine individual Commissioners on the proposals under their responsibility. The European Parliament should have the power to vet and veto the appointment of each and every Commissioner and, if necessary, sack individual Commissioners.
● Make sure that European Union bodies are more open. All EU institutions should conform to the principles of freedom of information. The Council of Ministers should meet in public whenever it discusses legislation and publish a record of its proceedings. The political leader of the country holding the Presidency of the European Council should be obliged to appear before the plenary session of the European Parliament both before and after all meetings of the European Council.
● Maintain the veto in areas of vital interest to the UK. We favour the application of majority voting in the Council where necessary to ensure that the EU functions effectively. But we will maintain a veto on the constitution, defence, own resources, budgetary and tax matters and regulations on pay and social security.
● Improve Westminster's scrutiny of European legislation and of the activities of UK ministers attending the Council of Ministers. There should be no substantial initiatives for European legislation in the Council of Ministers which have not been scrutinised by the UK Parliament. Ministers, including the Prime Minister, should give evidence before a European Union Affairs Committee in Westminster prior to European Council meetings and any significant meeting of ministers.

- Increase the transparency of the European Central Bank. The Board of the Bank should publish its minutes and votes, following the practice of the Bank of England's Monetary Policy Committee.
- Support a European Common Foreign and Security Policy that includes a significant defence capability consistent with our membership of NATO and other international institutions.
- Hold meetings of the European Parliament only in Brussels to end the waste of time and money incurred by holding meetings in Strasbourg.
- Push for early enlargement of the EU. The nations of central and eastern Europe have now been waiting over ten years for the opportunity to benefit from EU membership. We will seek to ensure that there is no further slippage in accession schedules dependent upon meeting the Copenhagen criteria such as guaranteeing democracy, the rule of law and human rights.

### Setting You Free

- Remove unnecessary regulations and reduce administrative costs. We support moves to streamline the role of the EU Commission and to strengthen measures against fraud. We will push for obligatory regulatory impact assessments on all new EU proposals with a direct bearing on businesses. We will also stop the practice of 'goldplating' EU regulations, whereby the UK government unnecessarily adds requirements to minimum EU standards.

### Green Action
### Putting the Environment at the Heart of Europe

All EU policies should be analysed for their likely environmental impact, with results reported to the European Parliament. This is particularly important for EU overseas aid, where we will support the establishment of a specialised European aid agency. All member states must comply fully with EU environmental standards, and the European Court of Justice should apply higher fines to those failing to comply. We will support the initiative started at the Cardiff summit to integrate environmental objectives into all EU activities - particularly in the area of trade policy, where the Commission has sole competence to negotiate on the EU's behalf.

### Strengthening Europe's Voice on the Global Environment

We will argue for the EU to play a greater role in raising environmental standards world-wide, through providing support for the UN Environment Programme and for the enforcement of environmental conventions, such as those protecting endangered species, combating climate change, and controlling the trade in GM products.

### Freedom, Justice, Honesty
## DEFENCE AND INTERNATIONAL INSTITUTIONS

Britain can achieve far more by working with others than working alone. An internationalist approach is the best way to protect our freedom and our interests. We will work to build effective international and regional organisations to promote peace and freedom throughout the world, combat poverty and disease and tackle global environmental problems.

Liberal Democrats will:

- Promote a foreign policy based on democracy, human rights and good governance
- Seek to make international institutions more able to address global security, trade and environmental issues
- Resist further erosion of Britain's defence capability while co-operating more closely with the country's allies

Events in one nation can have a profound impact on life in other countries. The world is no longer one of self-contained nation states. Britain has too often given aid and comfort to authoritarian regimes which oppress their people and threaten world stability. And as Britain's own defence capability has weakened, the country has been slow to pool resources with its allies.

### Foreign Policy

Britain stands at the centre of a web of global institutions. Our membership of the UN Security Council, the Commonwealth, the EU, NATO, and other global bodies gives Britain a key role in world affairs. But with power comes responsibility.

We must not turn a blind eye to injustice, nor support authoritarian regimes which oppress their people and threaten world stability. Britain's influence should be used to fight for human rights and equitable and peaceful relationships between nations.

The Liberal Democrat approach puts democratic values, human rights and good governance at the top of the foreign policy agenda. We will:

- End subsidies for arms sold to foreign regimes. We will put an end to the use of Export Credit Guarantees to support arms exports. We will establish a Parliamentary Arms Export Committee to monitor arms exports and scrutinise individual licence applications. We will require arms brokers to register under a Code of Conduct, and revoke the licences of those who break the code.
- Take account of human rights and development needs in government policy. We will audit relevant government departments to ensure that policies on issues such as aid, arms sales and credit guarantees conform to the standards we have set.

- Give priority to conflict prevention. It should focus on traditional threats to security but also the consequences of environmental degradation, resource depletion, volatile markets and unfair trade. Preventive diplomacy will be given a higher priority in the budgets of the Foreign and Commonwealth Office, Department for International Development and Ministry of Defence.
- Continue the fight against slave labour. We will co-operate with international bodies like the International Labour Organisation to stamp out slavery.
- Maintain funding for the BBC World Service and the British Council. We will ensure that these two organisations, which have a vital role in spreading the values of freedom and democracy, receive proper funding.

### International Security

We favour greater international co-operation to make the world a safer place and to uphold human rights in other countries. We will:

- Seek to strengthen the powers of the UN. The UN needs a more active role in holding member states to account for gross and persistent breaches of the Universal Declaration of Human Rights. Too many UN Conventions and Security Council resolutions are flouted and ignored. We propose that the Secretary General conducts an audit to determine outstanding obligations and the action needed to comply with them.
- Ensure that the United Nations has the resources to act. We will promote the establishment of a Staff College based in Britain to train UN peacekeepers. We also advocate the formation of a UN Rapid Reaction Disaster Task Force to tackle both man-made and natural disasters.
- Work with Britain's partners in the Commonwealth to make it more effective in promoting conflict resolution, good governance and democratic values.
- Support the International Criminal Court. If it is powerful and well resourced, the Court will enhance the cause of human rights. We will press opponents of the court to recognise its authority.

### Defence

We are proud of Britain's record of defending democracy. British armed forces rightly enjoy the respect of the world. It is essential to preserve that reputation. But as the country's own defence capability has shrunk since the end of the Cold War, it has been slow to pool resources with allies. Britain's capabilities must continue to adapt to meet the challenges of the 21st Century. We will:

- Resist further erosion of Britain's defence capability. We will maintain the current level of spending and resist any further reductions.
- Promote flexibility, mobility, rapid deployment and joint operations as the basis of Britain's defence policy, to enable the UK to honour Britain's commitments to the EU, NATO, the Commonwealth and the UN.
- Promote equal opportunities and family welfare in the armed forces. We will oppose unfair discrimination in the forces. We will review welfare policies in order to set minimum and consistent standards that can be applied at home and abroad for service families.
- Work for the elimination worldwide of all nuclear weapons. We will press for a new round of multilateral arms reduction talks, but will retain the UK's minimum nuclear deterrent for the foreseeable future.
- Oppose the National Missile Defence System (NMD). The system currently being proposed by the USA represents a threat to international stability and arms control agreements.
- Put in place a moratorium on the use of Depleted Uranium Shells until there is clear evidence regarding the health risks involved.

### Trade, Aid and International Development

Genuinely liberal trade benefits all the countries of the world, rich and poor. We will press for a fairer global trading system, and do more to assist poor nations. We advocate effective aid policies to address the problems of developing countries and promote democracy and good governance. We will:

- Promote genuine liberal trade. The removal of barriers to trade has stimulated economic growth and prosperity throughout much of the world, and the World Trade Organisation has helped establish and maintain international rules which guarantee equal treatment for all members, large or small. However, trade liberalisation has sometimes been pursued at the expense of other objectives, such as environmental protection or public health. We will work to reform the WTO so that environmental objectives and principles are fully integrated into its activities and poorer countries are helped to participate fully within it.
- Encourage fair competition. We would press for a global competition authority within the WTO to encourage co-ordination of the anti-monopoly activities of individual nations to tackle the growing concentration of corporate monopoly power more effectively. We want world-wide agreement to reduce subsidies, common in areas such as fossil fuel production, agriculture, forestry and fisheries: this would encourage trade, open markets to poorer countries' exports and reduce environmental damage.
- Honour the UK's commitment to meet the UN target of increasing overseas aid to 0.7% over the next ten years. We support the moves already made by the British Government to reduce the debts of the poorest countries. But Britain could lead more rapid action on debt relief by bodies such as the International Monetary Fund and the World Bank. Their Poverty Reduction Strategy Programmes should attach at least as much importance to governments taking action to tackle poverty as to liberalising their economies.

- End links between aid and trade. Tied aid is a form of protectionism which inhibits development. We will subject all aid programmes to thorough assessment for their environmental, social and human rights consequences.
- Direct aid towards women. Women in developing countries face discrimination and economic exclusion. All aid packages should address gender inequality, with a high priority for family planning and maternal health services.
- Step up the fight against HIV/AIDS. The AIDS pandemic is a global emergency which undermines economic development and threatens international security. We will increase backing for the development of an AIDS vaccine. Working with bodies such as the churches, we will support large-scale AIDS/HIV education programmes and press for mother-to-child AIDS treatment drugs to be made available cheaply.
- Promote universal primary education. Education is essential to economic development. We will spearhead initiatives to increase the resources for basic education in developing countries. In return for financial support recipient countries should be obliged to reduce expenditure on arms.
- Implement the OECD convention on bribery. We will allow UK registered companies to be prosecuted for bribery offences committed overseas.

### Setting You Free
- Stop using taxpayers' money to support the arms trade by ending subsidies for arms sold to foreign regimes.

### Green Action

### Global Climate Change
We will place Britain at the forefront of climate change negotiations, pressing other nations to ratify and implement the 1997 Kyoto Protocol by the Rio+10 world summit in mid 2002. We will seek to extend its terms and targets further. We will ensure that Britain achieves its target well before the deadline, and establishes a new target of a 20% reduction in $CO_2$ emissions by 2010.

### Introduce Stronger Environmental Objectives
We will campaign to introduce stronger environmental objectives into the Common Agricultural Policy, lending and investment policies of the IMF, World Bank and regional development banks. WTO rules should respect environmental principles as long as these are applied in a non-protectionist way.

### Promote Sustainable Development
We will ensure that environmental and social sustainability is a prime objective of aid and technology transfer policies.

### Improve Environmental Governance
The Rio+10 summit in 2002 is an opportunity to improve the international community's ability to tackle environmental threats. We want a substantial increase in resources for the UN Environment Programme and for the implementation of environmental agreements. We also advocate a UN Economic and Environmental Security Council for Sustainability.

# OTHER MANIFESTOS
## Summarised by Ruth Winstone

## ULSTER UNIONIST PARTY

The first UUP manifesto since the creation of the politically inclusive Northern Ireland Assembly in 1998 commits the party to the strong ties between the Assembly and Westminster. The interests of Unionists and nationalists are best served, it believes, by working together in Northern Ireland, not by a united Ireland. The failure of paramilitaries to decommission compromises the "partnership between equals" agreed in 1997, and the UUP refuses to bury or ignore the issue. In this connection the party also opposes community policing which it believes would accommodate terrorism within a two-tier police force.

An Anti-Intimidation Unit for victims, together with changes to the law on evidence and criminal assets, are supported by the UUP.

Northern Ireland is experiencing record economic growth, but the region has been beset by foot-and-mouth disease and depletion of its fishing stocks. The UUP supports a ten-year agriculture business plan with farm diversification, and renegotiation of fishing rights with the EU.

The UUP believes that a review of public administration should lead to better management of health services, while primary care co-operatives exercising local financial control will help to reverse the decline.

The high standards of education in Northern Ireland are compromised by a bureaucratic funding formula, which the UUP would reform. The 11-plus examination would be maintained but the "lower ranges of the ability spectrum" are the target of improvement by shifing the emphasis from GCSEs to vocational courses. The UUP opposes preferential treatment for Irish-medium schools.

## DEMOCRATIC UNIONIST PARTY

The DUP manifesto for the general election reiterates the party's opposition to what it believes is appeasement of republicanism, betrayal of Unionism and false pledges by the UUP in the wake of the Belfast agreement. "No more concessions to the IRA and no more rewards for Sinn Fein/IRA" is the message from which other attitudes to the agreement flow. The party would like to see the Royal Ulster Constabulary (RUC) retained in name and emblems, the Parades Commission wound up, and the balance in favour of Ulster Scots language and culture redressed. The Human Rights Commmission, it believes, is unrepresentative of those opposed to the Belfast agrement.

The DUP wants equal funding regardless of the students the schools principally serve, and would like to see specialist schools at post-primary level for different abilities.

The DUP would abolish full-time tuition fees and allow non-repayable means-tested grants and set up a student endowment fund.

It would augment its free transport for the elderly with other measures such as a tax-free pension, the restoration of the earnings link, a minimum income standard, and the abolition of standing charges on bills. The DUP believes that under the control of the IRA/Sinn Fein the health service in Northen Ireland has favoured "grandiose and expensive cross-border services" at the expense of local services.

The DUP agricultural policies include a scheme to help new farmers and those who wish to retire and an easing of farmland planning regulations to enable farming families to build homes in the countryside.

The removal of red tape and a single development agency in place of three existing ones to attract inward investment are part of the DUP's business strategy; the DUP opposes the climate change levy and aggregates tax which place businesses competing with those in the Irish Republic at a disadvantage.

## SOCIAL DEMOCRATIC AND LABOUR PARTY

Support for a new Bill of Rights and a human rights court is at the heart of the SDLP's human rights policy for Northern Ireland. The party believes that non-prison secure accommodation for under-18s and restorative justice schemes are priorities. Illegal weapons must be "put verifiably beyond use" and the SDLP is unequivocal in condemning punishment beatings. It seeks full implementation of the Patten Report on the police, reform of the Special Branch and public inquiries into controversial murders. It has a programme of reconciliation including practical support for victims and bereaved families.

A radical overhaul of sex offences laws in Northern Ireland, and protection of groups from discrimination and attacks, via a single equality Bill and anti-racial legislation, are priorities in the "creation of a fairer, more equal society". Culture policy endorses special recognition of the Irish language and Ulster Scots artistic endeavours, and all-island coverage of RTE television. The party's social policy includes higher benefit levels, a minimum income, £5 per hour minimum wage, and an integrated health strategy to address Northern Ireland's poor health record. It would also like to see the end of selection at age 11 and coeducation. Among its environmental policies are support for an independent environmental protection agency and for a green economy task force. The SDLP agrees with the "polluter pays" principle in areas such as packaging, water and air pollution; action to meet the Kyoto targets; and promotion of organic farming. The Barnett formula to calculate Northern Ireland's allocation of resources from Westminster would be reformed, The party is an enthusiastic supporter of the EU and the euro.

# SINN FEIN

Sinn Fein seeks a constitution court, co-ordinated environmental policies, an island-wide education approach and promotion of the Irish language. It welcomes the Patten Report on policing, insisting on neutral names, symbols and emblems, and disbandment of the Special Branch, powers of independent inquiry, and reduction in powers of the RUC Chief Constable and the Secretary of State for Northern Ireland.

A department of equality would promote an end to unemployment and discriminatory practices. Education in an all-Ireland context would include abolition of the 11-plus and more support for special needs. The party is pursuing its objective of an all-Ireland health service, democratised and with inequalities eradicated.

Sinn Fein would promote mixed and organic farming along with retraining and early retirement for farmers. Its wider environmental programme includes green taxes, the "producer pays" for pollution principle, a zero-waste agency across Ireland, and financial help to introduce cleaner technologies.

Child abuse would be combated by an all-Ireland register of paedophiles, and increased funding of children's services. The party would abolish tuition fees and restore a means-tested student maintenance grant.

Sinn Fein promotes a liberal programme on asylum-seekers and refugees. An amnesty, anti-racial discrimination laws, no detentions, and abolition of the voucher system are among measures to secure a multicultural society.

# ALLIANCE PARTY OF NORTHERN IRELAND

The "cultural war" between Unionism and nationalism is, in the view of the Alliance Party, undermining the Belfast agreement to which the Alliance Party is committed. It wants a criminal justice strategy between police and Customs and Excise to tackle drug trading; it supports Patten Report reforms of the police service, and a protocol to allow police either side of the border to cross in pursuit of suspects. The Alliance would like tax-varying powers for the Assembly, and a weighted-majority form of power-sharing.

# UNITED KINGDOM UNIONIST PARTY

The UKUP is opposed to the Belfast agreement on the grounds that it has "violated the basic principles of democracy, breached the rule of law, and placed the representatives of armed terrorists in government". Central to its policies is the constitutional position of Northern Ireland. It believes that increased central government involvement and investment, not devolution, is required.

# PROGRESSIVE UNIONIST PARTY

The PUP combines a commitment to, and strengthening of, the present constitutional position of Northern Ireland within the United Kingdom. It opposes what it calls the "contract culture" in local authority provision, and would like to see a revamping of the system of child support, the end of the Social Fund, an increase in benefit for lone parents, and the abolition of VAT on fuel and other necessities of life. It supports a written constitution and Bill of Rights for Northen Ireland.

# SCOTTISH NATIONAL PARTY

The drive to independence for Scotland is the main plank of the SNP's Westminster election strategy. The party pledges its Members of Parliament to a "contract with the people" to promote and protect Scottish interests, argue for more powers for the Scottish Parliament and secure a referendum on independence.

An independent SNP government would deliver enhanced health, education and social welfare. SNP health policies range from the setting up of a cross-party national healthcare commission overseeing health strategy in NHS Scotland, to free fruit in all schools and free dental checks.

A Scottish fund for future generations would divert surplus oil revenues to public services. The use of PFI and PPP in public infrastructure projects would be replaced by a Scottish trust for public investment to provide modern and reliable transport systems for businesses and more investment in NHS Scotland and housing.

The SNP would introduce proportional representation, votes at 16 and a moratorium on further changes to educational practice.

The party is committed to increasing the minimum wage and abolishing the age differential. The party is committed to producing 25 per cent of Scotland's electricity from renewable sources by 2010 and will call a halt to nuclear power stations.

The SNP rejects an EU superstate and would join the single currency only with public consent via a referendum. Opposition to a US missile defence system and the removal of Trident would be part of the SNP's defence policy. However, the SNP would have to negotiate phased withdrawal from Nato. A Scottish Defence Force would be principally defensive, the share of UK resources having been negotiated.

One thousand more policemen and greater legal responsibility of parents for antisocial offspring are part of the SNP's law policy. The party commits itself to a 10p per gallon cut in fuel taxation, met by an extra 5p per pound tax on incomes over £100,000. A small-business rates-relief scheme will be considered. Compensated tie-up schemes would keep the fishing industry viable and the return of 6,000 square miles of fishing grounds would be demanded. Streamlining benefits payments through the creation of one agency, instead of the existing three agencies, restoring the earnings link to old-age pensions, reviewing financial support for carers, and restoration of benefits for 16 to 17-year-olds form the basis of the SNP's social security policy. While not ruling out full public ownership of Railtrack, the SNP would initially take shares in the company; control of air traffic in Scotland would remain a public sector function.

## PLAID CYMRU — THE PARTY OF WALES

Plaid Cymru rejects the "Blair-Brown policy agenda" which it says has perpetuated the economic damage to Wales inflicted by previous Conservative Governments. It proposes more public spending on health (in particular on cancer and heart disease), higher taxes on income over £50,000, removal of means-tested help for Wales's disproportionately high elderly population, and a link between pensions and earnings. The Barnett formula for calculating Wales's budget should be replaced and the Assembly's political powers strengthened in line with the Scottish Parliament. The public control of Railtrack and a green renewable energy policy, in a global context, are essential to the Principality's economic wellbeing.

Wales's agricultural community would be given help through schemes for young farmers and early retirement; and cheaper housing in the private or enlarged council sector would help to alleviate poverty. Delays in compensating Wales's miners suffering industrial diseases would be reduced. On education, teachers' pay would be increased, performance-related pay ended and tuition fees abolished.

The party is unequivocally behind Britain joining the euro at an appropriate exchange rate, a common foreign and external security policy for Europe, and against an American missile defence scheme.

## GREEN PARTY

A fundamental shift in economic policy from growth and consumption to production for need is required to avoid an inheritance of environmental devastation, the Green Party says. Duties to protect ecologically sound products and services, "eco-tax" on products, higher fuel duty and a local land value tax, and fundamental reform of the World Trade Organisation's "harmful global trade practices" are among the Greens' policies. A non-means-tested citizen's income for all, to replace existing pensions and benefits, would be paid for by progressive taxation.

Transport policy is critical to the Greens' manifesto. They would renationalise Railtrack, end roadbuilding projects, and use the £59 billion budget to reduce car use and increase less harmful transport systems. Greens would impose higher taxes on aviation fuel.

The "anachronistic" European common agricultural policy should be phased out in favour of subsidies dependent on environmental and animal welfare criteria. The party's organic food target is 30 per cent of food production by 2010 and 50 per cent reduction in pesticide use by 2005. It would unequivocally ban engineering of farm animals and the import and production of GM food.

The party believes that reduction of greenhouse gas emissions globally by 80 per cent by the year 2050 is needed to avoid climate disaster. Carbon cuts would be tied in with development of renewable sources. Greens would like to see a waste reduction, refuse and recycling Bill to stimulate recycling of 60 per cent of household waste by 2007. The party does not believe that toxicity, warfare or other tests should be carried out on animals and would like to see them ended within five years. Hunting with hounds and badger culling should be ended. The "war on the natural world" will be harmful to birds and insects, but the loss will be reduced by bio-action plans. The Greens reject the superstate model; transnational issues such as environmental pollution, distribution of resources and animal rights should be agreed, by "qualified majority voting at the Council of Ministers in co-decision with the European Parliament". Other decisions should be subject to national veto.

The party would decriminalise all drugs, while a drugs commission considered which to legalise and how to regulate supply. Finally, there is a *cri de coeur* for proportional representation.

## COMMUNIST PARTY OF BRITAIN

The interests of Labour's "traditional supporters" are at the heart of the Communist Party's socialist manifesto and a return to wealth redistribution and greater public ownership of national assets are, unsurprisingly, the cornerstones of its programme. A windfall tax on the super-profits of banks and oil companies, and an increase in corporation tax on business profits and higher incomes are proposed. The party specifies a return of rail and buses and all the utilities to public ownership, reversing the privatisation of the previous 22 years and preventing any further selling-off. The Communists also oppose all privatised education.

The party would nationalise oil, steel, shipbuilding, technology, aerospace and telecommunications, and introduce planning agreements to other "strategically important" companies in the private sector. The party is opposed to the single European currency, and the independence of the Bank of England.

A 35-hour working week would extend to all workers, and the minimum wage would rise to two thirds of average male earnings. An immediate £28 per week rise in the state pension and free long-term nursing home care for the elderly are specific commitments. The party would repeal all immigration, nationality and asylum laws which it regards as racist, and make racist attacks a specific legal offence. The party's foreign policy condemns global capitalism and deplores a new arms race aimed at socialist China, North Korea and Cuba.

## SOCIALIST ALLIANCE

The manifesto of the Socialist Alliance reflects the coalition of socialist groups and individuals brought together for the 2001 election. On the general slogan of People before Profit, the candidates for the party are committed to receiving an average working wage if elected as MPs. Many policies are aimed at reversing the changes of the past 20 years, including ending all privatisation, and renationalising railways and utilities. The party would introduce a 35-hour maximum working week and a national minimum wage of £7.40 an hour. The "right to buy" option on council housing would be revoked; comprehensive education would be restored and measures to promote educational "choice" ended.

The party would reverse welfare state reforms, and raise the state pension to £150 for a single person. It aims for unilateral nuclear disarmament, removal of British troops from Iraq, the Balkans and Northern Ireland, and ending of Third World debt.

## UNITED KINGDOM INDEPENDENCE PARTY

This claims to be the only political party contesting the general election that "will never abolish the pound for the euro and will never abandon British common law, the right to trial by jury or the presumption of innocence".

It believes in freedom for the individual, businesses and local communities. It believes in freedom also from "patronising political-correctness intolerance or injustice". The cornerstone of its policies is Britain's withdrawal from the European Union. This it would achieve by repeal of the European Communities Act of 1972. This Act, together with subsequent legislation and commitments such as the Charter of Fundamental Human Rights, limits the UK's right to free trade, free speech, and threatens its legal and parliamentary system, the party says.

Removing bureaucracy in education authorities, the NHS, and social services, and simplifying and reforming state provision by, in certain cases, providing a "basic income", and compulsory private pension fund contributions, form part of the party's social reforms.

## LIBERAL PARTY

The offspring of the old Liberal Party continues some philosophical tenets of its parent. It believes in a free market economy with progressive tax rates, and a guaranteed old-age pension; it proposes a written constitution and would license drugs, and resist ID cards and curfews. Rationing of road transport and tax breaks for green vehicles, plus an environmentally friendly infrastructure for industry are among its policies. It would end live-animal experimentation and blood sports, and promote a return to non-intensive farming practices, supporting small farms and local markets. The party opposes the EU, and would replace it with a looser commonwealth of Europe which co-operated on environmental and peace policies. A world government is a long-term goal with unilateral nuclear disarmament and strengthening the UN at the heart of its foreign policy.

## SCOTTISH SOCIALIST PARTY

Comprising a number of socialist groups and individuals in Scotland, the Scottish Socialist Party is in favour of an independent republic of Scotland. The long-term vision is the ending of global capitalism in favour of global socialism, in which states co-operate "to end poverty, starvation, disease, war and the threat of environmental catastrophe".

Control of the economy and defence is seen as essential in an independent socialist state. The party would introduce a £7-an-hour minimum wage and reform taxation to raise more from corporations and wealthier earners. Any investment into services via PFI, PPP or other privatisation schemes would be halted, and all private medicine incorporated into the NHS.

## BRITISH NATIONAL PARTY

The BNP would halt all further non-white immigration and promote a non-white Britain by deporting illegal immigrants and introducing a system of voluntary resettlement. British people, it believes, should have a homeland and retain their unique identity and should be given preference in jobs. All vital national assets should be restored to British ownership.

The party would seek British withdrawal from the European Union and Nato and cancellation of the Belfast agreement. It would retain the nuclear deterrent and introduce National Service for young people. Capital punishment for premeditated murder, and as an option in cases of serious sex attacks by adults on young children, would be restored.

## PROLIFE ALLIANCE

The full protection of all human life from the one-cell embryo stage until natural death is the cornerstone of the Alliance manifesto.

This means not only repealing the 1967 Abortion Act and outlawing all abortion except when the baby's death is brought about indirectly, but also repealing the Human Fertilisation and Embryology Act 1990, and outlawing "voluntary, non-voluntary and involuntary euthanasia". The promotion of abortion and sterilisation abroad through aid programmes is condemned. The Alliance would outlaw cloning, embryo experiments and reproductive technologies whereby more than one embryo is created and transferred to the mother's body. Sex education would be scrutinised and the tax and benefit system would encourage marriage and family life.

# SOCIALIST LABOUR PARTY

The party, which was formed by Arthur Scargill to oppose nationalisation after the Labour Party scrapped Clause Four of its constitution, is fighting "for an end to hardship, inequality, injustice and despair . . . and above all for a socialist Britain". It demands a free National Health Service, free and high-quality education, a £30-a-week immediate rise in the single pension, the end of "right to buy" housing policy together with building or refurbishing one million homes a year for the next five years, introduction of a four-day working week and withdrawal from the European Union.

# THE CO-OPERATIVE PARTY

This party, which believes that more can be achieved working together than working alone, is closely allied to the Labour Party and supports that party in its aims.

# THE COUNTRYSIDE PARTY

This party aims to preserve country sports, sustain farming, safeguard rural employment, improve the rural transport system and seek financial guarantees for new rural businesses.

# THE NATIONAL FRONT

The Front, which is what remains after the split in 1980 eventually led to the formation of the British National Party, believes that Britain is threatened by non-white immigration and that the policies of the mainstream parties are inadequate to resist this perceived threat.

# MEBYON KERNOW — THE PARTY FOR CORNWALL

Having seen a Scottish Parliament and a Welsh Assembly established since the 1997 general election, Mebyon Kernow — the Party for Cornwall — has stepped up its demand for a Cornish assembly, rejecting the "artificial southwest region" status which it believes central government has imposed on the Cornish people. It describes its credentials as green, left-of-centre and decentralist.

# OFFICIAL MONSTER RAVING LOONY PARTY

The memory of the much-lamented Screaming Lord Sutch (now spiritual leader of the Official Monster Raving Loony Party) is marked in the party's manifesto by a proposal for a commemorative Sutch Column in Trafalgar Square (renamed Loony Square). Policies are strong on the environment. Building on flood-plains in the light of global warming would be restricted to houseboats, motorists would be offered horses to tow them during fuel crises, and a new small VW car (the "Dung Beetle") would be developed to run on farmyard effluent.

The divide that separates North from South in Britain would become a square-root, while on the European front, the party's answer to EU-style identity cards is to issue small mirrors to aid in self-identification.

Not averse to joining the hunting controversy, the party wants to see foxes hunted by Old English sheepdogs and dachshunds (to even the odds). Free Viagra for the over-69s, and free prescriptions for all, form the main plank of the health programme.

There is an authoritarian flavour to the party's law and order policies. Penalties on mobile phone users will include being squirted with coloured silly-string, and dogs will be required to wear nappies, a policy of which the new joint leader of the party, the feline Cat-Mandu, will no doubt approve.

Finally, a strong commitment to sport includes the introduction of witch-ducking in the Olympics, and making it an offence for anyone born south of Crewe to support Manchester United.

# INDEX TO CANDIDATES

# INDEX TO CANDIDATES

# RECORD OF BY-ELECTIONS IN THE PARLIAMENT OF 2001-